NEW REVISED & EXPANDED EDITION!

The Official NRA Guide to Firearms Assembly

RIFLES AND SHOTGUNS

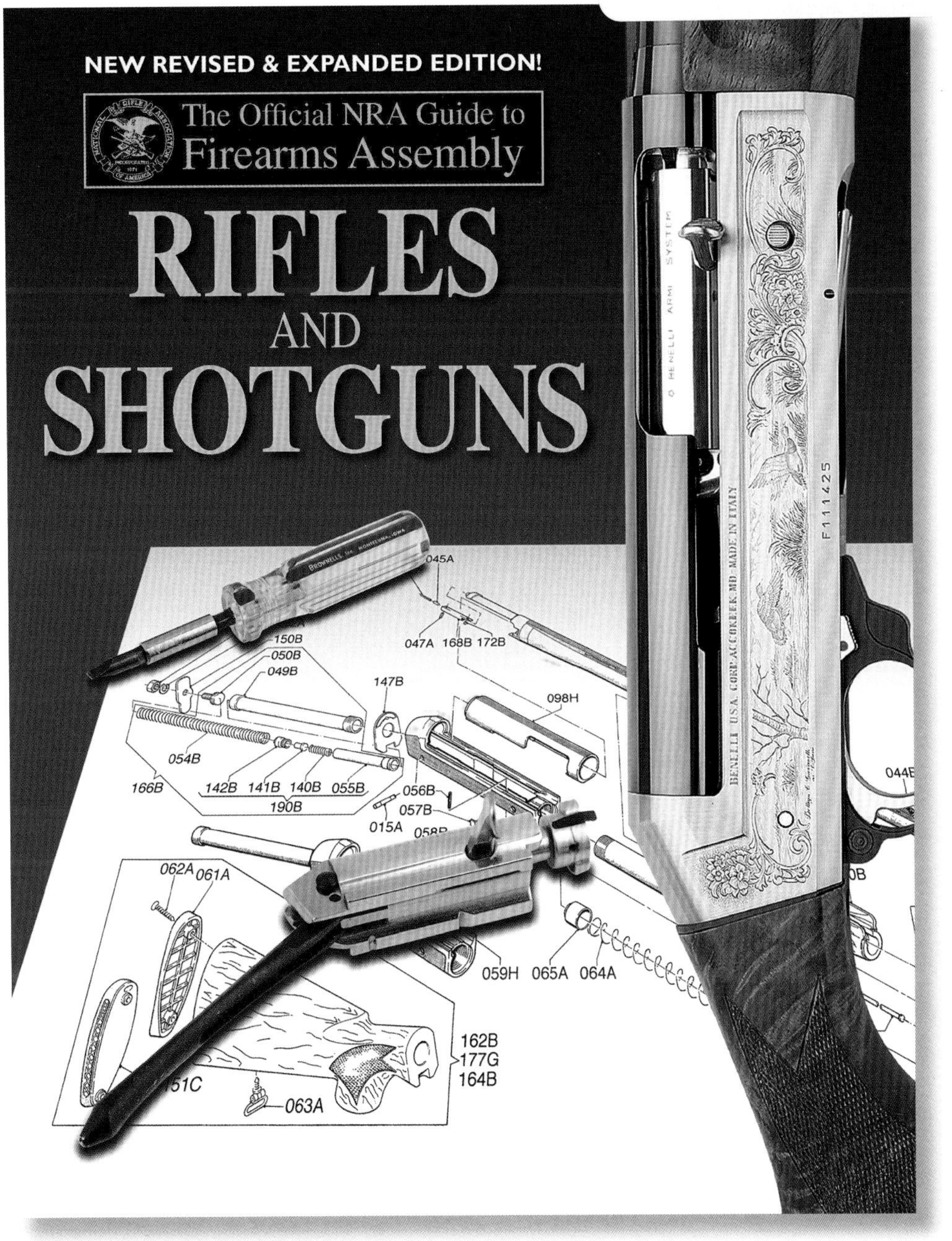

**Edited by Joseph B. Roberts, Jr.
and Harris J. Andrews**

A Publication of the
National Rifle Association of America

BK01616
ISBN-13: 978-0-88317-334-3
ISBN-10:0-88317-334-4
Library of Congress Control Number: 2007936924

Printed in the United States of America

Published by the National Rifle Association of America
11250 Waples Mill Road, Fairfax, VA 22030-9400

Wayne R. LaPierre, NRA Executive Vice President

Produced by NRA Publications
Joe H. Graham, Executive Director
Lourdes F. Kite, Deputy Executive Director
John R. Zent, Editorial Director
Harry L. Jaecks, Art Director
Michael J. Sanford, Production & Advertising Operations Director

For information, contact the National Rifle Association
11250 Waples Mill Road, Fairfax, Virginia 22030-9400.

FOREWORD

A modern firearm, or an antique one for that matter, tends to be among the most complex and advanced artifacts produced by any industrialized society. With their multitude of finely machined, interconnected parts and the stresses to which they are subjected by the nature of their function and operation — intense internal pressures, mechanical wear, recoil stress, moisture, oxidation and abuse by careless or inattentive owners — all firearms need regular servicing and, sooner or later, repairs. Many gunsmiths make a good part of their living by servicing and repairing guns brought into their shops by frustrated owners. With this compilation of articles we are not trying to put a dent in any gunsmith's livelihood. As a matter of fact, every worthwhile gunsmith I know has greasy, shopworn copies of previous editions of the *NRA Firearms Assembly Guides* ready at hand. But we do hope to help gun owners better understand their guns, and how to take them apart for maintenance and simple repair.

Cartridge and rifle innovator Charles Newton is credited with the first illustrated view of his High Power Rifle in the 15th edition of the Newton Arms Co. catalog, likely from 1915, with clear concise instructions on disassembly. He is, according to former *American Rifleman* Technical Editor Pete Dickey, "the father of the Exploded View."

American Rifleman printed its first "Exploded View" in 1952. Written and illustrated by the late E.J. Hoffschmidt, it gave a brief history of the Browning Hi Power, with an "Exploded View" parts drawing that showed all the parts and their relationship to each other, along with detailed and illustrated disassembly instructions. Back then, this was a pretty revolutionary concept. Most makers would merely have a photograph or a line drawing of the parts, and a list with prices so you could order replacements. Some credit *Rifleman's* "Exploded Views" with the clear, concise disassembly instructions found in most owner's manuals today.

Over the years, hundreds of "Exploded Views" of rifles, shotguns, pistols and revolvers have appeared in the pages of *American Rifleman*, written by dozens of writers and illustrators—myself included—and the vast majority of them are included here. To this day, they are the most commonly requested articles of the tens of thousands *Rifleman* has published over the years. You get most everything you need; the gun's background, when it was made, how to take it apart and a complete listing of all the parts. And in this book, they are all together.

One of the best features of this book is the appendix at the end giving brand names and model numbers that generally follow the guns included in the book. Those listed are mechanically and operationally similar to those covered here, but might be different enough to require gunsmith attention if you are not careful. When in doubt—or if you are taking apart a gun for the first time—take digital photos or make simple hand sketches of the parts in relation to each other as you remove each one. It's a good idea, even if you have the "Exploded View." Also, there are a number of guns here that only give fieldstripping directions. That's for good reason, as anyone who has unwittingly fully disassembled a Browning Auto-5 can attest. I've done it, and don't recommend it to even those I dislike. Some guns have tricks, some require special jigs and tools, and some are just a bear even if you know what you are doing.

For many men, reading the instructions is the last resort. As one who has taken guns apart weekly for more than 15 years, I can assure you that, unless you want to bring a bag of jumbled parts to a smirking gunsmith, the directions are, indeed, the place to start.

Mark A. Keefe, IV
Editor-In-Chief
American Rifleman
Fairfax, Virginia

CAUTION: The material contained herein is reprinted from past issues of the *American Rifleman* magazine, a copyrighted publication of the National Rifle Association of America (NRA). Therefore, while technically sound and historically relevant, it may have been updated by research more recent than the original date of publication. All technical data in this publication reflect the limited experience of individuals using specific tools, products, equipment and components under specific conditions and circumstances not necessarily reported in this publication, and over which NRA has no control. The data have not otherwise been tested or verified by the NRA. The NRA, its agents, officers and employees accept no responsibility for the results obtained by persons using such data and disclaim all liability for any consequential injuries or damages.

CONTENTS

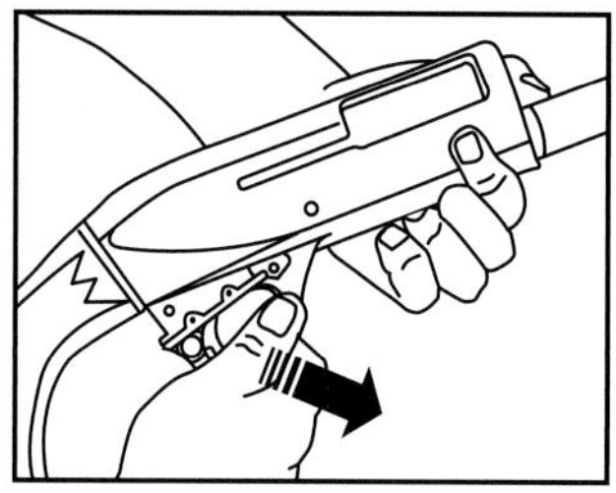

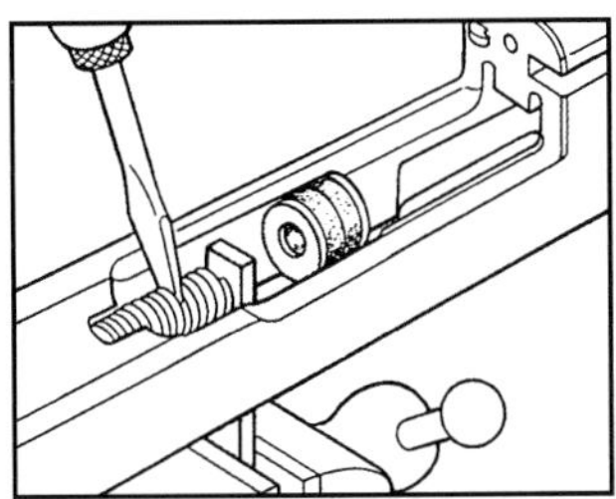

WHAT THE NRA IS & WHAT IT DOES

The National Rifle Association was organized as a non-profit, membership corporation in the State of New York in November 1871, by a small group of National Guard officers. The object for which it was formed was the improvement of its members in marksmanship, and to promote the introduction of the system of aiming drill and rifle practice as a part of the military drill of the National Guard.

In 1877, its name was changed to the National Rifle Association of America (NRA). During its years of existence, NRA Headquarters has been located in New York, New Jersey, Washington, D.C., and, since 1994, in Fairfax, Virginia.

The NRA represents and promotes the best interests of gun owners and shooter-sportsmen and supports their belief in the ideals of the United States of America and its way of life. It is dedicated to firearms safety education as a public service, marksmanship training as a contribution to individual preparedness for personal and national defense, and the sports of shooting and hunting as wholesome forms of recreation. It stands squarely behind the premise that ownership of firearms must not be denied to law-abiding Americans.

The purposes and objectives of the National Rifle Association of America are:

- To protect and defend the Constitution of the United States, especially with reference to the inalienable right of the individual American citizen guaranteed by such Constitution to acquire, possess, collect, exhibit, transport, carry, transfer ownership of, and enjoy the right to use arms, in order that the people may always be in a position to exercise their legitimate individual rights of self-preservation and defense of family, person, and property, as well as to serve effectively in the appropriate militia for the common defense of the Republic and the individual liberty of its citizens;
- To promote public safety, law and order, and the national defense;
- To train members of law enforcement agencies, the armed forces, the militia, and people of good repute in marksmanship and in the safe handling and efficient use of small arms;
- To foster and promote the shooting sports, including the advancement of amateur competitions in marksmanship at the local, state, regional, national, and international levels;
- To promote hunter safety, and to promote and defend hunting as a shooting sport and as a viable and necessary method of fostering the propagation, growth and conservation, and wise use of our renewable wildlife resources.

INTRODUCTION

Disassembling a rifle or shotgun seems easy enough. The carefully designed and finely machined parts should go together in a logical order and it should simply be a matter of unscrewing the right screws, driving out a pin or so, and pulling the thing apart. Unfortunately, it isn't always that easy! That unexpected heavy spring under brutal tension; a cluster (assembly in firearms trade parlance) of minute, interlocked parts and springs; a pin precisely milled to only drive in one direction; can all contrive to make even field stripping some rifles or shotguns an exercise in frustration and occasionally a small scale disaster.

A clear understanding of the interior design of a firearm and how its multitude of parts interact is vital for anyone trying to disassemble and then successfully reassemble it. Having access to a clear, well-labeled "exploded view" diagram is the next best thing to having an experienced gunsmith sitting at one's elbow. The logical, perspective-view schematic diagrams contained in this book clearly show the construction and relationship of components of hundreds of antique and modern firearms.

Most of the exploded views included in *The NRA Official Guide* were laboriously drawn by hand by highly experienced professional draftsmen using traditional drafting and inking tools. Modern engineers, however, use sophisticated computer drafting programs or "CAD" (Computer Assisted Drawing) systems to produce mechanical drawings. Whether drawn by hand or by machine, the scaled, detailed views are key to understanding the "guts" of any rifle or shotgun.

In addition, the *Official Guide* contains illustrated, step-by-step disassembly instructions and brief historical and technical descriptions of each firearm. The instruction sections include photographs of the primary models of the long arm in question and a selection of color photographs of various models included in the book.

Drawn from the files of the National Rifle Association's *American Rifleman* magazine, this collection was originally published in 1959. These articles were the product of the knowledge and skills of the magazine's contributors — gunsmiths, firearms aficionados, collectors and hunters — and they provide valuable information on many of the important, popular and innovative firearms of the last two centuries. The book has been revised and expanded since, and the latest revision simply adds to the scope and usefulness of a well-respected guidebook and shop companion.

This new edition, *The Official NRA Guide to Firearms Assembly: Rifles and Shotguns,* has been upgraded with new information and additional new entries covering current popular and interesting pistols and revolvers. Each rifle or shotgun features an exploded-view diagram and supporting, step-by-step instructions detailing the process for field stripping and disassembly. In many cases articles provide useful reassembly tips and cautions concerning the mechanical "quirks" of various guns.

ACKNOWLEDGEMENTS

The following authors and editors, along with the NRA Technical Staff, wrote and illustrated the articles printed in *American Rifleman* magazine that formed the text contained in the original editions of *Firearms Assembly: The NRA Guide to Rifles and Shotguns.*

Art Blatt
Pete Dickey
John Doughty
John F. Finnegan
Frank G. Hart
Edward J. Hoffschmidt
Robert W. Hunnicutt
John Karns
Andy Kendzie
Ludwig Olson
Stephen Otway
Arthur Pence
Dennis Riordan
Robert N. Sears
Edward A. Tolosky
John Traister
James M. Triggs
Stephen K. Vogel
Thomas E. Wessel
Doug Wicklund

GALLERY OF RIFLES & SHOTGUNS

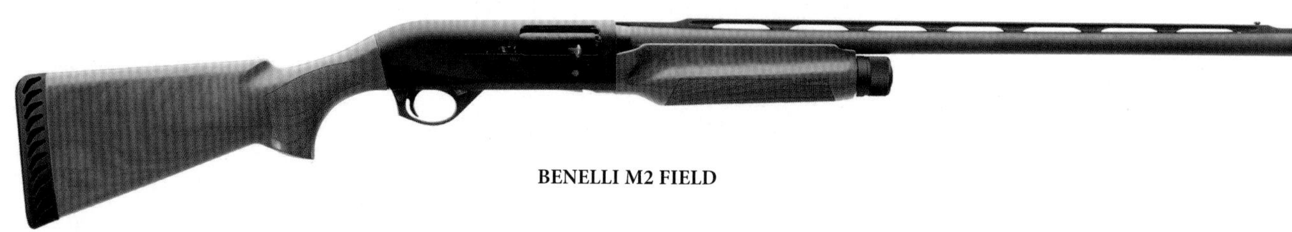
BENELLI M2 FIELD

BENELLI SUPER BLACK EAGLE II

BERETTA AL 391

BERETTA 682 GOLD

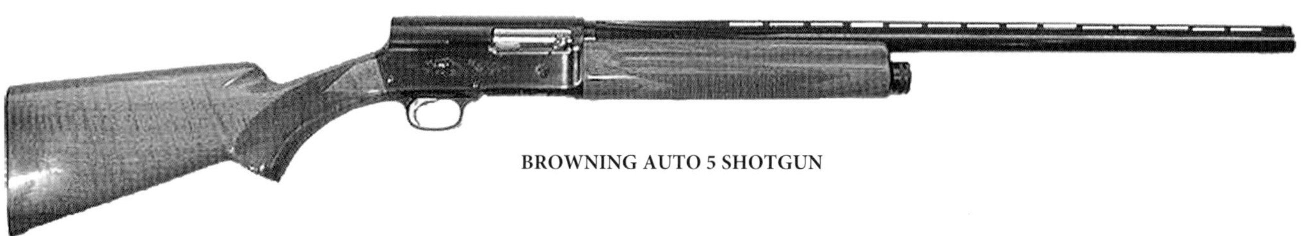

BROWNING AUTO 5 SHOTGUN

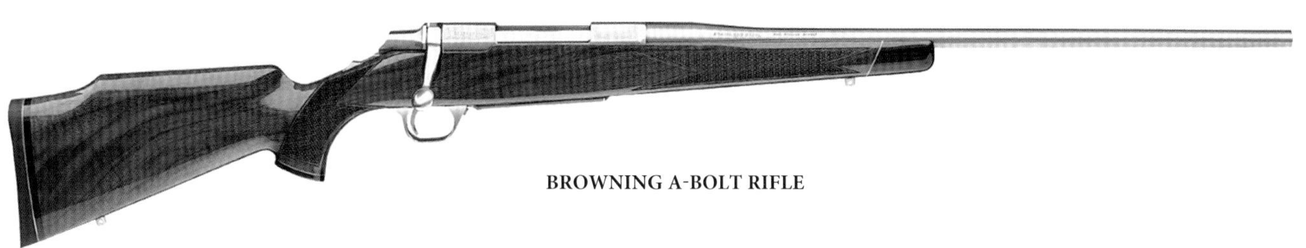

BROWNING A-BOLT RIFLE

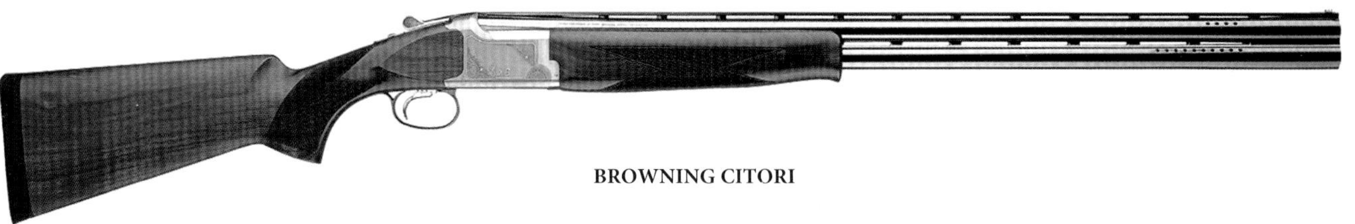

BROWNING CITORI

BUSHMASTER M4A3

GERMAN MODEL 1888 MAUSER RIFLE

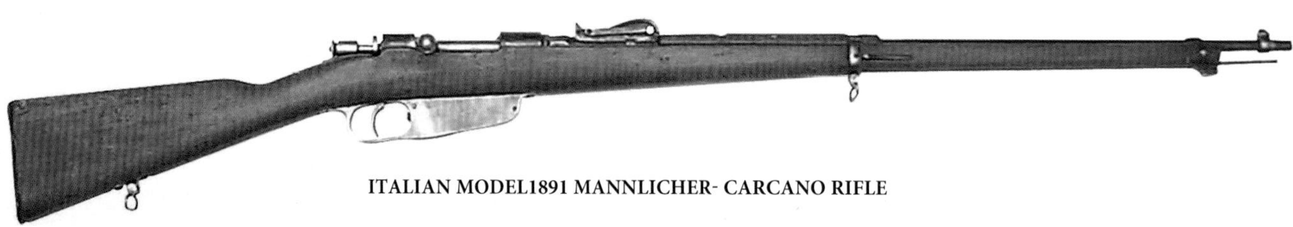

ITALIAN MODEL1891 MANNLICHER- CARCANO RIFLE

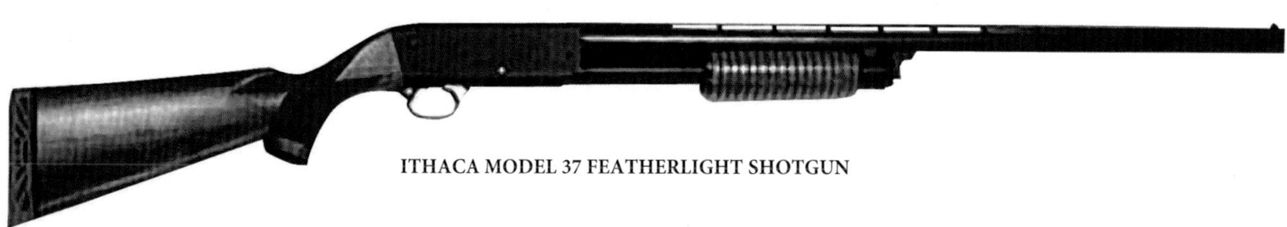

ITHACA MODEL 37 FEATHERLIGHT SHOTGUN

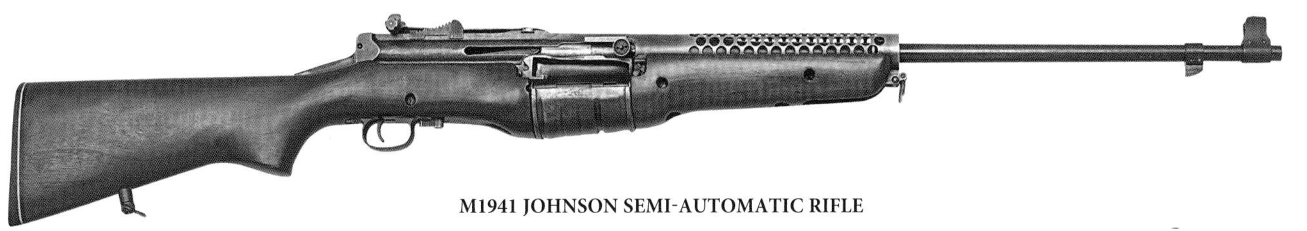

M1941 JOHNSON SEMI-AUTOMATIC RIFLE

KENTUCKY RIFLE

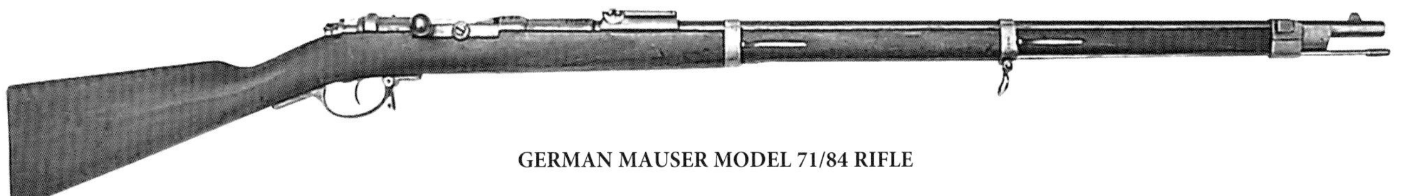

GERMAN MAUSER MODEL 71/84 RIFLE

RUSSIAN MOSIN-NAGANT MODEL 1891 RIFLE

MOSSBERG MODEL 500 SHOTGUN

OLYMPIC OA-93-CARBINE

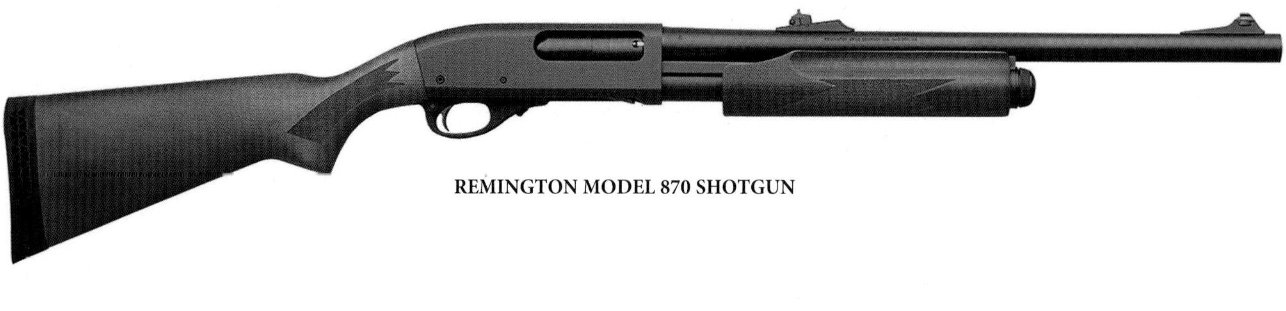

REMINGTON MODEL 870 SHOTGUN

REMINGTON MODEL 11-87 SHOTGUN

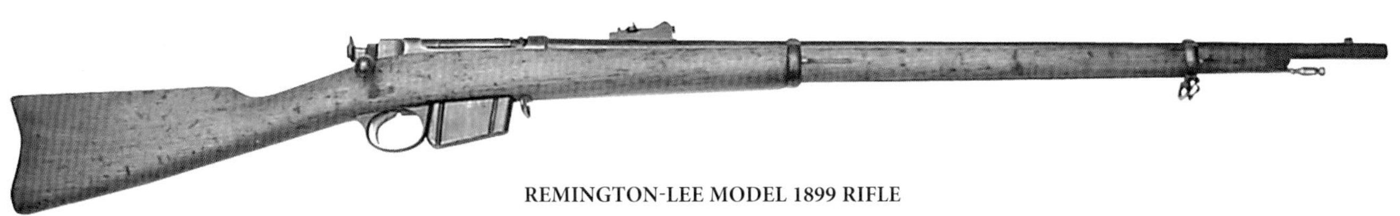

REMINGTON-LEE MODEL 1899 RIFLE

RUGER MODEL 96 RIFLE

SHARPS 1859 CARBINE

SHARPS-BORCHARDT MODEL 1878

L.C. SMITH HAMMERLESS GRADE 1 SHOTGUN

U.S. CAL. .30 M-1 GARAND RIFLE

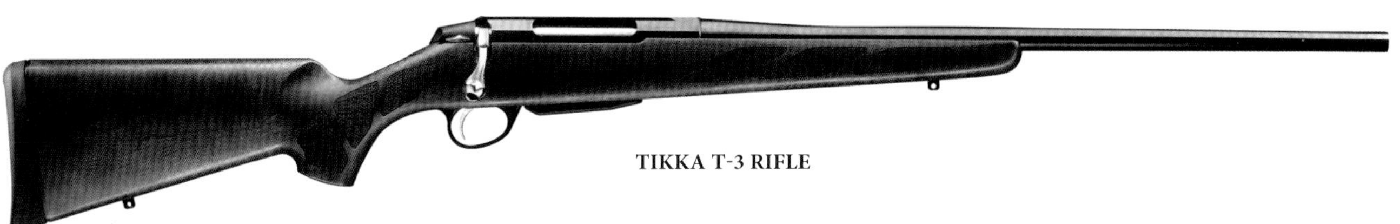

TIKKA T-3 RIFLE

WINCHESTER LEVER ACTION SHOTGUN

WINCHESTER MODEL 1873 RIFLE

WINCHESTER MODEL 1889 RIFLE

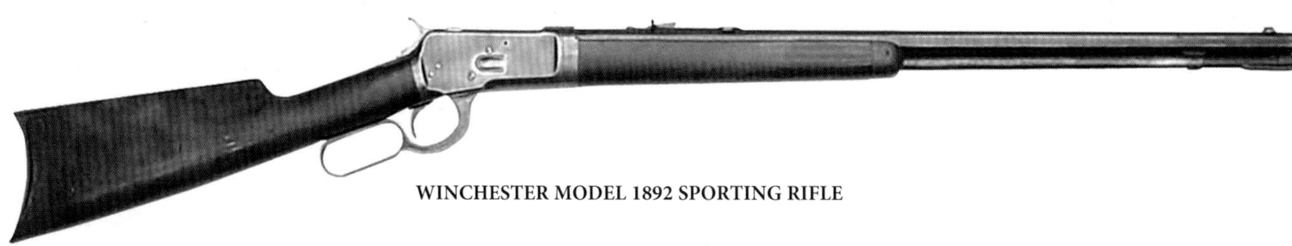
WINCHESTER MODEL 1892 SPORTING RIFLE

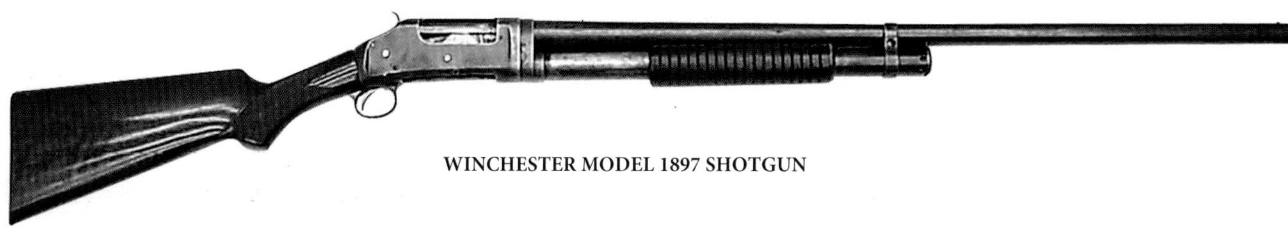
WINCHESTER MODEL 1897 SHOTGUN

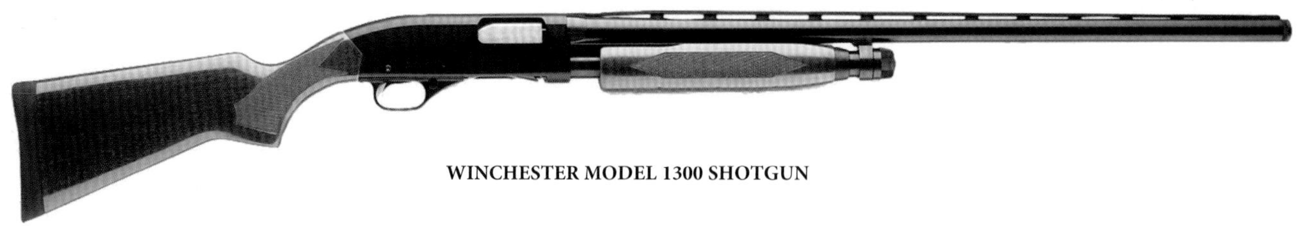
WINCHESTER MODEL 1300 SHOTGUN

FIREARMS DISASSEMBLY INSTRUCTIONS WITH EXPLODED VIEWS

WARNING: Before attempting to field strip or disassemble ANY firearm, always keep your finger off the trigger and hold the weapon with the muzzle pointed in a safe direction.

ALWAYS assume that a firearm is loaded and capable of being discharged until you have personally verified that it is not loaded.

ALWAYS open and inspect any loading port, remove any magazine, open the action and inspect the chamber and loading areas before beginning to disassemble any firearm.

ANSCHÜTZ 1422/1522D RIFLES

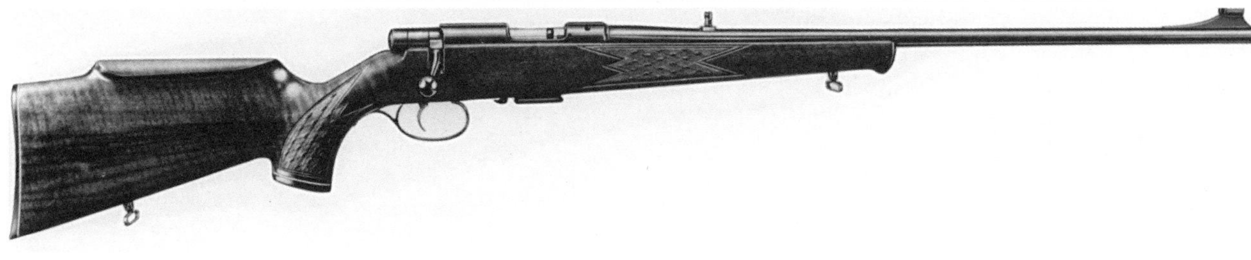

PARTS LEGEND

1. Bolt assembly
2. Spring clamp
3. Extractor
4. Cartridge retainer
5. Bolt body
6. Catch bolt
7. Catch bolt spring
8. Bolt handle
9. Spring support, front
10. Firing pin spring
11. Spring support. rear
12. Firing pin
13. Signal pin with spring
14. Cover sleeve
15. Safety
17. Dummy screw (4)
18. Bolt guide
19. Grooved pin
20. Parallel pin (2)
21. Receiver
22. Compression spring
23. Bolt stop
24. Magazine guide
25. Magazine retainer
26. Parallel pin
27. Torsional spring
28. Guide tongue
29. Cheese head screw
    29a. Toothed lock washer
30. Shoulder screw
31. Parallel pin
33. Bead
34. Countersunk head screw (2)
35. Safety plug
36. Front sight hood
37. Front sight base
38. Barrel
39. Folding sight
    39a. Rear sight blade
    39b. Rear sight blade screws (2)
40. Tangent sight
    40a. Sight elevator
    40b. Adjusting screw
    40c. Sleeve
    40d. Rear sight blade
    40e. Pan head screw (2)
41. Abutment
42. Trigger assembly
43. Compression spring
44. Parallel pin
45. Trigger bracket
46. Round head rivet
47. Trigger support with trigger
48. Compression screw
49. Adjusting screw
50. Set screw
51. Toothed lock washer
52. Hexagon nut
53. Cheese head screw
55. 5-shot magazine
56. 10-shot magazine
57. Magazine housing
58. Magazine housing
59. Magazine follower
60. Follower spring
61. Follower spring
62. Magazine floor
63. Screw nut
64. Stock with partial fittings
65. Front swivel
66. Hexagon nut
    66a. Toothed lock washer
67. Floor plate
68. Raised countersunk head screw
69. Raised countersunk head screw
70. Raised countersunk head screw
71. Raised cheese head screw
72. Trigger guard
73. Raised countersunk head screw
74. Rear swivel
75. Butt plate
76. Countersunk oval head wood screw (2)
77. Double set trigger assembly
78. Compression spring
79. Parallel pin
80. Parallel pin
81. Trigger bracket
82. Release lever
83. Trigger spring
    83a. Cheese head screw
84. Set trigger housing
85. Parallel pin
86. Parallel pin
87. Double set trigger spring
88. Adjusting screw
    88a. Safety plug
89. Front trigger
90. Rear trigger

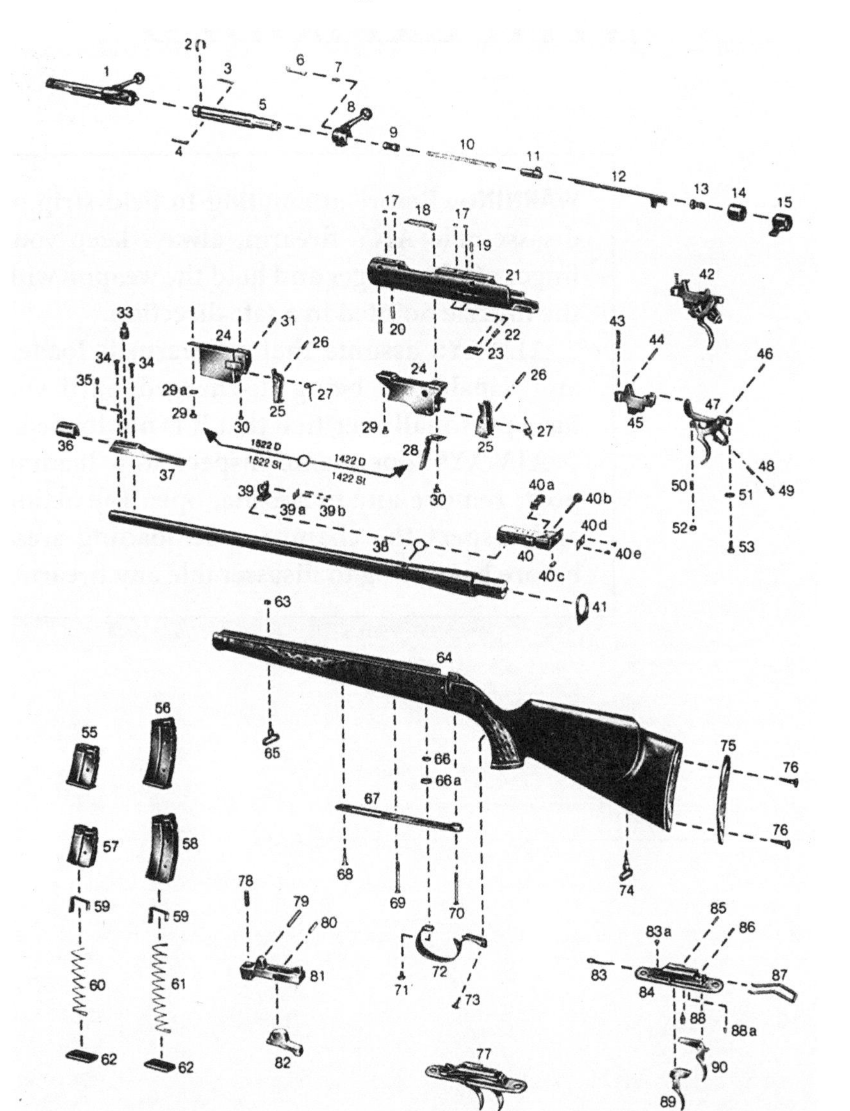

The Anschütz line of small-caliber sporter rifles was introduced in 1954 with the Model 1422 D, marketed in the United States as the Savage-Anschutz Model 54 Sporter.

The Model 1432 D debuted the next year in .22 Hornet, and appeared in Mannlicher-stocked garb in 1957 as the Model 1433 D. The .22 Win. Mag. Model 1522 D appeared in 1960, while the Model 1532 D in .222 Rem. was first sold in 1962. It was styled the Savage-Anschütz Model 153 in this country.

Anschutz added "Classic" models of all four rifles in 1982.

The sporters all share the Model 54 action, which dominated smallbore rifle competition for almost three decades until it was superseded by the Anschütz 1800-series action.

DISASSEMBLY

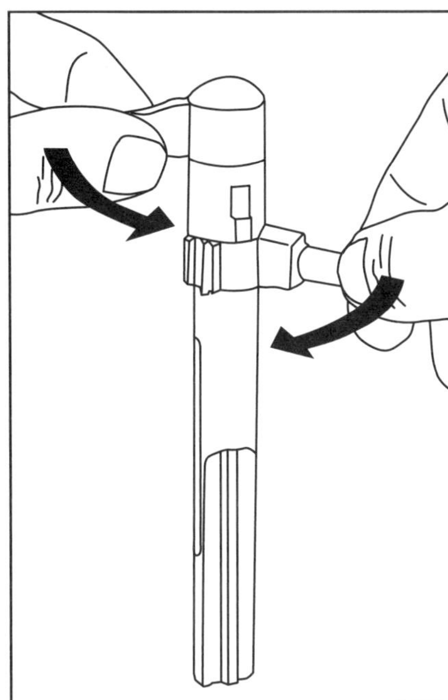

1 Be sure the rifle is pointed in a safe direction. the magazine is removed and the chamber is empty. Raise the safety to the horizontal position, depress the bolt stop and retract the bolt from the receiver. Turn the bolt handle clockwise and the wing safety counter-clockwise as far as they will go.

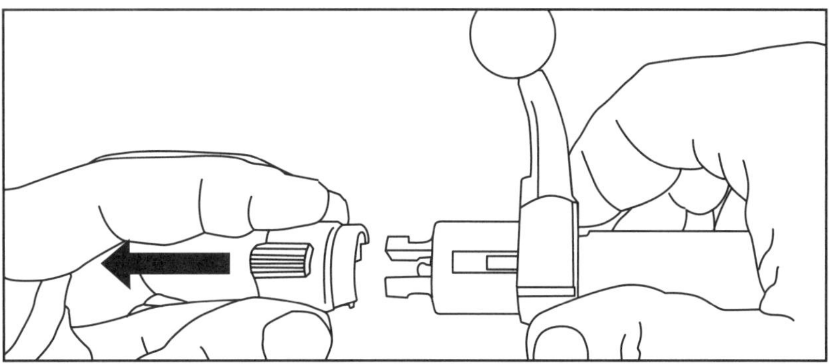

2 In 1532-series rifles, depress the catch at the base of the bolt handle. Hold the bolt with the safety up and remove the safety along with the cocking indicator and spring.

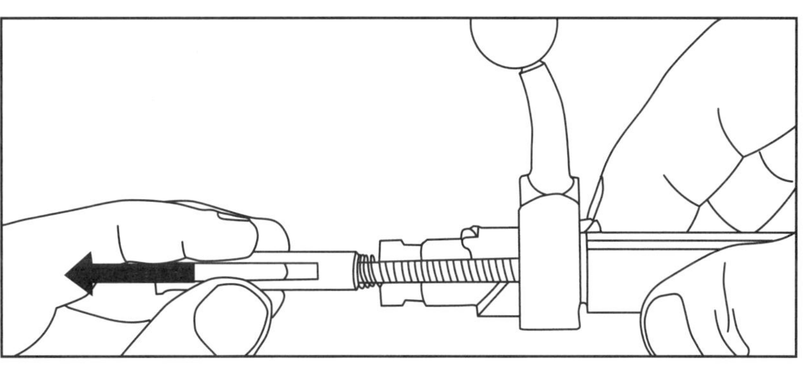

3 After removing the cover sleeve, remove the firing pin assembly and the bolt handle assembly.

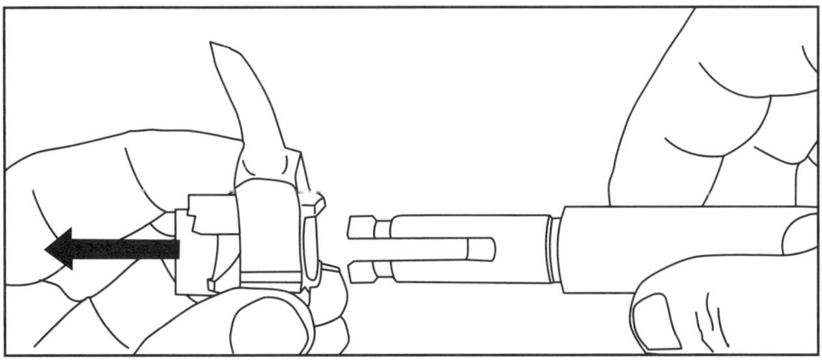

4 To reassemble the bolt, reverse the procedure. To uncock the bolt. lift the bolt handle as high as it will go, depress the trigger fully and turn the bolt handle down. The cocking indicator should not project from the rear of the bolt. To dismount the barreled action from the stock, remove the countersunk head screws (Nos. 69 and 70) from either end of the trigger guard. Further disassembly should not be necessary for routine maintenance. To reassemble, reverse the procedure, insuring that no moving parts are contacting the inside walls of the stock. Be sure to tighten the takedown screws equally with a screwdriver.

ARMALITE AR-7 .22 RIFLE

PARTS LEGEND

1. Front sight
2. Front sight roll pin
3. Barrel
4. Barrel nut
5. Bolt
6. Firing pin roll pin
7. Extractor
8. Extractor spring
9. Charging handle
10. Extractor roll pin
11. Firing pin
12. Bolt action springs (2)
13. Bolt spring guide
14. Receiver
15. Safety
16. Safety ball detent
17. Rear sight screw
18. Rear sight
19. Safety snap ring
20. Magazine
21. Trigger
22. Trigger spring support pin
23. Magazine latch
24. Magazine latch spring
25. Ejector
26. Hammer and trigger spring
27. Hammer
28. Hammer pivot pin
29. Receiver side plate
30. Receiver side plate screw
31. Stock
32. Stock take down screw
33. Stock take down screw nut
34. Nut roll pin
35. Stock butt cap

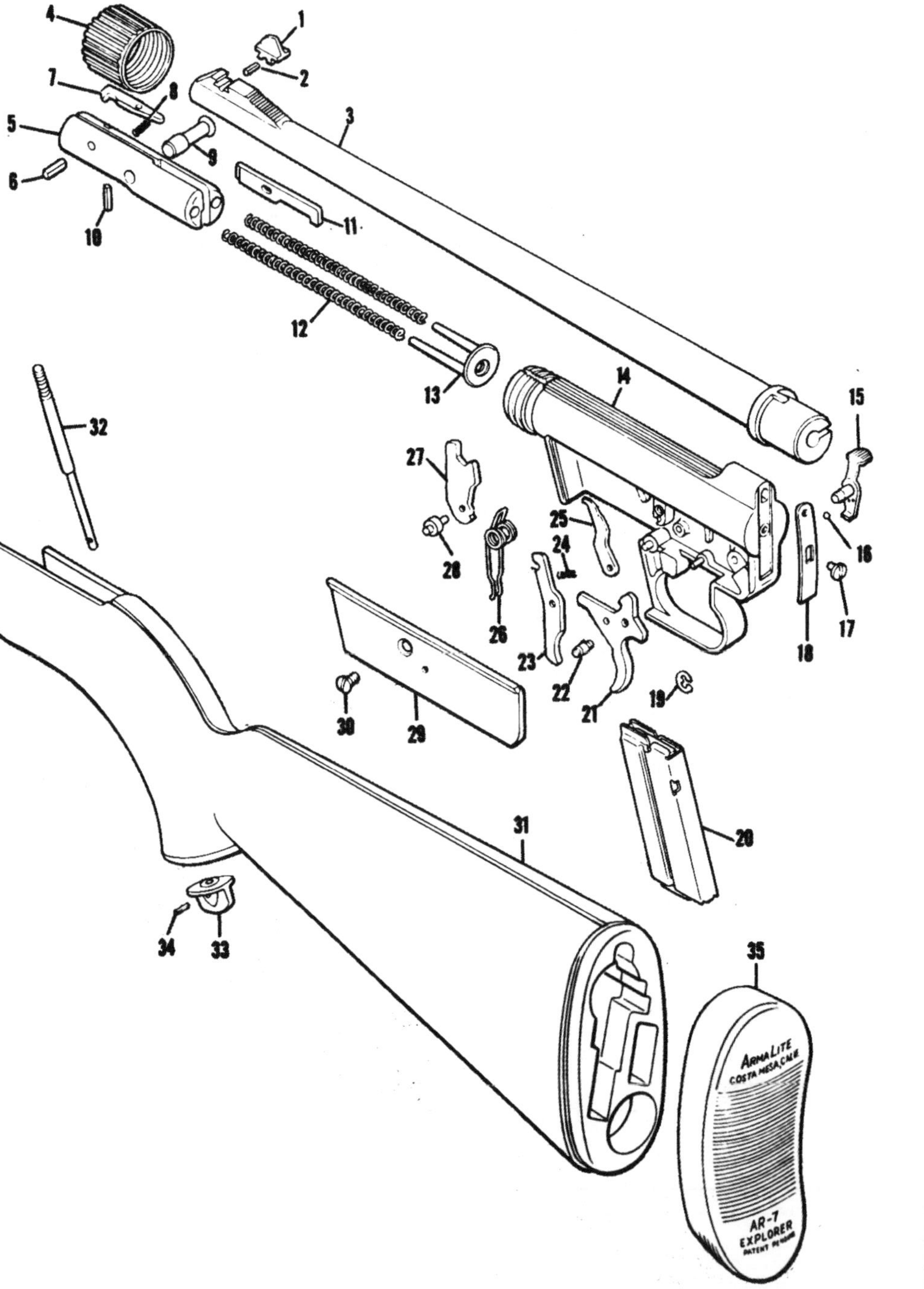

The AR-7 Explorer rifle was introduced in 1960 by Armalite Inc., of Costa Mesa, Calif. An outgrowth of a U.S. Air Force program to select an aircrew survival rifle, the AR-7 is a blowback operated selfloader chambered for the .22 Long Rifle cartridge. Extremely light in weight, the rifle has an aluminum alloy receiver and a plastic buttstock in which the disassembled barrel and action can be stowed.

The 16-inch-long barrel is constructed of steel reinforced aluminum and is secured to the receiver by a knurled nut. Cartridges are fed from an 8-round detachable box magazine.

With the butt cap in place on the stock, the AR-7 rifle will float in water in both the stored and ready for use modes. It weighs but two pounds, 14 ounces and when assembled is 35⅛ inches in overall length.

Ammlite produced the AR-7 until 1973, when they sold manufacturing rights to Charter Arms Corp., of Stratford, Connecticut and, in 1990, Charter Arms sold the rights to Survival Arms, in Cocoa, Florida. Since 1997, the AR-7 has been produced by Henry Repeating Arms of Brooklyn, New York and AR-7 Industries of Meriden, Connecticut..

DISASSEMBLY

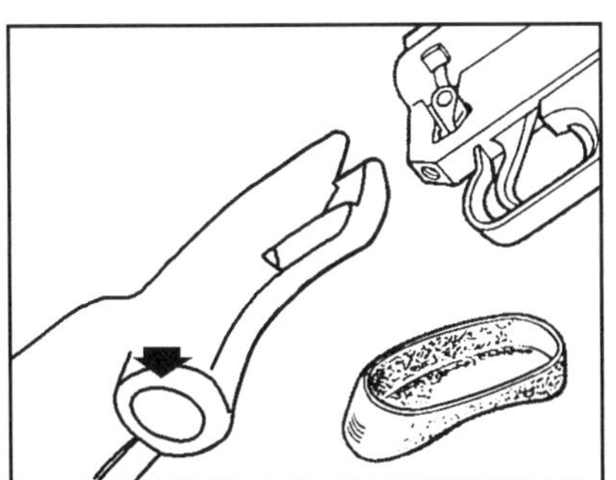

1 The AR-7 is easy to assemble and take down. Remove stock butt cap (35) and withdraw barrel, receiver assembly, and magazine. Insert rear of receiver (14) into its corresponding slots in front of stock (31). Turn stock takedown screw (32) in base of pistol grip until it threads into receiver and locks the two together.

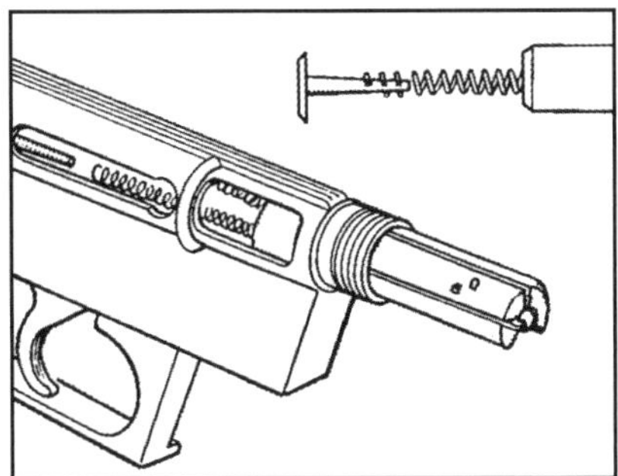

2 After stock and receiver have been assembled, barrel can be installed. When joining barrel (3) to receiver, be sure key on barrel lines up with slot in receiver. Then push them together and thread barrel nut (4) over receiver until it is hand tight.

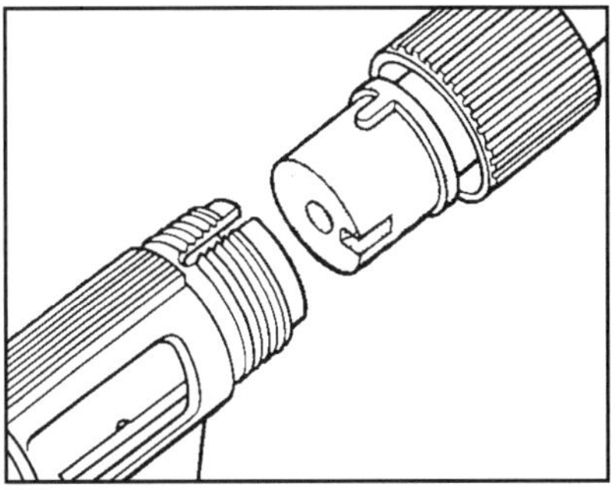

3 The charging handle (9) must be pushed crosswise into bolt when receiver is stowed in stock. The charging handle can only be removed when barrel is out. Insert a finger or dowel into front of receiver. Push bolt (5) back slightly until charging handle lines up exactly with circular cutout in receiver, and then pull charging handle out.

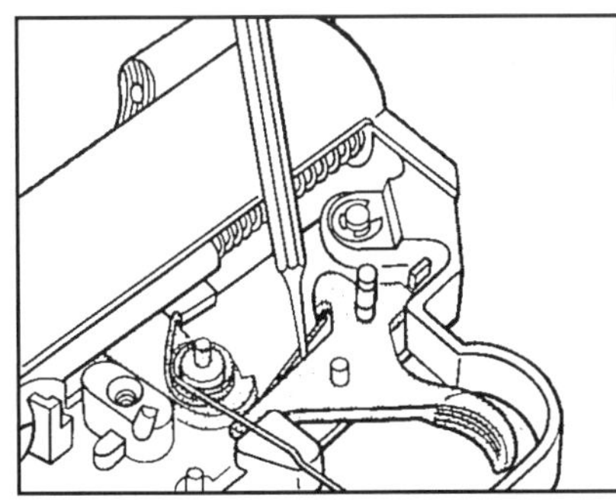

4 To remove bolt, first cock gun and remove charging handle. Insert a finger into receiver and press bolt back slightly to free it; then ease it out through front of receiver. When replacing bolt, be sure plastic rods on bolt spring guide (13) slide inside bolt action springs (12); then push bolt in and replace cocking handle.

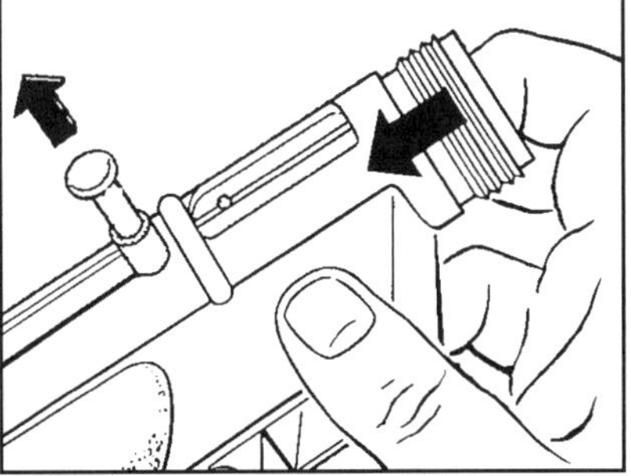

5 To expose the mechanism, first uncock gun; then remove the receiver side plate screw (30) and receiver side plate (29). Before removing internal parts, unhook hammer and trigger spring (26). When replacing parts, install hammer (27) and hammer and trigger spring; then trigger (21). Hold inside leg of spring up as shown and push trigger spring support pin (22) half way through trigger. Release inside leg of spring and lift outer leg over trigger spring support pin.

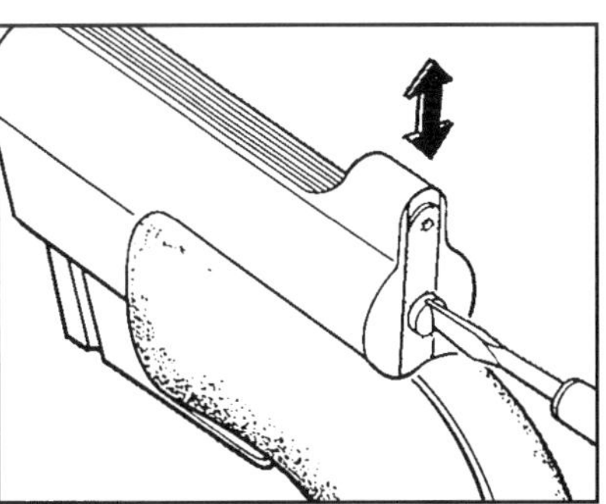

6 To adjust rear sight, loosen rear sight screw (17) and move rear sight (18) up or down.

BALLARD RIFLE

PARTS LEGEND

1. Barrel
2. Front sight
3. Receiver
4. Rear sight
5. Rear sight screw (2)
6. Stock lug
7. Forearm
8. Forearm insert
9. Forearm screw
10. Lever link
11. Breechblock, left
12. Breechblock, right
13. Firing pin
14. Hammer
15. Mainspring
16. Trigger spring
17. Trigger
18. Block screw (3)
19. Hammer screw
20. Rear block screw
21. Finger lever
22. Lever link screw
23. Extractor
24. Lever screw
25. Stock insert
26. Stock bolt
27. Buttplate
28. Buttplate screw (2)

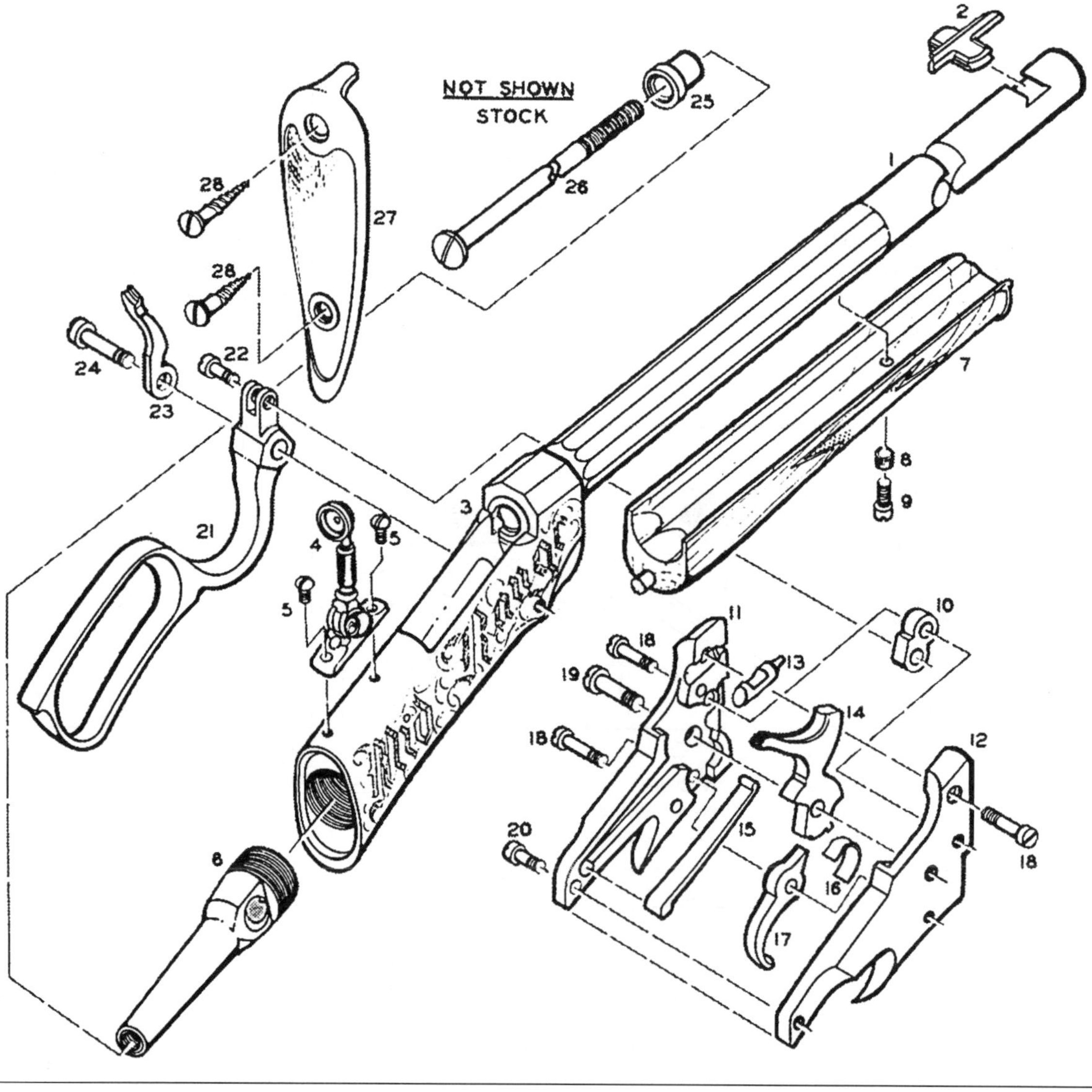

NOT SHOWN
STOCK

On Nov. 5, 1861, C. H. Ballard of Worcester, Mass., was granted U. S. Patent No. 33.631 protecting a lever-operated, single-shot rifle action. The initial manufacture of Ballard-action rifles was by Ball & Williams, of Worcester, Massachusetts. During the Civil War the firm sold 20,000 Ballard rifles to the State of Kentucky and furnished the U. S. Government 1509 carbines and 35 rifles. In 1866 production of Ballard rifles was taken over by the Merrimack Arms & Mfg. Co. of Newburyport, Massachusetts, and in 1869 by the Brown Mfg. Co. of the same city, which ceased production of Ballard rifles in 1873.

In 1875 Ballard rifle production was resumed by J. M. Marlin of New Haven, Conn. In 1881 this firm became the Marlin Firearms Co., but there was no break in production of Ballard rifles. The exact date that Marlin discontinued Ballard rifle production is unknown, but 1891 appears to be the final year.

During a production period that spanned 30 years the Ballard rifle earned an enviable reputation for both accuracy and reliability. Ballard actions were often used as the basis of custom target rifles and it is not uncommon to encounter .22 caliber match rifles with Ballard actions in regular use by top-flight competitors.

Early Ballard rifles are relatively crude in comparison with the late models produced by the Marlin Firearms Co., but the basic action style remained substantially unchanged. Early Ballards were made for rimfire cartridges and some incorporated an auxiliary nipple, which permitted use of loose powder and ball ignited by percussion cap. An improvement by Marlin was a reversible firing pin to allow use of both center-fire and rimfire cartridges.

Receivers and breechblocks of rimfire rifles were usually of casehardened cast iron, but these parts were often forged for use with larger center-fire cartridges. Several different types of extractors, finger levers, and set trigger arrangements will be noted in the various models and makes of the Ballard rifle. Factory chamberings ranged from the .22 short up to and including the powerful .45-100-2⅞-inch Sharps.

DISASSEMBLY

1 To disassemble the Ballard rifle, first open action, then remove lever screw (arrow-24). Holding extractor (23) in place with left thumb, pull action down and forward and thence away.

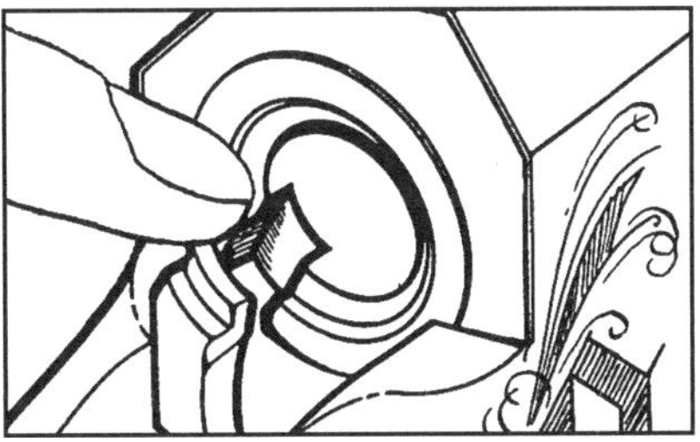

2 Remove extractor by flicking it out with a finger tip.

3 Next, holding action firmly, remove block screw (18) which retains lever link (10) in forward recess of breech-block. The finger lever (21), lever link, and lever link screw (22) may be lifted away from breechblock.

4 Remove hammer screw (19), rear block screw (20), and 2 remaining block screws (18). Using a small length of ¾ inch wide hardwood slat, pry halves of breechblock (11 and 12) apart by inserting slat into forward recess and twisting. This will separate breechblock and expose all internal working parts.

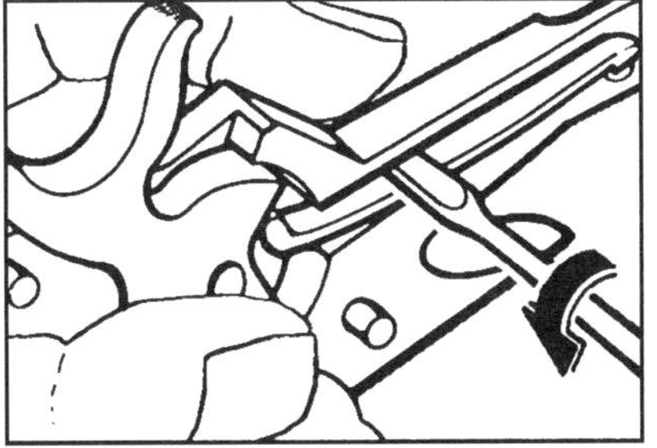

5 Continue by lifting away firing pin (13). Relieve spring tension on hammer (14) by placing a screwdriver blade against topmost surface of mainspring recess and top surface of mainspring, then twist slightly to depress mainspring. Hammer may be lifted out and away. Remove trigger (17) and trigger spring (16). Reassemble in reverse order.

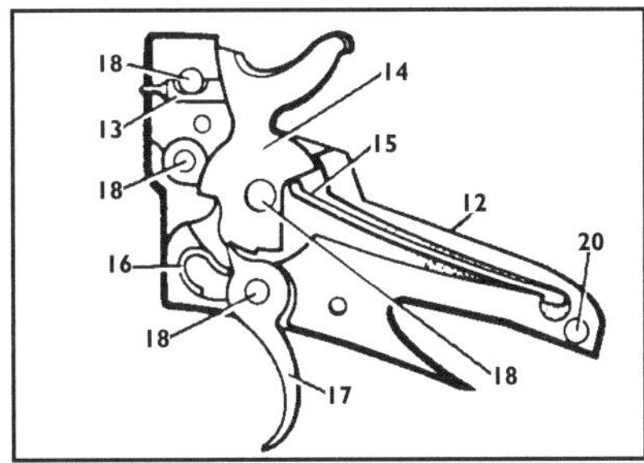

Side view of right breechblock half shows relative position of component parts.

BARRET 95 RIFLE

PARTS LEGEND

1. Lock pins (2)
2. Lock knob
3. Bipod assembly
4. Front lock pin
5. Recoil pad
6. Recoil pad screws (20
7. Bipod shim bushings (2)
8. Yoke mounts (2)
9. Yoke mount nuts (2)
10. Yoke mount washers (2)
11. Pistol grip
12. Pistol grip screw
13. Pistol grip washer
14. Safety
15. Safety spring
16. Safety detent
17. Magazine catch
18. Magazine catch spring
19. Magazine catch pin
20. Trigger pins (2)
21. Sear pin
22. Trigger over-travel screw
23. Sear spring
24. Trigger spring
25. Sear
26. Trigger complete
27. Barrel spring screws
28. Scope base screws
29. Muzzle brake shim kit
30. Muzzle brake screw
31. Barrel complete
32. Barrel extension screws (not shown)
33. Barrel screws
34. Upper receiver complete
35. Barrel nut
36. Scope base mounting rail
37. Muzzle brake
38. Ejector pin
39. Firing pin pin
40. Extractor
41. Extractor spring
42. Extractor plunger
43. Firing pin
44. Cocking piece
45. Bolt carrier
46. Bolt carrier pin
47. Bolt carrier hair pin
48. Firing springs
49. Bolt complete
50. Ejector
51. Ejector spring

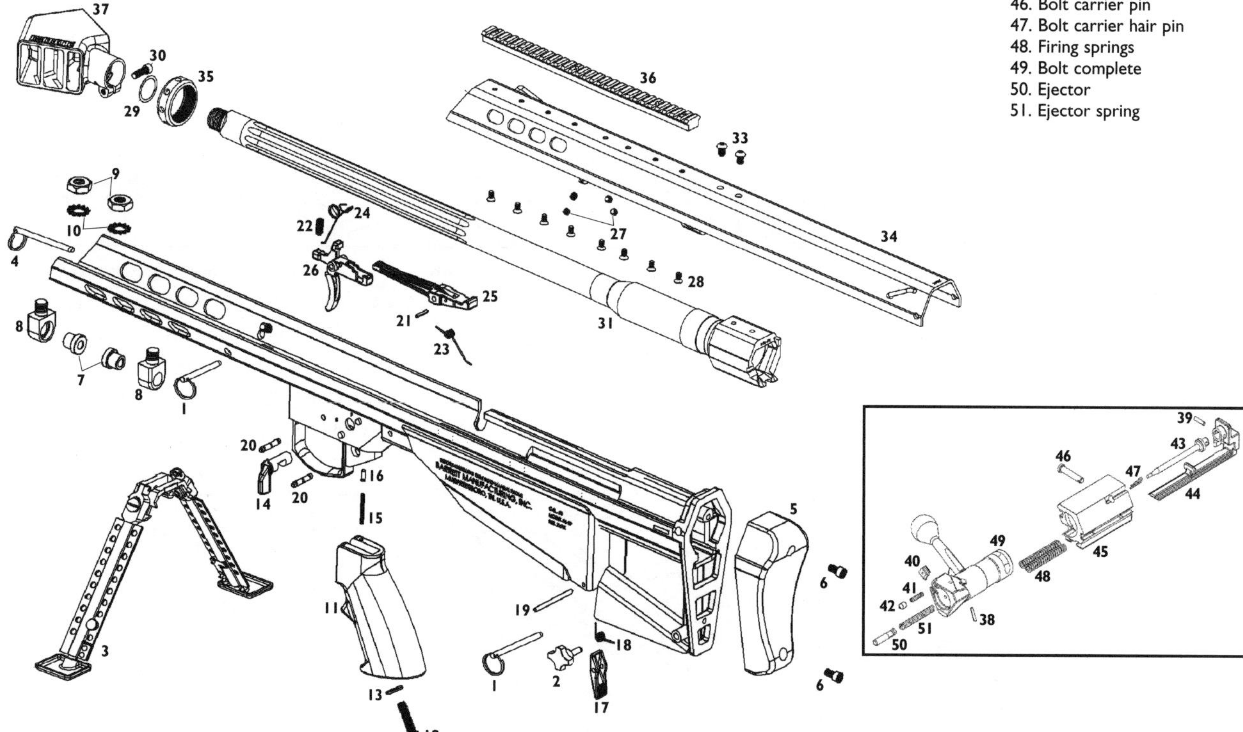

In 1982, firearms designer Ronnie Barrett built a handmade prototype for a shoulder-fired, .50 caliber rifle in his Murfreesboro, Tennessee one-bay garage. Barrett's prototype led to the production in 1986 of the short-recoil, semi-automatic Model 82 rifle. A bolt-action version, the Model 90, was replaced in 1995 by the Model 95 and was subsequently adopted as a long-range sniper rifle, designated the XM107, by the U. S. Army.

The Model 95 is an extreme large bore, magazine-fed bolt-action rifle, firing the .50 caliber BMG round originally intended for the Army's Browning .50 caliber Machine Gun. It has a bullpup design with an overall length of 45 inches and a 29-inch match-grade, chrome-chambered, fluted barrel. The buttplate, magazine well, and trigger housing act to reinforce the lower receiver and the upper receiver is reinforced by a steel, M1913 optics rail. The rifle is supported by a lightweight front bipod and optional adjustable rear monopod. The rifle can be fitted with the Barrett Optical Ranging System, an integrated electronic ballistic computer coupled to the rifle telescope.

BARRET

DISASSEMBLY

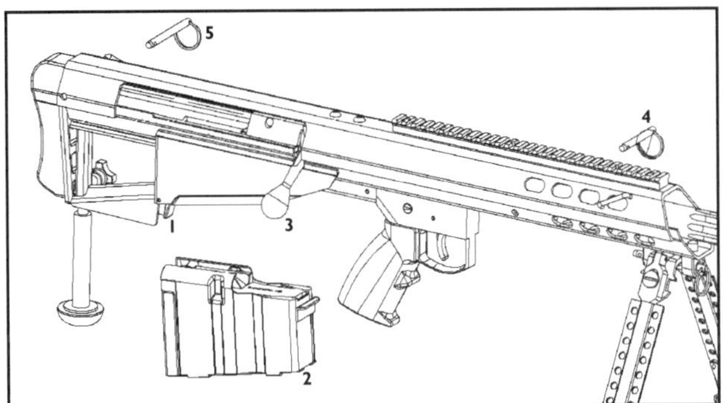

1 After deploying bipod legs to upright position, let rifle rest on its butt so that it is freestanding. Depress the magazine catch (1) and remove magazine (2) from the rifle. Unlock the bolt (3) by lifting the bolt handle upward and pulling it to the rear. Withdraw the mid lock pin (4) and rear lock pin (5) from the receiver.

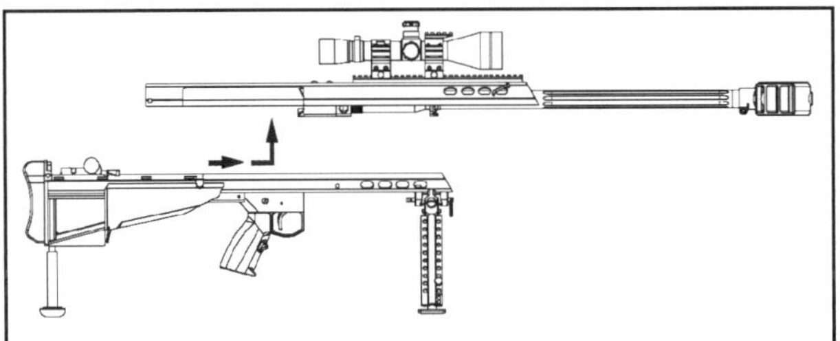

2 Grasp the upper receiver and barrel. Slide them forward about ½ inch (13 mm). Then lift the upper receiver assembly off lower receiver assembly. NOTE: No further disassembly of the upper receiver is necessary.

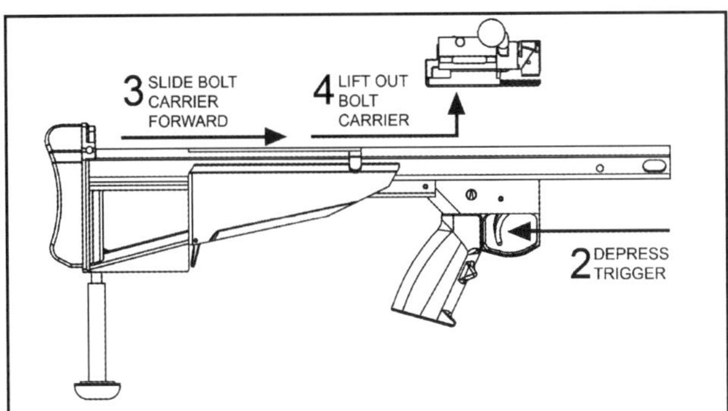

3 To remove the bolt carrier from the lower receiver assembly, place the safety switch on "FIRE," pull the trigger, then slide bolt carrier forward and lift it off the rails.

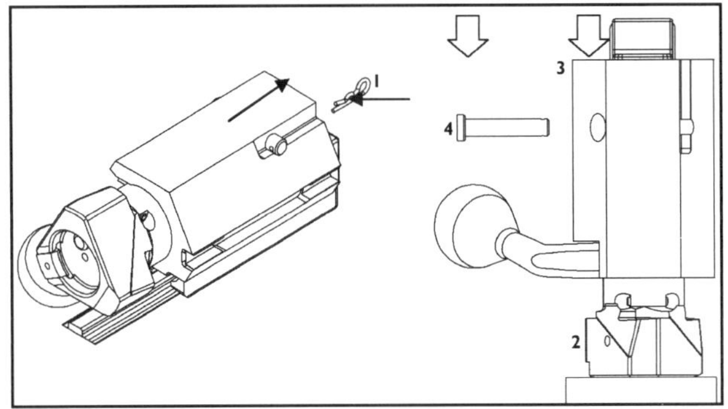

4 De-cock action by lowering the bolt handle. Remove the hair pin (1). While compressing the bolt (2) into bolt carrier (3), remove the bolt pin (4). Now remove the bolt from the bolt carrier assembly.

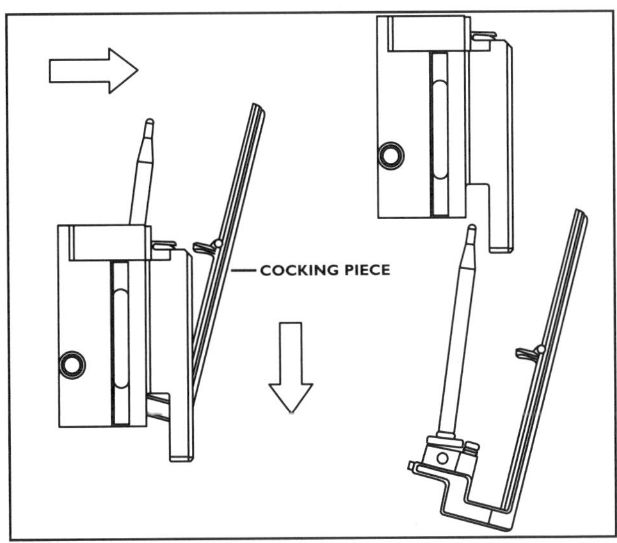

5 Pivot the cocking piece so that spring retainer clears the bolt carrier, then remove it from the rear of the bolt carrier. Remove the two firing springs. No further disassembly of bolt carrier assembly is necessary. NOTE: Removal of the firing pin from the cocking piece isn't necessary as long as the firing pin is freely pivoting on its retaining pin. Ensure the firing pin can move freely about ¾ inch (20mm).

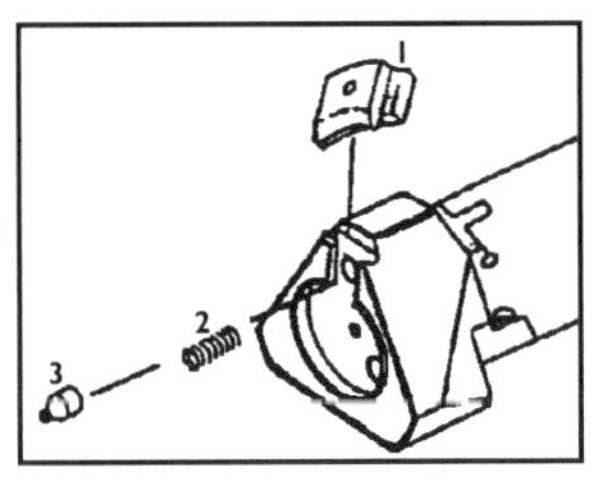

6 WARNING: The extractor is under spring pressure and is held in place by the ejector pin. Wear safety glasses when removing the ejector pin. NOTE: Removal of the extractor is not recommended unless it is broken or does not move freely back and forth. To remove the extractor (1), depress the extractor plunger by inserting a 1/16 inch (1.5 mm) pin punch or the end of a paper clip (2) through the extractor hole while simultaneously sliding the extractor away from the firing pin hole. Slide the extractor (1) out of its slot. The extractor spring (2), and the extractor plunger (3) can then be removed, but be careful to contain the spring and plunger.

BENELLI M2 SHOTGUN

PARTS LEGEND

1. Trigger group assembly
2. Hammer
3. Hammer spring cap
4. Hammer spring
5. Hammer disconnector
6. Disconnector plunger
7. Safety plunger springs
8. Hand safety plunger
9. Trigger
10. Trigger pin
11. Trigger spring
12. Safety spring retaining pin
13. Hand safety button
14. Trigger guard
15. Trigger guard pin
16. Trigger pin bushing
17. Carrier
18 Trigger guard pin spring
19. Bolt stop tooth
20. Bolt stop tooth pin
21. Carrier spring
22. Bolt latch pin
23. Disconnector pin
24. Bolt group
25. Firing pin
26. Bolt
27. Link
28. Firing pin retaining pin
29. Link pin
30. Bolt handle
31. Locking head pin
32. Locking head
33. Extractor spring
34. Extractor
35. Extractor pin
36. Inertia pin
37. Firing pin spring
38. Bolt handle retaining spring
39. Bolt handle pin
40. Bolt handle spring retaining spring
41. Front sight
42. Ejector pin
43. Ejector pin spring
44. Ejector pin spring retaining pin
45. Recoil spring tube
46. Stock retaining nut screw
47. Elastic washer
48. Stock retaining nut
49. Recoil spring
50. Carrier latch pin
51. Carrier latch
52. Carrier latch spring
53. Receiver assembly
54. Self-threaded screw (not shown)
55. Swivel plate (not shown)
56. Magazine spring
57. Magazine follower
58. Magazine tube
59. Ring
60. Magazine tube plug
61. Fore-end retaining cap
62. Cap ball spring
63. Cap retaining ball
64. Ring
65. Cartridge drop lever
66. Cartridge drop lever spring
67. Rear sight protection guard (not shown)
68. Ring (not shown)
69. Magazine spring seal ring
70. Fore-end slide bushing
71. Washer
72. Spring washer
73. Elastic ring
74. Washer
75. Cast change shim
76. Drop change shim
77. Spacer
78. Locking plate.
79. Gel butt plate
80. Carrier latch pin (not shown)
81. Three round limiter for short tube (not shown)
82. Locking head assembly
83. Kit, light loads booster
84. Ejector frame (not shown)
85. Fore-end assembly
86. Ejector retaining rivet
87. Retaining ring
88. Light load assembly
89. Internal choke
90. Disconnector Spring
91. Chevrons assembly
92. Comb insert

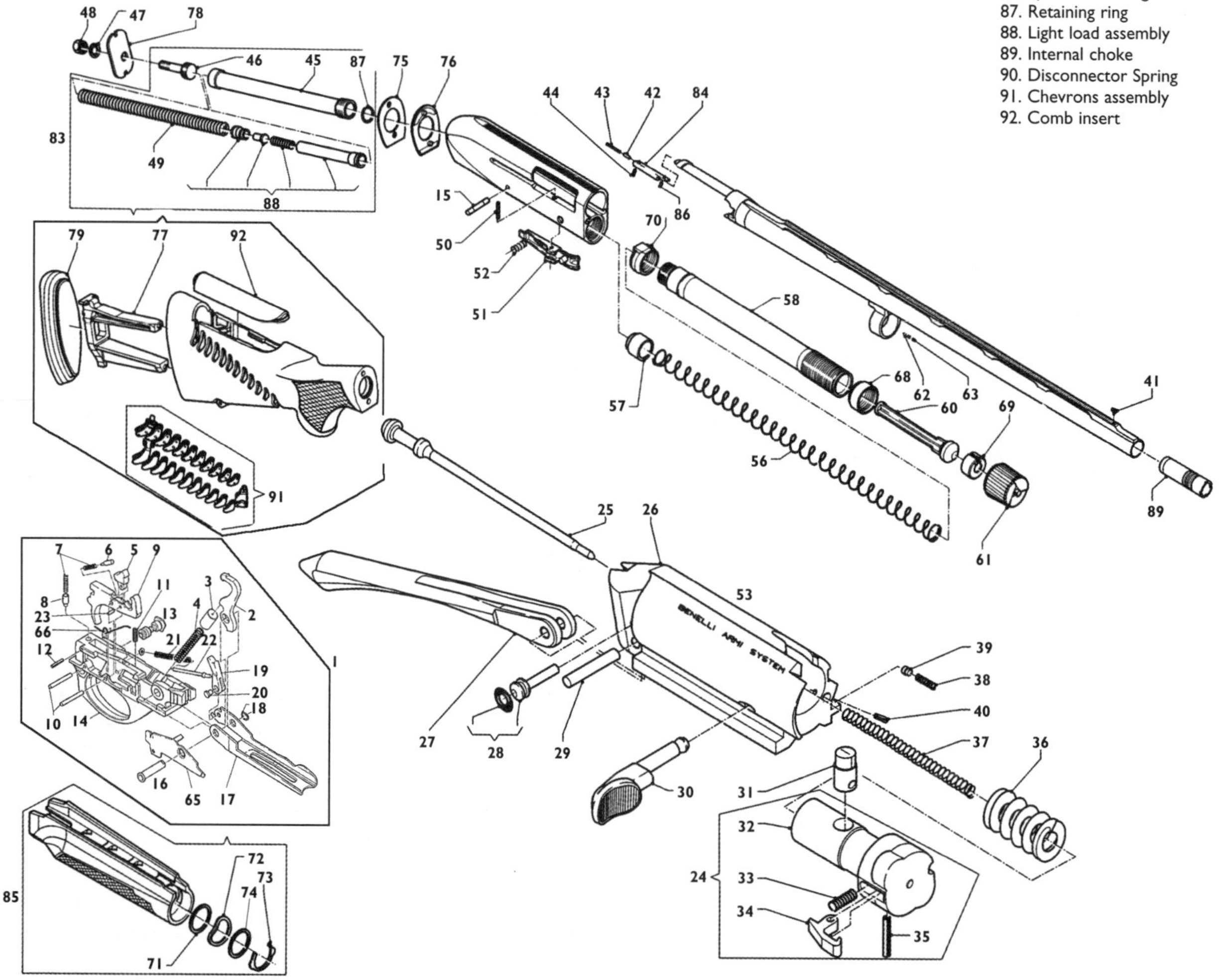

In 1967 Armi Benelli, a subsidiary of the Benelli motorcycle manufacturing firm located in Urbino, Italy, began small-scale production of shotguns. In 1983 the company was acquired by Beretta. The M-2 Field, introduced in 2003, was a redesign of Benelli's M1 autoloading shotgun.

In common with several other Benelli semi-automatic shotguns, the M-2 action, developed by Bruno Civolani, operates on an inertial principle using a fixed barrel and the kinetic energy of the recoil to cycle the action. This operating system incorporates a revolving bolt head with two locking heads. The system operates using a spring inserted between the locking head and bolt. As the shotgun recoils, the inert breech bolt moves forward to compress the spring. The fully compressed spring then propels the breech bolt to the rear extracting the spent shell before reloading another on the return movement.

The M-2 is fitted with the Benelli "Comfortech" recoil reduction system that incorporates chevron-shaped flexible inserts into the sides of the polymer stock, which allow the polymer stock to flex. There are also two gel pads, on the butt and comb, and a recoil tube assembly in the stock.

DISASSEMBLY

Slacken the screw and remove the barrel-magazine tube retaining ring from its seat on the magazine tube (only in versions equipped with long magazine tube or with magazine tube extension).

NOTE: during removal, expand the retaining ring slightly so that it can be slid over the magazine tube without binding.

Unscrew the fore-end cap and remove from magazine tube.

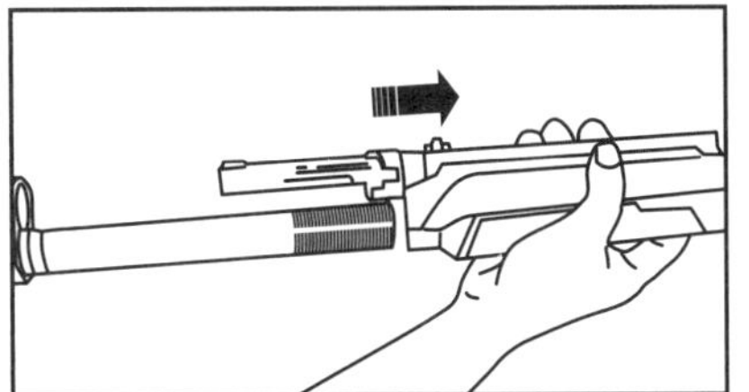

1 Take the gun in one hand and with the other, open the bolt; should the bolt fail to engage, move the cartridge drop lever as arrowed and repeat the operation. Keeping a grip on the shotgun with one hand, with the other take hold of the barrel-fore end unit and detach it completely from the receiver by pulling it forward and making it slip off the magazine tube. Separate the fore-end from the barrel-breech unit, by slipping it out of the barrel guide ring. Take a firm hold of the bolt handle and simultaneously press the carrier slowly forward until it stops.

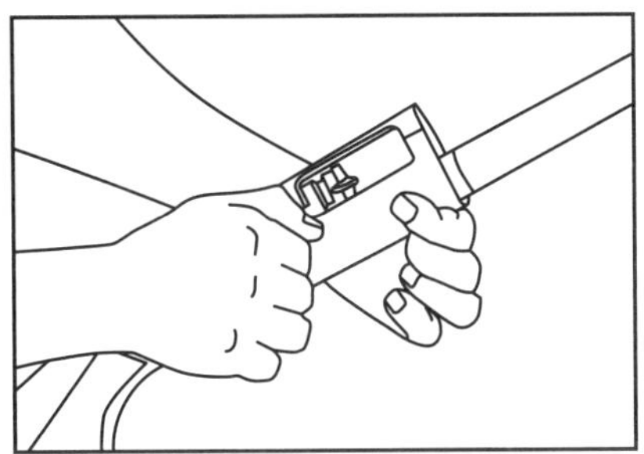

2 Pull the bolt handle off with a firm tug.

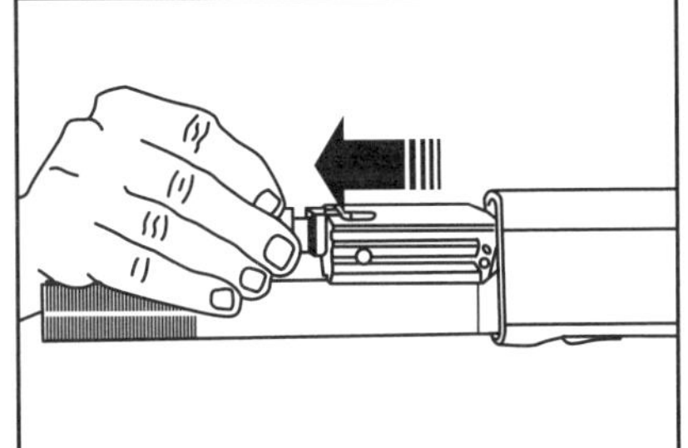

3 Pull the bolt assembly out of the receiver, sliding it along its guides.

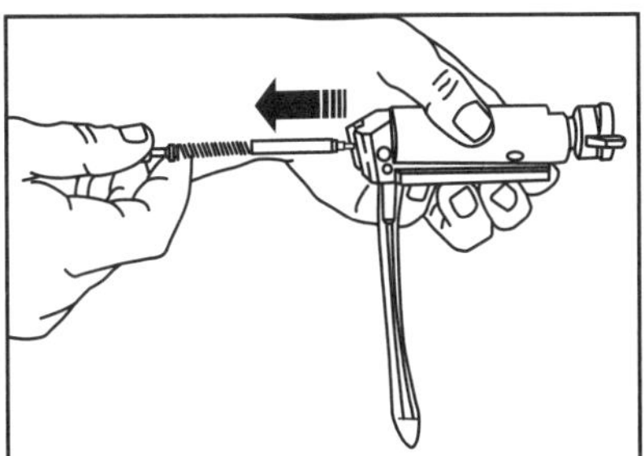

4 Remove the firing pin retaining pin from the bolt assembly, while holding the firing pin and firing pin spring in place. Remove the firing pin and firing pin spring from the bolt.

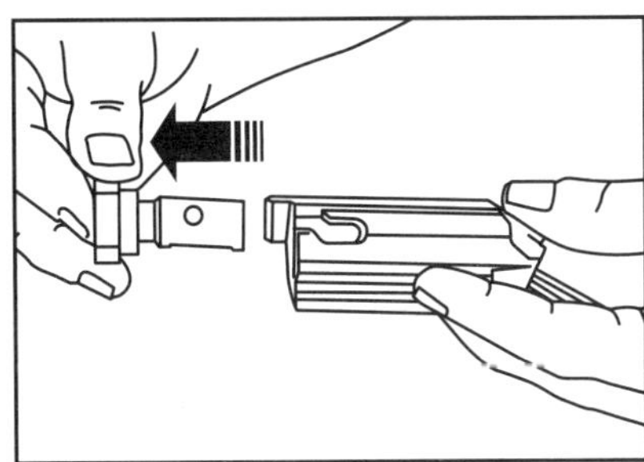

5 Remove the locking head pin from the bolt. Remove the bolt locking head from the bolt.

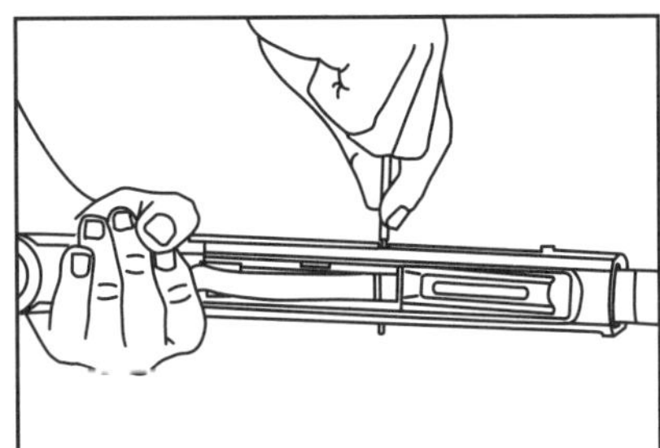

6 Remove the inertia spring from its seat in the bolt. Extract the trigger group stop plug from the stock-receiver unit, thrusting it from right or left with the point of the same firing pin or punch.

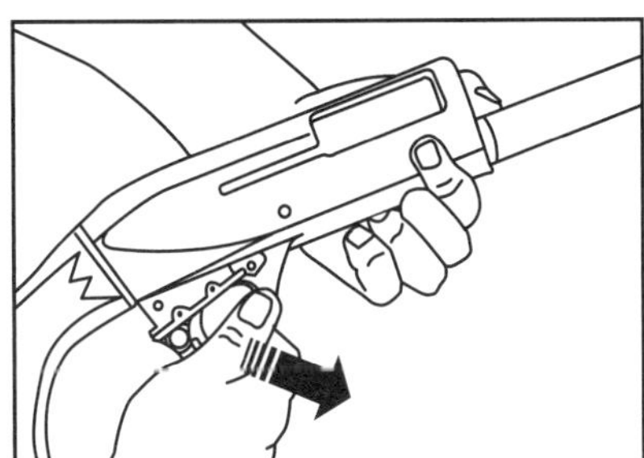

7 Press the carrier release button and extract the trigger guard assembly towards the front. The shotgun is now completely stripped. All the parts that require routine maintenance and cleaning are disassembled.

BENELLI SUPER BLACK EAGLE II

PARTS LEGEND

1. Trigger group assembly
2. Hammer
3. Hammer spring cap
4. Hammer spring
5. Hammer disconnector
7. Safety plunger spring
8. Hand safety plunger
9. Trigger
10. Trigger pins
11. Trigger spring
12. Safety spring retaining pin
13. Hand safety button
14. Trigger Guard
15. Trigger guard pin
16. Trigger pin bush
17. Carrier
18 Trigger guard pin springs
19. Bolt stop tooth
20. Bolt stop tooth pin
21. Carrier spring
22. Bolt latch pin
23. Disconnector pin
24. Bolt group
25. Firing pin
26. Bolt
27. Link
28. Firing pin retaining pin
29. Link pin
30. Bolt handle
31. Locking head pin
32. Locking head
33. Extractor pin
34. Extractor
35. Extractor pin
36. Inertia spring
37. Firing pin spring
38. Bolt handle retaining spring
39. Bolt handle pin
40. Bolt handle spring retaining spring
41. Front sight
42. Ejector pin
43. Ejector pin spring
44. Ejector pin spring retaining pin
45. Recoil spring tube
46. Stock retaining nut screw
47. Elastic washer
49. Stock retaining nut
50. Recoil spring
51. Carrier latch pin
52. Carrier latch
53. Carrier latch sprint
54. Receiver assembly
55. Self-threaded screw (not shown)
56. Swivel plate (not shown)
57. Magazine spring
58. Magazine follower
59. Magazine tube
60. Intermediate sight
61. Magazine tube plug (not shown)
62. Fore-end cap
63. Cap ball spring
64. Cap retaining ball
65. Ring (not shown)
66. Cartridge drop lever
67. Cartridge drop lever spring
68. Carrier pin
69. Rear sight guard (not shown)
70. Rear sight assembly (not shown)
71. Rear sight screw (not shown)
72. Ring
73. Magazine spring seal ring
74. Fore-end slide bushing
75. Washers
76. Spring washer
77. Elastic ring
78. Elastic ring
79. Cast change shim
80. Drop change shim
81. Spacer
82. Locking plate
83. Butt plate
84. Intermediate sight
85. Disconnector spring
86. Three round limiter
87. Stock assembly
88. Locking head assembly
89. Kit, light loads booster
90. Ejector frame
91. Fore-end assembly
92. Ejector retaining rivet
93. Retaining ring
94. Light load assembly
95. Internal choke

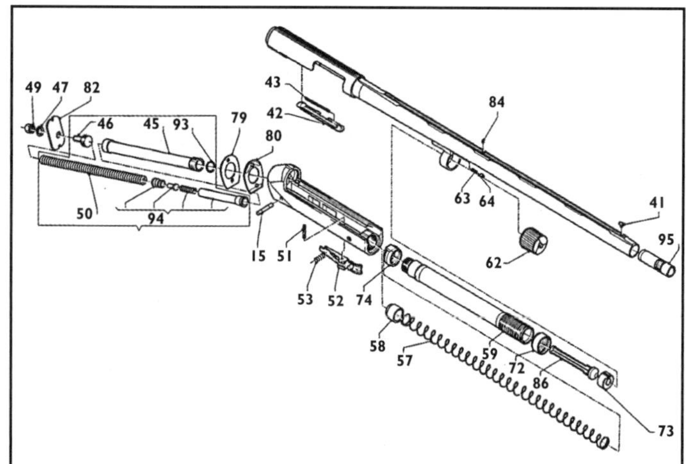

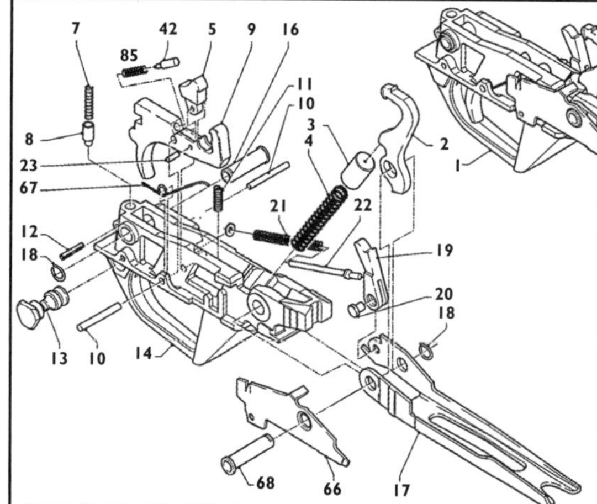

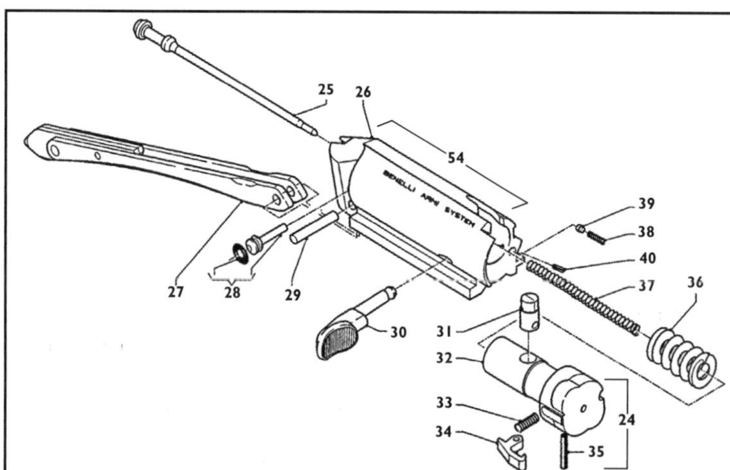

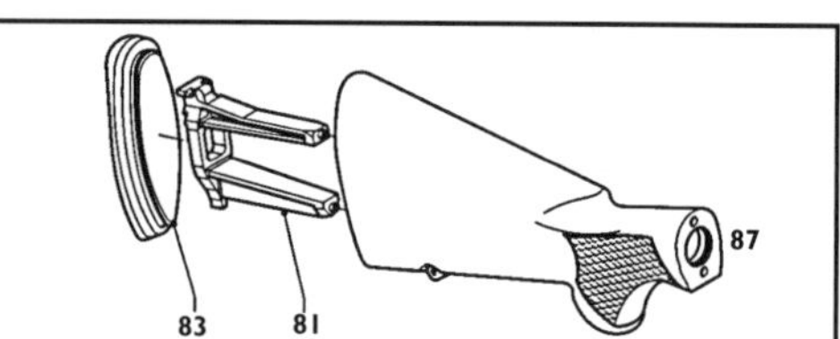

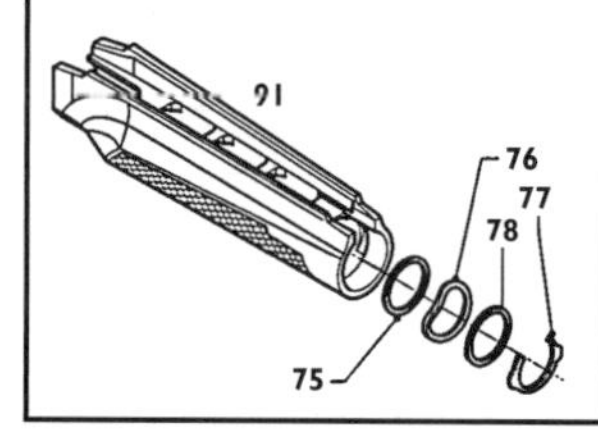

The Benelli Super Black Eagle shotgun, introduced in 1989, was designed to operate with the inertial operating system developed by Bruno Civolani. This action uses a fixed barrel and the kinetic energy of the recoil to cycle the action. It was one of the first semi-automatic shotguns capable of firing 2¾-, 3-, and 3½-inch shells.

In 2004, Benelli introduced the Super Black Eagle II, featuring the ComforTech recoil reduction system, with gel pads on the butt and comb and flexible inserts in a polymer stock. The Comfor Tech system is intended to reduce recoil without adding parts or weight. The barrel of the Super Black Eagle II is treated with the "Crio" process where the finished barrel is subjected to a temperature of -300 F. This is intended to "freeze" the steel and homogenize the stress patterns left by hammer forging.

DISASSEMBLY

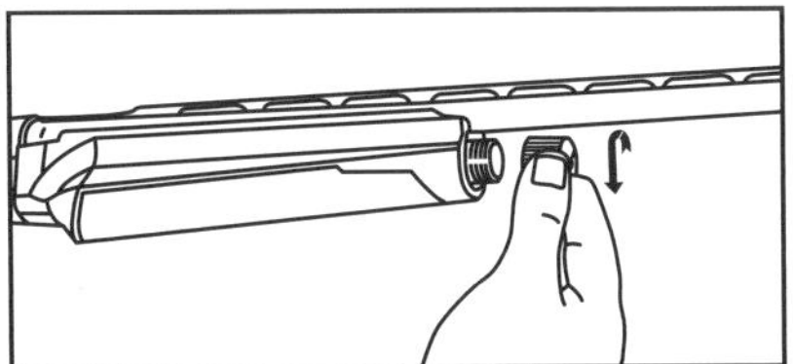

1 Open the bolt by pulling back the bolt handle (30) until the bolt is locked open. Should the bolt fail to engage, move the cartridge drop lever (66) as arrowed and repeat the operation. Pull the bolt handle off with a firm tug. Unscrew the fore-end cap (79) and remove from magazine tube (59).

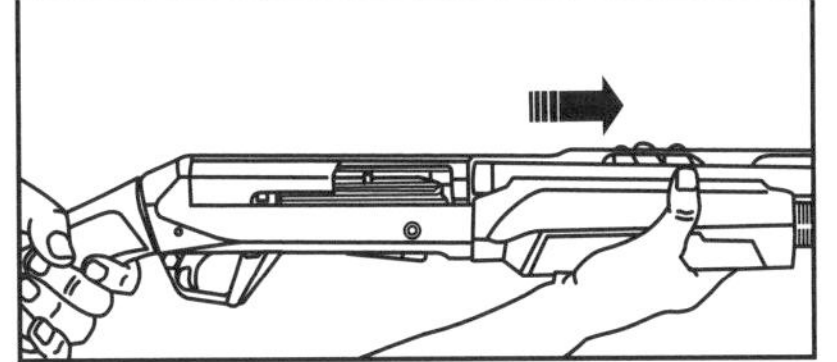

2 While resting the stock against your hip, grab the stock-receiver unit with a hand and the barrel-cover-fore-end unit with the other hand.

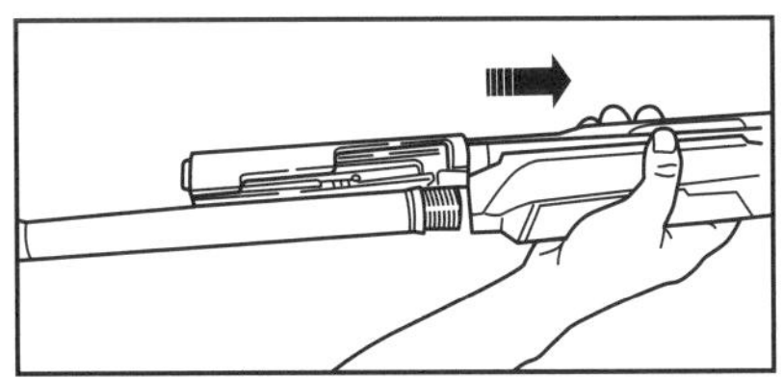

3 Pull the latter forward and completely off the magazine tube.

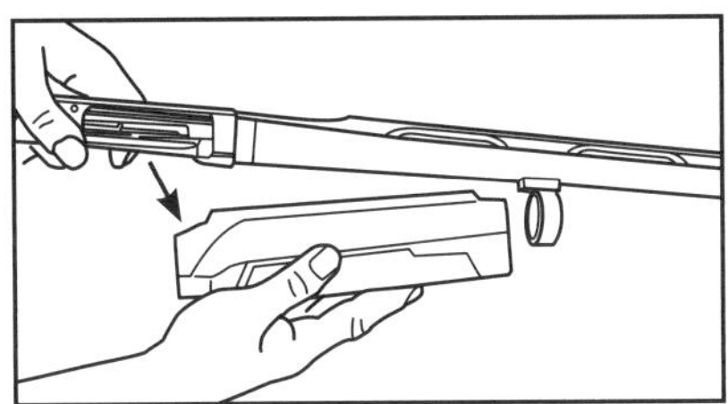

4 Rotate the barrel-cover-fore-end unit (91) downward from the rear and separate it from the barrel by pulling it out of the barrel guide ring.

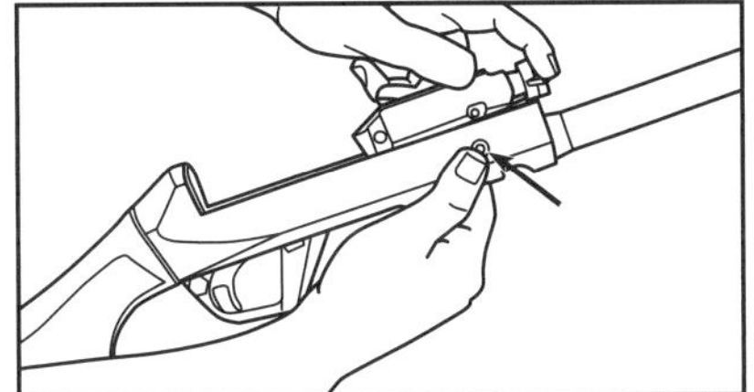

5 While holding the bolt assembly with your hand so as to counter-balance the thrust of the recoil spring (50), push the carrier release button and ease the bolt forward until the recoil spring no longer pushes it forward. Pull the bolt assembly out of the receiver, sliding it along its guides.

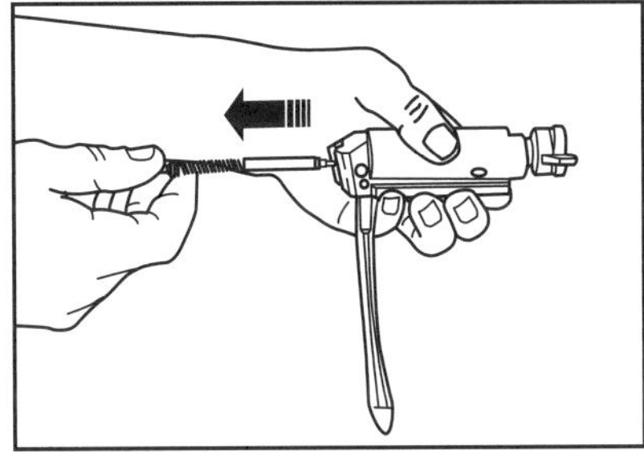

6 Remove the firing pin retaining pin (28) from the bolt assembly, while holding the firing pin (25) and firing pin spring (37) in place. Remove the firing pin and firing pin spring from the bolt.

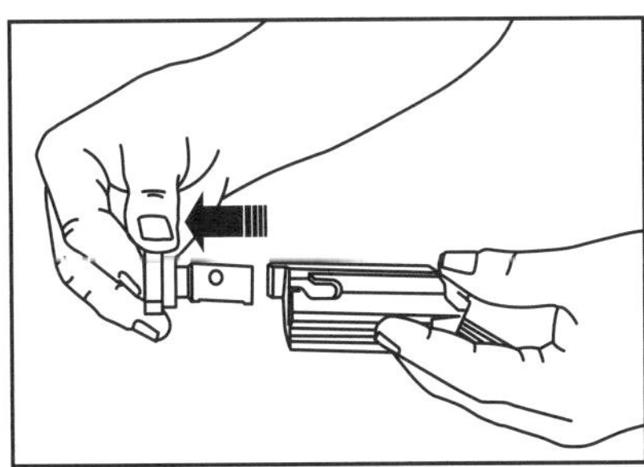

7 Remove the locking head pin from the bolt. Remove the bolt locking head from the bolt. Remove the inertia spring (36) from its seat in the bolt.

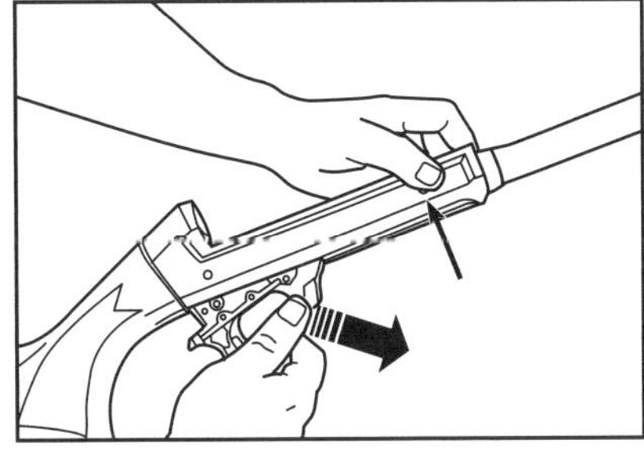

8 Extract the trigger group stop plug from the stock-receiver unit, thrusting it from right or left with the point of a firing pin or punch. Press the carrier release button and extract the trigger guard assembly toward the front. The shotgun is now completely stripped. All the parts that require routine maintenance and cleaning are disassembled.

BERETTA 682 GOLD SHOTGUN

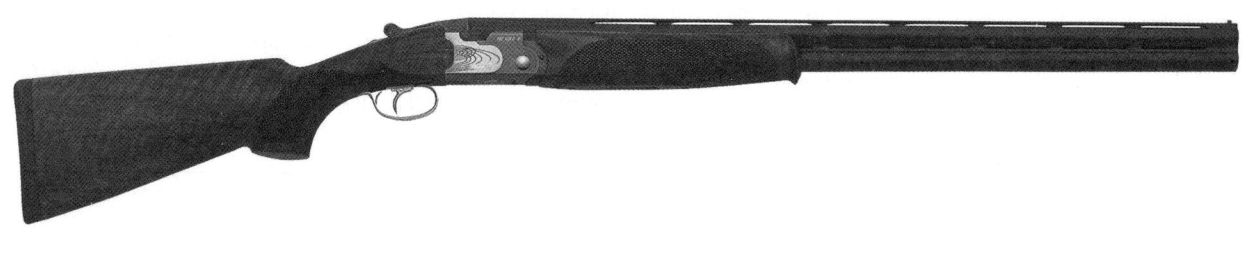

PARTS LEGEND

1. Barrels
2. Front sight
   2a. Intermediate sight
3. Ejector spring
4. Locking shoulder, lower
5. Locking shoulder, upper
6. Ejector plunger
7. Upper ejector
8. Lower ejector
9. Locking shoulder retaining screw
10. Stock
11. Fore-end
12. Fore-end nuts (2)
13. Fore-end iron screw, front
14. Fore-end iron screw, rear
15. Fore-end iron
16. Trigger pin
17. Fore-end iron catch spring
18. Spring pin
19. Fore-end iron catch
20. Fore-end iron lever pin screw
21. Fore-end iron lever plunger
22. Fore-end iron lever spring
23. Fore-end iron lever pin
24. Fore-end iron lever
25. Fore-end iron lever
26. Action body
27. Hinge pins (2)
28. Top lever
29. Locking latch
30. Top lever spring plunger
31. Top lever spring
32. Top lever pin
33. Spring washer
34. Top lever screw
35. Locking latch release plunger
36. Locking latch clamping lever spring
37. Locking latch clamping lever plunger
38. Locking latch clamping lever
39. Locking latch clamping lever pin
40. Firing pin right
41. Firing pin left
42. Firing pin spring
43. Spring pin
44. Cocking lever pin
45. Cocking lever spring
46. Cocking lever spring plunger
47. Cocking lever, right
48. Cocking lever, left
49. Cocking rod
50. Safety spring
51. Safety spring screw
52. Safety pin
53. Safety, single trigger
54. Stock bolt plate screw
55. Trigger plate screw
56. Trigger plate screw
57. Recoil pad screws (2)
58. Trigger plate
59. Hammer spring guide
60. Hammer spring
61. Hammer spring guide bush
62. Hammer spring guide nut
63. Hammer pin
64. Hammer
65. Hammer
66. Trigger body
67. Sear
68. Sear pin
69. Sear spring
70. Washer
71. Spring pin
72. Inertia block pin
73. Adjustable trigger
74. Concave washer
75. Trigger guard
76. Trigger guard screw
77. Trigger spring
78. Trigger plate screw retaining screw
79. Convex washer
80. Trigger retaining screw
81. Stock
82. Selector lever pin
83. Safety
84. Detent
85. Selector lever spring
86. Inertia block lever pin
87. Inertia block lever pawl
88. Inertia block lever spring
89. Inertia block lever
90. Inertia block rest
91. Spring pin
92. Inertia block
93. Spring pin
94. Inertia block spring
95. Conneting lever (upper)
96. Conneting lever (lower)
97. Stock adjustment mechanism
98. Fixed mechanism, adjustable stock
99. Stock bolt screw
100. Guiding bushing
101. Spring washer
102. Adjustable comb

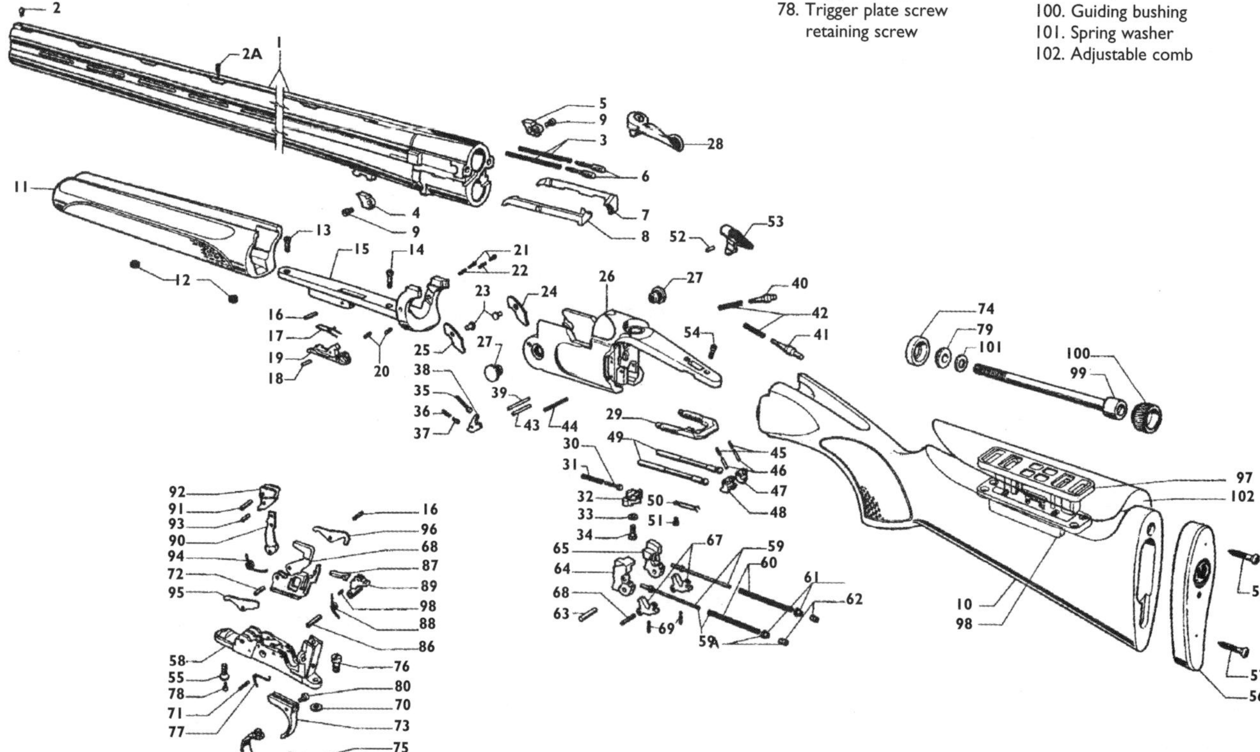

Beginning in 1985, Beretta introduced the 682 Gold series of high-grade over/under trap shotguns. Offered primarily in 12 and 20 gauge, some configurations are offered in 28 gauge and .410 bore. Gold series shotguns are fitted with nickel-alloy steel receivers, single selective triggers and automatic ejectors. Barrels come with ventilated ribs and various fixed or screw-in choke combinations.

The 682 Gold E Trap version illustrated here, introduced in 2002, is chambered for 3-inch, 12-gauge loads with 30- or 32-inch over-bored barrels. The single selective trigger is adjustable. All Gold Es have adjustable stocks. Gold E shotguns are available in combo models with two interchangeable barrel sets, skeet versions and a sporting model offered with a 28-, 30-, or 32-inch barrel with extended screw-in choke tubes.

DISASSEMBLY

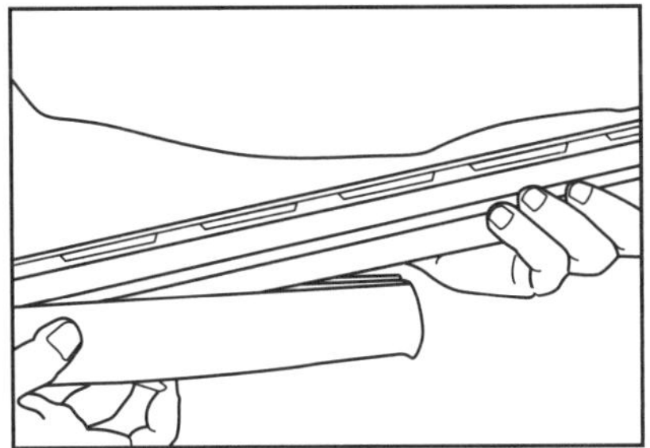

1 Check to ensure the chamber is empty. Remove the fore-end (11) from the barrels (1) by pulling the fore-end catch lever down. CAUTION: Do not pull the fore-end too far down before pulling it forward to remove it.

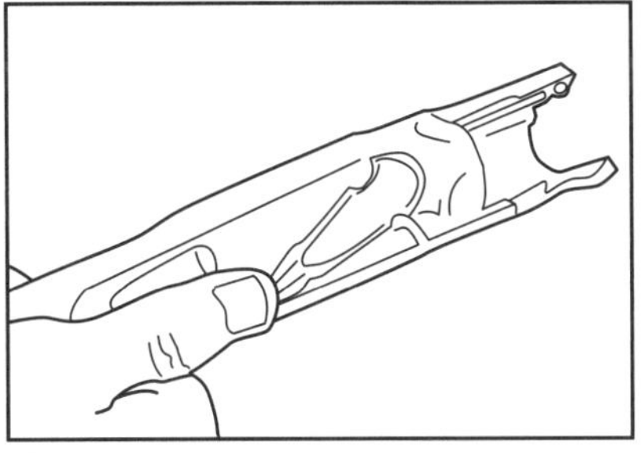

2 Move the top lever (28) to the right. Fully open the chamber by pivoting the muzzle end of the barrels downward. Lift the barrels out of the receiver .

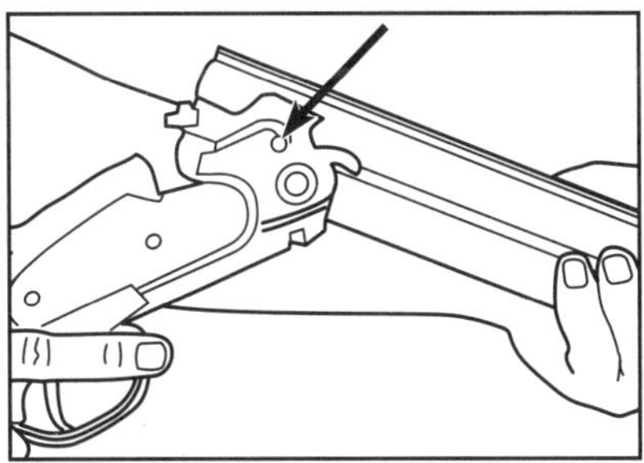

3 Disengage Monobloc recesses from hinge pins. The top lever remains open.

NOTE: Place the top lever in the centered position when the shotgun is being stored disassembled. Move the top lever to the right and depress the top lever plunger (30). Once the top lever plunger is completely depressed, release the top lever to its centered position. CAUTION: No further disassembly of component parts is recommended unless done by a competent gunsmith.

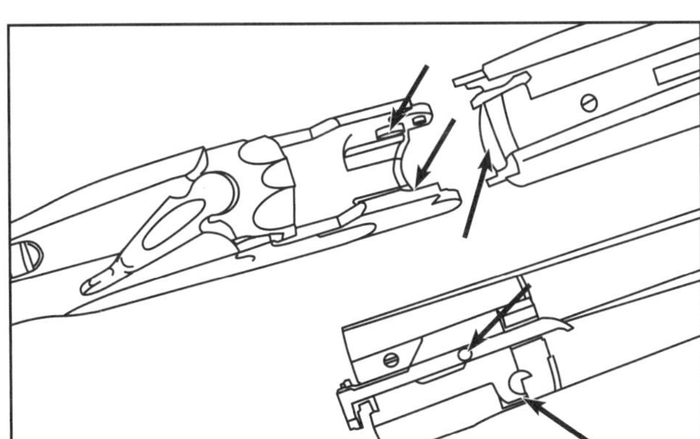

4 CAUTION: The hinge pin area is a very important mating surface. The receiver and fore-end iron are subject to very high loads: improper lubrication of these components can cause seizing of parts or malfunctioning of the shotgun. (The areas to lubricate are indicated by the arrows.) Before using this shotgun, make sure that lubricant is present as instructed.

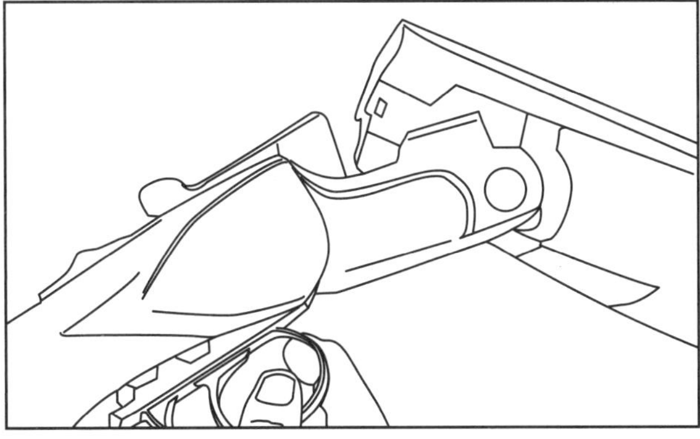

5 **Optional Interchangeable Trigger Group**

Push the safety/selector lever all the way forward, past the "ready to fire" position. You will expose a white dot at the base of the lever and hear a distinctive "click."

Rotate the top lever to the right and partially open the barrels. CAUTION: At this point, the trigger group is not locked in place but retained by a spring plunger and may drop out of the receiver if the gun is struck or if it is dislodged by contact with other objects.

Grab the trigger group by the trigger guard and gently pull it downward to remove it from the receiver. NOTE: To remove the trigger group it is necessary to pull it lightly. If a light pull does not release the trigger group, close the gun and repeat the operations above.

BERETTA AL 391 SHOTGUN

PARTS LEGEND

1. Barrel
2. Front sight
3. Stock
4. Butt plate
5. Butt plate screw
6. Stock swivel base assembly
7. Stock cap guide
8. Stock cap
9. Stock cap screw
10. Front spacer
11. Stock bolt tube
12. Recoil spring guide
13. Recoil spring
14. Recoil spring cap
15. Drop plate
16. Stock retaining nut washer
17. Stock retaining nut
18. Receiver
19. Ejector spring guide
20. Ejector spring
21. Ejector
22. Ejector spring pin
23. Cut-off
24. Cut-off spring
25. Cut-off spring pin
25. Cut-off plunger
26. Cut-off plunger spring
27. Cut-off plunger spring
28. Cut-off pin
29. Cut-off pin spring pin
30. Trigger plate retaining pin
31. Magazine tube cap plunger guide
32. Magazine tube cap plunger spring
33. Magazine tube cap retaining plunger
34. Cartridge latch body
35. Cartridge latch
36. Cartridge latch spring
37. Cartridge latch pin
38. Cartridge latch body spring
39. Cartridge latch body pin
40. Cartridge latch body pin stop spring pin
41. Magazine follower
42. Magazine spring
43. Magazine reducer plug
44. Magazine tube
45. Magazine tube cap
46. Magazine reducer plug retaining washer
47. Operating rod
48. Piston
49. Piston bush
50. Piston bush ring
51. Piston bush snap ring
52. Fore-end flange sleeve
53. Fore-end flange sleeve magnet
54. Fore-end
55. Fore-end cap
56. Front swivel
57. Breech bolt slide
58. Breech bolt connecting rod
59. Breech bolt connecting rod pin
60. Cocking handle plunger spring
61. Cocking handle plunger
62. Cocking handle plunger retaining spring pin
63. Breech bolt
64. Locking block
65. Firing pin spring
66. Firing pin
67. Firing pin retaining pin
68. Extractor spring
69. Extractor plunger
70. Extractor
71. Extractor pin
72. Cocking handle
73. Trigger plate
74. Ambidextrous safety
75. Safety spring
76. Safety spring plunger
77. Trigger
78. Trigger spring
79. Trigger spring guide plunger
80. Sear
81. Sear spring
82. Sear plunger
83. Trigger bush
84. Trigger pin
85. Hammer
86. Right brace
87. Left brace
88. Hammer spring guide
89. Hammer spring
90. Hammer spring guide plunger
91. Hammer spring guide pin
92. Hammer bush
93. Hammer bush retaining spring ring
94. Carrier catch plunger pin
95. Carrier catch plunger
96. Carrier catch plunger pin
97. Carrier
98. Carrier lever
99. Carrier lever spring
100. Carrier lever spring guide plunger
101. Carrier lever pin
102. Carrier swivel joint
103. Carrier spring guide
104. Carrier spring
105. Spring guide swivel joint
106. Carrier pin
107. Valve shaft
108. Valve
109. Valve centering ring
110. Valve nut
111. Valve counter nut
112. Valve spring
113. Trigger retaining pin
114. Recoil absorber

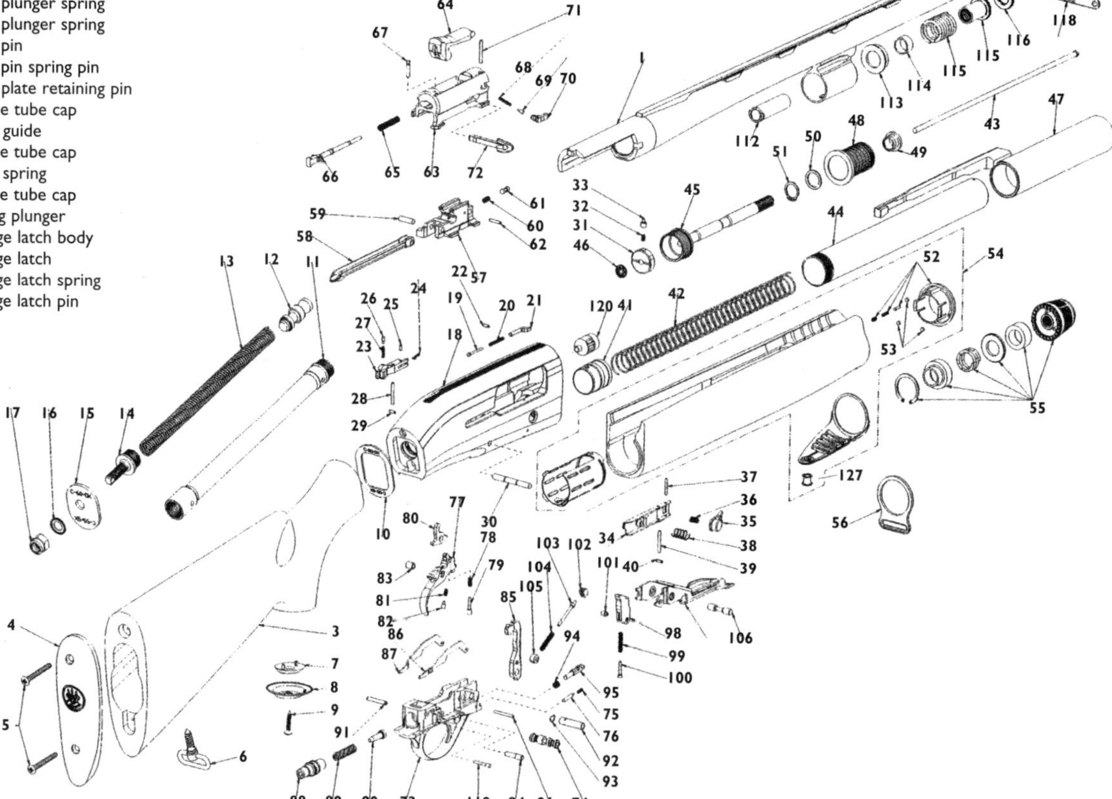

The Beretta AL 391 family of gas operated, semi-automatic shotguns consists of the Urika, Xtrema, and Xtrema 2 models. The Urika was first offered in 2000 followed by the Xtrema series beginning in 2002.

The 391s are manufactured in 12- and 20-gauge versions with light alloy receivers. The gas cylinder and piston are self-cleaning with a self-cleaning exhaust valve that expels excess gas allowing the AL 391 series to accept a wide variety of ammunition including 2¾- and 3-inch shells. The 391s vary in weight from 6.6 to 7.7 lbs. The shotguns have cross-bolt safeties and a magazine cut-off device that can be engaged when the breech bolt is closed.

The style of the AL 391 Xtrema was created for Beretta by Giugiaro Design, an industrial design company founded by automobile designer Giorgetto Giugiaro. As befits its name, the AL 391 Xtrema is specially treated with corrosion resistant materials to withstand use under harsh weather conditions. The exposed metal surfaces are blued, or black anodized in the case of the aluminum alloy receiver, and treated with a proprietary "Aqua Technology" coating. The breech bolt assembly, trigger and carrier are similarly treated. Many internal parts are either nickel or chrome plated, while other internal surfaces are specially coated with ceramics, titanium or chrome.

The Xtrema2 is an updated version of the Xtrema. In order to reduce wear and make the gun easier to clean, Beretta engineers reduced the number of springs and o-rings used in constructing the Xtrema. The shotgun also features Beretta's "Kick Off" anti-recoil device consisting of two oil-operated hydraulic absorbers mounted in the stock. The stock and forend are made of fiberglass-reinforced polymer.

DISASSEMBLY

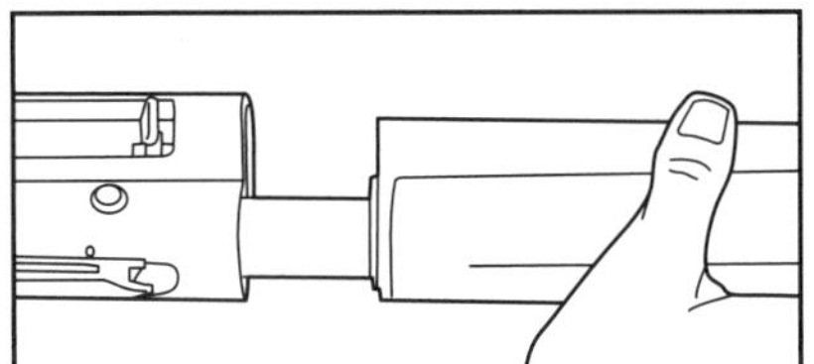

1 Retract the breech bolt until it hooks into the open position. Unscrew (counterclockwise) the fore-end cap from the firearm and remove the front swivel, if mounted. With one hand hold down the barrel and with the other hand slide the fore-end off the magazine tube.

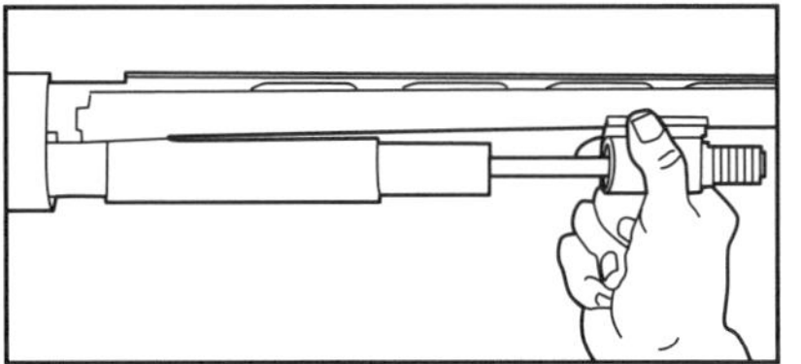

2 Grasping the barrel and holding the piston inside the gas cylinder with the right thumb to prevent dropping it, slide the barrel assembly forward off the stock/receiver assembly.

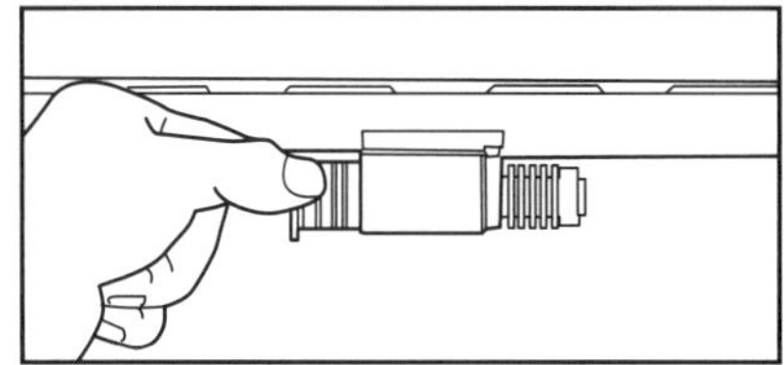

3 Slide the piston off the gas cylinder.

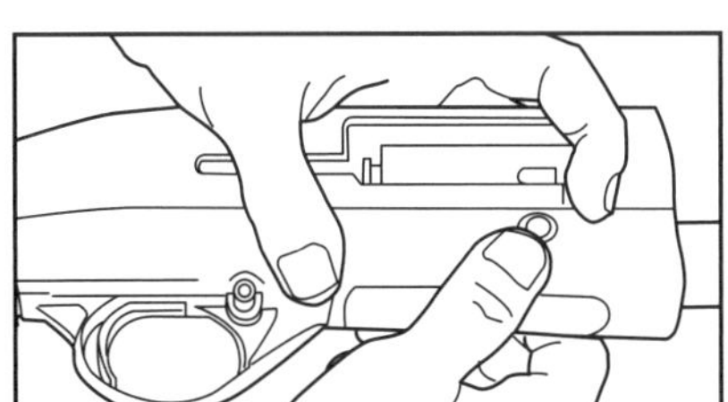

4 Holding the cocking handle with the index or middle finger of the left hand, depress the breech bolt release button and allow the breech bolt to slide slowly forward until it stops. Extract the cocking handle from the breech bolt slide.

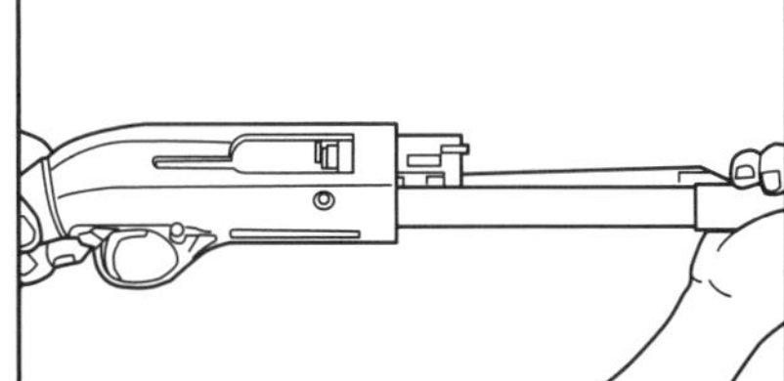

5 Holding the stock/receiver assembly on a table with the loading gate facing upward, slide the operating rod sleeve forward off the magazine tube to extract the breech bolt assembly from the receiver. The breech bolt assembly, no longer held by the operating rod, will divide into: breech bolt with firing pin, locking block, extractor, springs and pins. magazine catch (19) in frame while in-serting magazine catch pin (20).

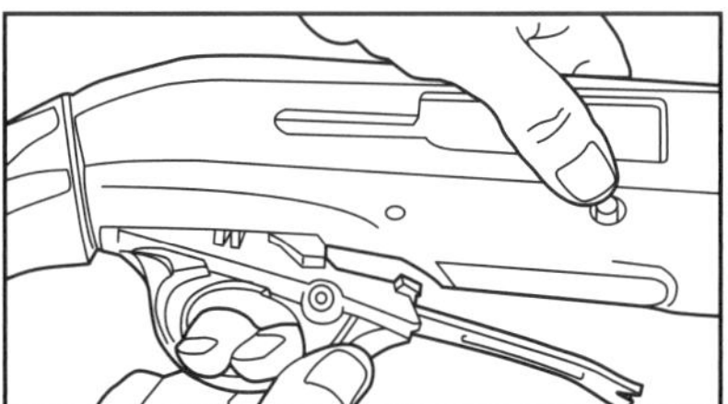

6 Engage the safety (the hammer is cocked). Depress the carrier stop push-button. Push out the trigger plate retaining pin by pressing it with a drift punch or other similar object. Keeping the breech bolt release button pressed, extract the trigger plate by pulling on the trigger guard with a forward and downward movement. magazine catch (19) in frame while in-serting magazine catch pin (20).

BREDA 12-GAUGE MARK II SHOTGUN

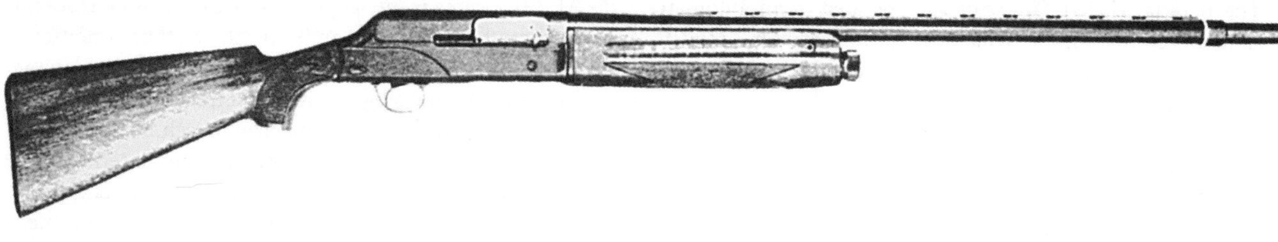

PARTS LEGEND

1. Barrel
2. Barrel extension *
3. Ejector, with fixing rivets (2) *
4. Front sight base*
5. Front sight
6. Choking tube retaining spring
7. Choking tube
8. Receiver cover
9. Receiver
10. Magazine cut-off lever
11. Cut-off plunger*
12. Cut-off plunger spring*
13. Cut-off plunger spring screw*
14. Magazine ring washer*
15. Magazine ring*
16. Magazine tube*
17. Recoil spring
18. Recoil spring washer
19. Beveled brake ring
20. Bronze friction brake
21. Magazine spring follower
22. Magazine spring
23. Magazine reducer (2 shell)
24. Magazine spring retainer
25. Magazine cap
26. Magazine cap retainer screw*
27. Magazine cap plunger*
28. Magazine cap retainer spring*
29. Carrier latch button
30. Carrier latch lever
31. Carrier latch spring
32. Right magazine shell latch lever
33. Right magazine shell latch spring
34. Shell latch-carrier latch pin (2)
35. Left magazine shell latch lever
36. Left latch spring
37. Reversible safety lever disassembly pin
38. Action spring tube lock washer *
39. Action spring tube lock nut *
40. Action spring tube *
41. Action spring follower
42. Action spring
43. Action spring guide
44. Stock lockwasher
45. Stock spring washer
46. Action spring tube plug
47. Trigger guard
48. Hammer pin
49. Hammer
50. Trigger
51. Trigger spring
52. Trigger pin
53. Hammer spring
54. Safety plunger spring
55. Safety plunger
56. Safety plunger plastic washer
57. Carrier
58. Carrier dog
59. Carrier dog plunger
60. Carrier dog spring
61. Carrier dog pin
62. Carrier rocker arm
63. Carrier rocker spring
64. Carrier rocker pivot
65. Carrier rocker pin
66. Bolt
67. Locking block
68. Left extractor
69. Left extractor spring
70. Extractor pin (2)
71. Right extractor spring
72. Right extractor
73. Bolt pawl spring
74. Bolt pawl
75. Bolt pawl pin
76. Bolt plate
77. Operating handle
78. Firing pin retaining pin
79. Link pin
80. Operating handle latch
81. Link spring
82. Firing pin
83. Firing pin spring
84. Bolt link
85. Pistol grip stock
86. Buttplate
87. Buttplate screw (2)
88. Fore-end
89. Fore-end yoke *

* To be factory disassembled only
Permanent assembly to carrier rocker arm (Part 62)

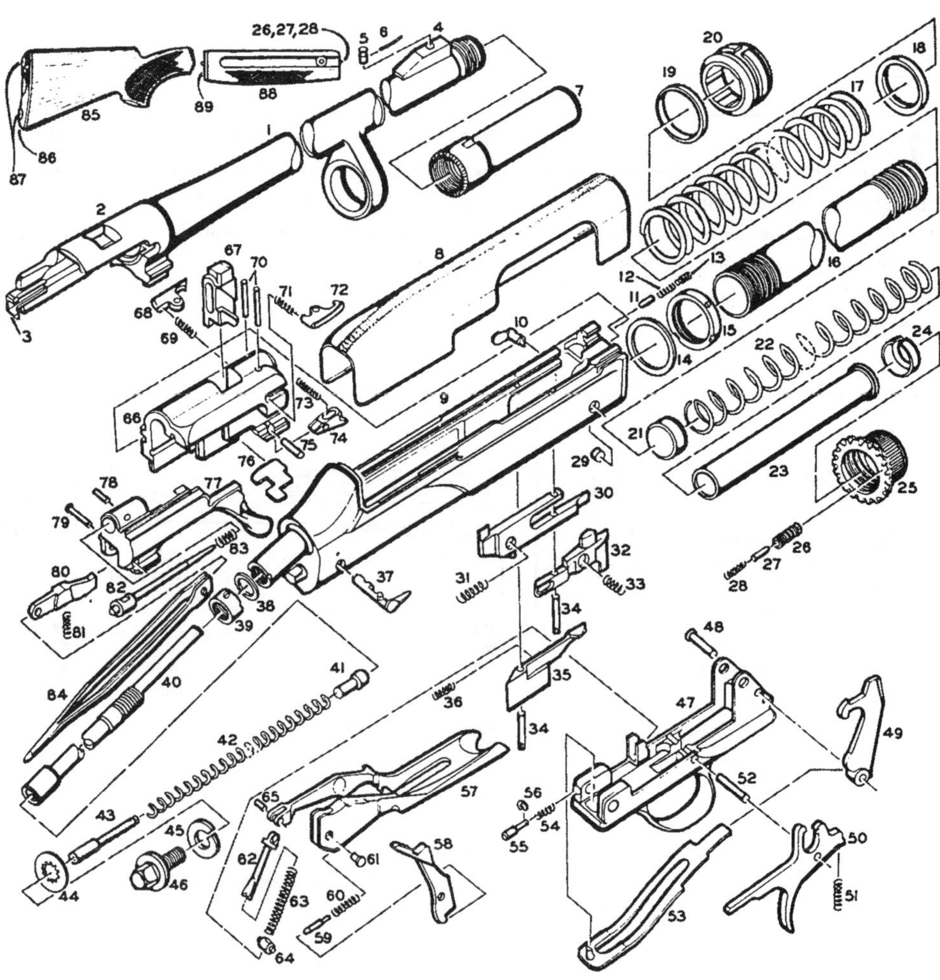

The Breda 12-ga. Mark II semi-automatic shotgun is manufactured in Italy by Breda Meccanica Bresciana. There were 7 distinct production series in the 12-ga. Breda shotgun prior to introduction of the Mark II version in 1957. Production of the first series was in 1948. The Mark II series, designated 1008A, covers Breda 12-ga. shotguns numbered from 40,001 and includes the Breda Superlight model, also introduced in 1957, which is serially numbered from 500,001.

The Breda Mark II shotgun design is essentially a modification of the Browning long-recoil system where the friction brake requires adjustment for light and heavy loads. Conversion kits alter 12-ga. standard models to 12-ga. Magnum.

The magazine cut-off is operated manually by pushing the lever on the left side of the action to the forward position. Shells will not feed from the magazine into the chamber unless the cut-off lever is moved to its rearward position. Provision of the magazine cut-off permits the user to maintain a full magazine of shells in reserve. To unload the gun, engage the safety, and move the cut-off lever to its forward position. Then clear the chamber by retracting the operating handle to rear latched position. With gun inverted, depress carrier latch button and push carrier down to locked position. Move cut-off lever to rearward position. With index finger, depress the bolt pawl which will release all shells in the magazine.

DISASSEMBLY

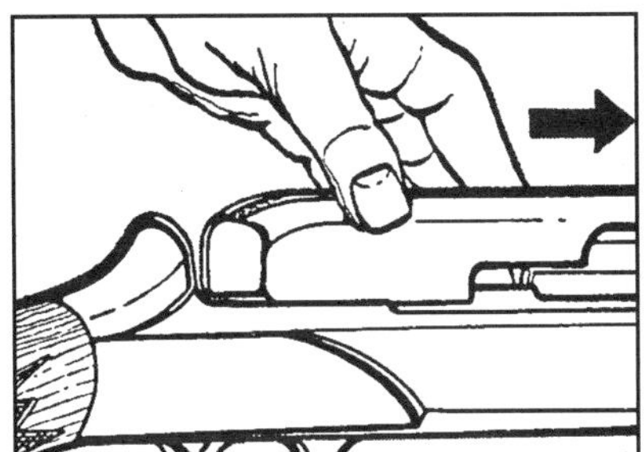

1 To disassemble, engage safety, open bolt (66), press fore-end toward receiver (9), and unscrew magazine cap (25). Remove fore-end and barrel assembly (1). Remove bronze friction brake (20), beveled brake (19), recoil spring washer (18), and recoil spring (17) from magazine tube (16). Press carrier latch button (29) and guide bolt closed. Slide off receiver cover (8).

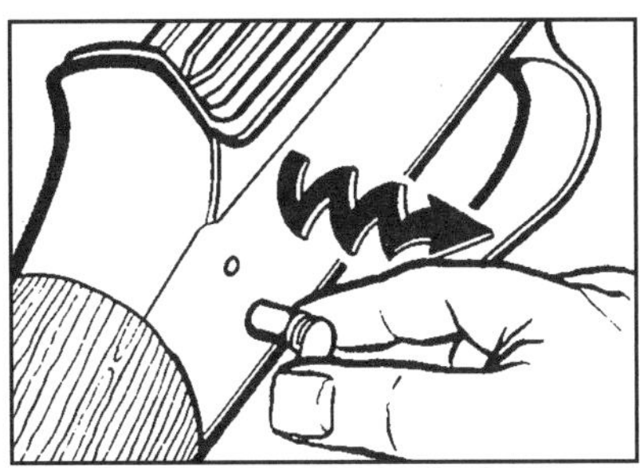

2 Push frimly on pin end of safety lever pin (37) (opposite side of receiver from safety lever portion) using magazine cap (25) as a thimble for thumb. Twist safety lever off engaged position and down clear of receiver. Pull out with twisting movement. With carrier latch button (29) depressed, grasp trigger guard (47) and swing assembly free, sliding the trigger assembly out of the action.

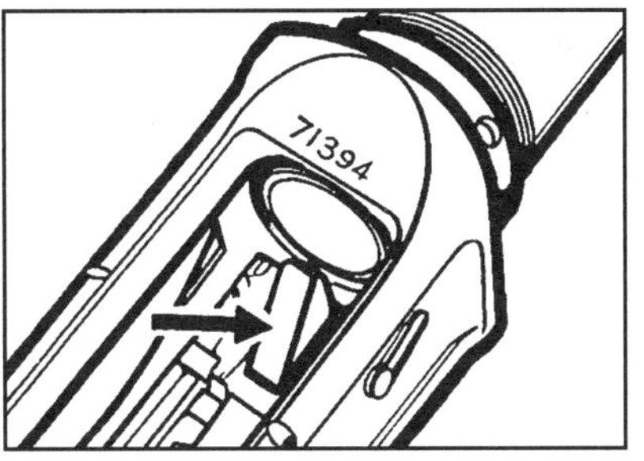

3 Depress bolt pawl (74-arrow) with index finger of the right hand and at same time slightly pull bolt rearward using operating handle (77) until pawl clears top of action. Press pawl against face of magazine tube (16) and slide bolt assembly forward through action slots over magazine tube. This frees the bolt assembly from the action body.

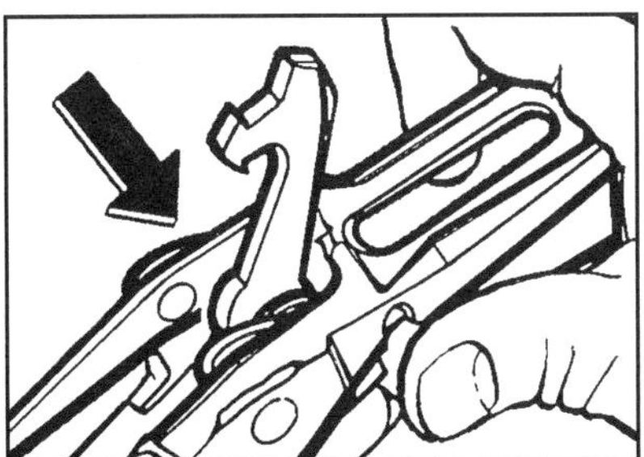

4 Grasp rear portion of trigger guard (47) with left hand, and with right hand move carrier (57) downward and then away from lugs on guard as shown. Lift carrier away, together with carrier rocker arm assembly (62, 63, 64, 65). Drift out hammer pin (48) and remove hammer (49) and hammer spring (53). Drift out trigger pin (52) and remove trigger (50) and trigger spring (51).

5 Hold bolt (66) upside-down and push bolt link (84) down and forward. Slide out bolt plate (76). Pull link back and slide out link, operating handle (77), and firing pin (82). This enables the locking block (67) to drop out. Other bolt disassembly is obvious. When reassembling the bolt, reinsert bolt plate (76) in direction indicated by arrow stamped on the bolt plate.

6 To remove parts from magazine tube, pry out magazine spring retainer (24). The magazine reducer (23), magazine spring (22), and magazine spring follower (21) may be withdrawn. To remove stock, remove buttplate screws (87) and buttplate (86). Using a 9/16 T-handle socket wrench, turn out the action spring tube plug (46). Maintain pressure on the wrench to prevent the action spring (42) from flying out.

BROWNING A-BOLT RIFLE

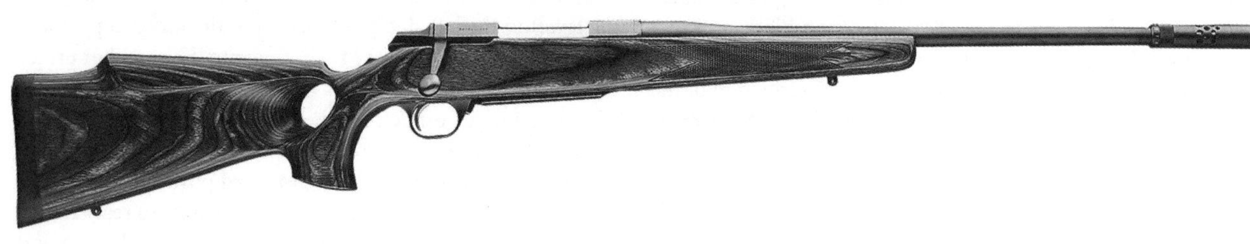

PARTS LEGEND

1. Barrel mounting screw
2. Barrel/receiver
3. Bolt assembly
4. Bolt body
5. Bolt handle
6. Bolt head
7. Bolt head key pin
8. Bolt retainer
9. Bolt retainer pin
10. Bolt retainer pin guide
11. Bolt retainer screw
12. Bolt retainer spring
13. Bolt shroud
14. Bolt sleeve
15. Butt plate
16. Butt plate screws
17. Ejector
18. Ejector pin
20. Extractor
21. Extractor spring
22. Firing pin
23. Firing pin sear pin
24. Firing pin spring
25. Firing pin washer
26. Gas stop assembly
27. Magazine base
28. Magazine body
30. Magazine floor plate hinge
31. Magazine floor plate hinge pin
32. Magazine floor plate hinge spring
33. Magazine floor plate latch
34. Magazine floor plate latch pin
35. Magazine floor plate latch spring
36. Safety stud
37. Magazine follower
38. Magazine follower rivet
39. Magazine follower spring
40. Magazine ramp
41. Magazine ramp rivet
42. Magazine retainer spring
43. Magazine spring pin
44. Magazine spring strut inner
45. Magazine spring strut outer
46. Magazine strut pin
47. Magazine strut spring
48. Mechanism housing
49. Mechanism housing assembly
50. Mechanism housing screw
51. Trigger w/sear & screw
52. Mechanism housing screw washer
53. Mechanism housing set pin
54. Safety
55. Safety blocking pin
56. Safety lever
    56a. Safety lever pin
57. Safety lever spring
58. Safety link
59. Safety link roll pin
60. Safety pin
61. Safety pin snap ring
62. Safety selector
63. Safety spring
64. Sear
65. Sear pin
66. Sear screw
67. Sear spring
68. Sling eyelet assembly front
69. Sling eyelet front and rear
70. Sling eyelet rear
71. Stock
72. Trigger guard
73. Trigger guard screw rear
74. Trigger pin
75. Trigger pull adjustment screw
76. Trigger spring
77. Bolt sleeve screw
78. Firing pin sear
79. Trigger w/sear and screw

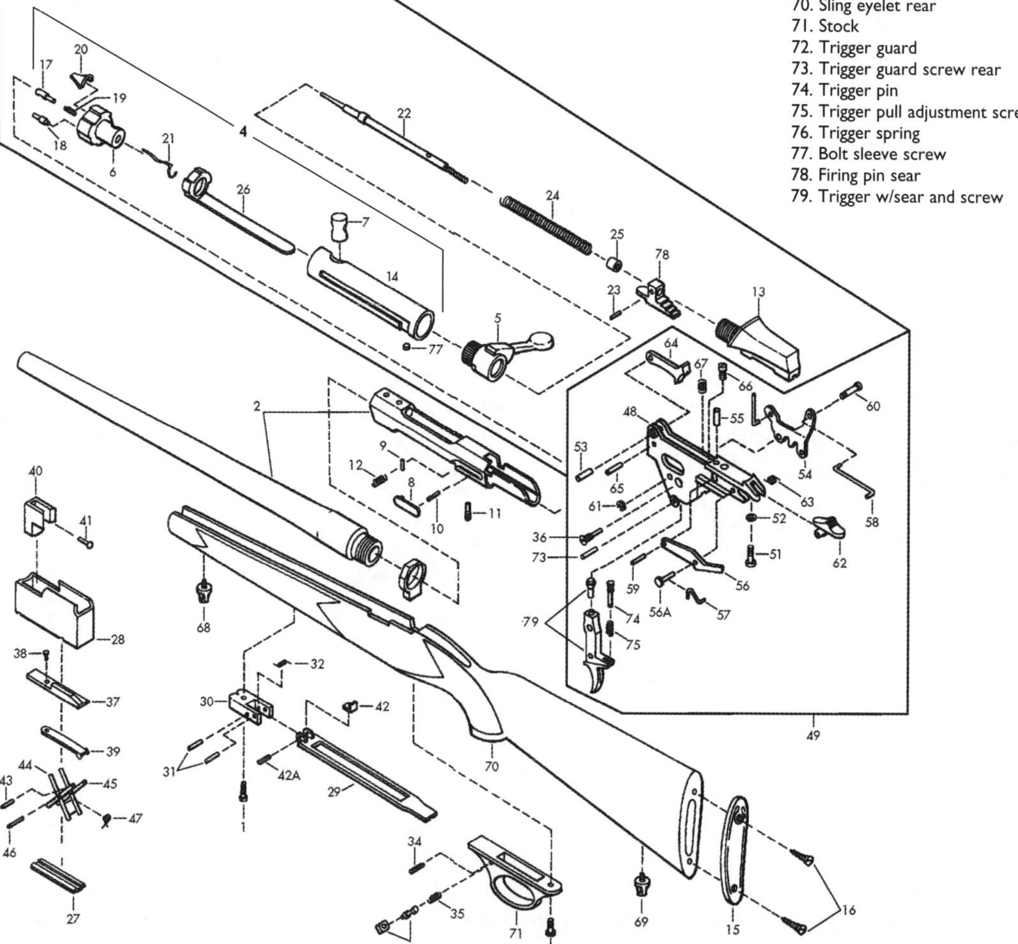

Browning began production of the A-Bolt rifle in 1985. The rifle used a non-rotating bolt sleeve with a rotating head and three locking lugs. The A-Bolt uses a detachable box magazine and a cartridge depressor remains independent of the bolt position to allow the bolt to move easily over the rounds in the magazine.

In 1994 designers produced the A-Bolt II series with a series of alterations and added the Browning Ballistic Optimizing Shooting System (BOSS) permitting adjustments to compensate for bullet weight. The A-Bolt II rifles are manufactured by the Miroku Corporation in Nangoku, Japan and are offered in various models and calibers, including the White Gold Medallion, Medallion, Hunter, Micro Hunter, Eclipse Hunter, and Stalker. The Stainless Stalker model was among the first rifles to be offered with a composite stock.

DISASSEMBLY

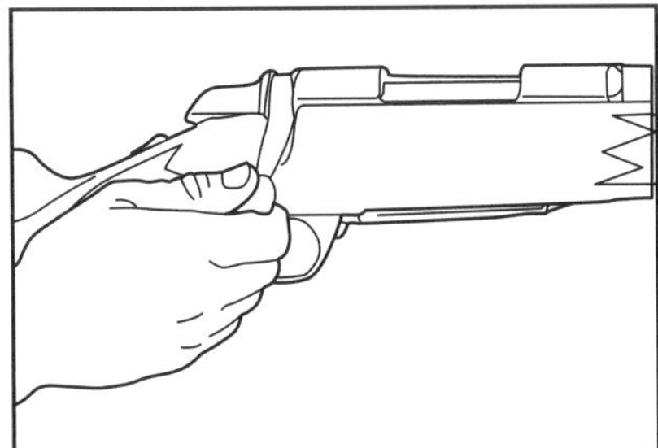

1 Check to make certain that there are no cartridges in the chamber or magazie and place the safety in the "off safe" position. Lift the bolt handle (5) up to unlock action and begin to withdraw the bolt toward the rear of the receiver.

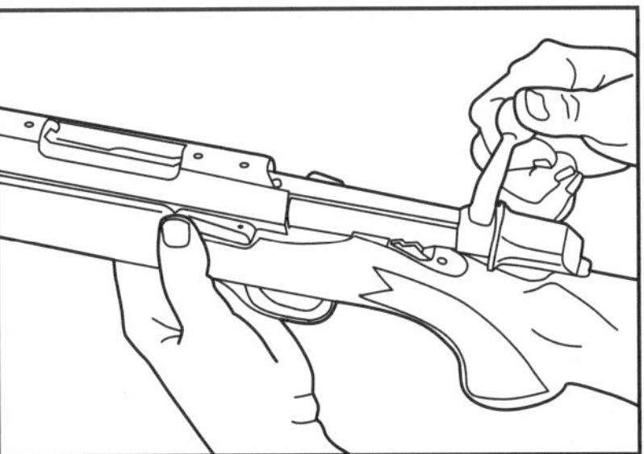

2 Press in on the forward end of the bolt retainer (8) — the horizontal bar on the left side of the receiver — with the left hand and draw the bolt (3) to the rear, completely removing it from the receiver (2) and the rifle..

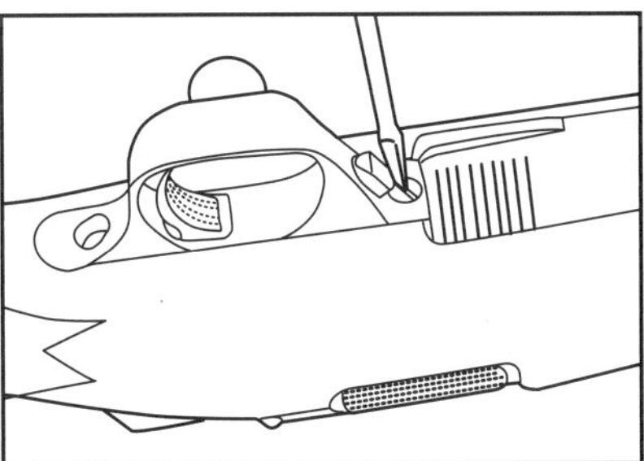

3 The rigger pull can be adjusted within a range of approximately 3.5 to 6.5 pounds. To adjust the triger pull, lower the magazine floorplate (29) and carefully remove the trigger guard screws (or rear trigger guard screw) with a standard screwdriver.

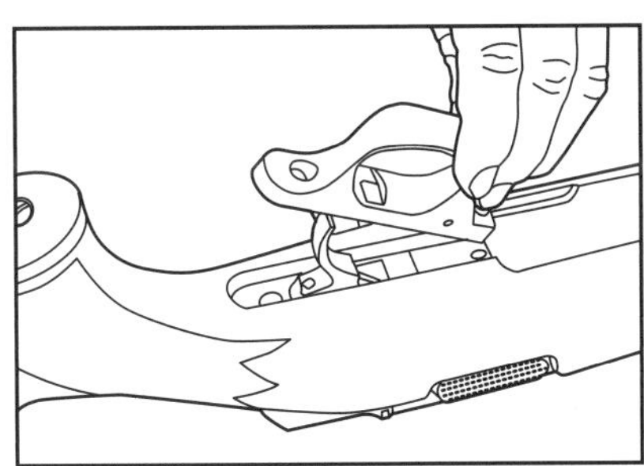

4 Lift the trigger guard (72) out of the stock exposing the trigger.

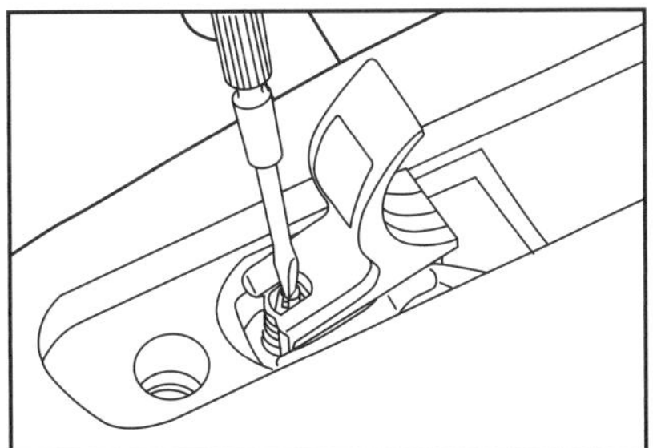

5 The trigger pull adjustment screw (75) is located at the rear of the trigger assembly. To decrease the weight of the trigger pull, turn the adjustment screw in a clockwise direction using a small screw driver. To increase the trigger pull, turn the adjustment screw counterclockwise. NOTE: If the trigger pull is increased too much, the trigger cannot be pulled.

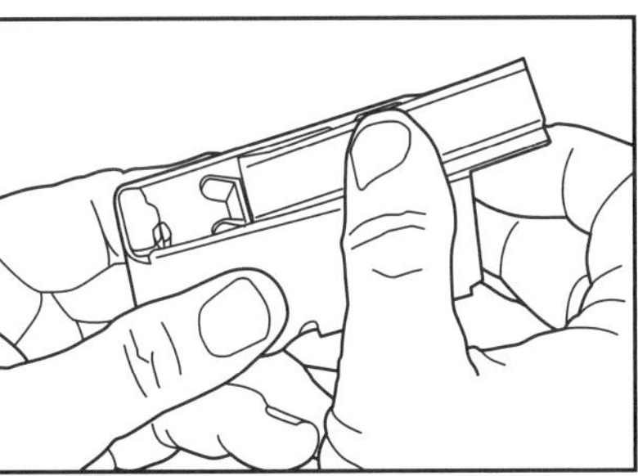

6 Disassemble the box magazine for cleaning, first remove the detachable box magazine from the rifle. Slide the magazine base (27) out to the rear. The magazine spring (44 & 45) and follower (37) can then be easily removed for inspection.

BROWNING AUTO-5 SHOTGUN

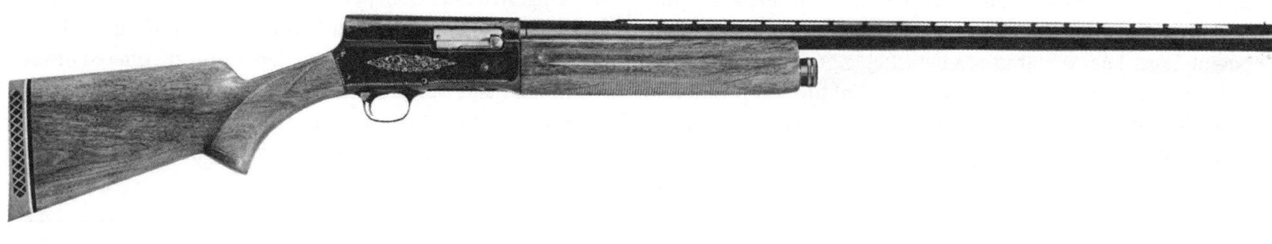

PARTS LEGEND

1. Action spring
2. Action spring follower
3. Action spring plug
4. Action spring plug pin
5. Action spring tube
6. Barrel/extension assy.
7. Breechblock
8. Buttplate
9. Buttplate screws (2)
10. Buttstock
11. Carrier assy.
12. Carrier dog
13. Carrier dog follower
14. Carrier dog pin
15. Carrier dog spring
16. Carrier latch assy.
17. Carrier latch button
18. Carrier screws (2)
19. Carrier spring
20. Cartridge stop
21. Cartridge stop pins (3)
22. Cartridge stop spring
23. Ejector
24. Ejector rivet
25. Extractor, left
26. Extractor, right
27. Extractor pins
28. Extractor spring, left
29. Extractor spring, right
30. Firing pin
31. Firing pin stop pin
32. Forearm
33. Friction piece, bronze
34. Friction ring
35. Friction spring
36. Hammer assy.
37. Hammer pin
38. Link
39. Link pin
40. Locking block
41. Locking block latch
42. Locking block latch pin
43. Locking block latch spring
44. Lock screws (5)
45. Magazine cap
46. Magazine cap detent
47. Magazine cap detent plunger
48. Magazine cap detent spring
49. Magazine cutoff
50. Magazine cutoff spring
51. Magazine cutoff spring screw
52. Magazine follower
53. Magazine spring
54. Magazine spring retainer
55. Magazine tube
56. Mainspring
57. Mainspring screw
58. Operating handle
59. Receiver
60. Recoil spring
61. Safety, crossbolt
62. Safety ball
63. Safety sear
64. Safety sear pin
65. Safety sear spring
66. Safety sear spring follower
67. Sight bead
68. Tang screw
69. Trigger
70. Trigger pin
71. Trigger plate
72. Trigger plate screw, front
73. Trigger plate screw, rear
74. Trigger spring pin retainer
75. Trigger spring retainer pin

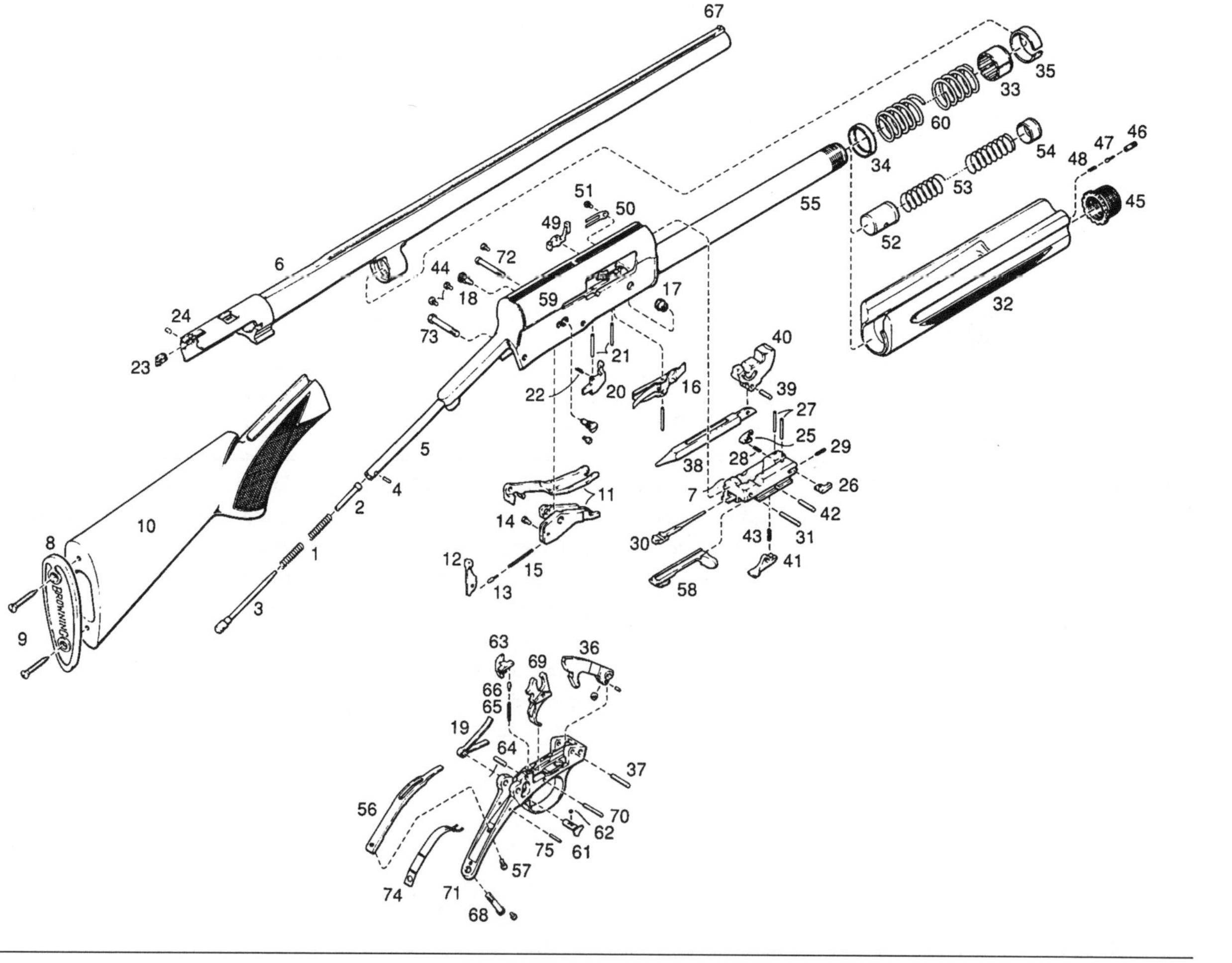

Known variously as the Browning Automatic, Automatic-5, Auto-5 or simply the A-5. John M. Browning's long-recoil-operated selfloader, patented in 1900, was the first successful semi-automatic shotgun produced and is still one of the most popular. Its full story appears in Colonel W.R. Betz's feature article in the August 1985 *American Rifleman*, and it is only necessary here to touch on its long history.

Belgium's Fabrique Nationale (FN) began full production of Browning's design in 1903, manufacturing it in 12-gauge only. The 16-gauge FN version followed in 1909, but 20-gauge Belgian-made guns did not appear until 1958. FN's production was interrupted by both world wars and ceased soon after production was initiated in Japan in 1971 by SKB and by 1976, production was fully transferred to Miroku. Regular production ended in 1989. In 1999 Browning issued a "Final Tribute" limited edition model of 1000 guns.

In 1905, concurrent with FN's early production, John Browning licensed the Remington Arms Company to make a similar autoloading shotgun without the magazine cutoff. Remington's Model 11 in 12-gauge was produced from 1906 until 1948, with 16- and 20-gauge versions available by the 1930s. In addition, from 1946 to 1951, while FN was reorganizing after the war, Remington produced guns with cutoffs in all three gauges to order for Browning Arms. These were advertised as "The American Brownings."

Another American-made version of the no-cutoff Browning was made after the original patents expired. The Savage Arms Model 720 (and its several variants) was produced between 1930 and 1949 in 12 and 16 gauge. Aside from these mentioned in the article, various close copies have been produced by smaller companies in Europe and Asia.

Since their inception, the Browning A-5s have been produced with many different mechanical and cosmetic variations. The shape and location of the manual safety has changed several times and ventilated ribs are now almost always present on the barrels that have been fully interchangeable within the same gauge/chamber-length groups since 1950.

A "quick loading" feature was incorporated in the 1960s that, with the bolt open, permitted initial chamber loading by inserting the first round into the magazine, where it would automatically cycle into the chamber and close the bolt. Previously it had been necessary to drop a round into the ejection port and push the carrier latch button in order to release the bolt and chamber the round.

Another significant change in design came with the introduction of 3-inch Magnum chamberings in 1958. For guns so-chambered, the "shock absorber" system of arranging the friction rings differently for light and heavy loads was modified. (The correct placement of rings and brakes for the two systems is shown in the inserts.)

DISASSEMBLY

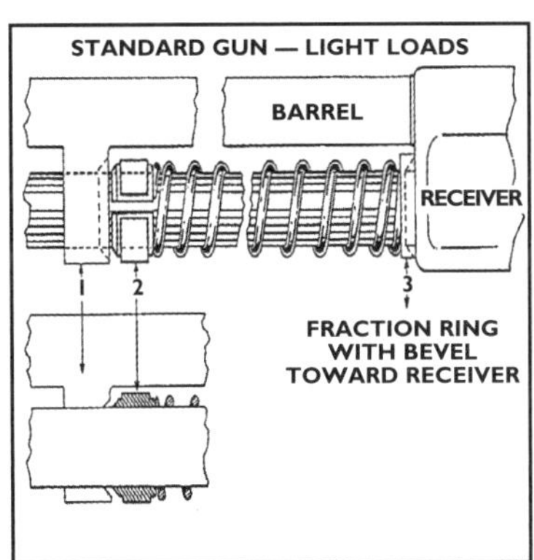

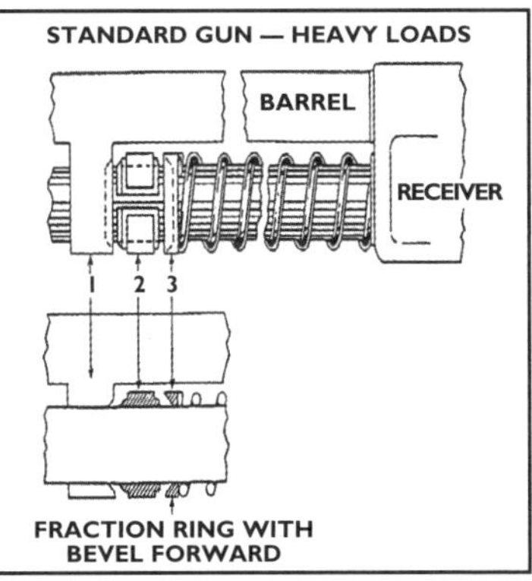

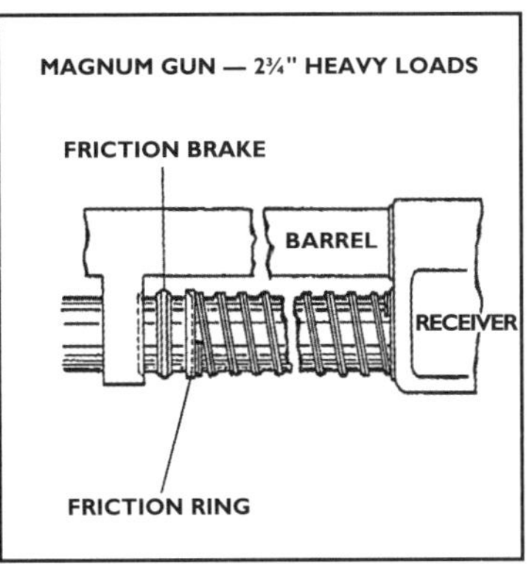

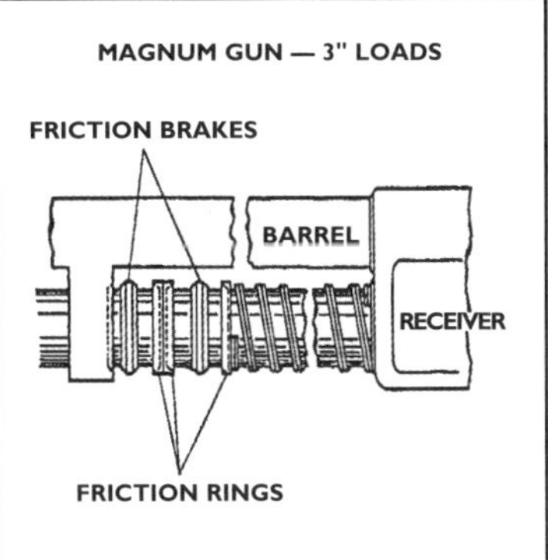

FIELD STRIPPING

Many A-5s have served for generations without full disassembly, and, because of the many (separate) parts and assemblies involved, only field stripping is sanctioned by Browning and covered here.

With the safety (61) engaged, retract the operating handle (58) to lock back the breechblock (7) and make sure the chamber and magazine are empty. Place the butt on the floor and push the barrel (6) slightly to the rear to relieve pressure on the magazine cap (45) so that it can then be unscrewed. Slowly relieve pressure on the barrel that will move forward and can be removed together with the forearm (32). Now the recoil spring (60) and friction piece, ring and spring (33-35) will be exposed. **Inserts** show the components in standard and magnum versions.

NOTE: With the barrel removed, care must be taken to avoid pressing the carrier latch button (17) that would release the spring-driven breech block suddenly with possible damage to the receiver. If it is necessary to close the breechblock for cleaning, grasp the operating handle before pushing the carrier latch button and ease the breechblock forward.

BROWNING BAR-22 RIFLE

PARTS LEGEND

1. Barrel
2. Barrel pin
3. Bolt
4. Bolt return spring
5. Buttplate
6. Buttplate screw
7. Buttstock
8. Carrier
9. Carrier pin
10. Carrier spring
11. Cocking handle
12. Ejector bar
13. Extractor
14. Extractor pin
15. Extractor spring
16. Extractor spring follower
17. Feed guide retaining screw
18. Feed guide assembly
19. Firing pin ejector
20. Firing pin ejector pin
21. Firing pin ejector spring
22. Firing pin ejector spring follower
23. Forearm
24. Forearm bracket
25. Forearm escutcheon
26. Forearm screw
27. Magazine assembly
28. Magazine tube bracket
29. Magazine tube bracket pin
30. Magazine tube bracket screw
31. Magazine tube outer
32. Magazine tube retaining screw
33. Mechanism housing
34. Mechanism housing pin
35. Receiver cover
36. Safety
37. Safety spring
38. Safety spring follower
39. Safety spring pin
40. Sear
41. Sear pin
42. Sear stop pin
43. Sear spring
44. Sear spring screw
45. Sear lever
46. Sear lever pin
47. Sear lever spring
48. Sight front
49. Sight base front
50. Sight base screw front
51. Sight assembly rear
52. Slide arm
53. Slide arm stud
54. Slide arm weight
55. Stock bolt
56. Stock bolt lock washer
57. Stock bolt washer
58. Striker
59. Striker guide pin
60. Striker spring
61. Striker spring guide
62. Takedown screw
63. Top ramp
64. Trigger
65. Trigger pin
66. Trigger spring

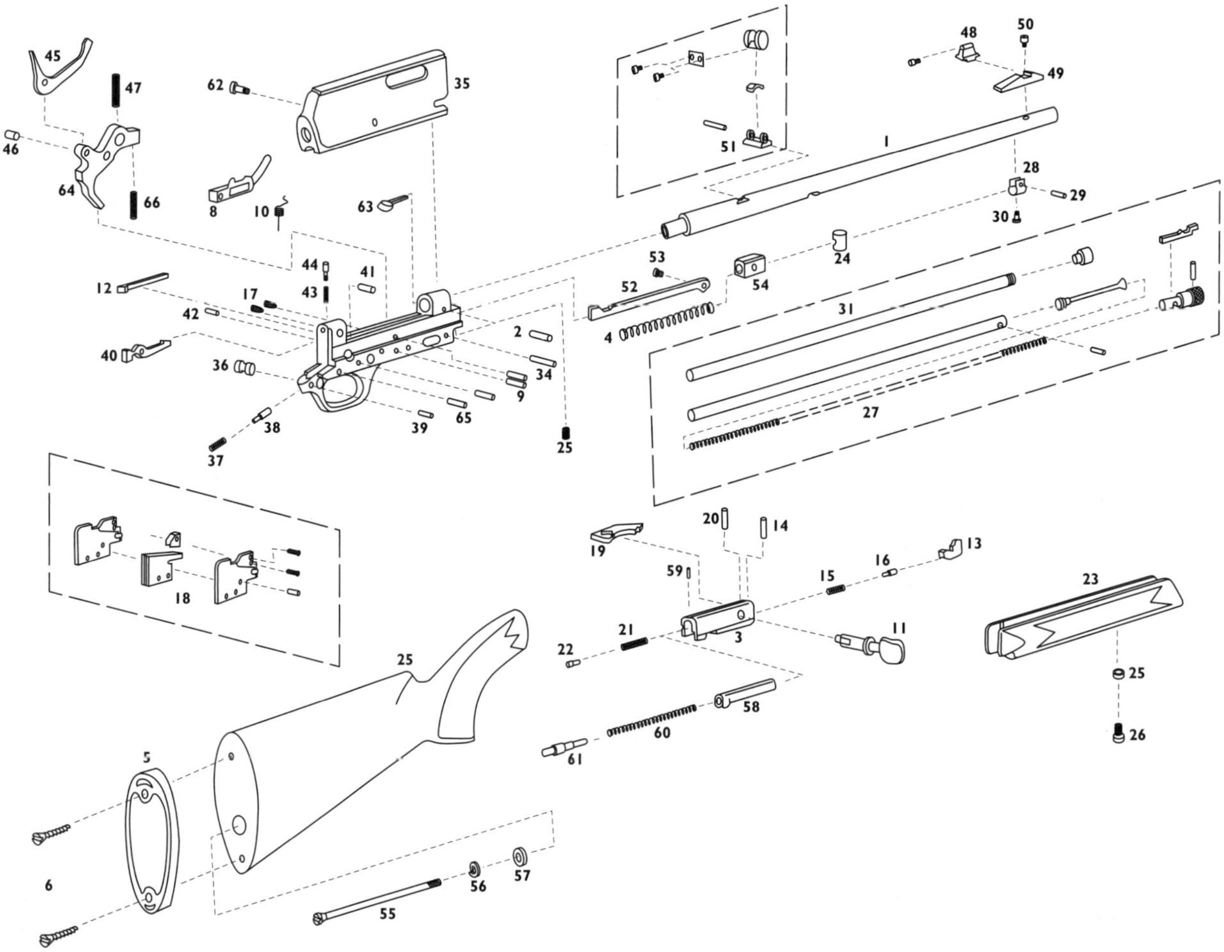

Browning s BAR-22 was introduced in 1977 as a companion to the BAR centerfire rifle introduced 10 years earlier. Of straight blowback operation, the BAR-22 was a self-loading, .22 rimfire rifle manufactured for Browning by B.C. Miroku Firearms Co., of Koehi, Japan.

The rifle's construction is unusual in that what appears to be the receiver is actually only a cover. Removing the cover exposes the breechbolt and firing mechanism, which are retained in a mechanism housing, or receiver, made integral with the trigger guard. Most BAR-22 parts are interchangeable with its counterpart, the BPR-22 (Browning Pump Rifle). The pump version, which has a greater number of parts, fires from a locked breech rather than a blowback action. It was made for the .22 Winchester Magnum Rimfire cartridge as well as for .22 Long Rifle.

The BAR-22 had a 20⅛ barrel and a tubular magazine with a capacity of 15, .22 Long Rifle cartridges. Overall length was 38¼ inches. Weight was 6½ pounds. Both the BAR and BPR were available in a Grade II version featuring fancy wood and engraved small game scenes on their receiver covers.

Standard sights were an adjustable folding leaf rear and a rampmounted front blade. Receiver covers were grooved for tip-off telescopic sight mounts. Serial numbers were stamped on the lower right wall of the receiver cover. BAR-22s were discontinued in 1985, BPRs in 1982.

DISASSEMBLY

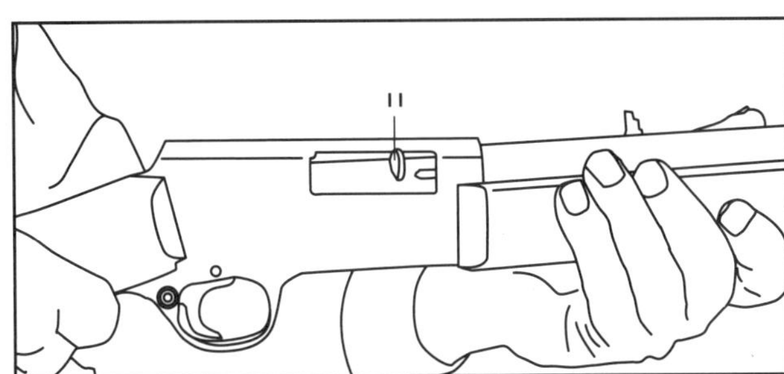

1 Make sure the magazine and chamber are empty and close the action. Remove the takedown screw (62) from the left side of the receiver. This allows the butt stock and receiver cover to be tipped upward slightly. The cocking handle(11) may then be removed from the bolt. Pull rearward and upward on the pistol grip to slide receiver cover and buttstock off of the mechanism housing.

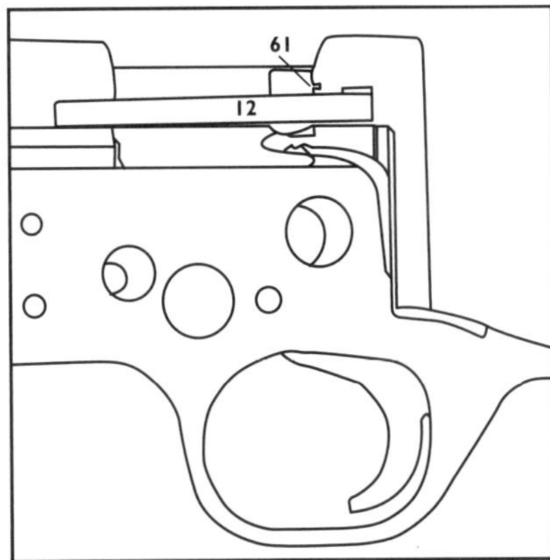

2 Remove the ejector bar (12) from the left side of the mechanism housing. Remove the striker spring (60) and guide (61) by pushing the guide forward until it can be lifted up and out of the housing.

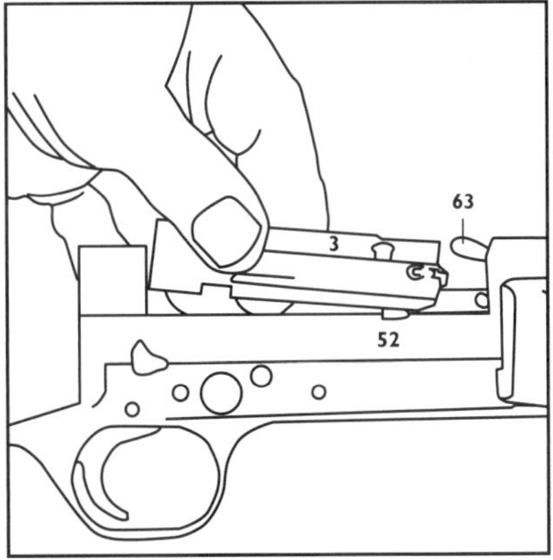

3 Raise the rear end of the bolt (3) straight upward. A click will be heard when the bolt is released from the slide arm (52). The striker (58) will now fall out of the bolt.

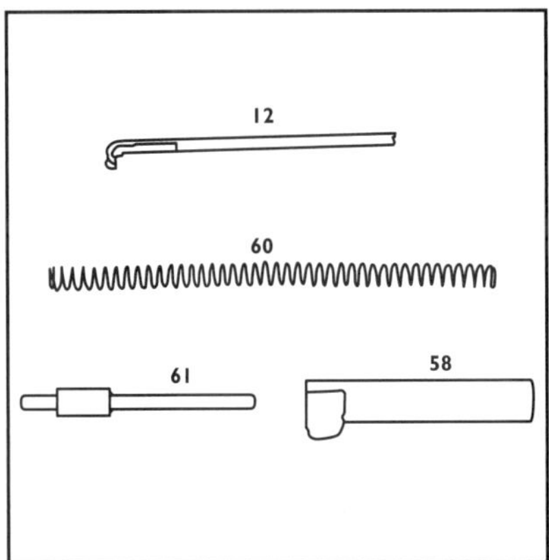

4 Remove the top ramp (63) which guides the cartridges into the chamber by pulling it rearward. Further disassembly is not ordinarily required or recommended. Clean the action and parts with solvent. Then dry them and apply a very light coat of oil.

BROWNING BAR HIGH-POWER RIFLE

PARTS LEGEND

1. Action bar-right or left
2. Action spring
3. Action spring guide
4. Barrel
5. Bolt
6. Bolt cover
7. Bolt sleeve
8. Buffer
9. Buffer plate
10. Buttplate
11. Buttplate screws
12. Buttstock
13. Cam pin
14. Disconnector
15. Disconnector pin
16. Disconnector spring
17. Disconnector spring plunger
18. Ejector
19. Ejector retaining pin
20. Ejector spring
21. Extractor
22. Extractor spring
23. Firing pin
24. Firing pin retaining pin
25. Firing pin spring
26. Forearm
27. Forearm escutcheon
28. Gas cylinder
29. Gas piston
30. Gas piston stop pin
31. Gas regulator
32. Gas regulator gasket
33. Hammer
34. Hammer pin
35. Inertia piece
36. Magazine body
37. Magazine floorplate
38. Magazine floorplate pivot pin
39. Magazine floorplate spring
40. Magazine follower
41. Magazine follower spring
42. Magazine follower rivet
43. Magazine latch
44. Magazine latch spring
45. Magazine latch spring plunger
46. Magazine latch stop pin
47. Magazine retaining spring
48. Magazine retaining spring pin
49. Mainspring-right or left
50. Mainspring guide-right or left
51. Mainspring pin-hammer
52. Mainspring pin-trigger guard
53. Operating handle
54. Operating handle lock
55. Operating handle lock pin
56. Operating handle lock spring
57. Receiver
58. Safety cross-bolt
59. Safety spring
60. Safety spring plunger
61. Safety spring retaining pin
62. Sear
63. Sear pin
64. Sight bead, front
65. Sight hood. front
66. Sight ramp, front
67. Sight assembly, rear
68. Sling eyelet, front
69. Sling eyelet washer
70. Sling eyelet, rear
71. Stock bolt
72. Stock bolt washer
73. Stock bolt plate
74. Support rail-right or left
75. Telescope mount filler screws
76. Timing latch
77. Timing latch retaining pin
78. Trigger
79. Trigger pin
80. Trigger guard

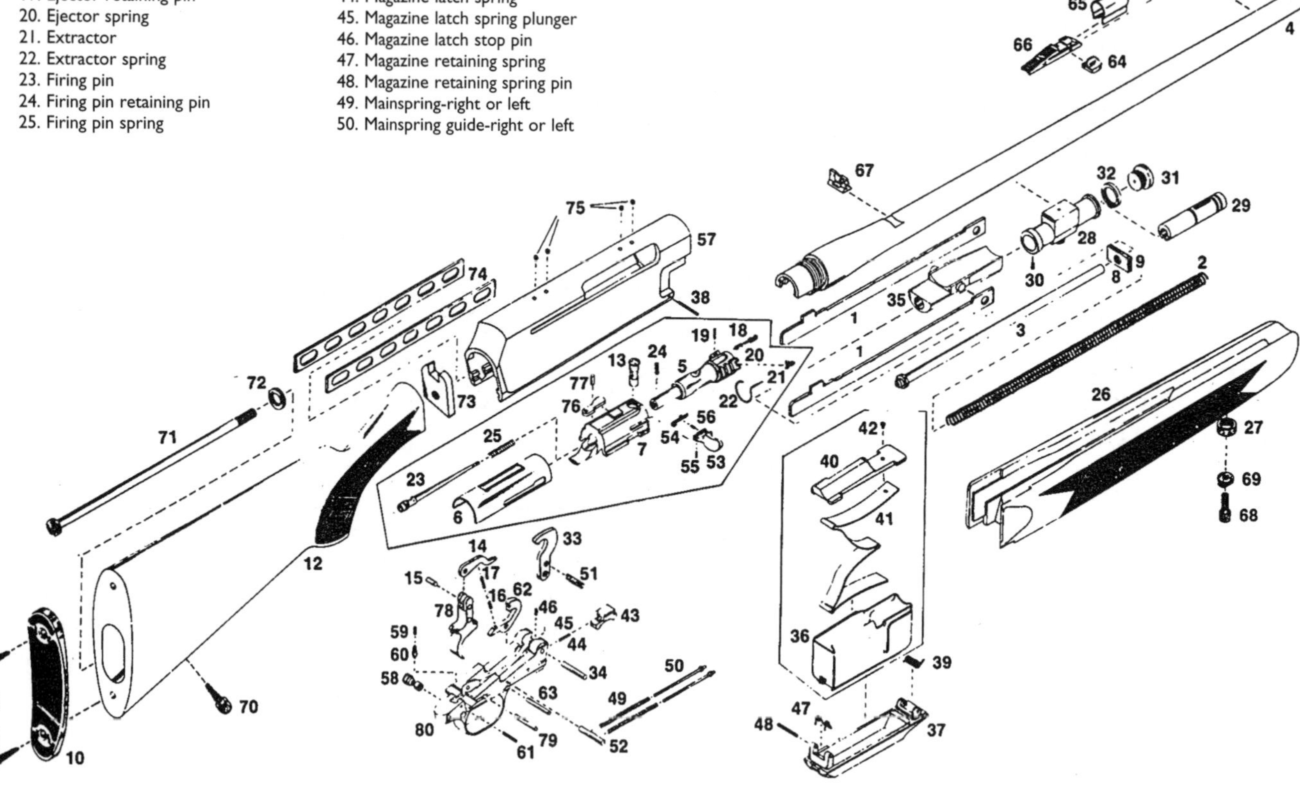

The Browning self-loading centerfire hunting rifle was a spinoff of Fabrique Nationale's (FN) development of military weapons.

It has a gas operated mechanism with a rotating bolt head that engages shoulders in the rear of the barrel. Its box magazine can, but need not, be detached from the hinged floorplate for loading. M. Ernest Vervier was its principal designer.

When it was introduced in 1967, the rifle was available in Grades I (no engraving) and II (lightly engraved), chambered for the .30-06 cartridge. By the following year chamberings included .243 Winchester, .270 W.C.F., .308 Winchester, 7mm Remington and the .300, and .338 Winchester Magnum cartridges. More elaborately decorated versions, the Grades III through V, appeared in Browning's 1971 catalog. Grades II and V were discontinued in 1975.

Since 1976 BARs have been made at an FN facility in Portugal. The .338 Winchester Magnum was dropped from production at that time as were the .243 and .270. All three chamberings were returned to the line in 1990, and the .280 Remington was added. Grade III rifles and the Grade IV magnum were produced until 1984. Grade IV rifles in standard calibers were made until 1989. The BAR Mark II series was introduced in 1993 and is still in production.

When chambered for magnum cartridges, Browning BARs are fitted with a recoil pad and have 24-inch barrels. Barrels for standard-cartridge rifles are 22 inches long.

Browning's referral to this self-loading hunting rifle as the BAR has caused some confusion on the part of old soldiers to whom the initials identify the U.S. military's M1918 series of selective fire and fully automatic rifles. The Model 1918 BAR (Browning Automatic Rifle) and its successors were designed by John M. Browning and were mainstay weapons of U.S. soldiers in World Wars I and II, and in Korea.

DISASSEMBLY

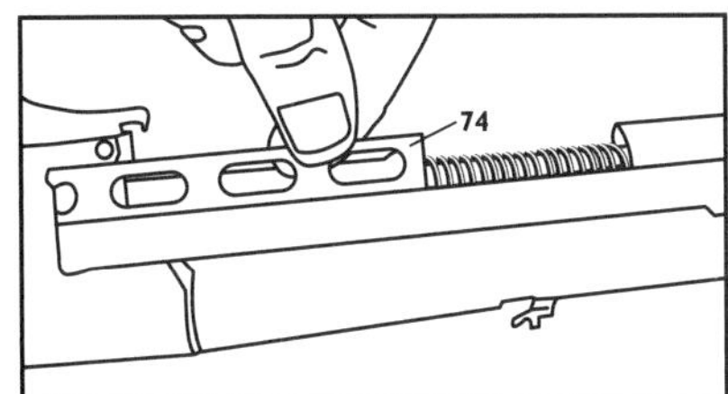

1 Close the bolt and pull the support rails (74) forward from their slots in the receiver (No.1). The action bars (1) are removed by pulling their forward ends away from the round connecting studs on the inertia piece (35), forward out of the receiver (No.2).

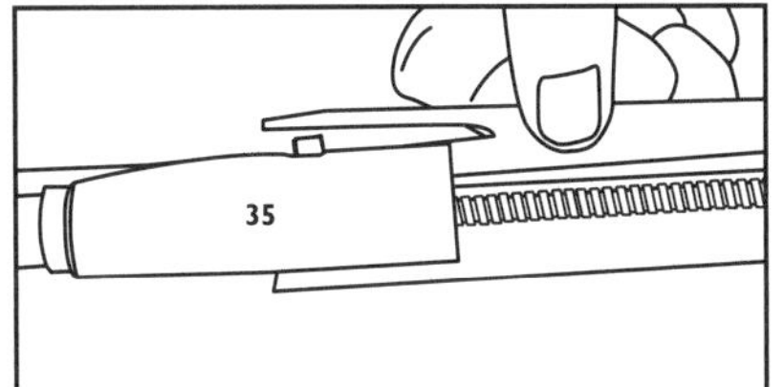

2 Remove the gas regulator (31) from the front end of the gas cylinder (No. 3) with a ⅝-inch wrench. The gas regulator will be very securely tightened in the gas cylinder and care must be taken to engage the wrench securely.

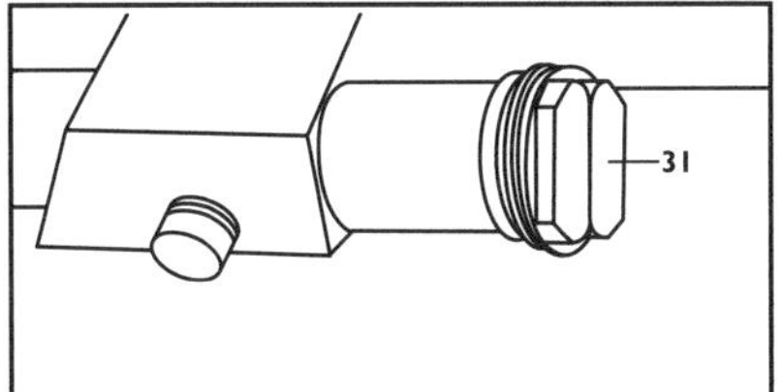

3 Pull the inertia piece back toward the receiver until rear face of the gas piston (29) can be pushed forward out of the gas cylinder with a small punch (No.4). A fouled gas system may require driving the gas piston forward with a hammer and drift punch. Use care to avoid scoring the parts. If the gas piston will not move with moderate force, put nitro-solvent around the piston, wait about 15 minutes and try to push it out with the punch.

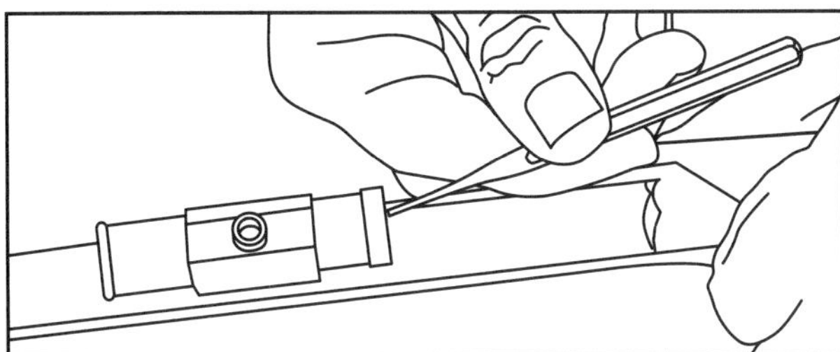

4 Grasp the receiver and pull the action spring guide (3) forward toward gas cylinder until it is clear of its recess in the receiver. The rear end of the action spring guide can then be moved to one side (No.5), then rearward to remove it with the action spring (2) and inertia piece.

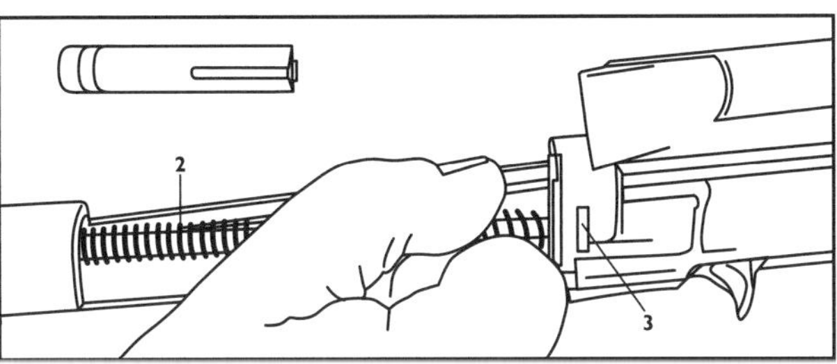

5 Residue in the gas cylinder and on the gas piston should be thoroughly removed with nitro-solvent or bore cleaner. Heavy residue can be removed by scrubbing the gas cylinder with a 20-ga. bronze wire bore-brush and solvent. The gas piston, gas cylinder and other parts of the gas system should be wiped with a very lightly oiled cloth after cleaning. The gas cylinder interior and the gas piston should not be oiled beyond this.

BROWNING BL-22 RIFLE

PARTS LEGEND

1. Bolt
2. Firing pin spring
3. Extractor spring
4. Extractor plunger
5. Extractor
6. Firing pin
7. Rear sight assembly
8. Barrel
9. Bolt cover plate
10. Bolt actuating pin
11. Firing pin retaining pin
12. Ejector
13. Ejector spring
14. Action screw
15. Magazine tube retaining screw
16. Receiver
17. Front sight
18. Magazine assembly
19. Outer magazine tube
20. Forearm
21. Forearm band pin
22. Forearm band
23. Muzzle clamp
24. Muzzle clamp screw
25. Buttplate screw (2)
26. Buttplate
27. Buttstock
28. Stock bolt
29. Stock bolt lock washer
30. Stock bolt washer
31. Hammer and mainspring guide
32. Mainspring
33. Mainspring follower
34. Carrier spacer
35. Carrier pin
36. Carrier spring
37. Carrier guide pin
38. Carrier
39. Locking block
40. Cocking lever link
41. Frame insert pin
42. Sear link
43. Trigger
44. Sear link spring
45. Trigger spring
46. Frame
47. Sear spring
48. Sear
49. Hammer pin
50. Sear pin
51. Cocking lever pin
52. Cocking lever link pin
53. Cocking lever
54. Sear link pin
55. Trigger pin

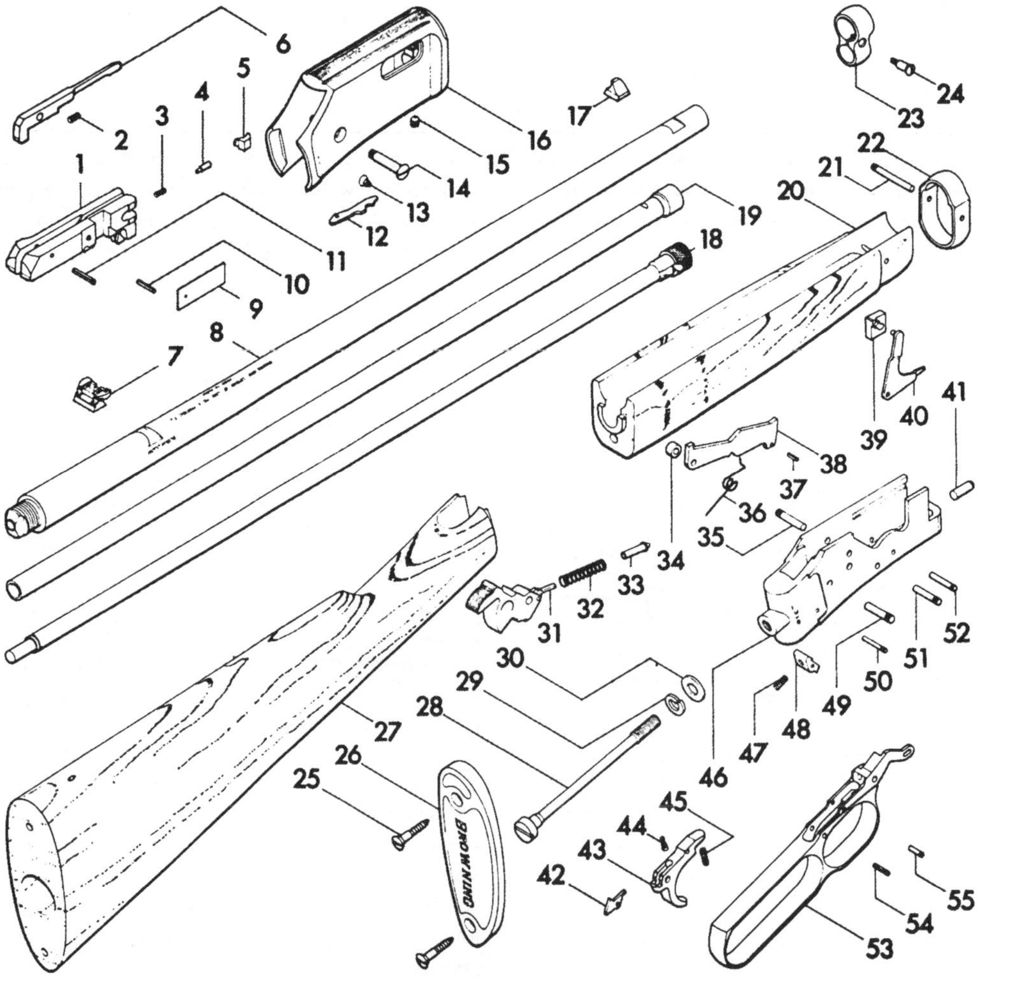

Browning Arms Co. added the BL-22 lever-action .22 caliber repeating rifle to its line of sporting arms in 1969. Generally similar in appearance to the Winchester lever-action repeaters developed by John M. Browning in the late 1800s, this small-game and plinking rifle is produced for Browning in Japan. It weighs only about five lbs., and fires .22 Long Rifle, Long, and Short Regular and high speed cartridges interchangeably, without adjustment. The capacity of its tubular under-barrel magazine is 15 Long Rifles, 17 Longs and 22 Shorts.

An excellent feature of this compact repeater is its short lever throw of only 33 inches, which makes for easy, rapid operation. Another fine feature is that the trigger is mounted on the lever and moves with it. This prevents the user's finger from being pinched between the lever and the trigger.

The exposed-type hammer has a half-cock notch designed to catch the hammer if it slips from the grasp when the rifle is being thumb cocked. The half-cock is not intended as a position of rest while handling or storing the rifle. The manufacturer suggests that the hammer be placed in fired position when the rifle is carried or stored.

Cartridge cases are ejected through a small port on the right side of the receiver. The receiver top is grooved for ease in attaching a clamp-on scope mount and the open sights fixed on the barrel consist of an adjustable, fold-down U-notch rear sight and a bead front sight.

Most exposed metal parts have a high-luster blue finish and the walnut buttstock and forearm are gloss-finished. There are two grades of this rifle. Grade I lacks engraving or checkering, and Grade II has hand engraving on the receiver, gold-plated trigger, and checkered buttstock and forearm.

DISASSEMBLY

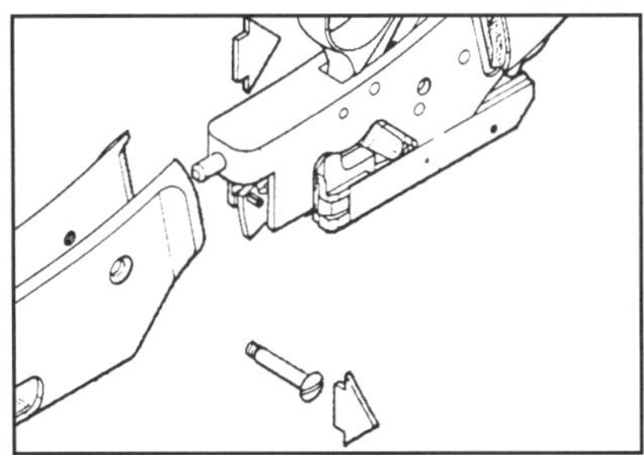

1 After removing the magazine assembly (18) check to see that no cartridges are in the rifle. Open the cocking lever (53) and remove the action screw (14). Turn the rifle upside down and pull the buttstock (27) and action assembly straight back out of receiver (16).

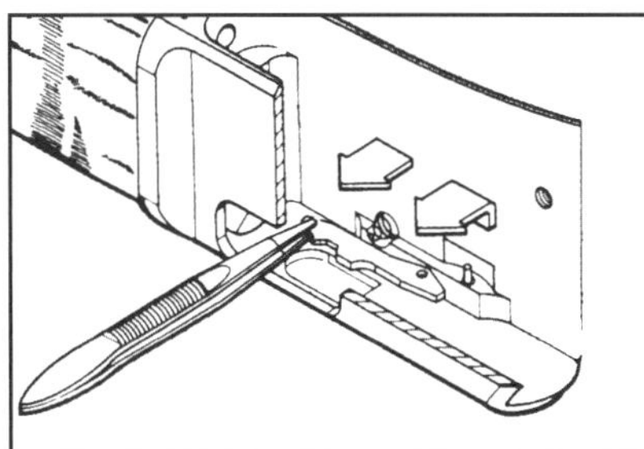

2 Working through the ejection port with tweezers, lift the ejector (12) from its fixed receiver pin and remove. Then, draw the ejector spring (13) straight out of its receiver seat. The frame insert pin (41), as shown in illustration 3, may come out with frame (46) or remain in its hole. If loose, remove the pin to prevent loss.

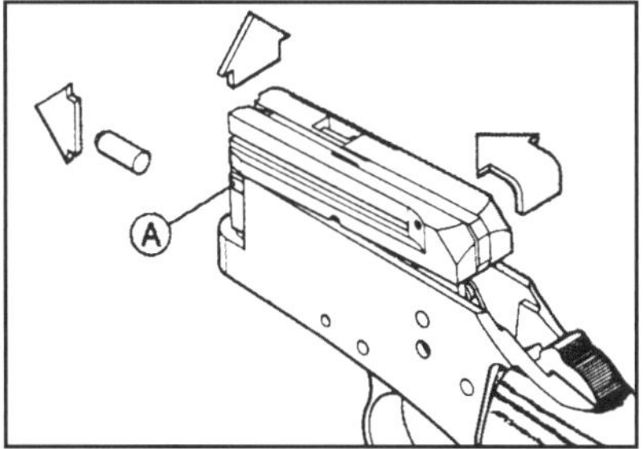

3 Close cocking lever. Lift rear of bolt (1) slightly and push forward until lug "A" emerges from front of frame. Lift off bolt, and remove locking block (39) from cocking lever link (40). Push front end of carrier (38) slightly to the left, and allow it to swing up on its spring. Do not lower hammer (31) while action is out of receiver. Drift out solid pins to emerge serrated end first.

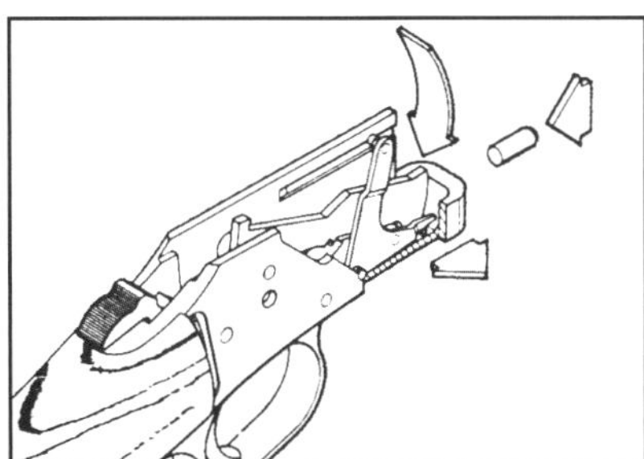

4 Begin reassembly by seating flat end of frame insert pin in its frame socket. Pivot carrier downward into frame, and move to the right, catching carrier guide pin (37) beneath tail of cocking lever link.

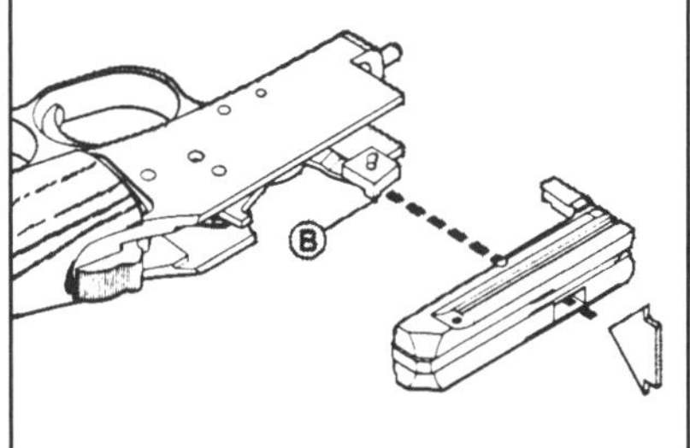

5 Turn right side of frame down, and place locking block over stud on cocking lever link, locating small triangular section of block "B" down and toward hammer. Install bolt over locking block, guiding block into its well within bolt. Start bolt lug into its frame groove, and slide bolt to the rear until it clears carrier hook and can be brought flush with frame. Then, open cocking lever fully.

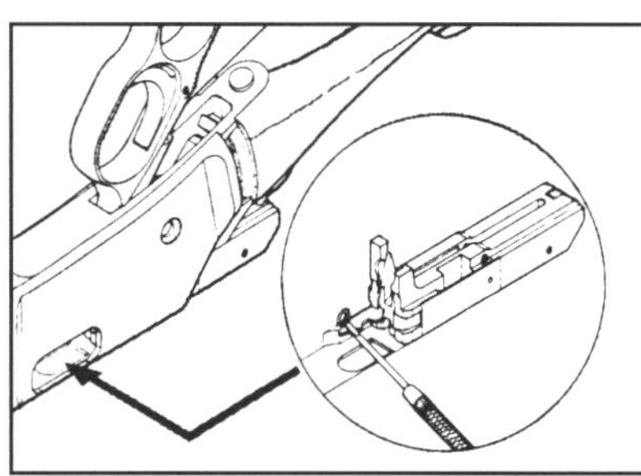

6 Insert ejector spring and ejector in receiver, positioning them as shown in illustration 2. Place action assembly in rear of receiver, sliding it forward on the bolt in a straight line. Tip of ejector spring must bear squarely on side of ejector. If necessary, position spring with a small screwdriver, working through ejection port. When action is fully home, replace action screw.

BROWNING BPS SHOTGUN

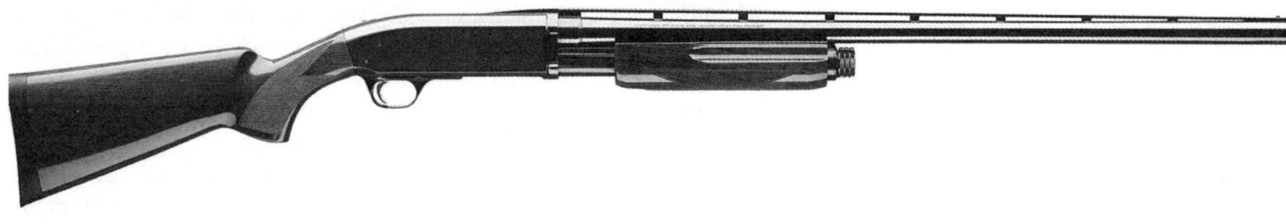

PARTS LEGEND

1. Action bar, right
2. Action bar, left
3. Action bar pin
4. Action slide lock release
5. Bolt
6. Buttstock
7. Carrier
8. Carrier pin
9. Carrier pin retainer
10. Cartridge stop, right
11. Cartridge stop, left
12. Disconnector
13. Extractor
14. Extractor pin
15. Extractor sping
16. Firing pin
17. Firing pin retaining pin
18. Forearm
19. Forearm screw
20. Forearm tube
21. Hammer
22. Hammer pin
23. Hammer spring
24. Hammer spring guide
25. Hammer spring pin
26. Lock
27. Lock pin
28. Magazine cap
29. Magazine cap stopper
30. Magazine cap stopper spring
31. Magazine follower
32. Magazine spring
33. Magazine spring retainer
34. Magazine tube
35. Receiver
36. Safety
37. Safety adjusting screw
38. Safety nut
39. Safety plunger
40. Safety spring
41. Sear
42. Sear adjusting screw
43. Sear pin
44. Sear spring
45. Selector
46. Selector retainer
47. Sight bead (front)
48. Slide
49. Slide lock pin
50. Slide lock spring
51. Slide lock stop
52. Stock bolt
53. Stock bolt lock washer
54. Stock bolt washer
55. Trigger
56. Trigger adjusting screw
57. Trigger guard
58. Trigger guide bushing
59. Trigger guide bushing spring
60. Trigger guide pin
61. Trigger pin
62. Trigger pull screw
63. Trigger spring
64. Trigger spring follower

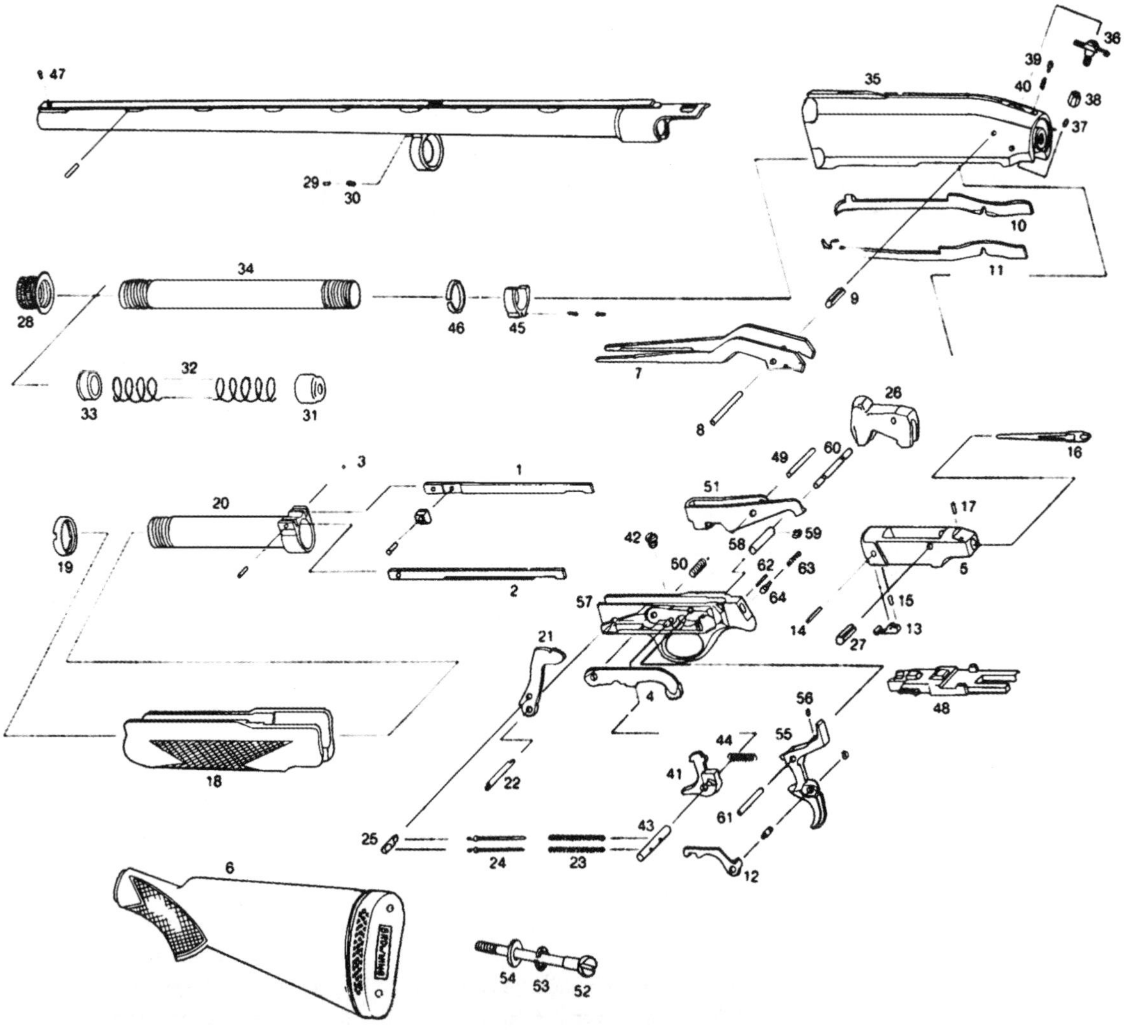

The Browning BPS shotgun, introduced in 1977, is chambered for 12-gauge, 2¾- and 3-inch ammunition and 3½-inch magnum. It was the first Browning-designed pump-action shotgun to bear the company's name.

Many famous shotguns, including the legendary Winchester Model 97, were designed by John M. Browning and sold to other gun manufacturing companies. A few other noteworthy examples of his original thinking are the Stevens Model 520, the Remington Model 17 and the Ithaca Model 37. These last two models share a common underloading and ejection port with the BPS.

The BPS, first produced in three grades — Field, Trap and a Buck Special — is now offered in at least nine. These include Upland Special, Rifled Deer Hunter, Trap, Micro and BPS 10-Gauge Stalker models. Current manufacture BPS guns come with either wood or synthetic stocks. Several barrel lengths are offered along with a rifled deer barrel and 12- and 20-gauge BPS shotguns include an interchangeable choke tube system. Most barrels are fitted with a ventilated rib.

The BPS has a magazine cutoff device located on the bottom of the magazine tube forward of the receiver. This cutoff has a two-position selector ring marked "S" for single-shot functioning or "R" for repeating. Rotating the selector to the "S" position enables the shooter to exchange shells in the chamber without disturbing the magazine contents. Magazine capacity for various models is 2¾ inch: four; 3 inch: three and 3½ inch: three.

DISASSEMBLY

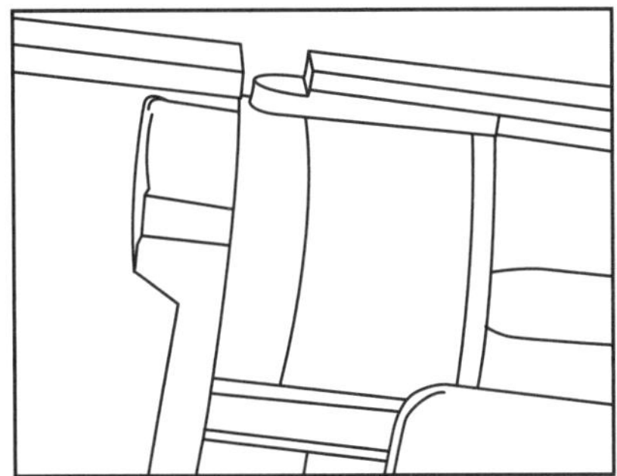

1 First, make sure that the chamber is empty, and check to be certain that there are no shells remaining in the magazine. To remove the barrel, unscrew the magazine cap (28). Initially, resistance to turning will be felt due to tension applied to the cap by the magazine cap stopper spring (30). Press up on the action slide lock release (4) and pull the forearm (18) fully to the rear. The barrel can then be withdrawn from the receiver. Note that the tail end of the ventilated rib fits into a recess at the front of the rib extension. This keeps the barrel and receiver in proper alignment.

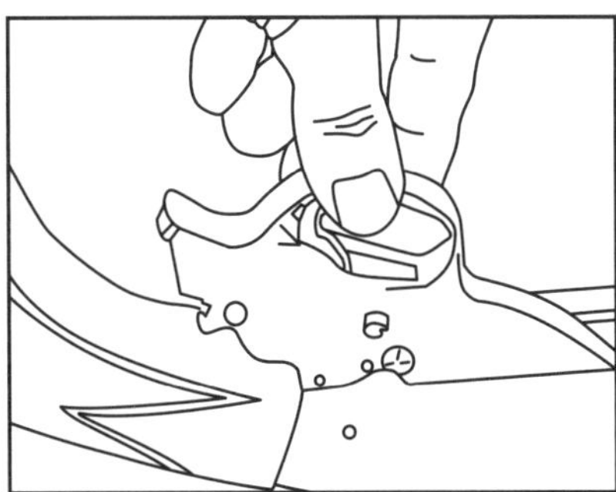

2 The trigger assembly is attached to the receiver by the trigger guide pin (60). This non-directional pin is located at the lower rear portion of the receiver and is the larger of the two pins found in the receiver. To remove the trigger assembly, the trigger guide pin (60) is removed by using a ⅛-inch drift and a light mallet. The trigger assembly is then pulled to the rear, up and out of the receiver. Lift out the right and left cartridge stops (10 and 11) from the inside walls of the receiver.

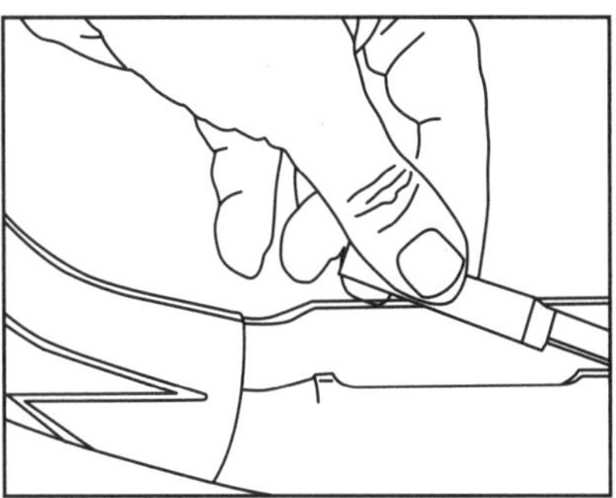

3 To disengage and remove the forearm and action bars (1 and 2), the slide (48) must first be removed. Pull the forearm fully to the rear and tilt the front of the slide up and then lift it out of the receiver. The forearm (18) and the action bars (1 and 2) are then pulled out of the receiver. The bolt (5) is lifted straight up and out of the receiver.

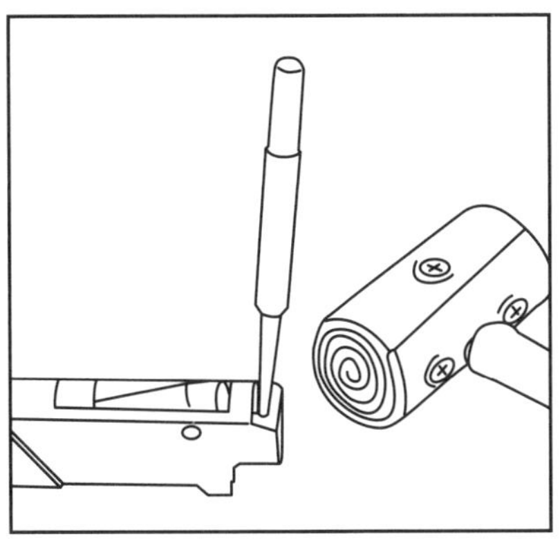

4 To remove firing pin (16), the firing pin retaining pin (17) at the top rear of the bolt must be driven out. This allows the firing pin to be withdrawn from the firing pin guide hole. The extractor (13) is removed by tapping out the extractor pin (14) located at the lower front portion of the bolt. CAUTION: The extractor spring (15) is heavily compressed. The carrier (7) is secured to the receiver with the carrier pin (8). NOTE: This pin is staked in place and removal of it and the carrier should be done only by a competent gunsmith. The magazine tube (34) and its follower (31), spring (32) and spring retainer (33) should be routinely cleaned. To disassemble, pry out the magazine spring retainer (33) using a flat-bladed screwdriver tip. CAUTION: The magazine spring (32) is under compression and care should be taken to prevent it from flying out of the magazine tube. After removing the magazine spring, tilt the front of the tube down and the magazine follower will slide out. Further disassembly should only be undertaken by a gunsmith.

BROWNING B-SS SHOTGUN

PARTS LEGEND

1. Buttplate
2. Buttplate (2)
3. Cocking lever (right)
4. Cocking lever (left)
5. Cocking lever screw (2)
6. Cocking lever screw lock screw (2)
7. Cocking lever spring (2)
8. Connector
9. Connector pin
10. Connector spring
11. Ejector (right)
12. Ejector (left)
13. Ejector stop screw
14. Ejector hammer (right)
15. Ejector hammer (left)
16. Ejector hammer housing
17. Ejector hammer housing pin
18. Ejector hammer spring
19. Ejector hammer spring guide
20. Ejector hammer sear (right)
21. Ejector hammer sear (left)
22. Ejector hammer sear pin
23. Ejector hammer sear spring
24. Ejector trip
25. Ejector trip screw
26. Firing pin (2)
27. Firing pin bushing (2)
28. Firing pin spring (2)
29. Forearm
30. Forearm bracket
31. Hammer (2)
32. Hammer pin
33. Inertia block
34. Inertia block spring
35. Locking bolt
36. Mainspring (2)
37. Mainspring guide (2)
38. Safety
39. Safety pin
40. Safety spring
41. Safety lever
42. Safety lever screw
43. Safety push rod
44. Sear (right)
45. Sear (left)
46. Sear pin
47. Sear spring (2)
48. Sight bead front
49. Sear spring plunger (2)
50. Stock
51. Stock bolt
52. Stock bolt washer
53. Stock bolt lock washer
54. Takedown lever
55. Takedown lever pin
56. Takedown lever spring
57. Takedown lever spring screw
58. Takedown lever bracket
59. Takedown lever bracket screw (rear)
60. Takedown lever bracket screw (front)
61. Tang screw
62. Top lever
63. Top lever screw
64. Top lever spring
65. Top lever spring screw
66. Joint pin (not shown)
67. Top lever dog shaft
68. Trigger
69. Trigger pin
70. Trigger guard
71. Trigger guard screw (1 or 2)
72. Trigger plate
73. Trigger plate screw (2) (Selective Trigger Models)
74. Inertia block
75. Inertia block pin
76. Inertia block pivot
77. Inertia block pivot holder pin
78. Inertia block spring
79. Inertia block stop
80. Inertia block stop spring
81. Safety
82. Safety spring
83. Safety lever
84. Sear lever
85. Sear lever pin
86. Selector
87. Selector button
88. Selector button pin
89. Selector plunger
90. Selector plunger spring
91. Selector plunger spring stop pin
92. Snap link
93. Trigger gold plated
94. Trigger plate
95. Trigger spring
96. Trigger spring pin

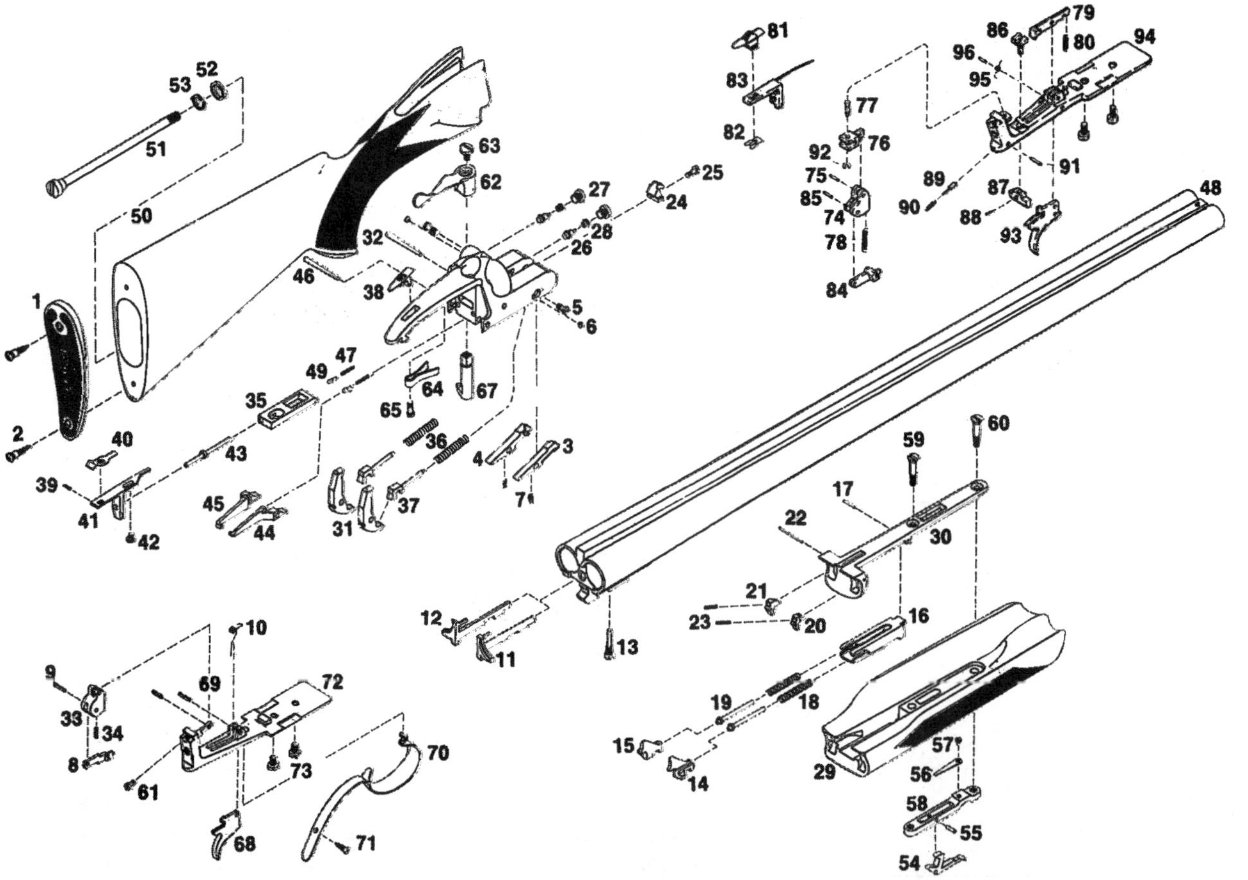

The Browning B-SS (Browning Side-by-Side) was introduced in 1971 bored for the 12-gauge shell only. One year later, Browning offered the B-SS in 20-gauge as well. Both gauges are chambered for either the 2¾- or 3-inch shells.

Early models — up to 1976 — were equipped with non-selective mechanical triggers. The first pull of the single trigger fired the right (more open choke) barrel. and the second pull fired the left (tighter choke) barrel. In 1977, Browning upgraded the B-SS by adding a barrel selector switch which is located at the rearmost portion of the trigger guard. In 1983 a sidelock model was introduced.

The B-SS is equipped with an automatic safety that engages whenever the action is fully opened. Automatic, selective ejectors are standard on all models. In the event that only a single shot is fired, only the fired shell will be ejected from the chamber after opening the action. The other ejector raises the unfired shell head about ¼ inch for manual removal.

The Browning is built on a true box-lock action. The barrels are held together at their breech ends by chopper lumps.

The B-SS stock is available with either a full pistol grip or a straight wrist. Three barrel lengths are available in 12-gauge — 26, 28 or 30 inches, and either 26- or 28-inch lengths in 20-gauge. A trio of chokes are available — improved cylinder, modified and full.

The French walnut stock and fore-end are checkered in an 18 lines-per-inch pattern. Grade II versions have a fancier grained stock and fore-end and 20 lines-per-inch checkering. Browning discontinued the B-SS shotgun in 1987.

DISASSEMBLY

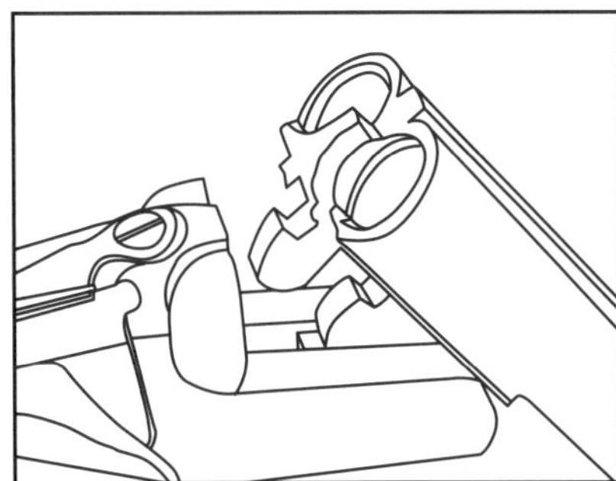

1 Remove the forearm (29) by pulling the takedown lever (54) out of its bracket (58) and simultaneously applying pressure at the tip of the forearm to pry it away from the barrels. Pull the entire forearm forward and down away from the frame. Set the forearm aside and grasp the barrels in one hand while moving the top lever (62) to the right, carefully allowing the barrels to pivot out of the receiver.

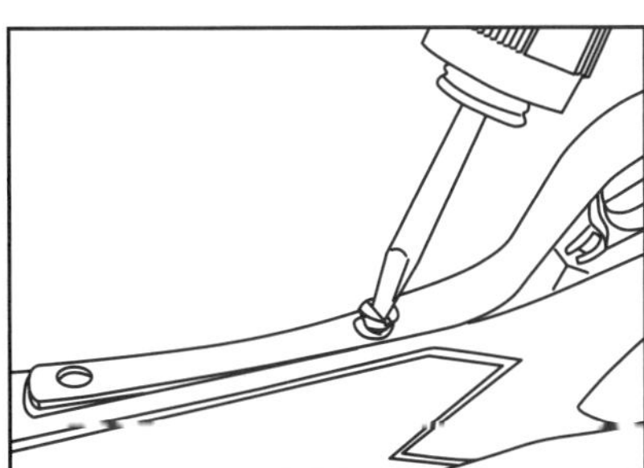

2 To remove the stock, first remove the buttplate screws (2) and buttplate (1) with a properly fitting screwdriver. The Sporter models have a hard-rubber buttplate, while field grade shotguns are generally equipped with a soft rubber recoil pad. These recoil pads are equipped with blind holes and it's important to first determine whether or not the internal screws have Phillips or slotted heads. Use a waxed or soaped Phillips screwdriver to determine the type of screw used by the factory. The stock is held in place with a through-bolt (51) that has a slotted head. A long, heavyduty screwdriver is needed to loosen this bolt. The trigger guard (70) should be removed after the stock bolt. The screws holding the trigger guard have fine slots, and a specially ground screwdriver tip should be used.

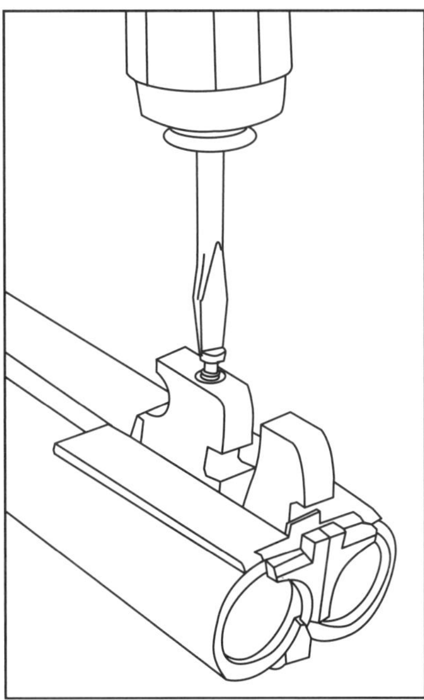

3 After removing both screws (pistol grip models have only one trigger guard screw), the trigger guard is then turned 90 degrees to the right and withdrawn from its corresponding groove slightly ahead of the trigger. To remove the ejectors (11 & 12), use the same fine-bladed screwdriver and remove the ejector stop screw (13) entirely from the under locking lug. This screw should be checked for rust and should carry a small amount of oil.

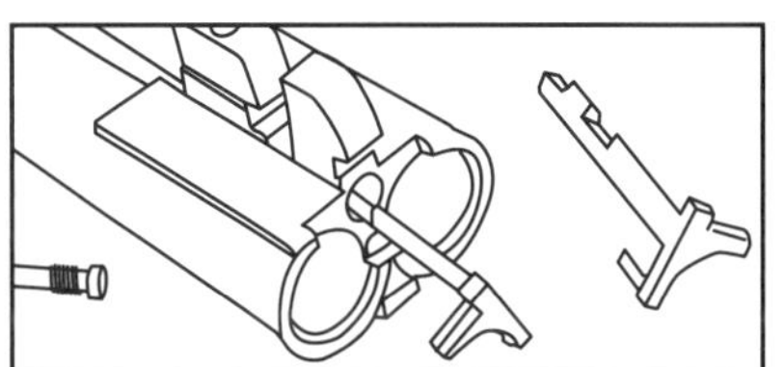

4 The twin ejectors can then be withdrawn from the holes in the barrel assembly. They should be thoroughly cleaned and lightly oiled to prevent rust.

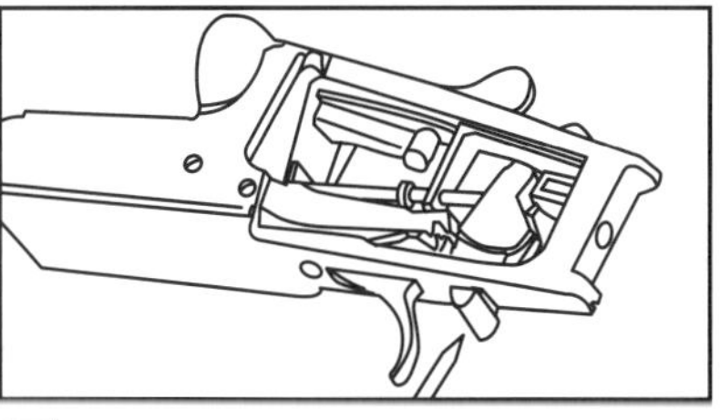

5 Later model B-SS shotguns are equipped with a barrel selector lever that is located behind the trigger. The B-SS has mechanical triggers. and in the event that the first barrel misfires, a second pull on the single trigger will fire the other barrel. Pointer indicates barrel selector. NOTE: Further disassembly is not recommended by the factory.

BROWNING .22 AUTOMATIC RIFLE

PARTS LEGEND

1. Barrel
2. Front sight
3. Barrel adjusting ring
4. Barrel lock ring
5. Barrel lock
6. Barrel lock spring
7. Barrel lock spring plunger
8. Cartridge guide
9. Receiver
10. Magazine spring
11. Forearm
12. Inner magazine tube
13. Magazine handle pin
14. Magazine follower
15. Magazine handle
16. Magazine follower spring
17. Magazine follower stop
18. Forearm retaining stud
19. Forearm escutcheon
20. Forearm screw
21. Rear sight
22. Firing pin spring
23. Firing pin spring guide
24. Breechblock
25. Extractor spring retaining pin
26. Extractor
27. Extractor spring
28. Extractor spring retainer
29. Firing pin
30. Recoil spring
31. Recoil spring guide
32. Trigger pin
33. Safety, cross-bolt
34. Trigger guard
35. Trigger
36. Safety spring
37. Safety spring plunger
38. Disconnector pin
39. Sear spring
40. Disconnector
41. Trigger spring
42. Sear
43. Cartridge guide spring
44. Cartridge stop
45. Sear spring pin
46. Sear pin
47. Stock screw
48. Outer magazine tube
49. Buttplate
50. Buttplate screw (2)
51. Magazine stop plate screw (4)
52. Magazine stop plate

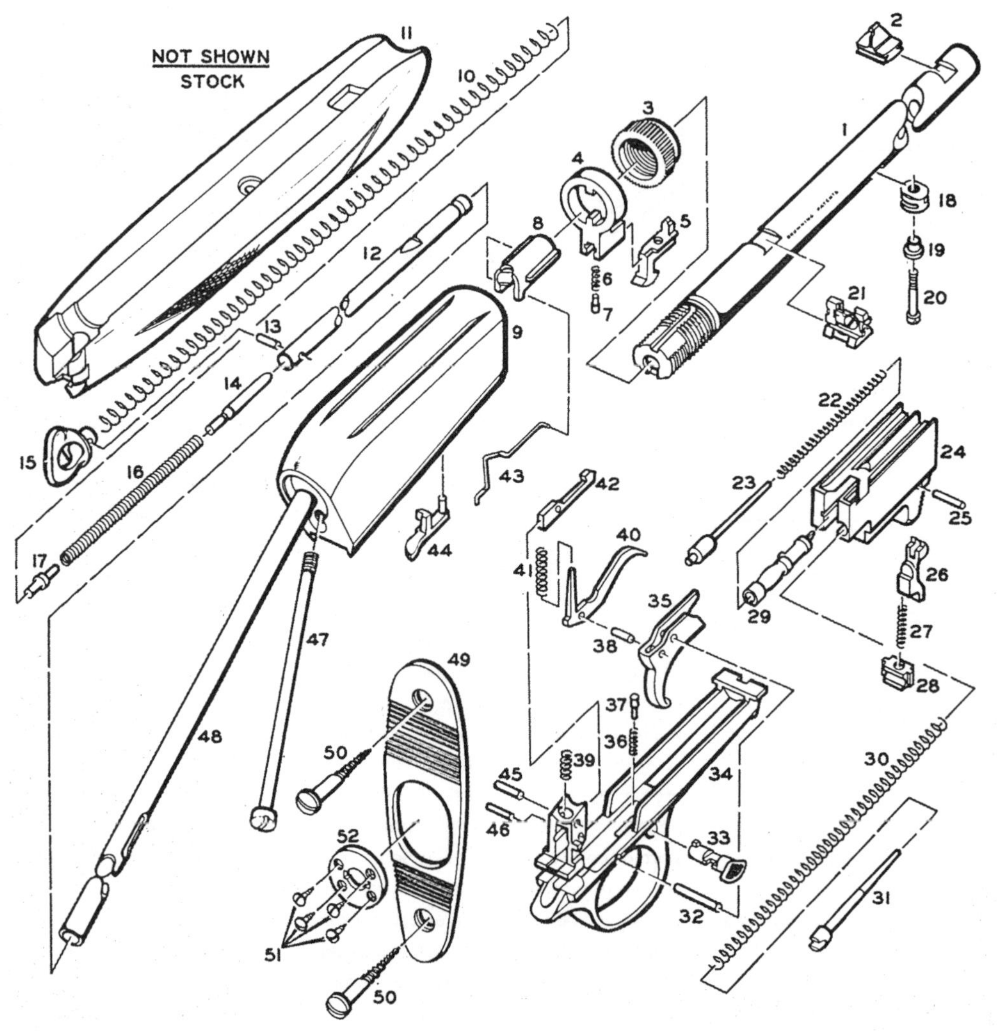

In 1914 the Belgian firm of Fabrique Nationale began production of a cal. .22 rifle designed in 1913 by John M. Browning. This rifle was semiautomatic with straight blowback operated breech. Of hammerless construction, it had a tubular magazine in the buttstock. The top and sides of the receiver were completely enclosed. Ejection of fired cases was from bottom of the receiver. It was readily taken down for cleaning or storage.

In 1922 Remington Arms Co. of Ilion, New York, began production of a similar rifle under license from FN. Designated Model 24, it had a loading port in the right side of the buttstock, but was otherwise mechanically similar to the FN rifle. The Model 24 had a 19-inch barrel and was chambered for both .22 Short and Long Rifle cartridges and was offered in several grades, and a special version was made for use in commercial shooting galleries.

The Model 24 was discontinued in 1935 to be replaced that year by the Model 241. The Model 241 had a larger forearm and buttstock which made it more suitable for adult use.

Barrel length was increased to 24 inches to improve the rifle's balance. The action was adapted for both standard and high-velocity 22 Short and Long Rifle cartridges and, like the Model 24, was available in several grades as well as a gallery model. Production of the Model 241 ceased in 1951.

Browning has sold its .22 Automatic Rifle almost continuously since 1914. In 1956 major improvements were made that gave the Browning product a strong resemblance to the Model 241. Chief among these was the addition of a loading port on the right side of the buttstock and the enlargement of both the buttstock and the fore-end. Barrel length of the Browning rifle remains at 19½ inches. Browning production was moved to the B. C. Miroku Co., in Japan in 1976.

DISASSEMBLY

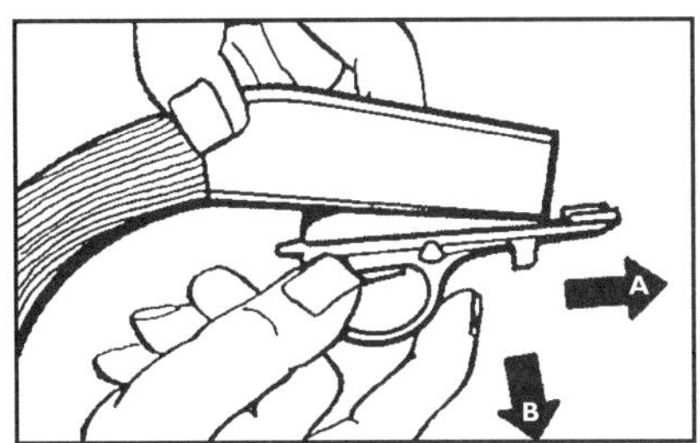

1 To remove barrel and forearm assembly from receiver, hold rifle upside down and push barrel lock (5) forward. Draw breech-block (24) back ¼ inches or more by the finger piece and hold with thumb. Give barrel a ¼-inch turn clockwise and separate the assemblies. For further disassembly, remove inner magazine tube (12) and assembly by turning magazine handle (15) ¼-inch turn and withdrawing assembly to rear until it catches against magazine stop plate (52). Turn assembly ¼ inches again and pull it from the stock. Push trigger guard (34) forward about ¾ inch (A), retract breech block (24) and hold in rearward position. Pull rear end of trigger guard out of receiver (B) about 1 inch and draw mechanism out and away.

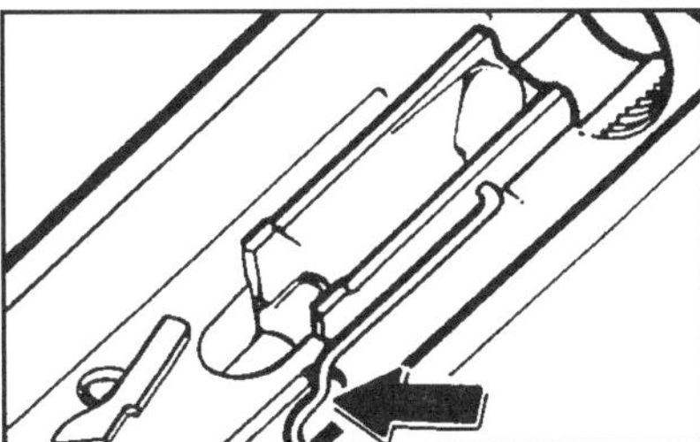

2 Remove stock screw (47) and stock. Place blade of a screwdriver against rear of cartridge guide spring (43) and pry spring out of cartridge guide slot in receiver (9). Slide cartridge guide (8) out of front end of receiver. Using thin-nosed pliers, grasp front end of cartridge stop (44) and lift it out of receiver.

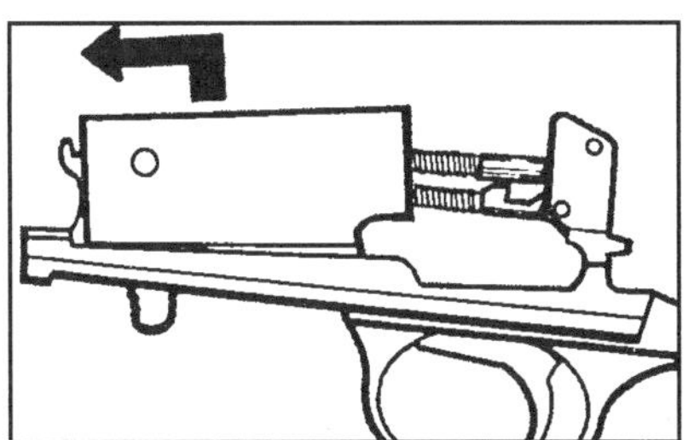

3 Continue by pulling trigger (35) to release firing pin (29). Lift breech block out of trigger guard and allow it to move slowly forward to prevent escape of recoil spring (30) and firing pin spring (22). When breech block is out, firing pin, firing pin spring guide (23), firing pin spring, recoil spring and recoil spring guide (31) may be lifted away.

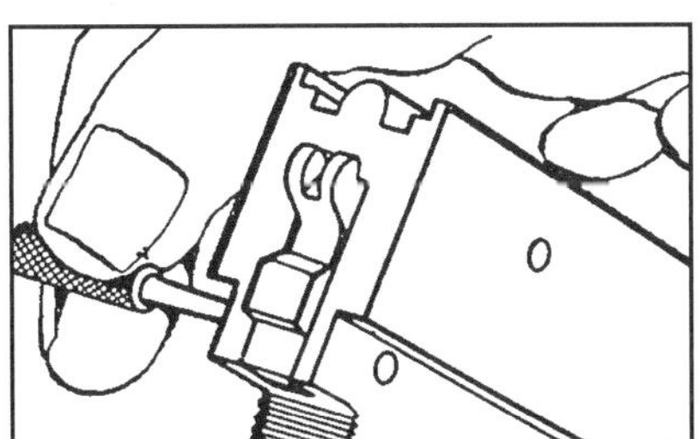

4 Drift out extractor spring retaining pin (25) and remove extractor (26), extractor spring (27), and extractor spring retainer (28).

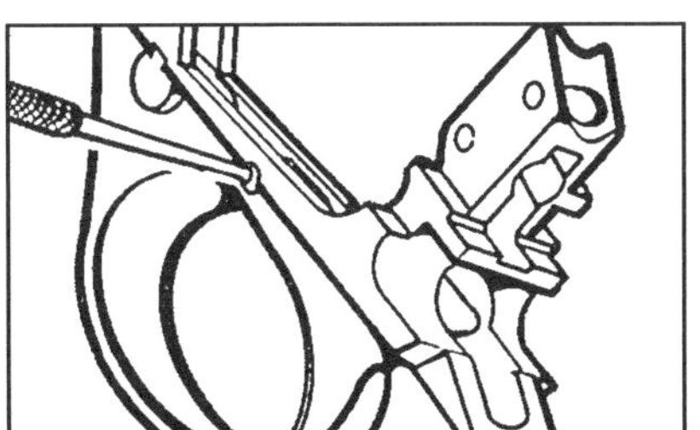

5 Next, drift out sear spring pin (45) from left to right and remove sear spring (39). Drift out sear pin (46), also from left to right, and slide sear (42) out of its housing to front. Drift out trigger pin (32) from left to right and remove the trigger and disconnector (40) through the top of the trigger guard. Drift disconnector pin (38) from left to right out of trigger.

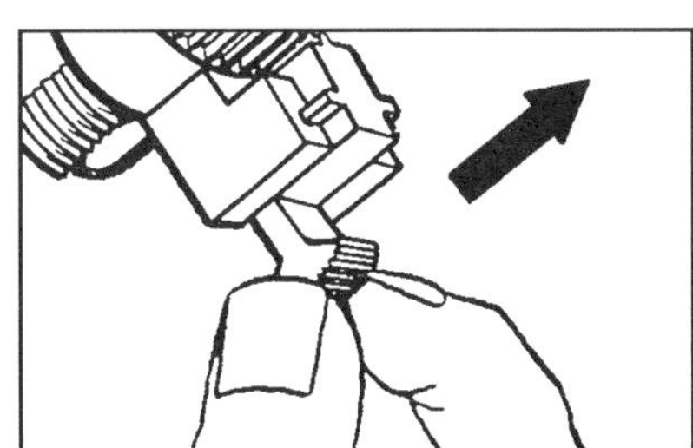

6 Remove forearm screw (20) and forearm (11). Slide barrel lock (5) forward and away. Barrel lock spring (6) and barrel lock spring plunger (7) can now be removed from barrel lock ring (4). Using a leather or plastic mallet, tap off the barrel lock ring and unscrew the barrel adjusting ring (3). Reassemble in reverse order.

BROWNING CITORI SHOTGUN

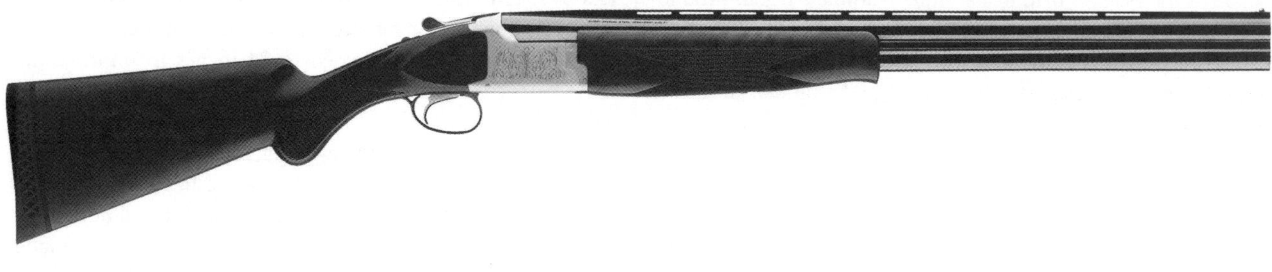

PARTS LEGEND

1. Buttplate
2. Buttplate screw
3. Cocking lever
4. Cocking lever lifter
5. Cocking lever lifter pin
7. Cocking lever pin
8. Connector
9. Connector stop pin
10. Drop stop adjustment set screw*
11. Ejector extension, left
12. Ejector extension, right
13. Ejector extension screw
14. Ejector hammer, left
15. Ejector hammer pin
16. Ejector hammer, right
17. Ejector hammer spring
18. Ejector hammer spring plunger
19. Ejector hammer spring receiver
20. Ejector hammer spring receiver screw
21. Ejector retaining pin (screw)
22. Ejector, right & left
23. Ejector sear
24. Ejector sear pin all
25. Ejector sear/cocking lever lifter spring
26. Ejector trip rod, left
27. Ejector trip rod, right
28. Firing pin over
29. Firing pin retaining pin
30. Firing pin spring under
31. Firing pin under
32. Forearm bracket
33. Forearm screw
34. Forearm
    34a. Forearm screw escutcheon
35. Hammer left
36. Hammer pin
37. Hammer right
38. Impact ring retaining screw*
39. Inertia block
    39a. Inertia block pin
40. Link
41. Link pin inertia block
42. Link pin receiver
43. Locking bolt
44. Mainspring
45. Mainspring plunger all
46. Recoil pad*
47. Recoil reducer (not shown)
48. Recoil reducer pad plate *
49. Recoil reducer pad plate set screw *
50. Recoil reducer stock plate plate screw*
51. Recoil reducer stock*
52. Rib assembly*
53. Rib elevator detent spring*
54. Rib elevator nut*
55. Rib elevator screw*
56. Rib elevator screw pin*
57. Rib elevator spring
58. Rib elevator spring follower*
59. Rib pivot*
60. Rib pivot pin*
61. Rib vibration damper*
62. Sear, left
63. Sear pin
64. Sear, right
65. Sear spring
66. Selector ball spring type
67. Selector ball type
68. Selector block
69. Selector safety
70. Selector spring
71. Selector spring detent pin
72. Selector/take down lever spring screw
72. Sight bead front
73. Sight white center all
74. Sight white front
75. Stock adjustment nut*
76. Stock adjustment plate*
77. Stock adjustment plate set screw*
78. Stock adjustment plate stud*
79. Stock adjustment stud screw*
80. Stock bolt
81. Stock bolt lock washer
82. Stock bolt washer
83. Stock
84. Takedown lever
85. Takedown lever bracket
86. Takedown lever bracket screw front
87. Takedown lever bracket screw rear
88. Takedown lever bracket screws, front & rear blue*
89. Takedown lever pin
90. Takedown lever spring
91, Top lever, 16-gauge*
92. Top lever
93. Top lever dog
94. Top lever dog screw
95. Top lever spring
96. Top lever spring retainer
97. Top lever spring retainer screw
98. Trigger
99. Trigger guard
100. Trigger guard wood screw
102. Trigger piston
103. Trigger piston pin
104. Trigger piston spring

* (not shown in exploded view)

The Browning Citori Over/Under 12 gauge shotgun was introduced in 1973 and is manufactured in a number of models and grades. The action was fitted with selective hammer ejectors and a single selective, single trigger. The barrels are locked by a traditional tapered under-lug and bolt system and pivot on a full-length, replaceable hinge pin. The chambers are chrome-plated and the barrels accept Browning Invector Plus interchangeable choke tubes. Various models include the Citori 20-gauge skeet (1975); the Citori Sideplate (1980); Citori Grade VI and Grade I Superposed (1983); Citori Upland Special and Sidelock 20-gauge (1984); Grade III Citori (1985); Citori Sporting Clays (1989).

Citori shotguns are marketed under the headings of Field, Target and High-Grade. Field guns include the 525, Lightning, White Lightning, Superlight Feather and Lightning Feather. The Target group includes the Citori Sporting, Lightning Sporting, XS Sporting, XT Trap, XS Pro-Comp, and XS Skeet. High Grade Models include the Citori Grand Lightning, Grade III Lightning and Grade VI Lightning. Lightning models are distinguished by a rounded semi-pistol grip buttstock, fluted comb and rounded forend.

DISASSEMBLY

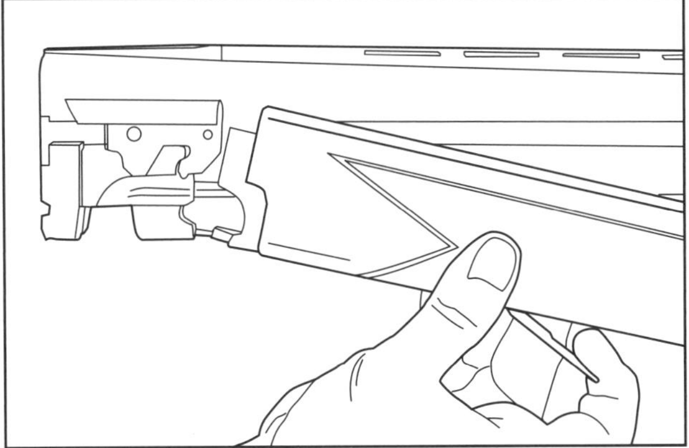

1 Close the action if it is not already and anchor the buttstock (83) against your upper leg and lift outward on the takedown lever (84) .At the same time, grasp the forearm (34) and,with the help of the left hand pivot the forearm away from the barrels and remove the forearm.

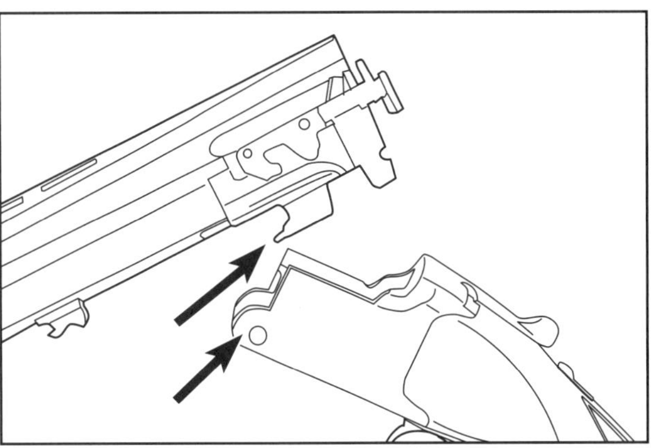

2 Break the action of the gun open. Carefully disengage the barrel lug from the hinge pin and lift the barrels upward and out of the action.

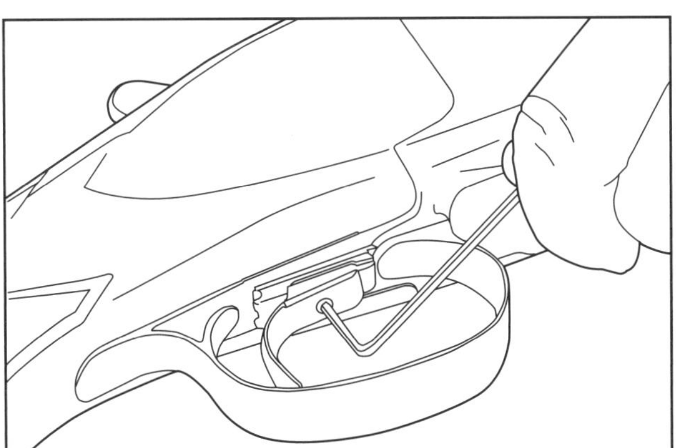

3 All Citori sporting models are supplied with three different styles of trigger shoes.To remove the trigger shoe, loosen the center screw with the provided 5/64" Allen wrench. Loosen the screw so the trigger shoe slides easily on the trigger plate. Keep the screw threaded at least one thread into the trigger plate so the screw is not lost.

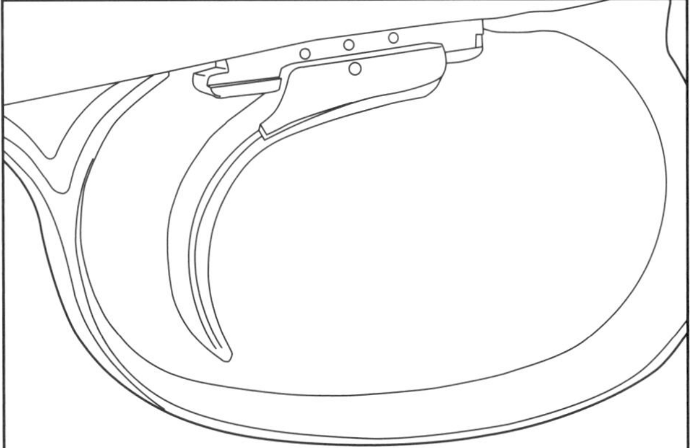

4 Slide the trigger shoe forward to the end of the trigger plate. Press the rearward end of the trigger plate down with your finger and gently slide the trigger shoe off the trigger plate.

BROWNING DOUBLE AUTOMATIC

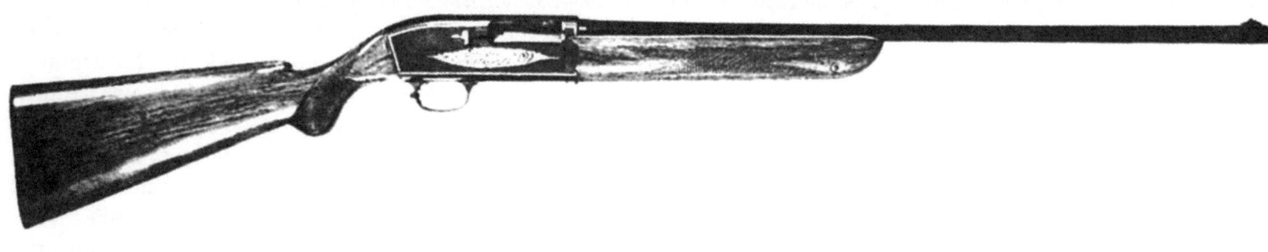

PARTS LEGEND

1. Receiver
2. Friction brake, bronze buffer
3. Recoil spring
4. Forearm pivot pin stop
5. Carrier latch spring
6. Carrier latch stabilizer spring
7. Carrier latch stabilizer
8. Carrier latch
9. Link hook spring
10. Link hook spring plunger
11. Link hook pin
12. Link hook
13. Inertia block core
14. Inertia block core spring
15. Inertia block
16. Action spring, inside
17. Stock bolt
18. Action spring, outside
19. Stock bolt lock washer
20. Stock bolt washer
21. Action spring tube cap
22. Action spring tube
23. Barrel
24. Operating handle
25. Firing pin
26. Firing pin stop plate
27. Locking block latch
28. Firing pin spring
29. Sight bead
30. Link
31. Extractor pin
32. Extractor spring guide
33. Breechblock
34. Extractor spring
35. Extractor
36. Link pin
37. Locking block
38. Forearm escutcheon (2)
39. Sight base*
40. Barrel lock
41. Barrel lock guide
42. Forearm latch
43. Forearm latch spring (2)
44. Forearm plate
45. Ejector*
46. Forearm
47. Barrel extension*
48. Breechblock buffer
49. Breechblock buffer pin (found on early production guns only)
50. Buttplate
51. Buttplate screw (2)
52. Friction brake ring
53. Friction brake bronze, posterior
54. Friction brake washer (2)
55. Friction brake bronze, anterior
56. Barrel guide
57. Orienting ring
58. Adjusting cap
59. Forearm pivot pin
60. Disconnector
61. Trigger
62. Disconnector pin
63. Disconnector spring
64. Disconnector spring plunger
65. Safety retaining pin
66. Safety finger piece
67. Safety spring
68. Trigger pin
69. Sear spring guide
70. Sear spring
71. Sear
72. Trigger guard
73. Hammer pin
74. Sear pivot
75. Mainspring guide (2)
76. Mainspring (2)
77. Mainspring yoke
78. Hammer
79. Carrier
80. Carrier dog
81. Carrier dog pin
82. Carrier dog spring
83. Carrier pin
84. Carrier dog spring guide
85. Carrier spring guide
86. Carrier spring
87. Trigger guard fastening guide, right
88. Trigger guard fastening guide, left
89. Recoil spring tube*
90. Carrier latch guide pin
91. Recoil spring tube pin
92. Locking block latch rivet

*Factory assembled component, do not disassemble.

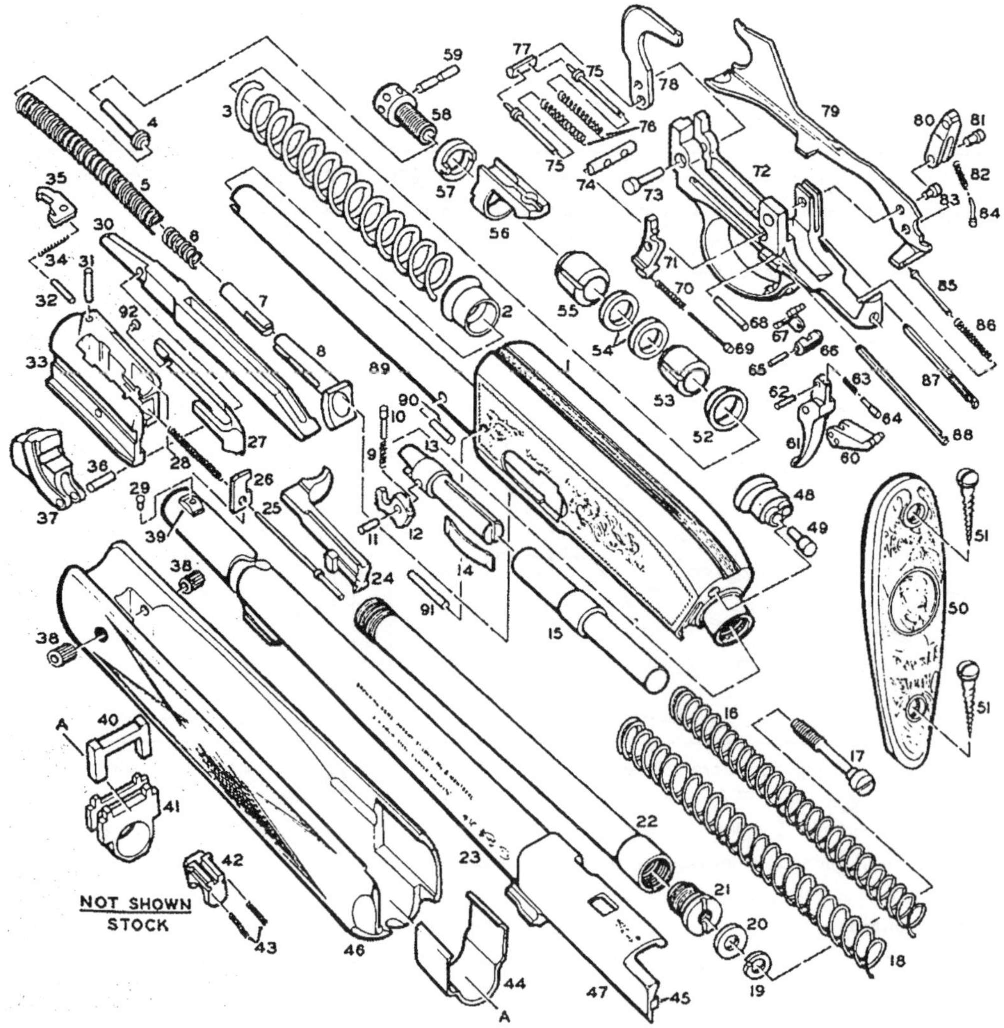

NOT SHOWN
STOCK

BROWNING

The Browning 12-gauge Double Automatic Shotgun, introduced early in 1955, was designed by Val M. Browning, son of firearms inventor John M. Browning. Manufactured in Belgium by Fabrique Nationale (FN), this gun is designated "Double Automatic" because it will hold only two shells and is a self-loader. Unlocking of the breech is accomplished by an inertia block housed in a tube in the buttstock. Rearward movement of the barrel in recoil is only about ⅞ inch. All types of 2¾-inch factory loads, including 2¾-inch Magnum, can be fired without adjustment.

Initially the Double Automatic was offered as a Standard Model, weighing 7 pounds, 11 ounces and a lighter, "Twelvette" model, weighing 6 pounds, 14 ounces. The weight saving was obtained through the use of an aluminum alloy receiver.

A later version, with an aluminum alloy receiver and 26-inch barrel, the "Twentyweight," was first offered in 1956. The name derives from the fact that, though a 12-gauge, its nominal weight is only six pounds, about that of a 20-gauge gun.

Aluminum receiver models were made in several anodized color combinations, and all guns have decorative engraving on the side of the receiver. Production of the Double Automatic ceased in 1971.

DISASSEMBLY

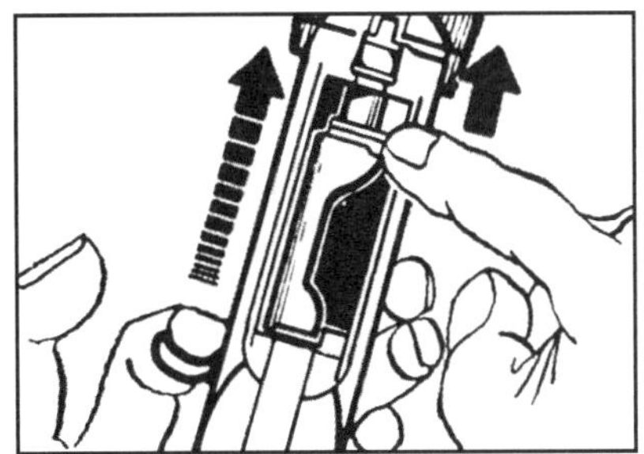

1 Commence disassembly of Browning Double Automatic by first insuring that breechblock (33) is retained in rearward position. Pull forearm latch (42) rearward and press forearm (46) completely down. Withdraw barrel (23). Next, while holding operating handle (24), push forward on carrier latch (8), then allow breech block to move gently forward.

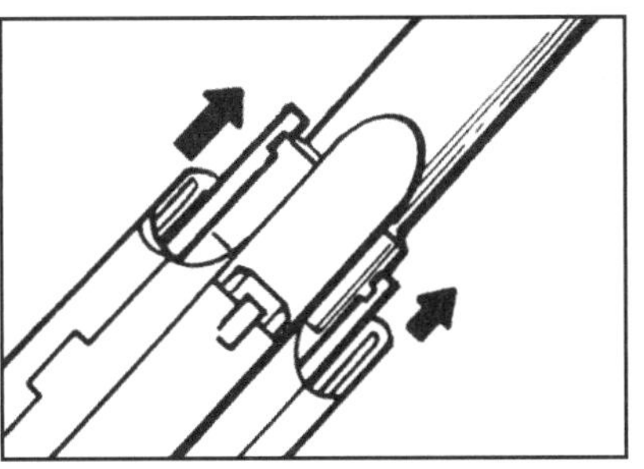

2 Remove butt plate screws (51), buttplate (50), and stock bolt (17). Remove stock rearward and away from receiver (I). Insert a small screwdriver into rear of receiver and engage notch at rear inside of each trigger guard fastening guide (87) and (88). Withdraw guides a short distance with a screwdriver so they may be pulled completely out with pliers. Remove trigger guard (72) from receiver. In reassembling, care should be exercised to replace short fastening guide on right side and long one on left, with notches of each facing inward.

3 Turn the gun over and unhook the inertia block (15) from link (30) and push the inertia block rearward and rotate it slightly. It will hook to the receiver.

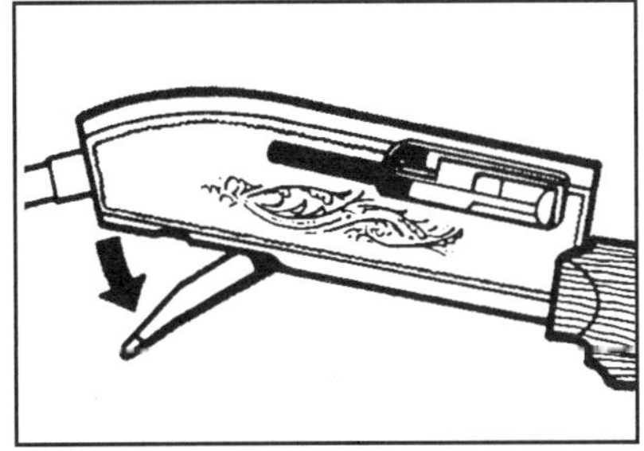

4 Link may now be swung on its pivot [link pin (36)] so that rear end swings out of receiver. Place rear of forearm down (in barrel unlatching position).

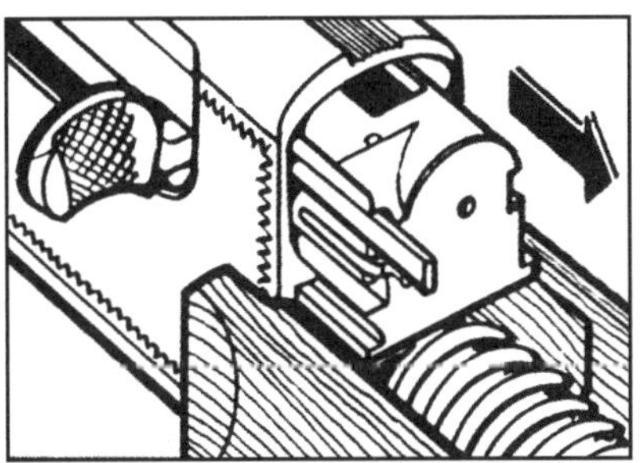

5 Remove breech block assembly through front of receiver, leaving operating handle (24) inside receiver. Now lift away operating handle.

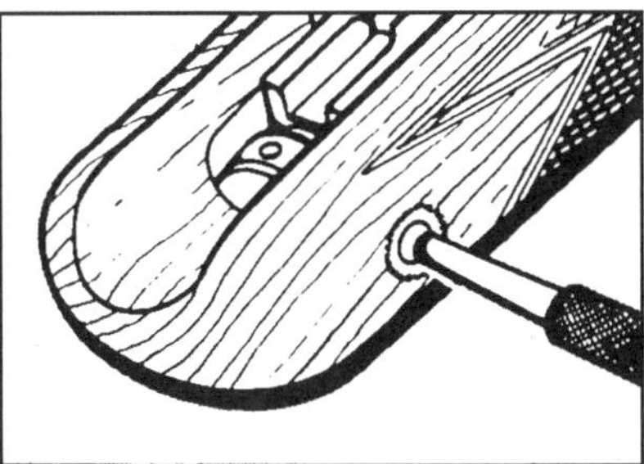

6 To dismount recoil mechanism, drift out forearm pivot pin (59) and remove forearm. Unscrew adjusting cap (58), using care that carrier latch spring (5) and forearm pivot pin stop (4) do not flip away when cap is unscrewed. At this point, other disassembly is immediately obvious. Reassemble the gun in reverse order. When re-installing anterior bronze friction brake, (55) insure that smaller diameter portion is facing front.

BROWNING GOLD SEMI-AUTO

PARTS LEGEND

1. Front sight
2. Ejector
3. Receiver w/ magazine tube
4. Magazine tube
5. Magazine follower
6. Magazine spring
7. Magazine cap retainer
8. Magazine spring retainer
9. Magazine cap
10. Magazine three-shot adapter
11. Piston assembly
12. Piston outer ring
13. Piston valve inner ring
14. Sleeve bar
15. Return spring
16. Carrier latch
17. Carrier latch pin clip
18. Carrier latch pin
19. Carrier latch spring
20. Breechblock buffer
21. Trigger guard buffer
22. Action spring tube
23. Action spring plunger
24. Action spring
25. Action spring retainer pin
26. Action spring retainer
27. Stock bolt plate
28. Stock bolt washer
29. Stock bolt screw
30. Bolt
31. Extractor pin
32. Extractor
33. Firing pin retaining pin
34. Firing pin spring
35. Firing pin
36. Breechblock assembly
37. Cartridge stop
38. Cartridge stop pin
39. Cartridge stop spring
40. Bolt cam
41. Bolt cam retaining pin
42. Link
43. Link pin
44. Operating handle
45. Trigger guard
46. Hammer
47. Hammer link
48. Hammer link pin
49. Mainspring plunger
50. Mainspring
51. Mainspring plunger pin
52. Trigger
53. Trigger guard & sear pin
54. Disconnector
55. Disconnector pin
56. Disconnector spring/trigger spring
57. Sear
58. Sear pin
59. Sear spring
60. Safety
61. Safety plunger
62. Safety plunger spring
63. Hammer pin & trigger guard bushing
64. Trigger guard pin retainer
65. Dog assembly
66. Carrier dog upper stop
67. Carrier dog spring guide
68. Carrier dog spring
69. Carrier dog lower stop
70. Carrier
71. Carrier spring
72. Trigger guard pin
73. Forearm
74. O-ring
75. O-ring retainer
76. Buttstock
77. Recoil pad vent
78. Recoil pad screw
79. Extractor plunger
80. Barrel

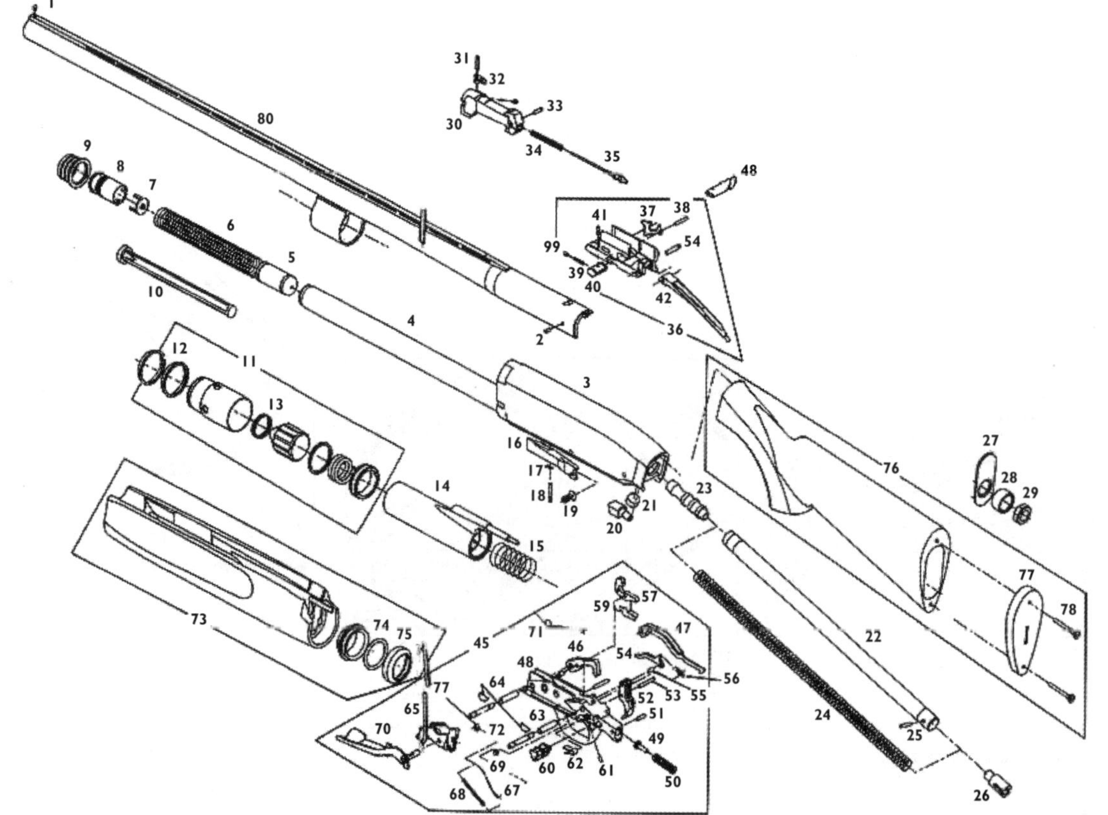

The first of the highly successful Browning Gold series of semi-automatic shotguns was introduced in 1994 in 12 and 20 gauge. The Gold models featured a self-regulating gas system designed to accept a wide range of shells, from magnum to standard, interchangeably. All Browning Gold models are built on aluminum receivers and all 12 and 20 gauge models have back-bored barrels.

During more than a decade of production, Browning has produced numerous variations of the Gold, ranging from dedicated target models to field guns, in 20, 12, and 10 gauge. The target models are chambered for 2¾ inch shells, while the field models are chambered in three or three and one-half inch versions. Some of the many models include Gold Sporting Clays (1997), Gold Hunter and Stalker (1998), The Gold Fusion (2001), Gold Classic high grade (2002), Gold Evolve (2004) and the Gold Superlight (2006). Gold models have been offered with wood, synthetic and camo stocks and different barrel lengths and configurations ranging from target to rifled slug.

Components for Browning Gold 12- and 20-gauge shotguns are made in Belgium by FN and assembled in Portugal, while Gold 10-gauge shotguns are manufactured by Miroku in Japan.

DISASSEMBLY

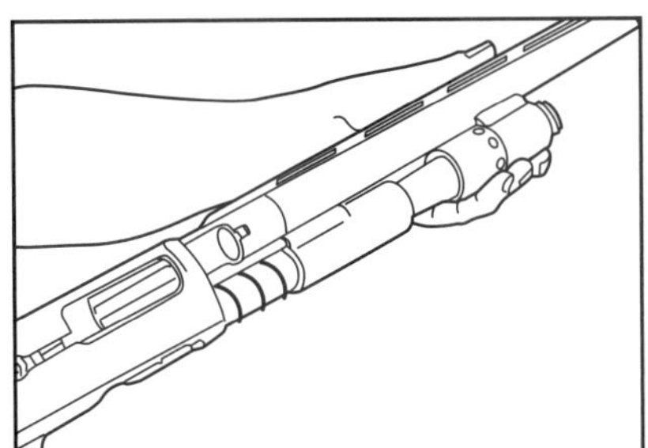

1 Unscrew the magazine cap and remove it. Remove the forearm by sliding it forward off the magazine tube. For cleaning, remove the barrel, piston and piston sleeve by sliding them forward off the magazine tube. If you are disassembling for storage, return the piston and piston sleeve onto the magazine tube. Reinstall the forearm over the magazine tube and screw on the magazine cap. You will then have two compact units: the barrel, and the action with forearm and stock. CAUTION: After the barrel has been removed from your gun, leave the bolt in the open position. Do not press the carrier release button.

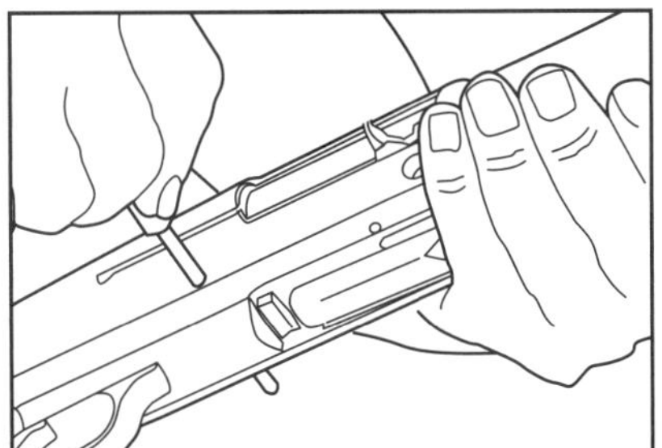

2 While holding the bolt handle, release the bolt to its forward position by depressing the carrier release button. Again use caution when releasing the bolt assembly to its forward position. If you allow the bolt assembly to slam closed with the barrel removed, you can damage the receiver.

With the gun inverted, (trigger guard up) use a drive punch or similar object to push upward on the trigger guard pins, using caution not to scratch the receiver. Trigger guard pins may be removed from either side of the receiver. Push the trigger guard pins through the other side of the receiver. It may be necessary to pull on the trigger pins to remove them from the receiver.

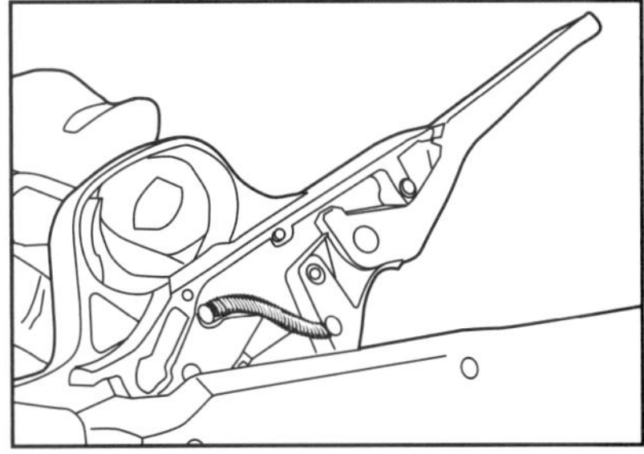

3 Grasp the trigger guard and pull it up and out of the receiver. Perform any cleaning of the parts and receiver cavity as necessary. CAUTION: Do not disassemble the trigger group beyond this point.

NOTE: Before removing the bolt assembly it is recommended to first remove the trigger group, as explained in step 2.

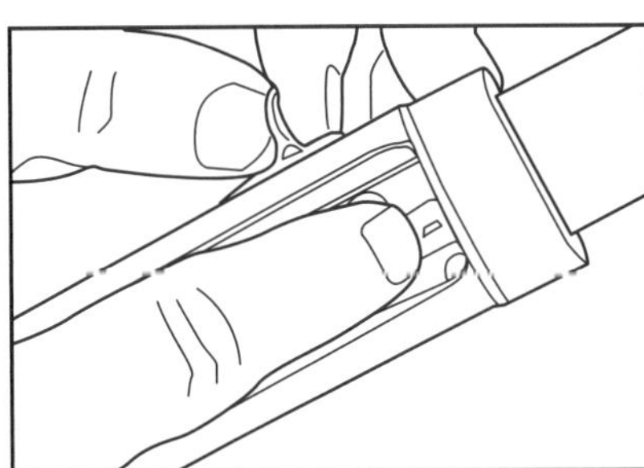

4 With the gun inverted (trigger guard up position), push down on the cartridge stop while pulling outward on the bolt handle. Remove the bolt handle from the bolt.

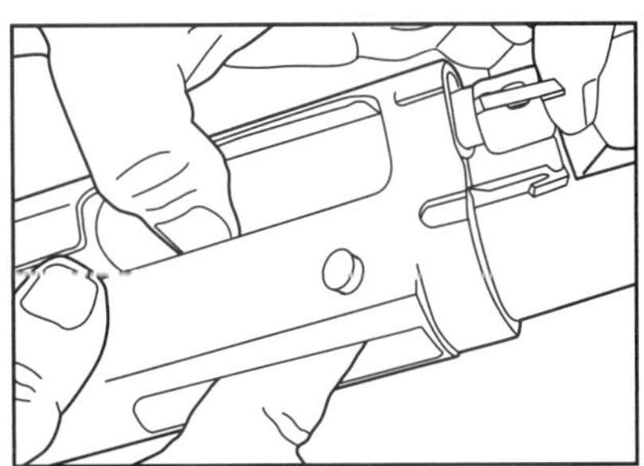

5 While keeping the cartridge stop depressed, slide the bolt slide forward and out the receiver.

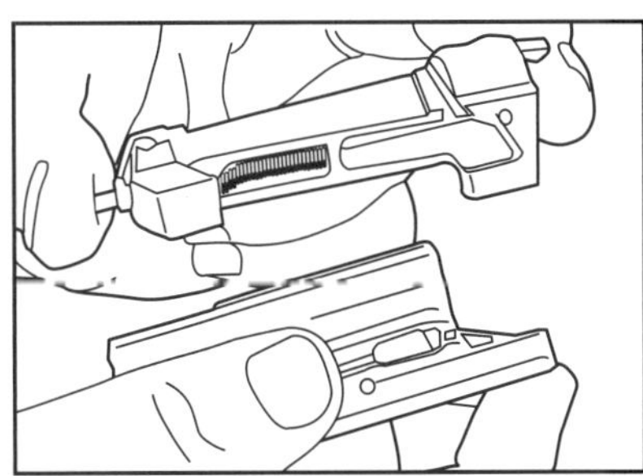

6 The bolt and bolt slide can be separated for cleaning. Perform any cleaning of the bolt and receiver cavity as necessary.

BROWNING SUPERPOSED SHOTGUN

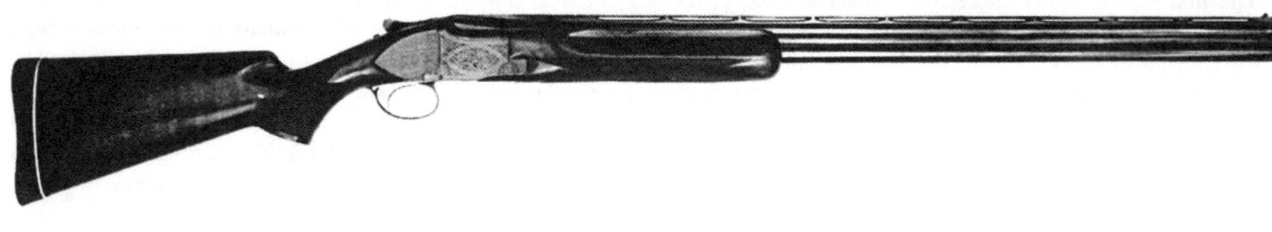

PARTS LEGEND

1. Barrels
2. Bead sight
3. Forearm
4. Forearm screw
5. Barrel plate wood, right
6. Barrel plate wood, left
7. Barrel plate screw (2)
8. Ejector extension, right
9. Ejector, right
10. Ejector extension stop screw (2)
11. Ejector stop screw (2)
12. Ejector extension, left
13. Ejector, left
14. Receiver
15. Top-lever
16. Top-lever spring
17. Top-lever spring retaining screw
18. Top-lever spring retainer
19. Firing pin spring, under
20. Firing pin, under
21. Firing pin, over
22. Top-lever dog
23. Top-lever dog screw
24. Selector, safety
25. Selector block
26. Tang-piece screw, top
27. Tang-piece screw, bottom
28. Trigger spring
29. Selector spring
30. Trigger pin
31. Trigger guard, pistol grip
32. Trigger guard screw (2)
33. Locking bolt
34. Tang piece
35. Stock bolt washer
36. Stock bolt lock washer
37. Stock bolt
38. Trigger ¾" rear
39. Trigger piston spring
40. Trigger piston
41. Trigger piston pin
42. Mainspring (2)
43. Mainspring guide (2)
44. Inertia block
45. Inertia block spring
46. Inertia block spring guide
47. Connector
48. Hammer, right
49. Hammer, left
50. Sear, right
51. Sear, left
52. Sear spring (2)
53. Sear pin
54. Firing pin retaining pin (2)
55. Hammer pin
56. Ejector trip rod, right
57. Ejector trip rod, left
58. Cocking lever
59. Cocking lever pin
60. Takedown lever latch
61. Takedown lever latch spring
62. Cocking lever lifter
63. Cocking lever lifter pin
64. Takedown lever pin
65. Ejector hammer, left
66. Ejector hammer, right
67. Ejector hammer pin
68. Ejector hammer sear (2)
69. Ejector hammer sear pin (2)
70. Ejector hammer sear spring (2)
71. Forearm bracket
72. Takedown lever latch pin
73. Ejector hammer spring guide (2)
74. Ejector hammer spring (2)
75. Buttplate
76. Buttplate screw (2)
77. Takedown lever

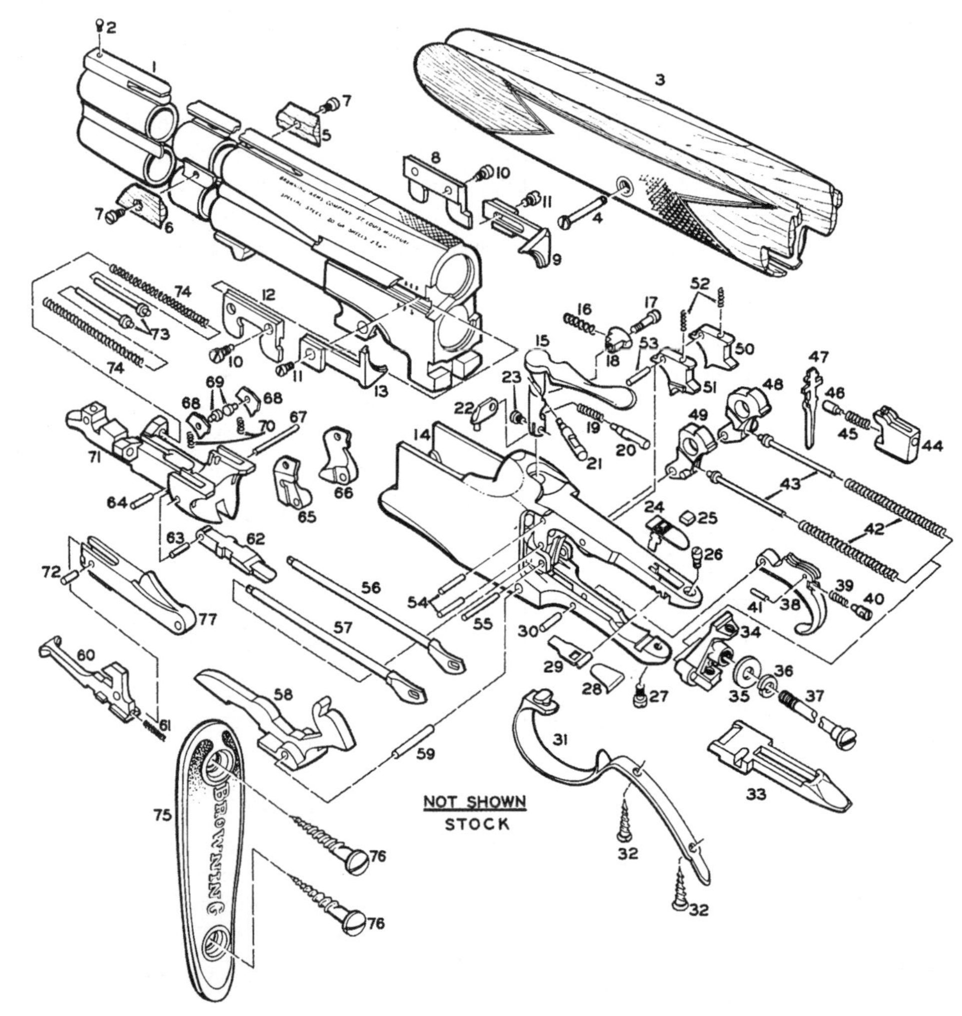

BROWNING

The Superposed was the last product of small-arms designer John M. Browning and its manufacture was just beginning at the time of Browning's death in 1926. It has proved to be one of the most successful guns of its kind.

Unique, original design features of the Superposed are the single underbolt, the fore-end which remains attached to the barrels when the gun is taken down, and the trigger. The gun was originally manufactured with conventional double triggers. These were replaced in later production by a "Twin-Single" trigger, a most unusual arrangement of two triggers which could be used as conventional double triggers or either as single triggers. Eventually a single trigger was standardized in which selection of the barrel to be fired was made by moving the safety slide to one side or the other. The Superposed has always been made with automatic ejectors.

The Browning superposed was discontinued in 1976 and replaced in the Browning line by, first, the Liege and later the Citori. FN, however, continued to make Superposed guns for sale in Europe, and in 1985 Browning resumed importation of custom-built, high-grade guns. The current model, the B-125, is assembled and finished in FN's custom shop in Herstal, Belgium. Hunting, Sporting Clay and Trap models are available.

DISASSEMBLY

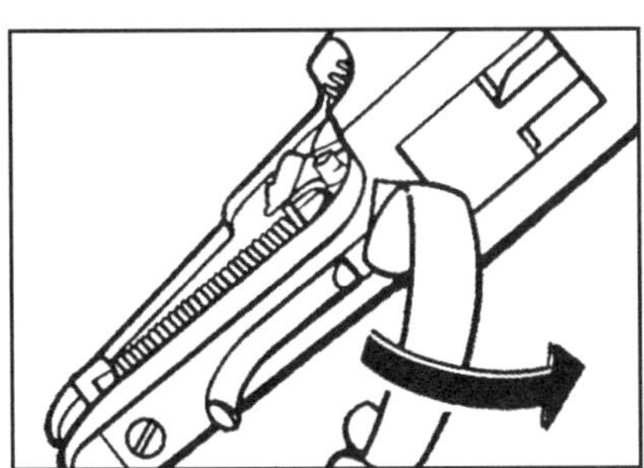

1 Turn gun bottom side up, press back and lift up takedown lever latch (60). Turn gun right side up and push forward on forearm (3), then unlock gun by pushing top-lever (15) to right. Lower buttstock and remove barrels (1) from receiver (14). Remove front and rear trigger guard screws (32), buttplate screws (76), and buttplate (75). Using a long screwdriver, remove stock bolt (37) together with lockwasher (36) and washer (35). Remove stock. Continue by turning trigger guard (31) one-quarter turn right (see arrow), lift up and away.

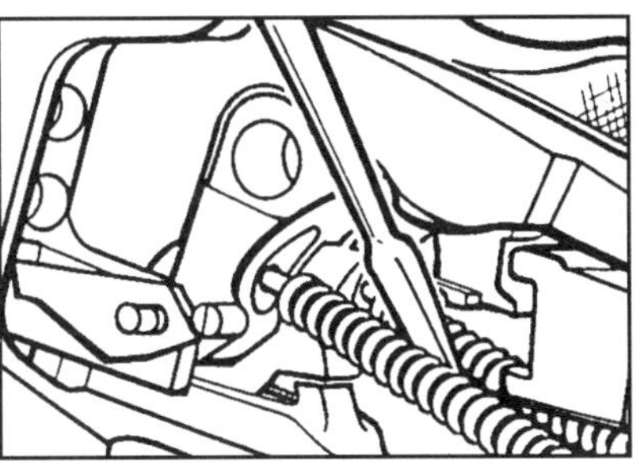

2 With receiver placed solidly on bench, reach through action with screwdriver to mainspring (42) on far side. Raise mainspring out of its socket in hammer (48 or 49), using near mainspring as fulcrum. Push directly down on mainspring guide (43) and slide it off edge of hammer. Turn action over and repeat for corresponding parts except use locking bolt (33) as fulcrum.

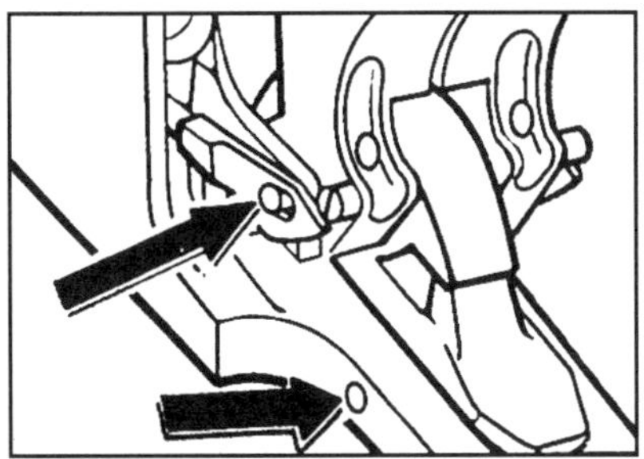

3 Drift out trigger pin (30, lower arrow) and pull trigger (38) down out of trigger slot. Hold inertia block (44) and pull trigger with other hand. Inertia block will rise off of connector (47). Remove trigger assembly and inertia block. Drift out hammer pin (55, top arrow); remove hammers (48 & 49) and ejector trip rods (56 & 57). Raise selector spring (29) from slot with knife blade and rotate one-quarter turn right or left. Remove selector safety (24) and block (25).

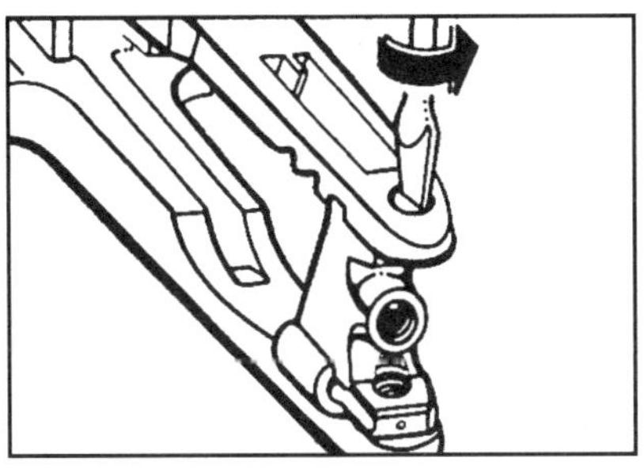

4 Continue by removing top and bottom tang-piece screws (26 and 27, see arrow) and, using a plastic hammer, drive out tang piece from left or right.

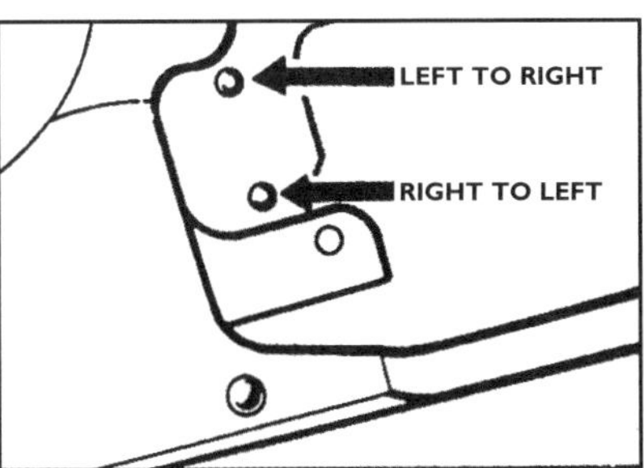

5 Drift out over firing pin retaining pin (54, upper arrow) from left to right and remove over firing pin (21). Turn receiver over and repeat for under firing pin retaining pin (54, lower arrow) from right to left. Remove under firing pin (20) and under firing pin spring (19). Remove top-lever spring retaining screw (17), top-lever spring retainer (18) and top-lever spring (16, arrow Illustration 6).

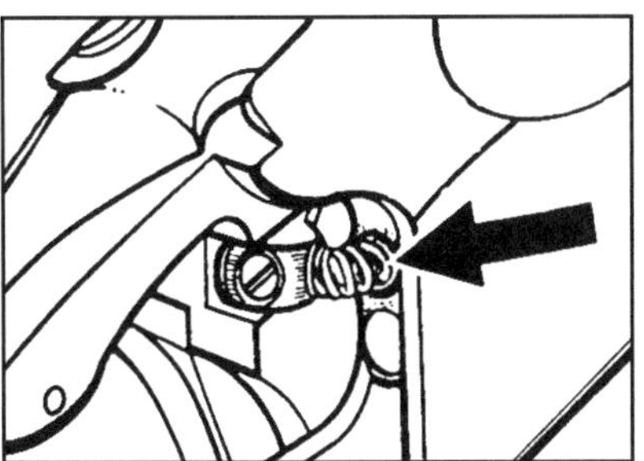

6 Drift out cocking lever pin (59) from left to right. If pin has been reversed, it will lodge tighter. Drive it out the other way. Remove cocking lever (58), lift top-lever (15) up and grasp rear of locking bolt (33); draw it rearward from receiver. Drift out top-lever by placing drift on top-lever dog (22). Top-lever dog rotates on top-lever dog screw (23) and clears hole in receiver. Remove top lever.

BSA MARTINI-INTERNATIONAL MK III

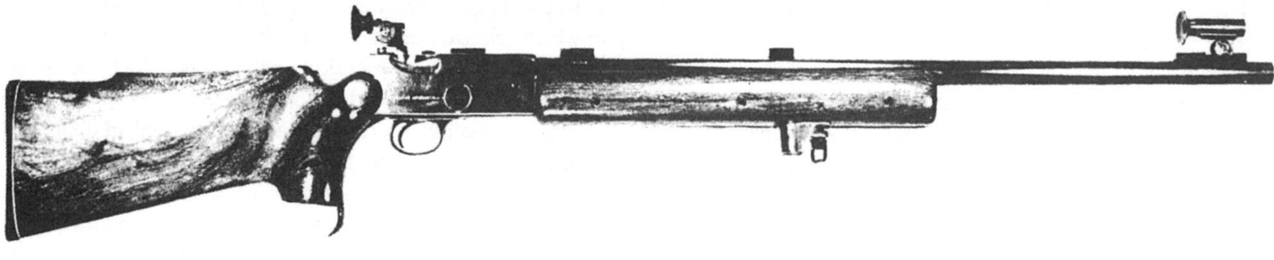

PARTS LEGEND

1. Barrel *
2. Foresight stool
3. Stool fixing screw (9)
4. Body
5. Fore-end support *
6. Guard keeper screw
7. Stock bolt
8. Stock bolt washer
9. Stock bolt nut
10. Pivot pin*
11. Barrel fixing screws (2) *
12. Backsight plate screw (2)
13. Backsight attachment plate
14. Backsight tube stool
15. Rear telescope stool
16. Front telescope stool
17. Left fore-end grip
18. Right fore-end grip
19. Fore-end grip screw (6)
20. Fore-end screw bush (6)
21. Handstop swivel screw
22. Handstop
23. Swivel assembly
24. Buttplate spacer
25. Buttplate
26. Buttplate screw (2)
27. Trigger frame
28. Cocking lever
29. Axis pins, large (3)
30. Tumbler
31. Striker retaining screw
32. Striker spring
33. Striker
34. Breechblock
35. Trigger
36. Axis pin, small (4)
37. Trigger spring
38. Trigger adjusting screw
39. Trigger stop screw
40. Locking screw (2)
41. Hammer
42. Hammer bush*
43. Hammer spring
44. Ejector spring
45. Ejector lever spring
46. Ejector release lever
47. Ejector lever axis pin
48. Ejector
49. Sear spacing collar (2)
50. Sear
51. Butt

*Factory assembled, do not disassemble

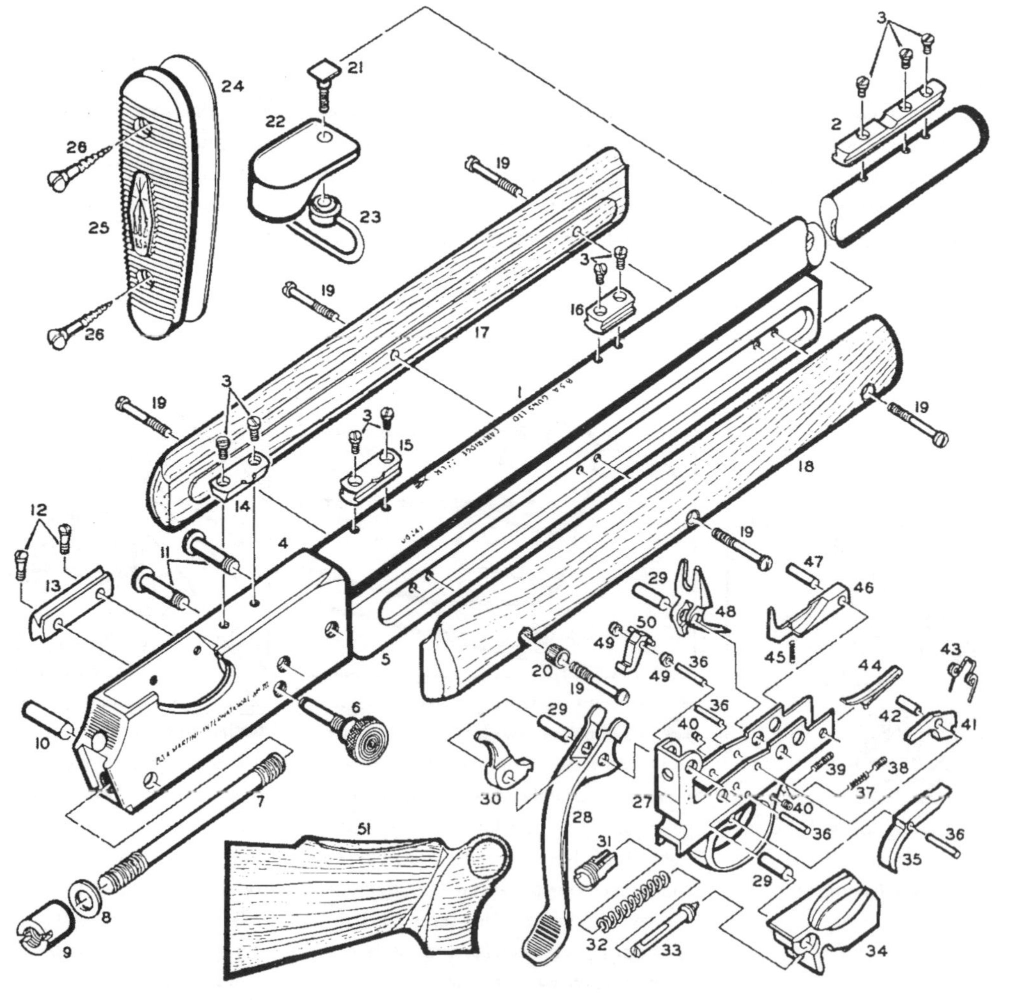

The BSA Martini-International Mk III match rifle was first made available for general sale in May 1960. Chambered for the cal. .22 long rifle cartridge, the Mk III rifle is the latest of a long series of Martini-action precision target rifles made by the English firm of BSA Guns Ltd. The Mk III rifle replaced the BSA Mk II model introduced after World War II.

The action stems from H. L. Peabody's 1862 patent for a lever-operated falling breechblock granted in 1862. A Peabody rifle was tested by the United States military but failed to win acceptance. However, Peabody military rifles were manufactured by the Providence Tool Co., under various foreign contracts, including Canada and Turkey.

In 1867 the Swiss Republic adopted a Peabody-action rifle with a hammerless modification by Swiss inventor, Friedrich Martini.

The Peabody-Martini action is well suited for rimfire target rifles and the compact design provides solid support for the cartridge and very fast lock time. In the current Mk III the action mechanism can be easily withdrawn from the receiver for routine inspection or cleaning. The fullfloated barrel has a long, 3-inch bearing in the receiver which enhances the rigidity of the barrel-receiver assembly. The under-lever loading principle and feed groove in the breech block permit convenient loading in the prone position. The French walnut stock assembly is a Monte Carlo pattern based on a design by Al Freeland. Production of the Mk III ceased around 1967.

DISASSEMBLY

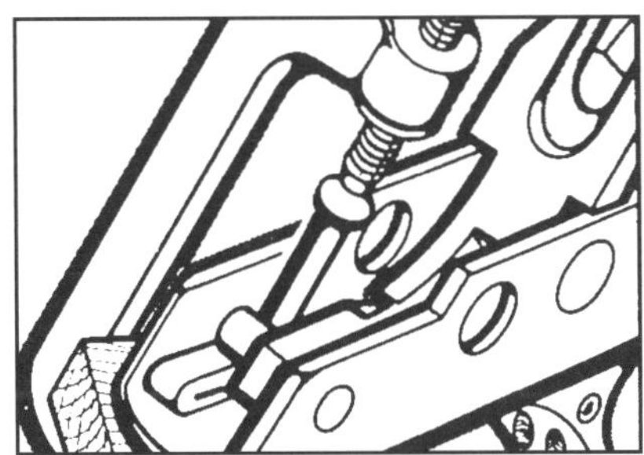

1 Disassemble BSA Mk III by first pressing cocking lever (28) to full ejection position and unscrewing guard keeper screw (6).

Trigger frame (27) carrying complete mechanism may be removed by exerting downward pressure on trigger guard. Place a 1-inch length of 3/16-inch drill rod against ejector spring (44) and apply machinists clamp as shown using block of soft wood against bottom surface of trigger frame. This relieves tension on ejector (48) and ejector lever axis pin (47). Drift out this pin and ejector axis pin (29) and remove ejector, ejector spring, ejector release lever (46), and ejector lever spring (45) being careful not to lose the latter.

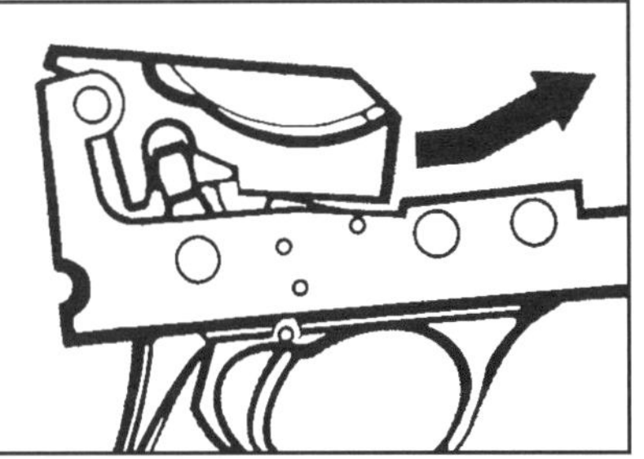

2 Drift out breechblock axis pin (29) and, with breech block (34) still in ejection position, pull breechblock firmly forward, upward, and away. This requires some tricky manipulation to get the feel in order to release breechblock from tumbler (30) and cocking lever.

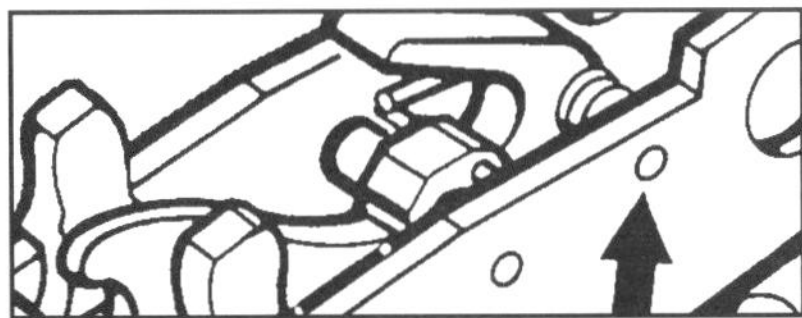

3 Next—carefully drift out hammer axis pin (36, arrow) and lift out hammer (41) with hammer bush (42) and hammer spring (43) attached.

4 Drift out cocking lever axis pin (29) and lift out tumbler (30) and remove cocking lever through top of trigger frame. Cocking lever must be turned sideways when bringing handle portion through trigger frame.

5 Drift out sear axis pin (36) and axis pin, small (36, upper arrow) and remove sear (50) and sear spacing collars (49). Drift out trigger axis pin (36, lower arrow) and lift trigger (35) out from top of frame being careful not to lose trigger spring (37) which will drop out when frame is turned upside down.

6 Using a wide-blade screwdriver, unscrew striker retaining screw (31) and tap out striker spring (32) and striker (33). Reassemble mechanism in reverse. When hammer has been replaced, hammer spring prongs can be engaged to sear pinions by inserting a small screwdriver under each side of hammer axis pin and gently prying spring prongs upward and over sear pinions.

BULLARD MODEL 1886 LEVER-ACTION

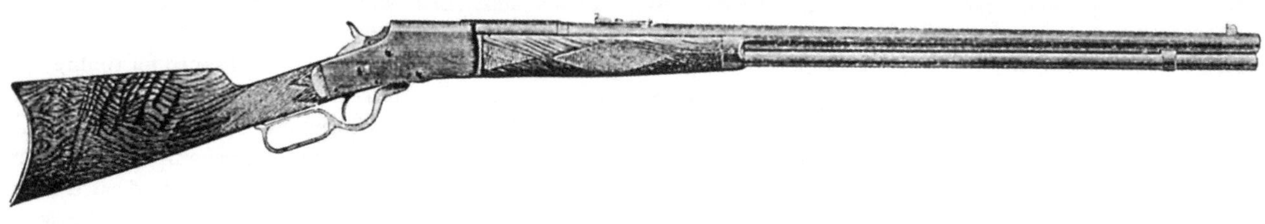

PARTS LEGEND

1. Receiver
2. Barrel
3. Buttstock (not shown)
   3a. Forestock (not shown)
4. Sideplate
5. Sideplate screw
6. Magazine lifting spring
7. Lower gear rack
8. Lower gear rack screw
9. Lower tang
10. Rear tang screw
11. Trigger
12. Trigger pin
13. Trigger spring
14. Trigger spring pin
15. Mainspring
16. Hammer
17. Stirrup
18. Stirrup pin
19. Hammer pin sleeve
20. Lever link
21. Lever link pin
22. Lower tang screws (2)
23. Breechblock pin
24. Breechblock retainer screw
25. Mainspring screw tension
26. Hammer screw
27. Breechblock
28. Striker pin
29. Striker retainer pin
30. Bolt
31. Extractor
32. Extractor pin
33. Firing pin
34. Firing pin spring
35. Firing pin retaining pin
36. Lever
37. Lever pin
38. Lever pin screw
39. Pinion gear link retainer
40. Retainer pin
41. Retainer plunger
42. Retainer plunger spring
43. Pinion gear link
44. Pinion gear assembly pin
45. Pinion gear assembly
46. Lever arm, left hand
47. Lever arm, right hand
48. Cartridge carrier lifter arm
49. Cartridge carrier
50. Floorplate
51. Floorplate spring
52. Floorplate spring pin
53. Floorplate pin
54. Magazine tube
55. Magazine follower
56. Magazine spring
57. Magazine cap
58. Magazine cap screw
59. Nose cap
60. Nose cap base
61. Nose cap screws (2)
62. Front magazine tube ring
63. Dustcover
64. Dustcover retainer
65. Dustcover retainer screw
66. Rear sight
67. Front sight
68. Blank tang sight mounting screws (2)
69. Buttplate
70. Buttplate screws (2)

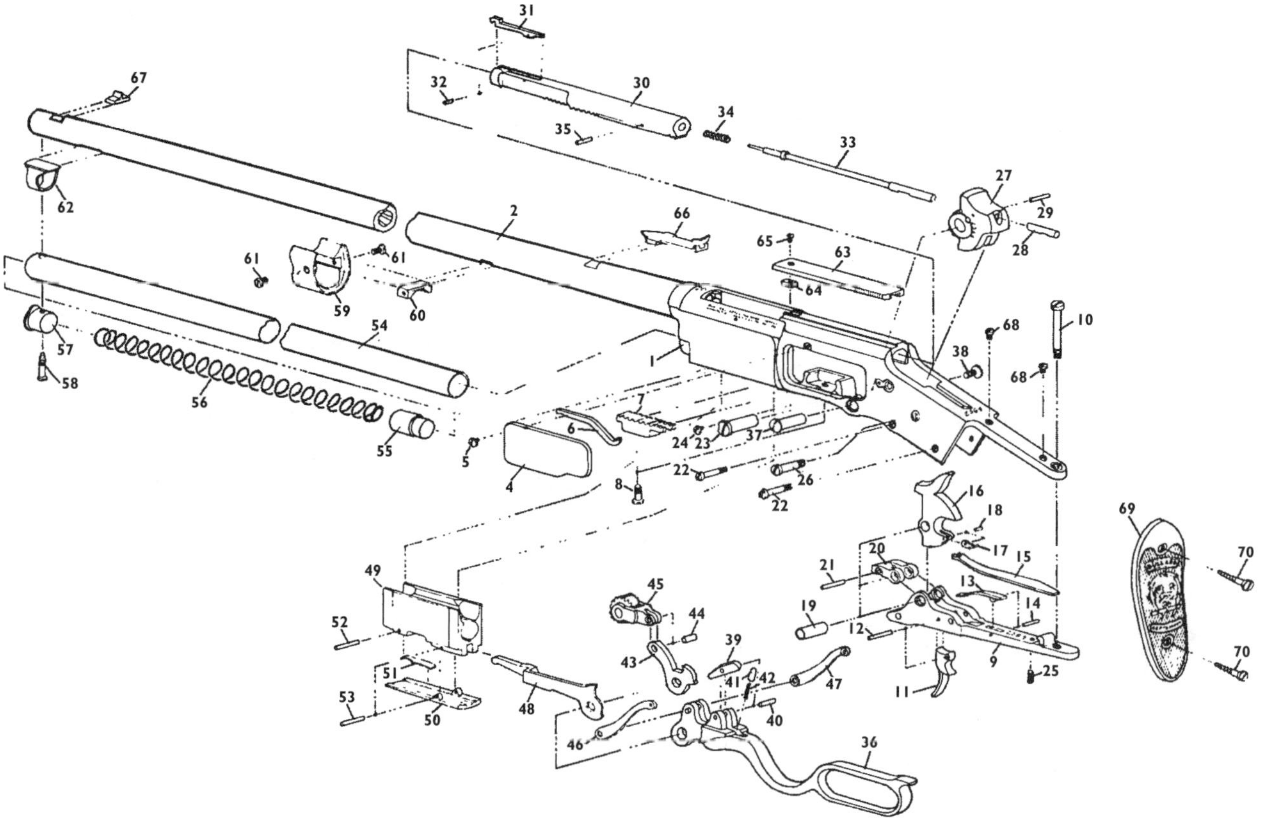

The Model 1886 Bullard lever-action rifle was produced by the Springfield, Massachusetts-based Bullard Repeating Rifle Co., headed by James R. Bullard, former chief mechanic for Smith & Wesson. Bullard formed his own company in 1880 to manufacture a single-shot rifle of his own design and expanded into manufacture of lever-action rifles six years later. The Bullard Model 1886 was intended to compete directly with Marlin's 1881 repeater and Winchester's Model 1886.

The 1886 Bullard has a complex mechanism, using gears and compound levers to accomplish many of the tasks performed by cams or direct leverage in other designs. It is, however, a robust complexity. The hammer, for example, is cocked by two links operated by the finger lever, instead of by direct action of the bolt. The Bullard's bolt is moved by a rack and pinion gear, rather than being pinned to the finger lever. And, the breech block works independently of the bolt and contains an interrupter to avoid firing with the mechanism unlocked.

The major disadvantage of the Bullard design — in addition to a greater number of parts — was the extreme length of its receiver. Though, the rack and pinion gear made its action smooth and easy to operate.

Bullard lever-actions were made from 1886 to 1890, a total production of about 12,000. They were offered in .32-40, .38-45, .40-75, .40-90, .45-85, and .50-115 Bullard Express.

DISASSEMBLY

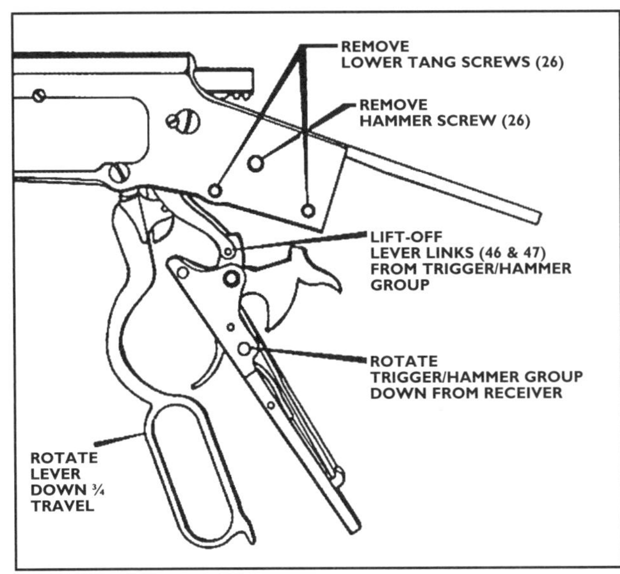

1 Check the rifle to insure it is unloaded. Remove the buttstock by removing the rear tang screw (10). Gently tap buttstock from upper and lower receiver tangs. Cock the hammer (16) and pull the lever (36) down approximately ¾ of its total travel. Remove the hammer screw (26) and lower tang screws (22). Rotate the assembled trigger (11) and hammer down and out of the receiver. Lift off the ends of the lever arms (46 and 47) from the lever link pin (21) on the lever link (20).

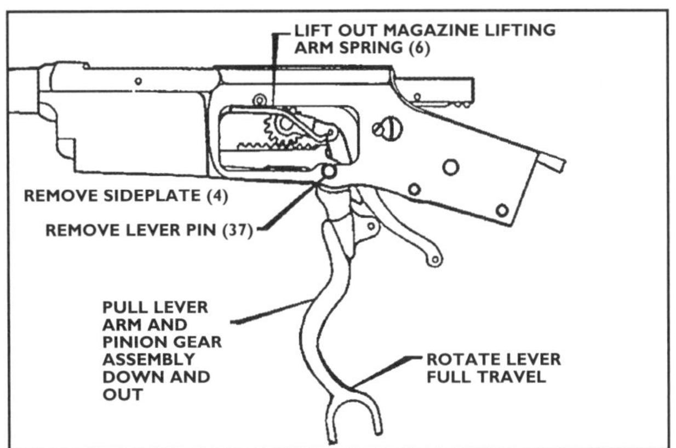

2 Remove sideplate screw (5), gently tap walls of receiver (1) and sideplate (4) to loosen sideplate, and gently pry sideplate from the receiver. Lift out magazine lifting spring (6). NOTE: Check orientation of this spring with cartridge carrier lifting arm (48) before removal. Remove lever pin (37) and lever pin screw (38). Pull the lever and pinion gear assembly (45) down and out from receiver frame. Disconnect lever from pinion gear assembly. Lift out cartridge carrier lifting arm. Push bolt (30) forward to remove breechblock (27). Remove dustcover (63) by removing retaining screw (65). Align hole in the bolt with the access hole in receiver. Insert a drift punch into the hole and push the extractor pin (32) out of the bolt. Remove the pin punch and lift out the extractor (31). NOTE: Extractor pin will not completely clear the bolt body, but will move sufficiently to allow removal of the extractor. Once the extractor is removed, push the extractor pin back into the bolt, then pull the bolt from the receiver. This will allow the pinion gear assembly to drop out through the bottom of the receiver.

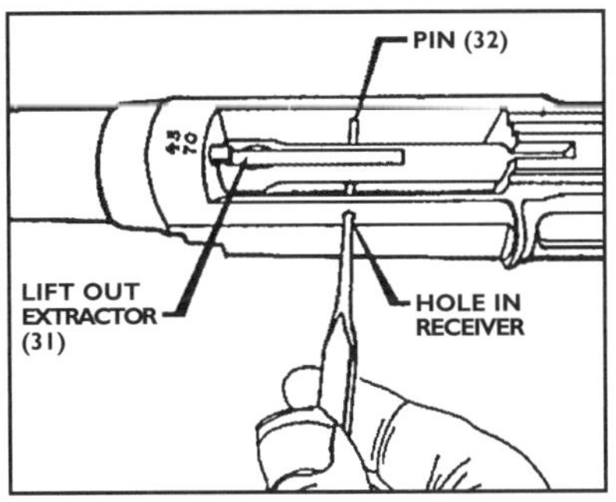

3 Remove the magazine cap screw (58). Then lift the magazine cap (57) out of the magazine tube (54). Pullout the magazine spring (56) and follower (55). Push down on the cartridge carrier (49) and remove it from the receiver. Remove the lower gear rack screw (8) and the lower gear rack (7).

To disassemble the trigger and hammer, cock the hammer, place a clamp on the mainspring (15). press the trigger (11) and release the hammer. Loosen the mainspring tension screw (25), remove the clamp and lift off the mainspring. Push the hammer pin sleeve (19) out of the lower tang (9), lift out the hammer. Remaining parts can be removed by driving out the appropriate retaining pins.

Other sub-assemblies are readily disassembled. Assemble in reverse order. Do not install the extractor unit after the pinion gear, bolt and lower gear rack are installed and alligned.

BUSHMASTER M4 A3 RIFLE

BUSHMASTER

PARTS LEGEND

1. Barrel
2. Front sight base
3. Front sight post
4. Front sight detent
5. Front sight detent spring
6. Gas tube roll pin
7. Barrel subassembly
8. Crush washer
9. Flash suppressor (Izzy)
10. Front sight tape pins
11. Gas tube
12. Handguard, upper
13. Handguard, lower
14. Front sling swivel
15. Front sling swivel rivet
16. Hand guard snap ring
17. Weld spring
18. Delta ring
19. Barrel indexing pin
20. Barrel extension
21. Barrel nut
22. Charging handle latch roll pin
23. Charging handle latch
24. Charging handle latch spring
25. Charging handle
26. Firing pin
27. Bolt carrier key screws
28. Bolt carrier key
29. Firing pin retaining pin
30. Cam pin
31. Bolt carrier
32. Bolt gas rings
33. Bolt
34. Extractor spring insert
35. Extractor spring
36. Extractor
37. Extractor pin
38. Extractor roll pin
39. Ejector roll pin
40. Ejector spring
41. Ejector
42. Forward assist plunger
43. Pawl detent
44. Pawl spring
45. Pawl spring pin
46. Forward assist pawl
47. Forward assist spring
48. Forward assist spring pin
49. Upper receiver
50. Carry handle
51. Clamping bar
52. Thumb nut assemblies
53. Cross bolts
54. Rear sight elevation spring
55. Index screw
56. Index, elevation
57. Elevation knob
58. Elevation spring
59. Ball bearing
60. Index spring
61. Rear sight windage knob
62. Rear sight windage knob pin
63. Rear sight windage screw
64. Rear sight base
65. Rear sight helical
66. Rear sight ball bearing
67. Rear sight aperture
68. Rear sight flat spring
69. Ejection port cover pin
70. Ejection port cover spring
71. Ejection port cover
72. Lower receiver
73. Hammer with J-pin
74. Hammer spring
75. Hammer pin
76. Trigger pin
77. Trigger guard assembly
78. Trigger guard pivot roll pin
79. Safety selector lever
80. Bolt catch
81. Bolt catch roll pin
82. Bolt catch spring
83. Magazine catch
84. Magazine release button
85. Magazine catch spring
86. Buffer retainer
87. Buffer retainer spring
88. Takedown pin spring
89. Takedown pin detent
90. Takedown pin
91. Safety detent
92. Safety detent spring
93. Pivot pin
94. Pivot pin detent
95. Pivot pin spring
96. Disconnector spring
97. Disconnector
98. Trigger
99. Trigger spring
100. Pistol grip
101. Lock washer
102. Pistol grip screw
103. Action spring
104. Buffer assembly
105. Six-position carbine receiver extension
106. Receiver extension nut
107. Buttstock collar tube lock
108. Buttstock slide lock pin
109. Telestock latch
110. Lockpin nut
111. Roll pin
112. Rear sight helical spring
113. Cover retaining ring
114. Bolt catch plunger
115. Lockpin spring

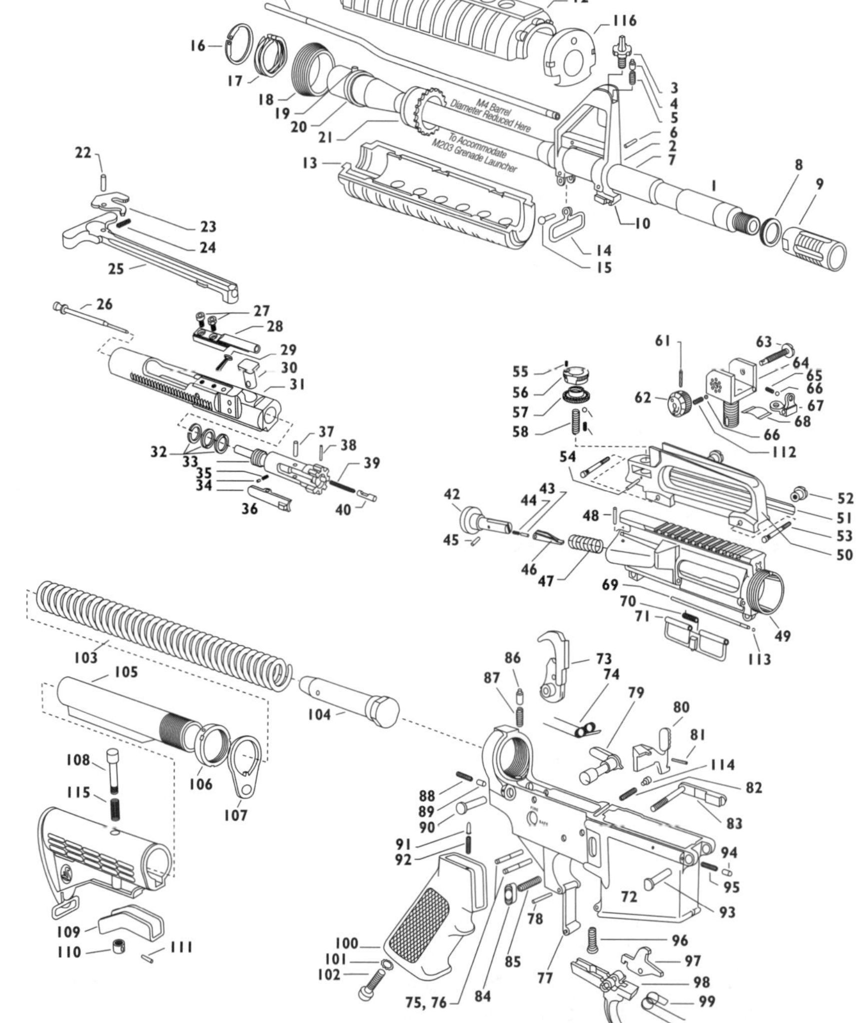

The Bushmaster M4 A3 is a lightweight, gas operated semi-automatic rifle. XM15 Models have forged aluminum upper and lower receivers. The Bushmaster uses an M-16-style 30-round detachable magazine. Bushmaster produces versions with injection molded carbon composite receivers. Barrels on the XM15 and Carbon 15 models are either chrome lined, chrome molybdenum, vanadium steel or stainless steel. They are usually button rifled, 1 turn in 9 inches, with a right hand twist.

All models feature pistol grips and can be fitted with either 6-position telescoping buttstocks or solid A2 buttstocks. The removable forends are vented to allow for heat dissipation.

DISASSEMBLY

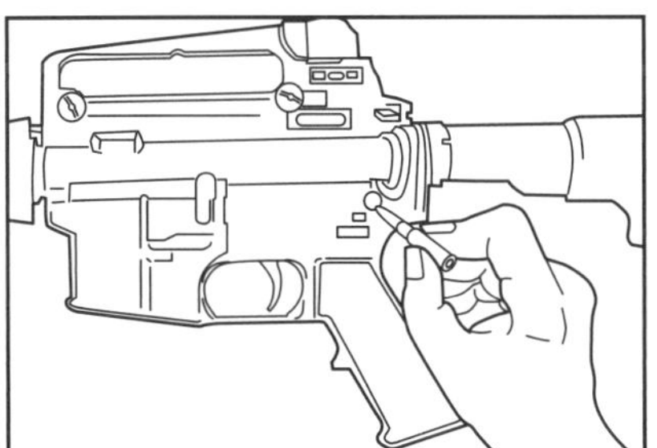

1 Push in takedown pin (a bullet tip can help) as far as it will go. Pivot upper receiver (49) from lower receiver (72).

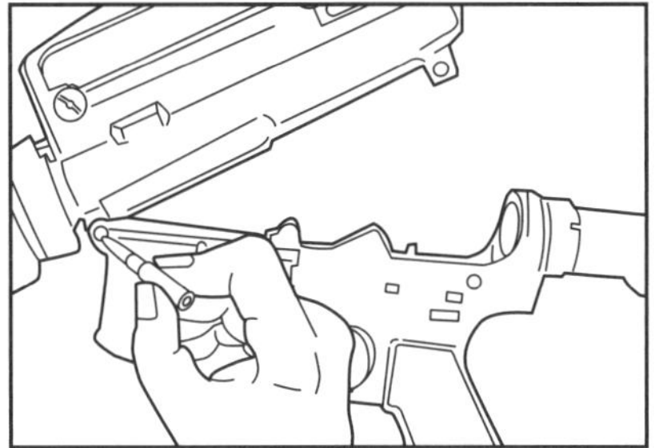

2 Push in pivot pin (93) (a bullet tip can help). Separate upper and lower receivers. Pull back charging handle (25) and bolt carrier (31).

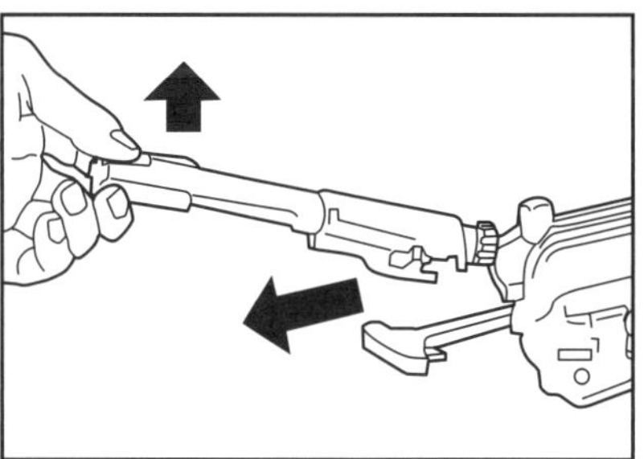

3 Remove bolt carrier and bolt (33).

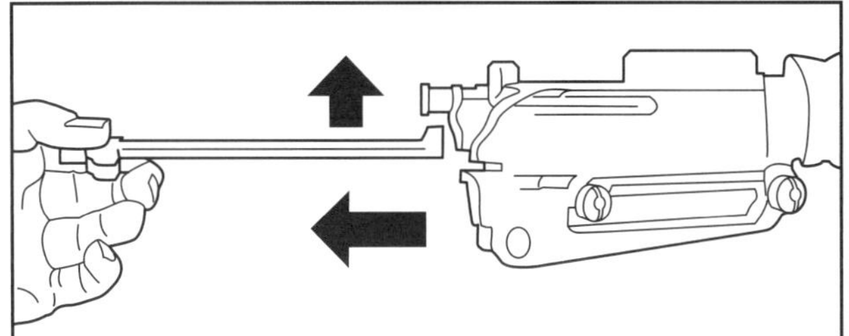

4 Remove charging handle by pulling back and up until "ears" clear cutouts in receiver. Remove firing pin retaining pin (29). A bullet tip can help push it out of the bolt carrier. Drop firing pin (26) out of rear of bolt carrier. Do not open or close split end of firing pin retaining pin, and do not substitute a common cotter pin on reassembly. Push bolt in to locked position. Remove cam pin (30) by rotating ¼ turn and lifting out.

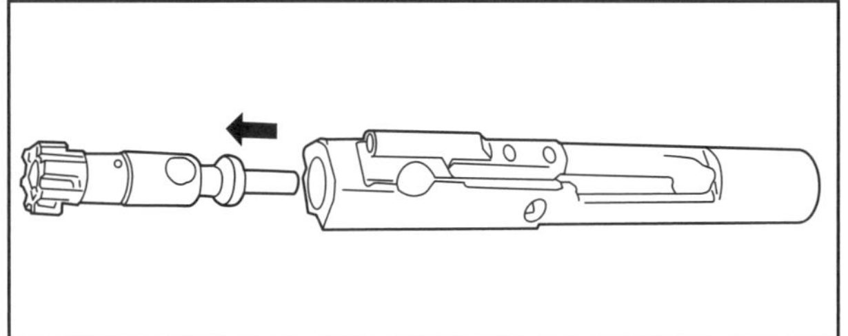

5 Remove bolt assembly from bolt carrier by pulling straight out. Remove extractor pin (37) by pushing out with a punch or the tip of a bullet.

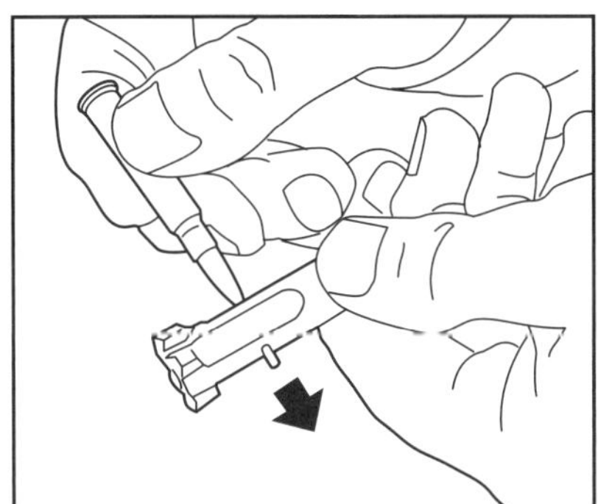

6 Push extractor pin out. NOTE: Press rear of extractor (36) to check spring function. Remove extractor from spring.

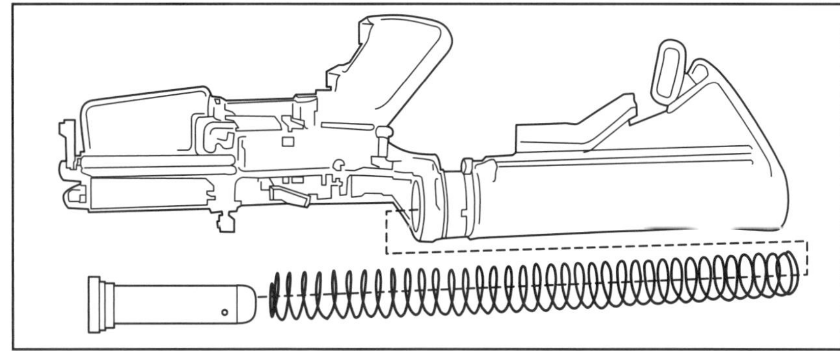

7 With hammer cocked, depress buffer retainer (86) with punch or bullet tip to release buffer (104) and action spring (103). CAUTION! Buffer is under tension from action Spring. NOTE: Hammer needs to be cocked to allow buffer and spring to clear receiver. Pull out buffer and action spring for cleaning.

CHINESE AKS OR TYPE 56S RIFLE

PARTS LEGEND

1. Accessories case spring
2. Bore brush
3. Combination tool
4. Jag
5. Accessories case
6. Accessories case cap
7. Bolt
8. Bolt carrier
9. Buttplate
10. Buttplate cover
11. Buttplate cover base
12. Buttplate cover pin
13. Buttplate cover spring
14. Buttplate screws (2)
15. Buttstock
16. Cleaning rod
17. Rear sight elevating slide catch
18. Rear sight elevating slide catch spring
19. Extractor
20. Extractor pin
21. Exractor spring
22. Firing pin
23. Firing pin spring
24. Firing pin retaining pin
25. Front sight base
26. Front sight base pins (2)
27. Front sight
28. Front sight adjusting block
29. Gas piston
30. Gas piston pin
31. Gas port block
32. Gas port block retaining pin
33. Hammer
34. Hammer pin
35. Hammer spring
36. Barrel pin
37. Lower handguard
38. Lower handguard band
39. Lower handguard clamp
40. Lower handguard lock
41. Lower handguard ferrule
42. Magazine
43. Magazine catch
44. Magazine catch pin
45. Magazine catch spring
46. Barrel bushing
47. Barrel bushing lock
48. Barrel bushing lock spring
49. Pistol grip
50. Pistol grip escutcheon
51. Pistol grip screw
52. Pistol grip base
53. Pistol grip cap
54. Bayonet
55. Bayonet pivot pin
56. Receiver pin lock spring
57. Rear sight base
58. Rear sight elevating slide
59. Rear sight pin
60. Rear sight leaf
61. Rear sight spring
62. Receiver and barrel assembly
63. Receiver cover
64. Front recoil spring guide
65. Rear recoil spring guide
66. Front guide retainer
67. Recoil spring
68. Safety lever
69. Disconnector
70. Disconnector spring
71. Safety lever stop
72. Front swivel
73. Rear swivel
74. Rear swivel screws (2)
75. Trigger/sear
76. Trigger guard
77. Front trigger guard rivets (2)
78. Rear trigger guard rivet
79. Trigger pin
80. Upper handguard/gas cylinder
81. Handguard latch
82. Tang screws (2)

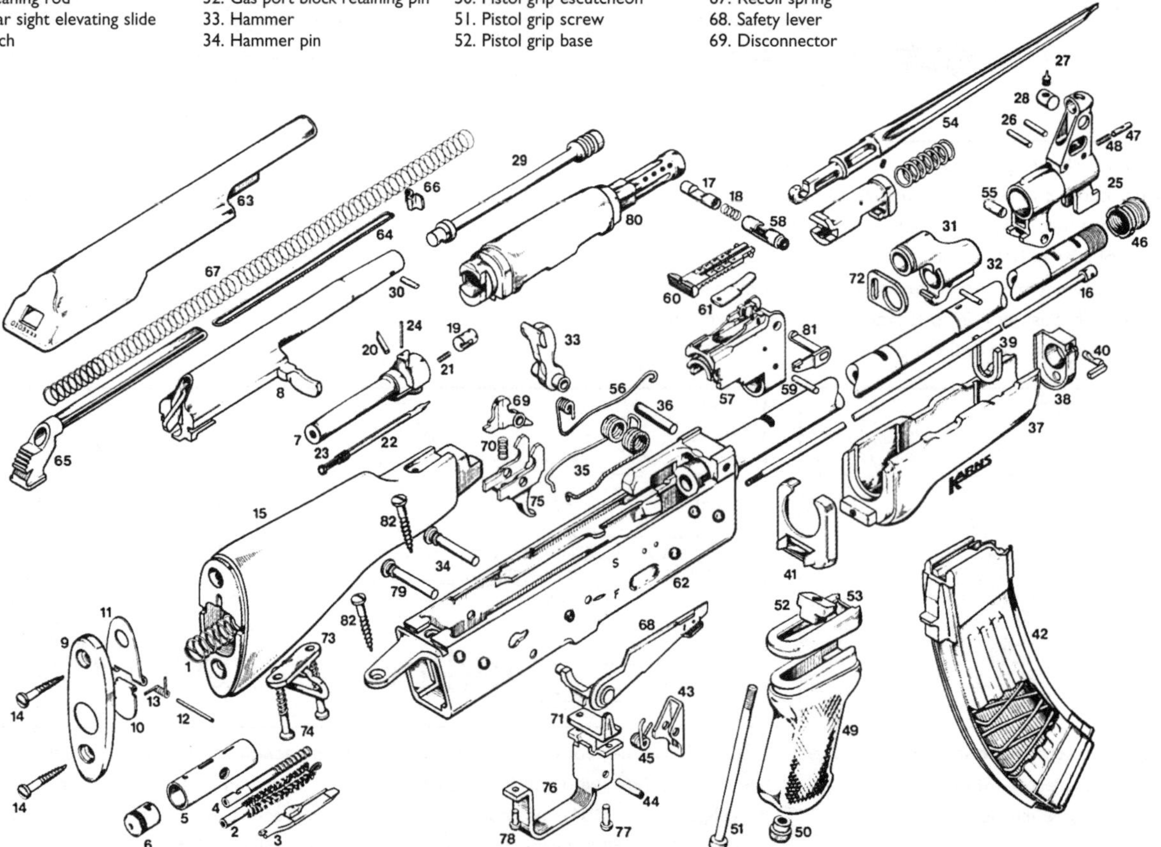

The AKS rifle is a Chinese production variant of one of the world's most successful small arms designs, the Russian *Avtomat Kalashnikova Obrazetza 1947g*, popularly known as the AK-47. The AK was designed in the mid-1940s by M.T. Kalashnikov. The earliest version, produced from 1948 to 1951, utilized a receiver built from steel stampings. This version was superseded in late 1951 by a model featuring a machined steel receiver. Two variants of the machined-receiver guns appeared, differing primarily in the manner of buttstock attachment.

As good as it was, the AK-47 was supplanted in the early 1960s by the AKM which, among other changes, reverted to the stamped-steel construction used in the first model AK receiver. This, with other changes, reduced the AKM's weight by 2½ lbs.

Use of the AK/AKM spread rapidly to Soviet allies and military assistance customers. In 1956, the People's Republic of China adopted the AK designating it the Type 56 Assault Rifle.

The Chinese retained the "Type 56" label for domestic production versions of the stamped-receiver AKM. These are the Type 56 submachine gun and Types 56-1 and 56-2 guns, with folding stocks. In addition, China North Industries Corp. (NORINCO) makes a semi-auto Sporting Rifle, Type 56S or AKS.

The rifle illustrated is an AKS made using the AKM receiver, an AK receiver cover and AK internal parts. Though there are minor mechanical differences between versions of M. T. Kalashnikov's rifle disassembly instructions for the AKS should suffice for any of these semi-automatic rifles.

DISASSEMBLY

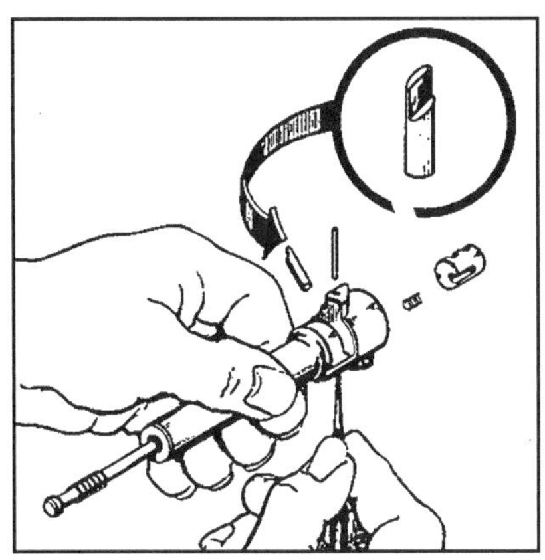

To field strip, remove magazine (42). Push forward on the takedown latch (65) where it passes through the rear of the receiver cover (63) and unlatch the receiver cover. Lift the cover up and to the rear, clear of the receiver (62), and set it aside.

Push forward on the takedown latch, until the rear recoil spring guide moves forward, clear of its seat in the receiver. Lift assembled recoil spring (67), front and rear guides (64 & 65) and front guide retainer (66) out of the receiver and withdraw assembly from its seat in the bolt carrier. Lift out the combined gas piston (29), bolt carrier (8) and bolt (7), by drawing it rearward until the carrier clears the guide ribs at the back of the receiver.

Remove bolt from carrier by pushing it down the carrier camway to the locked position. Rotate the bolt counterclockwise so that its locking cam clears the camway and pull it forward out of the carrier.

Remove upper handguard/gas cylinder (80) by rotating handguard latch (81) approximately 90° clockwise, until the flat surface atop the latch bar is parallel with the rear of the gas cylinder. Lift the back of the handguard free of the rear sight base (57) and pull handguard/gas cylinder clear.

Reassemble in reverse order noting:
a. The bolt locking cam must be turned into the locking camway at the rearmost (locked) position and then slid up the camway to the unlocked position before the bolt and carrier are reinstalled in receiver.

b. When replacing the bolt and carrier assembly in the receiver, start the gas piston into the rear of the gas cylinder then lower the rear of the carrier into the disassembly clearance at the rear of the guide ribs in the receiver. Maintain slight downward pressure on the carrier to overcome resistance by the hammer (33) and hammer spring (35) and slide the carrier and bolt forward.

Further disassembly: Remove accessories case (5) from butt trap. Remove buttplate screws (14), buttplate (9), and the buttplate cover (10) and associated parts. *Do not remove the accessories case spring* (1). Remove butt stock (15) by removing the tang screws (82). Slide the buttstock rearward out of the receiver. Unscrew pistol grip screw (51) and remove pistol grip (49). Lift the pistol grip base (52) out through top of receiver.

To remove lower handguard (37), withdraw cleaning rod (16). Turn lower handguard lock (40) 90° clockwise and drive it from left to right out of the lower handguard band (38). Slide the lower handguard band forward to release lower handguard. NOTE: *The left end of the lower handguard lock is peened to prevent loosening or and loss.*

To disassemble the bolt, use the drift on the combination tool to push the firing pin retaining pin (24) from the bottom of the bolt out through the top of the locking cam. Allow firing pin (22) and firing pin spring (23) to drop out of the back of the bolt. Using thumb to take up the tension on extractor (19) and extractor spring (21), push extractor pin (20) out of the bolt. Lift extractor and extractor spring out of their well in the bolt face.

To disassembe trigger mechanism: Lower hammer (33) until it rests on the hammer stop bar fixed behind the magazine well. Move safety lever to "Safe" position.

With a screwdriver blade or drift, reach into receiver behind the hammer and push the receiver pin lock spring (56) down out of the locking groove in the headed, left end of the hammer pin (34). Simultaneously, push the hammer pin from right to left and, by manipulating the hammer and hammer spring (35), free the head of the hammer pin from the left side of the receiver and pull it out. Twist hammer and spring ¼ turn counterclockwise. Free legs of the hammer spring from trigger/sear (75) and lift hammer and spring from the receiver.

Push and turn the receiver pin lock spring out from under the hammer stop bar and rotate it upward to release the trigger pin (79). Push the trigger pin out from right to left, manipulating the headed, left end clear of the receiver in the same way it was done with the hammer pin. Lift the trigger, disconnector (69) and disconnector spring (70) out of the receiver.

Remove the safety lever (68) and receiver pin lock spring (56) by rotateing the safety lever counterclockwise until the lug on the safety lever aligns with the takedown slot in the receiver. Pull the safety lever to the right, out of the receiver and lift the receiver pin lock spring out of the interior of the receiver.

COLT AR-15 RIFLE

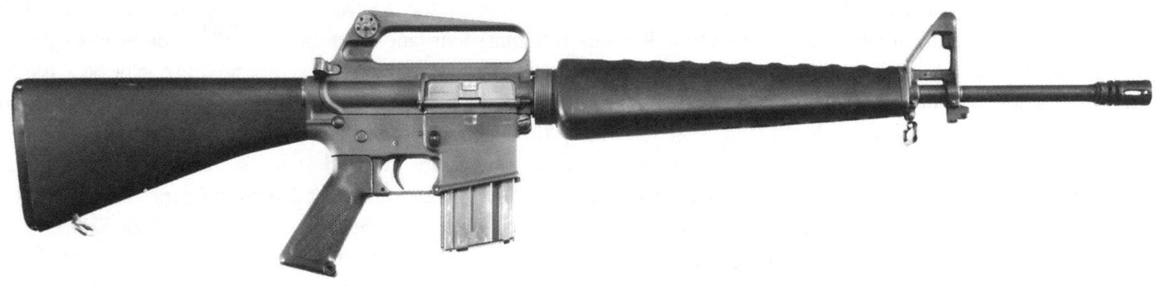

PARTS LEGEND

1. Magazine box
2. Magazine clip rivet (3)
3. Magazine clip
4. Magazine bottom plate
5. Magazine spacer
6. Magazine spring
7. Magazine follower
8. Pistol grip screw
9. Lock washer
10. Pistol grip
11. Buttstock
12. Rear swivel
13. Swivel base pin
14. Swivel base
15. Lower buttplate screw
16. Upper buttplate screw
17. Buttplate frame
18. Trapdoor latch
19. Latch spring
20. Latch pin
21. Trapdoor
22. Receiver extension
23. Buffer spring
24. Lower receiver
25. Buffer retainer spring
26. Buffer retainer
27. Bumper
28. Buffer spacer
29. Buffer weight (5)
30. Buffer disc (5)
31. Buffer body
32. Safety detent
33. Safety/ejector detent spring
34. Trigger guard
35. Detent spring pin
36. Guard detent
37. Detent spring
38. Guard pivot pin
39. Trigger pin
40. Trigger spring
41. Trigger
42. Disconnect spring
43. Disconnect
44. Hammer pin
45. Hammer pin retainer
46. Hammer
47. Hammer spring
48. Pivot pin screw
49. Bolt catch pin
50. Bolt catch
51. Bolt catch spring
52. Bolt catch plunger
53. Pivot pin
54. Mag. catch spring
55. Mag. catch button
56. Takedown pin
57. Takedown pin detent
58. Takedown pin spring
59. Safety
60. Magazine catch
61. Mag. catch shaft
62. Firing pin
63. Firing pin retainer
64. Bolt cam pin
65. Carrier screws (2)
66. Bolt carrier key
67. Bolt carrier
68. Bolt rings (3)
69. Bolt
70. Extractor
71. Extractor pin
72. Ejector pin
73. Ejector spring
74. Ejector
75. Extractor spring
76. Extractor plunger
77. Charging handle
78. Handle latch pin
79. Handle latch spring
80. Handle latch
81. Rear sight screw
82. Sight tension spring
83. Rear sight
84. Windage drum spring
85. Windage drum detent
86. Windage drum
87. Windage drum pin
88. Port cover spring
89. Port cover rod
90. Rod retaining ring
91. Upper receiver
92. Port cover detent
93. Detent spring
94. Detent spring retainer
95. Detent retainer
96. Port cover
97. Handguard, right
98. Handguard liner, right
99. Liner rivet (10)
100. Barrel
101. Barrel extension
102. Barrel index pin
103. Liner rivet (10)
104. Handguard liner, left
105. Handguard, left
106. Front sight post
107. Front sight detent
108. Front sight spring
109. Gas tube pin
110. Front sight housing
111. Sight taper pins (2)
112. Front swivel rivet
113. Front swivel
114. Gas tube plug
115. Gas tube
116. Handguard cap
117. Flash suppressor
118. Lock washer
119. Barrel nut
120. Handguard slip ring
121. Slip ring spring assy.
122. Handguard snap ring

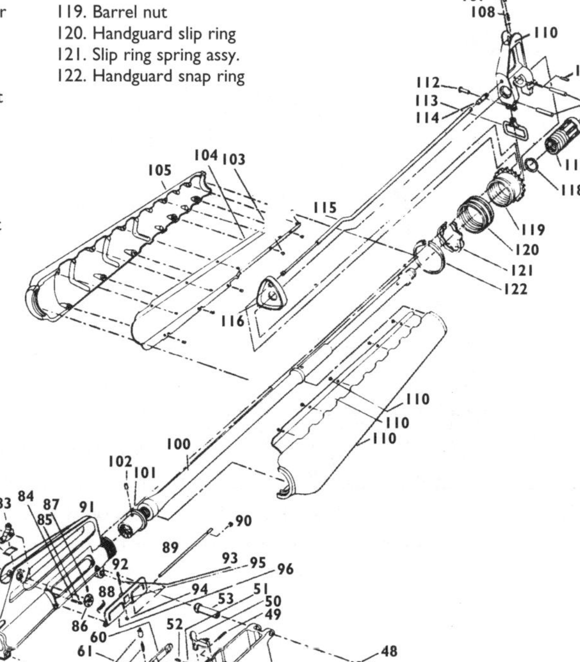

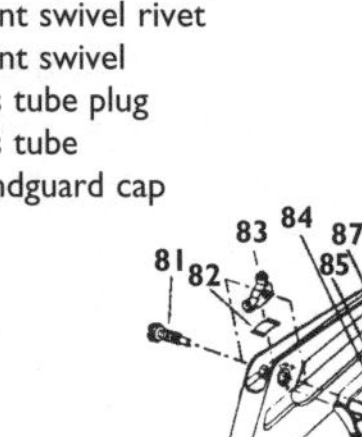

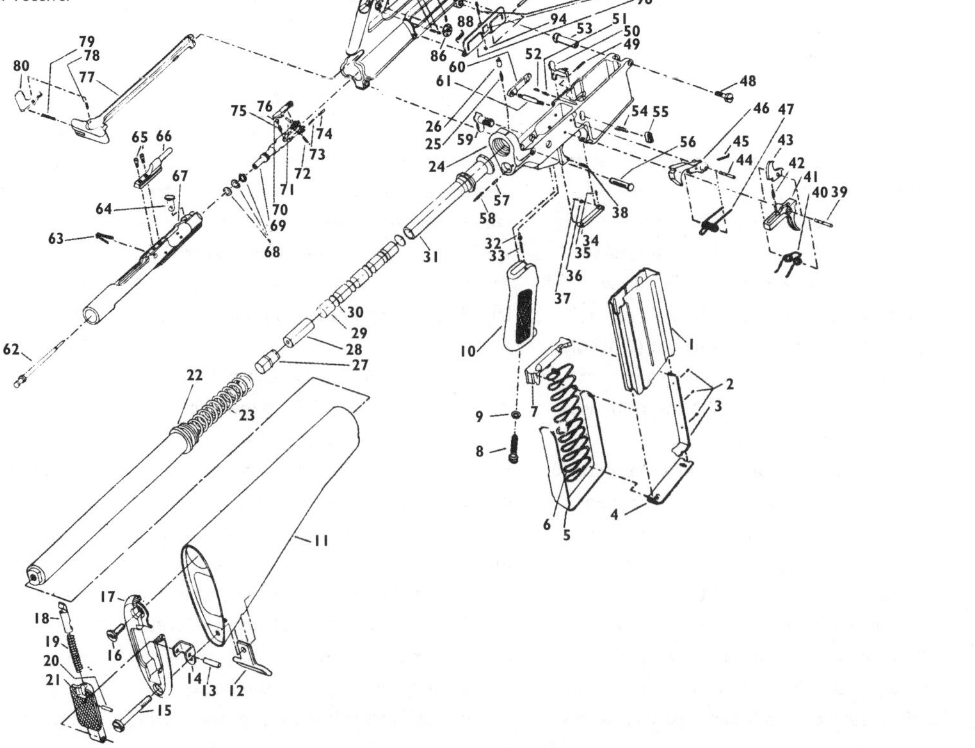

The AR-15 is the semi-automatic — sometimes called "Civilian" version — of the U.S. military M16 rifle of the same caliber. It differs from the M16 in that it is manufactured without provision for a full-automatic sear and with a two position selector (fire and safe), rather than the M16 three position selector (safe, semi and auto). The later MI6AI Service rifle is equipped with a forward assist plunger on the right side of the receiver, but this is lacking in the MI6 and the AR-15.

The AR-15, then, is a semi-automatic, gas-operated, magazine-fed rifle, suitable for military match-type shooting and popular as a small game hunting rifle. It was introduced by Colt in 1963, and, in addition to its sporting use, the AR-15 has considerable appeal as a police or guard rifle, where full-automatic capability is not required.

The AR-15 is made up of more than 150 parts, many of which are pre-assembled by the factory into component groups. A simple appearing handguard, for instance, is actually a two-part riveted assembly comprised of 24 separate pieces. The buffer assembly (over a dozen parts) may be removed easily from the buttstock as a unit, but should not be broken down to its component parts.

There are also various screws with thread-locking material installed and a number of rollpins and rivets, the removal of any of which would tend to lessen its effectiveness on reinstallation. In some cases it might become necessary to replace pins, rivets or springs after removal, and for this reason it is recommended that the AR-15 be field-stripped only, with further disassembly left in the hands of a competent gunsmith.

DISASSEMBLY

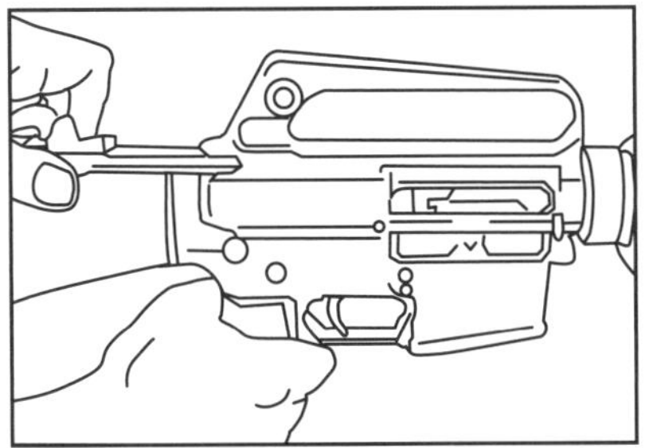

1 Depress the magazine catch button (55) and wlthdraw the magazine box (1). Depress the handle latch (80) and retract the charging handle (77). Examine chamber to make sure it is clear of a cartridge. Release the charging handle.

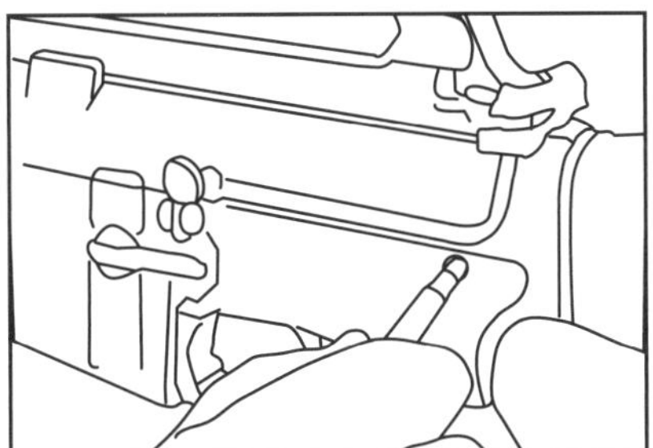

2 With the tip of a cartridge push the takedown pin (56) located above the safety lever through the receiver from left to rlght. The barrel unit may now be "broken open" from the stock in the same way that a double-barrel shotgun is broken open.

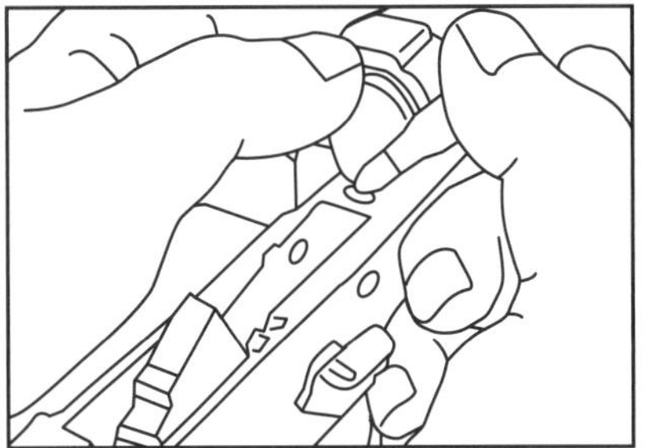

3 The buffer body (31) and all its attendant parts are easily withdrawn by pressing down the buffer retainer (26). The buffer assembly is, of course, under some tension, and care should be exercised In Its removal. It is not recommended that the trigger or hammer parts be removed, but their placement is evldent with the action open.

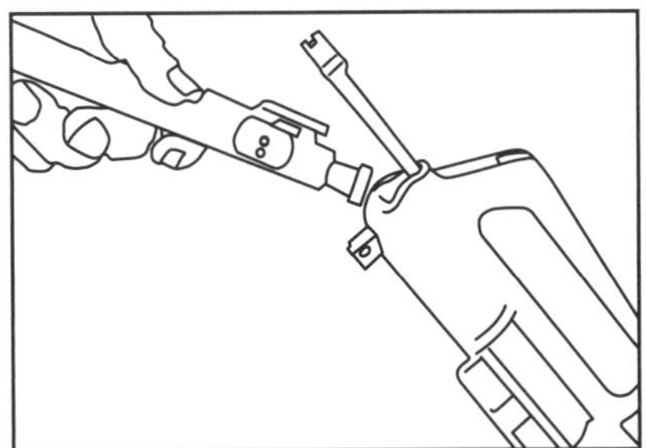

4 Withdraw the bolt carrier (67) from the upper recelver (91). This will require the retraction of the charging handle which, after the bolt carrier's removal, can be taken out completely, if required.

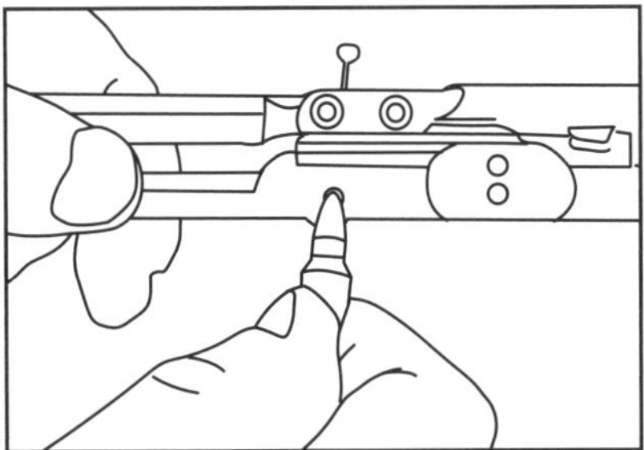

5 The bolt itself (69) containing extractor, ejector, firing pin and associated parts, is removed from the carrier by first pushing out the firing pin retainer (63) and pulling the exposed firing pin (62) to the rear and out.

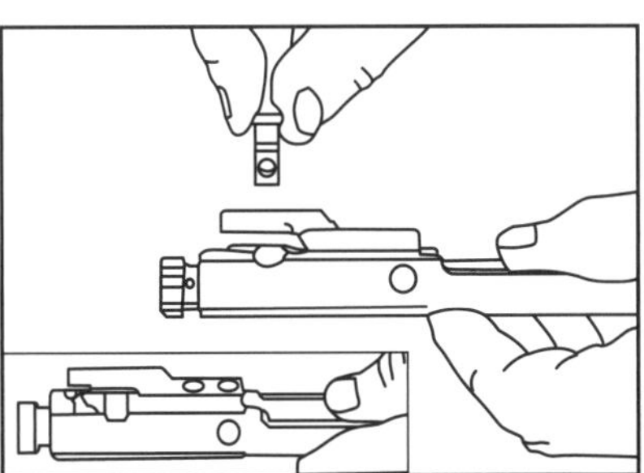

6 Push bolt to the rear and turn bolt cam pin (64) until it is free of the bolt carrier key (66) and can be lifted out; the bolt can be withdrawn exposing the extractor and ejector retaining pins. Their removal is not recommended, nor is that of the three bolt rings (68). Remove handguard by pulling back on the handguard slip ring (120) and separating the two handguard halves (97 & 105).

COLT LIGHTNING RIFLE

PARTS LEGEND

1. Receiver
2. Barrel
3. Buttstock (not shown)
4. Slide grip, right (not shown)
4a. Slide grip, left (not shown)
5. Bolt
6. Extractor
7. Extractor pin
8. Firing pin
9. Bolt roller bearing
10. Roller bearing pin
11. Locking brace
12. Locking brace pin
13. Firing pin lever
14. Firing pin lever pin
15. Ejector/bolt guide, right
16. Ejector/bolt guide, left
17. Ejector bolt guide screw
18. Magazine gate latch
19. Magazine gate latch spring
20. Magazine gate spring screw
21. Magazine guide screw
22. Trigger guard/frame
23. Slide
24. Magazine gate
25. Magazine gate pin
26. Slide locking latch
27. Magazine gate spring
28. Magazine gate spring screw
29. Slide lock
30. Trigger
31. Trigger pin
32. Trigger spring
33. Trigger spring screw
34. Cartridge carrier
35. Carrier screws (2)
36. Hammer
37. Hammer pin
38. Mainspring roller bearing
39. Mainspring roller bearing pin
40. Mainspring
41. Mainspring screw
42. Slide grips screws (4)
43. Tang screw
44. Receiver screws (2)
45. Rear sight
46. Rear sight elevator
47. Front sight
48. Magazine tube
49. Magazine tube follower
50. Magazine tube spring
51. Magazine tube cap
52. Magazine cap screw
53. Magazine barrel lug
54. Buttplate
55. Buttplate screws

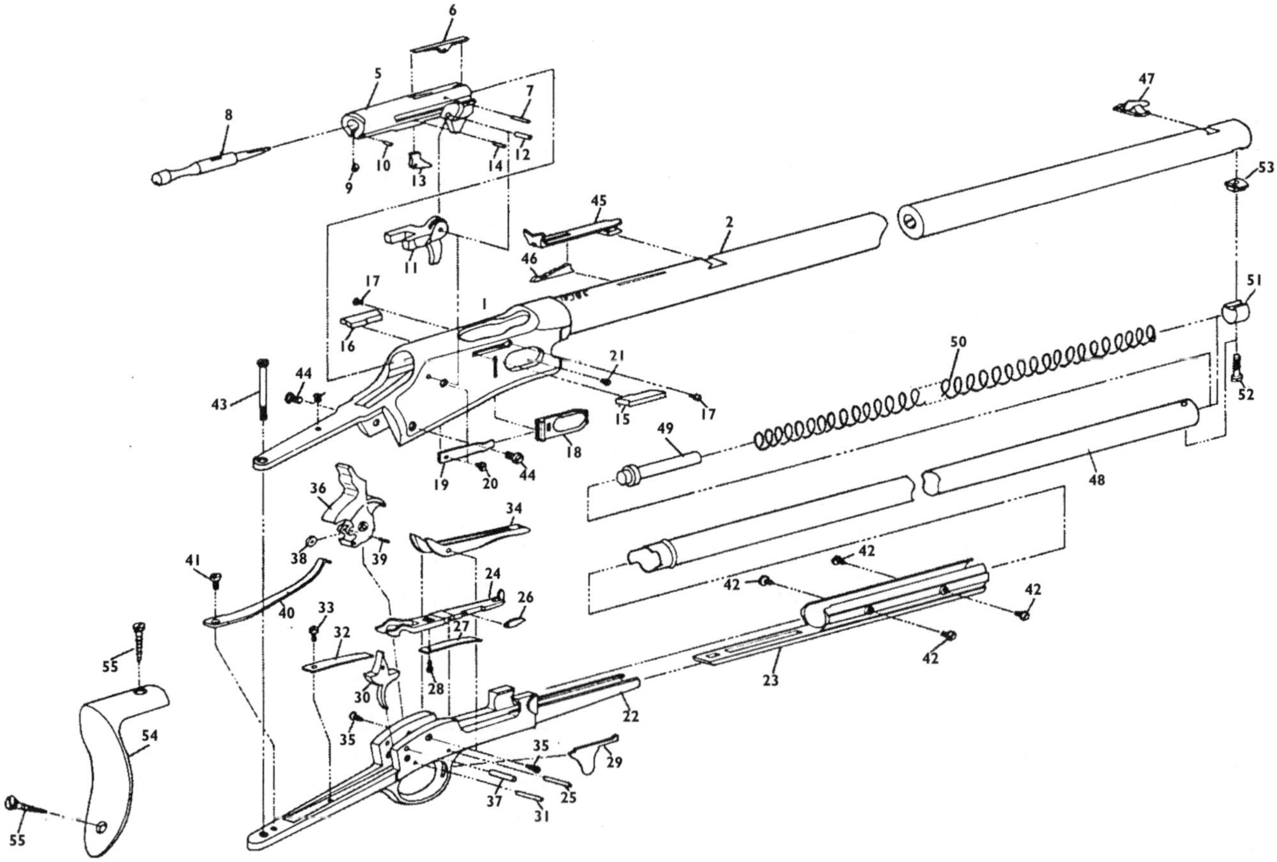

The Colt Lightning Magazine Rifle was introduced to the world's shooters in 1884. Based largely on two patents by W. H. Elliot, the Lightning was a tube-magazine, slide-action repeater. It was Colt's alternative to Winchester's Model 1873, matched to the calibers of the Single Action Army revolvers.

Eventually offered in three frame sizes, the first guns were on a medium-sized frame in .44-40, .38-40 and .32-20. Barrels were available in 26-inch rifle length (round or octagonal) and 20-inch carbine. Rifle magazines held 15 and the carbine 12.

The medium-frame Lightning was sufficiently successful and a small-frame version, chambered for .22 rimfire, was introduced in 1887. Small-frame Lightnings were made with 24-inch round or octagon barrels, with a standard half magazine holding 15 .22 Long or 16 .22 Short cartridges.

That same year, Colt offered a large-frame version, chambered for heavy cartridges such as .38-56, .45-85 and .50-95. Large-frame guns were sold as 28-inch barreled rifles and 22-inch barrel carbines, with 26 inches standard for .50-95 rifle barrels. Barrels were available in round or octagon.

Serial numbers for Lightnings began with I for each frame size and continued up to 89,777 for medium-frame models, 89,912 for .22s and 6496 for large-frame guns.

The Lightning design is complex, requiring a large number of precisely made and fitted parts. Colt met the challenge of craftsmanship, and Lightnings, particularly the small- and medium-frame guns, are rugged, reliable arms. What could not be met was the challenge of the marketplace.

Large-frame guns were discontinued in 1894. The two remaining models survived into the 20th century. Medium-frame production ceased in 1902 and small frames in 1904.

DISASSEMBLY

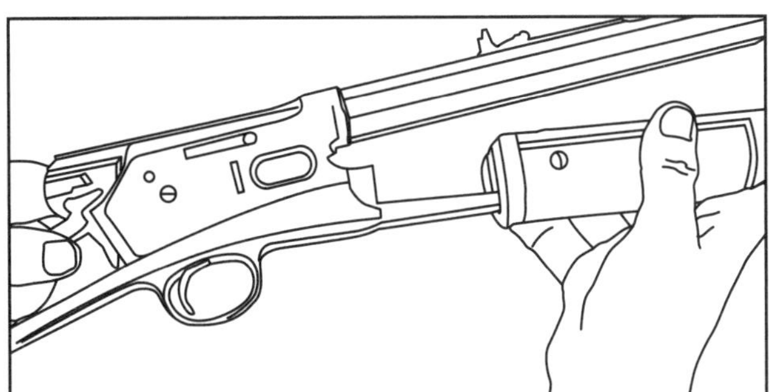

1 Remove tang screw (43) and buttstock (3). Take out magazine cap screw (52) and remove the magazine cap (51), being careful to hold the magazine spring (50) in the magazine tube (48). Holding the magazine spring, lift the magazine tube clear of the magazine lug (53) and pull it forward, out of the slide assembly.

Remove the receiver screws (44). Draw the slide (23) about half way to the rear, keeping the cartridge carrier (34) in the "down" position. With a soft-faced hammer, drift the trigger guard/frame (22) forward until the two semicircular fillets that mate with the receiver (1) are clear of their recesses, then pull the slide grip away from the barrel (2) rotating the trigger guard/frame out of the receiver (above). Slide the assembled bolt (5) and locking brace (11) to the rear of the receiver.

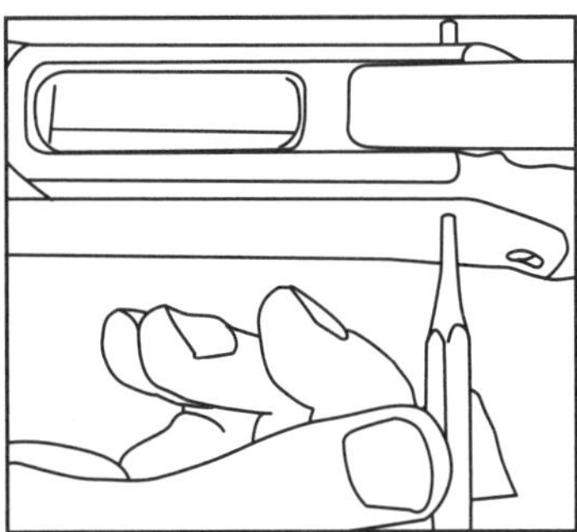

2 Drive out the locking brace pin (12) by inserting a pin punch through the small hole in the upper left-hand side of the receiver and pushing the pin from left to right (above). Lift the locking brace out through the bottom of the receiver and slide the bolt out through the rear of the receiver.

When disassembling the receiver, check orientation and fit of all parts. Take care in replacing the ejector/bolt guides (15 & 16) to insure that the contour cuts in the guides match case rim orientation. Other components must fit flush with interior receiver walls.

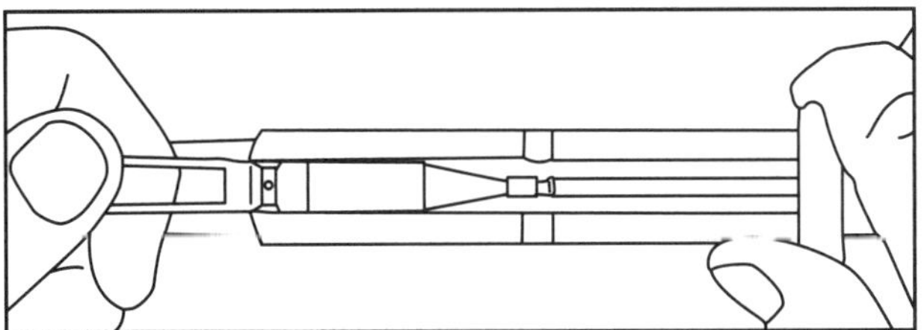

3 Bolt disassembly is not recommended as the pins are peened in place. If the bolt is disassembled, all pins must be replaced flush with the bolt surfaces to avoid drag in the receiver. To disassemble the trigger guard/frame assembly, push the slide (23) fully forward and lower the hammer (36) to the uncocked position. Then remove the mainspring screw (41) and mainspring (40). Remove the trigger spring screw (33) and trigger spring (32).

Use a pin punch to drive the headed hammer pin (37), from left to right, out of the frame. Lift the hammer to the rear and out of the frame. Remove the carrier screws (35) and lift the carrier (34) out of the frame.

With a pin punch, drive out the magazine gate pin (25). Lift the rear tangs of the magazine gate (24) out of the frame and draw the gate and slide to the rear until the cartridge stop on the magazine gate, which passes up through the long slot on the slide, drops into the trigger slot in the frame. This allows the magazine gate to be disengaged from the slide and lifted out of the frame (Fig. 3).

Drive the headed trigger pin (31) from left to right, out of the frame and lift the trigger (30) out of the frame.

FIREARMS INTERNATIONAL BRONCO

PARTS LEGEND

1. Barrel
2. Front link
3. Rear link
4. Barrel support rod
5. Link pin (2)
6. Front link screw
7. Support rod pin
8. Rear sight
9. Rear sight screw
10. Extractor rod
11. Extractor spring
12. Extractor
13. Extractor pin
14. Breechblock
15. Locking rod
16. Breech body pin
17. Cocking lever
18. Firing pin
19. Cocking lever spring
20. Firing pin bushing
21. Firing pin spring
22. Firing pin washer
23. Cocking lever pin
24. Spacer tube (.22 Mag.)
25. Stock/receiver
26. Stock rod
27. Safety
28. Safety spring
29. Safety ball
30. Sear
31. Trigger spring
32. Trigger
33. Trigger & sear pin (2)
34. Stock pin
35. Locking arm stop pin (2)
36. Support rod locking bolt
37. Support rod locking arm
38. Locking bolt washer
39. Locking bolt screw (2)

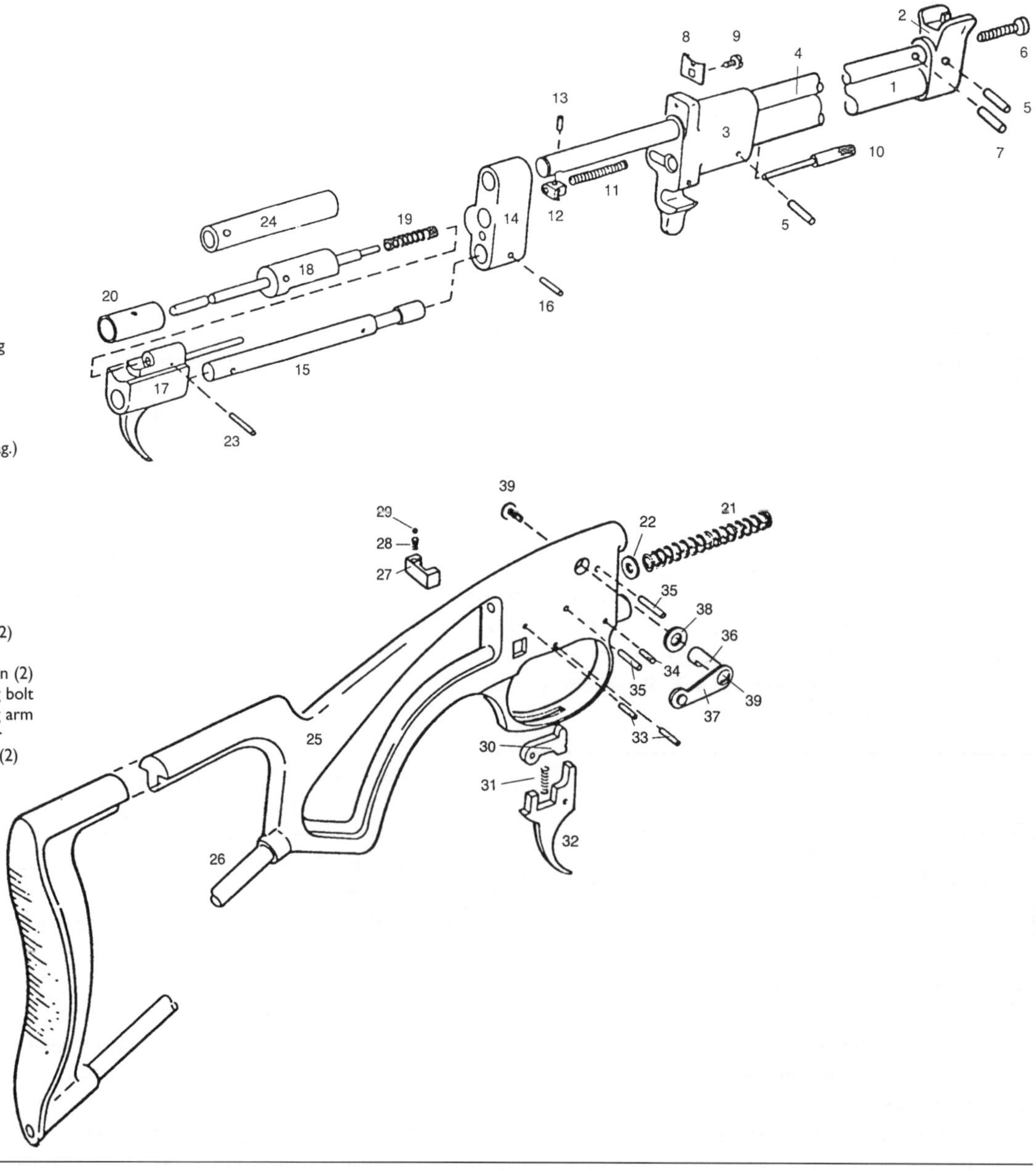

Introduced in 1967, the Bronco .22 was an updated version of the Hamilton Model 7 rifle originally made circa 1900. Both had all-metal frames and manual extractors and both were intended to be the cheapest .22 rifles on the market.

In 1900, the Hamilton sold for about $2.00 or was given away as a sales premium, a box of .22 Shorts for it cost about 15¢. In 1967, (when .22 Shorts had risen to 75¢ per box), Firearms International offered its Bronco at $9.95. Using .22 Short ammunition as a guide to the prices of the times, the Bronco cost the same in real dollars as the old Hamilton, and the Bronco could handle .22 Shorts and Long Rifles as well.

Firearms International's factory in Accokeek, Maryland was hard-pressed to keep up with the initial demand for the 3 lb. 16½-inch barrelled rifles, but their low cost, the real reason for existence, came to be their downfall.

The 1968 Gun Control Act required serial numbering on each receiver, and this proved to be one of the most expensive manufacturing operations on the gun. In 1969 the retail price rose to $14.95. The distributor then paid $8.97 and the dealer $11.21.

The GCA, of course, also required the manufacturer, distributors and dealers to keep detailed records of every firearm transaction and the buyers had to fill out 4473 Forms. Where the Broncos had sold well as "impulse items," they now required more paperwork and trouble than the modest markups permitted. Sales plummeted, and in less than a decade the Bronco was discontinued.

In their brief history, the Bronco rifles were made as solid-frames, then as takedowns; with brown-painted, diecast zinc receivers/stocks. After 1970, when Garcia Corp. took over Firearms International, rifles were produced with a black crinkle finish, in the .22 Short/Long/Long Rifle version mentioned above, and as a .22 Magnum version with a strengthening spacer placed between the breechblock and the receiver.

That wasn't the limit of the Bronco line. Concurrently with the .22s, a beefed up version with a 20-inch barrel was made, chambered for the .410 cartridge (solid or takedown). In 1975, a .410/.22 combination gun was made in limited quantity (including 200 sold through Sarco of Stirling, New Jersey) and was later remarketed (in its standard 22-inch barrel lengths), as the Bauer Rabbit.

Disassembly of the Bronco .22 is a tedious affair because of the many pins used in its construction. Pages could be written on the disassembly, but they would boil down to placing the rifle on a padded surface and, starting at the muzzle, working backwards to drive out every pin in sight separating the components as they were freed. That, in reverse order, was how the rifles were assembled and that's how they are taken apart.

On the models equipped with takedown levers, the takedown is effected by engaging the crossbolt safety above the trigger, pulling back the cocking lever, pivoting the barrel unit, turning the takedown lever and pulling the barrel unit away from the stock/action unit.

DISASSEMBLY

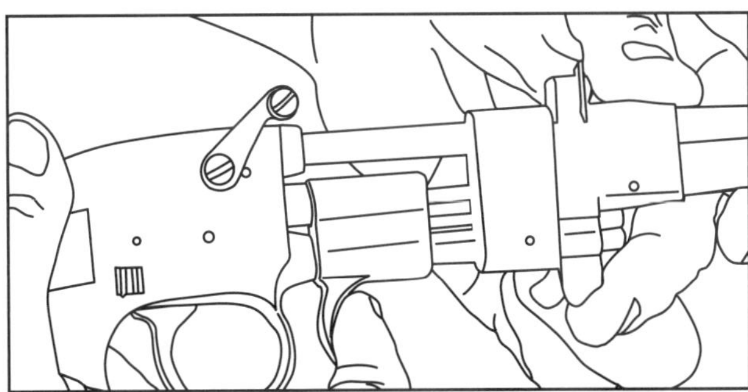

1 The Bronco is taken down by turning up the support rod locking arm (37) and retracting the cocking lever (17).

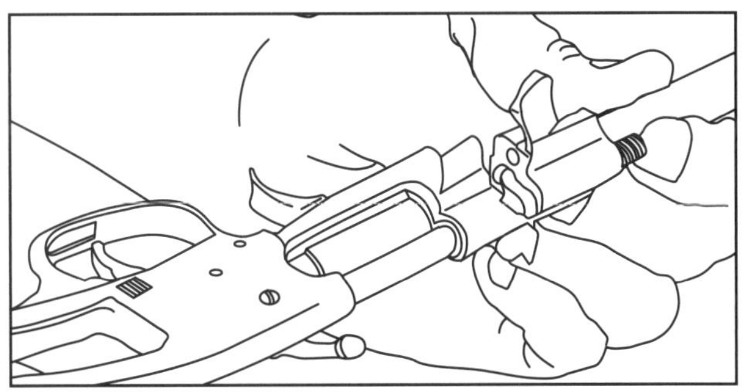

2 Then the breechblock (14) is rotated clockwise exposing the chamber and the manual extractor (12).

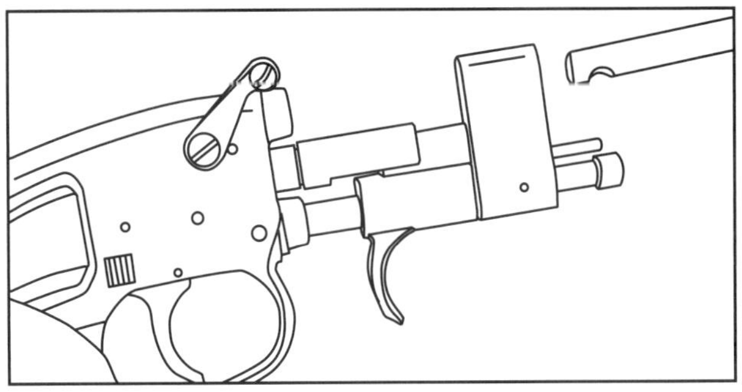

3 In reassembly, make certain the notch on the underside of the barrel support rod(4) points down.

F.I. COMBO PISTOL/RIFLE

PARTS LEGEND

1. Frame
2. Ejector
3. Hammer stop pin
4. Slide
5. Rear sight
6. Extractor
7. Extractor spring
8. Extractor pin
9. Firing pin
10. Firing pin spring
11. Firing pin stop plate
12. Recoil spring
13. Recoil spring guide
14. Recoil spring washer
15. Recoil spring guide nut
16. Safety/slide lock
17. Barrel
18. Hammer
19. Hammer pin
20. Hammer link
21. Hammer link pin
22. Hammer spring
23. Hammer guide
24. Magazine catch
25. Magazine catch button
26. Magazine catch spring
27. Magazine catch washer
28. Sear
29. Sear pin
30. Sear spring
31. Trigger
32. Trigger pin
33. Trigger bar
34. Trigger bar spring
35. Trigger bar plunger
36. Trigger bar pin
37. Magazine safety
38. Magazine safety spring
39. Magazine safety stop
40. Magazine safety pin
41. Magazine
42. Grip plates (pair)
43. Grip plate screws (4)

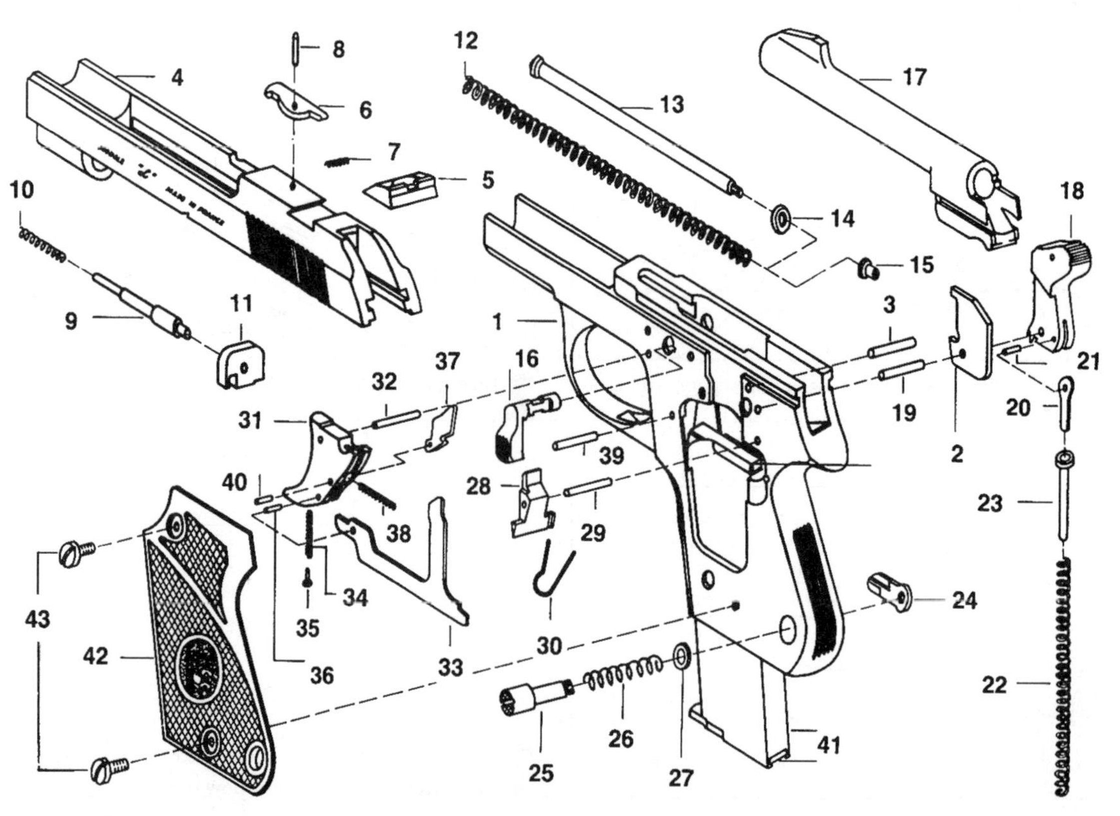

Many NRA members were introduced to the Combo by the Feb. 29, 1960, issue of *Newsweek* that contained this in its business section. "Pistol-Packing Rifle: A gun that converts from a pistol to a rifle in ten seconds has been developed by Firearms International Corp. of Washington, D.C. The Combo consists of a 22-caliber pistol and a rifle unit with stock, rifle barrel, sights, and operating rod. To convert to a rifle, you remove the barrel from the pistol, insert the rest of it into the rifle. Price: $64.95."

The pistol mentioned by *Newsweek* in its unusual burst of gun promotion was the Unique Model L, made by Manufacture d'Armes des Pyrenees Françaises of Hendaye, France, in .32, .380 ACP, and .22 Long Rifle. In .22 caliber it was used as the basis of the Combo throughout its eight-year production life. *Newsweek's* U.S.-made rifle was only provisional, however, with a one-piece stock lacking a separate handguard.

Despite its novelty and despite the fact that in addition to a steel-framed version it was offered for a time with an aluminum-framed Model L pistol anodized in pastel colors, the Combo was no toy but a good choice for anyone wanting a U.S.-made rifle barrel/stock unit, coupled with the excellent Unique Model L pistol. By 1969, when its price had risen to $80, the Combo disappeared from the U.S. market. The 1968 Gun Control Act prohibited the further importation of the pistol because of its small size.

In France, Unique-made rifle units complemented Unique pistols for European sales. Two distinct French variants have been noted: one, also called 'Combo," had optional open sights; the other, the Konvert, had a receiver sight but no handguard, and a trap in the butt for the pistol barrel.

There were rumors in the early 1960s that the U.S. Combo was a "pistol with a shoulder stock," thus coming under the National Firearms Act. Prior to its manufacture, however, the ATF ruled that the Combo could only be used either as a conventional pistol or (when its short barrel had been removed and the remainder of the gun affixed to the stock unit) as an 18-inch-barrelled rifle. There was no practical way to use the fully assembled 3-inch-barrelled pistol with the stock.

DISASSEMBLY

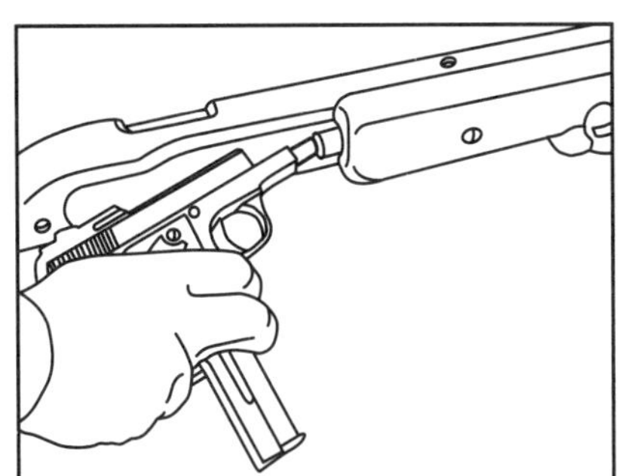

1 Rotate the safety/slide lock (16) to the rear to cover the red dot on the frame (1). Retract the slide (4) that will be held back by the safety/slide lock. Depress the magazine catch button (25) and withdraw the magazine (41). Slide, or, with a block of wood, tap the barrel (17) to the rear and out of the frame. Note that the barrel's rearward movement would be blocked either by the magazine or by the safety/slide lock if it is in forward (fire) position.

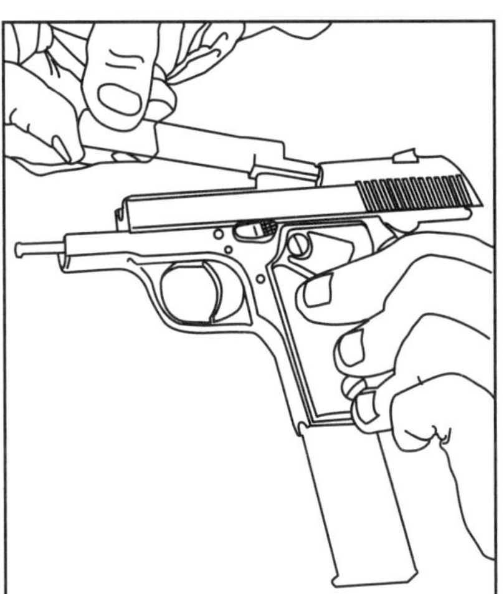

2 Grasp the slide serrations and turn down the safety/slide lock. Guide the slide forward off the frame. The recoil spring assembly (1215) will now be free and field stripping is complete. Detail stripping is not recommended as some parts, such as the magazine catch assembly (24-27), are staked together.

If required, the firing pin (9) can be removed by first pushing it in with a thin punch and then driving its stop plate (11) down and out of the slide. When replacing the firing pin, make sure the longitudinal groove on its shaft faces toward the top.

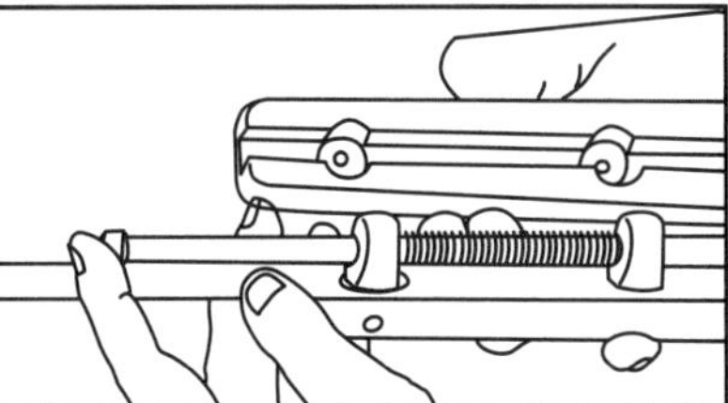

3 Dismantling the stock unit is straightforward but not recommended. Access to all parts — the rifle barrel, the operating rod with its return spring and their mounting bosses, screws and pins — is achieved by removing the two screws that retain the lower handguard.

Removal of the handguard also exposes the screws that retain the action cover plate that houses the adjustable rear sight and incorporates dovetail grooves for optional scope mounting.

FN SEMI-AUTOMATIC RIFLE (SAFN)

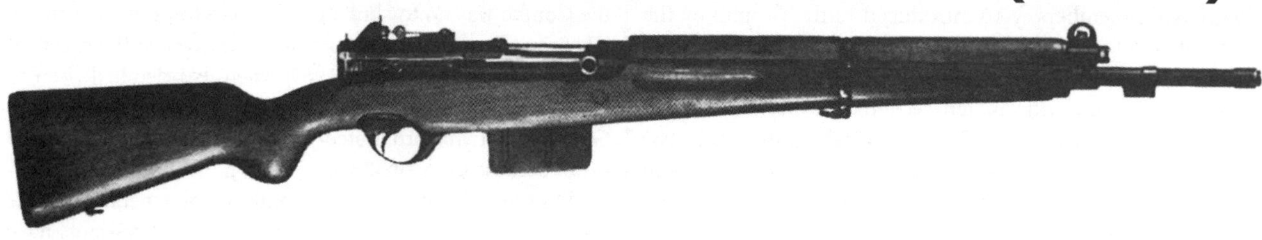

PARTS LEGEND

1. Receiver cover assembly
2. Bolt carrier catch stop
3. Bolt carrier catch spring
4. Rear sight
5. Rear sight spring
6. Bolt carrier catch
7. Inner recoil spring guide
8. Outer recoil spring
9. Inner recoil spring (2)
10. Firing pin extension
11. Sliding dust cover
12. Firing pin
13. Firing pin spring
14. Firing pin safety stop
15. Receiver
16. Bolt
17. Extractor
18. Extractor spring
19. Bolt carrier
20. Piston spring
21. Piston
22. Rear handguard
23. Barrel
24. Gas cylinder
25. Front handguard
26. Gas adjusting sleeve
27. Gas cylinder plug
28. Front sight
29. Muzzle cap
30. Buttplate screw (2)
31. Buttplate
32. Butt swivel screw (2)
33. Butt swivel
34. Trigger guard
35. Auxiliary sear spring
36. Auxiliary sear spring plunger
37. Auxiliary sear
38. Trigger
39. Bolt stop retainer
40. Bolt stop retainer plunger spring
41. Trigger spring plunger
42. Trigger spring
43. Bolt stop assembly
44. Outer hammer spring
45. Bolt stop retainer plunger
46. Ejector
47. Inner hammer spring
48. Hammer and hammer spring guide
49. Lower band swivel
50. Lower band
51. Stock
52. Stock end cap screw
53. Magazine follower
54. Stock end cap
55. Rear guard screw
56. Safety
57. Center guard screw
58. Magazine catch spring
59. Magazine catch
60. Trigger pin
61. Hammer pin
62. Guard screw stop screw (3)
63. Front guard screw
64. Magazine catch pin
65. Magazine box
66. Magazine follower spring

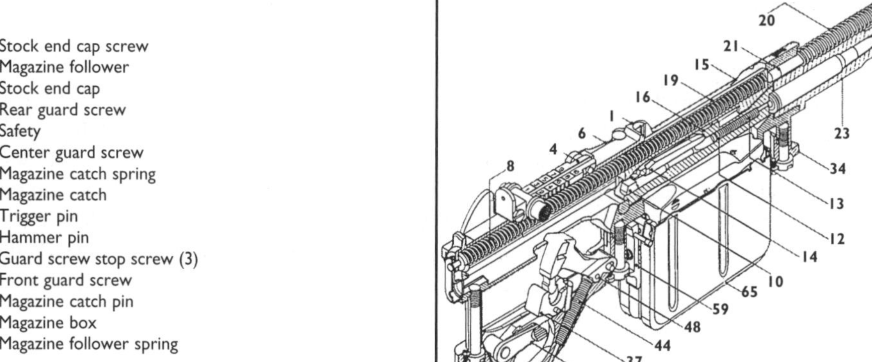

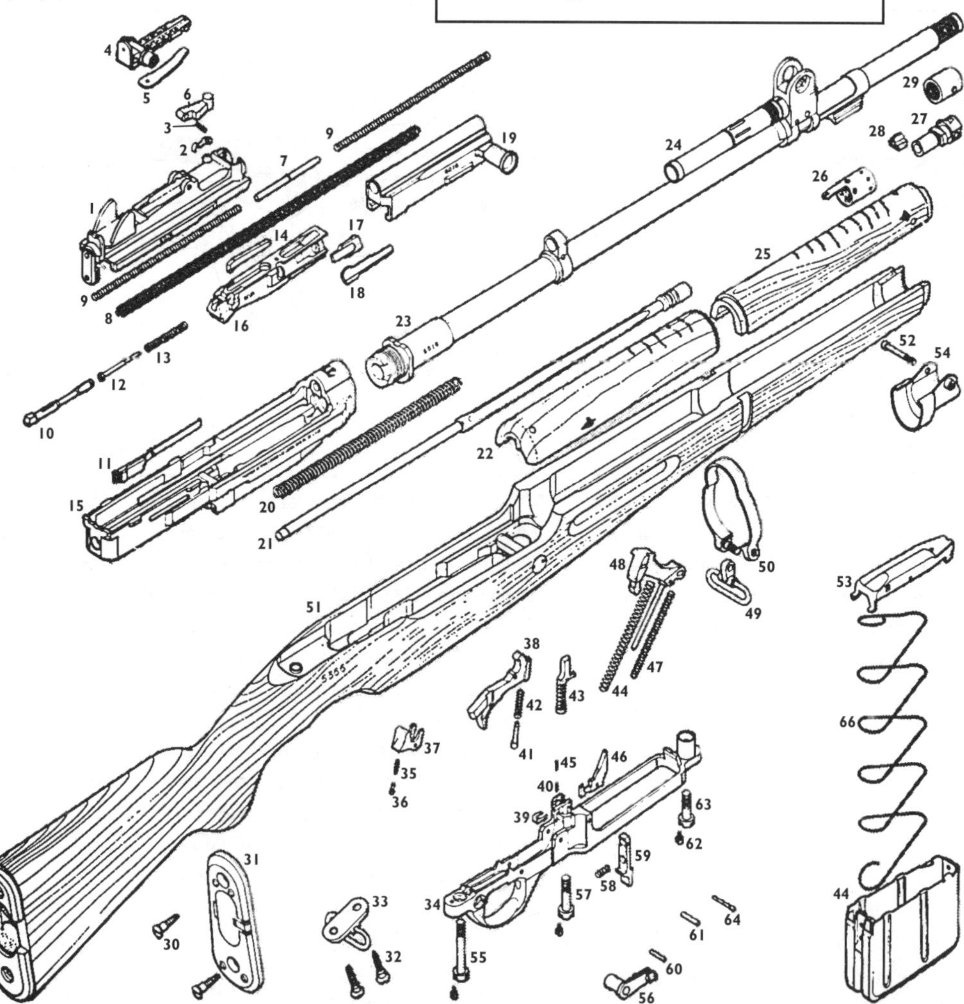

Developed in the 1930s by arms designer Dieudonne Saive, the Belgian made, gas-operated semi-automatic military rifle, produced by *Fabrique Nationale* (FN), replaced the bolt-action Mausers used by Belgium and other nations after World War II. This rifle is often called the SAFN (Semi-Automatic FN) or ABL (*Armee Belge Leger*). It was chambered in 7 mm. Mauser, .30-06, 7.65 mm. Mauser, and 8 mm. Mauser. The Belgian Model 1949 and models adopted by Luxembourg, Brazil, Colombia, Argentina and the Belgian Congo are in .30-06. Venezuela selected 7 mm. Mauser and the Egyptian 8 mm. Mauser.

The rifle has a fixed barrel with the gas mechanism above it, a tilting breech-bolt, and a one-piece stock. Two five-round Mauser strip clips are used to charge the 10-round semi-fixed box magazine. A bolt carrier catch on the receiver cover holds the action open when the gun is empty to allow for loading.

The rifle has a manual safety and when the hammer is cocked, the tip of the hammer spring guide projects from the bottom of the trigger guard as a cocking indicator.

The SAFN is fitted with an adjustable tangent-type aperture rear sight. The blade front sight, mounted on the gas cylinder bracket, has sideguards. Exposed metal parts of the SAFN have a black enamel or paint finish. The SAFN was discontinued in the late 1950s when a number of nations adopted the FN Light Automatic Rifle.

DISASSEMBLY

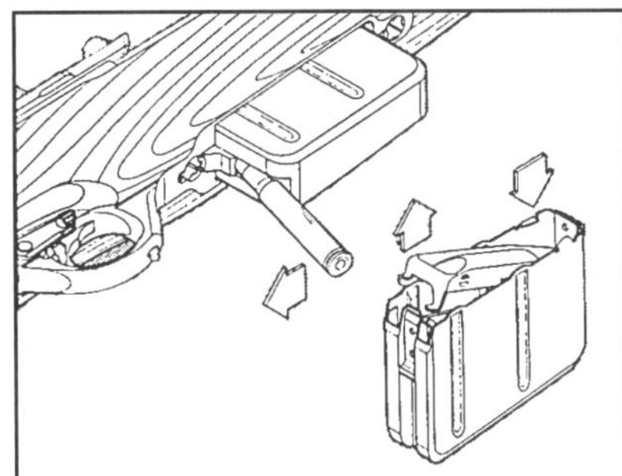

1 Make certain that the rifle is unloaded. Insert a cartridge nose in channel at rear of magazine box (65), pry back magazine catch (59) and remove magazine. Press front end of follower (53) downward until its rear hook disengages from the magazine box. Then, ease out follower and follower spring (66).

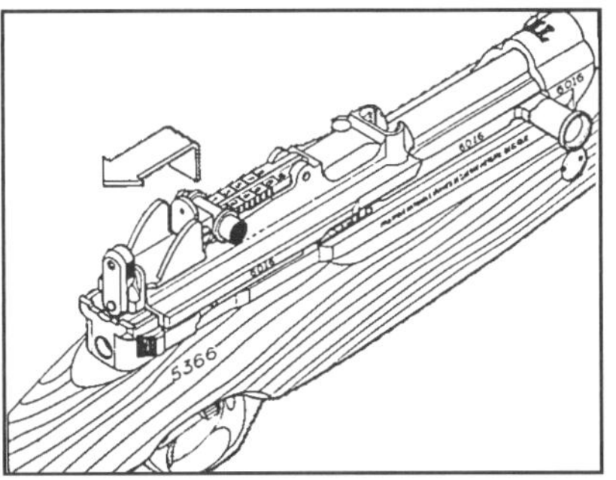

2 Pull operating handle of bolt carrier (19) fully to rear and release to cock rifle. Turn locking key at rear of receiver cover assembly (1) upward, and push cover forward until it strikes its stop. Lift rear end of cover to disengage from receiver (15), and ease off to the rear. Recoil springs (8, 9) come off with cover.

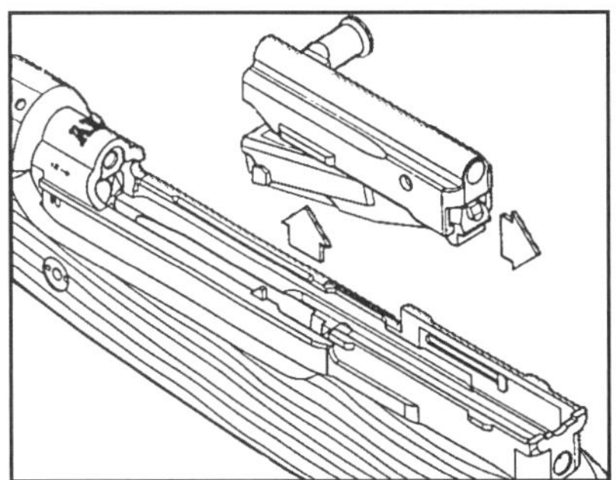

3 Pull operating handle back until bolt carrier guides align with dismount cuts in receiver. Lift off carrier and bolt (16), and separate by pulling bolt rearward out of carrier.

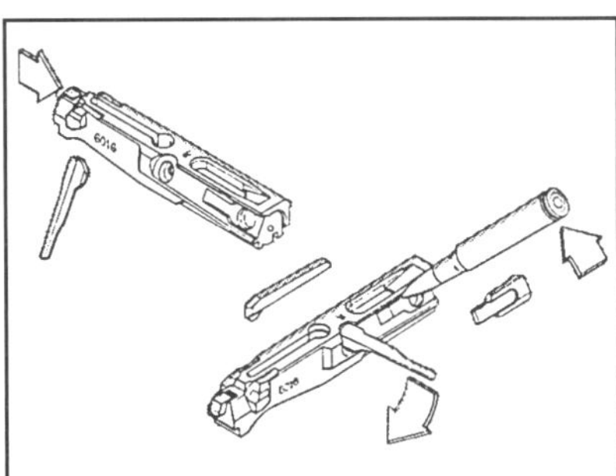

4 Lift firing pin safety stop (14) out of bolt. Using a cartridge point, flex extractor spring (18) out of extractor (17), and rotate the spring 1/4 turn downward. Remove extractor. Press firing pin extension (10) fully forward into bolt and pull out extractor spring. Remove firing pin extension, firing pin (12), and firing pin spring (13).

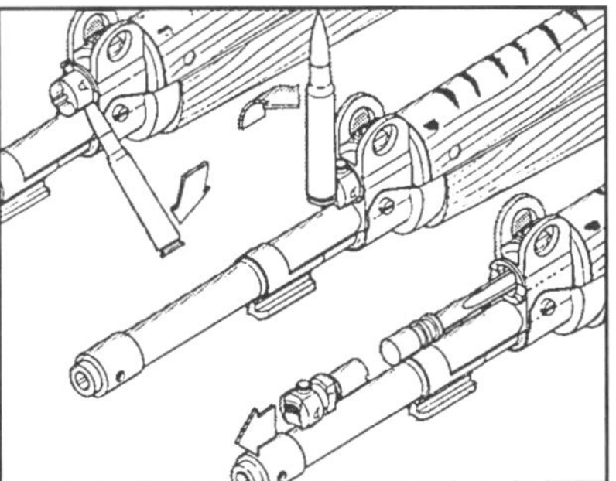

5 Press in the detent of gas cylinder plug (27) with a cartridge point, and rotate the plug 1/4 turn clockwise, using first the nose, then the rim of the cartridge. Remove the plug and depress muzzle to allow piston (21) and piston spring (20) to slide out. Reassemble rifle in reverse. On replacing gas cylinder plug, letter "A" (in Arabic on the Egyptian model) must face up. When opposite side of plug faces up, the gas port is blocked so that rifle can be used for launching grenades.

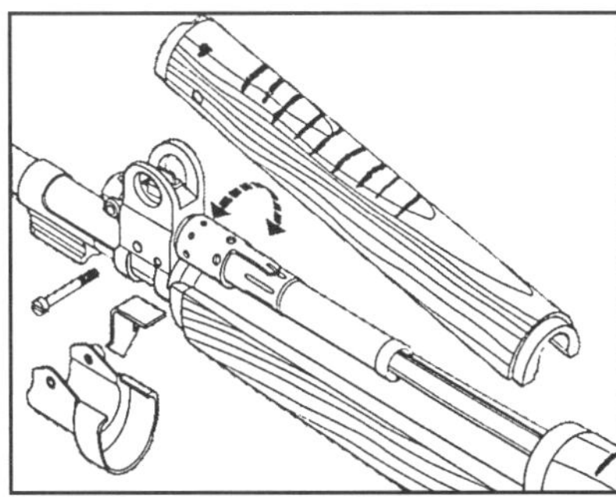

6 To adjust gas cylinder, remove stock end cap screw (52), slide stock end cap (54) forward and remove it. Lift forward end of front handguard (25) and slide forward out of lower band (50). Turn gas adjusting sleeve (26) right to increase gas pressure, left to decrease. Cases must eject smartly, but not violently.

FOX MODEL B SHOTGUN

PARTS LEGEND

1. Barrel assembly
2. Front sight
3. Rear sight
4. Extractor
5. Cocking plunger retaining screw
6. Cocking plunger spring
7. Cocking plunger
8. Extractor screw
9. Top snap trip
10. Top snap trip spring
11. Frame
12. Top snap
13. Top snap screw
14. Top snap plunger
15. Top snap plunger collar
16. Top snap plunger spring
17. Safety spring
18. Safety button
19. Safety plunger
20. Safety lever
21. Safety lever pin
22. Stock bolt washer
23. Trigger spring, left
24. Trigger spring, right
25. Trigger, left
26. Trigger, right
27. Trigger pin
28. Sear pin
29. Cocking lever and hammer pin
30. Sear, left
31. Sear, right
32. Sear spring
33. Cocking lever spring
34. Cocking lever spring pin
35. Cocking lever
36. Trigger guard
37. Trigger guard screw
38. Hammer, left
39. Hammer, right
40. Mainspring plunger (2)
41. Firing pin retaining screw (2)
42. Firing pin (2)
43. Mainspring (2)
44. Firing pin spring (2)
45. Stock bolt
46. Fore-end
47. Fore-end screw, front
48. Fore-end insert
49. Pistol grip cap
50. Pistol grip cap screw
51. Fore-end iron
52. Fore-end spring pin
53. Ejector screw
54. Fore-end screw, rear
55. Fore-end spring
56. Fore-end spring spring
57. Ejector
58. Buttplate
59. Buttplate screw (2)

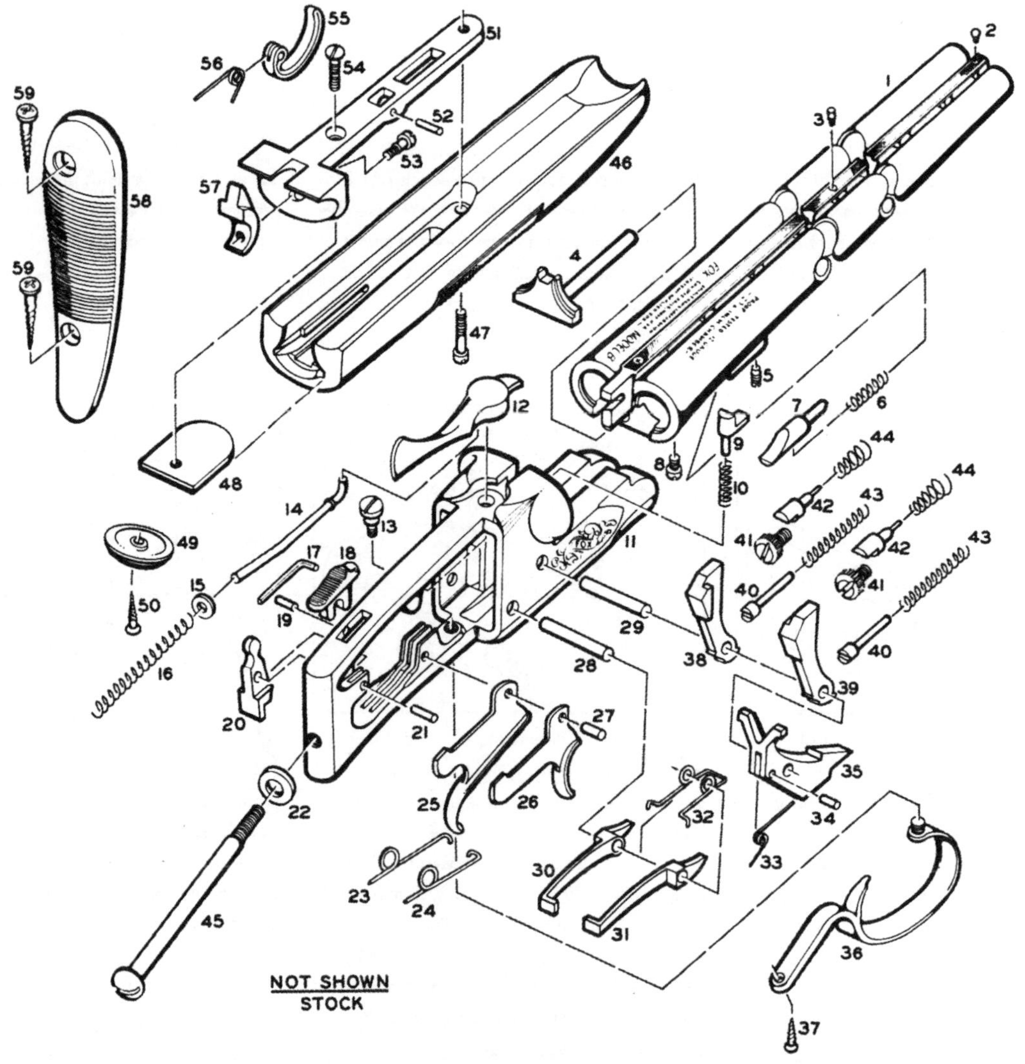

NOT SHOWN
STOCK

The Fox Model B is a moderately priced side-by-side double-barrel shotgun with concealed hammers. Introduced in 1939 by Savage Arms Corp, this gun bears the name of the famous Fox shotguns which were produced for many years by the A.H. Fox Gun Co. in Philadelphia, Pennsylvania. In 1930 Savage purchased the Fox company, and the Model B was the last shotgun to be marked with the Fox name.

There are several variants of the Model B. Early guns had double triggers and the later version, the B-ST, had a single, non-elective trigger. Beavertail fore-ends were standard in late production guns, as was a ventilated rib. The last model, the BSE, which was discontinued in 1989, featured selective automatic ejectors. Model B guns were made in 12-, 16- and 20-gauge, and .410-bore. They had a color case hardened box lock frame, automatic push-button safety and walnut stocks and fore-ends. Both the grip and foreend were checkered and the buttstock was a pistol grip type. Barrels were available in 26-, 28- and 30-inch lengths in the usual combinations of improved cylinder, modified and full chokes. The B De Luxe model had a chrome-finish frame and trigger guard.

In early models, the fore-end is held onto the fore-end iron by two wood screws. In some later guns, two machine screws are used instead. In the last guns made, the rear fore-end screw engages a threaded hole in a flat steel fore-end insert.

DISASSEMBLY

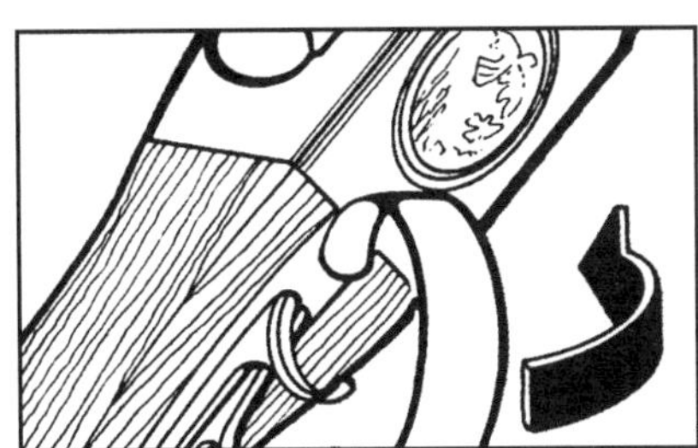

1 Remove trigger guard screw (37) and unscrew trigger guard (36) from frame (11). Remove buttplate screws (59) and buttplate (58). Then remove stock bolt (45), stock bolt washer (22), and stock. Remove fore-end (46) by pulling down on its front end, open action by pushing to right on top snap (12), and remove barrel assembly (I) from frame.

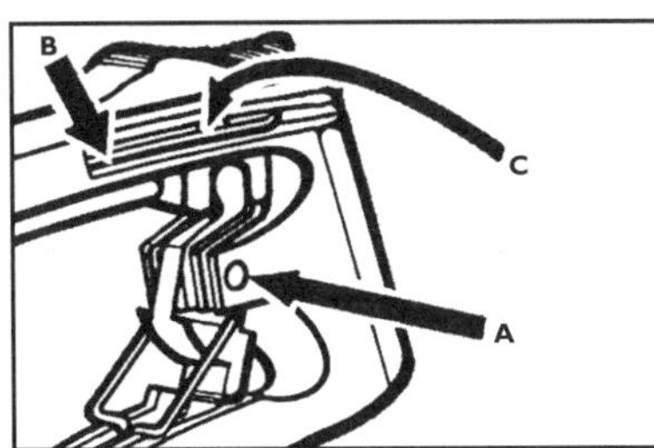

2 Remove triggers (25 & 26) after drifting out trigger pin (27) from right to left. (A) Drive out safety lever pin (21), and remove trigger springs (23 & 24) and safety lever (20). (B) Pry out safety spring (17), (C) remove safety plunger (19), and safety button (18).

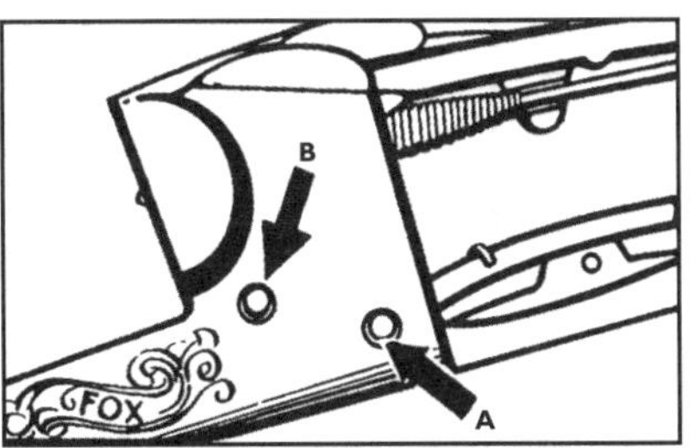

3 (A) Drive out sear pin (28), and remove sears (30 & 31). Remove sear spring (32) from under cocking lever spring (33). (B) Drift out cocking lever and hammer pin (29) and take out hammers (38 & 39), mainsprings (43), mainspring plungers (40), and cocking lever (35). Turn out firing pin retaining screws (41) and withdraw firing pins (42) and firing pin springs (44).

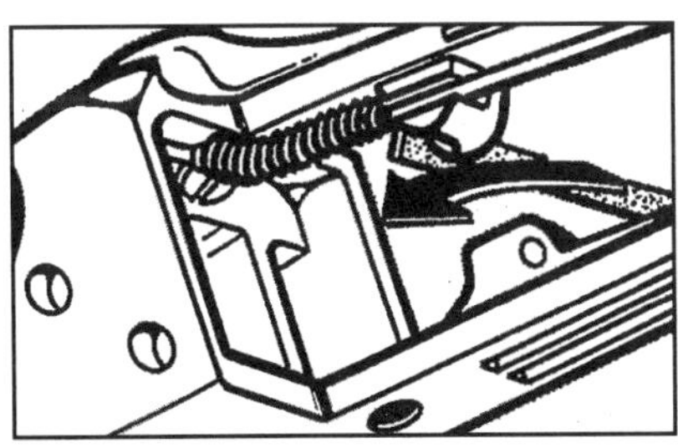

4 Depress top snap trip (9) so that top snap (12) can move to its central position. Using a screwdriver, force top snap plunger spring (16) forward and to left out of lug in top tang of frame. Remove top snap plunger (14), top snap plunger collar (15), and top snap plunger spring. Using an offset screwdriver, remove top snap screw (13) and lift out top snap (12), top snap trip (9), and top snap trip spring (10).

5 Remove cocking plunger retaining screw (5-upper arrow), cocking plunger (7), and cocking plunger spring (6). Remove extractor screw (8-lower arrow), and withdraw extractor (4).

A
40
29
28
30 & 31

6 When replacing hammers, a special tool (A) is required — an angled piece of steel or brass with the short end shaped to the back of the hammer. The lower point is shaped to enter the hammer sear notch. Clamp frame in vise with padded jaws so that rear of frame is up, and place mainsprings and mainspring plungers into frame.

Position a hammer so that its projection at lower front engages notch in mainspring plunger, and push hammer toward front of frame with tool to align hole in hammer with hole in frame. Insert punch through frame hole and hammer, pass punch through cocking lever, put in second hammer, press it forward with tool, and insert punch through holes in second hammer and other side of frame. Then drive in hammer pin, pushing out punch.

FRANCHI AUTOMATIC SHOTGUN

PARTS LEGEND

1. Barrel
2. Barrel ring*
3. Front sight and base *
4. Barrel extension *
5. Ejector *
6. Breechbolt
7. Extractor
8. Extractor plunger
9. Extractor spring
10. Firing pin limit stop
11. Operating handle
12. Firing pin spring
13. Firing pin
14. Locking block
15. Link pin
16. Link
17. Locking block lever pin
18. Locking block lever
19. Locking block lever spring
20. Rear nylon ring
21. Rear nylon ring spring
22. Front nylon ring
23. Fore-end cap retaining spring
24. Receiver
25. Magazine tube
26. Magazine tube blocking spring
27. Recoil spring
28. Friction ring
29. Friction piece
30. Friction spring
31. Fore-end cap
32. Magazine spring retaining ring
33. Magazine spring
34. Magazine follower
35. Trigger guard pin (2)
36. Action spring follower
37. Action spring tube
38. Action spring tube fastener
39. Eccentric washer
40. Elastic washer
41. Stock retaining screw
42. Action spring
43. Carrier latch button
44. Carrier latch
45. Carrier latch spring
46. Pin (2) (for parts 44, 47, & 49)
47. Auxiliary shell latch
48. Magazine shell latch & auxiliary shell latch spring
49. Magazine shell latch
50. Detent (2) (for parts 44, 47 & 49)
51. Trigger guard
52. Auto safety spring plunger
53. Auto safety spring
54. Auto safety spring guide
55. Hand safety spring follower
56. Hand safety spring
57. Hand safety
58. Trigger guard pin, large (2)
59. Trigger guard pin detent (2)
60. Trigger pin
61. Auto safety pin
62. Sear pin
63. Hammer pin
64. Hammer spring tube
65. Hammer spring
66. Hammer spring follower
67. Hammer
68. Hand safety retaining pin (2)
69. Trigger
70. Trigger lever retaining pin
71. Trigger lever spring
72. Trigger lever spring ball
73. Trigger lever
74. Trigger lever pin
75. Sear spring
76. Sear
77. Carrier spring stem pivot point
78. Carrier spring
79. Carrier spring stem
80. Carrier spring retaining washer & detent
81. Carrier plate, left
82. Carrier dog spring follower
83. Carrier dog spring
84. Carrier dog
85. Carrier
86. Carrier plate, right
87. Carrier dog spring guide pin
88. Auto safety
89. Buttplate
90. Buttplate screw (2)
91. Pistol grip stock
92. Pistol grip cap
93. Pistol grip cap screw
94. Fore-end

* Permanent factory assembly to other major part. Do not disassemble.

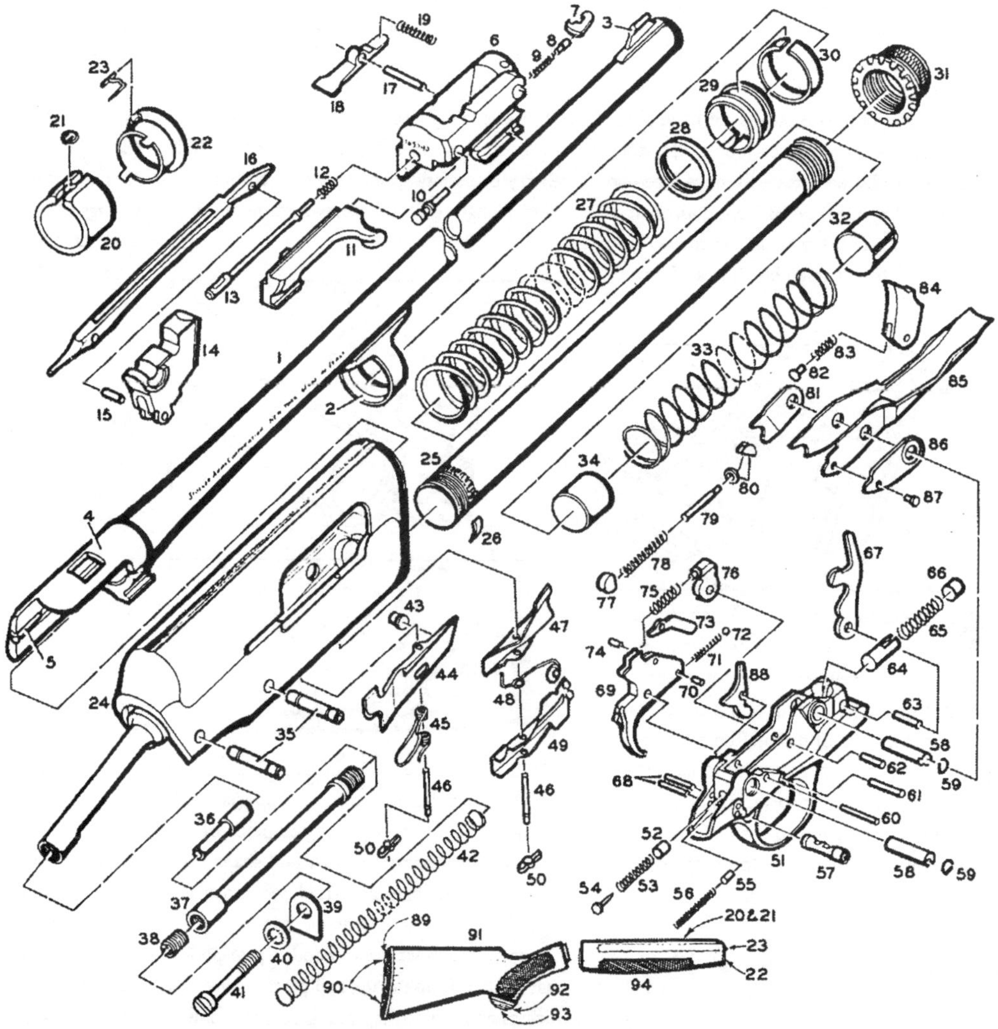

The Franchi semi-automatic shotgun was made in Brescia, Italy, by the firm of Luigi Franchi. The action design is based upon the time-tested Browning long-recoil system. Both steel and lightweight-alloy receiver models are offered in 12- and 20-gauge. Standard and magnum chamberings are optional in both gauges. Barrels have chrome-plated bores and are available in 24-, 26-, 27-, 28-, 30-, and 32-inch lengths, in ribless, matted rib, and ventilated rib styles.

When this gun is new, or when light loads are shot, the inside bevel of the friction ring should be toward the recoil spring. When heavy loads are shot, the friction ring should be reversed so that its inside bevel is toward the friction piece. When magnum gauge models are used with magnum loads, the inside bevel of the friction ring should be toward the friction piece.

The manufacturer suggests that the recoil spring of this gun be replaced after firing from 3000 to 4000 rounds.

DISASSEMBLY

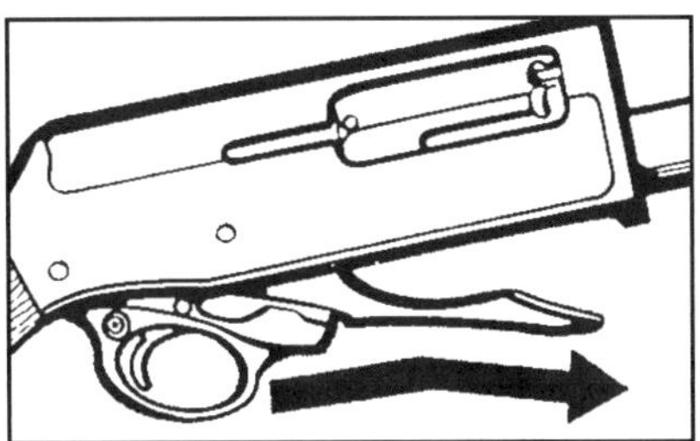

1 Disassemble arm by first cocking breech-bolt (6) and unscrewing fore-end cap (31). Remove fore-end (94), barrel (1), friction piece (29), friction ring (28) and recoil spring (27). Bring breechbolt forward. Press out trigger guard pins (35) from left side of receiver (24) using a wood dowel. Remove trigger guard (51) by pulling it forward and then down.

2 Hold the shotgun in an upright position and depress the action spring follower (36) in order to release the link (16), which will swing out by slightly inclining the shotgun. Push the breechbolt forward out of the receiver. The operating handle (11) will drop away as the breechbolt passes through forward section of the receiver.

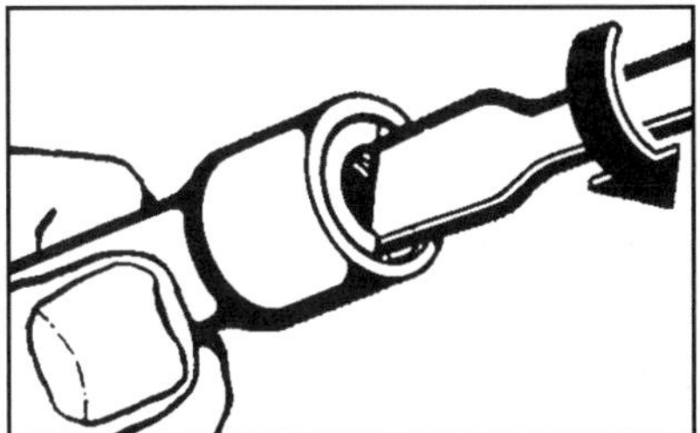

3 Remove buttplate screws (90) and buttplate (89). Unscrew stock retaining screw (41) using long-shanked screwdriver and remove elastic washer (40), eccentric washer (39), and stock (91). Grasp action spring tube (37) firmly and unscrew action spring tube fastener (38) maintaining steady inward pressure to prevent action spring (42) from flying out (Fig. 3). Remove spring and spring follower.

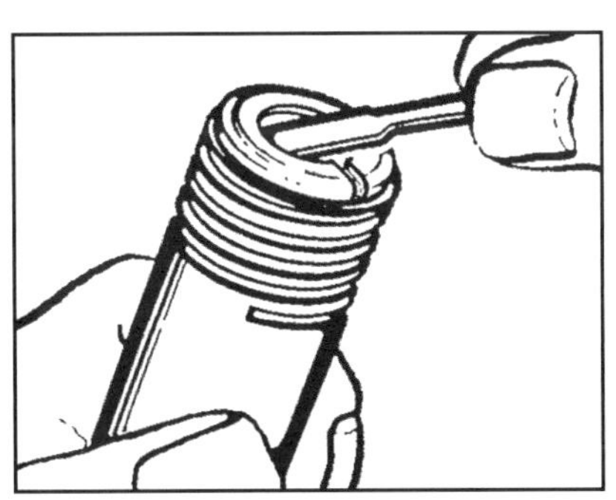

4 Carefully pry out magazine spring retaining ring (32) and remove magazine spring (33) and follower (34).

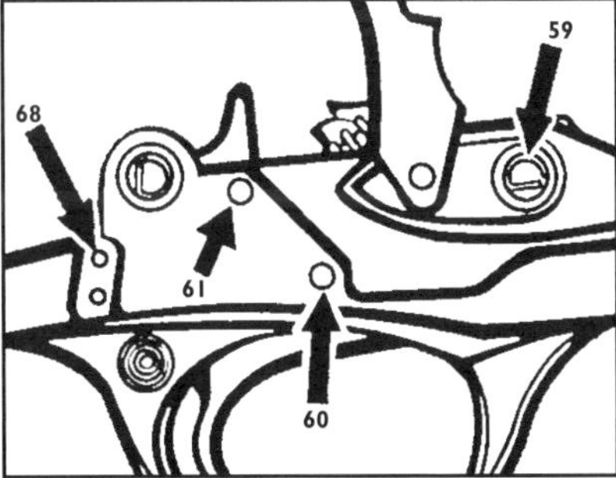

5 Disassemble firing mechanism by first drifting out upper hand safety retaining pin (68). Remove auto safety spring guide (54), spring (53), and plunger (52). Then drift out auto safety pin (61) and lift out auto safety (88). Drift out trigger pin (60) from left to right and remove sear spring (75). Remove forward trigger guard pin detent (59) and slide large trigger guard pin (58) out forward. Lift away carrier (85) and attached parts. Drift out sear pin (62) and remove sear (76). Lift out trigger (69). Drift out hammer pin (63) and remove hammer (67). Further disassembly of firing mechanism is obvious. Reassemble in reverse.

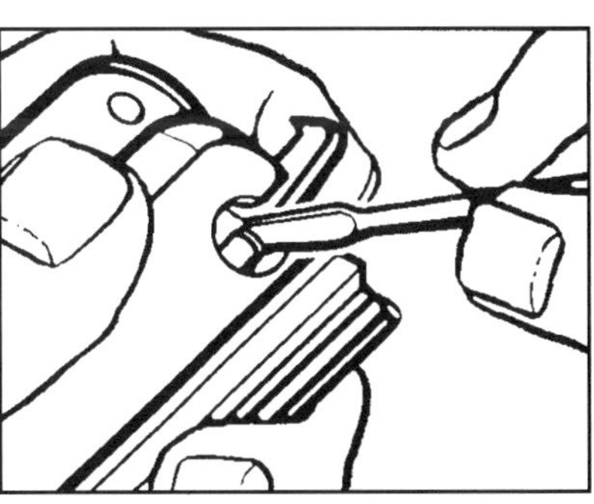

6 Disassemble breechbolt by pushing out firing pin limit stop (10). Withdraw firing pin (13) and firing pin spring (12). Push out locking block lever pin (17) and remove locking block lever (18) and spring (19). Rotate locking block (14) and remove it together with link from breech bolt. Insert small screwdriver between extractor (7) and plunger (8), depressing plunger and unhooking extractor. Release pressure on screwdriver slowly and remove plunger and extractor spring (9). Reassemble arm in reverse.

FRENCH MODEL 1936 RIFLE

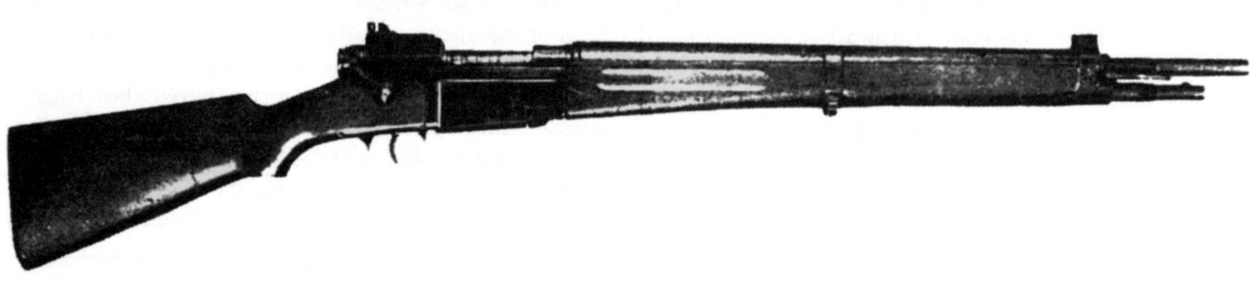

PARTS LEGEND

1. Handguard
2. Fore-end
3. Bayonet
4. Rear sight leaf
5. Rear sight pin
6. Rear sight spring
7. Rear sight slide
8. Barrel and action
9. Front band
10. Front band screw
11. Middle band
12. Middle band screw
13. Handguard support
14. Follower
15. Follower spring
16. Floorplate
17. Latch pin
18. Latch spring
19. Floorplate latch
20. Sear pin
21. Sear spring
22. Sear
23. Bolt stop spring
24. Trigger pin
25. Bolt stop-ejector
26. Trigger
27. Bolt
28. Extractor
29. Firing pin
30. Firing pin spring
31. Bolt head
32. Trigger guard
33. Guard screw
34. Buttstock
35. Buttplate screw (2)
36. Buttplate

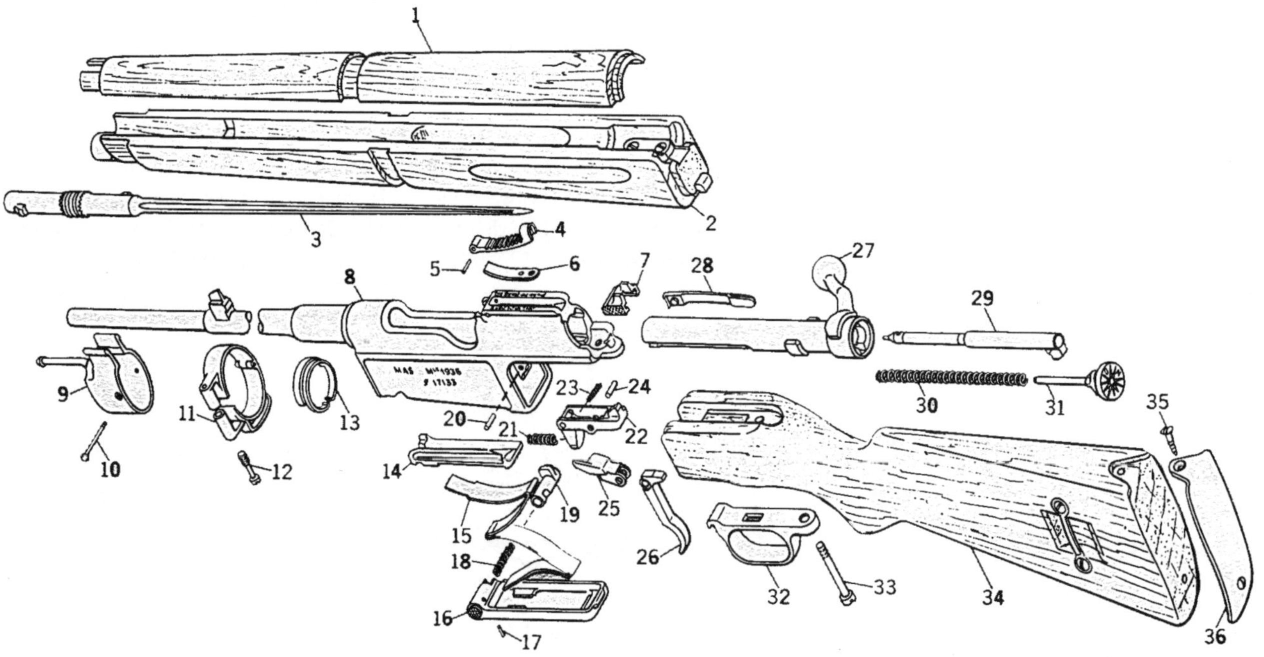

Adopted by France in 1936, the Model 1936, 7.5 mm. bolt-action rifle was introduced to replace the series of 8 mm. Lebel and Berthier bolt-action rifles.

The Model 1936 rifle was developed and manufactured by *Manufacture D'Armes St. Étienne*, a French government arsenal in St. Etienne. The initials of the manufacturing arsenal are stamped on the receivers of Model 1936 rifles adjacent to the model designation. Thus, the unofficial but commonly accepted designation for this arm is MAS Model 1936. A folding stock version made for use by airborne troops was designated the Model 1936 CR 39.

The rimless 7.5 mm. Model 1929 C ball cartridge is assembled with a 139-grain pointed bullet and its muzzle velocity in a 19.6-inch barrel is 2690 f.p.s.

The Model 1936 rifle can be loaded through the top of the receiver with 5-round stripper clips. The striker mechanism cocks on opening of the bolt. Dual locking lugs on the bolt engage locking recesses within the receiver bridge. Handle of the bolt is bent forward to place the knob opposite the trigger. The firing pin assembly is concealed within the bolt, and there is no visible means of determining whether the action is cocked or not. There is no mechanical safety or magazine cutoff.

Cartridges are staggered in the integral magazine box and are forced upward by the follower and follower spring attached to the magazine floorplate. The magazine floorplate assembly is detached from the action by depressing a spring plunger.

Other notable features of the Model 1936 rifle are the cruciform needle bayonet housed in the fore-end, the two-piece stock, and the simple means of adjusting the aperture rear sight for elevation.

DISASSEMBLY

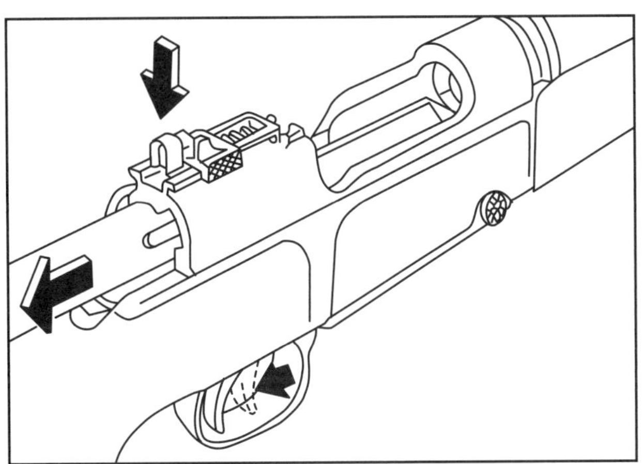

1 The trigger controls the bolt stop ejector (25). To remove the bolt, pull it to the rear and pull back hard on the trigger (26). To raise or lower the rear sight, push the rear sight leaf (4) down and move the rear sight slide (7) to the desired position.

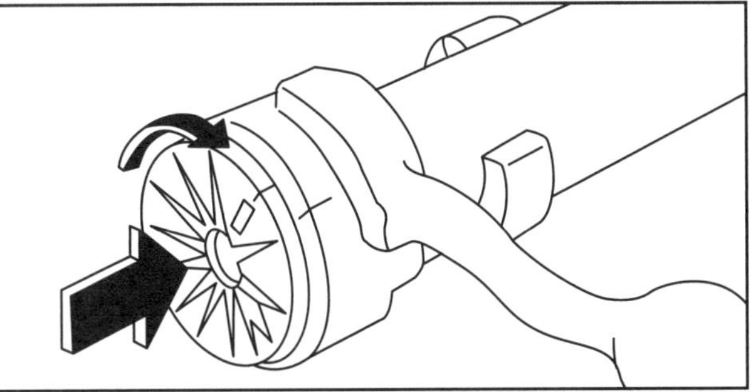

2 To disassemble the bolt, push in on the bolt head (31) and rotate it clockwise until the letter "D" on the bolt head lines up with the line on the bolt (27). Do this carefully, since the bolt head is under spring tension. With the bolt head out, the firing pin spring (30) and firing pin (29) can be removed.

3 The extractor (28) does not rotate around the bolt. It is machined to fit into a dovetail slot in the bolt. To remove the extractor, push it out as shown until the small boss on the extractor is clear of the hole in the bolt. Then pry the extractor up and out of its slot. To replace the extractor, tap it in with a brass or plastic hammer until it stops. Then push the boss clear of the bolt face and drive it down until it snaps into place.

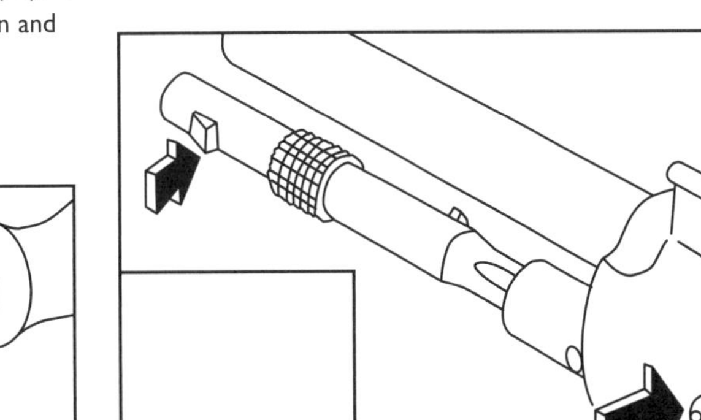

4 To further disassemble the rifle, it is necessary to make a special tool to remove the screws. Grind a screwdriver as shown in the insert. The two prongs must fit the notches in the screw head. Then the screws can be removed in the same manner as a normal slotted-head screw. Push in small latch to remove the bayonet (3) from its socket.

GERMAN MODEL 1888 RIFLE

PARTS LEGEND

1. Firing pin nut
2. Receiver
3. Bolt stop pin
4. Bolt stop
5. Bolt stop spring
6. Safety
7. Safety spring
8. Cartridge clip
9. Cocking piece
10. Firing pin spring
11. Firing pin
12. Bolt
13. Rear sight hinge pin
14. Sight spring
15. Sight spring screw
16. Fixed range leaf
17. Fixed range leaf spring
18. Adjustable range leaf and slide
19. Extractor
20. Bolt head
21. Ejector
22. Barrel jacket
23. Front sight
24. Barrel
25. Upper band
26. Upper band screw
27. Lower band spring
28. Stock
29. Lower band
30. Trigger guard
31. Sear pin
32. Sear spring
33. Sear
34. Trigger pin
35. Trigger
36. Front guard screw
37. Dust cover screw
38. Follower axle screw
39. Follower spring
40. Follower spring guide
41. Clip latch screw
42. Magazine follower
43. Dust cover
44. Rear guard screw
45. Clip latch
46. Clip latch spring
47. Buttplate
48. Buttplate screw (2)
49. Assembled bolt

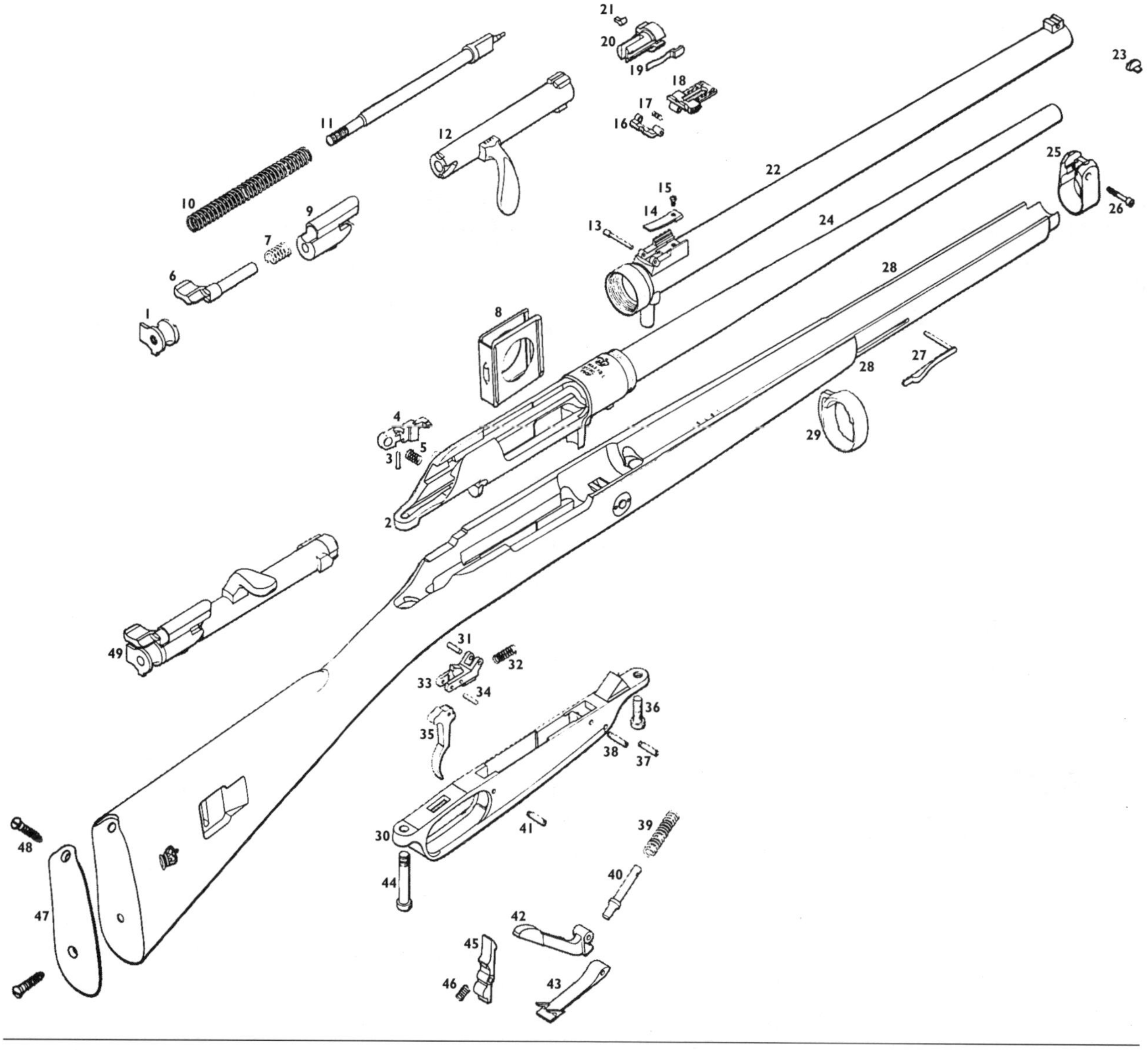

Developed by the Rifle Testing Commission at Spandau near Berlin, the German Commission Model 1888 bolt-action rifle and carbine fired the 7.9 mm. (8 mm.) Model 1888 rimless, smokeless powder cartridge loaded with a round-nose jacketed bullet. The Model 1888 incorporated a separate, non-rotary bolt head and several other features of the Model 1871 and 1871/84 German service rifles and a Mannlicher-type box magazine. The Model 1888 is often called a Mannlicher 88, or Mauser-Mannlicher.

The single-column, fixed magazine is loaded from the top with a five round, sheet-steel clip which was reversible to facilitate loading. One of the more unusual features of the Model 1888 is a sheet steel tube handguard that extends full length of the barrel.

Rifle and carbine versions feature the same action, except the rifle has a horizontal bolt handle while the carbine has a turned-down flat handle for mounted use. There is also a Model 1891 short rifle version intended for foot artillery and special troops.

The Model 1888 was produced in large quantity by German government arsenals at Spandau, Erfurt, Danzig and Amberg, by Ludwig Loewe & Co., Berlin, C. G. Haenel and V. C. Schilling in Suhl, Oesterreichisehe Waffenfabriks-Gesellschaft (Austrian Arms Co.) Steyr, Austria, and by firms in Belgium and China. Ludwig Loewe & Co. was a principal German producer.

Although replaced as a first-line German arm in 1898 by the Mauser Model 1898 rifle, the Model 1888 was used exclusively as a substitute standard by Germany until the end of World War I. Austria-Hungary, Yugoslavia, Ethiopia, China and various South American nations also used the Model 88. Model 1888 rifles were used by China Peru and Brazil. Some Model 1888s were chambered for the 7 mm. Mauser cartridge.

Most "88"rifles are in 8 mm. Mauser and those modified to fire the pointed 1905 "Spitzer" (pointed) bullet bear an "S" on the receiver ring. It is not advisable, however, to fire "S" cartridges in a Model 1888, as this round gives considerably higher pressure than the Model 1888 round-nose cartridge.

DISASSEMBLY

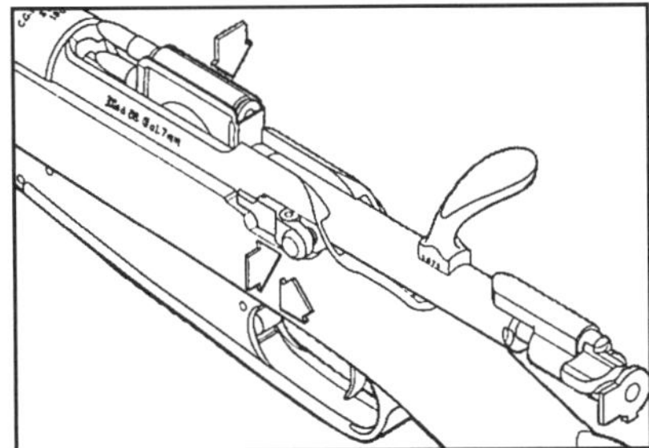

1 Remove bolt by depressing bolt stop (4) and sliding bolt out of receiver (2).

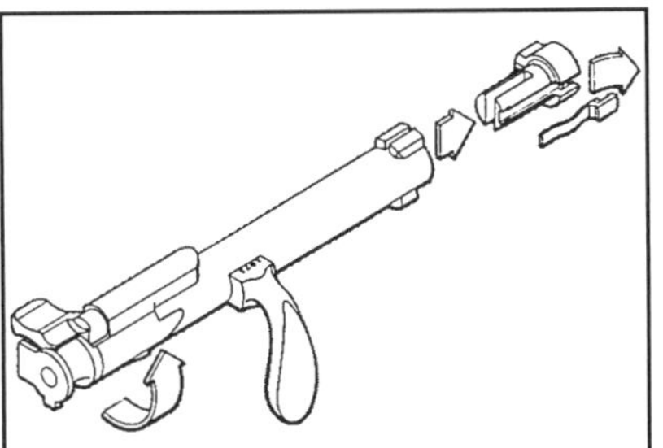

2 To strip bolt, hold it firmly and rotate cocking piece (9) a quarter turn to left. Pull bolt head (20) forward out of bolt. Remove extractor (19) by sliding it forward and outward from bolt head. NOTE: Ejector (21) is retained by peening the bolt head and should be removed only for repair.

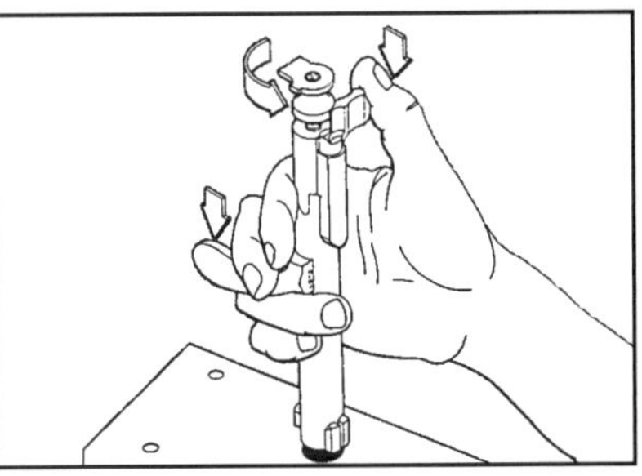

3 Place nose of firing pin (11) against a wood block and hold downward on bolt. Depress safety with thumb and unscrew firing pin nut (1). Ease pressure on bolt and lift off safety, safety spring (7) and cocking piece (9). Firing pin and firing pin spring (10) come out through front of bolt.

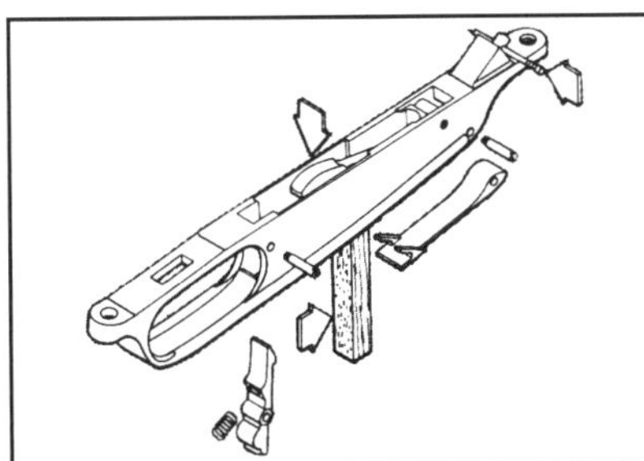

4 Unscrew front and rear guard screws (36 & 44) and remove trigger guard (30). Remove clip latch screw (41) to free clip latch (45) and spring (46). Depress magazine follower (42) flush with top of trigger guard, and insert a wire brad through hole in follower spring guide (40). Remove dust cover screw (37). Use wooden block and hammer to loosen dust cover (43).

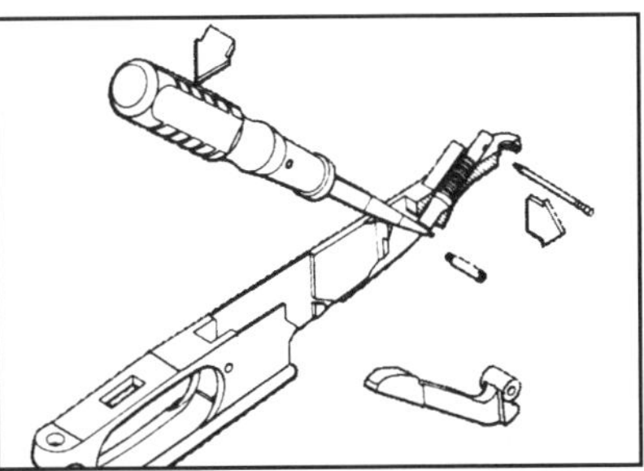

5 Remove follower axle screw (38) and pull follower out through bottom of guard. Place wide screwdriver blade between head of follower spring guide and web of trigger guard and lift guide enough to remove brad. Ease pressure on screwdriver and remove spring guide and follower spring (39).

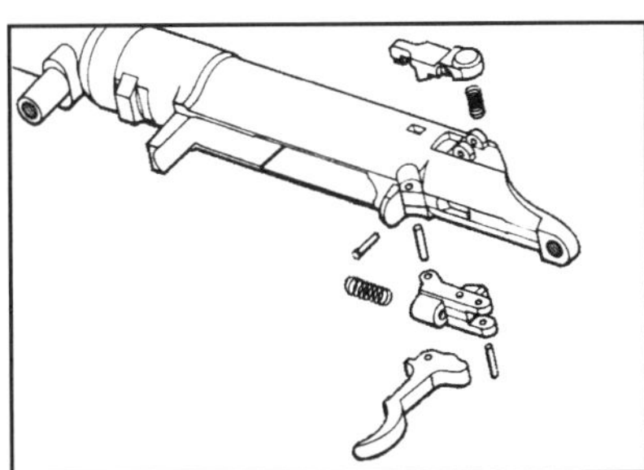

6 Remove upper band screw (26) and slide off upper band (25). Depress lower band spring (27) and remove lower band (29). Lift barrel and receiver assembly out of stock (28). Drive bolt stop pin (3) downward to free bolt stop and spring (5). Drift out sear pin (31) to remove sear (33) and sear spring (32). Trigger (35) is detached from sear by driving out trigger pin (34).

GERMAN MODEL 43 RIFLE

PARTS LEGEND

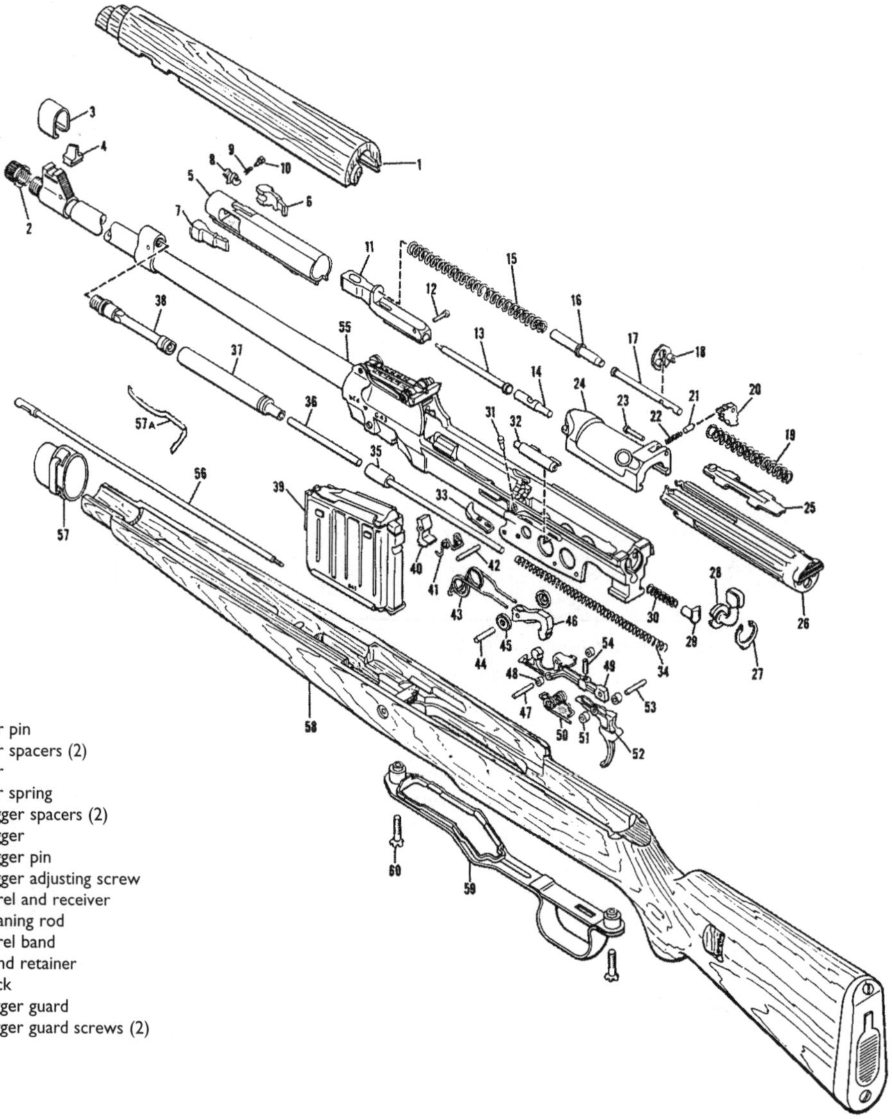

1. Handguard
2. Thread protector
3. Sight hood
4. Front sight
5. Bolt
6. Locking lug, right
7. Locking lug, left
8. Extractor
9. Extractor spring
10. Extractor retainer
11. Firing pin housing
12. Firing pin retainer
13. Firing pin
14. Firing pin extension
15. Recoil spring, front
16. Spring guide, front
17. Recoil spring guide, rear
18. Bolt housing retainer
19. Recoil spring, rear
20. Bolt carrier latch
21. Latch plunger
22. Latch spring
23. Bolt carrier latch pin
24. Bolt carrier
25. Sliding dust cover
26. Bolt housing
27. Safety retainer
28. Safety
29. Safety plunger
30. Safety spring
31. Ejector pin
32. Ejector spring housing
33. Ejector
34. Actuator rod spring
35. Actuator rod
36. Connecting rod
37. Gas cylinder
38. Gas piston
39. Magazine
40. Magazine catch
41. Magazine catch spring
42. Magazine catch pin
43. Hammer spring
44. Hammer pin
45. Hammer washers (2)
46. Hammer
47. Sear pin
48. Sear spacers (2)
49. Sear
50. Sear spring
51. Trigger spacers (2)
52. Trigger
53. Trigger pin
54. Trigger adjusting screw
55. Barrel and receiver
56. Cleaning rod
57. Barrel band

57a. Band retainer

58. Stock
59. Trigger guard
60. Trigger guard screws (2)

The most successful of several German semi-automatic rifles introduced during World War II was the Model 43, 8 mm. Mauser developed by Walther. Initially designated *Gewehr* 43 (Rifle 43) and later *Karabiner* 43 (Carbine 43), this rifle was used principally for sniping. It is well suited for this as it is very accurate and is adapted to a detachable 4X scope.

The gas system of the Model 43 is like that of the Soviet Tokarev semi-automatic rifle and is unusual in that the piston is fixed and the cylinder movable. The 10-round magazine is detachable. The non-rotary bolt with forward dual locking lugs was copied from the German Model 41 (W) rifle.

There is no provision for attaching a bayonet and the fore-end is relatively short. The M 43 rifle is fairly heavy because of its laminated beechwood stock.

M 43s were made for cheap, easy manufacture. All, except a few early Models, appear very crude and employ many sheet steel parts. Despite this lack of refinement, this rifle is serviceable and efficient, and well suited for the job it was intended to perform.

DISASSEMBLY

1 Press magazine catch (40) forward and remove magazine (39). In replacing magazine, insert upper front portion all the way into opening in stock, and then swing rear upward until latched. Pull bolt carrier (24) to rear as far as it will go and press inward on right side of bolt carrier latch (20) to engage latch with shoulder on bolt housing (26). Rotate safety (28) all the way right to engaged position. Press forward on rear recoil spring guide (17) with thumb as shown, simultaneously lift rear of bolt assembly and remove from receiver. Rifles of later manufacture do not have the bolt carrier latch. To disassemble, remove magazine, cock rifle by pulling bolt carrier to rear and letting it go forward, engage safety and, while holding bolt carrier about .4 inches to rear, press forward on rear recoil spring guide, lift upward on rear of bolt housing and remove from receiver. Pull the bolt carrier to the rear, remove the bolt carrier and bolt from the receiver, and lift the carrier off bolt.

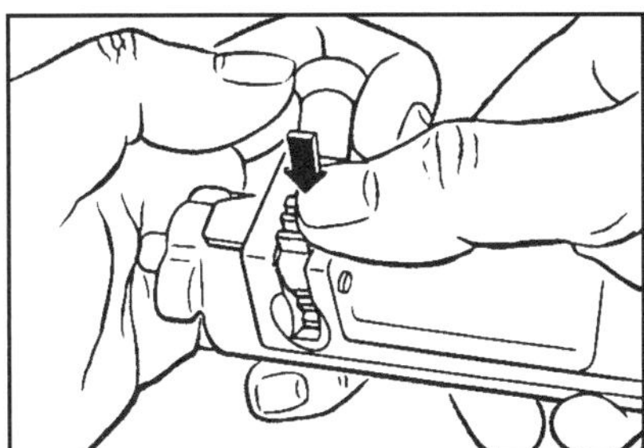

2 Great care must be taken in disassembly and assembly of bolt components of rifles with bolt carrier latch, as the parts are under heavy spring pressure. Hold bolt assembly in left hand as shown with rear of bolt housing against palm of hand and left index finger looped around handle of bolt carrier. Pull bolt carrier slightly to rear and at same time depress top of bolt carrier latch with right thumb. Grip bolt carrier in right hand, and ease carrier forward to separate from bolt housing. Lift the bolt carrier off bolt, and pull the assembled front and rear recoil springs with the guides forward out of the bolt housing.

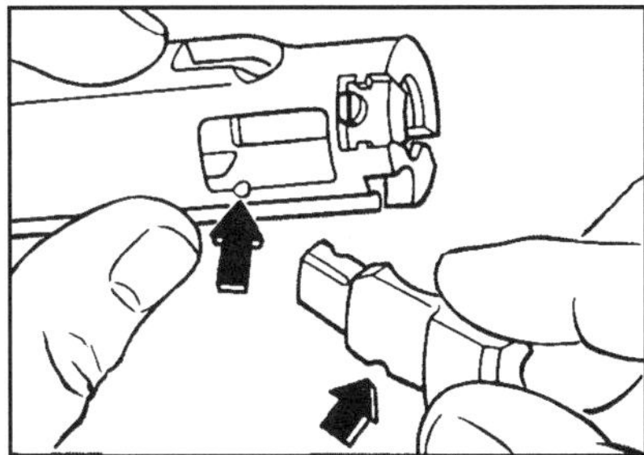

3 Pull firing pin housing (11) rearward from bolt, remove locking lugs (6 & 7), drift firing pin retainer (12) almost completely out of firing pin housing and remove firing pin (13) and firing pin extension (14). To remove late-manufacture spring-loaded firing pin retainers, depress retainer from left side. In replacing locking lugs, note that right locking lug (6) has a small notch to clear a projection on bolt. In reassembly, be sure to replace locking lugs. To remove extractor (8), use small screwdriver to depress extractor retainer (10) and rotate counter-clockwise ¼ turn until it releases. Slide extractor out of bolt.

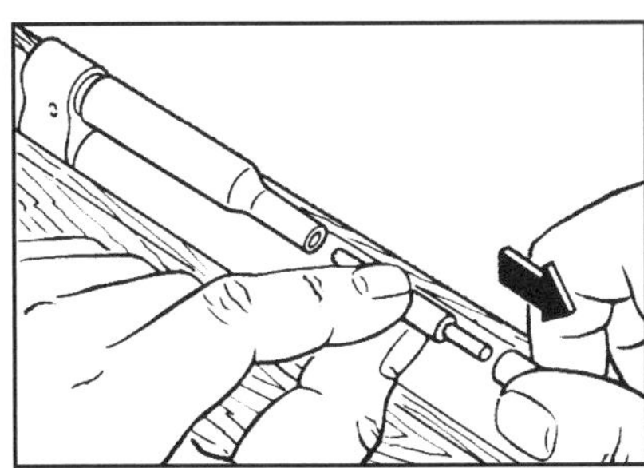

4 To disassemble gas system, use punch or small screwdriver to depress band retainer (57a) on right of barrel band (57). Slide barrel band forward off handguard (1). If bolt assembly is in rifle, insert empty magazine, and latch bolt in open position. Pull back actuator rod (35), lift out connecting rod (36), ease actuator rod forward, and remove it and actuator rod spring from receiver. Slide gas cylinder (37) rearward off gas piston (38).

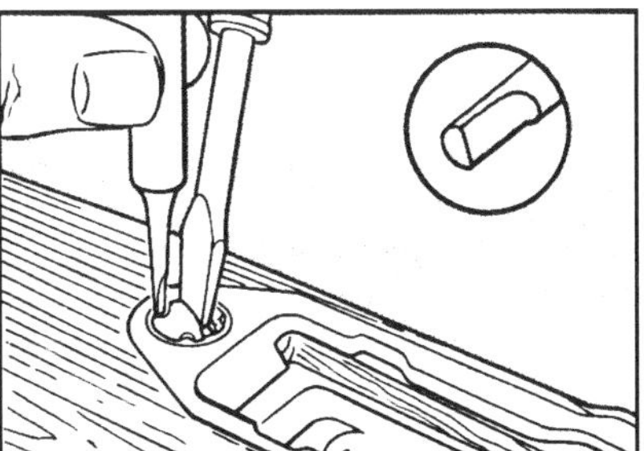

5 Front and rear trigger guard screws (60) are locked by spring-loaded pins in trigger guard (59). The pins engage notches on screw heads and must be depressed with a small-diameter punch or specially shaped punch (see inset). After turning out screws, hold magazine catch forward, lift off trigger guard, and separate stock from barrel and receiver.

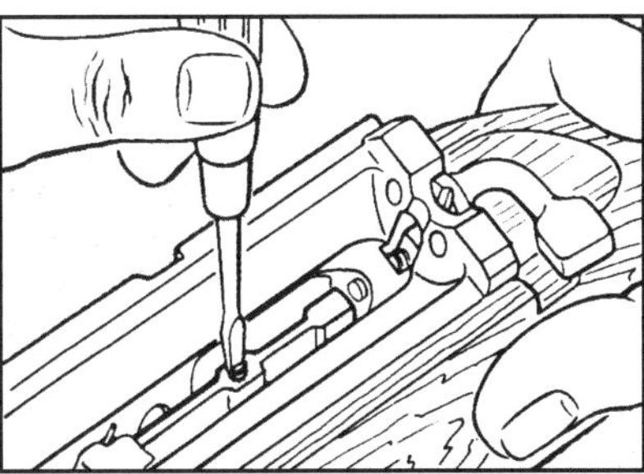

6 Unlike most military rifles, the Model 43 has an adjustable trigger pull. When the bolt assembly is removed, a trigger adjusting screw (54) in the sear (49) can be turned to minimize the amount of creep in the final stage of the pull.

GERMAN MODEL 98/40 RIFLE

PARTS LEGEND

1. Safety
   1a. Safety spring
2. Firing pin nut
3. Cocking piece
4. Bolt (stripped)
5. Firing pin spring
6. Firing pin
7. Ejector screw
8. Ejector
9. Bolt head
10. Extractor spring
11. Extractor
12. Bolt (assembled)
13. Bolt stop
14. Bolt stop pin
15. Bolt stop spring
16. Receiver
17. Sear spring
18. Sear safety pin
19. Sear pivot pin
20. Trigger pin
21. Sear
22. Trigger
23. Magazine box
24. Barrel assembly
    24a. Front sight cover
25. Handguard
26. Bayonet stud
27. Front band
28. Rear band
29. Rear band screw
30. Front band screw
31. Cleaning rod
32. Stock
33. Connector
34. Buttstock
35. Stock bolt
36. Buttplate
37. Buttplate screw (2)
38. Trigger guard
39. Rear guard screw
40. Front guard screw
41. Floorplate
42. Magazine spring
43. Magazine follower
44. Magazine catch
45. Magazine catch spring
46. Magazine catch pin

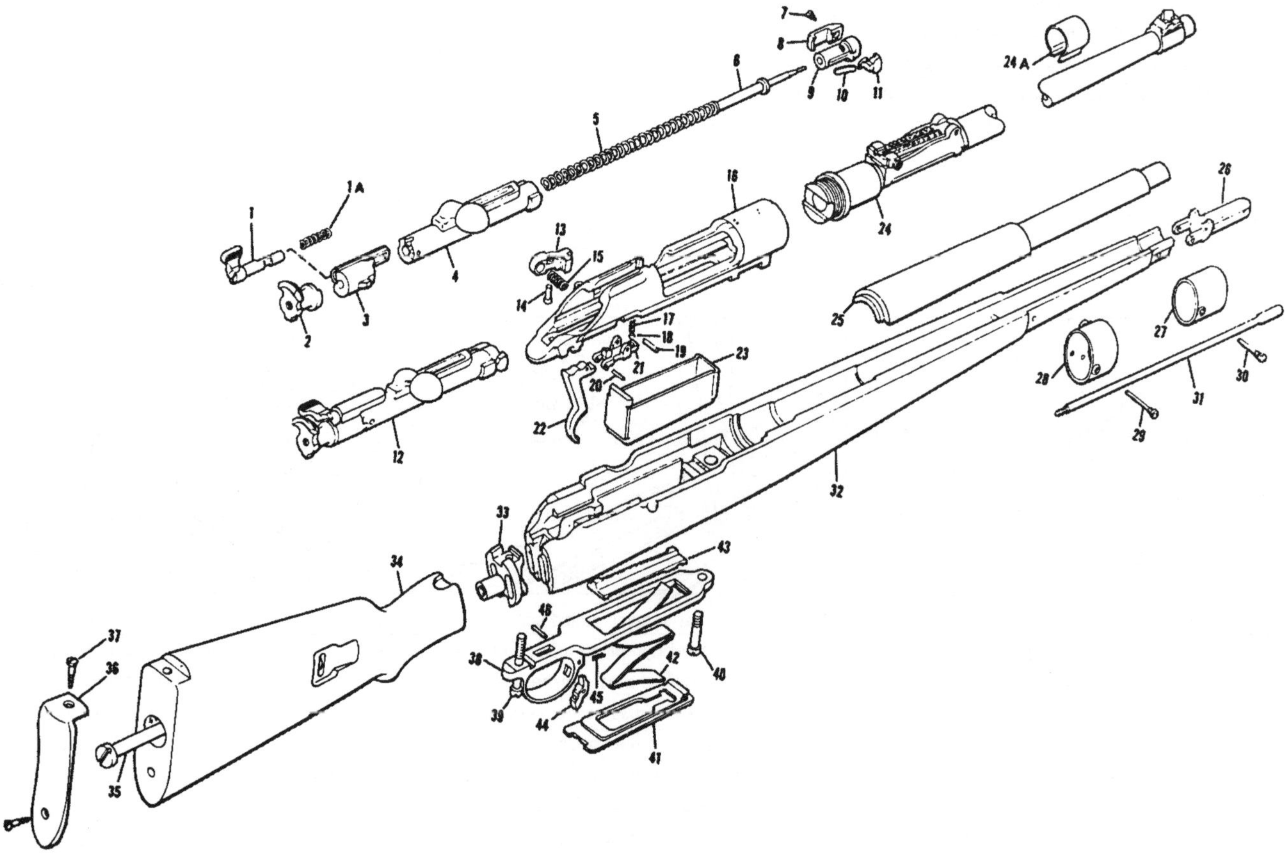

One of the substitute standard rifles adopted by Germany in 1940 was the Model 98/40. Produced in Budapest, Hungary, this rifle was developed from the Hungarian Model 35, a Mannlicher-type turnbolt rifle with protruding box magazine and 2-piece stock. The 98/40 is similar to the Hungarian Model 35 except that it is adapted to the 8 mm. Mauser cartridge, employs a Mauser type magazine flush with the stock, has a turned-down bolt handle, and is adapted to a German sling and bayonet.

The Germans adopted this rifle because they needed a large supply of rifles in a hurry. They utilized existing production facilities wherever these were available.

The 98/40 is sturdy and reliable, but its forward-positioned bolt handle makes it inferior to the Mauser 98 for rapid-fire shooting.

Early 98/40 specimens show excellent workmanship and finish. Later specimens of the 98/40 are not as well finished, but they are serviceable.

DISASSEMBLY

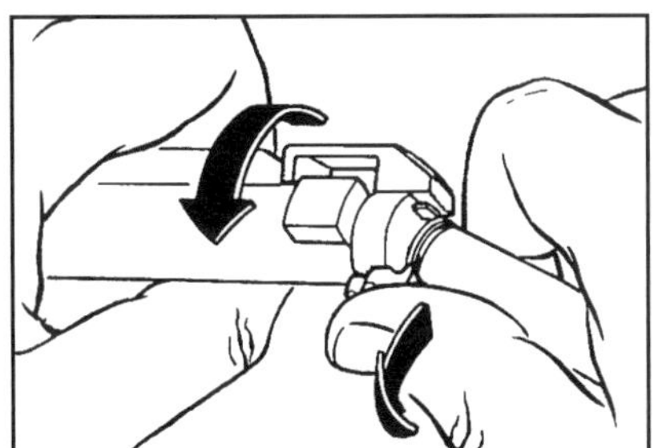

1 Remove bolt assembly while pushing in bolt stop (13). Push the extractor (11) outward so that bolt head assembly can be rotated a quarter turn to align ejector (8) with the rib on bolt. Pry extractor out a bit further with a cartridge case, and pull bolt head free of bolt.

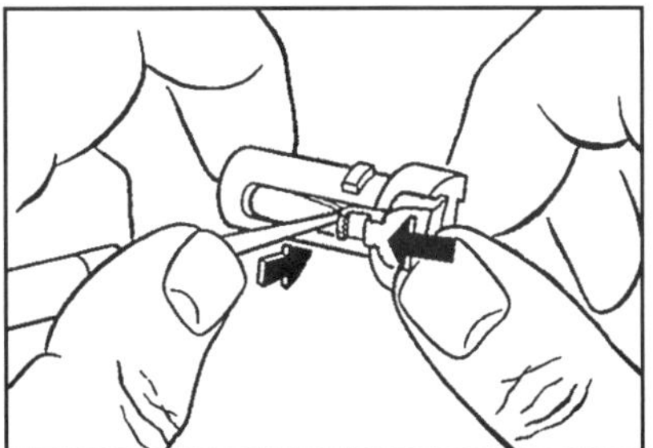

2 Remove ejector screw (7) and ejector (8). Then remove extractor (11) by pushing extractor spring (10) in until it is free of notch in underside of extractor. Push extractor to rear and remove from bolt head (9). Lift out extractor spring.

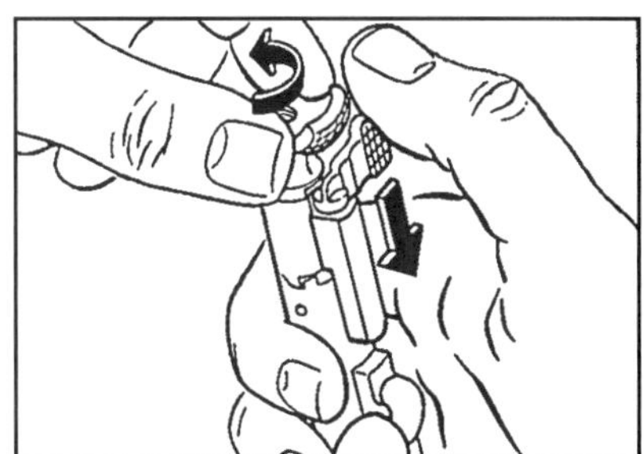

3 After bolt head has been removed, firing pin (6) and spring (5) can be removed by holding firing pin point against a wood block, grasping bolt firmly, pushing down on safety with thumb, unscrewing firing pin nut (2), and removing cocking piece. Be careful as firing pin is under spring tension. Hold bolt tight and ease it off firing pin. In reassembly, align flat on firing pin with flat in cocking piece.

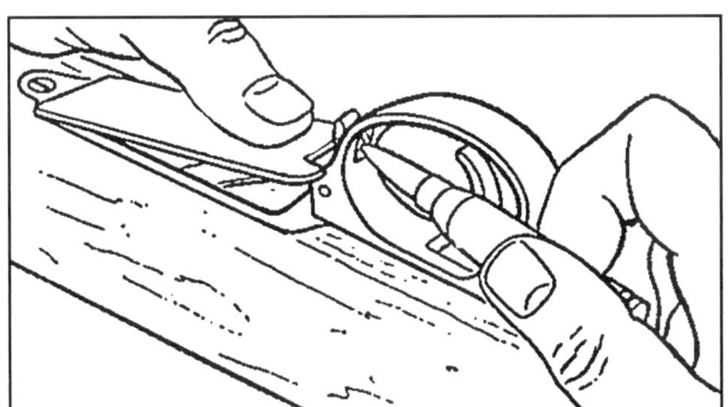

4 Magazine floorplate (41), follower (43), and spring (42) can be removed by pressing in on magazine catch (44) with bullet point or a thin punch.

5 To remove buttstock (34), take off buttplate (36). Use long screwdriver to remove stock bolt (35). Connector (33) can be removed only when receiver and trigger guard (38) are separated, since it is held by rear guard screw (39).

H&R MODEL 65 "REISING" RIFLE

PARTS LEGEND

1. Barrel
2. Receiver
3. Stock (not shown)
4. Bolt
5. Firing pin spring
6. Firing pin
7. Bolt pin
8. Extractor
9. Extractor pin
10. Extractor spring
11. Hammer
12. Hammer spring
13. Bumper plug
14. Ejector*
15. Bolt stop
16. Bolt stop catch
17. Bolt stop screw
18. Bolt stop screw
19. Action bar
20. Retracting spring
21. Retracting spring guide
22. Magazine guide studs (2)*
23. Magazine guide
24. Magazine catch spring
25. Magazine catch
26. Magazine catch washer
27. Magazine catch screw
28. Retaining nut washers (2)
29. Retaining nuts (2)
30. Takedown screw
31. Takedown screw washer
32. Stock plate brads (2)
33. Stock plate
34. Trigger mounting block*
35. Sear pin
36. Trigger pin
37. Sear
38. Sear spring
39. Disconnector
40. Disconnector pin
41. Disconnector spring
42. Trigger
43. Disconnector-sear pin
44. Trigger spring plunger
45. Trigger spring
46. Sear adjusting screw
47. Adjusting screw set screw
48. Safety
49. Safety screw
50. Trigger guard
51. Front trigger guard screws (2)
52. Rear trigger guard screw
53. Front sight
54. Front sight set screw
55. Rear sight
56. Rear sight screws (2)
57. Magazine assembly
58. Sling swivels (2)
59. Buttplate
60. Buttplate screws (2)

* Permanent assembly or subassembly. Do not attempt to disassemble.

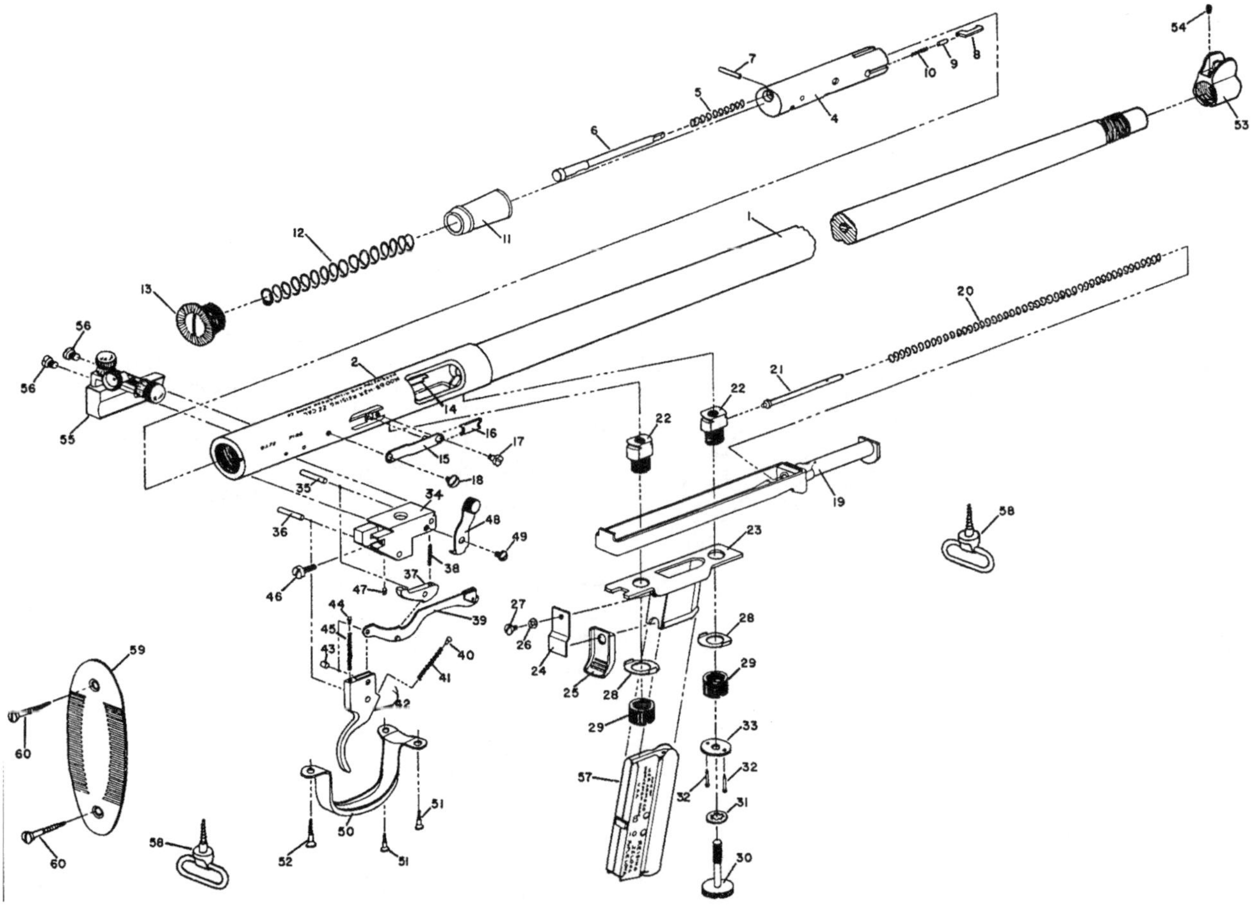

The H&R Model 65, .22 caliber rifle was the wartime outgrowth of H&Rs experience in the production of military small arms. Based on Eugene G. Reising's 1940 patent, H&R developed and sold about 100,000 "Reising" Model 50 and 55 submachine guns to the U.S. Marine Corps, Great Britain, the Soviet Union, and for use by domestic security guards.

The popularity of Reising guns for security use led, in 1943, to the production of the semi-automatic, .45 caliber Model 60 Reising and the .22 caliber Model 65. The Model 65 was manufactured as a military trainer during the war and for civilian purchase following the end of hostilities. Civilian Model 65s differ from military versions primarily in the configuration of the front sight and in the weight of the barrel. Two variations were listed in 1946, the Model 65 "General" and the Model 165 with a sporter-style stock. By 1948 the Model 165 was being marketed as "The Leatherneck" and was fitted with Redfield aperture rear sights and a 10-round detachable box magazine.

Restyled Leathernecks appeared in various catalogs as Models 150 (five-shot magazine, open sights) and 151 (Redfield rear sight) between 1949 and 1954, at which time both models seem to have been discontinued by H&R.

DISASSEMBLY

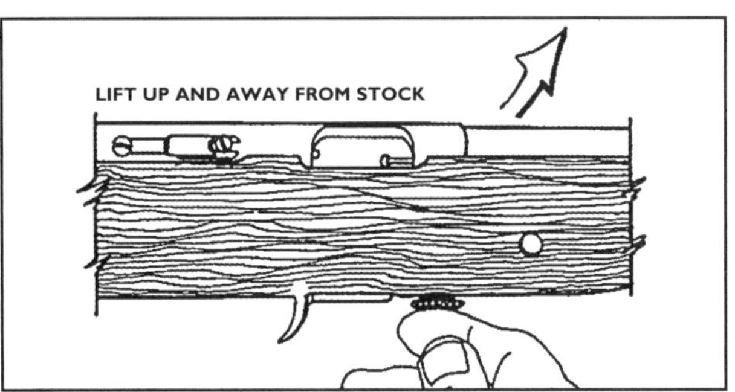

1 Remove the magazine (57). Open the bolt (4) by pushing the action bar (19) rearward and check to insure that the chamber is clear. Close the action. Loosen the take- down screw (30) and lift the barrel-receiver assembly out of the stock (3).

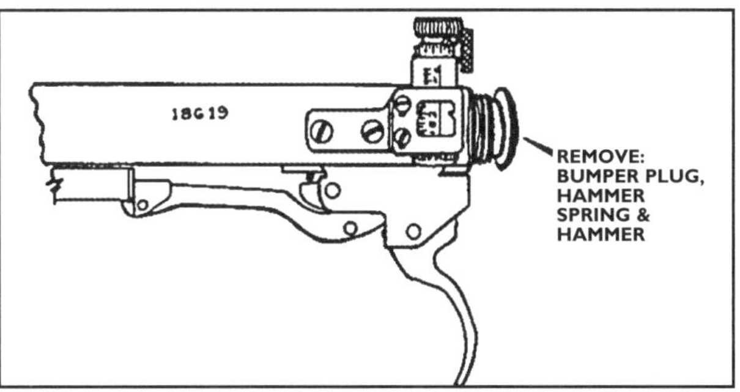

2 Remove the bumper plug (13), hammer spring (12), and hammer (11). To remove the hammer, press the trigger (42) lowering the sear (37) and allowing the hammer to slide to the rear out of the receiver (2).

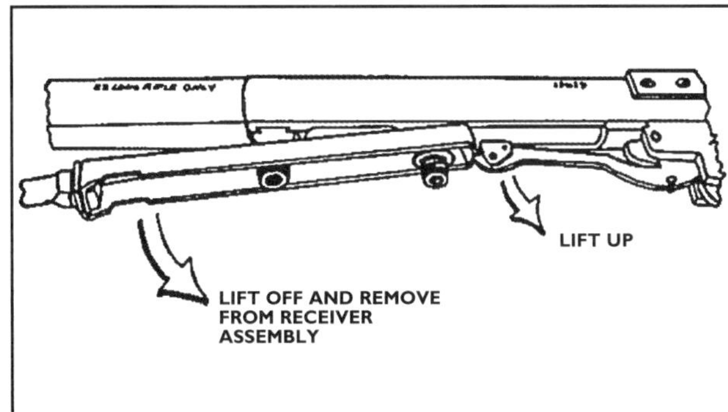

3 To remove the bolt, unscrew both retaining nuts (29) and lift off the retaining nut washers (28) and magazine guide (23). Push back on the action bar, compressing the retracting spring (20). Note the small holes in the leading end of the retracting spring guide (21). Insert the end of a wire paper clip into one of these holes, after compressing the spring, to retain the retracting spring. Slide the action bar forward and remove the retracting spring and guide from the action bar. The end of the retracting spring guide is indexed into a hole in the forward magazine guide stud (22). Lift up the disconnector (39) and at the same time lift off the action bar, disengaging it from its slot in the bottom of the bolt.

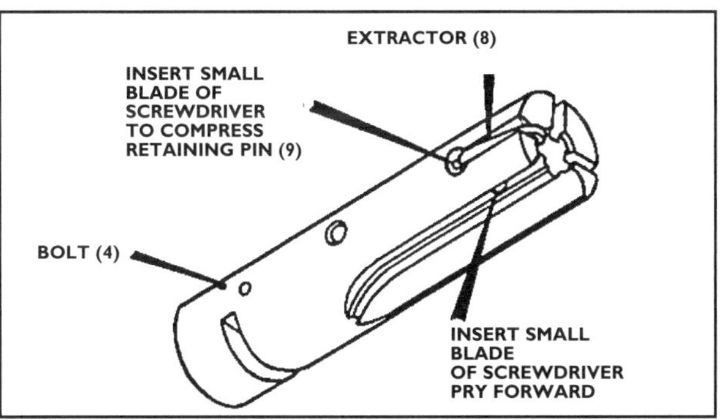

4 Slide the bolt to the rear and out of the receiver, after pressing the trigger and lowering the sear to allow the bolt to clear.

For cleaning purposes, no further disassembly is necessary.

To disassemble the bolt, remove the bolt pin (7) and slide out the firing pin (6) and firing pin spring (5). Remove the extractor by inserting a small screwdriver blade between the extractor (8) and the extractor pin (9) and compressing the extractor spring (10). Simultaneously insert a second screwdriver blade into the access hole underneath the bolt and pry the extractor out of its slot in the bolt. CAUTION: Do not attempt to remove the magazine guide studs (22), the mounting block (34), or ejector (14). These parts or assemblies are press-fitted or dovetailed into the receiver and are permanently installed in their respective positions.

H&K USC CARBINE

PARTS LEGEND

1. Upper receiver
2. Front sight
3. Front sight roll pin
4. Sight support
5. Flat spring
6. Rear sight
7. Windage adjustment screw
8. Rear sight spring
9. Sight support spring
10. Elevation adjustment screw
11. Roll pin, sight support
12. Cocking lever
13. Cocking lever spring
14. Cocking lever support
15. Roll pin, cocking lever support
16. Barrel
17. Barrel roll pin
18. Ejector
19. Hand stop
20. Hand stop insert plate
21. Hand stop cylindrical screw
22. Buttstock
23. Buffer
24. Bolt
25. Extractor
26. Firing pin assembly
27. Firing pin spring
28. Firing pin retaining pin
29. Recoil spring assembly
30. Lower receiver
31. Trigger
32. Trigger spring
33. Axle (3)
34. Sear, complete
35. Sear spring
36. Locking lever spring
37. Locking lever
38. Bolt
39. Locking lever housing
40. Elbow spring right
41. Elbow spring left
42. Hammer
43. Hammer spring, left
44. Hammer spring, right
45. Notched disk
46. Compression spring
47. Index plate
48. Axle, locking lever
49. Safety lever, left
50. Safety lever, right
51. Magazine release
52. Magazine release spring
53. Magazine release axle
54. Bolt catch
55. Bolt catch spring
56. Bolt catch roll pin
57. Buttstock Allen screws (2)
58. Magazine housing
59. Follower
60. Magazine spring
61. Locking plate
62. Floor plate
63. Picatinny rail, short
64. Cylindrical screws (2)
65. Picatinny rail, long
66. Cylindrical screws (2)
67. Carrying sling

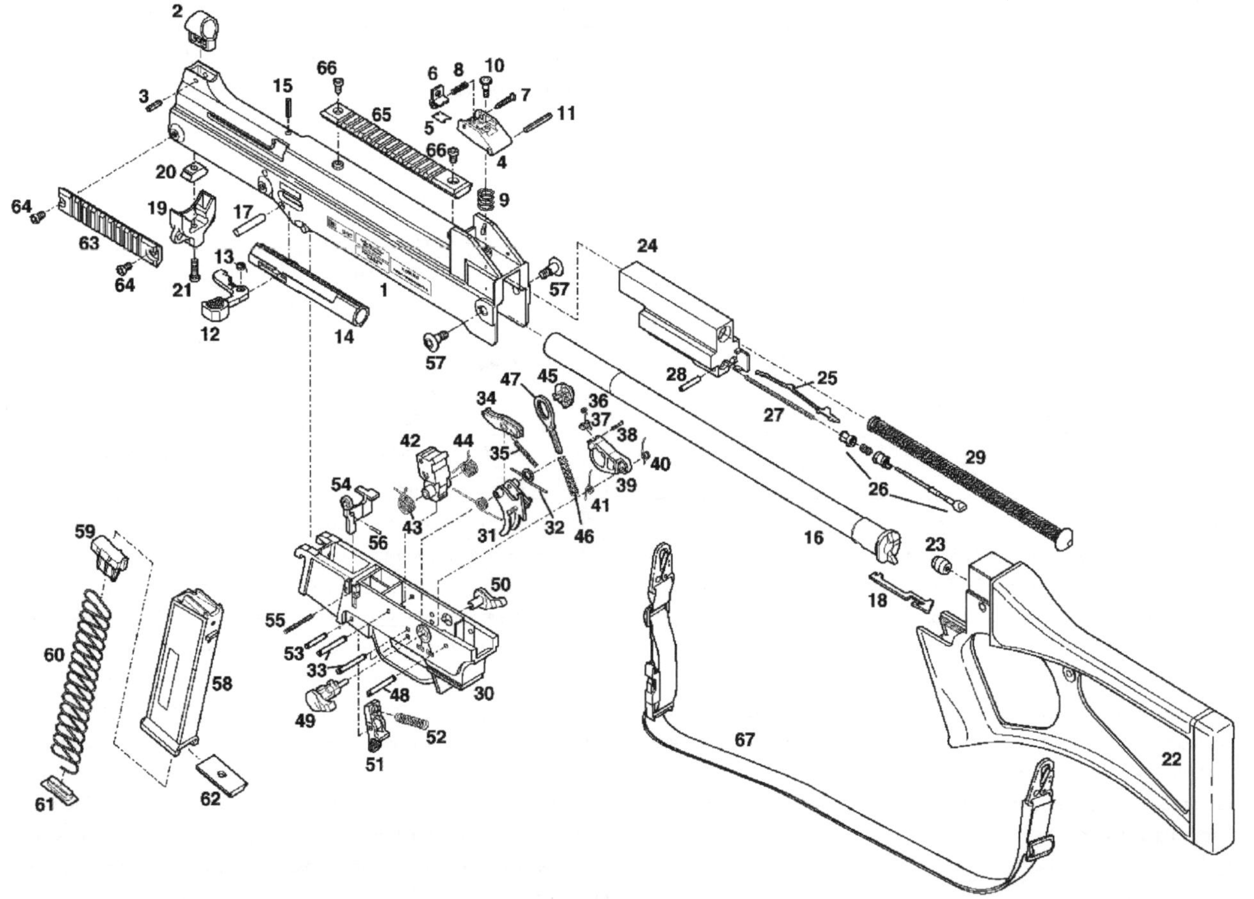

The USC or Universal Self loading Carbine is a civilian version of the fully-automatic Heckler & Koch UMP *Universale Maschinenpistole* (Universal Submachine Gun), part of H&K's line of military and police arms. The UMP, originally intended as a replacement for the 9mm Heckler & Koch MP5, fired a more powerful cartridge but was lighter and less expensive. The UMP was designed to operate like the MP5 but has not replaced it in the military and police markets.

As a firearm intended for the civilian market, the USC's trigger group and action do not permit full-automatic fire. The USC was designed to conform to the standards of the United States Assault Weapons Ban of 1994. Design changes included a "thumbhole" style stock, a longer (16-inch) barrel and a 10-round magazine. Both the USC and its parent, the UMP, are constructed mostly of reinforced polymers to decrease weight and reduce the number of parts subject to corrosion.

Chambered for the .45 ACP cartridge, the USC uses a simple blowback operating system, firing from a closed bolt position. The USC is 35.43 inches long and weighs approximately 6 lbs. The sights consist of an aperture rear sight and front ring with a vertical post. The USC has hard points for the attachment of Picatinny rails (top of the receiver, right, left, and the bottom of the handguard) for accessories such as optical sights, flashlights, or laser sights.

DISASSEMBLY

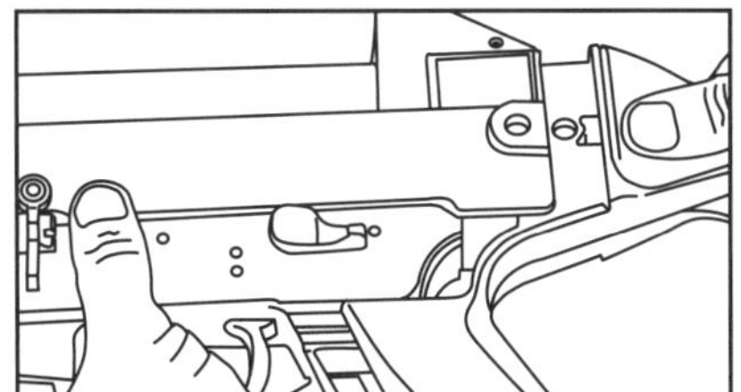

1 To strip the carbine into assembly groups: Remove magazine. Pull the cocking lever rearward one or more times to insure the chamber is empty. Lock cocking lever into the indent in the cocking lever housing to lock the bolt open to inspect the chamber live rounds. Detach carrying sling. Use the 5mm Allen wrench of the H&K Tool and remove the hex headed Allen screws located on the left and right sides of at the rear end of the receiver. Pull the buttstock straight backwards out of the guiding rails of the lower the receiver.

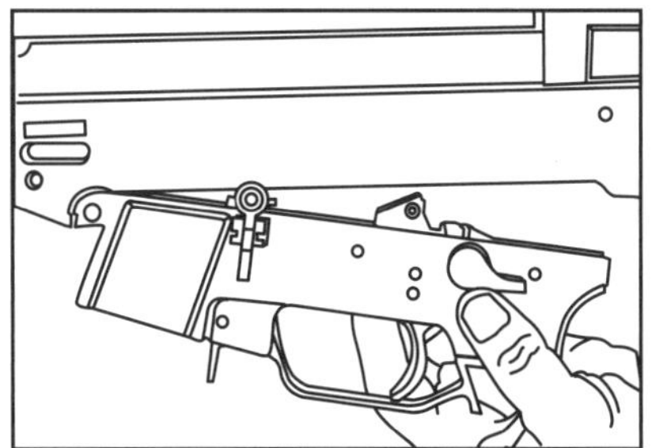

2 Swivel the lower receiver downwards at an angle of approximately 45° and detach it from the support bolts of the upper receiver.

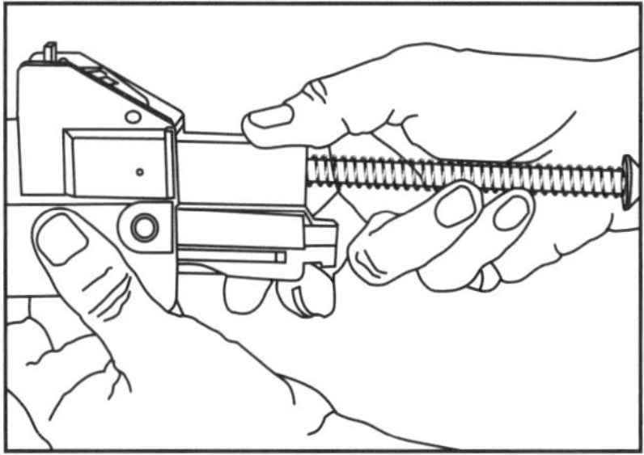

3 Pull back the cocking lever and remove the recoil spring assembly and the bolt to the rear.

4 To disassemble the bolt, push and hold the firing pin forward. Pull out firing pin assembly retaining pin to the left.

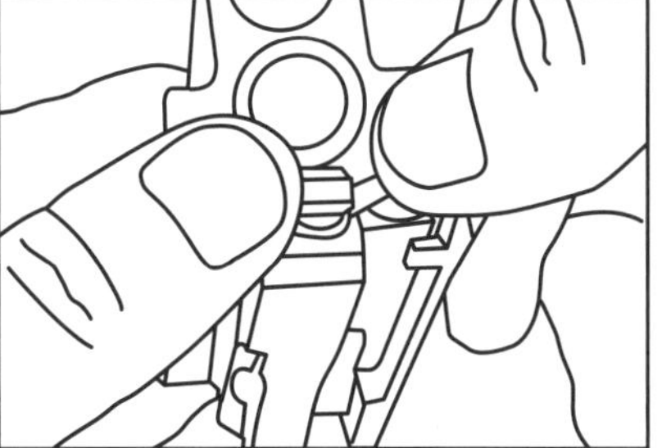

5 Remove firing pin assembly and firing pin spring to the rear. To do this, push the locking catch to the right (arrow, Fig. 4). With your thumb, prevent the firing pin assembly and firing pin spring from springing out. CAUTION: Never disassemble the firing pin. It is possible to assemble the firing pin assembly incorrectly and in doing so, disabling the USC firing pin safety.

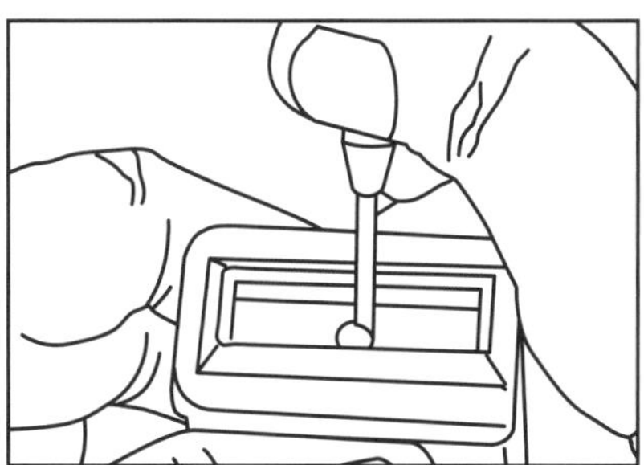

6 To disassembly the magazine, depress locking plate through magazine floor plate and slide magazine floor plate to the rear. Detach magazine floor plate to the rear. Remove follower spring with locking plate and follower. CAUTION: Magazine floor plate is under spring tension. With your thumb secure locking plate with follower spring to prevent it from springing out.

HOPKINS & ALLEN MODEL 922 RIFLE

PARTS LEGEND

1. Receiver
2. Barrel
3. Forestock (not shown)
   3a. Buttsock (not shown)
4. Breechblock
5. Firing pin
6. Firing pin retracting spring
7. Firing pin retaining pin
8. Upper link pin
9. Link
10. Trigger guard/lever
11. Lower link screw
12. Lever roller
13. Lever roller pin
14. Lever spring
15. Lever spring screw
16. Extractor
17. Extractor screw
18. Lever screw
19. Hammer screw
20. Trigger
21. Trigger pin
22. Hammer
23. Hammer roller pin
24. Hammer roller
25. Mainspring
26. Mainspring screw
27. Trigger spring
28. Trigger spring screw
29. Takedown screw
30. Rear sight
31. Front sight
32. Receiver tang screws (2)
33. Forestock screw
34. Buttplate
35. Buttplate screws (2)

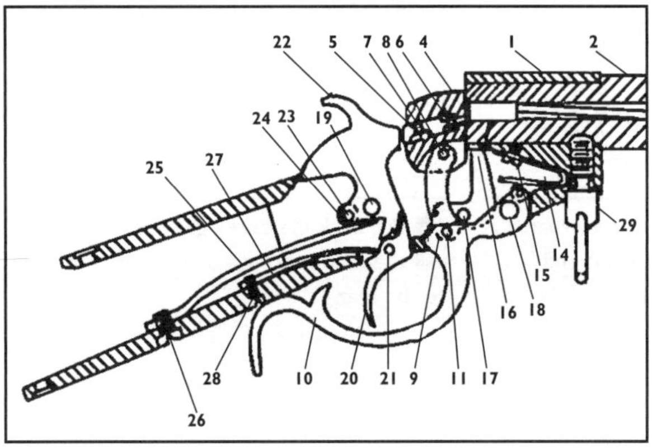

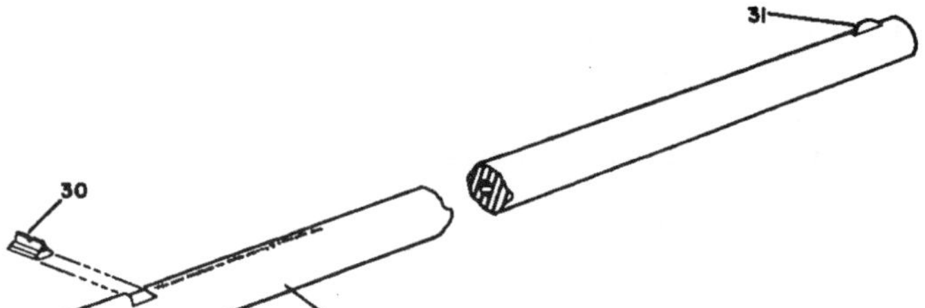

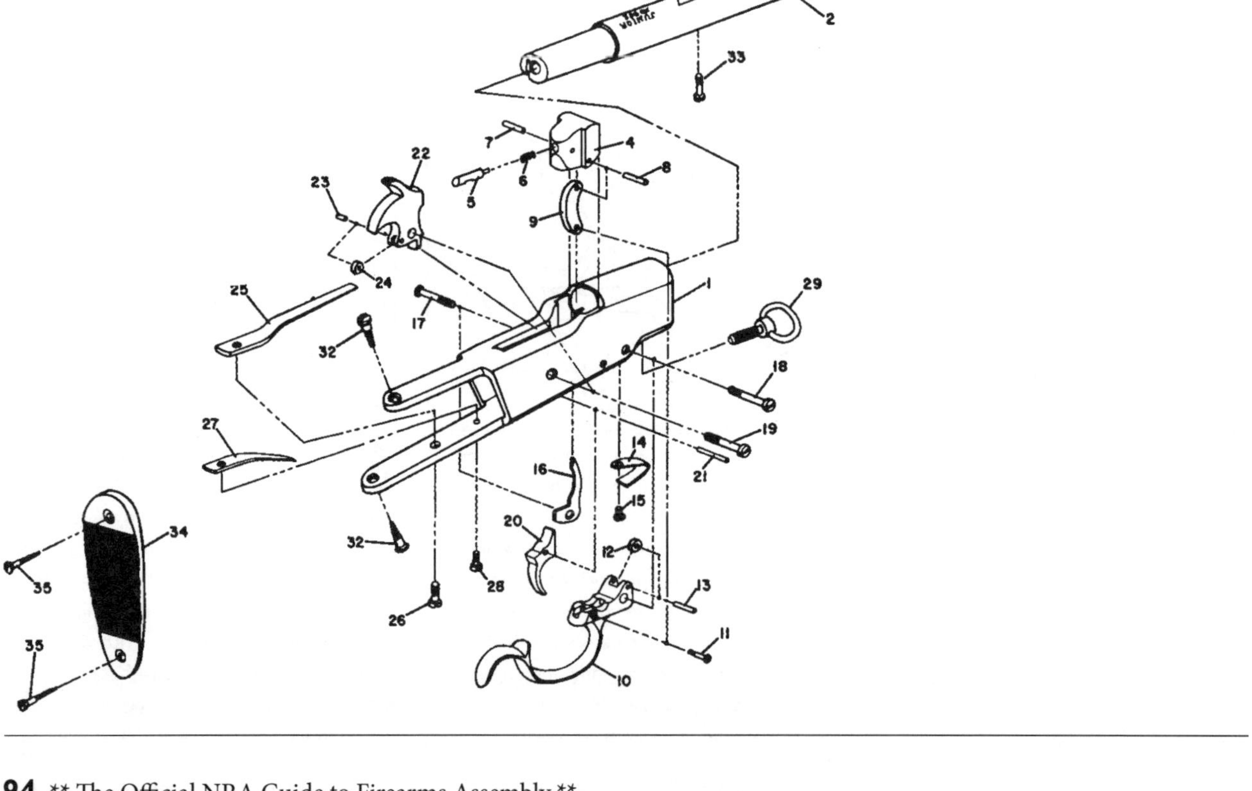

In 1868, when the Hopkins & Allen Manufacturing Co. was founded in Norwich, Connecticut, its principal products were cheap, small-frame, spur-trigger revolvers. Apart from these small handguns, Hopkins & Allen also manufactured most of the revolvers sold by Merwin-Hulbert & Co. including the firm's large-frame Army and Pocket revolvers.

At the end of Hopkins & Allen's second decade in 1887, the firm's management purchased the assets of Bay State Arms Co., including W. H. Davenport's patents for a falling-block, single-shot action suitable for rifles and shotguns. Three years later, in 1890, Hopkins& Allen entered the long gun market, offering a series of rifles based on the Bay State/Davenport action. One of these became the Model 922 "Junior Rifle."

The "Junior" is an underlever, falling-block rifle with a receiver made from a casehardened, malleable iron casting. The barrel is a slip fit in the receiver, held in place by a takedown screw. Nine-Series rifles feature a rebounding hammer, and the receiver features high sidewalls to surround the block. The block moves in slots milled into opposing sides of the interior receiver walls.

Hopkins & Allen had good luck with the Junior Rifle, even if luck in other respects was not so good. The last five years of the 19th century were particularly hard, despite generally steady sales. In 1897 Merwin-Hulbert went bankrupt, and Hopkins & Allen was left with the lion's share of M-H's unpaid bills. When this debt was finally paid, Hopkins & Allen's $90,000 claim netted them just $9,000.

Then on February 4, 1900, the Hopkins & Allen plant burned to the ground — a half million dollar loss. Undaunted, management began to rebuild and, in the process, acquired Forehand Arms Co. When the new plant opened its doors, Model 922 Junior Rifles were among the first guns shipped.

The nine-series expanded in the early 20th century. Before rising labor cost closed the plant for good Hopkins & Allen made the 922 (.22 RF. 22- or 24-inch round barrel). 925 (.25 RE). 932 (.32 RF). and 938 (.38 RF). l.ater, octagonal barreled models, the 19-Series, using the same action, were sold.

At a time, when .22 rifles could be had at prices from $1.00 and up. The Junior Rifle fell into the offerings of the great mass of competitors near the bottom of the price range. The 1907 Hopkins & Allen catalog lists the 922 at a price of $5.50.

DISASSEMBLY

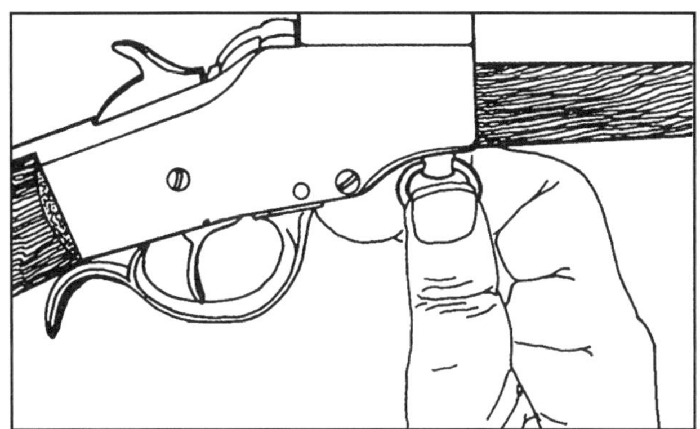

1 Check the rifle to insure that it is unloaded. Loosen the takedown screw (29) and remove the barrel (2) and forestock assembly.

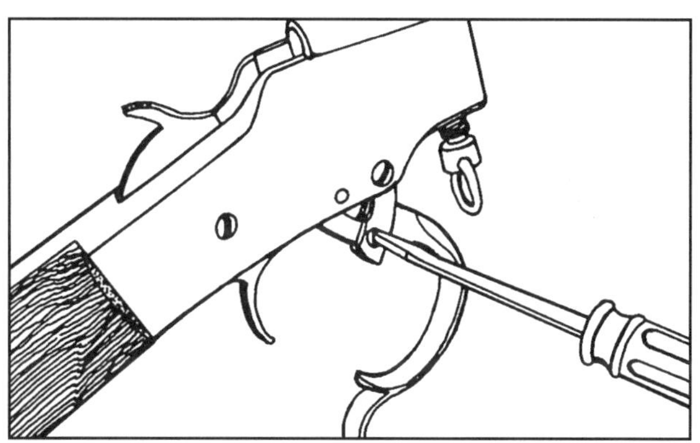

2 Open the breech by pulling downward on the trigger guard/lever (10). Remove the lower link screw (11).

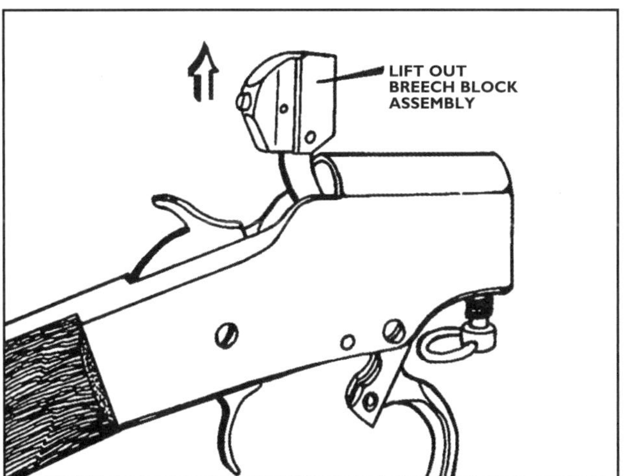

3 Allow the trigger guard/lever to hang free and push upward on the link (9). Lift the breechblock (4) out through the top of the receiver (1). Remove the lever screw (18) and lift out the trigger guard/lever. Remove the extractor screw (17) and lift out the extractor (16). From underneath the receiver, remove the lever spring screw (15) and lift out the lever spring (14).

Remove the receiver tang screws (32) and gently tap the buttstock (3a.) rearward until it clears the receiver tangs and can he removed. Remove the mainspring screw (26) and lift out the mainspring (25).

Remove the hammer screw (19) and lift out the hammer (22). Remove the trigger spring screw (28) and the trigger spring (27). Use a drift punch to drive out the trigger pin (21) and lift out the trigger. All other parts are readily disassembled.

ITALIAN CARCANO RIFLE

PARTS LEGEND

1. Cocking piece nut retainer
2. Retainer spring
3. Retainer pin
4. Cocking piece nut
5. Cocking piece
6. Safety catch
7. Firing pin spring
8. Firing pin
9. Bolt
10. Extractor
11. Assembled bolt
12. Carbine barrel and receiver
13. Sear pin
14. Ejector
15. Sear spring
16. Bolt stop
17. Trigger
18. Sear
19. Trigger pin
20. Plunger and spring
21. Bayonet hinge
22. Bayonet
23. Front band
24. Front band screw
25. Handguard
26. Carbine stock
27. Follower
28. Follower spring
29. Follower housing
30. Follower hinge pin
31. Housing retainer screw
32. Front guard screw
33. Trigger guard & magazine
34. Clip latch pin
35. Clip latch
36. Clip latch spring
37. Rear guard screw

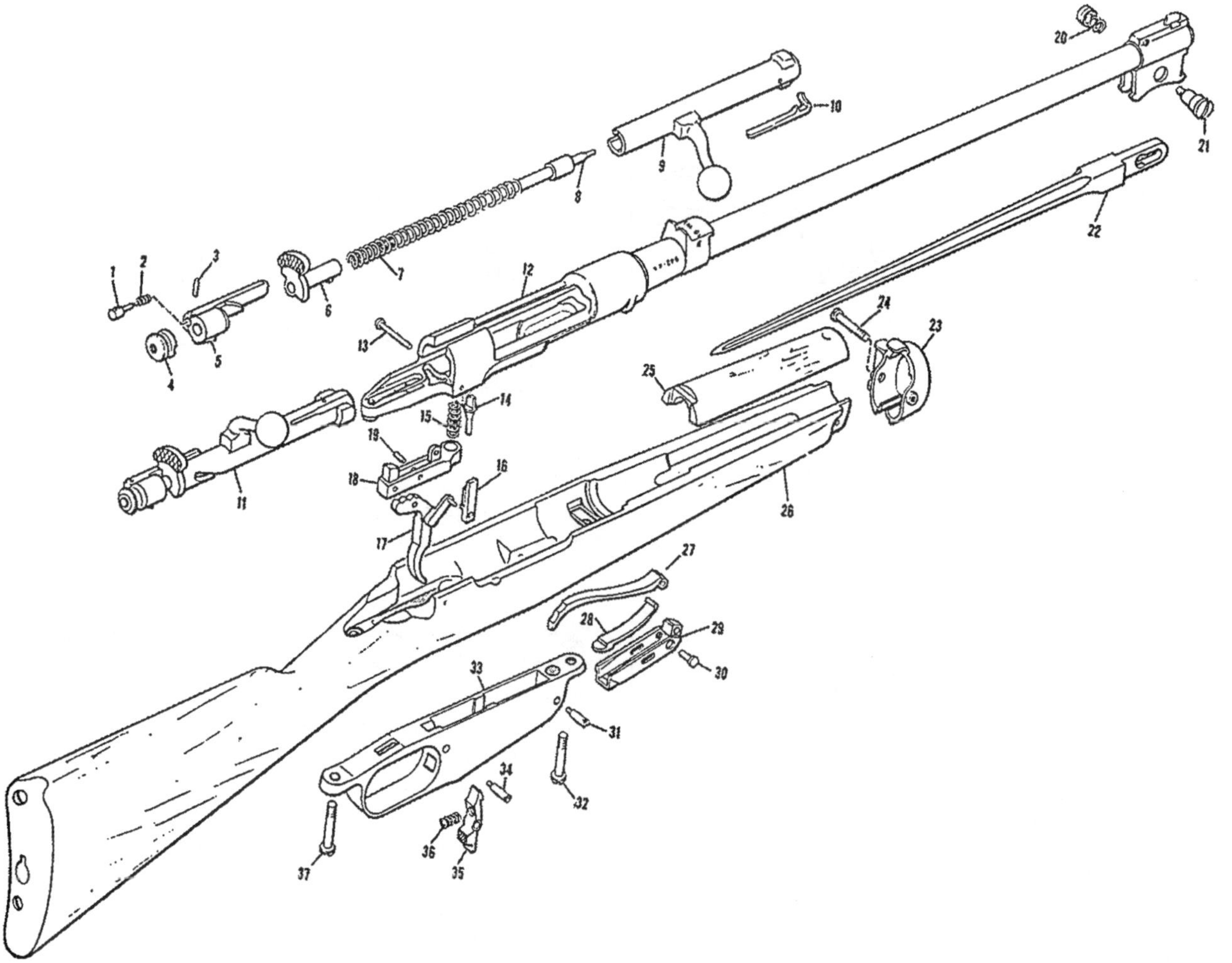

In the 1890's Italy desired a modern smokeless-powder military rifle to replace the obsolete Vetterli-Vitali. The new rifle, developed by Lieutanant Colonel Salvatore Carcano and Colonel G. Parravicino, incorporated Mauser features in the action with a Mannlicher-type feed system. It was made in several models, including a rifle and carbine and the above illustrated 1938 short rifle.

The Carcano is a robust and solid weapon. The bolt design, with solid head and fixed extractor, is extremely simple. There is no third locking lug, but the bolt handle locks forward of the receiver ring and acts as a safety lug.

A disposable clip is a necessary part of the feed system. A 6-shot-capacity steel or brass clip is retained by a latch in the magazine well. The spring-loaded follower forces the cartridges up into the path of the bolt. While the system lends itself to rapid loading and unloading, the gun becomes a single-shot if only loose ammunition is available.

Mannlicher-Carcano rifles and carbines are commonly found in two calibers, 6.5 mm. and 7.35 mm. In the late 1930s, the 6.5 mm. cartridge case was redesigned to accept a 7.35 mm. bullet. Although the 7.35 mm. cartridge was a better military round, Italy went back to the 6.5 mm. before the end of World War II.

Carcano rifles usually show a great deal of rough hand finishing. The safety catch is awkward and trigger pull uniformly hard. Cal. 6.5 mm. Carcanos are rifled with a progressive twist, but cal. 7.35 mm. rifles have a constant rifling twist.

DISASSEMBLY

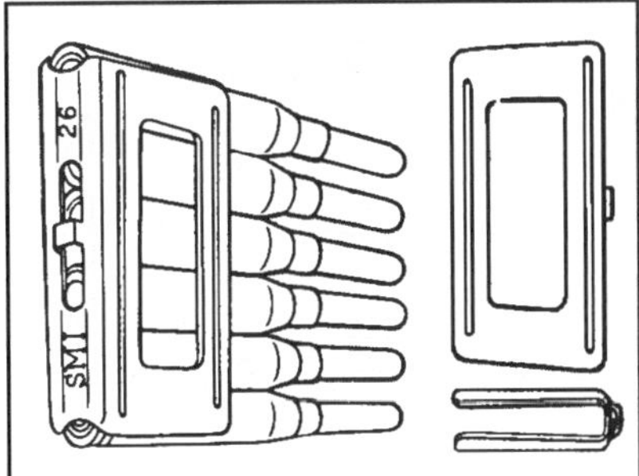

1 A 6-shot clip is a necessary part of the Mannlicher-style feed mechanism. The packet of cartridges is pressed into the magazine well until caught by the latch. To unload gun, open bolt and press clip latch (35). The empty clip falls out bottom of magazine as last round is fed.

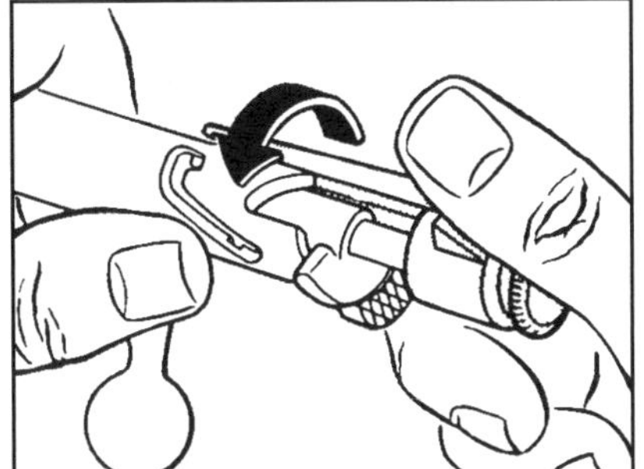

2 The Carcano has a simple bolt stop (16). To remove bolt, pull it to rear and at same time pull trigger. To disassemble bolt, rotate cocking piece (5) to fired position as shown. This relieves tension on firing pin spring (7).

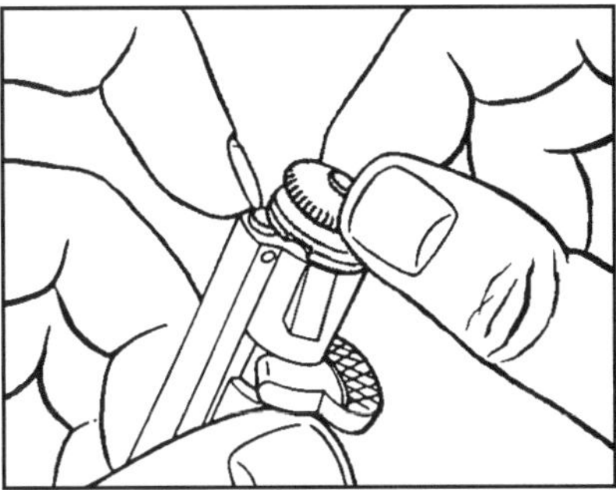

3 Although it is possible to remove the entire firing pin assembly by rotating the safety catch as illustrated in Fig. 4, it is safer to disassemble the firing mechanism in the bolt. To do so, push down cocking piece nut retainer (1) and unscrew cocking piece nut (4).

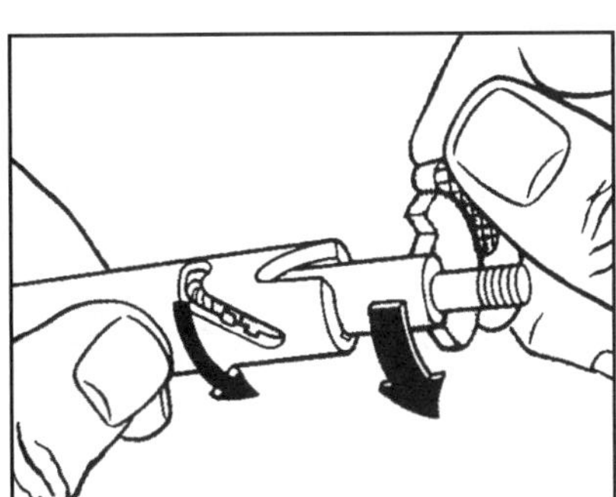

4 After cocking piece nut and cocking piece have been removed, push safety catch (6) forward slightly until the small lug is free of its bayonet-type notch in the bolt. Rotate safety and ease it down the cam groove until it drops into small notch near end of cam groove. Turn small lug into this notch and pull safety free of bolt. Then remove firing pin (8) and spring (7).

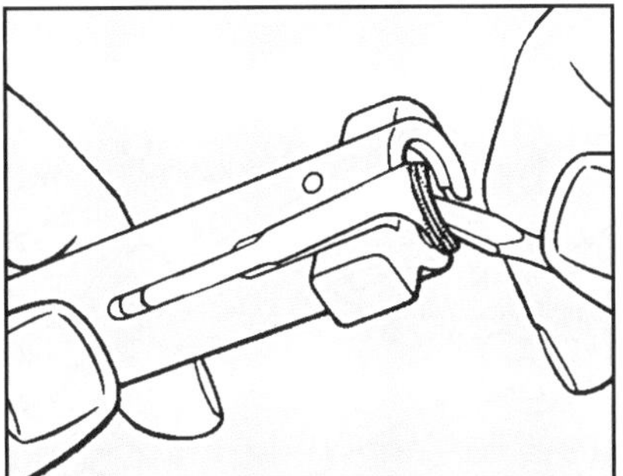

5 Extractor should not be removed unless absolutely necessary. Tail of extractor is peened or hammered to the bolt to help retain it. If peened too tightly, it may snap off if an attempt is made to pry it out as shown. The round hole in the bolt and small slot beneath extractor are the only outlets provided for gas escape.

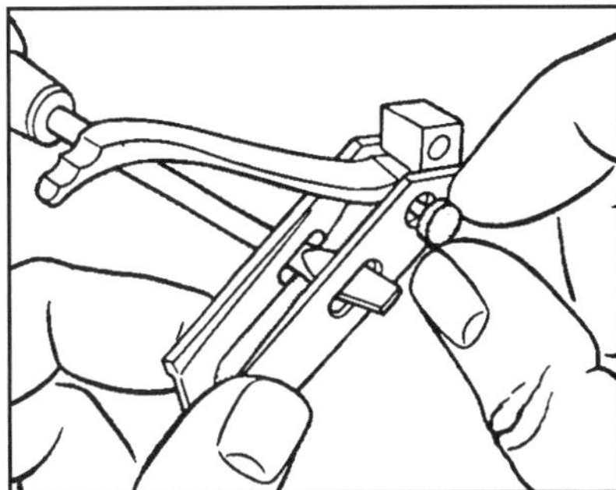

6 Follower (27) is operated by a very powerful spring (28). To replace follower hinge pin (30), it is necessary to compress this spring to align the pin. To do so, insert a screwdriver through slots in follower housing (29). Drive it in until follower spring is compressed enough to allow follower some freedom of motion.

ITHACA MODEL 37 FEATHERLIGHT

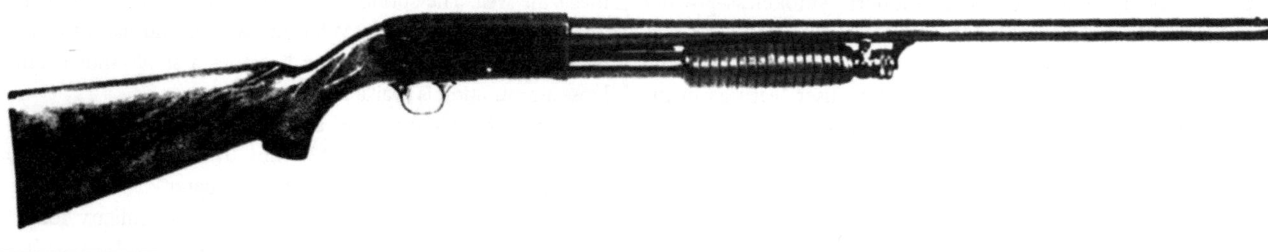

PARTS LEGEND

1. Barrel
2. Magazine nut pin*
3. Magazine nut
4. Magazine nut pin check screw*
5. Magazine nut pin catch spring*
6. Magazine nut pin check spring cap*
7. Yoke screw
8. Yoke
9. Magazine spring
10. Magazine spring cup
11. Receiver and magazine tube
12. Slide handle assembly
13. Spring shell stop (left)
14. Spring shell stop spring
15. Spring shell stop screw
16. Positive shell stop (right)
17. Trigger plate screw
18. Hammer pin
19. Trigger pin
20. Safety
21. Safety catch spring
22. Safety catch
23. Mainspring cup
24. Mainspring
25. Mainspring cap
26. Stock bolt
27. Stock washers
28. Mainspring stop
29. Trigger plate
30. Slide stop spring (bottom)
31. Trigger spring
32. Trigger
33. Slide pin
34. Slide pin spring
35. Slide
36. Slide pin check pin
37. Hammer bar
38. Hammer bar pin
39. Hammer
40. Slide stop
41. Slide stop release spring (top)
42. Carrier
43. Bottom extractor
44. Bottom extractor spring
45. Positive extractor spring cap
46. Positive extractor spring
47. Positive extractor (top)
48. Extractor hinge pin (bottom)
49. Firing pin check pin
50. Firing pin spring
51. Firing pin
52. Breechblock
53. Stock
54. Buttplate and screws
55. Carrier screw (2)
56. Carrier screw lock screw (2)

* Not used in guns made after 1954

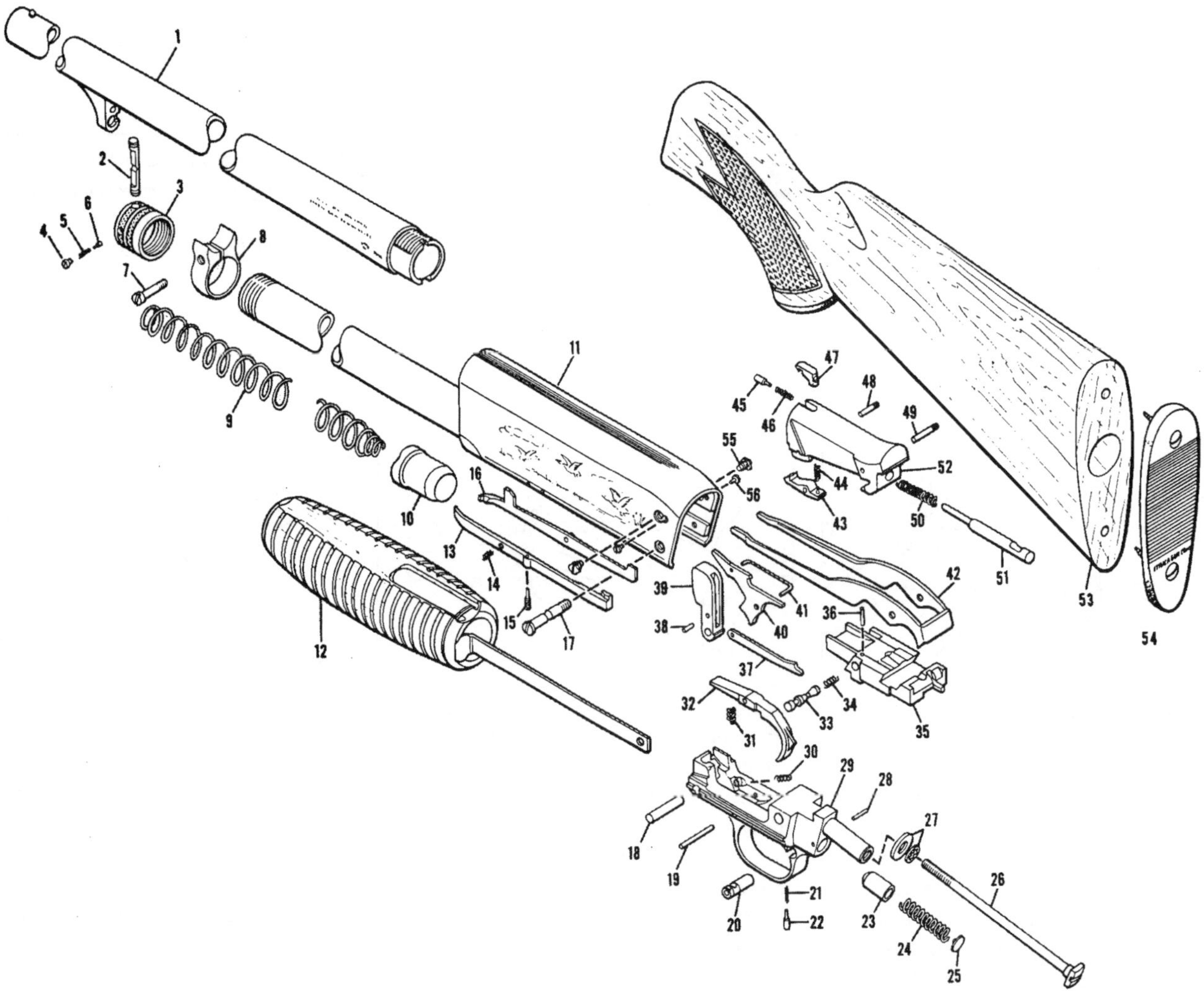

The Ithaca Gun Co. of Ithaca, New York, began manufacturing firearms in a small wood building on the banks of Fall Creek in 1880. Their first model was a 12-gauge hammer gun, and from this they developed a series of single- and double-barrel shotguns. Ithaca's reputation rests on their trap and double-barrel guns, and the Model 37 Featherlight slide-action shotgun.

The Featherlight, first offered in 1937, won immediate acclaim since it was a good pound lighter than its nearest competitor. Rather than use light alloys, Ithaca shed weight by reducing the number of operating parts wherever possible.

The bolt on the Model 37 bolt has no locking lugs or separate locking block. When the action is closed, the slide tips the end of the bolt up as it is pulled forward. When the end of the bolt is locked into the top of the receiver, the slide supports it from below to prevent unlocking.

The Model 37's bottom ejection system prevents rain from getting into the action and makes it a favorite with left-handed shooters. Model 37 Featherlight shotguns are made in 20, 16, and 12 gauge with barrel lengths that range from 20 inches for the riot gun, to 30 for trap or duck hunters.

DISASSEMBLY

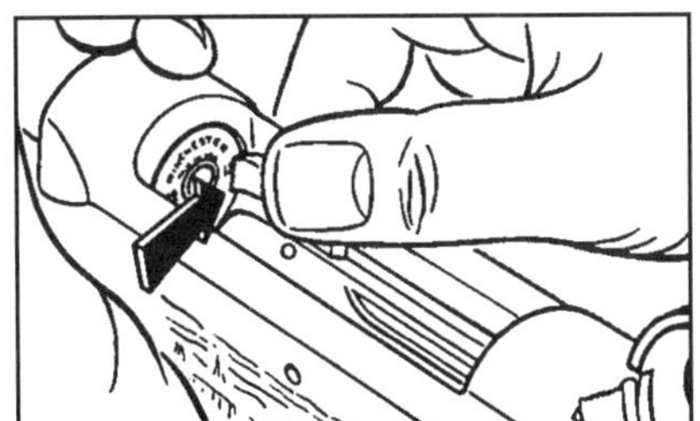

1 Before attempting to remove barrel, unload magazine and chamber. To empty magazine, push in spring shell stop (13) on inside of receiver as shown. Ease rounds out one by one. Pull back on slide release on forward side of trigger guard and pull back slide handle to empty chamber.

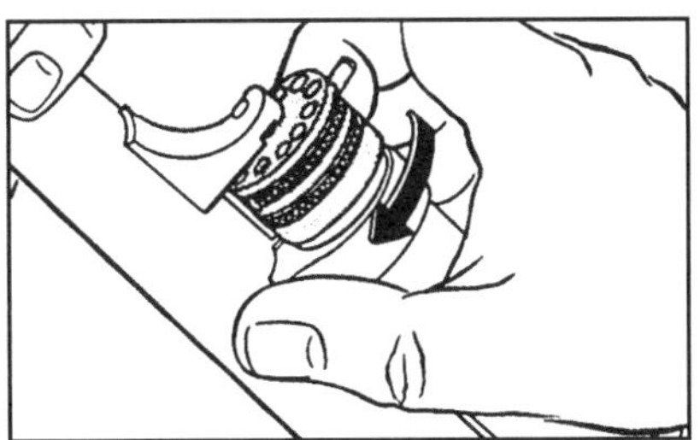

2 To remove barrel (1), pull back on slide release on forward side of trigger guard and pull slide handle assembly (12) to rear to open breech. Pull up magazine nut pin (2) and use it as a lever to rotate magazine nut (3) until projection on it is free of barrel lug. (Magazine nut pin furnished only on guns built prior to 1955.) On later built guns having no pin, simply rotate magazine nut in direction shown.

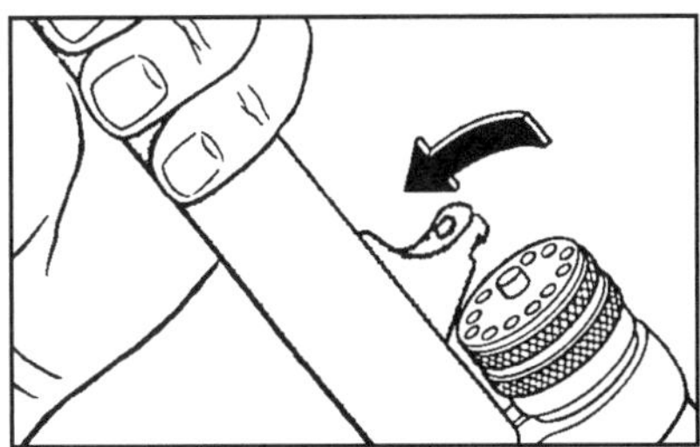

3 Barrel is joined to receiver by an interrupted thread. When magazine nut is free of barrel lug, give barrel ¼-turn in direction shown and pull it free of receiver. Magazine tube and slide handle assembly remain attached to receiver.

4 Stock (53) must be removed before disassembling action. First remove buttplate screws and buttplate. Stock is attached to receiver by a long bolt (26) which has a square head with slot so that it can be removed with a long screwdriver or socket wrench.

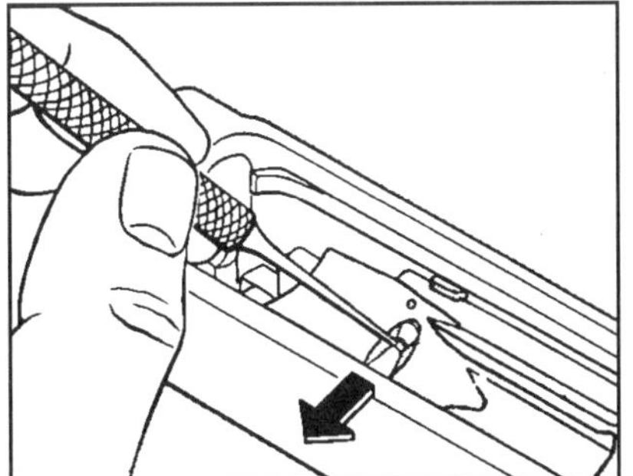

5 With stock removed, remove trigger plate screw (17) and pull trigger plate group to rear and out of receiver. Remove two carrier screw lock screws (56) and carrier screws (55) from receiver. Hold receiver bottom up with magazine to left, and with punch or fingernail pull slide pin (33) toward body until slide bar can be pulled forward from engagement with slide (35). Pull slide, breechblock (52), and carrier (42) together to rear, out of the receiver.

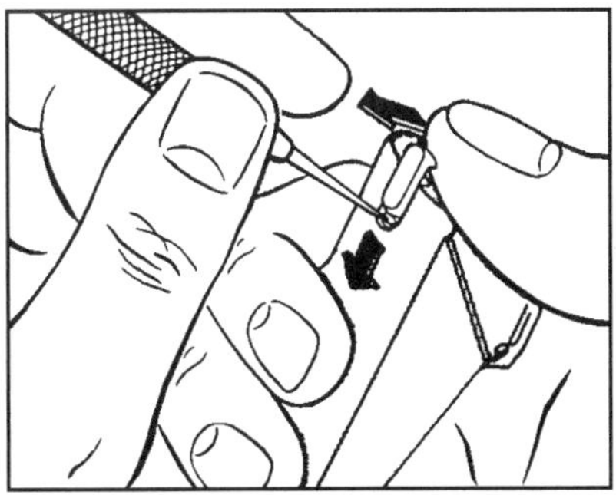

6 The positive extractor (47) is retained by a powerful spring. To remove it, use a thin punch to push spring plunger back. At same time, push extractor out of its seat as shown. Bottom extractor (43) can be easily removed by driving out its hinge pin (48). To remove firing pin from breechblock, first drive out firing pin check pin (49). Then firing pin and spring (51 & 50) can easily be removed. Reassemble in reverse order.

ITHACA SINGLE BARREL TRAP

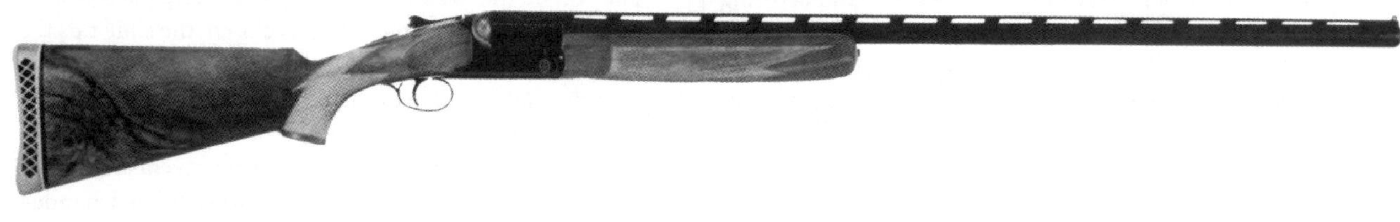

PARTS LEGEND

1. Frame
2. Trigger plate
3. Sear spring
4. Trigger plate screws (3)
5. Trigger
6. Trigger pin
7. Trigger spring
8. Rear tang screw
9. Tang wood screw
10. Trigger guard
11. Trigger guard screws (2)
12. Cocking rod
13. Cocking cam
14. Cocking cam pin
15. Top-lever
16. Action bolt
17. Action bolt cam
18. Action bolt spring
19. Action bolt spring cap
20. Action bolt spring stop
21. Top-lever screw
22. Trip machine screw
23. Trip spring
24. Mainspring
25. Mainspring cap
26. Firing pin
27. Firing pin check screw
28. Sear
29. Sear pin retainer springs (2)
30. Hammer pin set screw
31. Hammer
32. Hammer pin bolt assembly
33. Frame and lock mechanism, complete assembly
34. Stock
35. Recoil pad bolt screw
36. Recoil pad screws (2) (Not shown)
37. Gold oval (shield) inlay
38. Grip cap
39. Grip cap screw machine screw
40. Barrel
41. Bead-type front sight
42. Middle sight (ivory bead)
43. Fore-end
44. Fore-end long machine screw collar
45. Fore-end long machine screw
46. Fore-end iron round nut
47. Kicker
48. Kicker spring
49. Kicker retainer
50. Kicker sear locking screw
51. Kicker sear and retainer springs (2)
52. Kicker sear and retainer pin
53. Fore-end fastener
54. Fore-end bolt spring
55. Kicker retainer pin
56. Fore-end fastener
57. Fore-end bolt guide
58. Fore-end latch escutcheon
59. Fore-end, short machine screw
60. Fore-end latch escutcheon
61. Fore-end latch escutcheon flat-head wood screw
62. Fore-end latch
63. Fore-end latch lever and latch spring pin (2)
64. Fore-end latch spring
65. Fore-end machine screw round nut
66. Extractor
67. Extractor check screw
68. Extractor check locking screw

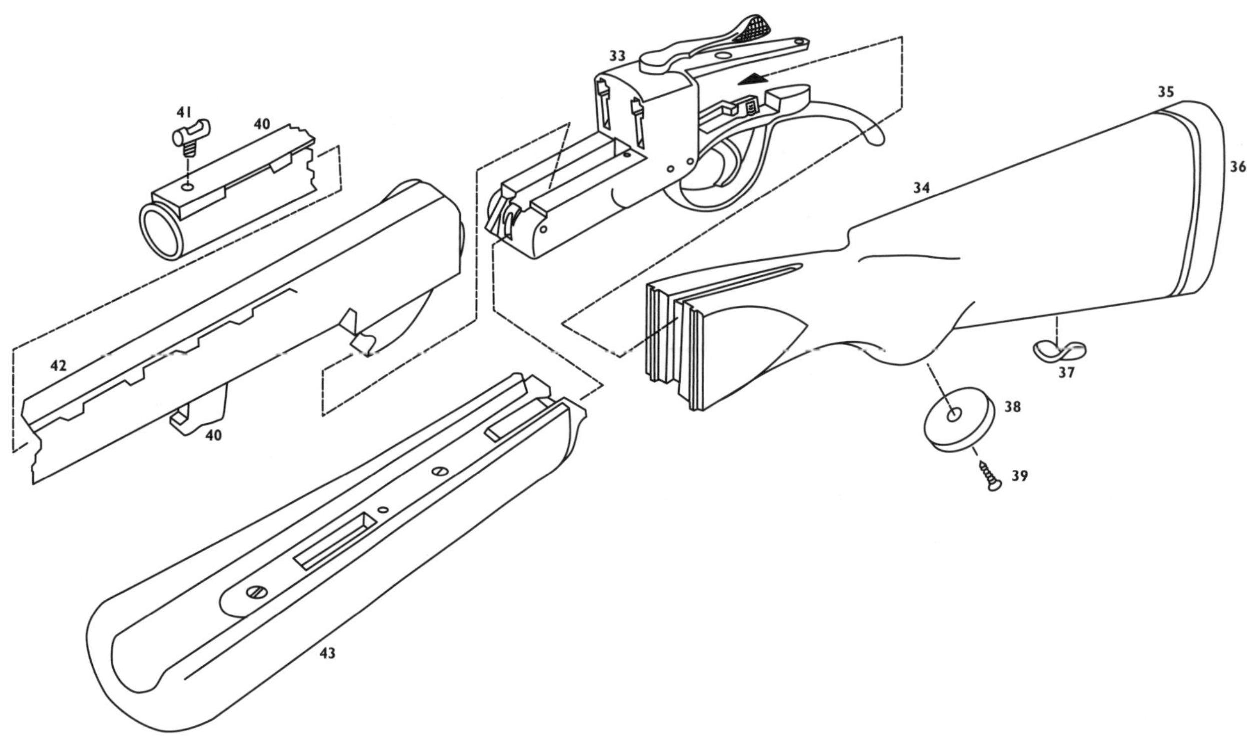

From 1911 until 1922 the Ithaca Gun Co., of Ithaca, New York made a very fine, hand built, single barrel shotgun, designed and intended especially for trap shooting. Known as the "Flues" model , after its designer Emil Flues, the gun earned an enviable reputation within America's trapshooting fraternity. The Flues model Ithaca was superseded in production in 1922, at serial number 400,000, by a re-designed gun popularly known as "the Knick", again after its designer, Frank Knickerbocker. The Knick was made on special order, cataloged in "5E" and "Dollar" grades, until 1944. Ithaca closed its doors in 2005.

DISASSEMBLY

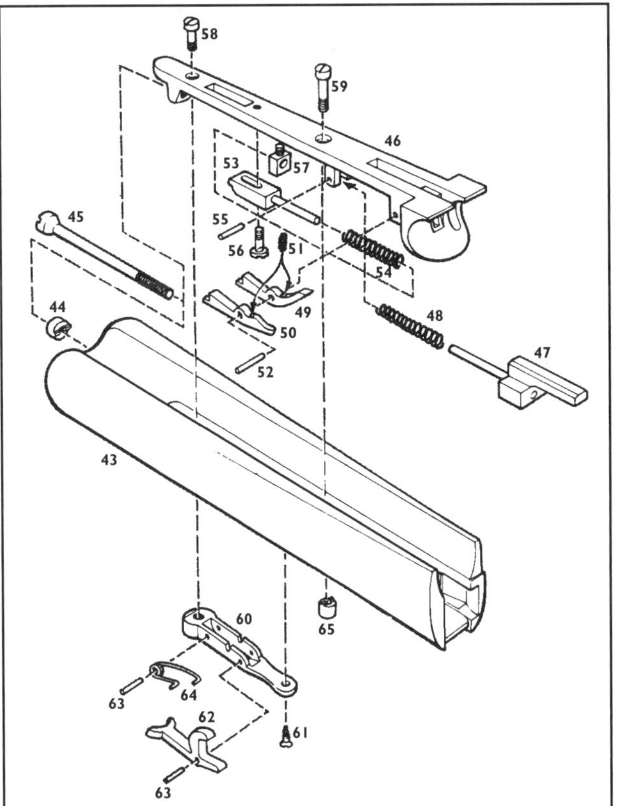

1 To take the gun down, lift fore-end latch (62) and pull fore-end (43) down and back, freeing it from the barrel and frame. Move top lever (15) to right and tilt barrel (40) down. Lift barrel up off frame assembly (33). Reassemble in reverse order. To disassemble fore-end assembly, remove fore-end latch escutcheon machine screw (58) and short fore-end machine screw (59) from top of fore-end iron (46). Fore-end iron may be lifted out of fore-end. Fore-end iron and spring (54) may be removed by unscrewing fore-end fastener bolt screw (56). Kicker spring (48) may be removed after drifting out pin (55). Kicker retainer (49) and kicker sear (50) and springs (51) may be removed by drifting out pin (52).

Remove fore-end latch escutcheon flat head wood screw (61). Remove fore-end latch escutcheon (60) from bottom of fore-end by knocking out gently with a punch or small screwdriver from top through fore-end latch escutcheon machine screw hole. Latch (62) and spring (64) may be removed by drifting out pins (63).

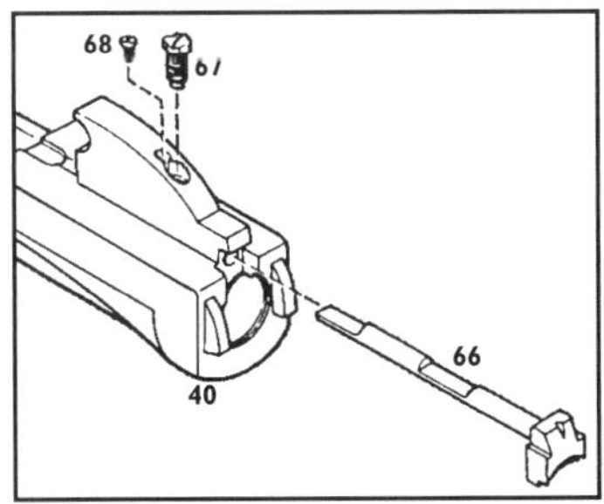

3 To disassemble extractor mechanism invert breech end of barrel. Remove extractor check locking screw (68) and unscrew extractor check screw (67). Pull extractor (66) out rear of barrel.

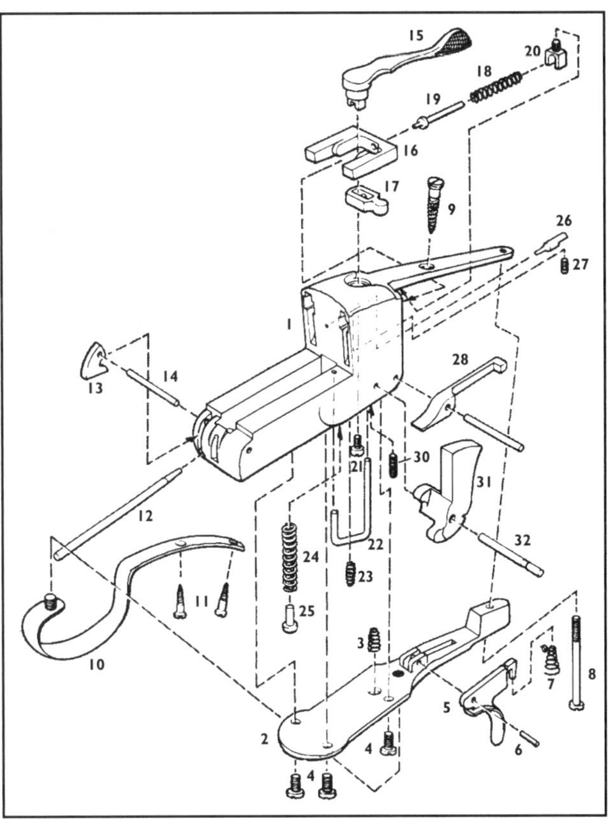

2 To disassemble frame and lock mechanism, take down gun as described in Fig. 1. To remove stock (34) move top lever (15) to side and unscrew tang wood screw (9). Unscrew two trigger guard wood screws (11). Spring out rear end of trigger guard (10) slightly and unscrew trigger guard from trigger plate (2). With the trigger guard removed, the rear tang screw (8) can be removed from underside of trigger plate. Remove three trigger plate screws (4). Rapping stock lightly with heal of hand will loosen trigger plate so it can be removed from bottom of frame (1). Do not attempt to pry trigger plate out of frame. Stock can be drawn off frame to rear. Trigger (5) can be removed from trigger plate by drifting out trigger pin (6). Remove trip spring (23) and trip (22) from underside of frame. Drift out cocking cam pin (14) and remove cocking cam (13) and cocking rod (12) from front end of frame. Drift out sear pin (29) and remove sear (28). Remove hammer pin set screw (30) from underside of frame and drift out hammer pin (32). Remove hammer (31), mainspring (24), and mainspring cap (25) from frame. Compress action bolt spring (18) with end of screwdriver and slip spring and cap (19) out of seat in action bolt spring stop (20). Unscrew action bolt spring stop from underside of top tang. Remove top-lever screw (21) from underside of frame and lift top-lever out top of frame. Action bolt (16) with cam (17) can be slid out of frame top rear.

JAPANESE ARISAKA TYPE 38 6.5MM

PARTS LEGEND

1. Safety catch
2. Firing pin spring
3. Firing pin
4. Bolt
5. Extractor
6. Completely assembled bolt
7. Bolt stop spring
8. Bolt stop
9. Bolt stop and ejector screws
10. Ejector
11. Carbine receiver and barrel
12. Upper tang
13. Tang screw
14. Sear
15. Trigger
16. Trigger pin
17. Sear pin
18. Sear spring
19. Magazine follower
20. Magazine spring
21. Magazine box
22. Trigger guard
23. Front guard screw
24. Rear guard screw
25. Floorplate
26. Floorplate release
27. Floorplate catch
28. Floorplate catch spring
29. Floorplate release pin
30. Lower tang
31. Carbine stock
32. Upper handguard
33. Barrel seat
34. Lower band
35. Front band
36. Cleaning rod

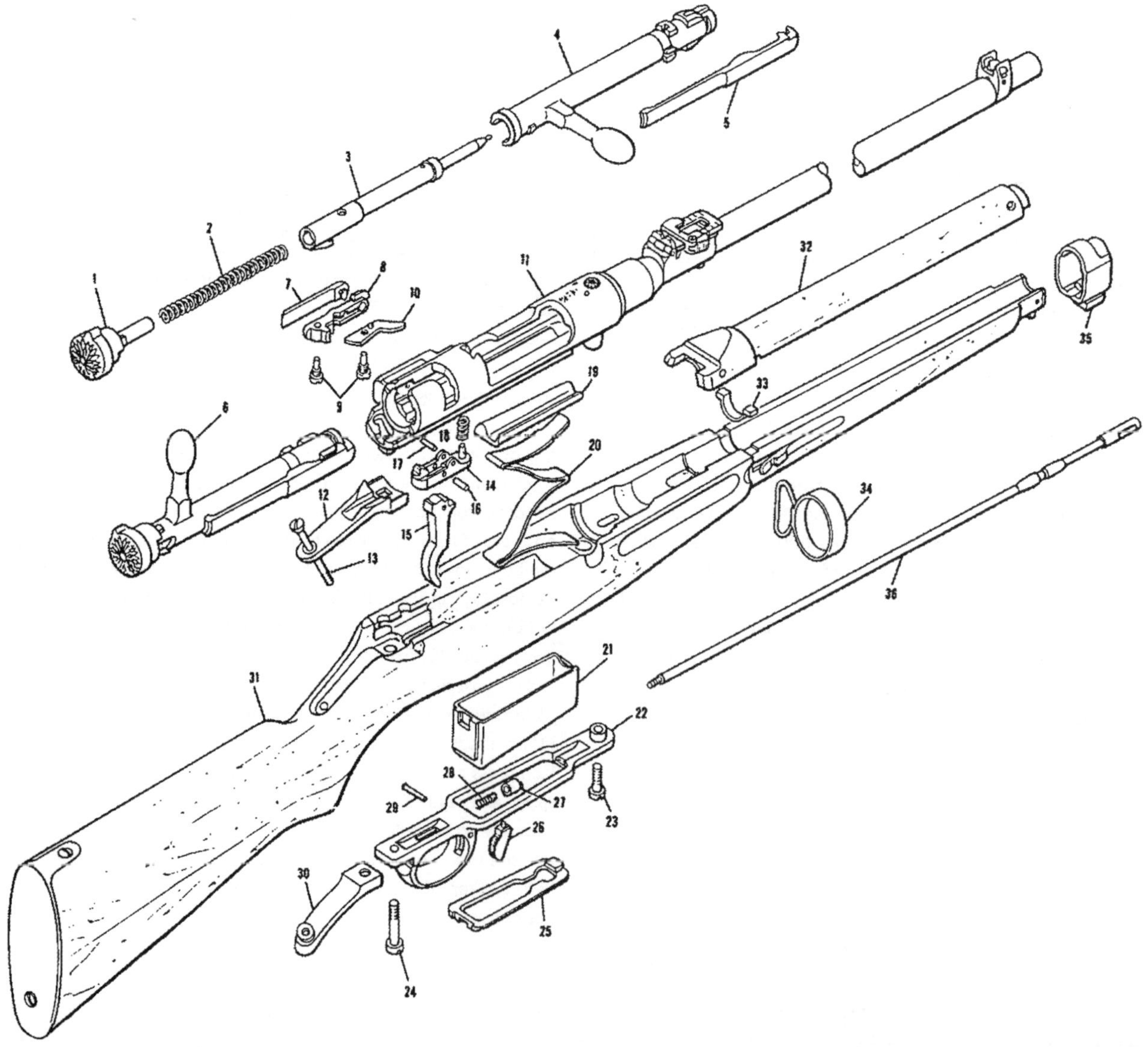

Few guns have been as maligned as the Japanese Model 1905 (Type 38) rifle. During the early stages of World War II, ill-informed observers dismissed the gun as junk and argued that its 6.5 mm. cartridge was inadequate for military use. Few critics took the time to find out how good the gun and cartridge really were.

The Arisaka is a modified Mauser, developed under the direction of Colonel Nariaki Arisaka, superintendent of the Tokyo Arsenal, and officially designated as the Type 38 (1905). The rifle's inherent safety features include two gas escape holes in the receiver and a large combination safety catch and gas shield. The bolt has two large, solid, front locking lugs and the bolt handle engages a cut in the receiver to act as a third lug.

The bolt has another lug about ¼ inch behind the left front locking lug. It acts as a bolt stop and serves as a guide-rib to prevent the bolt from jamming when the locking lugs pass the clip-loading cutaway on the receiver. It also cams the ejector into the path of the bolt. The ejector is not a spring-operated Mauser type, but rather it pivots on a separate screw; when the bolt is pulled back, the bolt lug strikes the rear of the ejector, camming it into the bolt cut in the receiver.

The Type 38's butt is made in two pieces dovetailed together, allowing for the use of smaller blanks and providing stronger grain direction through the grip. Two steel tangs extending back from the action strengthen the grip area.

The Type 38 Arisaka was made in several models, ranging from a carbine to long rifle. Shortly before the beginning of World War II, the 6.5 mm. rifle was superseded by the Type 99 (1939) rifle in 7.7 mm. Most Type 99 parts are not interchangeable with those of the Type 38 rifle.

DISASSEMBLY

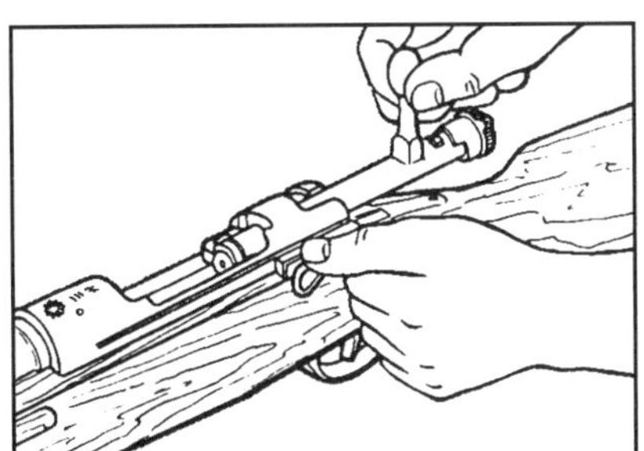

1 To remove assembled bolt (6), first pull it all the way to rear. Then pull bolt stop (8) out to clear stop lug on bolt. Unlike other Mauser rifles, it is not necessary to engage safety in order to disassemble bolt outside receiver.

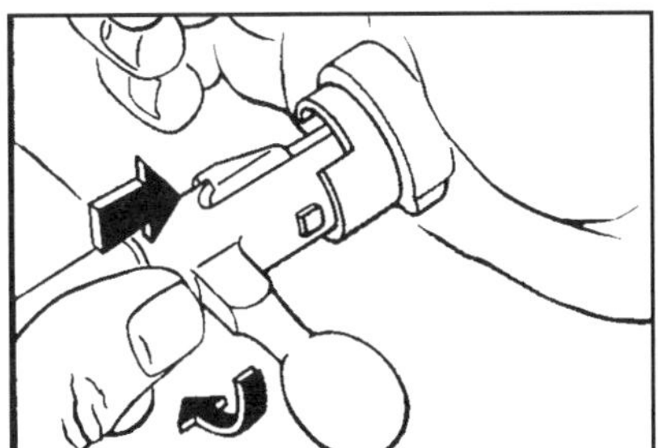

2 To disassemble bolt, hold it as shown and push safety catch (1) in as far as it can go. Rotate bolt ¼-turn and ease out safety catch, firing pin (3), and firing pin spring (2). When reassembling, sear notch must be seated in shallower notch in bolt so that firing pin does not protrude. Then push in safety catch.

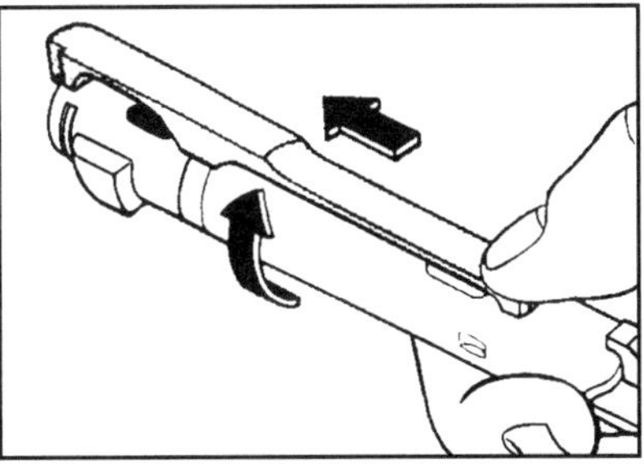

3 Extractor (5) is attached to bolt in typical Mauser style. To remove it, rotate extractor until small guide rib which rides in groove in front end of bolt is free of groove. Push extractor forward until it snaps free of extractor collar.

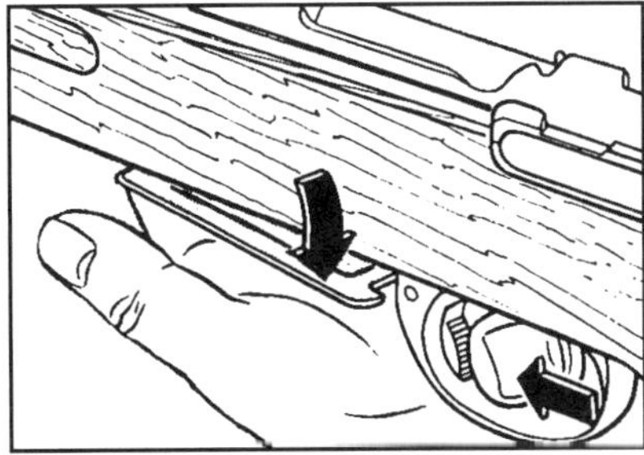

4 To empty magazine without running cartridges through gun, release floorplate (25) by depressing floorplate release (26) in as far as it will go. Floorplate, magazine spring (20), and follower (19) are now detached from magazine.

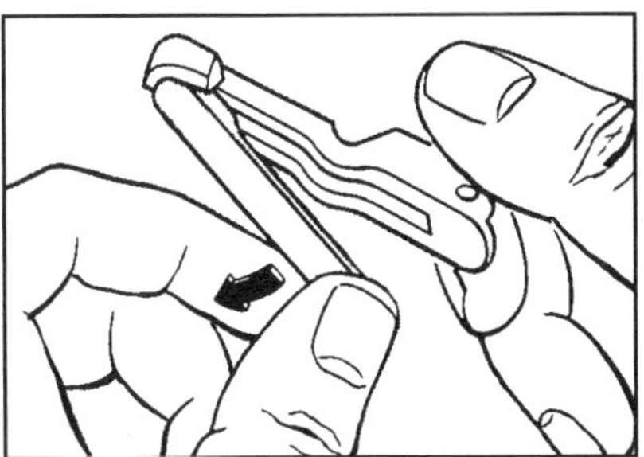

5 To remove bolt stop screw (9), action must be removed from stock. To remove bolt stop spring (7), rotate it 90° as shown and pull it free of bolt stop (8).

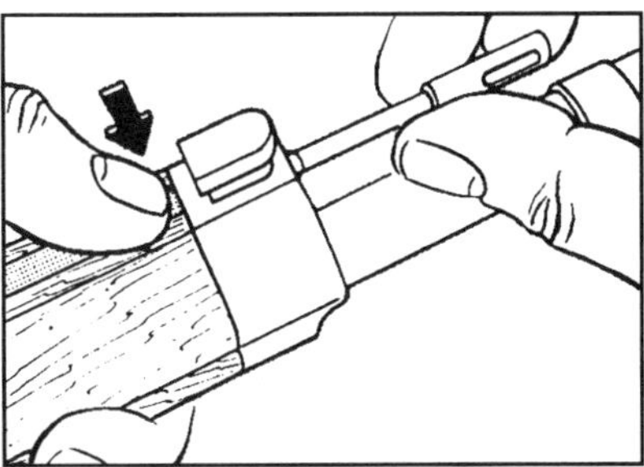

6 All Japanese cal. 6.5 mm. rifles are equipped with a full-length cleaning rod for threading to a handle in the soldier's cleaning kit. To remove cleaning rod (36), push in on long spring that retains front band (35). To remove band (35), remove rod and depress spring as far as possible, and then gently drive off front band.

JAPANESE PARATROOP TYPE 2 RIFLE

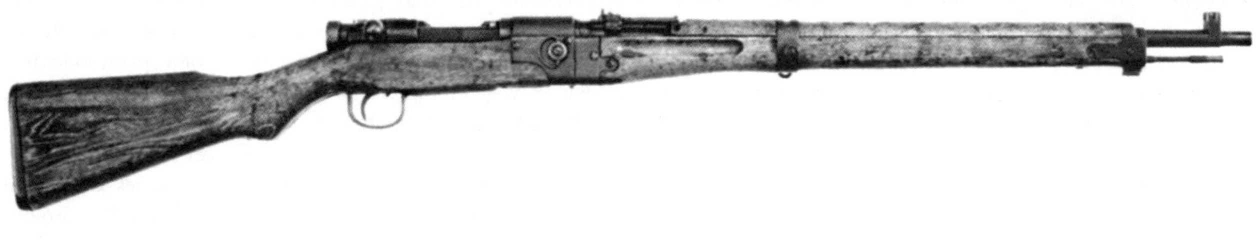

PARTS LEGEND

1. Receiver assembly, Type 2
2. Barrel assembly, Type 2
3. Rear sight
4. Front sight base
5. Front sight
6. Cleaning rod
7. Tang
8. Bolt stop
9. Bolt stop screw
10. Ejector
11. Bolt stop spring
12. Ejector spring
13. Bolt
14. Extractor
15. Striker
16. Striker spring
17. Bolt cap/safety
18. Trigger
19. Trigger pin
20. Sear
21. Sear spring
22. Sear pin
23. Barrel key wedge
24. Barrel key stop screw
25. Barrel key cap
26. Barrel key screw
27. Barrel key pin
28. Trigger guard
29. Tang screw
30. Rear guard screw
31. Front guard screw
32. Magazine floorplate
33. Floorplate pin
34. Floorplate latch
35. Floorplate latch spring
36. Floorplate latch screw
37. Magazine box
38. Magazine follower
39. Follower spring
40. Buttplate
41. Lower buttplate screw
42. Upper buttplate screw
43. Stock swivel
44. Swivel screws (2)
45. Forestock locating stud
46. Buttstock collar
47. Buttstock collar screws (5)
48. Forestock collar
49. Forestock collar screws (2)
50. Handguard collar
51. Middle band
52. Middle band screw
53. Upper band
54. Cleaning rod latch screws (2)
55. Upper band screw
56. Upper band cap
57. Breech cover

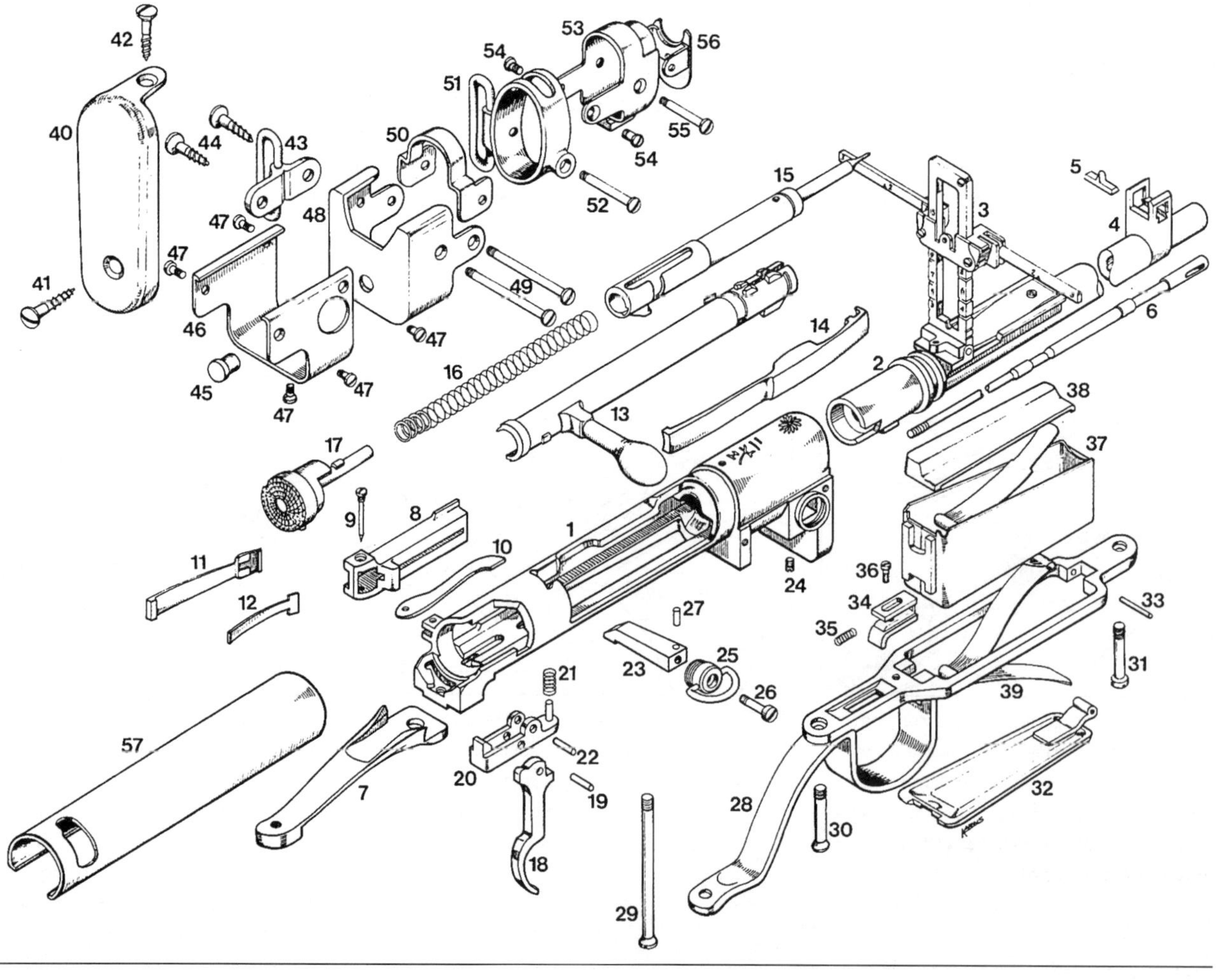

The Japanese Type 99 rifle and its variant Type 2 Paratroop model represent the culmination of a design series that began with the adoption of the Types 29 and 30 bolt-action rifles in 1896-1899. Named for the head of the design commission, the Arisaka rifles are Mauser-like, having the basic Mauser turning bolt and staggered-column box magazine, but include a number of original mechanical features.

The Type 99 rifle and the Type 2 Paratroop model answered both a need for increased production and changes in tactical requirements. The Type 99 rifle introduced the more powerful 7.7x58 mm. cartridge to replace the earlier 6.5 mm. Arisaka round. The 99 also substituted several easier-to-make parts, simplified some of the production machining and replaced some forged parts with stamped sheet-metal fittings.

The Type 2, with its dismountable barrel, was selected as the best of three experimental takedown rifles intended for airborne troops. Wing sights, graduated in kilometers for aerial targets, are seen on some Japanese rifles.

DISASSEMBLY

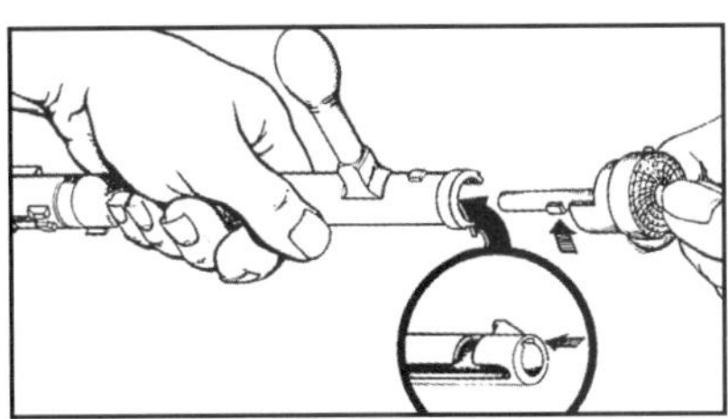

1 To dismount the barrel assembly of the Type 2 Paratroop rifle, turn the barrel key cap (25) counterclockwise until it is free of the threaded retainer in the receiver extension. Pull the cap and barrel key wedge (23) out of the receiver until the assembly stops against the internal key stop screw (24). Pull the barrel assembly forward, straight out of the receiver.

Begin disassembly of the Type 99/Type 2 rifle for routine care and cleaning by insuring that the rifle is unloaded. Press inward on the cleaning rod latch underneath the forestock about 1 inch below the upper band (53), and withdraw the cleaning rod (6).

Disassemble the magazine by pulling the magazine floorplate latch (34), located inside the trigger guard (28), to the rear, allowing the floorplate (32) to swing forward and down out of the magazine box (37). Slide the follower spring (39) and follower (38) out from under the tab at the front of the floorplate and set them aside. Close and latch the floorplate.

Open the bolt (13), and pivot the bolt stop (8) away from the receiver and withdraw the bolt. (Except for a few late war models, Type 99 and Type 2 rifles have a provision for a sliding breech cover (57) to protect the action from dirt and debris. This will slide off the rear of the receiver when the bolt is removed.)

Hold the bolt in one hand, rotate extractor (14) to the right, around the bolt body, until it is clear of the guide groove just ahead of the locking lugs. Push forward on the extractor and slide it off of the extractor collar. The extractor collar is easily damaged, remove it only if replacement is necessary.

Support the bolt by resting the bolt face on a solid surface. Push down on the bolt cap (17) and turn it 90° clockwise to disengage it from the bolt body. Lift the cap clear of the body and withdraw the striker (15) and striker spring (16) from inside the bolt. Reassemble in reverse order. Note, when reassembling the bolt, the cocking stud on the striker must rest on the shallower of the two notches in the rear of the bolt body.

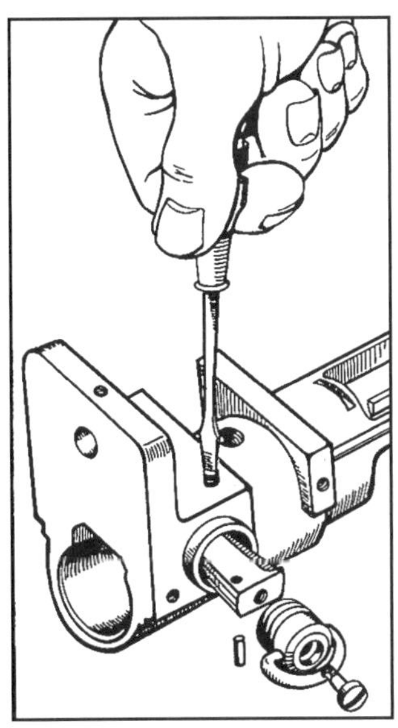

2 To disassemble the receiver and buttstock assembly, remove the tang screw (29) and the front (31) and rear (30) guard screws and lift the trigger guard (28), magazine floorplate, and magazine box (37) out of the buttstock. Pull the barrel key wedge out of the receiver and drive the barrel key pin (27) out of the wedge. Remove the barrel key screw (26) and barrel key cap (25) from the end of the wedge.

Remove the five screws that hold the buttstock collar (46) in place and slide the buttstock collar forward, off of the receiver extension. Lift the buttstock off of the receiver. Take care not to lose the tang (7), which may remain in its mortise in the wrist of the stock, or the forestock locating stud (45), which rides in a clearance hole through the receiver extension.

Turn the barrel key stop screw (24) out of its seat in the flat underside of the receiver extension (Fig. 2) until the barrel key wedge (23) will slide past it and out of the receiver. It is not necessary to remove the key stop screw.

Disassemble the barrel and forestock assembly by removing the forestock collar screws (49), the middle band screw (52), the cleaning rod latch screws (54) and the upper band screw (55). Then remove the appropriate bands and the forestock and handguard from the barrel.

Remove the assembled bolt stop (8) and ejector (10), by taking out the bolt stop screw (9) and lifting the bolt stop and ejector off of the receiver. Slide the ejector forward out of the bolt stop. Drift the bolt stop spring (11) forward out of its seat in the bolt stop and remove the ejector spring (12) from its recess in the bolt stop spring.

Drift out the sear pin (22) and remove the trigger assembly, being careful not to lose the sear spring (21). Drift out the trigger pin (19) to separate the trigger (18) from the sear (20). Drift out the floorplate pin (33) and separate the floorplate from the trigger guard. Remove the floorplate latch screw (36) from the trigger guard to release both the floorplate latch (34) and its spring (35).

J.C. HIGGINS MODEL 33 RIFLE

PARTS LEGEND

1. Barrel
2. Front sight ramp*
3. Front sight
4. Receiver
5. Trigger guard retaining pin
6. Receiver tang
7. Stock bolt washer
8. Stock bolt lock washer
9. Stock bolt
10. Stock washer
11. Rear sight
12. Rear sight elevator
13. Magazine support
14. Magazine support pin
15. Magazine tube
16. Receiver shoe
17. Receiver shoe screw
18. Inside magazine tube
19. Magazine cap
20. Magazine cap pin
21. Magazine spring
22. Magazine follower
23. Action bar
24. Action bar stud*
25. Forearm stud
26. Forearm screw
27. Bolt
28. Extractor, left
29. Extractor retaining pin
30. Extractor retaining roll pin
31. Firing pin retaining pin
32. Extractor, right
33. Firing pin
34. Firing pin spring
35. Extractor spring
36. Buttplate screws (2)
37. Buttplate
38. White plastic buttplate spacer
39. Trigger guard
40. Trigger guard retaining pin spring*
41. Action bar locking lever
42. Action bar locking lever stud*
43. Action bar locking lever spring
44. Safety button
45. Safety button plunger
46. Safety button plunger spring
47. Hammer spring pin
48. Hammer spring
49. Hammer spring guide
50. Hammer strut pin
51. Hammer
52. Hammer pin
53. Trigger
54. Trigger pin
55. Trigger spring
56. Sear pin
57. Sear spring
58. Sear
59. Disconnector
60. Disconnector hinge pin*
61. Disconnector spring
62. Disconnector spring retaining washer*
63. Disconnector spring retaining pin
64. Cartridge lifter spring
65. Cartridge lifter spring retaining pin
66. Cartridge lifter
67. Cartridge lifter pin
68. Magazine throat retaining pin
69. Magazine throat, right
70. Magazine throat, left
71. Buttstock
72. Pistol grip cap and screw
73. Fore-end

* Factory assembled to other major part. Do not disassemble.

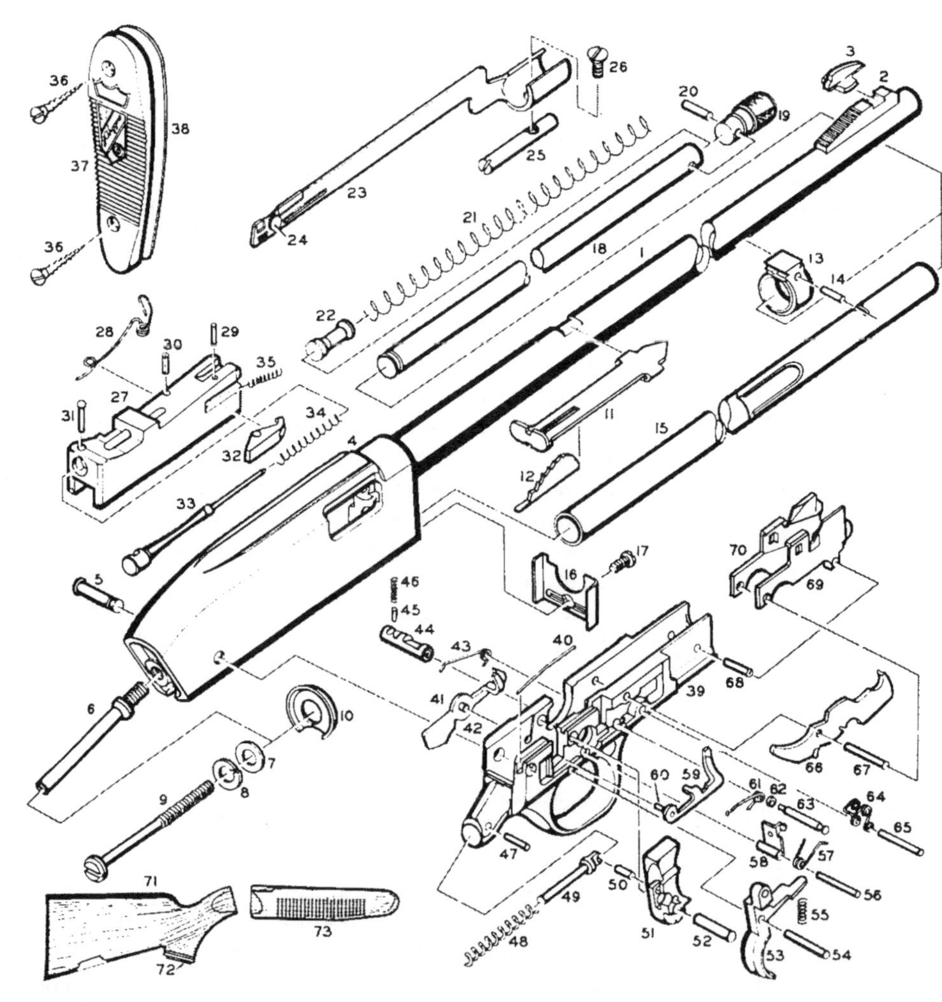

The J.C. Higgins Model 33 slide-action rifle, introduced in 1955, was produced by the High Standard Manufacturing Co. of Hamden, Connecticut, for sale by Sears, Roebuck & Co. Of hammerless design, and fed by a tubular magazine, the Model 33 could handle .22 Short, Long or Long Rifle cartridges interchangeably, in both standard and high-velocity loadings. Magazine capacity was 25 Short, 20 Long or 17 Long Rifle cartridges. The Model 33 weighed 5 lbs, 2 ozs, and had an overall length of 41¾ inches. Barrel length was 23¼ inches.

The Model 33 used an aluminum alloy in the construction of its receiver and trigger guard assembly. The receiver was grooved for tip-off scope mounts. Stocks were of American walnut.

Sears, Roebuck terminated its relationship with High Standard in 1962, effectively causing the discontinuance of the Model 33. High Standard, however, made the rifle under its own name, as the Sport King Pump, until 1975.

DISASSEMBLY

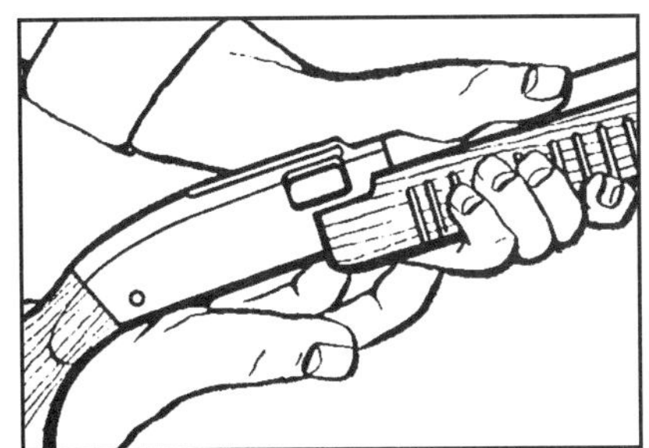

1 Disassemble Model 33 by turning gun upside-down and, using a pencil, push out trigger guard retaining pin (5) from left to right. Grasp trigger guard (39) and pull up and toward buttstock (71). Entire trigger guard assembly will come out as a unit. While gun is still upside-down, place right hand over bottom of receiver (4) from where trigger guard assembly was removed. Turn gun over. With left hand, pull fore-end (73) slowly rearward and bolt (27) will drop out into right hand.

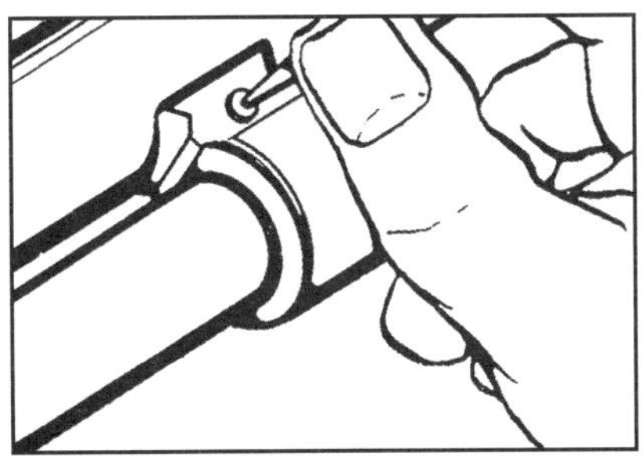

2 Withdraw inside magazine tube (18). Drift out magazine support pin (14) and slide magazine tube (15) forward out of receiver and magazine support (13). Fore-end (73) with action bar (23) attached will now be free of gun.

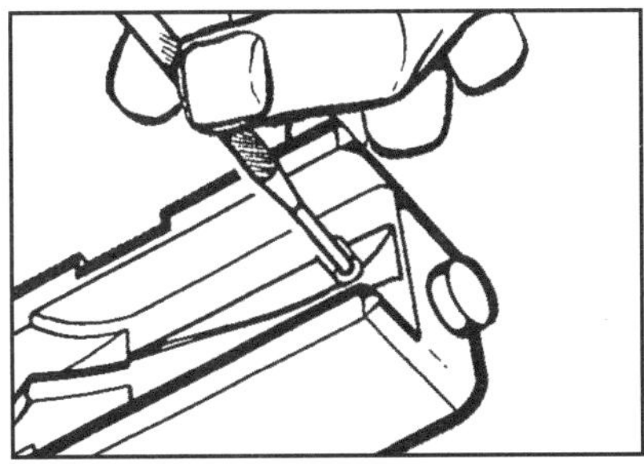

3 Disassemble bolt by drifting out firing pin retaining pin (31) from underside of bolt as shown. Withdraw firing pin (33) and firing pin spring (34). Drift out extractor retaining roll pin (30) and remove left extractor (28). Drift out extractor retaining pin (29) and remove right extractor (32) and extractor spring (35). Reassemble bolt in reverse.

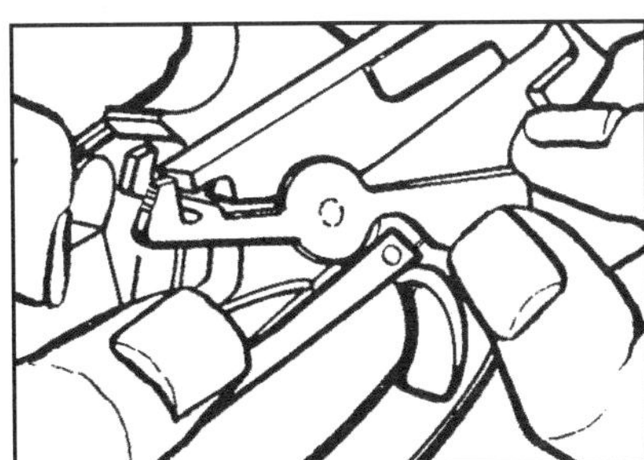

4 Disassemble trigger mechanism by depressing action bar locking lever spring (43) with thumb and lifting out action bar locking lever (41). Remove disconnector (59) in similar fashion. Drift out magazine throat retaining pin (68) and cartridge lifter pin (67). Lift away right and left magazine throats (69 & 70) and cartridge lifter (66). Drift out cartridge lifter spring retaining pin (65) and remove cartridge lifter spring (64).

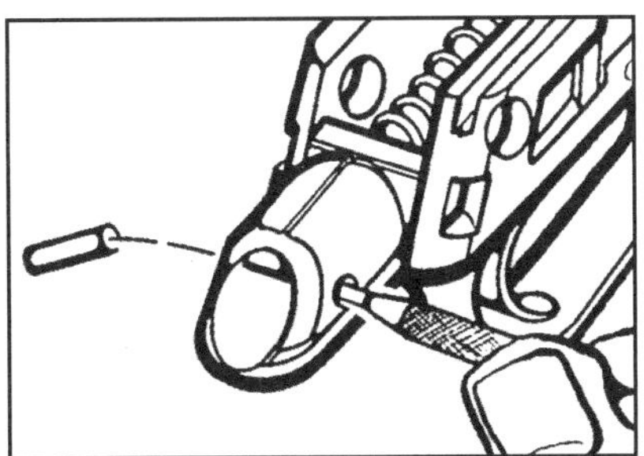

5 Continue by drifting out hammer spring pin (47) over cotton waste to prevent loss of hammer spring (48) and hammer spring guide (49). This relieves tension on hammer (51).

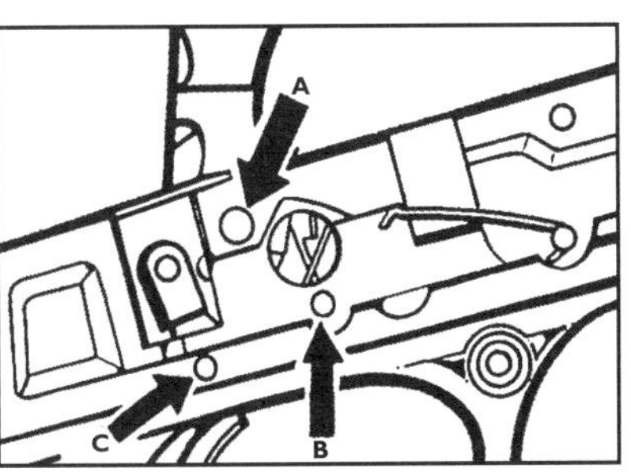

6 Next, drift out hammer pin (52) and remove hammer. Drift out sear pin (56) and remove sear (58) and sear spring (57). Drift out trigger pin (54) and remove trigger (53) and trigger spring (55). Do not remove disconnector spring retaining pin (63) unless absolutely necessary as disconnector spring retaining washer (62) is press fitted to pin and may become loose if repeatedly removed. Reassemble trigger guard and gun in reverse.

JOHNSON M1941 SEMI-AUTOMATIC

PARTS LEGEND

1. Barrel and collar
2. Receiver
3. Rear sight elevator
4. Rear sight assembly
5. Bolt stop plate and plunger
6. Ejector
7. Ejector pin retainer spring
8. Ejector hinge pin
9. Spring retaining pin
10. Magazine retainer pin
11. Latch spring guide
12. Barrel latch
13. Return spring plunger
14. Barrel return spring
15. Latch hinge pin
16. Detent retainer pin
17. Detent
18. Detent spring
19. Cross pin, front
20. Cross pin, rear
21. Bolt catch
22. Bolt
23. Bolt stop
24. Firing pin spring
25. Firing pin
26. Operating handle
27. Extractor
28. Locking cam unit
29. Firing pin stop
30. Hinge pin
31. Link
32. Mainspring follower
33. Hammer spring
34. Hammer strut
35. Hammer strut pin
36. Hammer
37. Sear
38. Trigger pin link pin
39. Trigger spring
40. Spring plunger
41. Safety catch cam
42. Trigger
43. Trigger pin
44. Sear stop pin
45. Hammer hinge pin
46. Sear housing
47. Magazine cover hinge pin
48. Magazine cover
49. Magazine cover spring
50. Magazine axis
51. Magazine spring
52. Magazine follower
53. Magazine housing
54. Fore-end
55. Recoil stop screw
56. Recoil stop
57. Recoil stop screw
58. Fore-end screw
59. Washer
60. Buttstock
61. Upper buttplate screw
62. Buttplate
63. Buttplate screw
64. Mainspring tube cap and buffer assembly
65. Mainspring
66. Trigger guard wood screw
67. Trigger guard screw
68. Trigger guard and safety assembly
69. Recoil stop screw
70. Recoil stop
71. Recoil stop screw
72. Stock screw
73. Washer

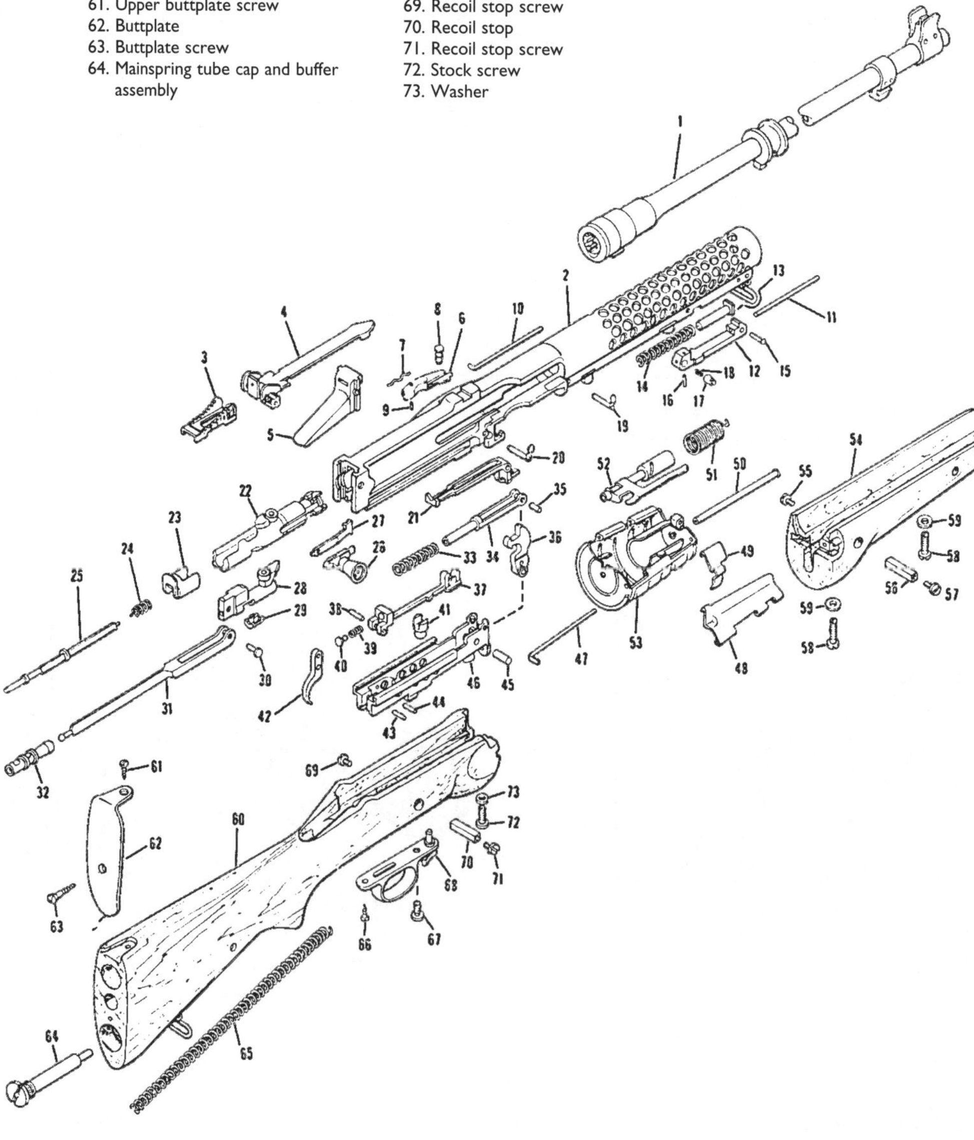

JOHNSON

The Johnson rotary-magazine, semiautomatic recoil-operated rifle was invented just prior to World War II by firearms designer Melvin M. Johnson. Working with Marlin Firearms, Johnson submitted a prototype military rifle to the Army Ordnance Board in 1938. In 1940, however, the Board rejected the rifle as too heavy, and unreliable with a fixed bayonet.

Johnson refined his design, renaming it the Model 1941. That same year he received an order from the Netherlands Purchasing Commission for 70,000 rifles, chambered for .30-06 caliber, to be issued in the East Indies.

Soon after production started, the newly created Marine Corps parachute echelons became interested in the Model 41 due to the ease of removing the barrel. It was adopted and saw action with Marine Raider forces in the Solomon Islands. The Marines procured their rifles from Dutch government in exile, which banned their export after the Japanese had overrun the Dutch East Indies. The only other military order for Model 41 rifles came from the Chilean government, which ordered 1,000 in 7mm. in 1943.

Total production of the Model 41 rifles is believed to be around 30,000. In 1953, the Winfield Arms Co. bought the Dutch rifles as surplus for importation to the U.S. In addition, Winfield offered sporterized Johnson rifles in .270 Winchester, 7 mm. Mauser, and .30- 06 calibers.

DISASSEMBLY

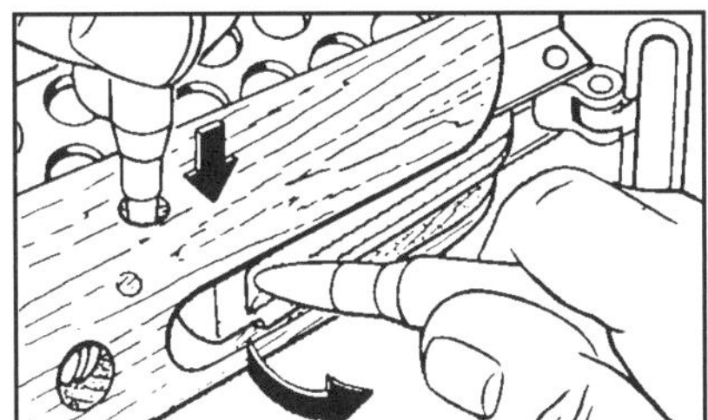

1 To remove the barrel, disengage the barrel latch detent (17) by inserting bullet end of cartridge in the hole in the fore-end as shown. While the detent is depressed, push the barrel back slightly, permitting the barrel latch to drop downward on its hinge. If the latch does not fall, assist by inserting bullet of another round in the hole in the underside of the latch (12). Then press backward on the operating handle (26) with the right forefinger to unlock the bolt from the barrel, and withdraw the barrel from the receiver.

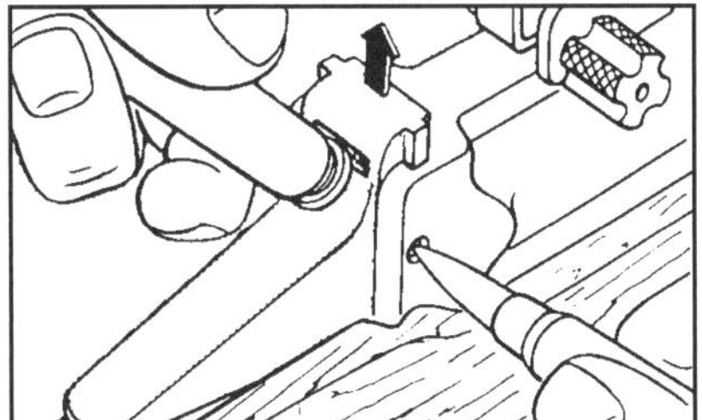

2 Remove the bolt stop plate (5) by pushing in on the plunger, which extends through right rear side of receiver. Use the rim of another cartridge to lift the bolt stop plate out of its slot in the receiver. Then the bolt stop (23) can be removed from the rear of the receiver.

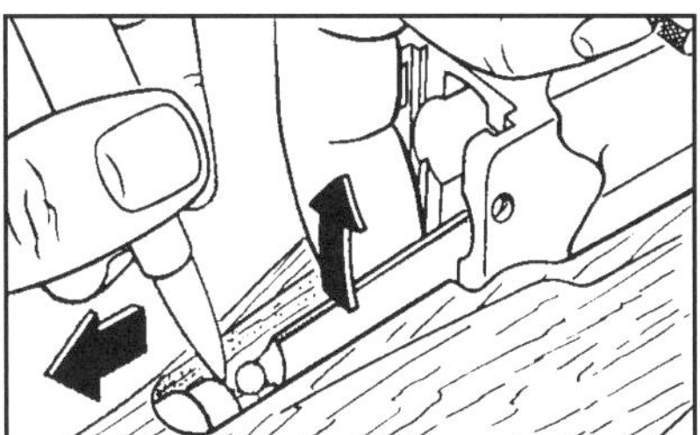

3 Before the bolt assembly can be removed, the link (31) must be disconnected from the mainspring follower (32). Depress the follower with a cartridge or screwdriver and lift up on the link. Then pull the bolt assembly back about 2 inches.

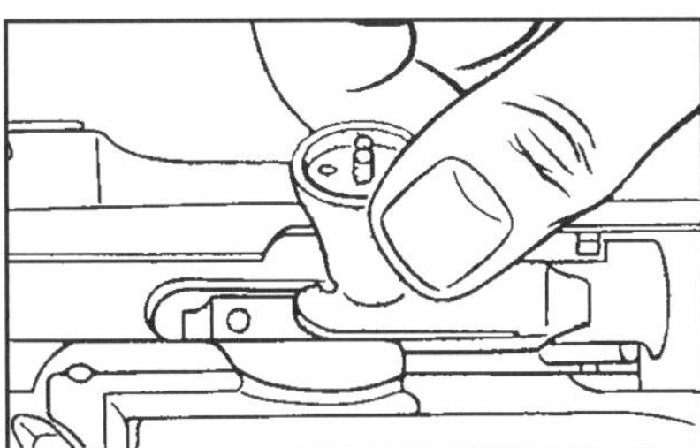

4 When the bolt is back 2 inches, grasp the link to hold the bolt group in place and at the same time pull up on the operating handle spindle and push operating handle forward until it clears the shoulder in the extractor, then lift out. Lift out the extractor (27). Next, pull rearward on link to remove bolt group from receiver.

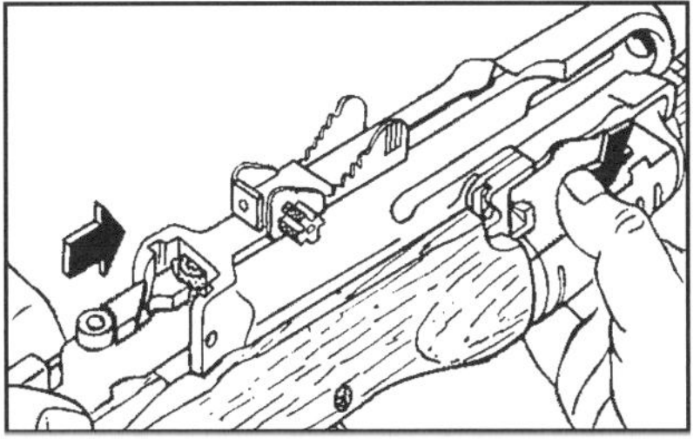

5 When reassembling the gun, assemble bolt (22) and firing pin assembly before inserting them in the receiver (2). Be sure cams and rollers line up as bolt slides in. To get bolt forward, depress bolt catch (21) by pushing in magazine cover (48).

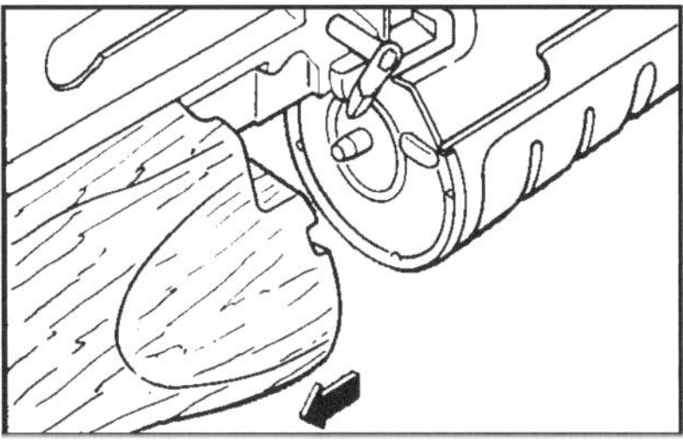

6 The buttstock (60) and trigger assembly are retained by the rear cross pin (20). To remove the cross pin, push in on the spring end and rotate it about 45° to the open section on the receiver and pry it out of the receiver. Sliding buttstock and trigger assembly to rear exposes magazine assembly retaining pins.

L.C. SMITH DOUBLE-BARREL

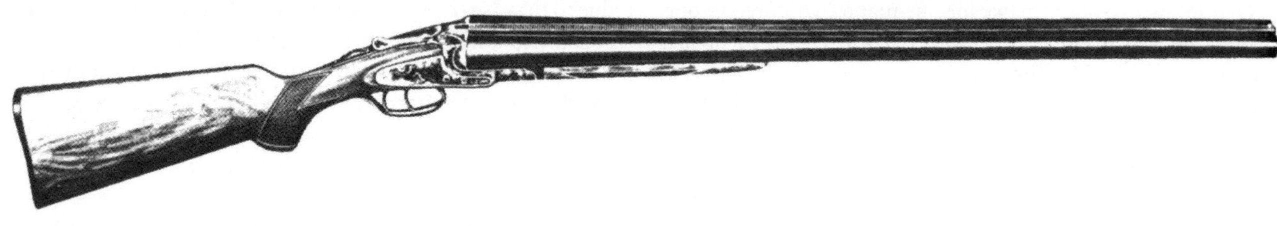

PARTS LEGEND

1. Barrels
2. Front sight
3. Extractor
4. Extractor screw
5. Trip
6. Bolt
7. Coupler
8. Coupler screw
9. Top-lever
10. Frame
11. Cocking rod (2)
12. Fore-end iron
13. Fore-end spring pin
14. Extractor actuator bar
15. Extractor actuator
16. Extractor actuator pin
17. Extractor actuator spring
18. Rear fore-end screw (2)
19. Fore-end spring
20. Fore-end spring retracting spring
21. Fore-end screw (2)
22. Fore-end
23. Trip spring
24. Bolt spring
25. Right lifter
26. Firing pin (2)
27. Trigger plate screw
28. Left lifter
29. Safety button and pin
30. Safety spring
31. Safety spring screw
32. Trigger plate screw bushing
33. Grip cap
34. Grip cap screw
35. Buttplate
36. Buttplate screw (2)
37. Lockplate, right
38. Lockplate retaining screw (2)
39. Lockplate connector screw
40. Mainspring retaining screw (2)
41. Sear pin
42. Mainspring (2)
43. Hammer, right
44. Sear, right
45. Bridle, right
46. Bridle screw (4)
47. Hammer pin (2)
48. Trigger guard
49. Trigger guard screw
50. Lockplate, left
51. Sear, left
52. Bridle, left
53. Hammer, left
54. Trigger plate
55. Trigger plate retaining screw, front
56. Top-lever screw
57. Trigger pin
58. Selector
59. Safety stud screw
60. Safety stud
61. Trigger plate retaining screw, rear
62. Selector spring
63. Selector spring screw
64. Sear plate
65. Firing plate
66. Spur spring screw
67. Recoil weight spring
68. Recoil weight pin
69. Recoil weight
70. Spur spring
71. Spur link
72. Spur link pin (2)
73. Spur
74. Spur ball
75. Trigger
76. Cocking plate screw
77. Cocking plate

Note: Left lock shown partially assembled for clarity.

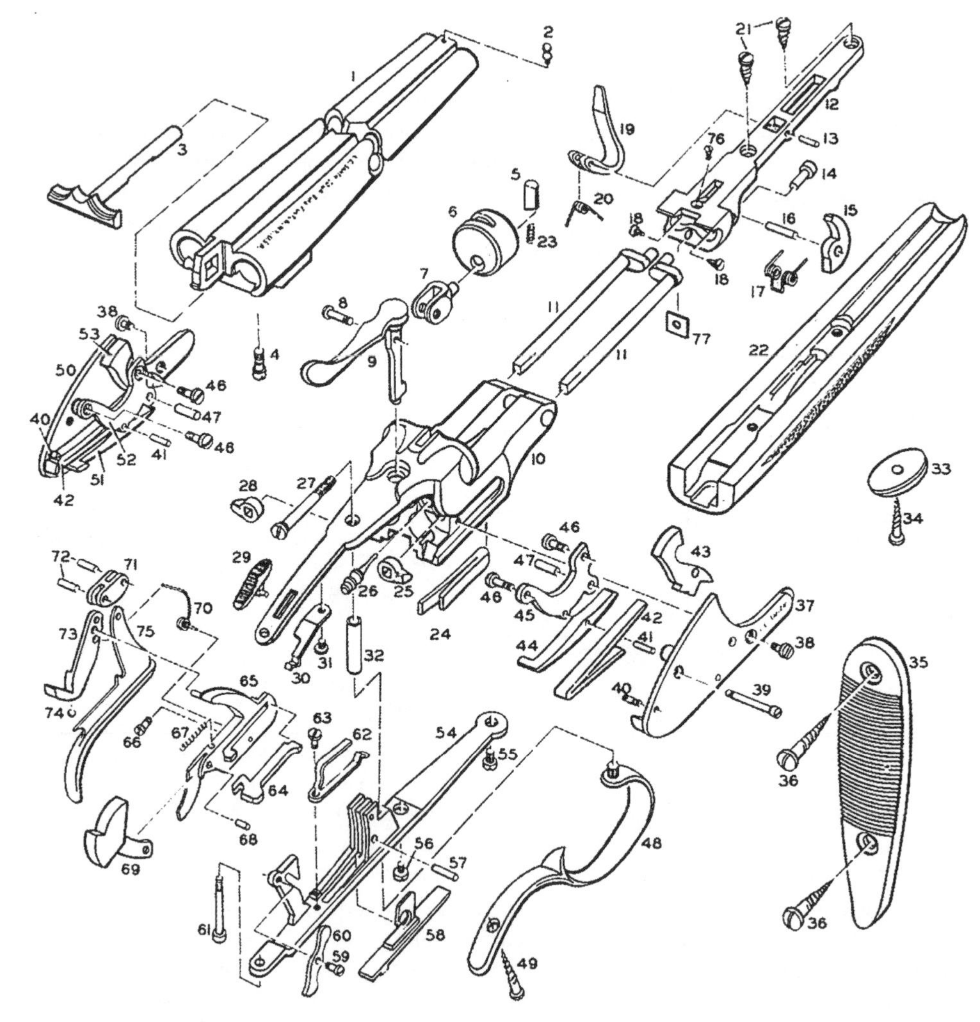

L. C. Smith shotguns were manufactured by the Hunter Arms Co., Inc., of Fulton, New York, beginning in about 1889. They were based on models first introduced in about 1880 by L. C. Smith at the W. H. Baker Co. of Syracuse, New York. By 1881, Smith had become proprietor of the Baker Gun Co. selling double barrel hammer guns and later introducing hammerless doubles. In 1888 Smith sold the company to John Hunter, Sr.

During its half century of existence, the Hunter Arms Co. also manufactured Fulton, Hunter, and other shotguns, including many private-brand shotguns, for distribution in addition to their L. C. Smith guns.

L. C. Smith double-barrel guns are distinguished among United States shotguns by their side-lock construction, in which the lock parts are carried on side-plates inletted partly in the action body and partly in the stock. The company early adopted the Baker top-bolt for holding the gun closed. This bolt, later used also by Fox and Ithaca, was a rotating cylinder slotted to engage a heavy extension of the top rib between the barrels, the engaging surfaces being sloped so as to tighten automatically.

L. C. Smith doubles were produced in a number of grades, all of the same basic design but differing in features (single trigger, beaver-tail fore-end, and ventilated rib) and in quality of wood and workmanship, including finish and engraving.

At end of World War 11 the Hunter Arms Co. was purchased by Marlin Firearms Co., and, under the operating name of L. C. Smith Gun Co., produced a few grades of L.C. Smith guns until about 1950, when production ended.

DISASSEMBLY

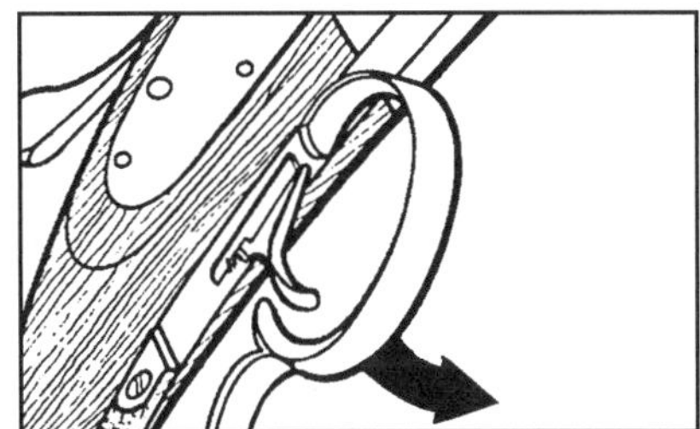

1 With gun closed, remove fore-end by pulling front end away from barrels. Press top-lever to right, lower buttstock, and lift barrels off action. Leave hammers cocked. Remove trigger guard screw (49) and unscrew trigger guard (48) counterclockwise.

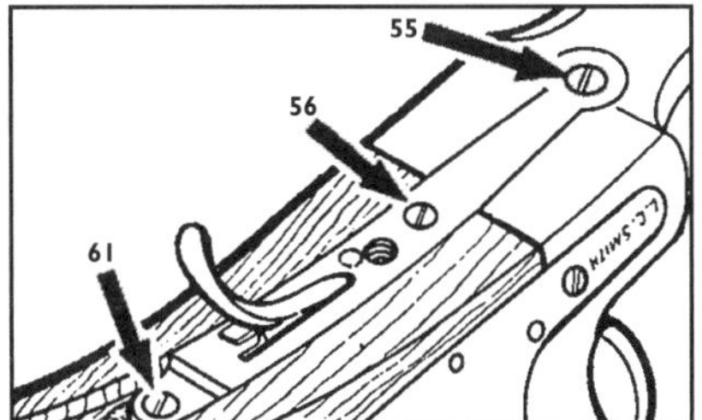

2 With top-lever (9) moved to right, remove trigger plate screw (27). Turn gun over and remove trigger plate retaining screws (55 and 61). Remove top-lever screw (56), and entire trigger mechanism may now be lifted away. Do not perform any further disassembly on this mechanism as it requires rather delicate balancing.

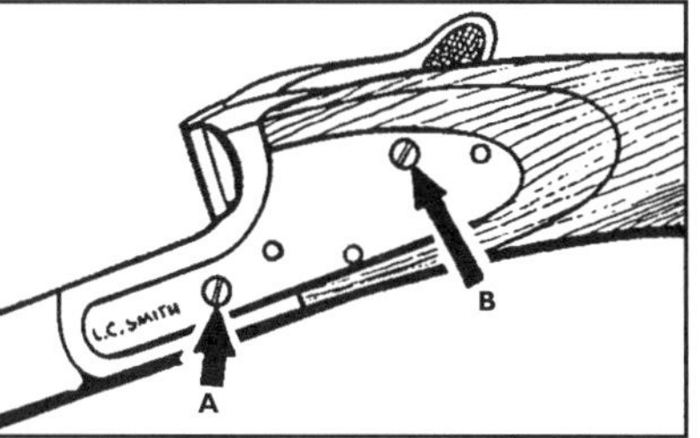

3 Remove lockplate retaining screws (38) from right and left sides of gun (see A) and lockplate connector screw (39) from right side of gun (see B). Right and left locks may now be removed, with slight tapping of frame (10) with heel of hand if required to loosen them. Be careful not to trip sears (44 and 51).

4 Up-end frame and firing pins (26) will drop out. Place small steel rod against exposed long end of bolt spring (24) and padded steel bar against frame on opposite side. Apply a C-clamp and take up tension on bolt spring. With clamp in place, remove coupler screw (8) and coupler (7), and then top-lever (9). Release tension on bolt spring but do not remove it as it is impossible to replace without a special jig. Bolt (6), trip (5), and trip spring (23) may now be removed.

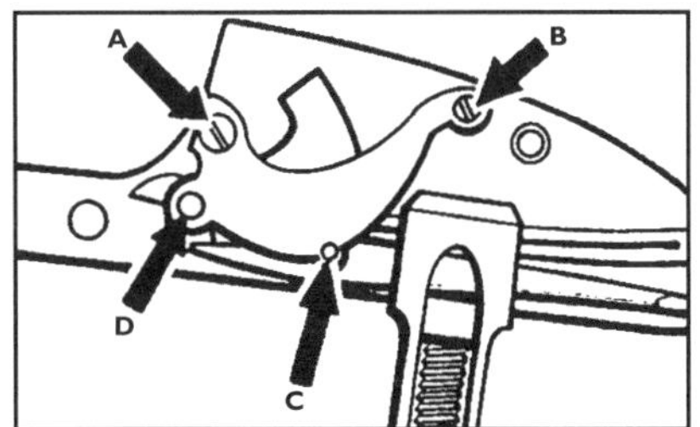

5 To disassemble either lock assembly, apply mainspring vise (such as Civil War type) between sear and mainspring (42) and take up all slack. Remove bridle screws (46) at A and B. Do not drift out sear pin C or trigger pin D. Remove bridle, mainspring, and sear as a unit (with vise), and hammer.

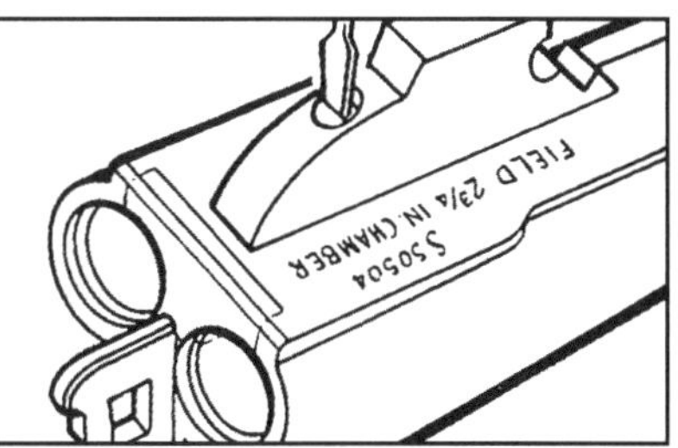

6 Unscrew extractor screw (4) and withdraw extractor. Reassemble gun in reverse order. After top-lever has been connected to its spring, and as trigger plate is being dropped into its recess in frame, a piece of tapered and hardened steel rod must be inserted in top-lever screw hole through clearance hole in trigger plate, and bottom of top-lever forced over until it drops into hole in trigger plate.

LEE-ENFIELD RIFLE NO. I, MARK III

PARTS LEGEND

1. Barrel
2. Foresight blade
3. Inner band
4. Inner band screw
5. Backsight assembly
6. Backsight protector
7. Backsight protector screw
8. Fore-end collar
9. Protector nut
10. Action body
11. Safety catch
12. Locking bolt
13. Safety catch washer
14. Safety spring
15. Safety spring screw
16. Back trigger guard screw
17. Stock bolt plate
18. Swivel screw (3)
19. Butt swivel bracket
20. Swivel bracket screw (2)
21. Sling swivel (2)
22. Stock bolt washer
23. Stock bolt
24. Stock bolt wad (leather)
25. Magazine catch pin
26. Retaining spring
27. Magazine catch
28. Retaining spring screw
29. Sear spring
30. Sear
31. Trigger pin
32. Trigger
33. Front trigger guard screw
34. Trigger guard
35. Magazine
36. Front trigger guard screw bushing
37. Buttplate trap
38. Buttplate trap pin
39. Buttplate screw (2)
40. Buttplate
41. Buttplate trap spring
42. Buttplate trap spring screw
43. Outer band
44. Fore-end stud spring
45. Fore-end stud
46. Back nose cap screw
47. Piling swivel
48. Nose cap
49. Nose cap nut
50. Front nose cap screw
51. Inner band screw spring
52. Ejector screw
53. Striker screw
54. Cocking piece
55. Breechbolt
56. Mainspring
57. Striker
58. Breechbolt head
59. Extractor screw
60. Extractor
61. Extractor spring
62. Cutoff
63. Cutoff screw
64. Buttstock
65. Fore-end
66. Rear handguard
67. Front handguard

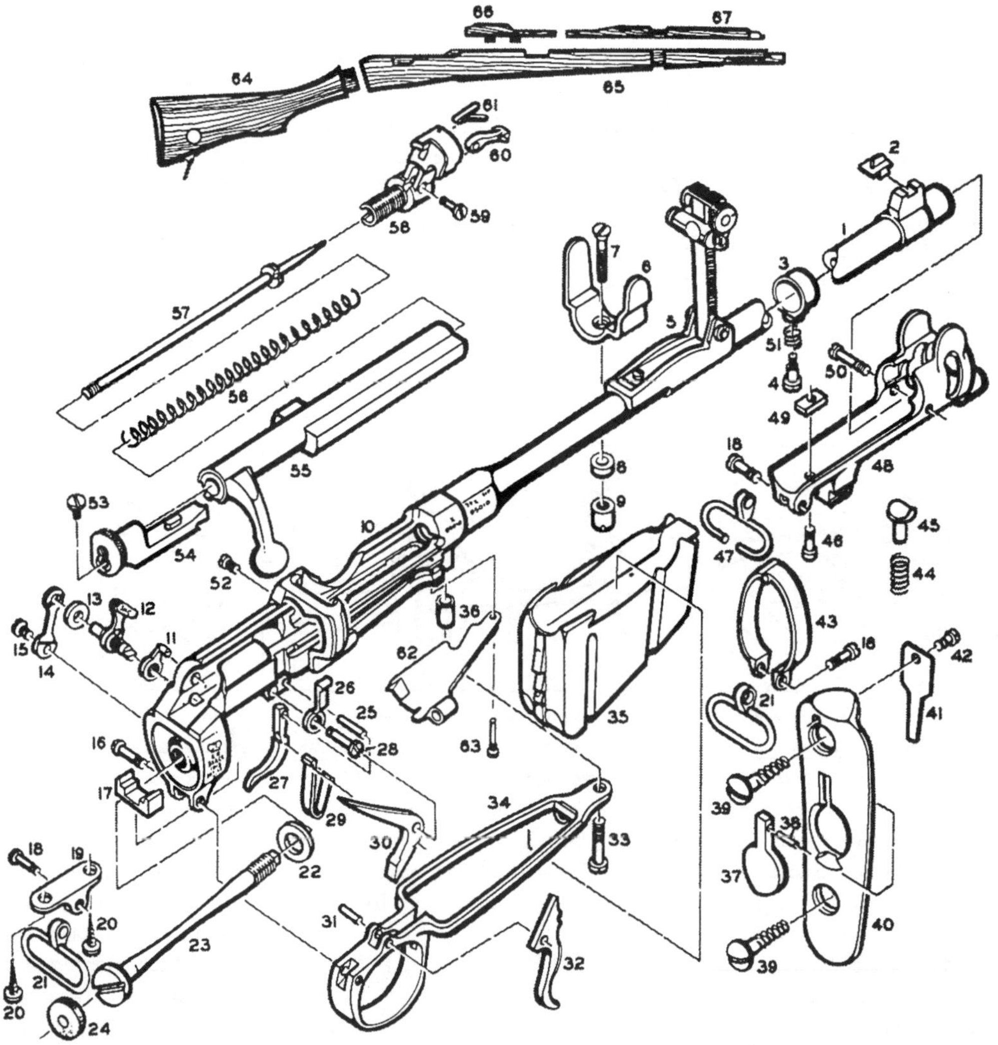

The caliber .303 British Short Magazine Lee-Enfield Rifle, Mark III was accepted for British military service in January, 1907. The new rifle was developed from the Short Magazine Lee Enfield Rifle, Mark I, which had been adopted in 1902.

The Mark III version is dimensionally similar to the earlier Mark I but is shorter and heavier, weighing 8 lbs. 10½ ozs.

The Mark III is fitted with a magazine cutoff so that contents of the 10-shot detachable box magazine could be held in reserve while the rifle was used as a single-loader. The receiver is fitted with a bridge-type charger guide with slots sloped to the front so that the empty charger is automatically ejected from the charger guide as the bolt is closed.

The Mark III has a fully adjustable rear sight and square-blade Patridge-type front sight. An additional dial sight is provided on early manufacture rifles for long-range firing. Before and after the First World War many changes were made in establishing specifications for the Mark III rifle.

In 1926, British Service rifles were redesignated and the Short Magazine Lee-Enfield Rifle, Mark III, officially became designated as the Rifle No. 1. Mark III.

DISASSEMBLY

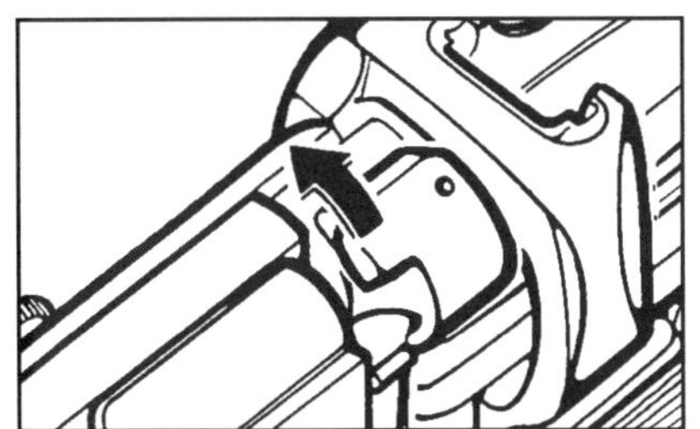

1 Commence disassembly by first removing magazine (35) and then rotating breechbolt (55) counterclockwise and withdrawing rearward as far as it will go. Disengage breechbolt head (58) from retaining spring (26) by rotating it as shown. It will disengage with an audible click. Withdraw bolt from action body (10).

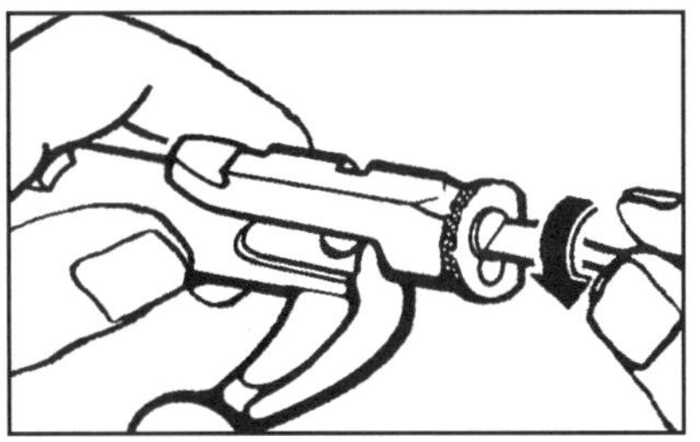

2 Disassemble breechbolt by removing striker screw (53), and then unscrewing breechbolt head from the other end of the breechbolt.

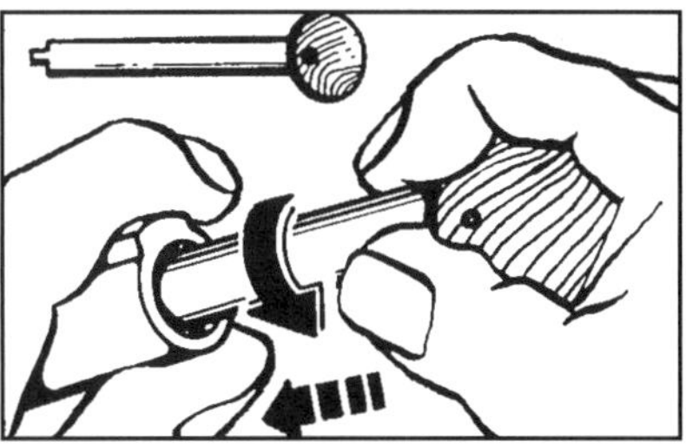

3 To remove striker (57), use an Enfield bolt-stripping wrench or improvise, using a 6-inch-long, ⅜-inch O.D. brass tube. File two opposing notches in one end as shown above, and affix a wooden ball on other end as a handle. Drill through handle and tube with ⅛-inch drill and insert pin. Insert tool into front end of breech bolt until notches engage notches in striker collar. Unscrew striker from cocking piece (54). Keep steady pressure to prevent mainspring (56) from expelling striker.

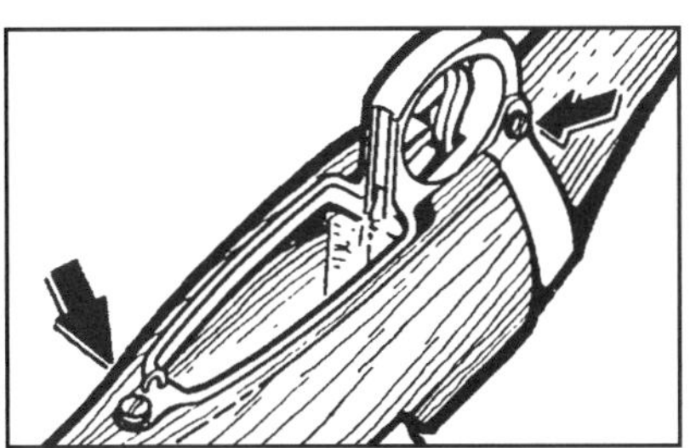

4 Remove back and front trigger guard screws (16 and 33, right and left arrows respectively). Lift away trigger guard (34). Remove back and front nose cap screws (46 and 50 respectively) and pull nose cap (48) forward off rifle. Remove inner band screw (4), and swivel screw (18) from outer band (43). Open and lift away outer band. Front handguard (67), fore-end (65), and rear handguard (66) may now be removed in that order.

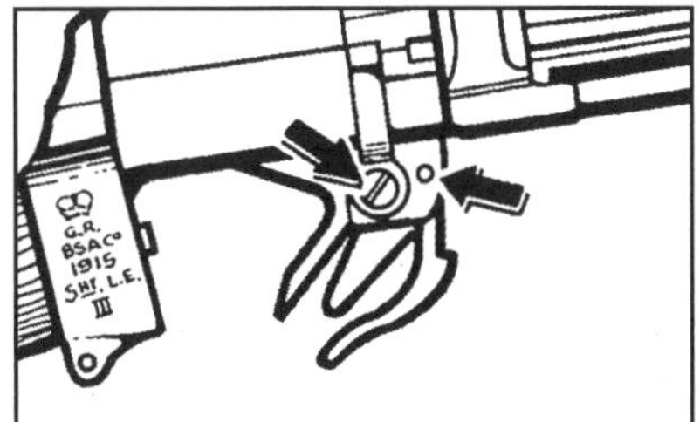

5 Remove retaining spring screw (28, left arrow) and lift away retaining spring (26), sear (30), and sear spring (29). Drift out magazine catch pin (25, right arrow), remove magazine catch (27).

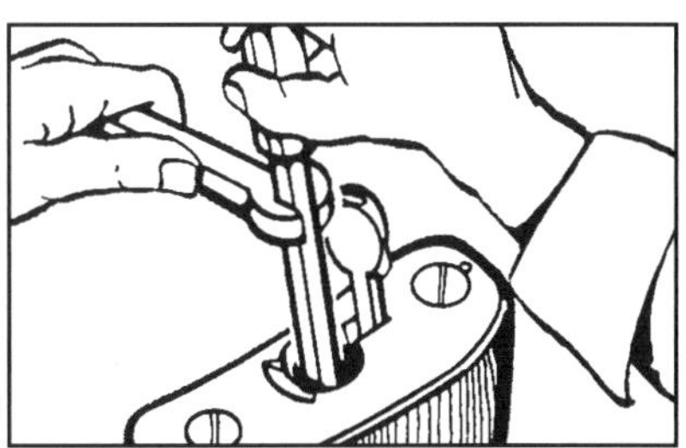

6 Should removal of buttstock (64) become necessary, open buttplate trap (37) and with a piece of bent wire fish out leather stock bolt wad (24). Insert long, square shanked screwdriver and engage slot in stock bolt (23). While applying downward pressure, place an appropriately sized open-end wrench against screwdriver shank and turn out stock bolt. A small quantity of penetrating oil may aid this operation as the bolts are often rusted in. Reassemble rifle in reverse.

LEE ENFIELD NO.4 RIFLE

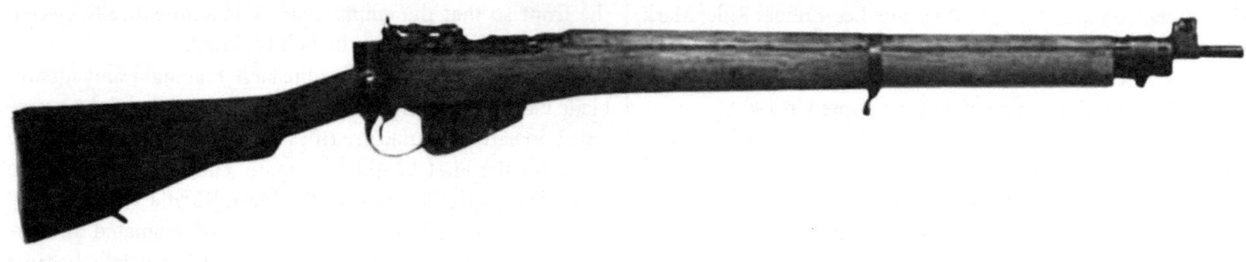

PARTS LEGEND

1. Striker screw
2. Cocking piece
3. Breechbolt (stripped)
4. Mainspring
5. Striker
6. Breechbolt head
7. Extractor
8. Extractor screw
9. Extractor spring
10. Bolt (assembled)
11. Locking bolt screw
12. Locking bolt spring
13. Locking bolt
14. Safety catch
15. Rear guard screw
16. Magazine catch screw
17. Ejector screw
18. Mk. III rear sight
19. Spacer
20. Rear sight hinge pin
21. Sight detent plunger
22. Detent spring
23. Hinge pin lock pin
24. Bolt release stop
25. Bolt release
26. Bolt release spring
27. Sear hinge pin
28. Magazine catch
29. Sear spring
30. Sear
31. Body, No. 4 Mk. I (receiver)
32. Trigger
33. Trigger pin
34. Trigger guard
35. Magazine
36. Front guard screw
37. Guard screw lock washer
38. Fore-end
39. Handguard, front
40. Swivel band
41. Swivel band screw
42. Sling swivel
43. Upper band screw
44. Upper band
45. Handguard, rear
46. Foresight protector screw
47. Foresight protector (Mk. II)
48. Stock bolt
49. Stock bolt lock washer
50. Buttplate
51. Buttplate screw (2)
52. Lower band

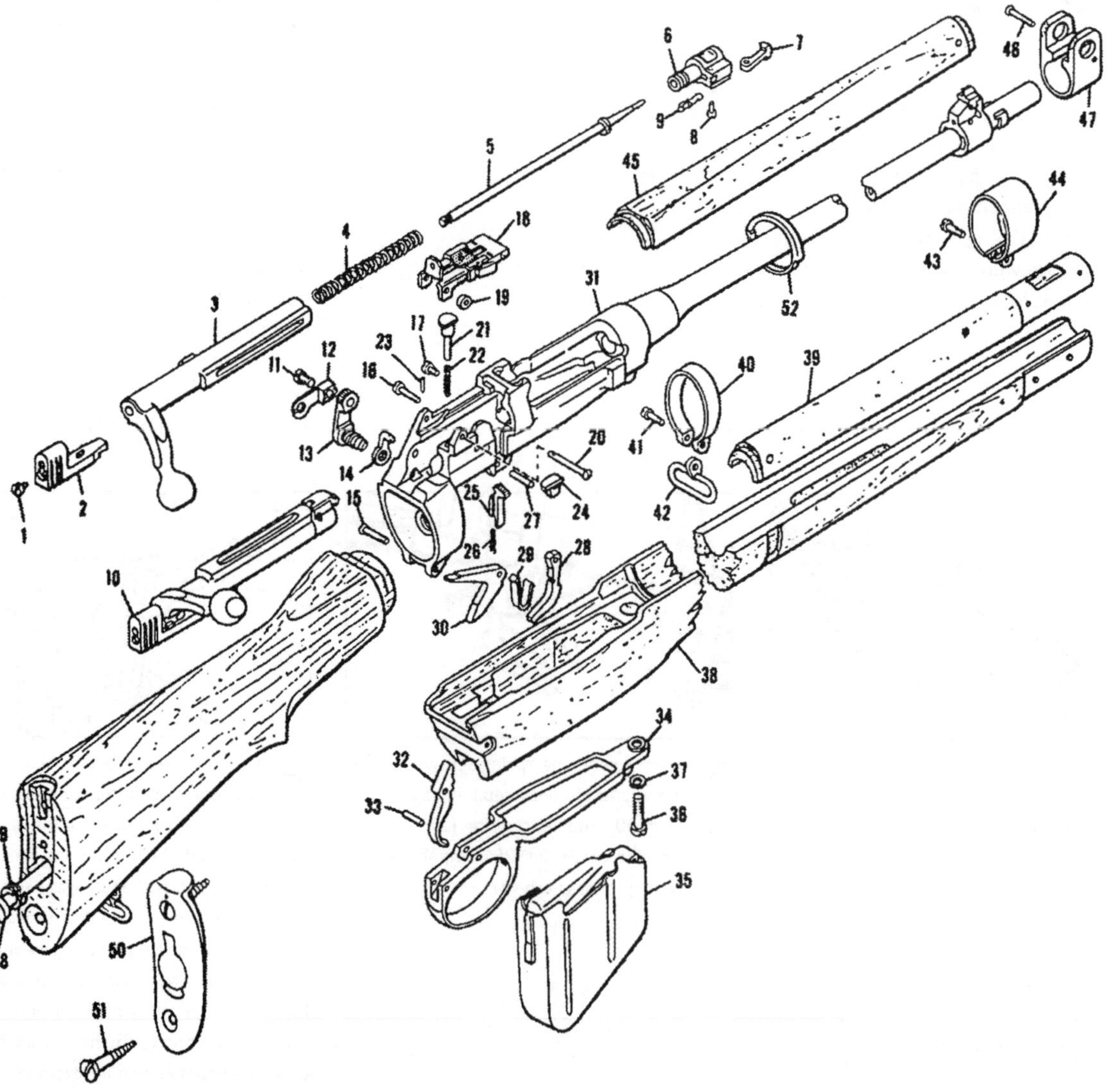

As a result of service in World War I the shortcomings of the British bolt-action Lee-Enfield Rifle Mk. 111* were recognized and, in the 1920s, the SMLE Mk. VI was designed to replace it. The British changed their system of rifle nomenclature and the SMLE Mk. VI became known as the Rifle No. 4 Mk. I.

The Rifle No. 4 Mk. I features an aperture rear sight, heavier barrel, simplified stock and improved bolt-retaining system. During World War II the design was simplified by eliminating the separate bolt release and labled the Rifle No. 4 Mk. 1*.

Since England's small arms production was greatly strained by wartime demands, the Stevens Arms Co., a division of Savage Arms Corp., manufactured No. 4 rifles under the Lend Lease Act. These rifles are found marked "U. S. Property."

Like other military rifles, the No. 4 rifle will be found in a variety of finishes, ranging from the usually finely made Canadian Long Branch Arsenal guns to the cruder Lee-Enfields turned out in England right after Dunkirk. A modified No. 4 rifle, shortened and lightened for jungle fighting, was designated Rifle No. 5 Mk. I. It has exactly the same mechanism as the No. 4 but is far handier. The Rifle No. 4 Mk. I (T) was fitted with a cheekpiece and the No. 32 telescope sight.

In an effort to improve the trigger arrangement, the Rifles No. 4 Mk. 1/2 and Mk. 1/3 had the trigger pivoted to the body (receiver) instead of to the trigger guard.

As a military weapon the Lee design was superior to many of its bolt-action contemporaries. It has a 10-shot magazine and a 20 percent shorter bolt stroke than the Mauser or Mannlicher, plus about 20 percent less bolt rotation. These features, combined with a smoothly working bolt, make the LeeEnfield excellent for rapid-fire. The Lee-Enfield has a few drawbacks, however, the rear locking arrangement is not quite so favorable for accuracy as the front locking type and the .303 cartridge is rimmed, making feeding critical although it simplifies the headspace problem.

DISASSEMBLY

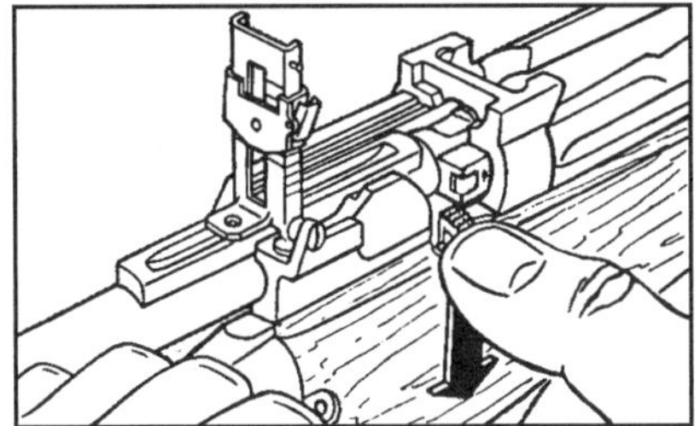

1 There are 2 types of bolt release in No. 4 rifles. To operate the type in the No. 4 Mk. I rifle, the rear sight (18) is lifted first and then the bolt release (25) is depressed. Pull the bolt all the way back and release the bolt release. Rotate breechbolt head (6) up in line with rib on bolt and pull it free of gun.

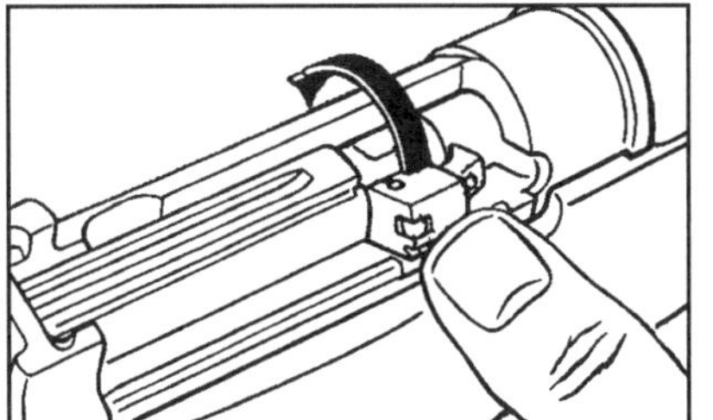

2 The bolt release in the No. 4 Mk. I* rifle is far simpler and eliminates three parts. Simply open the bolt and ease it back until breechbolt head rides out of its guide groove into the milled-away portion ¼-inch back from the end of the receiver ring. Rotate the breechbolt head upward and pull the bolt free of the gun. Flip up the rear sight if necessary.

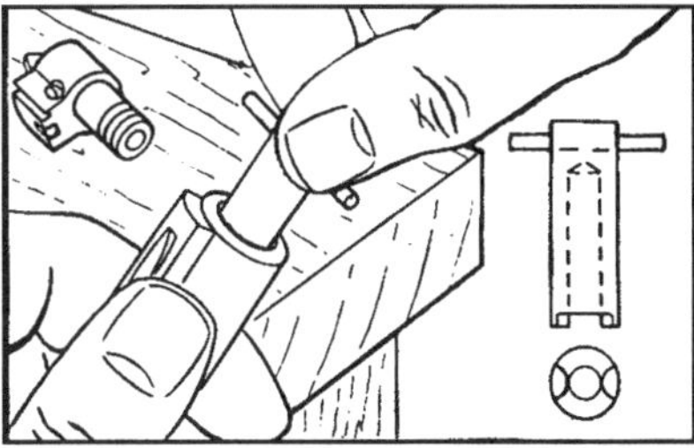

3 To remove striker (5), unscrew breechbolt head and striker screw (1) in cocking piece (2). Unscrew striker with a simple tool made for the purpose as shown (do not attempt to remove striker with pliers). This tool engages in the notches on striker shoulder. Striker can only be removed from front of bolt.

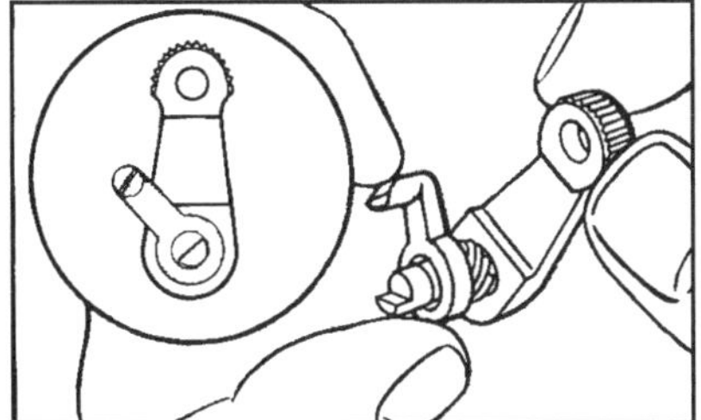

4 The locking bolt (13) has a multiple thread to move the safety catch (14) in and out of engagement. To operate properly, the pieces must line up when tightened together as shown in insert. To align the pieces, be sure flat on safety catch is roughly parallel to flat on locking bolt pin before engaging threads.

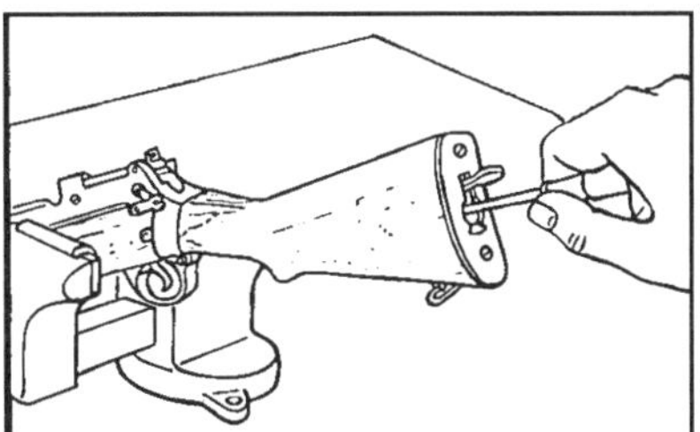

5 To remove buttstock, clamp rifle in padded vise, open trap in buttplate (50), remove felt wad, and unscrew stock bolt (48) with long screwdriver.

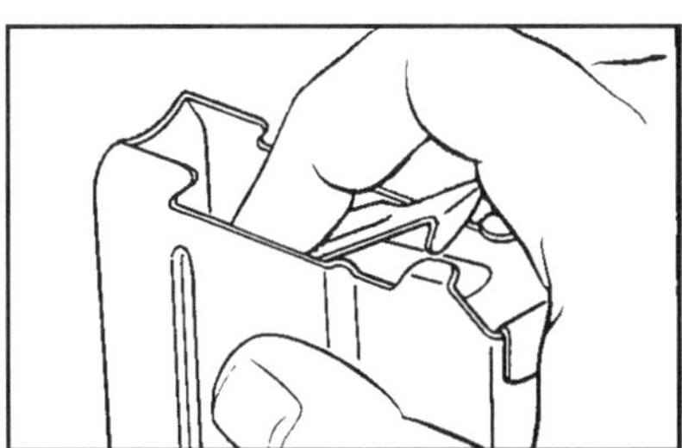

6 To remove magazine follower and spring, push rear of follower down far enough for the front end to clear tab-like projections on the magazine, then ease out follower and spring.

MADSEN MODEL 1958 RIFLE

PARTS LEGEND

1. Assembled bolt
2. Firing pin nut
3. Nut retainer
4. Nut retainer spring
5. Nut retainer pin
6. Cocking piece
7. Safety catch pin
8. Safety
9. Safety catch spring
10. Safety catch
11. Firing pin spring
12. Left locking seat
13. Bolt
14. Extractor
15. Receiver
16. Firing pin
17. Rear sight leaf spring
18. Sight slide catch
19. Leaf spring keeper
20. Sight slide spring
21. Sight slide
22. Sight leaf bushing
23. Sight leaf
24. Aperture set screw
25. Aperture
26. Windage screw flange
27. Flange pin
28. Windage screw
29. Leaf bushing lock screw
30. Windage scale
31. Windage knob pin
32. Windage index ball
33. Windage knob
34. Index spring
35. Index spring plug
36. Handguard clamp
37. Handguard
38. Barrel
39. Front sight hood
40. Sight post
41. Sight post lock screw
42. Upper band
43. Upper band spring
44. Stock
45. Lower band spring
46. Lower band
47. Right locking seat
48. Locking seat screw(2)
49. Front guard screw
50. Sear spring
51. Ejector/bolt stop
52. Sear
53. Sear pin
54. Ejector spring
55. Trigger pin
56. Trigger
57. Magazine floorplate
58. Floorplate catch
59. Floorplate catch spring
60. Floorplate catch guide bushing
61. Magazine spring
62. Magazine follower
63. Rear guard screw
64. Trigger guard

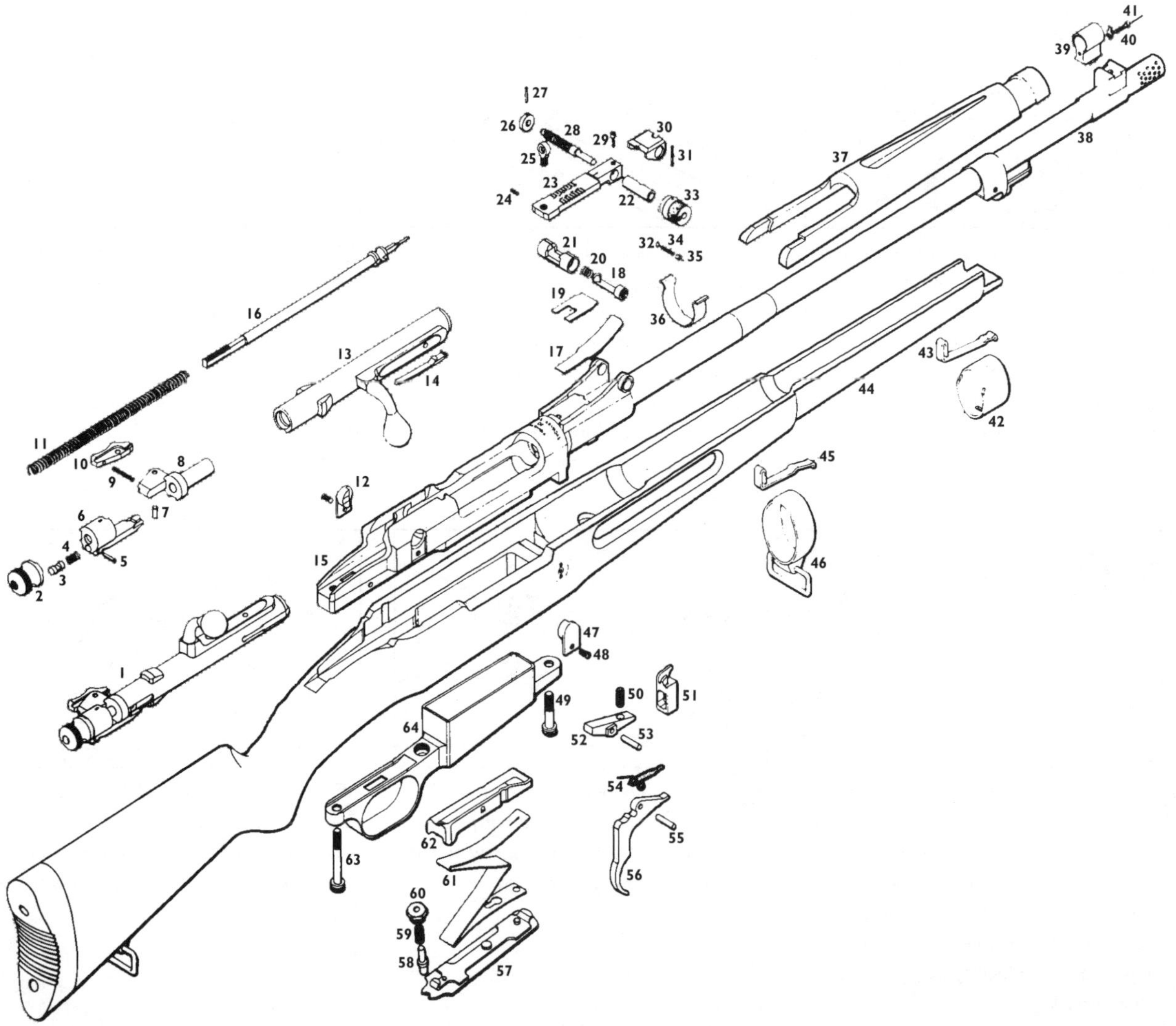

The bolt-action Madsen Model 1958 rifle, named after a former Danish war minister, was developed and produced by the *Dansk Industri Syndikat* of Copenhagen and it was intended chiefly for export to nations with limited financial means. The version of this rifle sold as surplus in the United States was produced for the Colombian Navy in .30-06 caliber, and is marked with the Colombian arms on the left of the stock.

The one-piece bolt has dual-opposed locking lugs and its turned-down handle serves as a safety lug. The firing mechanism cocks on opening the bolt and rearward motion of the bolt is stopped by a combination bolt stop and ejector, similar to that of the Italian Carcano rifle. Also similar to the Carcano is the one-piece firing pin with detachable cocking piece and firing pin nut. The safety is on the left rear of the bolt and a spring-loaded catch on the safety must he depressed before the safety can be engaged.

The 5-round, staggered-column, fixed box magazine can be loaded singly or by using a M1903 Springfield clip. Only cartridges with pointed bullets feed properly. The tangent type aperture rear sight has a large windage knob with micrometer click adjustments. The front sight has a square-top blade protected by a metal hood.

A special feature of this rifle is the small muzzle brake with several round gas ports. Another special feature is a thick rubber recoil pad fitted to the one-piece walnut stock. At the front of the fore-end is a combination nosecap and bayonet lug.

DISASSEMBLY

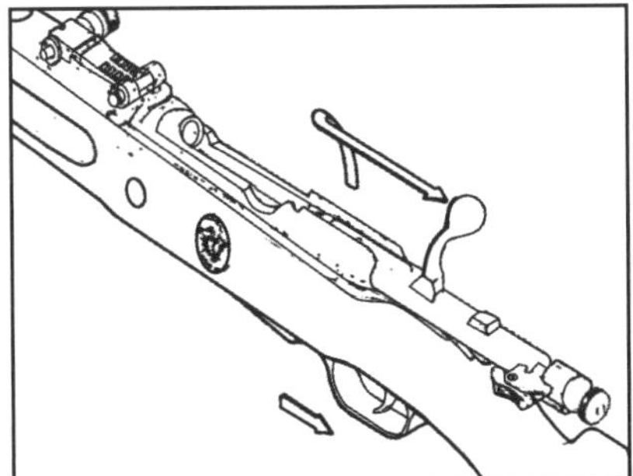

1 To field-strip the Madsen rifle, lift bolt handle, pull bolt (13) fully to the rear, and remove any cartridges. Depress trigger (56) and slide bolt assembly from receiver.

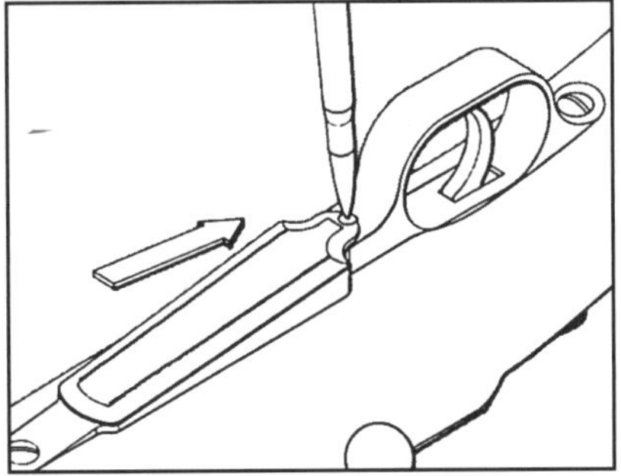

2 Strip the magazine by depressing floorplate catch (58) with tip of jacketed bullet or a punch, at the same time pushing rearward on magazine floorplate (57). Lift out floorplate, magazine spring (61), and follower (62). Further disassembly is not required for normal cleaning.

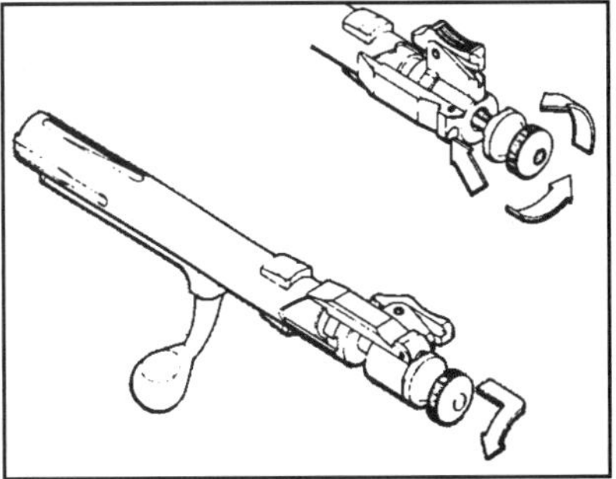

3 To strip bolt assembly, pull rearward on firing pin nut (2), and rotate firing mechanism ¼ turn to the left. This lowers the firing pin (16) and relieves most of the tension on firing pin spring (11). Depress firing pin nut retainer (3), and unscrew firing pin nut. Remove cocking piece (6) to rear.

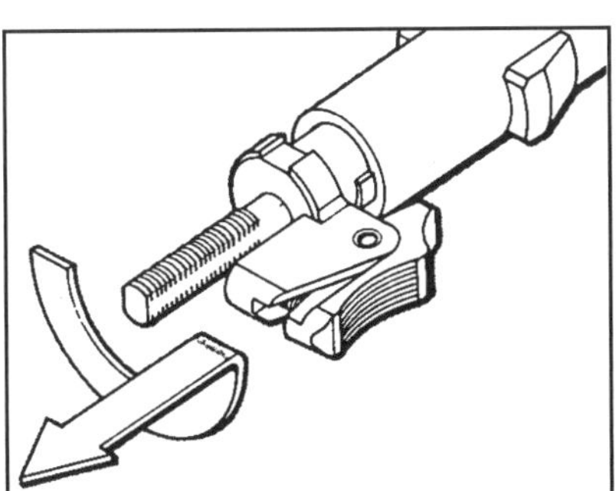

4 Grasp safety (8) firmly and rotate ½ turn to align it with bolt rib. Use caution, as safety is under spring tension. Ease safety out to the rear, and remove firing pin (16) and firing pin spring.

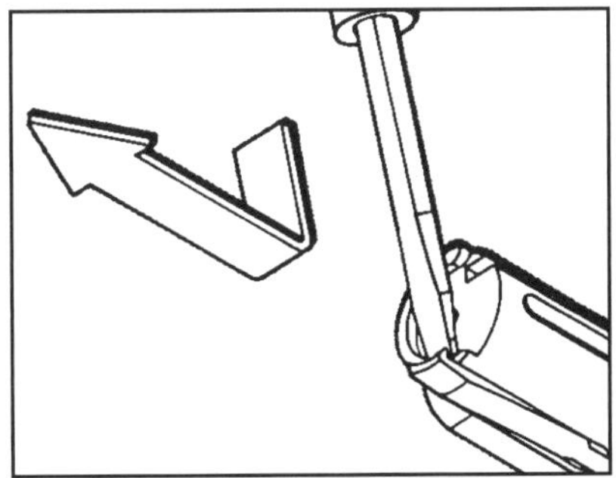

5 To remove extractor (14), place a small screwdriver beneath extractor claw and spring the extractor outward until its lug is free of retaining hole in bolt. Then pry extractor forward out of bolt. Reassemble in reverse. In doing so, screw on firing pin nut as far as it will go, and then back off slightly to engage one of its notches with firing pin nut retainer.

MANNLICHER-SCHÖNAUER RIFLE

PARTS LEGEND

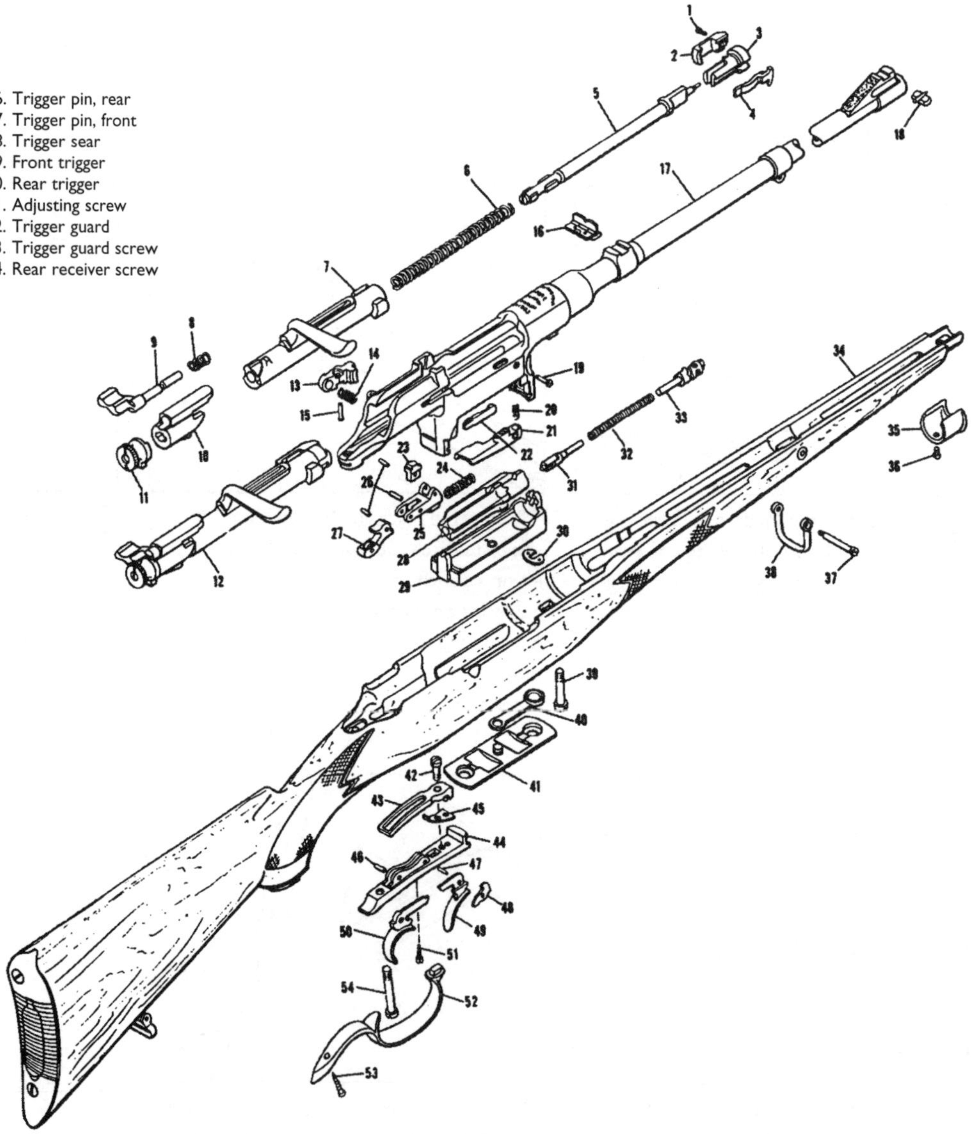

1. Ejector screw
2. Ejector
3. Bolt head
4. Extractor
5. Firing pin
6. Firing pin spring
7. Bolt, stripped
8. Safety catch spring
9. Safety catch
10. Cocking piece
11. Firing pin nut
12. Bolt, assembled
13. Bolt stop
14. Bolt stop spring
15. Bolt stop pin
16. Rear sight
17. Barrel and receiver
18. Front sight
19. Cartridge stop screw
20. Cartridge stop spring
21. Cartridge stop
22. Bolt tension spring
23. Sear
24. Sear spring
25. Sear carrier
26. Sear pins (3)
27. Trigger connection
28. Magazine follower
29. Magazine box
30. Floorplate spring retainer
31. Rear magazine bearing
32. Magazine spring
33. Front magazine bearing
34. Carbine stock
35. Fore-end cap
36. Fore-end cap screw
37. Front swivel screw
38. Front swivel
39. Front receiver screw
40. Floorplate spring
41. Floorplate
42. Set trigger mainspring screw
43. Set trigger mainspring
44. Set trigger housing
45. Set trigger sear spring
46. Trigger pin, rear
47. Trigger pin, front
48. Trigger sear
49. Front trigger
50. Rear trigger
51. Adjusting screw
52. Trigger guard
53. Trigger guard screw
54. Rear receiver screw

In 1900 the Austrian Arms Factory in Steyr, Austria, introduced a Mannlicher bolt-action rifle with a spool-type rotary magazine perfected by designer Otto Schönauer. A military version was adopted by Greece in 1903. That year, Steyr offered a sporting carbine chambered for the 6.5x53 mm. Mannlicher-Schönauer cartridge. (6.7x53 mm. M.S.). Later models included the Model 1905 rifle in 9x56 mm. M.S., the Model 1908 in 8x56 mm. M. S. (8.2x56 mm. M.S.) and the Model 1910, in 9.5x57 mm. M.S., the final model offered by Steyr prior to World War I.

Following World War I, Mannlicher-Schönauer rifles and carbines were offered in several new calibers, including .30-

06, 7x57 mm. Mauser, and 10.75x68 mm. Mauser.

Production of sporting rifles was discontinued during World War II and was not resumed until 1950 when Steyer resumed limited production of sporting rifles. Calibers offered in 1950 included .257 Roberts, .270 Win., and .30-06. In succeeding years other caliber were offered including 6.5x68mm., .243 Win., .308 Win., .257 Weatherby Mag., .338 Win. Mag. And .458 Win. Mag. Between 1950 and the end of production in 1971, there were a wide variety of design changes to Steyer rifles and carbines including alterations of the receiver to accommodate scope mounts, changes in the bolt handle and stock, and the abandonment of the rotary magazine.

DISASSEMBLY

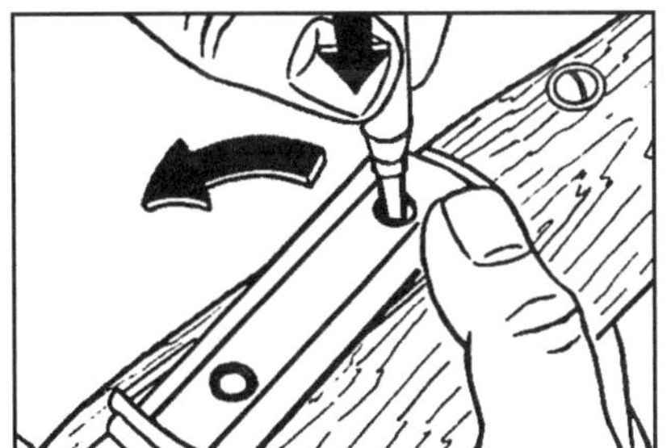

1 The magazine can be unloaded by removing the magazine assembly. To remove the magazine assembly, insert a cartridge point into the front hole in the floorplate (41). Depress the floorplate spring (40) and rotate the plate until it is free of the undercuts in the receiver, then lift out.

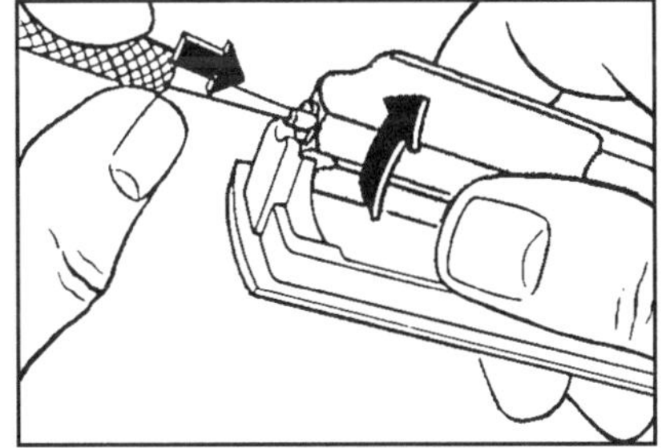

2 To remove the follower (28), use a thin punch to depress the rear magazine bearing (31) or front magazine bearing (33). When bearing is clear of its seat, lift out the follower. At this point the follower still contains the front and rear bearings and the magazine spring (32).

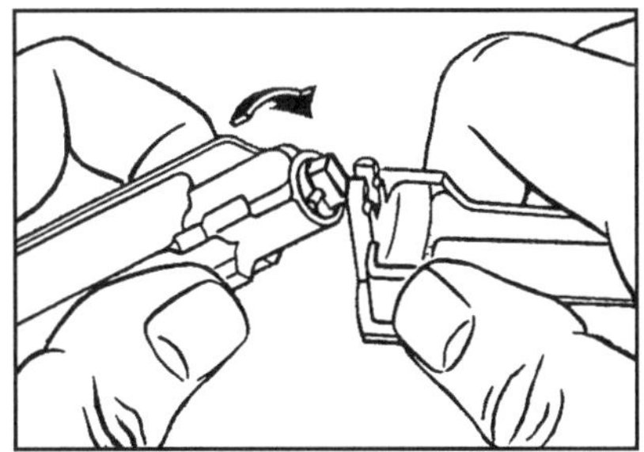

3 To remove the magazine spring and magazine follower bearings, use the magazine box (29) as a wrench. Insert the tapered magazine bearing (33) into the notch and turn the follower as shown. This unlocks the bearing. It can be pulled out with the magazine spring and rear bearing.

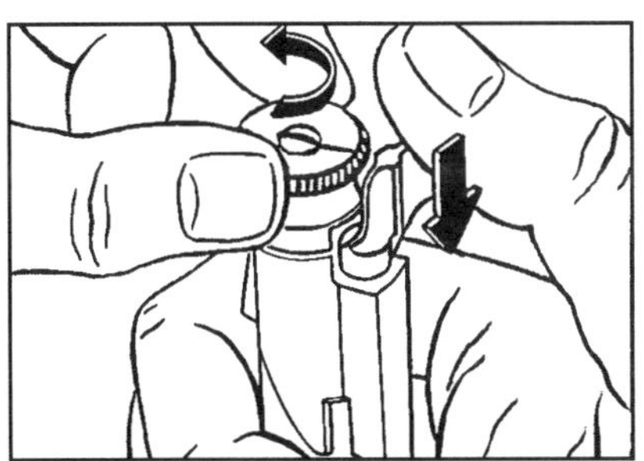

4 To remove the bolt (12), pull it to the rear and depress the bolt stop (13). To disassemble the bolt, rotate the cocking piece (10) until it snaps all the way forward and firing pin protrudes from the bolt face. Depress safety catch (9) and turn the firing pin nut (11) counterclockwise 90° until it unlocks. Ease off the firing pin nut and cocking piece with the safety catch.

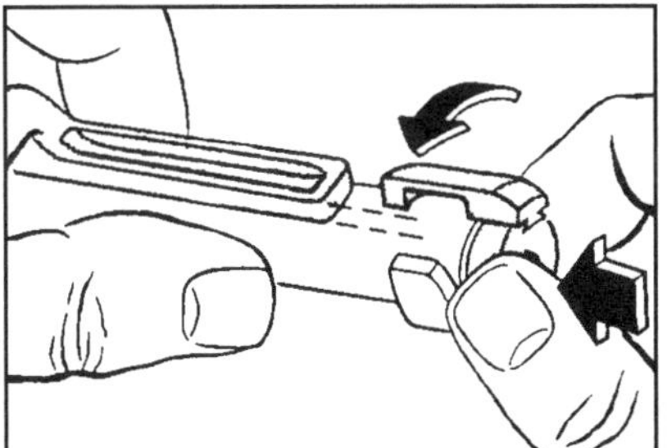

5 After the cocking piece assembly has been removed, the firing pin (5) and firing pin spring (6) can be removed. Remember the firing pin is under heavy spring pressure, therefore hold the bolt head tight when turning it as shown. Align the ejector (2) with the rib on the bolt and ease off the bolt head (3).

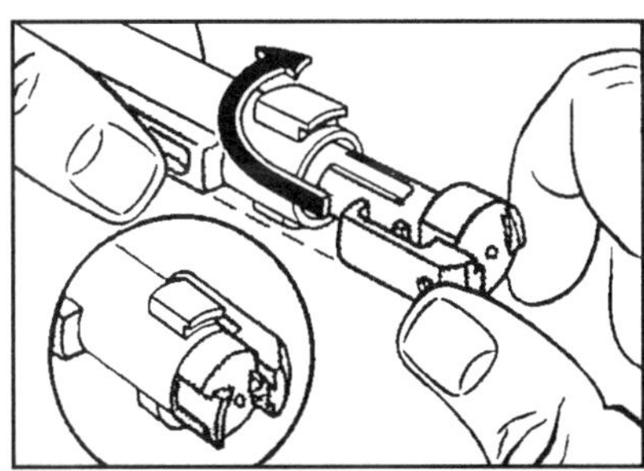

6 To replace the firing pin assembly, insert the pin (5) and spring (6) into the bolt. Put the bolt head (3) over the firing pin and push the bolt head into the bolt, lining up the ejector (2) with the rib on the bolt. Then turn the ejector 180° opposite the bolt rib. The cocking piece can be reassembled by reversing the steps.

MARLIN MODEL 39-A RIFLE

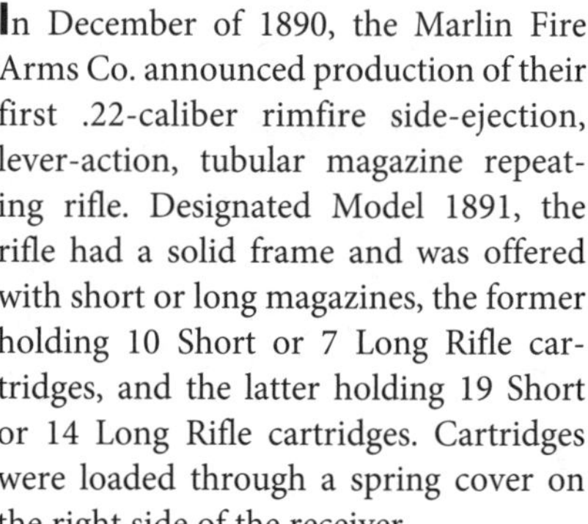

PARTS LEGEND

1. Barrel
2. Front sight insert
3. Front sight ramp screw (2)
4. Front sight ramp hood
5. Front sight ramp
6. Rear sight
7. Rear sight elevator
8. Magazine tube band pin
9. Magazine tube band
10. Forearm tip tenon
11. Forearm tip tenon screw (2)
12. Forearm tip with swivel
13. Magazine tube, outside
14. Magazine tube plug
15. Magazine tube plug pin
16. Magazine tube, inside
17. Magazine tube spring
18. Magazine tube follower
19. Firing pin
20. Breech bolt
21. Extractor
22. Receiver, left side
23. Cartridge cutoff spacer
24. Cartridge cutoff
25. Ejector spring
26. Ejector base
27. Cartridge guide spring
28. Ejector
29. Ejector lock rivet *
30. Ejector pin
31. Adapter base dummy screw (2)
32. Cartridge guide spring screw
33. Ejector base screw (2)
34. Cartridge cutoff screw
35. Hammer
36. Hammer screw
37. Hammer rod pin
38. Hammer rod
39. Mainspring
40. Mainspring adjusting plate
41. Cartridge stop
42. Finger lever spring
43. Finger lever spring screw
44. Cartridge stop pin
45. Finger lever screw
46. Carrier screw
47. Tang screw
48. Receiver, right side
49. Carrier
50. Carrier rocker
51. Carrier rocker spring
52. Carrier rocker screw
53. Thumbscrew
54. Receiver peep sight dummy screw (2)
55. Cartridge stop spring
56. Trigger spring
57. Trigger spring pin
58. Trigger pin
59. Trigger
60. Finger lever
61. Buttplate
62. Buttplate screw (2)
63. Rear swivel

* Permanent sub-assembly of ejector base.

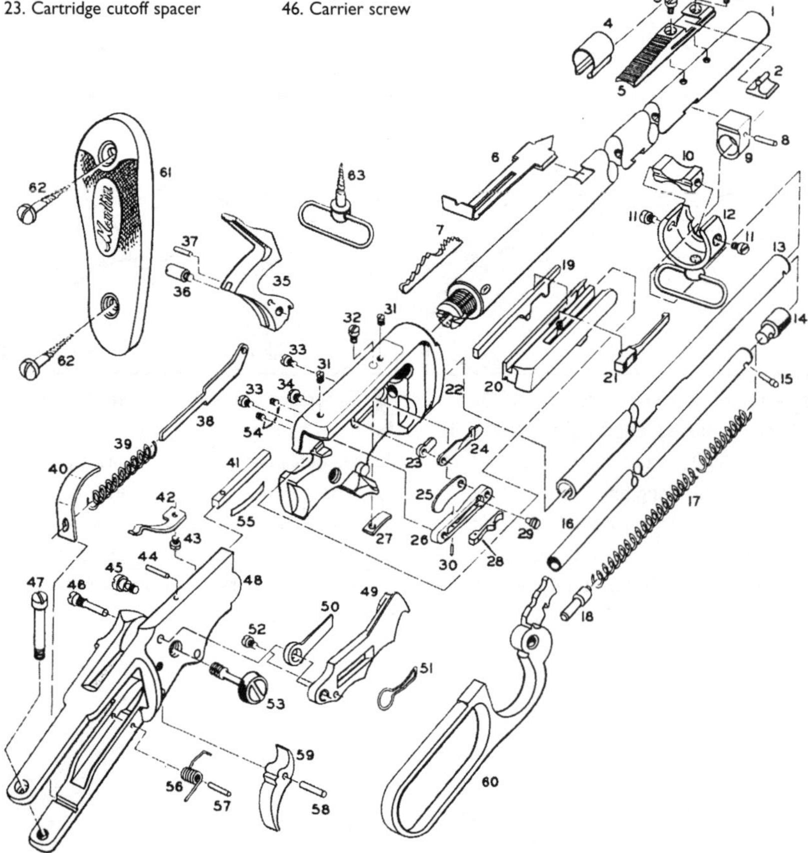

In December of 1890, the Marlin Fire Arms Co. announced production of their first .22-caliber rimfire side-ejection, lever-action, tubular magazine repeating rifle. Designated Model 1891, the rifle had a solid frame and was offered with short or long magazines, the former holding 10 Short or 7 Long Rifle cartridges, and the latter holding 19 Short or 14 Long Rifle cartridges. Cartridges were loaded through a spring cover on the right side of the receiver.

Shortly after its introduction, the Model 1891 was modified so that it could be loaded through the front end of the magazine tube and the magazine was increased in length to hold 25 Short, 20 Long, or 18 Long Rifle cartridges. Optional barrel lengths were 24, 25, and 26 inches in round, half-octagon, or full-octagon.

The Model 1891 rifle was also offered in .32 caliber, convertible for either center-fire or rimfire cartridges by changing firing pins.

The Model 1891 rifle was replaced by the Model 1892. Mechanical differences between the two models were minor. The sear and trigger of the Model 1892 were integral, and not separate as in the Model 1891. There were additional changes in the firing pin, breech bolt and trigger spring. Standard barrel length for the Model 1892 was 24 inches, but longer barrels could be furnished. Barrels were round, half-octagon, and full-octagon.

A take-down version, the Model 1897, was introduced in that year. It was made to the same general specifications as the Model 1892 and was available in regular and deluxe grades. A special l6-inch barrel "bicycle model" was also offered. Production of both Model 1892 and Model 1897 rifles was discontinued in 1915 when the firm was sold by the

Marlin family to the Marlin-Rockwell Corp.

After World War I, Marlin-Rockwell made an unsuccessful attempt to produce sporting arms. Following bankruptcy, assets of the firm were purchased by Frank Kenna, a New Haven industrialist. Advised by a group of former Marlin employees that there were sufficient remaining pre-war rifle parts to resume production, Kenna reorganized the Marlin Firearms Co., and shortly thereafter the Model 1897 rifle was redesignated Model 39. The initial production rifles were assembled from Model 1897 parts.

The Model 39 was offered in pistol-grip style onlywith a 24-inch octagon barrel. In 1939 an improved version of the Model 39, designated Model 39A, was introduced with a shotgun-type pistol-grip buttstock and semi-beavertail forearm. A 24-inch tapered round barrel was standard. The mainspring and trigger spring were of coil type.

In 1954 a 20-barrel, carbine version, the "Mountie," was introduced, with a straight-grip stock. The 39-A was produced in two major variants. The 39-AS and the 39-TDS. Acurrent version, the Golden 39-A, was introduced in 1957.

DISASSEMBLY

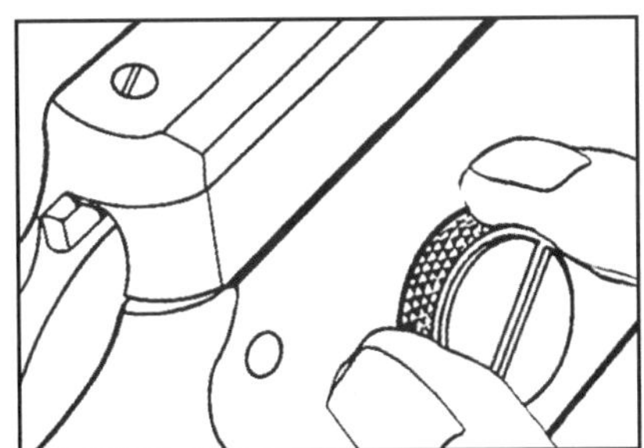

1 To disassemble Marlin 39-A, first close action, then manually cock hammer (35) and unscrew thumbscrew (53).

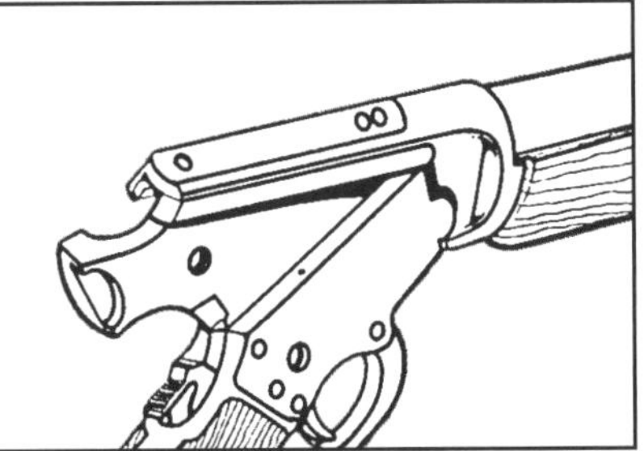

2 The 2 portions of the receiver (22 & 48) will come apart at the joints by forcing the buttstock (right side) portion to the right.

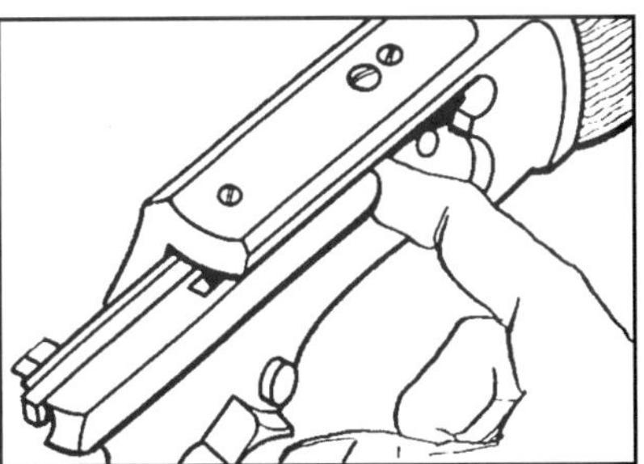

3 Breech bolt (20) can be removed by sliding it rearward as far as it will go and then lifting it away. Depress wing of ejector (28) into ejector base (26) and rotate ejector lock rivet (29) to retain ejector in depressed position. Disassembly thus far will suffice for cleaning and oiling. To reassemble, first insure that hammer is cocked. Next, turn ejector lock rivet (29) to free ejector wing, replace breech bolt, and slide it forward. Open finger lever (60) slightly (approximately ⅛ to ¼), place buttstock (right side) portion of receiver into left side so that the lip on the front end fits into recess in left side. Screw down the thumbscrew as far as it will go.

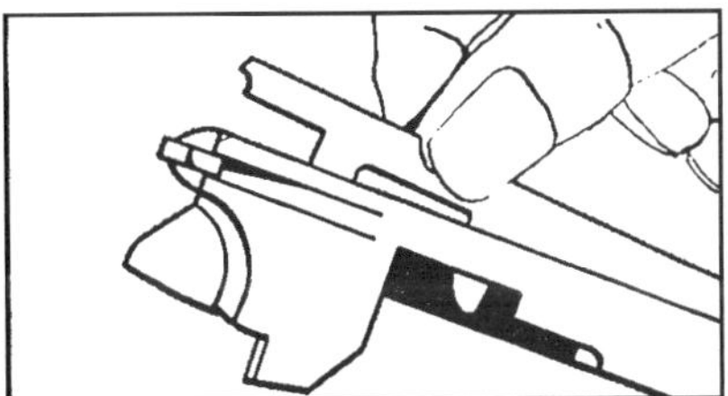

4 Further disassembly is accomplished by removing the firing pin (19), which simply may be lifted away from the bolt.

5 To remove the buttstock, unscrew the tang screw (47) and lift the stock away to the rear.

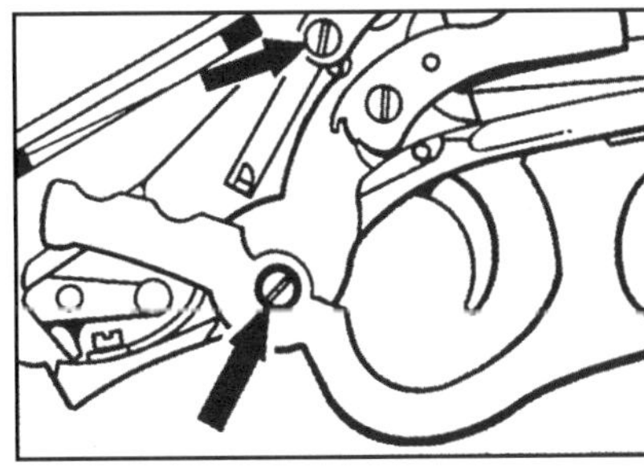

6 Next, unscrew finger lever screw (45—lower arrow) and lift away finger lever. Following that, unscrew carrier screw (46—upper arrow) and lift out carrier (49).

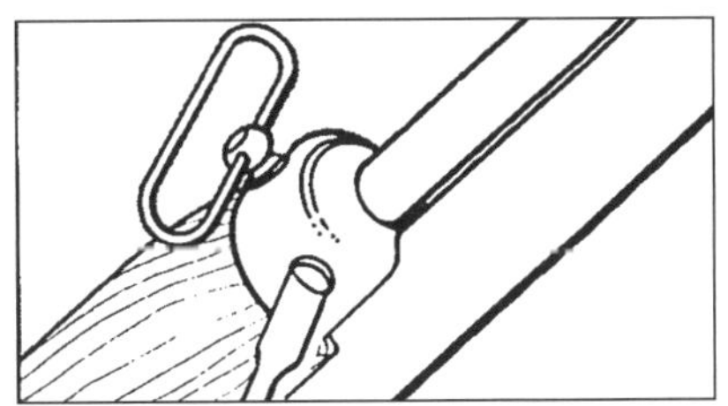

7 The forearm may be removed by unscrewing the 2 forearm tip tenon screws (II) and sliding forearm tip (12) forward. The forearm may now be lifted away. Reassemble in reverse order.

MARLIN MODEL 90 ST SHOTGUN

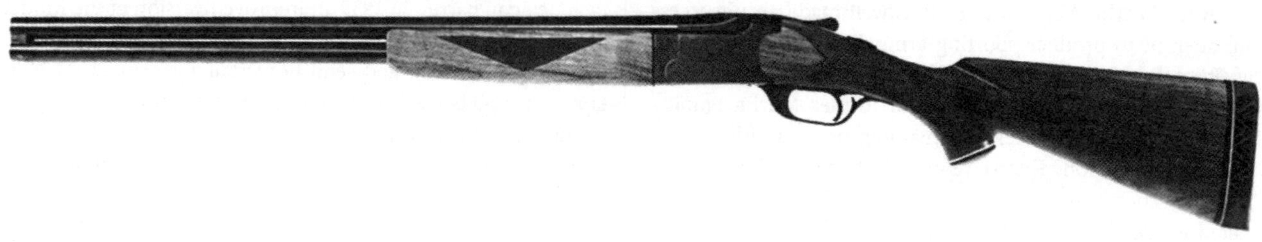

PARTS LEGEND

1. Barrel
2. Front sight
3. Extractor
4. Extractor retaining screw (2)
5. Forearm
6. Fore-end iron
7. Forearm screw (2)
8. Fore-end iron catch
9. Fore-end iron catch pin
10. Fore-end iron catch spring
11. Fore-end iron catch screw lockwasher
12. Fore-end iron catch screw
13. Extractor lever (2)
14. Extractor lever pin
15. Locking bolt
16. Top-lever link
17. Top-lever link pin
18. Single trigger slide
19. Single trigger
20. Cocking lever
21. Cocking lever pin
22. Cocking lever spring
23. Single trigger pin, front
24. Trigger guard pin
25. Safety button
26. Safety button spring
27. Inertia weight
28. Inertia weight plunger spring
29. Inertia weight plunger
30. Inertia weight pin
31. Trigger guard
32. Single trigger pin, rear
33. Trigger guard screw
34. Frame
35. Buttstock screw
36. Buttstock lockwasher
37. Buttstock washer
38. Inerta weight stop plate
39. Inertia weight stop plate pin
40. Safety button spring screw
41. Sear spring (2)
42. Sear, bottom
43. Sear, top
44. Sear link
45. Sear box
46. Firing pin guide
47. Sear box pin
48. Sear pin (2)
49. Cocking rod
50. Safety button rod
51. Sear box screw
52. Firing pin spring (2)
53. Positioner
    53A. Positioner spacer
54. Firing pin, bottom
55. Firing pin, top
56. Top-lever
57. Top-lever spring
58. Cocking cam
59. Cocking rod retaining screw
60. Top-lever retaining screw
61. Recoil pad
62. Recoil pad screw (2)
63. Slide spring
64. Slide spring guide
65. Sear link pin

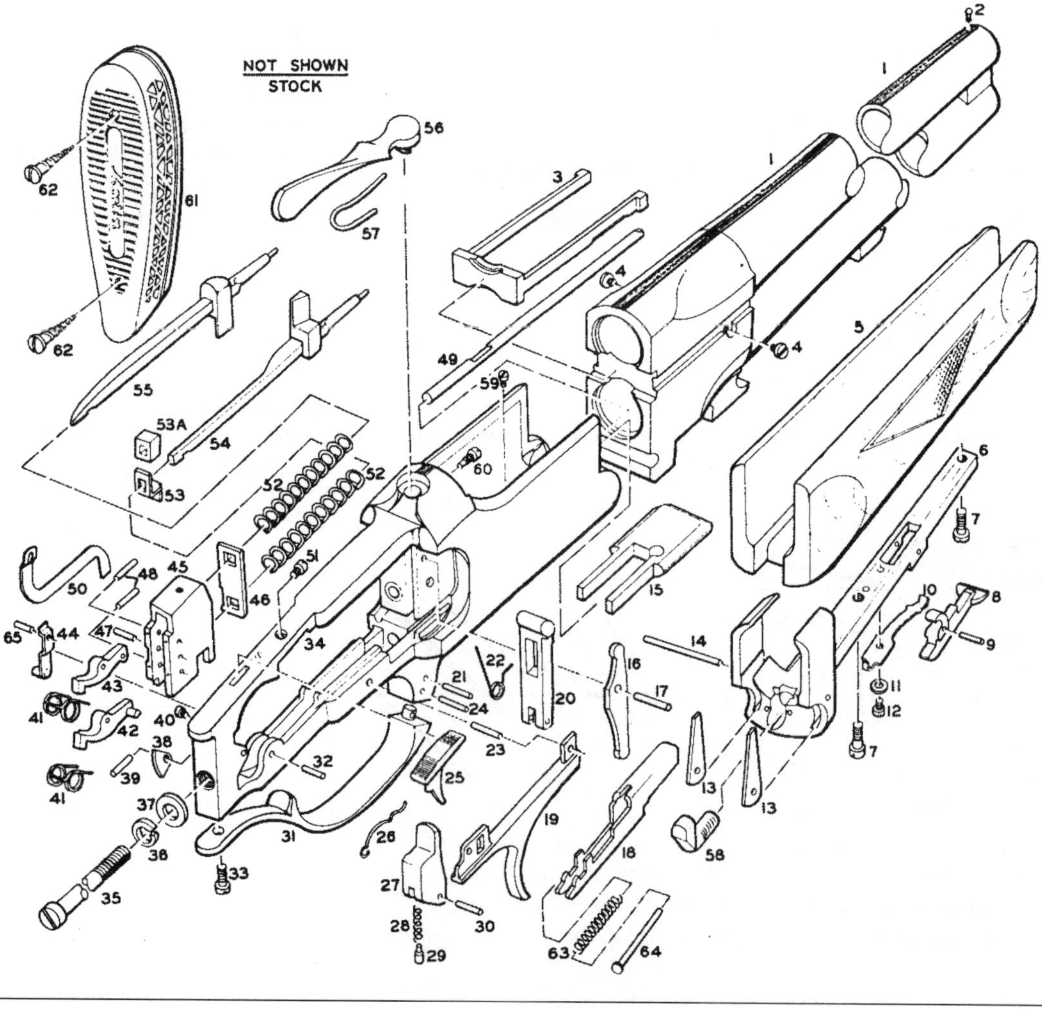

NOT SHOWN
STOCK

In 1937, Marlin Firearms Co. began production of the Model 90 double trigger over-under shotgun. Early production guns had a low fore-end iron which did not rise even with front of frame side members as in later guns. Pre-war production was in 12-gauge on a large frame, with somewhat smaller frames used on 16- and 20-gauge models. A few guns were made in .410-bore on a small sized frame.

Rifle-shotgun combinations were also made in .30 Winchester/20-gauge, and also .410-bore with rifle barrels chambered for .22 rimfire, .22 Hornet, or .218 Bee. Special hardened recoil plates were fitted to standing breeches for center-fire rifle cartridges and small-diameter firing pins were installed to prevent puncturing of primers. In 1951 a pull-down pivoted catch on the fore-end iron replaced the flat spring catch used on earlier models.

In 1954 a non-selective, single trigger version was introduced which fired the lower barrel first. Designated Model 90 ST, it had an anti-doubling mechanism operated by an inertia weight. In event of a recoil-induced involuntary trigger release and involuntary second pull after firing the first barrel, counter recoil moves the entire gun with reference to the inertia weight so that it swings under the inertia stop in the frame. At the same time the sear slide moves forward to engage the upper sear, thus losing contact with the lower sear. If the trigger is involuntarily pulled at this time, trigger motion is blocked by the inertia weight so that a deliberate release and second pull of the trigger is necessary to fire the upper barrel. The Model 90 ST was discontinued in 1960.

DISASSEMBLY

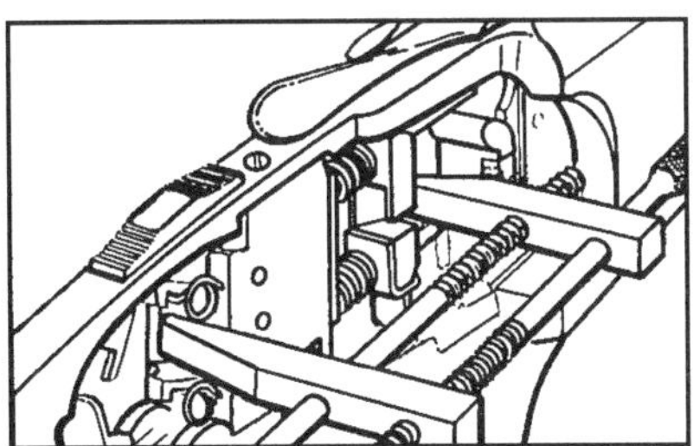

1 To disassemble Model 90 ST, first cock the arm to compress firing pin springs (52), set safety button (25) to "S" (Safe), and remove forearm (5) and barrel (1). Next, remove recoil pad screws (62) and recoil pad (61). Using a long-shanked screwdriver, remove buttstock screw (35), buttstock washer (37), and buttstock lock-washer (36). Pull stock away from frame (34). Place a felt-padded machinists clamp between cocking arms on the firing pins (54 and 55) and rear surface of sear box (45). Remove sear box screw (51) and lift away entire sear box assembly to right.

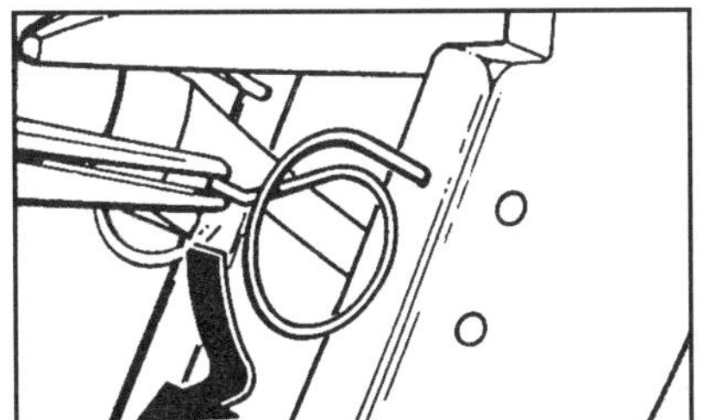

2 Manually trip sears (42 and 43) and slowly open clamp to release tension on firing pin springs. Using long-nosed pliers, carefully unhook sear springs (41) from rear notch of each sear and lift springs away. Drift out sear pins (48) and remove sears, sear link (44), firing pin guide (46),. firing pins, positioner (53), and positioner spacer (53A).

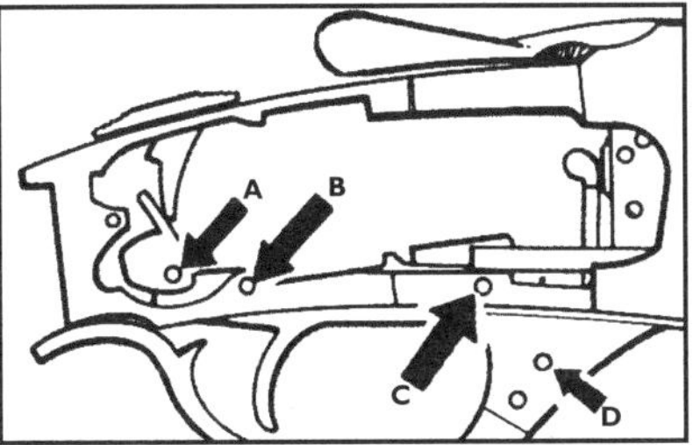

3 Remove safety button spring screw (40) and lift away safety button spring (26) and safety button rod (50). Next, (A) drift out inertia weight pin (30) and remove inertia weight (27), inertia weight plunger spring (28), and inertia weight plunger (29), being careful not to lose the latter two parts. Then (B and C) drift out single trigger pin, rear (32), and single trigger pin, front (23). Remove single trigger slide (18) and single trigger (19). (D) Drift out cocking lever pin (21).

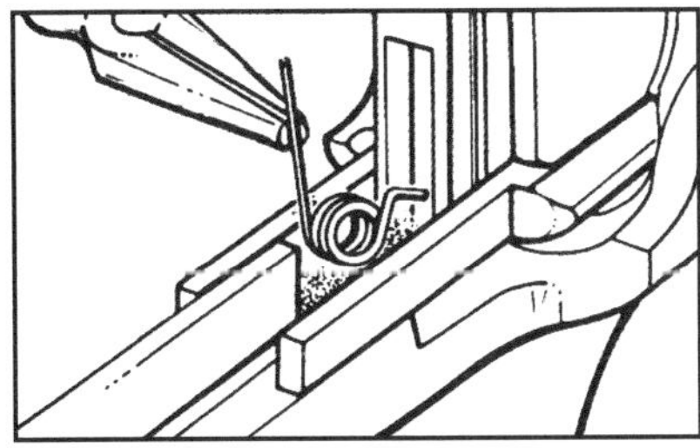

4 Using long-nosed pliers, remove cocking lever spring (22) and cocking lever (20). Drift out top-lever link pin (17). Remove top-lever link (16) and withdraw locking bolt (15) from front of frame.

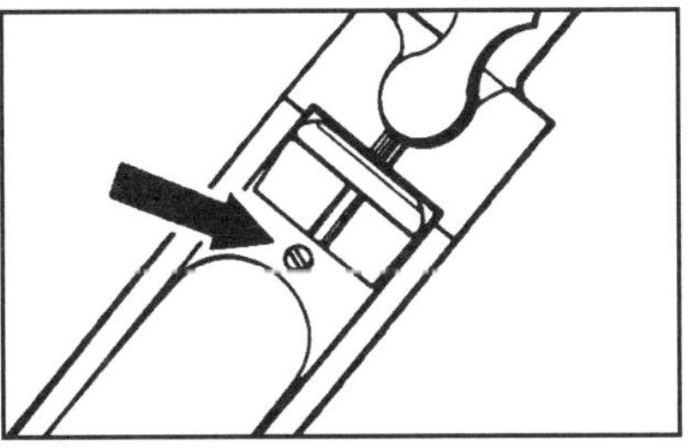

5 Remove cocking rod retaining screw (59) (arrow) and withdraw cocking rod (49). Reassemble Model 90 ST in reverse order.

MARLIN MODEL 336 RIFLE

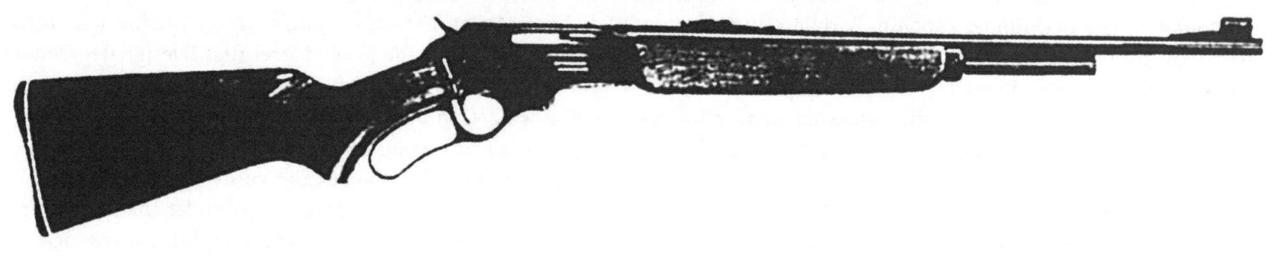

PARTS LEGEND

1. Receiver
2. Receiver dummy screws (6)
3. Breech bolt
4. Extractor
5. Rear firing pin retaining pin (long)
   5a. Front firing pin retaining pin (short)
6. Front firing pin
7. Rear firing pin
8. Firing pin spring
9. Hammer
10. Hammer rod
11. Hammer rod pin
12. Mainspring
13. Mainspring adjusting plate
14. Hammer screw
15. Tang screw
16. Trigger guard plate
17. Trigger guard plate screw
18. Trigger guard plate support screw
19. Carrier rocker
20. Carrier rocker spring
21. Carrier rocker rivet
22. Carrier
23. Carrier screw
24. Locking bolt
25. Ejector and ejector spring
26. Loading spring
27. Loading spring screw
28. Trigger
29. Trigger pin
30. Sear
31. Trigger safety block
32. Trigger safety block spring
33. Trigger safety block pin
34. Finger lever
35. Finger lever plunger
36. Finger lever plunger spring
37. Finger lever plunger pin
38. Finger lever screw
39. Barrel
40. Rear sight
41. Rear sight elevator
42. Front sight
43. Front band
44. Front band screw
45. Magazine tube
46. Magazine tube follower
47. Magazine tube spring
48. Magazine tube plug
49. Magazine tube plug screw
50. Forearm
51. Rear band
52. Rear band screw
53. Buttplate
54. Buttplate screws (2)
55. Buttstock (not shown)

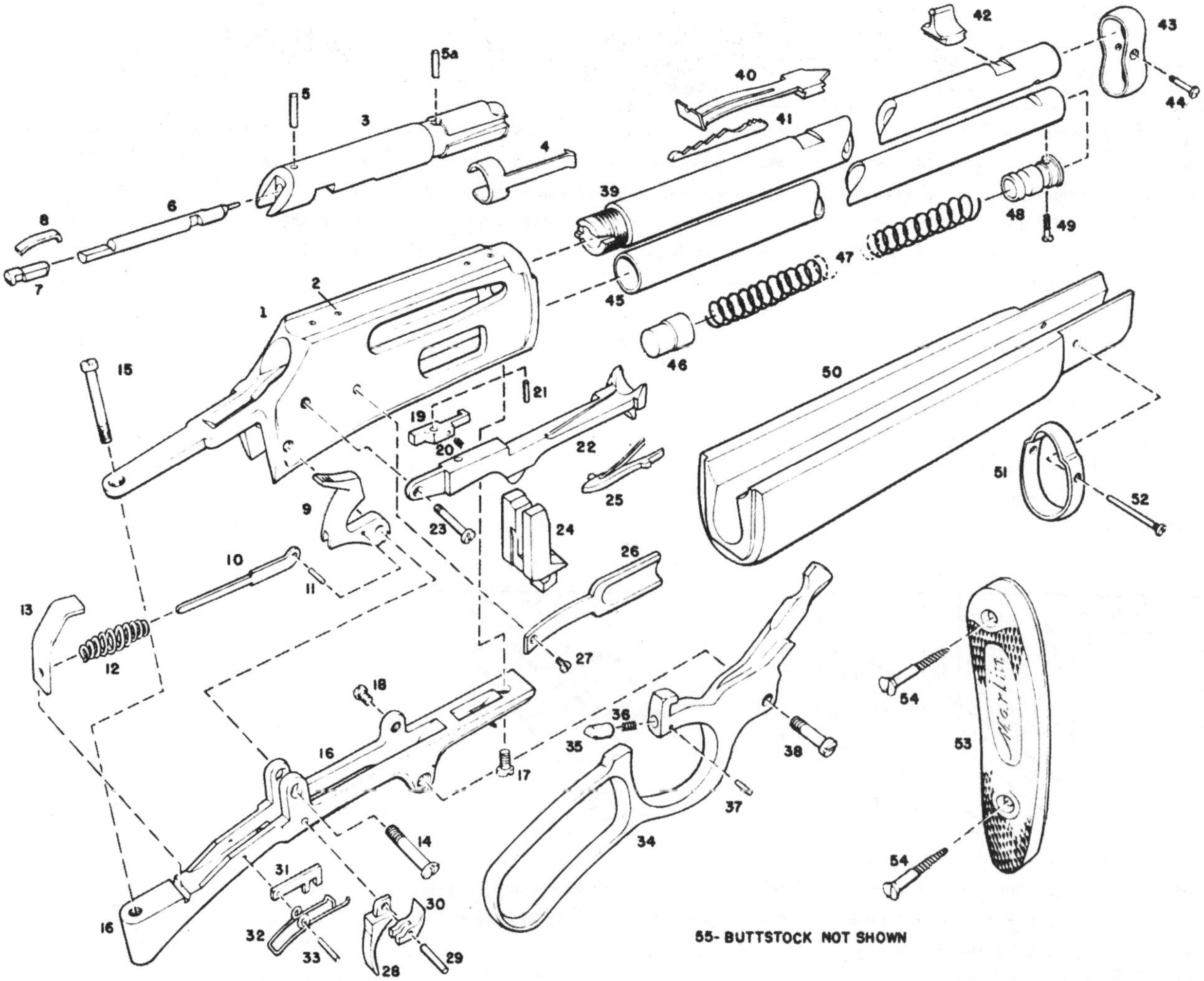

55- BUTTSTOCK NOT SHOWN

It was in 1889, or well over half a century ago, that the Marlin Firearms Company introduced the first successful side-ejection tubular-magazine lever-action rifle with solid receiver. The basic design has been improved several times through the years, with the last significant change made in 1948 with the introduction of the Model 336 series of rifles and carbines. Of major interest is that all guns of this modern series have round barrels and a round breech bolt of alloy steel. This in contrast with the "square" breech bolt of previous Marlin lever-action rifles.

The fact that the Model 336 ejects spent cartridges to the side rather than out the top of the receiver is of importance to the shooter who wants to mount a scope sight directly over the bore of his rifle. This is not feasible with top-ejection arms, which must be fitted with a relatively awkward offset side mount if a telescope sight is desired.

The Model 336 is available in a variety of calibers including .219 Zipper, .30-30, .32 Special, and .35 Remington. The carbine versions feature 20-inch barrels and the rifles are offered with 24-inch barrels. With the exception of the straight-grip "Texan" carbine in .30-30 or .35 Remington caliber, all offerings in the 336 line have pistol grip buttstocks. Checkering on pistol grip and forearm plus detachable shooting sling are features of the deluxe grade carbine and rifle.

DISASSEMBLY

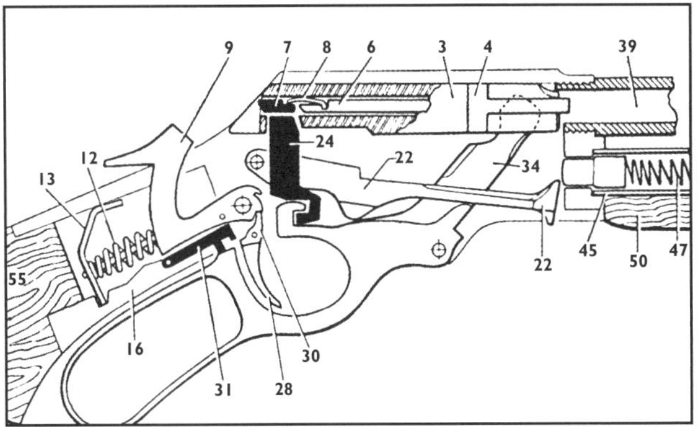

The proper relationship of all ports within the receiver with the action closed, cocked, and properly locked.

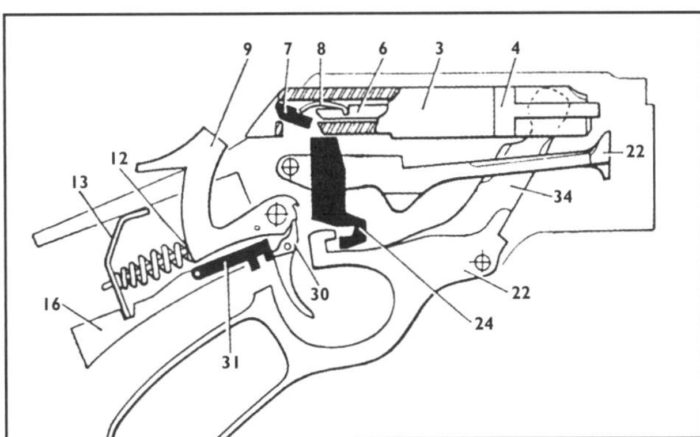

The finger lever is opened slightly and the action is not locked. Note that when the locking bolt (24) is not fully engaged with the breech bolt (3), due to the finger lever being partially or fully opened, the rear and front firing pins (7 & 6) are not in alignment and a blow of the hammer cannot be transmitted to the front firing pin. Note that, in addition, when the lever is opened only slightly, the trigger safety block (31) drops and the trigger cannot be pulled. Before the gun can be fired, the trigger block must be raised by the fully closed lever and the rear firing pin must be fully elevated into alignment with the front firing pin by the fully seated locking bolt.

Disassemblly Procedure For Normal Cleaning: For normal cleaning and inspection of the bore from the breech, it is only necessary to open the finger lever (34) halfway, remove finger lever screw (38), and pull finger lever down and out of action. Thereafter, pull breech bolt (3) all the way out of the receiver and remove the ejector (25) from its slot in left side of the receiver.

Complete Disassembly: Remove finger lever plunger (35) and spring (36) by driving out plunger pin (37). Remove tang screw (15) and pull off buttstock (55). Remove the mainspring (12) and mainspring adjusting plate (13) by lowering hammer (9) carefully to its foremost position and thereafter tipping the top of the mainspring adjusting plate forward and sideward from under top tang.

Remove the hammer screw (14) and, pressing trigger slightly, remove the hammer (9) upward. Drive out hammer rod pin (11) and remove hammer rod (10). Remove trigger guard plate screw (17) and trigger guard plate support screw (18). Drop trigger guard plate (16) out bottom of receiver. Remove trigger (28) and sear (30) from trigger guard plate by driving out trigger pin (29). Removed trigger safety block (31) and spring (32) by driving out trigger safety block pin (33).

Remove carrier screw (23) on right side of receiver and drop carrier (22) and locking bolt (24) from bottom of receiver. Remove loading spring screw (27) and loading spring (26) from right side.

Remove magazine tube plug screw (49) and draw magazine tube plug (48) out of magazine tube. Withdraw magazine tube spring (47) and follower (46) from magazine tube (45). Remove front band screw (44) and slide off front band (43). Remove rear band screw (52) and loosen rear band (51). Slide forearm (50) up on barrel slightly and withdraw magazine tube from receiver. Remove forearm by sliding off rear band.

To strip the breech bolt (3), remove front and rear firing pins (6 & 7) and firing pin spring (8) by driving out the front firing pin retaining pin (short) (5a) and rear firing pin retaining pin (long) (5). Pry the extractor (4) gently from its slot with a small screwdriver.

Reassemble in reverse order. Before re-installing breech bolt, be sure that ejector is placed back in its slot in the receiver and that the stud on the ejector is in place in its hole in the receiver wall. Slide breech bolt halfway into the receiver and insert the finger lever into its slot in the trigger guard plate so that its upper end engages the slot in the breech bolt.

MARLIN MODEL 1881 RIFLE

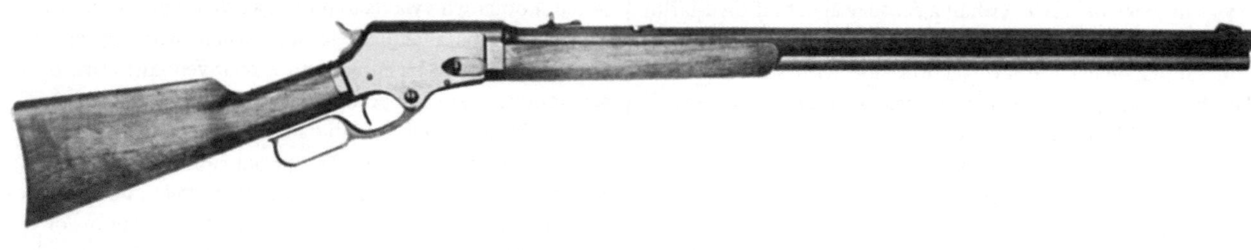

PARTS LEGEND

1. Barrel
2. Breechbolt
3. Buttplate
4. Buttplate screws (2)
5. Buttstock
6. Carrier block
7. Carrier block pins
8. Ejector
9. Ejector pin
10. Extractor
11. Extractor screw
12. Firing pin
13. Firing pin retaining pin
14. Fore-end
15. Fore-end tip
16. Fore-end tip screw
17. Front set trigger
18. Front set trigger pin
19. Front set trigger screw
20. Front set trigger spring
21. Hammer
22. Hammer bushing
23. Hammer fly
24. Hammer screw
25. Lever
26. Lever pin
27. Lever pin screw
28. Lever spring
29. Lever spring screw
30. Magazine follower
31. Magazine tube
32. Magazine tube plug
33. Magazine spring
34. Magazine stud
35. Magazine stud screw
36. Mainspring
37. Mainspring screw
38. Mortise cover
39. Mortise cover screw
40. Rear sight
41. Rear sight blade
42. Rear sight blade screw
43. Rear sight elevator
44. Rear set trigger
45. Rear set trigger pin
46. Rear set trigger spring
47. Rear set trigger spring screw
48. Receiver
49. Sear
50. Sear pin
51. Sear spring
52. Side cover
53. Side cover spring
54. Side cover spring abutment
55. Side cover spring guide
56. Tang sight plug screws (2)
57. Trigger plate
58. Trigger plate pin
59. Trigger set screw
60. Front sight
61. Front sight screw
62. Upper tang screw

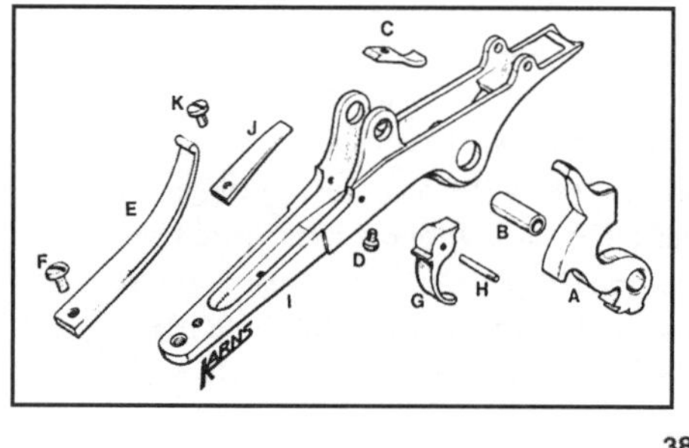

Standard Trigger Group Parts Legend

A. Hammer
B. Hammer bushing
C. Lever spring
D. Lever spring screw
E. Mainspring
F. Mainspring screw
G. Trigger
H. Trigger pin
I. Trigger plate
J. Trigger spring
K. Trigger spring screw

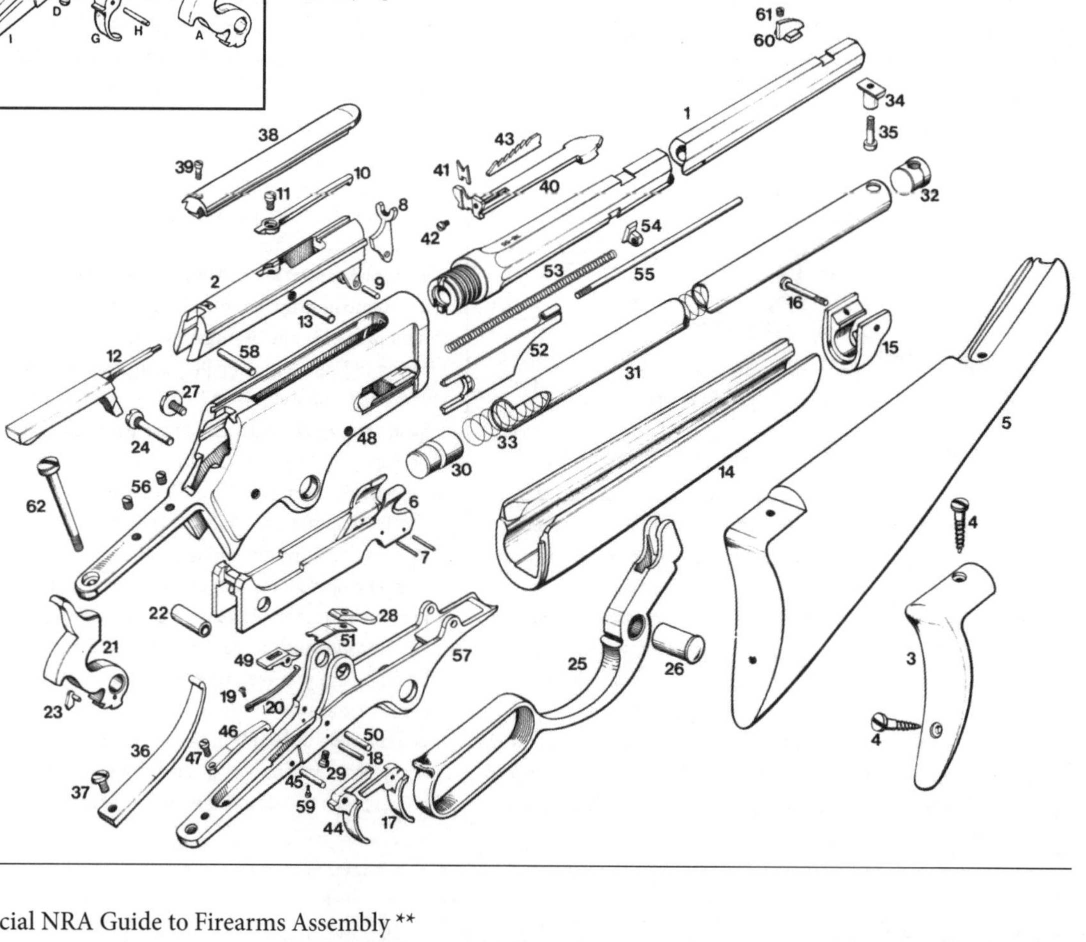

In 1881 J. M. Marlin introduced a center-fire lever-action repeating rifle featuring side loading and top ejection. This was the first production rifle of his own design and incorporated the tubular magazine concept with an octagon barrel fitted to a large-frame receiver. These rifles were originally chambered in both .45-70 and .40-60.

The Model 1881 was produced in four distinct variations. The first was a large-frame rifle with a "heavy receiver" and a stepped lower profile. These early production guns are identified by this step behind the front receiver flange that increased the depth of the receiver below the loading port.

A second heavy receiver variation eliminated the stepped profile. To reduce weight, Marlin introduced a third variation, the "light receiver," with a short barrel and narrow receiver flanges. The fourth version was the same receiver on a smaller scale. Reduced in both size and weight, this "small receiver" version was offered only in .32-40 and .38-55.

In addition to the four sizes, Marlin offered various barrel weights and lengths, set triggers, half magazines, pistol-grip stocks, buttplates, checkering and engraving. With these options the possible configurations were virtually limitless.

Contributing further to the possible variations was the design of both the carrier and ejector. Early production guns featured a simple bar ejector which was replaced by an improved Y-shaped version. The carrier was modified to improve the feeding function. Several design changes, including the addition of wedges, split carrier bodies and carrier spring fingers, contributed to internal variations of the '81.

These changes were initiated to address malfunctions in the feeding mechanism. Both the improved ejector and the split carrier with its parting wedge are evident in the small receiver version. The larger frame guns including both the heavy and light receiver versions were fitted with carriers with the added spring fingers. The Model 1881, with these improvements, continued in production until 1891, with estimated production totals of more than 20,000.

DISASSEMBLY

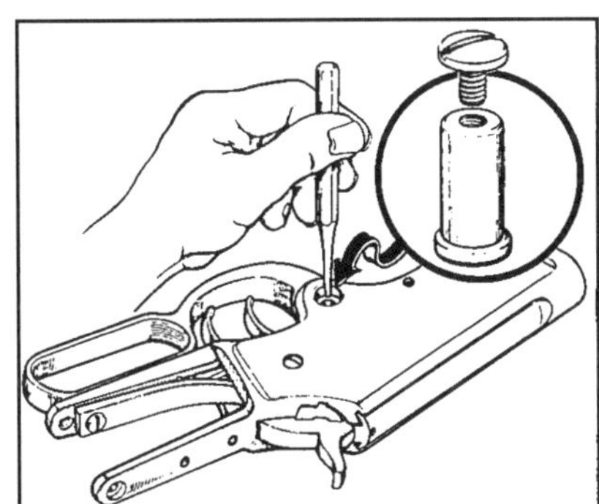

1 Lower the lever and check both the chamber and magazine to be sure the gun is not loaded.

Remove the upper tang screw (62) and slide the buttstock (5) off the receiver. Unscrew the lever pin retaining screw (27) and drift out the headed lever pin (26) from left to right.

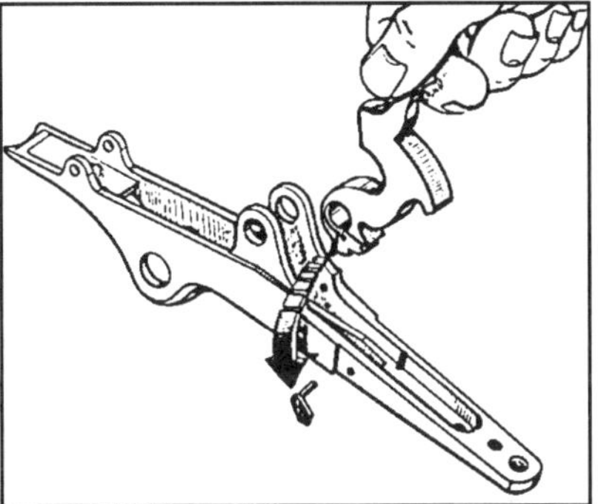

2 Pull the lever (25) down and out from the bottom of the receiver.

Remove the hammer screw (24) from the left side of the receiver. Drift out the trigger plate pin (58) and remove the trigger plate (57) from the bottom of the receiver. The hammer (21) with hammer bushing (22) and the set trigger group remain intact on the trigger plate and are removed as an assembly. This permits the set trigger function to be checked before disassembly of the trigger group.

If further disassembly of this lock group is required, support the hammer while pulling the trigger to release mainspring tension. Then remove the mainspring screw (37) and mainspring (36). Drift out the hammer bushing (22) and lift out the hammer (21). Exercise caution to avoid losing the fly (23) which pivots freely in a recess on the left side of the hammer.

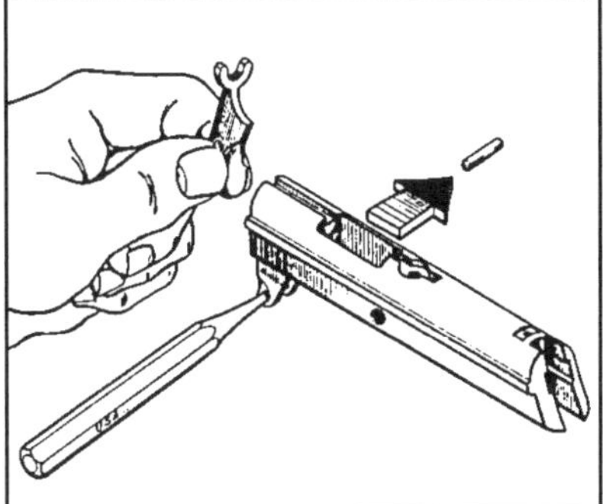

3 Now both the front and rear trigger springs (20 & 46) may be displaced by removing their respective screws (19 & 47). Next remove the lever spring screw (29) to free both the lever spring (28) and the sear spring (51). To facilitate reassembly, note the relationship of these springs as they are removed. Drift out the sear pin (50) and remove the sear (49). Now both the front and rear triggers (17 & 44) may be removed by drifting out their respective pins (18 & 45).

Slide the breechbolt (2) from the receiver (48). Remove the mortise cover screw (39) to separate the mortise cover (38) from the bolt. Unscrew the extractor screw (11) and lift out the extractor (10). Drift out the firing pin retaining pin (13) and withdraw the firing pin (12) from the back of the bolt. If repair or replacement is required, drift out the staked ejector pin (9) to remove the ejector (8) from the front of the bolt.

MAUSER MODEL 71/84 RIFLE

PARTS LEGEND

1. Ejector
2. Bolt head
3. Extractor
4. Firing pin
5. Firing pin spring
6. Bolt body
7. Retainer pin
8. Bolt stop
9. Bolt stop screw
10. Cocking piece
11. Firing pin nut
12. Safety catch
13. Safety catch spring
14. Rear guard screw
15. Cutoff spring screw
16. Cutoff spring
17. Cutoff lever
18. Cartridge lifter detent
19. Detent retainer screw
20. Cartridge stop pin
21. Cartridge stop
22. Barrel and receiver
23. Magazine tube
24. Magazine spring
25. Magazine follower
26. Cartridge lifter
27. Cartridge lifter hinge
28. Hinge lock screw
29. Sear hinge pin
30. Cutoff cam
31. Sear spring
32. Sear
33. Trigger pin
34. Trigger
35. Stock
36. Forward band
37. Cross key
38. Key-retaining screw
39. Middle band
40. Rear band
41. Band spring
42. Band spring screw
43. Center trigger guard screw
44. Trigger guard
45. Front guard screw

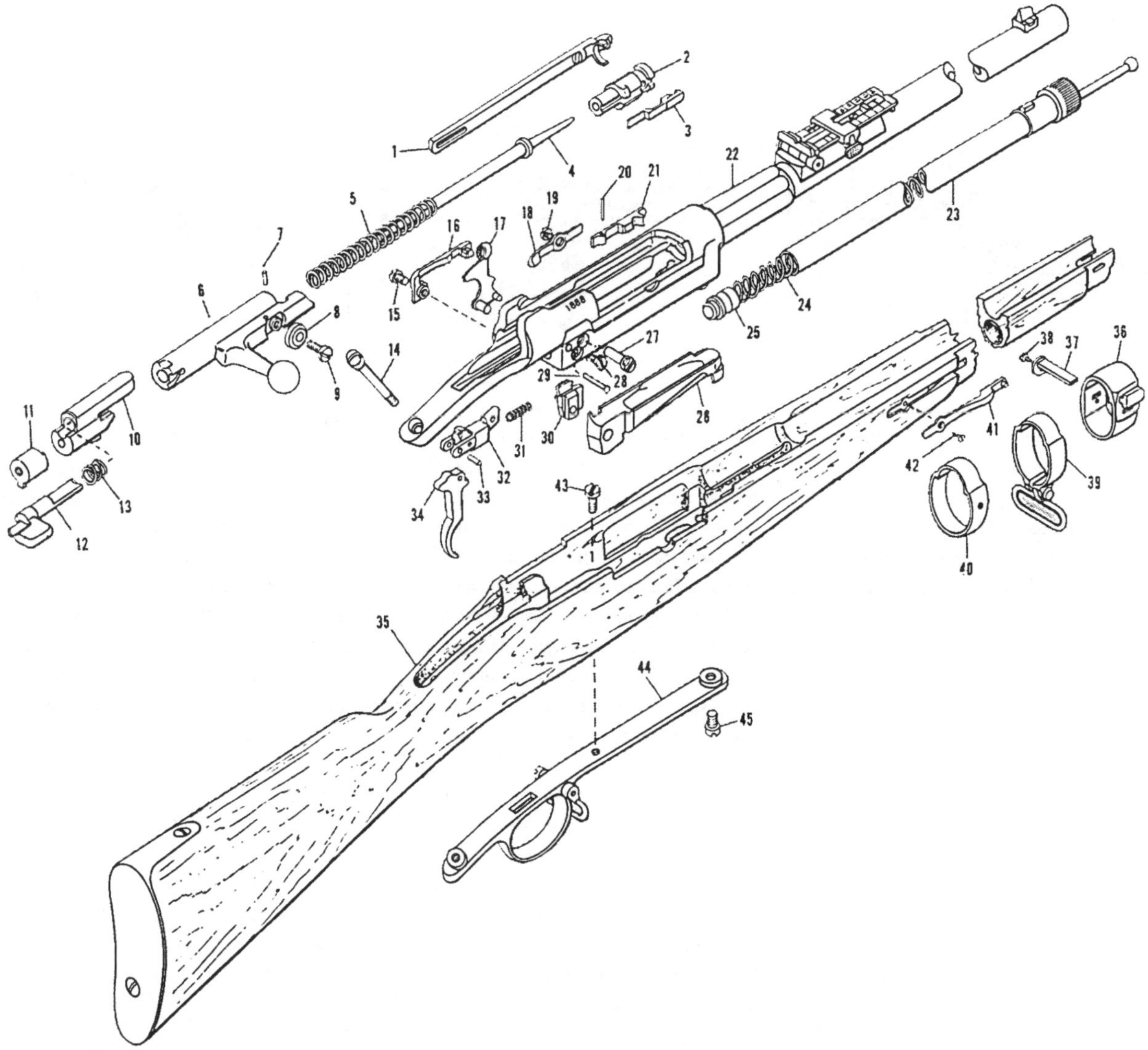

In 1871 the German Army adopted the 11 mm. Model 71 single-shot rifle that used a brass case in lieu of the old paper-covered needle-gun cartridge. When the decision was made to adopt a magazine rifle, Mauser submitted a design that combined the Model 71 bolt system with a tube magazine.

When the Model 71/84 was accepted by the German armed forces, production was instituted on a royalty basis at the government arsenals at Amberg, Spandau and Erfurt. By 1887 the entire German Army had been armed with the repeating rifle, but its success was short lived. The invention of smokeless powder made it obsolete, and the gun was replaced by the 8 mm. Model 88. During World War I, however, German Colonial troops in East Africa were armed with 71/84s.

To load the gun, open the bolt, and push the cutoff to the rear. The cartridge lifter can then be depressed and the cartridges fed into the magazine tube. The rifle is equipped with a cutoff that allows the 8-round magazine to be held in reserve while the gun is operated as a single-shot weapon.

DISASSEMBLY

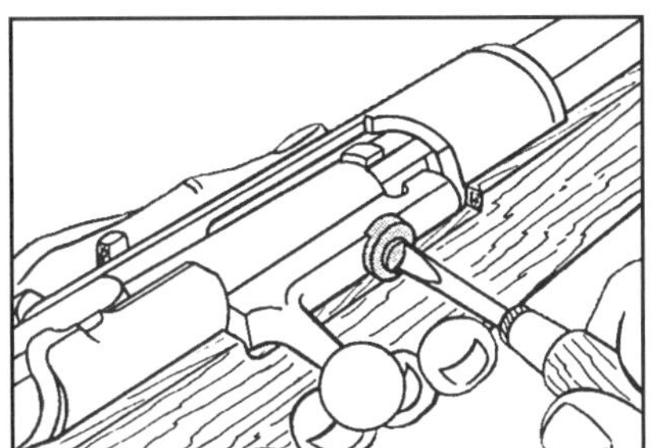

1 The first step in the removal of the Mauser 71/84 bolt is to loosen the bolt stop screw (9). This will allow the round washer-like bolt stop (8) to move upward and clear the receiver bridge. Do not try to remove the bolt stop screw. It cannot be removed unless the retainer pin (7) is knocked out and this is rarely necessary. Then push the cutoff lever (17) all the way forward.

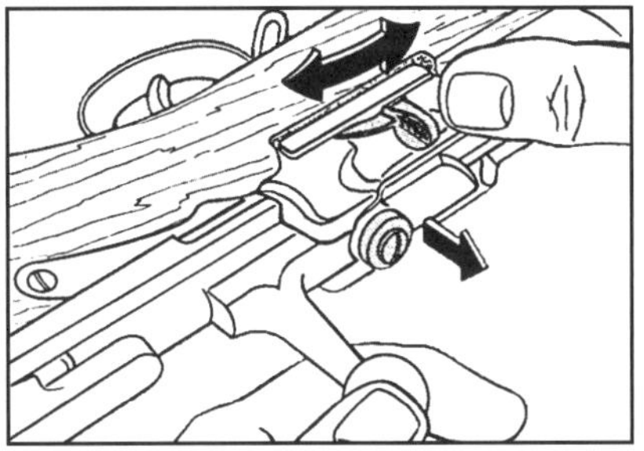

2 Turn the weapon on its side to keep the bolt stop (8) from falling back on the bolt and preventing its removal. Push the cutoff lever (17) back about ⅛-inch or enough to cam the cutoff spring tail (16) out of the path of the bolt. Pull bolt to rear and out of gun. ***Caution:*** *Do not open or close the bolt violently when the bolt stop is loose as the ejector will batter the part of the cutoff spring that protrudes through the receiver.*

3 To disassemble the bolt, the ejector (1) must be removed. This can be lifted off easily since it is only held on by a half-moon spring. Next, turn the cocking piece (10) assembly until the cocking piece cam drops into its cam groove on the bolt (6). Then push down the safety catch (12) as shown until it is free of the notch in the firing pin nut (11). Screw the firing pin nut off the firing pin and remove the cocking piece.

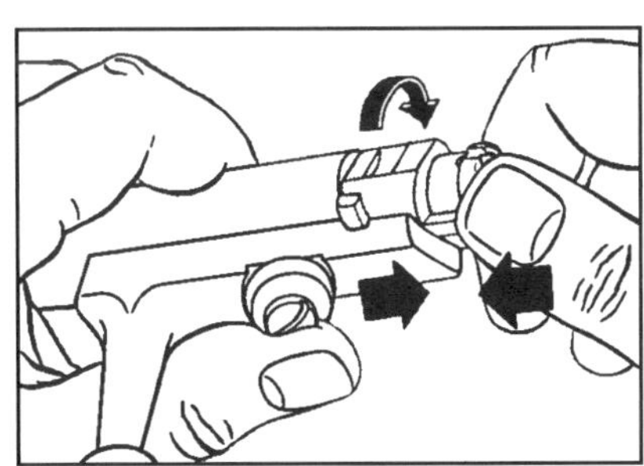

4 Once the ejector has been removed, the bolt head (2) can be disassembled regardless of whether the firing pin nut is on or off. The bolt head is retained by a lug that engages in the rib on the bolt. To remove the bolt head, simply turn it clockwise until the lug is free, then pull the bolt head out. If the firing pin nut (11) has been removed, the bolt head must be pushed toward the bolt while turning, since the head will be under heavy spring pressure as soon as the lug clears the bolt rib.

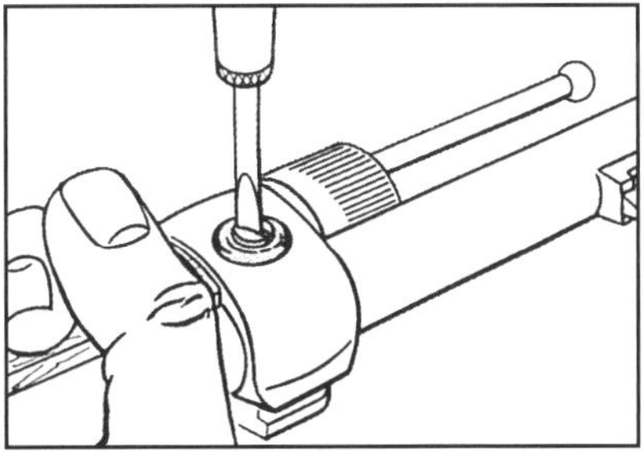

5 The bands must be removed to disassemble the gun. The front band (36) is retained by a cross key (37). The key is in turn retained by a lock screw (38). Therefore, remove the lock screw and drive the key out. The magazine tube can be pulled out when the key is removed.

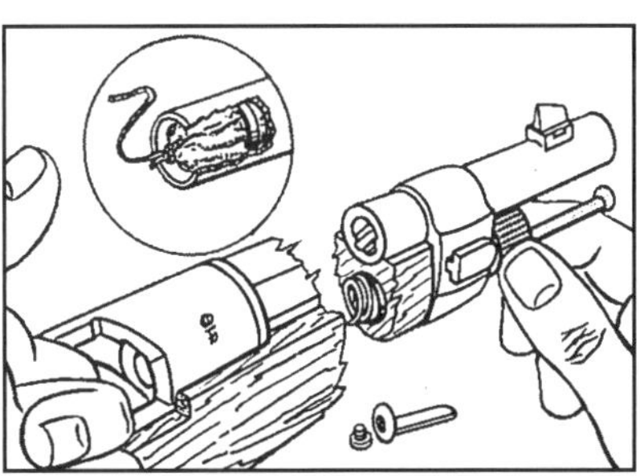

6 Difficulty will sometimes be encountered when replacing the magazine tube. If so, depress the cartridge lifter (26) and push the follower forward well into the magazine tube with the little finger. At the same time push the magazine tube into its seat in the receiver or tie a string to a piece of rag and stuff it in the tube to hold the magazine follower (25) and spring assembly a short distance down the tube. The magazine tube can then be easily reassembled into its seat in the receiver and the rag pulled out freeing the magazine follower.

MAUSER 98 RIFLE

PARTS LEGEND

1. Cocking piece
2. Safety catch
3. Bolt sleeve
4. Bolt sleeve stop spring
5. Bolt sleeve stop
6. Firing pin spring
7. Firing pin
8. Bolt (stripped)
9. Extractor collar
10. Extractor
11. Bolt (complete)
12. Bolt stop screw
13. Bolt stop and spring
14. Ejector
15. Receiver (stripped)
16. Bonnet
17. Stock
18. Magazine follower
19. Sear spring
20. Sear
21. Sear and trigger pins
22. Trigger
23. Latch retainer pin
24. Magazine and trigger guard
25. Look screw
26. Front guard screw
27. Magazine follower spring
28. Magazine floorplate
29. Magazine latch spring
30. Magazine latch
31. Rear guard screw
32. Buttplate

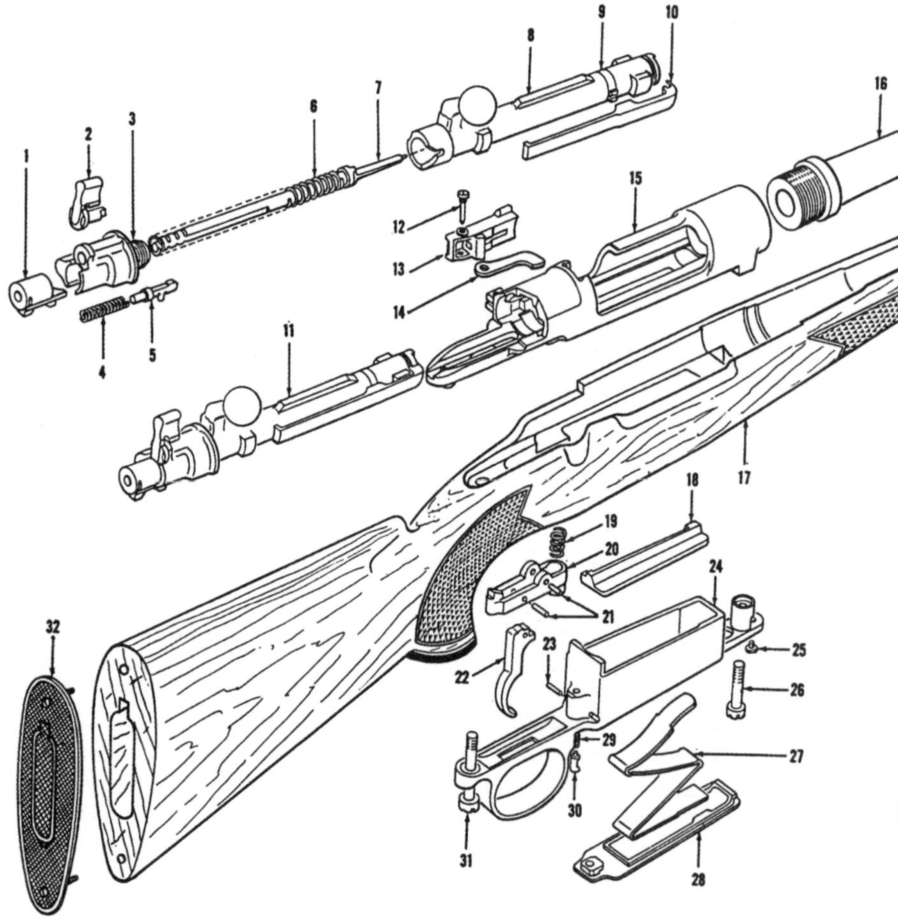

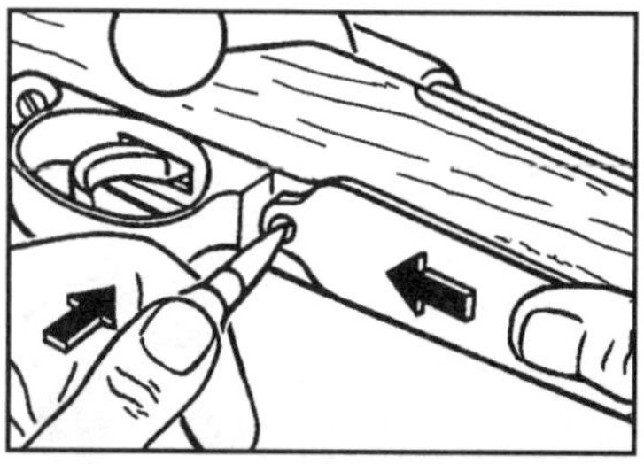

The military-type magazine floor-plate release is by far the common type, but genuine Mouser sporters rarely use it. They normally had a lever or push-latch release.

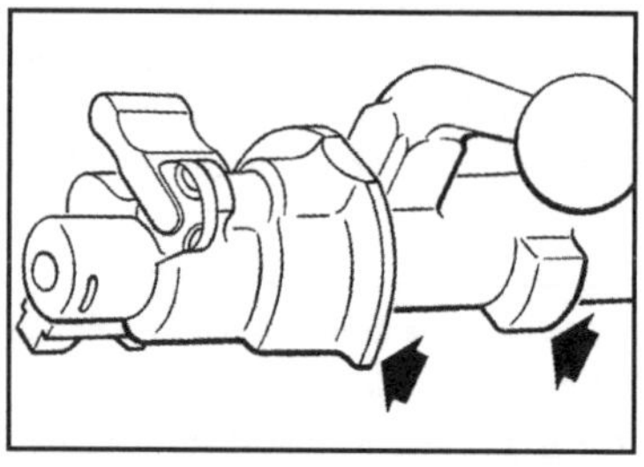

Two of the features that make the Mouser 98 so popular with shooters are the large gas shield and the third locking lug near the rear end of the bolt.

Of all of Paul Mauser's many patents and designs, the one that made his name renowned was the 1898 rifle, which has been manufactured since that date to the present. The *Gehwere 98* rifle, noted for its strength, simplicity and ease of manufacture, became the standard by which all other bolt-action rifles were measured. Mauser actions have been manufactured in many countries in varying degrees of quality but few, if any, can surpass the pre-World War II products of the Oberndorf works.

Pre-war Oberndorf actions were manufactured in three basic lengths: short, standard, and magnum. The receivers themselves were machined for 14 specific cartridges, ranging from the #6 action, designed for the 6.5 x 54, to the #20 action, designed to handle the .416 Rigby.

The pre-war Oberndorf military rifles were well made and finished but they lacked the refinement found in the sporting guns. The Mauser 1898 action had so many improvements that it rendered the earlier Model 95 actions virtually obsolete. The best of these was the addition of a third, or safety, locking lug at the rear of the bolt. Another safety feature is the large gas shield located at the front of the bolt sleeve (see illustration).

The firing pin offers greater safety than most others, in that the shoulder that the firing pin spring rests against has two flanges. These flanges take such a position when the bolt is even partly open that, should the firing pin break at the rear, it cannot go forward and fire the cartridge in the chamber. The firing pin can go fully forward only when the bolt is completely closed and the flanges on the firing pin line up with the cuts on the inside of the bolt.

Features such as these have made the Mauser 1898 action the most widely used design in military and sporting arms.

DISASSEMBLY

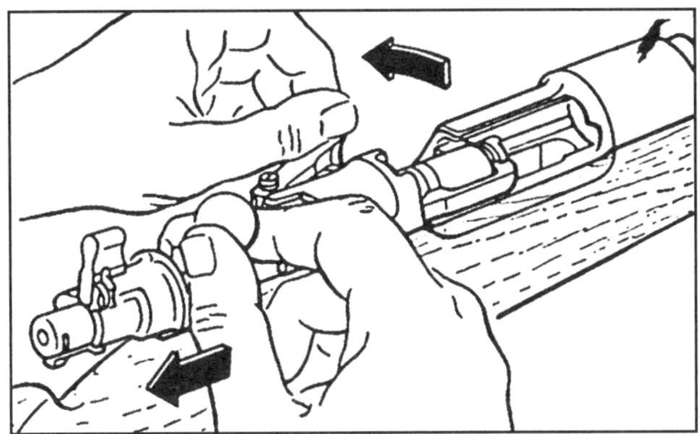

1 To take down the Mauser bolt (11), lift the bolt handle, pull it back to be sure the chamber is empty. Close it, and turn the safety catch (2) to the vertical position. Open the bolt again, and pull it back until it stops. Next, push the forward end of the bolt stop (13) out as far as it can go. You con now pull the bolt assembly out of the rifle.

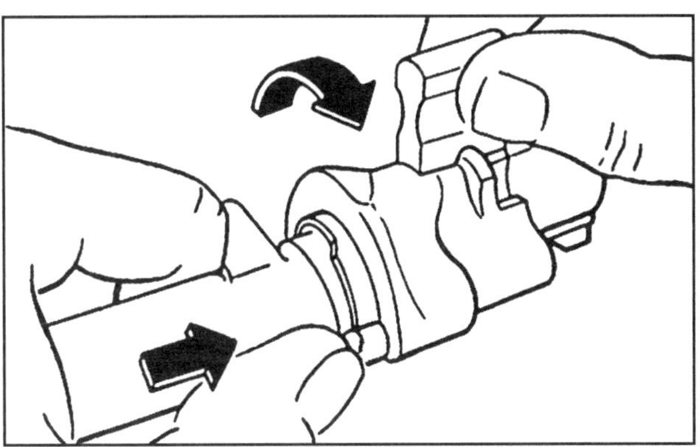

2 To remove the bolt sleeve and firing pin assembly (1-7), push the bolt sleeve stop (5) in as shown. When the stop pin is pushed in far enough, you will be able to screw the assembly out. As you start to turn it, it will be necessary to press the stop pin again to get it around the bolt handle.

3 To remove the extractor (10), turn the extractor away from the bolt handle as far as it will go. Then, using a screwdriver, pry the front end of the extractor up and out of its groove in the bolt. Revolve it a bit further until it is in between the locking lugs. Tap the end of the extractor on the edge of the bench as shown. The extractor will snap free, exposing the extractor collar (9). Do not remove the extractor collar unless absolutely necessary.

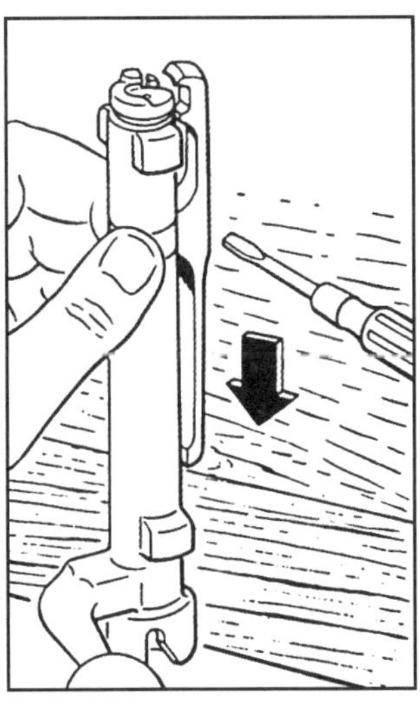

4 To disassemble the belt sleeve, first rest the point of the firing pin (7) against a block of soft wood to prevent it from getting damaged. Next, grasp the bolt sleeve as shown and press down hard until the cocking piece (1) is clear of the bolt sleeve. Turn the cocking piece one-quarter turn as shown, and lift it off. Ease up on the pressure and remove the bolt sleeve (3) and firing pin spring (6). Perform this operation away from your face, for the firing pin spring is very powerful.

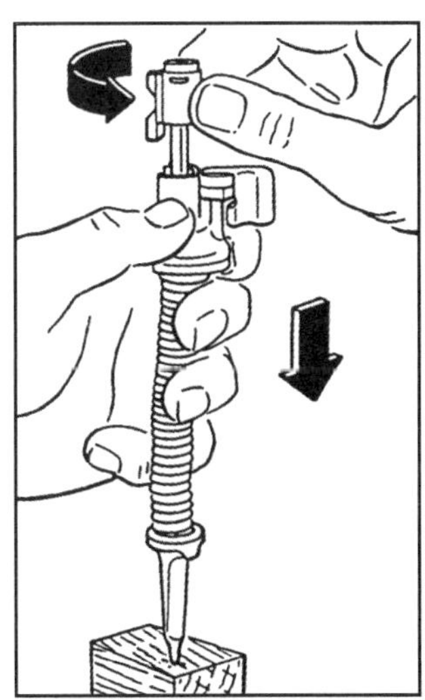

MAUSER 1891 RIFLE - ARGENTINE

PARTS LEGEND

1. Barrel
2. Front sight
3. Rear sight
4. Rear sight spring screw
5. Rear sight spring
6. Rear sight pin
7. Receiver
8. Bolt stop spring screw
9. Bolt stop spring
10. Ejector
11. Bolt stop
12. Bolt stop pin
13. Sear
14. Sear spring
15. Sear pin
16. Trigger pin
17. Trigger
18. Rear guard screw bushing
19. Top buttplate screw
20. Buttplate
21. Rear buttplate screw
22. Trigger guard
23. Rear guard screw
24. Magazine latch pin
25. Magazine latch
26. Magazine latch spring
27. Magazine catch
28. Front guard screw
29. Follower screw
30. Magazine
31. Floorplate pin
32. Floorplate
33. Floorplate spring
34. Follower pin
35. Follower arm
36. Follower spring
37. Magazine follower
38. Rear swivel
39. Rear swivel screw (2)
40. Front swivel
41. Front swivel screw
42. Lower band
43. Front swivel nut*
44. Lower band spring
45. Upper band
46. Upper band spring
47. Front plate
48. Front plate screw (2)
49. Cleaning rod
50. Cleaning rod stop
51. Extractor
52. Bolt
53. Bolt sleeve
54. Safety
55. Safety detent
56. Safety detent spring
57. Safety detent screw
58. Mainspring
59. Firing pin
60. Cocking piece
61. Stock
62. Handguard

* Permanently assembled to other part.

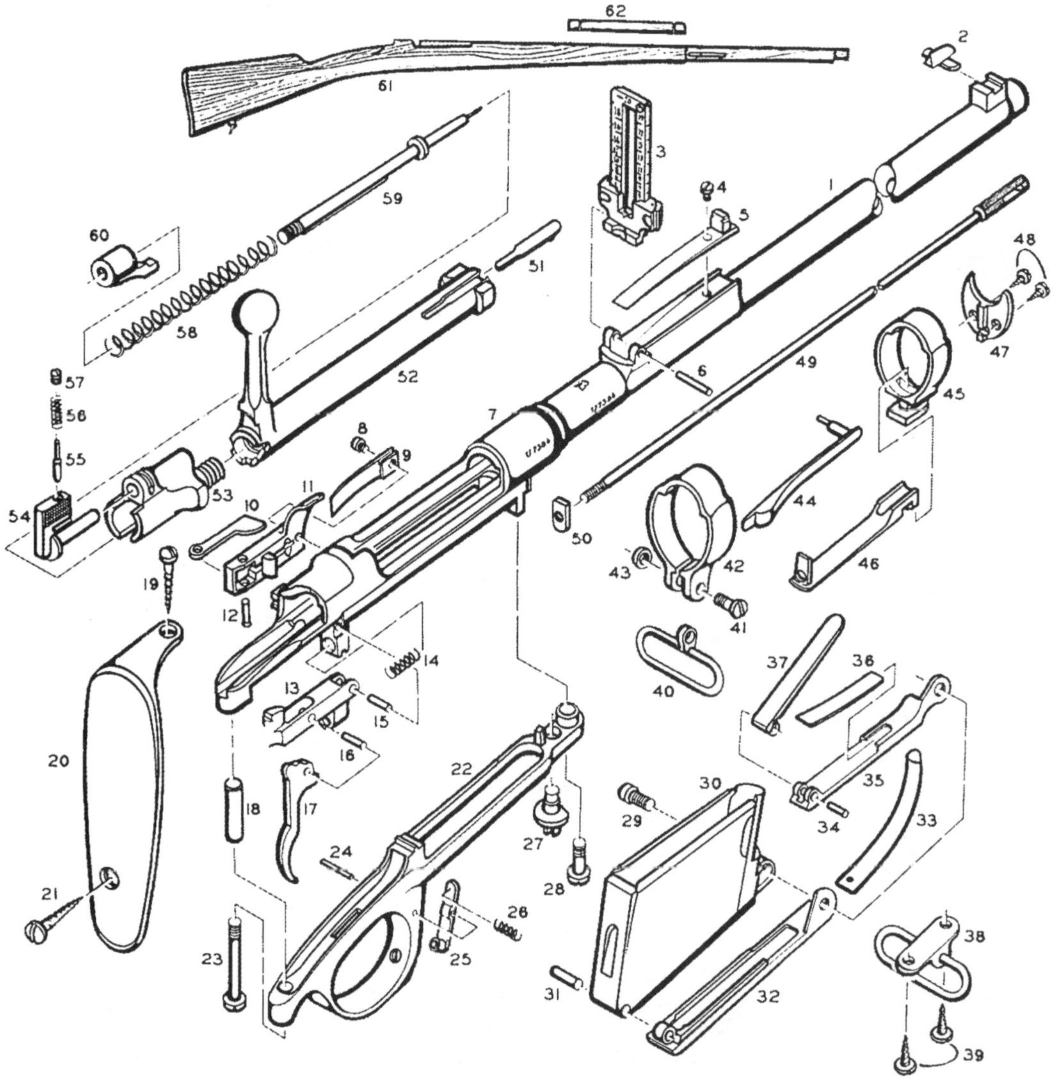

The Argentine Model 1891 Mauser military rifle was adopted in 1991, and the initial production contract for 180,000 rifles and 30,000 carbines was granted to Ludwig Loewe & Co. of Berlin. Additional 1891 rifles were made later for Argentina by Deutsche Waffen und Munitionsfabriken (DWM) in Berlin. DWM had taken control of Loewe in 1896.

The Argentine Model 1891 rifle was essentially identical in design to the earlier Turkish Model 1890 rifle and was chambered for the same cartridge. These arms were chambered for the 7.65 mm. Mauser cartridge loaded with a 212-grain, round-nose bullet with a muzzle velocity of approximately 2060 feet per second. Later Argentine Service ammunition was loaded with 154-grain pointed bullets.

The action cocks on closing of the bolt. There is no auxiliary bolt safety lug as in the later Mauser Model 1898. The stepped barrel contour of the Turkish rifle was retained in the Argentine version. Inletting cuts in the stock fore-end for the barrel shoulders are relieved to prevent binding of the barrel as it elongates from heating in rapid fire. This design feature was carried over to later Mauser bolt-action military rifles.

DISASSEMBLY

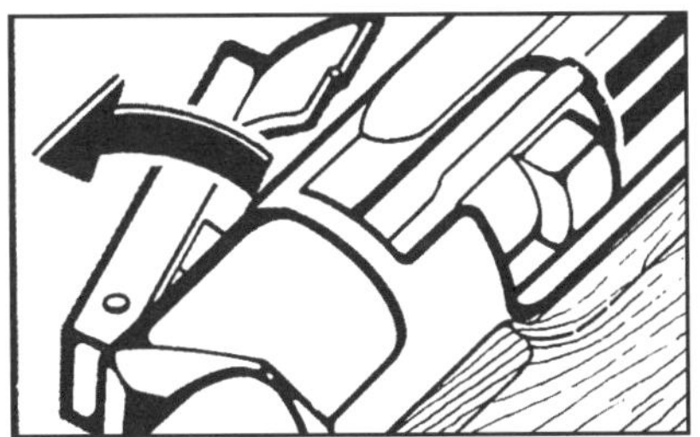

1 Remove bolt assembly from receiver by rotating both safety (54) and then bolt (52) counterclockwise and withdrawing rearward as far as assembly will go. Pull bolt stop (II) to the left and remove bolt.

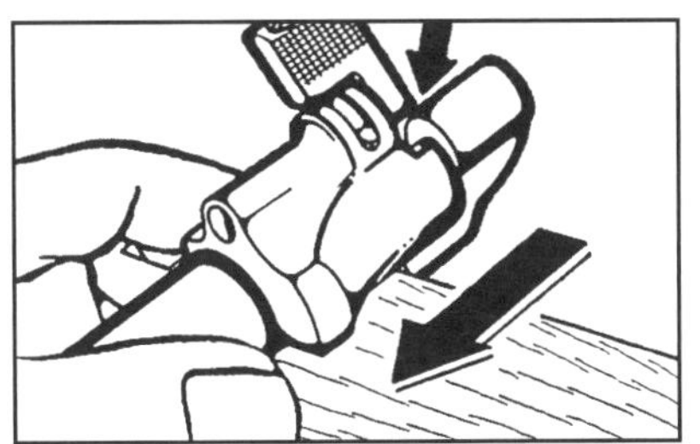

2 Engage nose of cocking piece (60) on edge of bench and pull bolt away until a coin can be inserted between cocking piece and bolt sleeve (53, upper arrow). Unscrew firing mechanism from bolt without dislodging coin. Hold firing mechanism vertically with point of firing pin on a hardwood block, and press down on safety until bolt sleeve clears cocking piece. Unscrew cocking piece from firing pin, allow bolt sleeve to move up gradually under mainspring pressure, and remove bolt sleeve and mainspring from firing pin. Remove safety detent screw (57) and tap out safety detent (55) and safety detent spring (56). In reassembly, screw on cocking piece so that its rear surface is flush with the outer rear edge of the firing pin.

3 Turn rifle over. Give magazine catch (27—arrow, upper right) a half-turn counterclockwise. Depress magazine latch (25—arrow, lower left) and remove the magazine (30).

4 Remove follower screw (29) and swing floorplate (32) down. Using a small pick, push follower arm (35) pivoting leg up into magazine. Follower assembly may now be removed from magazine.

5 Unscrew and remove cleaning rod (49). Depress upper band spring (46) with thumb and slide upper band (45) off front end of barrel (I). Loosen front swivel screw (41), depress lower band spring (44), and remove lower band (42). Remove rear and front guard screws (23 and 28 respectively) and lift away trigger guard (22). Entire barrel and receiver assembly may now be separated from stock (61). Do not remove handguard (62) unless necessary as it is held in place with carefully twisted copper wire.

6 Drift out sear pin (15) and remove sear (13) with trigger assembly attached. Sear spring (14) will drop away at this point. Remove the trigger pin (16) and lift out the trigger (17). Reassemble rifle in reverse.

MAUSER - SWEDISH MODEL 96

PARTS LEGEND

1. Bolt with extractor collar
2. Extractor
3. Firing pin
4. Firing pin spring
5. Bolt sleeve
6. Cocking piece
7. Safety
8. Handguard
9. Stock
10. Handguard band
11. Cleaning rod
12. Lower band
13. Upper band
14. Barrel and receiver
15. Bolt stop
16. Ejector
17. Bolt stop screw
18. Bolt stop and ejector spring
19. Follower
20. Magazine spring
21. Trigger guard
22. Front guard screw
23. Floorplate
24. Floorplate catch
25. Catch spring
26. Rear guard screw
27. Trigger
28. Sear
29. Trigger pin
30. Sear pin
31. Sear spring
32. Assembled bolt

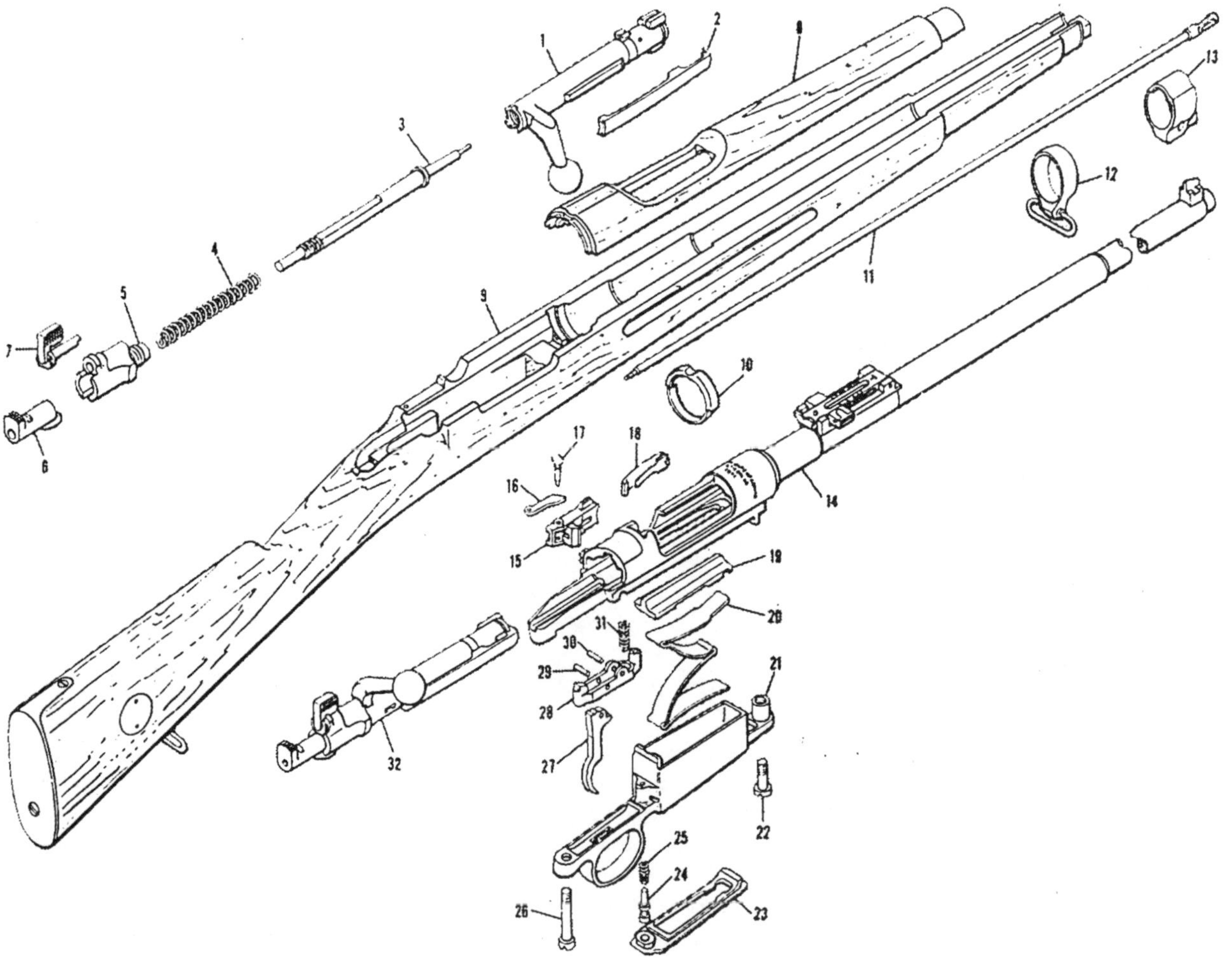

MAUSER

The Swedish 6.5 mm. Mauser rifle was one of the many arms developed by German arms designer Paul Mauser. It is made for the 6.5x55 mm. cartridge, and was produced in several models, the 1894 carbine and 1896 infantry rifle being most common. This rifle was produced in Sweden by the Carl Gustafs Government Rifle Factory and the Husqvarna Arms Co. Earlier specimens were made in Germany by Mauser.

This rifle is an improvement on the Model 1893 Spanish rifle, the first Mauser with a staggered-column internal box-magazine. Improvements include a guide rib on the bolt, deep rounded cut in left receiver wall to facilitate magazine loading, and a thumb-piece which permits the firing pin to be eased forward. Overall, the rifle is simple, reliable, highly accurate, and famous for its fine-quality workmanship and finish.

Besides the Model 1894 carbine and 1896 rifle, there is a Model 1938 short rifle and 1941 sniper rifle. All models are mechanically alike and adapted to the 6.5x55 cartridge.

In addition to its use by Sweden, Finland employed this rifle in the 1939-40 Russo-Finnish War, and a quantity was purchased by Denmark following World War II.

DISASSEMBLY

1 After checking to make sure that chamber and magazine are unloaded, cock rifle by rotating bolt to open position, pulling back several inches, and then closing it. Turn safety (7) to vertical middle position, pull outward on bolt stop (15) with thumb, and remove bolt from receiver. In replacing bolt, it is unnecessary to pull out bolt stop, which will be automatically forced aside as bolt is pushed into receiver. Follower (19) must be pushed down to allow bolt to go forward.

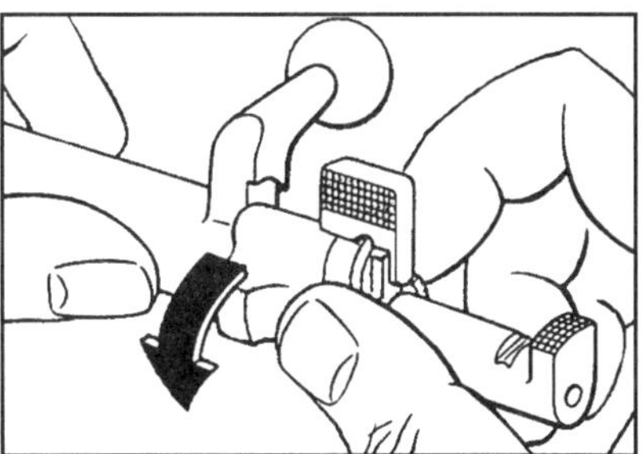

2 With safety in middle position, grasp bolt sleeve (5) and unscrew firing mechanism from bolt.

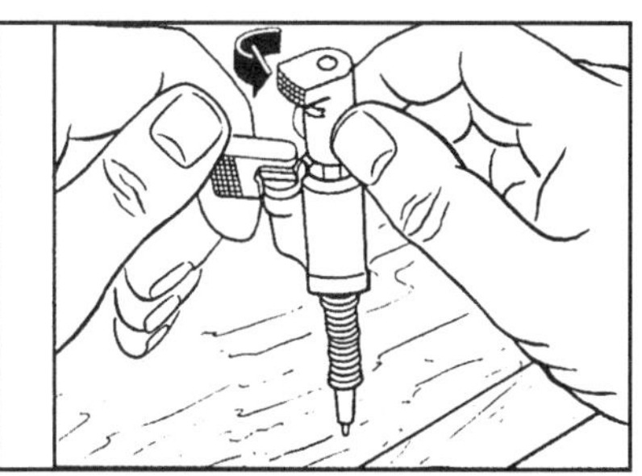

3 Rest firing pin point against a wooden block. Grasp bolt sleeve and safety (7) tightly, and push down on safety with thumb until cocking piece (6) is clear of bolt sleeve. Rotate cocking piece a quarter turn in either direction, and lift it off firing pin (3). Slowly allow firing pin spring (4) to expand and remove bolt sleeve and firing pin spring from firing pin. Turn safety all the way to the right, and remove it from bolt sleeve.

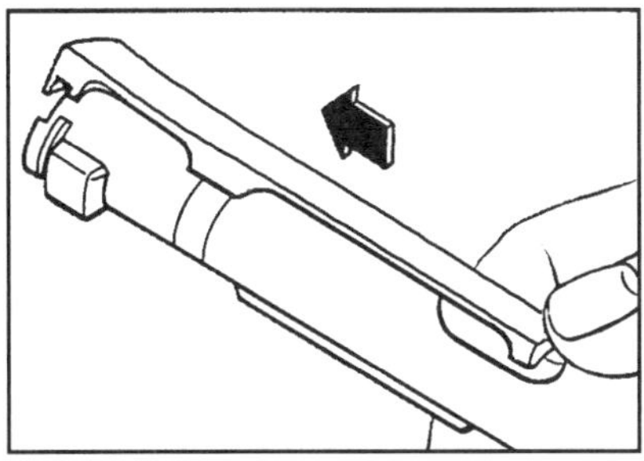

4 Rotate extractor (2) until its tongue runs out of the extractor groove on bolt head. Push extractor forward with thumb to free it from extractor collar on bolt. Do not remove extractor collar. To replace extractor, engage undercuts on its lower suface with lugs of extractor collar. Push extractor to rear, lift its tongue over front edge of bolt, and rotate extractor until tongue is in extractor groove on bolt.

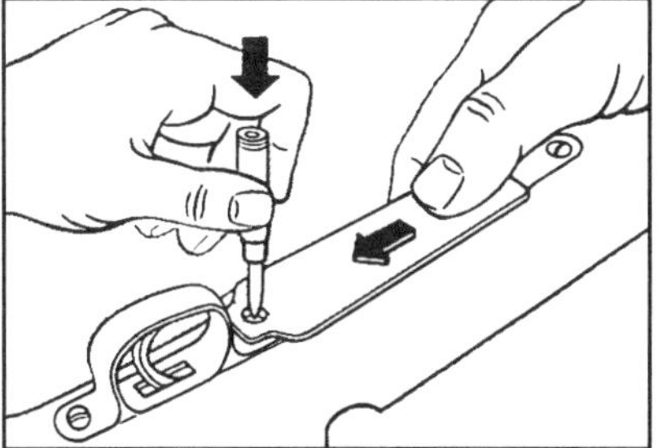

5 To disassemble magazine, use a cartridge nose to depress floorplate catch (24), and at the same time push floorplate (23) rearward until disengaged from undercuts in trigger guard. Lift floorplate with attached magazine spring and follower out of trigger guard, and slide magazine spring out of undercuts on floorplate and follower. In reassembly, first engage narrow end of magazine spring in undercuts of follower.

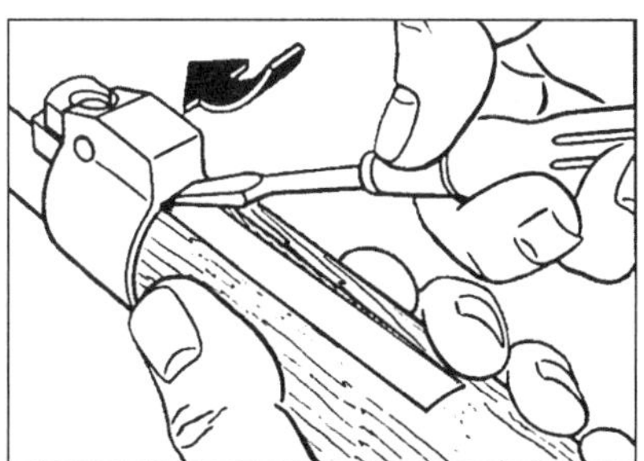

6 To remove stock and handguard, it is necessary to remove the lower band (12) and upper band (13). Use a screwdriver to depress band-retaining springs and push bands forward. Cleaning rod (11) must be unscrewed and removed before attempting to depress upper band spring. Raise rear sight leaf to vertical position, and lift off handguard (8). Unscrew front and rear guard screws (22 & 26), and separate barrel and receiver (14) and trigger guard (21) from stock.

MOISIN NAGANT MODEL 1891 RIFLE

PARTS LEGEND

1. Cocking piece
2. Bolt
3. Firing pin spring
4. Firing pin
5. Bolt connector and guide bar
6. Bolt head
7. Extractor
8. Bolt (assembled)
9. Rear guard screw
10. Ejector spring retaining screw
11. Ejector spring and feed interrupter
12. Ejector
13. Receiver
14. Barrel assembly
15. Handguard
16. Front and rear barrel bands
17. Front sight
18. Trigger
19. Trigger hinge pin
20. Trigger spring and bolt stop
21. Bolt stop retaining screw
22. Magazine and trigger guard
23. Front guard screw
24. Magazine follower
25. Magazine follower spring assembly
26. Follower hinge pin
27. Lower magazine follower spring
28. Spring retaining screw
29. Magazine floorplate
30. Floorplate latch
31. Floorplate latch screw
32. Follower hinge pin (upper)
33. Stock
34. Buttplate

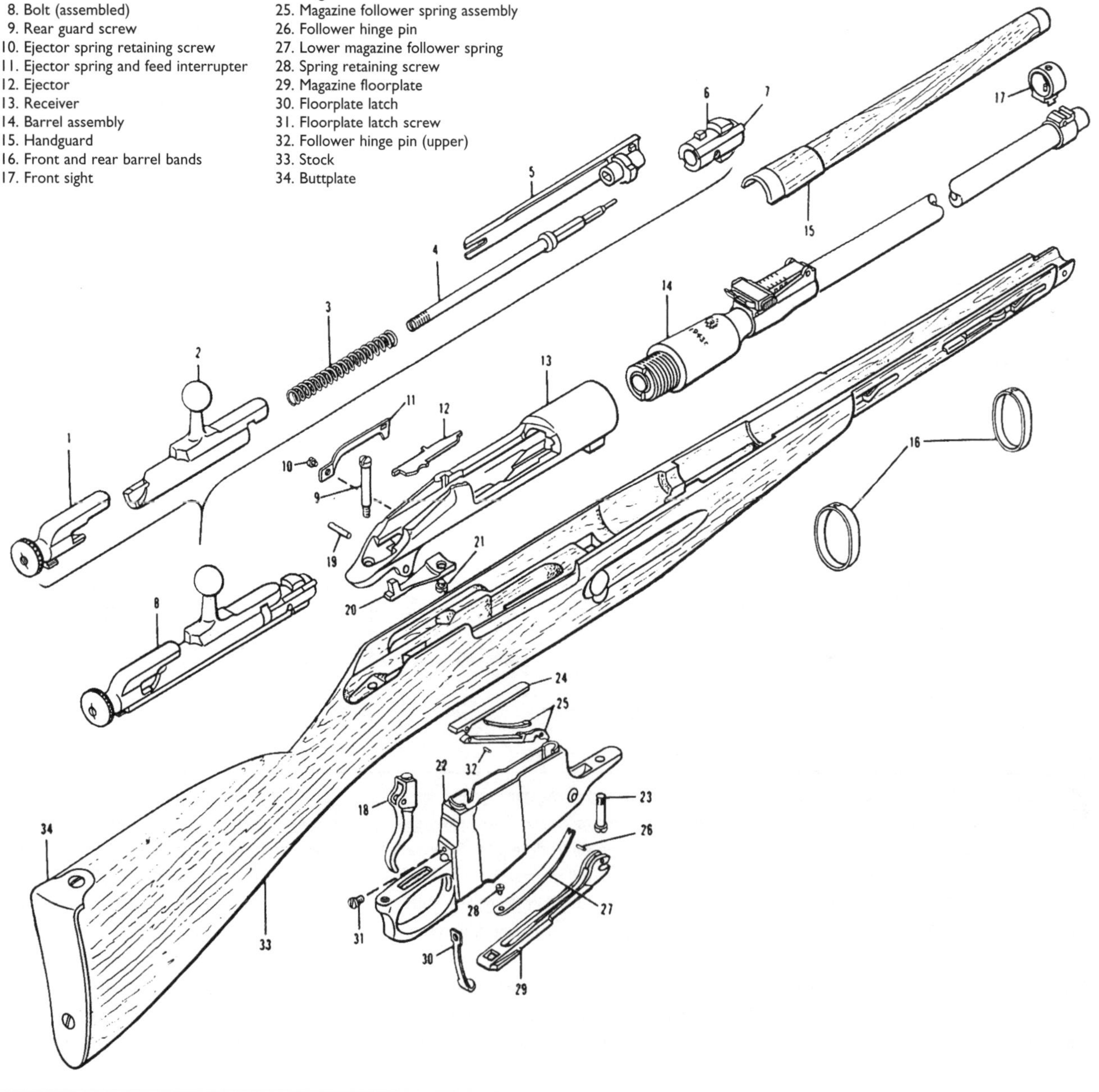

Adopted for use by Czarist Russian armies in 1891, the Moisin-Nagant rifle was among the earliest military rifles designed for smokeless powder. As such it is a peer of the Krag-Jorgensen, the British Lee-Enfield Mks I and II, the German Model 1888 Commission Rifle and the French Mannlicher-Berthier.

The Russian Model 1891 rifle was designed by Colonel Serge Moisin, of the Imperial Russian Army, in collaboration with the renown Belgian arms designer, Emile Nagant. The term three-line , sometimes used to describe these rifles, indicates that the nominal bore diameter is 0.300 inch, based on a native Russian unit of measure equal to 0.1 inch.

Moisin-Nagant rifles have been manufactured in Russia, Switzerland, France, Finland, China and North Korea, and in the United States by Remington and New England Westinghouse. American-made Moisin rifles, not delivered because of the Russian Revolution in 1917, were purchased by the U.S. government, used for training during World War I and finally, in the 1920s and '30s, sold to NRA members by the Director of Civilian Marksmanship (D.C.M.).

The earliest Model 1891 rifles had octagon-shaped receivers whereas subsequent versions had round receivers. Numerous variations exist, including rifles and carbines made by several users (the specimen illustrated in a Russian made Model 91-30). Several nations furnished their snipers with specially adapted, telescopically sighted versions of this rifle. Like the U.S. M1903 rifle, specially constructed Moisin-Nagant rifles have been used successfully by both Russian and Finnish International and Olympic shooters.

Along with at least one of its contemporaries, the Moisin-Nagant remained in limited service in several of the world's military forces until well past the mid-century mark.

DISASSEMBLY

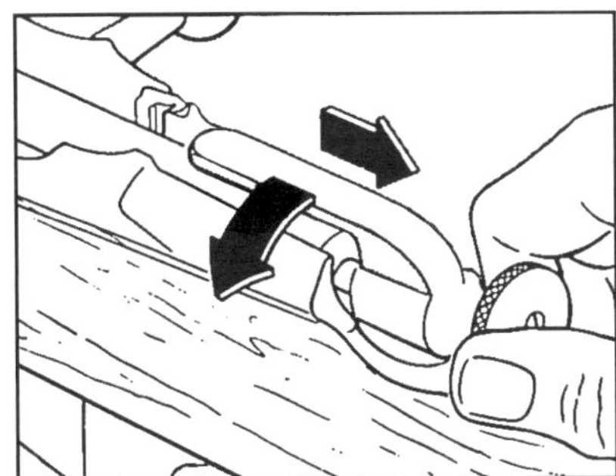

1 To apply safety catch, pull back cocking piece (1) far enough to allow it to be rotated as shown, over back edge of receiver.

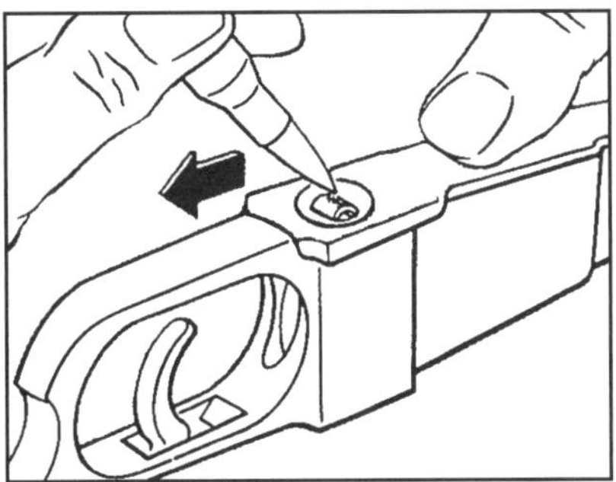

2 This rifle has a simple magazine floorplate release. Using a cartridge or finger, pull back floorplate latch (30). Then swing magazine floorplate (29) open.

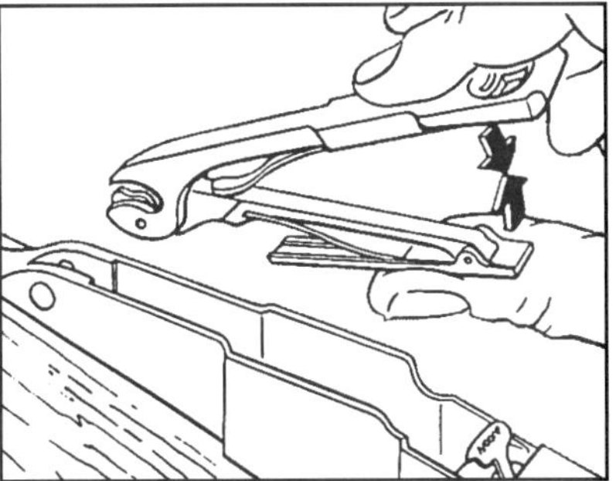

3 To remove magazine floorplate (29) and magazine follower (24), squeeze floorplate and follower together as shown. This will open hinge at end of floorplate and allow it to be pulled free of hinge pin that is riveted through magazine.

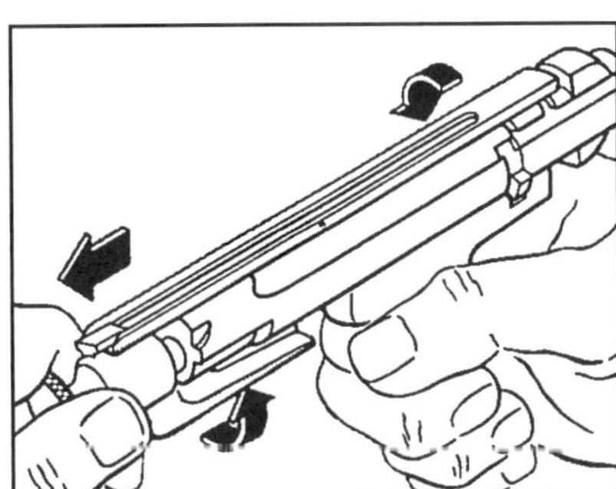

4 To strip bolt (8), grasp as shown. Pull back cocking piece (1) far enough to disengage it from end of bolt. Rotate it as shown, allowing it to go forward. Now slide bolt head (6) and bolt connector and guide bar (5) off bolt body (2).

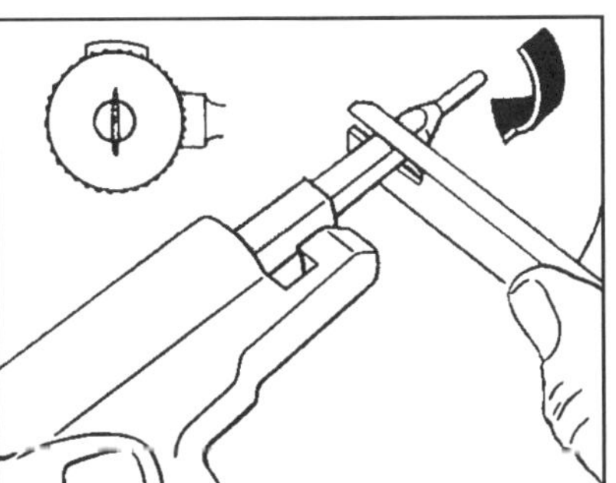

5 Since firing pin (4) is screwed into cocking piece (1), they sometimes bind. End of bolt connector and guide bar (5) can be used as a wrench to screw out firing pin (4). When reassembling bolt, be sure marks on firing pin and cocking piece line up.

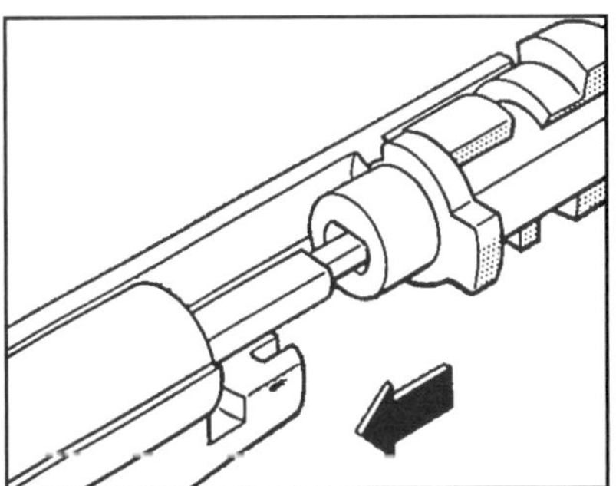

6 To reassemble bolt, screw firing pin (4), firing pin spring (3), bolt (2), and cocking piece (1) together. Line up open end of guide bar with lug on cocking piece, then rotate bolt head until it lines up as shown. Push it all together and rotate cocking piece back to cocked position.

MOSSBERG MODEL 144-LS .22 RIFLE

PARTS LEGEND

1. Receiver
2. Barrel
3. Barrel band
4. Sight assembly
5. Ejector
6. Receiver peep sight assembly
7. Receiver sight base
8. Receiver sight lock screw
9. Receiver sight base mounting screws (2)
10. Bolt body
11. Extractor, left
12. Extractor, right
13. Firing pin
14. Bolt lever
15. Mainspring plunger
16. Mainspring
17. Mainspring cap
18. Takedown stud
19. Bracket
20. Safety
21. Safety screw
22. Trigger
23. Trigger pin
24. Trigger pull adjusting screw
25. Trigger pull adjusting spring
26. Trigger pull adjusting plunger
27. Angle bar & adjusting bracket
28. Magazine latch
29. Bracket screw
30. Buttplate
31. Buttplate screws (2)
32. Butt swivel assembly
32a. Butt swivel screws (2)
33. Trigger spring plunger
34. Trigger spring
35. Stock
36. Trigger guard
37. Rear trigger guard screw
38. Front trigger guard screw
39. Magazine stock plate
40. Takedown screw
41. Magazine assembly
42. Adjustable forearm plate
43. Adjustable forearm stop nut
44. Adjustable forearm stop
45. Adjustable forearm stop screw
46. Forearm swivel screw
47. Forearm swivel
48. Adjustable forearm plate

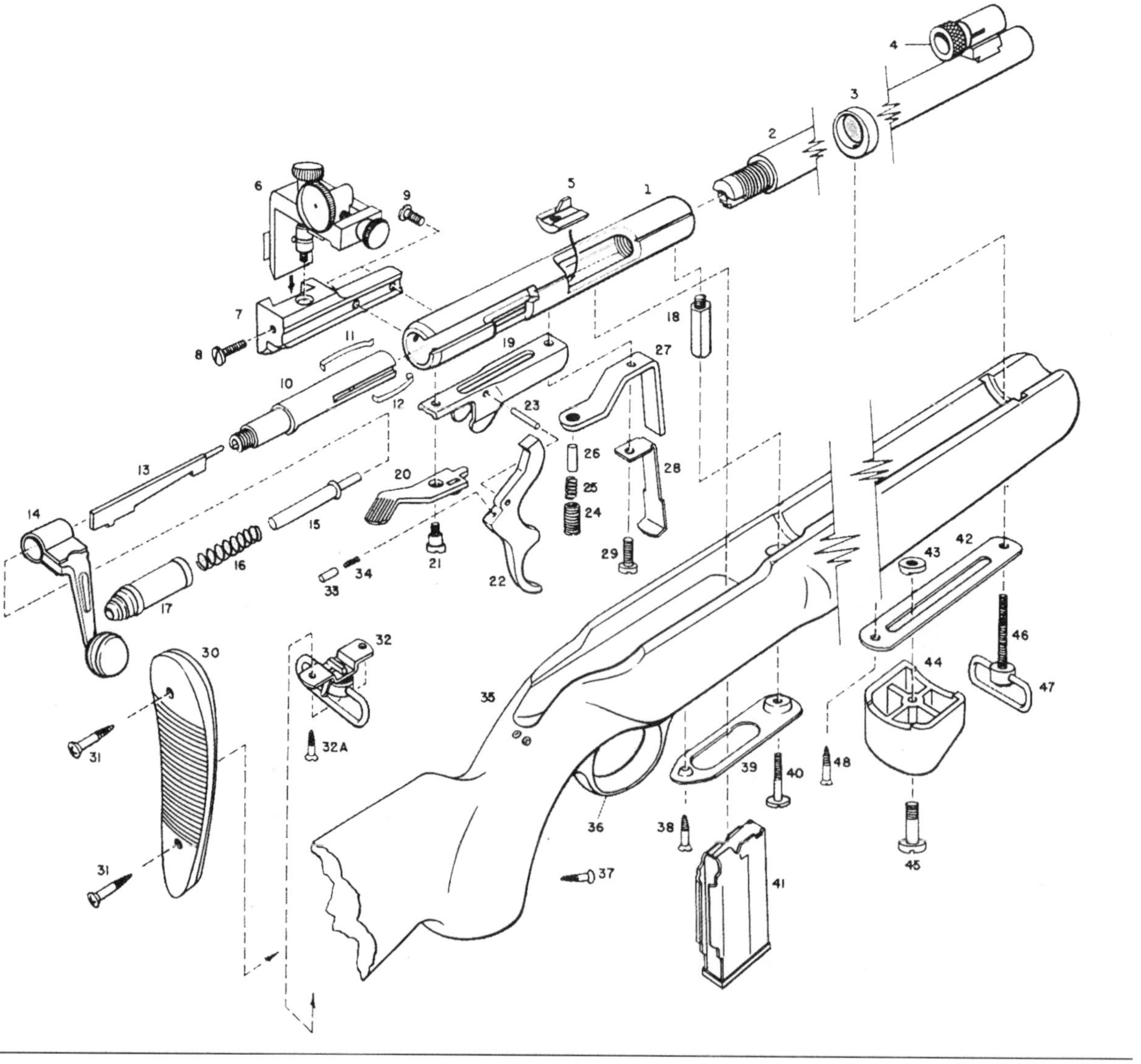

The Mossberg Model 144, .22 caliber target rifle was introduced in 1954 by O.F. Mossberg. Weighing eight pounds, it was a moderately priced target rifle intended for basic marksmanship training and beginning rifle competition.

The bolt action of the Model 144 was similar to that of the Mossberg Model 44-US, a training rifle used by the Army during World War II. The 144 had a 26-inch, medium weight barrel and a target-style stock with a high comb, pistol grip and beavertail fore-end. The rifle featured dual extractors and a seven-round detachable box magazine.

Model 144 rifles were initially produced with Mossberg sights, and later with Lyman front and rear sights. After 1960 144s were fitted with Lyman front and Mossberg rear sights. The Model 144 was discontinued in 1985.

DISASSEMBLY

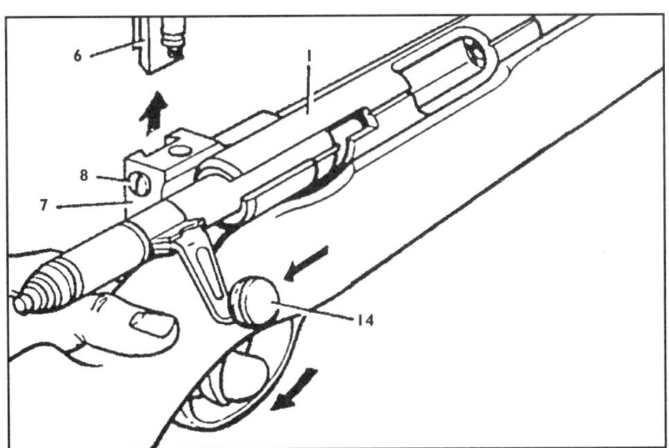

1 To remove bolt from receiver, open bolt and be sure rifle is unloaded. Press magazine latch (28) rearward and remove magazine assembly (41) from rifle. Loosen receiver sight lock screw (8) in sight base (7). Lift receiver peep sight assembly (6) up out of base. Pull back trigger and slide bolt out of receiver to rear. Unscrew takedown screw (40) and forearm swivel screw (46), and remove action and barrel assembly from stock.

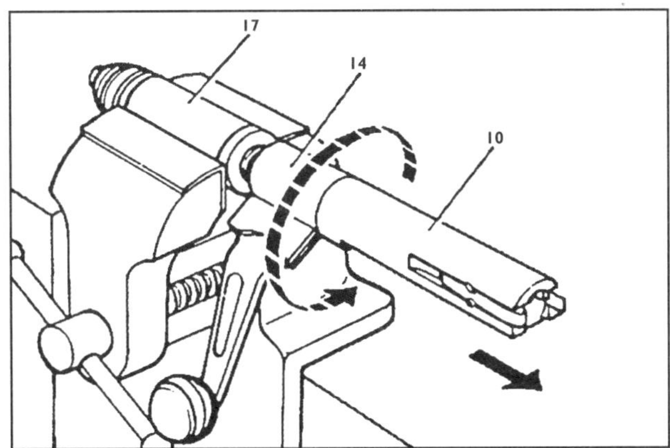

2 To disassemble the bolt, clamp the mainspring cap (17) in a padded vise as shown. Use bolt lever (14) for handle and unscrew bolt body (10) from the cap and remove the bolt body, mainspring (16), plunger (15), firing pin (13), and bolt lever (14). Note that left and right extractors (11 & 12) are retained in the bolt body by permanent crimps punched into the bolt body. Removal of the extractors is not recommended.

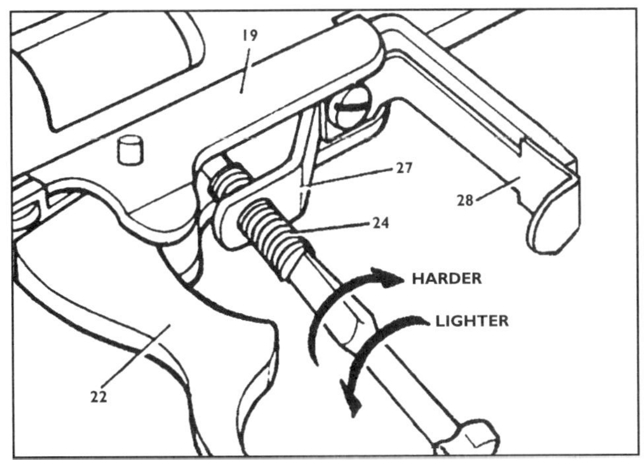

3 Turn in trigger pull adjusting screw (24) for a harder trigger pull and turn out for a lighter pull as shown. Adjusting for a pull lighter than three pounds should not be attempted. Remove trigger and safety assembly by unscrewing safety screw (21) and bracket screw (29). Remove ejector (5) from inside of receiver (I), and drop bracket (19) from bottom of receiver with angle bar (27) and magazine latch (28). Trigger (22) can be removed by drifting out trigger pin (23). Take care not to lose trigger spring and plunger (34 & 33).

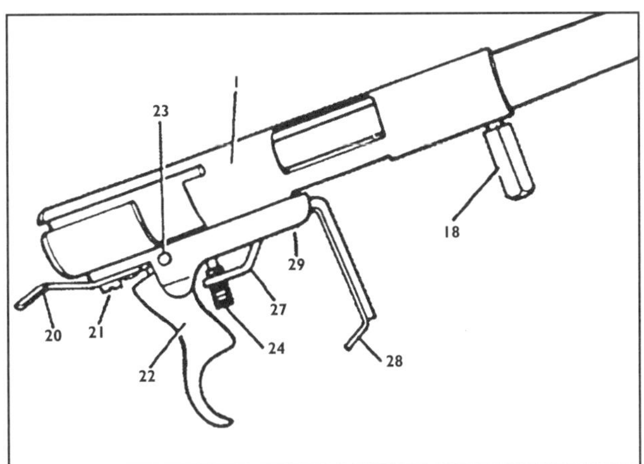

4 This drawing shows the proper arrangement of lock mechanism parts when they are assembled.

MOSSBERG MODEL 500 SHOTGUN

PARTS LEGEND

1. Barrel assembly
2. Mid-point bead
3. Front sight
4. Takedown screw (model 500)
5. Choke tube
6. Receiver
7. Scope mount dummy screws
8. Ejector
9. Ejector screw
10. Elevator
11. Cartridge stop
12. Cartridge interrupter
13. Bolt assembly
14. Bolt slide
15. Trigger housing assembly
16. Trigger housing pin
17. Stock
18. Recoil pad
19. Spacer
20. Recoil pad screw
21. Stock bolt
22. Lock washer
23. Ejector follower
24. Magazine spring
25. Limiting plug
26. Retaining "O" ring
27. Magazine tube
28. Action slide assembly
29. Forearm
30. Action slide tube nut
31. Rifled barrel
32. Front sight assembly
33. Rear rifle sight assembly
34. Magazine cap (model 590)
35. Retaining washer
36. Front swivel stud
37. Heat shield
38. Heat shield spacer
39. Head shield screw/nuts
40. Speedfeed, stock
41. Speedfeed, recoil pad
42. Speedfeed, recoil pad screws
43. Speedfeed, stock bolt
44. Lock washer
45. Flat washer
46. Stock swivel, Q.D. post
47. Speedfeed, followers
48. Speedfeed, springs

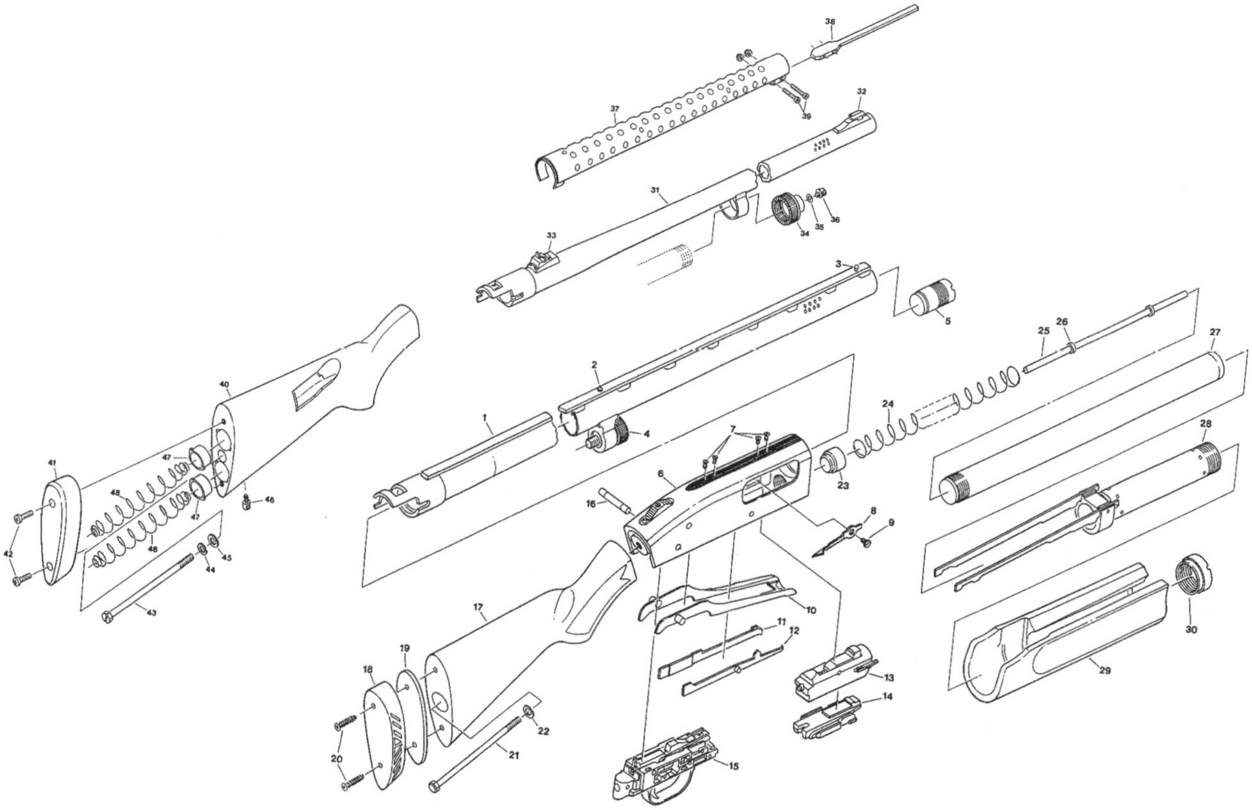

The Mossberg 500 pump-action shotgun, manufactured by O.F. Mossberg & Sons, was first marketed in 1962. The design included a lightweight aluminum receiver and has been produced in 12 and 20 gauge and .410 bore. The Mossberg 500 has been manufactured in as many as 17 models, including a 12 gauge/.50 caliber muzzleloading version. Barrels for the 500 are interchangeable and have been produced in several variations in lengths ranging from 18½ to 32 inches. In 1979 the Model 500 was adopted for general issue by all major branches of the United States armed forces. It was replaced by a variant, the Model 590, in 1987.

DISASSEMBLY

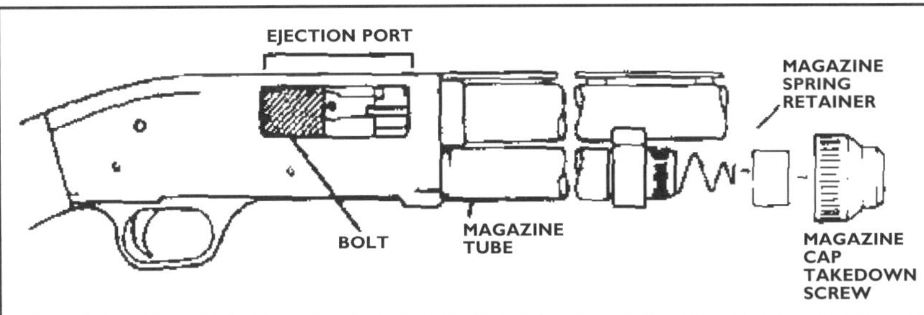

1 Depress the action lock lever and open the action by sliding the forearm fully rearward. Move the forearm slowly forward from the fully rearward position until the front of the bolt is in the middle of the ejection port. Loosen the takedown screw by turning it counterclockwise until the screw threads are completely disengaged from the end of the magazine tube. Remove the barrel from the receiver with a gentle back-and-forth rotational movement while pulling the barrel out of the receiver assembly.

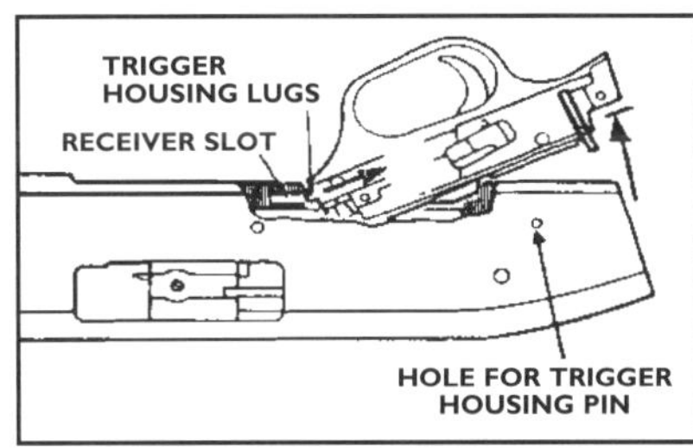

2 Position the shotgun with the trigger guard upward. With a blunt object (no greater than 3/16-inch [4.76 mm] diameter), push out the small diameter trigger housing retainer pin located on the slide of the receiver, approximately a ½-inch (12.7 mm) below the rear of the trigger guard.

Remove the trigger housing assembly by lifting the rear portion upward first.

The trigger housing assembly is a complex assembly and must not be disassembled. Disassembly should only be performed at an authorized Product Service Center or by a qualified gunsmith.

CAUTION: Pay special attention to the position of the bolt, bolt slide and action slide bar assembly during this portion of the disassembly, as the parts must be in the same relationship during reassembly.

3 Remove the cartridge interrupter from the ejection port side and cartridge stop from the opposite side. (It may be necessary to tap the sides of the receiver lightly to release these parts).

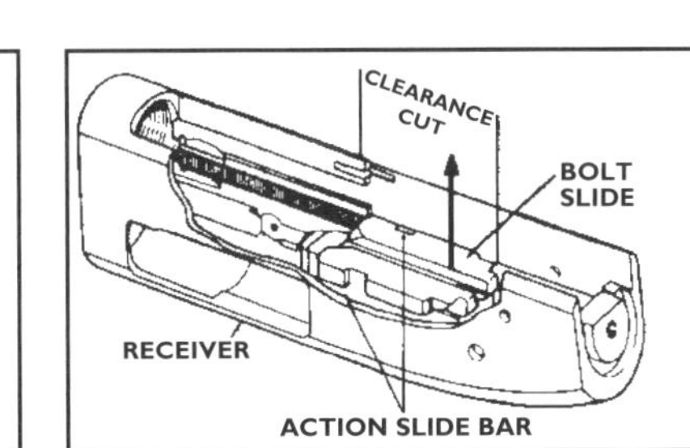

4 Move the forearm/action slide assembly rearward so that the bolt assembly and bolt slide are three quarters of the way rearward. When the bottom of the bolt slide is aligned with the clearance cuts in the sides of the receiver, lift the bolt slide upward and out of the receiver.

Remove the bolt assembly by sliding it forward and out of the receiver assembly through the barrel opening at the front of the receiver.

NOTE: The safety button located on the upper rear of the receiver must be fully rearward in the "on" (safe) position to remove the elevator assembly.

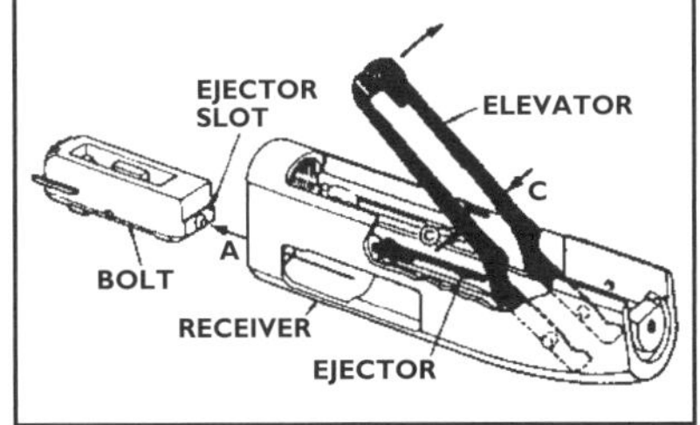

5 Pivot the front portion of the elevator upward out of the receiver. Squeeze the two arms that form the open end of the elevator assembly together sufficiently to disengage and remove the elevator from the receiver.

Remove the forearm/action slide assembly by sliding it forward and off the magazine tube.

NAVY ARMS MODEL 66 RIFLE

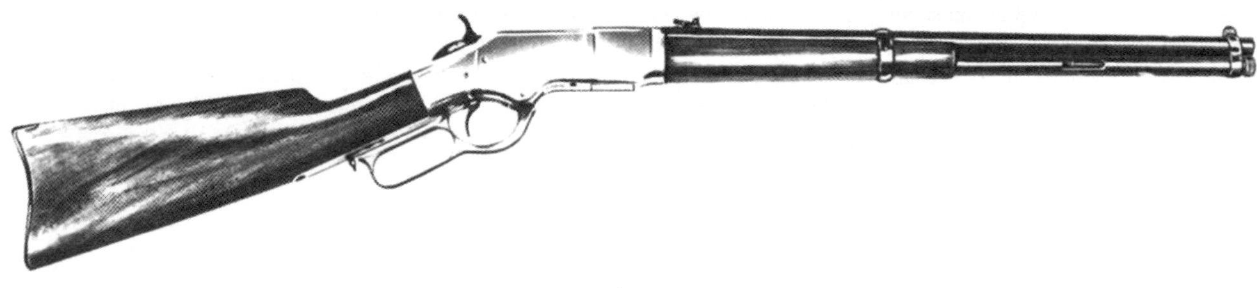

PARTS LEGEND

1. Front band
2. Band screw
3. Barrel
4. Rear sight
5. Magazine tube
6. Magazine tube Button
7. Button retaining screw
8. Magazine follower
9. Forend band
10. Band screw
11. Forend
12. Extractor
13. Extractor pin
14. Bolt
15. Left front link
16. Connecting pin
17. Right front link
18. Link pin
19. Right rear link
20. Left rear link
21. Link pin
22. Firing pin spring
23. Firing pin
24. Firing pin extension
25. Right side plate
26. Link hinge pin
27. Hammer
28. Hammer link
29. Tang screw
30. Hammer spring
31. Buttstock
32. Buttplate screw
33. Buttplate
34. Receiver
35. Tang screw
36. Hammer spring screw
37. Sear spring
38. Grip safety
39. Safety hinge pin
40. Sear
41. Trigger
42. Trigger pin
43. Hammer screw
44. Spring retaining screws (2)
45. Cartridge lifter spring
46. Lever spring
47. Lever
48. Link operating pin
49. Feed Block Lifter
50. Feed Block
51. Cartridge Stop
52. Stop Screw
53. Left Side Plate
54. Lever Screw
55. Side Plate Screw
56. Link Pin

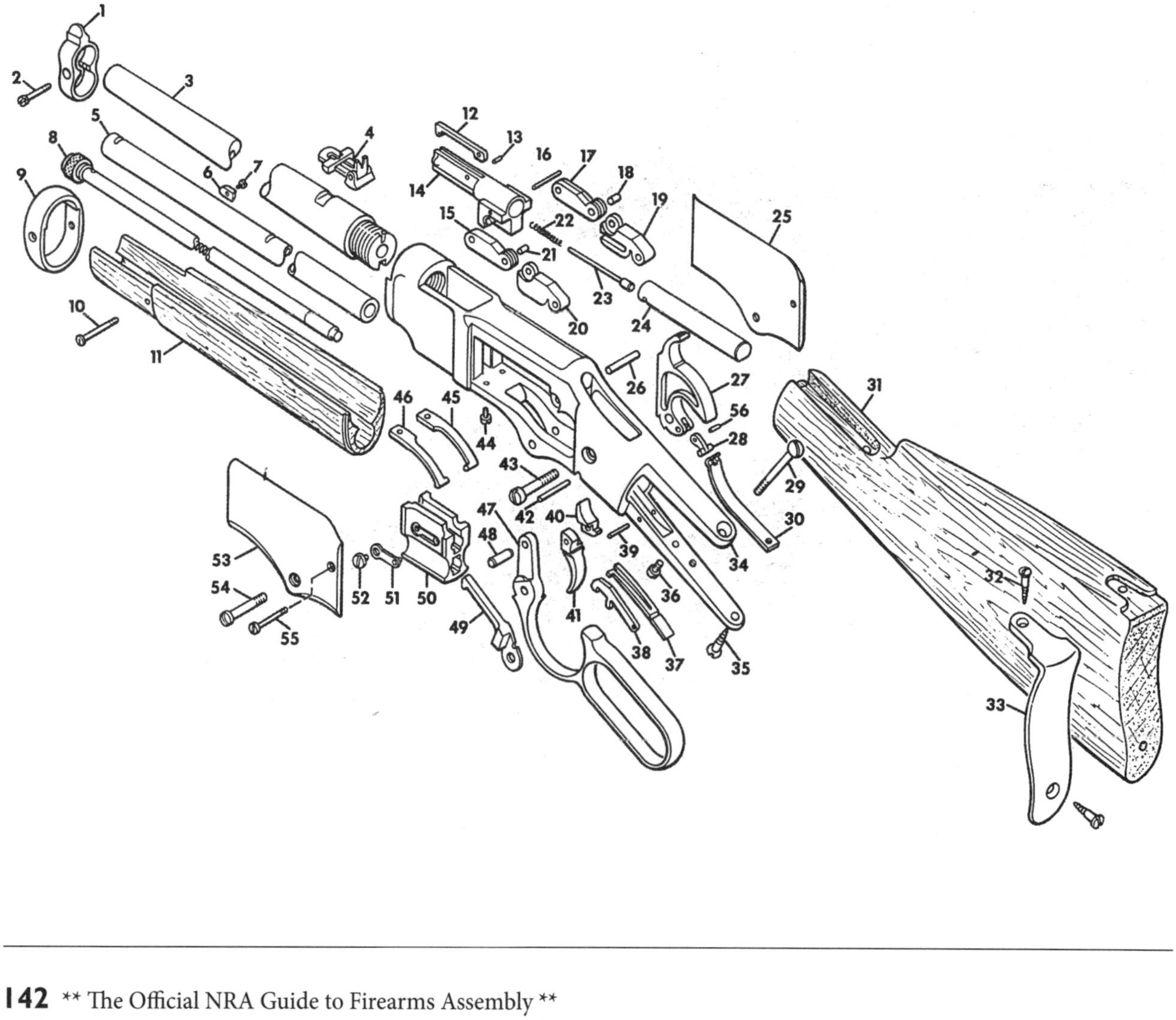

The Navy Arms Model 66 Yellowboy was made as a replica of one of the most significant firearms in American history — the Winchester Model 1866. Chambered in .22 Long Rifle, the Model 66 Yellowboy was made for Navy Arms by the Italian firm of A. Uberti, and was first produced in 1966, the centennial of the original Winchester. This lever-action rimfire featured a 19-inch blued barrel set in a polished brass frame, and was available with three styles of engraving.

The gun was later made in .38 Special and .44/40 as well as the .22 Long Rifle, and there was a Trapper's Model which sported a 16-inch barrel. When Navy Arms saw the production costs climb too high, the Model 66 was set aside and Uberti ceased production. Approximately 20,000 guns were made in all, with the last one being produced in 1978.

DISASSEMBLY

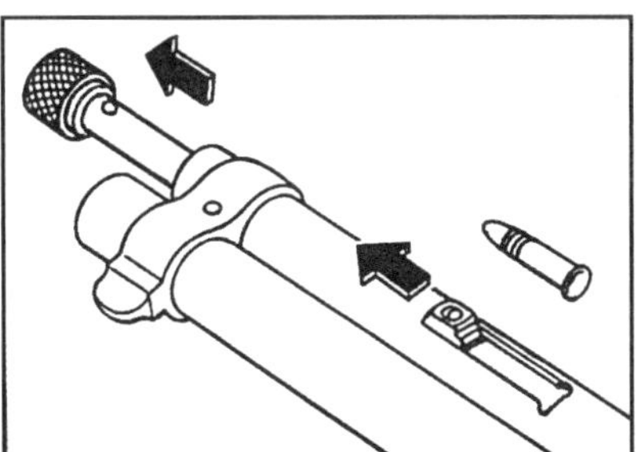

1 To load Model 66 .22 lever-action, first push back the button (6) that covers the opening in the magazine tube. Seventeen .22 long rifle cartridges can then be inserted as shown. When the tube is loaded, push the follower assembly in and rotate it one quarter turn to lock it in place.

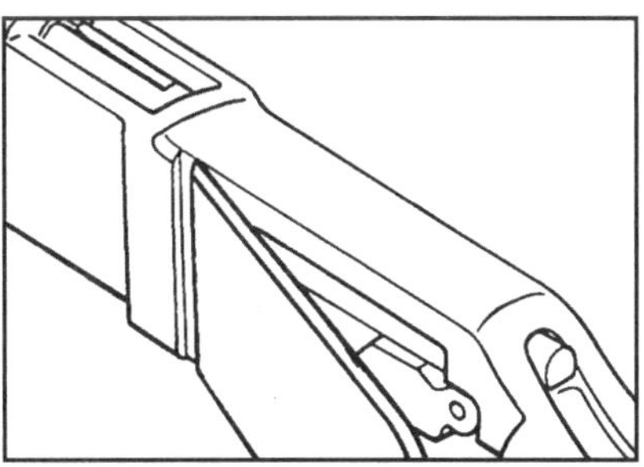

2 To disassemble the mechanism, the side plates (25) and (53) must be removed. Begin by removing the lever hinge screw (54), then unscrew the side plate screw (55) a few turns and tap it gently. This will loosen the right side plate (25). Then remove the screw (55) entirely and lift off the left plate. (When reassembling, insert the front edge of the sideplate under the lip of the receiver and replace screws.)

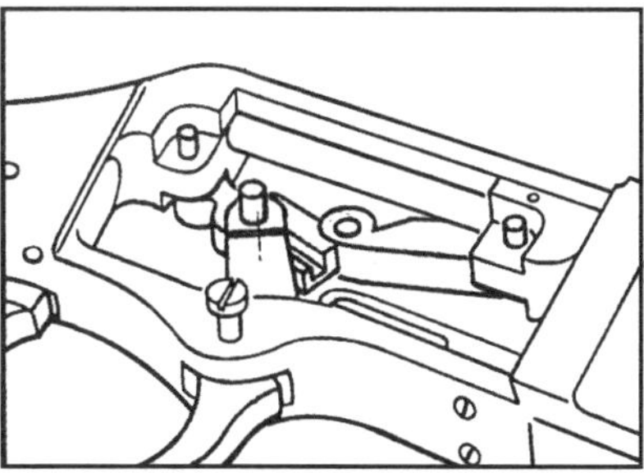

3 After the side plates are removed, the pair of left and right links (15, 20, 17 & 19) can be lifted off the hinge pins on the bolt (14) and the link hinge pin (26). When replacing the links, insert the lever screw (54) in order to line up the lever. Insert the operating pin (48) and install the links. Hold the links on the operating pin while the hinge screw is removed and the side plates installed. Then replace the lever hinge screw.

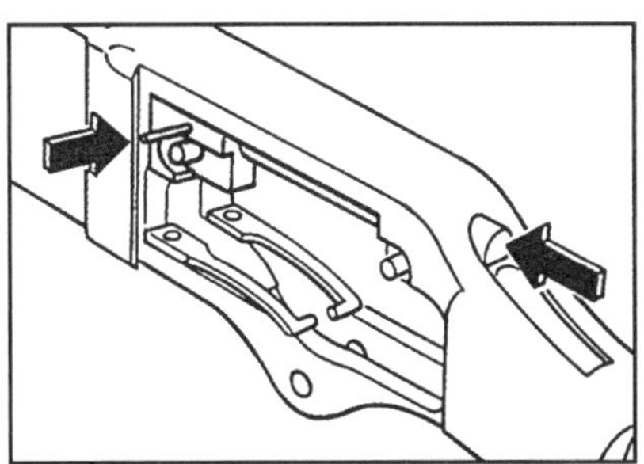

4 The bolt (14) and the firing pin extension (24) are held together by a long, thin connecting pin (16). To remove the bolt or the firing pin (23) and spring (22), push out this connecting pin (16). Remove the firing pin extension (24) through the back of the frame. Then pull the bolt rearward and allow the end to drop.

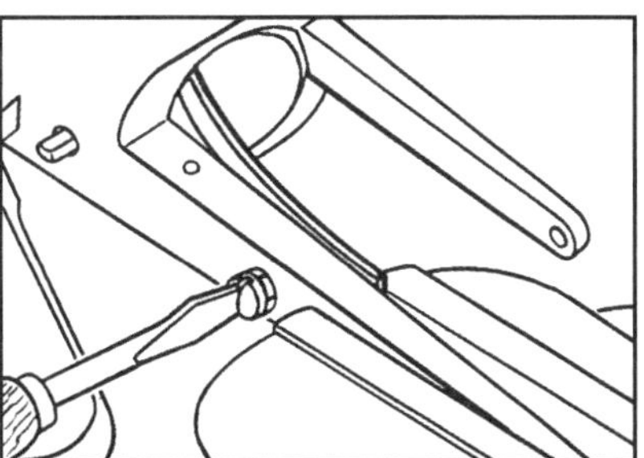

5 To remove the hammer spring (30), the buttstock must first be removed. To do this, first remove the upper tang screw (29) and the lower tang screw (35). Using the heel of the hand, hit the butt stock gently until it can be pulled free. Pull down the lever and remove the hammer spring screw (36). When replacing the hammer spring, first hook it on to the hammer link, line up the screw holes, and with the spring and receiver secured in a padded vise, turn the screw until it has caught the threads in the spring.

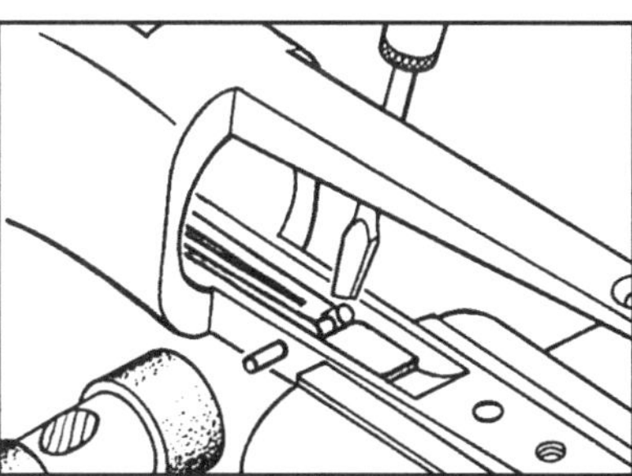

6 The Model 66 has a built in safety device. When the hammer is cocked, the trigger cannot be pulled until the lever is squeezed up against the tang. In order to remove this grip safety (38), or the sear and trigger spring (37), drive out the safety hinge pin (39). Since the sear and trigger spring is very stiff, it may be necessary to push down on the incoming end of the pin with a screwdriver to align it with the hole on the opposite side of the tang.

N.E.F. "PARDNER" SHOTGUN

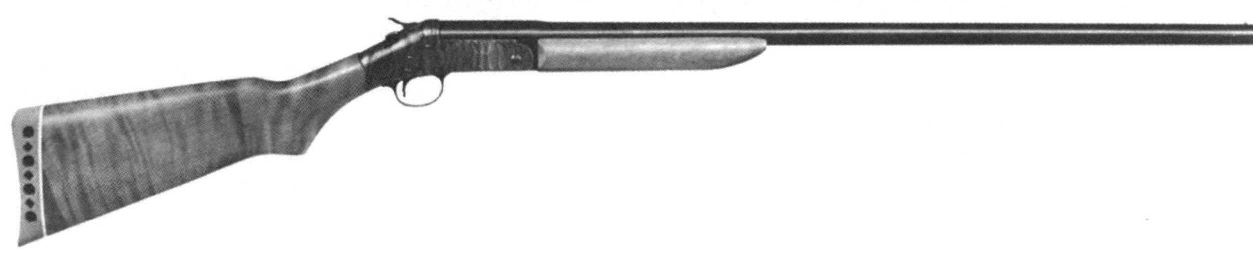

PARTS LEGEND

1. Barrel
2. Barrel catch
3. Barrel catch spring
4. Buttplate
5. Buttplate screws (2)
6. Ejector
7. Ejector latch
8. Ejector latch stop pins (2)
9. Ejector latch spring
10. Ejector spring
11. Ejector stop pin
12. Firing pin
13. Firing pin spring
14. Fore-end
15. Fore-end screw
16. Fore-end spacer
17. Fore-end spacer screws (2)
18. Frame
19. Front sight
20. Hammer
21. Hammer spring
22. Lifter spring
23. Release lever
24. Release lever/firing pin retaining pin
25. Buttstock
26. Striker/lifter
27. Through bolt
28. Through bolt washer
29. Trigger
30. Trigger extension
31. Trigger guard
32. Trigger guard pin, front
33. Trigger guard pin, rear
34. Barrel catch pin
35. Hammer pin
36. Trigger spring

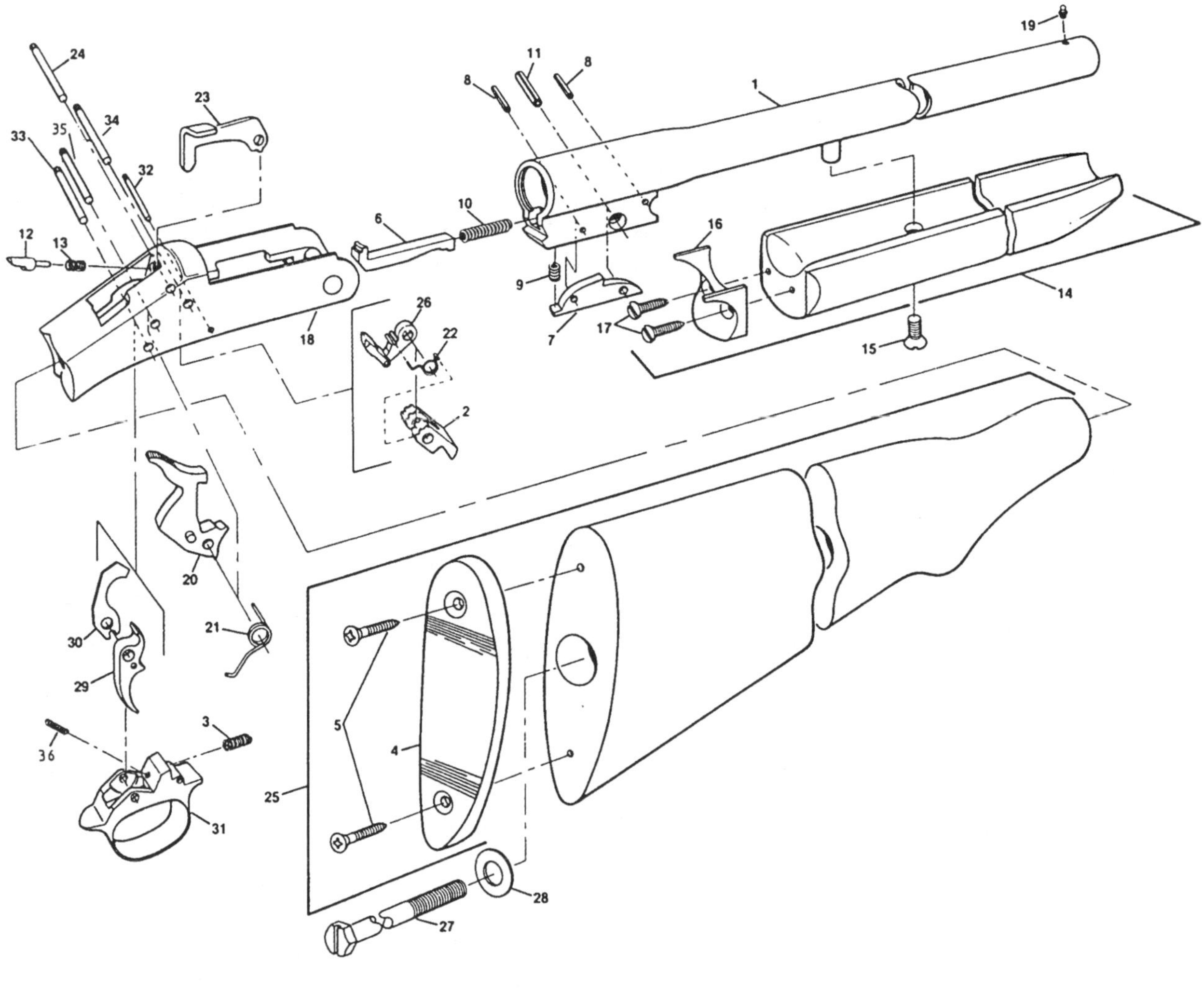

The Pardner, produced by the New England Firearms Co., Inc (N.E.F.)., of Gardner, Massachusetts, since 1987, marks the rebirth of a long line of American-made, single-shot shotguns and traces its ancestry back to Harrington & Richardson's popular Topper and further back to the first H&R single-shots made in 1901. It is made at the H&R 1871, Inc. facility and on the same machinery used to manufacture earlier H&Rs. Like the Topper, the Pardner is an inexpensive smoothbore.

The H&R Toppers, in one variation or another, were sold in 10-, 12-, 16-, 20-, 28-gauge, and .410-bore. When fitted with rifle barrels they became H&R Single Shot Rifles. The N.E.F. Pardner was offered only in 12 and 20 gauge and .410 bore. Standard production features of the first Pardners included a forged iron, color case-hardened frame, a blued barrel, and a walnut-finished stock. A "youth" model with shortened stock was also advertised.

In use, depressing a frame-mounted release lever (or rotating a top lever in earlier Topper models) cams open a single locking bolt, allowing the barrel to be pivoted open. As the barrel opens, a spring-loaded ejector throws the fired shell clear of the gun. Disassembly of the Pardner duplicates the procedures used with the Topper itself.

DISASSEMBLY

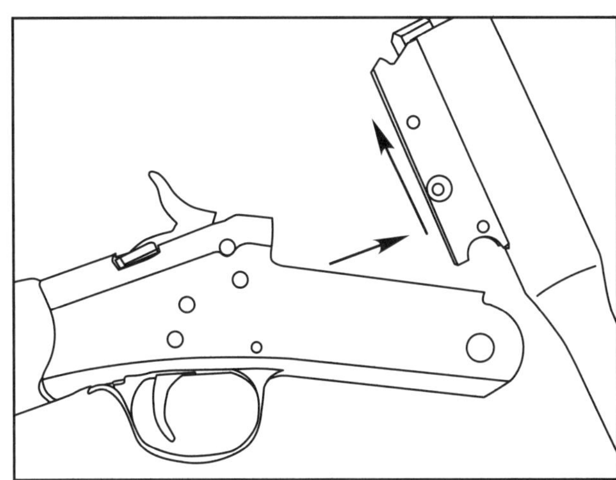

1 Begin disassembly by depressing the release lever (23) to open the action and determine that the chamber and bore are clear. Close the action. Remove the fore-end screw (15) and lift the fore-end (14) away from the barrel. Press the release lever and rotate the barrel assembly up and away from the frame (18). For cleaning purposes no further disassembly is required or advised.

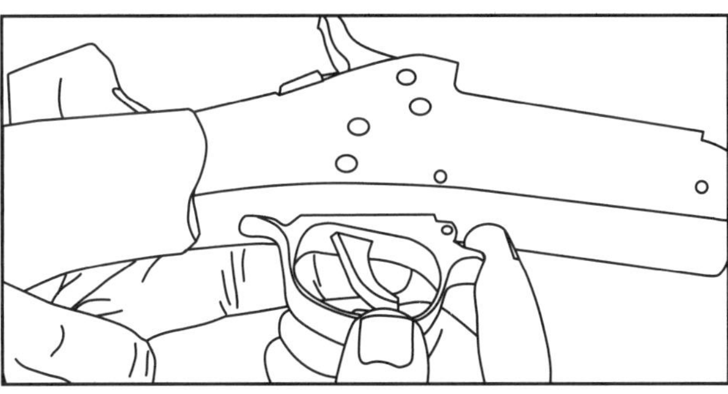

2 To disassemble the frame assembly, first remove the buttplate (4). Insert a long-bladed screwdriver into the stock access hole to remove the through bolt (27) and its washer (28). From the right side of the frame drive out the trigger guard pins (32 & 33) and pull down on the trigger guard (31) to remove the trigger (29), trigger extension (30), the trigger spring (36) and the barrel catch spring (3).

3 Tap out the hammer pin (35) and remove the hammer (20) and hammer spring (21) through the trigger guard opening. Drive out the barrel catch pin (34) and remove the striker/lifter assembly (26) with the lifter spring (22) and barrel catch (2). Drift out the release lever/firing pin retaining pin (24), taking care to restrain the firing pin (12) and spring (13). Remove the release lever (23). The relative positions of the internal parts are shown here.

To disassemble the barrel assembly, drive out the ejector latch stop pins (8) and the ejector stop pin (11). Pull down on the ejector latch (7) while restraining the ejector (6). After the latch is removed with its spring (9), release tension on the ejector to remove it and its spring (10).

NEWTON BOLT-ACTION RIFLE

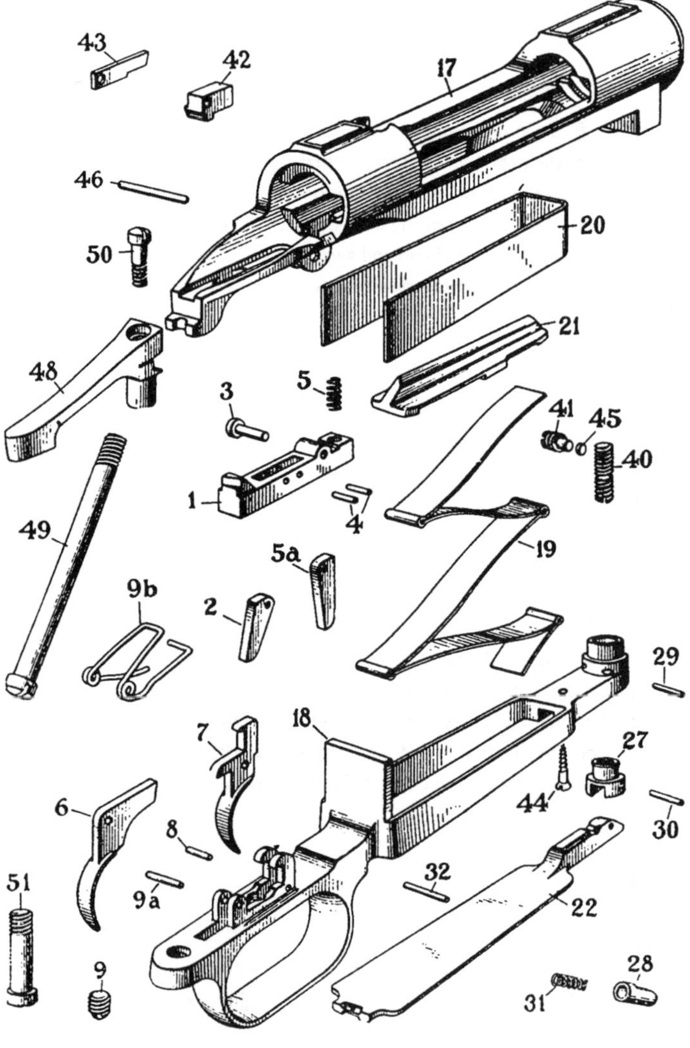

PARTS LEGEND

1. Sear
2. Rear knock-off
3. Sear pin
4. Knock-off pins (2)
5. Sear spring
   5a. Front knock-off
6. Set trigger
7. Front trigger
8. Front trigger pin
9. Trigger adjusting screw
   9a. Rear trigger pin
   9b. Set trigger spring
10. Sleeve
11. Safety
12. Sleeve locking bolt
13. Sleeve locking bolt spring
14. Rear sleeve poppet
15. Sleeve poppet spring
16. Front sleeve poppet
17. Receiver
18. Guard
19. Magazine spring
20. Magazine box
21. Magazine follower
22. Magazine floor plate
27. Front receiver screw nut
28. Magazine floorplate catch
29. Front receiver screw nut pin
30. Magazine floorplate pin
31. Magazine floorplate catch spring
32. Magazine floorplate catch pin
33. Bolt
34. Extractor
35. Extractor collar
36. Firing pin
37. Firing pin nut
38. Cocking head
39. Main spring
40. Front receiver screw
41. Front receiver screw binding screw
42. Bolt stop
43. Ejector
44. Front guard screw
45. Front receiver screw binding screw plug
46. Bolt stop pin
48. Upper tang
49. Upper tang truss bolt
50. Upper tang adjusting screw
51. Rear receiver screw

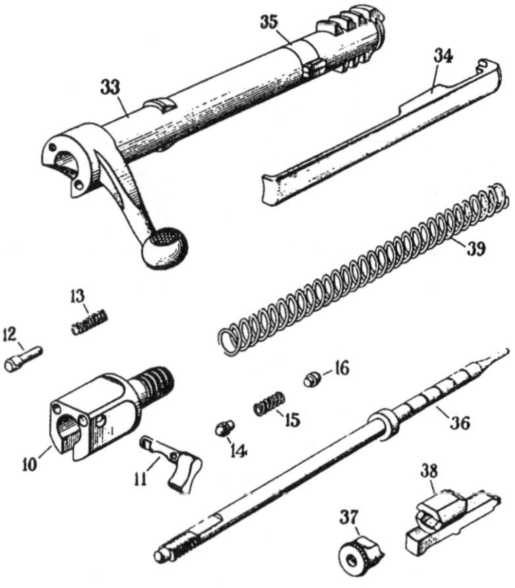

Charles Newton (1870-1932) was a pioneer in the allied fields of firearms design and ammunition development. A lawyer by training, he was an entrepreneur, engineer and experimenter; and was a contemporary of American experimental firearms notaries such as Dr. F.W. Mann, Harry Pope and A.O. Niedner. During his career, Newton gave American riflemen a bevy of cartridges, including the .250-3000 Savage, the .22 Hi-Power (or "Imp") and the original .25-06.

When World War I ended the flow of Mauser rifles to his company, Newton devised his own, sophisticated bolt-action sporting rifle called the original Newton High Power Rifle. It was announced to the sporting public in *Arms and the Man* (later *American Rifleman*) in July 1915.

Newton's contributions to the firearms industry are well documented in the book by Bruce Jennings, Jr. — *Charles Newton: Father of High Velocity.* The instructions for disassembly of the Newton High Power Rifle were first published in the 15th edition of the Newton Arms Co., catalog in 1915. It is the earliest set of illustrated parts lists and take-down instructions that we could find. Its existence entitles Charles Newton, in addition to other honors, to be known as "the father of the Exploded View."

DISASSEMBLY

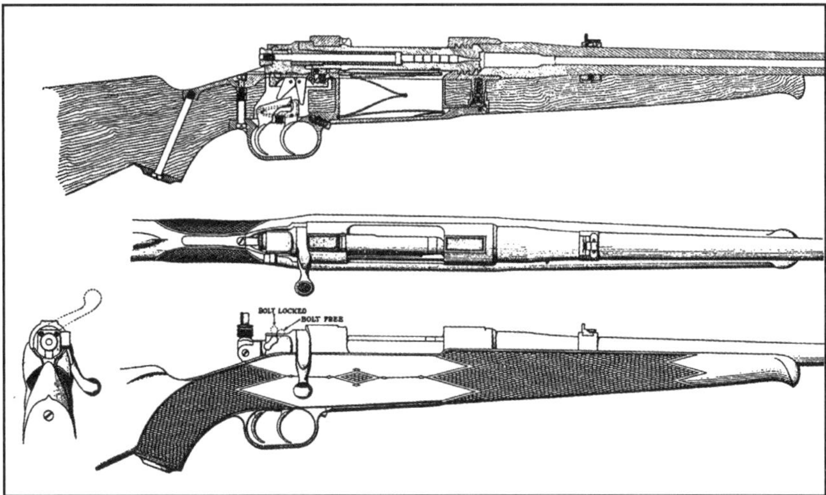

To remove the bolt from the arm: Turn up the bolt handle and draw backward on the bolt, at the same time pressing backward on the front trigger. The backward pressure on the front trigger causes the forward portion of the sear to rise up and engage a detent finger on the lower side of the bolt stop, which is located under the rear receiver bridge. This prevents the bolt stop from rising and permits withdrawing the bolt completely from the rifle. This pressure must be applied before the bolt stop has entered into the notch of the lower side of the bolt.

To take down the arm for carrying: Press in the magazine floor plate catch immediately in front of the trigger guard until it releases the rear end of the magazine floor plate, which is thrown down by the pressure of the magazine spring; swing the floor plate which is pivoted in the front receiver screw nut, down to its lower position, and, using it as a lever, un-screw the nut off the front receiver screw and the barrel will unhook and the barrel and receiver together tip upward and off the stock, leaving the guard with its trigger mechanism, magazine, etc., with the stock. Press the forearm screw nut up into the guard forging at its front end until it is flush, then press the magazine floor plate up close against the magazine until it is caught by the magazine floor plate catch.

To dismount the bolt: Cock the rifle by raising the bolt handle and turning it down again into place. Turn the safety up and forward until at an angle of 45° in front of the perpendicular. This will permit the bolt handle to rotate while the bolt handle is locked. Raise the bolt handle and withdraw the bolt completely from the rifle. The sleeve may then be unscrewed from the bolt by rotating it from left to right, as it is a left hand screw.

To dismount the sleeve: Remove the bolt and remove the sleeve from the bolt as above stated. Throw the safety back to the firing position, which is to the rear and 45 degrees below the horizontal, which relieves the strain on the main spring. Rest the point of the firing pin upon some hard substance and press the sleeve forward, thus compressing the main spring until the V-shaped projections on the sides of the firing pin nut are clear of their seats in the cocking head. Unscrew the firing pin nut from the rear end of the firing pin. This separates the firing pin, main spring, cocking head and firing pin nut from the sleeve proper.

To dismount the safety mechanism: Having dismounted the sleeve, turn the leaf of the safety until it projects directly to the rear and pull it out to the right. The sleeve locking bolt with its spring and the poppets bearing against the safety and rear end of the bolt, with their springs, may be pushed out with a ... small drift.

To remove the rear tang from the stock: First remove the rear receiver screw, then unscrew the rear tang screw running from the center of the pistol grip into the rear end of the receiver tang until it is free of the tang, then press upward on the end of this screw and it will force the rear tang upward and out of its seat in the stock.

To remove the extractor from the bolt: Remove the bolt from the rifle. Turn the extractor around to that side of the bolt which is to the left when the bolt is in position and to the bottom when it is being withdrawn. This will free the jaw of the extractor from the groove next to the bolt head. Push the extractor forward and it will slide off the bolt.

OLYMPIC OA-93 CARBINE

PARTS LEGEND

1. Scope mount nuts
2. Scope mount screws (2)
3. Charging screw
4. Charging screw sleeve
5. Charging lever block
6. Recoil rod link
7. Link pin
8. Scope mount base
9. Ejection cover
10. Ejection cover hinge pin
11. Ejection cover hinge pin clip
12. Ejection cover spring
13. Bolt carrier
14. Bolt carrier key
15. Bolt
16. Bolt cam pin
17. Firing pin
18. Firing pin retaining pin
19. Upper receiver
20. Ejector
21. Ejector-spring
22. Ejector roll pin
23. Flash suppressor washer
24. Brennan flash suppressor
25. Vortex flash suppressor
26. Hand guard
27. Barrel
28. Recoil spring
29. Recoil rod
30. Bolt carrier key screw
31. Gas tube
32. Gas tube roll pin
33. Sling swivel
34. Sling swivel pin
35. Sling swivel stud
36. Recoil spring housing
37. Recoil rod locking pin
38. Detent pin
39. Locking pin spring
40. Front sight taper pins (2)
41. Lower receiver
42. Pistol grip screw
43. Grip screw washer
44. Pistol grip
45. Safety spring
46. Safety detent
47. Trigger
48. Trigger spring
49. Trigger pin
50. Hammer pin
51. Trigger guard
52. Trigger guard roll pin (not shown)
53. Disconnector
54. Disconnector spring (not shown)
55. Takedown pin
56. Takedown pin detent
57. Takedown pin detent spring
58. Magazine catch button
59. Magazine catch spring
60. Magazine catch
61. Bolt catch
62. Bolt catch plunger
63. Bolt catch roll pin
64. Bolt catch spring
65. Safety selector
66. Hammer
67. Hammer spring
68. Takedown pin, rear
69. Takedown pin detent, rear
70. Takedown pin detent spring
71. Set screw
72. Folding stock bolts (2)
73. Folding stock
74. Folding stock spacer
75. Locking ring

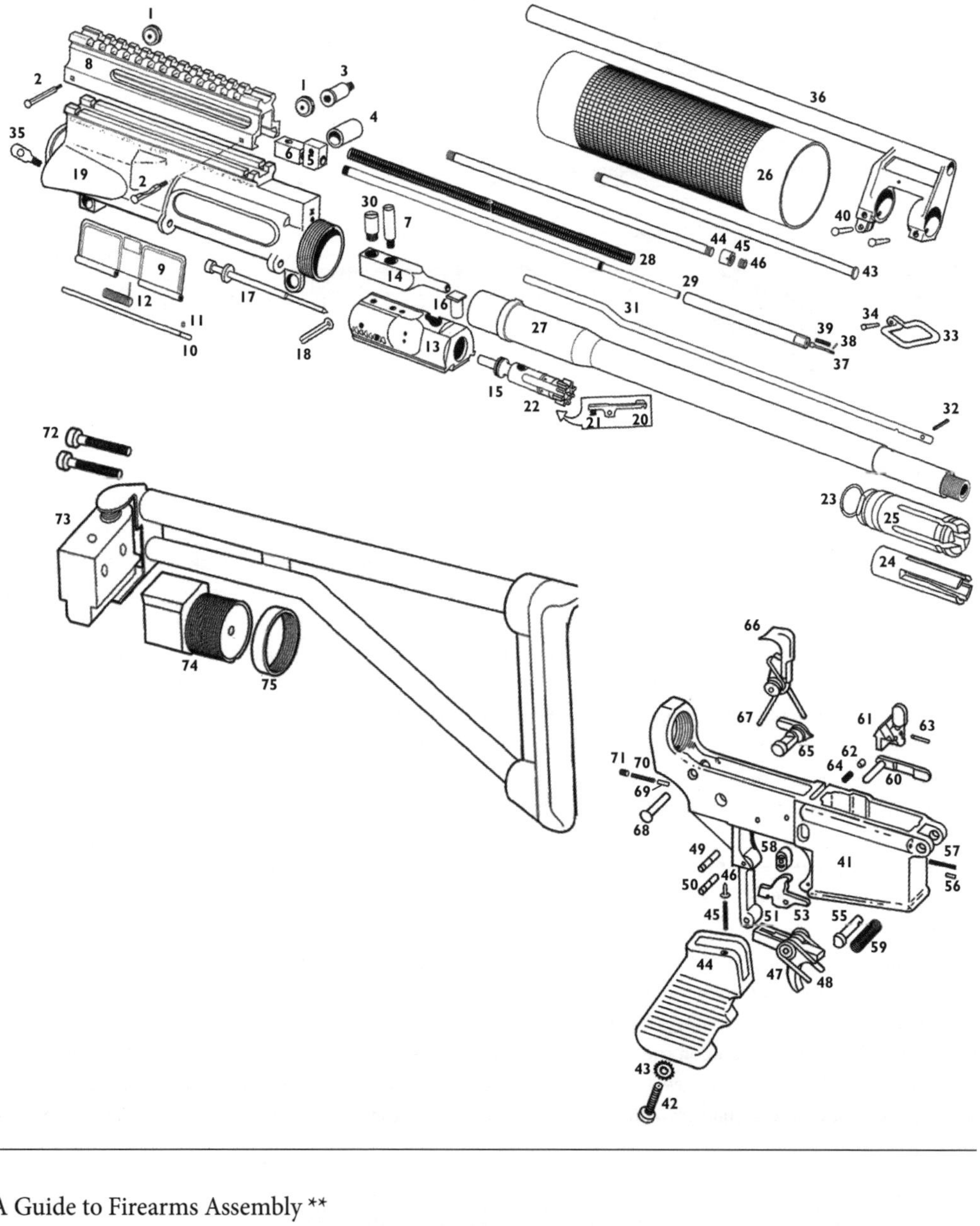

In 1956, Olympic Arms began operation as the Schuetzen Gun Works, manufacturing rifle barrels in Colorado Springs, Colorado. By 1975 the company moved to Olympia, Washington, changing its name to Olympic Arms in 1982. In 1987 the company purchased Safari Arms, adding a line of M1911 pistols to its AR-15 products. Olympic has added numerous alternate features to many of their AR-15 style rifles, including flat top receivers and free-floating aluminum handguards.

Olympic's AO-93 Carbine is a gas operated semi-automatic AR-15 style carbine with a folding stock. It has a 16-inch chromemoly steel barrel and a free-floating aluminum tube handguard. The receivers of the OA-93 series are forged and machined aluminum and the flat top upper receivers are fitted with a Picatinny rail. The OA-93 Carbine weighs 7.33 lbs and is 35.75 inches in length overall. All steel parts are Parkerized. The carbines are chambered for the 5.56 NATO cartridge.

DISASSEMBLY

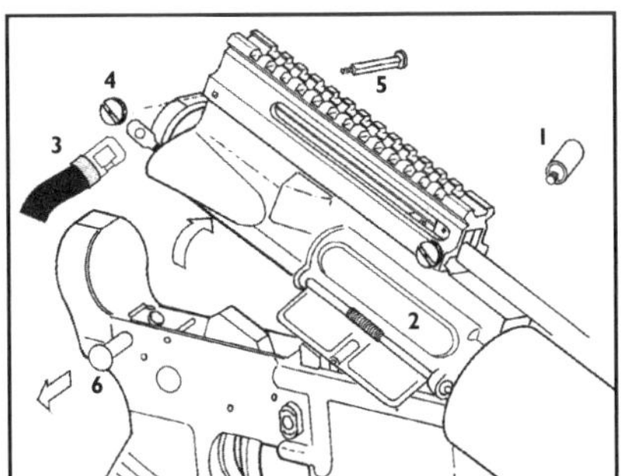

1 Remove rear knurled locking nut (4), using a large standard screwdriver. Push out rear locking pin (5). Push out takedown pin (6) as far as it will go and pivot upper receiver away from lower.

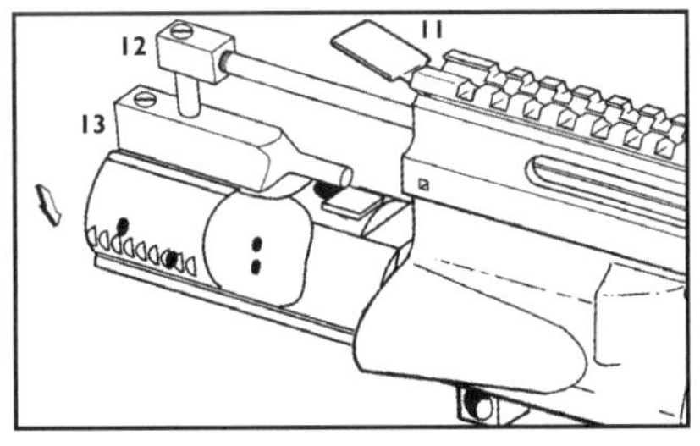

2 Grasp knurled recoil rod locking pin (7) and pull out until detent pin (8) clears slot in recoil plug, then twist so that detent pin rests clear of slot. Grasp recoil plug (9) by the flat edges and unscrew from recoil rod (10). Lift access hatch (11) at rear of scope mount. Slide out bolt carrier and recoil assembly (12). Drop bolt carrier, carrier key and linking pin (13) free of recoil assembly.

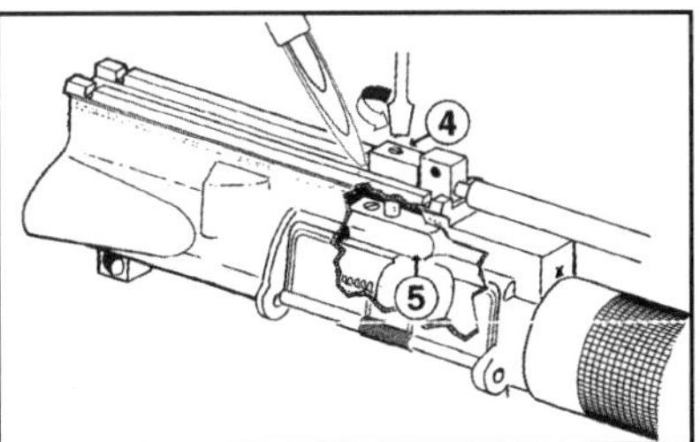

3 Use a hex wrench to remove the charging lever (1) and a large screwdriver to remove the front knurled locking nut (2), and push out front locking pin (3). Note that forward pin is radiused on the side facing up, while the rear pin is not. Slide off scope mount base. To remove link pin: Use a propane torch to apply heat to the base of the link pin (1) to soften the Red Loctite. Unscrew link pin from bolt carrier key. NOTE: the recoil assembly is under tension. Do not attempt to remove the recoil rod link. If you must remove it, be aware that the spring and recoil rod will shoot out violently when the block is removed.

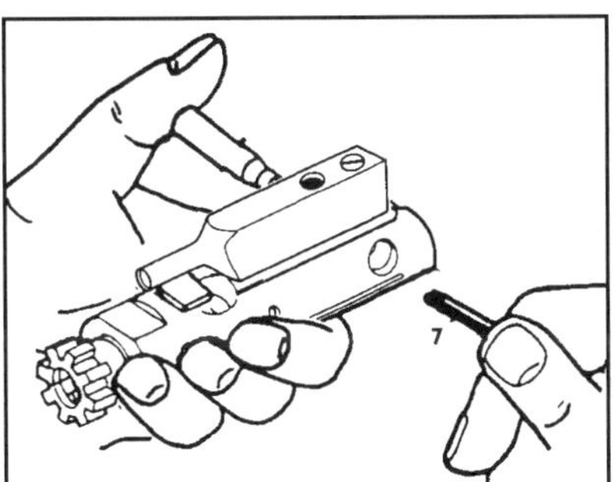

4 Move bolt assembly (6) forward to unlocked position and remove firing pin retaining pin (7). Do not open or close split end of firing pin retaining pin (7). Push in on bolt assembly (6) to put in locked position.

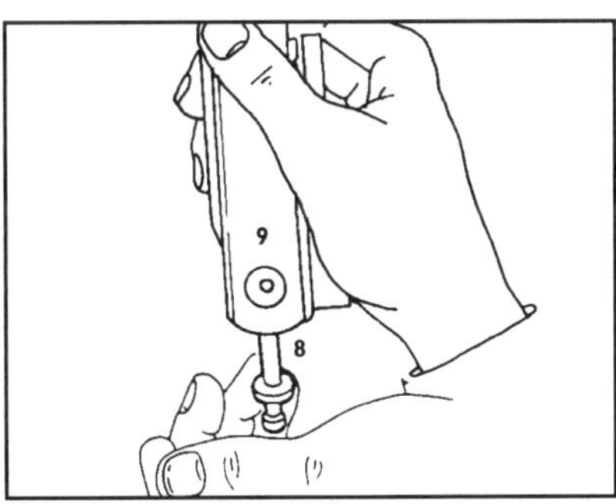

5 Catch firing pin (8) as it drops out of rear of bolt carrier assembly (9).

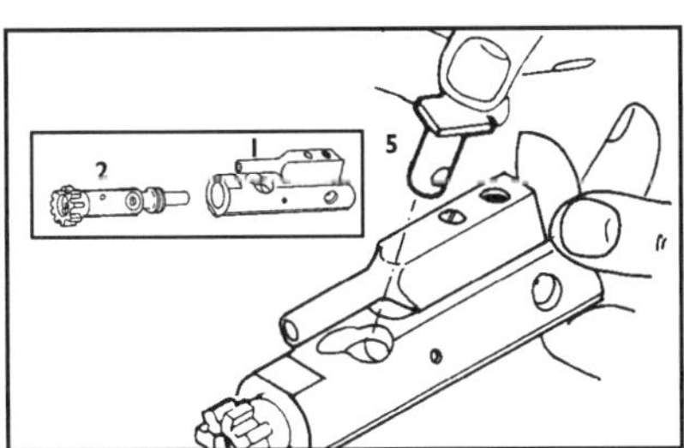

6 Give bolt cam pin (5) a quarterturn and lift out. Remove bolt assembly (2) from bolt carrier assembly (1).

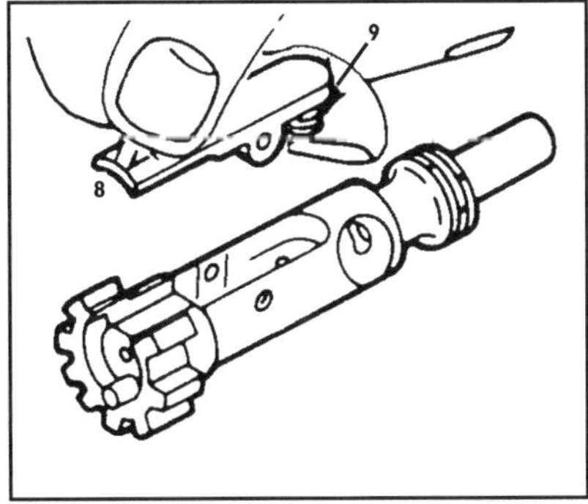

7 Disassemble extractor and spring assembly only when dirty or damaged. Use dummy round to remove extractor pin (7). Do not separate insert from spring assembly (9). Remove extractor (8) and spring assembly (9). Do not remove spring assembly (9) from extractor (8). NOTE: Lower receiver should only be disassembled by a qualified gunsmith. Reassemble rifle in reverse order. Use Red Loctite to reinstall link pin.

PARKER DOUBLE-BARREL SHOTGUN

PARTS LEGEND

1. Barrels
2. Front sight
3. Cocking link
4. Cocking link spring pin
5. Cocking link spring
6. Cocking link screw
7. Bolt plate
8. Bolt plate retaining pin
9. Extractor screw
10. Extractor
11. Buttplate
12. Buttplate screw (2)
13. Top-lever spring shell
14. Top-lever spring
15. Top-lever spring plunger
16. Top-lever
17. Cocking crank
18. Joint pin screw
19. Joint pin
20. Cocking crank pin stop screw (2)
21. Cocking crank pin
22. Hammer fastening screw (2)
23. Hammer screw (2)
24. Unhooking pin screw
25. Joint roll
26. Unhooking pin spring
27. Unhooking pin
28. Receiver
29. Top-lever retaining screw
30. Tang screw, front
31. Safety slide pin
32. Safety slide
33. Safety slide spring
34. Safety lever jacket
35. Safety lever pin
36. Safety lever
37. Safety pin
38. Bolt
39. Sear spring
40. Sear pin
41. Trip
42. Trip spring
43. Trip spring plunger
44. Sear, left
45. Sear, right
46. Cocking slide
47. Mainspring (2)
48. Mainspring plunger (2)
49. Hammer, left
50. Hammer, right
51. Hammer stirrup (2)
52. Mainspring pin (2)
53. Trigger pin
54. Trigger, left
55. Trigger, right
56. Unhooking slide screw
57. Trigger plate screw (3)
58. Trigger plate
59. Tang screw sleeve
60. Trigger spring
61. Trigger spring screw
62. Unhooking slide
63. Unhooking slide spring
64. Unhooking slide plunger
65. Tang screw, rear
66. Guard bow
67. Guard bow screw
68. Fore-end
69. Fore-end iron
70. Fore-end plunger box pin
71. Fore-end screw (2)
72. Fore-end plunger box
73. Fore-end plunger spring
74. Fore-end plunger
75. Fore-end plunger roll
76. Fore-end plunger roll pin

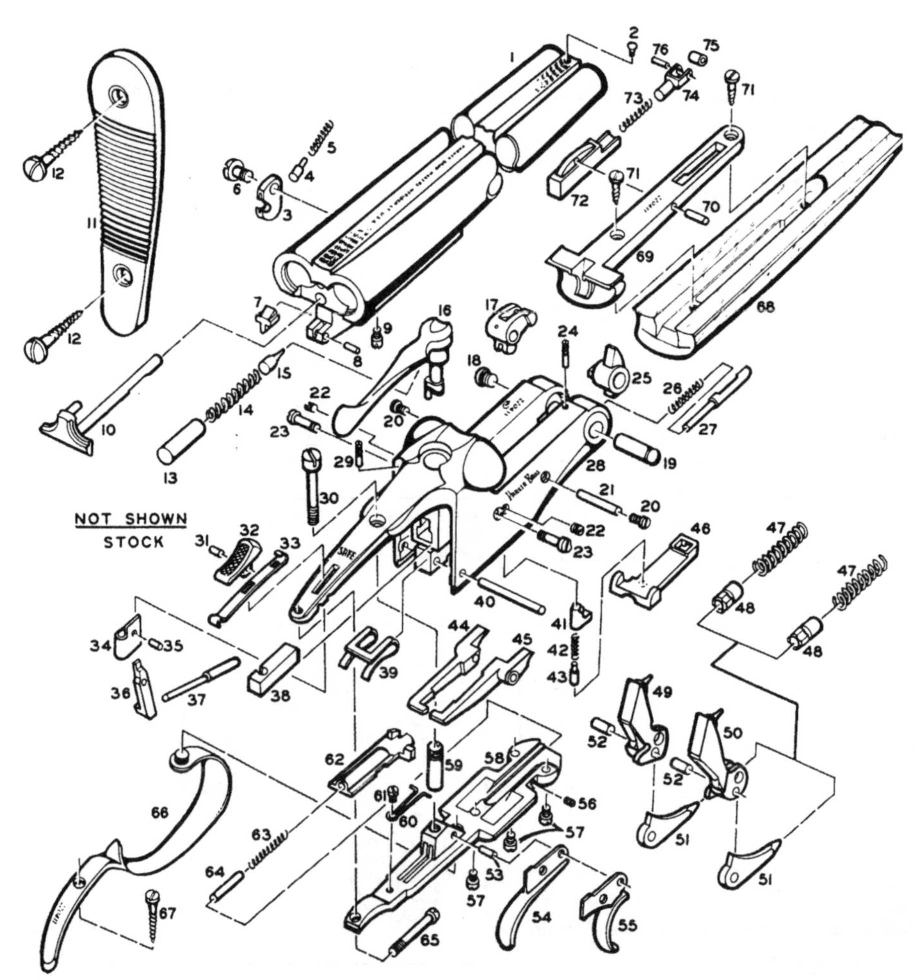

In 1832 Charles Parker of Meriden, Connecticut, organized the Parker Co. to make coffee mills and subsequently bench vises. In 1860 the firm was reorganized to become Parker, Snow, Brooks & Co. On September 28, 1863, the firm signed a contract with the government to make 15,000 Model 1861 rifled muskets at $19 each. This contract was fulfilled. Upon termination of the Civil War, Charles Parker became president of the Meriden Mfg. Co., a position he held until 1868 when the firm of Parker Brothers was organized.

Their first shotgun was made in 1868 and was known as the 'Parker Brothers.' Of hammer type, it featured a lifter bolting device, and the fore-end was attached to the barrels with a cross-key. In 1879 an improved fore-end assembly based on the Deeley & Edge system was made standard. A hammerless lock was adopted in 1889, with automatic ejectors first offered in 1902. The Parker single trigger was introduced in 1922.

On June 1, 1934, the assets of the Parker firm were purchased by Remington Arms Co., Inc., but with the advent of World War II production of Parker shotguns was discontinued and was not resumed with the coming of peace.

The Parker shotgun was essentially machine made, although much hand-fitting was involved in its production. Forgings were machined slightly oversize and then hand fitted by filing and scraping. The reputation of the Parker shotgun was founded on uniformly excellent quality and durability as well as fine balance and handling qualities. Parkers were offered in several grades, and all but the cheapest Trojan grade could be ordered built to customers specifications. Regardless of price, the Parker shotgun justly earned its title of "Old Reliable."

DISASSEMBLY

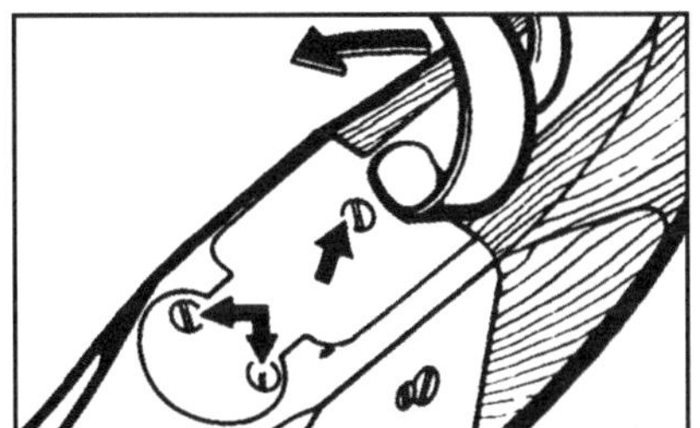

1 Commence disassembly by removing fore-end assembly and barrels (1). Remove guard bow screw (67) and rear tang screw (65). Unscrew guard bow (66) and remove three trigger plate screws (57, arrows). Turn gun right side up and push top-lever (16) to right. Remove front tang screw (30).

2 Tap out trigger plate (58) and attached assembly. Use a small wood dowel inserted into forward part of receiver (28) and just in front of cocking crank (17) where a portion of the foremost surface of trigger plate may be seen. Lift trigger plate assembly away, while lifting out cocking slide (46). Trip (41) and its internal assembly will also drop out. Trip sears (44 & 45), drift out sear pin (40), and remove sears. This will permit removal of stock.

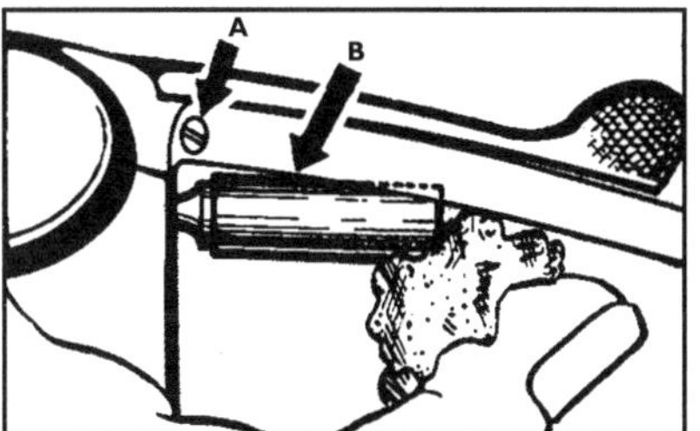

3 Continue (A) by removing top-lever retaining screw (29). Using a piece of cotton waste for padding, place thumb against top-lever spring shell (13) and fingers against face of receiver. Pry shell away from tang at (B) using a small screwdriver or hardwood wedge. Withdraw top-lever spring shell, spring (14), and plunger (15). Top-lever (16) may now be lifted out, and bolt (38) withdrawn rearward from receiver.

4 Next, remove hammer fastening screws (22) and hammer screws (23). Hammers (49 & 50), hammer stirrups (51), mainspring plungers (48), and mainsprings (47) will drop out. It is best to hold a large cloth at rear of receiver while doing this to prevent loss of parts which are under spring tension.

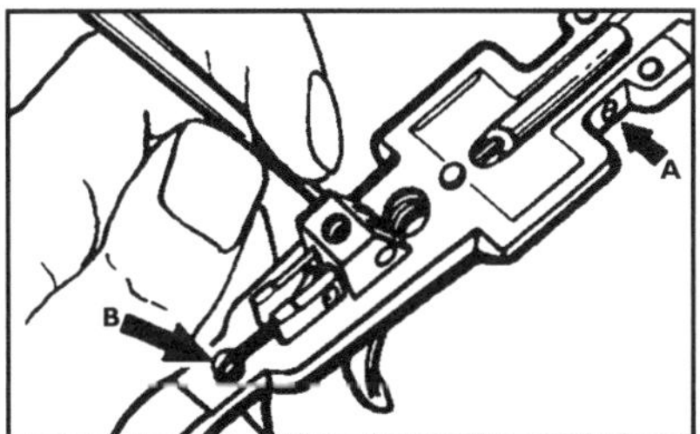

5 Remove (A) unhooking slide screw (56) and withdraw unhooking slide (62) and assembly from front end of trigger plate. (B) Remove trigger spring screw (61) and trigger spring (60). Drift out trigger pin (53) and remove triggers (54 & 55).

6 Remove extractor screw (9) and slide extractor out and away rearward. Remove cocking link screw (6) and cocking link (3), link spring pin (4), and link spring (5). Removal of extractor or cocking link is not dependent on prior removal of one or the other.

PEABODY RIFLE

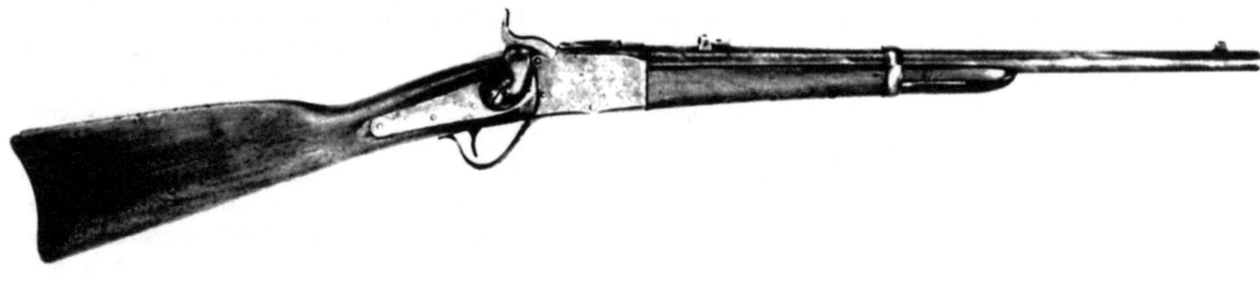

PARTS LEGEND

1. Receiver
2. Barrel
3. Buttstock (not illustrated)
   3a. Forestock (not illustrated)
4. Breechblock
5. Firing pin
6. Firing pin spring
7. Brace lever spring
8. Brace lever screw
9. Brace lever
10. Extractor
11. Extractor mounting plate
12. Extractor screw
13. Breechblock screw
14. Breech lever screw
15. Brace lever roller
16. Roller screw
17. Sideplate screw
18. Swivel bar plate
19. Swivel bar plate screws (2)
20. Buttstock screw
21. Lockplate
22. Tumbler
23. Mainspring stirrup
24. Stirrup screw
25. Bridle
26. Sear
27. Mainspring
28. Mainspring screw
29. Bridle/sear screws (3)
30. Lockplate screw
31. Lockplate screw bushing
32. Hammer
33. Hammer screw
34. Trigger plate
35. Trigger
36. Trigger screw
37. Rear trigger plate screw
38. Front trigger plate screw
39. Breech lever
40. Rear sight
41. Rear sight spring
42. Sight mounting screws (2)
43. Front sight
44. Stock stud
45. Nose cap screw
46. Nose cap
47. Band springs (22)
48. Upper band
49. Lower band
50. Buttplate
51. Buttplate screws (2)
52. Ramrod
53. Extractor mounting plate screw

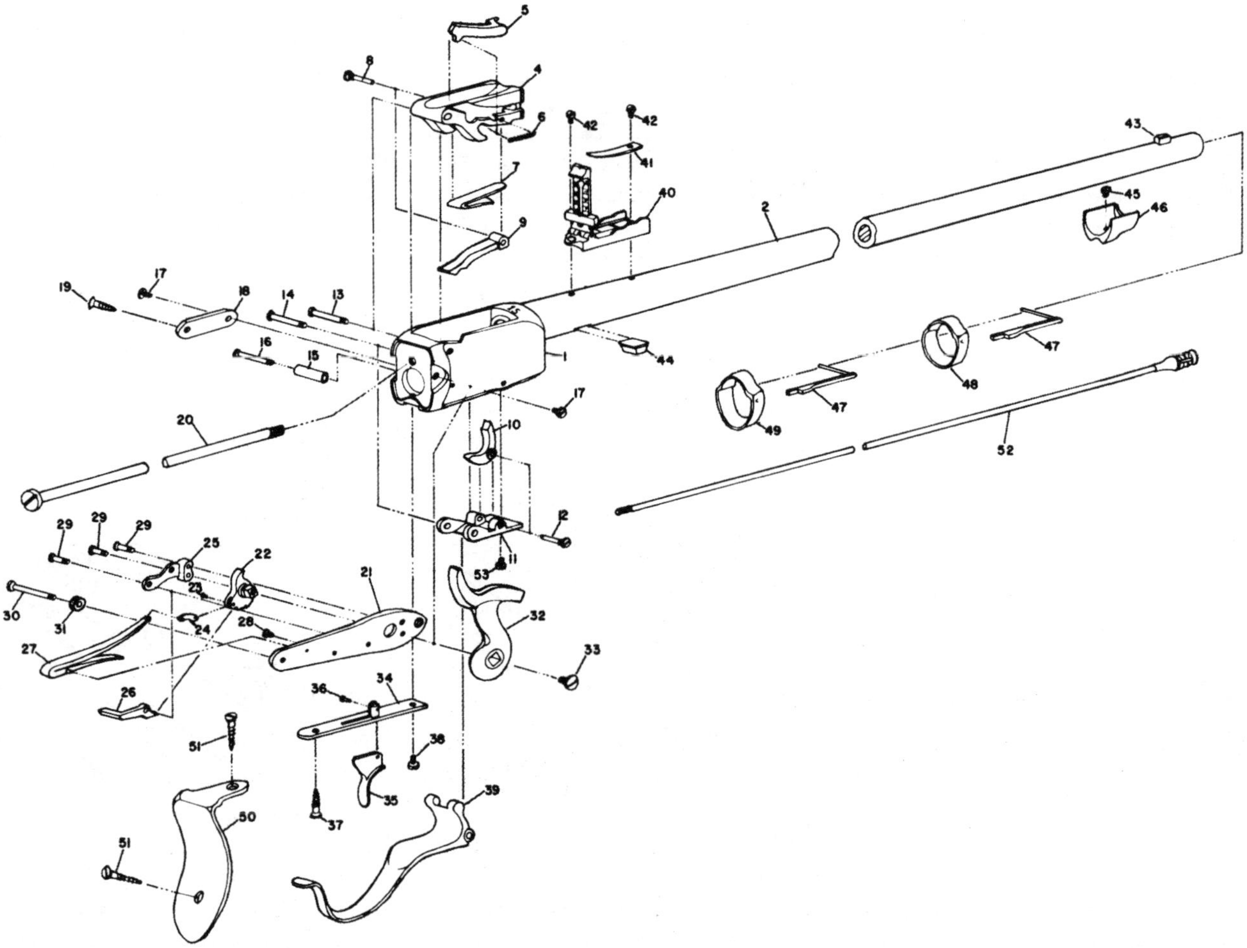

Consigned today to relative obscurity, the sturdy side-hammered single shot rifles built on Henry O. Peabody's 1862 patent are truly epochal firearms. As pioneer metallic-cartridge breechloaders, Peabody rifles were at once the strongest, least complicated, and most adaptable. In their final form, as modified by Friedrich Martini, Peabodys are the basis for some the world's finest target rifles and pistols.

Peabody arms were manufactured by the Providence Tool Co. and the earliest were chambered for the Spencer carbine cartridge. Samples were submitted to the Chief of Ordnance for testing at the Watertown Arsenal. Despite positive results in several tests conducted between 1865 and 1872, the rifle was rejected because it could not be produced at any government manufactory without extensive retooling.

Failure to sell the Peabody to the Army, however, did not spell the immediate demise of the Peabody rifle. The Canadian government purchased 3,000 Peabody rifles in .50-60 Peabody caliber in 1865 and New York, Connecticut and Massachusetts bought quantities of Peabody rifles for their state militias. In 1867 the Swiss bought 15,000, in .41 caliber rimfire. Romania took delivery of a total of 25,000 rifles during the 1860s, chambered for a .45 cal. center-fire cartridge. More Peabodys went to military authorities in Spain, Cuba, Mexico and France. Most were chambered in 11 mm. Spanish, though the 39,000 guns sent to France in 1870 must have been chambered for the French service cartridge.

Civilian versions of the Peabody never gained any real popularity. Sporting Peabodys were made in .45 and .50 caliber rimfire and later for .45 and .50 bottleneck center-fire cartridges. The company went out of business in the 1870s.

DISASSEMBLY

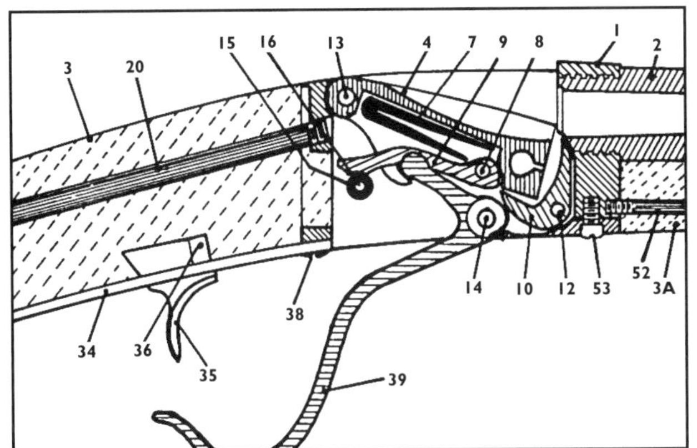

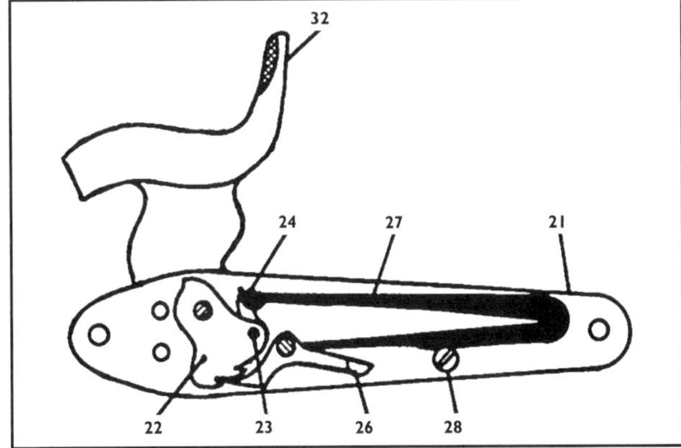

1. Half cock the hammer (32). Lower the breech lever (39), dropping the breechblock (4) to expose the chamber. Leave the breech open. Remove the barrel bands (48-49) and the fore-end.
2. Unscrew and remove the breech lever screw (14). NOTE: The breech lever is under tension from the brace lever (9) and brace lever spring (7), and it may be necessary to drive the disengaged screw from right to left out of the receiver (1). Remove the breech lever.
3. Invert the rifle and remove the extractor mounting plate screw (53). NOTE: The extractor mounting plate (11) is a tight friction fit. It may be necessary to tap it lightly with a soft-faced hammer to slide it to the rear. Remove the extractor mounting plate and extractor (10) and extractor screw (12).
4. Loosen breechblock screw (13) until the threaded section is disengaged from the receiver. Apply thumb pressure to the breechblock, at the hinging point, to relieve tension from the brace lever spring. Remove the breechblock screw.
5. Rotate the front of the breechblock downward until the brace lever is clear of the brace lever roller (15) and push the breechblock out the bottom of the receiver. Take care when removing the breechblock to capture the firing pin (5) and firing pin spring (6) — present in some, but not all, models — fitted in a slot in the right side of the breechblock.
6. Disassembly of the breechblock, brace lever and brace lever spring is not recommended. Should it be necessary, use a padded hand vise to clamp the brace lever in place in the breechblock. Remove the brace lever screw (8) and slowly open the hand vise to release the brace lever spring tension. Reassembly requires the use of the hand vise to compress the brace lever spring beneath the brace lever until a slave pin can be inserted and to hold the assembly in position until the brace lever screw is replaced.
7. Remove the brace lever roller screw (16) and brace lever roller (15) from the receiver.
8. Remove the lock by taking out the lockplate screw (30) and the sideplate screw (17) located in front of the hammer. Lift the lock from its mortise in the receiver and buttstock (3).
9. Remove the front (38) and rear (37) trigger plate screws and lift the trigger plate out of its mortise in the receiver and buttstock.
10. If desired, or required, the butt-stock is removed by removing the buttplate screws (51), and buttplate (50) and loosening the buttstock screw (20). NOTE: The swivel ring and bar fitted on carbines must be removed before attempting to detach the buttstock.
11. Reassemble in reverse order, except the fore-end must be replaced after the breechblock is installed and before replacing the extactor mounting plate.

REMINGTON MODELS 8 & 81 RIFLES

PARTS LEGEND

1. Receiver
2. Action spring tube
3. Action spring follower
4. Action spring
5. Action spring plug
6. Action spring plug pin
7. Trigger plate screw
8. Peep sight plug screw
9. Bolt carrier latch screw
10. Barrel lock screw
11. Bolt assembly (complete)
12. Operating handle
13. Operating handle plunger
14. Operating handle plunger spring
15. Operating handle bushing
16. Link (See Fig. 4 for link pin "C")
17. Safety detent ball
18. Hammer pin
19. Bolt carrier latch spring
20. Bolt carrier latch
21. Barrel lock
22. Barrel lock spring
23. Magazine indicator
24. Magazine indicator spring
25. Magazine indicator thumbpiece
26. Safety
27. Safety rocker
28. Safety rocker stop screw (Note: permanently installed inside receiver—removal is not recommended)
29. Barrel
30. Barrel jacket
31. Barrel jacket plug
32. Barrel jacket plug screw
33. Front sight assembly
34. Buffer spring
35. Recoil spring case
36. Recoil spring
37. Barrel nut washer
38. Barrel nut
39. Barrel jacket bushing
40. Bar sight assembly
41. Bar sight mounting screws (2)
42. Trigger plate
43. Trigger spring
44. Mainspring
45. Mainspring screw
46. Tang screw
47. Trigger
48. Trigger pin
49. Hammer
50. Hammer bushing
51. Hammer roll
52. Hammer roll pin
53. Magazine assembly
54. Magazine side spring, right
55. Magazine side spring, left
56. Fore-end
57. Fore-end screw
58. Fore-end escutcheon
59. Takedown screw
60. Takedown screw washers
61. Takedown lever pin
62. Takedown lever
63. Buttplate
64. Buttplate screws (2)
65. Buttstock (not shown)

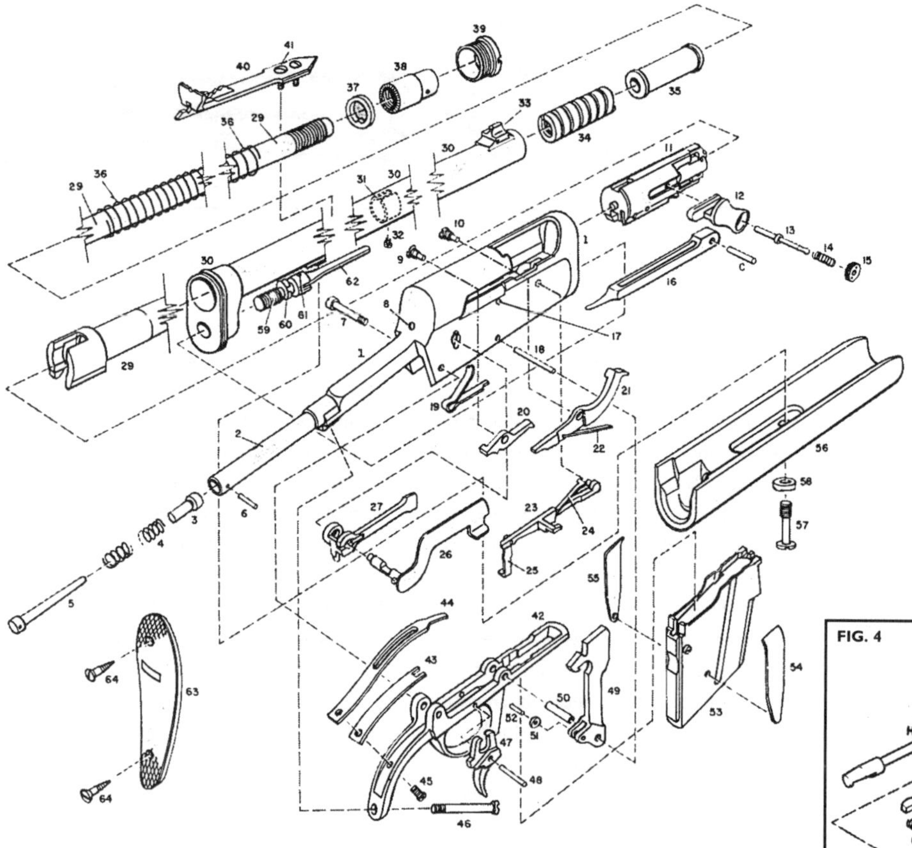

BOLTS ASSEMBLY PARTS LEGEND

A. Bolt carrier
B. Firing pin retaining pin
C. Link pin
D. Cam pins (2)
E. Bolt lock
F. Bolt lock pin
G. Bolt lock spring
H. Firing pin
J. Firing pin buffer spring
K. Firing pin spring
L. Extractor
M. Ejector
N. Ejector spring
O. Ejector pin
P. Bolt

FIG. 4

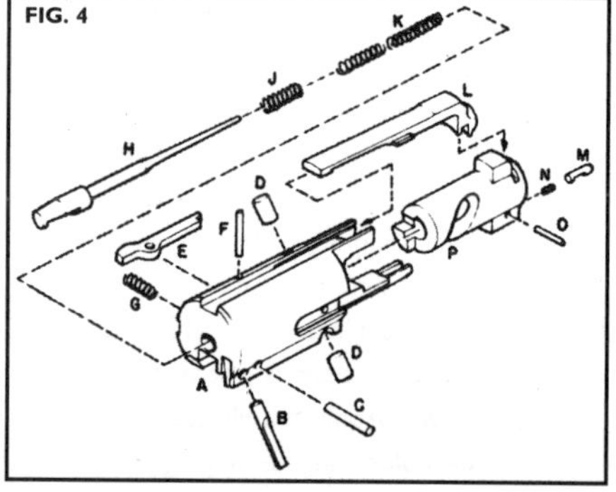

The Remington Model 81 Woodsmaster autoloading rifle was produced from 1936 until 1950. Except for minor differences, it is mechanically identical to the Remington Model 8, 5-shot autoloading rifle produced between 1906 to 1936. The design was based on John M. Browning's 1900 patent and the Model 81, with its locked breech, long-recoil action, was America's first successful high power autoloading rifle.

The Model 8 was chambered for the .25, .30, .32, and .35 caliber Remington rimless cartridges and was designed for clip loading. The Model 81 rifle was chambered for the same cartridges, (production in .25 Remington was limited), and was also offered in .300 Savage. The Models 8 and 81 sporting rifles were furnished with fixed magazines though a Model 81 Police Special was offered with 15-round detachable magazine.

DISASSEMBLY

To take down rifle, press safety (26) down and retract operating handle (12), locking bolt carrier assembly to rear. Unscrew fore-end screw (57) and remove fore-end (56) by pulling downward and forward. Swing takedown lever (62) sideways and unscrew takedown screw (59). Pull barrel jacket (30) and barrel (29) assembly forward out of receiver (1).

To disassemble barrel jacket, a special spanner wrench is required. Use spanner wrench to unscrew barrel nut (38), preventing breech end of barrel from turning by holding a large screwdriver in slot of breech end of barrel. Pull barrel to rear out of barrel jacket and hold so that muzzle end of barrel is clear of front face of barrel jacket bushing (39). Unscrew bushing from barrel jacket with spanner wrench, taking care not to allow compressed recoil spring (36) to escape. Remove recoil spring, barrel nut washer (37), recoil spring case (35), and buffer spring (34) from barrel jacket. Removal of plug (31) is not recommended.

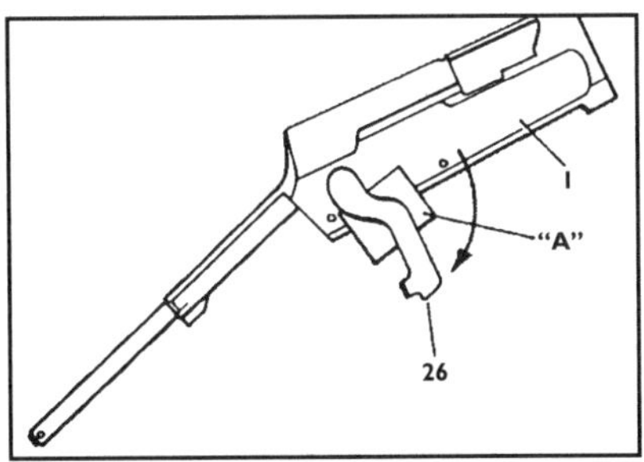

1 When removing safety (26), slip a piece of paper or cardboard between safety and receiver as shown at "A."

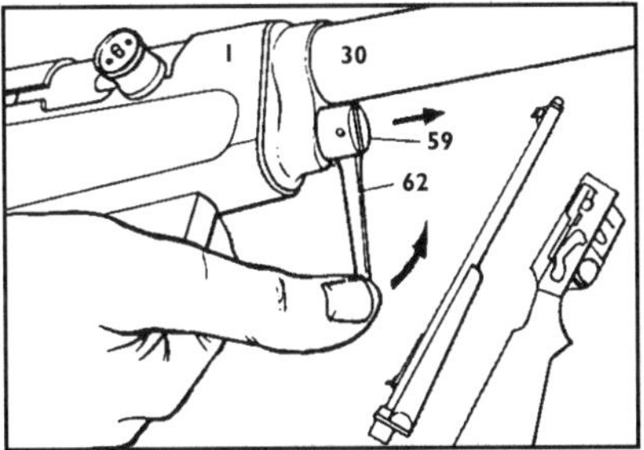

2 After removing fore-end, swing take-down lever (62) sideways and unscrew takedown screw (59) as shown. Pull barrel jacket and barrel assembly out of receiver to front.

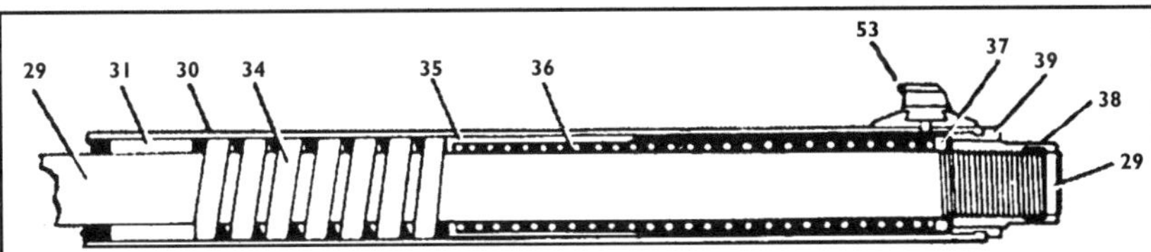

3 Section showing assembly of parts inside barrel jacket. Take care to reassemble parts in proper order. When replacing barrel nut washer (37) over muzzle, line up tongue in washer with keyway on barrel before screwing on barrel nut (38).

4 (See Fig. 4 on previous page). To remove bolt carrier-bolt assembly from receiver, push down front end of barrel lock (21) to release bolt carrier (A) which will stop on magazine indicator (23). Lift operating handle plunger (13) and slide operating handle assembly (12) forward and out of bolt carrier. Push down magazine indicator thumbpiece (25) on left side of receiver, releasing bolt carrier, which will spring out front end of receiver. Take care to catch bolt carrier-bolt assembly on release. To disassemble bolt carrier and bolt assembly, drive out link pin (C) and remove link (16). Drive out firing pin retaining pin (B) and remove firing pin (H) and firing pin buffer spring (J) from rear of bolt carrier. Remove 2 cam pins (D) and pull bolt (P) with extractor (L) forward out of bolt carrier. Remove firing pin spring (K). Drift out bolt lock pin (F) and remove bolt lock (E) and spring (G). Drift out ejector pin (O) and remove ejector (M) and spring (N) from bolt. When reassembling bolt carrier and bolt mechanism, be sure that rear end of link is seated in action spring follower (3) at rear of receiver.

To remove trigger and hammer mechanism, remove tang screw (46) and pull off buttstock. Remove trigger plate screw (7) and drive out hammer pin (18). Pull rear end of trigger plate (42) down and out of receiver. Push magazine assembly (53) up through trigger plate, releasing left and right side springs (54 & 55). Uncock hammer (49) and remove by carefully drifting out hammer bushing (50). Remove mainspring screw (45) and lift out mainspring (44) and trigger spring (43). Drive out trigger pin (48) and remove trigger (47). Reassemble in reverse order.

To disassemble receiver components, turn receiver upside down. Depress front end of bolt carrier latch spring (19) from under stud inside receiver and slide rear end of spring off its rear stud. Slide bolt carrier latch (20) off bolt carrier latch screw (9) in left receiver wall. Slide barrel lock (21) off barrel lock screw (10) in left receiver wall. It is not necessary to remove screws (9 & 10) from receiver. Remove magazine indicator assembly (23) from its pivot stud in receiver side wall. Lift safety (26) away from receiver and slip a piece of cardboard or heavy paper between safety and receiver to protect finish. Swing safety down below receiver as shown in Fig. 4. Drive out safety pivot from left to right and remove safety from right. Drop out safety rocker (27). Reassemble in reverse order.

REMINGTON MODEL 10 SHOTGUN

PARTS LEGEND

1. Action bar
2. Action bar lock, complete
3. Action bar lock pin
4. Barrel adjusting bushing
5. Barrel
6. Barrel adjusting bushing lock
7. Barrel adjusting bushing lock screw
8. Breechbolt
9. Buttplate
10. Buttplate screws (2)
11. Carrier, complete
12. Carrier stop
13. Cocking head
14. Cocking head pin
15. Extractor
16. Extractor spring
17. Firing pin
18. Firing pin bushing
19. Firing pin bushing pin
20. Fore-end
21. Fore-end nut
22. Front sight
23. Guard
24. Guard screw
25. Guard screw check screw
26. Mainspring
27. Magazine follower
28. Magazine lever
29. Magazine lever detent
30. Magazine lever detent pin
31. Magazine lever pin
32. Magazine lever spring
33. Magazine plug
34. Magazine plug screw
35. Magazine spring
36. Magazine tube
37. Receiver
38. Safety slide
39. Safety slide ball
40. Safety slide pin
41. Safety slide spring
42. Sear
43. Sear spring
44. Sear spring screw
45. Sear pin
46. Stock
47. Stock bolt
48. Stock bolt washer
49. Tang screw
50. Tang screw check screw
51. Trigger
52. Trigger pin
53. Trigger spring
54. Action bar lock button
55. Action bar lock button spring
56. Extractor pin

Note: Many design changes were made in the Model 10 over the years, and parts in some specimens may be different than those listed above.

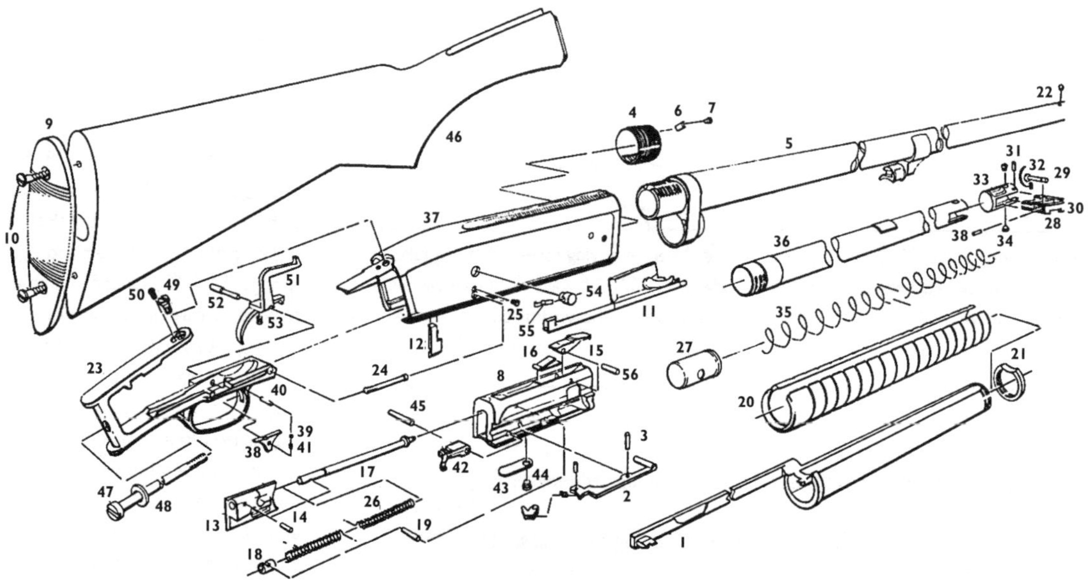

Remington entered the slide-action shotgun field in 1907 with a 12-gauge repeater characterized by handsome lines and several interesting features. Produced under John D. Pedersen's patents, this solid breech, hammerless action takedown shotgun featured a five-shot tubular magazine. The receiver is closed except for a bottom loading and ejection port.

Among several other features of this striker-fired repeater is a recoil lock which prevents opening of the action by a rearward pull on the fore-end until the latter is released by the recoil of firing. This is designed to prevent accidents from hangfires. Other interesting features are the short 7⁄16-inch travel of the firing pin for a fast lock time, and the slide safety in the forward part of the trigger guard.

First introduced as the Model 1908, the designation was later changed to the Model 1910. Several grades in various barrel lengths and chokes were offered. According to the Remington 1918-19 catalog, the No. 10A Standard Grade was a plain gun without checkering and engraving. Other grades are the No. 10B Special with checkered pistol grip and fore-end, No. 10S Trap Special with straight-grip stock, No. 10C Trap, No. 10D Tournament, No. 10E Expert, and No. 10F Premier. There is also a No. 10R Riot Grade with 20-inch barrel, and a version of this gun, fitted with a hand-guard and bayonet attachment, was produced for the U.S. Army.

Checkering, engraving and select walnut are special features of the higher grades. The highest grade is the No. 10F listed at $183.50 in the 1918-19 Remington catalog. The Model 1910 was superseded in 1929 by the Remington Model 29.

DISASSEMBLY

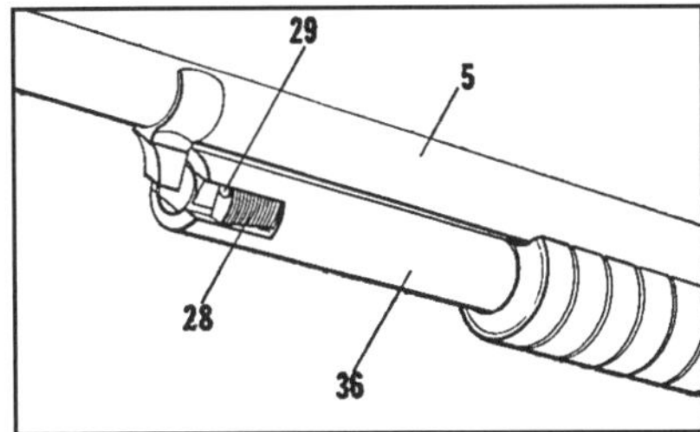

1 Remove any shells from magazine and chamber. Press magazine lever detent (29) inward upon magazine lever (28). Magazine lever is then unlocked and can be turned crossways so it protrudes from right side of magazine tube (36).

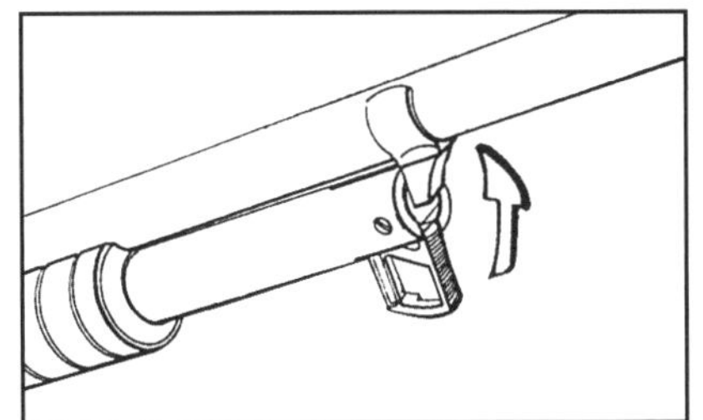

2 Rotate magazine lever downward. This will turn magazine tube one quarter turn to unlock tube from receiver (37).

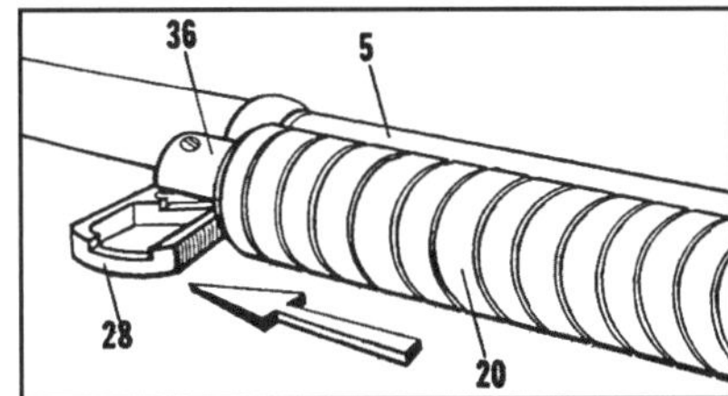

3 With magazine lever in down position, slide magazine tube forward so that lever slot in front of tube moves forward over lug on barrel (5). Rear of magazine will then be free of receiver. Slide fore-end (20) forward until end of attached action bar (1) is free of breech- bolt (8) and receiver.

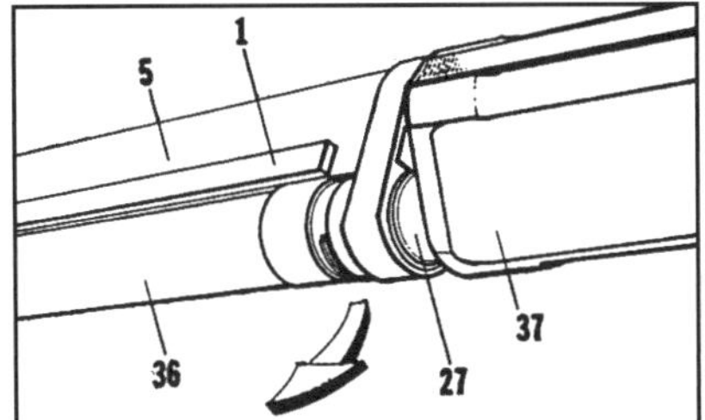

4 Hold fore-end and magazine tube foward. Turn barrel, fore-end, and magazine tube as a complete unit one quarter turn clockwise (as viewed from rear) to disengage barrel threads from threads in receiver. Pull barrel, tube, fore-end, and action bar forward away from receiver. This is sufficient disassembly for routine cleaning and lubrication. Before reassembly of barrel to receiver, lower firing pin (17) by pulling trigger.

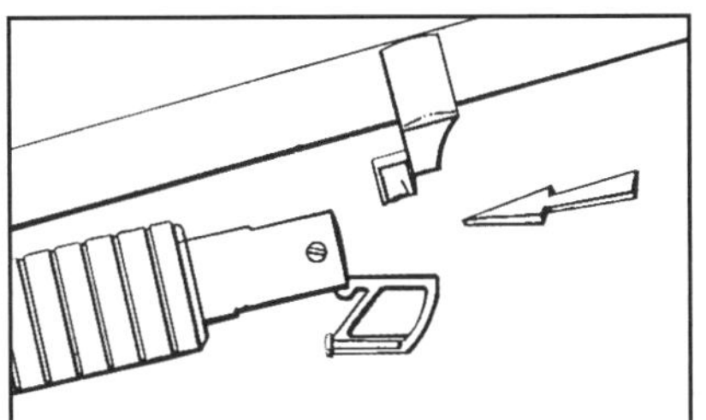

5 Use small screwdriver to press magazine lever detent inward upon magazine lever, and turn lever free from end of magazine tube. Hold lever forward and slide tube rearward until separated from barrel lug. Then pull combined tube and fore-end forward to disengage action bar from yoke at rear of barrel.

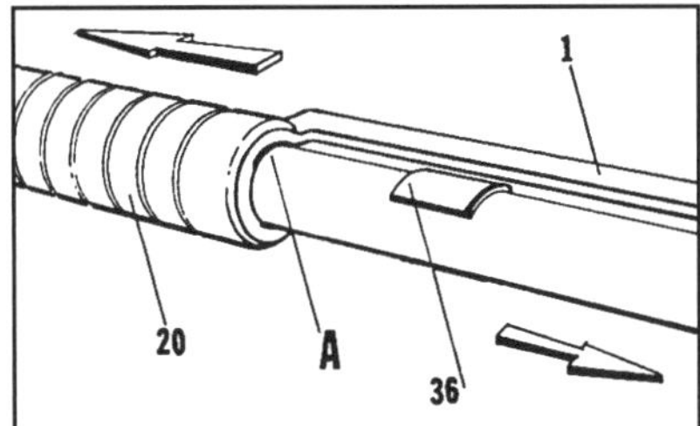

6 Press magazine lever detent inward, and turn lever to re-engage fully into end of tube. Fore-end must be turned until lugs on tube match slots in action bar (see A). Pull action bar and fore-end forward off magazine tube.

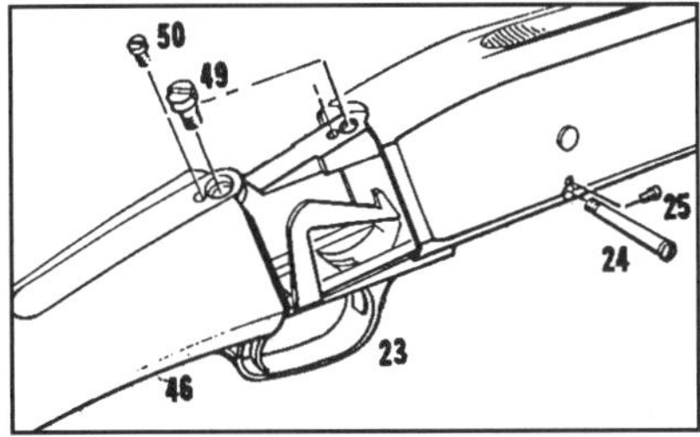

7 To remove guard (23) and stock (46) from receiver, unscrew guard screw check screw (25), guard screw (24), tang screw check screw (50), and tang screw (49). Pull guard and stock rearward away from receiver.

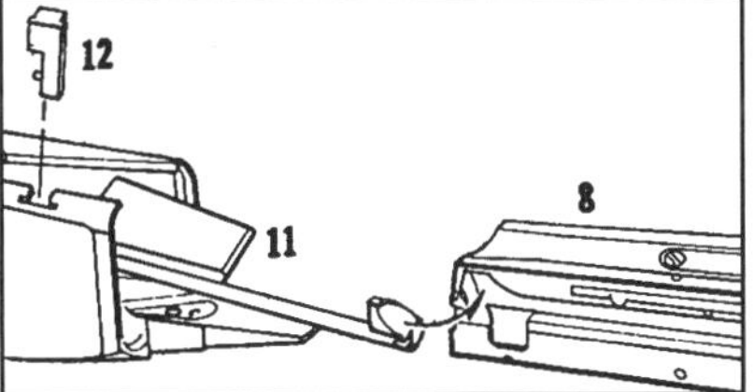

8 Use small screwdriver to pry carrier stop (12) from bottom of receiver. While depressing action bar lock button (54), lift breechbolt (8) out of engagement with recoil shoulder, and move breechbolt rearward until it and the carrier (11) are out of receiver. Uncock firing pin by depressing sear (42), and remove sear spring screw (44) and sear spring (43). Remove sear, firing pin, and extractor (15) with spring (16) after driving out pins which retain these parts. Reassemble in reverse. In so doing, engage rear end of carrier in recess on side of breechbolt and hold these parts together while sliding them into receiver. Also, press forward on rear of carrier while inserting carrier stop.

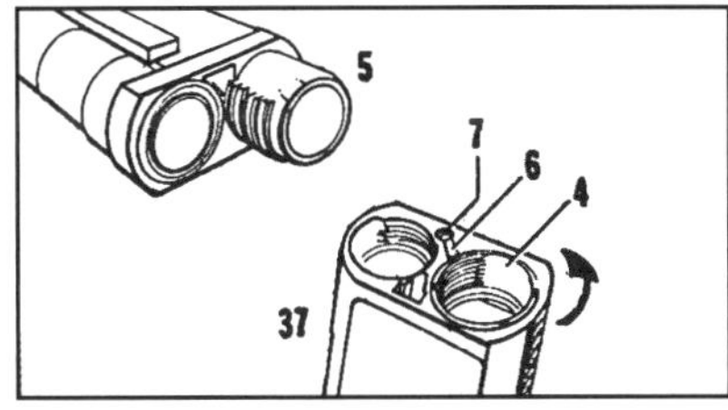

9 If barrel becomes loose in receiver, remove barrel and magazine assembly and unscrew barrel adjusting bushing lock screw (7) four turns. Slide barrel adjusting bushing lock (6) out of engagement with barrel adjusting bushing (4) and turn bushing slightly in direction of arrow until barrel will tighten in receiver. Qualification marks on bottom of gun should align. Slide bushing lock against corrugations in bushing, and tighten lock screw.

REMINGTON MODEL 11 SHOTGUN

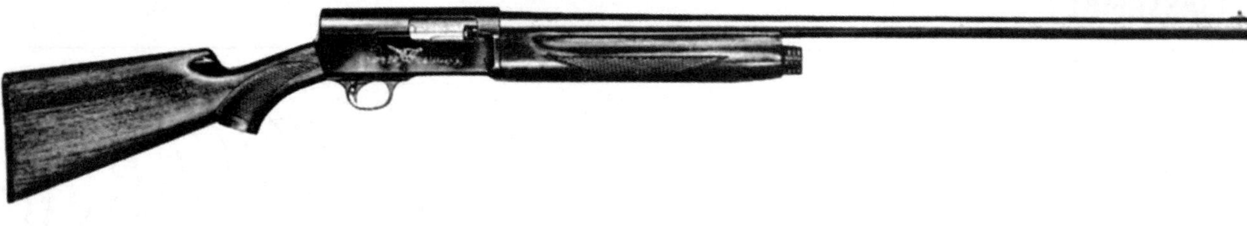

PARTS LEGEND

1. Barrel
2. Bead sight
3. Front sight
4. Barrel extension *
5. Barrel guide *
6. Ejector *
7. Receiver
8. Action spring tube
9. Action spring follower
10. Action spring
11. Action spring plug pin
12. Action spring plug
13. Fiber cushion *
14. Fiber cushion rivet *
15. Carrier screws (2)
16. Carrier screw locking screws (2)
17. Trigger plate pin
18. Trigger plate pin locking screw
19. Trigger plate screw
20. Carrier latch pin lock screw
21. Carrier latch pin
22. Carrier latch
23. Carrier latch spring
24. Carrier latch button
25. Carrier spring
26. Cartridge stop pin lock screw
27. Cartridge stop spring
28. Cartridge stop
29. Cartridge stop pin
30. Breechbolt
31. Locking block
32. Link pin
33. Extractor pin
34. Extractor spring
35. Extractor plunger
36. Extractor
37. Locking block latch spring
38. Locking block latch
39. Locking block latch pin
40. Firing pin retaining pin
41. Operating slide
42. Firing pin retractor spring
43. Firing pin
44. Link
45. Mainspring
46. Trigger spring
47. Tang screw bushing
48. Trigger plate
49. Mainspring screw
50. Tang screw locking screw
51. Tang screw
52. Safety sear spring follower
53. Safety sear spring
54. Safety sear
55. Hammer pin
56. Trigger pin
57. Safety sear pin
58. Safety
59. Safety ball
60. Trigger
61. Hammer roll
62. Hammer
63. Hammer roll pin
64. Carrier
65. Carrier dog pin
66. Carrier dog spring
67. Carrier dog spring follower
68. Carrier dog
69. Pistol grip cap
70. Pistol grip cap screw
71. Fore-end
72. Buttplate screw (2)
73. Buttplate
74. Magazine spring retainer
75. Magazine spring
76. Magazine follower
77. Magazine tube
78. Fore-end guide ring
79. Fore-end guide ring screw
80. Friction ring
81. Recoil spring
82. Friction piece
83. Friction spring
84. Magazine cap
85. Magazine cap stop plunger spring
86. Magazine cap stop plunger
87. Magazine stop screw
88. Magazine cap stop plunger tube

* Permanent factory assemble

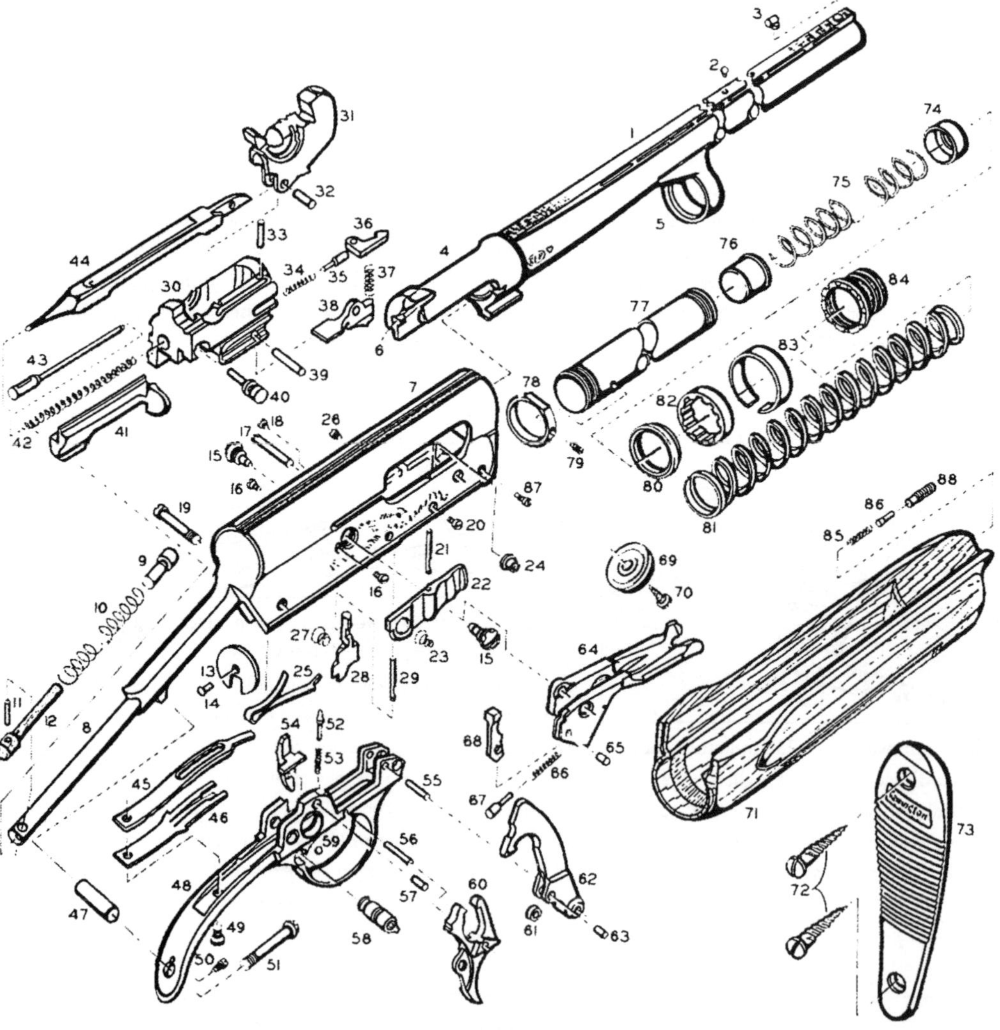

In 1900, John M. Browning was granted U. S. Patent No. 659.507 for a locked-breech, long recoil operated semi-automatic shotgun mechanism. Browning first offered this design to Winchester Repeating Arms Co., as he had done with his arms designs in previous years, but on a royalty basis instead of outright sale as had been his practice. The parties could not reach an agreement, and Browning terminated his 17-year relationship with Winchester.

At that time, no other American arms maker was in a position to produce this shotgun, so Browning went to Belgium where he arranged for its manufacture by Fabrique Nationale d'Armes de Guerre in Liege. Initial production by the FN firm was in 1903.

In 1905 Remington Arms was licensed to manufacture the Browning shotgun in the United States. It was introduced that year as the Remington Model 11 and was offered in 12, 16, and 20 gauge and in several grades with various barrel lengths and chokes. The Model 11 No. 0 Riot Grade shotgun with 18½-inch barrel in 12 gauge only was offered the following year.

The Model 11 Police Special with 18½-inch barrel in 12-gauge was introduced in 1921. The barrel was especially bored for buckshot loads and the gun was furnished with sling swivels.

Remington's Model 11 Riot gun was also introduced in 1921. It was furnished with 20-inch cylinder-bored barrel in 12, 16, and 20 gauge.

A 3-shot version of the Model 11 was introduced in 1931. Designated Sportsman Model, it was available in various barrel lengths and grades in 12, 16, and 20 gauge.

Production of the Model 11 shotgun terminated in 1948 and was replaced the following year by the Model 11-48.

DISASSEMBLY

1 Push barrel (1) slightly rearward into receiver (7) to relieve pressure on the fore-end (71), and unscrew magazine cap (84). Release barrel and remove fore-end and barrel from magazine tube (77). Slide friction ring (80), friction piece (82), and recoil spring (81) forward off magazine tube. Remove tang screw locking screw (50) and tang screw (51) from lower tang. Pull stock off rearward. Remove the trigger plate screw (19, right arrow). Remove trigger plate pin locking screw (18) and drift out the trigger plate pin (17, left arrow) from right to left. Lift out trigger plate (48). It is best to label each of the small locking screws as they are removed from the gun to avoid mixing them.

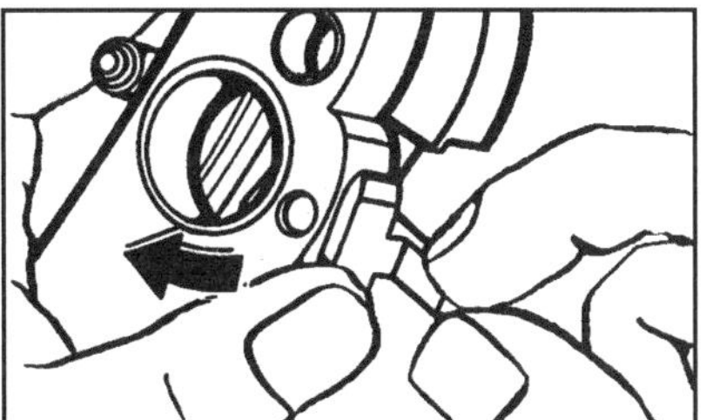

2 Cock the hammer (62), depress safety sear spring follower (52) as shown, and slide safety sear (54) off its stud toward the left side of the trigger plate. Remove safety sear spring follower and safety sear spring (53) from hole in top right side of trigger plate. Uncock hammer letting it forward slowly.

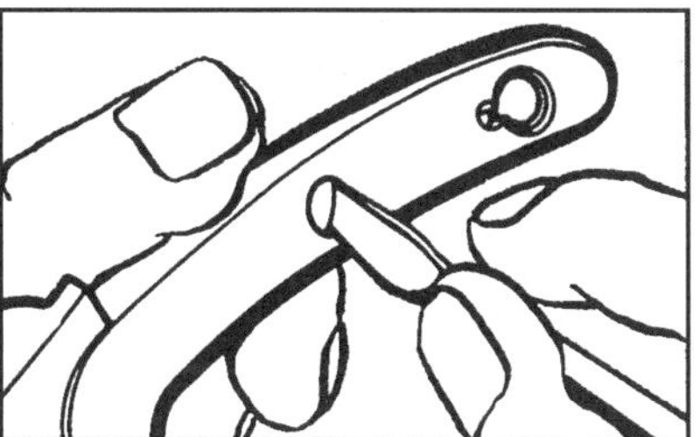

3 Remove mainspring screw (49) from bottom of tang and lift away mainspring (45) and trigger spring (46) from slot in top of tang. Remove safety ball (59) from hole in bottom of slot just in rear of trigger (60).

REMINGTON MODEL 11 SHOTGUN

DISASSEMBLY CONTINUED

4 Drive out the hammer pin (55) and remove hammer (62) together with hammer roll (61) and attached hammer roll pin (63). Drift out the trigger pin (56) as shown and remove trigger (60). Slide out safety (58).

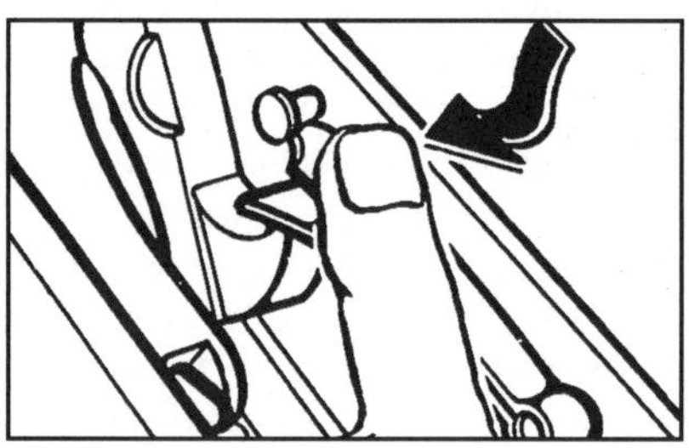

5 Press front end of carrier spring (25) from under head of stud in left side of receiver and lift away spring.

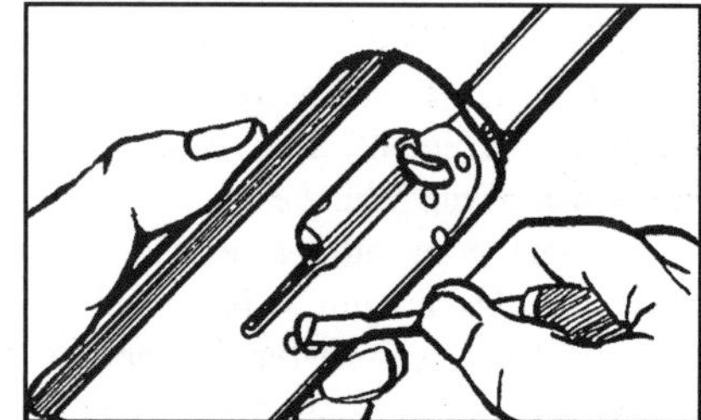

6 Remove 2 carrier screw locking screws (16) and 2 carrier screws (15) from sides of receiver and lift carrier out of the bottom of receiver.

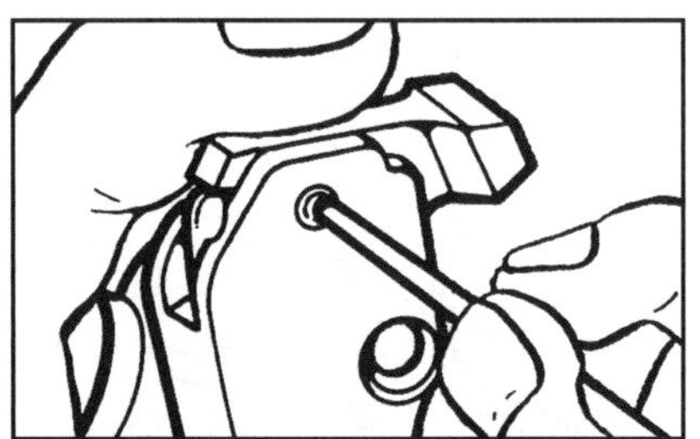

7 Drive carrier dog pin (65) from rear of carrier, holding carrier dog (68) with thumb as shown, to prevent loss of carrier dog spring follower (67) and carrier dog spring (66). These 2 latter parts may be eased out.

8 Compress action spring plug (12) with thumb and push out action spring plug pin (11). Carefully release action spring (10) and remove it with action spring plug and attached action spring follower (9) from action spring tube (8).

9 Move breechbolt (30) rearward in receiver until locking block latch pin (39) in breechbolt lines up with hole in left side of receiver (arrow), opposite lower edge of ejection port. A pen flashlight will greatly aid in alignment. Drift out locking block latch pin from right side of receiver and remove locking block latch (38) and locking block latch spring (37) from bottom of breechbolt.

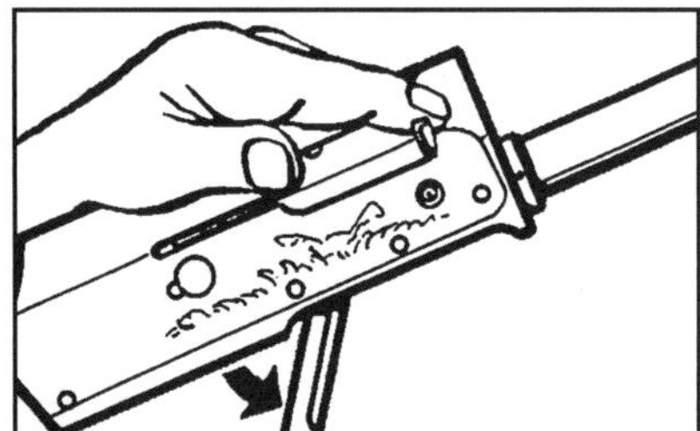

10 Swing link (44) toward bottom of receiver, hold operating slide (41), and push breechbolt forward from receiver through barrel opening in front end of receiver. Remove operating slide through ejection port.

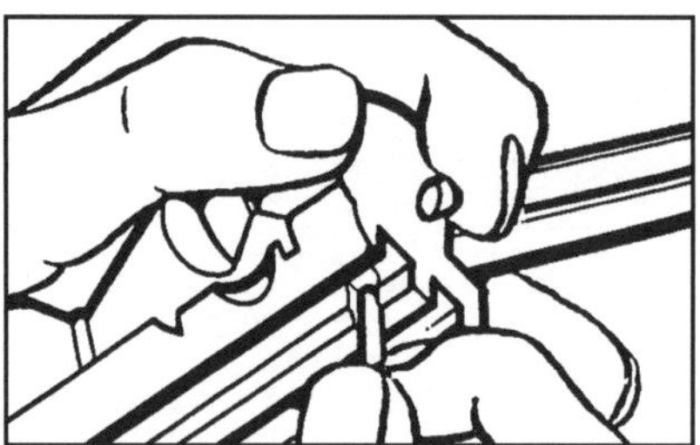

11 Compress firing pin (43) with index finger as shown and drift out firing pin retaining pin (40) from left to right. Remove the firing pin and the firing pin retractor spring (42).

12 Lift locking block (31) with link attached through top of breechbolt. Drive out extractor pin (33) from bottom to top, remove extractor (36), extractor plunger (35), and extractor spring (34).

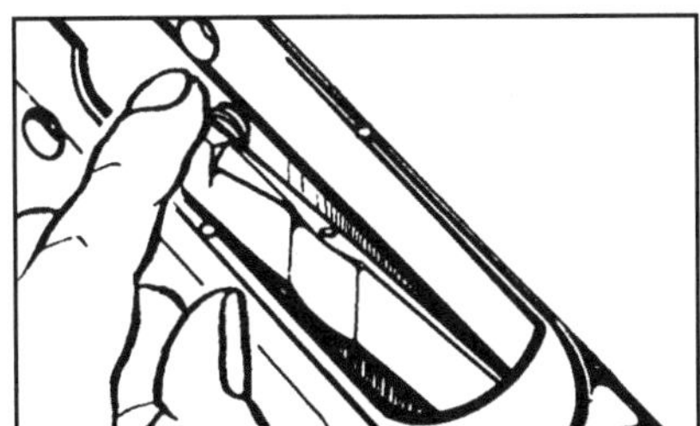

13 Remove carrier latch pin lock screw (20) and carrier latch pin (21) from lower right edge of receiver. Remove carrier latch (22) using index finger, with carrier latch spring (23) attached. Remove carrier latch button (24).

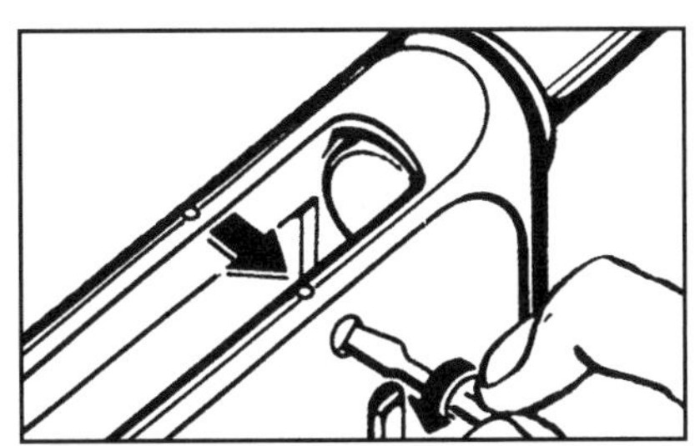

14 Remove cartridge stop pin lock screw (26) and cartridge stop pin (29) from lower left edge of receiver. Remove the cartridge stop (28) with the cartridge stop spring (27) attached.

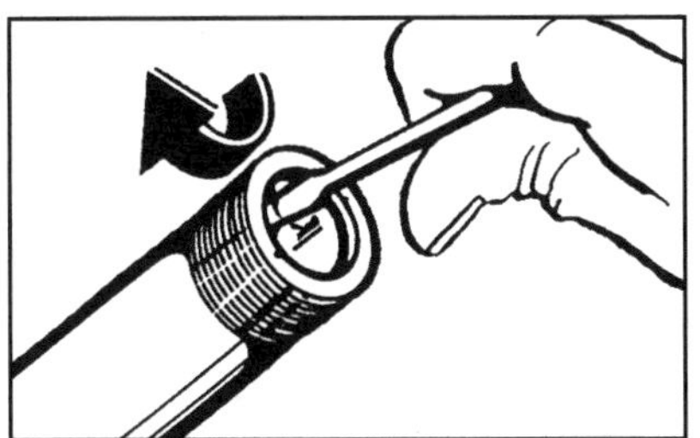

15 Pry out magazine spring retainer (74) from front end of magazine tube (77). Do carefully to control magazine spring (75) and prevent it from flying out of tube. Remove magazine spring and slide magazine follower (76) from tube end.

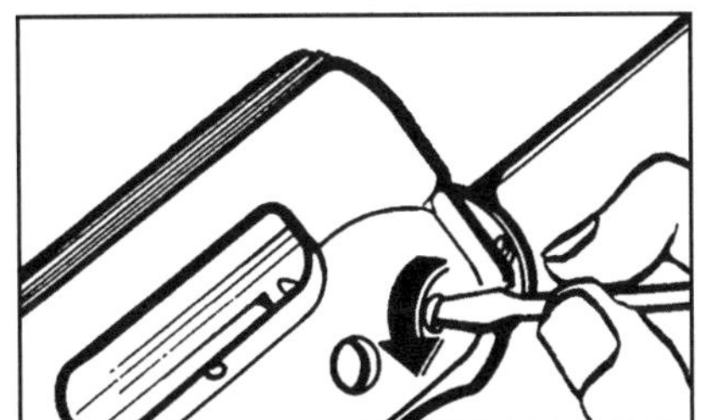

16 Remove magazine stop screw (87) from right front side of receiver. Unscrew magazine tube.

17 Reassemble arm in reverse order. When replacing locking block latch (38), align hole in breechbolt with hole in left side of receiver. Insert locking block latch pin (39) to hold breechbolt in place. Insert locking block latch spring (37) and locking block latch (38). Drive pin all the way in with small drift as shown.

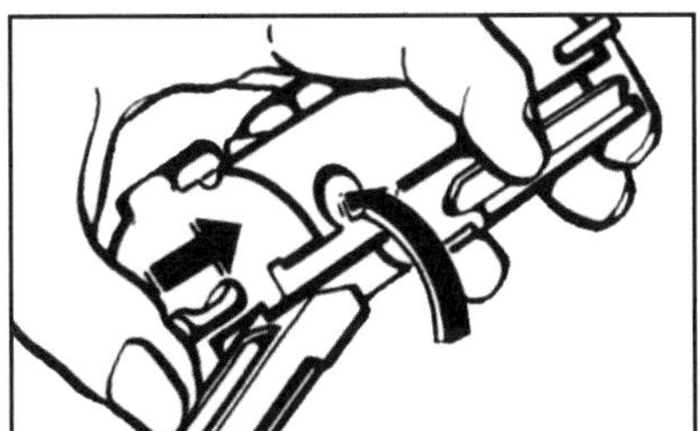

18 When replacing firing pin (43) and firing pin retractor spring (42), place spring over firing pin and insert in hole at rear of breechbolt (30). Insure that indented surface of firing pin faces top of breechbolt. Compress with thumb. Insert firing pin retaining pin (40, arrow).

REMINGTON MODEL 11-48 SHOTGUN

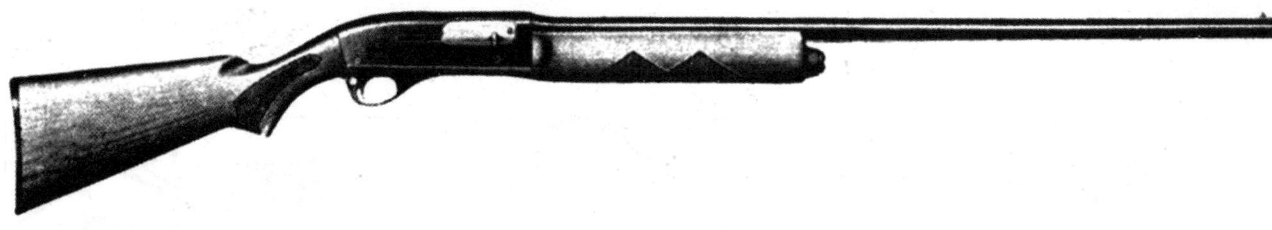

PARTS LEGEND

1. Action spring
2. Action spring follower
3. Action spring plug
4. Action spring plug pin
5. Action spring tube nut
6. Action spring tube nut lock washer
7. Action spring tube nut washer
8. Barrel assembly
9. Breechbolt
10. Buttplate
11. Buttplate screw (2)
12. Carrier assembly
13. Carrier dog follower
14. Carrier dog follower spring
15. Carrier latch assembly
16. Carrier latch button
17. Carrier latch pin
18. Carrier pivot tube
19. Connector, left
20. Connector, right
21. Connector pin
22. Disconnector
23. Extractor
24. Extractor plunger
25. Extractor spring
26. Firing pin
27. Firing pin retaining pin
28. Firing pin retractor spring
29. Fore-end assembly
30. Fore-end detent
31. Fore-end detent spring
32. Friction piece
33. Front sight
34. Front sight base
35. Hammer
36. Hammer pin
37. Hammer pin washer
38. Hammer plunger
39. Hammer spring
40. Link, left
41. Link, right
42. Link pin
43. Locking block
44. Locking block pin
45. Magazine cap
46. Magazine follower
47. Magazine spring
48. Magazine spring retainer
49. Operating handle
50. Receiver assembly
51. Recoil spring and ring assembly
52. Safety
53. Safety detent ball
54. Safety spring
55. Safety spring retaining pin
56. Sear
57. Sear pin
58. Sear spring
59. Shell latch
60. Slide
61. Stock bearing plate
62. Trigger
63. Trigger pin
64. Trigger plate
65. Trigger plate pin bushing
66. Trigger plate pin detent spring, front (2)
67. Trigger plate pin detent spring, rear
68. Trigger plate pin, front
69. Trigger plate pin, rear

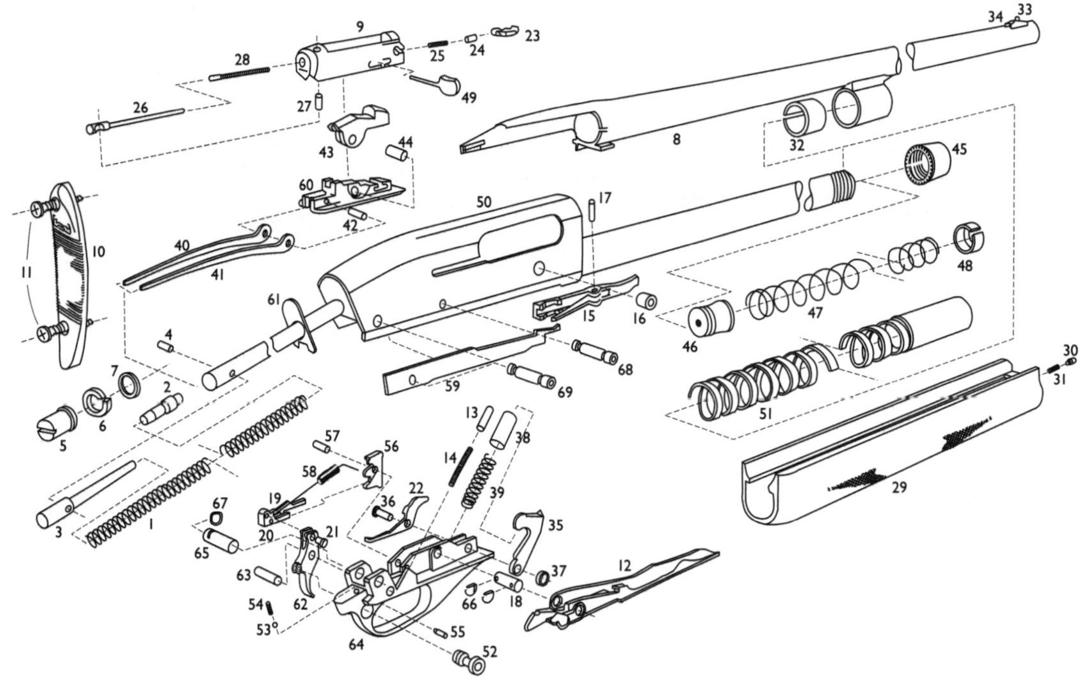

The first Remington shotgun of this type was the long-recoil operated Model 11 designed by John M. Browning and introduced in 1905. This was followed in 1931 by the Sportsman Model, a slightly modified 3-shot version of the Model 11. While the Model 11 and Sportsman were excellent guns, they were quite expensive to produce and had a square-hack receiver that did not appeal to some shooters.

In 1949, Remington introduced a new autoloader to replace the Model II. Designated the Model 11-48, the new gun was based on the Model II, but was re-engineered to facilitate production and featured a new receiver design that was nicely rounded and sloped on the upper rear.

The Model 11-48 was offered in 12, 16, and 20 gauge chambered for 2¾-inch shells, and with various barrel lengths and chokes. The magazine capacity was four shells. Later, the gun was available in 28 gauge and .410 bore for skeet shooting, and a 12 gauge version with rifle sights designed for slugs was offered as the "Rifled Slug Special." The Sportsman 48 version had a two-shot magazine. The Sportsman 48 was discontinued in 1960 and the Model 11-48 was last listed in 1968.

DISASSEMBLY

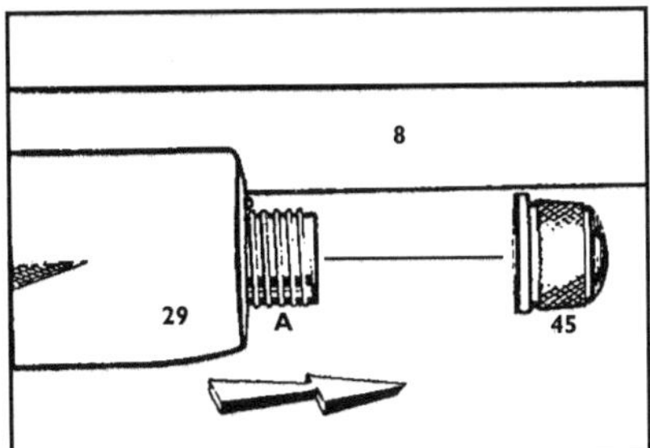

1 Before disassembling the Model 11- 48, engage safety (52) on safe by pushing to right, and unload magazine and barrel. Red band marking will not show when safety is on. Unscrew magazine cap (45) from end of magazine tube (A). Pull fore-end assembly (29) forward and remove from gun.

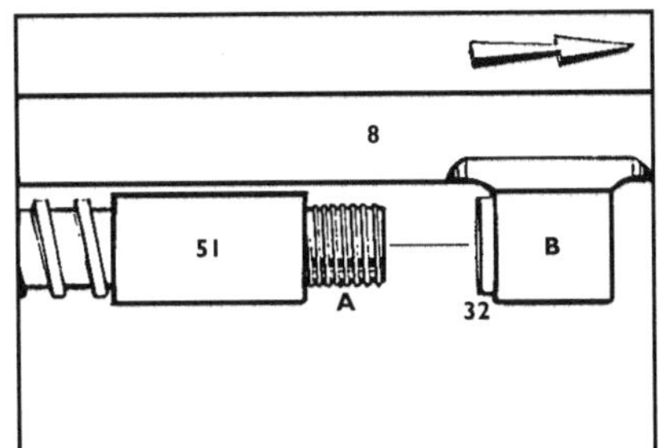

2 Pull barrel assembly (8) forward and separate from magazine tube and receiver (50). Friction piece (32) will remain in barrel guide ring (B).

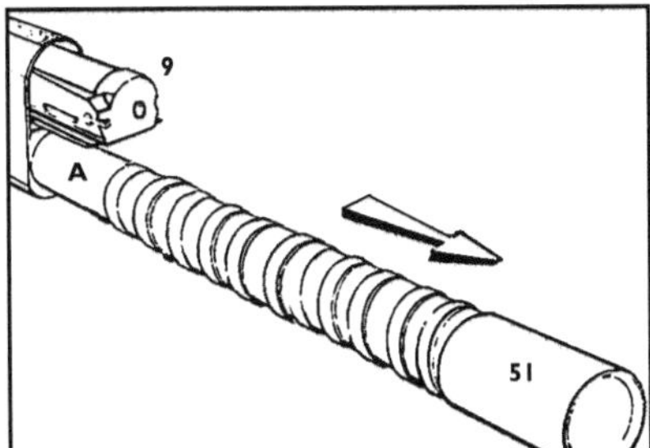

3 Twist recoil spring clockwise, and pull recoil spring and ring assembly (51) forward off magazine tube. Pull operating handle (49) outward to disassemble from breechbolt (9). Move breechbolt with attached slide (60), locking block (43), and links (40 & 41) forward out of receiver. Replace magazine cap on magazine tube for safe retention of magazine spring (47).

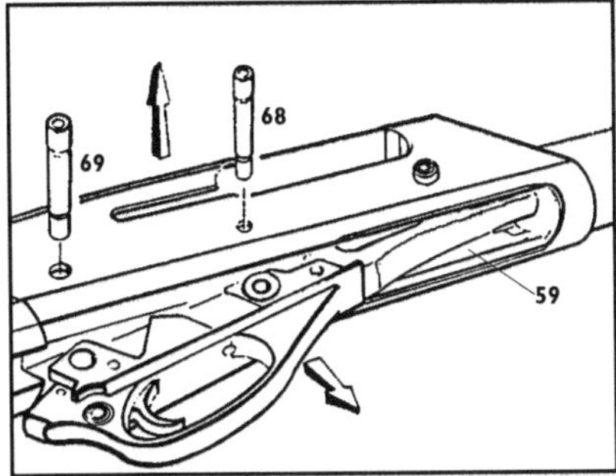

4 Barrel assembly and breechbolt may or may not be removed from gun to take out trigger plate assembly. Close action if breechbolt is not removed. Cock hammer, engage safety on safe, and tap out trigger plate pins (68 & 69). Lift out trigger plate assembly. Shell latch (59) will fall free of receiver.

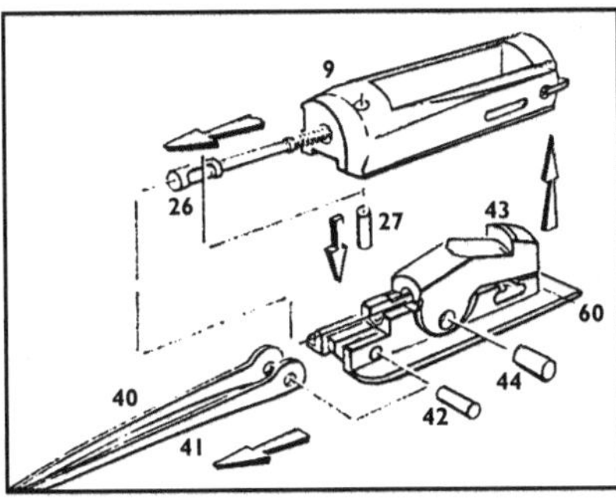

5 Lift rear of breechbolt. Tap firing pin retaining pin (27) downward and disassemble firing pin (26) and firing pin retractor spring (28) from rear of breech-bolt. Lift breechbolt from slide. Tap out locking block pin (44). Lift locking block from slide. Separate links from slide after removing link pin (42).

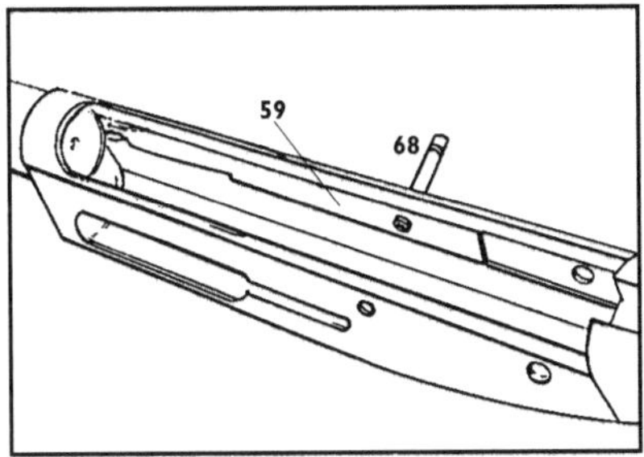

6 Reassemble in reverse. To reassemble shell latch, locate it in channel in left of receiver. Align hole in shell latch flush with front trigger plate pin in receiver. Check to be sure that back end of disconnector (22) is below the left connector (19). Then, position rear of trigger plate assembly in receiver, drop front into place, and insert pins.

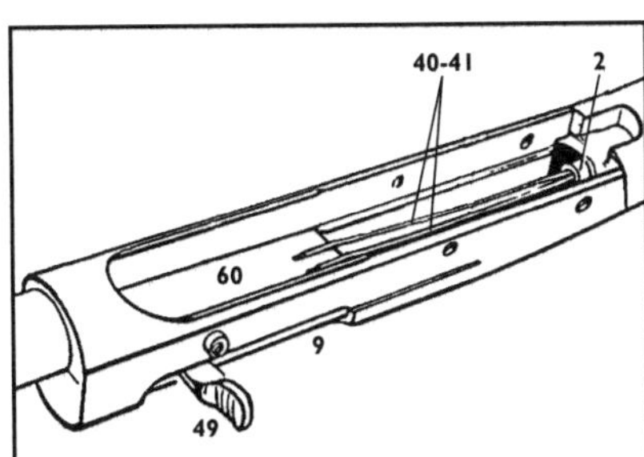

7 Replace the breechbolt assembly into the receiver from the front. Align the slide with the channels in receiver. Push the assembly rearward into the receiver and locate rear of both links in action spring follower (2). Insert operating handle in the handle slot in the breechbolt.

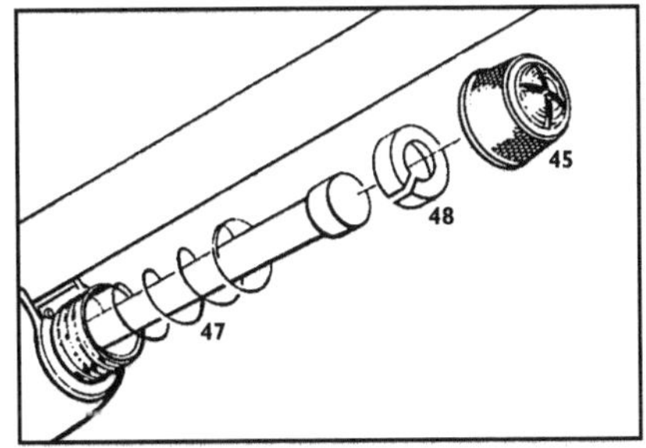

8 Wood plug to reduce total capacity of gun to three shots as required by Federal Migratory Bird Regulations, may be installed after removing magazine cap and prying out magazine spring retainer (48). Take care in doing this as this spring is under tension. Position wood plug as shown and replace parts.

REMINGTON

REMINGTON MODEL 11-87 SHOTGUN

PARTS LEGEND

1. Action bar assembly
2. Action bar sleeve
3. Action spring
4. Action spring follower
5. Action spring plug
6. Action spring plug pin
7. Action spring tube
8. Action spring tube nut
9. Action spring tube nut washer
10. Action spring tube nut lock washer
11. Barrel assembly
12. Barrel seal

12a. Barrel seal activator (Super Magnum only)

13. Breech bolt
14. Breech bolt buffer
15. Breech bolt return plunger
16. Breech bolt return plunger retaining ring
17. Carrier
18. Carrier assembly
19. Carrier dog
20. Carrier dog pin
21. Carrier dog washer
22. Carrier dog follower
23. Carrier dog follower spring
24. Carrier latch
25. Carrier latch pin
26. Carrier latch spring
27. Carrier latch spring
28. Carrier pivot tube
29. Carrier release
30. Carrier release pin
31. Carrier release spring
32. Connector, left
33. Connector, right
34. Connector pin
35. Disconnector
36. Extractor
37. Extractor plunger
38. Extractor spring
39. Feed latch
40. Firing pin
41. Firing pin retaining pin
42. Firing pin retractor spring
43. Fore-end assembly
44. Fore-end support assembly
45. Front sight

45a. Gas cylinder collar (12 gauge only)

46. Grip cap
48. Hammer
49. Hammer pin
50. Hammer pin washer
51. Hammer plunger
52. Hammer spring
53. Interceptor latch retainer
54. Interceptor latch spring
55. Interceptor latch
56. Link
57. Locking block assembly
58. Magazine cap
60. Magazine follower
61. Magazine spring
62. Magazine spring retainer

62a. Middle sight

63. Operating handle
64. Operating handle detent ball
65. Operating handle detent spring
66. Piston 12 gauge
67. Piston seal
68. Receiver assembly

68a. Return plunger retaining pin

69. Recoil pad
70. Recoil pad screws (2)
71. Rubber grommet (not shown)
72. Safety mechanism
73. Safety mechanism detent plunger
74. Safety mechanism spring
75. Safety mechanism spring retaining pin
76. Sear
77. Sear pin
78. Sear spring
79. Slide block buffer
80. Stock assembly
81. Stock bearing plate
82. Trigger
83. Trigger pin
84. Trigger plate safety mechanism
85. Trigger plate pin bushing, rear
86. Trigger plate pin detent springs, front (2)
87. Trigger plate detent spring, rear
88. Trigger plate pin, front
89. Trigger plate pin, rear

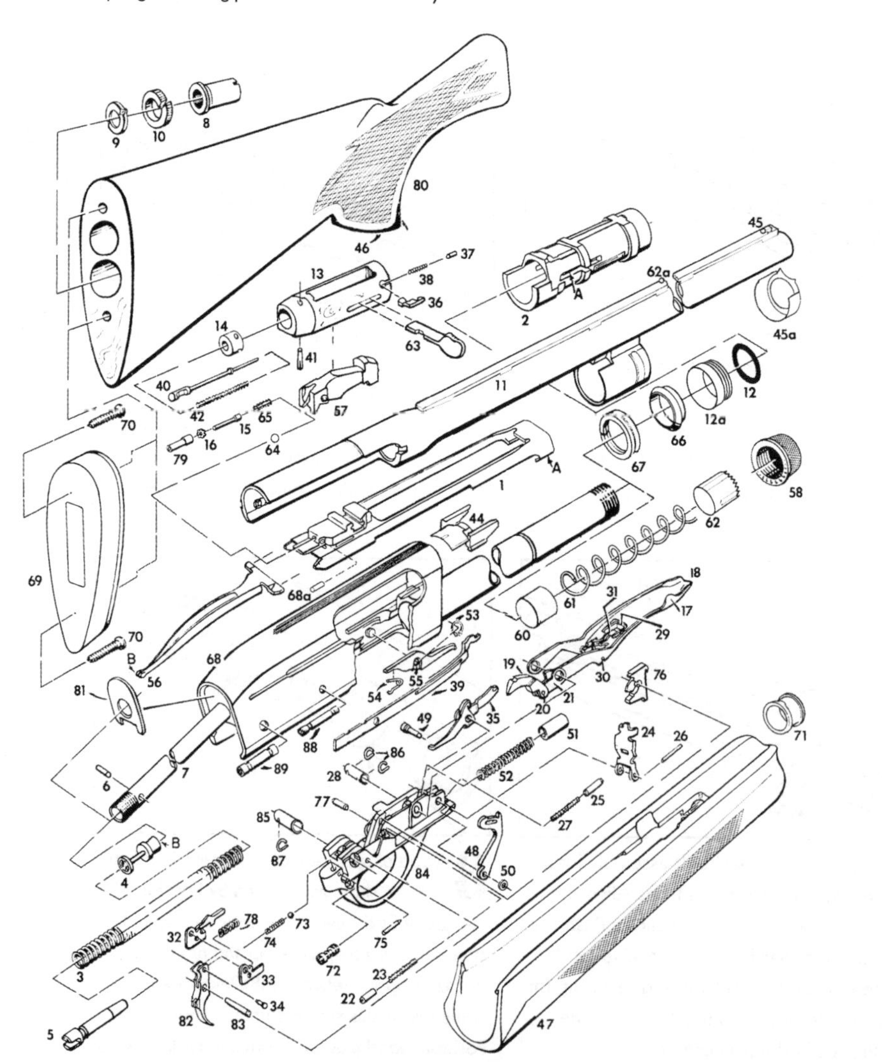

The Remington Model 11-87 is a pressure compensated autoloading shotgun introduced in 1987 by Remington Arms as an improved and strengthened version of their Model 1100 shotgun. The magazine fed 11-87 was technically similar to 1100 but was designed and strengthened to fire 3½-inch magnum shells.

About 20 hunting versions of the Model 11-87 have been produced along with police and tactical models. Most Police/Tactical models are fitted with magazine extension tubes. The 11-87 is similar to the Model 1100 in design but heavier and some parts, including barrels, are not interchangeable between models. The 11-87's gas cylinder is located around the front of the magazine tube and the piston is linked to the action by two action bars. Barrel locking is achieved by the single tilting locking piece. A 20-gauge model was introduced in 1999.

DISASSEMBLY

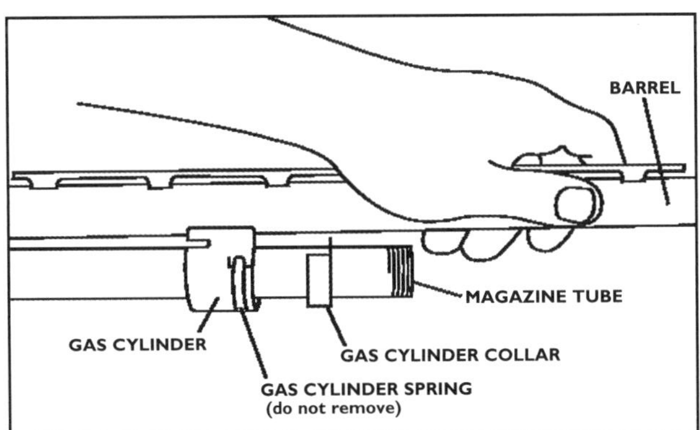

1 Remove the gas cylinder collar. Hold the barrel in front of the gas cylinder. Pull the barrel from the receiver.

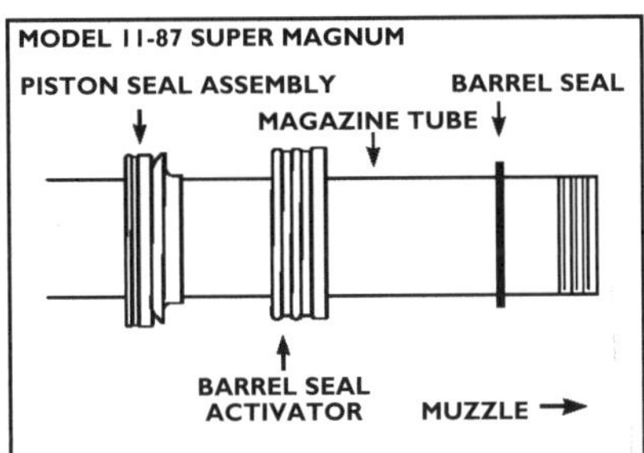

2 For 11-87 12-g auge Super Magnum: slide the barrel seal, barrel seal activator (when using 2¾-inch shells) and piston/piston seal assembly from the magazine tube. Important: A barrel seal activator is used on the M 11-87 Super Magnum when using 2¾-inch loads. Removal of the barrel seal activator is recommended when using 3- or 3½-inch loads.

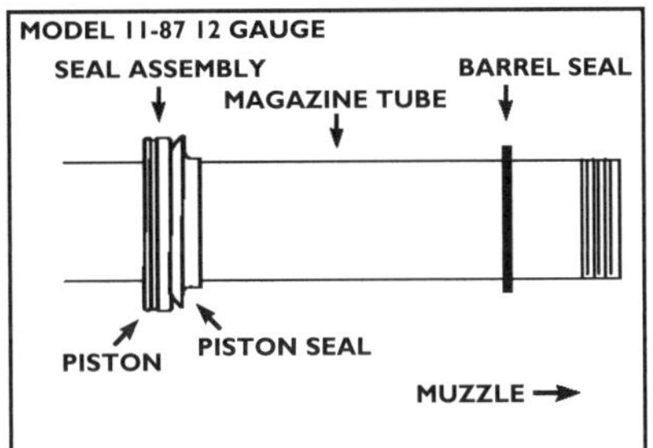

3 For 11-87 12-gauge (2¾-3-inch) only: slide the barrel seal and piston/piston seal assembly from the magazine tube.

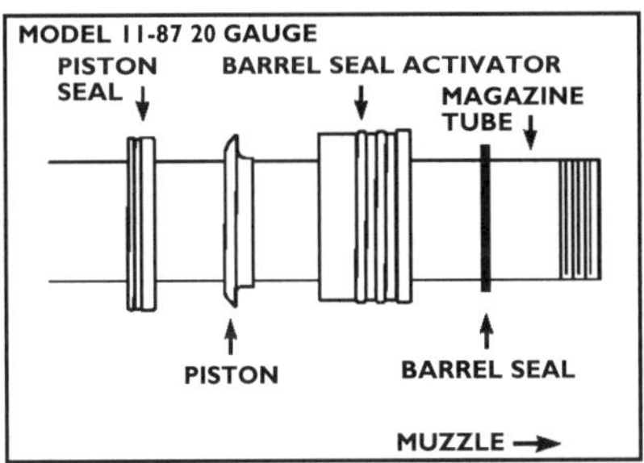

4 For 11087 20-gauge only: slide the barrel seal, barrel seal activator, piston and piston seal from the magazine tube.

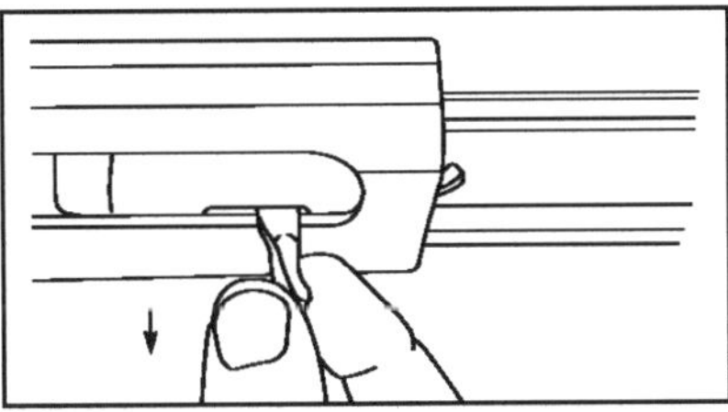

5 Hold the operating handle and close the action. Pull the operating handle from the bolt. Push the carrier release and push upward on the carrier.

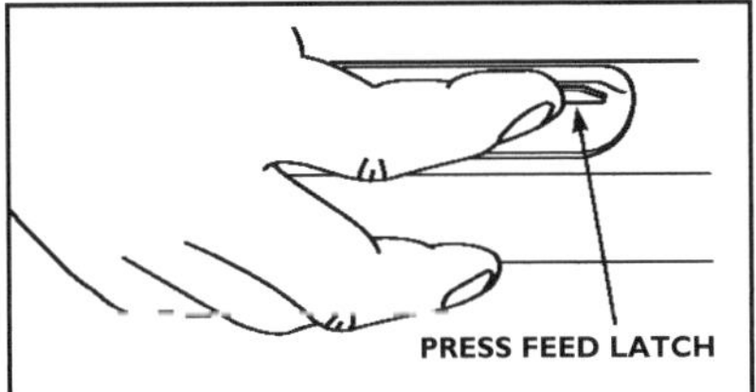

6 Reach in the bottom of the receiver. Press and hold the feed latch. Pull the action bar assembly from the receiver and the magazine tube. Release the feed latch. Lift the breech bolt assembly from the rear of the action bar assembly. Replace the magazine cap.

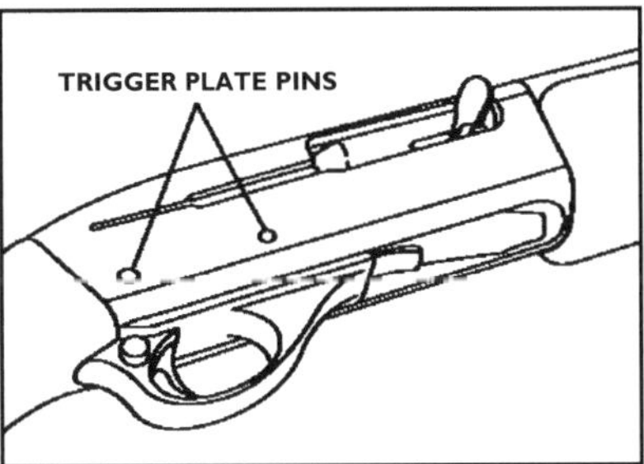

7 Tap out the front and rear trigger plate pins. Lift the rear of the trigger plate assembly, slide rearward and remove it from the receiver.

REMINGTON MODEL 12 RIFLE

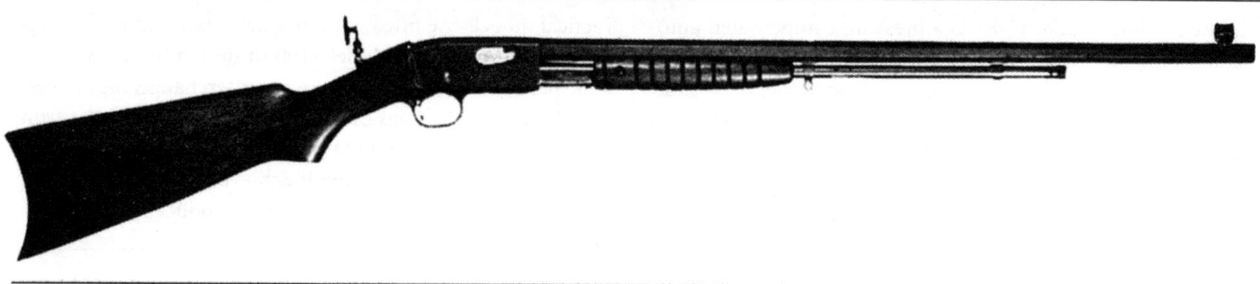

PARTS LEGEND

1. Firing pin spring
2. Firing pin spring guide
3. Firing pin pin
4. Ejector pin
5. Receiver bushing, plain
6. Takedown screw
7. Takedown screw retainer
8. Firing pin
9. Breechblock
10. Extractor spring
11. Extractor
12. Extractor plunger
13. Receiver bushing, threaded
14. Receiver
15. Magazine tube, inner, complete
16. Barrel
17. Front sight
18. Cartridge retainer
19. Carrier dog pin
20. Cartridge stop
21. Carrier dog spring
22. Carrier dog
23. Action bar plunger
24. Action bar plunger pin
25. Action bar spring
26. Magazine screw
27. Action bar
28. Magazine ring (2)
29. Magazine tube, outer
30. Fore-end screw (2)
31. Fore-end
32. Buttplate
33. Buttplate screw (2)
34. Stock
35. Stock bolt
36. Stock bolt washer
37. Ejector spring screw
38. Ejector spring
39. Rear sight
40. Rear sight screw (2)
41. Guard
42. Trigger
43. Trigger spring
44. Trigger spring case
45. Carrier
46. Safety plunger pin
47. Mainspring rod
48. Mainspring
49. Safety spring
50. Safety plunger
51. Safety
52. Hammer pin
53. Hammer bushing
54. Hammer
55. Trigger pin

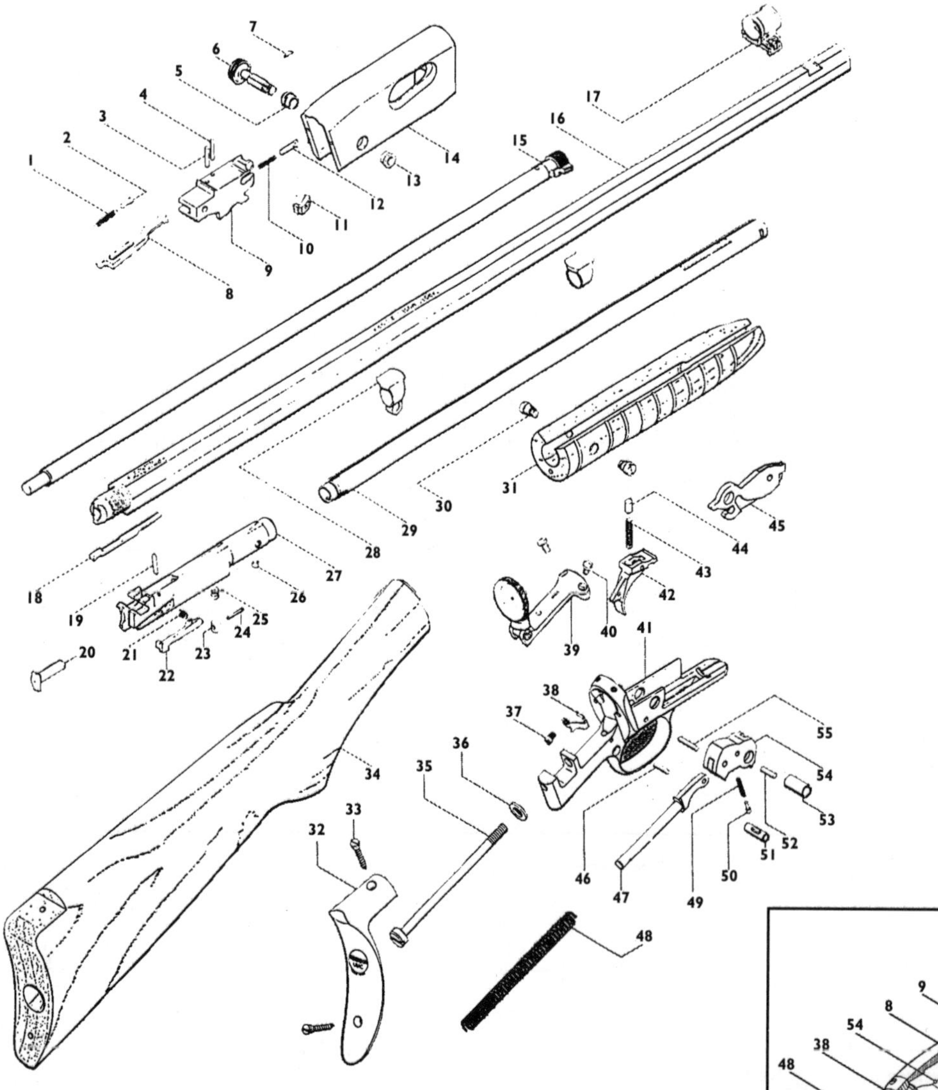

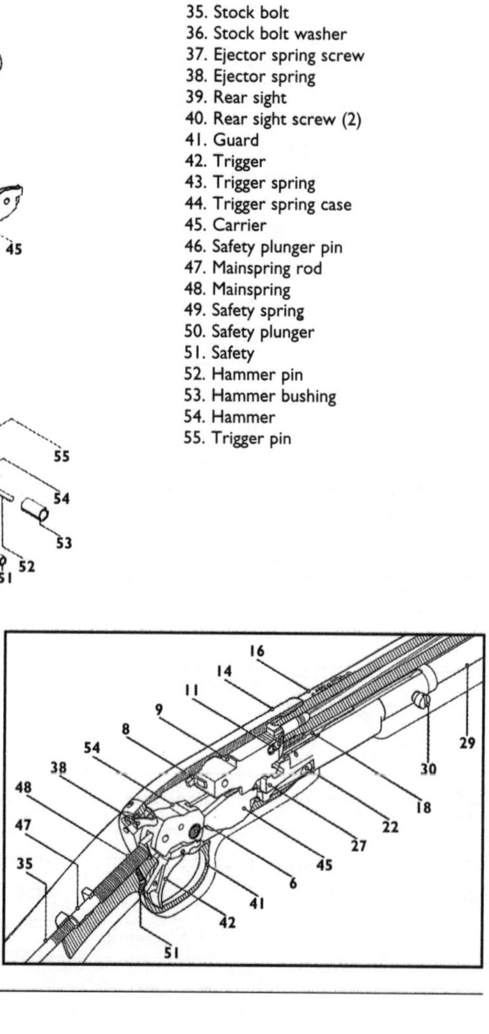

Developed by John D. Pedersen, the Remington Model 12, .22 caliber rimfire slide-action rifle was introduced in 1909. This concealed-hammer, takedown rifle has an under-barrel tubular magazine or can be loaded singly via the ejection port.

The most common Model 12 rifle is the No. 12A Standard Grade that fires .22 Short, Long, and Long Rifle cartridges. This version has a 22-inch round barrel and weighs 4½ lbs. Its magazine holds 16 Short, 12 Long, or 11 Long Rifle cartridges.

There are several other versions of the Model 12. The No. 12B Gallery Special Grade with 24-inch octagon barrel chambered for the .22 Short only and the No. 12C Target Grade, that fires .22 Short, Long, and Long Rifle. A variation of the 12C, the No. 12C NRA Target Grade, chambered in .22 Long Rifle, has a 24-inch octagon barrel and weighs six lbs. It is equipped with target sights and sling strap. Another variation of the 12C rifle is the No. 12CS Remington Special Grade for the .22 Remington Special (.22 W.R.F.) cartridge.

Deluxe versions include the No. 12D and 12DS Peerless Grade, No. 12E and 12ES Expert Grade, and the No. 12F and I2FS Premier Grades. The "S" denotes rifles chambered for the .22 Remington Special cartridge. The Model 12 was superseded in 1936 by the Remington Model 121 rifle.

DISASSEMBLY

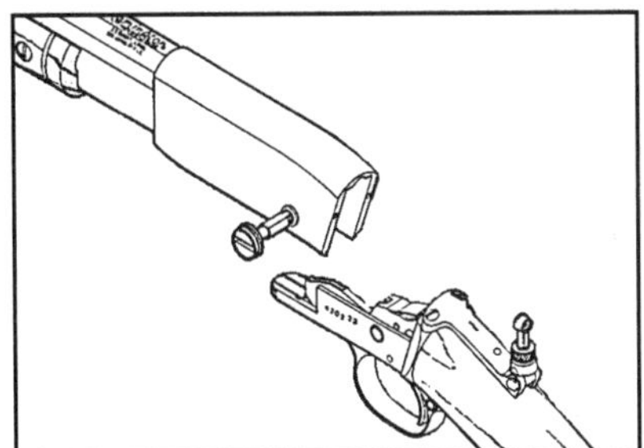

1 Before starting disassembly, unload the magazine and clear the chamber. Loosen takedown screw (6) and pull out to left as far as it will go. Hold rifle with left side down, and pull guard and stock assembly rearward out of receiver (14).

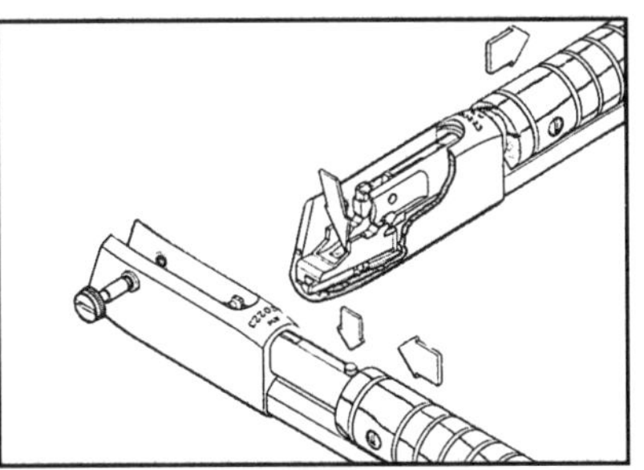

2 Invert receiver assembly and move fore-end (31) to rear, depressing action bar plunger (23) to clear the receiver. Press down at center of breechblock (9) while sliding fore-end forward to remove breechblock. This is sufficient for cleaning. On reassembly, cock hammer (54) and depress rear of breech-block to engage with action bar (27).

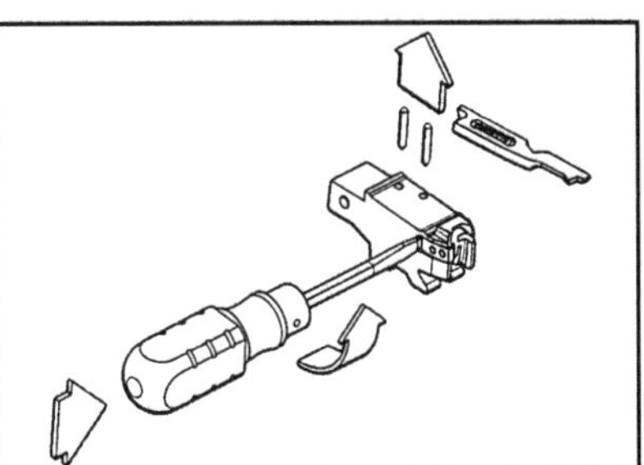

3 To remove extractor (11), insert thin-bladed screwdriver between extractor and extractor plunger (12). Turning the blade slightly forces plunger back against spring (10), and moves rear of extractor out of breechblock. Drive ejector pin (4) and firing pin pin (3) upward to release firing pin (8).

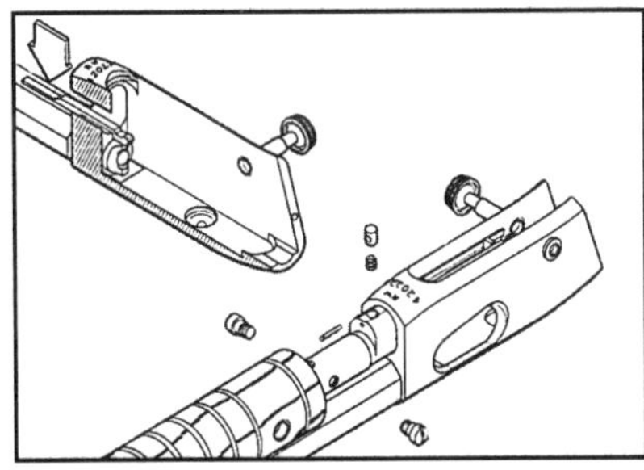

4 Depress latch of inner magazine tube (15) and pull tube out forward. Unscrew fore-end screws (30). Then, push fore-end (31) forward slightly over outer magazine tube (29). Depress action bar plunger and pull out its pin (24). Ease out plunger and spring (25). Pull action bar assembly out through rear of receiver, releasing fore-end and cartridge retainer (18). In reassembly, insert retainer in same position and carefully start action bar groove over it.

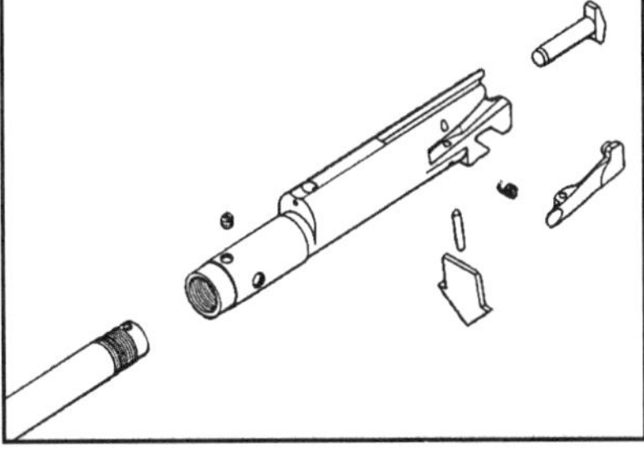

5 Remove magazine screw (26) and unscrew outer magazine tube. Holes in magazine tube and action bar must align when the screw is replaced. Driving out carrier dog pin (19) releases carrier dog (22) and spring (21), which allows removal of cartridge stop (20).

6 Turn out screws (40) and remove tang sight (39). Unscrew buttplate screws (33) and take off buttplate (32). Insert long-shank screwdriver in stock hole and remove stock bolt (35) and washer (36); pull guard (41) from stock (34). Pull trigger (42) and lower hammer (54) with thumb. Force mainspring (48) forward and insert a short wire through hole in mainspring rod (47). Push out hammer bushing (53) to right and lift off hammer and rod, pushing out hammer pin (52) to separate them. Cup palm over top of guard to catch trigger spring case (44) and spring (43). Pull carrier (45) forward and off. Reassemble in reverse. Safety must be disengaged when inserting hammer bushing.

REMINGTON MODEL 14 RIFLE

PARTS LEGEND

1. Action bar
2. Action bar cover
3. Action bar cover screw
4. Action bar lock
5. Action bar lock pin
6. Action bar lock spring
7. Action bar lock spring case
8. Ammunition indicator
9. Barrel & receiver
10. Breech block
11. Butt plate
12. Butt plate screw (2)
13. Carrier
14. Carrier dog
15. Carrier dog pin
16. Carrier dog spring
17. Carrier friction plunger
18. Carrier friction spring
19. Carrier lever
20. Carrier lever pin
21. Carrier lever plunger
22. Carrier lever spring
23. Carrier pin
24. Cartridge stop
25. Ejector
26. Ejector rod
27. Extractor
28. Extractor plunger
29. Extractor spring
30. Firing pin & extension
31. Firing pin catch
32. Firing pin catch pin
33. Firing pin catch plunger
34. Firing pin catch spring
35. Fore-end
36. Fore-end screws (2)
37. Front sight
38. Guard
39. Loading door
40. Loading door pin
41. Loading door plunger
42. Loading door spring
43. Magazine follower
44. Magazine plug
45. Magazine plug screw
46. Magazine ring
47. Magazine screw
48. Magazine spring
49. Magazine tube
50. Main spring
51. Main spring plug
52. Rear sight base
53. Rear sight leaf
54. Rear sight leaf screw
55. Rear sight step
56. Receiver bushing, plain
57. Receiver bushing, threaded
58. Safety
59. Sear
60. Sear lock
61. Sear lock pin
62. Sear lock plunger
63. Sear lock spring
64. Sear pin
65. Stock
66. Stock bolt
67. Stock bolt lock washer
68. Stock bolt washer
69. Take-down screw
70. Trigger
71. Trigger bushing
72. Trigger spring
73. Trigger spring cap
74. Trigger spring rod
75. Unlocking plunger

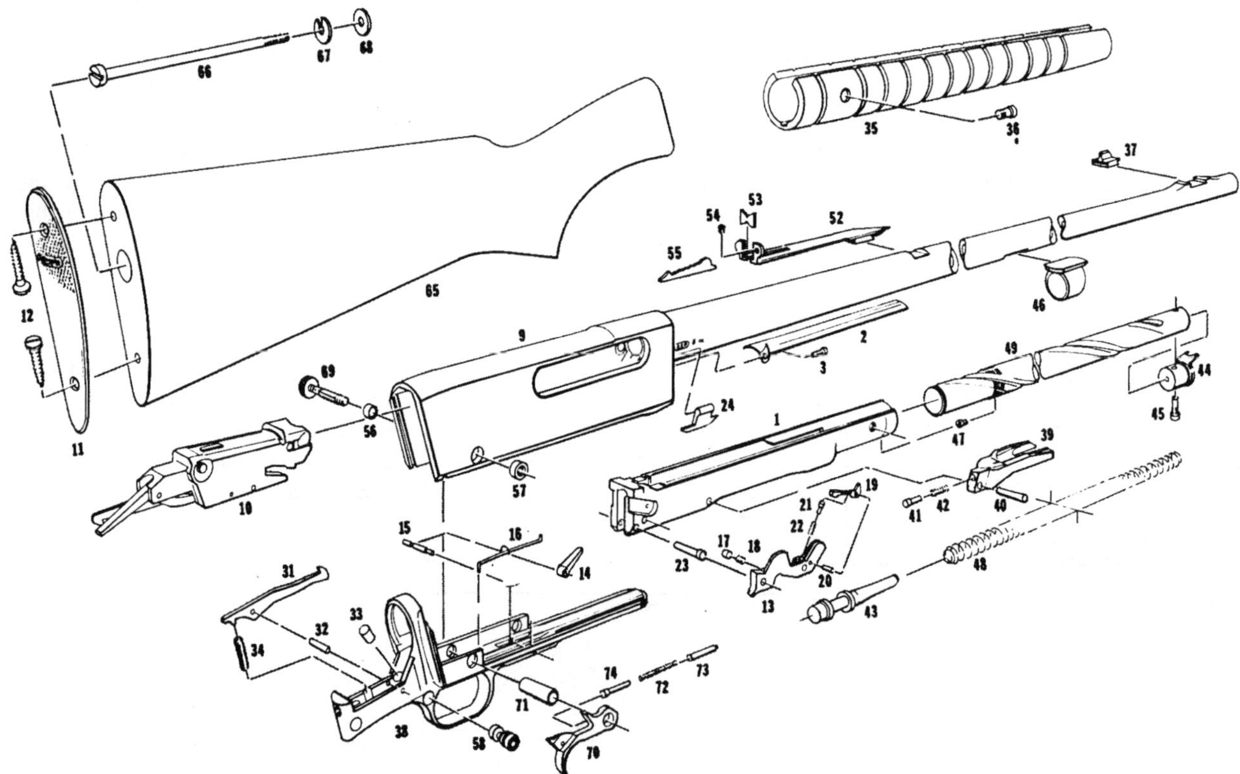

The Remington Model 14 and Model 14½ were among the first successful high powered pump-action rifles. Introduced in 1912, the guns were hammerless and featured a takedown design. Both models were offered in a carbine version, designated by Remington by the suffix "R."

The Model 14 and its carbine counterpart were produced in .25, .30, .32, and .35 Remington calibers, while the 14½ versions came in .38-40 and .44-40. The rifle was offered with a half-pistol grip while the carbine had a simple straight stock. Both models were stocked with walnut. The rear sight was step-adjustable for elevation on the Model 14 and screw-adjustable for elevation on the Model 14½.

A significant difference was in magazine design. The Model 14 featured a spiral magazine, a design that keeps the pointed bullet of one cartridge from resting on the primer of the cartridge in front of it. In the Model 14½, the flat nosed .38-40 and .44-40 cartridges did not call for such a device, and the magazine tube was not spiraled.

DISASSEMBLY

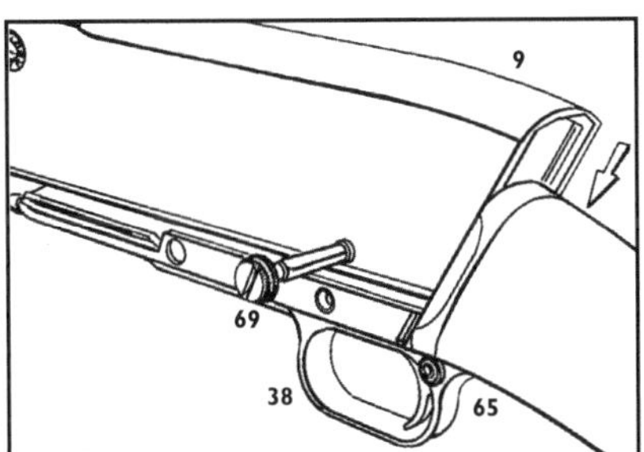

1 Close action and cock rifle before take-down. Unscrew takedown screw (69) and pull screw out to bushing in receiver. Holding the barrel and receiver (9) with one hand, push the stock (65) with trigger guard (38) toward the muzzle and simultaneously slide the stock assembly away from the receiver.

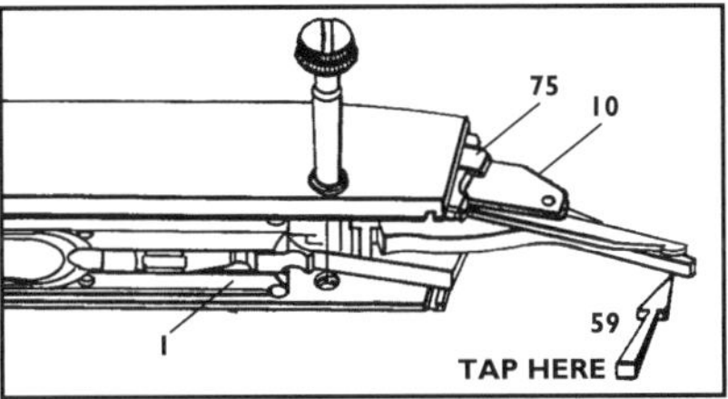

2 Turn rifle upside down. Open action by pressing unlocking plunger (75) (See Fig. 6) in breech block (10) and pulling forend to rear. Tip up rear of breech block (10), which protudes from rear of receiver. This will drop front of block into receiver well and release the action bar (1). Breech block may be uncocked by gently tapping end of sear (59). Sear protrudes from rear of block.

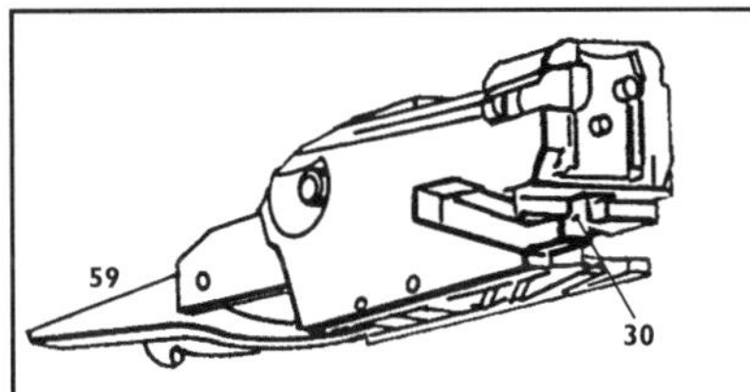

3 Breech block must be recocked to reassemble action bar. Place screwdriver or similar tool against firing pin (30) shoulder, which is exposed inside front of block. Press this shoulder until sear (59) within the block catches and cocks firing pin. To reinstall breech block, place in receiver allowing front of block to settle in well-hole of receiver (See Fig. 2). Pull action bar (1) back against block. Then push ejector (25) forward, to allow action bar to reengage breech block, and close action.

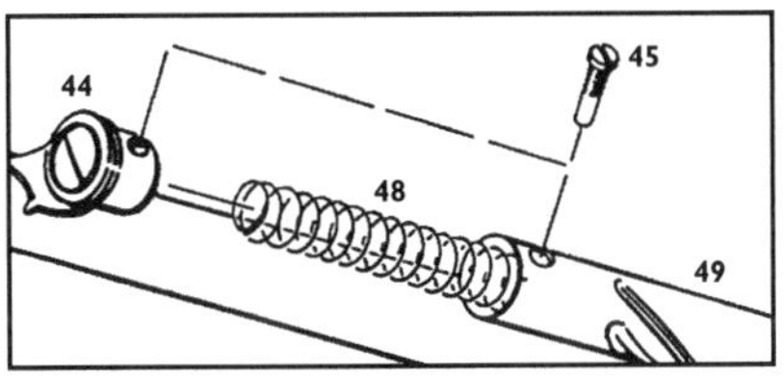

4 Unscrew magazine plug screw (45). Gently pry loose and remove magazine plug (44) from front end of magazine tube (49). Pull out magazine spring (48) and attached magazine follower from tube. Detach magazine spring from follower.

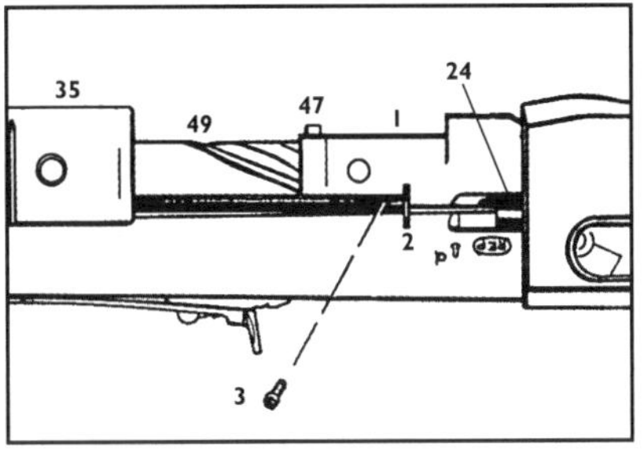

5 Unscrew forend screw (36) from each side. Slide forend (35) to front of magazine tube (49). Unscrew action bar cover screw (3) and slide action bar cover (2) forward and disengage from bar. Re-move loosened cartridge stop (24) located in front end of receiver. Slide action bar (1) with attached magazine tube (49) rearward in receiver. Pull forend from end of tube and remove action bar and tube from rear of receiver. Unscrew magazine screw (47) at bottom of bar. Screw out magazine tube from bar.

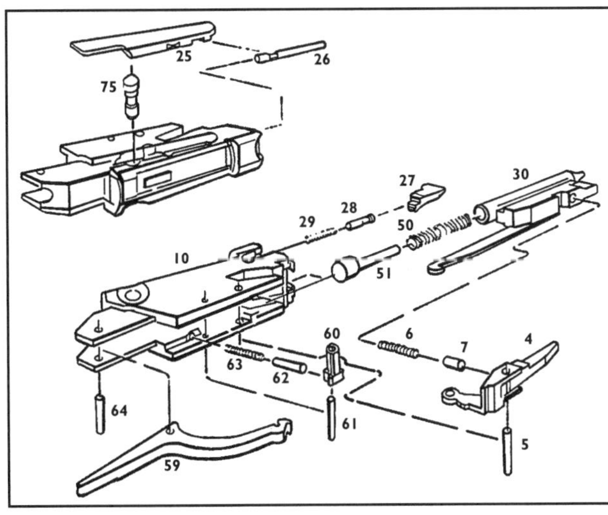

6 Drive out sear lock pin (61). Remove sear lock (60), sear lock plunger (62), and sear lock spring (63). Drive out action bar lock pin (5). Remove action bar lock (4), action bar lock spring (6), and action bar lock spring case (7). Uncock firing pin (if cocked) by gently tapping rear of sear (59). Drive out sear pin (64). Remove sear, firing pin and extension (30), main spring (50), and main spring plug (51). Slide ejector (25) rearward until small ellipse shape on ejector matches ellipse in breech block and remove ejector. Remove loose unlocking plunger (75). Gently pry between extractor (27) and extractor plunger (28) and detach extractor, extractor plunger, and extractor spring (29).

REMINGTON MODEL 25 RIFLE

PARTS LEGEND

1. Action bar assembly
2. Action bar cover
3. Barrel
4. Breechblock assembly
5. Buttplate
6. Buttplate screw (2)
7. Cartridge stop
8. Cartridge stop screw
9. Fore-end
10. Fore-end screw (2)
11. Fore-end locking screw (2)
12. Front sight
13. Front sight lock screw
14. Guard assembly
15. Magazine connector
16. Magazine follower
17. Magazine plug
18. Magazine plug screw
19. Magazine ring (2)
20. Magazine screw (2)
21. Magazine spring
22. Magazine tube
23. Plug screw (2)
24. Rear sight
25. Rear sight slide screw
26. Rear sight step
27. Receiver assembly
28. Stock
29. Stock bolt
30. Stock bolt lock washer
31. Stock bolt washer

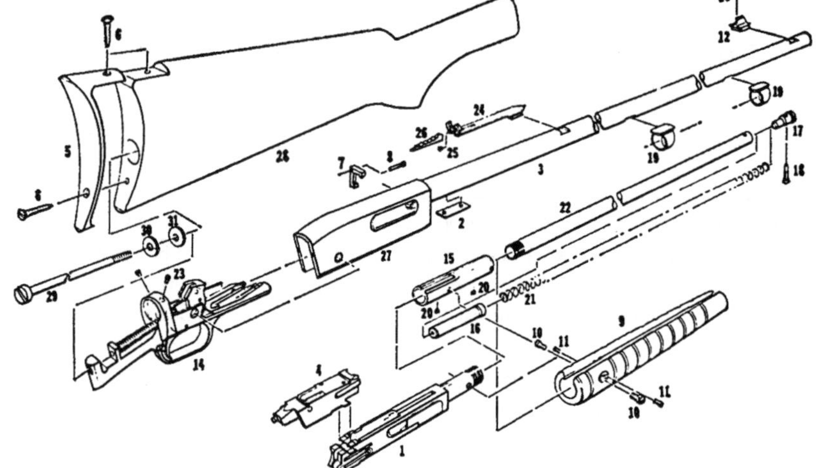

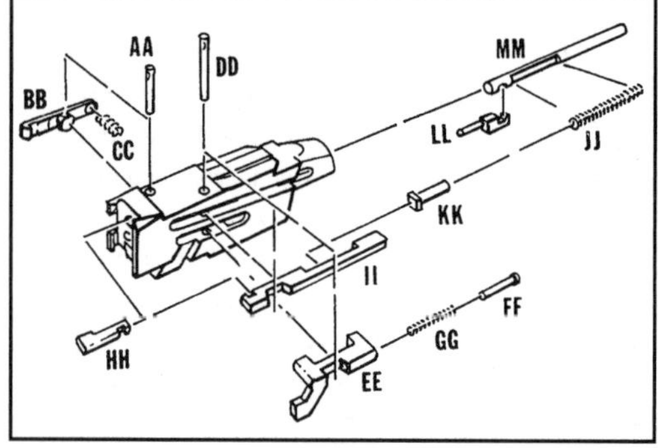

BREECHBLOCK ASSEMBLY

AA. Extractor pin
BB. Extractor
CC. Extractor spring
DD. Ejector pin
EE. Retractor
FF. Retractor plunger
GG. Retractor spring
HH. Ejector
II. Ejector rod
JJ. Firing pin spring
KK. Firing pin spring guide
LL. Firing pin, front
MM. Firing pin, rear

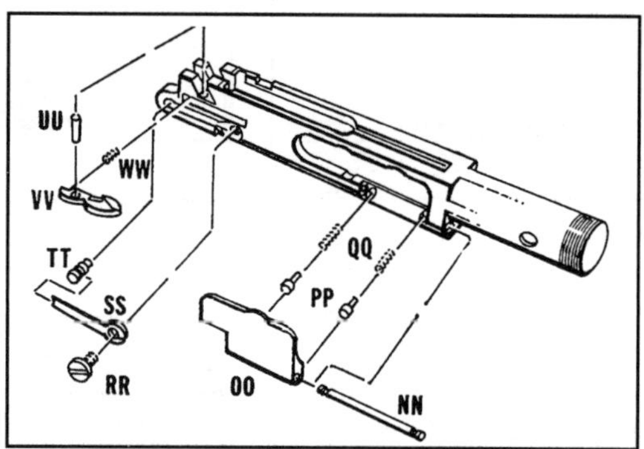

ACTION BAR ASSEMBLY

NN. Loading door pin
OO. Loading door
PP. Loading door plunger (2)
QQ. Loading door spring (2)
RR. Carrier dog spring screw
SS. Carrier dog spring
TT. Carrier dog
UU. Cartridge dog pin
VV. Cartridge dog
WW. Cartridge dog spring

Based on the patents of arms designers John D. Pedersen and Crawford C. Loomis, the Model 25 was introduced in 1923 and was offered in two center-fire chamberings: .25-20 Winchester and .32-20 Winchester. It provided more power than a rifle in .22 rimfire and was suitable for hunting coyote and fox.

In basic design, the Model 25 is similar to the Remington Model 12 and Model 14 slide-action rifles. This takedown-style repeater, with its 10-round tubular magazine, has a compact action that is closed at the rear. Cartridges are loaded through a door on the right side of the action bar and cases are ejected through a port in the right side of the receiver.

Rifle and carbine versions of the Model 25 were offered. The No. 25A Standard Grade rifle weighs 5½ lbs. and features a 24-inch barrel, American walnut stock with half-pistol grip and a rifle-style steel buttplate. The grooved fore-end is also American walnut. The No. 25R carbine has an 18-inch barrel and a straight-grip stock. It was described by the manufacturer as an excellent arm for saddle and automobile use.

There were also higher grades of the Model 25 rifle with checkered grip and fore-end of selected walnut, engraving on action and barrel, and hand-polished working parts. The Model 25 was discontinued in 1936.

DISASSEMBLY

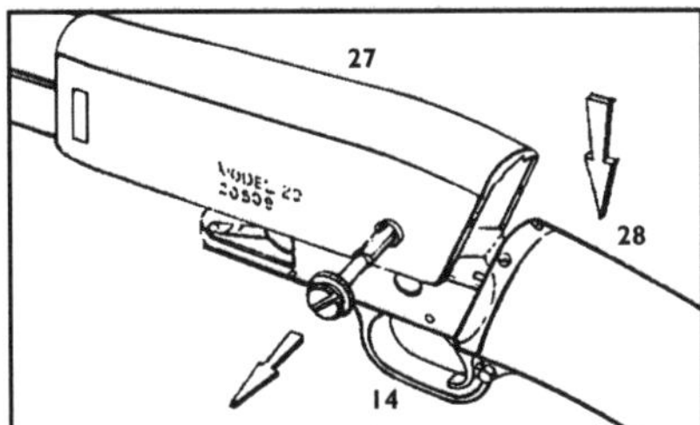

1 Before disassembling the rifle, make sure it is unloaded. Slide fore-end (9) to the rear and forward to cock action. Then, unscrew takedown screw and pull out from receiver assembly (27) as far as possible. Remove stock (28) and guard assembly (14) from receiver.

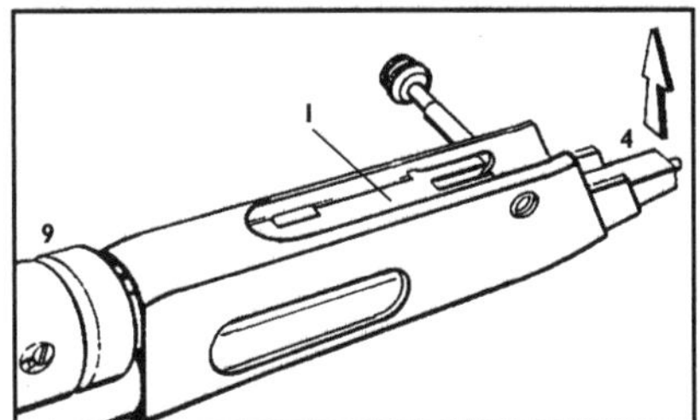

2 Slide fore-end rearward until breech-block assembly (4) protrudes from rear of receiver. Lift rear end of breech- block upward and slide fore-end forward. This will separate action bar assembly (1) from breechblock. Remove breech- block assembly from receiver.

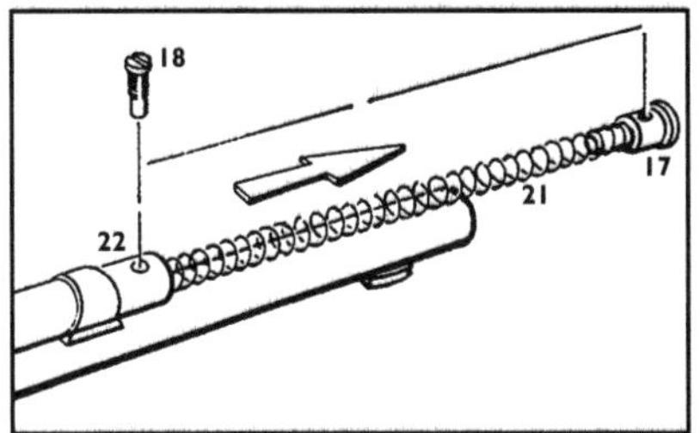

3 Unscrew magazine plug screw (18). Remove magazine plug (17) from front end of magazine tube (22). Also remove magazine follower (16) and magazine spring (21). Disassemble magazine spring from magazine plug and follower.

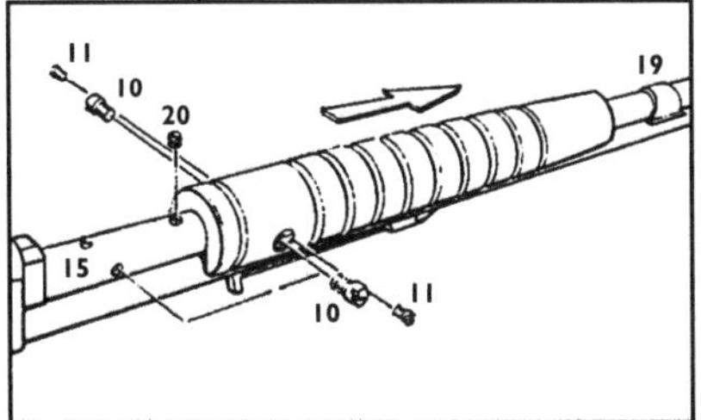

4 Slide fore-end rearward to receiver. Unscrew both fore-end locking screws (11). Then, unscrew both fore-end screws (10). Slide loosened fore-end forward to clear magazine connector (15). Unscrew exposed magazine screw (20) nearest fore-end. Turn out magazine tube, pull through magazine rings (19), and remove from gun. Slide fore-end off.

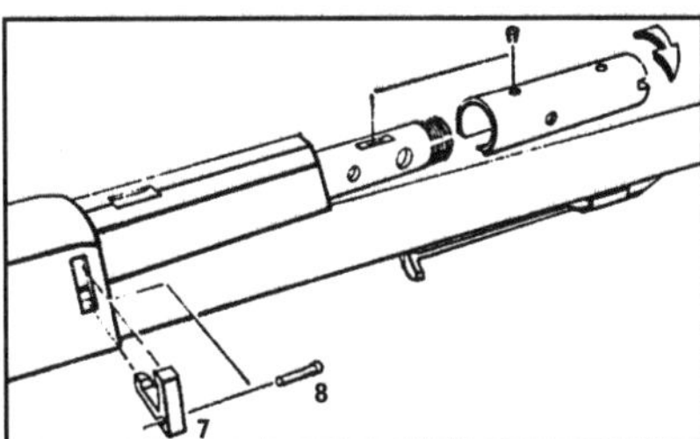

5 Slide action bar assembly fully forward, and unscrew magazine screw in magazine connector. Turn off magazine connector, and remove from action bar. Unscrew cartridge stop screw (8). Remove cartridge stop (7) from side of receiver. Cartridge stop can be removed only with action bar forward.

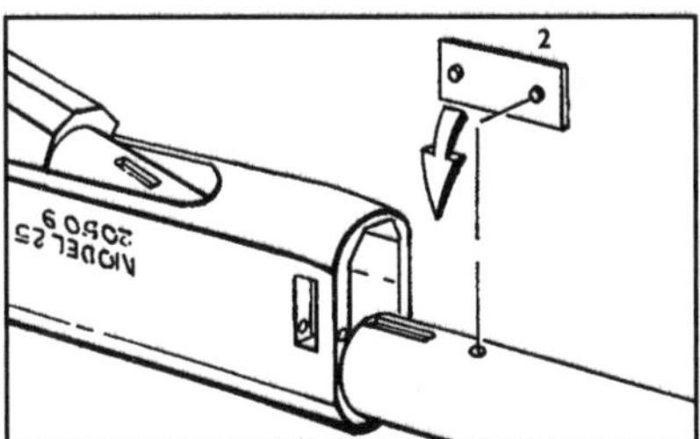

6 Pull action bar assembly rearward until bar can be disassembled from receiver. Lift action bar cover (2) from barrel.

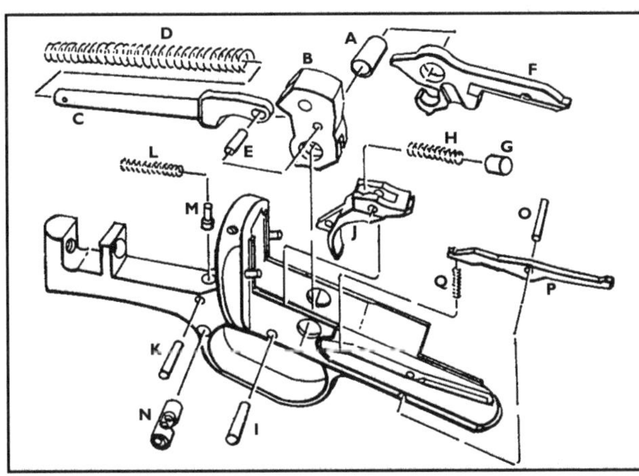

7 Hold hammer (B), pull trigger (J), and ease hammer forward. Force rear end of mainspring (O) forward and insert small pin through hole in end of mainspring rod (C) to hold mainspring forward on rod. Drive out hammer bushing (A). Remove hammer with mainspring rod and mainspring attached. Pull out small pin and remove mainspring from mainspring rod. Drive out hammer pin (E) to disassemble hammer from mainspring rod. Remove carrier (F), trigger spring case (G), and trigger spring (H). Drive out trigger pin (I), and remove trigger. Drive out safety plunger pin (K), and remove safety spring (L), safety plunger (M), and safety (N). Drive out timing lever pin (O), and remove timing lever (P) and spring (Q).

GUARD ASSEMBLY

A. Hammer bushing
B. Hammer
C. Mainspring rod
D. Mainspring
E. Hammer pin
F. Carrier
G. Trigger spring case
H. Trigger spring
I. Trigger pin
J. Trigger
K. Safety plunger pin
L. Safety spring
M. Safety plunger
N. Safety
O. Timing lever pin
P. Timing lever
Q. Timing lever spring

REMINGTON MODEL 30 RIFLE

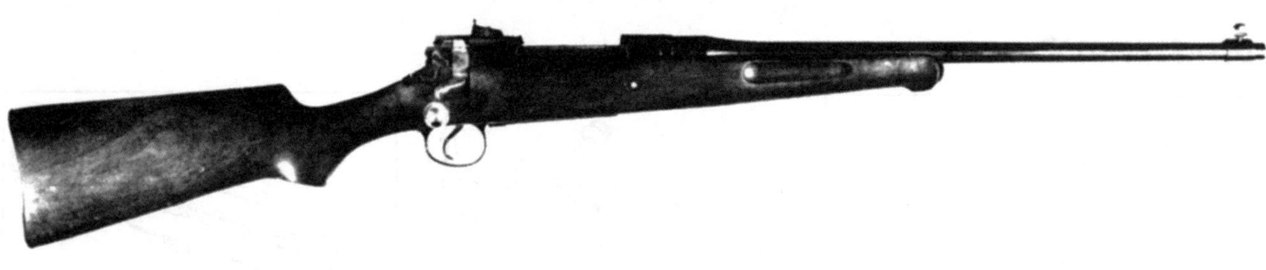

PARTS LEGEND

1. Barrel
2. Bolt
3. Bolt plug
4. Bolt stop
5. Bolt stop axis screw
6. Bolt stop spring
7. Bolt stop spring rest
8. Buttplate
9. Buttplate screw (2)
10. Cocking piece
11. Ejector
12. Extractor
13. Extractor ring
14. Firing pin
15. Front sight
16. Front sight band block
17. Front sight band block fixing key
18. Front sight band block fixing pin
19. Front sight screw
20. Front guard screw
21. Front guard screw collar
22. Locking bolt
23. Locking bolt spring
24. Magazine
25. Magazine bottom
26. Magazine catch
27. Magazine catch pin
28. Magazine catch spring
29. Magazine follower
30. Magazine follower spring
31. Magazine follower stop pin
32. Mainspring
33. Rear guard screw
34. Rear guard screw collar
35. Rear sight base
36. Rear sight base lock screw
37. Rear sight slide
38. Rear sight slide screw
39. Rear sight adjustment lock
40. Rear sight adjustment lock screw
41. Rear sight adjustment lock spring
42. Receiver
43. Safety catch
44. Safety hole plug
45. Safety hole plug screw
46. Sear
47. Sear axis pin
48. Sear spring
49. Stock
50. Stock bolt
51. Stock bolt nut
52. Stock pin
53. Trigger
54. Trigger axis pin
55. Trigger guard

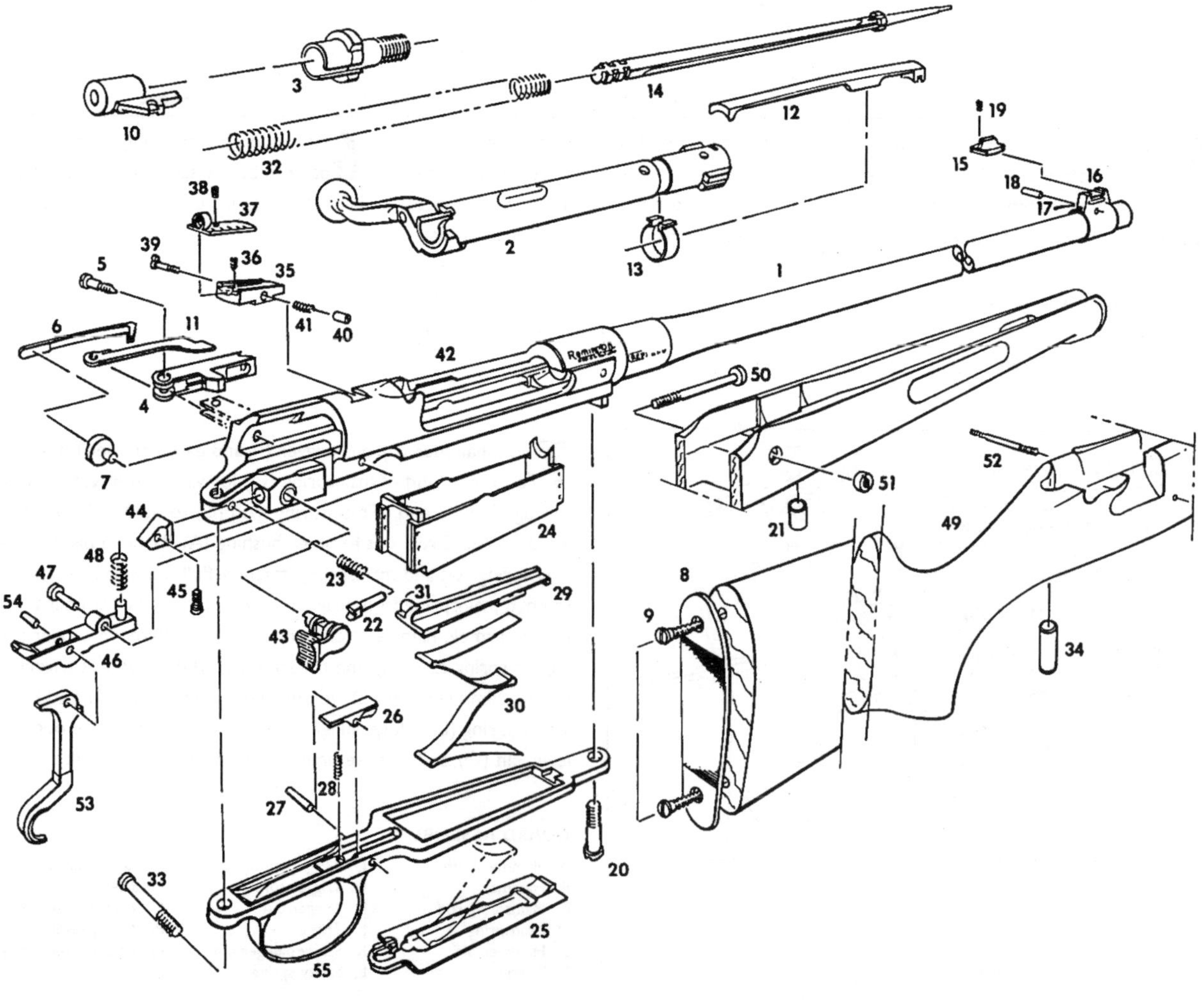

The Model 30 center-fire sporting rifle, introduced in 1921, was Remington's first entry into the bolt-action rifle field. This Mauser-type rifle had a modified Enfield action and was produced on machinery used by Remington during the war to manufacture the Model 1917 Enfield. Remington initially offered the Model 30 only in .30-06 caliber.

The Model 30 had a one-piece bolt with dual-opposed locking lugs. A safety lug was provided by the bolt handle which entered a notch in the receiver. The capacity of the staggered-column box magazine was five rounds.

The first version of the Model 30 cocked on closing the bolt, but in 1926, the action was modified to cock while opening the bolt. The new version, called the Model 30 Express rifle, had an open rear sight on the barrel. In addition to 30-06, the new rifle was chambered for .25, .30, .32 and .35 Remington cartridges. The barrel was 22-inches long, and the rifle weighed 7¼ lbs.

A further change occurred in 1930 with introduction of the Model 30S "Special Grade" rifle in .30-06 and 7 mm. Mauser with a 24-inch barrel, and .25 Remington with a 22-inch barrel. An NRA-style American walnut stock with checkered pistol grip and fore-end was an important feature of the Model 30S. The list of chamberings for later Model 30S rifles included .30-06 and .257 Roberts only.

Two other versions of the Model 30 were the Model 30A "Standard" Grade rifle and Model 30R carbine. The Model 30A had a 22-inch barrel, and was available in .30-06, 7 mm. Mauser and the four Remington chamberings. It featured an open rear sight, single-stage trigger and a walnut stock similar to that of earlier Model 30 rifles that preceded the 30S.

A Model 30R carbine had a 20-inch barrel, an un-checkered stock and was offered in .30-06 for use by forest rangers, guards or state police. In 1941, the Model 30 was discontinued.

DISASSEMBLY

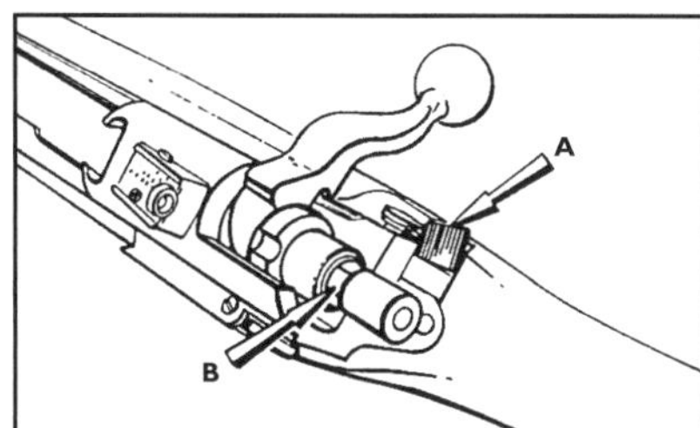

1 Rotate safety catch (43) to the rear safe position "A," and close bolt as far as possible. Safety catch engaging cocking piece (10) will cause separation to occur at "B." Insert washer or coin between cocking piece and bolt plug (3), and raise bolt handle.

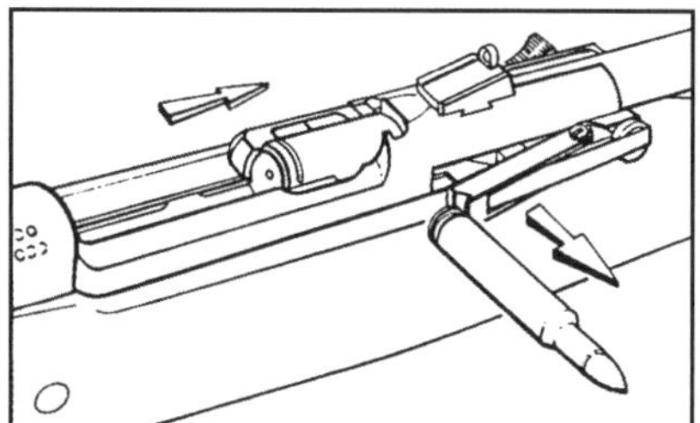

2 Rotate safety catch forward to fire position. Pivot bolt stop (4) to the left, and pull bolt assembly rearward out of receiver (42). Cartridge used as shown assists in pivoting bolt stop to left.

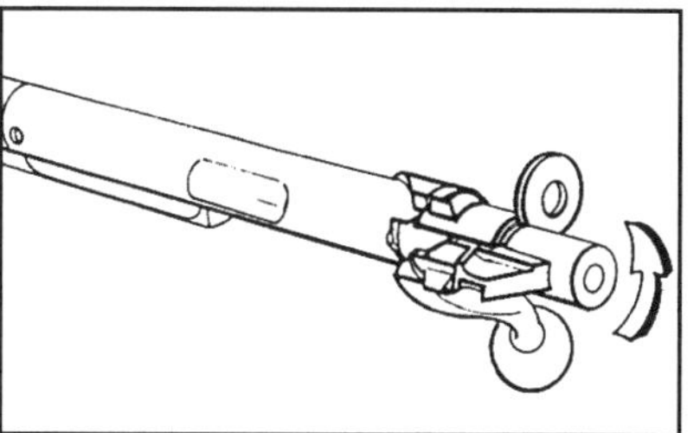

3 With washer or coin between cocking piece and bolt plug, unscrew firing mechanism from bolt.

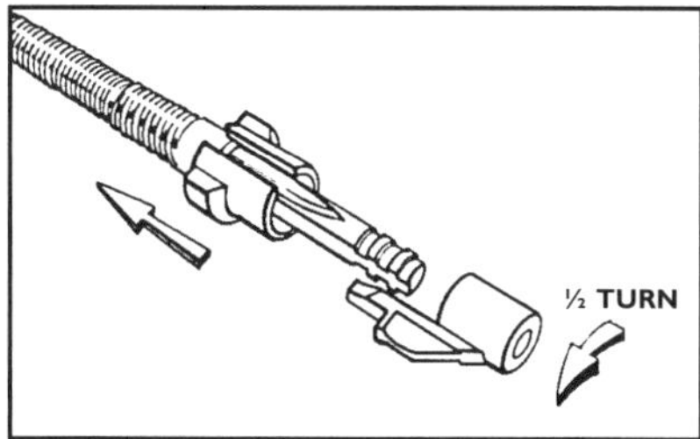

4 Press point of firing pin (14) against a wood surface. Push on bolt plug until it clears nose of cocking piece, rotate cocking piece ½ turn in either direction, and pull it rearward off firing pin. Ease bolt plug to rear slowly, and separate it and the mainspring (32) from firing pin. Hold bolt plug firmly, and keep it pointed in a safe direction as it is under heavy pressure of mainspring.

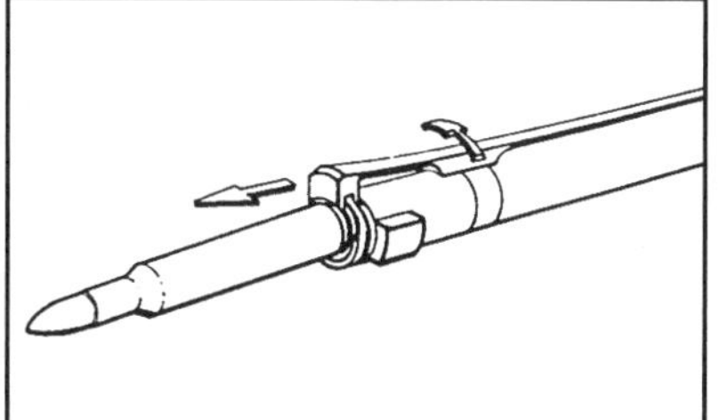

5 Rotate extractor (12) until it rests on ungrooved portion of bolt head between locking lugs. Position cartridge rim under extractor hook, and use cartridge to pull extractor forward off bolt. It is not advisable to remove extractor ring (13) as doing so may deform it.

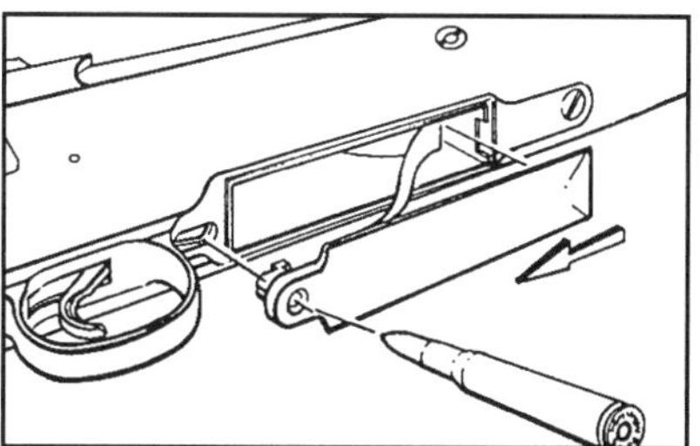

6 Use a bullet point or pointed tool to depress magazine catch (26), and slide magazine bottom (25) slightly rearward until it disengages from trigger guard (55) Remove magazine bottom with attached parts, and slide magazine follower spring (30) out of engagement with magazine bottom and magazine follower (29). Remove front guard screw (20) and rear guard screw (33). Pull out trigger guard and magazine (24), and separate stock (49) from receiver and barrel (I).

REMINGTON MODEL 31 SHOTGUN

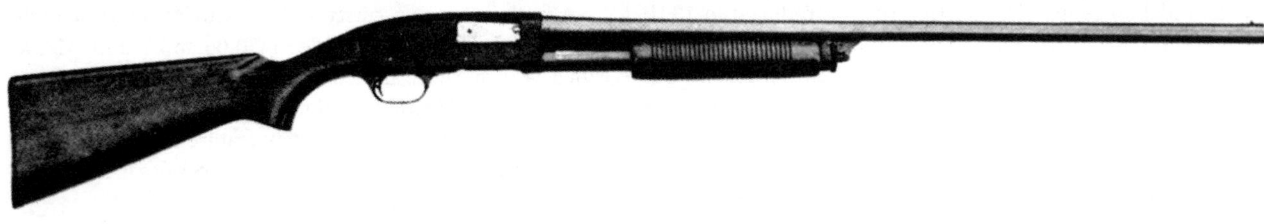

PARTS LEGEND

1. Barrel
2. Front sight *
3. Barrel lug *
4. Barrel lug stud pin
5. Barrel lock nut stop plunger pin
6. Barrel lug stud
7. Barrel lock nut stop plunger spring
8. Barrel lock nut stop plunger
9. Fore-end tube nut
10. Fore-end tube
11. Fore-end tube cap*
12. Action bar *
13. Magazine guide screw
14. Magazine guide
15. Barrel lock nut
16. Magazine plugt **
17. Barrel lock nut key (2)**
18. Magazine tube *
19. Magazine spring
20. Magazine follower
21. Barrel lock compensator screw
22. Barrel lock spring
23. Barrel lock compensator
24. Barrel lock
25. Barrel adjusting bushing lock screw
26. Barrel adjusting bushing lock **
27. Magazine lock **
28. Barrel adjusting bushing **
29. Receiver
30. Stock bolt stud **
31. Stock bolt washer
32. Stock bolt lock washer
33. Stock bolt
34. Buttplate screw (2)
35. Buttplate
36. Stock reinforcement ring *
37. Ejector
38. Ejector spring
39. Right cartridge stop
40. Left cartridge stop
41. Carrier
42. Trigger plate
43. Safety plunger
44. Safety spring
45. Safety
46. Mainspring pin
47. Trigger plate pin spring pin
48. Trigger plate stud (2)
49. Trigger plate pin spring
50. Left cartridge stop plunger screw
51. Left cartridge stop spring
52. Left cartridge stop plunger
53. Trigger lock plunger
54. Trigger lock spring
55. Action bar lock spring
56. Action bar lock
57. Hammer
58. Hammer link pin
59. Hammer pin
60. Trigger pin
61. Trigger lock pin
62. Hammer link
63. Mainspring follower
64. Mainspring
65. Trigger lock (shown rotated 120 degrees)
66. Trigger
67. Trigger spring
68. Slide
69. Extractor plunger
70. Right extractor spring
71. Right extractor
72. Breechblock
73. Firing pin retaining pin
74. Trigger plate pin
75. Firing pin
76. Firing pin spring
77. Left extractor spring
78. Extractor pin
79. Left extractor
80. Stock
81. Fore-end

* Permanent factory assembly
** Parts to be factory disassembled only.

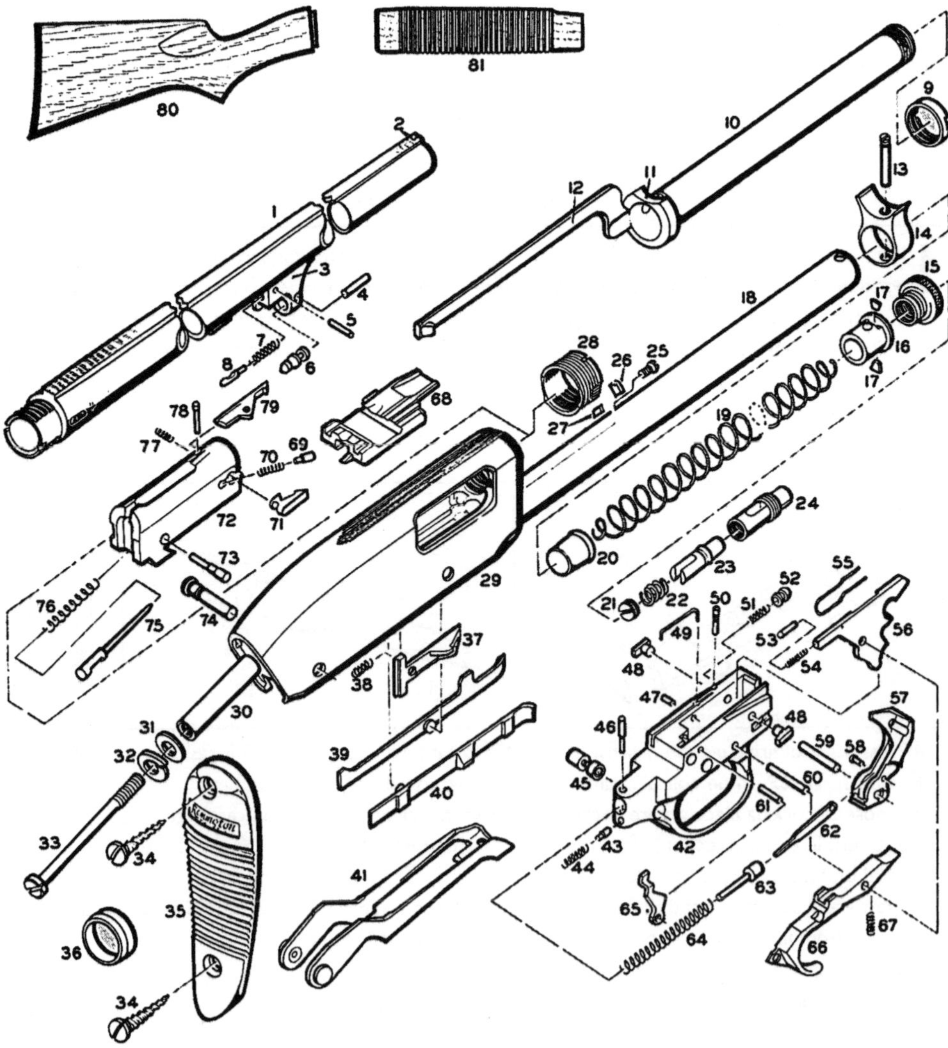

The Remington Model 31 slide-action shotgun was introduced in 1931. Made in 12, 16, and 20 gauge, in several grades, the Model 31 shotgun underwent several modifications during the course of production. The original 1931 series had a "spring-up" barrel lock assembly which was replaced in 1934 with a screw-up assembly, which was made smaller in 1941.

The initial series, made from 1931 until 1936, included 12-gauge guns while the second series, produced from 1936 until 1940, included 12-, 16- and 20-guage guns.

In the third series, introduced in 1941, the safety button was enlarged and numerous parts were changed, including the action bar lock, hammer, extractor and trigger lock and plate. The rifle was available in a lightweight version with aluminum trigger plate and receiver. The Model 31 was discontinued in 1949.

DISASSEMBLY

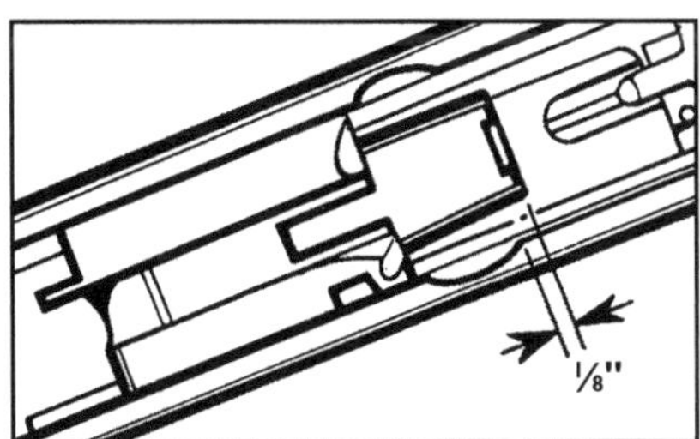

1 Open action partially, unscrew barrel lock nut (15) to left, turn barrel (l) 90 degrees left, and move it forward from receiver (29). Push out trigger plate pin (74) from right to left and turn gun bottom up. Slide trigger plate (42) forward until trigger plate studs (48) align with slots in sides of receiver and lift trigger plate out.

If gun is cocked, press action bar lock (56) to release trigger plate before moving it forward. Lift out right and left cartridge stops (39 and 40) from inside walls of receiver. Move fore-end (81) rearward until projection at rear of slide (68) is even with trigger plate holes in side of receiver. Pull upward on slide while moving fore-end forward to free action bar (12) from slide.

Holding slide up, disengage it from breechblock (72) and move block fully forward. Swing carrier (41) against block. Move slide until forward end is ⅛ inch forward of trigger plate stud slots as shown. Tip up right side of slide (side opposite action bar) and swing slide out sideways from receiver. This is effortless when slide is properly positioned; do not force it.

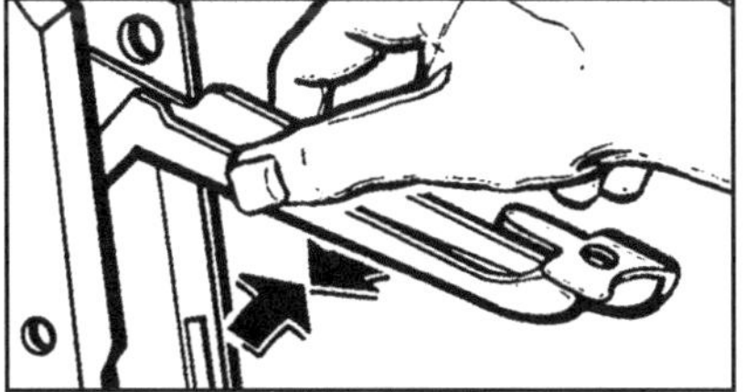

2 With fore-end and breechblock fully forward, swing front end of carrier outward until about perpendicular to receiver and press ends together to disengage pivots. Lift it away. Press ejector (37) fully into its slot and lift out breechblock. Swing ejector rearward and lift from its slot in side of receiver.

3 Remove magazine guide screw (13) from top of magazine guide (14-arrow), grasping hand around all parts at front end of magazine tube (18) to prevent loss. Pull barrel lock nut (15) carefully from tube to prevent magazine spring (19) from releasing too fast. Remove magazine spring and magazine follower (20) from tube. Pull magazine guide from tube and slide fore-end assembly off tube.

4 Drift out firing pin retaining pin (73) from left to right and remove firing pin (75) and firing pin spring (76) from back end of breechblock. Drift extractor pin (78) out bottom of breechblock and remove left extractor (79) and left extractor spring (77). Insert small screwdriver in back of right extractor (71) and pry back extractor plunger (69), then push screwdriver forward, pushing right extractor out of slot. Remove extractor plunger and right extractor spring (70).

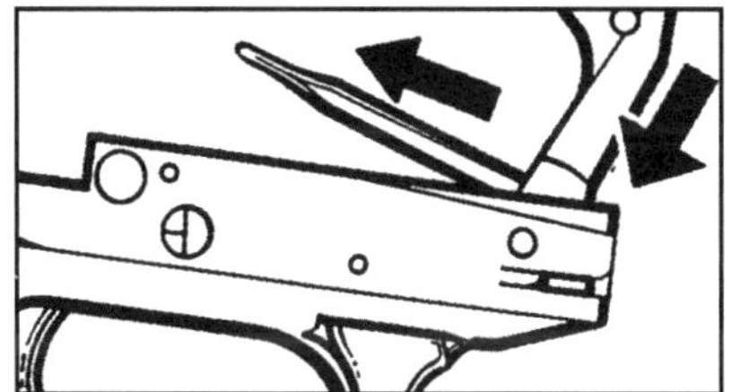

5 With hammer (57) down, drift out mainspring pin (46) and remove safety spring (44) and safety plunger (43). Remove mainspring (64) and mainspring follower (63) from upper hole. Remove safety (45). Drive out hammer pin (59) and push hammer forward and down until rear of hammer link (62) is out of slot in trigger plate. Pull hammer link rearward, disengaging hammer from action bar lock spring (55). Never lift hammer upward until it has been disengaged from this spring. Lift away hammer. Drift out trigger pin (60) and remove action bar lock with spring attached. Remove trigger lock plunger (53) and trigger lock spring (54).

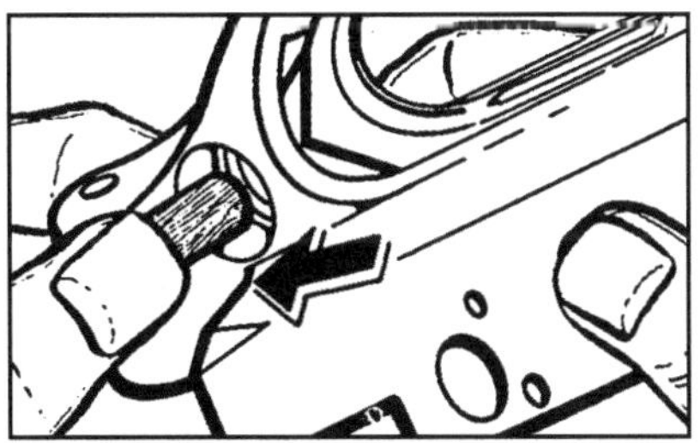

6 Reassemble gun in reverse. When reassembling mainspring, mainspring follower, safety spring, and safety plunger, it will facilitate reassembly to insert these parts first. Then, after replacing the mainspring pin, and using a short length of wood dowel to compress safety plunger, re-insert safety.

REMINGTON MODEL 33 RIFLE

PARTS LEGEND

1. Barrel
2. Bolt
3. Bolt extension sleeve pin
4. Ejector
5. Ejector pin
6. Extractor
7. Extractor pin
8. Extractor spring
9. Extractor spring plunger
10. Firing pin
11. Firing pin extension
12. Firing pin extension pin
13. Front sight
14. Mainspring
15. Mainspring plunger
16. Rear sight leaf
17. Rear sight step
18. Receiver
19. Retractor spring
20. Retractor spring plunger
21. Sear
22. Sear pin
23. Sear stop pin
24. Stock
25. Takedown screw
26. Trigger
27. Trigger guard
28. Trigger guard screw (2)
29. Trigger pin
30. Trigger spring

NOTE: Buttplate and screws are not shown.

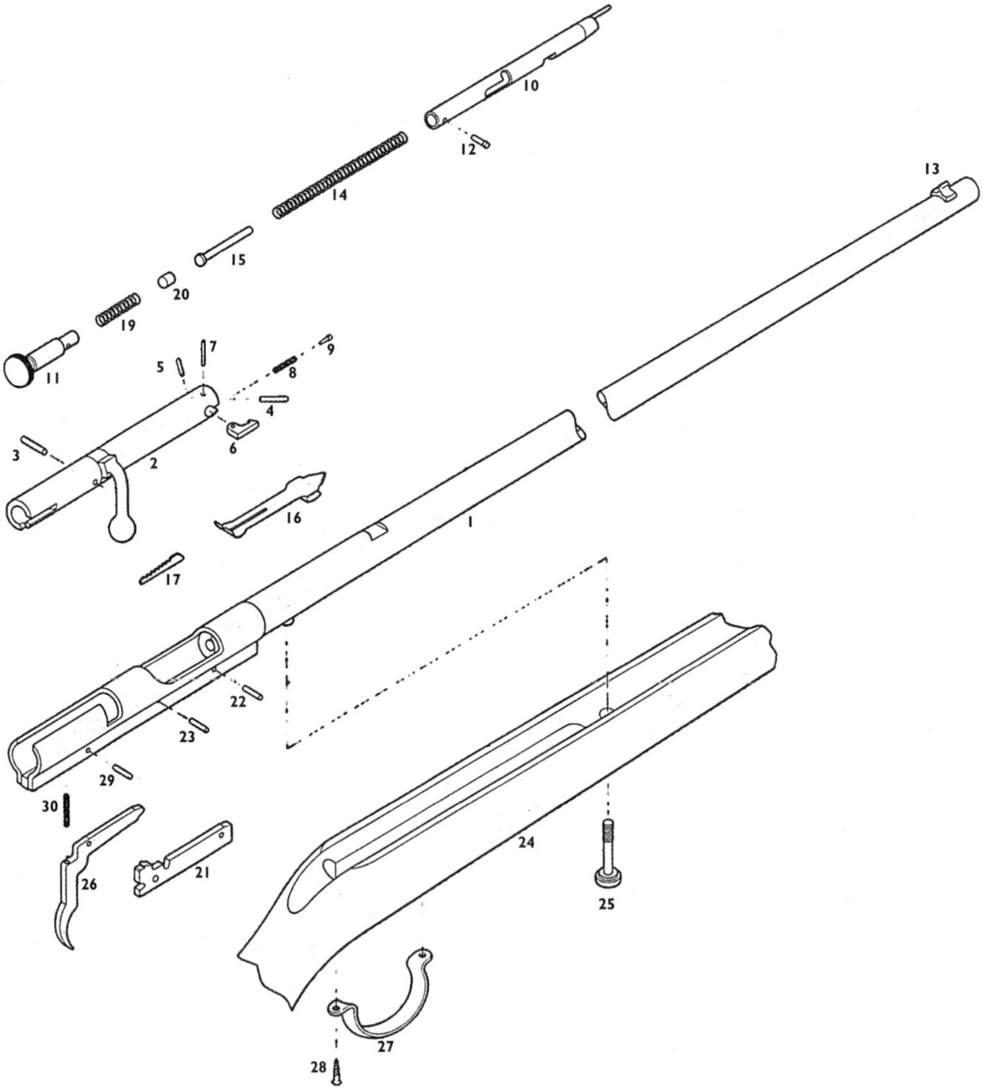

Remington's first single-shot, bolt-action, rimfire rifle was introduced in 1931. Designated the Model 33, it was a take- down rifle based on patents granted to Remington engineer C. C. Loomis. It fired .22 Short, Long, and Long Rifle standard-velocity and high-speed cartridges. A Remington advertising brochure published in 1934 proudly announced it as "the finest cal. .22 single-shot rifle ever offered at the price."

According to this brochure, the retail price of the Standard Grade Model 33 fitted with a white metal bead front sight and U-notch open rear sight was $5.50. When equipped with a Lyman No. 55 aperture rear sight, the rifle retailed for $7.70. There was also an NRA Junior Target Grade of the Model 33. This rifle was fitted with a Patridgetype blade front sight, Lyman No. 55 aperture receiver sight, sling swivels, and a 1-inch-wide adjustable leather sling. It was offered at $10.30 retail.

All grades of the Model 33 have a 24-inch, blued round barrel, a pistol grip walnut stock and weigh around 4½ lbs. The firing pin is cocked manually after closing the bolt. No safety lever is provided, but the firing pin can be pulled back and rotated to a safe position. An automatic rebounding lock prevents discharge if the firing pin should be hit accidentally.

Unlike many bolt-action rifles chambered for .22 rimfire ammunition, the Model 33 has dual-opposed locking lugs. One of these lugs is the root of the bolt handle.

In 1936, the Model 33 was replaced by the Remington Model 41 .22 rimfire rifle.

DISASSEMBLY

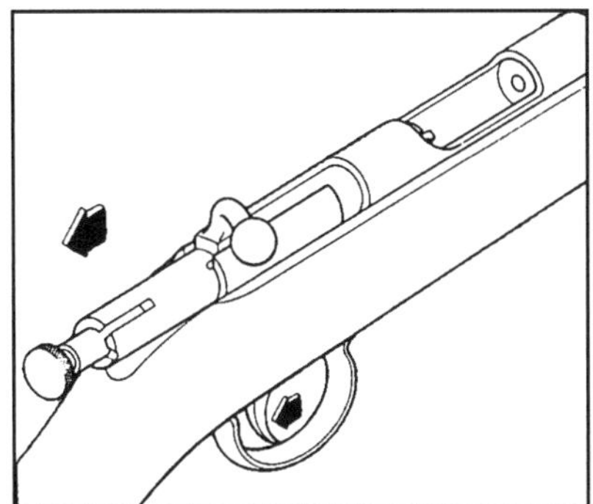

1 Before disassembly, open the action to make sure the rifle is unloaded. Lift bolt handle, pull trigger (26) and remove bolt assembly from receiver (18). Loosen take-down screw (25), and remove stock (24).

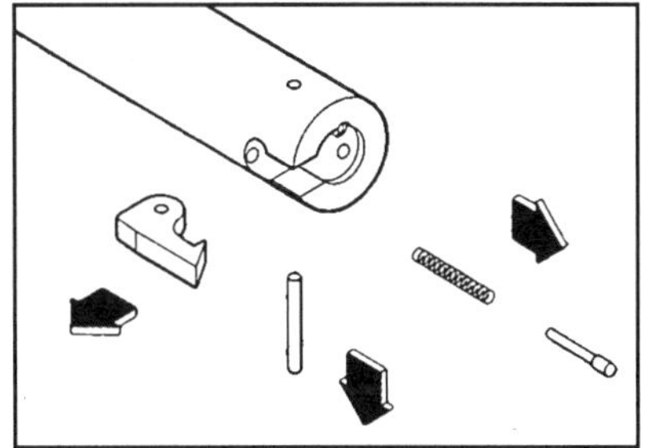

2 Drive out extractor pin (7), and remove extractor (6), extractor spring plunger (9), and extractor spring (8). Drive out ejector pin (5), and remove ejector (4) from front of bolt (2).

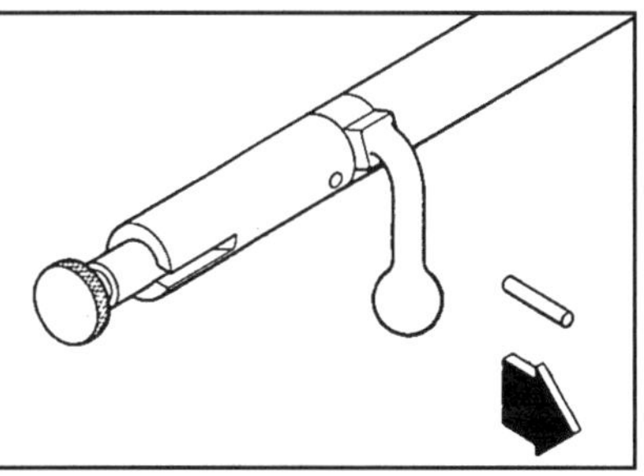

3 Drive out bolt extension sleeve pin (3), and pull firing pin assembly from bolt.

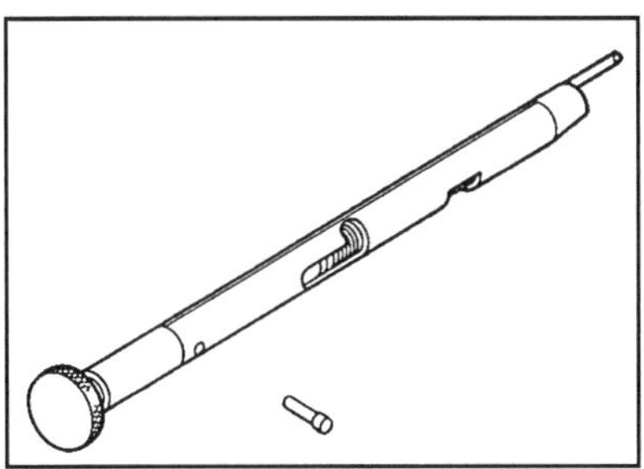

4 After driving out firing pin extension pin (12) from left to right, remove firing pin extension (11), retractor spring (19), and retractor spring plunger (20) from firing pin (10). Mainspring (14) and mainspring plunger (15) are permanently staked in place inside the firing pin. Disassembly of these parts should not be attempted.

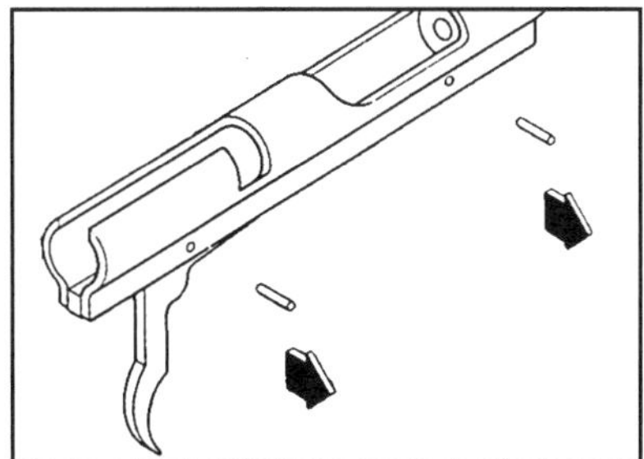

5 Drive out trigger and sear pins (22 & 29). Remove trigger (26), trigger spring (30), and sear (21) from bottom of receiver.

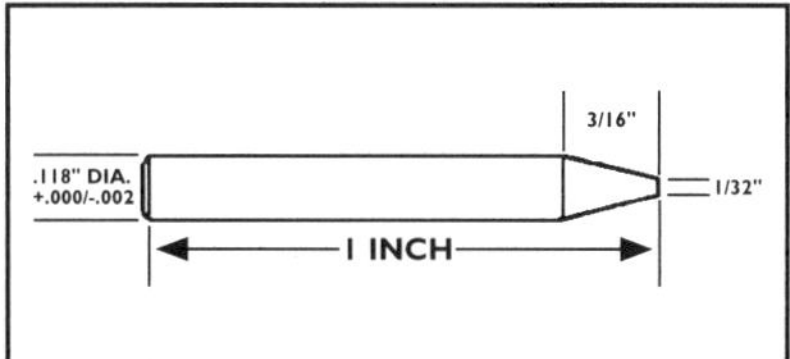

6 Reassemble in reverse. Replacement of firing pin assembly in bolt is best accomplished by making a special assembly pin from drill rod as illustrated. Insert reassembled firing pin assembly into bolt. Align small opening between mainspring plunger and retractor spring plunger with extension sleeve pin hole in bolt. Insert pointed end of special assembly pin into hole from right side of bolt and tap through. This will separate mainspring plunger and retractor spring plunger to allow passage of extension sleeve pin. Align and drive extension sleeve pin through from left to right.

REM. MODEL 37 RANGEMASTER

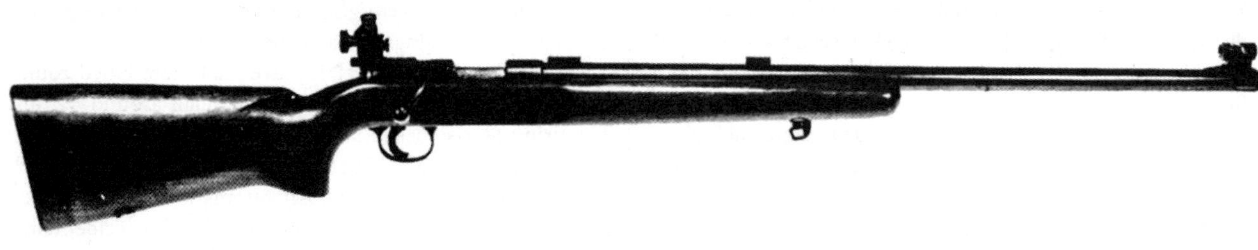

PARTS LEGEND

1. Receiver
2. Ejector
3. Bolt handle detent plunger
4. Bolt handle detent spring
5. Bolt handle detent screw
6. Barrel
7. Telescope base, rear
8. Telescope base screws, rear (2)
9. Telescope base, front
10. Telescope base screws, front (2)
11. Front sight base
12. Front sight base screws (2)
13. Front sight assembly (Redfield Olympic)
14. Receiver sight base
15. Receiver sight base screws (2)
16. Receiver sight (Redfield Olympic)
17. Safety
18. Safety shaft
19. Safety detent
20. Safety detent spring
21. Safety shaft lock screw
22. Bolt assembly, complete (See illustration on next breakdown)
23. Trigger housing
24. Trigger housing pins (2)
25. Bolt stop
26. Bolt stop pin
27. Bolt stop spring
28. Sear
29. Sear spring
30. Sear screw
31. Sear guide pin
32. Trigger adjusting screw, rear
33. Trigger adjusting screw, front
34. Trigger adjusting screw
35. Trigger
36. Trigger pin
37. Trigger spring
38. Magazine lock plunger
39. Magazine lock plunger spring
40. Magazine lock bracket
41. Magazine lock bracket screws (2)
42. Magazine lock
43. Magazine lock pin
44. Front guard bow screw nut
45. Rear guard bow screw bushing
46. Front guard bow extension screw bushing
47. Stock
48. Guard bow
49. Rear guard bow screw
50. Front guard bow screw
51. Guard bow extension
52. Magazine lock button
53. Magazine lock button bushing
54. Front guard bow extension screw
55. Loading platform (magazine assembly not shown)
56. Swivel base guide
57. Swivel base guide screws (2)
58. Front swivel assembly
59. Rear swivel (not shown)
60. Buttplate (not shown)
61. Buttplate screws (not shown)

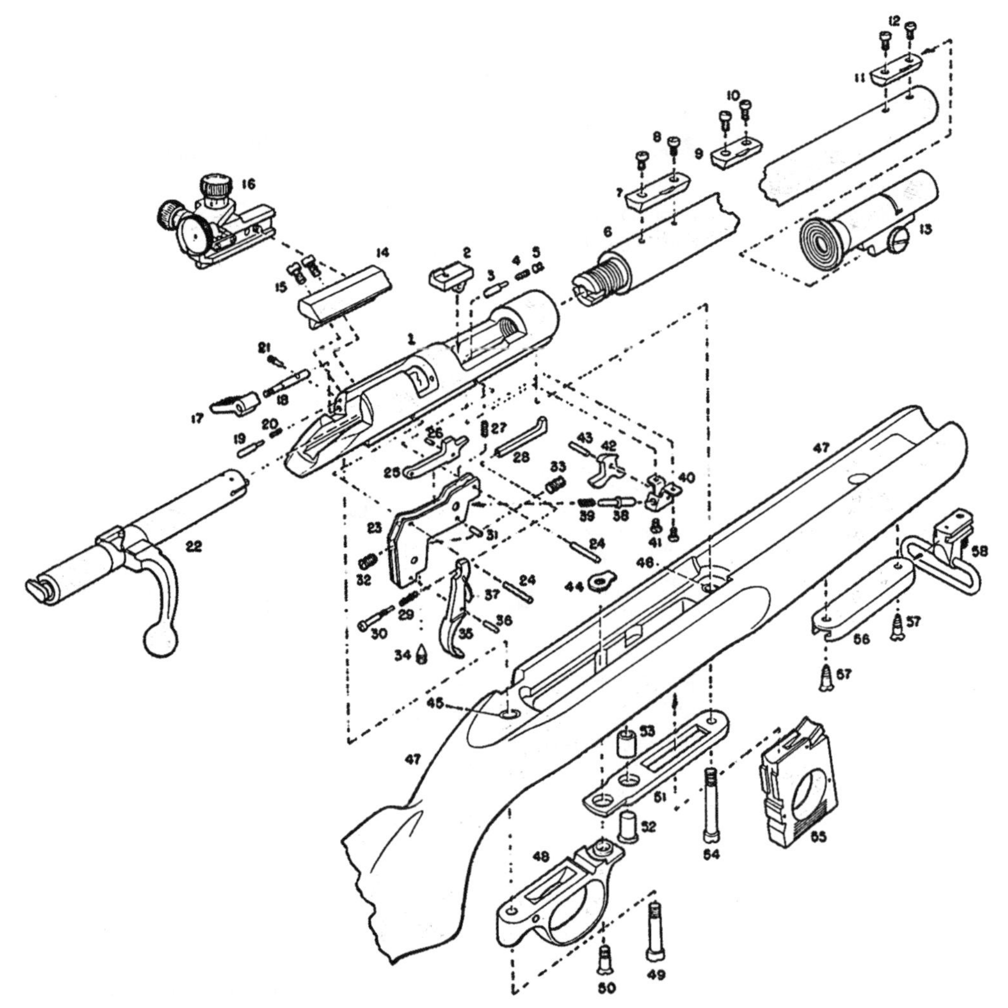

Prior to 1937 the Winchester Model 52 bolt-action target rifle virtually dominated the American .22 rim-fire smallbore rifle competition scene. However, at the 1936 National Matches held at Camp Perry, Ohio, Remington Arms Co. introduced a new deluxe smallbore target rifle obviously designed to compete with the already well-established Winchester product.

Called Model 37 Rangemaster, the new rifle had a heavy barrel, adjustable trigger, and high comb target stock, with semi-beavertail fore-end, barrel band, and adjustable fore-end stop. It also had a hardened bolt and receiver, twin extractors, twin locking lugs, a Remington-designed ¼-minute click aperture rear sight, and detachable Redfield globe front sight.

The sights were mounted so that line-of-sight with both metallic and scope sights was identical. The 5-shot, detachable clip-magazine was supplemented with a milled steel loading block to permit rapid single loading of cartridges. To round out the new rifle, the manufacturer furnished a high-grade, adjustable, leather shooting sling. The Model 37 was ready to shoot on an out-of-the-box basis.

The Model 37 scored well in the 1936 National Matches although used by only a few shooters. It did not become regularly available until 1937 when quantity production began.

In 1940, Remington produced the New Model Rangemaster, incorporating several improvements based on field testing and comments from customers. The stock was completely redesigned to incorporate suggestions made by smallbore shooter Thurman Randle. The barrel band was omitted and the fore-end was of full beavertail pattern.

A new trigger mechanism, based on a design by California inventor J. B. Sweany, was dubbed the "Miracle Trigger" by Remington. It was fully adjustable and gave almost imperceptible movement on release.

The Remington Model 37 was discontinued in 1955 upon introduction of the Model 40X rifle.

DISASSEMBLY

To remove bolt assembly (22): open bolt and, while pulling trigger, press down on bolt stop (25) through hole in top of ejector (2) with small punch or similar instrument. Draw bolt out of receiver (1).

To remove barrel and receiver from stock: press in magazine lock button (52) and remove magazine or loading platform (55) from underside of stock. Unscrew rear guard bow screw (49) and front guard bow extension screw (54). Lift barrel and receiver out of stock (47).

To remove trigger assembly: drift out two trigger housing pins (24). Remove ejector (2) from top of receiver and drop trigger housing (23) out bottom of receiver. Remove magazine lock plunger (38) and spring (39). To remove trigger (35), remove three adjusting screws (32, 33, 34). Remove sear screw (30) and sear spring (29). Drive out trigger pin (36) and bolt stop pin (26). Trigger, bolt stop (25), and sear (28) can now be removed from trigger housing. Magazine lock assembly is removed from underside of receiver by unscrewing two magazine lock bracket screws (41).

To remove safety (17): unscrew safety shaft lock screw (21) in left side of receiver and pull safety out to rear, taking care not to lose safety detent spring (20) and detent (19). Reverse procedure to reassemble.

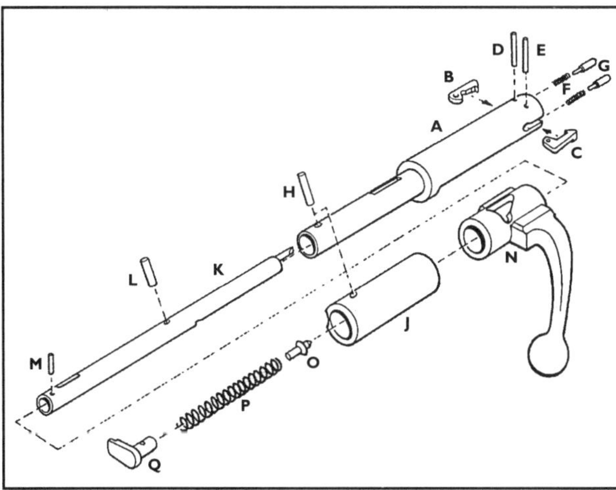

BOLT ASSEMBLY

A. Bolt
B. Extractor, left
C. Extractor, right
D. Extractor pin, left
E. Extractor pin, right
F. Extractor springs (2)
G. Extractor plungers (2)
H. Bolt sleeve pin
J. Bolt sleeve
K. Firing pin
L. Firing pin cam pin
M. Safety cam pin
N. Bolt handle
O. Mainspring plunger
P. Mainspring
Q. Safety cam

To disassemble bolt: remove bolt assembly from receiver. With bolt cocked, carefully drift out safety cam pin (M) and remove safety cam (Q) from rear of firing pin (K). Cover rear end of firing pin to prevent forcible ejection of mainspring and drift out bolt sleeve pin (H). Remove mainspring (P) and mainspring plunger (O) from firing pin. Remove firing pin from bolt (A). Remove bolt sleeve (J). Remove firing pin cam pin (L) and remove bolt handle (N) to rear of bolt. Extractors (B, C) can be removed by drifting out extractor pins (D, E) from bottom to top. After reassembling bolt handle and sleeve to bolt, insert mainspring and plunger into firing pin. Press mainspring into firing pin with blade of small screwdriver or similar tool and replace bolt sleeve pin over mainspring. With bolt cocked, replace safety cam and pin in rear of firing pin.

REMINGTON MODEL 40X TARGET

PARTS LEGEND

1. Barrel *
2. Receiver plug screws (6)
3. Telescope base, front
4. Telescope base screws (4)
5. Barrel bracket *
6. Receiver *
7. Telescope base, rear
8. Ejector
9. Ejector screw
10. Bolt stop
11. Bolt stop spring
12. Sear pin
13. Bolt stop pin
14. Trigger guide plate
15. Rear guard screw
16. Trigger guard
17. Center guard screw
18. Front guard screw
19. Receiver filler spring
20. Receiver filler piece
21. Safety pivot pin
22. Trigger pin
23. Bolt stop release
24. Trigger stop screws (2)
25. Trigger
26. Connector
27. Trigger adjusting screw
28. Trigger housing
29. Trigger spring
30. Trigger adjusting ball
31. Sear spring
32. Sear
33. Safety cam
34. Safety
35. Safety detent spring
36. Safety snap washer
37. Safety detent ball
38. Front swivel screw
39. Front swivel
40. Front swivel washer
41. Front swivel block
42. Front swivel base screw (2)
43. Front swivel base
44. Front swivel nut
45. Bedding detent springs (2)
46. Bedding detent balls (2)
47. Bedding screws (2)
48. Bedding escutcheon (2)
49. Butt pad screws (2)
50. Butt pad
51. Bolt body
52. Bolt pins (2)
53. Bolt head
54. Extractor springs (2)
55. Extractor plungers (2)
56. Extractor, left
57. Extractor, right
58. Mainspring
59. Firing pin*
60. Firing pin cross pin
61. Firing pin head
62. Bolt plug
63. Stock

* Denotes a permanent factory assembly.

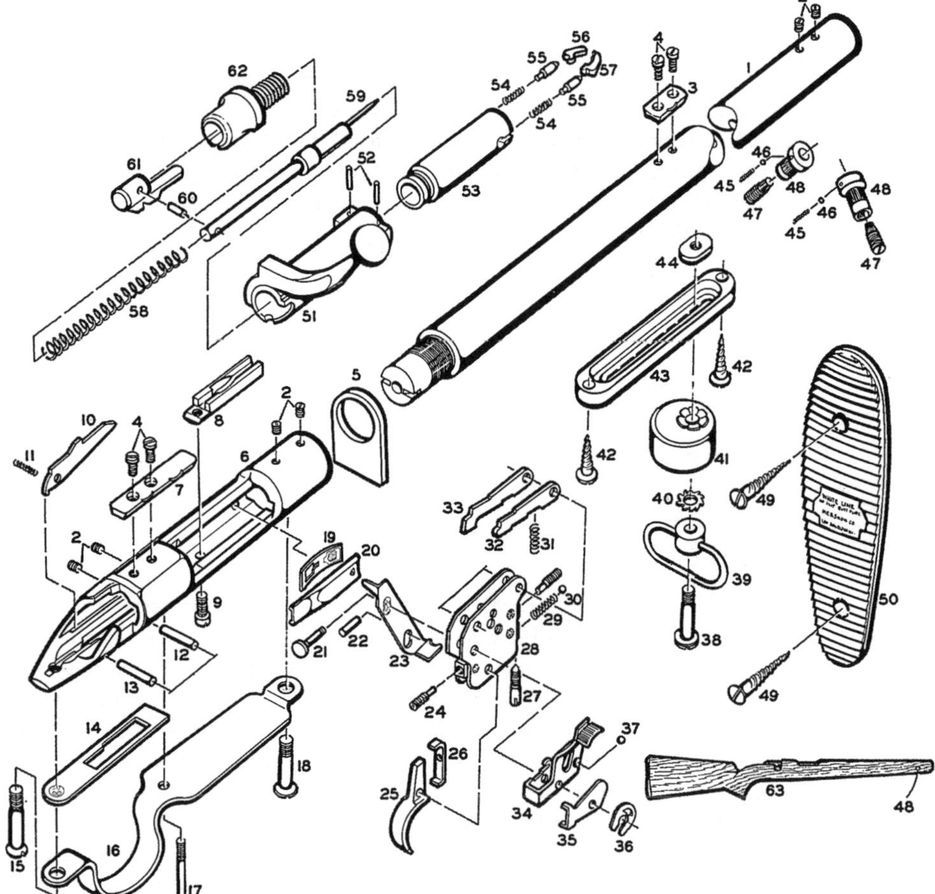

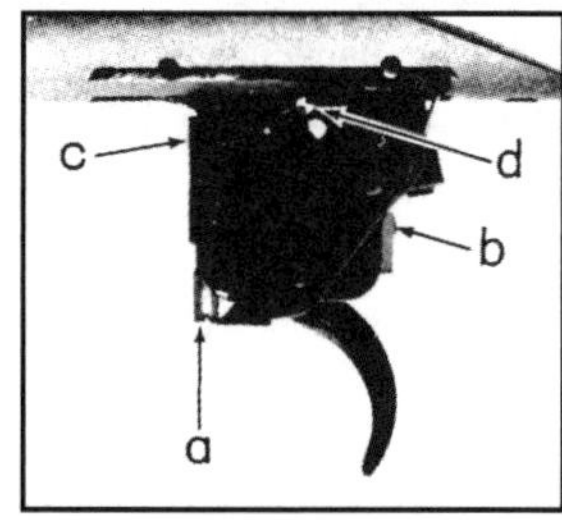

MODEL 40X ADJUSTABLE TRIGGER.
(a) Weight of pull adjustment screw. (b) Rear trigger stop screw for adjusting trigger travel. (c) Front trigger stop screw for adjusting trigger overtravel. (d) Inspection hole in trigger housing for viewing sear and connector engagement.

The Remington Model 40X small-bore target rifle was introduced in 1955. Chambered for the .22 Long Rifle cartridge, the 40X is a single-shot rifle with a speed lock firing mechanism. The bolt has two lugs located at the front of the bolt body that bear against the receiver bridge and a mortise in the bottom of the receiver. The designation "40X" was expanded in 1961 to include centerfire rifles in the series.

The 40X trigger is adjustable for weight of pull, take-up, and overtravel. Adjustment for weight of pull is made by turning an external screw within the trigger guard loop, forward of the trigger. Adjusting take-up (slack) and overtravel requires that the barreled action be removed from the stock. To adjust take-up, turn the trigger stop screw, located at the rear of the trigger housing, clockwise until the firing pin falls without the trigger being pulled. Then back off the stop screw ⅛-turn at a time until the firing pin stays cocked.

Adjustment for overtravel is made using the trigger stop screw in the front of the trigger housing. Turn the stop screw clockwise until the rifle will not fire when the trigger is pulled. Then, continuing to hold the trigger, back off the stop screw until the firing pin releases. Add ⅛ of a turn to take up slack in the threads. Use a thread sealant to lock screws in place.

DISASSEMBLY

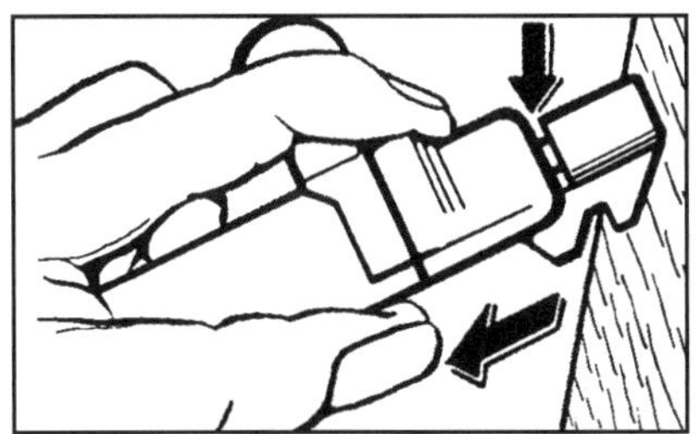

1 Disassemble Model 40X by pushing safety (34) to fire position, press upward on bolt stop release (23), raise bolt handle, and withdraw bolt assembly from receiver (6). Engage rearmost notch of firing pin head (61) on edge of bench, or grip flat undersection of firing pin head in vise, and pull back until coin can be inserted between firing pin head and bolt plug (62, upper arrow). Unscrew bolt plug with firing pin mechanism from bolt body.

2 Drift out firing pin cross pin (60) using drift or long slave pin which takes place of the cross pin in the firing pin head. Be careful not to dislodge the coin at this time as the mainspring (58) will cause the parts to fly with great force.

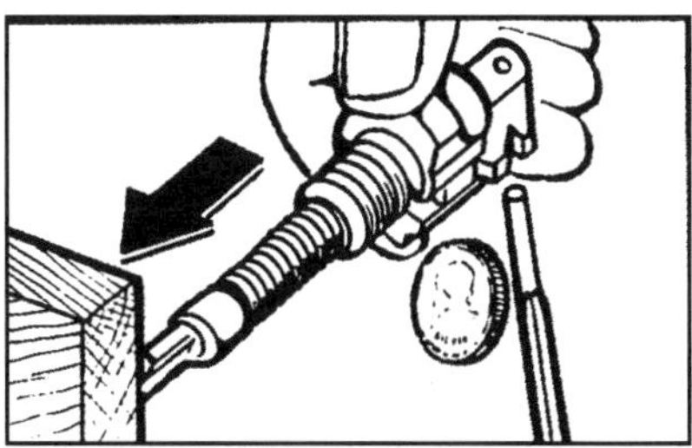

3 Insert front end of firing pin assembly into a ¼-inch hole drilled in a hardwood block held firmly in a vise. Exert forward pressure on bolt plug (62) until drift and coin drop away. Slowly release tension rearward on mainspring. Further disassembly is immediately apparent.

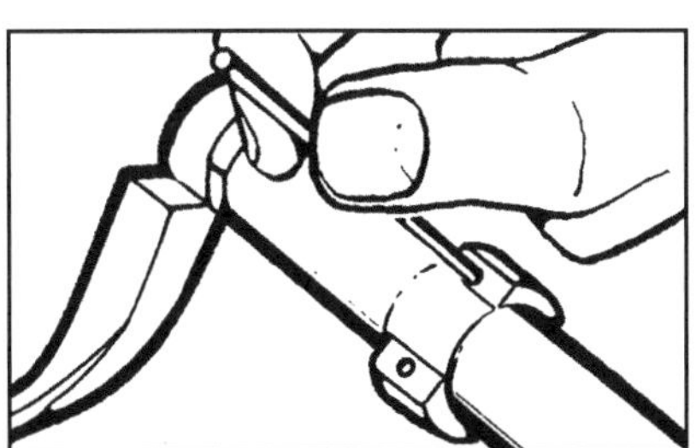

4 Using a small drift, remove bolt pins (52) from locking lugs on bolt body (51). Pull away bolt ahead (53).

5 To remove extractors (56 & 57), insert small screwdriver blade between extractor plunger (55) and rear shoulder of extractor. Force plunger rearward in bolt head and away from rear shoulder of extractor. Pry up and raise rear of extractor from slot in bolt head, then pivot extractor in slot and remove from bolt head. Extractor plunger and extractor spring (54) can be removed at this time. Instructions are for right or left extractor.

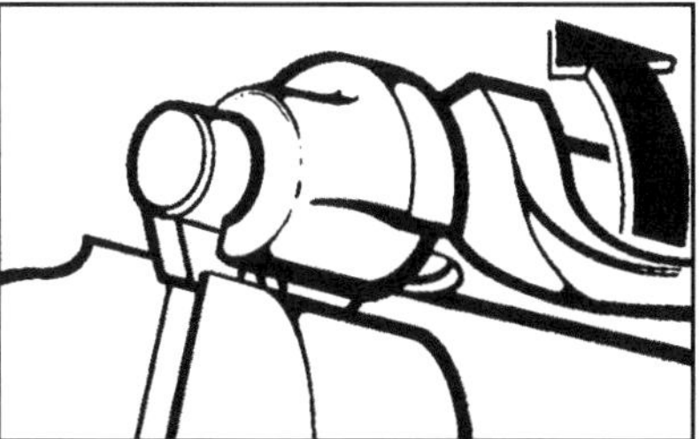

6 Bolt assembly cannot be reassembled to rifle unless firing pin is in retracted position. If firing pin has been released forward, retract it by gripping flat undersection of firing pin head tightly in a vise and raising bolt handle upward. This will cam bolt body forward and retract firing pin. Reassemble arm in reverse order. Do not disassemble trigger housing.

REMINGTON MODEL 58 SHOTGUN

PARTS LEGEND

1. Action bar assembly
2. Action spring
3. Action spring stop
4. Barrel assembly
5. Breechbolt
6. Buffer
7. Buttplate
8. Buttplate screws (2)
9. Carrier assembly
10. Carrier dog follower
11. Carrier dog follower spring
12. Carrier latch
13. Carrier latch pin
14. Carrier latch spring
15. Carrier pivot tube
16. Connector, left
17. Connector, right
18. Connector pin
19. Disconnector
20. Extractor
21. Extractor plunger
22. Extractor spring
23. Firing pin
24. Firing pin retaining pin
25. Firing pin retractor spring
26. Follower latch
27. Follower latch pin (2)
28. Follower latch spring
29. Fore-end
30. Fore-end ring
31. Fore-end ring washer
32. Front sight
33. Grip cap
34. Hammer
35. Hammer pin
36. Hammer pin washer
37. Hammer plunger
38. Hammer spring
39. Locking block assembly
40. Magazine cap assembly
41. Magazine cap detent
42. Magazine cap detent spring
43. Magazine follower
44. Magazine spring
45. Magazine spring pin
46. Operating handle
47. Piston assembly
48. Piston ring
49. Receiver assembly
50. Receiver stud
51. Safety
52. Safety detent ball
53. Safety spring
54. Safety spring retaining pin
55. Sear
56. Sear pin
57. Sear spring
58. Shell latch, left
59. Shell latch, right
60. Stock assembly
61. Stock bearing plate
62. Stock bolt
63. Stock bolt lock washer
64. Stock bolt washer
65. Trigger
66. Trigger pin
67. Trigger plate
68. Trigger plate pin bushing
69. Trigger plate pin detent spring, front (2)
70. Trigger plate pin detent spring, rear
71. Trigger plate pin, front
72. Trigger plate pin, rear

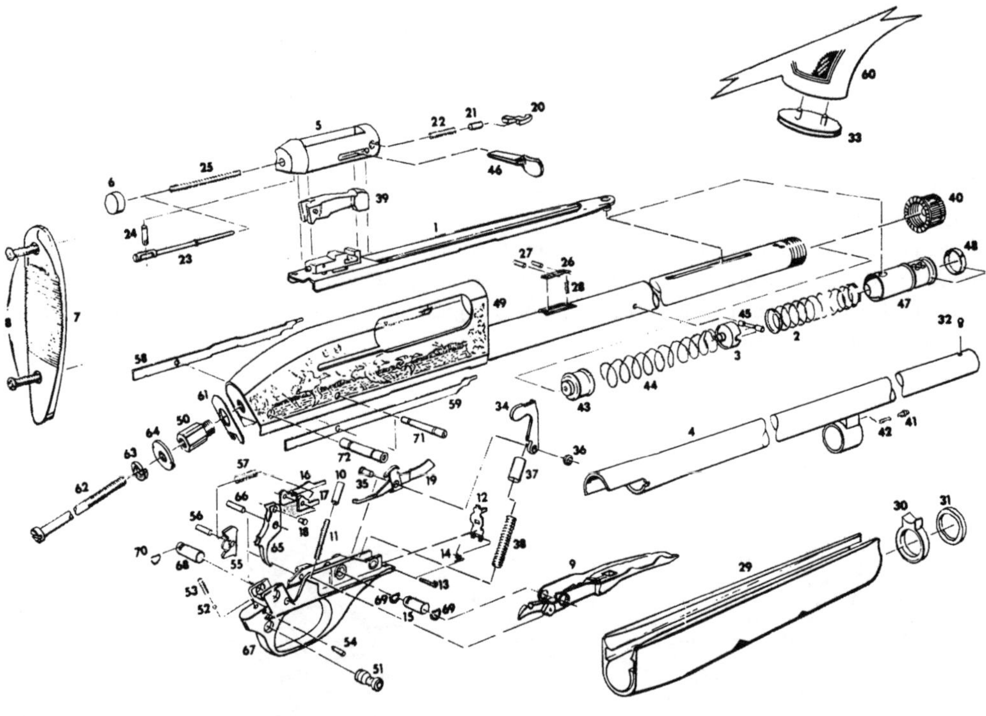

The Sportsman 58 autoloader with 'Power-Matic' action was the first gas-operated semi-automatic shotgun produced by Remington. Introduced in 1956. this gun was offered in field, trap, and skeet versions, and various grades. Choice of gauges was 12, 16, and 20 with 2¾-inch chamber length. There was also a 12-gauge Magnum version chambered for three-inch Magnum loads. Interchangeable barrels with various lengths and chokes were offered.

During firing, a portion of the powder gas passes through two orifices in the barrel and impinges on the piston assembly in the front of the magazine tube. As the piston moves rearward, it drives back the action bar assembly and breechbolt. The compressed action spring then returns the parts forward. Due to the gas-operated action, the felt recoil seems soft and the functioning cycle is smooth and fast.

A selector on the front of the magazine cap assembly must be turned to adjust the action for light and heavy loads. Capacity of the gun is three shells, two in the magazine plus the round in the chamber.

In 1963, an improved Remington semi-automatic shotgun, the Model 1100, was introduced, and shortly thereafter the Sportsman 58 was discontinued.

DISASSEMBLY

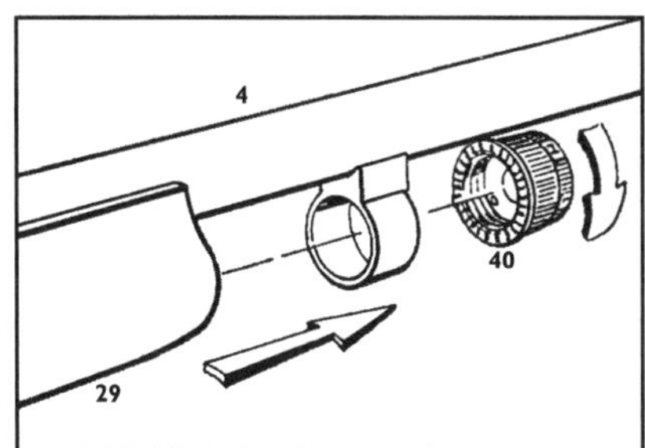

1 Before starting to disassemble the Model 58, engage safety (51) on safe and unload magazine and chamber. Remove magazine cap (40) and pull barrel (4) and fore-end (29) forward out of gun. Separate fore-end from barrel.

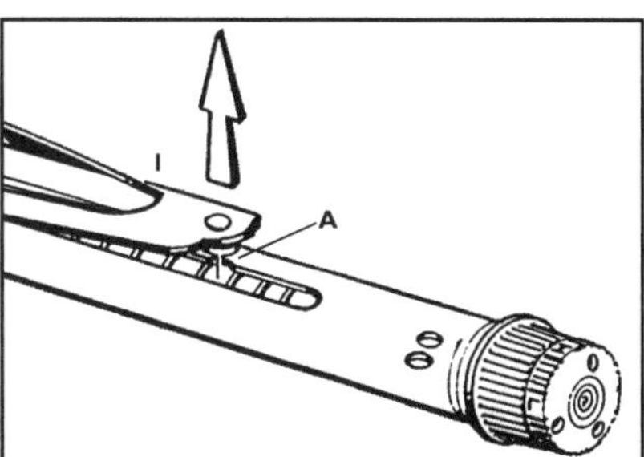

2 Replace magazine cap and close action. Then, pull action bar assembly (1) to rear until action bar stud aligns with stud notch (A) in magazine tube. Lift action bar assembly up through notch and position stud on tube. Unscrew magazine cap assembly. Piston assembly (47) and action spring (2) will disassemble from open end of magazine tube.

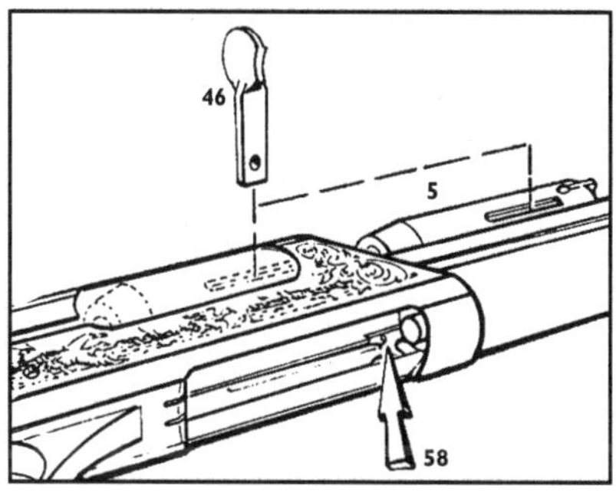

3 To remove breechbolt (5) and action bar assembly, pull out operating handle (46). Depress left shell latch (58). Then, pull action bar assembly forward to disassemble action bar and breechbolt from gun.

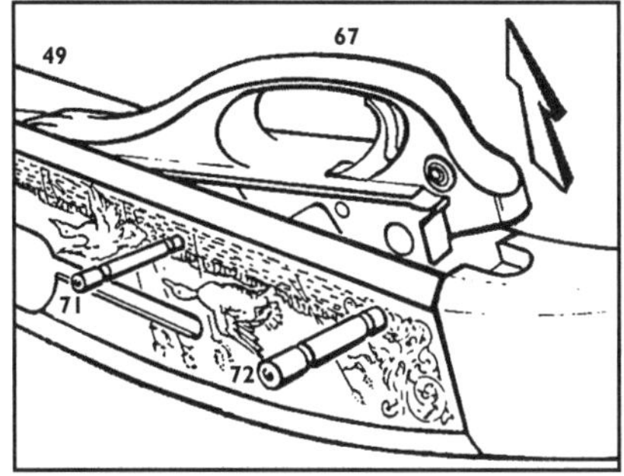

4 Tap out front trigger plate pin (71) and rear trigger plate pin (72), and lift trigger plate (67) with assembled parts out of receiver (49).

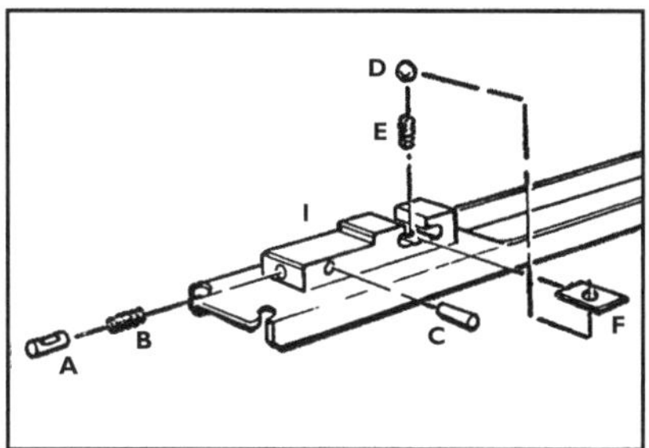

5 Exploded view of action bar assembly (1):

- A Bolt return plunger
- B Bolt return slide plunger spring
- C Bolt return plunger pin
- D Operating handle plunger
- E Operating handle plunger spring
- F Operating handle plunger retainer

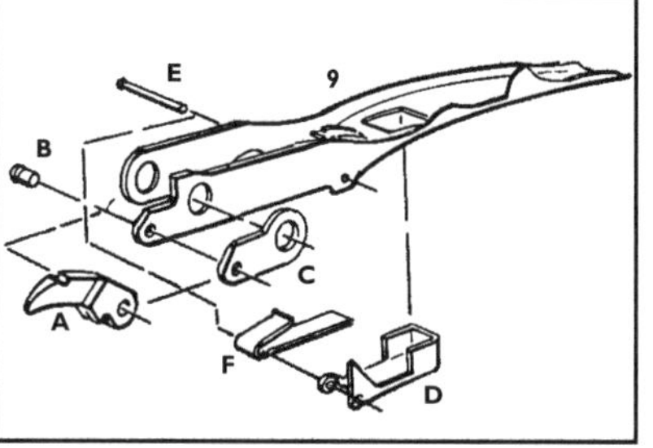

6 Exploded view of carrier assembly (9):

- A Carrier dog
- B Carrier dog pin
- C Carrier dog washer
- D Carrier release
- E Carrier release pin
- F Carrier release spring

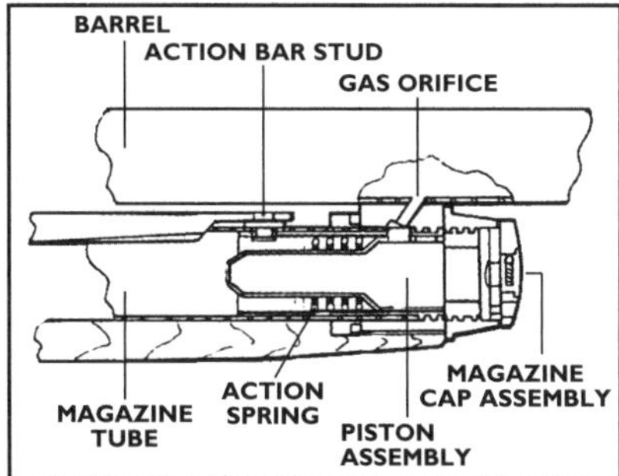

7 After shot leaves barrel, a measured portion of residual gases is exhausted downward through two orifices in barrel. Metered gases thus supply energy to piston assembly for opening action. The action spring then closes action. Excess gas in piston assembly is vented through magazine cap by load selector on cap (see Fig. 8).

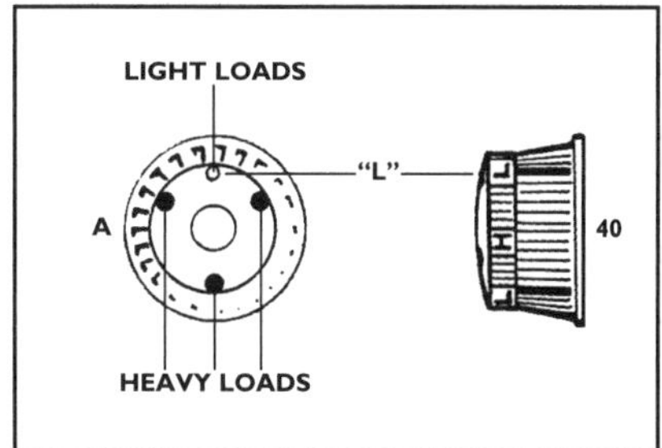

8 Magazine cap assembly (40). Inside view is at A. When using light loads, selector on cap is turned to "L" marking, and one small vent is opened to vent any excess gas. Using heavy loads, selector on cap is turned to "H" marking. Three larger vents will then be open.

REMINGTON MODEL 510 RIFLE

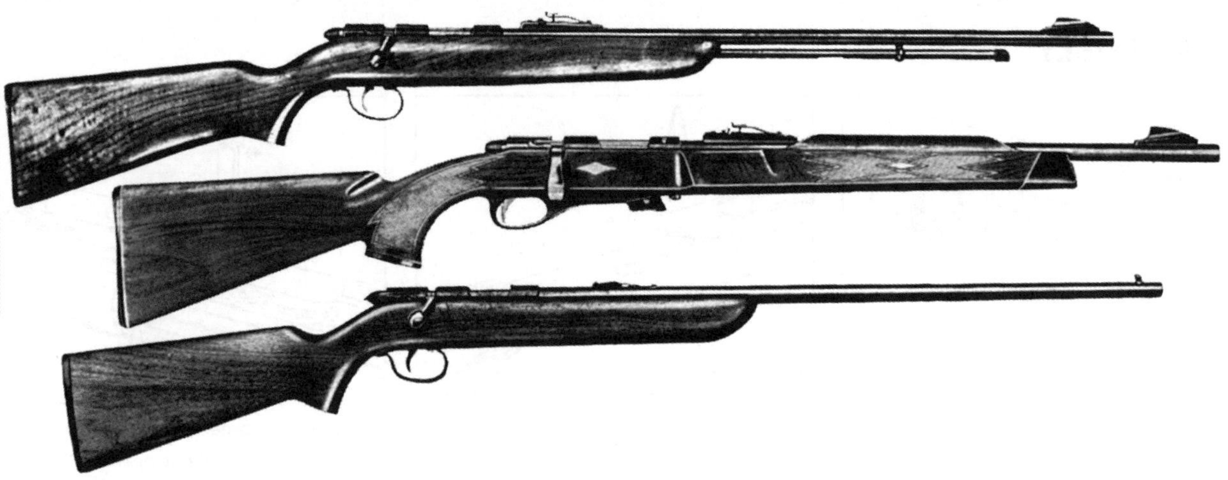

PARTS LEGEND

1. Barrel
2. Bolt
3. Bolt handle assembly
4. Bolt sleeve
5. Bolt sleeve pin
6. Ejector
7. Ejector screw
8. Extractor, left
9. Extractor, right
10. Extractor pin (2)
11. Extractor spring
12. Firing pin assembly
13. Firing pin cam pin
14. Front sight
15. Mainspring
16. Mainspring plunger
17. Rear sight
18. Rear sight screw (2)
19. Rear sight step

2
2

22. Receiver insert retaining pin (2)
23. Safety
24. Safety indicator
25. Safety lever
26. Safety screw
27. Sear pivot screw
28. Sear spacing collar
29. Stock
30. Takedown screw
31. Takedown screw escutcheon
32. Trigger assembly
33. Trigger guard
34. Trigger guard screw (2)
35. Trigger pin
36. Trigger spring
37. Trigger spring plunger

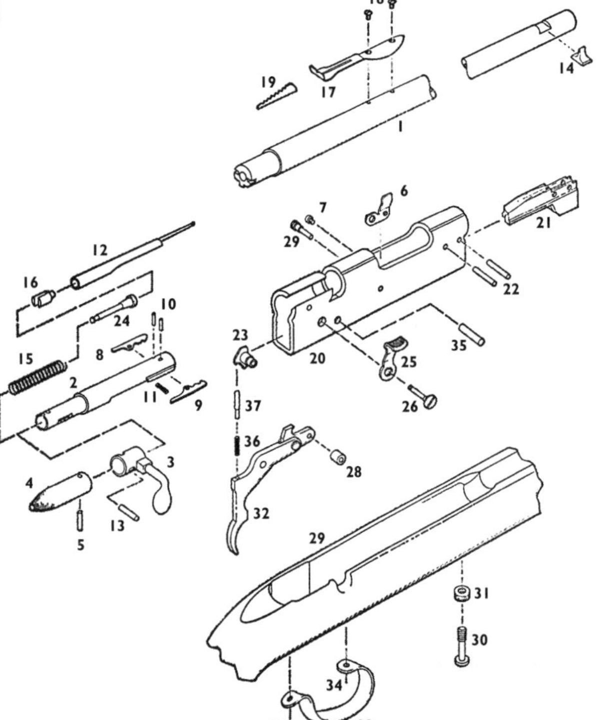

MODEL 511 PARTS LEGEND

A. Magazine lock
B. Magazine lock screw
C. Magazine lock spacer
D. Receiver insert, front
E. Receiver insert, rear

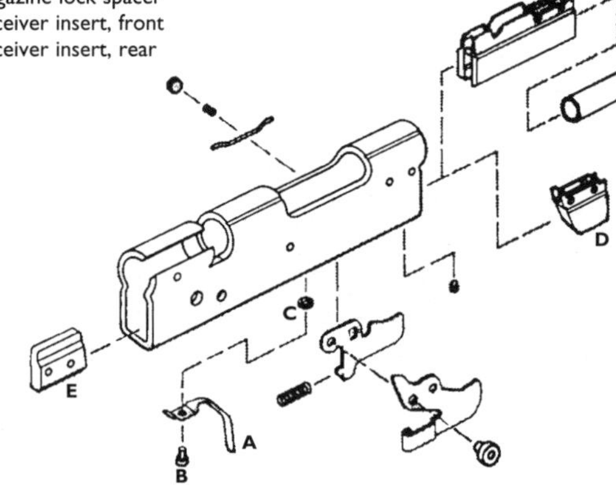

MODEL 512 PARTS LEGEND

AA. Receiver insert
BB. Cartridge retainer
CC. Cartridge retainer spring
DD. Cartridge retainer spring screw
EE. Cartridge stop
FF. Carrier
GG. Carrier spacer bushing
HH. Carrier tension spring
JJ. Magazine
KK. Magazine screw

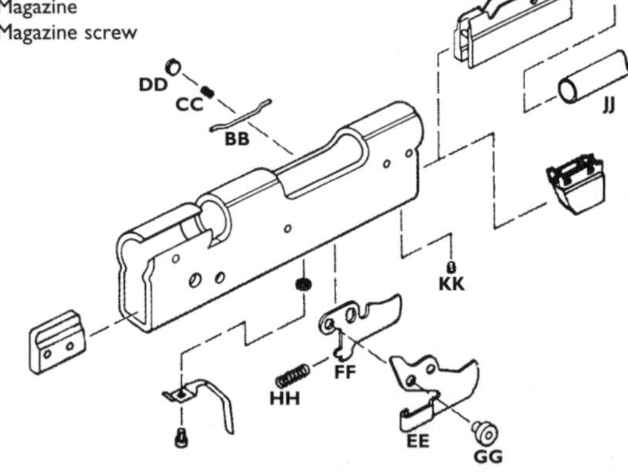

Introduced in 1939, the Remington Model 510 Targetmaster .22 caliber rimfire bolt-action rifle was a single-shot arm intended for informal target shooting and small game hunting. Chambered for .22 Short, Long, and Long Rifle cartridges, the 510 was also available in smoothbore for shot cartridges.

Remington followed the Model 510 with two new .22 bolt-action repeaters, the Model 511 Scoremaster with detachable box magazine and the Model 512 Sportmaster with tubular magazine. The rifles accepted .22 Short, Long, and Long Rifle and were similar to the Model 510, to facilitate production.

In 1962, the Models 510, 511, and 512 were replaced by the Nylon 10 single-shot, Nylon 11 box-magazine, and Nylon 12 rifles. These rifles featured one-piece nylon stocks.

In 1964 the nylon series rifles were replaced by the Models 510X, 511X, and 512X rifles with walnut stocks. The 510 series was discontinued in 1967.

DISASSEMBLY

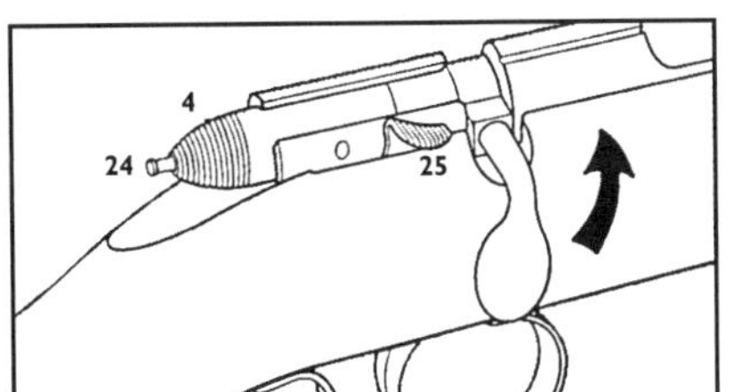

1 To disassemble rifle, lift bolt handle (3), push safety lever (25) forward, pull trigger, and withdraw bolt assembly from rifle. When replacing bolt assembly, firing mechanism must be cocked. This is indicated by red band on safety indicator (24) at rear of bolt sleeve (4). If mechanism is uncocked, cock it by pushing bolt into receiver (20) as far as possible, and lifting bolt handle. With safety lever forward, hold trigger rearward, and slide bolt assembly into rifle. In the Model 510, forward motion of bolt will be stopped by safety (23). Release trigger and turn safety lever rearward. Push bolt assembly forward, and lower bolt handle.

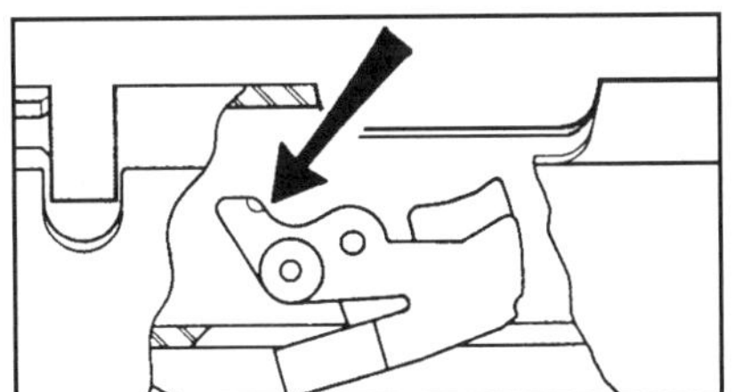

2 When replacing Model 512 bolt assembly, cartridge stop (EE) must be in upward position. If not, reach into receiver opening with small tool and press downward on rear of stop. In all three models, firing mechanism will uncock if safety lever is forward and bolt handle is lowered while pulling trigger.

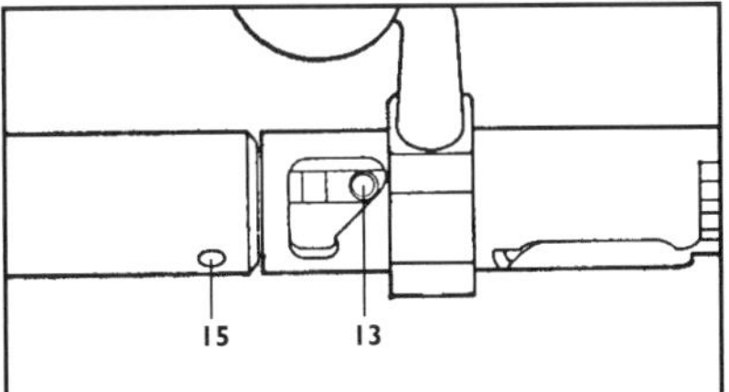

3 To strip bolt assembly, uncock by rotating bolt handle until firing pin cam pin (13) moves to forward position at base of handle. Tap out bolt sleeve pin (5). Use care as bolt sleeve is under tension of mainspring. Remove bolt sleeve, mainspring (15), and safety indicator. Slide mainspring plunger (16) from bolt (2). Push out firing pin cam pin, and remove bolt handle assembly and firing pin assembly (12). Drive out extractor pins (10) and remove extractors (8 & 9), and extractor spring (11).

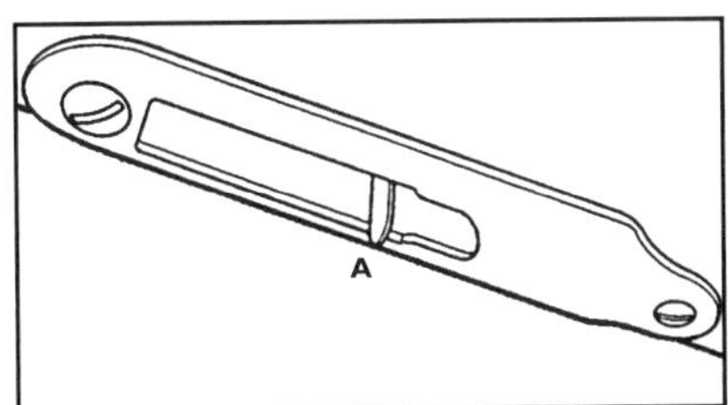

4 Loosen takedown screw (30) and remove barrel and action from stock (29). In Model 511, press magazine lock (A) rearward and remove magazine before removing barrel and action. Unscrew safety screw (26) and safety lever (25). Remove safety (23), trigger spring plunger (37), and spring (36) from receiver. Then, unscrew sear pivot screw (27). In Model 510, remove sear spacing collar (28). In Model 512, remove cartridge stop (EE), carrier (FF), carrier spacer bushing (GG), and carrier tension spring (HH).

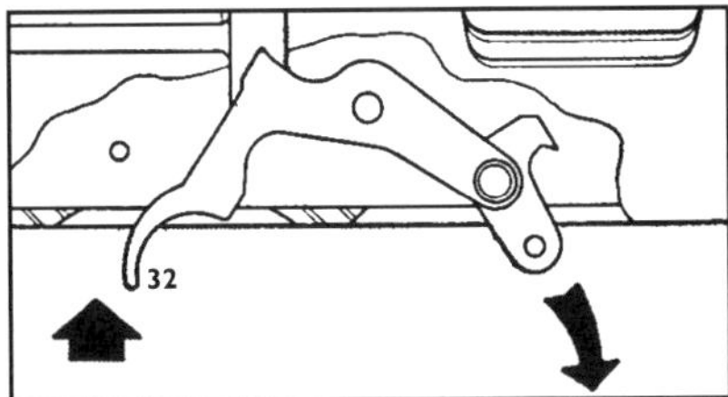

5 Drive out trigger pin (35). Push trigger assembly (32) upward into receiver. Then, push assembly forward and remove sear first through bottom of receiver. In Model 511, unscrew magazine lock screw (B), and remove magazine lock and spacer (C). Magazine lock of early Model 511 rifles is attached directly to stock from inside and comes out with stock. Slide rear receiver insert (E) forward in receiver before removing trigger assembly. Remove insert from receiver.

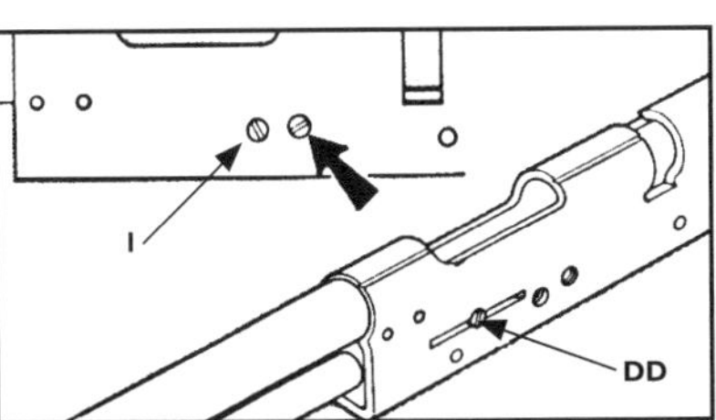

6 Unscrew ejector screw (7) and remove ejector (6). When replacing sear pivot screw, assemble to full depth, back off one-half turn and re-stake in place (arrow). In Model 512, unscrew cartridge retainer spring screw (DD) and remove cartridge retainer spring (CC) and cartridge retainer (BB) from left of receiver. Unscrew magazine screw (KK) and remove magazine (JJ).

REMINGTON MODEL 514A RIFLE

PARTS LEGEND

1. Barrel
2. Barrel lock screw
3. Bolt assembly
4. Bolt detent ball
5. Bolt detent retainer
6. Front sight
7. Rear sight leaf
8. Rear sight screw (2)
9. Rear sight step
10. Receiver
11. Stock
12. Takedown screw
13. Takedown screw escutcheon
14. Trigger
15. Trigger guard
16. Trigger guard screw (2)
17. Trigger pin
18. Trigger spring

Note: Buttplate and screws not shown.

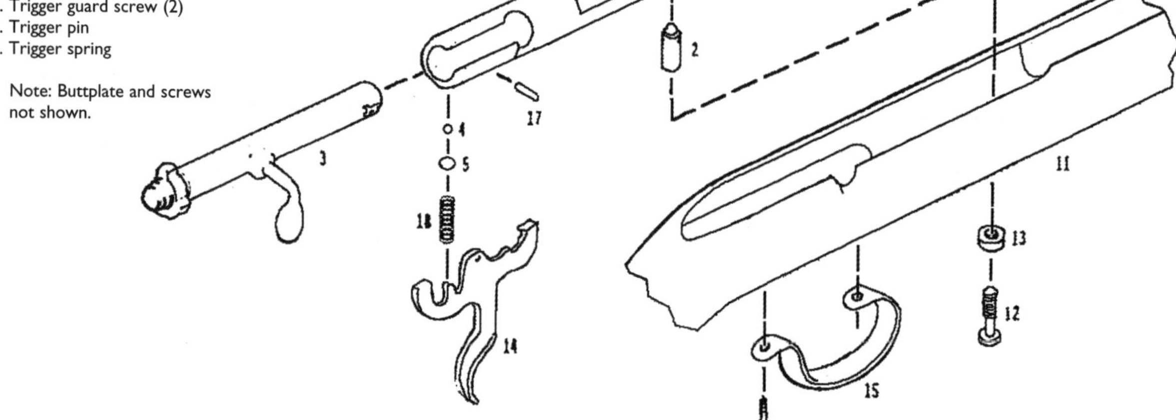

BOLT ASSEMBLY PARTS LEGEND

19. Bolt
20. Ejector
21. Ejector pin
22. Ejector spring
23. Extractor
24. Extractor plunger
25. Extractor spring
26. Firing pin
27. Mainspring
28. Safety
29. Safety screw

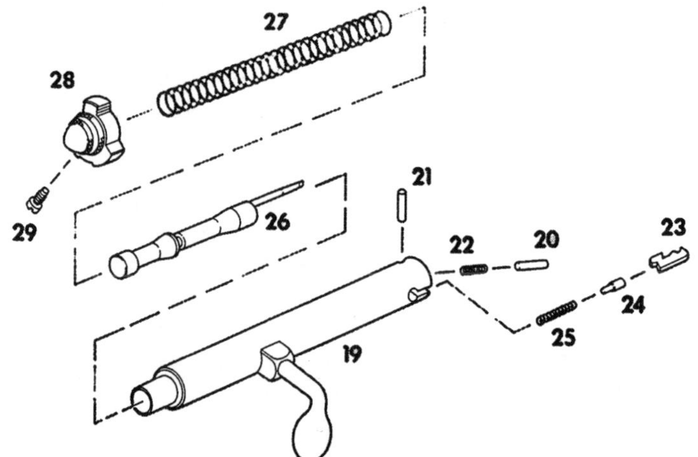

Introduced in 1948, the Remington Model 514 was offered as a simple, reliable and inexpensive .22 rimfire, single-shot rifle. It was initially marketed as the 514A with an open rear sight, and as the 514P, with an aperture rear sight fitted on the receiver. Both versions had 24¾-inch barrels and walnut stocks.

During the years that it was produced, there were several variations of the 514. The 514P was dropped in the 1950s, as was a youth model, the 514BC ("boy's carbine"). The 514BC, with its 20-inch barrel and shortened (12½-inch pull) stock, was replaced, after several years of absence, by the 514 Boy's Rifle in 1962. For a few years in the 1960s the 514A and 514 BC were fitted with 20-inch barrels. About 1967 the 24¾-inch barrel again became standard for both rifles. All variations of the Model 514 were discontinued in 1971.

DISASSEMBLY

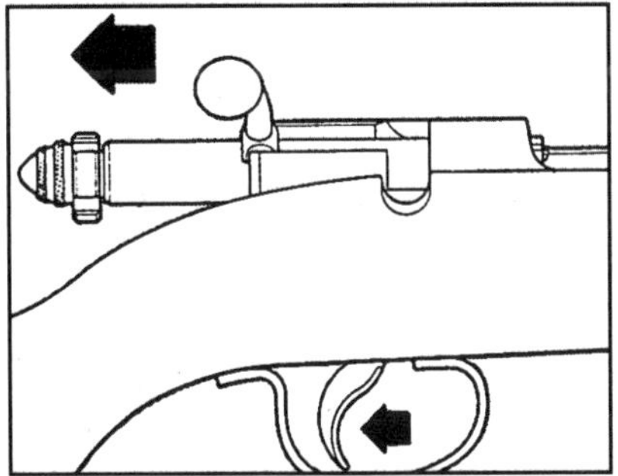

1 Lift bolt handle and pull bolt assembly (3) rearward. Check chamber to make sure rifle is not loaded. Pull trigger (14) and remove bolt assembly from rifle.

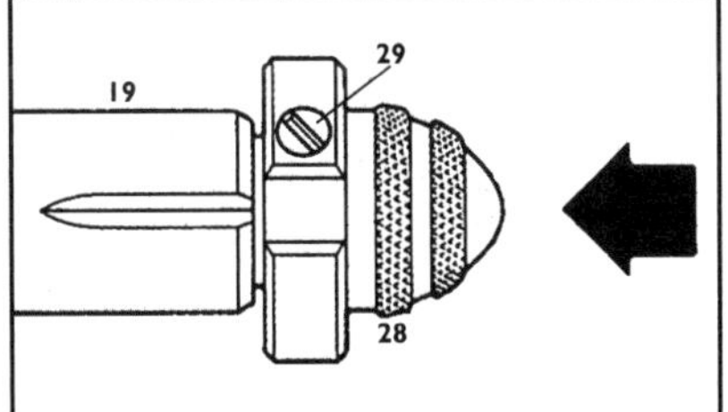

2 To disassemble bolt assembly, push and hold safety (28) forward against tension of mainspring (27), and unscrew safety screw (29). Slowly release forward pressure on safety and remove safety from bolt (19). Remove mainspring. Drive out ejector pin (21) and remove ejector (20) and ejector spring (22) from face of bolt. Disassembly of extractor (23) is not recommended unless necessary for repair or replacement. Force small screwdriver or knife blade between extractor and extractor plunger (24), and push plunger rearward. Pry extractor out of its slot in bolt. CAUTION: Extractor plunger is under spring load and may fly out of bolt with force when extractor is removed. Care should be taken to prevent this. Remove extractor plunger and spring (25).

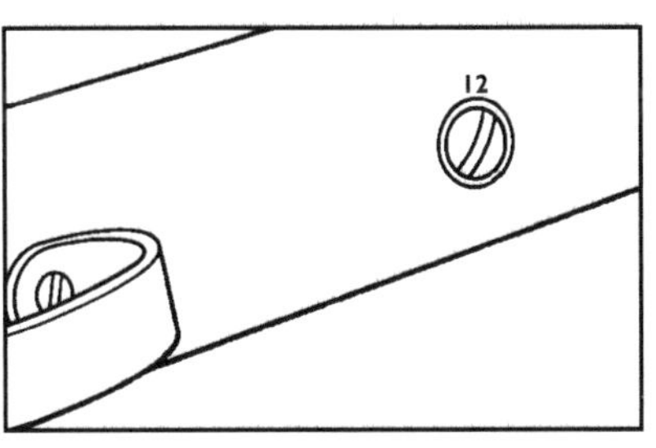

3 Unscrew takedown screw (12) until action can be lifted from stock (11). Leave screw in stock to prevent loss.

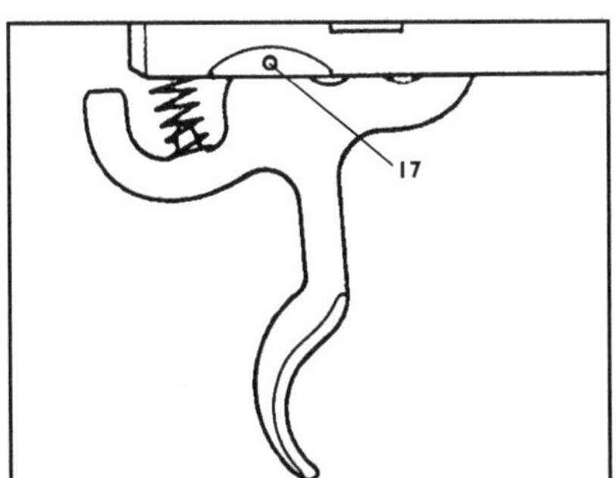

4 Drive out trigger pin (17). Remove trigger, trigger spring (18), bolt detent retainer (5), and bolt detent ball (4). Use care when disassembling these parts since retainer and ball may fall out of receiver when pressure of trigger spring is removed. NOTE: When reassembling safety to bolt, make sure that safety screw is screwed into safety as far as possible.

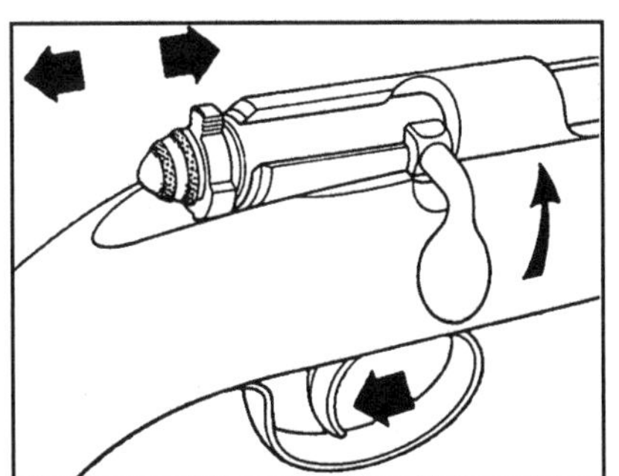

5 Tension should be relieved from mainspring when rifle is not in use. This is done by lifting bolt handle and allowing bolt assembly to travel rearward approximately ⅝-inch. After making sure there is no cartridge in chamber, hold trigger rearward and move bolt assembly forward approximately ¼-inch. Release trigger and close bolt.

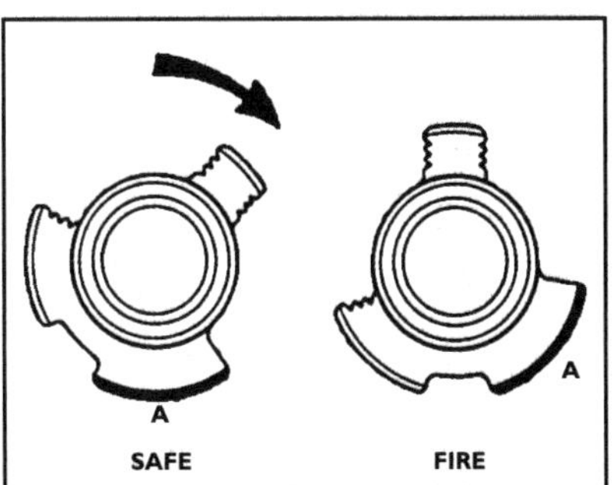

6 Rifle is on safe when safety is rotated to right (clockwise) about ⅛ of a turn. The red safety indicator (A) is then concealed. Safety is in fire position when red indicator is visible on right side.

REMINGTON MODEL 521T RIFLE

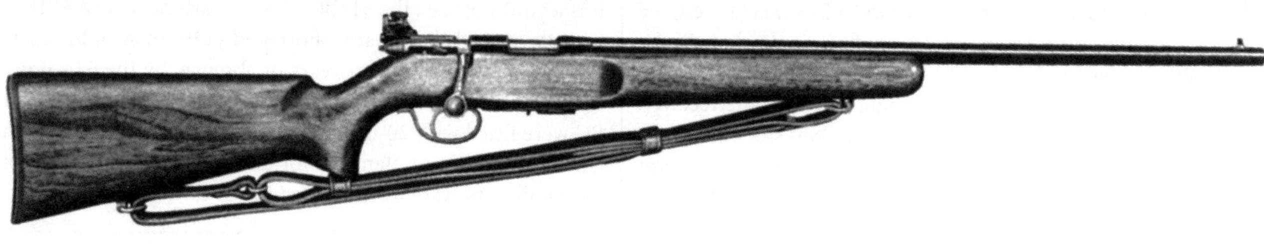

PARTS LEGEND

1. Barrel
2. Front sight
3. Stock
4. Takedown screw escutcheon
5. Takedown screw
6. Magazine guide plate
7. Magazine guide plate screw
8. Magazine lock
9. Magazine lock screw
10. Trigger guard
11. Trigger guard screw (2)
12. Front swivel base
13. Front swivel base screw (2)
14. Front swivel
15. Front swivel screw
16. Magazine assembly
17. Sling strap assembly
18. Rear swivel
19. Buttplate screw (2)
20. Buttplate
21. Bolt sleeve
22. Mainspring
23. Safety indicator
24. Mainspring plunger
25. Firing pin cam pin
26. Firing pin
27. Bolt handle
28. Bolt
29. Bolt sleeve pin
30. Extractor, left
31. Extractor, right
32. Extractor pin (2)
33. Extractor spring
34. Sear pivot screw
35. Sear
36. Trigger
37. Sear stud
38. Trigger spring
39. Trigger spring plunger
40. Ejector screw
41. Ejector
42. Receiver insert, rear
43. Trigger pin
44. Safety
45. Safety lever
46. Safety screw
47. Receiver
48. Barrel lock pin (2)
49. Receiver insert, front
50. Barrel filler block
51. Rear micrometer sight, Lyman 57RS

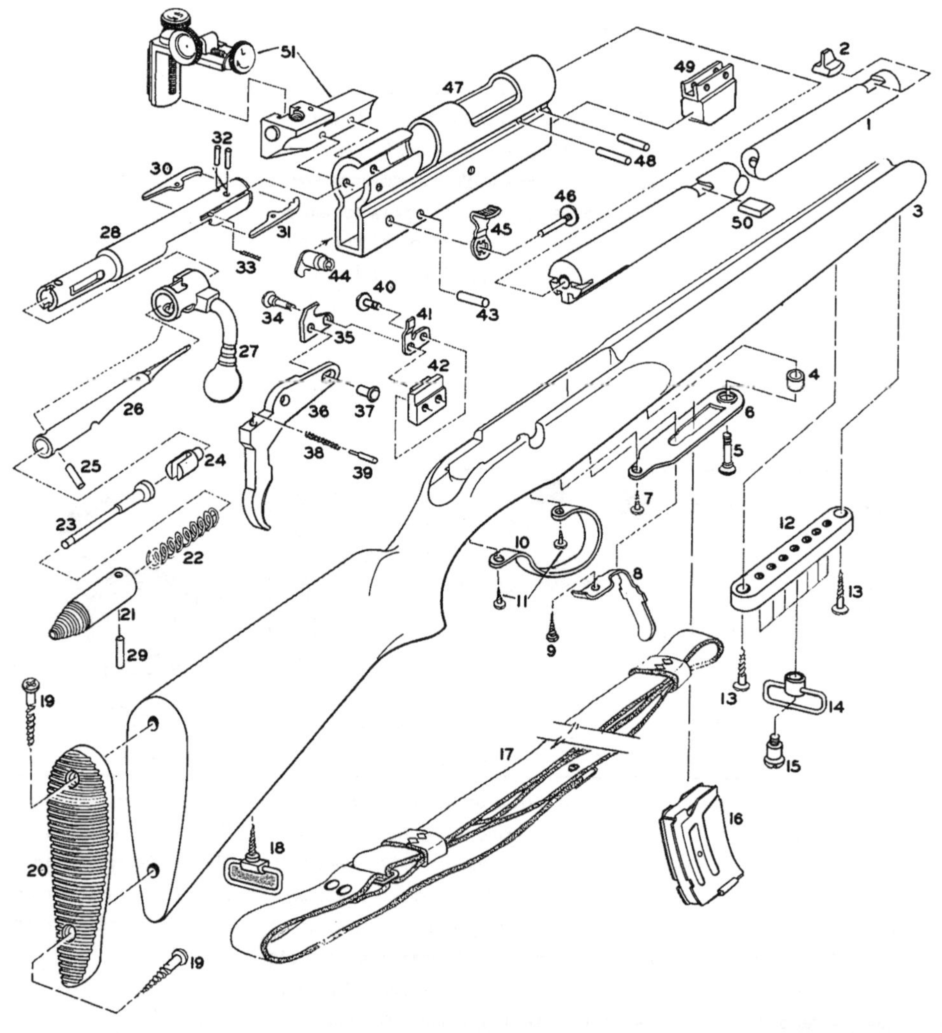

The Remington Model 521T smallbore target rifle, chambered for the .22 Long Rifle cartridge, was first offered by Remington Arms Co., in 1947. Designed for young target shooters, this moderately-priced rifle filled the gap between the more expensive and heavier Remington Model 513T and Model 40X target rifles.

The 521's tumbolt action featured dual locking lugs and extractors and was of the cock-on-opening type. A safety indicator pin protruded from the end of the bolt to show that the action was cocked. A detachable box magazine held six cartridges.

The American walnut stock was a high-comb target type with the full, close pistol grip and beavertail fore-end preferred by many target shooters. Sling swivels were standard and the front swivel was adjustable to seven positions to accommodate differences in arm length. A 1-inch, military style, leather sling was furnished with each rifle.

The 521T was equipped with a Patridge-style, blade front sight and a Lyman 57R5 aperture rear with ¼-minute adjustments for elevation and windage. The overall length of the rifle, with its 25-inch barrel, was 43 inches — weight was about seven pounds.

The Model 521T, or 513TL as it was cataloged later, was discontinued in 1969.

DISASSEMBLY

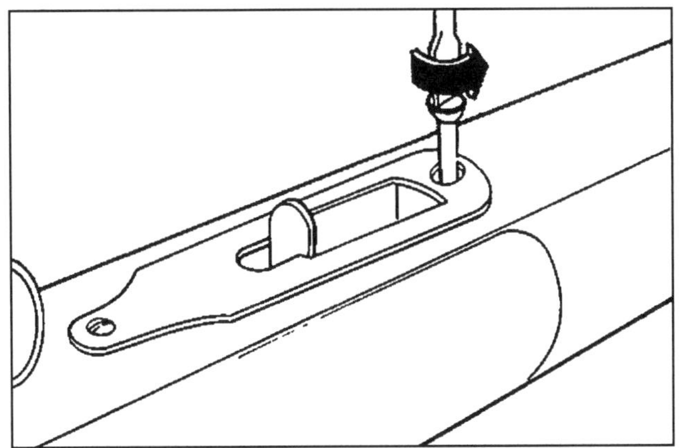

1 Takedown of Model 521T is accomplished by removing box magazine (16) and loosening takedown screw (5) just forward of magazine opening in magazine guide plate (6). Stock can now be removed from action.

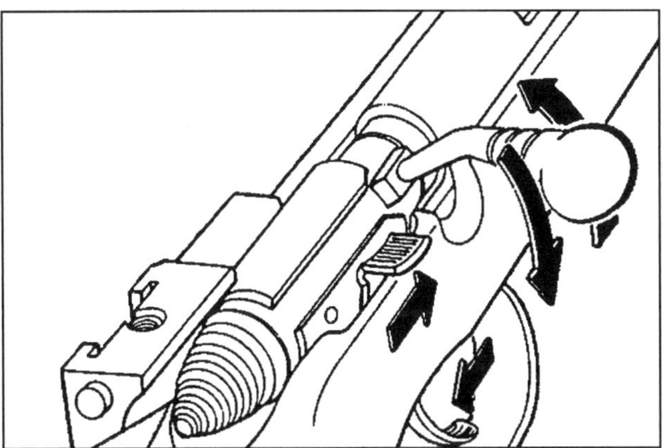

2 CAUTION: Insure there is no cartridge in chamber prior to this operation. Tension on mainspring (22) may be relieved when the rifle is not in use by rotating bolt handle (27) upward, then pushing safety lever (45) forward to "Fire" position while holding trigger (36) back and simultaneously rotating bolt handle downward.

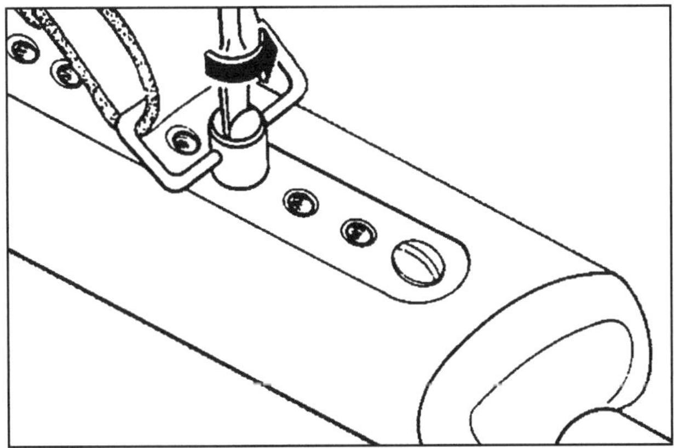

3 Position of front swivel (14) can be changed to any one of 7 holes in front swivel base (12) by unscrewing front swivel screw (15) and repositioning it where desired.

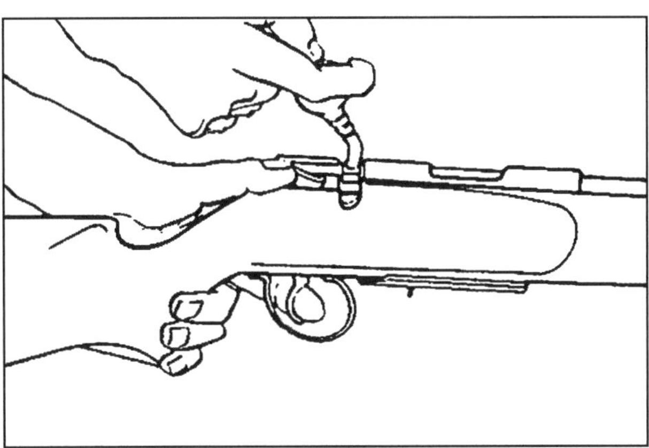

4 To remove bolt (28), press release button on micrometer sight (51) and raise or remove it. Open action, push safety lever (45) to "Fire" position, hold trigger full rearward, and pull bolt from receiver. This is sufficient disassembly for cleaning.

REMINGTON MODEL 540X RIFLE

PARTS LEGEND

1. Barrel
2. Barrel assembly pin (2)
3. Barrel plug screw (4)
4. Bolt assembly pin
5. Bolt body assembly
6. Bolt head
7. Bolt plug
8. Bolt stop
9. Bolt stop release
10. Bolt stop spring
11. Butt pad assembly
12. Butt pad base
13. Butt pad base screw (2)
14. Buttplate tube assembly
15. Cocking piece
16. Ejector
17. Extractor left hand
18. Extractor right hand
19. Extractor spring
20. Firing pin
21. Front sight base
22. Front sight base screw (2)
23. Floor plate
24. Floor plate screw
25. Housing
26. Housing lock screw
27. Housing pin
28. Loading platform
29. Loading platform screw
30. Mainspring
31. Rail
32. Rail screw (2)
33. Receiver assembly
34. Receiver plug screw (3)
35. Safety
36. Safety detent
37. Safety detent spring
38. Safety pivot pin
39. Safety pivot pin retaining washer
40. Safety retainer screw
41. Sear
42. Sear pin
43. Stock assembly
44. Striker
45. Striker assembly
46. Striker cross pin
47. Striker washer
48. Takedown screw (2)
49. Trigger
50. Trigger adjustment screw
51. Trigger adjustment spring
52. Trigger engagement screw
53. Trigger pin
54. Trigger spring
55. Trigger spring retaining pin
56. Trigger stop screw
57. Trigger guard
58. Trigger guard screw
59. Tube clamp screw (2)
60. Tube screw
61. Tube screw washer

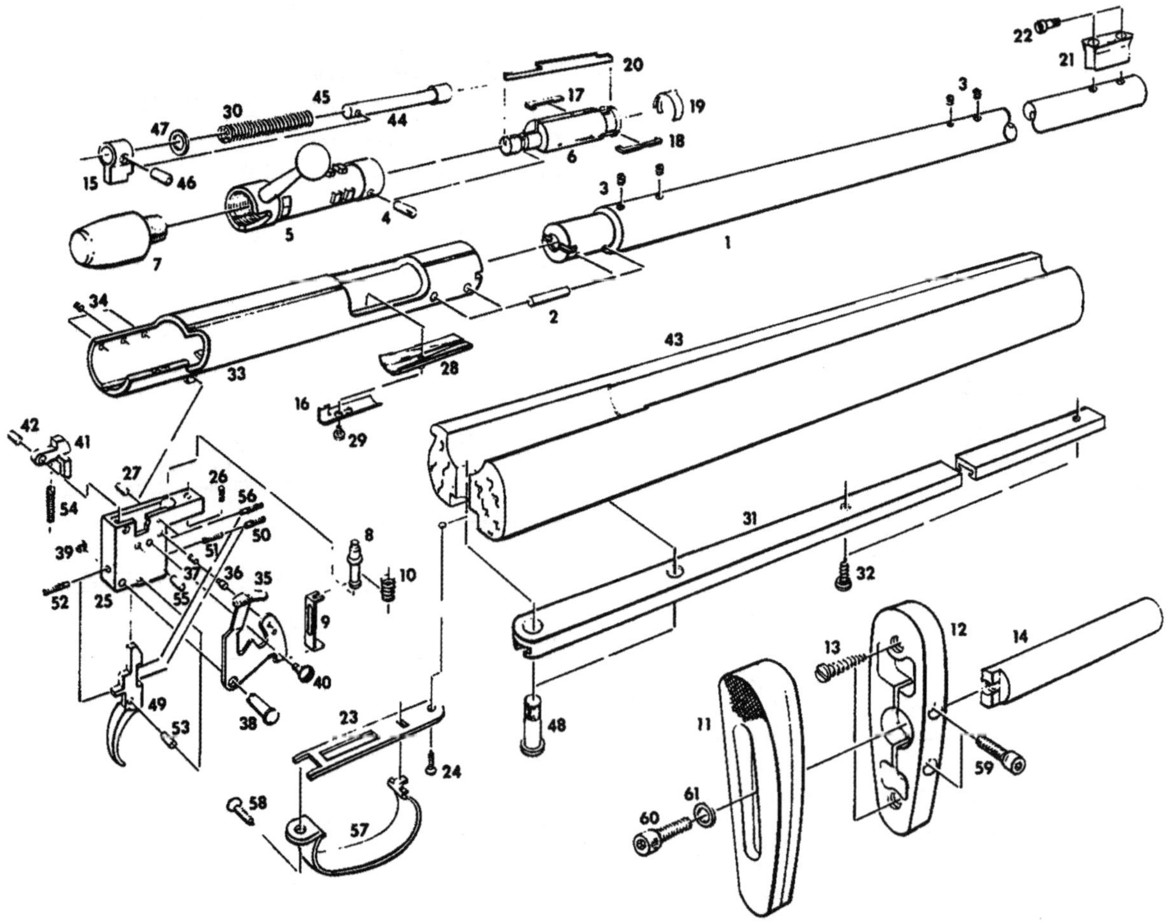

The Remington Model 540X .22 caliber, single-shot, bolt-action target rifle was introduced in 1969. Chambered for the .22 Long Rifle cartridge, it weighs only about 9 lbs. complete with sling and iron sights, it is capable of firing 1-inch, 10-shot groups at 100 yds. with match ammunition.

An important reason for this rifle's fine performance is its high-quality, 26-inch, medium-weight barrel which is full floating in the fore-end. Some other important reasons for the fine performance are secure lock-up of the six-lug bolt and extremely fast lock time of only 1.4 milliseconds.

A nylon plastic loading tray in the receiver bottom guides the cartridge into the chamber without deforming the bullet. The trigger mechanism of the Model 540X is adjustable for weight of pull, sear engagement and overtravel.

Sights consists of a Redfield No. 75 micrometer aperture rear sight and No. 63 globe front sight with interchangeable inserts. The barrel is drilled and tapped for scope blocks, and the receiver is grooved for clamp-on scope mounts. The rifle was available with or without iron sights.

The one-piece birch stock has a cheek-piece, full pistol grip, shelf for the right thumb and a wide palm groove behind the grip. A full-length accessory rail in the bottom of the semi-beavertail fore-end adapts the rifle for use with a handstop-swivel block and palm rests.

The buttplate is adjustable for length of pull, vertical movement, and right or left cant. Length of pull is adjustable from approximately 12¾ to15½ inches. In 1975, the Model 540X rifle was replaced by the Model 540XR.

DISASSEMBLY

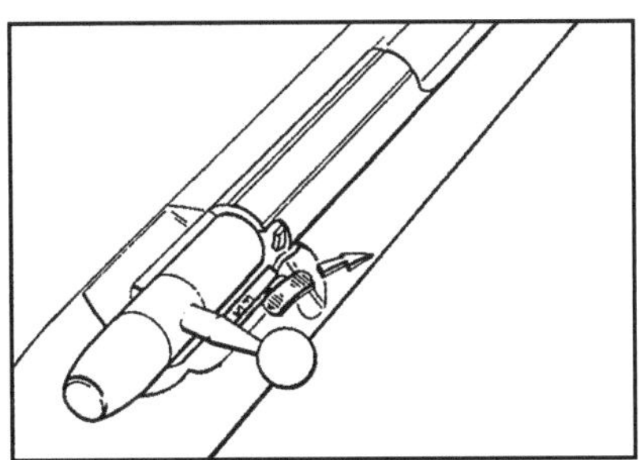

1 Pull bolt all the way to the rear and make sure rifle is unloaded. Push safety (35) completely forward beyond "F" marking on receiver (33), and remove bolt assembly from rifle.

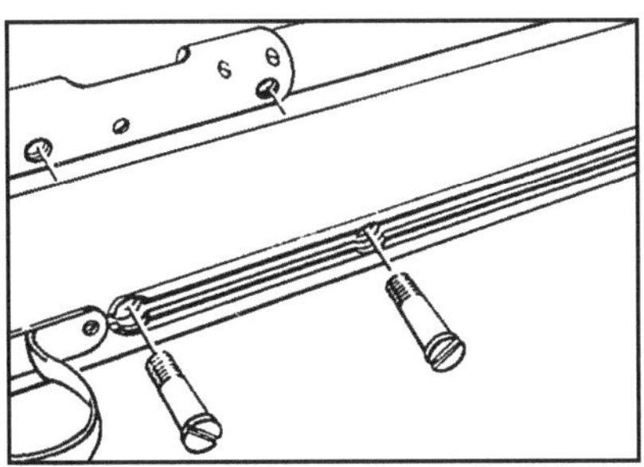

2 Unscrew takedown screws (48), and remove stock assembly (43) from barreled action.

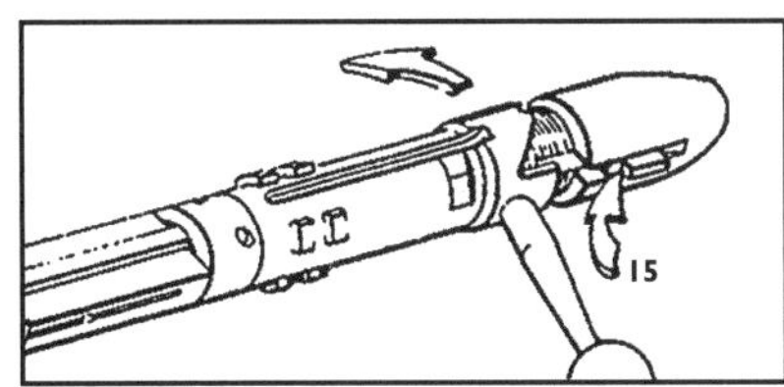

3 Clamp bolt plug (7) in a padded vise. Push cocking piece (15) rearward into bolt plug with a punch or screwdriver, and unscrew bolt body assembly (5) from bolt plug, and remove striker assembly (45). Clamp striker (44) in a padded vise, drive out striker cross pin (46) with a punch, and remove cocking piece, striker washer (47), and mainspring (30). CAUTION: Cocking piece is under spring pressure. Drift out bolt assembly pin (4), and separate bolt head (6) from bolt body. Use small screwdriver to pry extractor spring off bolt head. Remove firing pin (20) and extractors (17 & 18).

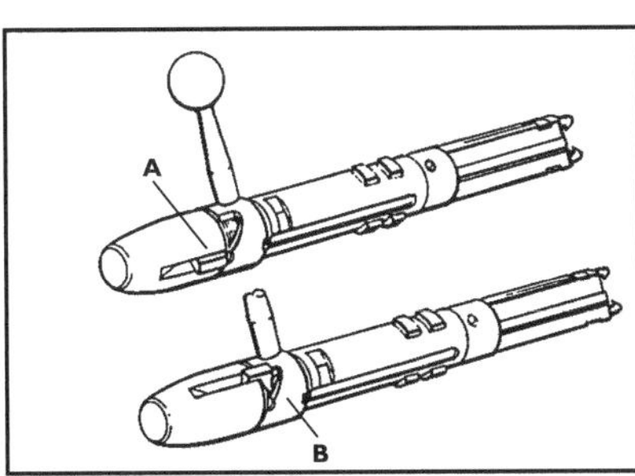

4 Firing mechanism must be cocked before replacing bolt in receiver. Cocking piece must be engaged in notch (position A) at rear of bolt body assembly. If cocking piece is in position B, push it rearward with screwdriver or punch, and turn bolt to engage cocking piece with notch. Also, rib on bottom of bolt head must be aligned with groove on bolt body assembly. Start bolt assembly in receiver with handle at two o'clock position, press safety all the way forward, and push bolt toward barrel.

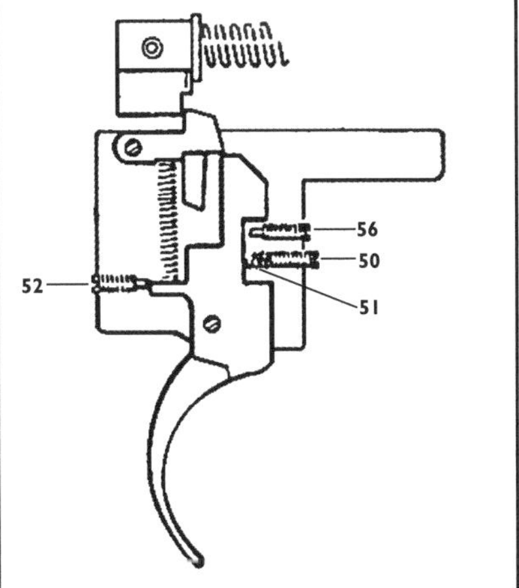

5 Turn trigger adjustment screw (50) in against spring (51) to increase weight of pull, or out to lighten pull. It is recommended that trigger engagement screw (52) and trigger stop screw (56) not be turned as they are adjusted properly at the factory.

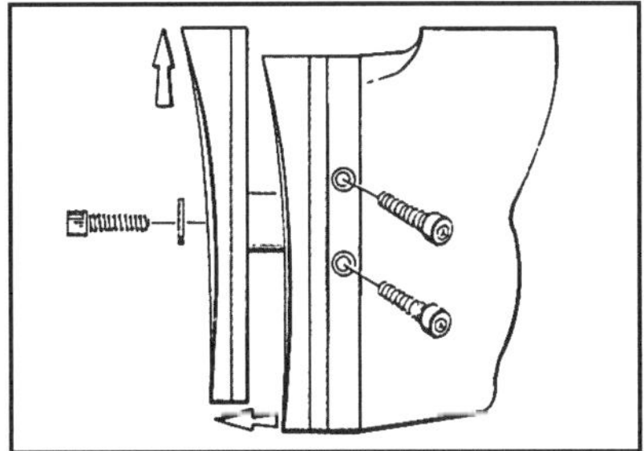

6 Buttplate assembly is adjustable for length of pull, vertical movement, and right or left cant by using an Allen wrench. Adjustments can be made in vertical movement after loosening tube screw (60), and in length of pull and cant after loosening tube clamp screws (59). Retighten screws after making adjustments.

REMINGTON MODEL 550 A RIFLE

PARTS LEGEND

1. Action spring
2. Action-spring bushing
3. Action-spring guide
4. Barrel
5. Bolt
6. Bolt handle
7. Buttplate
8. Buttplate screws (2)
9. Carrier
10. Carrier-spacer bushing
11. Carrier-tension spring
12. Cartridge stop
13. Deflector
14. Deflector screw
15. Extractor
16. Extractor plunger
17. Extractor spring
18. Firing-pin assembly
19. Front sight
20. Inner magazine-tube assembly
21. Magazine ring
22. Magazine screw
23. Magazine-tube support screw
24. Mainspring
25. Mainspring plunger
26. Open sight leaf
27. Open sight screw (2)
28. Open sight step
29. Outer-magazine tube
30. Receiver assembly
31. Receiver-insert assembly
32. Receiver plug
33. Receiver-plug retainer
34. Receiver-plug retainer screw
35. Receiver-plug retainer-screw lock washer
36. Recoiling chamber
37. Safety
38. Safety lever
39. Safety screw
40. Sear assembly
41. Sear pin
42. Sear spring
43. Sear-spring case
44. Stock assembly
45. Takedown screw
46. Takedown-screw bushing
47. Trigger assembly
48. Trigger guard
49. Trigger-guard screw (2)
50. Trigger pin
51. Trigger spring
52. Trigger-spring plunger
53. Trigger-stop pin

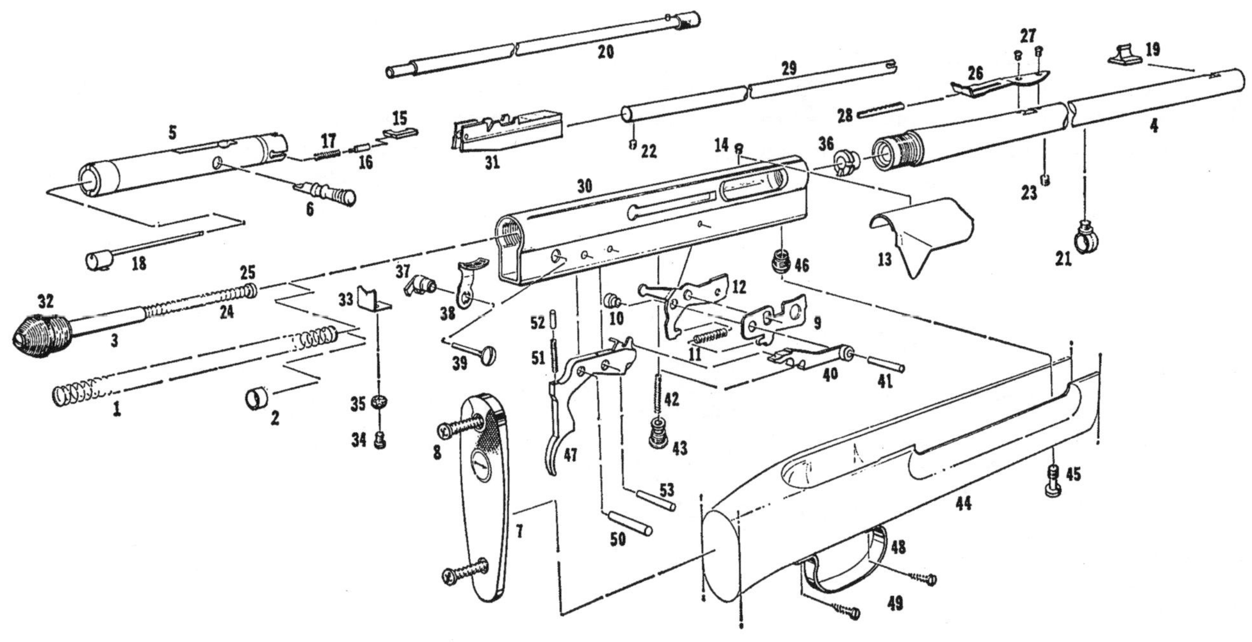

The Remington Model 550A semiautomatic rifle was introduced in 1941. Of takedown design, this blow-back-operated rifle for small game hunting and informal target shooting fires .22 short, long, and long-rifle regular and high-velocity cartridges interchangeably and without adjustment. Capacity of the tubular magazine under the 24-inch round barrel is 15 Long Rifle, 17 Long, or 22 Short cartridges.

An unusual feature of the Model 550A is its floating chamber (or power piston) which allows for reliable functioning with a wide variety of ammunition. Designed by David M. "Carbine" Williams, this device is a hollow piston that contains the chamber and fits in the breech end of the barrel.

When the rifle is fired, powder gas enters the space between the front of the hollow piston and barrel, and the gas pressure drives the piston rearward. This gives greater rearward force than would be obtained with a normal blowback system without the piston.

Another feature of this rifle is a sheet steel deflector fastened to the receiver adjacent to the ejection port. This prevents gas or partially-burnt powder from blowing toward the user.

The thumb-operated safety is on the right side of the receiver. When the safety is forward in fire position, a red dot on the receiver is exposed.

In addition to open sights on the barrel, the receiver has dovetail grooves on top to permit attachment of clamp-on telescope sight mounts. The one-piece American walnut stock is fitted with a checkered black plastic buttplate. Most metal parts are blued.

While the Model 550A is an excellent rifle, it does not have the trim lines of Remington's newer .22 rimfire auto-loaders. It was discontinued in 1970.

DISASSEMBLY

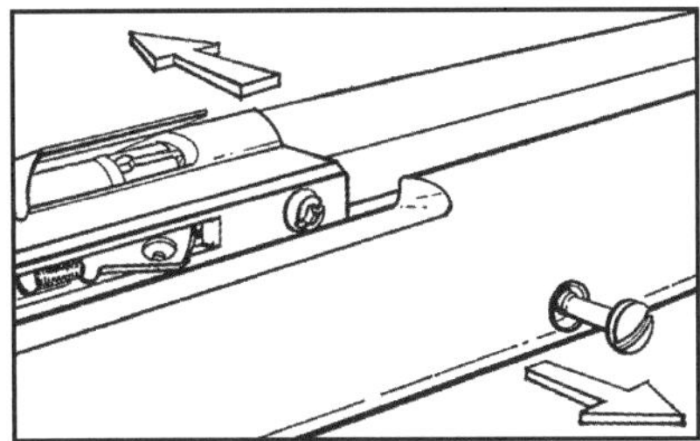

1 Before disassembling rifle, check chamber and magazine to be sure they are unloaded. Unscrew takedown screw (45) from bottom of stock. Remove stock assembly (44) from rifle.

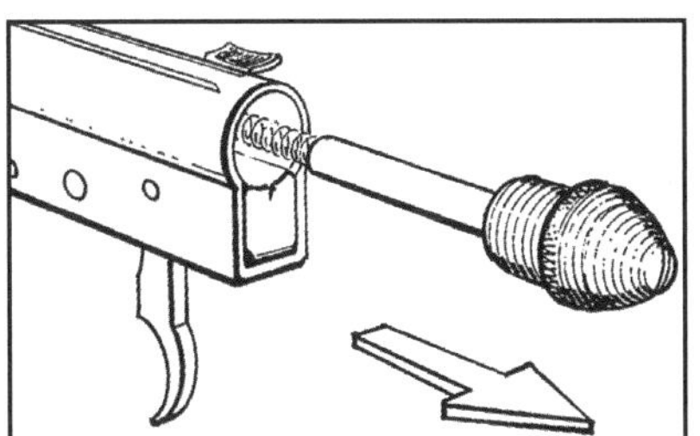

2 Loosen deflector screw (14), and remove deflector (13). Unscrew receiver plug (32) at rear of receiver (30), and remove plug along with action spring (1), action-spring bushing (2), action-spring guide (3), mainspring (24), and mainspring plunger (25).

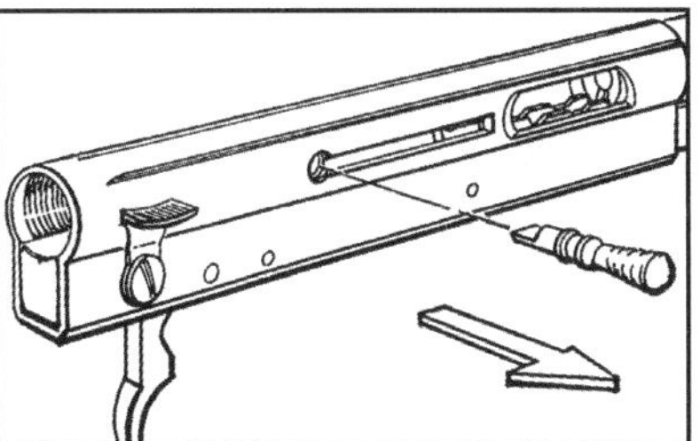

3 Pull bolt handle (6) back until handle aligns with semicircular cut at rear of handle slot in receiver. Pull handle outward and remove from rifle.

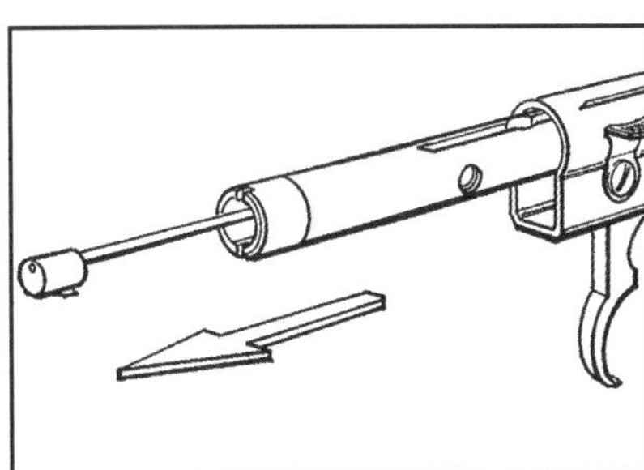

4 Slide bolt (5) from rear of receiver. Remove firing-pin assembly (18) from bolt. Pull trigger when replacing bolt.

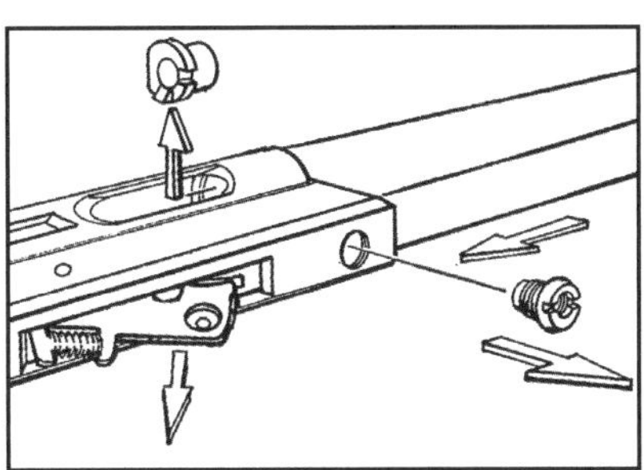

5 Push cartridge stop (12) and carrier (9) to lower position in receiver. Unscrew takedown-screw bushing (46), and remove from receiver. Then, push loosened receiver-insert assembly (31) and attached outer magazine tube (29) rearward into receiver. Recoiling chamber (36) can then be disassembled from breech end of barrel and removed through ejection port of receiver.

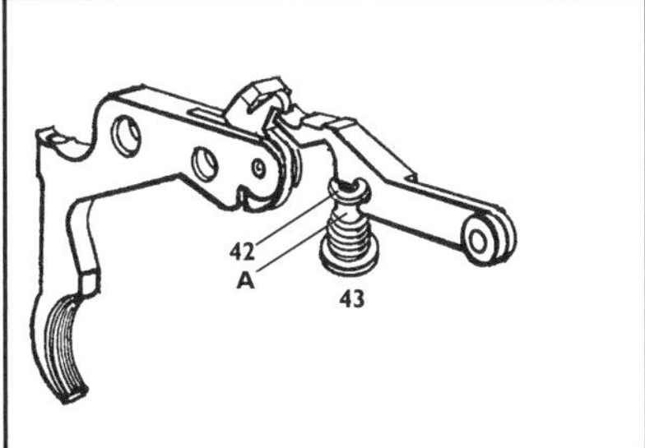

6 Sear-spring case (43) should not be removed except for replacement of parts. If removed, make sure engagement of sear assembly (40) with trigger assembly (47) is as shown. Also, be sure sear-spring case engages sear notch at "A," and sear spring (42) in case exerts pressure against sear. Do not cross-thread sear-spring case in receiver.

REMINGTON MODEL 552 RIFLE

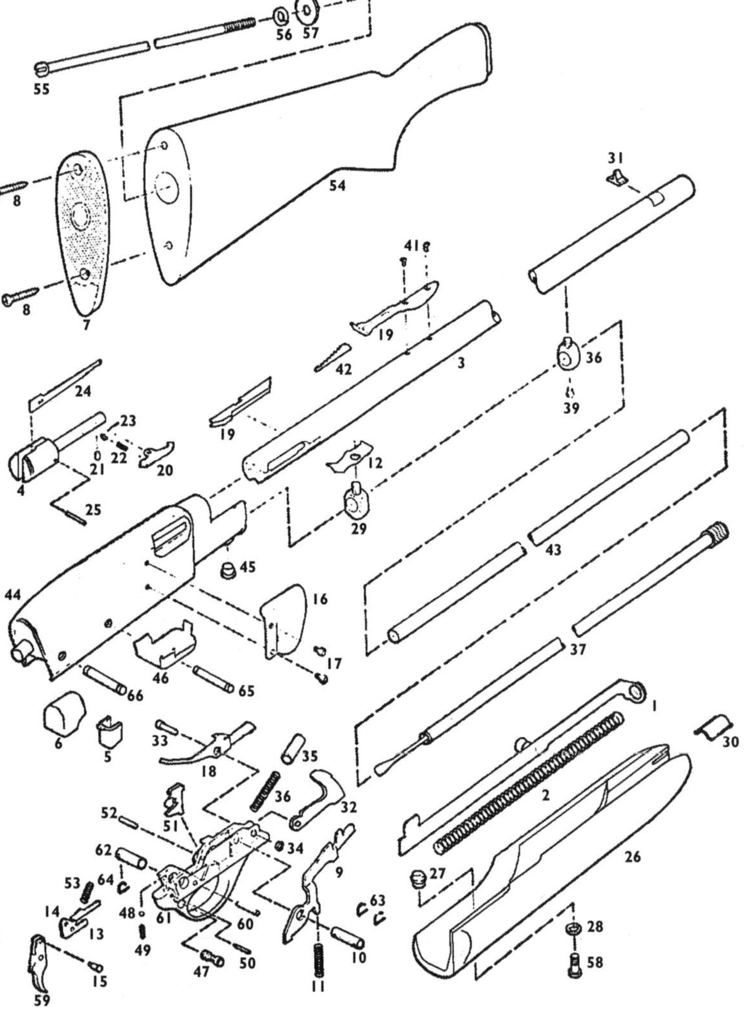

PARTS LEGEND

1. Action-bar assembly
2. Action spring
3. Barrel
4. Bolt
5. Bolt buffer
6. Buffer pad
7. Buttplate
8. Buttplate screws (2)
9. Carrier
10. Carrier-pivot tube
11. Carrier spring
12. Cartridge ramp
13. Connector, right
14. Connector, left
15. Connector pin
16. Deflector
17. Deflector screws (2)
18. Disconnector
19. Ejector
20. Extractor
21. Extractor pin
22. Extractor spring
23. Extractor-spring seat
24. Firing pin
25. Firing-pin retaining pin
26. Fore-end
27. Fore-end escutcheon
28. Fore-end escutcheon nut
29. Fore-end hanger
30. Fore -end support
31. Front sight
32. Hammer
33. Hammer pin
34. Hammer-pin washer
35. Hammer plunger
36. Hammer spring
37. Inner-magazine tube assembly
38. Magazine ring
39. Magazine screw
40. Open sight leaf (not shown)
41. Open sight screws (2)
42. Open sight step
43. Outer magazine tube
44. Receiver
45. Receiver bushing
46. Receiver cover
47. Safety
48. Safety-detent ball
49. Safety spring
50. Safety-spring retaining pin
51. Sear
52. Sear pin
53. Sear spring
54. Stock
55. Stock bolt
56. Stock-bolt lock washer
57. Stock-bolt washer
58. Takedown screw
59. Trigger
60. Trigger pin
61. Trigger plate
62. Trigger-plate pin bushing, rear
63. Trigger-plate pin detent spring, front (2)
64. Trigger-plate pin detent spring, rear
65. Trigger-plate pin, front
66. Trigger-plate pin, rear

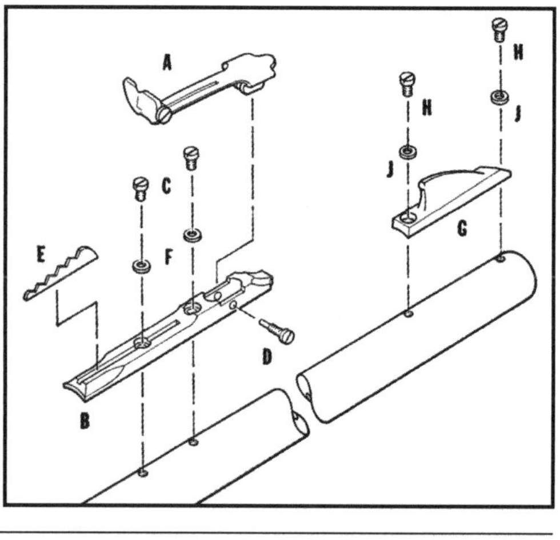

BDL GRADE SIGHTS PARTS LEGEND

A. Rear-sight assembly
B. Rear-sight base
C. Rear-sight base screw (2)
D. Rear-sight screw
E. Rear-sight step
F. Rear-sight washer (2)
G. Front sight
H. Front-sight screw (2)
J. Front-sight washer (2)

The Remington Model 552 Speedmaster .22 rimfire semi-automatic rifle was introduced in 1957. A blowback-operated autoloader designed for informal target shooting and small game hunting, it fires .22 Short, Long, and Long Rifle regular and high-velocity cartridges interchangeably. The 552 bolt is sufficiently light to permit functioning with low-power cartridges, and a buffer in the rear of the receiver cushions the bolt when high-power rounds are fired.

The Model 552 follows the "family of guns" concept in which several basic parts of one gun are interchangeable with those of other guns in the same family. This facilitates manufacture, and reduces material and machine requirements.

Made of black-finished lightweight alloy, the receiver is rounded on the upper rear and has dovetail grooves along its top for a clamp-on optical sight mount. The rifle has a metal bead front sight and adjustable U-notch open rear sight. The trigger plate is also black-finished lightweight alloy. The safety is a cross-bolt type. Fitted to the underside of the 23-inch, round tapered barrel is a tube magazine with capacity of 20 Short, 17 Long, and 15 Long Rifle cartridges.

In addition to standard grade, the Model 552 is produced in Carbine, BDL Deluxe and Gallery Special versions. The Gallery Special Rifle fires .22 Short cartridges only, and the Carbine version has a 21-inch barrel.

DISASSEMBLY

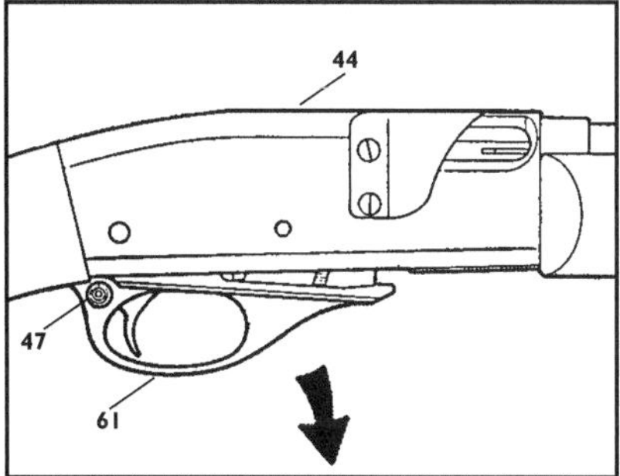

1 Before disassembly, open action and check barrel chamber and magazine to make sure rifle is unloaded. With safety (47) in safe position (red marking on safety will not show), cock action by pulling action bar (1) rearward. Drive out front and rear trigger-plate pins (65 & 66). Grasp trigger plate (61) and pull trigger-plate assembly from receiver (44).

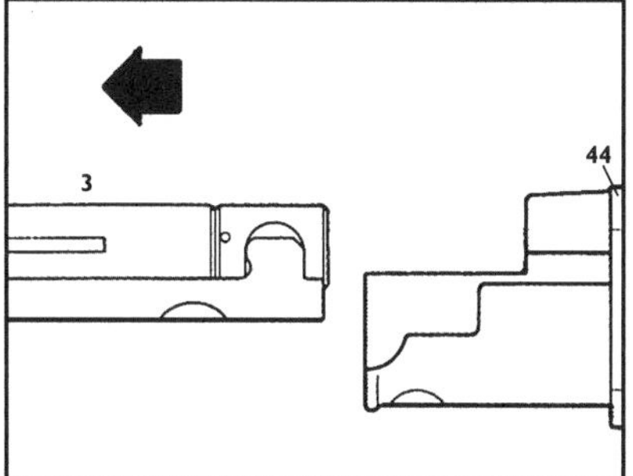

2 Unlock and remove inner-magazine tube assembly (37). Loosen take-down screw (58), lift rear of fore-end (26) away from barrel (3) slightly, and slide forward to clear front of receiver. Grasp fore-end and barrel firmly, and pull complete bolt, barrel, and fore-end group from receiver.

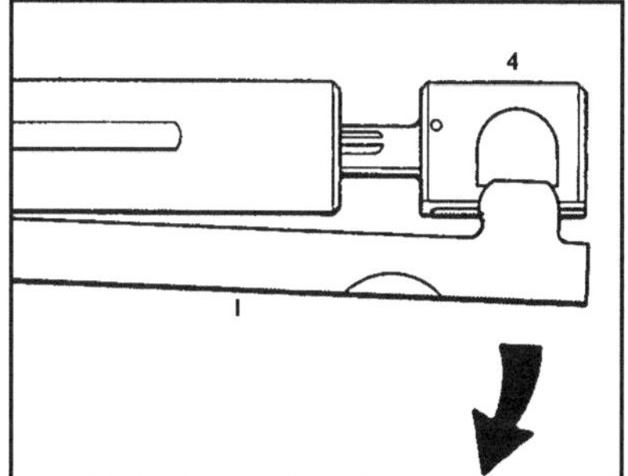

3 Disengage lug of action-bar assembly from slot in bolt (4). Ease action-bar assembly forward to relieve tension of action spring (2), and remove bolt assembly from barrel. This is sufficient disassembly for normal cleaning.

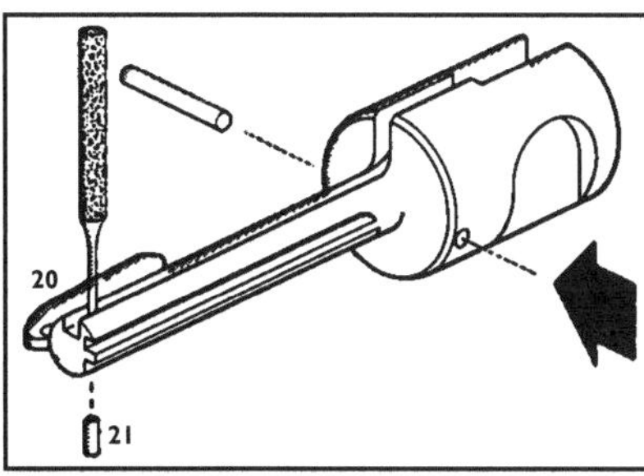

4 For further disassembly, drive firing pin retaining pin (25) from left to right out of bolt and remove firing pin (24). Drive extractor pin (21) from bolt, and remove extractor (20), extractor spring (22), and extractor-spring seat (23). Insert small flat tool into ejection slot at breech end of barrel. Push front end of ejector (19) outward, and remove from barrel.

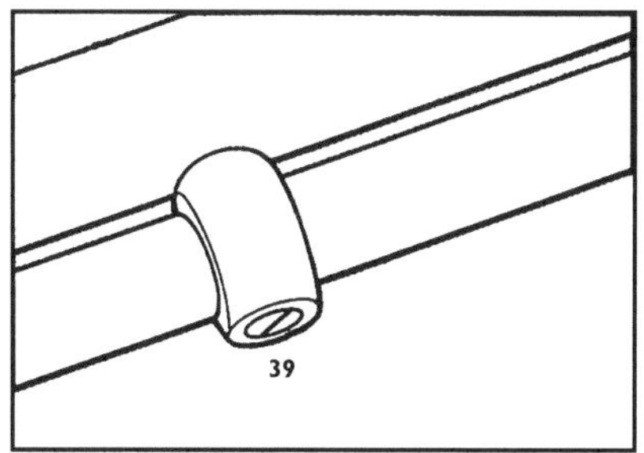

5 Unscrew magazine screw (39) from magazine ring (38), and remove outer magazine tube (43), fore-end, action-bar assembly, and action spring. Unscrew and remove fore-end hanger (29) and cartridge ramp (12) from barrel. Unscrew and remove buttplate screws (8) and buttplate (7). Reach into hole in rear of stock with a Tong-bladed screwdriver, and unscrew stock bolt (55). Remove stock bolt, stock-bolt washer (57), stock-bolt lock washer (56), and stock (54). Reassemble rifle in reverse. Bent rear tail of disconnector (18) must be under connector, left (14).

REMINGTON MODEL 572 RIFLE

PARTS LEGEND

1. Receiver
2. Barrel
3. Stock
4. Fore-end
5. Fore-end support
6. Barrel lock screw
7. Cartridge ramp
8. Fore-end hanger
9. Receiver bushing
10. Receiver cover
11. Trigger plate pin, front
12. Trigger plate pin, rear
13. Hammer plunger
14. Hammer spring
15. Trigger plate
16. Safety
17. Safety spring retaining pin
18. Safety plunger
19. Safety spring
20. Trigger
21. Trigger pin
22. Connector, left
23. Connector, right
24. Connector pin
25. Action bar lock
26. Carrier
27. Carrier spring
28. Carrier pivot tube
29. Trigger plate pin detent spring, front
30. Hammer
31. Sear
32. Sear pin
33. Sear spring
34. Locking bar
35. Locking bar spring
36. Locking bar retaining screw
37. Hammer pin
38. Magazine follower
39. Magazine follower spring
40. Inner magazine tube
41. Magazine plug
42. Outer magazine tube
43. Magazine ring
44. Magazine screw
45. Front sight
46. Action bar
47. Fore-end screw
48. Fore-end nut
49. Fore-end escutcheon
50. Bolt
51. Firing pin
52. Extractor, right
53. Extractor, left
54. Extractor pin
55. Extractor spring
56. Firing pin retaining pin
57. Open sight leaf
58. Rear sight screw (2)
59. Rear sight step
60. Trigger plate pin bushing, rear
61. Trigger plate pin detent spring, rear
62. Buttplate screw (2)
63. Buttplate
64. Stock bolt
65. Stock bolt lock washer (2)
66. Stock bolt washer
67. Ejector

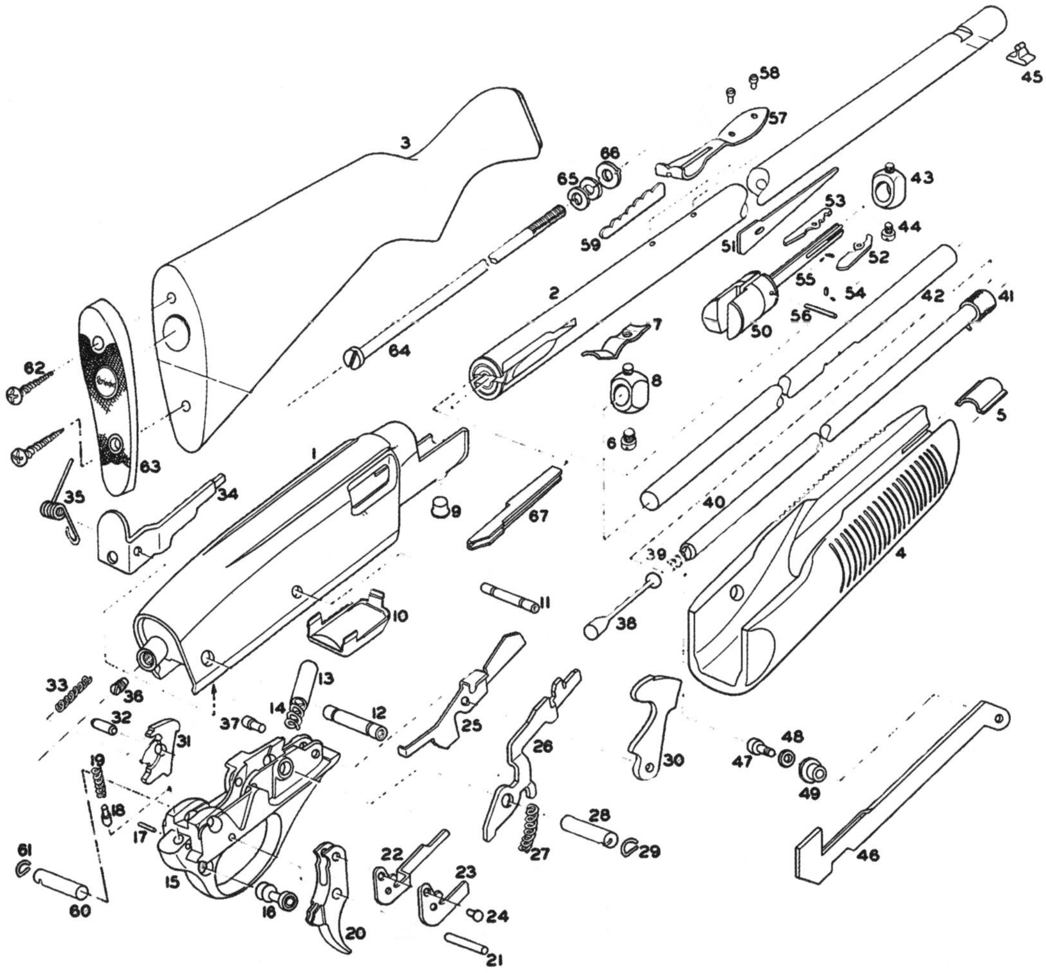

REMINGTON

The Remington Model 572 was introduced in early 1955 to meet the demand for a full size slide-action rifle chambered for .22 rimfire cartridge. An interesting feature of the rifle is its aluminum alloy receiver, grooved for tip-off scope mounts. Also, the 572 functions with .22 Short, Long or Long Rifle cartridges interchangeably without adjustment. Magazine capacities are 20, 17 and 15 cartridges, respectively. The 572 can be single-loaded by simply opening the breech and dropping a cartridge into the ejection port. Closing the action chambers the cartridge.

Initially, the 572 was offered with a steel barrel and walnut buttstock and fore-end. Smoothbore guns, a short, 21-inch barrel version and variants with anodized receivers in "Buckskin Tan," "Crow Wing Black" and "Teal Wing Blue." The current model is the 572BDL Deluxe.

DISASSEMBLY

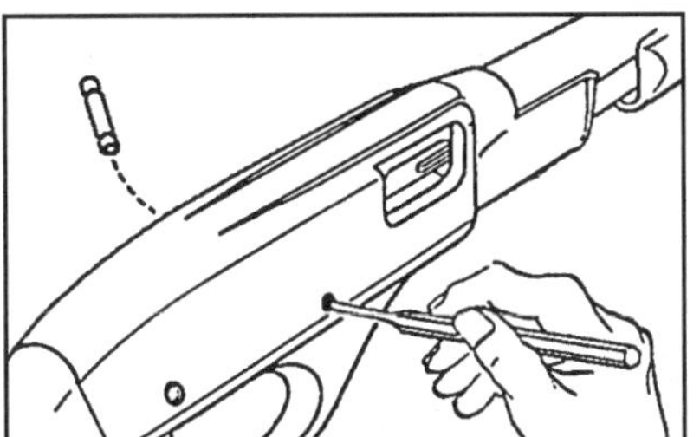

1 To disassemble rifle, drift out front and rear trigger plate pins (11 & 12) from either side of receiver (1). Use small punch. These pins are conically counterbored for this purpose. Lift out trigger plate (15) assembly.

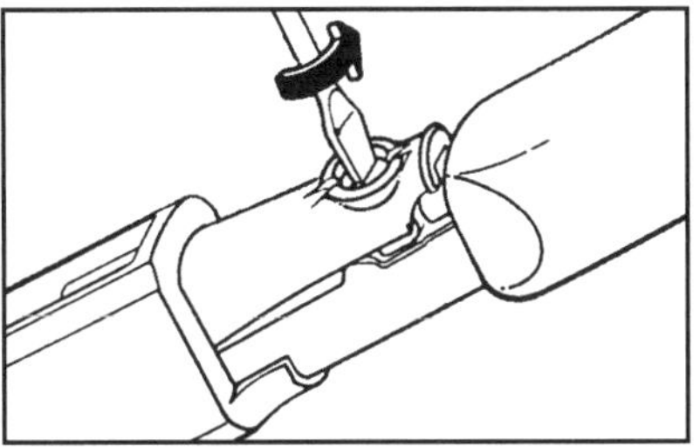

2 Pull fore-end (4) forward and turn rifle over. Using proper-size screwdriver, carefully remove barrel lock screw (6). CAUTION: Do not disturb receiver bushing (9) or the manner in which it is staked into receiver. Grasp fore-end assembly and barrel firmly and pull barrel and bolt assembly forward together.

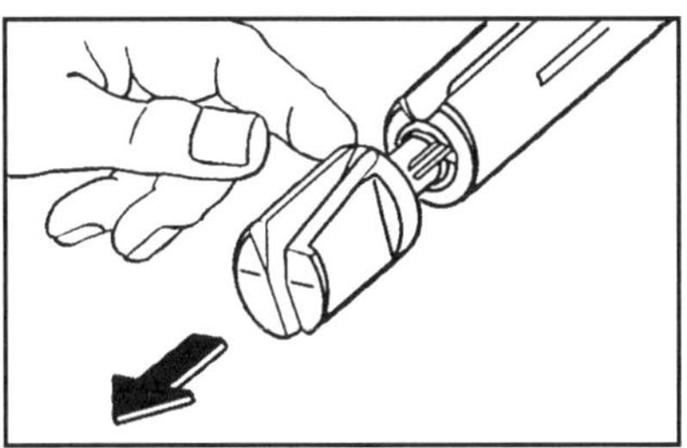

3 To remove bolt (50) from barrel, lift action bar (46) lug away from bolt and slide bolt from barrel.

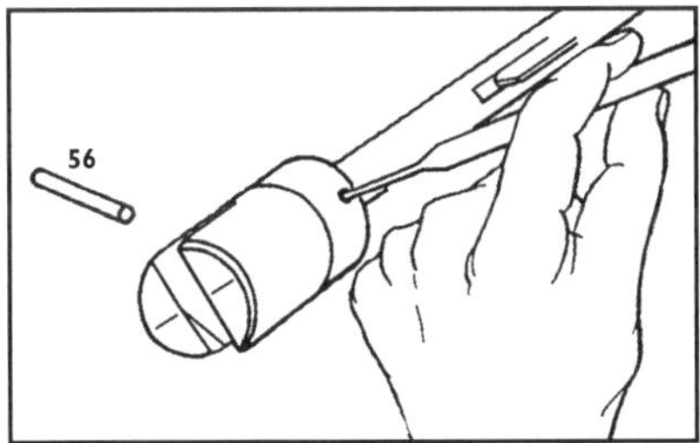

4 To remove firing pin (51), drift out firing pin retaining pin (56) with fine flat-nosed punch. Lift firing pin from bolt.

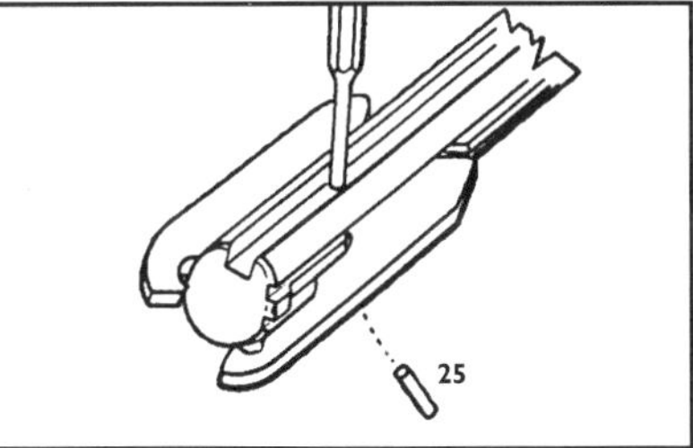

5 To remove extractors (52 & 53), drift out extractor pin (54) with fine punch. Extractors and extractor spring (55) can then be lifted away from bolt.

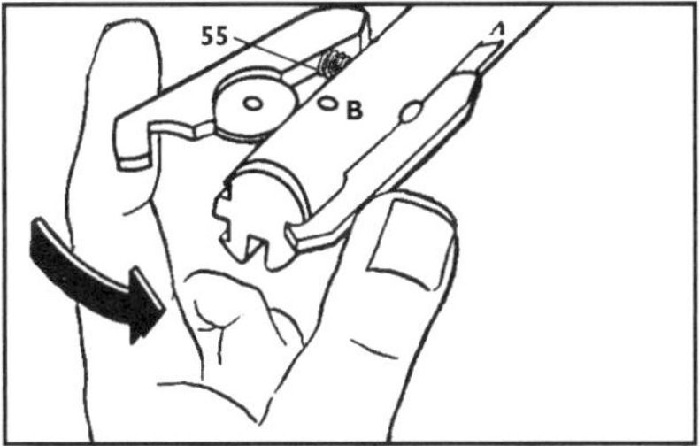

6 To reassemble extractors, insert right extractor (52) into bolt slot. CAUTION: Extractors must be reassembled to bolt with firing pin removed. Insert extractor pin (54) into pin hole (B) from bottom side of bolt so that it rests just inside corresponding extractor hole. Replace extractor spring, press in left extractor (53) and reset extractor pin through balance of the bolt.

REMINGTON MODEL 580 RIFLE

PARTS LEGEND

1. Barrel
2. Barrel assembly pin (2)
3. Bolt assembly pin
4. Bolt body assembly
5. Bolt head
6. Bolt plug
7. Bolt stop
8. Bolt stop spring
9. Cocking piece
10. Ejector
11. Elevation screw
12. Extractor, left
13. Extractor, right
14. Extractor spring
15. Firing pin
16. Floorplate
17. Floorplate screw
18. Front sight
19. Housing
20. Housing pin
21. Housing lock screw
22. Loading platform
23. Mainspring
24. Rear sight base
25. Rear sight eyepiece
26. Rear sight leaf
27. Rear sight screw
28. Receiver
29. Safety
30. Safety pivot pin
31. Safety pivot pin retaining washer
32. Safety plunger
33. Safety plunger spring
34. Safety retaining screw
35. Sear
36. Sear pin (u.) and Trigger pin (2)
37. Stock (not shown)
38. Striker assembly
39. Striker
40. Striker cross pin
41. Striker washer
42. Takedown screw
43. Takedown screw escutcheon
44. Trigger
45. Trigger guard
46. Trigger guard screw
47. Trigger spring

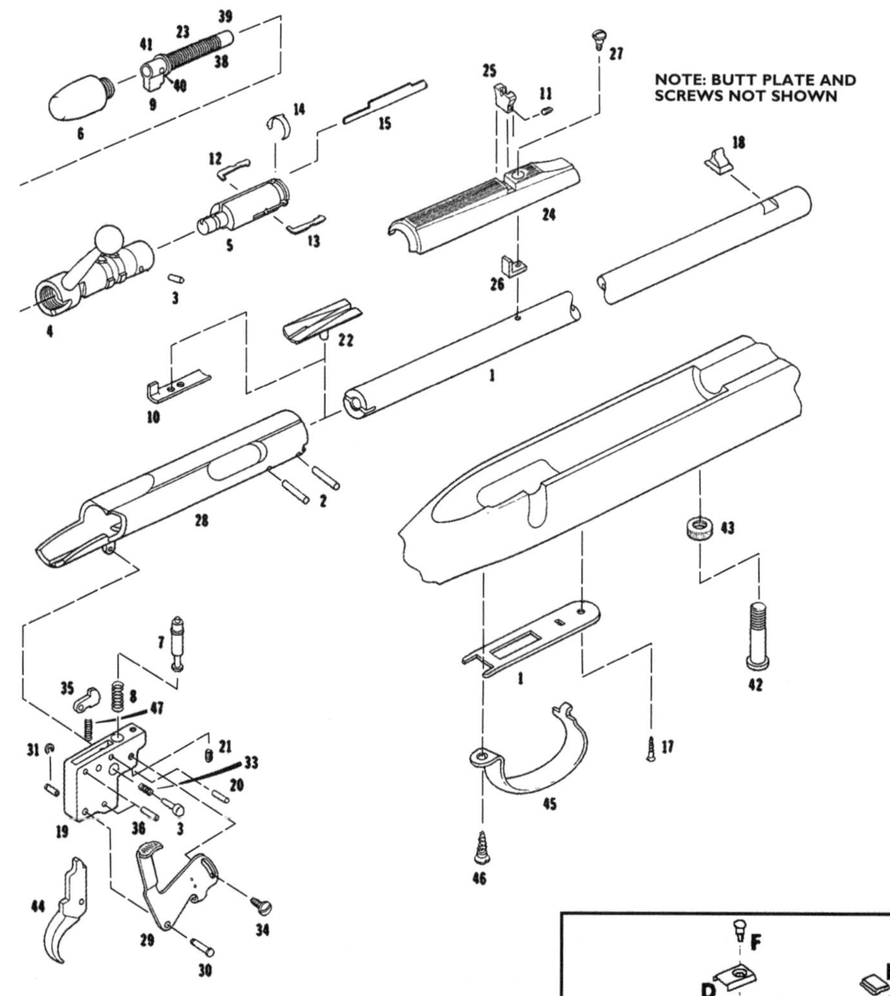

580 SMOOTH BORE PARTS LEGEND

A. Barrel
B. Front sight
C. Rear sight base
D. Rear sight base cover
E. Rear sight base locater
F. Rear sight base screw

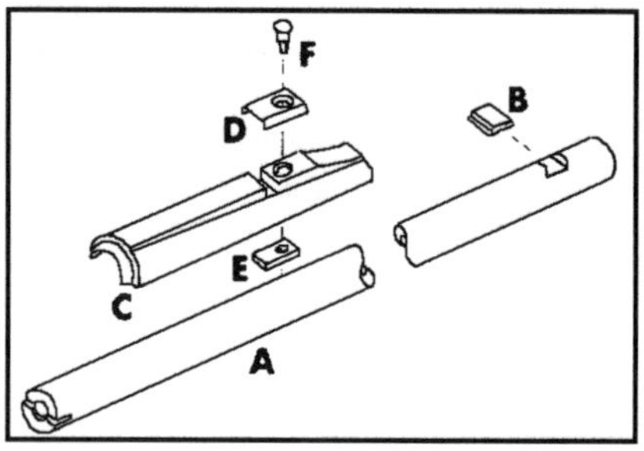

In 1967 Remington introduced a new "family" of .22 caliber rimfire bolt-action guns. This group consisted of three rifles and a single-shot smoothbore shotgun. The rifles were the Model 580 single-shot, the Model 581 with a detachable box magazine and the Model 582 with an under-barrel tube magazine. The rifles accepted .22 Long Rifle, Long, or Short cartridges. Except for its sights and a smoothbore barrel chambered for .22 shot cartridges, the Model 580 shotgun is identical to the Model 580 rifle. The rifles in this series were designed for small game or plinking, whereas the Model 580 Smooth Bore is suitable for small pests.

The bolt action used in this "family" of guns has a rear locking bolt with six locking lugs and a non-rotating bolt head. Except for their cartridge feeding systems, the Models 581 and 582 are mechanically identical to the single-shot Model 580 rifle and shotgun. The 580 was discontinued in 1978, the 581 and 582 in 1983.

DISASSEMBLY

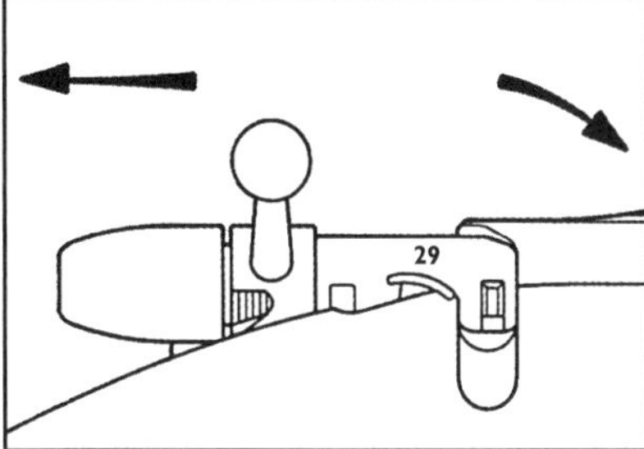

1 To disassemble, lift bolt handle and pull bolt rearward to bolt stop. Push safety (29) fully forward (past "fire" position) and remove bolt from receiver.

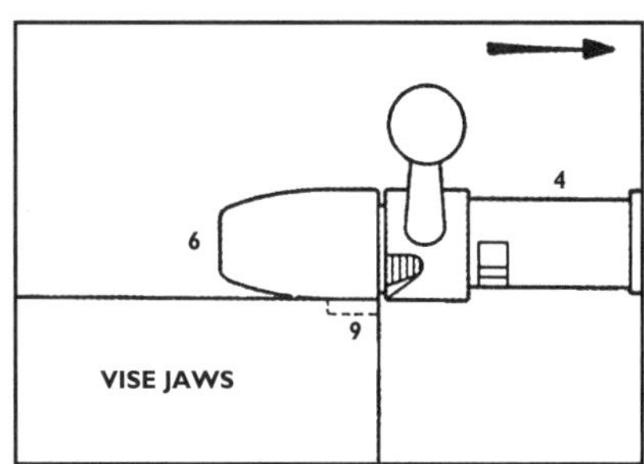

2 Clamp cocking piece (9) in vise jaws and move bolt assembly (4) forward as far as possible. Unscrew and remove bolt from bolt plug (6) and remove striker assembly (38). Pry ends of extractor spring (14) up and away from bolt head (5). Slide extractors (12 & 13) and firing pin (15) out of bolt head.

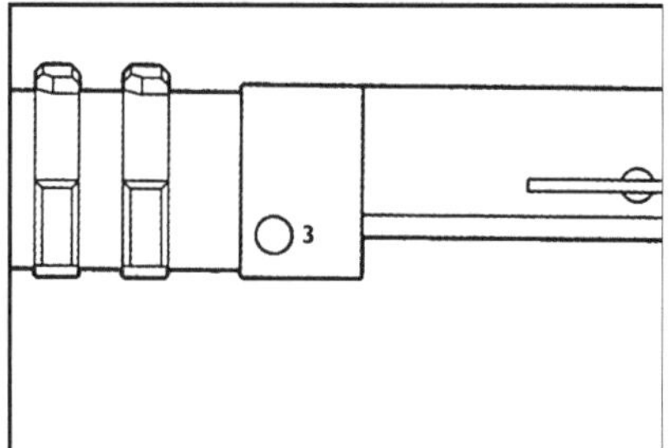

3 Drive out bolt assembly pin (3) and remove bolt head. Special factory processes are used to make up the striker assembly. Disassembly of this unit is not recommended. Unscrew take-down screw (42) and remove stock assembly (37). Unscrew rear sight screw (27) and remove rear sight assembly from barrel. Remove elevation screw (11) and lift eyepiece (25) from rear sight leaf (26). Remove rear sight leaf from rear sight base (24).

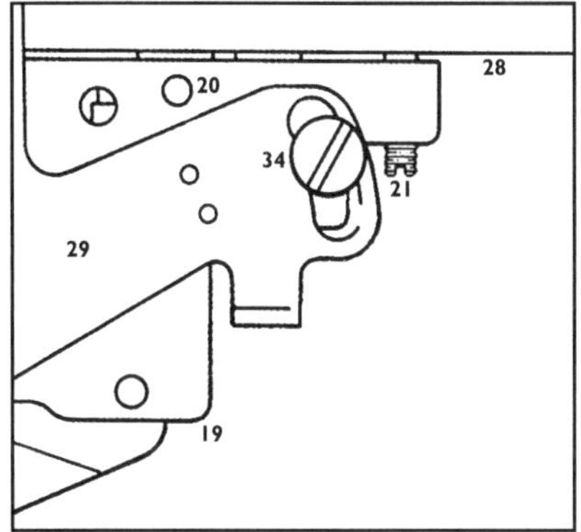

4 Back off housing lock screw (21) one complete turn. Drive out housing pin (20) and remove entire housing assembly from receiver (28). Lift sear and remove trigger spring (47) from housing (19). Push safety pivot pin retaining washer (31) from end of safety pivot pin and remove pin. Carefully unscrew and remove safety retaining screw (34) and safety (29). Safety plunger (32) is under spring load beneath safety. Take care when removing safety that plunger and spring do not spring free. Lift safety plunger and safety plunger spring (33) from housing. Bolt stop (7) and bolt stop spring (8) may then be removed. Remaining components comprise the trigger housing sub-assembly. This unit is factory assembled by precision equipment. Disassembly of this sub-assembly is seldom necessary and is not recommended.

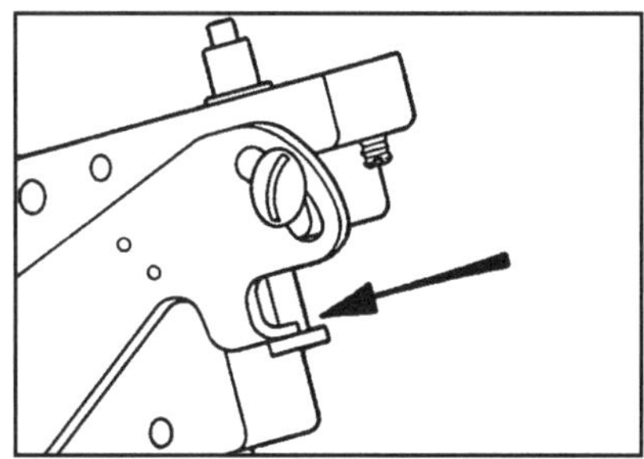

5 Reassemble in reverse order. Bent tab on bottom of safety must fit over flange on bottom of bolt stop (arrow). Adjust housing lock screw until assembly is snug. Bolt stop must work freely in receiver when activated by safety. Make sure that small tab on top of extractor spring faces forward and into firing pin slot on top of bolt head.

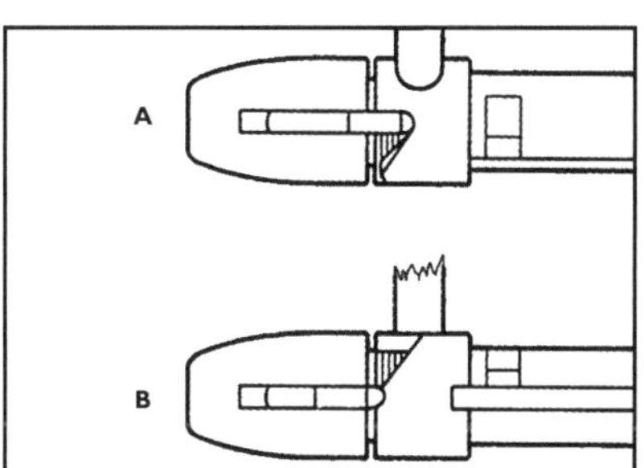

6 Bolt must be cocked to replace it in receiver. Should bolt become uncocked (A), cocking piece will snap forward into cocking cam at rear of bolt. To cock bolt, clamp cocking piece in vise jaws and rotate bolt handle until cocking piece snaps into small detent on rear edge of bolt (B).

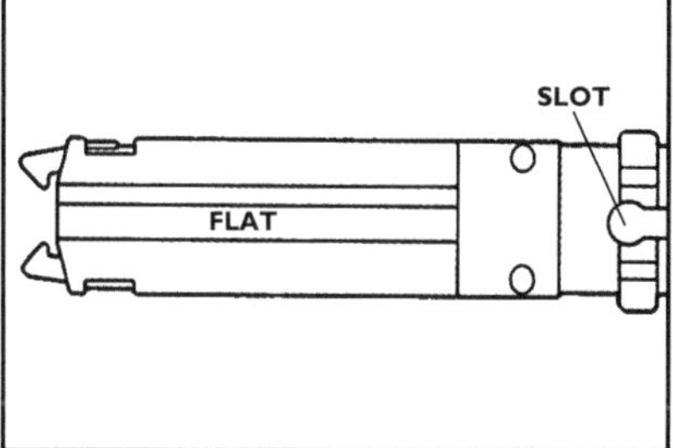

7 To replace bolt assembly in receiver, align bolt stop slot on bolt body with rib on bottom of bolt head. While holding safety in full forward position, and with firing pin on top of bolt in 12 o'clock position, insert and push bolt forward into receiver. Release safety and close bolt.

REMINGTON MODELS 591 & 592

REMINGTON MODEL 591 RIFLE

REMINGTON MODEL 592 RIFLE

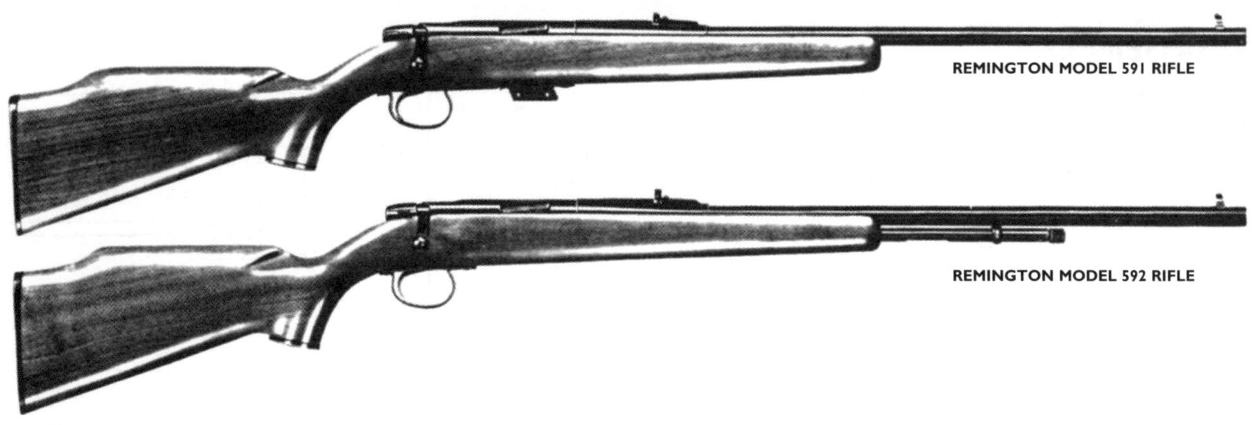

PARTS LEGEND

1. Barrel (592)
2. Barrel assembly pin (2)
3. Barrel bracket (592)
4. Bolt assembly pin
5. Bolt body assembly
6. Bolt head
7. Bolt plug
8. Bolt stop
9. Bolt stop spring
10. Buttplate
11. Buttplate screw (2)
12. Carrier (592)
13. Carrier pin (592)
14. Carrier spring (592)
15. Cartridge feed insert
16. Cartridge feed insert pin
17. Cocking piece
18. Ejector
19. Ejector cover
20. Ejector release
21. Ejector rivet
22. Ejector spring
23. Ejector spring guide
24. Elevation screw
25. Extractor
26. Firing pin
27. Firing pin retaining pin
28. Floor plate (592)
29. Floor plate screw (592)
30. Front sight
31. Grip cap
32. Grip cap screw
33. Housing
34. Housing lock screw
35. Housing pin (592)
36. Inner magazine tube pin (592)
37. Latch
38. Magazine assembly (591)
39. Magazine follower (592)
40. Magazine guide (591)
41. Magazine latch (591)
42. Magazine latch screw (591)
43. Magazine pin (592)
44. Magazine plate (591)
45. Magazine plate screw (591)
46. Magazine plug (592)
47. Magazine ring (592)
48. Magazine shoe (591)
49. Magazine spring (592)
50. Mainspring
51. Outer magazine tube (592)
52. Rear sight base
53. Rear sight eyepiece
54. Rear sight leaf
55. Rear sight rib
56. Rear sight screw (2)
57. Receiver assembly
58. Receiver cover
59. Receiver cover screw (4)
60. Safety
61. Safety pivot pin
62. Safety pivot pin retaining washer
63. Safety plunger
64. Safety plunger spring
65. Safety retaining screw
66. Sear
67. Sear pin
68. Stock
69. Striker
70. Striker cross pin
71. Striker washer
72. Takedown screw (592)
73. Takedown screw (591)
74. Takedown screw escutcheon (591)
75. Trigger
76. Trigger guard
77. Trigger guard screw
78. Trigger pin
79. Trigger spring
80. Windage screw

NOTE: Model number following name of part indicates part is for that model only. Parts 29 and 45 are alike except in name.

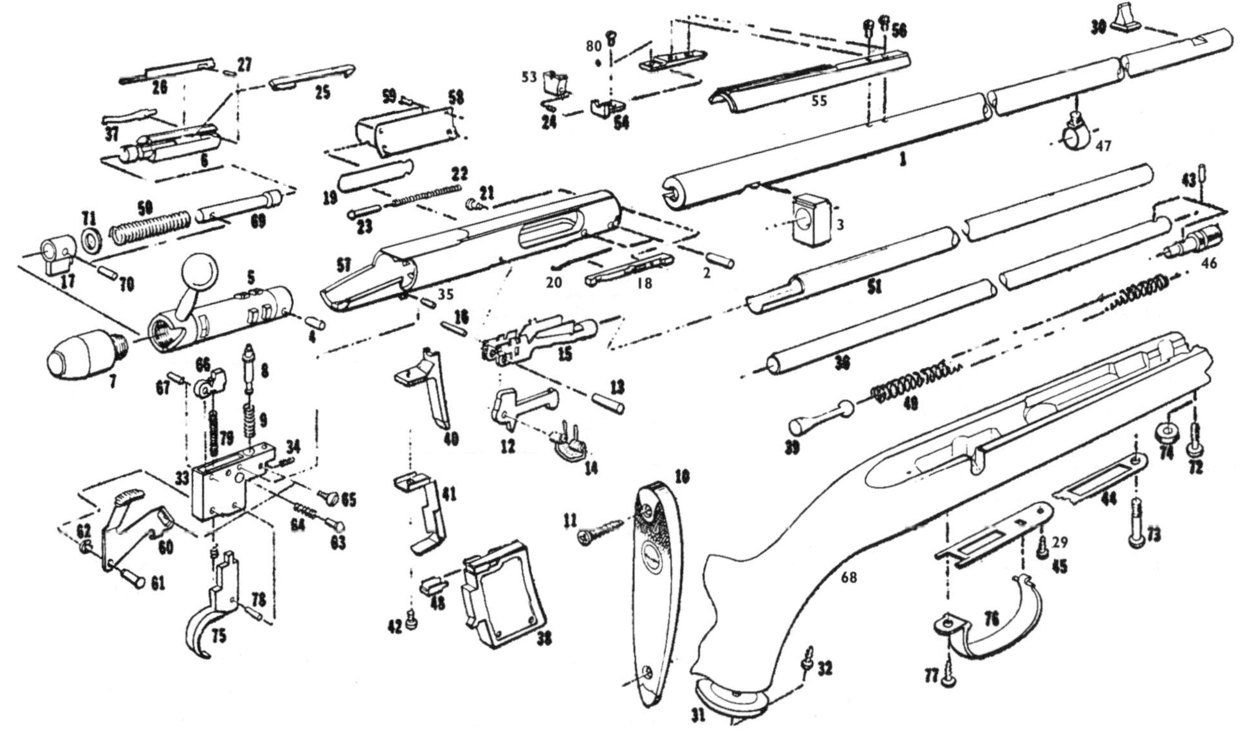

In 1959, Winchester-Western introduced the .22 WMR (Winchester Magnum Rimfire) cartridge. Designed for hunting small game and varmints, this round offered much higher ballistic performance than other .22 rimfire cartridges.

Remington's entry in this field was the 5 mm. Remington Rim Fire Magnum cartridge, introduced in 1970. It featured a bottleneck case and a 38-grain bullet (.2045-inch), slightly smaller than .22 caliber. Fired in a 24-inch barrel, its muzzle velocity is 2100 f.p.s., 100 f.p.s. faster than the .22 WMR.

Remington introduced two bolt-action repeating rifles chambered for the 5 mm., the Model 591 with detachable, four-round box magazine, and the Model 592 with a 10-round, tube magazine.

These rifles feaured an unusual extractor and ejector system. The extractor has a forward projecting hook which rests on a barrel ramp. As the bolt is opened, the spring-actuated ejector in the left side of the receiver is moved rearward by a latch on the bolt head. This starts extraction of the case, and the extractor then engages the rim to complete extraction.

The rifles are fitted with an adjustable, open rear sight and bead front sight. The top of the receiver is grooved for installation of clamp-on telescope sight mounts.

Both models have hardwood stocks with pistol grips and a Monte Carlo comb. The rifles were discontinued in 1974 and the ammunition is no longer available.

DISASSEMBLY

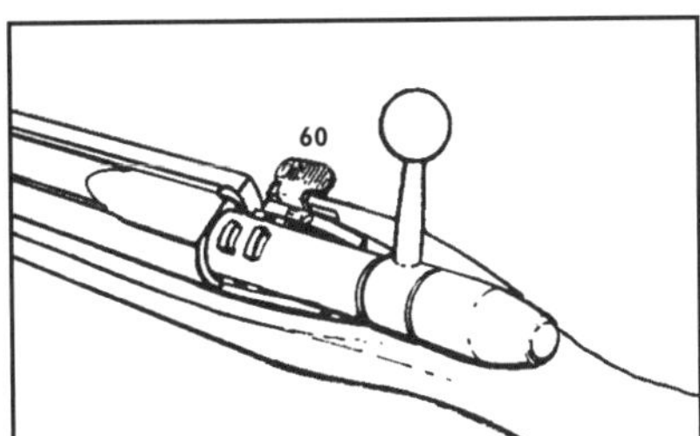

1 Prior to disassembly, unload rifle. Remove magazine assembly (38) from Model 591, and inner magazine tube (36) from Model 592. Tilt muzzle of Model 592 downward to unload tubular magazine. Replace inner magazine tube, and open and close action several times to remove any cartridges remaining in rifle. Then, remove inner magazine tube. Open bolt, and pull rearward to bolt stop (8). Push safety (60) completely forward, and remove bolt assembly from rifle.

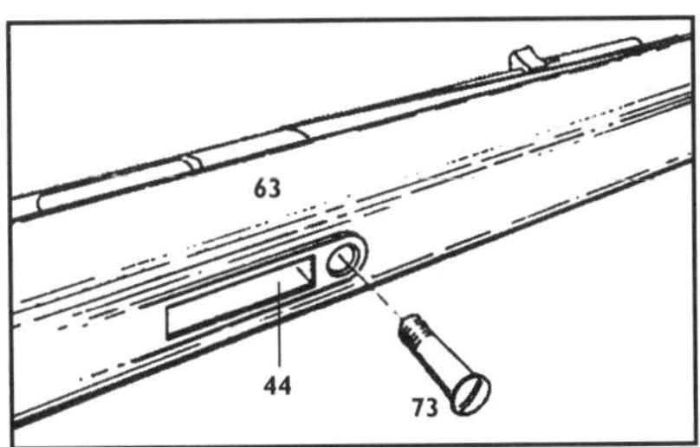

2 Unscrew takedown screw (73 for Model 591; 72 for Model 592), and remove stock (68) from barrel and action.

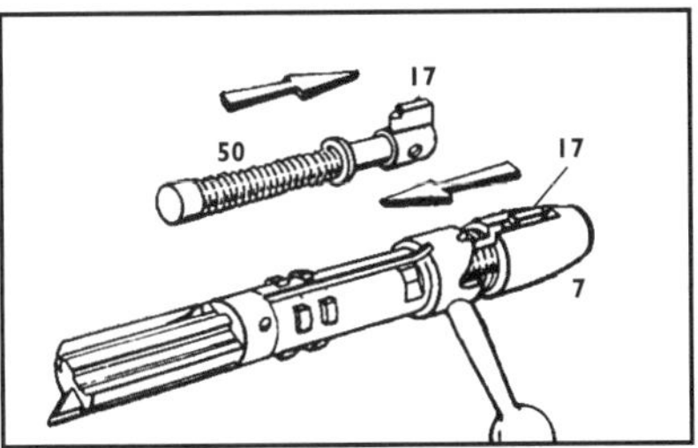

3 Use a drift punch and hammer to drive out bolt assembly pin (4), and separate bolt head (6) from bolt body assembly (5). Clamp a ¼-inch drift punch in a vise so that end of punch projects 1½-inch beyond vise jaws. Position front of striker (69) against punch, and push bolt body toward vise to move cocking piece (17) out of engagement with notch in bolt body. Then, unscrew and remove bolt plug (7) and striker assembly as a unit. While holding striker in a padded vise, drive out striker cross pin (70) with a punch, and remove cocking piece, striker washer (71), and mainspring (50). Take care in doing this since cocking piece is under heavy spring pressure.

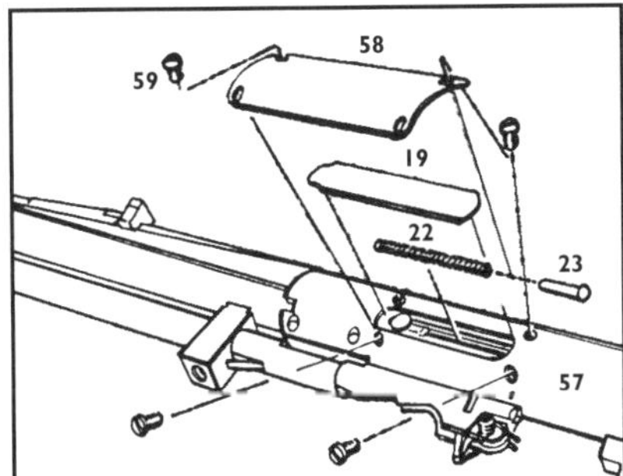

4 Unscrew four receiver cover screws (59), and remove receiver cover (58) from left side of receiver assembly (57). Pry out ejector cover (19), and remove ejector spring (22) and ejector spring guide (23). Reassemble in reverse.

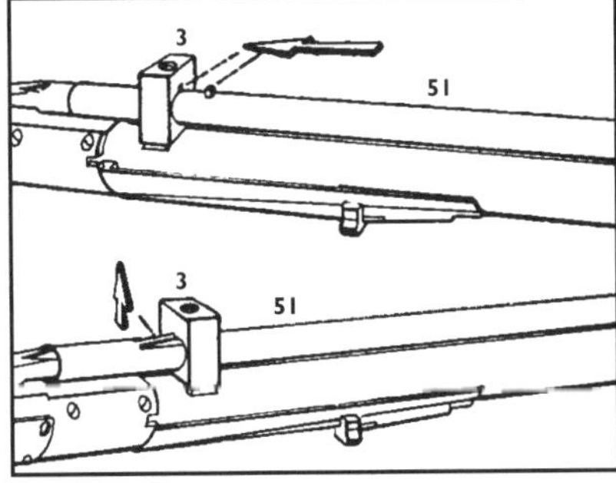

5 During reassembly of Model 592, small stud on outer magazine tube (51) must engage with groove in barrel bracket (3). Bend small tongue on tube so that it engages against rear of bracket and prevents tube from moving forward.

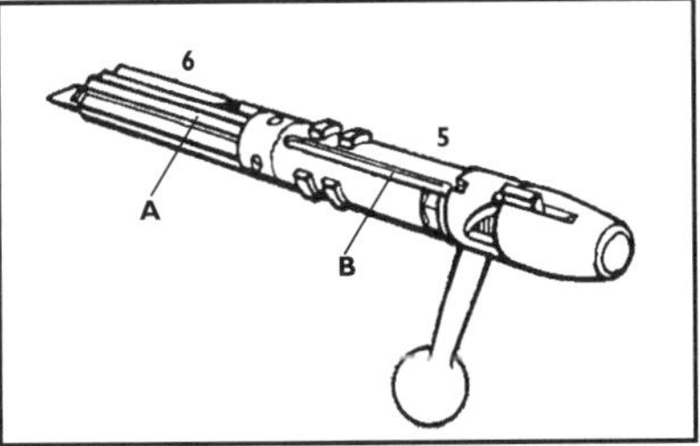

6 Firing pin must be cocked when replacing bolt in receiver. Align rib (A) on bottom of bolt head with groove (B) on bolt body assembly. Start bolt assembly in receiver with handle at two o'clock position, press safety forward and push bolt forward.

REMINGTON MODEL 597 RIFLE

PARTS LEGEND

1. Receiver
2. Trigger housing assembly
3. Barrel assembly
4. Bolt
5. Bolt guide rails (2)
6. Guide rail screws (2)
7. Action springs (2)
8. Magazine box assembly
9. Assembly pin
10. Bolt buffer
11. Pivot pin
12. Ejector
13. Hold-open pin
14. Hold-open
15. Hold-open spring
16. Firing pin
17. Firing pin spring
18. Firing pin retaining pin
19. Extractor spring
20. Extractor plunger
21. Extractor
22. Barrel clamp
23. Barrel clamp screw
24. Receiver plug screws (3)
25. Bolt handle
26. Front sight screw
27. Front sight
28. Bolt assembly
    *Bolt handle spring
    *Bolt spring rivet
29. Stock assembly
30. Butt plate
31. Grip cap
32. Takedown screw, front
33. Takedown screw, rear
36. Rear sight assembly
37. Rear sight aperture
38. Rear sght base
39. Rear sight base screw (2)
40. Rear sight slide
41. Elevation screw
42. Windage screw

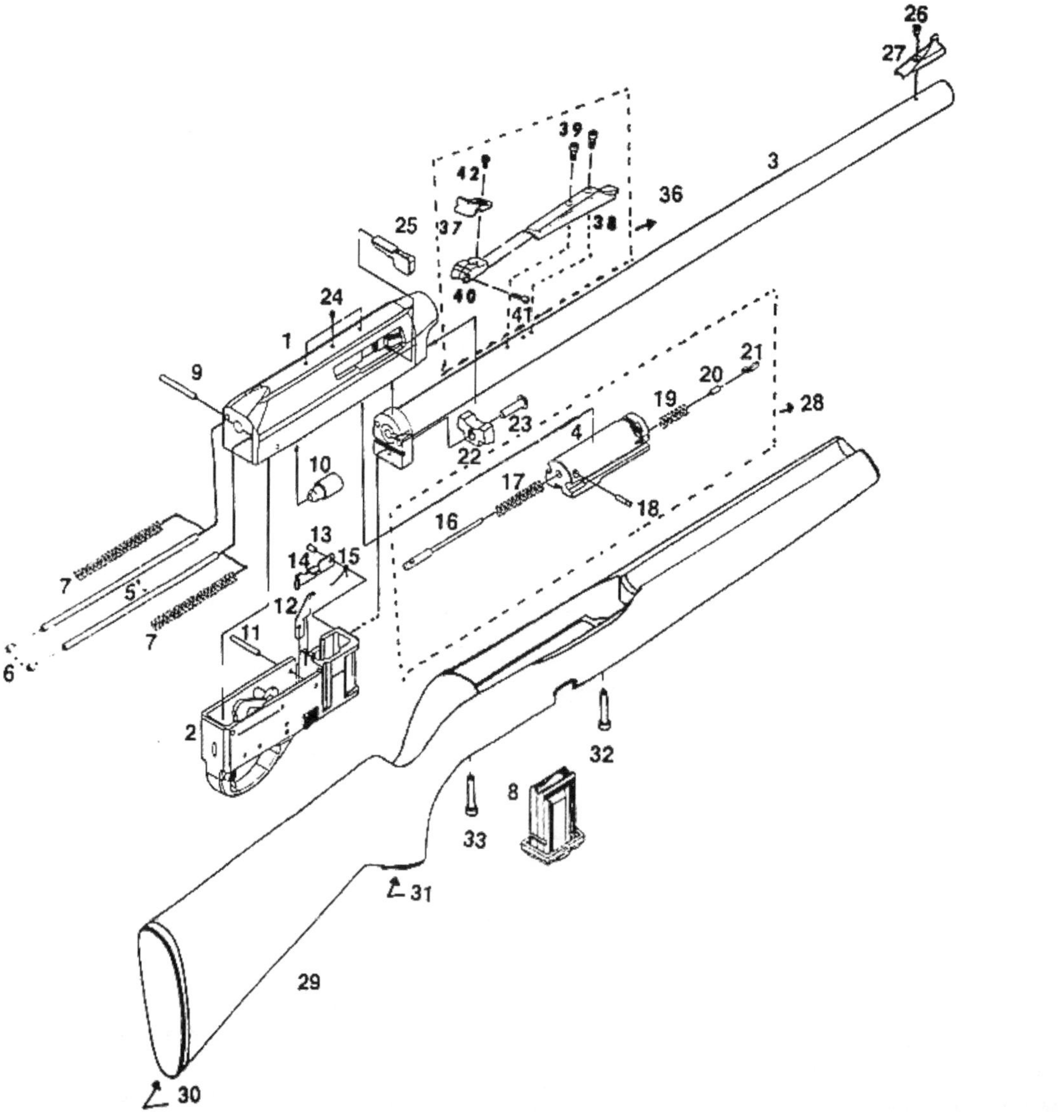

The Remington 597 is a semi-automatic, rimfire rifle chambered for .22 Long Rifle, .22 WMR and .17 HMR. Standard and magnum versions of the 597 have been in production since 1997, and a version chambered for .17 HMR was introduced by Remington in 2003. All 597s are built in Remington's Mayfield, Kentucky factory. The rifle's standard barrel length is 20 inches and a target model is available with a 20 inch bull barrel. It is available in a number of configurations with a choice of synthetic or laminated wood stocks.

The Remington 597 uses a 10-round removable box magazine for models loading .22 LR and an 8-round magazine for magnums. Early production magazines were made of plastic and were subject to fouling from oil, dirt, and unburned propellant, eventually resulting in ammunition feeding problems. To solve the feeding problem, a second generation of magazines was offered in 2000. These were manufactured from cast aluminum alloy with a plastic base cap and follower.

DISASSEMBLY

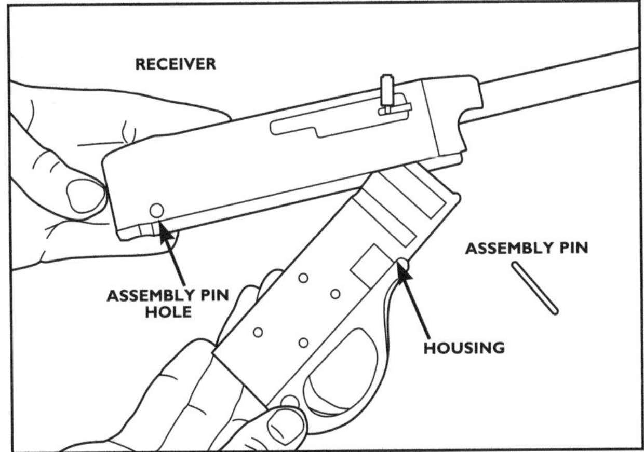

1 NOTE: The action has two (2) major parts, the receiver assembly and the housing assembly. Tap out assembly pin from either side. Rotate the housing downward, pivoting around front of housing, slowly separating the housing from the receiver.

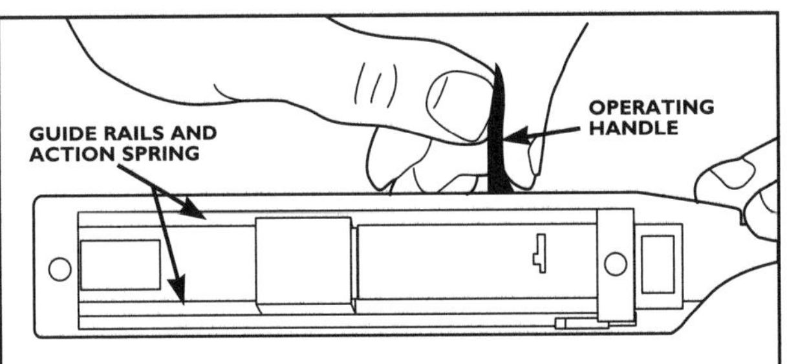

2 Remove two guide rail screws from rear of receiver. Cycle bolt several times until bolt guide rails protrude from rear of receiver. WARNING: Use extreme care when disassembling bolt guide rails as the action springs are under compression. Wear eye protection to avoid serious personal injury.

Pull bolt guide rails out. Care should be taken with guide rail springs. Pull out on operating handle to remove handle from bolt.

Remove bolt from receiver.

REMINGTON MODELS 600 & 660

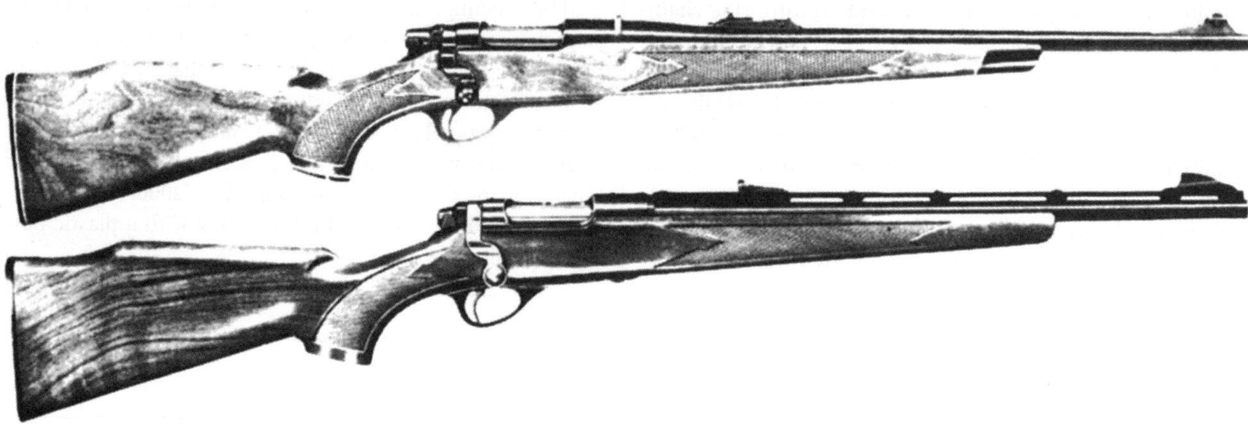

PARTS LEGEND

1. Barrel and receiver assembly
2. Bolt
3. Bolt plug
4. Bolt stop
5. Bolt stop pin
6. Bolt stop spring
7. Ejector
8. Ejector pin
9. Ejector spring
10. Extractor
11. Extractor rivet
12. Firing pin
13. Firing pin assembly
14. Firing pin head
15. Front guard screw
16. Front sight
17. Front sight ramp
18. Front sight ramp screw (2)
19. Magazine
20. Magazine follower
21. Magazine spring
22. Mainspring
23. Rear guard screw
24. Rear sight assembly
25. Rear sight base
26. Rear sight base screw (2)
27. Rear sight screw
28. Rear sight step
29. Rear sight washer (2)
30. Receiver plug screw (5)
31. Safety
32. Safety detent ball
33. Safety detent spring
34. Safety pivot pin
35. Safety snap washer
36. Sear safety cam
37. Sear pin (2)
38. Sear spring
39. Trigger
40. Trigger adjusting screw
41. Trigger adjusting screw, front
42. Trigger connector
43. Trigger guard
44. Trigger housing
45. Trigger pin
46. Trigger spring
47. Trigger stop screw

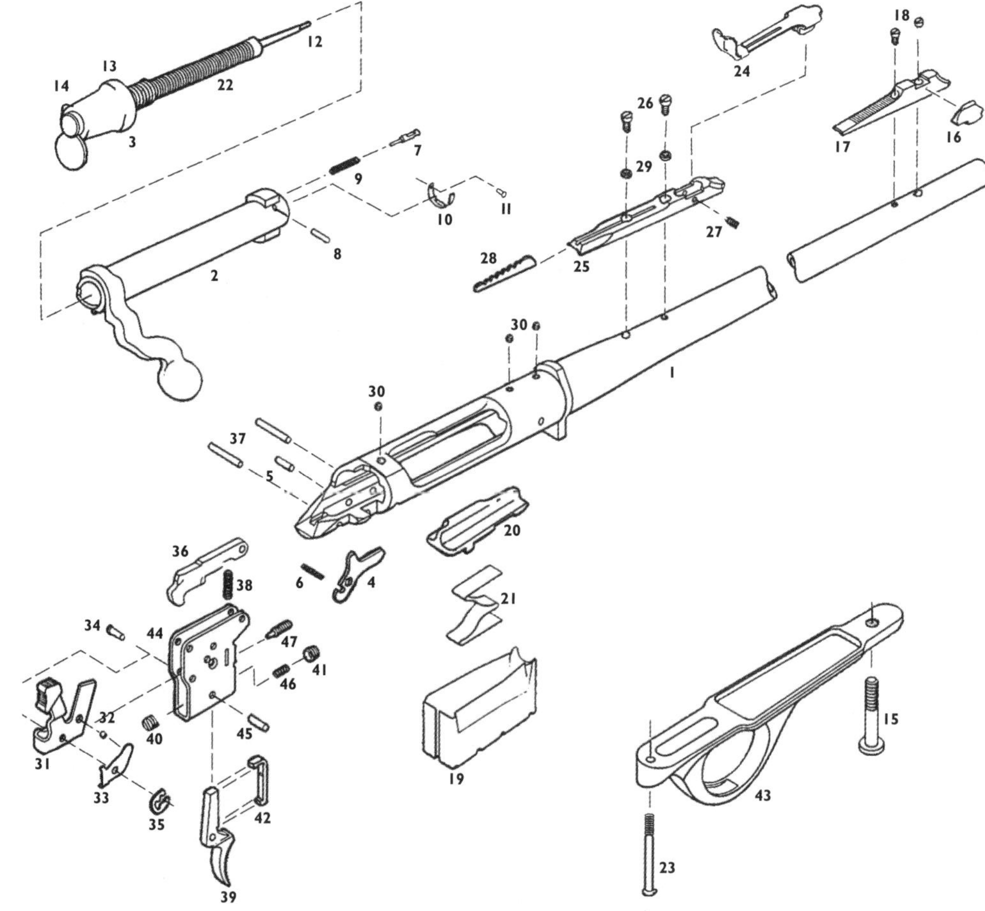

In 1964, Remington introduced the Model 600 center-fire bolt-action carbine. The 6-lb. rifle featured an 18½-inch barrel with a ventilated rib and open sights with a walnut stock with long fore-end and Monte Carlo comb. It was offered in .308 Win., .35 Rem., .222 Rem., 6 mm Rem. and .243 Win.

In 1965, a version of this carbine, chambered for the .350 Rem. Magnum cartridge, was introduced as the Model 600 Magnum. In 1966, it was offered in 6.5 mm. Rem. Magnum.

In 1968, Remington replaced the Models 600 and 600 Magnum with the Model 660 and Model 660 Magnum carbines. The new models were mechanically identical to the 600s and were offered in the same calibers with the exception of .35 Remington.

The 660s featured lengthened bolt sleeves, 20-inch plain barrels and improved open sights. The 660-series rifles remained in production until 1971. Remington's "Mohawk," rifles using 600/660 receivers and other parts, were distributed to retail store chains until about 1979.

DISASSEMBLY

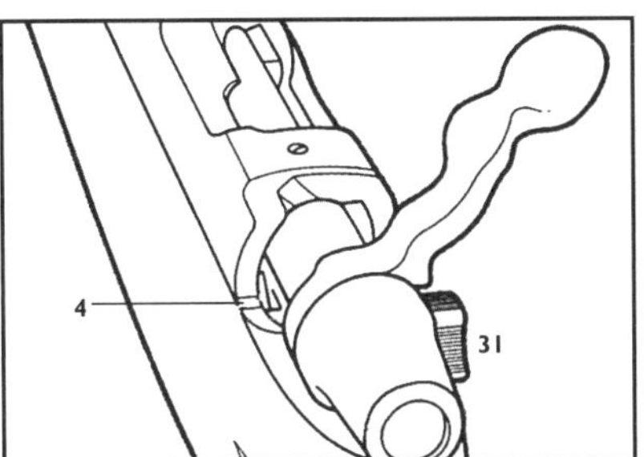

1 To disassemble, unlock bolt by pushing safety (31) forward to FIRE position. Raise bolt handle and pull bolt rearward. Check to see that chamber and magazine are unloaded. Using a small, flat key or screwdriver, press down on front of bolt stop (4) located in left rear of bolt channel in receiver. Withdraw bolt from receiver.

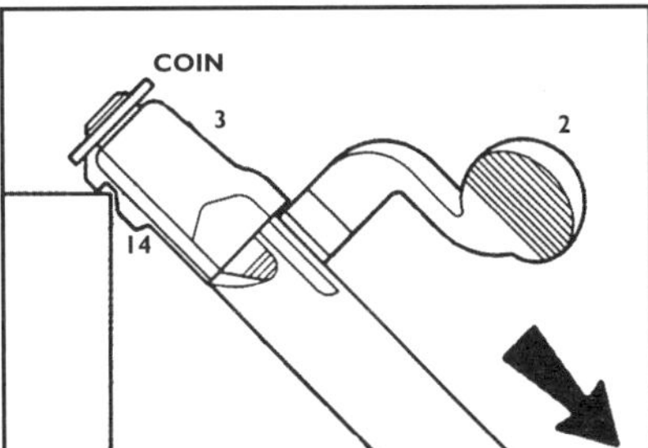

2 Clamp firing pin head (14) securely in vise jaws and move bolt (2) until coin or washer can be inserted into small slot in rear of firing pin head, (Model 660) or between firing pin head and bolt plug (3) in Model 600. Bolt can also be moved after hooking notch on bottom of firing pin head over a sharp corner. Unscrew and remove firing pin assembly (13) from bolt. Coin or washer must remain in slot or between firing pin head and bolt plug at all times when firing pin assembly is removed from bolt. Should coin become dislodged, difficulty will be experienced in replacing firing pin assembly. Further take down of firing pin assembly is not recommended and should be attempted only if necessary by a qualified gunsmith.

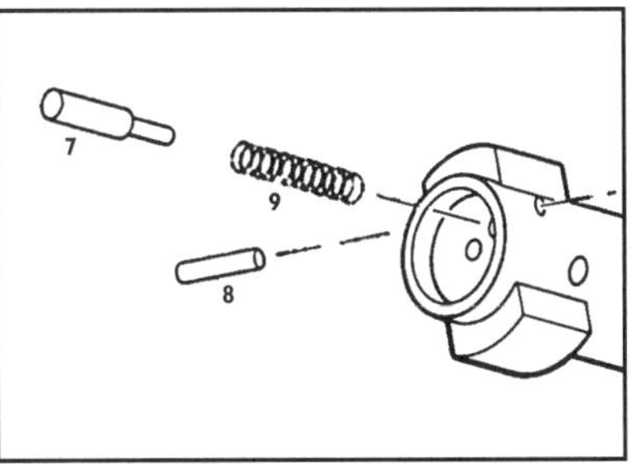

3 Drive out ejector pin (8) and remove ejector (7) and ejector spring (9) from bolt head. Do not attempt removal of extractor. Unscrew front and rear guard screws (15 & 23) and remove trigger guard (43) and stock. Action of Magnum model may require more effort to disassemble due to custom bedding in stock. Removal of stock and trigger guard is necessary only for replacement of parts or adjustment of trigger mechanism.

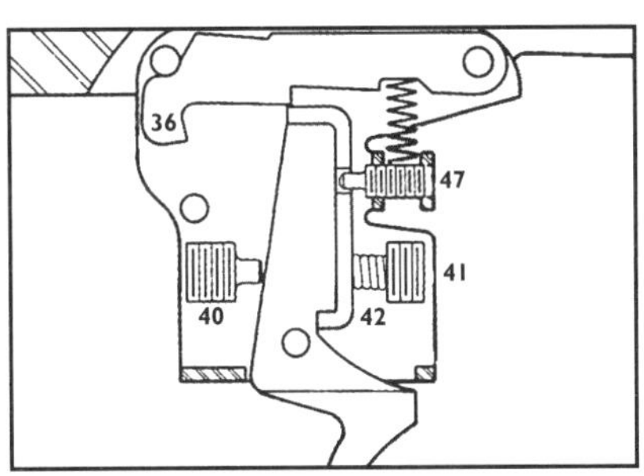

4 Trigger pull may be adjusted to desired weight by turning front trigger adjusting screw (41) clockwise to make pull heavier or counter-clockwise for a lighter pull. Do not adjust rear trigger adjusting screw (40). It is properly adjusted and sealed at the factory to provide correct engagement of trigger connector (42) and sear safety cam (36). To reduce trigger travel, place bolt in receiver and cock action. Turn trigger stop screw (47) clockwise until firing pin will not fall when trigger is pulled. Re-cock action and back off stop screw until firing pin falls. Adjusting in this manner will give minimum trigger overtravel.

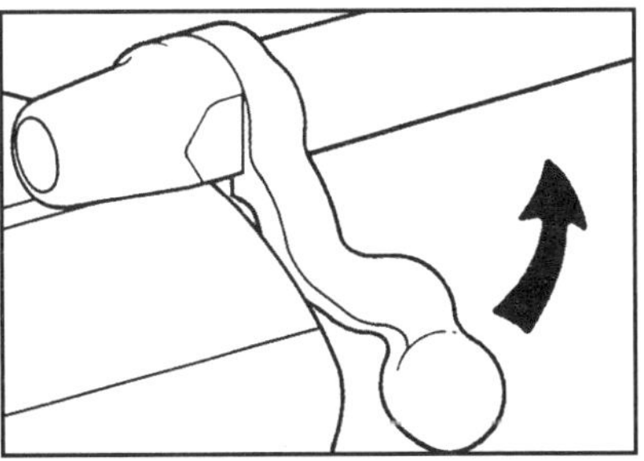

5 Reassemble rifle in reverse. Firing pin must be cocked before replacing bolt in rifle. If firing pin becomes Un-cocked, firing pin head will be deep inside bolt plug. To cock firing pin, clamp firing pin head in vise jaws and raise bolt handle until firing pin head snaps into small cocking notch on rear of bolt.

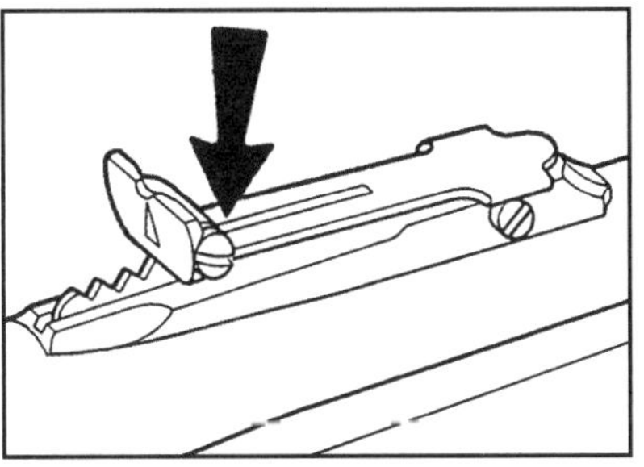

6 To adjust windage, turn windage screw (arrow). Turn screw clockwise to move rear sight eyepiece to left, and counter-clockwise to move eyepiece to right.

REMINGTON MODEL 700 RIFLE

PARTS LEGEND

1. Barrel and receiver assembly
2. Bolt assembly
3. Bolt plug
4. Bolt stop
5. Bolt stop pin
6. Bolt stop release
7. Bolt stop spring
8. Buttplate
9. Buttplate screw (2)
10. Ejector
11. Ejector pin
12. Ejector spring
13. Elevation screw
14. Extractor
15. Extractor rivet
16. Firing pin
17. Firing pin cross pin
18. Firing pin head
19. Front guard screw
20. Front sight
21. Front sight ramp
22. Front sight ramp screw (2)
23. Magazine
24. Magazine follower
25. Magazine spring
26. Magazine tab screw
27. Mainspring
28. Rear guard screw
29. Rear sight eyepiece
30. Rear sight base
31. Rear sight base screw (2)
32. Rear sight slide
33. Receiver plug screw (6)
34. Safety
35. Safety detent ball
36. Safety detent spring
37. Safety pivot pin
38. Safety snap washer
39. Sear safety cam
40. Sear pin
41. Sear spring
42. Stock
43. Takedown screw
44. Takedown screw bushing
45. Trigger
46. Trigger adjusting screw
47. Trigger connector
48. Trigger engagement screw
49. Trigger guard
50. Trigger housing
51. Trigger pin
52. Trigger spring
53. Trigger stop screw
54. Windage screw

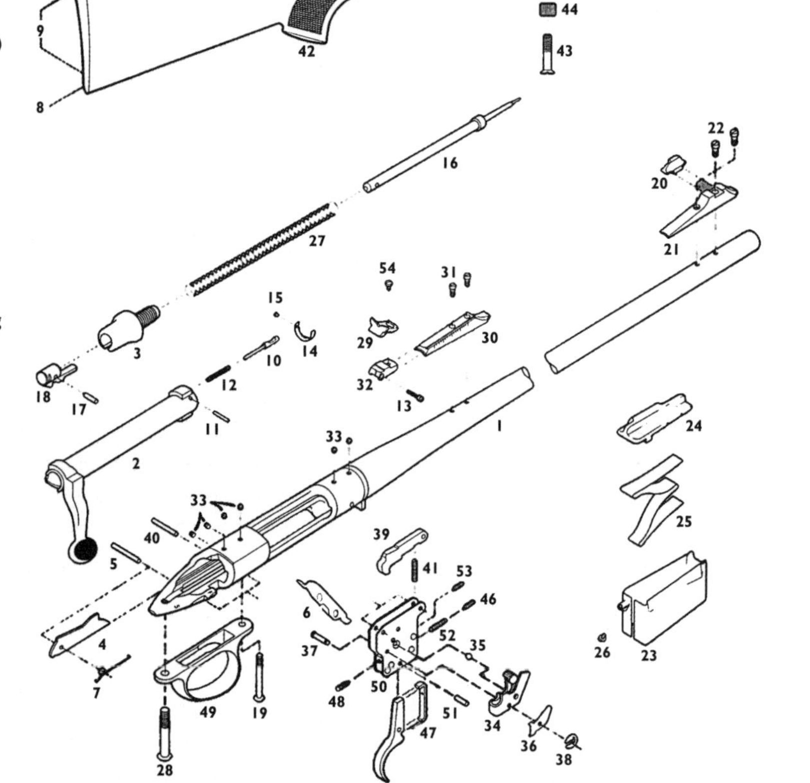

In 1962, the Models 721, 722, and 725 were replaced by the Remington Model 700 rifle, which was essentially an improved version of the Models 721 and 722. An improved Model 700 was introduced in 1974.

The Model 700 is offered in a wide range of popular chamberings from .17 Remington through .458 Winchester Magnum. It is produced in two action lengths, right- and left-hand versions and several grades. The short-action version is suitable for short and medium cartridges from .17 Remington through .308 Win., while long action version is adapted to .30-06 length cartridges and slightly longer.

Two grades of this rifle are the ADL Deluxe and BDL Custom Deluxe. Both feature one-piece walnut stocks with pistol grip, cheekpiece, Monte Carlo comb and checkering. The BDL Custom Deluxe grade rifle has cut checkering and a black plastic buttplate, grip cap, and fore-end tip.

Model 700 rifles in these two grades have 22- or 24-inch barrels and are fitted with a ramp-mounted gold-bead front sights and adjustable open rear sights. The lower-priced ADL grade has a blind-box magazine.

A BDL Varmint Special grade of this rifle is offered in varmint chamberings from .22-250 Rem. through 243 Win. Its receiver and 24-inch heavy barrel are fitted with dovetail-type target scope mount bases.

There is also a Custom Model 700C with 20-, 22-, or 24-inch barrel. The American walnut stock of this grade is hand checkered, and the rifle is available on special order only.

Action improvements in the 1974 version are an anti-bind feature to give smoother bolt operation, better bolt handle shape, and a stainless steel magazine follower.

REMINGTON

DISASSEMBLY

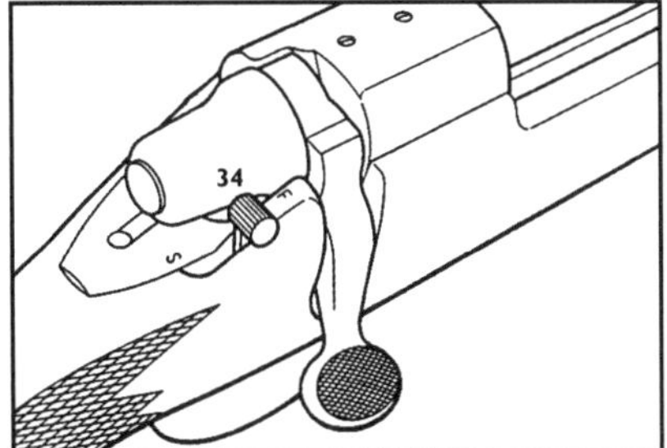

1 Before disassembly, check rifle to be sure that it is unloaded. Push safety (34) forward to fire position, unlock bolt (2), and pull it rearward to bolt stop (4). Press bolt stop release (6) upward, and withdraw bolt assembly from rifle.

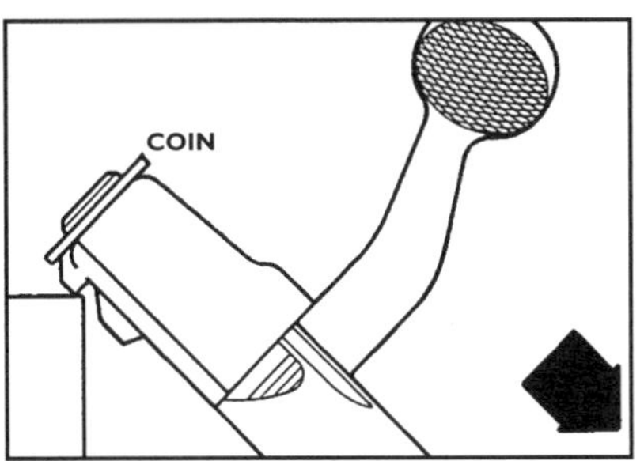

2 Hook firing pin head (18) on sharp corner of bench (or clamp in vise jaws), and pull bolt in direction shown until coin can be inserted in small slot on firing pin head. In earlier design where slot in firing pin head was omitted, coin may be inserted in space between bolt plug (3) and firing pin head. Hold bolt handle, and unscrew bolt plug to remove firing pin assembly from bolt. Place a metal sleeve (3⁄8-inch diameter, 7⁄8-inch long, with 3⁄16-inch hole through it lengthwise) over front of firing pin, and screw bolt plug back into bolt until coin is released. Drive out firing pin cross pin (17) with drift punch, and remove firing pin head. Unscrew bolt plug carefully as it is under force of mainspring (27). Remove bolt plug and mainspring from firing pin.

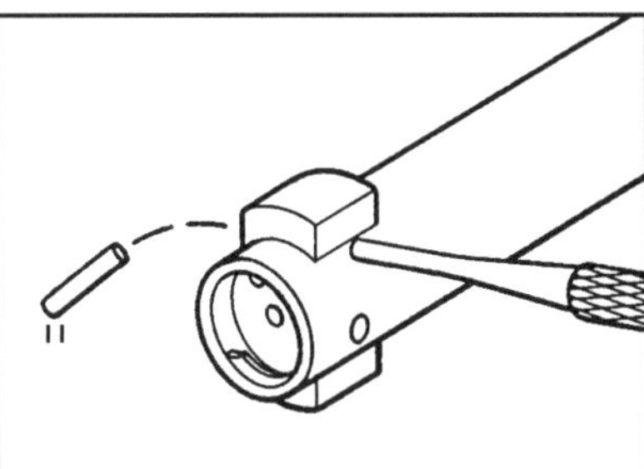

3 Drive out ejector pin (11), and remove ejector (10) and ejector spring (12) from front of bolt.

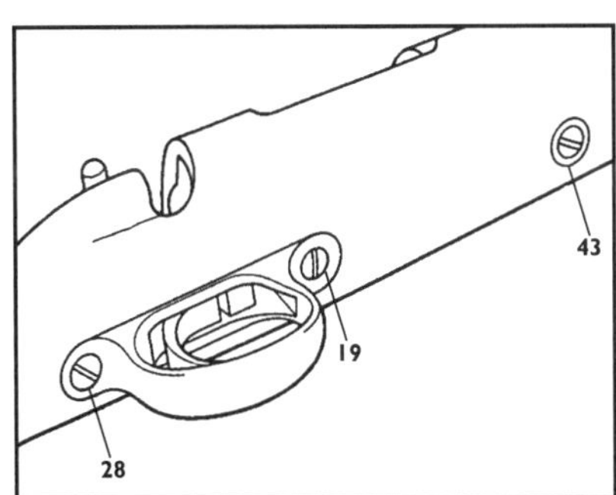

4 Unscrew takedown screw (43), and front and rear guard screws (19) and remove trigger guard (49), stock magazine (23), magazine spring and follower (24).

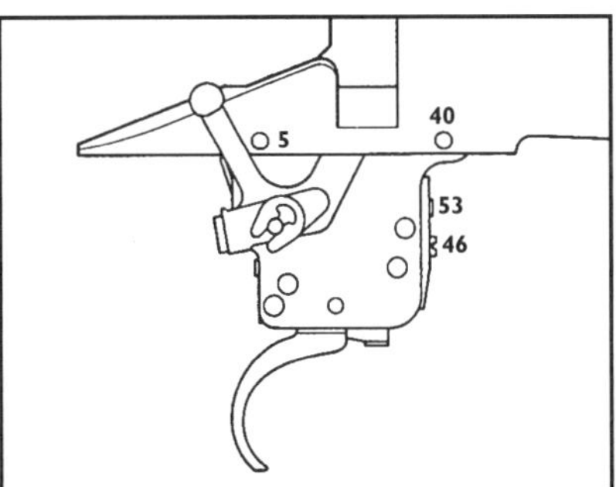

5 Drive out bolt stop pin (5), and remove bolt stop and bolt stop spring (7). Drive out sear pin (40), and remove trigger housing assembly unit, sear safety cam (39), and sear spring (41). Weight of trigger pull is adjustable by turning trigger adjusting screw (46) clockwise for a heavier pull, and counterclockwise for a lighter one. Overtravel can be reduced by turning trigger stop screw (53) clockwise until firing pin will not release when trigger is pulled. While keeping pressure on trigger, trigger stop screw is backed off until firing pin falls. Trigger stop screw is then backed off 1⁄16 turn.

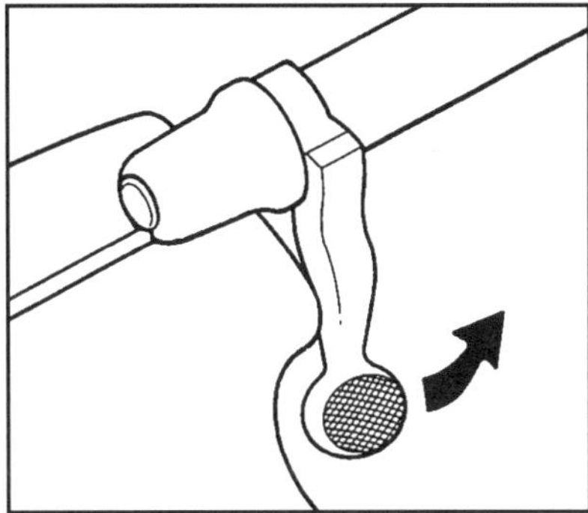

6 Reassemble in reverse. When reassembling firing mechanism, place metal sleeve over front of firing pin, reassemble mainspring and bolt plug on firing pin, and screw bolt plug into bolt. Then, replace firing pin head and firing pin cross pin on firing pin. While unscrewing bolt plug, insert coin between bolt plug and firing pin head, complete unscrewing plug, and remove metal sleeve. Screw firing pin assembly into bolt until front of firing pin head matches small cocking notch on rear edge of bolt. Remove coin to allow firing pin head to snap into cocking notch. With safety in forward (fire) position, replace assembled bolt in rifle. Firing pin must be cocked to replace bolt in rifle. If firing pin is uncocked, clamp firing pin head in vise, and rotate bolt handle upward until front of firing pin head engages cocking notch on bolt.

REMINGTON 721-722 RIFLES

PARTS LEGEND

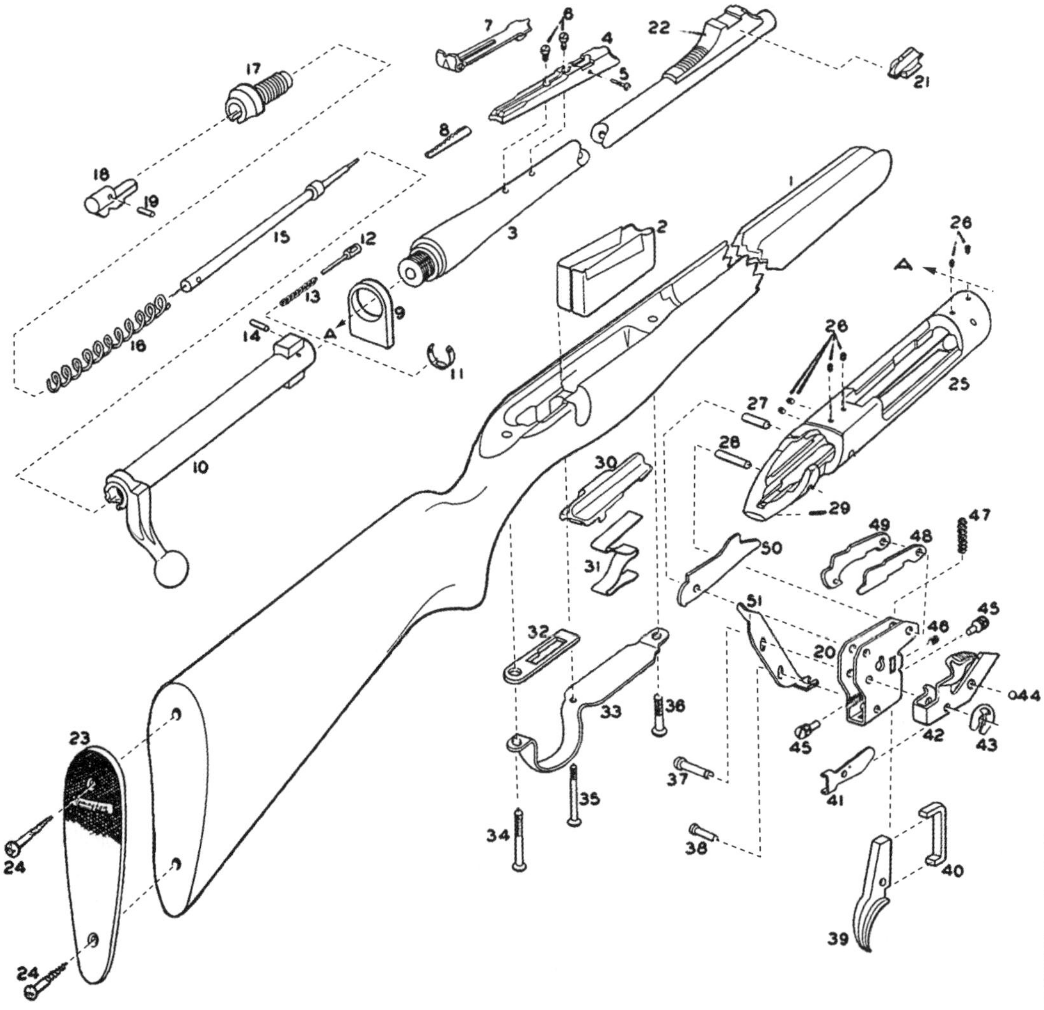

1. Stock
2. Magazine
3. Barrel
4. Rear sight base
5. Rear sight screw
6. Rear sight base screw (2)
7. Rear sight assembly
8. Rear sight step
9. Barrel bracket
10. Bolt
11. Ectractor
12. Ejector
13. Ejector spring
14. Ejector pin
15. Firing pin
16. Mainspring
17. Bolt plug
18. Firing pin head
19. Firing pin crosspin
20. Housing
21. Front sight
22. Front sight ramp
23. Buttplate
24. Buttplote screw (2)
25. Receiver
26. Receiver plug screw (6)
27. Sear pin
28. Bolt stop pin
29. Bolt stop spring
30. Follower
31. Magazine spring
32. Trigger guide plate
33. Trigger guard
34. Rear guard screw
35. Center guard screw
36. Front guard screw
37. Safety pivot pin
38. Trigger pin
39. Trigger
40. Trigger connector
41. Safety detent spring
42. Safety
43. Safety snap washer
44. Safety detent ball
45. Trigger adjusting screw (2)
46. Trigger stop screw
47. Sear spring
48. Sear
49. Safety cam
50. Bolt stop
51. Bolt stop release

One of the first new high power rifles offered after World War II was the bolt-action Remington Model 721, announced in the early spring of 1948. It was followed shortly by the Model 722 with an action ⅞-inch shorter than that of the Model 721. These rifles were designed for ease of manufacture, with receivers and bolt bodies machined from round bar stock. Striker mechanism is of speed-lock type with short firing pin fall and the single-stage trigger is adjustable.

The design of the bolt is particularly noteworthy as the cartridge head is almost completely shrouded by the counterbored bolt head. This was made possible by the unique circular-spring extractor fitted within the counterbore. The ejector, in the form of a small spring-loaded plunger, is also contained within the counterbore. Another noteworthy feature of the Model 721-722 action is the recoil lug, or barrel bracket, which is a simple flat piece installed between barrel and receiver.

To date, the Model 721-722 has been offered in .300 H&H Magnum, .30-06, .270 Win., .308 Win., .257 Roberts, .222 Rem., .222 Rem. Magnum and .244 Rem. Model 721/722 rifles in calibers .280 Rem. and 264 Win. Mag. are rare.

Both the Model 721 and the 722 were supplanted, in 1958, by the Model 725.

DISASSEMBLY

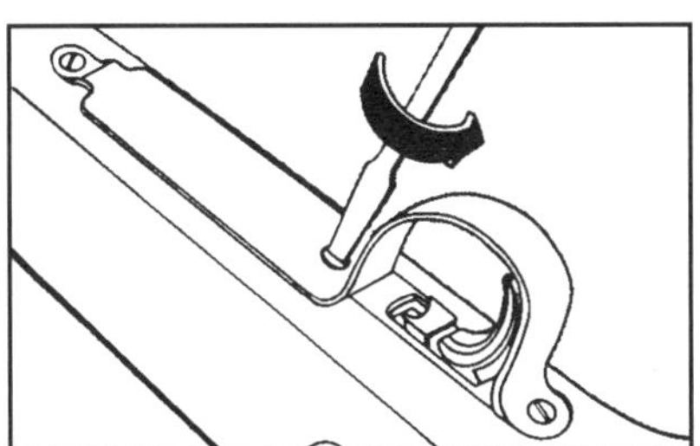

1 To remove barrel and action from stock: Remove front guard screw (36), center guard screw (35), and rear guard screw (34). Use proper size screwdriver to avoid burring screw slots. Next, lift away trigger guard (33), magazine spring (31), with follower (30), and trigger guide plate (32). Magazine (2) will remain either in receiver (25) or in stock (1). In reassembling barrel and action to stock, insure that magazine is reseated properly in receiver.

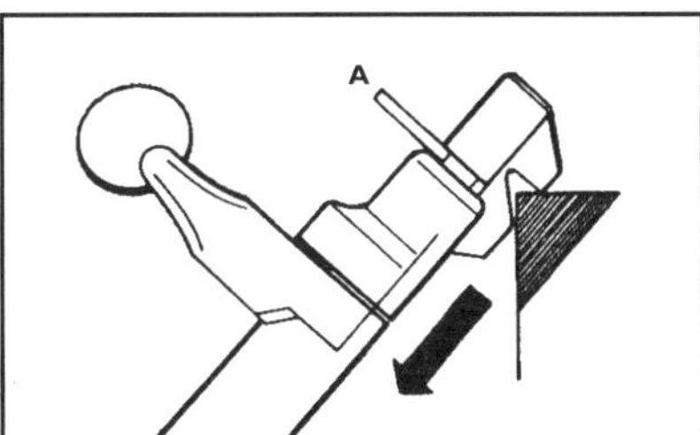

2 To remove firing pin assembly: Pull firing pin head rearward until a coin (A) can lie inserted between it and bolt plug (17). A convenient method is to catch notch on firing pin head on a sharp corner. Unscrew bolt plug to remove assembly from bolt (10). CAUTION: Do not disturb coin; should it be inadvertently knocked out, great difficulty will be experienced in repulling firing pin head.

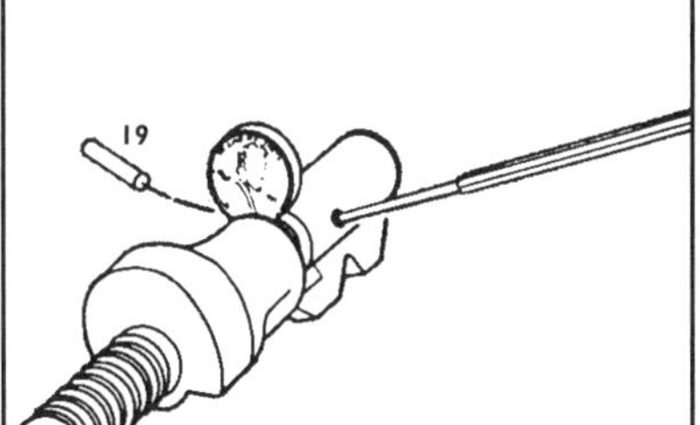

3 To further disassemble firing pin, drive out firing pin crosspin (19) using a flat-nosed center punch, leaving punch in hole to hold parts together. This prevents the mainspring (16) tension from forcing them apart.

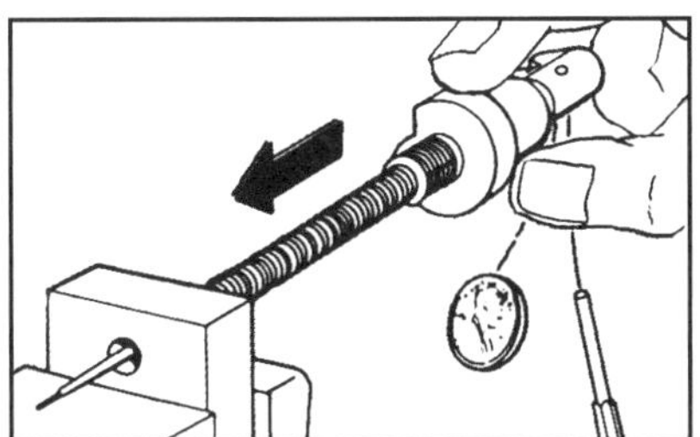

4 Next, using a small vise-held block of wood, which has been drilled through with a 3⁄16-inch drill, insert forward end of firing pin as shown and compress mainspring with bolt plug until coin, punch, and firing pin head can be removed, or drop away. Apply steady, even force to bolt plug. Slowly and carefully release mainspring tension. Assemble in reverse order.

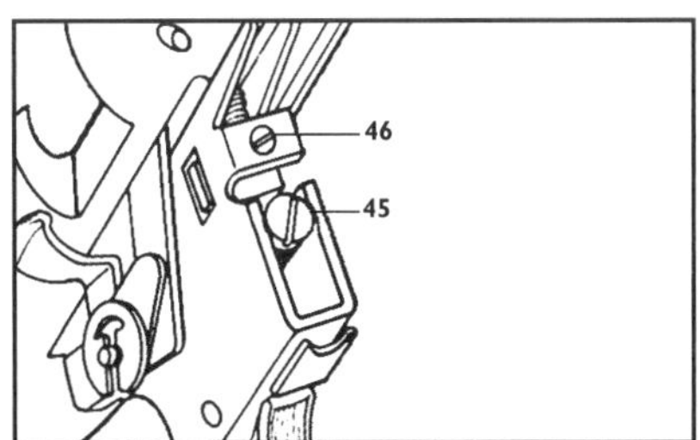

5 Pull of trigger (39) may be adjusted to desired weight by turning front trigger-adjusting screw (45) clockwise for a heavier weight adjustment and counterclockwise for a lighter weight adjustment. CAUTION: Do not adjust or remove rear trigger adjusting screw. Trigger travel may be reduced by turning trigger stop screw (46) clockwise until firing pin will not fall when trigger is pulled. Then, while keeping pressure on trigger, back off trigger stop screw, counterclockwise, until firing pin falls. This method of adjustment will allow least amount of overtravel.

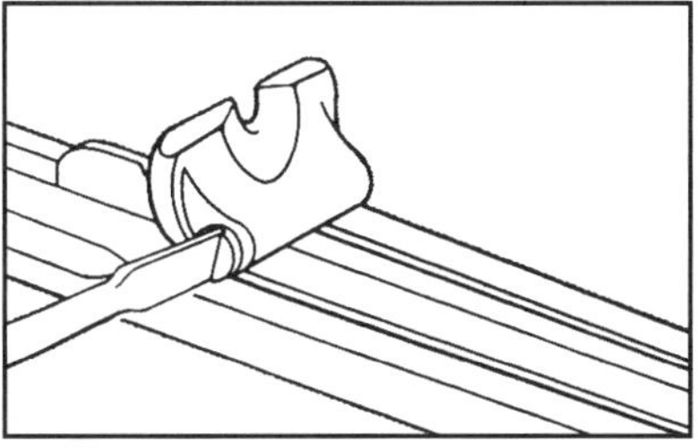

6 To adjust for windage, rear sight plate may be moved to left by turning the windage screw clockwise or to right by turning screw counterclockwise.

REM. MODELS 740-742 RIFLES

PARTS LEGEND

1. Barrel
2. Front sight ramp
3. Front sight
4. Rear sight base
5. Rear sight screw
6. Rear sight base screw (2)
7. Rear sight
8. Rear sight step
9. Firing pin retracting spring
10. Firing pin
11. Bolt carrier
12. Cam pin
13. Operating handle
14. Firing pin retaining pin
15. Operating handle retaining pin
16. Breech bolt
17. Extractor rivet *
18. Ejector retaining pin
19. Extractor *
20. Ejector spring
21. Ejector
22. Barrel extension *
23. Stock bolt
24. Stock bolt lock washer
25. Stock bolt washer
26. Receiver plug screw (4)
27. Breech ring *
28. Breech ring nut
29. Ejection port cover
30. Action tube support
31. Gas tube
32. Orifice screw
33. Orifice ball
34. Action tube support pin
35. Barrel lug
36. Action tube
37. Action bar rivet (2) *
38. Action bar sleeve
39. Fore-end bushing *
40. Fore-end screw
41. Fore-end reinforcement *
42. Action bar *
43. Action spring
44. Breech ring bolt
45. Front trigger plate pin
46. Receiver
47. Rear trigger plate pin
48. Stock bearing plate
49. Buttplate screw (2)
50. Buttplate
51. Receiver stud
52. Rear trigger plate pin bushing
53. Rear trigger plate pin detent spring
54. Safety spring
55. Safety plunger
56. Trigger plate
57. Sear pin
58. Sear
59. Safety
60. Safety spring retaining pin
61. Trigger pin
62. Front trigger plate pin bushing
63. Front trigger plate pin detent spring
64. Left connector
65. Trigger
66. Right connector
67. Connector pin
68. Sear spring
69. Magazine latch spring
70. Hammer pin
71. Magazine latch
72. Disconnector spring
73. Disconnector*
74. Hammer spring
75. Hammer plunger
76. Hammer
77. Fore-end
78. Fore-end cap
79. Magazine follower
80. Magazine spring
81. Magazine
82. Bolt release pin
83. Bolt release button
84. Bolt release *

* Factory assembled to other major part. Not recommended for field disassembly.

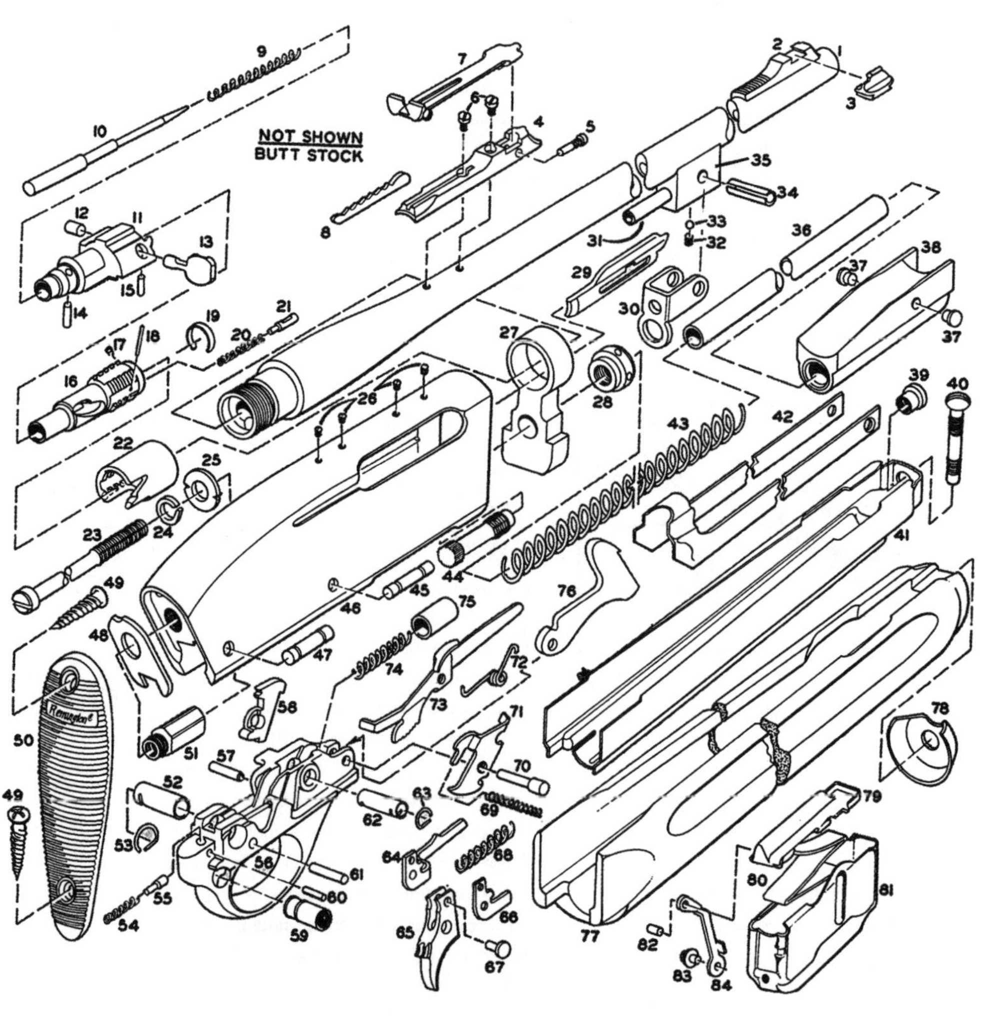

The Model 740 Woodsmaster center-fire rifle, offered in 1955 by Remington Arms Co., was essentially an autoloading version of the Model 760 slide-action rifle introduced in 1952. Of hammerless, solid-frame construction with side ejection, the Model 740 is gas-operated with dual action bars and multiple-lug rotating breech bolt locking into the barrel assembly. The detachable box magazine holds 4 cartridges. The safety is cross-bolt type, in rear of trigger guard.

The Model 740 was first offered in .30- 06 caliber but the list of chamberings was expanded to include the .308 Winchester, .280 Rem., and .244 Rem. Both standard and deluxe grades were available. At no extra cost buttstocks could be had with high comb for use with scope sights.

In 1960, the Model 740 was superseded by the Model 742, which appears identical, but which differs in details. The principal difference is that the barrel can be easily removed from the receiver. The earlier Model 740 rifles were quite sensitive to variations in the degree of tightness with which the fore-end screw was set up, and a spacing block had to be used to maintain an even tension.

In the later Model 740 rifles and in the Model 742 this is accomplished by making separate threaded portions, each thread having a different pitch. When the screw is tightened, the parts are drawn together by the differential action of the varying pitches and the fore-end tightens leaving a small clearance between its rear end and the front of the receiver.

Between 1960 and 1980 several minor mechanical changes were made that affect the 742's operation but not its assembly and disassembly. The 742 was discontinued in 1980 in favor of the Model 7400, introduced in 1982.

DISASSEMBLY

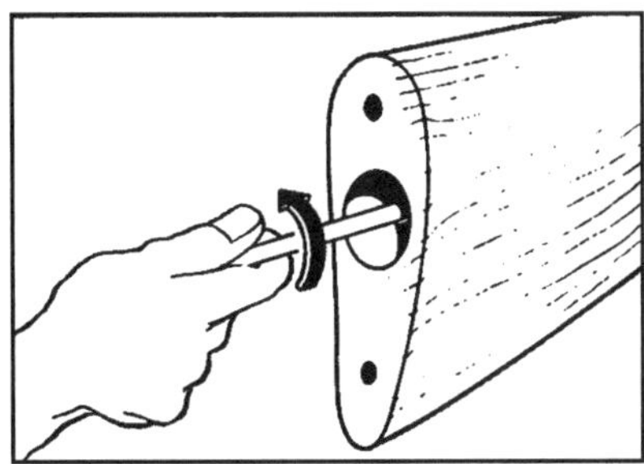

1 To remove stock, first remove buttplate screws (49) and then buttplate (50), using a Phillips-head screwdriver. Next, using a long-shanked screwdriver, remove stock bolt (23). Stock bolt lock washer (24), stock bolt washer (25), and stock may be pulled away from receiver (46).

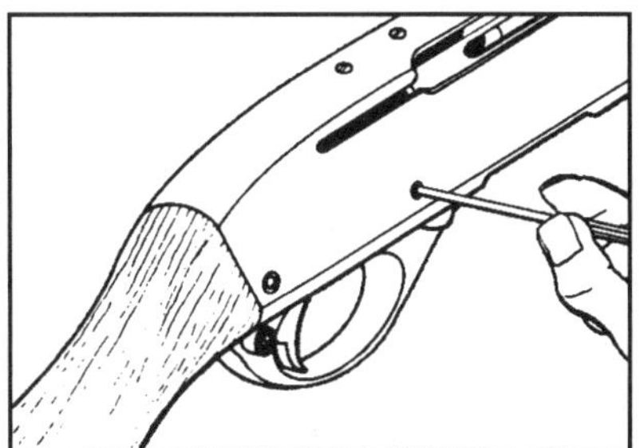

2 To remove trigger plate (56) and assembly, also known as the fire control mechanism, remove magazine (81) and drift out front and rear trigger plate pins (45 & 47). Use a flat-nosed punch.

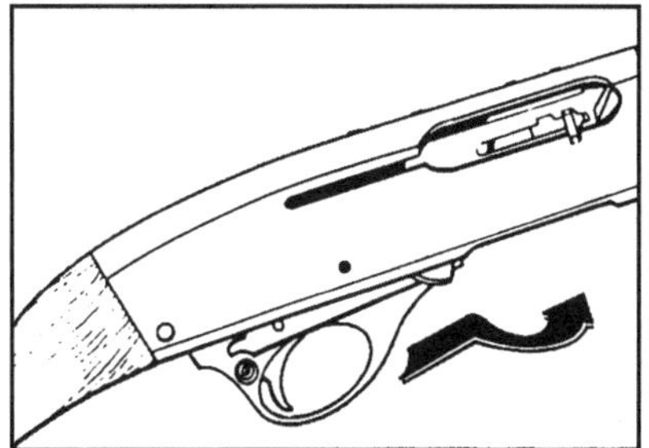

3 Next, lift out fire control unit by moving it slightly forward and tipping it slightly to clear disconnector (73). When reassembling, place safety (59) on "Safe" (red band not showing) and, with mechanism in cocked position, insert front end of trigger plate into bottom of receiver, rotating unit counterclockwise to clear disconnector. Push rearward, align holes, and drive in trigger plate pins.

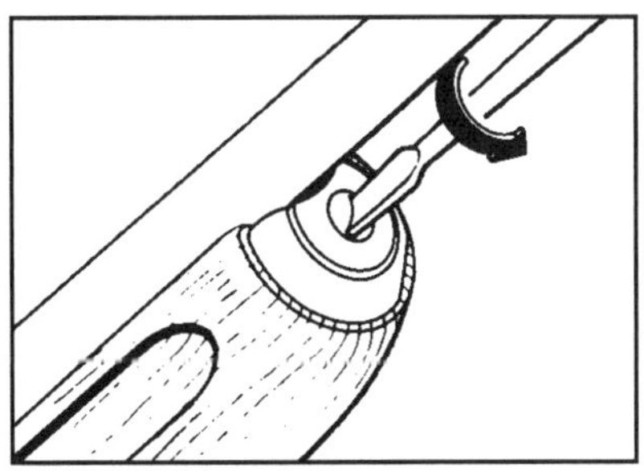

4 To remove the fore-end (77), unscrew the fore-end screw (40) and pull fore-end forward toward the muzzle and remove it from the gun.

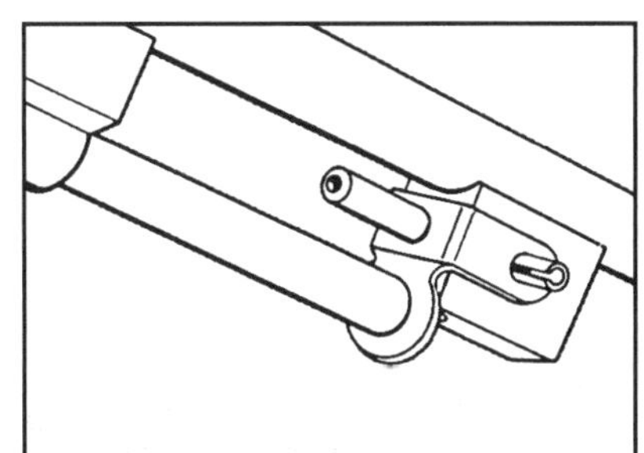

5 During cleaning, take care that jet on gas tube (31) is undamaged and not burred or closed at nozzle end. Proper functioning of the arm depends on this jet being undamaged. The jet is self-cleaning.

REMINGTON MODEL 760 RIFLE

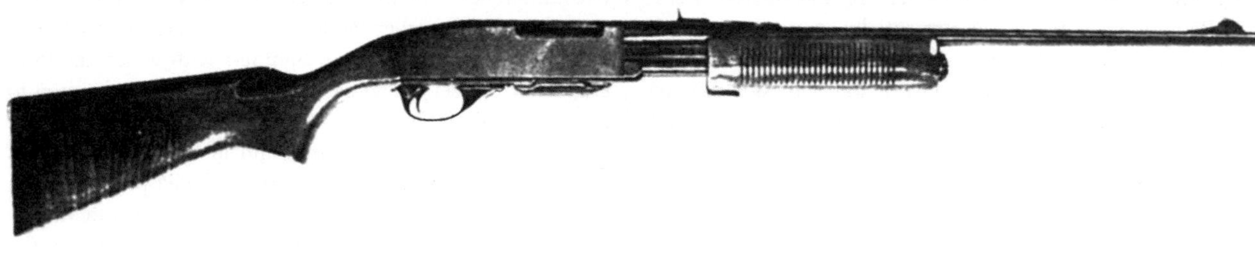

PARTS LEGEND

1. Barrel
2. Front sight ramp
3. Rear sight
4. Rear sight base screw (2)
5. Rear sight base
6. Rear sight screw
7. Rear sight step
8. Firing pin
9. Bolt carrier
10. Small cam pin
11. Large cam pin
12, Firing pin retaining pin
13. Breech bolt
14. Ejector retaining pin
15. Extractor
16. Ejector spring
17. Ejector
18. Barrel extension
19. Receiver stud
20. Stock bearing plate
21. Receiver
22. Receiver plug screw (4)
23. Barrel bracket
24. Action tube guard
25. Action tube cap
26. Front sight
27. Action tube
28. Barrel bracket nut
29. Fore-end tube nut
30. Fore-end tube
31. Fore-end tube yoke
32. Action bar rivet (2)
33. Fore-end
34. Ejection port cover
35. Action bar
36. Barrel bracket bolt
37. Front trigger plate pin
38. Rear trigger plate pin
39. Stock bolt washer
40. Stock bolt lock washer
41. Stock bolt
42. Action bar lock spring
43. Hammer spring
44. Hammer plunger
45. Sear
46. Sear pin
47. Rear trigger plate pin detent spring
48. Rear trigger plate bushing
49. Safety spring
50. Safety plunger
51. Trigger plate
52. Left connector
53. Trigger
54. Connector pin
55. Right connector
56. Sear spring
57. Safety
58. Safety spring retaining pin
59. Trigger pin
60. Front trigger plate pin bushing
61. Front trigger plate pin detent spring
62. Magazine latch
63. Magazine latch spring
64. Hammer pin
65. Hammer
66. Magazine
67. Magazine spring
68. Magazine follower
69. Buttplate screw (2)
70. Buttplate
71. Collar
72. Action bar lock
73. Magazine filler piece *

* Cals. .35 .244, .222 Remington, and .308 Winchester only.

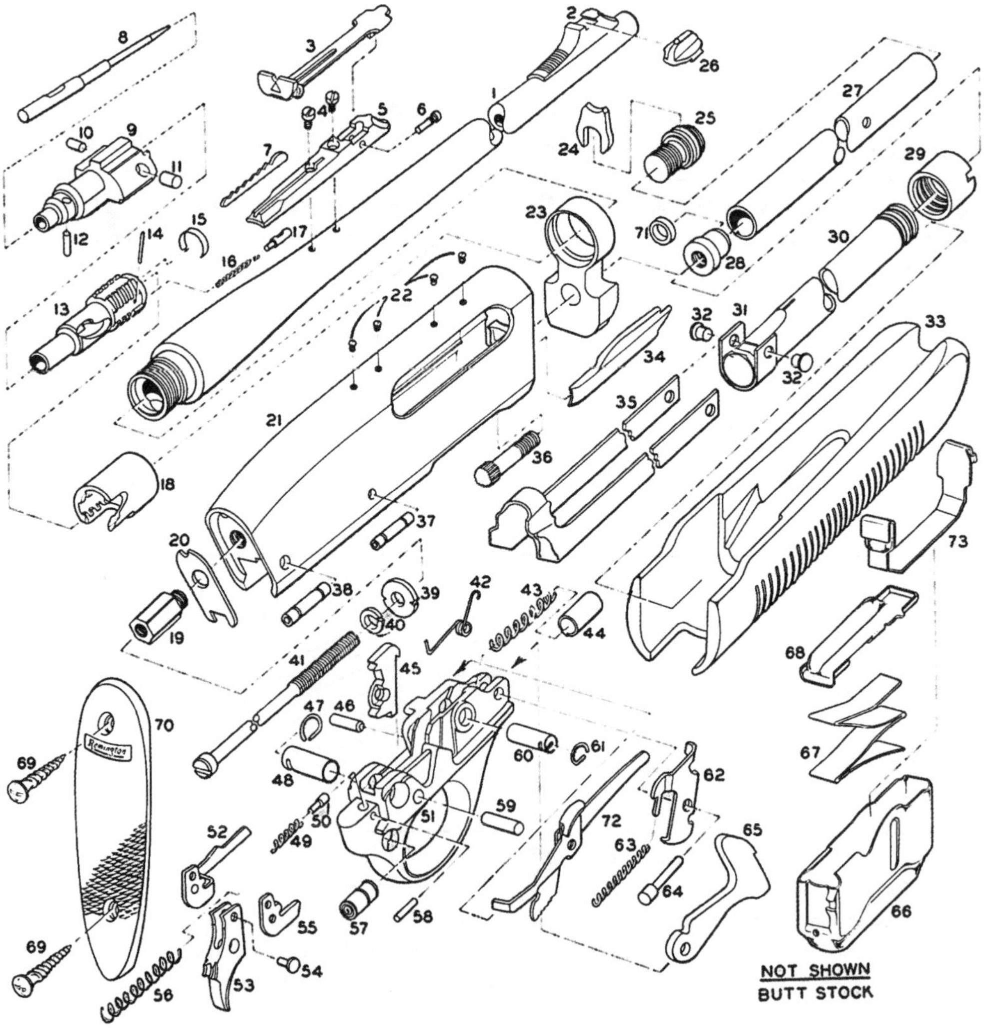

NOT SHOWN
BUTT STOCK

The Model 760 "Gamemaster" slide-action hammerless center-fire rifle, released by Remington in 1952, was introduced as a replacement for the Model 141 Gamemaster. Although both are slide-action rifles, they are mechanically dissimilar.

The Model 141's action and bolting system were not suitable for modern high-pressure cartridges and, as early as 1940, Remington engineers began working on a replacement. Shelved during World War II, this development program was reinstated after the war and the Model 760 was the end product. Initially chambered for .30-06, .300 Savage, and .35 Rem. cartridges, the list was expanded to include .222 Rem., .257 Roberts, .244 Rem., .270 Win., .280 Rem., and .308 Win.

The Model 760 is classed as a solid-frame rifle although the barrel does not screw directly into the receiver. The barrel screws into a barrel extension that carries the breech-bolt locking lug recesses. The barrel extension and barrel bracket are fitted very tightly to the barrel, and their removal requires perfectly fitted vise jaws to prevent deformation of these parts.

The breech bolt is an interrupted thread type, with four separate banks of multiple lugs. The bolt face is recessed and is fitted with the typical Remington horseshoe extractor and plunger ejector. The Model 760 was phased out in 1982.

DISASSEMBLY

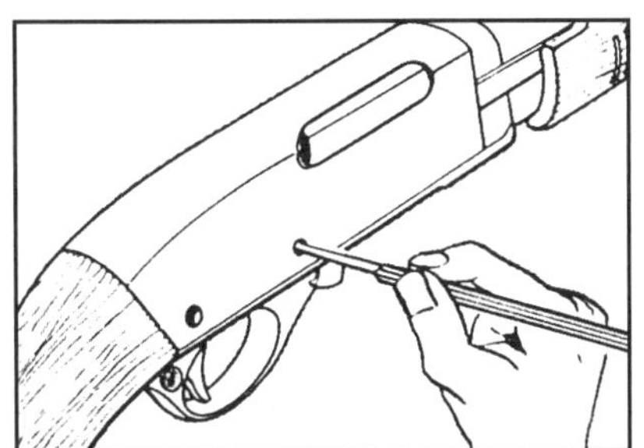

1 To remove trigger plate (51) and assembly—called the fire control mechanism by the manufacturer—place safety (57) on "Safe" (red band not showing), remove magazine (66) by pushing magazine latch (62) forward, then drift out front and rear trigger plate pins (37 & 38).

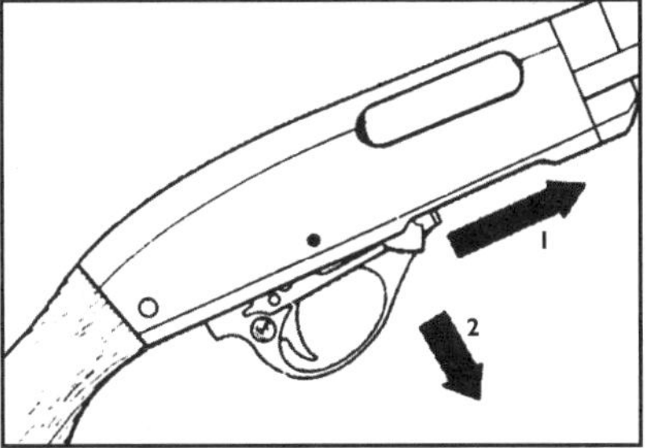

2 Lift out fire control mechanism by moving it forward and away from gun, tipping mechanism slightly to clear action bar lock (72). When reassembling, place safety on "Safe," open action half way, and with mechanism in cocked position, insert front of trigger plate into bottom of receiver (21). Rotate unit clockwise to clear action bar lock and slide unit fully into opening. Push it rearward and align pin holes. Insert front and rear trigger plate pins.

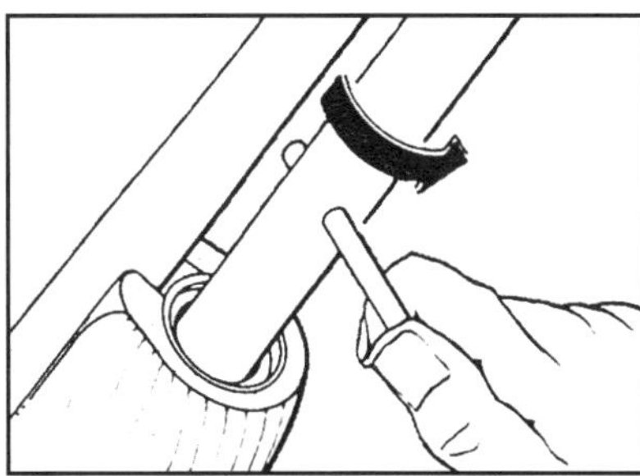

3 To remove barrel (l) and breech mechanism from receiver, remove magazine, press action bar lock, and open action. Make sure chamber is empty. Holding rifle on a flat padded surface with the magazine opening upward, insert a snug fitting steel pin into holes exposed in action tube (27). Turn as indicated until action tube can be removed.

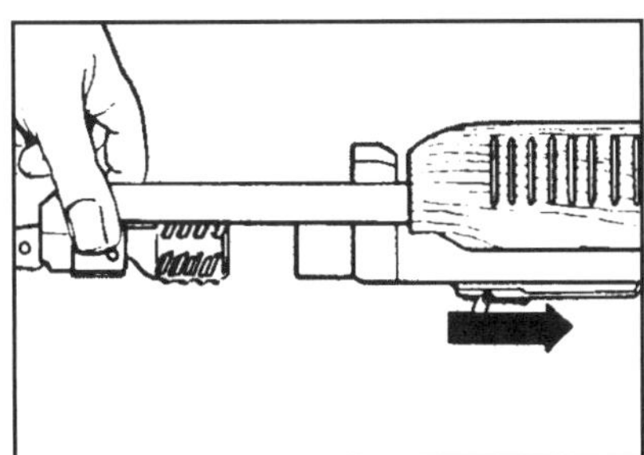

4 Continue by closing action. Remove barrel and breech mechanism by pulling forward out of receiver. Rest fore-end (33) on a flat surface and, holding bolt carrier (9), pull barrel forward until breech bolt (13) releases from barrel extension (18).

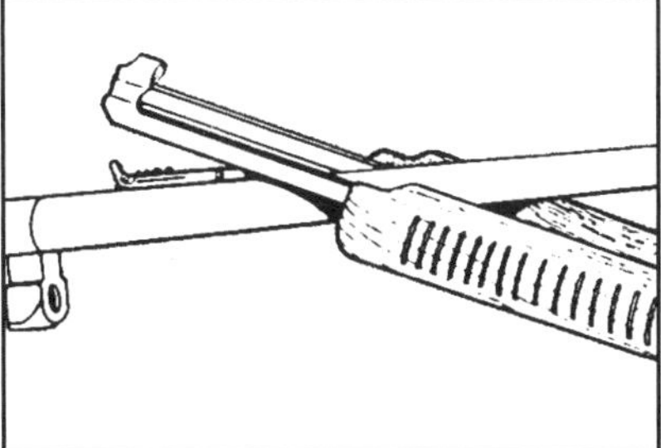

5 Push bolt carrier with assembled breech bolt free of action bar (35), then lift front end of barrel, and release downward between the double action bars.

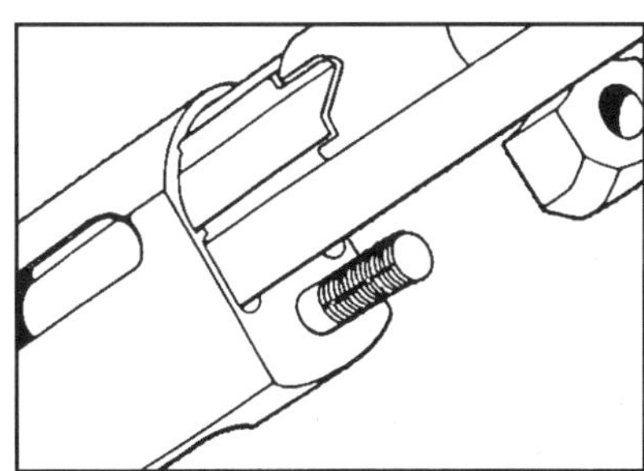

6 Reassemble in reverse order. When assembling barrel to fore-end assembly, do not spread action bars farther than necessary to position barrel bracket (23). When assembling barrel and breech parts to receiver, be sure indent in curved end of ejection port cover (34) is locked ahead of lug on bolt carrier. Cover should enter small slot in top of receiver freely. Do not force it.

REMINGTON

REMINGTON MODEL 788 RIFLE

PARTS LEGEND

1. Barrel assembly (includes receiver)
2. Bolt
3. Bolt assembly pin *
4. Bolt head *
5. Bolt plug
6. Bolt plug washer
7. Bolt stop
8. Bolt stop spring
9. Elevation screw
10. Ejector
11. Ejector pin *
12. Ejector spring *
13. Extractor *
14. Firing pin assembly
15. Firing pin
16. Firing pin cross pin
17. Firing pin head
18. Floor plate
19. Floor plate screw
20. Front guard screw
21. Front sight
22. Front sight screw
23. Housing lock screw
24. Housing pin
25. Magazine assembly
26. Magazine guide bar
27. Magazine guide bar screw
28. Mainspring
29. Rear guard screw
30. Rear sight base
31. Rear sight eyepiece
32. Rear sight leaf
33. Rear sight screw (2)
34. Receiver plug screw (3)
35. Rib (rear sight)
36. Rib spacer (rear sight)
37. Safety
38. Safety pivot pin
39. Safety pivot pin retaining washer
40. Safety plunger
41. Safety plunger spring
42. Safety retaining screw
43. Sear
44. Sear pin
45. Stock
46. Trigger
47. Trigger housing
48. Trigger guard
49. Trigger pin
50. Trigger spring

* Used on .30-30 and .44 Remington Magnum calibers only.
NOTE: Buttplate and buttplate screws not shown on drawing.

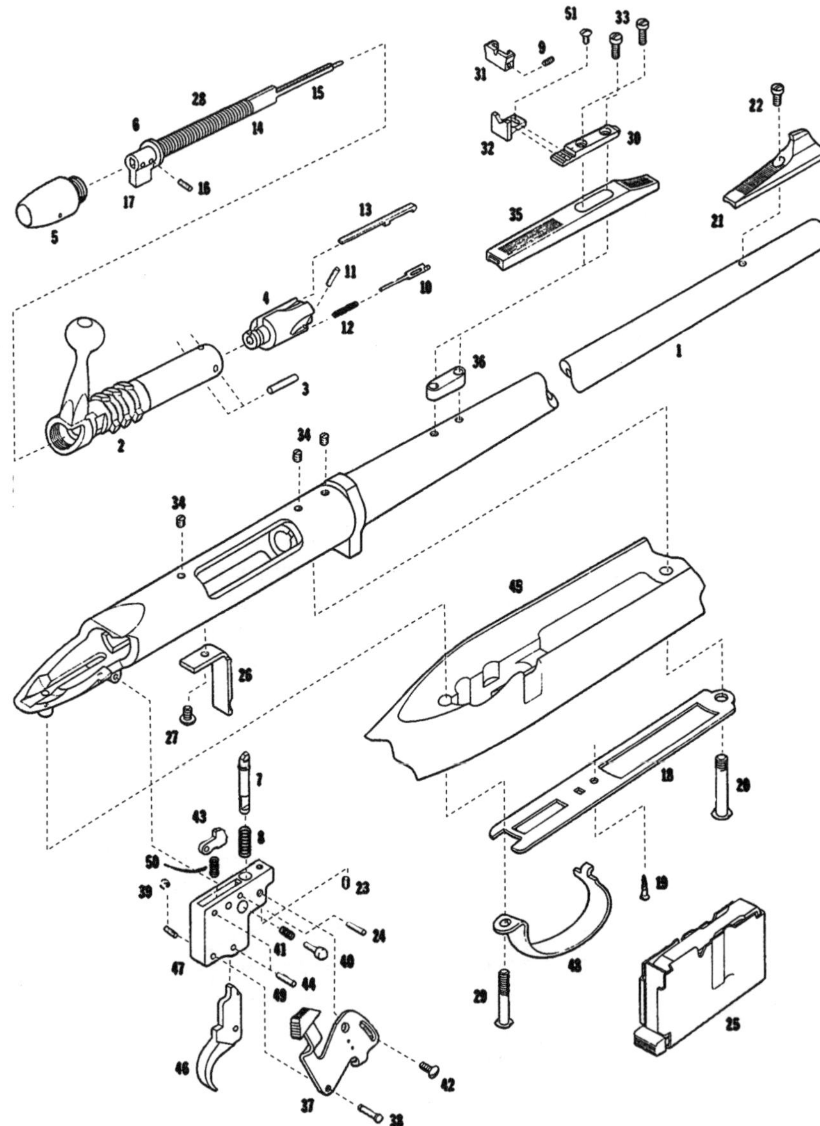

The Remington Model 788 bolt-action rifle was introduced in 1967. The Model 788 was chambered for a several centerfire deer and varmint cartridges including the .30-30, .44 Rem. Magnum, .222 Rem. and .22-250 Rem. The .308 Win. and 6 mm Rem. chamberings were added in 1969. A chambering for 7mm-08 was added later on. Calibers using rimmed cases were dropped from the line early in its production history.

The Model 788 featured a tubular receiver with nine locking lugs engaging locking recesses in the receiver bridge. The locking lugs are arranged in three series of three lugs each with each series spaced 120 degrees apart. Bolt rotation is 68 degrees instead of 90 degrees as in the usual turn-bolt action.

Two types of bolt head are used with this rifle. Type 1, with a rotating bolt head, is employed with the rimmed calibers. Type 2, of one-piece design, is used for rimless calibers.

The Model 788 was dropped from production in 1984.

DISASSEMBLY

1 Check action to make sure rifle is unloaded. Push in magazine latch and remove magazine. Lift bolt handle and pull bolt rearward to bolt stop. Rotate safety (37) forward as far as possible. This will depress bolt stop and allow removal of bolt from rifle.

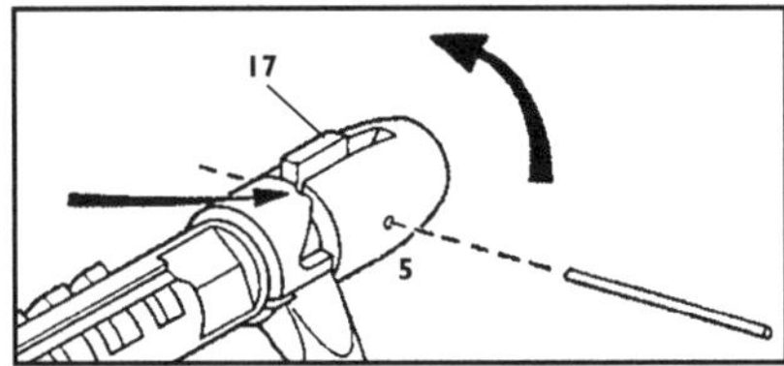

2 With bolt removed, grasp bolt plug (5) firmly and rotate clockwise until firing pin head (17) snaps out of cocking notch (arrow). Insert a small diameter slave pin through aligned holes in bolt plug and firing pin head. This pin holds firing pin head retracted into bolt plug. Unscrew bolt plug and remove firing pin assembly (14) (with bolt plug) from bolt.

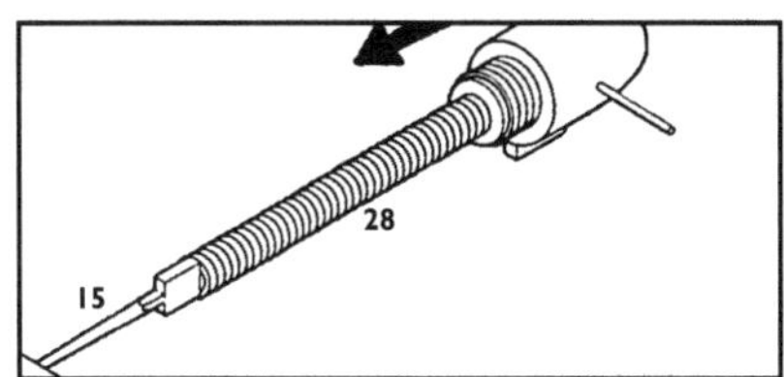

3 Support end of firing pin (15) against firm surface and exert forward pressure on bolt plug against tension of mainspring (28). This will relieve pressure on small slave pin, which can then be removed. Carefully release pressure on bolt plug and remove from firing pin assembly. Special factory processes are used to make up the firing pin assembly; disassembly is not recommended.

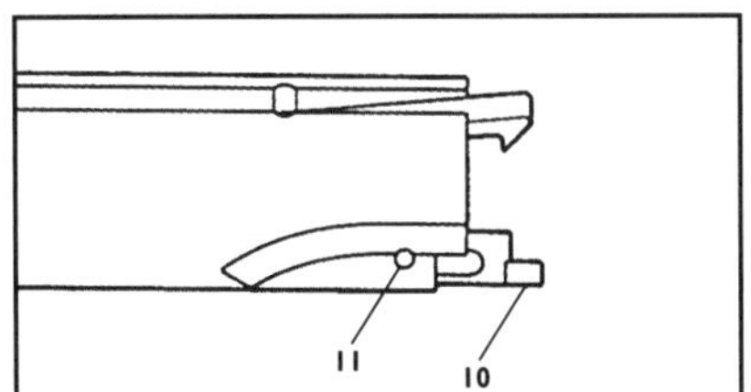

4 To disassemble ejector (10) (used on bolt Type I for rimmed calibers .30-30 and .44 Remington Magnum) drive out ejector pin (11) and remove ejector and ejector spring (12).

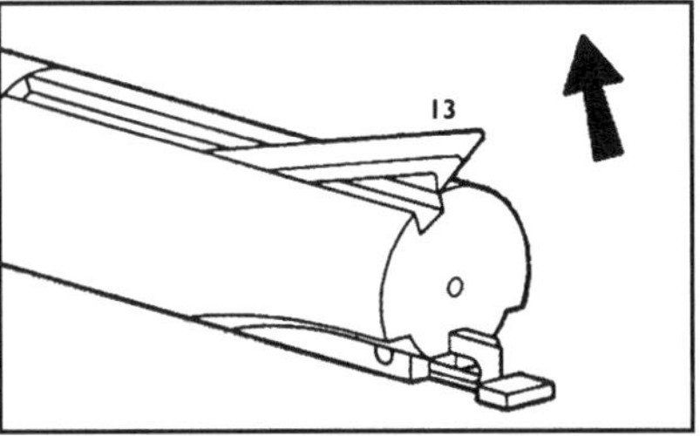

5 To disassemble extractor (13) (used on bolt Type I) grasp claw of extractor and lift up carefully to free stud on bottom of extractor from locating hole in bolt. When stud is clear, pull extractor forward and away from bolt. When reassembling, end of extractor should fit inside of bolt body between the two bolt assembly pins. Unscrew front and rear guard screws (20) and (29) and remove stock.

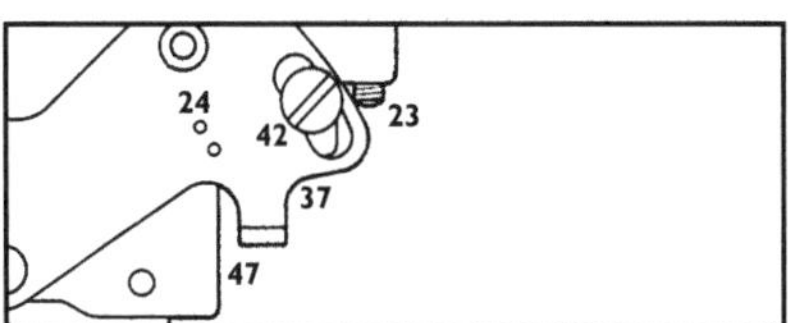

6 Back off housing lock screw (23) one complete turn. Drive out housing pin (24) through large hole in top of safety and remove complete housing assembly from receiver. Lift sear (43) and remove trigger spring (50) from housing (47). Push safety pivot pin retaining washer (39) from end of pivot pin (38) and remove pin. NOTE: Safety plunger is under spring load beneath safety. Carefully unscrew and remove safety retaining screw (42) and safety (37). Lift safety plunger (40) and safety plunger spring (41) from housing. Bolt stop (7) and bolt stop spring (8) may then be removed. Remaining components comprising the trigger housing sub-assembly are factory assembled and disassembly is not recommended.

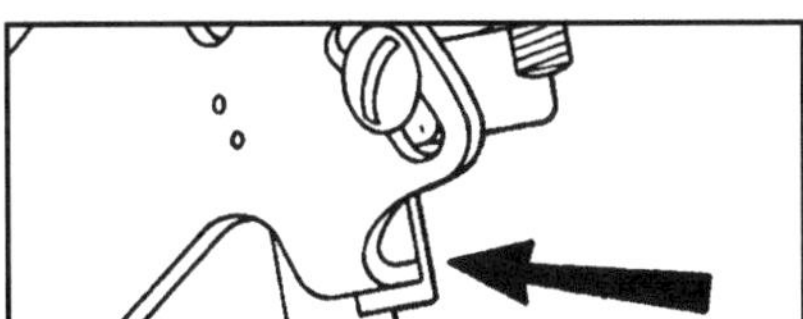

7 Reassemble rifle in reverse order. Bent tab on bottom of safety must fit into recess in bottom of bolt stop (arrow). Tighten housing lock screw until assembly is snug. Bolt stop must work freely in receiver when actuated by safety.

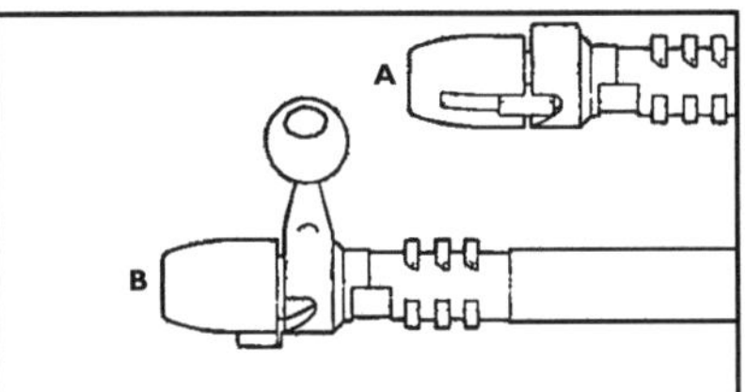

8 Bolt must be cocked to reassemble into rifle. When uncocked, firing pin head will snap forward into cocking cam at rear of bolt (A). Clamp firing pin head in vise jaws and raise bolt handle until firing pin head moves out of cocking cam and snaps into cocking notch on rear of bolt (B).

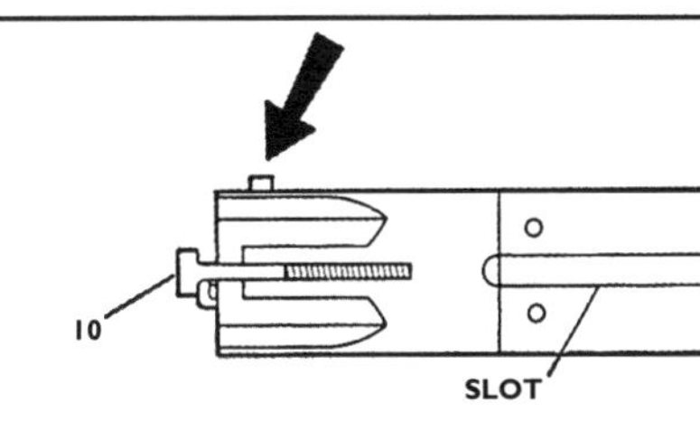

9 To reassemble Type No. I bolt assembly (rotary head) into receiver, align ejector (10) with slot on bottom of bolt body. With bolt head guide pin (arrow) in 9 o clock position, push bolt forward into receiver. For one piece bolt assembly (Type No. 2), simply place bolt into receiver with handle in 2 o clock position and push forward.

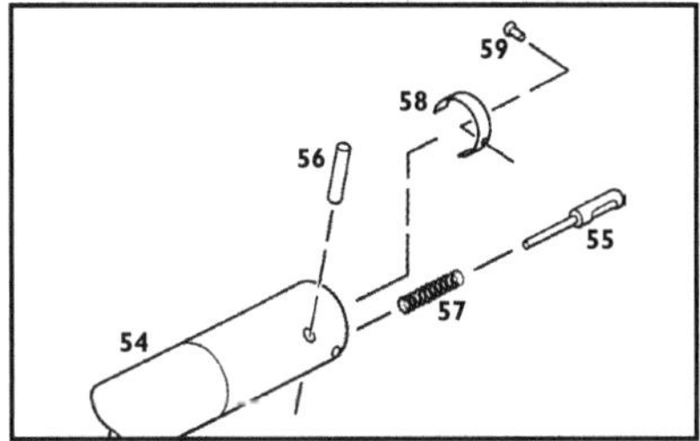

10 Extractor and ejector system used with bolt Type No. 2 for rimless calibers 6mm Rem., .308 Win., .243 Win., .222 Rem., and .22-250 Rem. Extractor is riveted to bolt in proper position at the factory. Disassembly is rarely necessary and should only be attempted by a qualified gunsmith.

REMINGTON MODEL 870 SHOTGUN

PARTS LEGEND

1. Barrel
2. Stock
3. Stock bolt washer
4. Stock bolt lock washer
5. Stock bolt
6. Barrel extension
7. Barrel guide ring *
8. Magazine cap detent spring
9. Magazine cap detent
10. Front sight bead
11. Magazine cap
12. Magazine spring retainer
13. Magazine tube *
14. Magazine spring
15. Receiver
16. Front ejector rivet
17. Magazine follower
18. Ejector
19. Ejector spring
20. Rear ejector rivet
21. Front trigger plate pin
22. Rear trigger plate pin
23. Stock bearing plate
24. Receiver stud
25. Buttplate
26. Buttplate screw (2)
27. Barrel support *
28. Action bar, left *
29. Action bar, right *
30. Fore-end tube
31. Fore-end tube nut
32. Fore-end
33. Left shell latch
34. Right shell latch
35. Hammer plunger
36. Hammer spring
37. Sear
38. Action bar lock spring
39. Hammer pin
40. Front trigger plate pin detent spring
41. Sear pin
42. Rear trigger plate pin detent spring
43. Trigger plate pin bushing
44. Safety spring retaining pin
45. Right connector
46. Left connector
47. Trigger
48. Connector pin
49. Safety plunger
50. Safety spring
51. Safety
52. Trigger pin
53. Trigger plate
54. Carrier pivot tube
55. Sear spring
56. Action bar lock
57. Carrier
58. Hammer
59. Carrier dog
60. Carrier dog washer
61. Carrier dog pin
62. Carrier dog spring
63. Carrier dog follower
64. Slide
65. Firing pin
66. Firing pin retractor spring
67. Locking block stud
68. Locking block
69. Firing pin retaining pin
70. Breech bolt
71. Extractor
72. Extractor spring
73. Extractor plunger

* Part is silver-soldered to other major part.

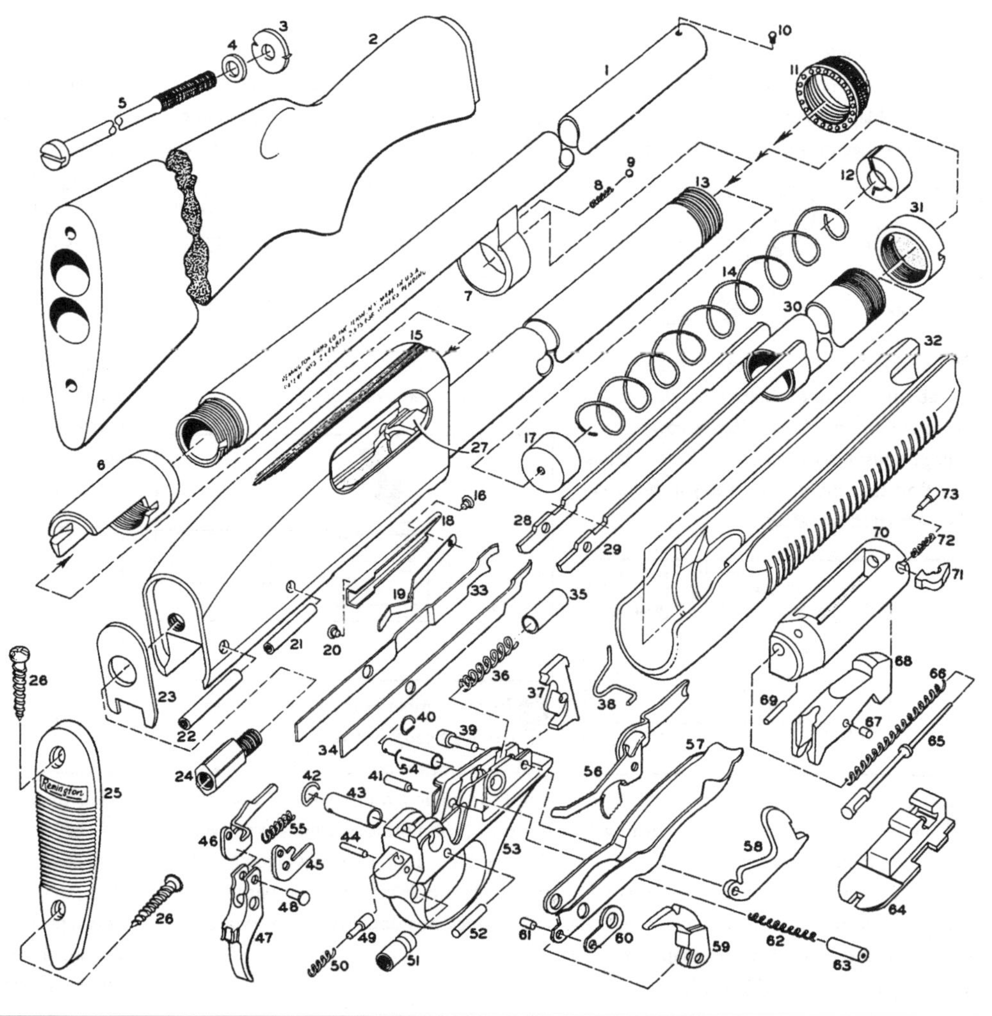

The Remington Model 870 Wingmaster side-ejection, slide-action shotgun was introduced in early 1950 by Remington Arms Co., Inc., of Ilion, New York, as a replacement for the Remington Model 31.

The Model 870 was once available in 20-, 16-, and 12-gauge chamberings with both 2¾-inch and 3-inch chambers available in 12 gauge. Magazine capacity is three, 3-inch Magnum shells, four of the 2¾-inch variety.

By 1988, with over 4,000,000 Model 870s sold, model variations had been reduced to 12- and 20-gauge guns, the latter with 3-inch chambers, only.

The Model 870 has been offered in several grades and with a wide choice of barrel lengths and chokes. Special, 12-gauge riot guns are made for use by security and law enforcement personnel. For the deer hunter Remington makes models with rifle sights and scope sight mounts to allow more precise aiming.

Disassembly of the Model 870 is extremely simple, which makes for great convenience in cleaning.

DISASSEMBLY

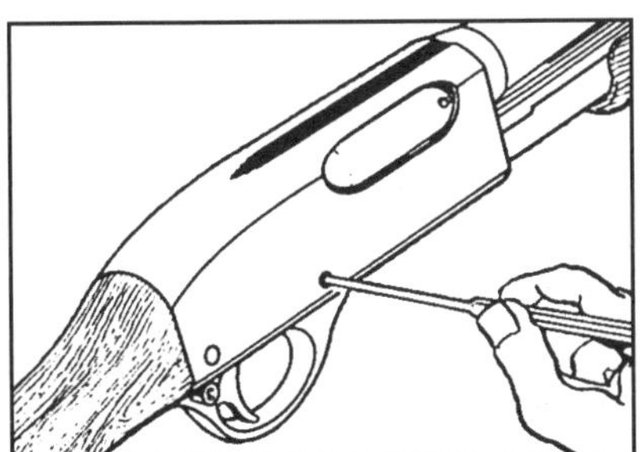

1 To remove trigger plate (53) and assembly, first set safety (51) on safe , then drift out front and rear trigger plate pins (21 & 22). When replacing these pins, trigger plate and receiver (15) holes must be properly aligned and show clear passage.

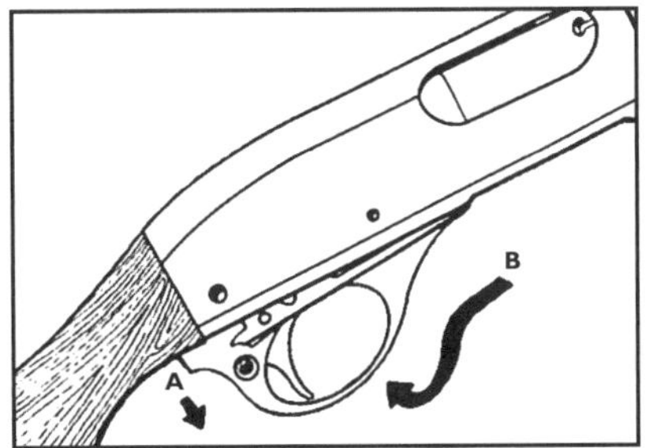

2 Next, lift rear end of trigger plate from receiver (A). Then, slide unit rearward (B), turning it clockwise to clear action bar lock (56). When reassembling trigger plate assembly, rear end of action bar lock must go below end of left connector (46) for gun to function properly.

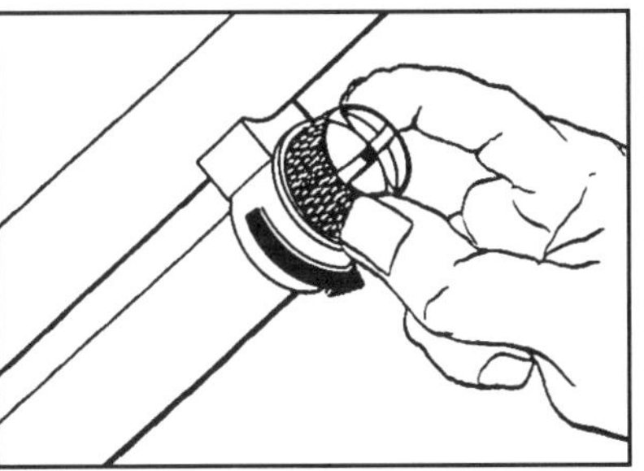

3 To remove barrel assembly, including barrel extension (6), if the gun is cocked, press action bar lock (56) upward. Move fore-end (32) half way back to open the action. Unscrew magazine cap (11), remove it, and then pull barrel assembly from receiver.

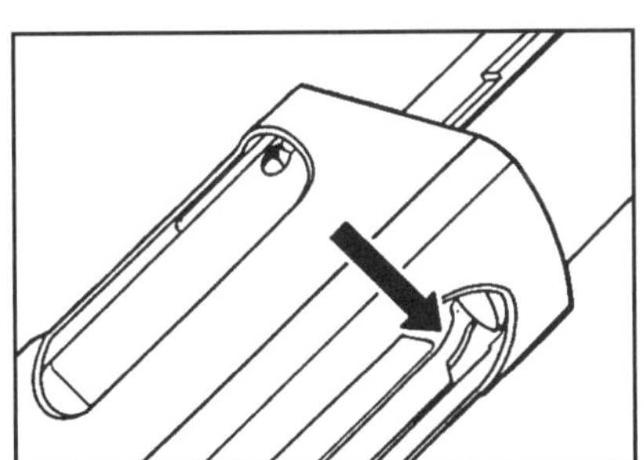

4 To remove fore-end assembly, including fore-end, breech bolt (70), locking block (68), slide (64), etc., press in front end of left shell latch (33) and slide the assembly forward off magazine tube (13). The barrel must be first removed to effect this operation.

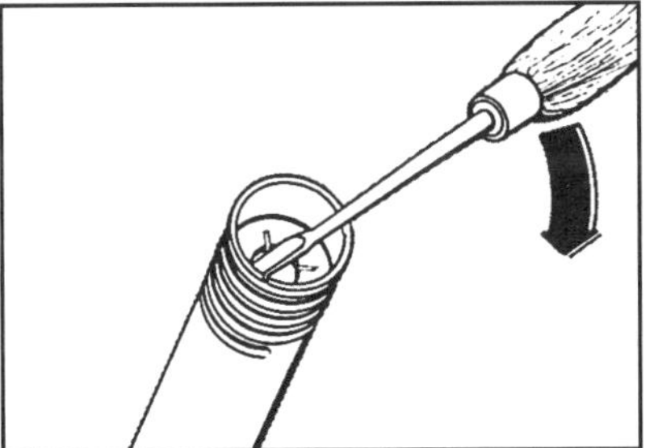

5 To remove magazine spring (14) and magazine follower (17), insert blade of a small screwdriver into hole in spring retainer (12) and pry retainer from magazine tube (13). Remove retainer slowly to relieve tension of magazine spring. Spring and follower may now be removed.

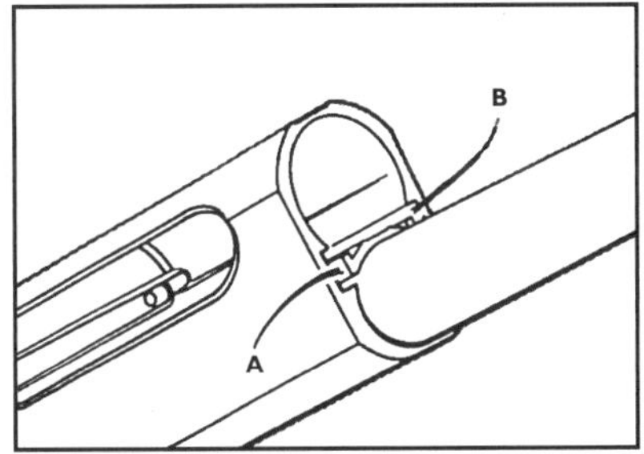

6 Assemble gun in reverse order. Assemble slide to action bars (28 & 29), together with breech bolt assembly. Assemble fore-end tube (30) over magazine tube and insert rear end of action bars (with slide and breech bolt assembly on them) into receiver grooves (A & B). Move assembly rearward gently until it contacts the front end of the right shell latch (34). Press in on right shell latch to clear action bar and slide fore- end gently rearward again until it contacts the left shell latch (33). Press in left shell latch and push fore-end rearward until it is stopped by the action bar lock (56).

REMINGTON MODEL 878 SHOTGUN

PARTS LEGEND

1. Action bar assembly
2. Action spring
3. Action spring stop
4. Barrel assembly
5. Breechbolt
6. Buttplate
7. Buttplate screw (2)
8. Extractor
9. Extractor plunger
10. Extractor spring
11. Firing pin
12. Firing pin retaining pin
13. Firing pin retractor spring
14. Fore-end
15. Fore-end ring
16. Fore-end ring washer
17. Locking block assembly
18. Magazine cap
19. Magazine follower
20. Magazine spring
21. Operating handle
22. Piston assembly
23. Receiver assembly
24. Receiver stud
25. Shell latch, right
26. Shell latch, left
27. Stock bearing plate
28. Stock bolt
29. Stock bolt lock washer
30. Stock bolt washer
31. Trigger plate assembly
32. Trigger plate pin, front
33. Trigger plate pin, rear

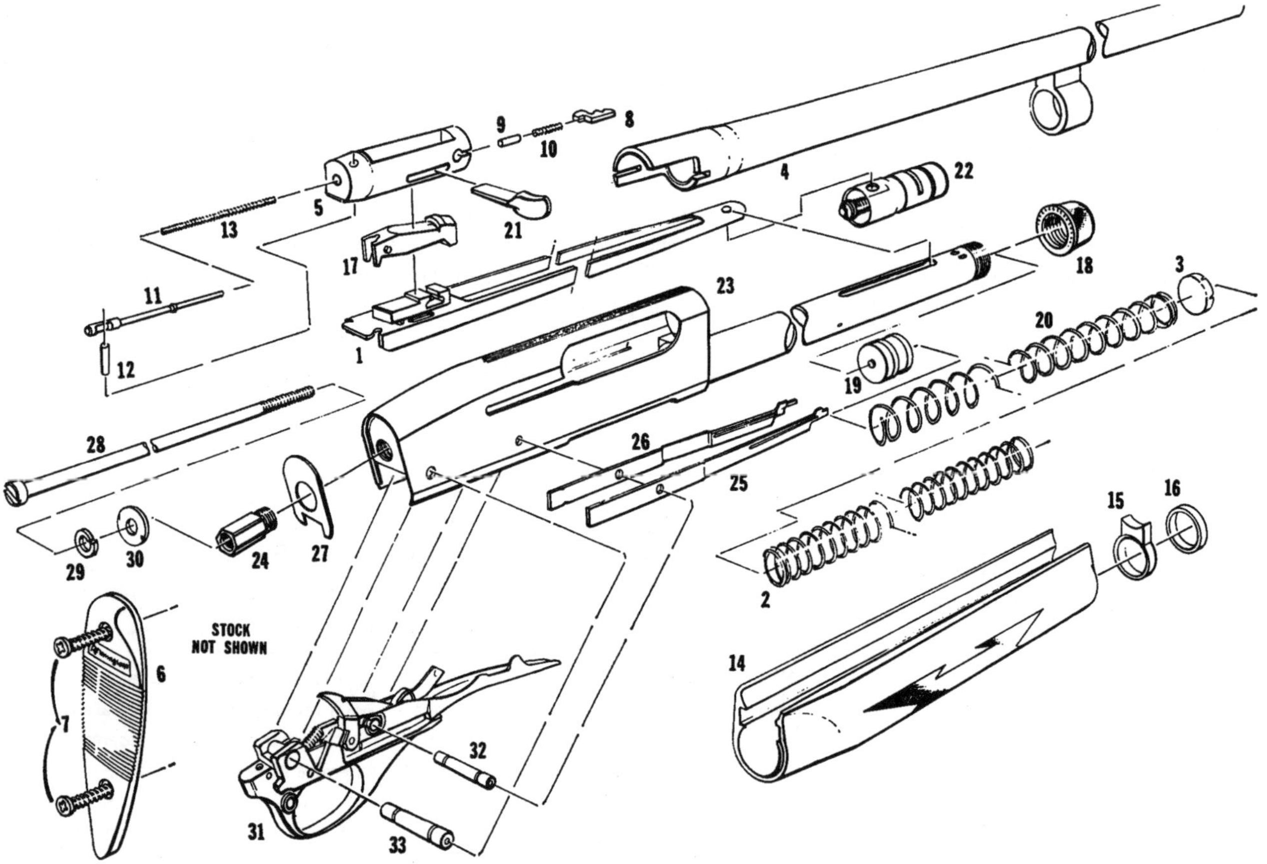

STOCK NOT SHOWN

Produced from 1959 to 1962, the Remington Model 878 "Automaster" semi-automatic shotgun with gas-operated action was designed to fire a variety of 12-ga. 2¾" loads from light to magnum without any change or adjustment by the user. This was made possible by a self-adjusting gas piston located in the front of the tubular magazine under the barrel.

After the shot load clears the barrel, a small amount of propellant gas is metered through two gas ports to the piston assembly. Piston inertia during initial recoil of the gun causes the piston to be displaced toward the muzzle, and this restricts the amount of gas entering the piston chamber. Amount of restriction is proportional to the recoil and, therefore, to the load being fired.

The Model 878 was offered in field and trap versions and several different grades. Interchangeable barrels with various lengths and chokes were available, but in 12-ga. only. Magazine capacity was two shells. With one shell in the chamber, total capacity of the gun was three rounds.

A commonly-encountered version of this gun is the 878A with uncheckered walnut stock and fore-end, and no engraving. Less frequently seen are higher grades with checkered stock and fore-end, and game scenes engraved on the receiver sides. Most higher grades of this gun also have a ventilated rib.

DISASSEMBLY

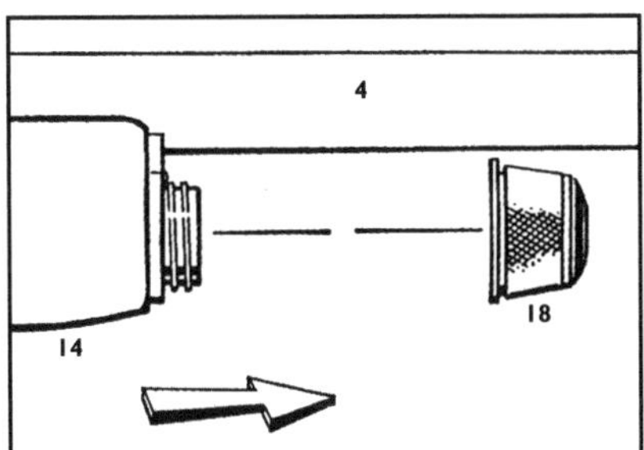

1 Before disassembling the Model 878, push safety on safe. Red band marking on safety will not show. Make sure magazine and chamber are unloaded. Open action to cock hammer, and close action by depressing carrier. (See arrow and CLOSE marking on bottom front of receiver.) Unscrew magazine cap (18) from end of magazine tube. Pull fore-end (14) and barrel assembly (4) out of gun.

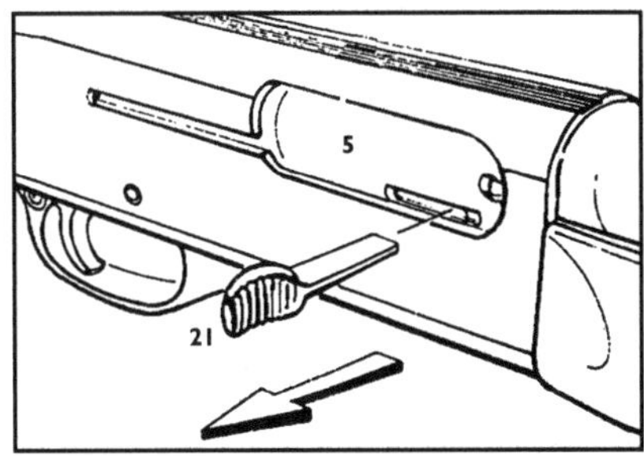

2 Pull operating handle (21) outward to disassemble from breechbolt (5).

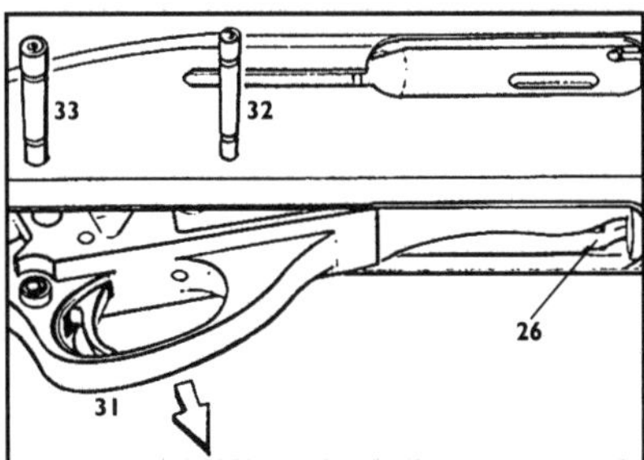

3 Tap out trigger plate pins (32 & 33). Pull out trigger plate assembly (31). Shell latch, left (26) may fall free. Align shell latch flush with front trigger plate pin when replacing trigger plate assembly, and be sure bent rear tail of disconnector is under left connector.

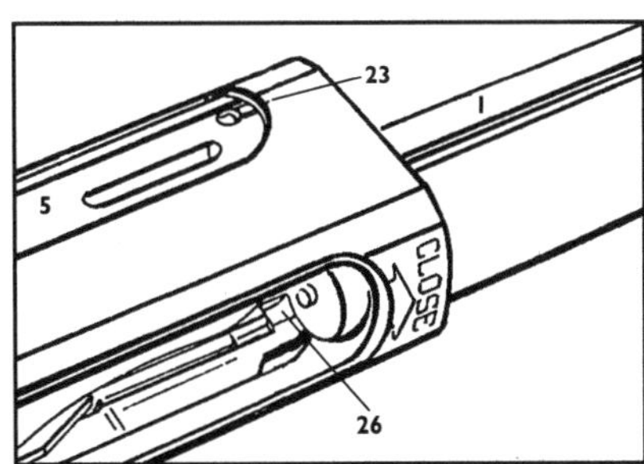

4 Push breechbolt forward in receiver assembly (23). Depress left shell latch to allow action bar assembly (1) to pass slightly forward on magazine tube.

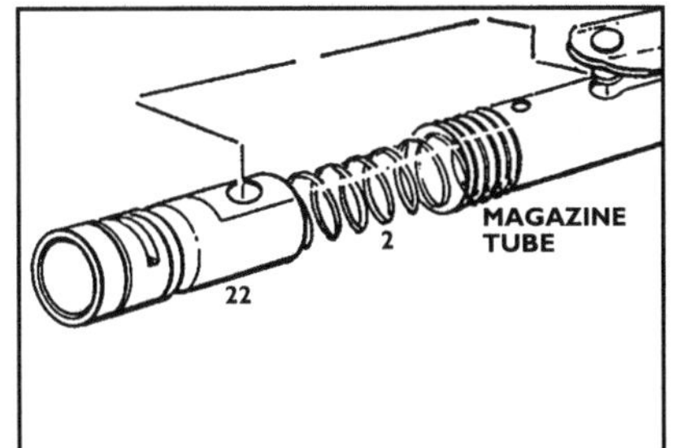

5 Move action bar assembly forward until stud on front of action bar aligns with stud removal notch, and lift out action bar. Piston assembly (22) and action spring (2) can then be removed from front of magazine tube.

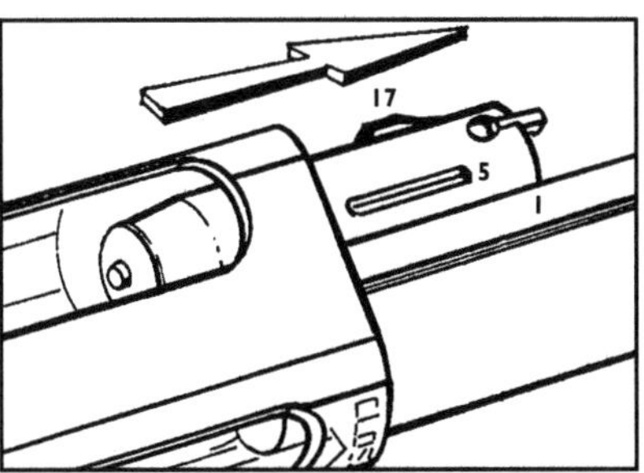

6 Pull action bar assembly and breechbolt out of receiver. Lift breechbolt with locking block assembly (17) from gun.

REMINGTON MODEL 1100 SHOTGUN

PARTS LEGEND

1. Action bar
2. Action bar sleeve
3. Action spring
4. Action spring follower
5. Action spring plug
6. Action spring plug pin
7. Action spring tube nut
8. Action spring tube nut lock washer
9. Action spring tube nut washer
10. Barrel
11. Barrel seal
12. Breechbolt
13. Breechbolt buffer
14. Breechbolt return plunger
15. Breechbolt return plunger retaining ring
16. Breechbolt return plunger spring
17. Buttplate
18. Buttplate screw (2)
19. Buttplate spacer
20. Carrier
21. Carrier dog
22. Carrier dog pin
23. Carrier dog washer
24. Carrier dog follower
25. Carrier dog follower spring
26. Carrier latch
27. Carrier latch pin
28. Carrier latch follower
29. Carrier latch spring
30. Carrier pivot tube
31. Carrier release
32. Carrier release pin
33. Carrier release spring
34. Connector, left
35. Connector, right
36. Connector pin
37. Disconnector
38. Ejector
39. Extractor
40. Extractor plunger
41. Extractor spring
42. Feed latch
43. Firing pin
44. Firing pin retaining pin
45. Firing pin retractor spring
46. Fore-end
47. Fore-end support assembly
48. Front sight
49. Front sight base
50. Grip cap
51. Grip cap inlay
52. Grip cap screw
53. Grip cap spacer
54. Hammer
55. Hammer pin
56. Hammer pin washer
57. Hammer plunger
58. Hammer spring
59. Interceptor latch
60. Interceptor latch retainer
61. Interceptor latch spring
62. Link
63. Locking block assembly
64. Magazine cap
65. Magazine cap detent
66. Magazine cap detent spring
67. Magazine cap plug
68. Magazine follower
69. Magazine spring
70. Magazine spring retainer
71. Operating handle
72. Operating handle plunger
73. Operating handle plunger retainer
74. Operating handle spring
75. Piston
76. Piston seal
77. Receiver assembly
78. Safety
79. Safety detent ball
80. Safety spring
81. Safety spring retaining pin
82. Sear
83. Sear pin
84. Sear spring
85. Stock
86. Stock bearing plate
87. Slide buffer
88. Trigger
89. Trigger pin
90. Trigger plate
91. Trigger plate pin bushing
92. Trigger plate pin detent spring, front (2)
93. Trigger plate pin detent spring, rear
94. Trigger plate pin, front
95. Trigger plate pin, rear

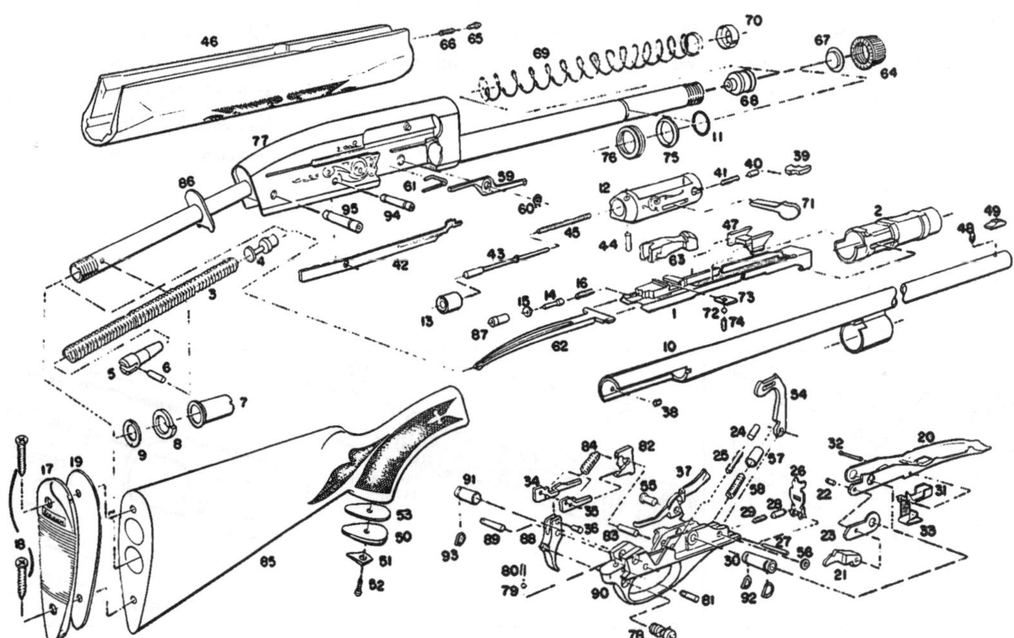

Introduced in 1963, the gas-operated Remington Model 1100 semi-automatic shotgun was offered in field, trap and skeet models, a rifled-slug "Deer" version and various grades.

Initially, the Model 1100 was offered in 12-gauge, 2¾-inch and 12-gauge, three-inch Magnum only. Later, it also became available in 16-, 20-, and 28-gauge, 2¾inch 20-gauge, three-inch Magnum and .410 bore 2½- and 3-inch. Interchangeable barrels with various chokes and lengths (25 inches only for 28-gauge and .410 bore.) A ventilated rib is standard on trap and skeet versions. Magazine capacity in most versions is four shells.

Most metal parts of the Model 1100 are steel with a high-luster blue finish. The stock and fore-end are mostly American walnut with impressed checkering on the pistol grip and fore-end. The receiver sides are decorated with roll engraving.

DISASSEMBLY

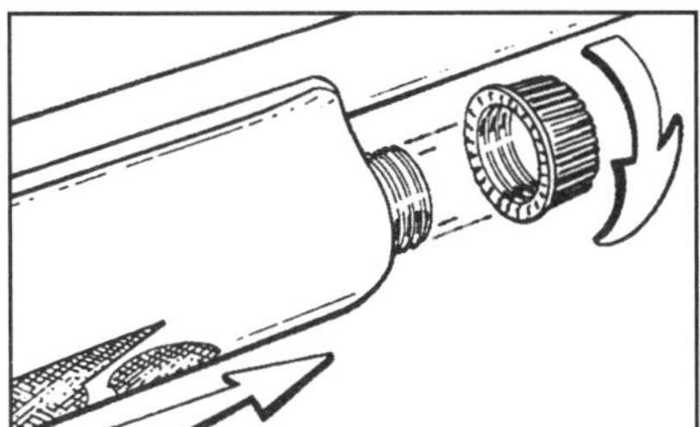

1 To field-strip for routine cleaning and lubrication, engage safety (78) on safe, and unload gun. Unscrew and remove magazine cap (64). Slide fore-end (46) forward and remove. Pull barrel (10) forward from receiver (77).

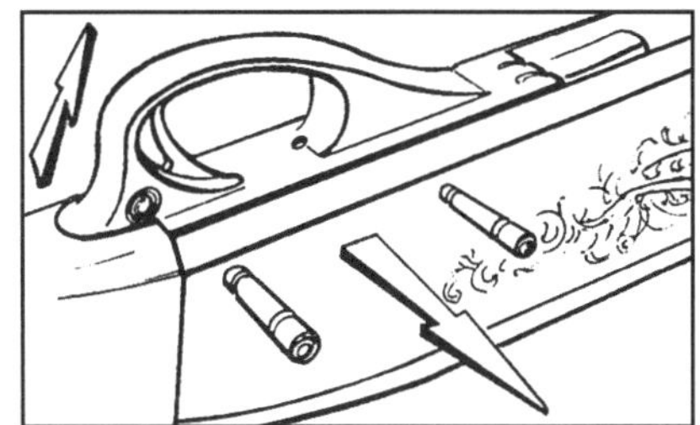

2 For further disassembly, cock gun and close action. Tap out trigger plate pins (94 & 95) from either side. Lift up and remove trigger plate assembly from receiver. When reassembling, guide disconnector (37) carefully into receiver to avoid damage.

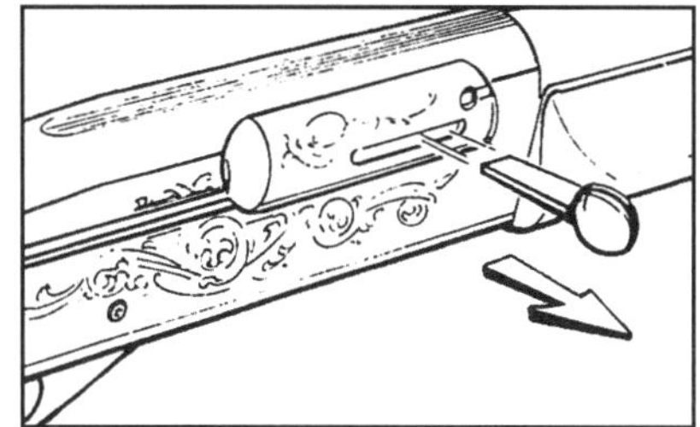

3 Remove operating handle (71) by pulling it to the right out of breech-bolt (12).

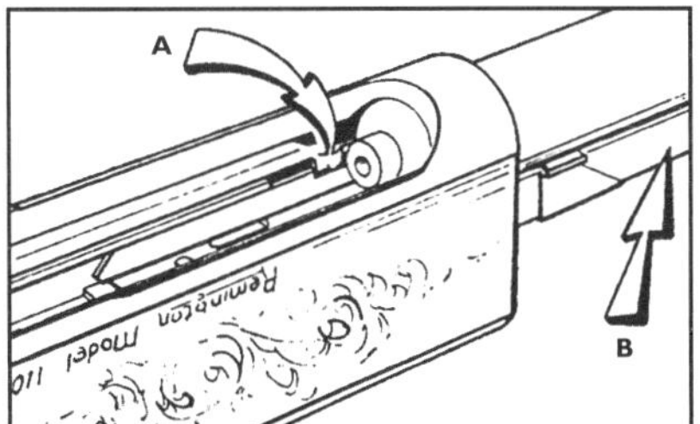

4 Remove barrel seal (11), piston (75), and piston seal (76). With action fully forward, depress feed latch (42) at A, and pull action bar (1) at B with breechbolt forward. Action bar sleeve (2), action bar, breechbolt with locking block (63) attached, and fore-end support (47) can now be disassembled from gun.

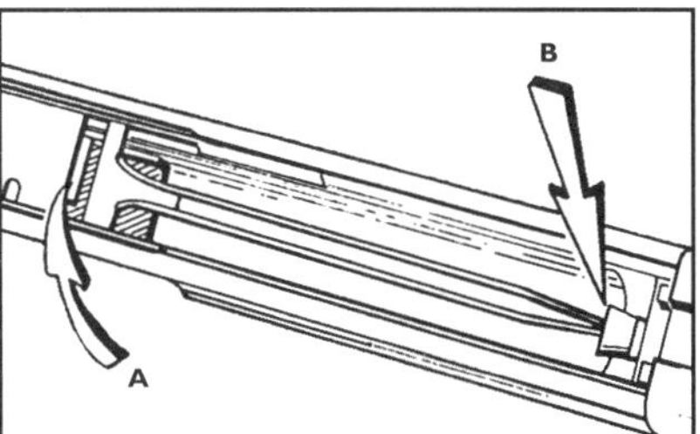

5 Link (62) can be removed after action bar at A is moved forward for disassembly. Squeeze sides of link lightly at rear with long-nose pliers, and pull forward to separate from action spring follower (4) at B. Tilt slightly to remove from gun.

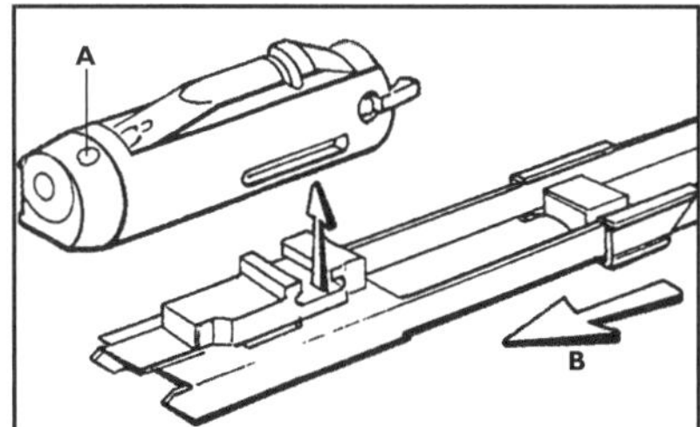

6 Lift up breechbolt and disassemble from action bar. Drive firing pin retaining pin (44) at A from breechbolt, remove firing pin (43), spring (45), and locking block. NOTE: Fore-end support assembly at B should slide easily to rear of action bar when fore-end is reassembled on gun.

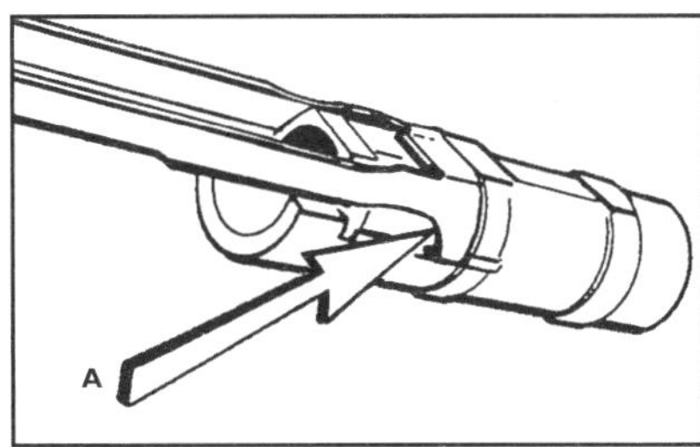

7 Action bar can be disassembled from action bar sleeve after removing action bar from receiver. Insert small tool under lip of bar at A. Pry up until bar disassembles from sleeve. Snap down on bar to reassemble on sleeve. In reassembly, guide breechbolt and action bar carefully in receiver until contact is made with feed latch. Depress feed latch; then, continue pushing breechbolt into receiver. Release latch, and make certain that rear of action bar aligns properly with front of link.

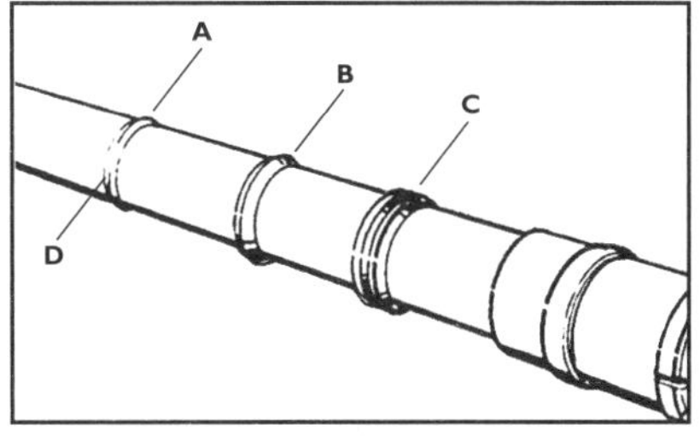

8 Barrel seal at A, piston at B, and piston seal at C in proper position on magazine tube. Barrel seal must position easily in recess of tube at D. Open action slightly when reassembling seals and piston on magazine tube.

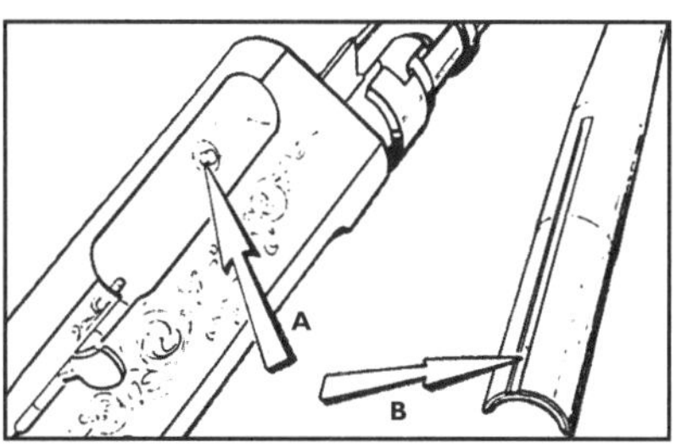

9 To replace barrel, open action. Align gas cylinder on middle of barrel over magazine tube; then, insert breech end of barrel in receiver. Align long slot at A on barrel with barrel lock (stud) at B in receiver. Slide barrel fully into receiver. Replace fore-end and magazine cap. Screw cap down tightly.

THE REMINGTON 3200 SHOTGUN

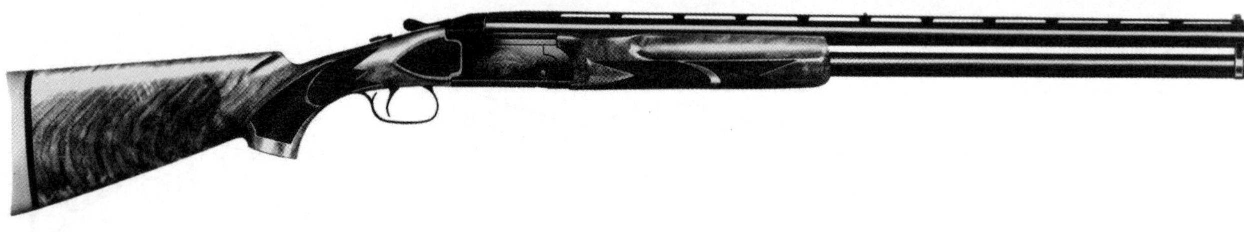

PARTS LEGEND

1. Barrel assembly*
2. Bottom tang *
3. Bottom tang screws (2)
4. Butt plate
5. Butt plate screw (2)
6. Connector
7. Connector pin
8. Ejector, left *
9. Ejector, right *
10. Ejector hammer, right
11. Ejector hammer, left
12. Ejector hammer pin
13. Ejector hammer pivot ring
14. Ejector hammer spring (2)
15. Ejector plunger assembly (2)
16. Ejector sear (2)
17. Ejector sear spring (2)
18. Ejector stop pin (2)
19. Ejector trip rod, left
20. Ejector trip rod, right
21. Firing pin (2)
22. Firing pin housing
23. Firing pin housing assembly pin
24. Firing pin retractor
25. Fore-end
26. Fore-end adjuster plate *
27. Fore-end adjuster plate lock nut
28. Fore-end adjuster plate stud *
29. Fore-end latch*
30. Fore-end latch cover*
31. Fore-end latch finger piece *
32. Fore-end latch spring (2) *
33. Fore-end screw, front
34. Fore-end screw, rear
35. Fore-end screw nut
36. Fore-end iron *
37. Frame *
38. Front sight
39. Hammer, right
40. Hammer, left
41. Hammer cocking cam
42. Hammer cocking cam pin
43. Hammer cocking cam spring
44. Hammer cocking rod
45. Hammer pin
46. Hammer plunger, right
47. Hammer plunger, left
48. Hammer spring (2)
49. Rear connector link
50. Safety selector assembly
51. Safety selector detent
52. Safety selector detent spring
53. Sear, left
54. Sear, right
55. Sear pin
56. Sear spring (2)
57. Sear spring plunger (2)
58. Selector block
59. Selector block guide
60. Selector block guide pin
61. Stock
62. Stock bolt
63. Stock bolt lock washer
64. Stock bolt washer
65. Tang block screw
66. Tang block slot nut
67. Tang connecting block
68. Tang strut
69. Tang strut pin (2)
70. Toggle block
71. Toggle block retaining pin
72. Toggle link
73. Toggle link screw
74. Toggle slide block
75. Toggle slide block stud
76. Top lock *
77. Top lock latch
78. Top lock latch pin
79. Top lock latch spring
80. Top lock lever
81. Top lock lever plunger
82. Top lock lever screw
83. Top lock lever spring
84. Top lock shim
85. Trigger
86. Trigger adjusting screw
87. Trigger adjusting screw nut
88. Trigger connector spring
89. Trigger connector spring pin
90. Trigger guard
91. Trigger guard pin, front
92. Trigger guard pin, rear
93. Trigger pin
94. Trigger stop screw
95. Trigger stop screw nut
96. Yoke
97. Yoke rod
98. Yoke rod buffer spring
99. Yoke rod buffer spring washer
100. Yoke rod nut (2)
101. Yoke rod spring
102. Ejector sear pin (2)

* These parts are manufactured to close tolerances and selectively assembled at the factory to assure proper function. Should any require service the gun must be returned to the factory

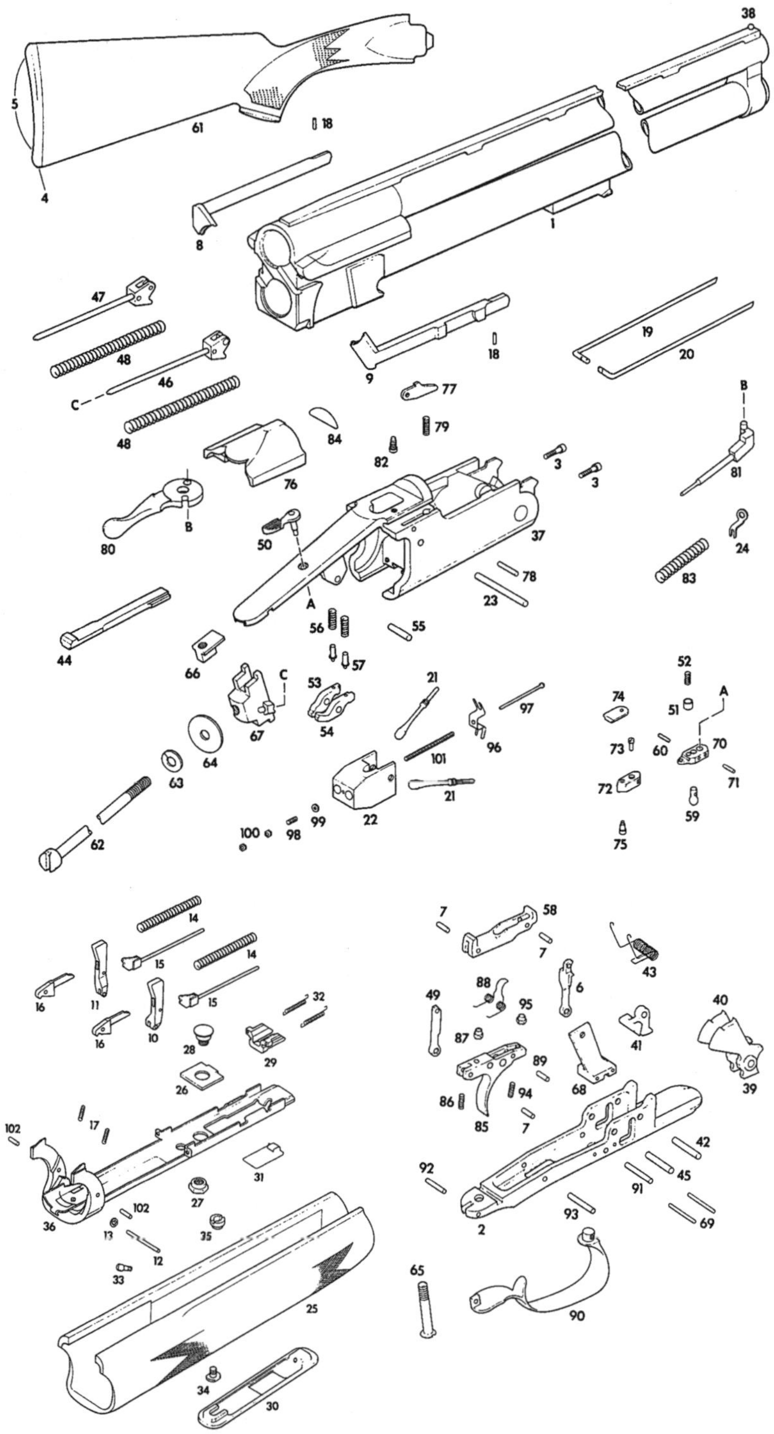

The Remington Model 3200 shotgun was introduced in 1973. It generally resembles the Model 32, an earlier Remington over-under made from 1932 until 1942. Both models have a separated barrel construction and are bolted by a sliding top lock.

Offered in 12-gauge only, the Model 3200 has a mechanically operated single trigger and selective ejectors. The thumb operated tang safety is pivoted from side to side rather than the more usual back and forth sliding movement. Swinging it left or right selects which barrel is fired first. The barrels are assembled to a monobloc which has large lugs on each side. These lugs engage shoulders in the frame to prevent the thrust of recoil from being transmitted to the hinge pin. In guns of early production the tang was assembled to the frame by a pin, and the front and rear fore-end screws were identical. These and other details have been modified to the construction shown here.

Though made in both field and target versions, the Model 3200 evolved into a very successful gun for either skeet or trap competition. The field guns were discontinued early in the gun's production history and a saturated market among target gunners led to its being discontinued altogether in 1984.

DISASSEMBLY

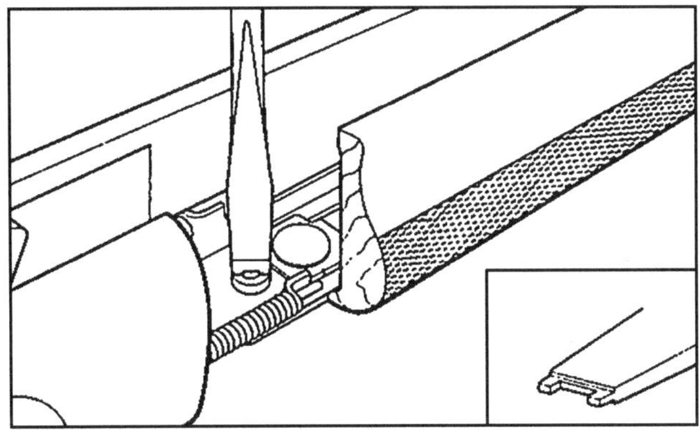

1 Make sure gun is unloaded. Close action, push fore-end latch (29) rearward and rotate fore-end downward slightly to disengage from barrel assembly (1). Pull forward and away from gun. Open action and rotate barrel assembly downward as far as possible. Move assembly rearward slightly to disengage from pivot pins in frame (37) and remove.

Unscrew fore-end screw nut (35), using altered screwdriver as shown, and front fore-end screw (33). Pull fore-end latch cover (30) and rear fore-end screw (34) from fore-end (25). Slide fore-end iron assembly unit from fore-end. Remove buttplate (4) and unscrew stock bolt (62). Further disassembly is not required for normal cleaning and lubrication.

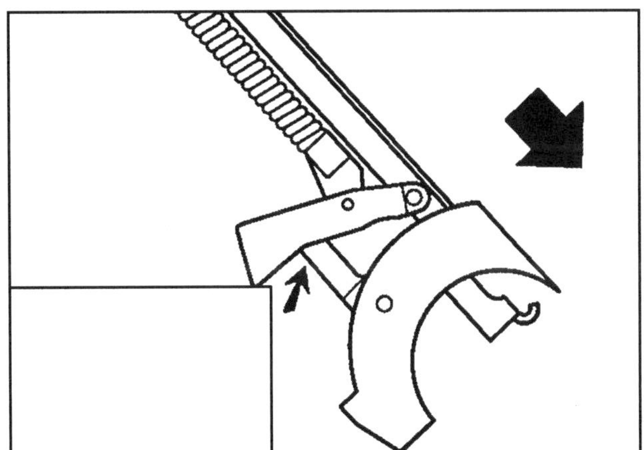

2 To take fore-end iron assembly apart, hook point of ejector hammers (10 & 11) on edge of bench, press ejector sears (16) downward and ease ejector hammers rearward. Grasp ejector plunger blocks forward of ejector hammers with long nosed pliers and pry free from engagement with pins in ejector hammers. Remove ejector plunger asemblies (15) and ejector hammer springs (14). Drive out ejector hammer pin (12) from right to left and remove ejector hammers and pivot ring (13). Remove ejector sears and springs (17). Press fore-end latch finger piece (31) forward to disassemble from fore-end latch (29). Unscrew and remove fore-end adjuster plate lock nut (27), stud (28) and fore-end adjuster plate (26). Disengage fore-end latch springs (32) from front of fore-end iron (36). Slide fore-end latch rearward and out and disengage springs from latch.

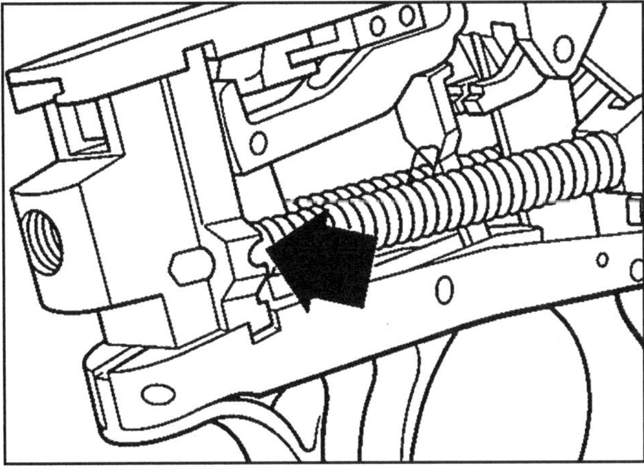

3 Insert 1⁄16-inch diameter pin to a depth of ¼ inch into small hole (arrow) in tang connecting block (67). Depress top lock latch (77) to release top lock (76). Pull trigger twice to fire hammers, rotate hammers forward and remove right and left hammer plunger assembly units. CAUTION: Do not disturb small pin at rear of assembly. Disassembly of these units is not necessary except for replacement of parts. Hammer springs (48) are under high compression and must be prevented from flying free when pins are removed from hammer plunger rods. Drive out front and rear trigger guard pins (91 & 92) and remove trigger guard (90). Rotate hammers to rear (cocked) position. Push right and left ejector trip rods (20) and (19) forward as far as possible, rotate bend ends upward through slots and remove. Unscrew tang block screw (65). Remove tang block slot nut (66) and tang connecting block.

THE REMINGTON 3200 SHOTGUN

DISASSEMBLY CONT'D

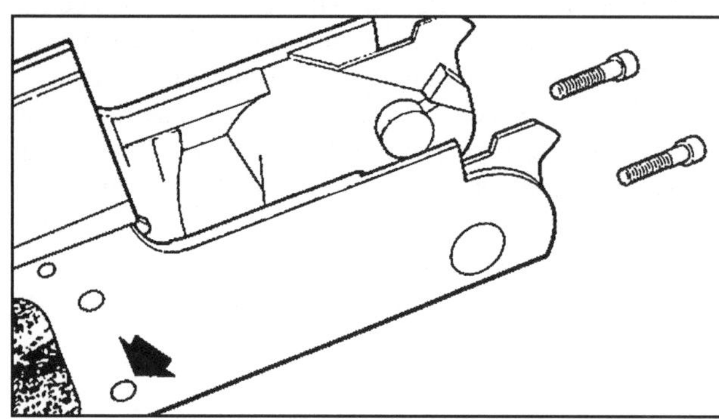

4 Unscrew bottom tang screws (3) or drive out assembly pin (arrow). NOTE: Do not attempt to remove the filler pins found in early guns modified by the factory. Drive out sear pin (55) and remove right and left sears (54) and (53), sear spring plungers (57) and sear springs (56). Hold selector block (58) rearward, grasp bottom tang assembly unit and pull rearward and out of frame. Remove hammer cocking rod (44). Drive out trigger pin and remove trigger assembly unit. Disassembly of this unit is seldom necessary and should not be attempted except by a qualified gunsmith. Drive out hammer pin (45) and remove right and left hammers (39) and (40). Drive out hammer cocking cam pin (42) and remove hammer cocking cam (41) and spring (43). Disassembly of tang strut (68) is not necessary.

To disassemble safety, provide support beneath side of toggle block (70) and drive out toggle block retaining pin (71) from left to right. Drive safety selector assembly (50) from toggle block. CAUTION: Safety selector detent (51), located between toggle block and top tang, is under compressed load of safety selector detent spring (52). Carefully slide remaining assembly from top tang.

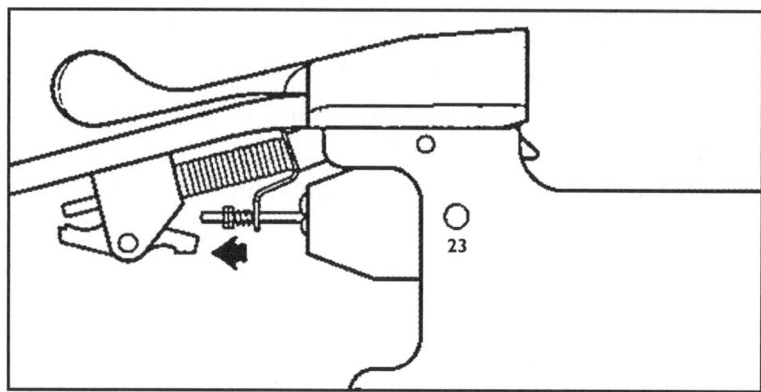

5 With top lock latched in rear position, drive out firing pin housing assembly pin (23). Grasp yoke rod (97) and retract and hold as far rearward as possible and pull firing pin housing assembly unit from frame. Unscrew yoke rod nuts (100) and remove firing pins (21), yoke (96), yoke rod buffer spring (98), washer (99), yoke rod and yoke rod spring (101).

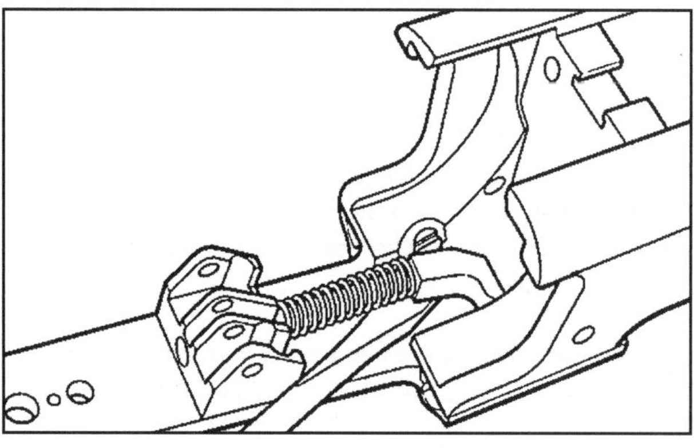

6 Release top lock lever to forward position. Using small screwdriver, pry stud on top lock lever plunger (81) from hole in top lock lever. Unscrew top lock lever screw (82). Depress top lock latch (77) and pull top lock and lever from frame. Remove top lock shim (84). Lift top lock latch spring (79) from frame. Drive out top lock latch pin (78) and remove latch. Pull top lock lever plunger, spring (83) and firing pin retractor (24) from top of frame.

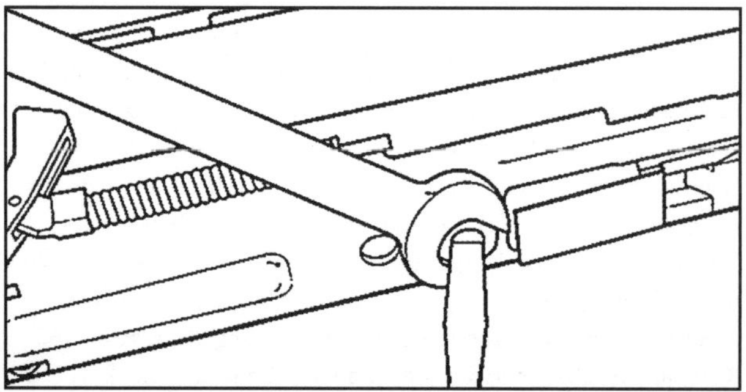

7 Wear between fore-end iron and frame is taken up by adjusting the fore-end adjuster plate. Remove fore-end and fore-end iron assembly. Replace fore-end iron assembly on gun. Loosen fore-end adjuster plate lock nut and rotate stud to right or left until desired tightness is obtained when action is opened. Hold stud in position, tighten lock nut and reassemble.

REMINGTON MODEL 7400 RIFLE

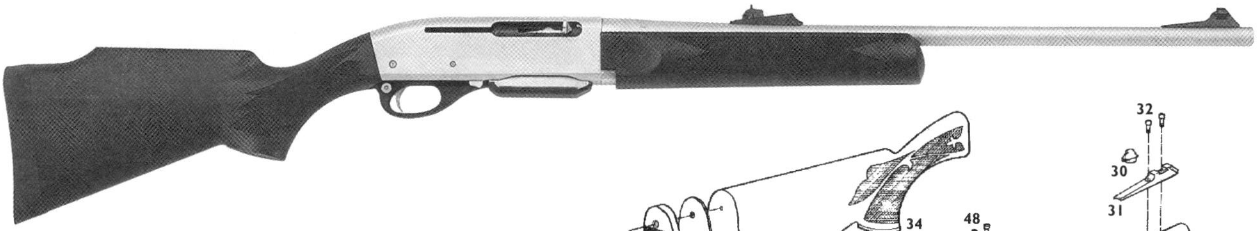

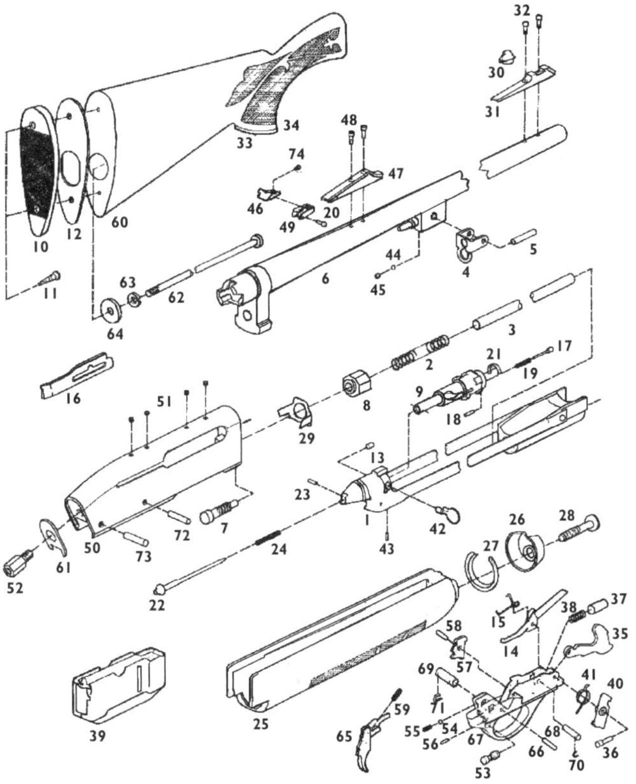

PARTS LEGEND

1. Action bar assembly
2. Action spring
3. Action tube
4. Action tube support
5. Action tube support pin
6. Barrel assembly
7. Barrel extension bolt
8. Barrel take down nut (.30-06)
9. Breech bolt
10. Butt plate frame
11. Butt plate frame screw
12. Plate insert
    Butt plate insert screw
13. Cam pin
14. Disconnector
15. Disconnector spring
16. Ejector port cover
17. Ejector
18. Ejector retaining pin
19. Ejector spring
20. Elevation screw
21. Extractor
22. Firing pin
23. Firing pin retaining pin
24. Firing pin retracting spring
25. Fore-end assembly and
    fore-end reinforcement assembly
26. Fore-end cap
27. Fore-end cap spacer
28. Fore-end screw
29. Fore-end spring
30. Front sight
31. Front sight ramp
32. Front sight ramp screw
33. Grip cap
34. not shown
35. Hammer
36. Hammer pin
37. Hammer plunger
38. Hammer spring
39. Magazine assembly
40. Magazine latch
41. Magazine latch spring
42. Operating handle
43. Operating handle retaining Pin
44. Orifice ball
45. Orifice screw
46. Rear sight aperture
47. Rear sight base
48. Rear sight base screw
49. Rear sight slide
50. Receiver assembly
51. Receiver plug screw
52. Receiver stud
53. Safety mechanism
54. Safety mechanism detent ball
55. Safety mechanism spring
56. Safety mechanism spring
    retaining pin
57. Sear
58. Sear pin
59. Sear spring
60. Stock assembly
61. Stock bearing plate
62. Stock bolt
63. Stock bolt lock washer
64. Stock bolt washer
65. Trigger assembly
66. Trigger pin
67. Trigger plate
    Trigger plate assembly
68. Trigger plate pin bushing, front
69. Trigger plate pin bushing, rear
70. Trigger plate pin detent spring, front
71. Trigger plate pin detent spring, rear
72. Trigger plate pin, front
73. Trigger plate pin, rear
74. Windage screw

The Remington Model 7400, designed by the Remington Arms Research & Development department and introduced in 1981, is an autoloading centerfire rifle with a gas-metered operating system.

The 7400 has been offered in the following chamberings: 6mm Remington (1981 – 1995), .243 Win. (1981 – Present), .270 Winchester (1981 – Present), 7mm Remington Express (1981 - 1987), .280 Remington (1988 – Present), .30-06 Sprg. (1981 – Present), .308 Winchester (1981 – Present) and .35 Whelen (1993 – 1995). Model variations include the Special Purpose marketed between 1993 and 1995, the Synthetic, first manufactured in1998 and the Weathermaster, introduced in 2004.

DISASSEMBLY

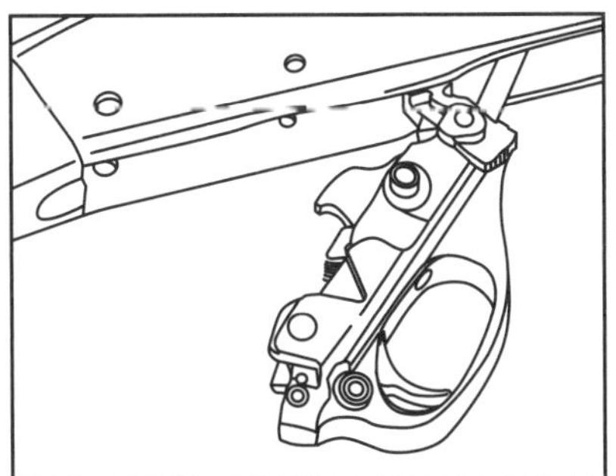

1 Move the rear end of the trigger guard assembly down and forward, then down out of the receiver.

2 Pull the action tube forward out, while releasing the bolt very slowly. This will release the action spring. The action spring will cause tension. The action spring can be removed from the action bar sleeve and taken out. CAUTION: Release the spring carefully.

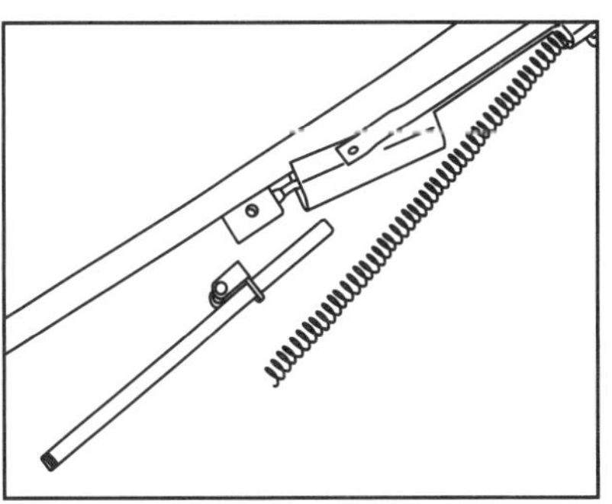

REMINGTON MODELS 1885 & 1899

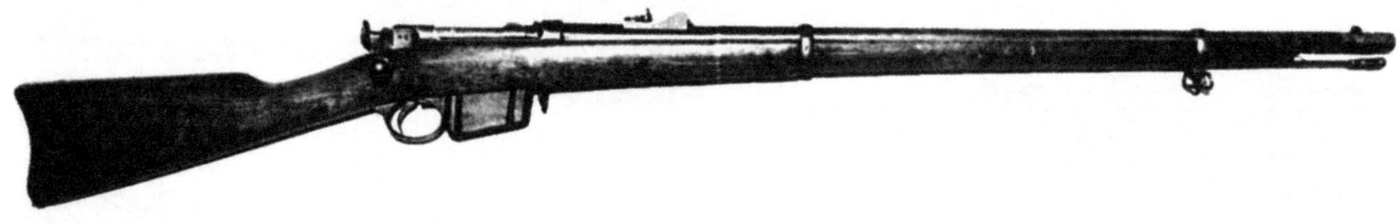

PARTS LEGEND FOR MODEL 1885

1. Barrel
2. Receiver
3. Stock (not shown)
4. Bolt head
5. Striker
6. Mainspring
7. Bolt
8. Cocking piece
9. Striker retaining nut
10. Extractor
11. Extractor locking spring
12. Trigger
13. Sear
14. Sear pin
15. Magazine catch
16. Magazine catch pin
17. Sear and magazine catch spring
18. Trigger pin
19. Trigger guard
20. Front screw, trigger guard
21. Tang screw, receiver
22. Magazine cutoff spring
23. Screw, magazine cutoff spring
24. Rear sight
25. Screws, rear sight (2)
26. Front sight
27. Pin, front sight
28. Middle band
29. Front band with sling swivel and stacking swivel
30. Band retaining springs (2)
31. Nose cap, stock
32. Screw, nose cap
33. Ram rod
34. Retaining nut, ram rod, press fit in stock
35. Buttplate
36. Screws, buttplate(2)
37. Magazine assembly

PARTS LEGEND FOR MODEL 1899

1. Barrel
2. Receiver
3. Stock (not shown)
   3a. Upper hand guard
4. Bolt head
5. Extractor
6. Striker
7. Mainspring
8. Bolt
9. Locking lever, Bolt assembly
10. Cocking piece
11. Striker retaining nut
12. Trigger
13. Sear
14. Sear pin
15. Magazine catch
16. Magazine catch pin
17. Sear and magazine catch spring
18. Ejector, cartridge
19. Ejector spring
20. Screw, ejector spring
21. Pin, ejector
22. Bolt stop
23. Pin, bolt stop
24. Pin, indexing, bolt stop
25. Retaining screw, Indexing pin
26. Magazine cutoff spring
27. Screw, magazine cutoff spring
28. Trigger pin
29. Trigger guard
30. Front screw, trigger guard
31. Tang screw, receiver
32. Rear sight
33. Screws, rear sight (2)
34. Front sight
35. Front sight pin
36. Middle band
37. Screw, middle band
38. Band retaining spring
39. Nose cap and bayonet stud
40. Screw, nose cap-bayonet stud
41. Front band with sling swivel
42. Ram rod
43. Retaining nut, ram rod,
44. Screws, buttplate(2)
45. Buttplate
46. Magazine assembly

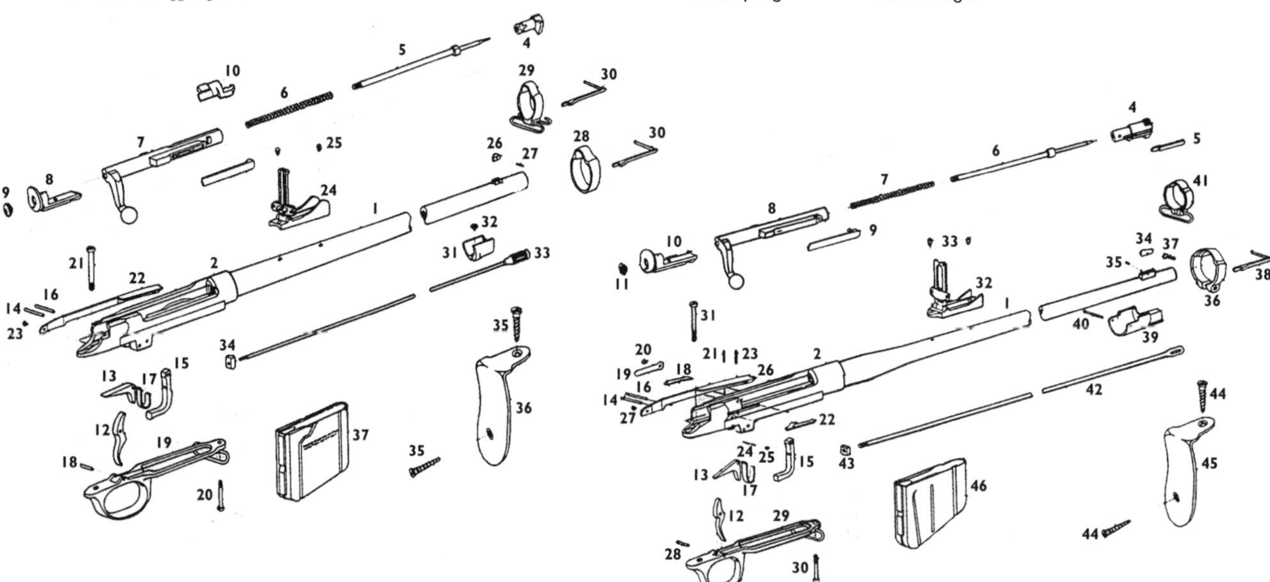

James Paris Lee, began this design in 1877 and ultimately assigned his 1879 patent to Remington. In 1882, Remington submitted two models of the Remington Lee rifle to the United States Army Ordnance Board, the Model 1879 and an improved version, the Model 1885. Remington was awarded a limited contract for Model 1885 rifles by the Navy.

When efforts to interest the military in the smokeless powder Model 1899 proved fruitless, Remington introduced the Lee system to the commercial market in target and sporting rifles.

Though similar in appearance, the Models 1885 and 1899 are different in nearly every detail. Except for small elements, none of the parts are interchangeable. Both rifles cock on closing the bolt. To engage the safety, simply pull back on the cocking piece, press the trigger and lower the cocking piece forward to engage a safety notch. A magazine cutoff blocks the magazine cutout when the five-round detachable box magazine is removed allowing the rifle to be loaded single shot.

Remington discontinued production of the Model 1899 in 1901. In the meantime, Lee had regained his patent rights and England adopted his system for their series of Lee-Enfield service Rifles that would serve the British military for more than half a century.

DISASSEMBLY FOR MODEL 1885

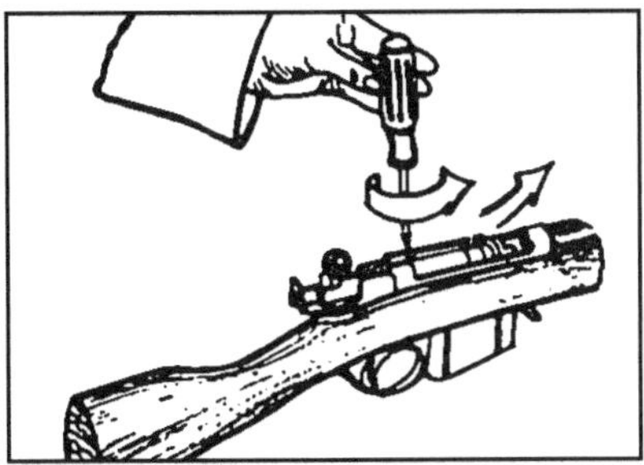

1 Remove magazine assembly by depressing magazine catch. Lift bolt handle and slide bolt rearward approximately 1 inch. Insert a screwdriver in the slot between the extractor locking spring and the front face of the bolt lug.

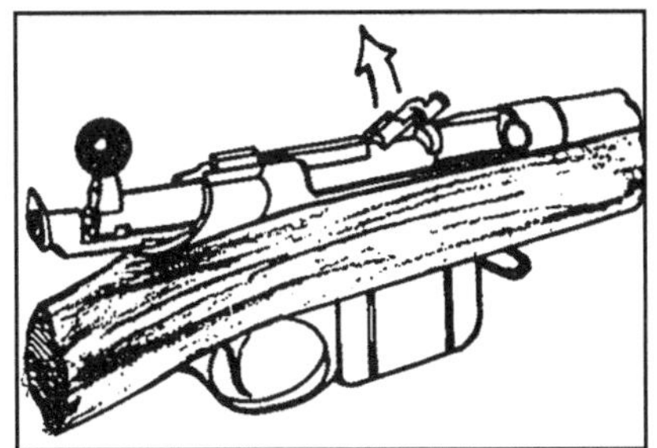

2 Rotate blade of screwdriver counterclockwise to force the extractor locking spring forward. Lift out from bolt assembly. Remove extractor by lifting away from bolt.

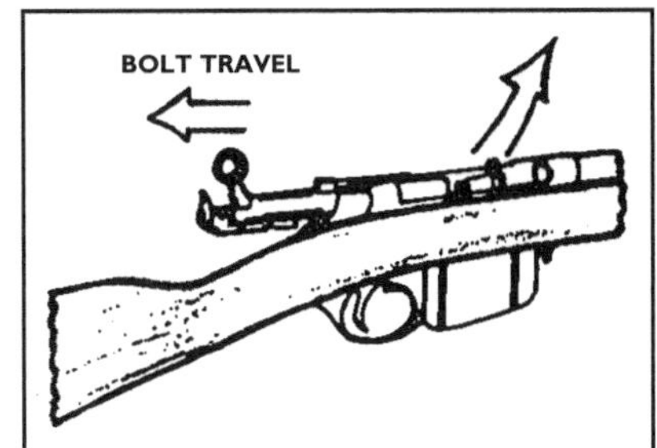

3 Slide bolt rearward approximately half the distance of the opening in the receiver. Rotate bolt head 60 degrees counterclockwise and slide out from bolt. Remove bolt assembly from receiver.

DISASSEMBLY FOR MODEL 1899

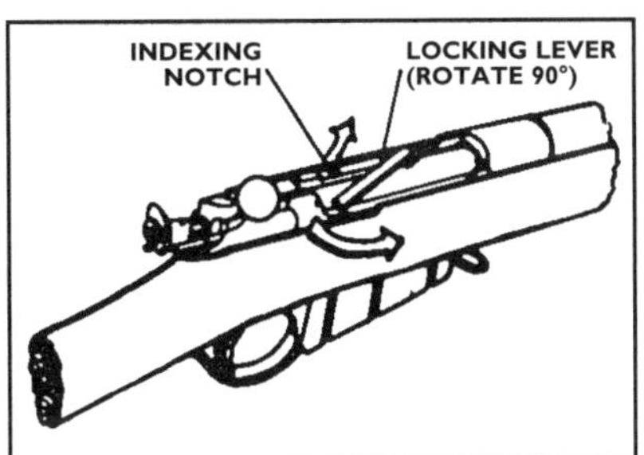

Remove magazine assembly by depressing magazine catch. Lift bolt handle and slide bolt rearward approximately one-half the distance of travel. Raise the locking lever slightly. CAUTION: Do not raise more than a 1/32 inch or the part will snap. Rotate counterclockwise 90 degrees. Remove from bolt. Slide bolt rearward and remove from receiver. Bolt head will be engaged by the bolt stop and remains in the receiver. Slide bolt head forward and lift out of receiver.

DISASSEMBLY COMMON TO BOTH MODELS

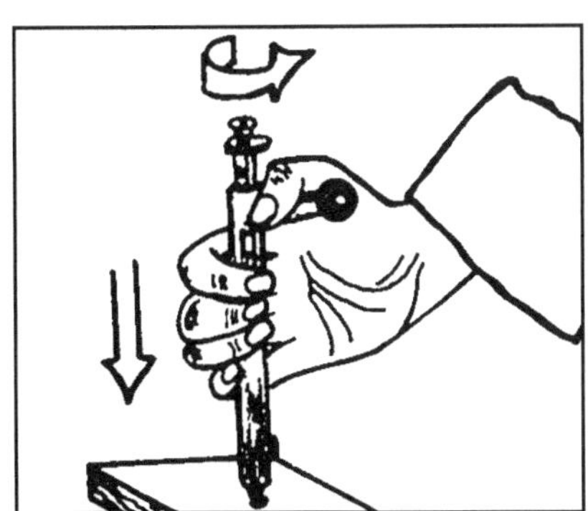

To disassemble bolt,
place it on a flat surface, preferably a wood block. This eliminates the possibility of damage to the striker. Grasping the bolt body and handle, push down, unscrew striker retaining nut, and slowly relieve tension on the mainspring. Remove cocking piece, striker and mainspring from bolt.

Remove ramrod from stock channel, using a small adjustable open-end wrench. Loosen the hex-head screw on the front band (M1899 only) and remove nose cap screw. Tap nose cap and front band from stock. Loosen middle band screw and depress band spring, then slide off middle band. Remove upper hand guard (M1899 only). Remove tang screw and trigger guard screw. Lift out barrel and receiver assembly and lightly tap stock with a rubber mallet to remove trigger guard.

To disassemble trigger guard,
drive out trigger pin and lift out trigger. Then drive out sear pin and remove sear. Sear and magazine catch spring will drop out. Drive out magazine catch pin and lift out magazine catch. Remove ejector screw and ejector spring. Drive out ejector pin and lift out magazine cutoff spring. Remove bolt stop retaining screw and indexing pin; drive out bolt stop pin and remove bolt stop.

CAUTION: Do not attempt to disassemble the magazine assembly.

REMINGTON NYLON 66 RIFLE

PARTS LEGEND

1. Action spring
2. Action spring plunger
3. Barrel
4. Barrel bracket
5. Barrel support
6. Barrel lock screw
7. Bolt
8. Bolt handle
9. Cartridge feed guide
10. Cartridge feed insert
11. Cartridge stop
12. Cartridge stop pin
13. Cartridge stop spring
14. Cover screw (2)
15. Disconnector
16. Disconnector pivot
17. Disconnector pivot spring
18. Disconnector pivot pin
19. Ejector
20. Extractor
21. Extractor plunger
22. Extractor spring
23. Firing pin
24. Firing pin retaining pin
25. Firing pin retractor spring
26. Firing pin stop pin
27. Firing pin striker
28. Firing pin striker spring
29. Front sight
30. Front sight screw (2)
31. Front sight washer (2)
32. Inner magazine tube assembly
33. Outer magazine tube
34. Receiver cover assembly
35. Rear cover screw bushing
36. Safety
37. Safety detent ball
38. Safety detent retaining pin
39. Safety detent spring
40. Safety lever
41. Safety lever pin
42. Safety lever cam pin
43. Sear
44. Sear assembly pin
45. Sear spring
46. Stock assembly
47. Striker spring sleeve
48. Trigger
49. Trigger assembly pin
50. Trigger guard
51. Trigger guard assembly pin
52. Trigger spring

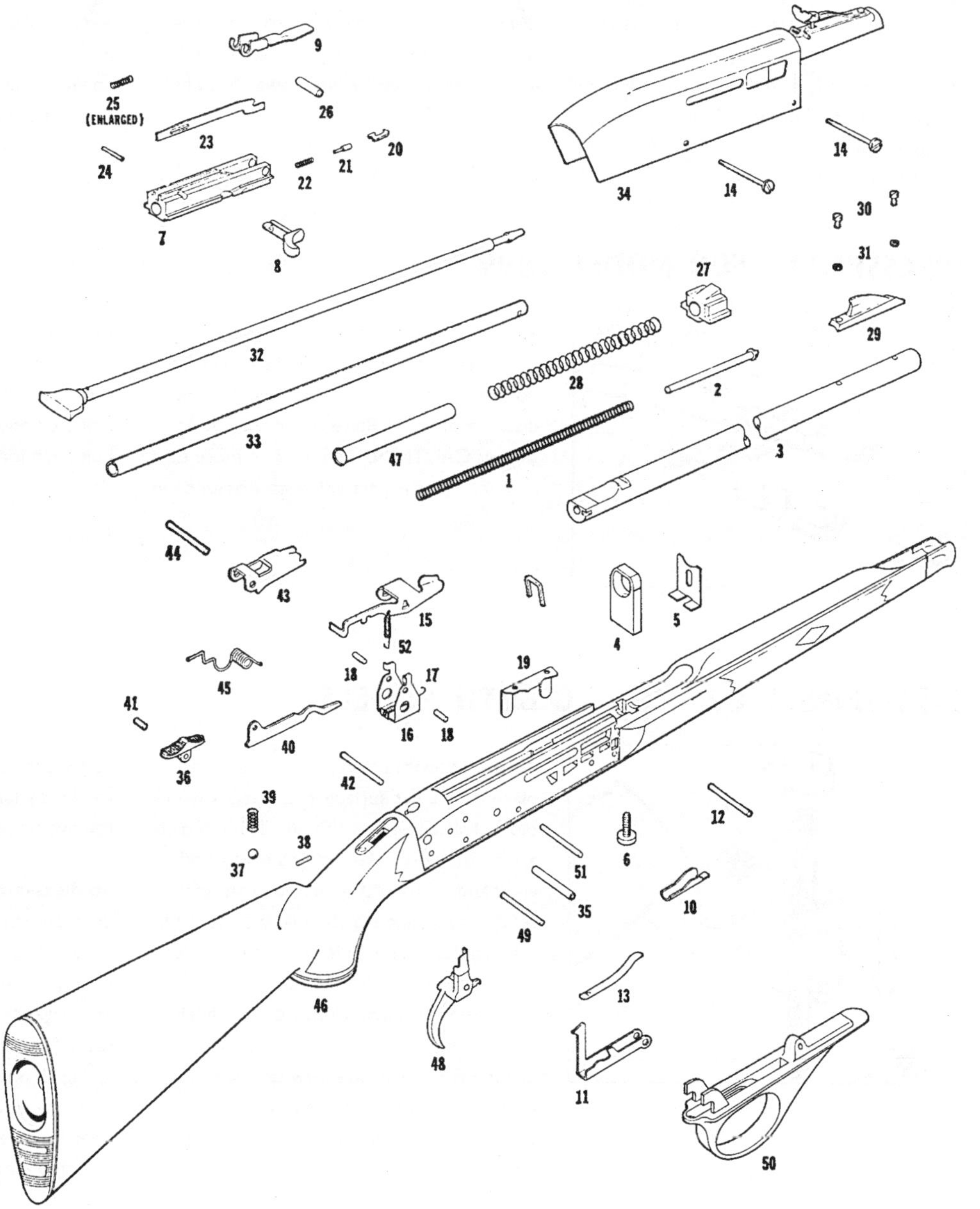

Introduction of the Remington Nylon 66 .22 caliber semiautomatic rifle in 1959 heralded a new concept in firearms. Featuring a one-piece stock, receiver and fore-end produced from structural nylon, this unusual blowbackoperated rifle was designed by a team of engineers headed by Wayne E. Leek. The designation Nylon 66 was taken from the name of the high-strength DuPont nylon selected for the rifle.

Chambered for .22 Long Rifle, the 4¼-lb. Nylon 66 has a 14-round tubular magazine in the buttstock. In addition to the stock, the bolt handle, safety, trigger, trigger guard, and several other parts are nylon. The barrel, breechbolt, receiver cover, striker, springs, and various small components are steel.

The rifle was first offered with a brown or green stock. A version was later offered with a black stock and chrome-plated barrel and receiver cover. Production of the Nylon 66 ended in 1989. Approximately 1,050,350 were produced in six grades.

DISASSEMBLY

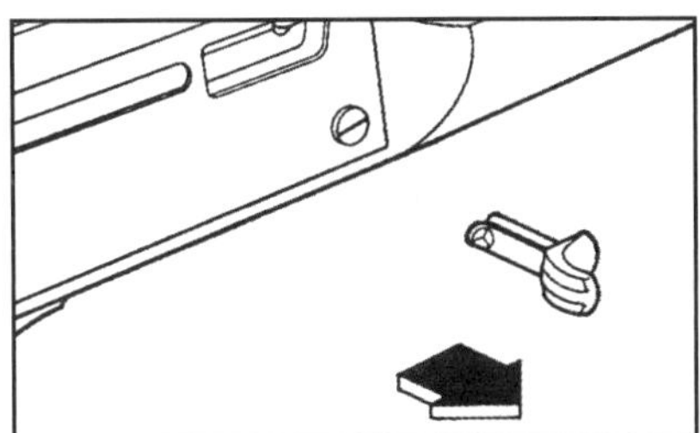

1 Before disassembly, make sure rifle is unloaded. Engage safety (36) on safe position to rear. Pull bolt handle (8) rearward, and check barrel chamber through open ejection port. Colored magazine follower should be visible. With action cocked, grasp bolt handle firmly and pull to right from rifle.

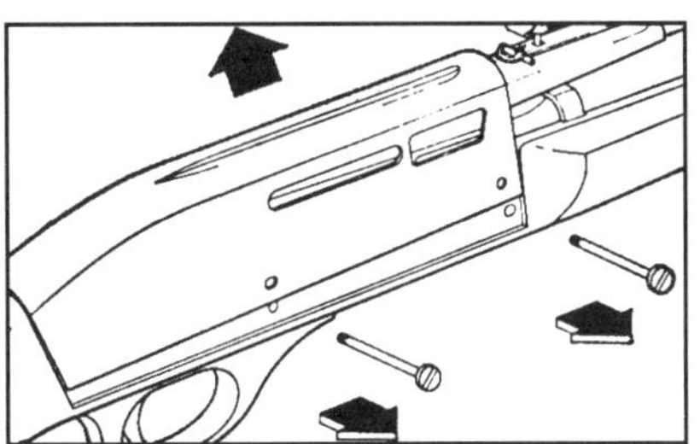

2 Unscrew and remove the two cover screws (14). Lift receiver cover assembly (34) from stock assembly (46). Replace bolt handle into hole in bolt (7) until handle is retained by pressure of action spring plunger (2).

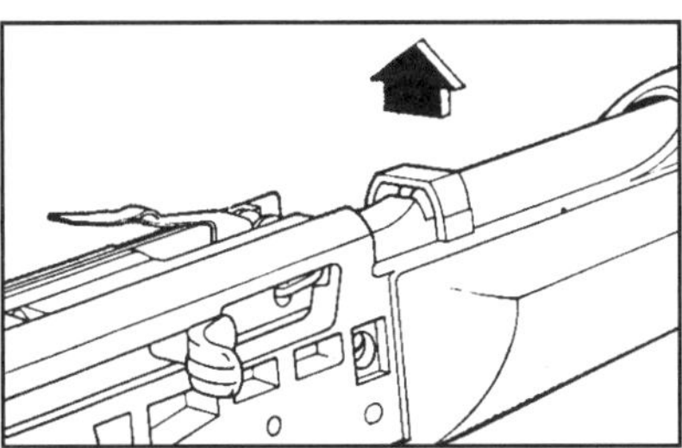

3 Loosen barrel lock screw (6) until barrel bracket (4) can be moved upward in stock assembly far enough to clear slot in top of barrel (3). Pull barrel forward from stock assembly.

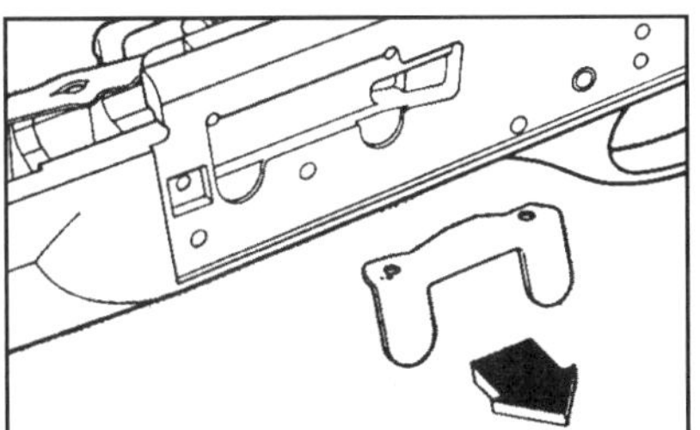

4 Remove ejector (19) from recess in left side of stock assembly. Remove barrel lock screw, barrel bracket, and barrel support (5) from stock assembly.

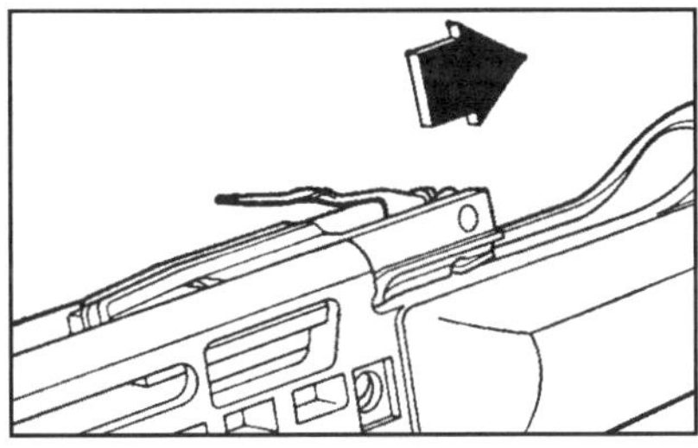

5 Remove bolt handle. Push bolt forward and remove from stock assembly. Action spring (1) and action spring plunger (2) are also disassembled from rifle at this time.

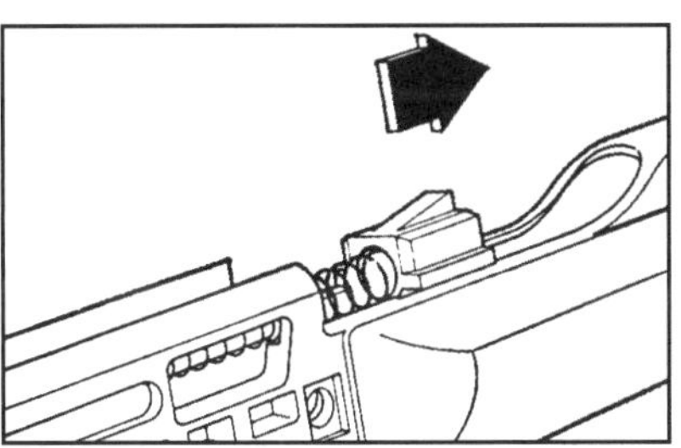

6 Push safety forward to fire position. Take care not to touch trigger (48) since firing pin striker (27) is under compressed load of firing pin striker spring (28). Hold cocked striker against pressure of spring, pull trigger, and ease striker forward until spring tension is relieved. Remove striker, spring, and striker spring sleeve (47). Drive out trigger guard assembly pin (51), and pull trigger guard (50) from stock assembly. This is sufficient disassembly for normal cleaning.

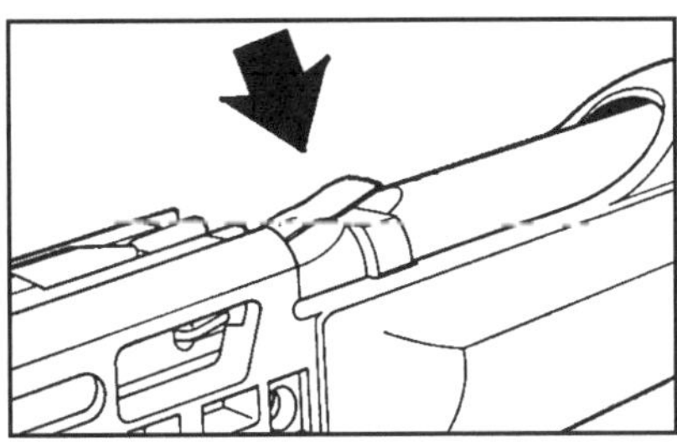

7 Reassemble in reverse. Place striker spring sleeve (with flanged end rearward) into hole in stock assembly. Replace spring over sleeve. Slide striker rearward along bolt rails in stock assembly until spring enters hole in rear of striker and rearward motion of striker is stopped by sear (43). Pull trigger. Push downward on front end of sear and move striker rearward over sear until cocked. Release trigger. Sear will hold striker cocked in rearward position. When reassembling receiver cover assembly to stock assembly, cartridge feed guide (9), must lie in forward position on barrel (arrow).

REMINGTON NYLON 76 RIFLE

PARTS LEGEND

1. Barrel
2. Barrel bracket
3. Barrel lock screw
4. Barrel support
5. Bolt
6. Bolt push rod assembly
7. Cartridge feed guide
8. Cartridge feed insert
9. Cartridge feed insert spring
10. Cartridge stop
11. Cartridge stop pin
12. Cartridge stop spring
13. Cover screw (2)
14. Disconnector
15. Disconnector pivot
16. Disconnector pivot pin, right hand
17. Disconnector pivot pin, left hand
18. Disconnector pivot spring
19. Ejector
20. Extractor
21. Extractor plunger
22. Extractor spring
23. Firing pin
24. Firing pin retaining pin
25. Firing pin stop pin, front
26. Firing pin stop pin, rear
27. Firing pin striker
28. Firing pin striker spring
29. Floor plate
30. Floor plate retaining pin (2)
31. Front sight
32. Front sight screw (2)
33. Front sight washer (2)
34. Gear
35. Lever
36. Lever latch
37. Lever latch screw
38. Lever pivot bushing
39. Lever pivot screw
40. Locking bar
41. Locking bar release lever
42. Locking bar spring (2)
43. Magazine lock
44. Magazine assembly
45. Outer magazine tube
46. Rack
47. Rear cover screw bushing
48. Receiver cover assembly
49. Safety
50. Safety lever
51. Safety lever cam pin
52. Safety lever pin
53. Safety detent ball
54. Safety detent retaining pin
55. Safety detent spring
56. Sear
57. Sear assembly pin
58. Sear spring
59. Stock
60. Striker spring sleeve
61. Trigger
62. Trigger assembly pin
63. Trigger cap
64. Trigger cap spring
65. Trigger cap retaining pin
66. Trigger spring

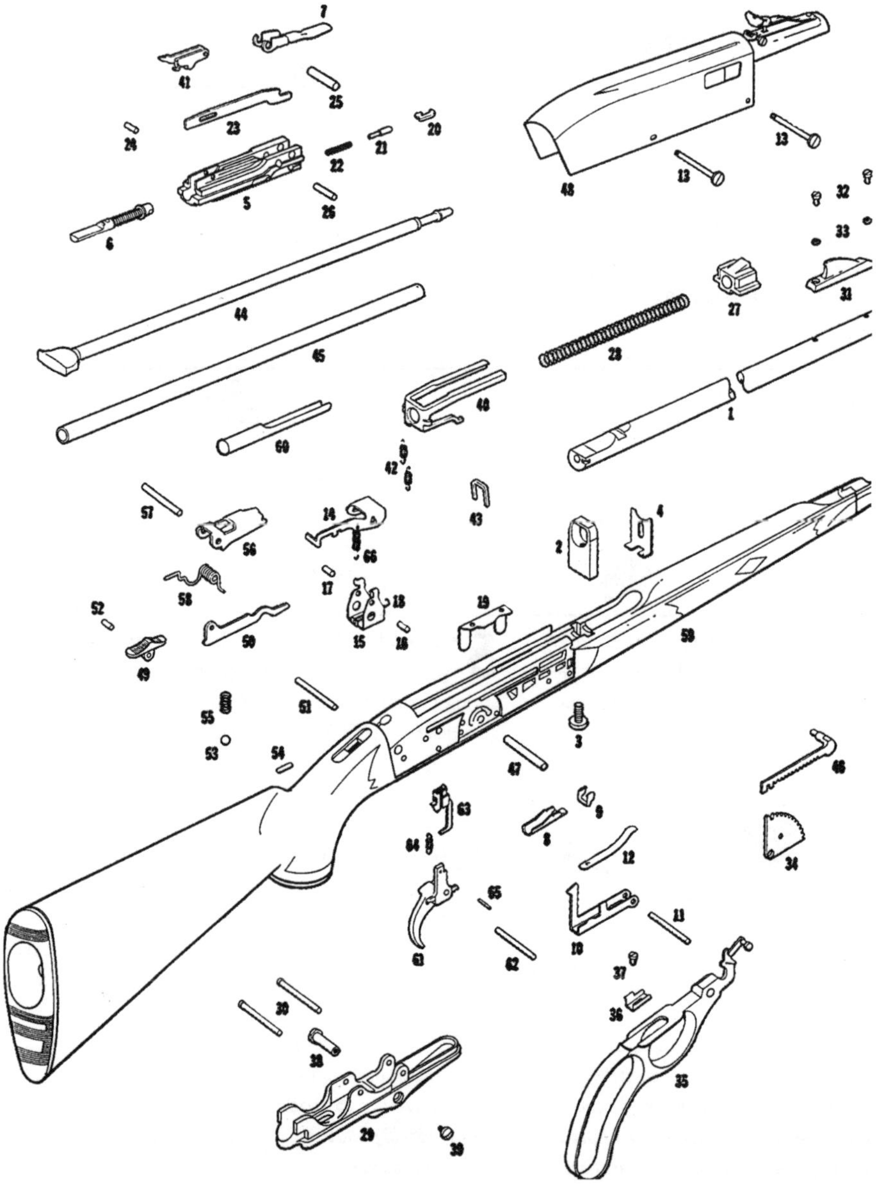

In 1962, the Remington Arms Co. introduced thei first lever-action repeater, the Nylon 76 Trail Rider rifle. Chambered for .22 Long Rifle, the Nylon 76 was designed for informal target shooting and small game. Except for its lever-operated action, it was similar to the Nylon 66 semi-automatic rifle. Like the Nylon 66, the Nylon 76 features a one-piece stock, receiver and fore-end of Du Pont structural nylon.

Other features of the Nylon 76 are its short-stroke finger lever which aids speed of operation and a 14-round tubular magazine in the buttstock. Working the lever rotates a gear which moves a rack connected with the breech bolt. The self-lubricating character of nylon reduced the need for oiling.

When first introduced, this rifle was offered with a brown stock and blued metal parts. A later version featured a black stock and chrome-plated barrel, lever and receiver cover. Both versions of the Nylon 76 were discontinued in 1964.

DISASSEMBLY

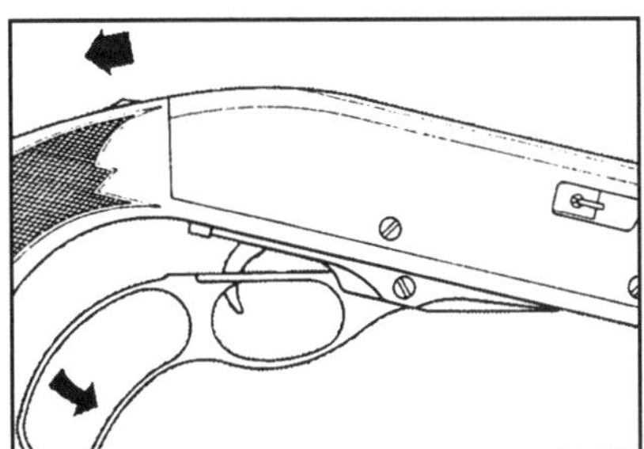

1 Make sure rifle is unloaded before starting disassembly. When action is open, colored magazine follower should be visible through ejection port. Push safety (49) to the rear on safe position, and work lever (35) to cock rifle. Unscrew and remove the two cover screws (13), and lift receiver cover assembly (48) from stock (59).

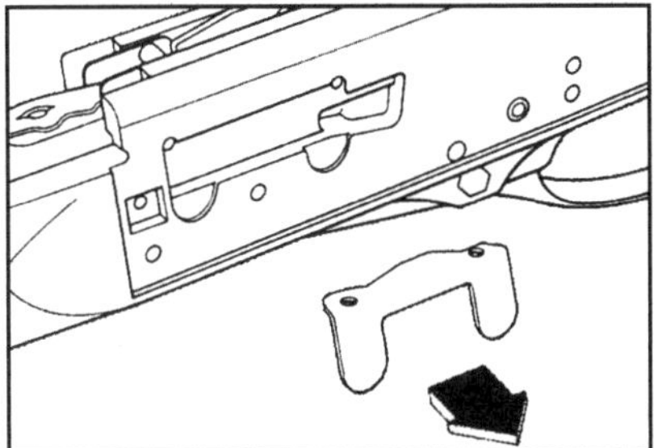

2 Remove ejector (19) from well in left side of stock. Pull loosened rack (46) out of bolt (5). Partially open lever, and lift gear (34) from rear cover screw bushing (47).

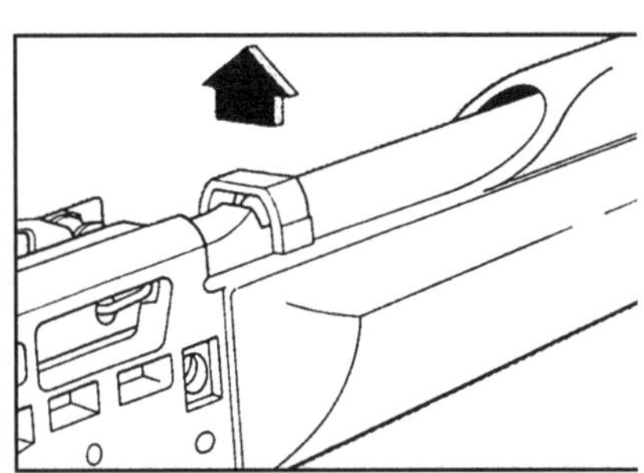

3 Remove barrel lock screw (3). Lift starting disassembly. When action is barrel bracket (2) to clear slot in top of barrel (1), and pull barrel forward, out of stock. Remove barrel bracket and barrel support (4).

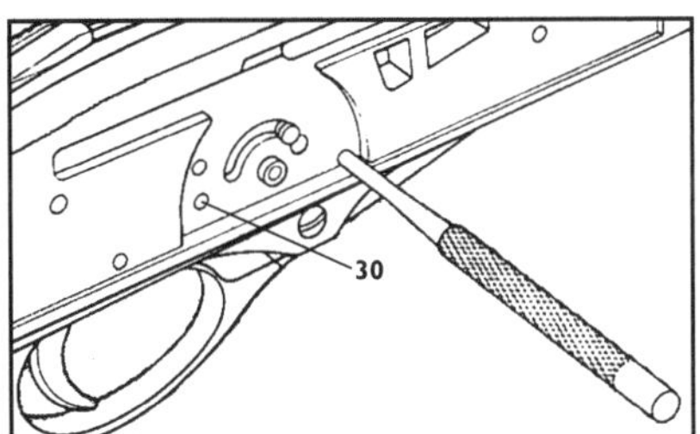

4 Pull bolt assembly forward out of the stock. Drive out the two floor plate retaining pins (30) from right to left.

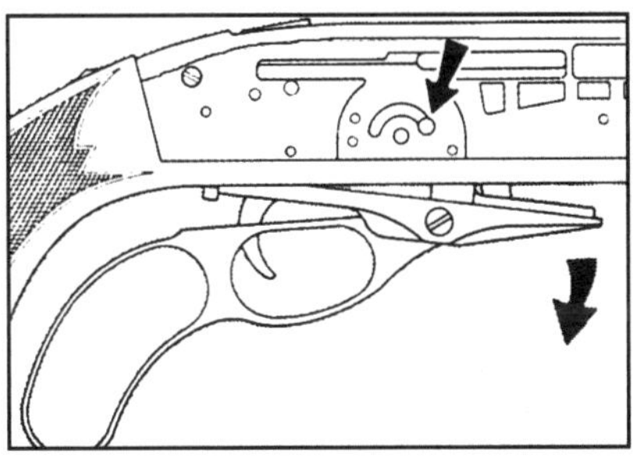

5 Pull front of floor plate (29) downward. Open lever to position lever connector stud into circular slot (arrow) in stock. Push stud inward until it becomes disengaged from slot. Open lever and remove floor plate lever assembly. This is sufficient disassembly for normal cleaning. Reassemble in reverse. Lever must be unlatched from floor plate. Replace rear of floor plate into stock. Extend lever arm and press into stock. Position lever connector stud into circular slot in stock, push front of floor plate up into stock and close Lever. Align holes in stock and floor plate and drive in floor plate retaining pins from left to right. When replacing bolt assembly, guide rear end of bolt push rod assembly (6) into striker spring sleeve (60). Lift front of locking bar (40) to enable locking bar release lever (41) to pass beneath.

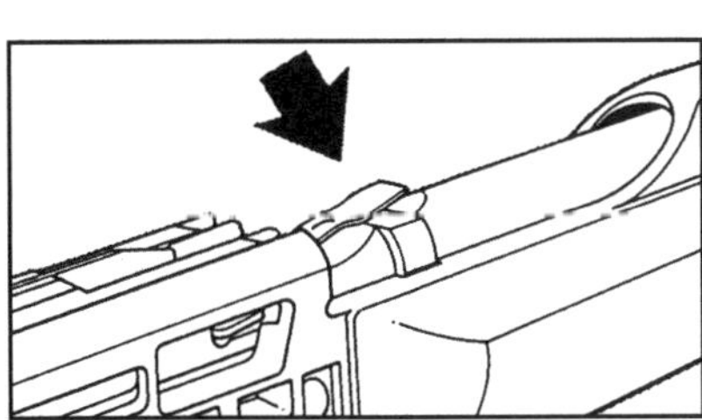

6 Cartridge feed guide (7) must face forward along barrel. Replace gear and rack. Stud on rack extends through stock and bolt into recess in bolt push rod.

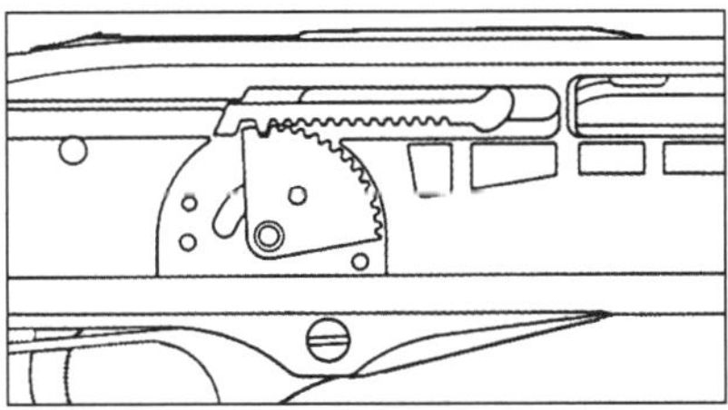

7 Engage large teeth of rack and gear. Hold both parts in place, replace ejector, and reassemble receiver cover assembly to stock.

REMINGTON ROLLING-BLOCK RIFLE

PARTS LEGEND

1. Receiver
2. Barrel
3. Rear sight assembly
4. Recoil stud
5. Recall stud screw
6. Stock tip
7. Stock tip screw
8. Front band
9. Front band screw
10. Middle band & swivel
11. Rear band
12. Rear band screw
13. Ramrod
14. Ramrod stop
15. Guard plate
16. Front guard plate screw
17. Rear guard plate screw
18. Lever spring
19. Lever spring screw
20. Mainspring
21. Mainspring screw
22. Trigger spring
23. Trigger spring screw
24. Locking lever
25. Locking lever screw
26. Trigger
    26a. Trigger pin
27. Breechblock
28. Firing pin
    28a. Firing pin retractor
    28b. Firing pin limit pin
29. Retractor pin
30. Extractor
    30a. Extractor screw
    31a. Breechblock pin
    31b. Hammer pin
32. Hammer
33. Button
34. Button screw
35. Tang screw
36. Buttplate
37. Buttplate screws (2)
38. Stock swivel
39. Stack swivel screws (2)
40. Fore-end
41. Stock

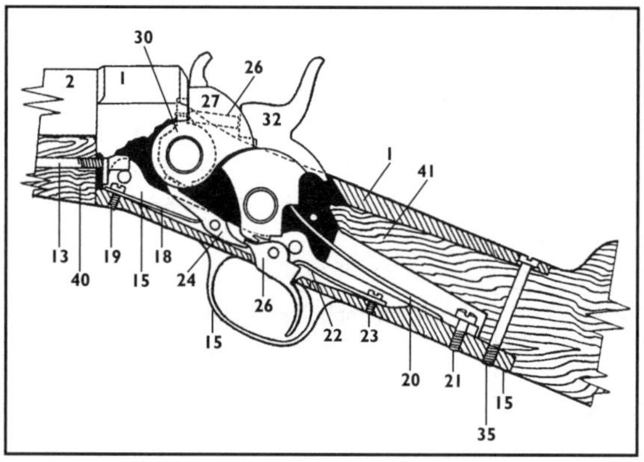

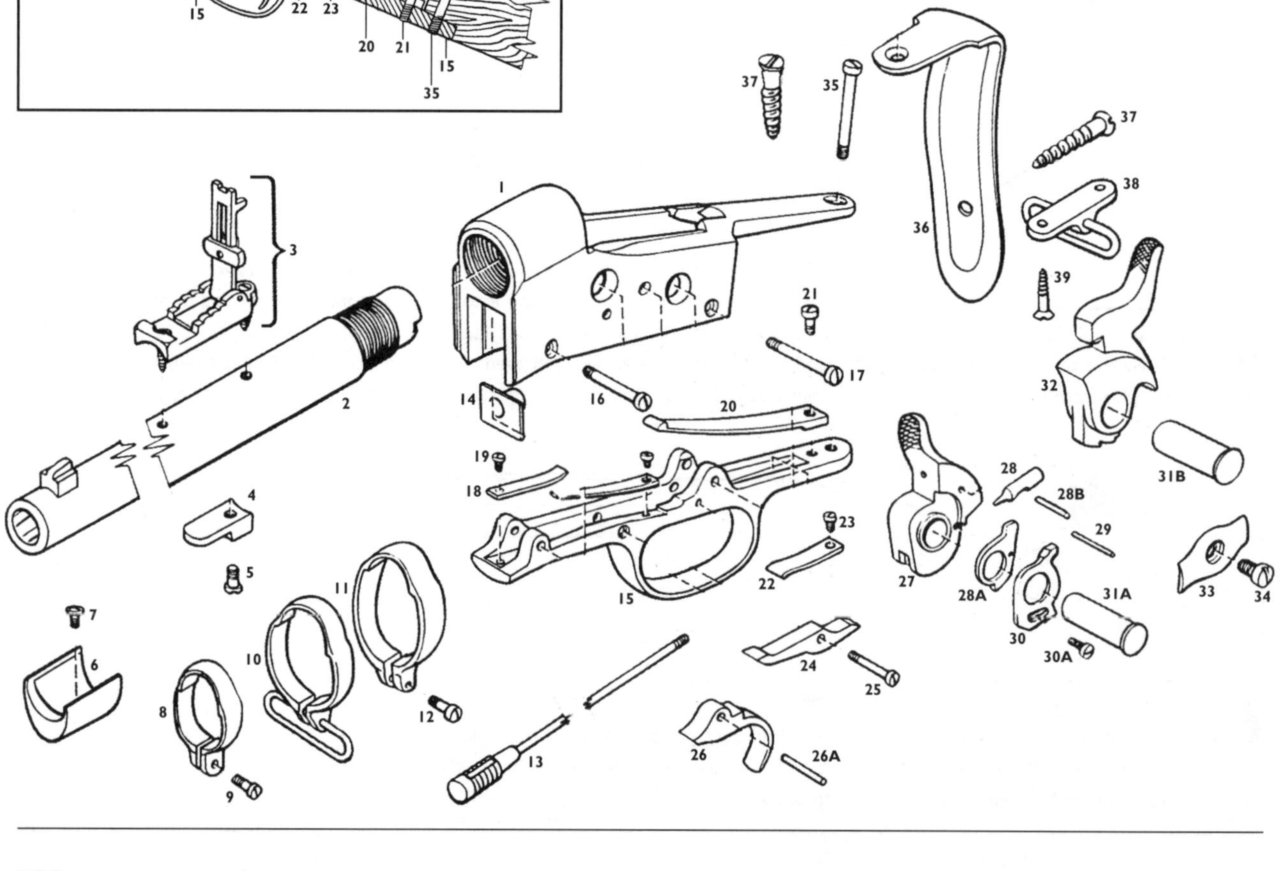

On Jan. 27, 1863, a U.S. patent was granted to Leonard Geiger for a hinged or "split-breech" gun action. This basic action, with many subsequent improvements, would remain in production through the 1930s.

The first arms made under the Geiger patent were 20,000 carbines chambered for the .56-50 Spencer rim-fire cartridge. Delivered in 1865, these carbines were purchased by the U.S. Government under a contract granted to E. Remington & Sons. At the time this contract was granted, Remington production facilities were so involved with other government commitments that the carbines were actually manufactured by the Savage Revolving Fire Arms Co., of Middletown, Connecticut, under Remington license and with Remington-designed machinery.

The original Geiger action was substantially improved by Remington employee Joseph Rider. His initial patent No. 45,123 was granted on Nov. 15, 1864. Rider's influence as co-inventor was so profound in respect to this action that Remington-Rider and Remington Rolling-Block are virtually synonymous to the arms student or collector.

A host of other inventors effected changes and improvements in the basic action during its long production history. It was in effect a workhorse in the Remington line, being used in rifles, shotguns, and single-shot pistols. That it successfully bridged the smokeless powder era is attested by the fact that the Remington Rolling-Block rifle was regularly chambered for such cartridges as the .30-30 Winchester, 8 mm. Lebel, 7 mm Mauser, and even the .30- 06. Some of the largest purchases of Remington single-shot rifles were by foreign governments desiring an inexpensive, serviceable, and a simple military weapon. Military rifles with the Remington-Rider action were made at Springfield Armory and by Denmark in the Danish government arsenal in Copenhagen. Rifles utilizing the basic rolling-block action are still made in Italy and imported into the U.S.

Rolling-block rifles are interesting curios but should not be seriously regarded as shooting rifles unless their use is limited strictly to fresh ammunition of characteristics consistent with the period of their original design and manufacture.

DISASSEMBLY

Loosen button screw (34) and remove button (33) from left side of receiver (1). Cock hammer (32) and push out breech-block pin (31A) from right to left. Lift out breech-block (27) with extractor (30) attached. Firing pin (28) can be removed from breechblock by drifting out firing pin retractor pin (29). Let hammer down all the way, remove hammer pin (31B) and lift hammer (32) out of receiver (1).

The wooden fore-end (not shown in exploded view) may be removed by withdrawing ramrod (13) and removing barrel bands (8, 10 & 11).

To remove buttstock (not shown in exploded view), take out tang screw (35) and pull buttstock off to rear. Remove front and rear guard plate screws (16 & 17) and drop guard plate (15) out of receiver (1). All parts and springs contained within the guard plate may be removed if necessary by withdrawing their respective screws and retaining pins.

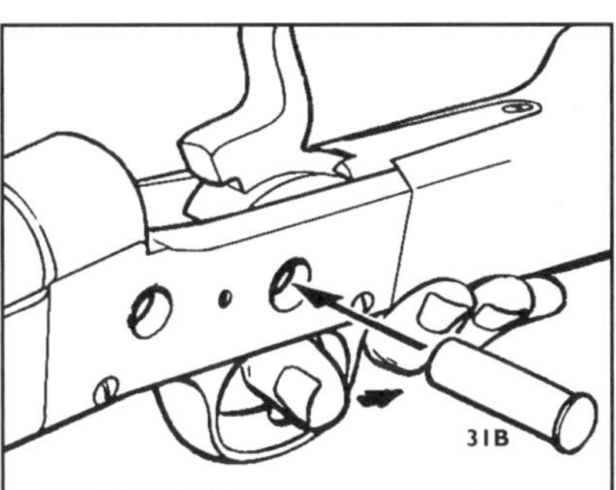

1 To replace hammer and breechblock in receiver, keep trigger pulled all the way back while inserting hammer with its nose forward in fired position as shown. Move hammer until its hole lines up with hammer pin holes in receiver. Slip hammer pin (31b) into hole in left of receiver, through hammer, and through hole in right of receiver. Cock hammer and replace breechblock and breech-block pin in like fashion

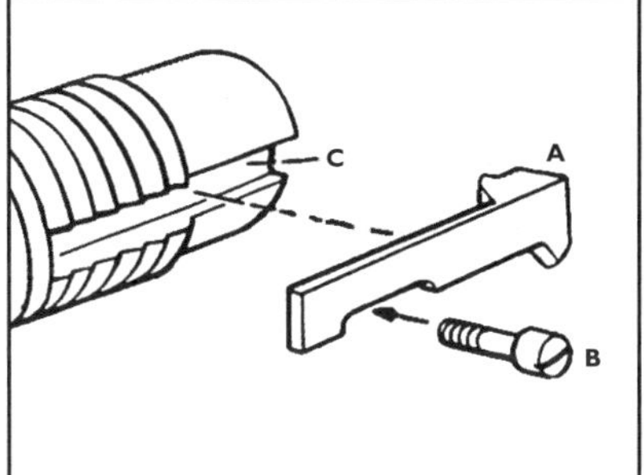

2 This shows type of extractor (A) used in Remington Railing-Black Rifle, U. S. Navy Model of 1869. Extractor is held in place in the slot (C) in the barrel by screw (B) which passes through receiver from the left side. This model also has a firing pin spring and firing pin retaining screw in the hammer nose. Also, in this Navy Remington the mainspring is provided with an anti-friction roller at the hammer end and a different type of ramrod stop is employed. Disassembly procedure for all rolling black rifles, with the exception of these few variations, remains the same

ROSSI PUMA CARBINE

PARTS LEGEND

1. Barrel
2. Front sight
3. Front sight pin
4. Front band
5. Front band screw
6. Magazine plug
7. Magazine plug screw
8. Magazine spring
9. Fore-end
10. Rear band
11. Rear band Screw
12. Magazine tube
13. Magazine follower
14. Rear sight assembly
15. Elevator
16. Receiver
17. Carrier
18. Carrier stop
19. Carrier stop spring
20. Carrier stop pin
21. Carrier screws (2)
22. Saddle ring
23. Saddle ring staple
24. Trigger
25. Trigger pin
26. Lower tang
27. Trigger spring
28. Trigger spring screw
29. Plug screw
30. Right cartridge guide
31. Cartridge guide screws(2)
32. Spring cover
33. Spring cover screw
34. Finger lever
35. Friction stud
36. Friction stud spring
37. Friction stud pin
38. Right locking bolt
39. Left locking bolt
40. Locking bolt pin
41. Locking bolt pin stop screw
42. Left cartridge guide
43. Cartridge stop
44. Cartridge stop pin
45. Cartridge stop spring
46. Ejector
47. Ejector spring
48. Ejector collar
49. Ejector guide
50. Ejector guide pins (2)
51. Extractor
52. Extractor Pin
53. Breechbolt
54. Firing pin
55. Firing pin stop
56. Lever/breechbolt pin
57. Hammer
58. Hammer strut
59. Hammer strut pin
60. Hammer screw
61. Mainspring
62. Stock
63. Buttplate
64. Buttplate screws (2)
65. Tang screw

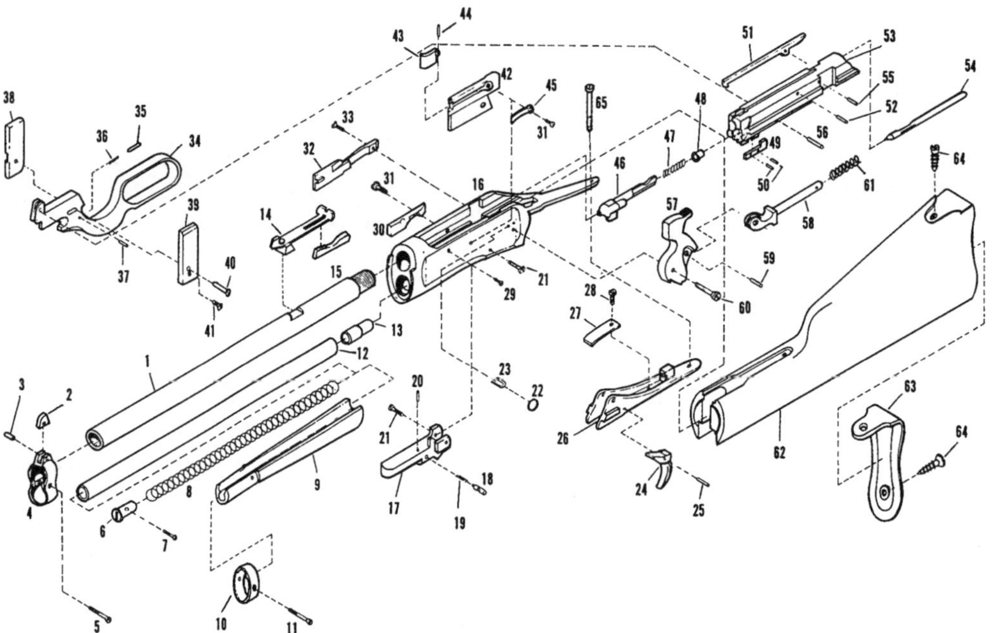

The first production units of the Brazilian-made version of the Winchester Model 1892 carbine were completed in August 1976. Exportation to the United States of the 20-inch barrelled, .357 Magnum/.38 Spl. model began shortly thereafter.

Until fairly recently this gun was referred to as the Rossi M92 SRC or Rossi Saddle Ring Carbine. The importer, Interarms, labled it the Puma, as it had been called by the manufacturer, Amadeo Rossi S.A.

The Rossi 92 line includes .44 Magnum/Special., 44-40 and .45 Colt and are offered with 16-, 20-, and 24-inch barrels. Interarms at one time offered a Hollywood-styled .357/.38 with 16-inch barrel and oversized finger lever. Beginning in 1986, all versions had a high-relief puma's head medallion affixed to the receiver forward of the saddle ring staple but this was subsequently removed. Rossi Model 92s have been distributed by Navy Arms and EMF.

While the Rossis greatly resemble the old Winchesters in appearance, function and construction, there are internal differences and most parts are not readily interchangeable.

To date, and unlike those made by Winchester, no rifle or takedown versions of the Puma have been made, though many engraved and plated models have been sold.

DISASSEMBLY

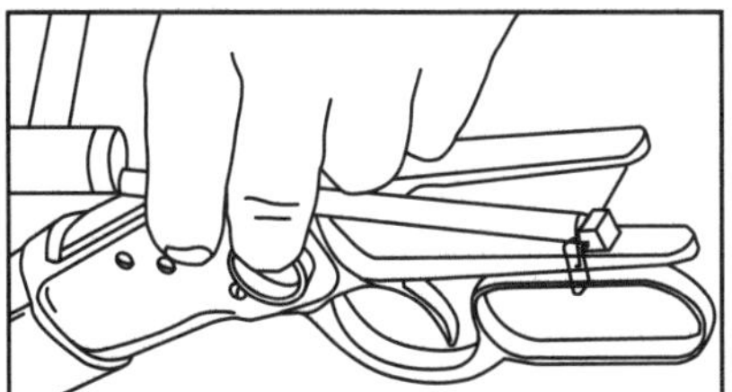

1 Open the finger lever (34) and check that chamber and magazine are unloaded. Remove the tang screw (65) and carefully work the buttstock (62) to the rear. There is no compartment or trap under the buttplate (63), but it and its two screws (64) may be removed if necessary.

If magazine removal is required, first restrain the magazine plug (6) that is under pressure from the magazine spring (8). Then remove the magazine plug screw (7) that will free the plug, spring and magazine follower (13).

Remove the front and rear barrel band screws (5 & 11), slide the bands (4 & 10) forward and remove the fore-end (9) and magazine tube (12). The front sight (2) is held in the front band by a small cross pin (3).

After removing its elevator (15) the rear sight assembly (14) can be drifted out and the barrel (1) can be removed, if absolutely necessary, with a proper barrel vise and receiver wrench.

To disassemble the action, hold the hammer (57) back between half- and full-cocked positions, so that the hole in the rod of the hammer strut (58) lines up with the notch in the forward part of the mainspring seat in the lower tang (26). Insert a paper clip through the rod's hole to retain the mainspring (61).

Now the hammer screw (60) is removed, the lower tang drifted rearward about ¼", and the hammer strut pin (59) drifted out. The strut/spring unit now may be angled out.

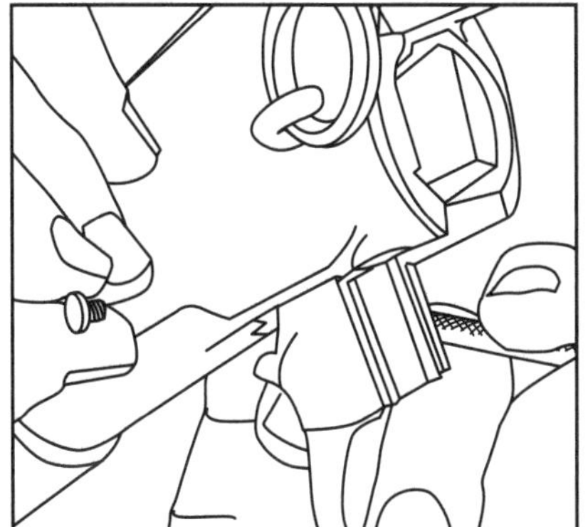

2 The hammer can now be removed from the top of the receiver (16) and the lower tang slid or driven completely out.

The lower tang contains the trigger (24), trigger pin (25), trigger spring screw (28) and the trigger spring itself (27). This may be a flat spring, as shown, or a formed wire spring as on earlier guns. Removal of all these parts is quite straightforward.

With the finger lever down, unscrew the locking bolt pin stop screw (41) and press out (Fig. 2) the slotted but unthreaded locking bolt pin (40). The right and left locking bolts (38 & 39) may now be pulled down and out of the bottom of the receiver.

From the left side of the receiver remove the plug screw (29) and, through the access hole on the right side of the receiver, use a drift punch to drive the lever/breechbolt pin (56) out through the plug screw hole on the receiver's left side. Note that to do this the breechbolt (53) must be fully forward so that the lever/breechbolt pin is in line with the two receiver holes.

The finger lever with its friction stud (35) and stud spring (36) will now be free and the breechbolt can be slid out of the receiver.

The breechbolt contains the extractor (51), extractor pin (52), firing pin (54), firing pin stop (55), ejector (46), ejector spring (47) ejector guide (49) and the guide s two pins (50). Disassembly of the breechbolt presents no problem but removal of parts and further disassembly of the receiver are not normally found to be necessary.

The spring cover (32), often called the loading gate, is held by its screw (33) on the right rear of the receiver. The saddle ring staple (23) has been installed by bending its arms apart inside the receiver. They should be straightened before attempting to pry the staple out.

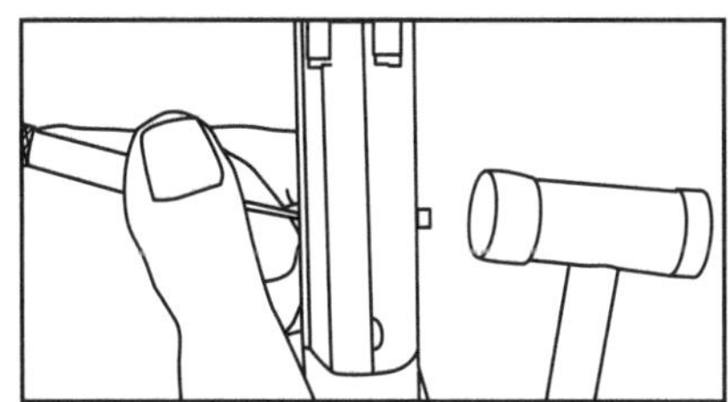

3 Remove the two carrier screws (21), which are the lowest ones on each side of the receiver. This releases the carrier (17) that, with its stop (18), stop pin (20) and spring (19) can now be pried rearward and out.

The right cartridge guide (30), being a solid piece with no complications or appendages, is easily removed by taking out its screw (31). The left cartridge guide (42), however, is relatively difficult to reinstall. It has fixed to it the cartridge stop (43) with its pin (44) but lying between it and the left receiver wall, with its convex side facing the inside of the receiver and its unperforated end under the rear lip of the cartridge stop is the cartridge stop spring (45). All these parts are released by removal of the left cartridge guide screw (31), but reassembly is tiresome because the cartridge stop spring is difficult to position correctly.

Aside from this, reassembly of the Rossi is uncomplicated and done in reverse order. It is helpful, when reinserting the lever/breech-bolt pin (56), to insert a drift pin through the access hole on the receiver's right side (Fig. 3) to cam the breech bolt forward and align the pin holes.

RUGER .44 MAGNUM CARBINE

PARTS LEGEND

1. Barrel
2. Rear sight
3. Front scope base hole plug screws (2)
4. Cartridge guide plate screws (2)
5. Rear scope base hole plug screws (2)
6. Cartridge guide plate
7. Ejector
8. Ejector screw
9. Piston
10. Piston block plug
11. Piston block plug taming pin (inner outer pins)
12. Front sight
13. Barrel band
14. Barrel band screw
15. Recoil block
16. Recoil block bolt washer
17. Recoil block bolt
18. Receiver cross pin
19. Bolt
20. Extractor
21. Extractor spring
22. Extractor pivot pin
23. Firing pin retaining pin
24. Firing pin retaining spring
25. Firing pin
26. Slide
27. Slide handle
28. Slide spring
29. Magazine tube
30. Magazine follower
31. Magazine spring
32. Magazine plug
33. Magazine plug cross pin
34. Buttplate
35. Buttplate screws (2)
36. Receiver
37. Disconnector plunger
38. Disconnector plunger spring
39. Disconnector plunger spring screw
40. Lifter cam
41. Lifter cam spring
42. Lifter cam pin
43. Hammer spring, left
44. Hammer spring, right
45. Hammer spring retaining pin
46. Safety
47. Safety detent plunger
48. Safety detent plunger spring
49. Trigger
50. Trigger cross pin
51. Sear
52. Sear spring
53. Disconnector
54. Trigger pivot pin
55. Hammer pivot pin
56. Hammer
57. Hammer roller
58. Hammer roller pivot pin
59. Lifter latch
60. Lifter latch pivot pin
61. Lifter latch spring
62. Lifter latch plunger
63. Lifter dog
64. Lifter dog pivot pin
65. Lifter assembly
66. Cartridge stop flat spring
67. Cartridge stop flat spring retaining pin
68. Cartridge stop
69. Flapper spring
70. Cartridge stop coil spring
71. Flapper
72. Cartridge stop pivot pin
73. Trigger guard (trigger mechanism housing)

Note: Parts 37-73 are contained in trigger guard assembly

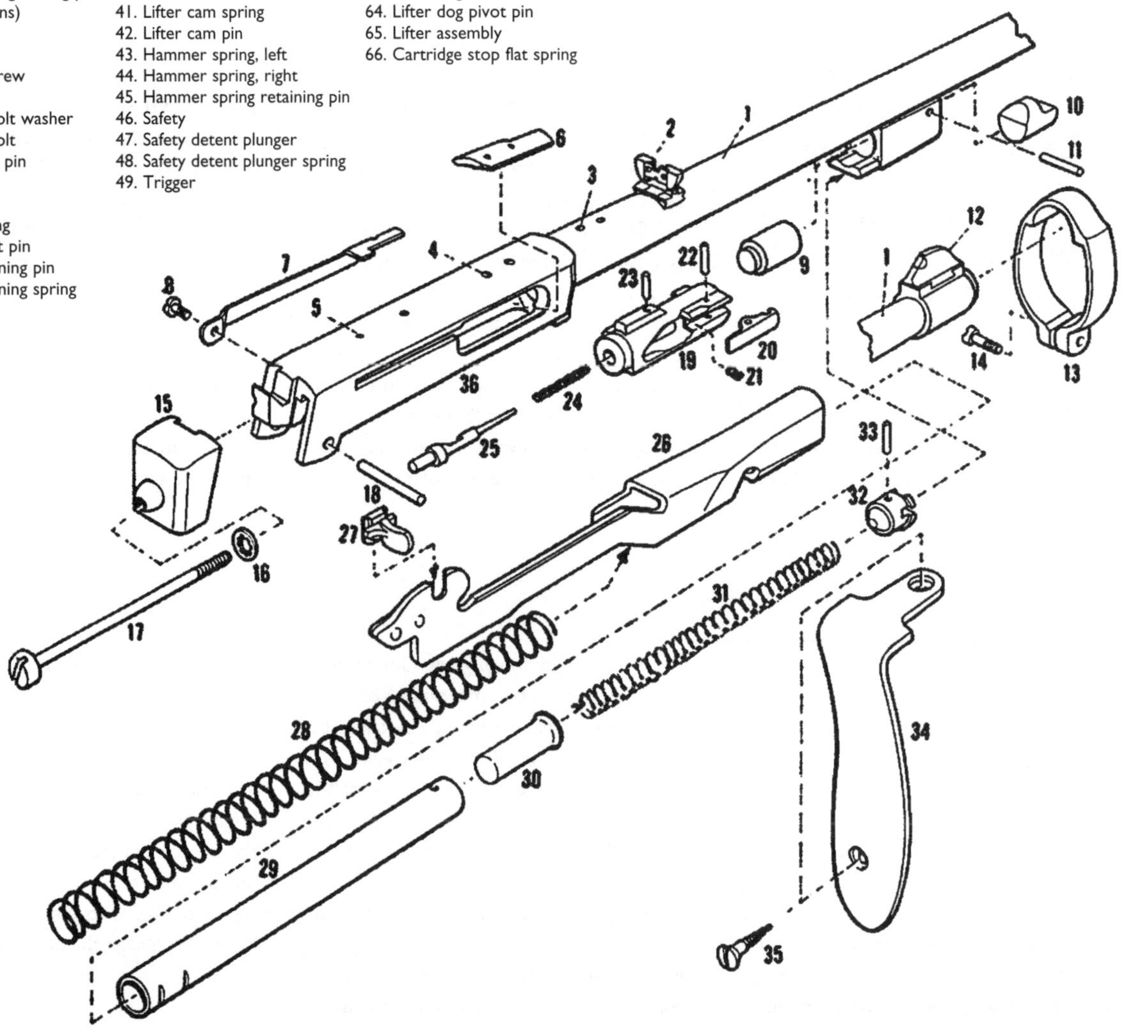

The Ruger .44 Carbine introduced in 1961 as the "Deerstalker," (the name was changed to Ruger .44 Carbine in 1962 after a production run of a little over 3,000), was the first factory-made shoulder arm to be chambered for the potent .44 Remington Magnum cartridge.

Designed for hunting deer-sized game at relatively short range, this gun is noteworthy for several design features. The 5 lb.-12 oz rifle is gas operated with a short-stroke piston. The receiver is machined steel and is closed on top. The receiver is drilled and tapped for commercial scope mounts. The tubular magazine holds 4 cartridges; with a cartridge in the chamber, capacity of the gun is 5 rounds. The 18½-inch barrel is rifled with 12 lands and grooves and a twist rate of 1:38. Ruger discontinued production the .44 Magnum Carbine in 1985.

DISASSEMBLY

Pull back slide handle (27) until it latches and check action to be sure carbine is unloaded. loosen barrel band screw (14) and slide barrel band (13) off stock and barrel to front. Pull barrel and receiver upward and disengage tenon at rear of receiver from recoil block (15) in stock. Recoil block may be removed from stock by first removing buttplate (34) and unscrewing recoil block bolt (17) through hole in butt.

Push out receiver cross pin (18) and pull trigger guard assembly to rear and out bottom of receiver. To remove slide (26) turn receiver upside down and pull slide back and upward slightly while holding compressed slide spring (28) to prevent its forcible ejection. Release slide spring and draw it out rear of slide. Disengage slide handle (27) from its slot in slide and remove. Disengage slot in face of magazine plug (32) from lip at rear of piston block (integral with under side of barrel) and withdraw slide with magazine assembly from barrel and receiver assembly. Piston (9) will drop out rear of cylinder block. Magazine assembly may be disassembled by drifting out magazine plug cross pin (33) and removing plug (32), spring (31), and follower (30) from magazine tube (29).

Bolt (19) is removed from receiver by first removing ejector screw (8) and ejector (7). Then rotate bolt slightly from its forward locked position and draw it to rear to position where bolt lugs will clear cuts in receiver. Then lift the bolt out of bottom of receiver.

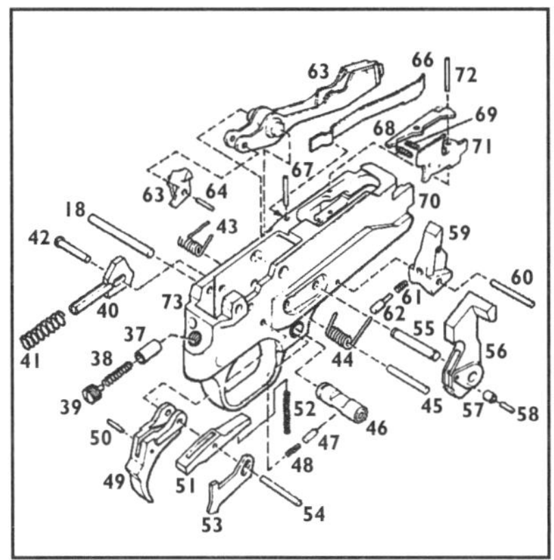

1 NOTE: Disassembly of trigger mechanism parts from housing (73) is not recommended and should only be undertaken at factory or by a qualified gunsmith when repair or replacement of parts is needed.

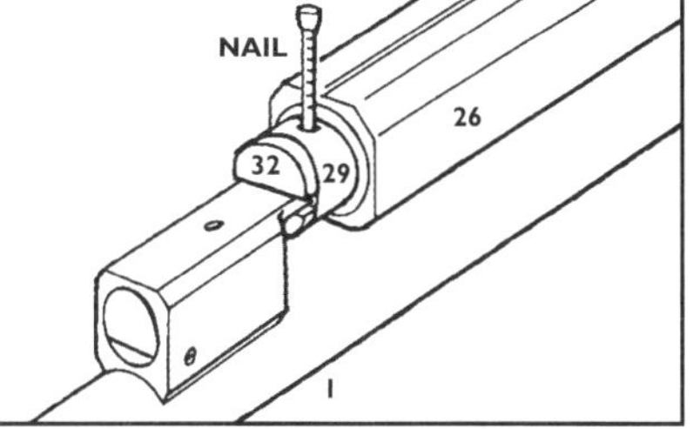

2 To reassemble slide and magazine assembly to barrel and receiver assembly, turn barrel and receiver assembly upside down and replace bolt in its forward (locked) position. Replace ejector (7) and ejector screw (8). Replace piston (9) in cylinder block with small end to rear. Replace magazine tube (29) in slide (26) and replace slide spring (28) in rear of slide. Seat slot in face of magazine plug (32) on lip at rear of piston block on underside of barrel as shown. Pull slide rearward (toward butt) slightly and insert a small nail in hole in magazine tube (29) as shown and move slide forward against nail.

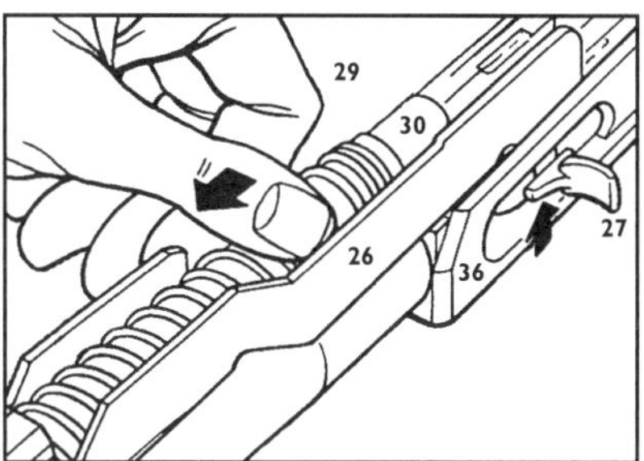

3 Position slide handle (27) through hole at the right side of receiver in its slot in the side as shown by the arrow (above). Pull slide spring forward (toward the muzzle) and over the magazine tube (29) until it clears the end of the magazine tube.

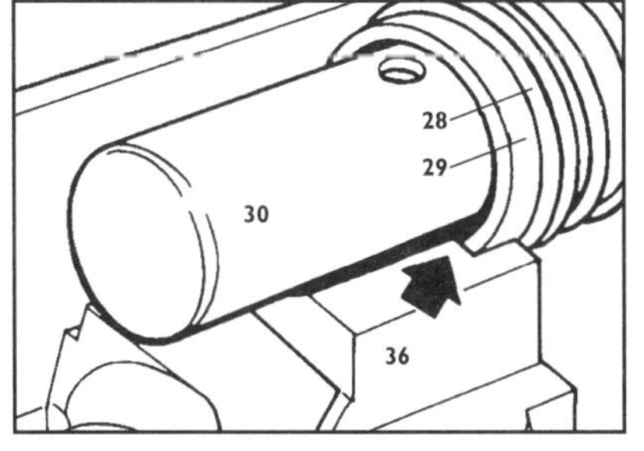

4 Press slide assembly into receiver and seat rear end of magazine tube in slot at front underside of receiver (36) as shown by arrow. Remove nail from forward end of magazine tube, allowing slide to come to its full forward (locked) position. While holding down slide assembly replace trigger guard assembly (73) in bottom of receiver and replace receiver cross pin (18) through rear of receiver and trigger guard. Retract slide assembly and replace barrel and receiver assembly in stock. Replace barrel band (13) and tighten barrel band screw (14).

RUGER MODEL 10/22 CARBINE

PARTS LEGEND

1. Receiver
2. Barrel
3. Rear sight assembly
4. Front sight
5. Barrel band
6. Barrel band screw
7. Barrel retainer
8. Barrel retainer screws (2)
9. Receiver cross pins (2)
10. Bolt stop pin
11. Escutcheon (contained in stock)
12. Takedown screw
13. Bolt assembly, complete (see Bolt Assembly)
14. Bolt handle assembly (bolt handle, recoil spring, guide rod, and bushing)
15. Magazine assembly (see Magazine Assembly)
16. Trigger guard assembly, complete (see Trigger Guard Assembly)
17. Buttplate
18. Buttplate screws (2) (Stock and stock swivels are not shown.)
19. Scope base adapter (available as optional extra)

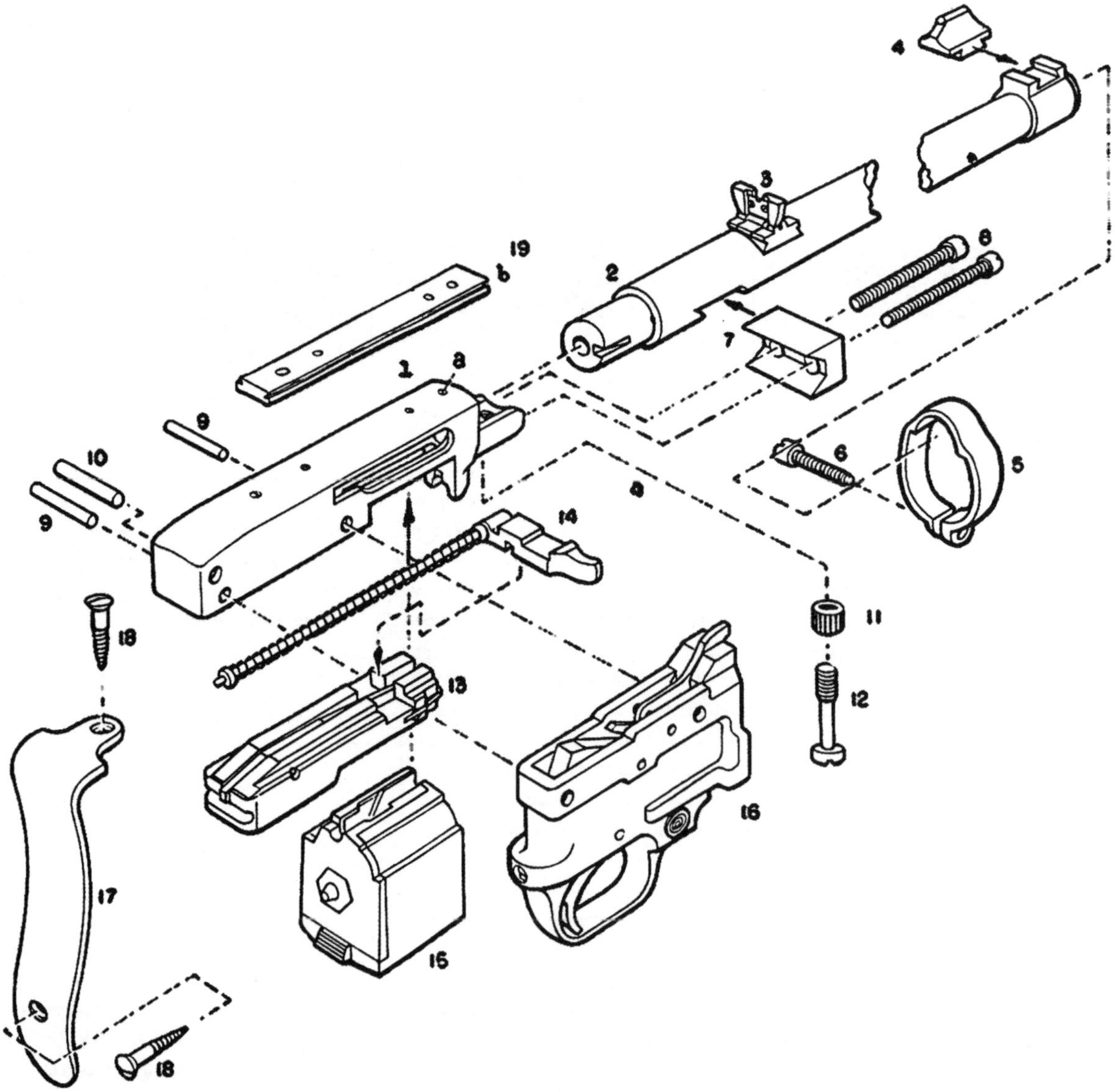

The Ruger Model 10/22 carbine, introduced in 1964, is chambered for the .22 Long Rifle cartridge, regular or high velocity. This semi-automatic blow-back-operated arm has a detachable 10-shot rotary box magazine.

The 10/22 is produced with wood stocks in several designs as well as laminated wood and black synthetic. Barrels are available in 16⅛-, 18½-, and 20-inch lengths. A 20-inch Bull barrel is also available.

Receiver and trigger guard of the Model 10/22 are machined from lightweight alloy. An unusual V-block arrangement secures the 18½-inch barrel to the receiver.

In 1998 Ruger introduced a magnum version, the 10/22 RBM, chambered for the .22 WMR cartridge with a steel receiver.

DISASSEMBLY

Press up on magazine latch, (6, Trigger Guard Assembly) and pull magazine (15) out from bottom of stock. Pull bolt handle (14) back and check action to be sure carbine is unloaded. Loosen barrel band screw (6) and slide barrel band (5) forward off stock. Unscrew takedown screw (12). Move safety (8, Trigger Guard Assembly) to centered position and lift barrel and assembly up out of stock from top. Drift out receiver cross pins (9) to left and drop trigger guard assembly (16) out bottom of receiver (l). Drift out bolt stop pin (10). Pull bolt assembly (13) to rear and lift out through bottom of receiver. Remove bolt handle (14) with recoil spring and guide assembly through side of receiver. NOTE: Bolt handle, recoil spring, guide rod, and bushing are a factory-staked assembly and further disassembly is not recommended. This completes disassembly for normal cleaning purposes.

To remove barrel, unscrew barrel retainer screws (8) and pull barrel (2) with barrel retainer (7) out of receiver (1) to front. NOTE: Disassembly of lock mechanism contained in trigger guard assembly (16) should only be undertaken by a competent gunsmith for repair or replacement of parts (See Trigger Guard Assembly). Reassemble in reverse order.

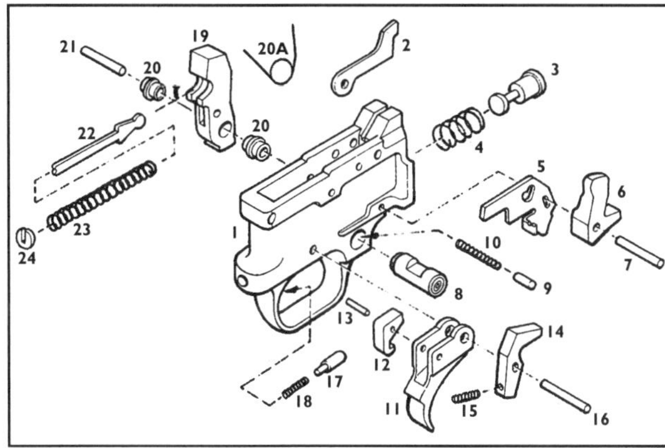

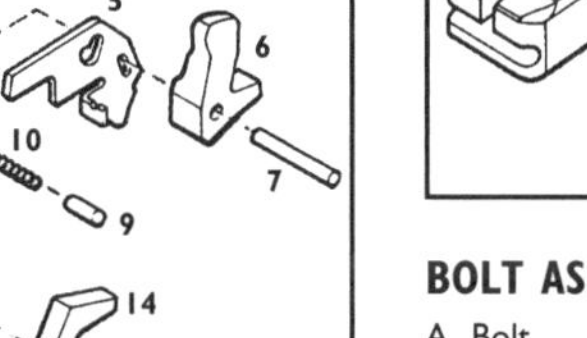

TRIGGER GUARD ASSEMBLY

1. Trigger guard
2. Ejector
3. Magazine latch plunger
4. Magazine latch plunger spring
5. Bolt lock
6. Magazine latch
7. Magazine latch pivot pin
8. Safety
9. Safety detent plunger
10. Safety detent plunger spring
11. Trigger
12. Disconnector
13. Disccnnector pivot pin
14. Sear
15. Sear spring
16. Trigger pivot pin
17. Trigger plunger
18. Trigger plunger spring
19. Hammer
20. Hammer bushings (2)
    20a. Bolt lock spring
21. Hammer pivot pin
22. Hammer strut
23. Hammer spring
24. Hammer strut washer

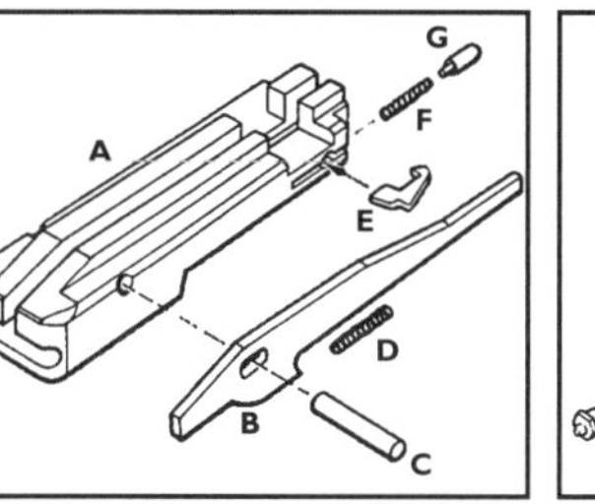

BOLT ASSEMBLY

A. Bolt
B. Firing pin
C. Firing pin stop pin
D. Firing pin rebound spring
E. Extractor
F. Extractor spring
G. Extractor plunger

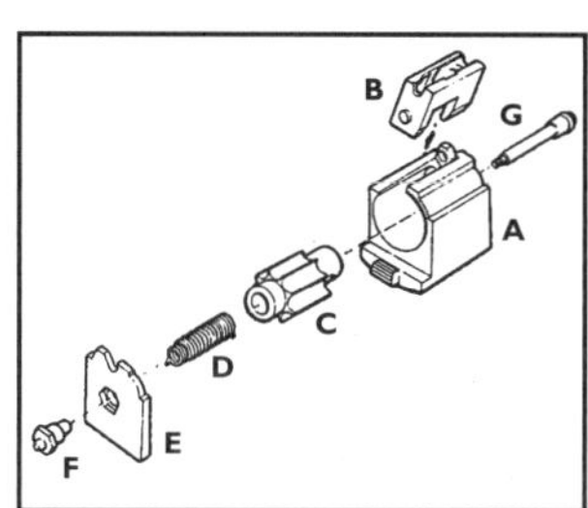

MAGAZINE ASSEMBLY

A. Magazine shell
B. Magazine throat
C. Magazine rotor
D. Rotor spring
E. Magazine cap
F. Magazine cap nut
G. Magazine screw

RUGER MODEL 77/22 RIFLE

PARTS LEGEND

1. Barrel
2. Barrel retainer, v-block
3. Barrel retainer screws
4. Bolt handle
5. Bolt lock plunger
6. Bolt lock plunger retainer
7. Bolt lock plunger spring
8. Bolt sleeve
9. Bolt stop
10. Bolt stop plunger
11. Bolt stop plunger spring
12. Breech block retainer
13. Cartridge support
14. Cartridge support plunger
15. Cartridge support spring
16. Cocking piece
17. Extractor (left side & right side)
18. Firing pin
19. Front mounting screw
20. Front sight
21. Magazine
22. Magazine latch lever
23. Magazine latch pivot pin
24. Magazine latch plunger
25. Magazine latch plunger spring
26. Pistol grip cap
27. Pistol grip cap medallion
28. Pistol grip cap screw
29. Rear mounting screw
30. Rear sight
31. Recoil pad
32. Recoil pad screws
33. Safety selector
34. Safety selector detent
35. Safety selector detent spring
36. Safety selector retainer
37. Scope ring clamp
38. Scope ring nut
39. Scope ring screws
40. Scope base & screws
41. Scope rings
42. Sear
43. Sear pivot pin
44. Sling swivel front screw, with nut
45. Sling swivel rear mounting stud
46. Stock
47. Striker
48. Striker cross pin
49. Striker spring
50. Trigger
51. Trigger guard assembly
52. Trigger pivot pin
53. Trigger sear/spring
54. Magazine well liner

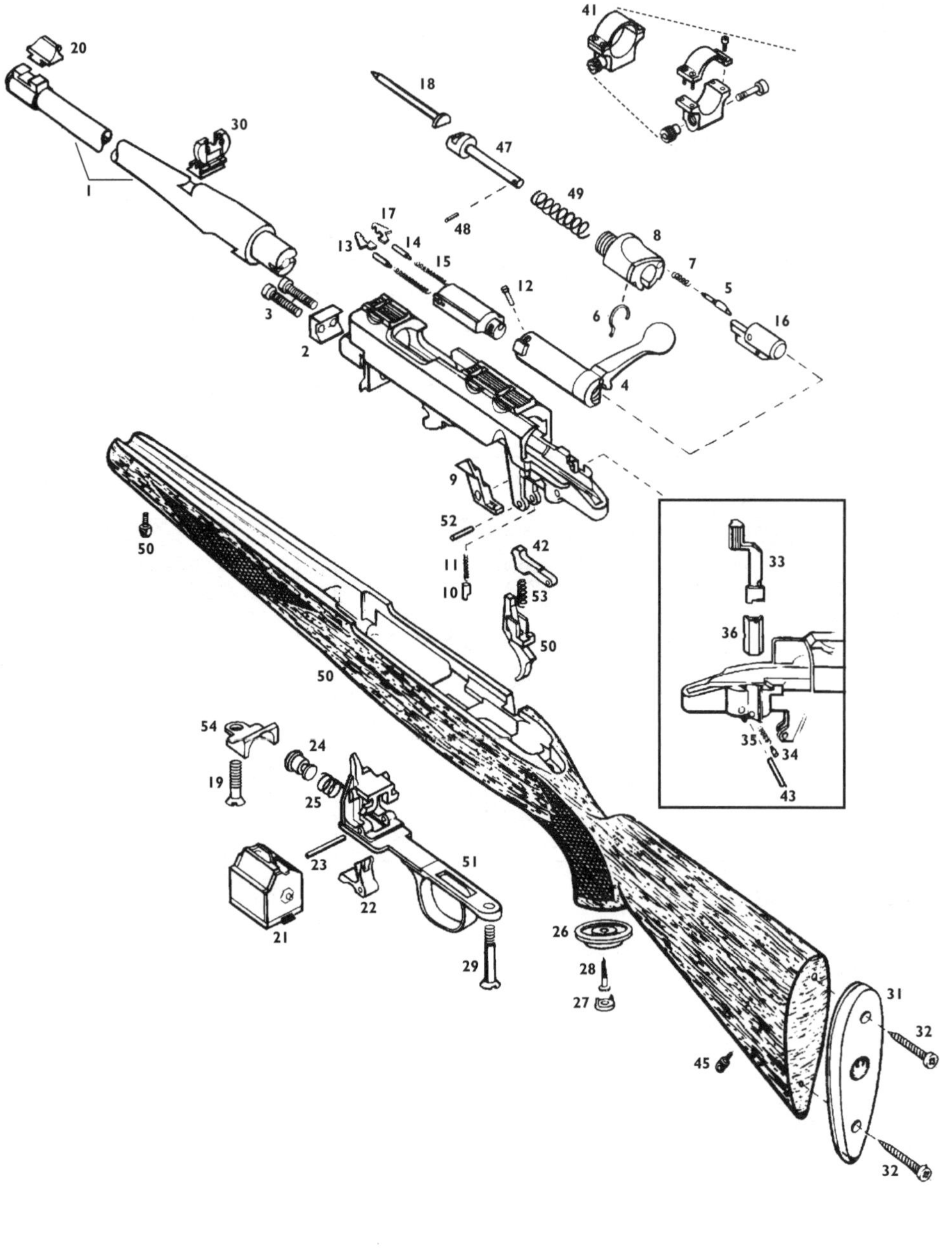

Ruger's first bolt action rifle, the Model 77, was introduced in 1968. The one-piece bolt (including the operating handle), receiver and other major parts are investment cast. The original Model 77 had a tang safety that connected to the trigger mechanism by a slender steel rod. In 1989 Ruger introduced the Model 77 Mark II with a redesigned trigger and safety. The Ruger Model 77/22 was first produced in 1983 and was similar in appearance to the Model 77 Mark II centerfire models. The 77/22 uses the same rotary detachable box magazine as the Ruger 10/22. The strong lockup of the basic 77/22 action allowed Ruger to introduce higher pressure chamberings, including .22 Hornet, .22 Magnum, and .44 Magnum (77/44). All Model 77 rifles have rotary magazines designed for the respective cartridges.

DISASSEMBLY

To remove the stock: Remove the rear mounting screw in the trigger guard. Swing the rear of the trigger guard out of the stock to clear trigger. Unhook trigger guard assembly from the receiver. Remove the trigger guard assembly. Remove the front mounting screw and magazine well liner. Very carefully lift the barrel/receiver from the stock.

To remove the barrel: Remove the (2) barrel retainer screws and barrel retainer. Slide the barrel forward to remove it from the receiver. NOTE: .22 Hornet and .44 Magnum caliber barrels are threaded into the receiver and should not be removed except by the factory.

To remove the trigger: (Safety Selector should be in the "Fire" position). While holding the trigger in place, press out the trigger pivot pin. CAUTION: Trigger is spring loaded and under tension. Remove the trigger and trigger/sear spring.

To remove the sear: Press out the sear pivot pin. Turn receiver upside down and slide sear forward. Sear will drop out of the top slot in the receiver.

To remove safety assembly: Rotate the safety selector so that the upper section is positioned fully over the center of the receiver tang. While holding the safety selector in place with thumb and forefinger, slide the retainer up out of receiver. (CAUTION: Safety selector is under spring tension from a spring and plunger acting against the lower section of the safety selector. The spring and plunger will jump out if not contained.) Lift out the safety selector.

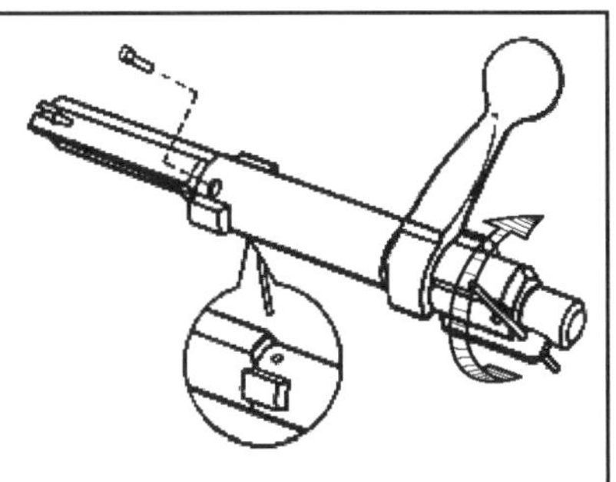

1 Be sure that the rifle is unloaded prior to disassembly. To remove the bolt: Lift the bolt handle up. Depress the bolt stop on the left side of the receiver. Withdraw the bolt from the rifle.

To disassemble the bolt: While holding the bolt handle, rotate the bolt sleeve clock-wise (as viewed from the rifle) to position shown above. Rotate the breach block until the head of the breechblock retaining pin is aligned with the larger holes in the bolt. Push out the breechblock retaining pin by inserting a pin through the small hole on the side opposite from the larger hole. The alignment must be precise to remove the retainer.

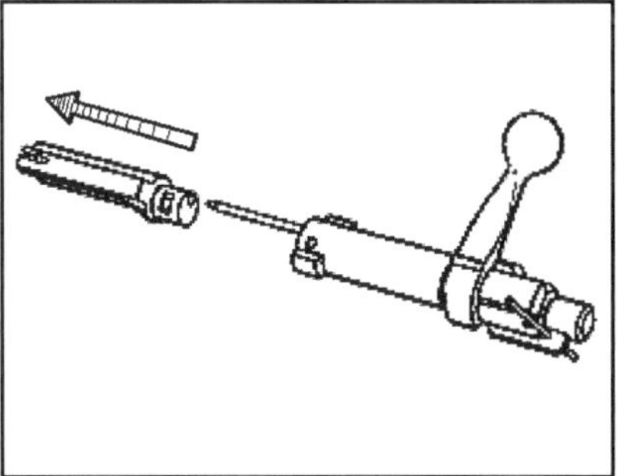

2 Remove the breach block assembly by sliding it forward out of the bolt. Insert a small pin (or suitable nail) into the "disassembly hole" in the striker/cocking piece assembly to hold it in the rear position. Note: The pin should be as close as possible in size to the hole diameter and at least 2 inches long so that it can be used to 'lever' the cocking piece to the rear when reassembling the bolt stop assembly into the bolt.

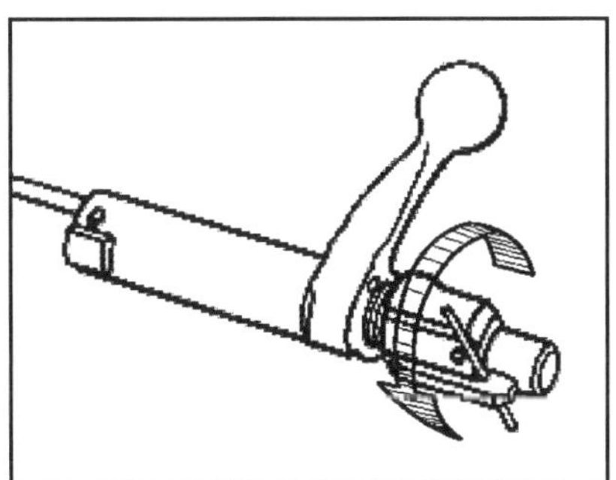

3 Unscrew the bolt sleeve.

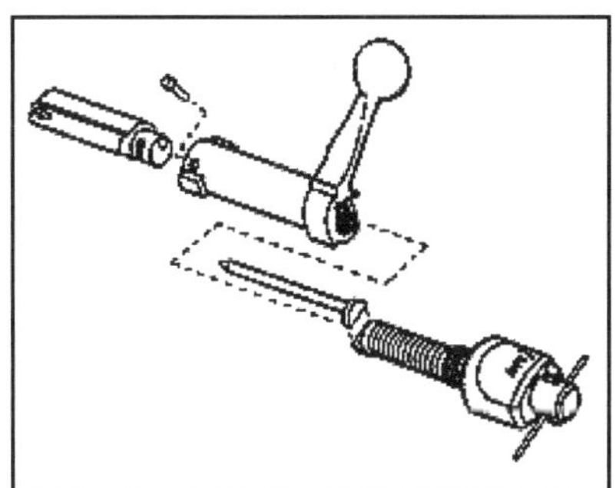

4 Remove the bolt sleeve assembly. The firing pin can now be removed from the bolt sleeve assembly.

RUGER MODEL 96 RIFLE

PARTS LEGEND

1. Barrel
2. Barrel band
3. Barrel band screw
4. Barrel retainer, v-block
5. Barrel retainer screws
6. Bolt
7. Bolt link pin
8. Butt plate
9. Butt plate screws
10. Cartridge support
11. Cartridge support plunger
12. Cartridge support spring
13. Ejector
14. Ejector pin
15. Extractor
16. Extractor spring
17. Firing pin
18. Firing pin spring
19. Firing pin retaining pin
20. Front sight
21. Hammer pivot pin
22. Hammer roller
23. Hammer roller pin
24. Hammer spring, right
25. Hammer spring, left
26. Hammer spring support pin
27. Indicator lifter
28. Indicator lifter pivot pin
29. Indicator pin
30. Indicator retainer
31. Indicator spring
32. Lever detent plunger
33. Lever detent plunger spring
34. Lever housing assembly
35. Lever/link pin
36. Lever locking link
37. Lever pivot bushing
38. Lever pivot screw
39. Magazine
40. Bolt stop pin
41. Lever assembly
42. Magazine latch pivot pin
43. Magazine latch plunger
44. Magazine latch spring
45. Receiver cross pin
46. Receiver cross pin
47. Safety button
48. Safety detent plunger
49. Safety detent plunger spring
50. Scope base adapter & screws
51. Scope base screws
52. Sear
53. Sear spring
54. Take-down screw
55. Trigger
56. Trigger pivot bearing
57. Trigger pivot pin
58. Trigger plunger
59. Trigger plunger spring

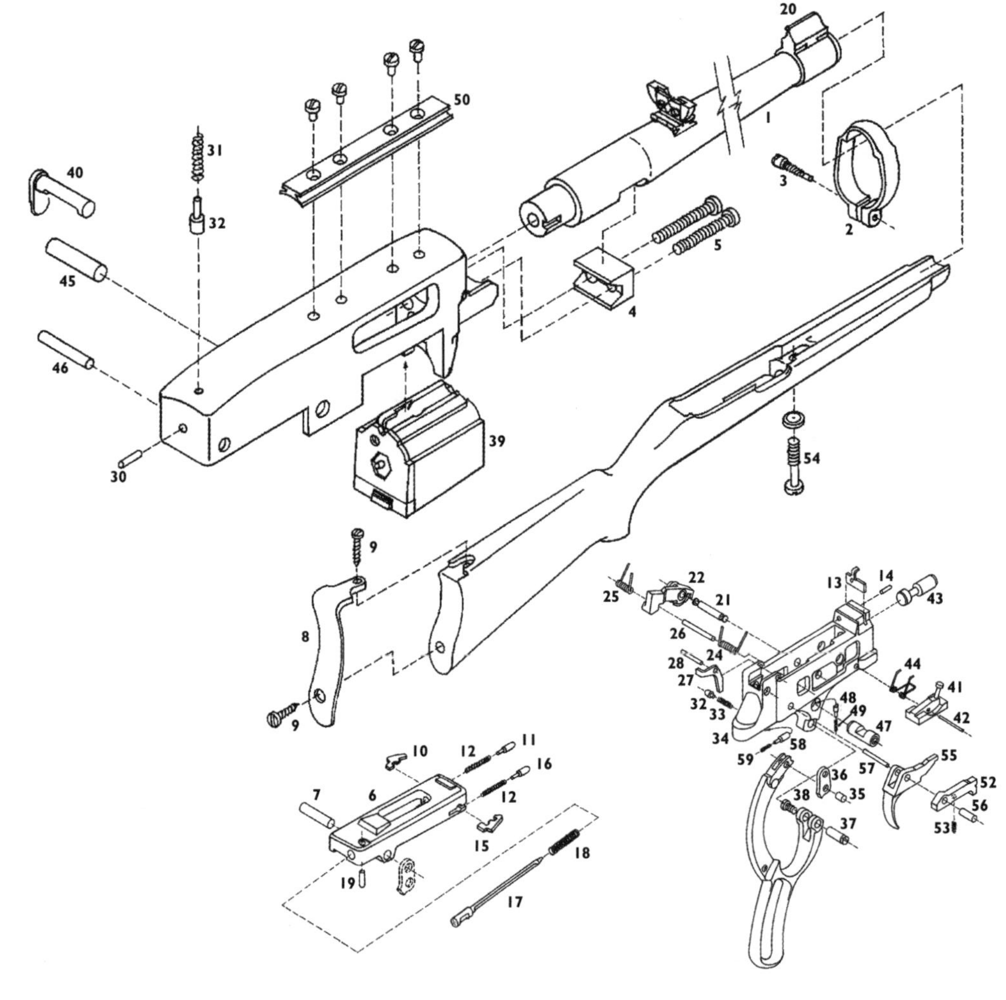

The Model 96 is a manually operated, short-throw lever action rifle introduced by Sturm, Ruger in 1996. The rifle weighs just under 6 pounds and is externally similar to the Ruger 10/22 semi-automatic rifle, but with a short-throw (54-degree), actuating lever. The Model 96 cocks on opening and the bolt locks on closing the lever when the rear portion tilts upward into a reinforced recess in the receiver. Cartridges are expelled by dual extractors.

The Model 96 uses a 4-, 9- or 10-shot Ruger rotary magazine, depending upon the caliber. It is chambered for .22 WMR, .22 Long Rifle, .17 HMR(Model 96/17) or .44 Rem. Mag. (Model 96/44) cartridges.

The rifle is equipped with a crossbolt safety in front of the trigger and features a cocking indicator in the form of a small brass pin that protrudes on top of the receiver. The Model 96 is provided with open sights, but the receiver has an integral raised portion along the top that is machined to receive the standard Ruger-style scope rings.

DISASSEMBLY

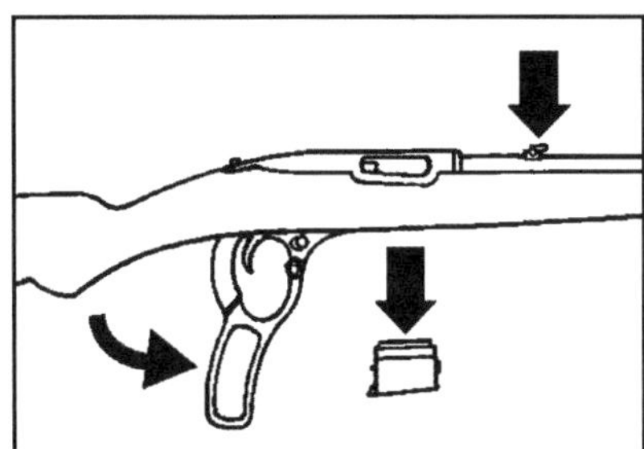

1 With the rifle pointing in a safe direction, remove the magazine. Fully open the lever and bolt to make certain there is not a cartridge in the chamber. The rear sight leaf should be down, and the internal hammer should be cocked. Keep the lever open and the safety "on."

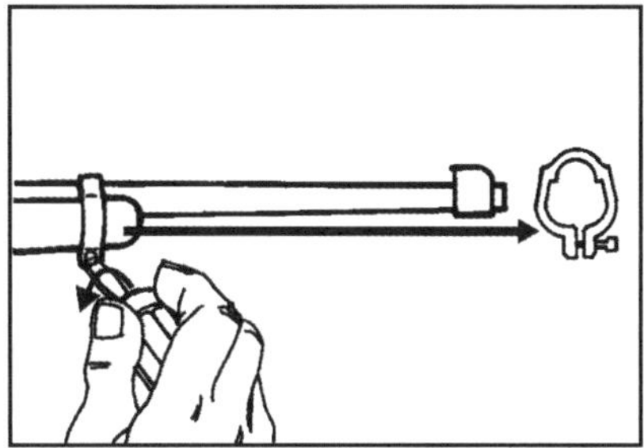

2 Loosen the barrel band screw and remove the barrel band.

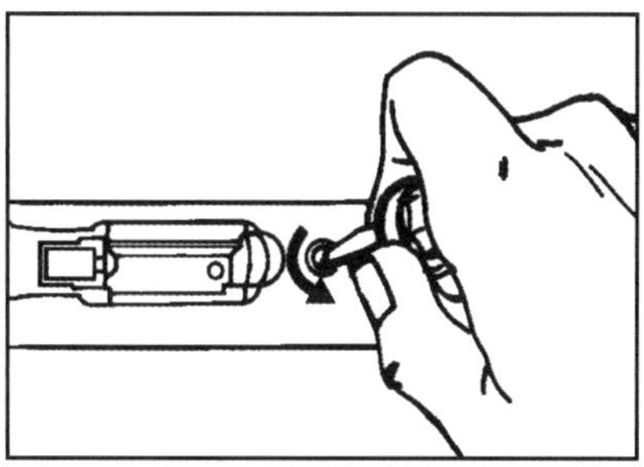

3 Loosen the take-down screw completely, but note that it will not come out of the stock. Position the safety so an equal amount of the button is exposed on each side. If the safety is not in the middle when the barrel-receiver assembly is lifted out of the stock, the stock will be damaged. Make sure the lever is open.

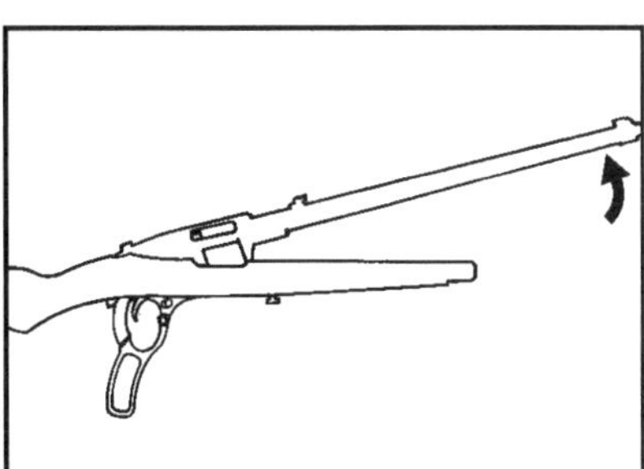

4 Swing the barrel-receiver assembly upward away from the forearm of the stock. Be careful the two receiver cross pins and bolt stop pin do not fall out.

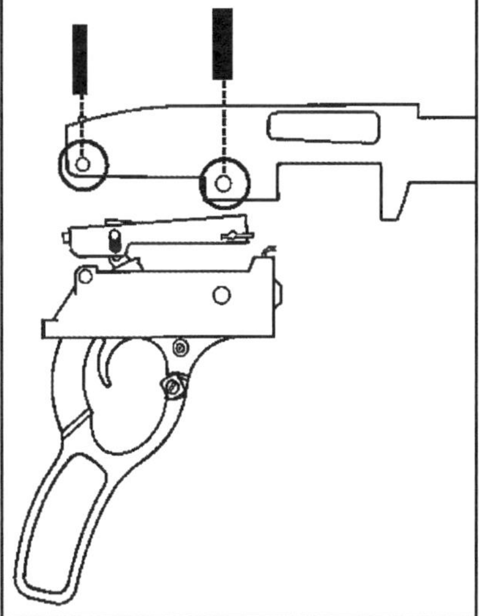

5 To remove the lever housing, again make sure the lever is fully open. Drift out the two larger diameter receiver pins with a small diameter screwdriver or punch. Do not drive out any of the smaller pins. Do not disassemble the components of the lever housing assembly. The bolt is removed together with the lever housing.

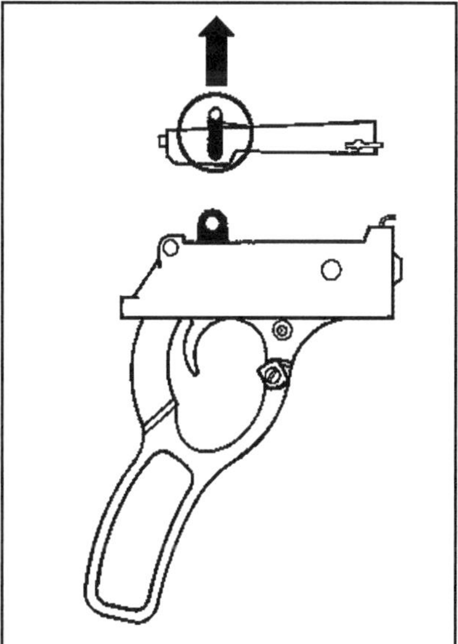

6 The bolt is separated from the lever by pushing out the bolt link pin.

RUGER MINI-14 CARBINE

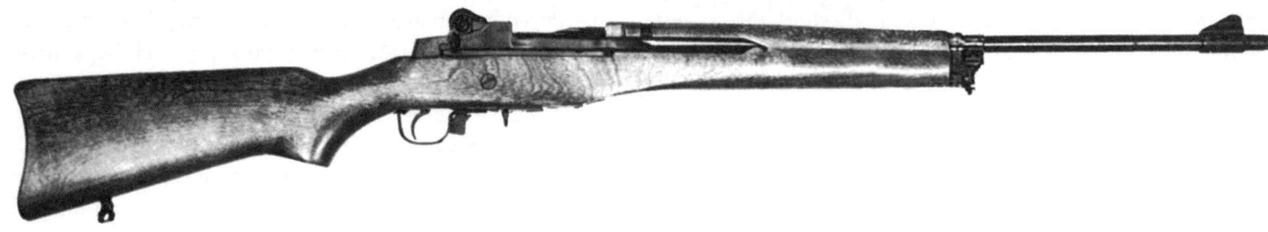

PARTS LEGEND

1. Barrel
2. Bolt
3. Bolt lock assembly (with buffer spring)
4. Bolt lock buffer spring
5. Bolt lock cover plate
6. Bolt lock plunger
7. Bolt lock plunger spring
8. Butt plate
9. Butt plate screw (2 req'd)
10. Ejector
11. Ejector spring
12. Extractor
13. Extractor plunger
14. Extractor spring
15. Firing pin
16. Forearm liner & stock cap assembly
17. Front sight
18. Front sight cross pin
19. Gas block (top & bottom)
20. Gas block screw (4 req'd)
21. Gas port bushing
22. Guide rod
23. Hammer
24. Hammer pivot pin
25. Hammer spring
26. Hammer strut
27. Hand guard assembly
28. Magazine bottom, 5-shot
29. Magazine bottom retainer, 5-shot
30. Magazine follower, 5-shot
31. Magazine shell, 5-shot
32. Magazine spring, 5-shot
33. Magazine catch, front
34. Magazine catch retaining pin
35. Magazine latch
36. Magazine latch pivot pin
37. Magazine latch spring
38. Piston
39. Rear sight assembly, complete (not illustrated)
40. Rear sight base
41. Rear sight plunger elevation detent plunger
42. Rear sight elevation detent spring
43. Rear sight elevation screw
44. Rear sight elevation plunger
45. Rear sight elevation plunger spring
46. Rear sight nut
47. Rear sight peep
48. Rear sight windage detent plunger
49. Rear sight windage detent spring
50. Rear sight windage screw
51. Rear sight windage screw pin
52. Receiver
53. Recoil spring
54. Safety
55. Safety detent spring
56. Safety spring retaining spring
57. Secondary sear
58. Secondary sear spring
59. Slide
60. Sling swivel, front
61. Sling swivel assembly, rear
62. Stock
63. Stock reinforcement
64. Stock reinforcement screw (2 req'd)
65. Stock reinforcement lock washer (2 req'd)
66. Trigger
67. Trigger bushing
68. Trigger guard
69. Trigger housing
70. Trigger pivot pin
71. Trigger spring

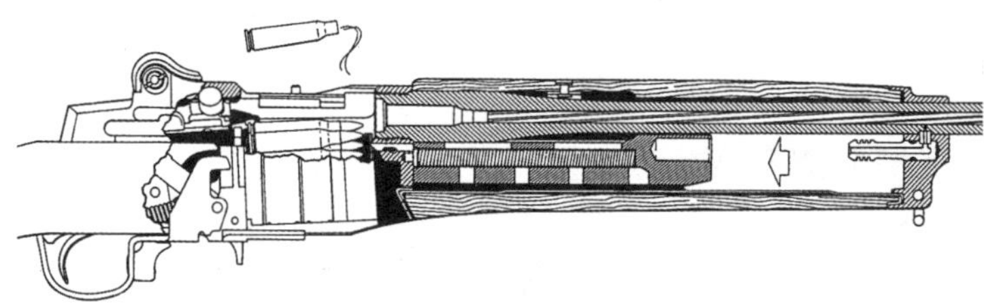

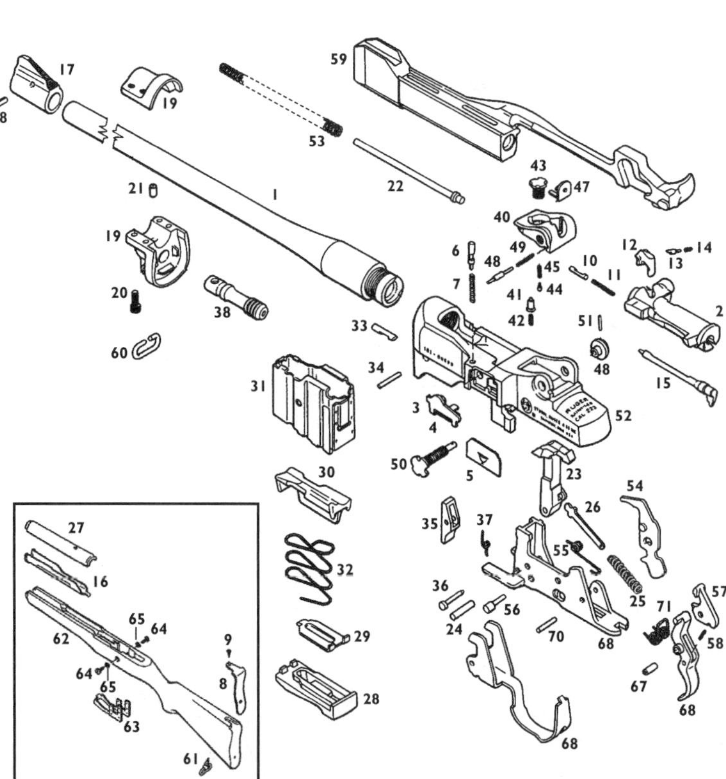

The .223 (5.56 mm.) Mini-14 resembles the U.S. M 14 rifle in appearance and incorporates the Garand rotating bolt principle.

The Ruger-designed gun was first produced in 1974 in Southport, Connecticut, where about 1000 were made before production was transferred to a larger plant in Newport, New Hampshire. All Southport guns and early runs made at Newport bear serial numbers with the 180 prefix. The Southport model can be identified by the sporting type, gold bead front sight.

In mid-1978, a refined Mini-14 replaced the "180-" prefix models. Current production Mini-14 carbines bear the serial number prefix "181-." The drawings and information which follow apply only to the "181-" Mini-14 series.

Although several specialized variations of the Mini-14 designed for use by law enforcement and government agencies will be encountered from time to time, these are virtually identical to the standard production guns with respect to disassembly procedures. Government service Mini-14 carbines are usually equipped with a flash hider and with a special front sight with protective steel "ears" on either side of the sight blade. Some service models use a ventilated upper handguard.

Several different magazines are offered for this rifle. The most frequently encountered is the five-shot and 10- and 20-round magazines are also common.

The Mini-14 is a strong and reliable rifle designed for ease of cleaning and maintenance. Only the simplest tools are required to field strip the arm for cleaning and lubrication.

DISASSEMBLY

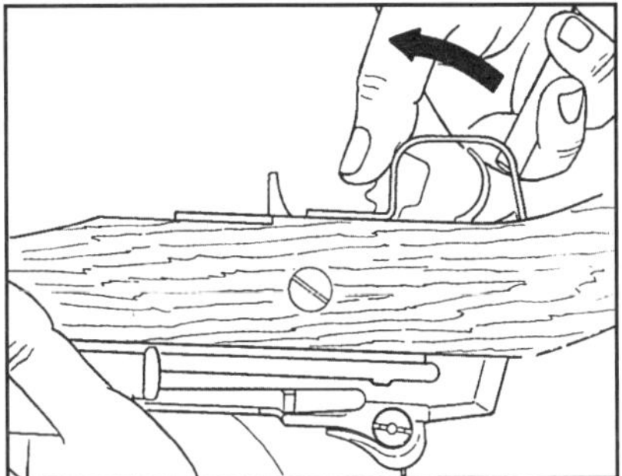

1 Push magazine latch (35) forward and, with a forward/down movement, remove the magazine. Pull slide (59) fully to rear. Check chamber to be sure carbine is unloaded and release the slide, which will ride forward under spring pressure. Place safety (54) in rear or "On" position (toward trigger). NOTE: Safety must be engaged and hammer cocked for disassembly or reassembly.

Holding the gun upside down, insert a small screwdriver or punch in the rear hole in the trigger guard (68) and, exerting forward pressure, unlatch the trigger guard, freeing its rear tab from the trigger housing (69).

2 Pull the entire trigger guard/ trigger group straight upward to remove.

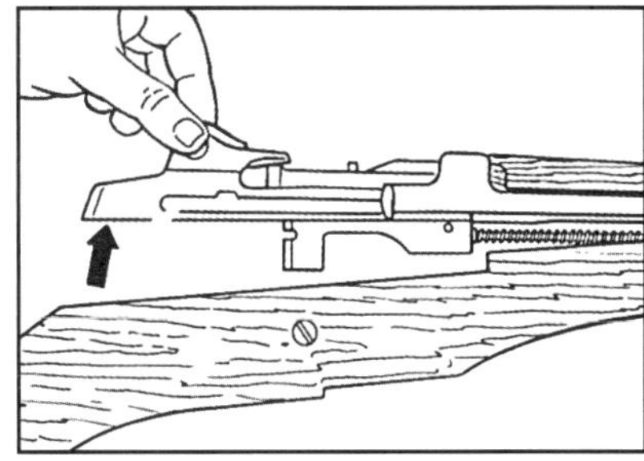

3 Holding the carbine with sights up, raise the rear of the receiver until it is just clear of the stock. Separate barreled action from stock (62).

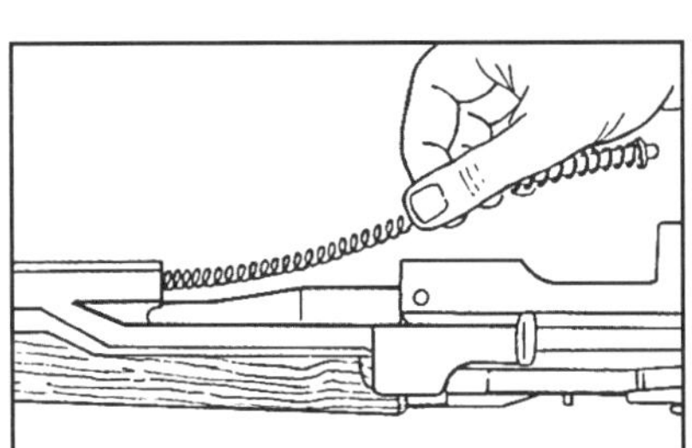

4 Grasp guide rod (22) and recoil spring (53) and pull toward muzzle until guide rod is free from its retaining recess in the front of the receiver. CAUTION: Spring is under compression Lift guide rod/recoil spring asembly clear of the receiver and withdraw the spring from the slide tunnel.

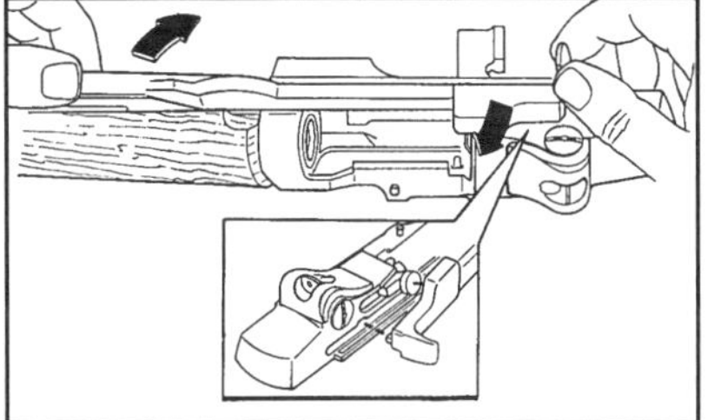

5 Pull slide (59) to the rear until retaining projections are aligned with corresponding notches in the receiver. Remove slide.

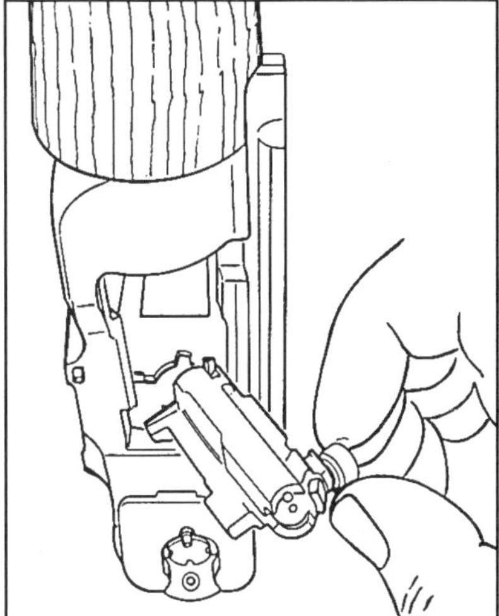

6 Move bolt (2) forward and pivot it upward. The firing pin (15) must be fully retracted for removal or replacement of bolt in receiver. Align tail of firing pin with slot in the interior of the receiver crossbridge. Remove bolt. NOTE: Force should not be used or required to remove or replace bolt.

Further disassembly is not recommended by the factory and is not required for cleaning/maintenance. Reassembly is accomplished by reversing the above procedures.

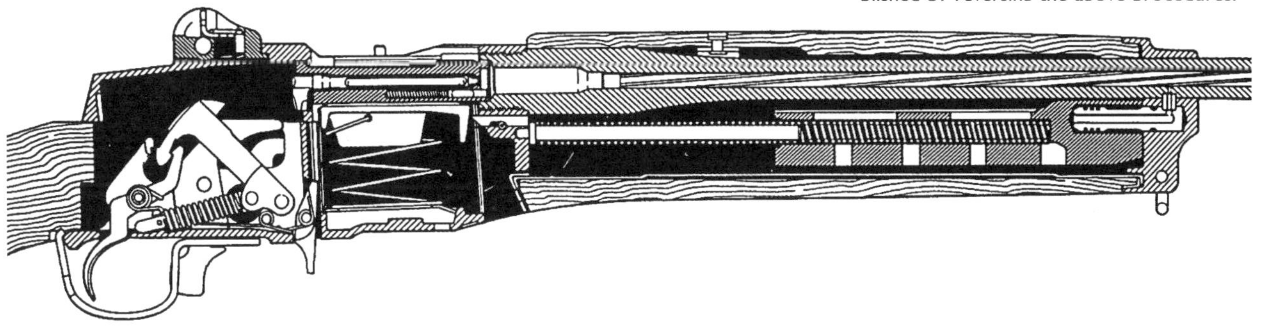

RUGER NO. 1 RIFLE

PARTS LEGEND

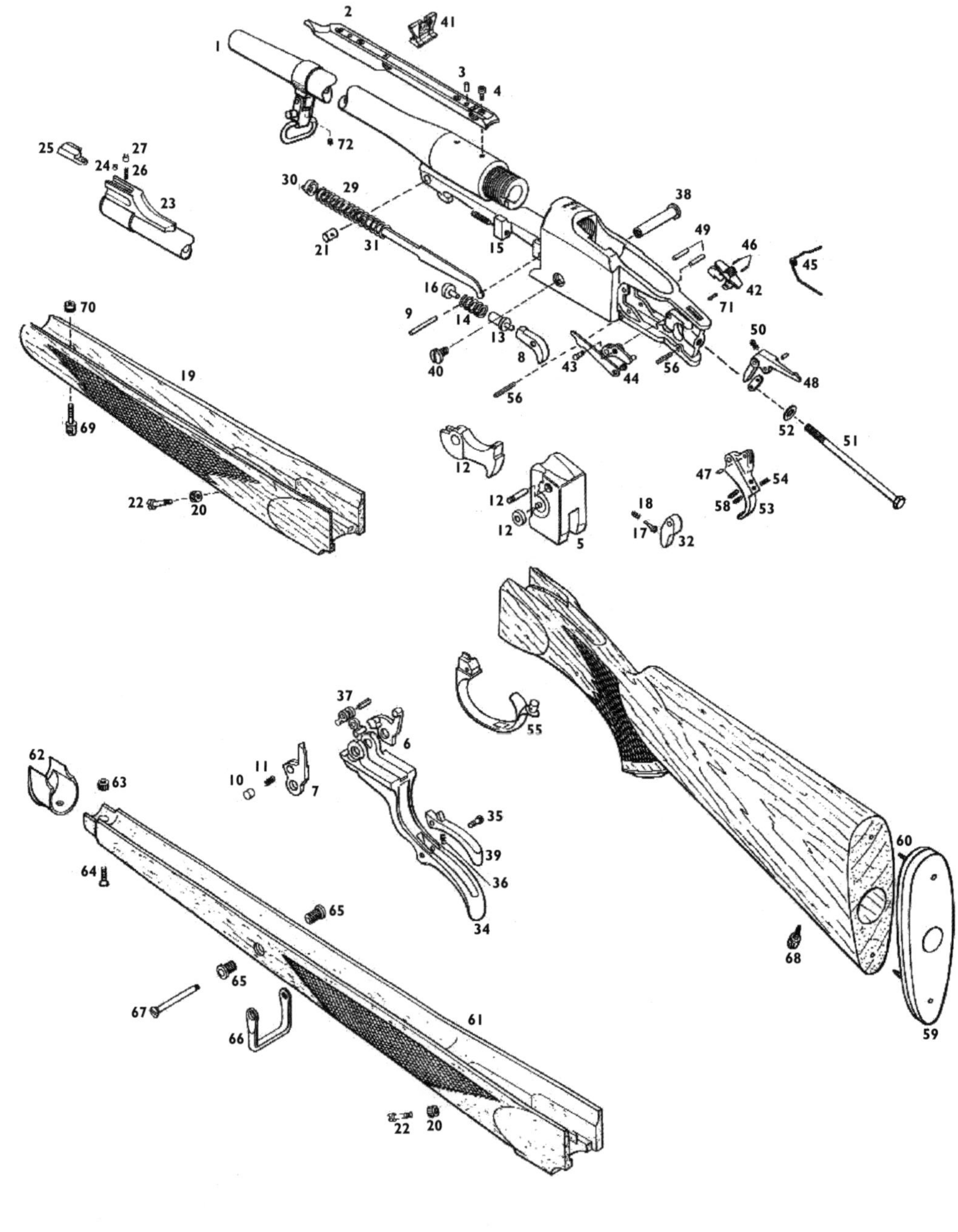

1. Barrel
2. Barrel rib
3. Barrel rib dowel
4. Barrel rib screw
5. Breech block
6. Breech block arm
7. Ejector
8. Ejector cam
9. Ejector cam pivot pin
10. Ejector plunger
11. Ejector plunger spring
12. Ejector roller
13. Ejector strut
14. Ejector strut spring
15. Ejector strut adjustment screw
16. Ejector strut swivel
17. Firing pin
18. Firing pin spring
19. Forearm
20. Forearm escutcheon
21. Forearm take down nut
22. Forearm take down screw
23. Front sight base
24. Front sight base set screw
25. Front sight blade assembly
26. Front sight plunger spring
27. Front sight retaining plunger
28. Hammer
29. Hammer spring
30. Hammer spring retaining washer
31. Hammer strut
32. Hammer transfer block
33. Hammer transfer block pivot pin
34. Lever
35. Lever latch pivot pin
36. Lever latch spring
37. Lever link and pin assembly
38. Lever pivot pin
39. Lever latch
40. Lever pivot screw
41. Rear sight
42. Safety
43. Safety arm pivot pin
44. Safety bar arm assembly
45. Safety detent spring
46. Safety retaining pins
47. Sear adjustment screw
48. Sear & trigger assembly
49. Sear pivot pin
50. Sear spring
51. Stock bolt
52. Stock bolt washer
53. Trigger
54. Trigger adjustment spring
55. Trigger guard
56. Trigger guard retaining pins
57. Trigger pivot pin
58. Trigger spring adjustment screw
59. Recoil pad
60. Recoil pad screws
61. Mannlicher fore-end (stock)
62. Muzzle cap
63. Muzzle cap escutcheon
64. Muzzle cap screw
65. Sling Swivel Escutcheons
66. Sling Swivel, front
67. Sling swivel screw
68. Sling swivel mounting screw, rear
69. Sling swivel screw, front
70. Sling swivel nut, front
71. Safety detent spring pin
72. Sling swivel band set screw

Introduced in 1967, the Ruger No. 1 is a single shot, Farquharson-style, hammerless falling block rifle. The action uses an under-lever that wraps around, but is separate from, the front of the trigger guard. The lever lowers the block for loading and cocks the rifle. The No. 1 uses a shotgun-style tang safety that acts on the hammer and sear. Ruger offers variations of the rifle with Alexander-Henry, Beavertail, or Mannlicher style forearms. The rifle is produced in more than 26 calibers from .204 Ruger to .458 Lott Magnum. Since its introduction the No. 1 Rifle has been offered in several variations including the Medium Sporter, Light Sporter, International, Standard, Tropical, and Varminter. In 1972, Ruger introduced the No. 3, a plainer version of the No. 1 with a Winchester Low Wall-style trigger guard/lever.

DISASSEMBLY

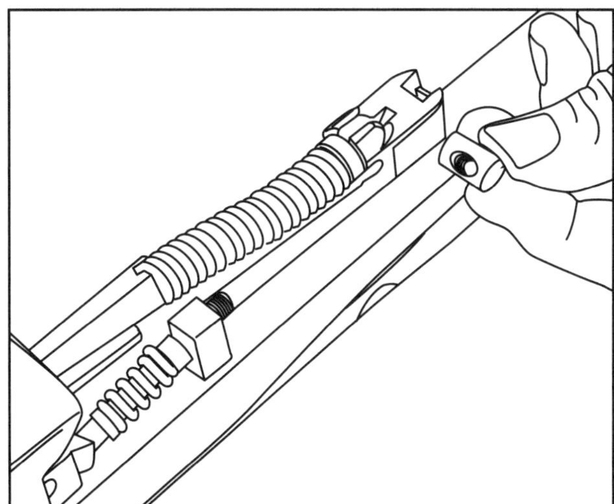

1 Remove the forearm takedown screw on the underside of the forearm and gently pull off the forearm by pulling it down and away from the receiver. Remove the forearm takedown nut.

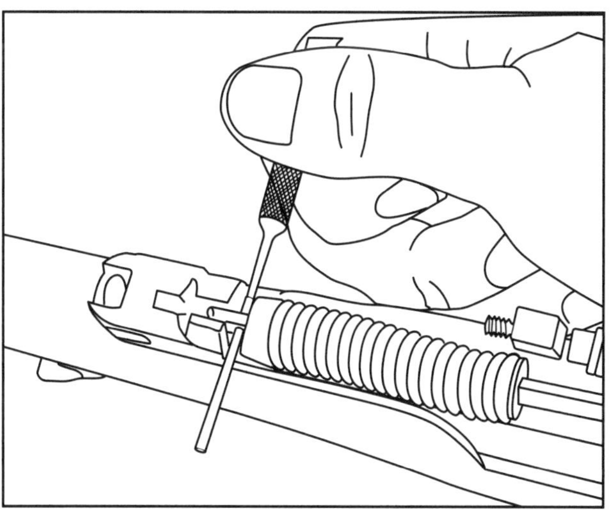

2 With hammer cocked, insert a "slave pin" through hole in hammer spring strut. Pull the trigger to release the hammer. Shift the hammer spring and strut assembly toward the rear, tip the front of the assembly downward and remove it toward the front. CAUTION: The hammer assembly is under tension, only disassemble it for repairs.

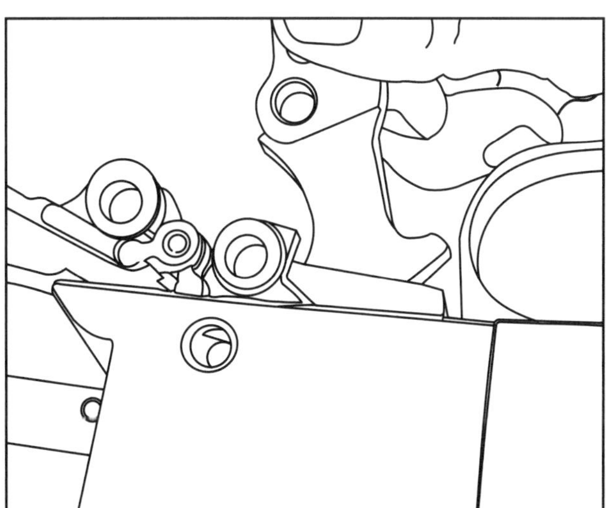

3 Lower the lever and unscrew the cap screw on the lever pivot. Push the pivot out.

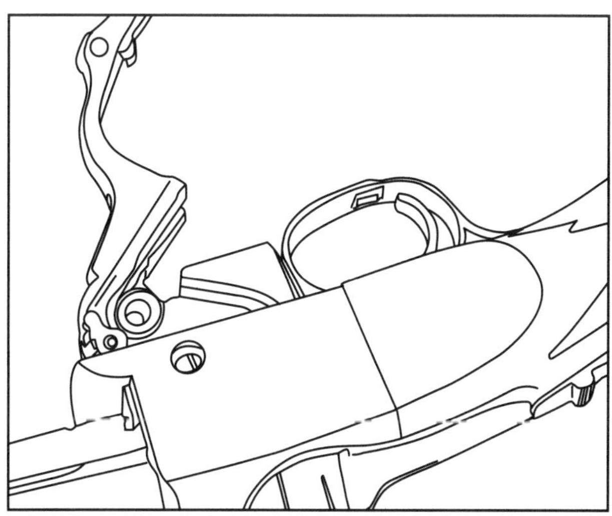

4 Remove the hammer. Push the breechblock back up, close the lever, and then re-open the lever about half way. Remove the breechblock, breechblock arm and the linkage as a unit from the bottom of the receiver. Remove the ejector, ejector plunger and ejector plunger spring.

SAKO CENTER-FIRE BOLT-ACTION

PARTS LEGEND

1. Bolt complete
2. Bolt stop, complete
3. Trigger mechanism
4. Stock
5. Trigger guard, complete
6. Cocking piece
7. Bolt sleeve
8. Firing pin
9. Firing pin spring
10. Bolt body
11. Bolt guard stop plate spring
12. Bolt guard stop plate
13. Bolt guard strip
14. Bolt guard stop spring
15. Bolt guard strip ring
16. Extractor catch spring
17. Extractor catch
18. Extractor
19. Firing pin locking screw
20. Bolt stop screw
21. Receiver
22. Bolt stop pin
23. Barrel
24. Front sight (not shown)
25. Swivel nut
26. Swivel
27. Butt plate
28. Spacer
29. Magazine follower
30. Trigger guard bushing
31. Magazine housing
32. Magazine spring
33. Trigger guard bottom plate
34. Adjuster screw
35. Adjuster bottom plate
36. Adjuster
37. Sight hood (not shown)
38. Rear guard screw
39. Front guard screw

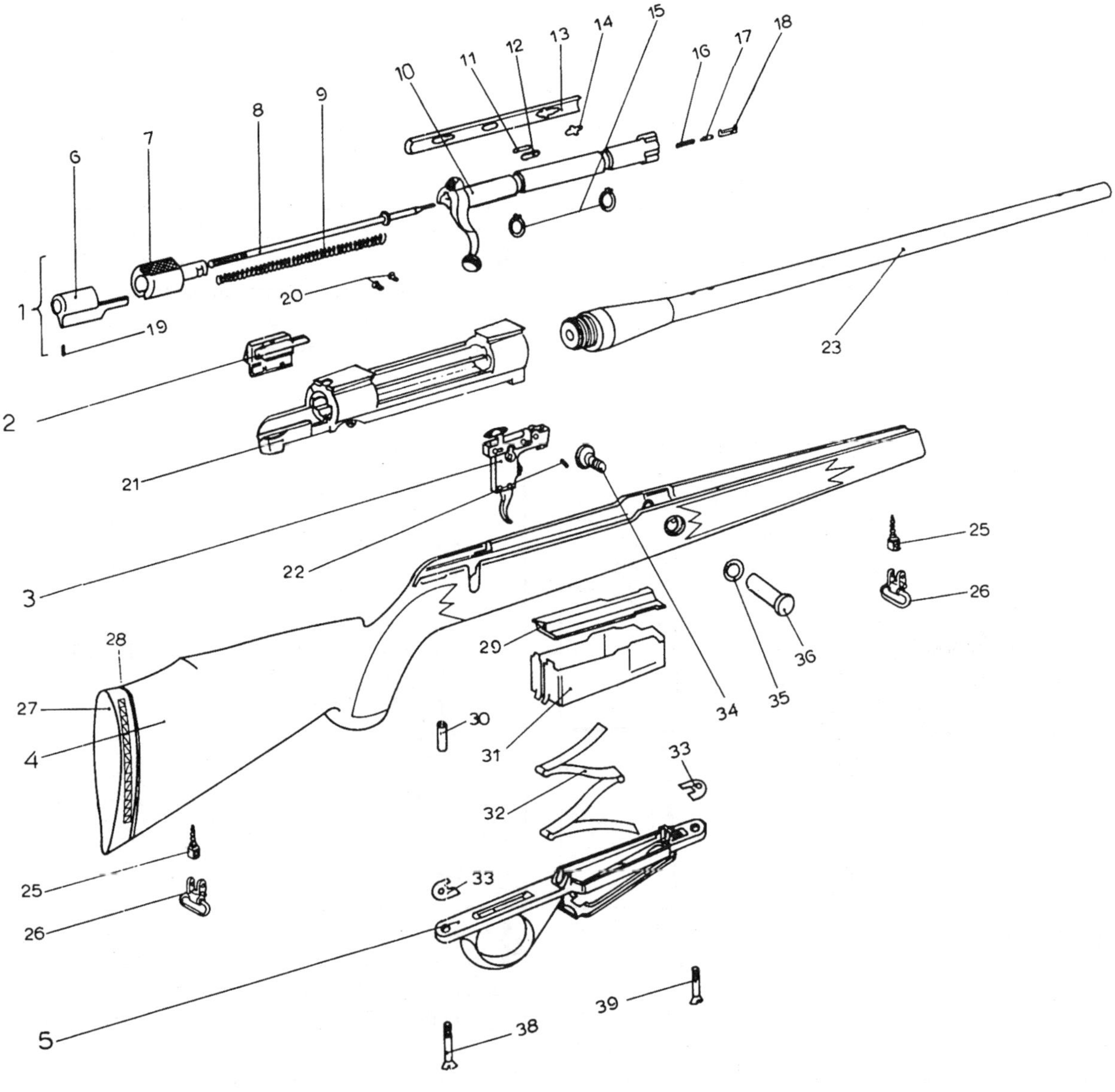

Oy Sako Ab of Riihimaki, Finland, is that country's largest firearm and ammunition manufacturer. Sako began production of commercial rifles after World War II, with the L46 rifle, later renamed the L461 "Vixen." Initially chambered for 7x33 Sako, the short action Vixens have been chambered for such calibers as .17, .222, .222 Mag. and .223. In 1957, Sako introduced a medium action, the L579 "Forester," for .220 Swift, .243, .244, and .308Win. A "long action" rifle, the L61 "Finnbear," was offered in 1961 in chamberings such as .270 and .30- 06 and medium length magnums; .300 Win. and .338 Win. Sako rifles were produced in factories in Riihimaeki, Hausjaervi and Tourula, Finland. Stoeger Industries distributed these rifles in the United States as AI, AII, and AIII rifles.

Construction and disassembly features of these rifles are similar. Basically a modification of the Mauser system, the older Sako rifles have one feature that must be noted. The firing pin is threaded into the cocking piece, and its protrusion from the bolt face is adjustable. If the firing pin is tampered with, it must be readjusted and secured by its locking screw. The factory recommends firing pin protrusion from .059 to .071 inches. Newer models of Sako rifles lack this adjustment.

In 1987 Sako joined with state owned Valmet to form Sako-Valmet. In 1999, the Rauma (a technology company) and Valmet merged and sold Sako to the Beretta Holdings Group that same year. All of Sako's older model rifles have been replaced by the Model 75 series.

DISASSEMBLY

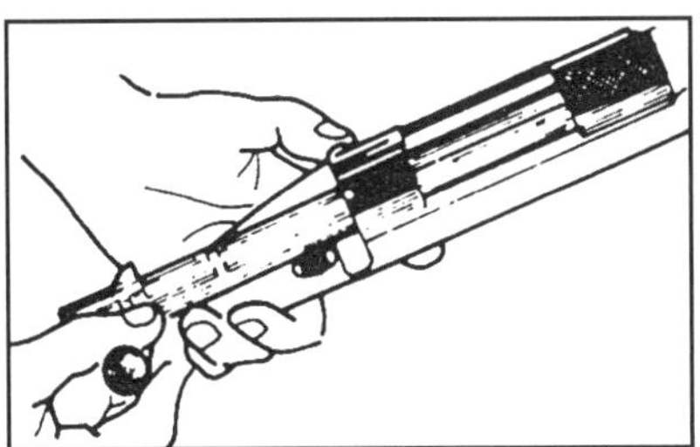

1 To remove the bolt, depress the bolt release button on the bolt stop assembly (2) with the left thumb, lift the bolt handle and withdraw the bolt from the rear of the receiver.

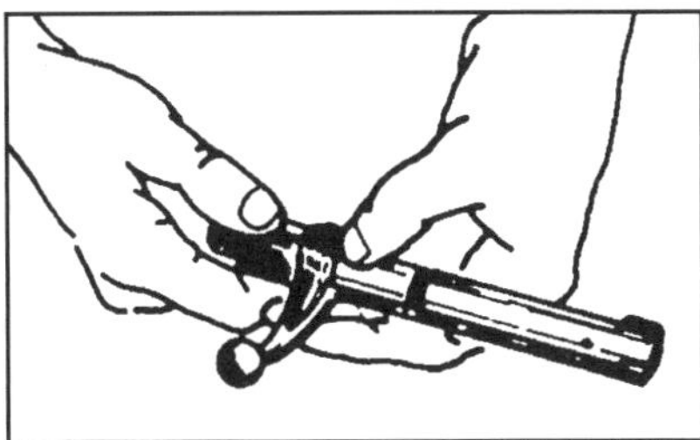

2 Hold the bolt body (10) in the left hand and, with the bolt rear pointing up.

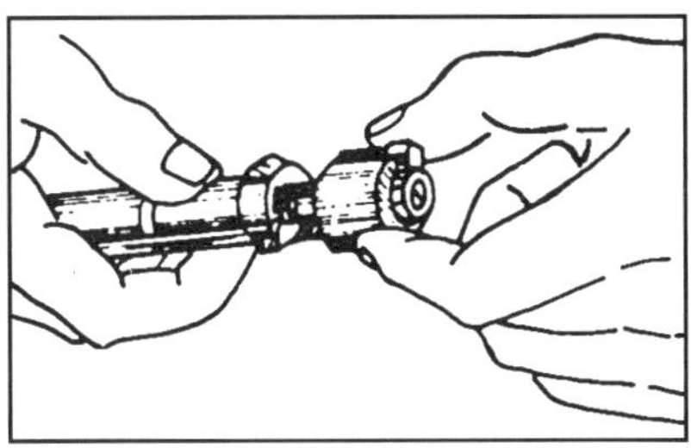

3 Turn the bolt sleeve (7) clockwise until it disengages from the body.

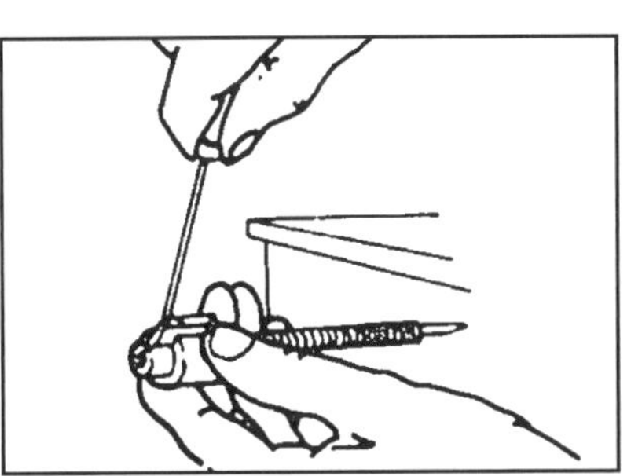

4 Loosen the firing pin locking screw (19) with a small screw driver. Hold the rear of the firing pin assembly in the left hand with the firing pin point bearing on a wooden surface to prevent parts loss or injury from spring pressure.

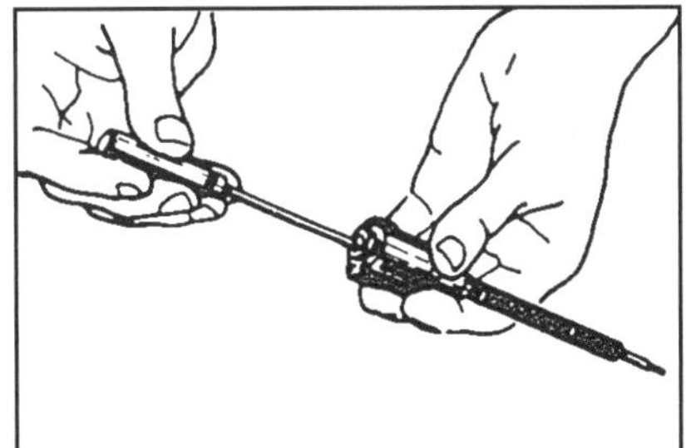

5 With a screwdriver, turn the slotted end of the threaded firing pin (8) downward out of the cocking piece.

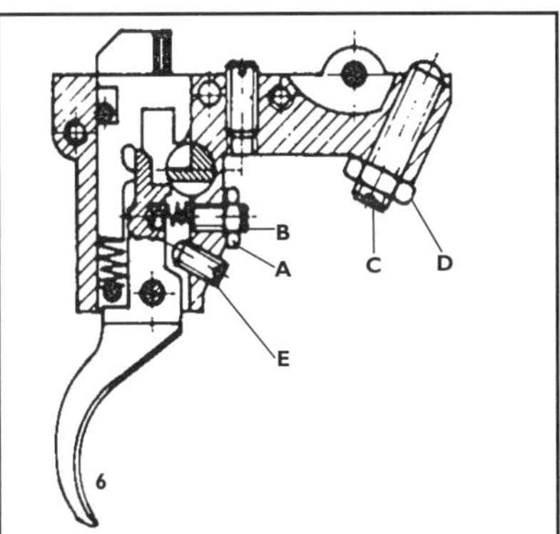

6 The Sako trigger is factory adjusted for sear engagement, attempts to change this adjustment could be hazardous and would void the guarantee. Weight of pull and blacklash can be adjusted simply and positively by the owner. To lessen weight of pull, loosen lock nut (A) and back of screw (B) until desired weight is reached. Retighten lock nut (A). To increase weight of pull, reverse above procedure. Backlash may be reduced, if required, by turning in screw (E). NOTE: Be sure screw (C) and lock nut (D) are tight before attempting adjustment.

SAVAGE MODEL 6 RIFLE

PARTS LEGEND

1. Barrel
2. Front sight
3. Rear sight
4. Rear sight step
5. Bumper spring
6. Bumper
7. Rear magazine mount
8. Front magazine mount
9. Outside magazine tube
10. Magazine plug
11. Magazine follower
12. Inside magazine tube
13. Magazine follower spring
14. Magazine plug pin
15. Stock
16. Buttplate
17. Buttplate screws (2)
18. Firing pin
19. Recoil plug
20. Hammer
21. Breech bolt spring rod
22. Breech bolt spring washer
23. Breech bolt spring
24. Hammer spring
25. Breech bolt
26. Long trigger guard screw
27. Short trigger guard screw
28. Trigger guard
29. Extractor
30. Takedown screw
31. Locking bolt plunger ball
32. Locking bolt plunger ball spring
33. Locking bolt
34. Receiver
35. Barrel pins (2)
36. Magazine guide
37. Cartridge guide spring
38. Magazine screws (2)
39. Lifter pin
40. Lifter spring
41. Right detent lever
42. Left detent lever
43. Release housing
44. Hammer spring washer
45. Release housing screw
46. Release plunger
47. Detent lever pin
48. Lifter
49. Lifter spacers (2)
50. Release plunger pin
51. Release lever
52. Release lever actuating pin
53. Trigger
54. Detent plunger spring
55. Detent plunger
56. Detent plunger pin
57. Trigger pin
58. Release lever pin
59. Safety screws (2)
60. Safety spring
61. Safety

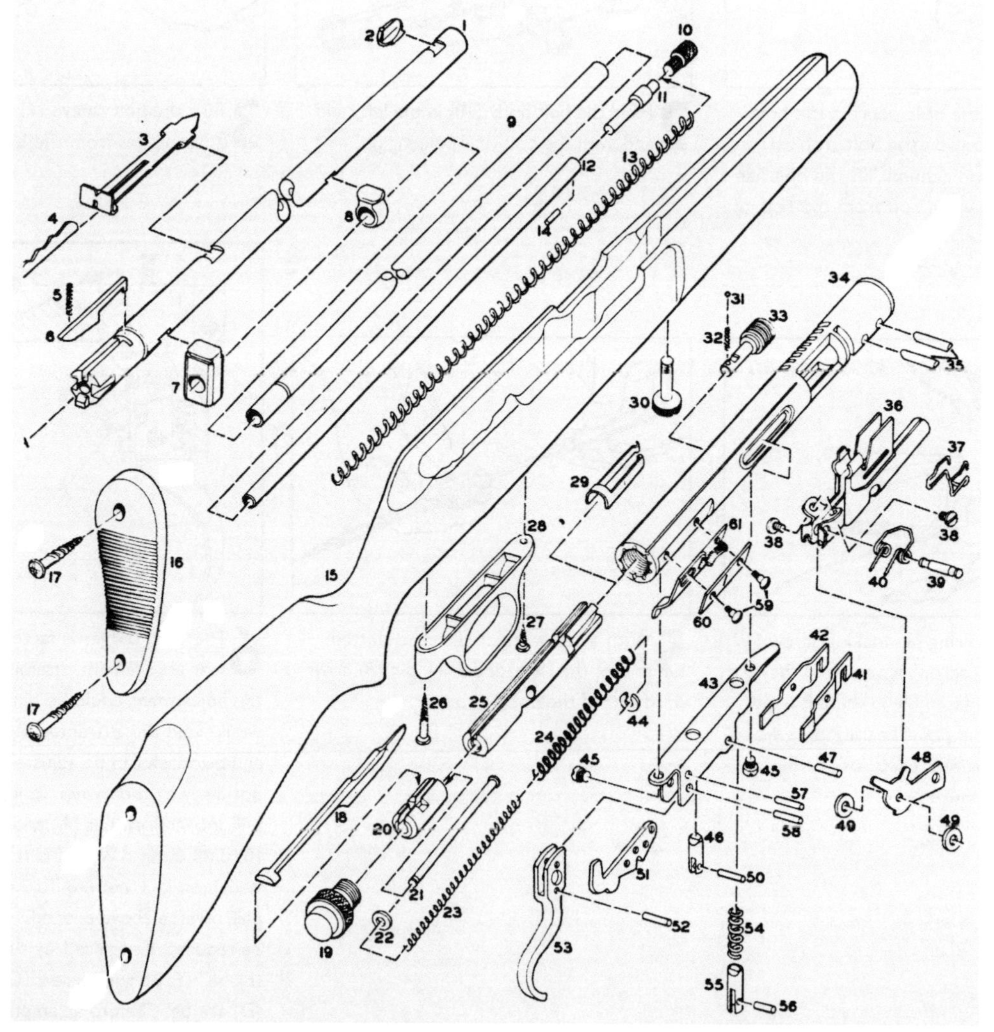

In 1938, Savage Arms Corp. introduced their Model 6 cal. .22 rimfire rifle with tubular magazine holding 15 long rifle, 17 long, or 22 short cartridges. It is essentially a straight-pull, locked breech, bolt-action rifle, but by adjustment will fire semi-automatically with regular or high-velocity .22 Long Rifle cartridges. It will not function semi-automatically with the .22 Long or Short cartridges as they develop insufficient power to operate the mechanism.

The shift from semi-automatic to manual action, or vice versa, is accomplished through the bolt handle. When the bolt handle is pulled outward, the gun functions semi-automatically, provided it is loaded with .22 Long Rifle cartridges. On firing, the bolt handle with attached breech bolt is blown to the rear, at the same time extracting and ejecting the fired cartridge case and cocking the hammer. In returning to battery, the bolt picks up and chambers a fresh round from the magazine to complete the operating cycle. When manual operation is desired, the bolt handle is pushed in when the breech bolt has been moved forward to closed position with a cartridge in the chamber. This locks the breech bolt shut, withdrawn and after discharging the cartridge it is necessary to pull outward on the bolt handle to unlock the action so that the breech bolt can be retracted to extract and eject the fired cartridge case. Cartridges can be either loaded singly into the chamber, or functioned through the tubular magazine.

From its inception until it was dropped, about 1968, only minor changes were made to the Model 6, the most visible of which was a streamlined recoil plug added in the 1960s.

Late-production Model 6 rifles feature grooved receivers for use with tip-off scope mounts.

DISASSEMBLY

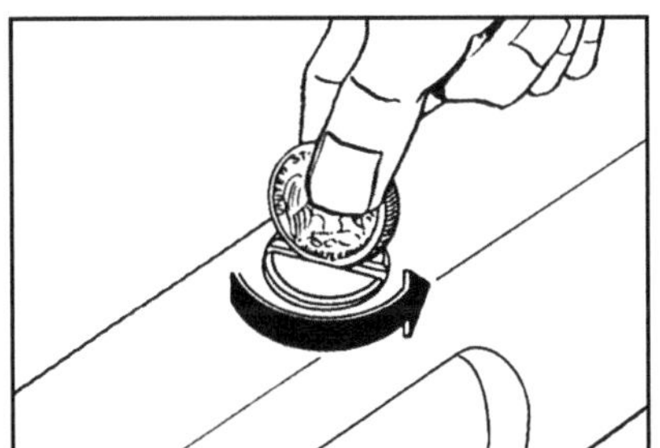

1 To disassemble barrel and action from stock (15), unscrew takedown screw (30) using a large coin such as a quarter. This precludes burring of the screw. After this disassembly, all working parts are exposed for lubricating, replacement, etc.

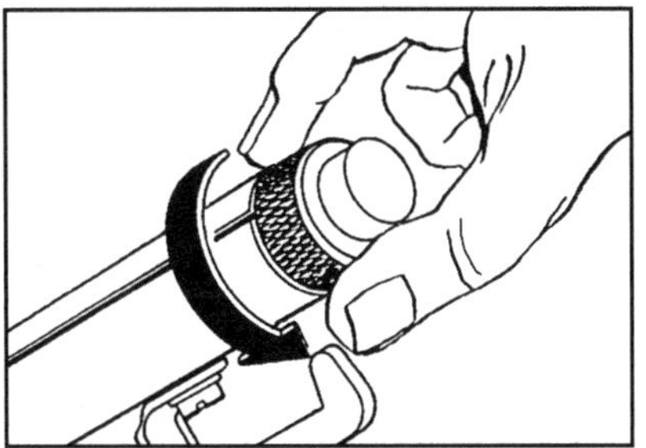

2 To disassemble action for cleaning, first insure that rifle is unloaded and that no cartridge is in the chamber. Next, move action to closed position and pull trigger (53). Unscrew recoil plug (19) at rear of receiver (34).

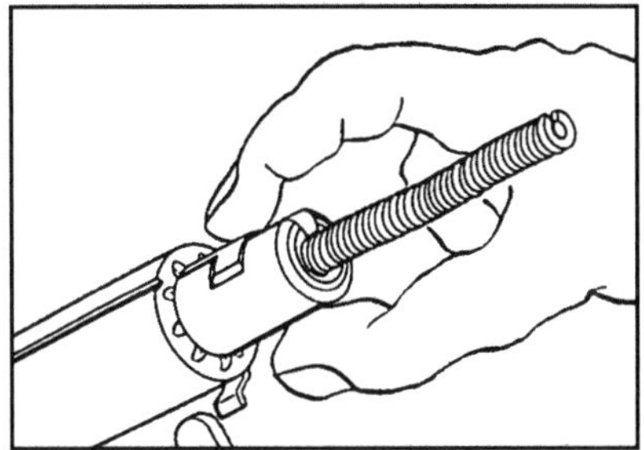

3 Withdraw hammer (20) and kindred assembly, and firing pin (18). The latter will drop away from hammer assembly when just about fully withdrawn.

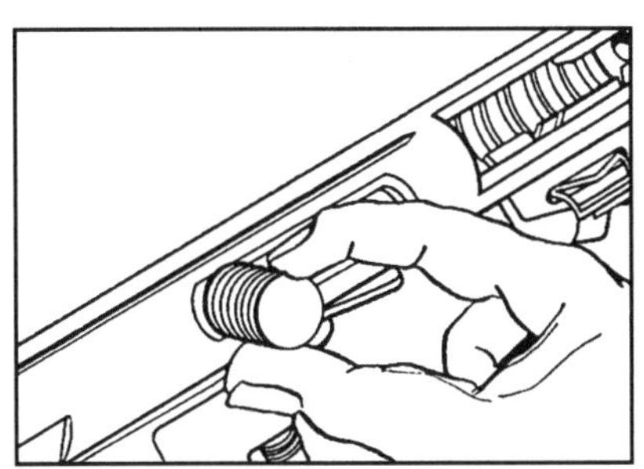

4 Now remove locking bolt (33) which was held in place by the firing pin.

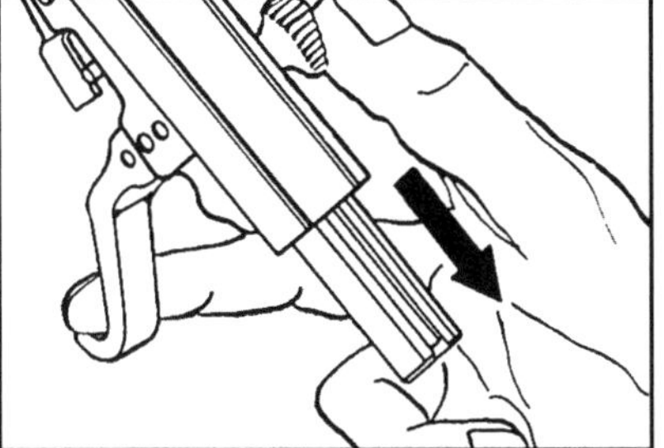

5 With a grip as shown, hold trigger back. This keeps left hand free to slide breech bolt (25) from rear of receiver, since, if properly lubricated, the oil will form a suction between the inside surface of receiver and breech bolt and thus prevent it dropping out. Assemble the Model 6 in reverse order, being sure to pull trigger prior to screwing in recoil plug.

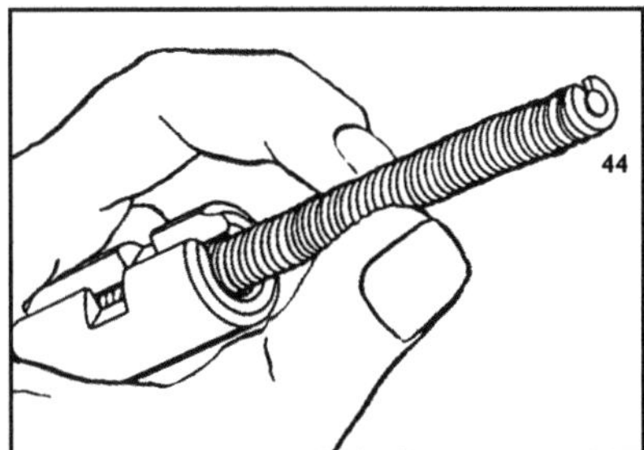

6 To further disassemble hammer assembly, grip assembly in left hand as shown using thumb and index finger to keep tension on breech bolt spring (23) and hammer spring (24). Then tap off hammer spring washer (44) and slowly release tension on both springs, which now may be removed. Breech bolt spring rod (21) and breech bolt spring washer (22) may also be removed. Gun is assembled in reverse order.

SAVAGE MODEL 24 COMBINATION

PARTS LEGEND

1. Frame
2. Stock bolt
3. Stock bolt washer
4. Trigger guard
5. Rear trigger guard screw
6. Front trigger guard screw
7. Selector button
8. Selector button plunger
9. Selector button plunger spring
10. Firing pin screw (.22)
11. Firing pin screw (.410)
12. Firing pin (.22)
13. Firing pin spring (.22)
14. Firing pin (.410)
15. Selector 24.
16. Top snap
17. Top snap sleeve
18. Top snap screw
    18a. Top snap plunger
19. Top snap plunger spring
20. Locking bolt plunger
21. Locking bolt plunger spring
22. Locking bolt assembly
23. Locking bolt pin
24. Hammer
25. Hammer pin
26. Trigger
27. Trigger spring
28. Trigger pin
29. Mainspring plunger
30. Mainspring
31. Mainspring plunger seat

BARREL AND FORE-END PARTS

A. Barrel
B. Rear sight assembly
C. Front sight assembly
D. Extractor screw
E. Extractor, .22
F. Extractor spring, .22
G. Extractor, .410
H. Extractor Stem, .410
J. Extractor lever spring
K. Extractor pin
L. Extractor lever
M. Extractor lever pin
N. Fore-end spring housing
O. Fore-end spring
P. Fore-end spring pin
Q. Fore-end spring spring
R. Fore-end spring spring pin
S. Fore-end spring housing screw, front
T. Fore-end spring housing screw, rear
U. Fore-end
V. Fore-end iron head
W. Fore-end iron head screws (2)

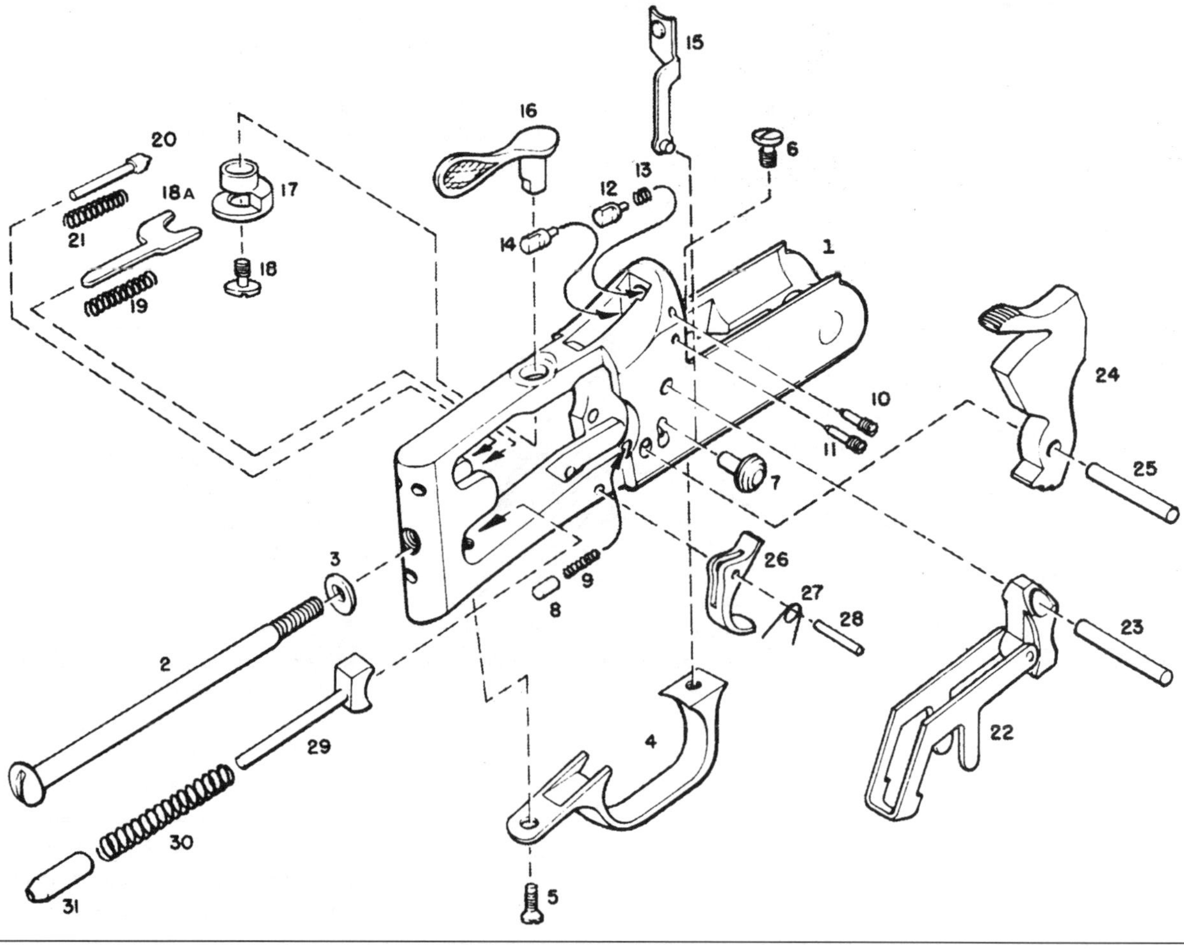

The Stevens .22-.410 over-under combination rifle and shotgun was first offered in 1939 by the I. Stevens Arms Co., (a subsidiary of the Savage Arms). This gun was chambered for the .22 Long Rifle cartridge and the 3-inch length of the .410 shotshell. Guns produced initially had walnut stocks and fore-ends, but stock assemblies of Tenite plastic were later made standard. During World War II the U. S. Air Force purchased 10,000 combination guns for issue as survival weapons.

Commercial production was resumed in 1945. In 1950 a slightly improved type with walnut stock assembly and somewhat heavier barrel replaced the original model. It was designated Savage Model 24. When the .22 Winchester Magnum Rimfire cartridge was introduced in 1959, the Model 24 was made available in this caliber also.

In 1962, the Model 24 was introduced in DL and MDL types, with fire selector button on left side of the frame rather than on the right. The Model 24 DL is chambered for the .22 Long Rifle cartridge and is available with optional shotgun barrel chambered for either the 20-gauge, 3-inch shell or the .410, 3-inch shell. The Model 24 MDL is chambered for the .22 Winchester Magnum Rimfire cartridge and with the same choice of shot-shell chamberings as the DL.

DISASSEMBLY

To remove fore-end (Fig. 1) grasp it at the tip and pull away from barrel. Move top snap (16) to side and open breech by tipping barrel downward. Unhook barrel lug from hinge pin at forward end of frame. Remove barrels from frame.

To remove buttstock, unscrew both butt-plate screws and remove buttplate. Unscrew stock bolt (2) through hole in butt of stock. Slide buttstock off frame to rear.

NOTE: Further disassembly of frame and lock parts is not recommended and should be unnecessary for normal cleaning purposes. Major parts are retained in frame by pivot pins. Firing pins are retained in frame by screws (10 & 11), which are staked at the factory making them rather difficult to remove.

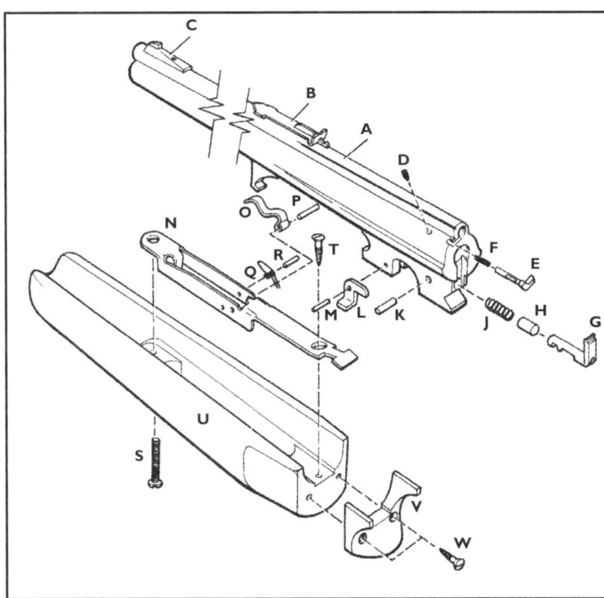

1 After removing fore-end (U) from underside of barrel (A) and separating barrel from frame, loosen extractor screw (D) and withdraw .22 extractor (E) and spring (F) from breech end of barrel. Drift out extractor pin (K) and remove .410 extractor (G) and stem (H) from breech end of barrel. Drift out extractor lever pin (M) and remove extractor lever (L) from lug under barrel. Remove extractor lever spring (J). NOTE: Extractor lever spring is inserted in barrel lug between front end of lug and arm on extractor lever (L). Fore-end parts are easily removed by removing screws S and T.

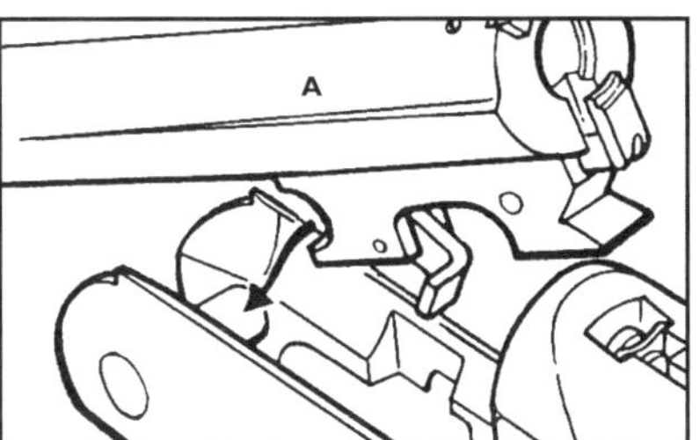

2 When reassembling barrel (A) to frame (1), hook cut-out at forward end of barrel lug onto hinge pin in forward end of frame as shown. Swing barrels upward, locking barrels to frame.

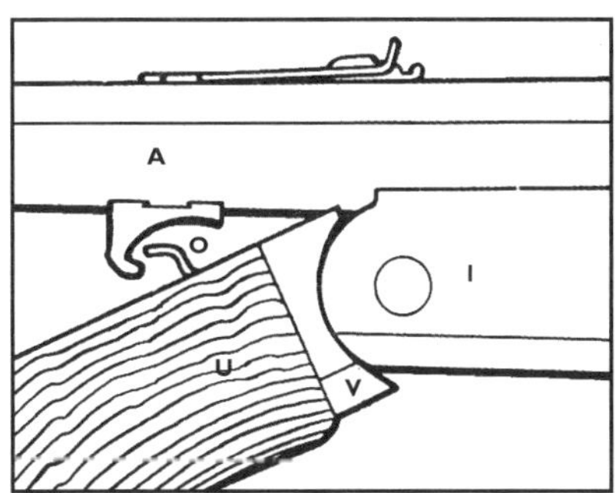

3 When reassembling fore-end (U) to underside of barrel (A), place rear of fore-end iron head (V) in position shown against front edge of frame. Note position of fore-end (O) in relation to hook on underside of barrel. Press fore-end up against underside of barrel until it locks in place.

SAVAGE MODELS 29A & 29B RIFLES

PARTS LEGEND

1. Receiver
2. Takedown screw
3. Takedown screw bushing
4. Cartridge stop
5. Cartridge stop pin
6. Barrel pin
7. Barrel
8. Rear sight assembly
9. Front sight
10. Operating handle bar assembly
11. Operating handle (wood)
12. Operating handle escutcheons (2)
13. Operating handle screws (2)
14. Breechbolt assembly (see Fig. 2)
15. Trigger guard assembly (see Fig. 1)
16. Outside magazine tube
17. Front magazine mount
18. Magazine tube retaining screw bushing
19. Magazine tube retaining screw
20. Inside magazine tube
21. Magazine plug pin
22. Magazine follower
23. Magazine follower spring
24. Magazine plug
25. Stock bolt
26. Stock bolt washer
27. Stock (not shown)
28. Buttplate (not shown)
29. Buttplate screws (2) (not shown)

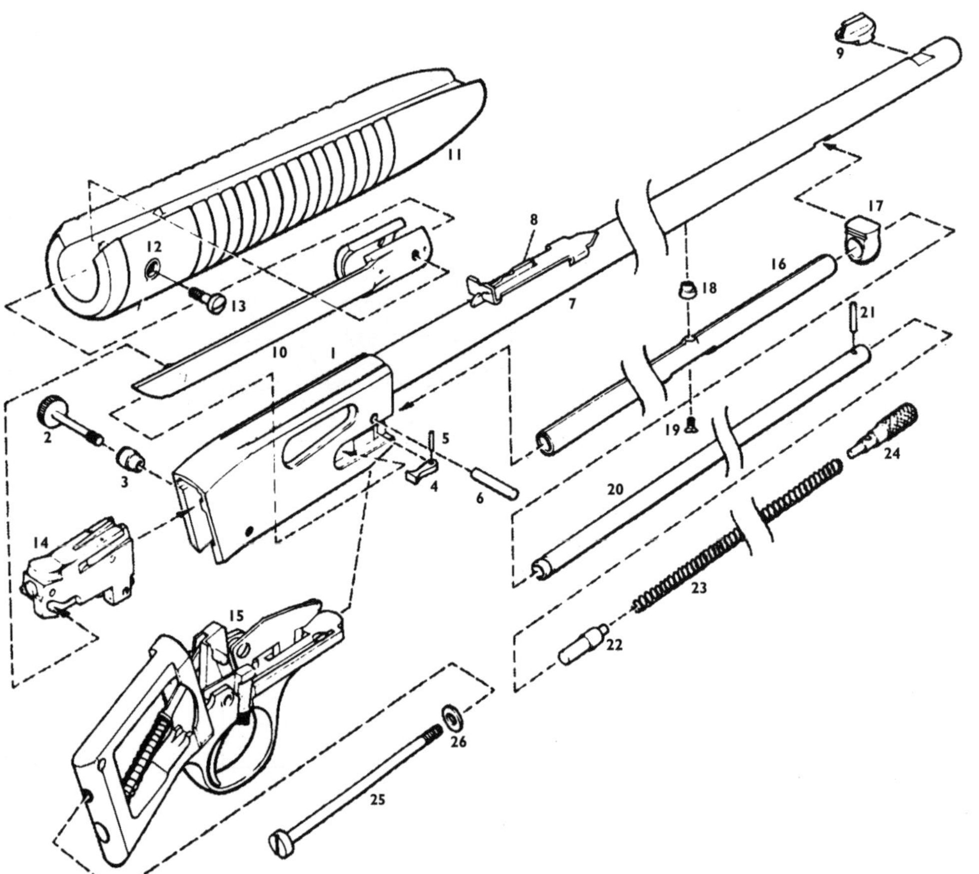

TRIGGER GUARD ASSEMBLY PARTS LEGEND

A. Trigger guard
B. Mainspring
C. Mainspring retainer washer
D. Mainspring plunger
E. Mainspring plunger pin
F. Hammer
G. Hammer bushing
H. Operating lock
J. Lifter
K. Lifter screw
L. Lifter spring
M. Operating lock spring
N. Operating lock spring screw
O. Trigger
P. Trigger pin
Q. Safety spring
R. Safety plunger
S. Safety

BREECHBOLT ASSEMBLY PARTS LEGEND

A. Breech-bolt
B. Extractor, left
C. Extractor, right
D. Extractor springs (2)
E. Extractor pins (2)
F. Cartridge guide
G. Cartridge guide pin
H. Cartridge guide spring
J. Operating plunger
K. Operating plunger pin
L. Operating plunger spring
M. Firing pin retaining pin
N. Firing pin
O. Firing pin spring

The Savage Model 29A hammerless slide-action .22 rimfire rifle was introduced in 1933. Receiver of this take-down rifle was grooved subsequently for use with tip-off scope mounts and the designation was then changed to Model 29B. The catalog designation 29G was at one time used to indicate the grooved receiver version which was actually stamped 29B. The tubular magazines of the Models 29A and 29B rifles will hold 14 long rifle, 16 long, or 20 short cal. .22 rimfire cartridges. Bead front sight and open elevator rear sight are standard. Buttstock and slide handle are of walnut. Total weight of the rifle is 5¾ lbs.; over-all length is 41 inches.

The original Savage Model 29 slide-action rifle (initially designated Model 1929) was introduced in 1929 and discontinued in 1933. Parts and service are no longer available from Savage.

The Model 29A rifle, which represents a complete redesign of the 1929 rifle, was itself dropped from production in 1967.

DISASSEMBLY

Close action and unscrew takedown screw (2) at left of receiver (1) until screw threads are clear of trigger guard (15). Pull receiver and barrel assembly forward, separating the trigger guard and stock assembly from the receiver.

To remove buttstock: Remove buttplate screws and buttplate and unscrew stock bolt (25) through hole at rear of stock. Remove stock bolt (25) and stock bolt washer (26). Separate trigger guard assembly (15) from stock.

To remove breechbolt assembly (14): Hold receiver inverted and make sure takedown screw is clear of inside of receiver. Pull operating handle (11) and operating handle bar assembly (10) to rearward position. Lift forward end of breechbolt upward and pull back out of receiver.

Remove inside magazine tube (20) and remove magazine tube retaining screw (19) through loading port in outside magazine tube (16). Press magazine tube away from barrel (7) slightly with fingers and remove magazine tube retaining screw bushing (18). Tap front magazine mount (17) out of dovetail in barrel from left to right and withdraw outside magazine tube (16). Push operating handle (11) to forward position and pull operating handle bar (10) out of receiver to side. Take care not to lose cartridge stop (4) and pin (5) which are now free to drop out of receiver. Reassemble in reverse.

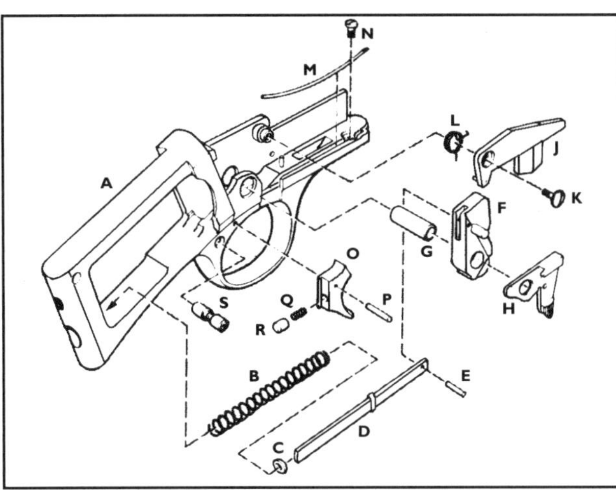

1 To disassemble trigger guard assembly, press in hammer bushing (G) until operating lock (H) can be lifted out. Remove operating lock spring screw (N) and operating lock spring (M). Place hammer (F) in fired position and push out hammer bushing (G) from right to left. Hold trigger to rear and lift out hammer, mainspring (B), and plunger (D).

Drop safety (S) out. Remove lifter screw (K), lifter (J), and lifter spring (L). Drift out trigger pin (P) from right to left and remove trigger (O). Remove safety spring (Q) and safety plunger (R) from trigger. Reassemble in reverse.

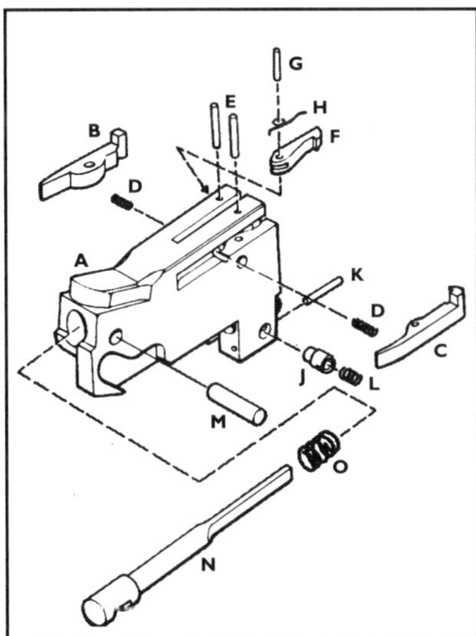

2 Drift extractor pins (E) up with punch through access holes in breechbolt (A) until ends of pins can be grasped with pliers and withdrawn. Remove left and right extractors (B & C) and extractor springs (D).

Using same procedure remove cartridge guide pin (G), cartridge guide (F), and cartridge guide spring (H) from left side of breechbolt. Operating plunger (J) and operating plunger spring (L) are removed after drifting out operating plunger pin (K). Drift out firing pin retaining pin (M) and remove firing pin (N) and spring (O) out rear. Reassemble in reverse.

3 To disassemble rifle, unscrew takedown screw (2) as far as possible and draw stock and trigger guard assembly (15 & 27) away from receiver (1). In reassembling, be sure lip at front end of trigger guard, shown at "A," enters its slot in front end of receiver as shown by arrow.

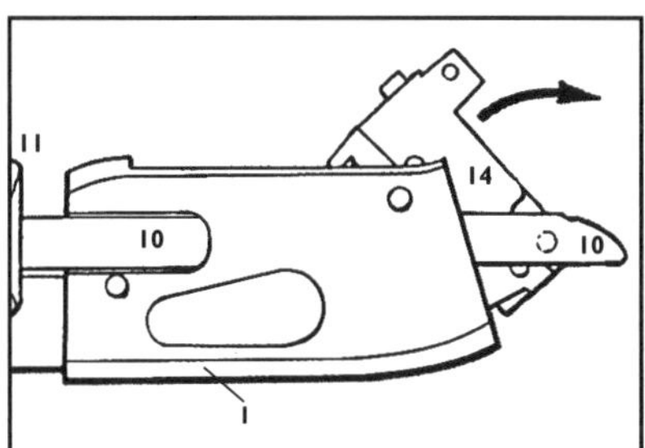

4 To remove breechbolt assembly (14) from receiver (1), draw operating handle (11) back with receiver inverted until breechbolt rises slightly. Grasp breechbolt and rotate upward in direction shown until pin on operating handle bar assembly (10) can he disengaged from slot.

SAVAGE MODEL 99 RIFLE

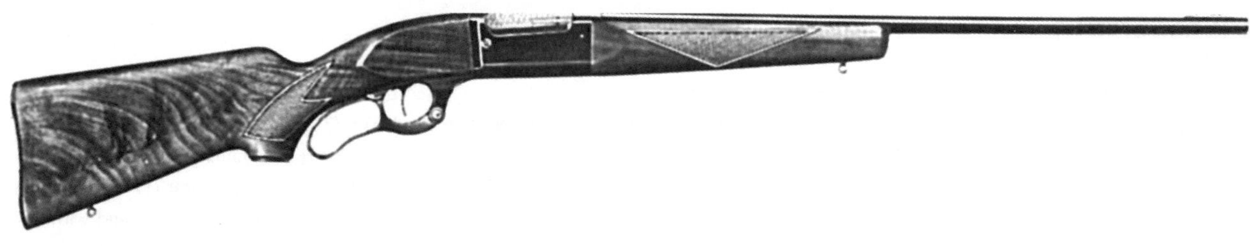

PARTS LEGEND

1. Barrel
2. Receiver
3. Front sight
4. Barrel stud
5. Fore-end escutcheon
6. Fore-end screw
7. Dummy screw—telescope (4)
8. Dummy screw—tang (2)
9. Sear screw
10. Hammer indicator pin
11. Cartridge guide
12. Cartridge guide pin (2)
13. Extractor
14. Automatic cutoff
15. Automatic cutoff spring
16. Breech bolt
17. Extractor pin
18. Hammer indicator spring
19. Hammer indicator
20. Hammer retractor spring
21. Hammer bushing screw
22. Hammer
23. Hammer bushing
24. Mainspring
25. Firing pin
26. Firing pin securing pin
27. Trigger spring screw
28. Trigger spring
29. Breech bolt stop screw
30. Breech bolt stop
31. Trigger pin
32. Stock bolt washer
33. Stock bolt
34. Lever lock—safety
35. Lever lock tension spring
36. Lever bushing
37. Lever lock pin
38. Trigger
39. Lever bushing screw
40. Sear
41. Lever
42. Sear screw nut
43. Carrier spindle support
44. Carrier
45. Carrier spring
46. Carrier spindle
47. Carrier spindle head
48. Carrier spindle nut
49. Rear sight
50. Rear sight step
51. Carrier spindle head screw
52. Pistol grip cap
53. Pistol grip cap screw
54. Buttplate
55. Buttplate screw (2)

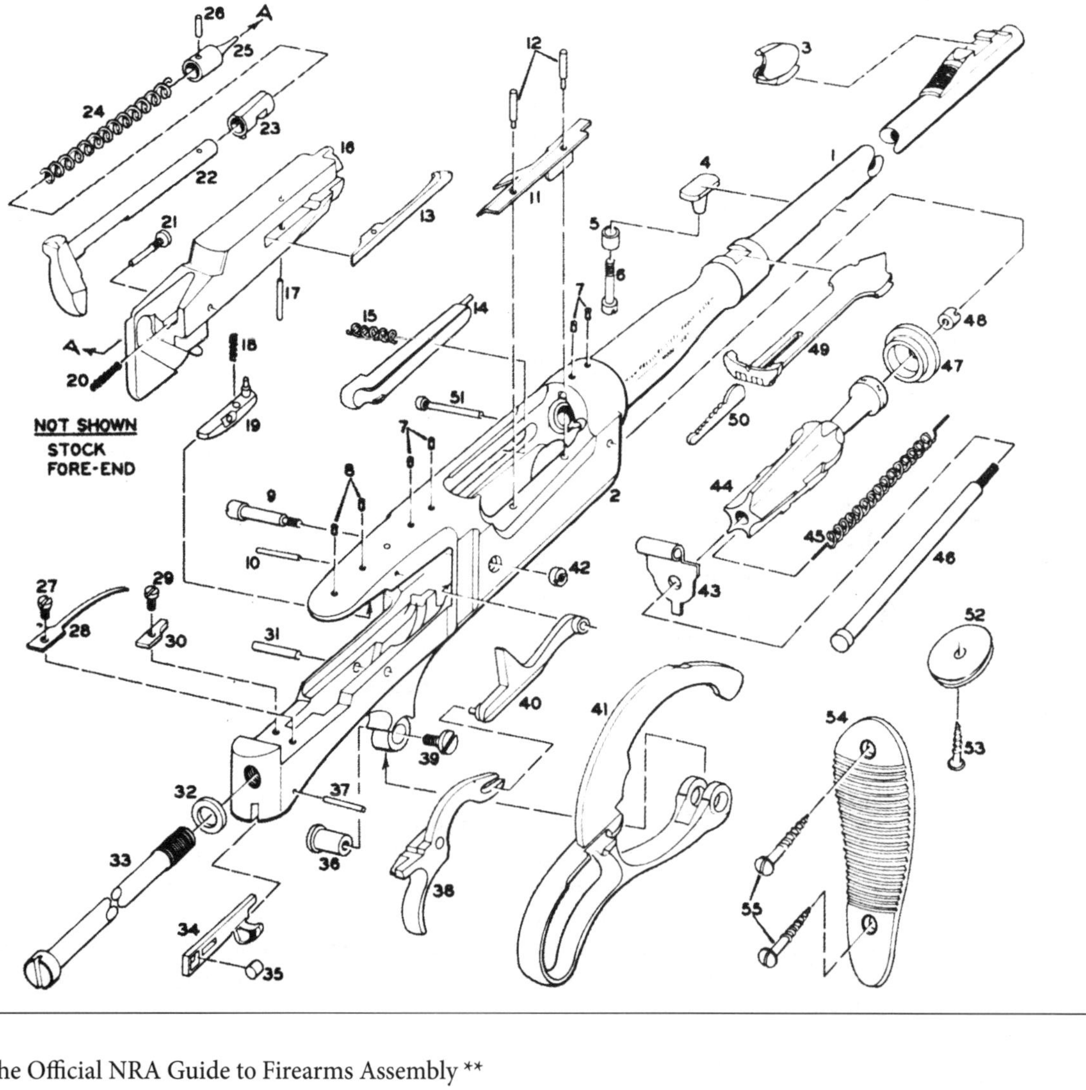

NOT SHOWN
STOCK
FORE-END

Savage Repeating Arms introduced the Model 1899 in .303 Savage caliber in January 1899. The rifle had a 5-round rotary magazine with a remaining-round indicator on the receiver.

The rifle was immediately popular with sportsmen worldwide, and became the mainstay of the Savage firearms line. Changes to the action over the years have been minor. The cocking indicator was dropped in favor of a small pin in the upper receiver tang and the rear of the breech bolt was rounded. Both solid-frame and takedown models have been made in many grades.

The 1899 was the first commercial rifle chambered for a high-velocity cartridge, the .22 Savage Hi-Power, and has been offered in several calibers, including: .300 Savage, .25-35 and .30-30 W.C.F., and .32-40. It was discontinued in 2000.

DISASSEMBLY

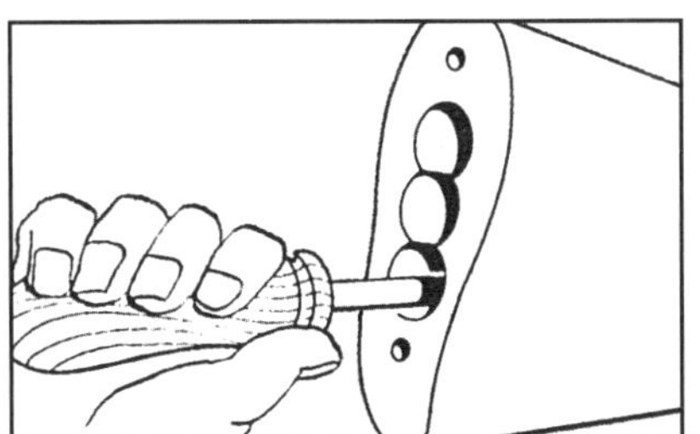

1 To disassemble the Model 99, unscrew 2 buttplate screws (55) and lift away buttplate (54). Then, using a long-shanked screwdriver, remove stock bolt (33) and stock bolt washer (32). Pull stock away from receiver (2). It may be necessary to tap the stock using palm of the hand. CAUTION: Tap stock straight to rear to avoid splitting.

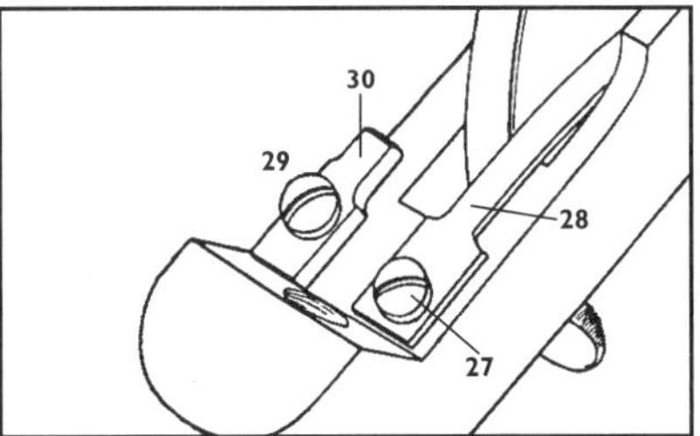

2 To further disassemble, remove breech bolt stop screw (29), breech bolt stop (30). bushing screw (39). Use a proper-size trigger spring screw (27), and trigger spring (28).

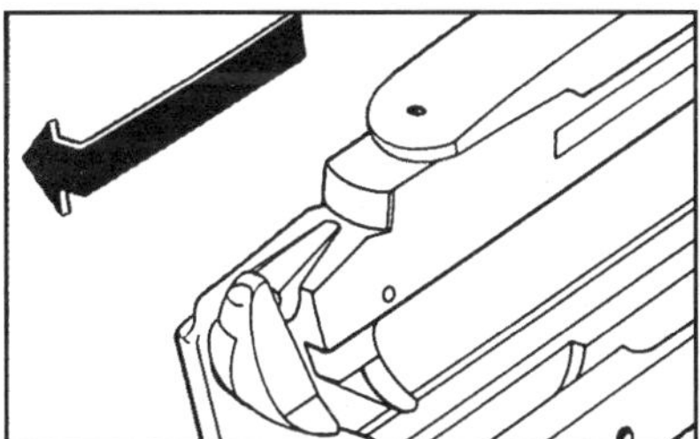

3 Open action with a downward motion of lever (41). Breech bolt (16) may now be removed by sliding it slightly rearward and thence left. Automatic cutoff (14) and automatic cutoff spring (15) will fall out at this time. (Lever not shown in drawing).

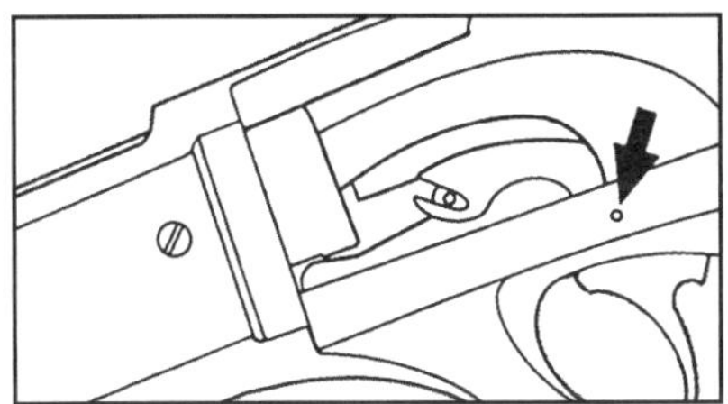

4 Next, using a flat-nosed punch, drift out trigger pin (31). This allows trigger (38) to be removed. Use a plastic dish or tray to hold disassembled parts to preclude their loss.

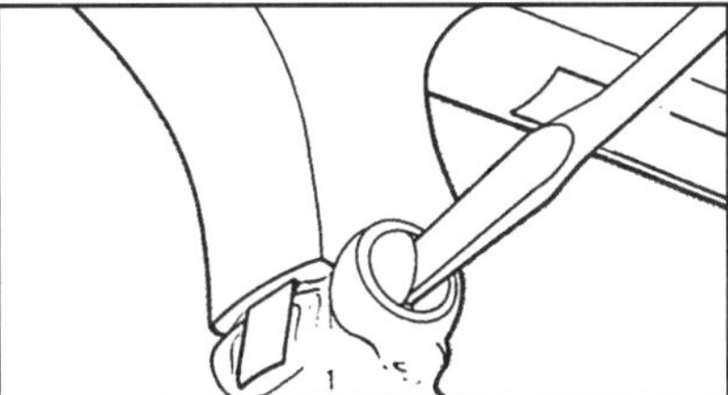

5 Continue disassembly by removing lever bushing screw (39). Use a proper size screwdriver to avoid burring screw. After lever bushing (36) has been pushed out, lever may be lifted free from underside of receiver.

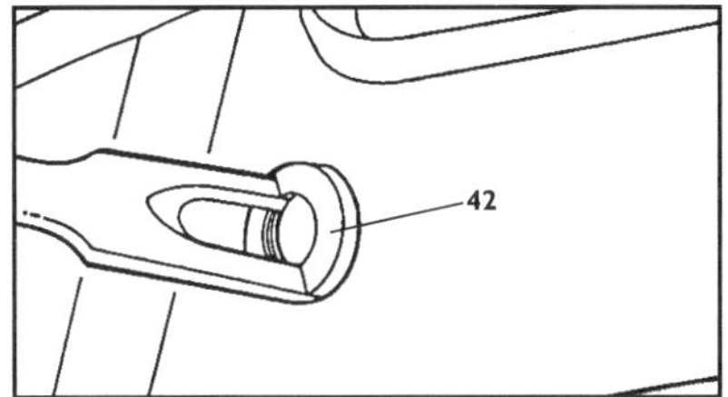

6 Remove sear screw nut (42) with a split-bladed screwdriver. Sear screw (9) and sear (40) may now be removed. It is not recommended that any of the carrier assembly be removed because of precise adjustment required to reinsert it.

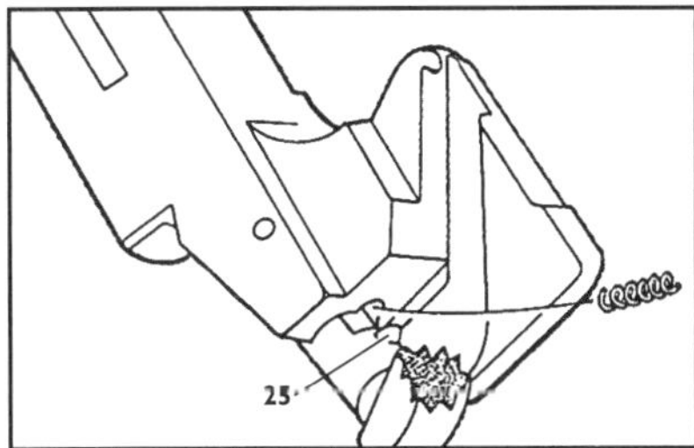

7 Remove firing pin-hammer assembly from breech bolt and unscrew hammer bushing screw (21). Assembly may then be withdrawn from breech bolt. Caution: Hammer retractor spring (20) will drop out as the complete assembly is removed. When reassembling, insert firing pin-hammer assembly into breech bolt to within ⅜ inch of rear bolt face. sembling, When in place, hammer assembly will easily slide in rest of the way and spring will bear on protruding lip (A) of hammer bushing (23). (Hammer shown partially cut away for clarity).

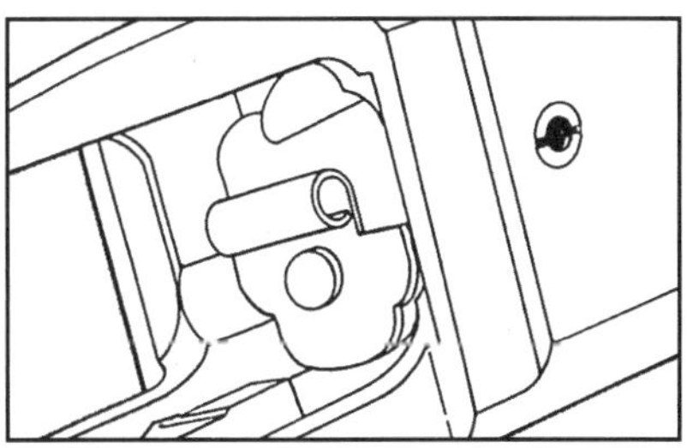

8 Accomplish reassembly of Model 99 in reverse order. When reassembling, ensure that carrier spindle support (43) is properly seated in receiver. Although the support is not removed, it may turn out of alignment when sear screw and other parts are removed.

SAVAGE MODEL 110 RIFLE

PARTS LEGEND

1. Barrel
2. Front sight
3. Front sight
4. Front sight
5. Front sight
6. Rear sight
7. Rear sight step
8. Barrel lock nut
9. Recoil lug
10. Receiver
11. Dummy screws, top (4)
12. Dummy screws, side (2)
13. Sear pin
14. Sear bushing
15. Sear spring
16. Sear
17. Trigger bracket
18. Safety bearing pin
19. Trigger pin
20. Trigger spring
21. Trigger spring plunger
22. Safety
23. Trigger pull adjusting screw cover
24. Trigger pull adjusting screw (2)
25. Trigger
26. Steel balls, 5/32-inch (3)
27. Trigger pin retaining spring
28. Trigger engagement adjusting screw
29. Magazine box
30. Magazine latch
31. Ejector
32. Ejector spring
33. Trigger guard screw
34. Trigger guard
35. Floorplate
36. Floorplate insert
37. Floorplate screw, front
38. Magazine follower
39. Magazine spring
40. Floorplate screw, rear
41. Buttplate
42. Buttplate screws (2)
43. Pistol grip cap
44. Pistol grip cap screw
45. Bolt handle slot liner
46. Bolt handle slot liner screw
47. Extractor
48. Bolt head
49. Bolt head retaining pin
50. Front baffle
51. Front baffle friction washer
52. Bolt body
53. Cocking piece pin
54. Rear baffle
55. Rear baffle spring
56. Striker stop nut
57. Striker stop nut lockwasher
58. Firing pin
59. Mainspring
60. Cocking piece lockwasher
61. Cocking piece
62. Cocking piece sleeve
63. Bolt handle
64. Bolt assembly screw washer
65. Bolt assembly screw
66. Bolt assembly screw springs (3)
67. Steel balls, 1/8-inch (3)

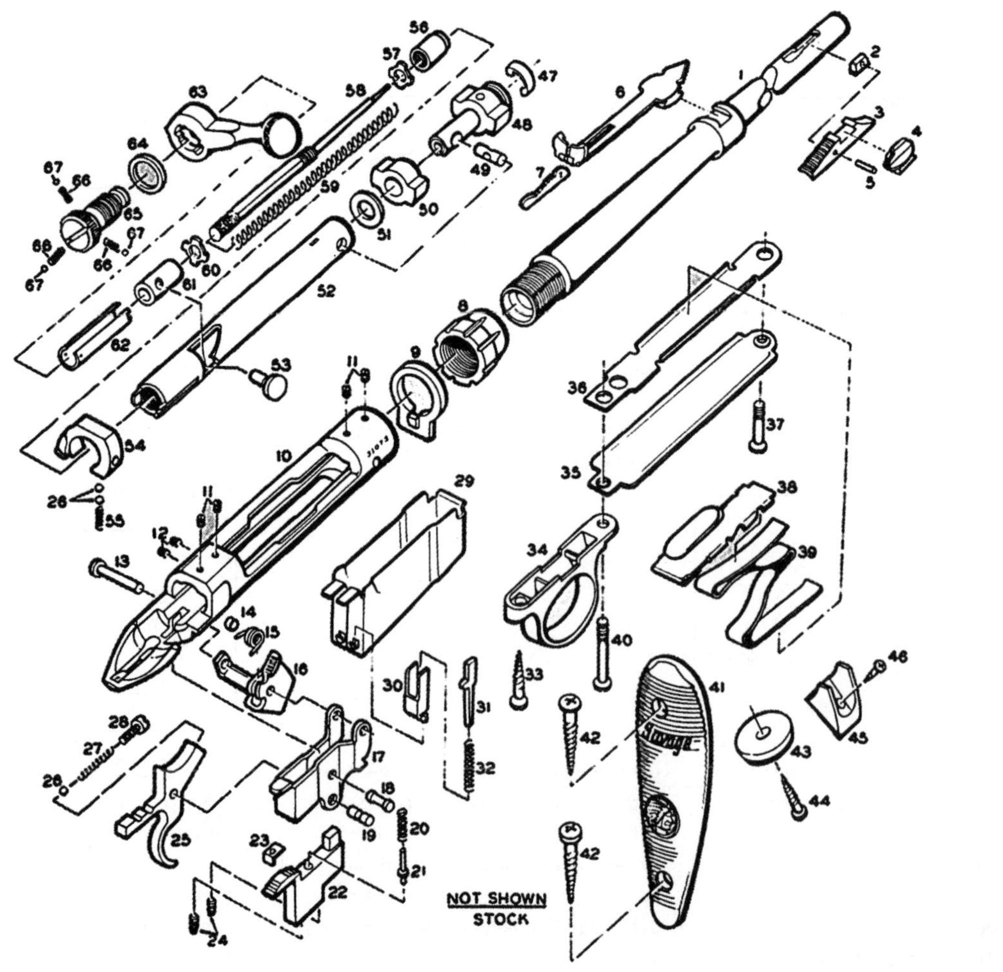

The Model 110 bolt-action high power sporting rifle, introduced early in 1958 by Savage Arms Corp., was designed for simplicity of manufacture. Initial chamberings were in .30-06 and .270 Win. The Model 110 has a Mauser-type action with staggered-column box magazine,

The rifle cocks on opening the bolt. An integral sleeve in rear of the barrel chamber completely shrouds the bolt face to reinforce the receiver ring in case-head area. A gas port between the locking lugs vents the interior of the bolt and aligns with gas port in the receiver ring. A double-lug front baffle on the bolt in rear of the front locking lugs blocks the locking lug slots in the receiver when bolt is closed. The tang safety locks both bolt and trigger when engaged. Magazine capacity of the Model 110 is 4 rounds.

In 1958 a short-action version designated Model 110 MC was introduced, chambered for .243 and .308 Win.

In 1959, left-hand versions of both short- and long-action models were announced under the designation of Model 110 MC-L. These versions were mechanically identical to corresponding right-hand models except for reversal of the bolt.

DISASSEMBLY

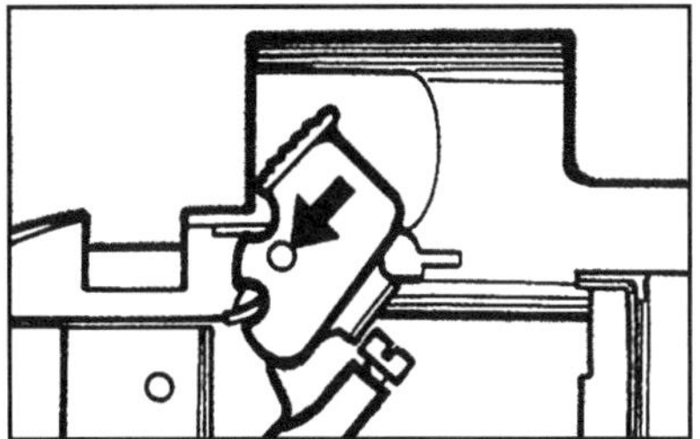

1 Commence disassembly of Savage Model 110 by removing bolt assembly from receiver by depressing cocking indicator and holding back on trigger while withdrawing bolt assembly. Remove front and rear floorplate screws (37) and (40), which will permit the floorplate (35), floorplate insert (36), magazine follower (38), and magazine spring (39) to be lifted away from bottom of gun and complete barrel and receiver assembly to be lifted away from the stock. Continue by pushing out sear pin (13-arrow) from right to left. Pull down on front end of trigger bracket (17) and unhook back end from receiver (10). Sear (16), sear spring (15), and sear bushing (14) may be removed at this time. Disassembly of trigger mechanism is immediately apparent.

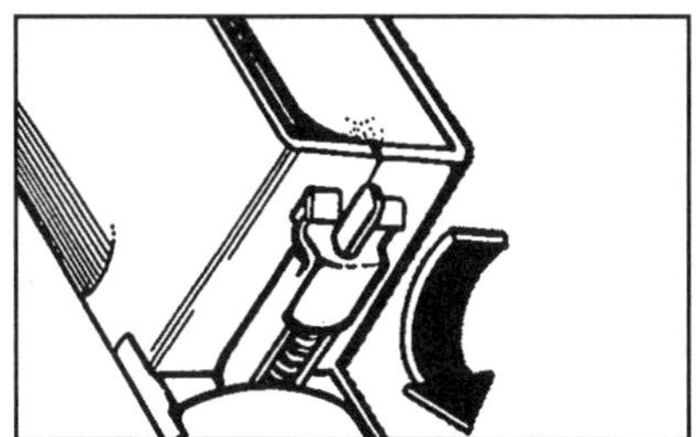

2 To remove magazine box (29), push down and back on magazine latch (30), disengaging hooks on lower edge of magazine box. Ejector (31) and ejector spring (32) are removed concurrent with removal of latch. Pull magazine box back and lift front end up above receiver and push box forward and away.

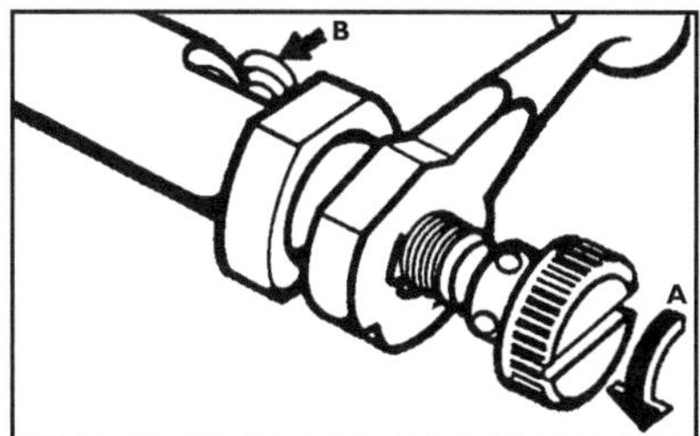

3 Disassemble bolt group by (A) removing bolt assembly screw (65) using coin as a screwdriver. Cocking piece sleeve (62) will be withdrawn as screw is removed, and (B) cocking piece pin (53) will drop out of bolt together with firing pin unit, which will also drop out by tapping rear of bolt body (52). Remove bolt handle (63) and rear baffle (54).

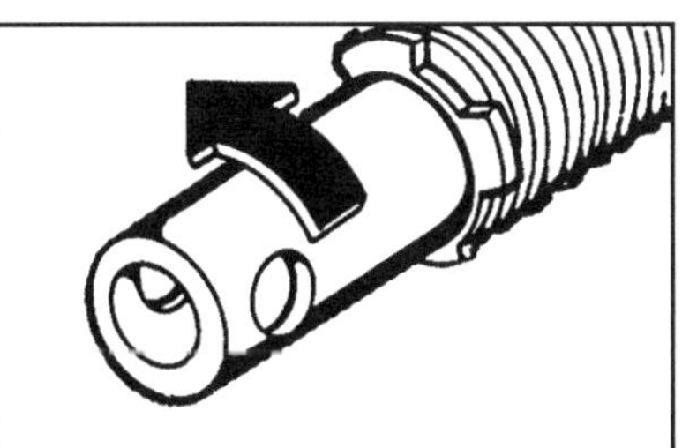

4 Remove mainspring (59) by unscrewing cocking piece (61) and removing cocking piece lockwasher (60). Do not disturb striker stop nut (56) as this nut is adjusted at the factory to give correct firing pin protrusion.

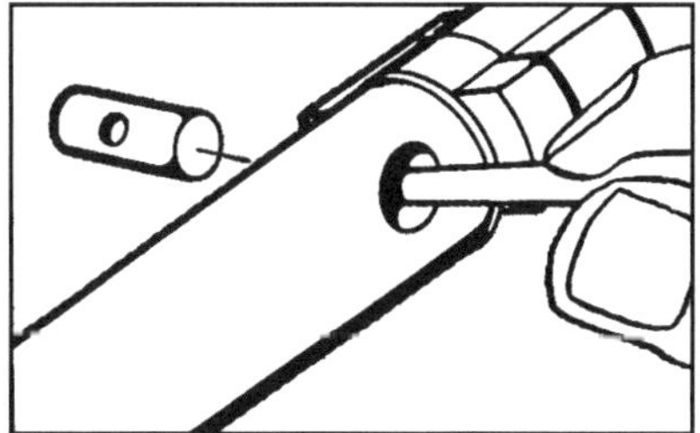

5 Next, drift out bolt head retaining pin (49) and lift bolt head (48), front baffle (50), and front baffle friction washer (51) away from bolt body (52).

6 Remove extractor (47), using a small screwdriver, by exerting a slight pressure out and counterclockwise on opposite end (small arrow) from large extracting lip. Reassemble in reverse order. To replace bolt in receiver, it must first be cocked Do this by placing cocking piece pin (53) against the edge of a square block, pushing down and rotating counterclockwise. This operation can be avoided by assembling bolt with cocking piece pin in rear (cocked) position. Hold back on the trigger when inserting the bolt in receiver.

SAVAGE MODEL 1903 SLIDE-ACTION

PARTS LEGEND

1. Receiver, right side
   la. Receiver, left side
2. Barrel
3. Stock (not shown)
   3a.Operating handle (wood)
4. Bolt
5. Firing pin
6. Pin, extractor
7. Extractor
8. Pin, firing
9. Hammer
10. Screw, hammer
11. Trigger
12. Pin, trigger
13. Ejector
14. Retaining screw, ejector
15. Ejector spring
16. Magazine catch
17. Spring, magazine catch
18. Pin, magazine catch
19. Safety
20. Safety connector bar
21. Pin, safety bar
22. Mainspring plunger
23. Retaining washer, mainspring
24. Mainspring
25. Spring, safety
26. Screw, safety spring
27. Screw, tang, stock
28. Screw, sight blank
29. Screw, sight blank
30. Operating handle
31. Spring, stop, operating bar
32. Pin, operating bar stop
33. Guide rod, operating bar
34. Mount, guide rod
35. Screw, retaining guide
36. Operating bar
37. Assembling screw
38. Screws (2), operating handle
39. Rear sight
40. Screw, rear sight
41. Base, rear sight
42. Screw, elevation rear sight
43. Front sight
44. Buttplate
45. Screws (2), buttplate
46. Magazine
47. Spring, magazine
48. Follower
49. Magazine floor plate

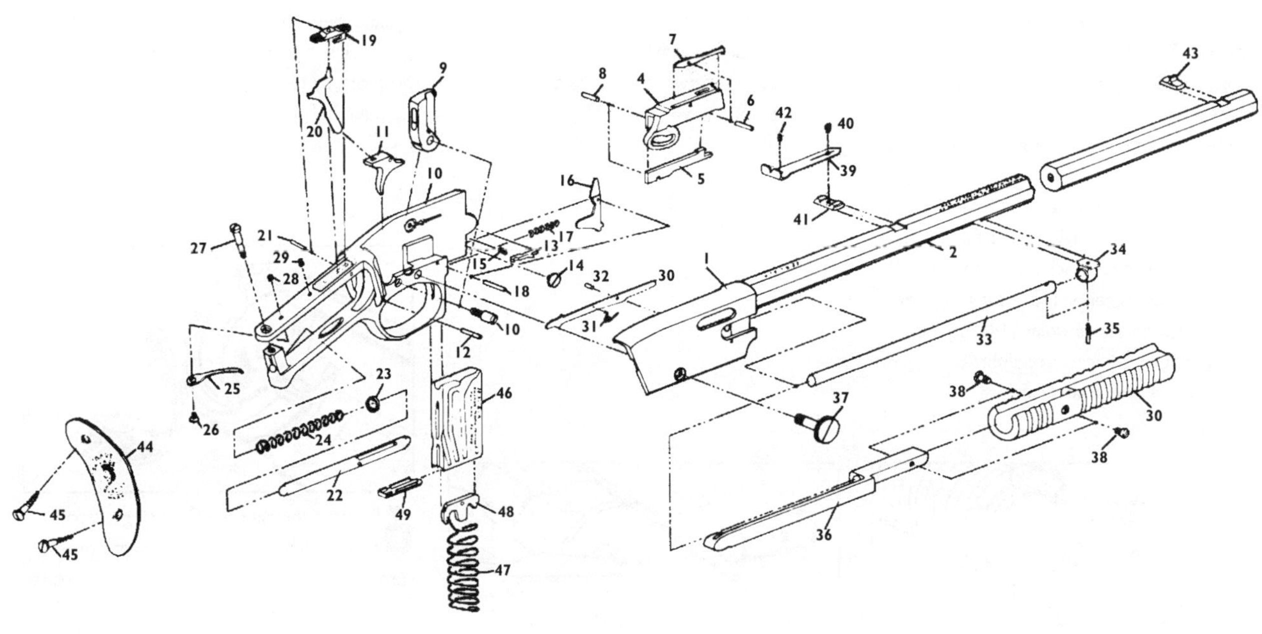

By the end of the 19th century, considerable progress had been made in improving the accuracy and performance of the .22 rimfire cartridge, greatly increasing consumer demand for quality .22 caliber rimfire rifles.

Savage Arms Company's contribution to the field was the introduction of the Model 1903 rifle. By that year, Savage Arms had gained a foothold in the marketplace with its Model 1899 lever-action rifle and hoped to expand its product line by offering a reliable .22 caliber rifle.

The Model 1903 is a hammerless, slide-action, magazine-fed repeating rifle. Its uncomplicated, sound design incorporates a positive slide safety and a simple takedown procedure. The Model 1903 was offered with a 24-inch octagon barrel. The magazine capacity was 7 rounds.

Later, Savage Arms introduced the Model 1909, which was basically the same design, except for a 20-inch barrel. The final variation of this design was the Model 1914, which was modified to incorporate a tubular feed magazine. The Model 1903 was discontinued in 1921. This model ranks as one of the most practical designs for a slide-action rifle.

DISASSEMBLY

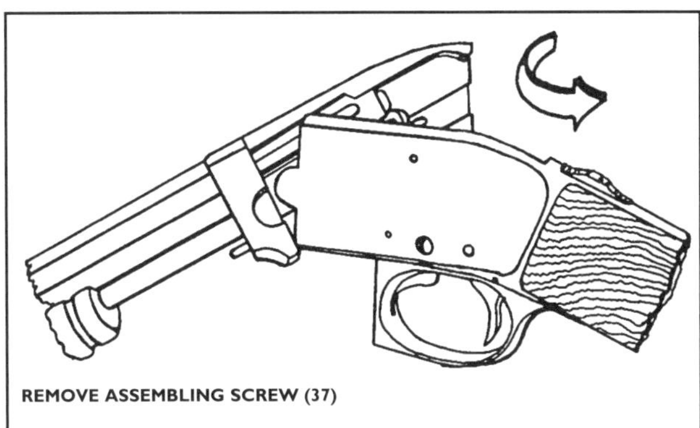

REMOVE ASSEMBLING SCREW (37)

1 Check the rifle to insure it is unloaded, remove magazine assembly from rifle, loosen and remove assembling screw (37). The two portions of the receiver (1) and (la) will come apart at the joints by forcing the buttstock portion (left side) up and to the left.

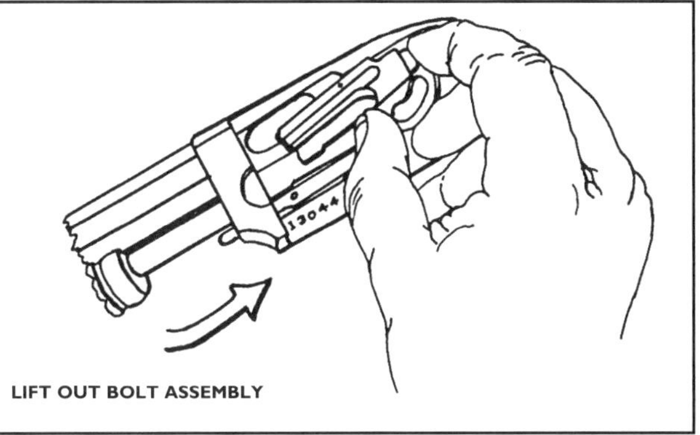

LIFT OUT BOLT ASSEMBLY

2 Press operating bar stop (30) and push operating handle (3a) half way to the rear. Lift out bolt assembly.

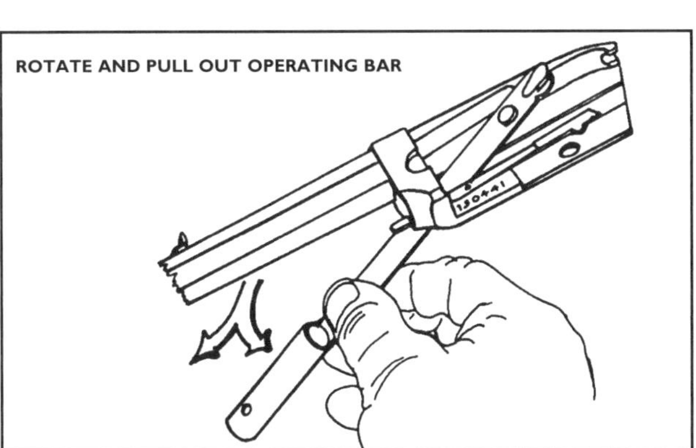

ROTATE AND PULL OUT OPERATING BAR

3 To disassemble right half of receiver assembly, remove retaining guide rod screw (35), slide operating bar guide rod (33) forward approximately ½ inch. Tap out guide rod mount (34), remove operating handle screws (38), and tap operating handle from operating bar (36). Pull out operating bar guide rod; rotate and pull operating bar down and out from body of receiver. Tap out operating bar stop pin (32) from receiver and lift out operating bar stop and operating bar stop spring (31). Note; Record orientation of spring; maintain same orientation in assembling.

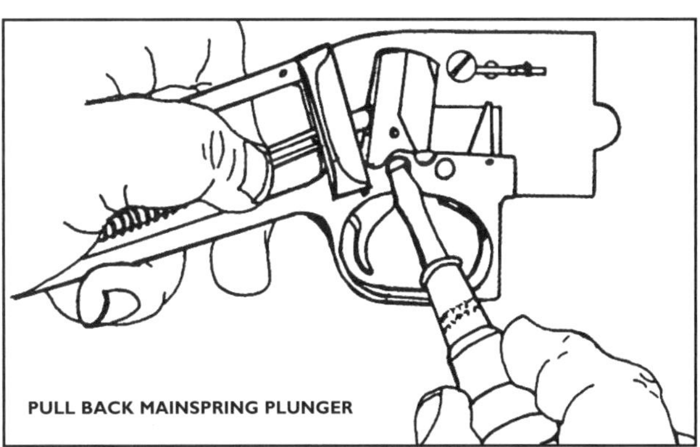

PULL BACK MAINSPRING PLUNGER

4 To disassemble left half of receiver assembly, remove tang stock screw (27) and tap off buttstock (3). Compress safety spring (25) and rotate end off one notched area of safety connector bar (20). Once spring is clear of safety connector bar, remove safety spring, drive out safety bar pin (21) and lift out safety (19), and safety connector bar. Pull back on mainspring plunger (22). While compressing mainspring (24), loosen and remove hammer screw (10): lift out hammer (9).

Relax pressure on mainspring plunger, and remove mainspring plunger, mainspring (24), and mainspring retaining washer (23). Remove ejector retaining screw (14) and lift out ejector (13) and ejector spring (15). Drive out magazine catch (18), lift out magazine catch (16) and magazine catch spring (17). Drive out trigger pin (12), and lift out trigger (11). All other parts are readily disassembled.

SAVAGE MODEL 1919 NRA RIFLE

PARTS LEGEND

1. Bolt
2. Safety
3. Cocking piece head
4. Bolt sleeve retaining collar
5. Mainspring bushing
6. Ejector pin
7. Ejector
8. Ejector spring
9. Mainspring
10. Cocking piece pin
11. Cocking piece (hammer)
12. Barrel
13. Bolt sleeve
14. Bolt pin
15. Bolt head
16. Extractor spring
17. Extractor pin
18. Firing pin stop pin
19. Extractor
20. Firing pin
21. Front sight
22. Front barrel band screw
23. Front barrel band
24. Stock
25. Middle barrel band swivel
26. Middle barrel band screw
27. Middle barrel band
28. Rear sight base screw
29. Elevation screw
30. Elevator
31. Aperture disc
32. Aperture disc screw
33. Windage screw
34. Windage yoke
35. Rear sight base
36. Magazine retainer, front
37. Magazine retainer, rear
38. Trigger spring box
39. Trigger spring
40. Trigger adjusting screw
41. Trigger pin
42. Trigger
43. Takedown screw, front
44. Magazine assembly
45. Takedown screw, rear
46. Trigger guard
47. Trigger guard screw
48. Buttplate screw (2)
49. Buttplate
50. Trigger plate
51. Stock swivel assembly

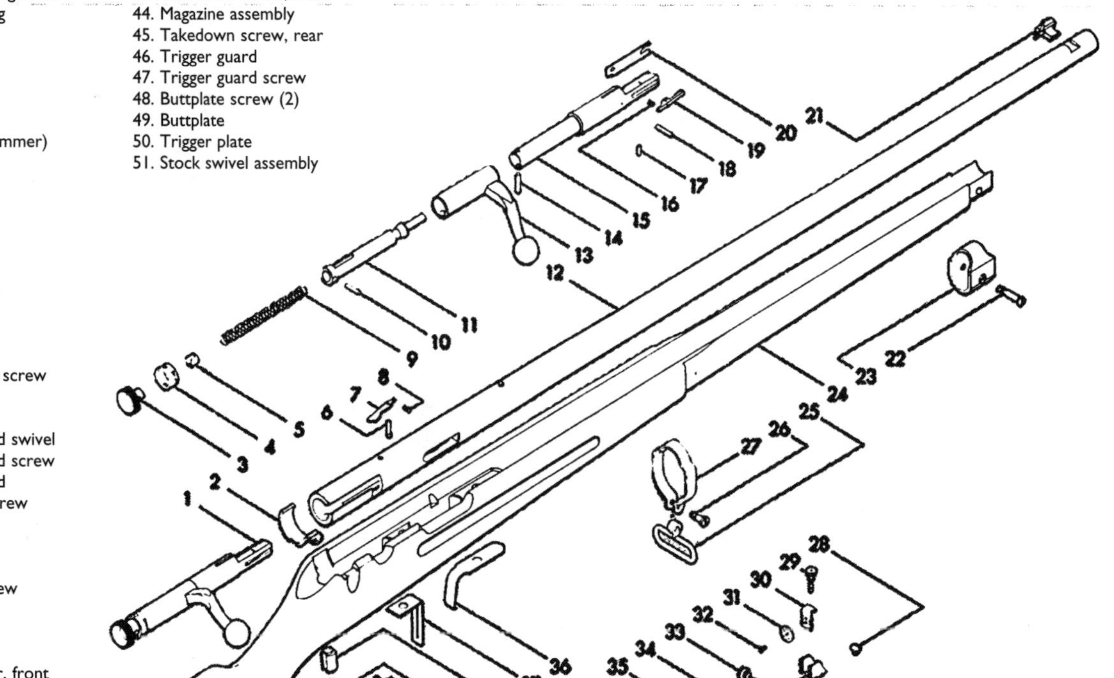

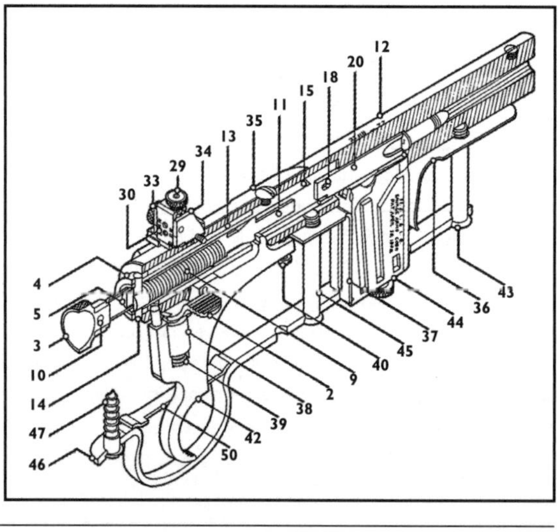

Following World War I, U.S. arms manufacturers introduced several models of commercial bolt-action rifles to meet popular demand. One of these rifles, the Savage Model 1919 NRA, was a military-style target rifle with a long fore-end. The NRA designation was explained by the mention that the rifle was suitable for firing from the standard positions in National Rifle Association matches. The Model 1919 was offered in .22 Long Rifle and .22 Short. The rifle chambered for .22 Short was made on special order only in very limited quantity.

The rifle had a 25-inch, round barrel and weighed approximately 7 lbs. with a 5-round detachable box magazine and the thumb-operated safety. A fully adjustable aperture rear sight was mounted on the upper rear of the action, and the front sight was dovetailed into the barrel.

An unusual feature was that the barrel and receiver were integral. Also unusual was the 2-point striker. The cartridge rim was struck in 2 positions to aid reliable ignition.

A later version of this rifle (serial numbers 25000 to 45000), had a single-point striker and twin-extractors. In 1933, this rifle was replaced by the Savage Model 19.

DISASSEMBLY

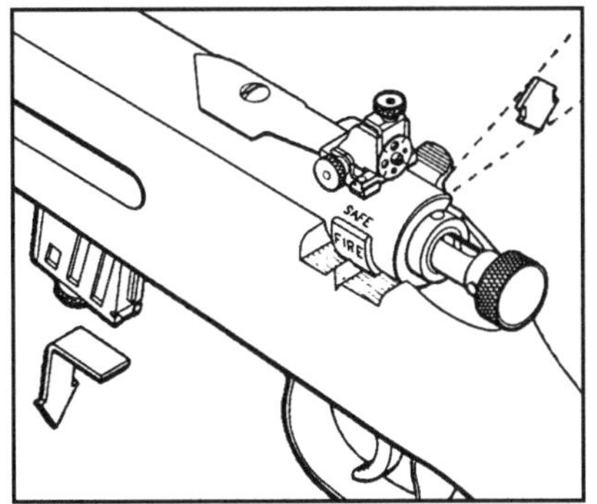

1 Lift thumbpiece of safety (2) to put rifle on safe. Depressing the thumbpiece disengages safety, and the word "FIRE" on left of safety is exposed. Remove magazine (44) by pressing knurled knob on its base forward and down. To remove bolt (1), disengage safety and pull bolt fully to the rear; then, pull trigger (42) and remove bolt.

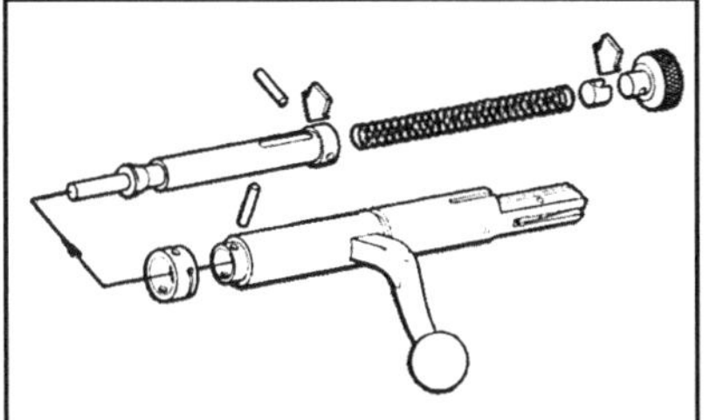

2 Disassemble bolt by drifting out bolt pin (14). Cocking piece (11), bolt sleeve retaining collar (4), and bolt sleeve (13) slide off to rear. Strip cocking piece by drifting out cocking piece pin (10). Hold cocking piece head (3) tightly while withdrawing the punch, as head is under spring tension. Ease off cocking piece head, mainspring bushing (5), and mainspring (9). Notch (arrow) in mainspring bushing must align with slots (arrow) in cocking piece when reassembled.

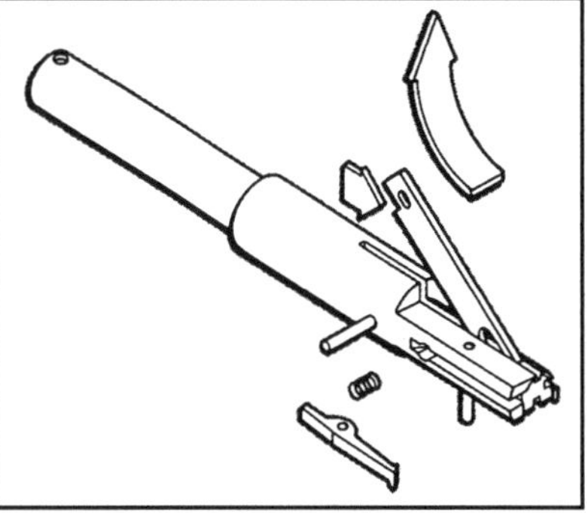

3 Drift out extractor pin (17) to release extractor (19) and extractor spring (16). Drift out firing pin stop pin (18), and lift firing pin (20) out of bolt head. Small notch (arrow) at rear of firing pin must face toward bottom of bolt on replacement.

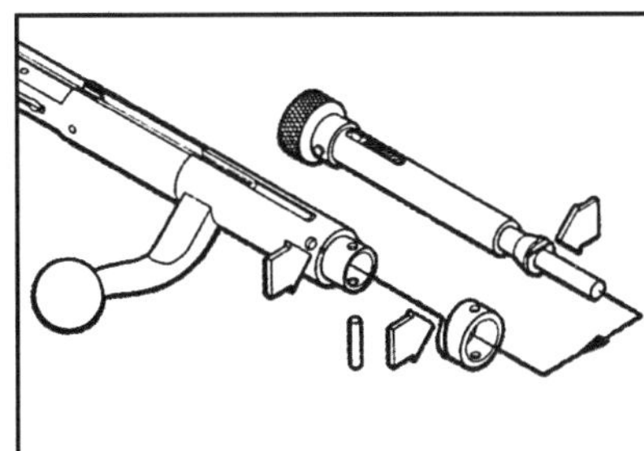

4 In reassembling the bolt, align the slots on the underside of bolt head and bolt sleeve. Replace bolt sleeve retaining collar so that the tip (arrow) of its integral spring seats in the small notch (arrow) on rear face of bolt sleeve. Before inserting cocking piece, align sear notch (arrow) with slots in bolt head and sleeve. A tapered punch is useful in lining up holes for replacement of bolt pin.

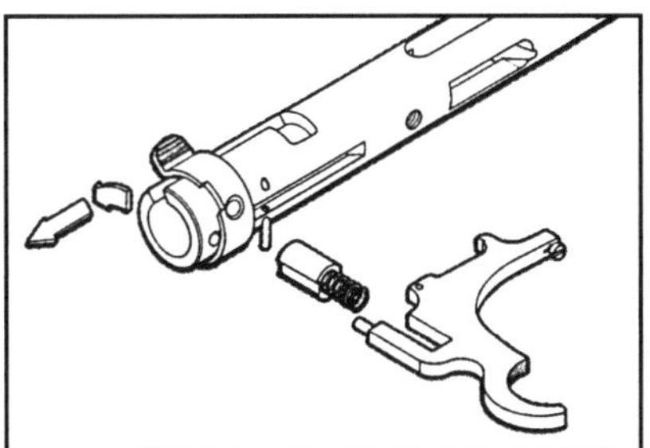

5 Remove front barrel band screw (22), loosen middle barrel band screw (26), and slide the bands (23, 27) forward off the barrel. Remove front and rear takedown screws (43, 45) and lift barrel out of stock. Drift out trigger pin (41) to remove trigger (42), trigger spring box (38), and trigger spring (39). Turn safety counterclockwise until its thumbpiece aligns with top of bolt handle cut in barrel extension. Slide safety off to rear.

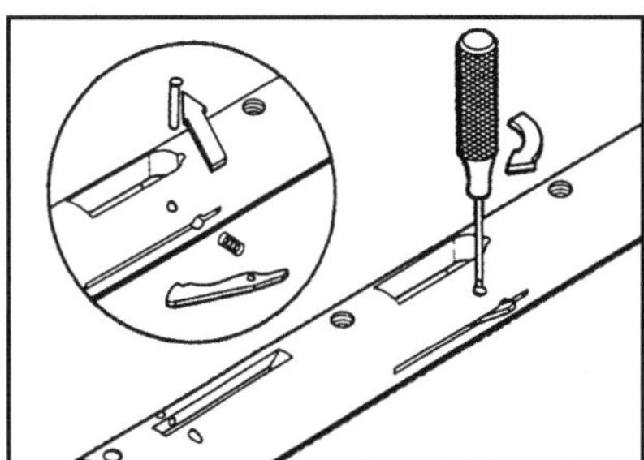

6 Ejector pin (6) is loosely fitted in a blind hole in barrel extension. Remove by turning L-shaped head of pin outward with a jeweler's screwdriver. Exposed head of pin provides a purchase for the thumbnail. It is pried out, releasing ejector (7) and ejector spring (8).

SAVAGE-STEVENS MODEL 94-C

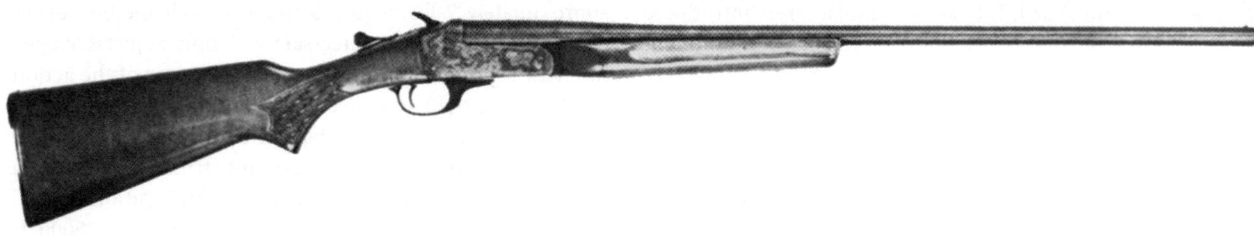

PARTS LEGEND

1. Top snap
2. Locking bolt plunger spring
3. Locking bolt plunger
4. Locking bolt assembly
5. Firing pin screw
6. Firing pin
7. Barrel
8. Front sight
9. Top snap plunger spring
10. Top snap plunger
11. Top snap sleeve
12. Hammer
13. Mainspring plunger seat
14. Mainspring
15. Mainspring plunger assembly
16. Top snap screw
17. Frame
18. Locking bolt, hammer pin
19. Trigger guard screw
20. Trigger spring
21. Trigger
22. Trigger pin
23. Extractor
24. Ejector spring
25. Ejector starter pin
26. Trigger guard
27. Trigger guard screw
28. Ejector hook
29. Extractor stop pin
30. Extractor lever pin
31. Fore-end spring
32. Fore-end spring spring
33. Fore-end spring spring pin
34. Fore-end spring housing screw
35. Fore-end spring housing
36. Fore-end spring pin
37. Fore-end iron head screw
38. Fore-end head
39. Fore-end wood
40. Fore-end screw
41. Butt plate screw
42. Butt plate
43. Stock
44. Stock bolt
45. Stock bolt washer

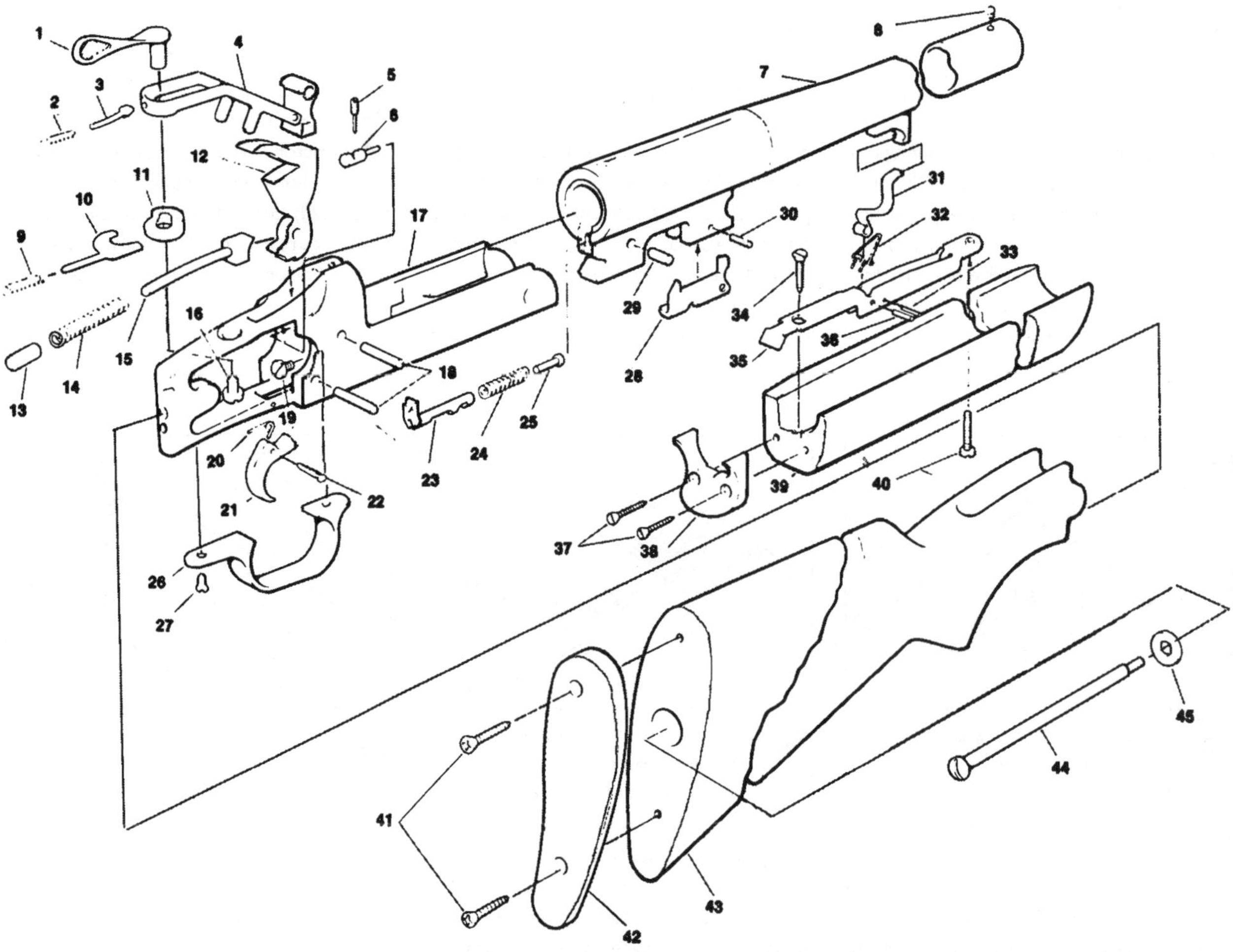

In 1920 the J. Stevens Arms & Tool Co. was purchased by the Savage Arms Co., who retained the Stevens name on many of their products. Around 1929, the first Model 94 shotgun was sold under the company's Springfield lable. It featured a two way top snap, rebounding exposed hammer, color case-hardened receiver and automatic ejector.

Nearly identical guns were marketed concurrently including the Springfield Model 944, a 4½-lb., .410; the 94-R, with large fore-end and Jostam recoil pad, and the 94-P with adjustable choke. Under the Stevens name were the Models 104 for 24, 28, 32 gauge, and .410, and Model 107 for large and small bores. After World War II the Springfield name was dropped. By the 1960s the shotguns were usually cataloged as the Savage-Stevens 94-C and the Youth Model, 94-Y (20 gauge or .410 bore). The last variant of the Model 94, which was discontinued in the 1980s, was the Model 94 Series P.

DISASSEMBLY

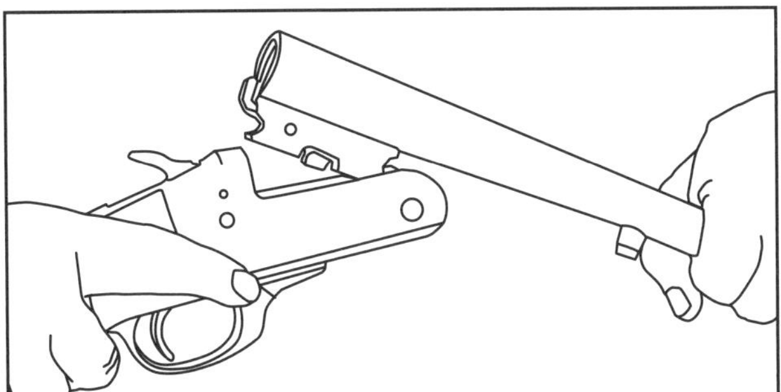

1 Remove fore-end by pulling the forward end down or, in some models, by removing the fore-end screw; push top snap (1) to either side and pivot barrel (7) down and off. This is all that is normally required for cleaning and maintenance. Remove buttplate screws (41) and buttplate (42), and with a long screwdriver loosen stockbolt (44) and remove stock (43). On some of the later variations further disassembly involves the removal of "groove pins" that are not intended for removal and replacement as a part of routine maintenance. Older guns are assembled with standard push pins. Pins are removed from left to right and installed from right to left.

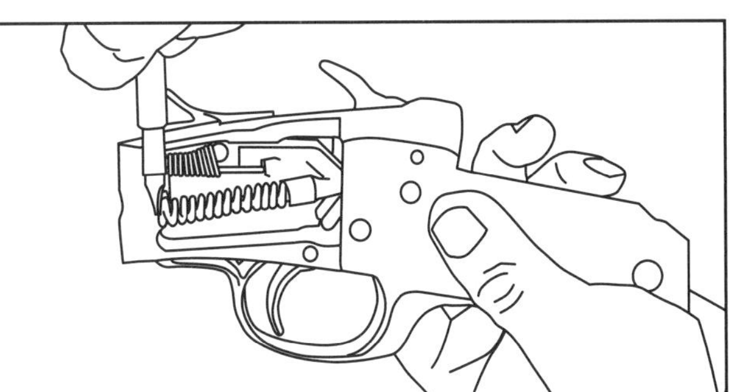

2 Drift out the trigger pin (22) and remove trigger (21) and trigger spring (20). On newer models the trigger spring is an unsecured coil spring and care must be exercised to retain it when the trigger is removed. Remove the mainspring (14) by using the blade of a screwdriver to compress it from behind and pivot it and the mainspring guide (mainspring plunger assembly, 15) and the mainspring plunger seat (13) to the side. The locking bolt plunger (3) and spring (2) are removed in the same manner. Notice the position of the bend in the locking bolt plunger (3); it must be in the same position for reassembly.

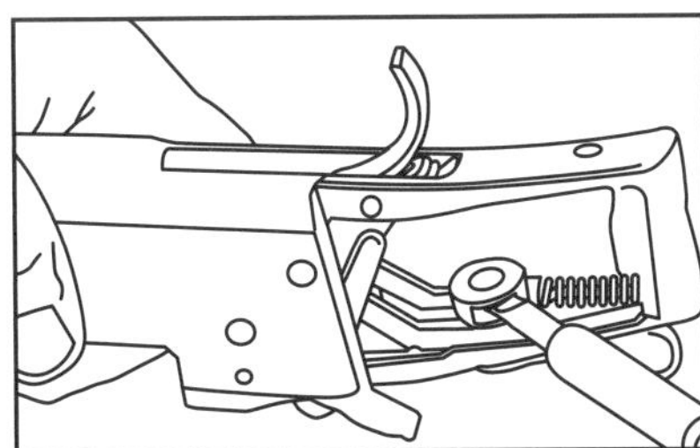

3 Remove the top snap screw (16) with a 90 degree screwdriver or similar tool. Gently pry the top snap sleeve (11) off the top snap (1), freeing the top snap plunger and spring. Drift out the locking bolt and hammer pins (18), and remove these parts. Remove the firing pin screw (5) and draw the firing pin (6) to the rear. On late models the firing pin is retained by a transverse pin and is spring retracted.

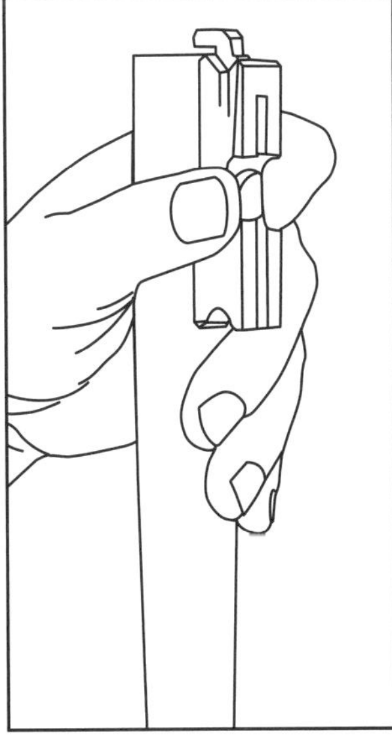

4 Remove the inner trigger guard screw (19) from the top; also remove the outer trigger guard screw (27) to free the trigger guard (26). The extractor (23) should be uncocked; if it is not, uncock it by lifting slightly the flange on the left side of the ejector hook (28). Then apply some pressure against the extractor (23) and drift out the extractor stop pin (29), being careful not to lose control of the ejector spring (24) and ejector starter pin (25). Drift out the extractor lever pin (30), and remove the ejector hook (28).

To remove the fore-end parts, take out the fore-end iron screws (37) and fore-end head (38), then the fore-end spring housing screw (34) and the fore-end screw (40). There remain only the fore-end spring (31) and the fore-end spring spring pin (33) to be removed. On current models the fore-end is retained by a single screw. Reassembe in reverse order.

SHARPS '59, '63 & CONVERSIONS

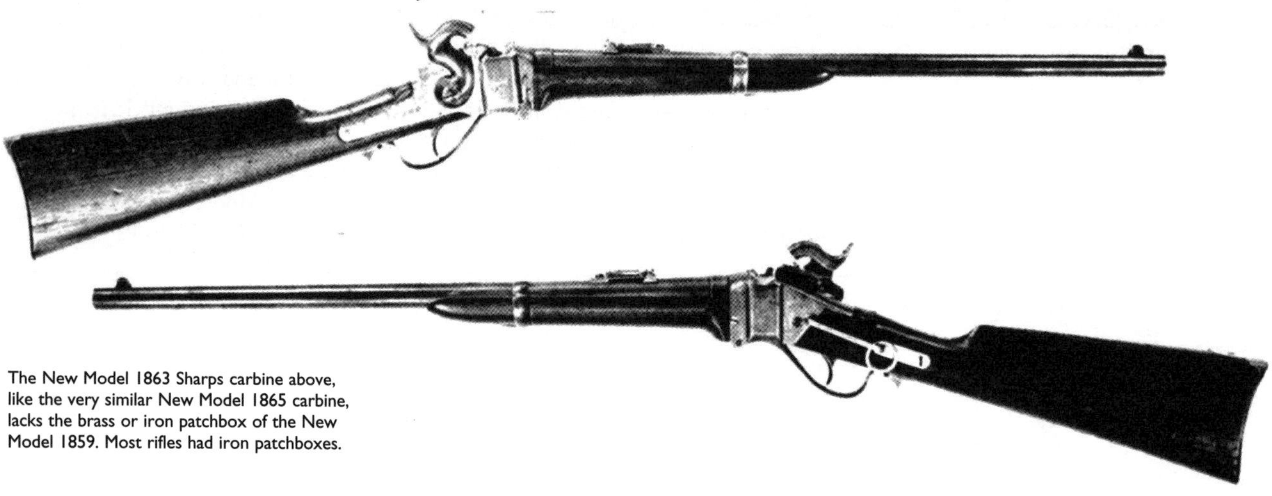

The New Model 1863 Sharps carbine above, like the very similar New Model 1865 carbine, lacks the brass or iron patchbox of the New Model 1859. Most rifles had iron patchboxes.

PARTS LEGEND

1. Receiver
2. Barrel
3. Buttstock (not shown)
   3a. Forestock (not shown)
4. Breechblock (Slide)
5. Firing pin
6. Firing pin screw
7. Upper toggle link screw
8. Lever toggle link
9. Lever pin
10. Extractor
11. Lever pin retainer plunger
12. Lever pin retainer spring
13. Lever pin retainer screw
14. Lever spring
15. Barrel stud
16. Lever spring screw
17. Stock bushing
18. Forestock screw
19. Lockplate
20. Hammer
21. Hammer screw
22. Tumbler
23. Stirrup screw
24. Stirrup
25. Mainspring
26. Mainspring screw
27. Bridle
28. Sear
29. Bridle screws (3)
30. Lockplate screws (2)
31. Lockplate base screw
32. Swivel bar screw
33. Swivel bar
34. Swivel ring
35. Tang screws (2)
36. Lever
37. Guard plate
38. Trigger
39. Lever catch
40. Lever catch spring
41. Lever catch spring screw
42. Lever catch screw
43. Rear guard screw
44. Front guard screw
45. Trigger screw
46. Rear sight
47. Rear sight base
48. Rear sight screw
49. Front sight
50. Front sight pin
51. Upper band
52. Upper band spring
53. Butt plate
54. Buttplate screws (2)

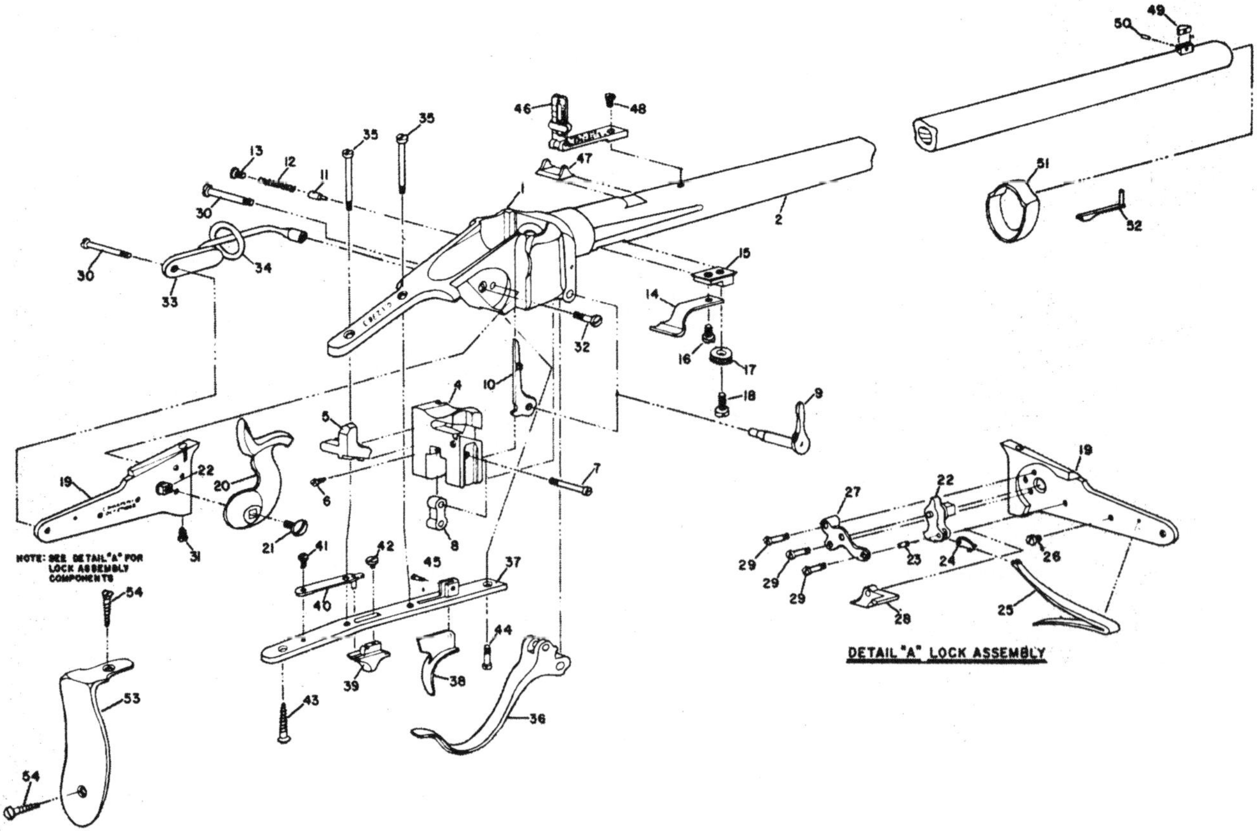

NOTE: SEE DETAIL "A" FOR LOCK ASSEMBLY COMPONENTS

DETAIL "A" LOCK ASSEMBLY

The United States government began buying breech-loading arms of Christian Sharps' design as early as 1851 with significant purchases of Sharps' New Model 1859 carbines and rifles on the eve of the Civil War. By the end of the Civil War, the Federal government held more than 65,000 Sharps 1859 and New Model 1863 carbines and rifles.

Having adopted the .50-70 cartridge as standard in 1866, the Army Ordnance Department sought an economical means to convert Sharps' proven design to cartridge use. Sharps agreed to undertake the conversion program and deliveries began in February 1868.

Carbines converted under this contract are of two versions, the Models 1867 and 1868. They are identified by the means of withdrawing the firing pin; a retracting spring in the 1867 model and a retracting cam in the 1868. Other alterations included the substitutuon of a new breechblock adapted for the .50-70 Government cartridge, removing the pellet primer mechanism, reshaping the hammer and lining the barrel with a .50 caliber rifled sleeve.

Sharps converted just over 32,000 carbines and rifles for the government before introducing its first dedicated metallic cartridge weapon, the Model 1869.

DISASSEMBLY

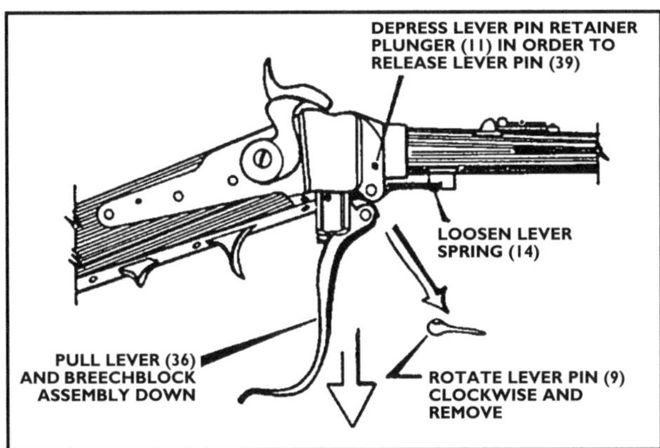

1 Disengage the lever catches (39) and push down on the lever (36) to lower the breechblock (4) and open the breech. Make sure the chamber and bore are clear.

To remove the breechblock, remove the upper band (51) and forestock screw (18). Lift off the forestock (3a). Release tension on the lever spring (14) by loosening the lever spring screw (16). It is not necessary to remove the lever spring. Depress the lever pin retaining plunger (11) located on the front right-hand side of the receiver (1) and rotate the lever pin one-quarter turn clockwise. Draw the lever pin out from the right side of the receiver and allow the lever to drop free of the receiver. By pulling down on the lever the breechblock and extractor (10) will be drawn out through the bottom of the receiver.

Separate the lever and breechblock by removing the upper toggle link screw (7) from the breechblock. Remove the firing pin screw (6) and firing pin (5).

Remove the buttstock (3) by removing the lockplate screws (30) — Note: on carbines, the rearmost lockplate screw passes through the rear of the swivel bar. Place the hammer (20) on half-cock and lift the lock out of its mortise in the buttstock and receiver. Remove the tang screws (35) and the front (44) and rear (43) guard screws and lift the guard plate (37) out of the stock. On carbines, remove the swivel bar screw (32) and swivel bar (33). Now slide the buttstock rearward, off the receiver tang.

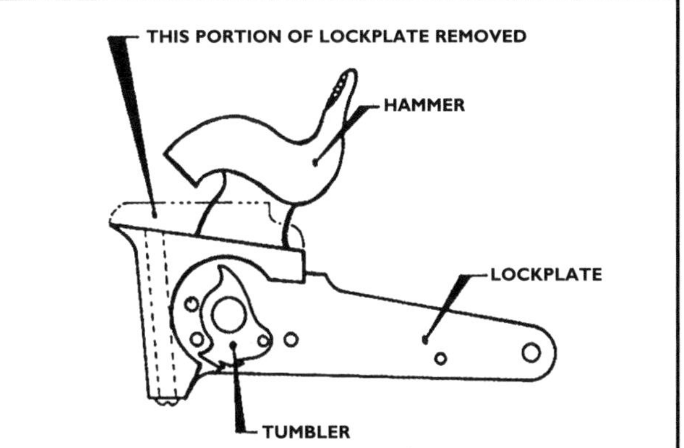

2 To disassemble the lock, lower the hammer. Loosen — do not remove — the mainspring screw (26) one or two turns, then raise the hammer to full cock. Place a clamp on the mainspring (25) at the mainspring screw and tighten. Depress the sear (28) and let the hammer all the way down. Lift the mainspring until the alignment pin on the spring is clear of its hole in the lock-plate, then rotate the spring clear of the stirrup (24) and sear, and remove it from the lock. The bridle (27) and sear are removed by loosening the appropriate screws. Removal of the hammer, hammer screw (21), and tumbler (22) is not recommended

Reassemble in reverse sequence.

SHARPS-BORCHARDT MODEL 1878

PARTS LEGEND

1. Receiver
2. Barrel
3. Forestock (not shown)
   3a. Buttstock (not shown)
4. Breechblock
5. Striker
6. Cross pin
7. Mainspring
8. Breech bushing
9. Breech bushing pin
10. Sear
11. Sear pin
12. Sear plunger
13. Sear plunger spring
14. Sear connecting bar
15. Trigger
16. Trigger pin
17. Safety lever
18. Safety lever pin
19. Safety catch
20. Safety catch plunger
21. Safety catch plunger spring
22. Extractor
23. Lever
24. Lever bearing roller
25. Lever roller pin
26. Lever pin
27. Lever pin screw
28. Lever spring
29. Barrel stud
30. Lever spring screw
31. Forestock screw
32. Forestock bushing
33. Breechblock screw
34. Link
35. Lever screw
36. Cocking cam plate, right
37. Cocking cam plate, left
38. Cam plate screws (4)
39. Receiver screws (2)
40. Rear sight
41. Rear sight screws (2)
42. Front sight
43. Nose cap
44. Nose cap screw
45. Upper band (with swivel)
46. Lower band
47. Band screws (2)
48. Ramrod
49. Buttstock screw
50. Buttplate
51. Buttplate screws (2)

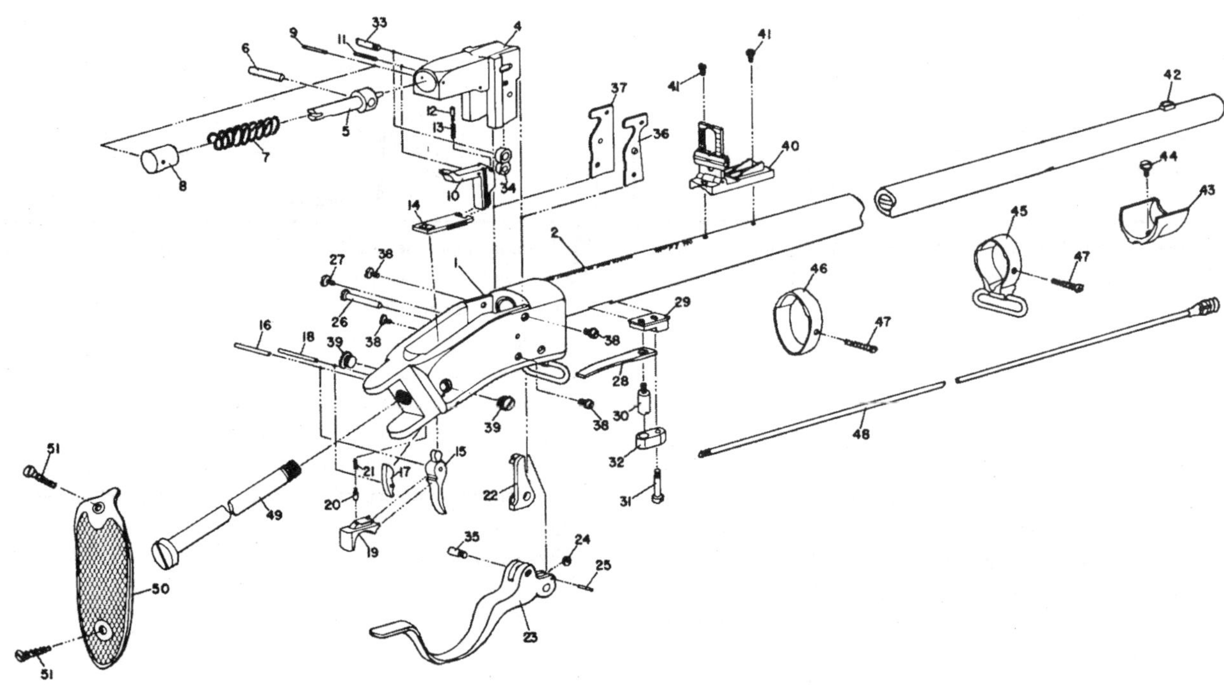

The Sharps Model 1878 single-shot rifle remains, even a century after its commercial demise, one of the best single-shot rifle designs ever produced. Strangely, it was too good for its own era, not gaining any appreciable popularity among shooters until some years after it was discontinued.

The 1878 was built around a hammerless self-cocking action designed and patented in 1876 by Hugo Borchardt. Borchardt, who had already designed a very workable — but never-to-be-produced — revolver for Winchester, and who would go on to design the pistol that is the basis from which the Luger was developed, assigned his patent to the Sharps Rifle Co. in the same year it was granted. The name by which the Model 1878 is commonly known, the Sharps-Borchardt, is drawn from the teaming of skills that resulted in its production.

The chief advantage of the Sharps-Borchardt (and, paradoxically the feature that denied the rifle any immediate success) was its hammerless action. In place of the separate lock and side-hammer of earlier Sharps guns, the Borchardt used a coil spring driven striker, encased in a shroud integral with the breechblock.

Borchardt, who would design the pistol that was the inspiration for the Luger "P-08" military pistol, assigned his rifle patent to the Sharps Rifle Co. in 1878.

The Sharps Rifle Co. made a number of attempts to sell the Borchardt as a military arm. The Imperial Chinese Army bought 300 for trial in 1877, and the states of Louisiana, Michigan, and South Carolina purchased quantities for issue to militia units. But, the United States Army, and most foreign military establishments, were already looking for repeating rifles. Despite the fact that nearly 75 percent of all Sharps-Borchardts were of military pattern, military sales were poor.

Sporting models of the Sharps-Borchardt, including the Sporting Rifle, were made for most of the more successful Sharps cartridges. Variations in barrel style — octagonal or round — and length, sights, stock configuration, and decoration were available within specific models or as options. Of all the Borchardts the "Long Range Target Rifles," with their checkered English walnut stocks, 32- or 34-inch, .45 caliber barrels, vernier rear sights and spirit-level windgauge front sights, were probably the finest.

Long Range rifles, and other civilian models, sold well in the eastern half of the country but were not popular in the West, where the greater portion of Sharps' market lay. Thus, the Borchardt, and the Sharps Rifle Co. were doomed. Production of the Borchardt ended in 1881. The company closed its doors a year later. It would be a quarter-century before custom makers A.O. Zischang, Axel Peterson, George Schoyen, and others, using the Borchardt as the basis for their Schuetzen-style target rifles, brought it the acclaim it deserved. Taken all together, the Sharps-Borchardt is an excellent example of single-shot rifle development in the United States.

Operation of the Sharps-Borchardt is relatively simple. Pulling the lever down drops the breechblock to expose the chamber for loading. As the breechblock clears the bottom of the chamber, the lever operates a single extractor, cocks the striker and engages a trigger block safety catch.

Returning the lever to its closed position raises the breechblock for firing. Since the block moves vertically, there is no assist in chambering.

DISASSEMBLY

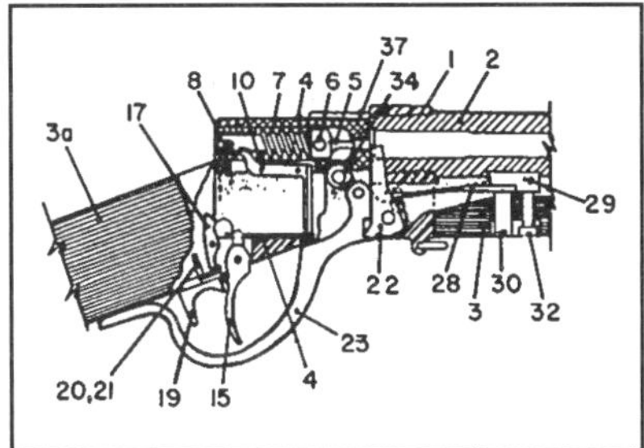

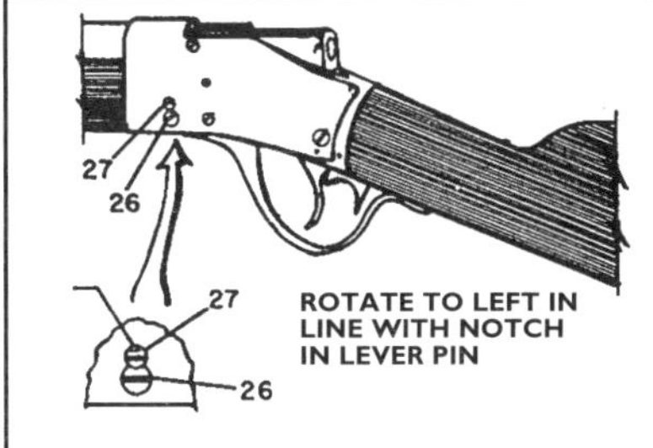

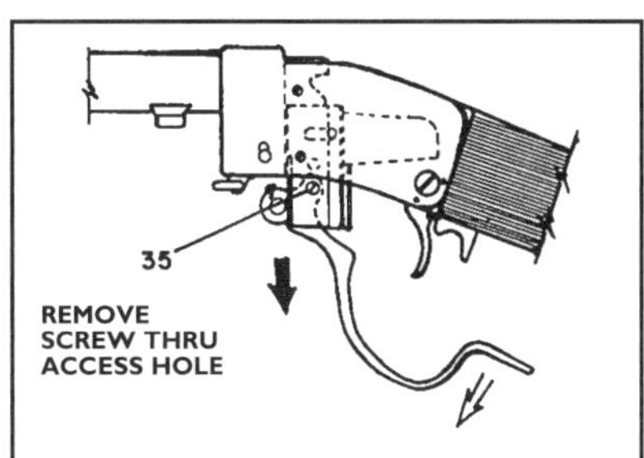

Begin disassembly by lowering the lever (23) and breechblock (4). Assure that the bore and chamber are clear. Raise the lever, closing the breech. Then:

1. Remove the buttplate screws (51) and buttplate (50). Loosen the buttstock screw (49) and remove the buttstock. Withdraw the ramrod (48), if applicable, and the band screws (47). Remove the upper (45) and lower (46) bands and forestock screw (31). Remove the forestock. Note: This procedure applies to military-style rifles and carbines. Civilian model fore-ends were attached by the forestock screw, or the forestock screw and a cross pin The lever spring screw (30) is accessible with the forestock in place.

2. Make sure the rifle is cocked. Loosen the lever spring screw to relieve tension on the lever spring (28). Lower the lever about half way and take out the lever pin (26). The lever pin is held in place by a lever pin screw (27). To release the lever pin, turn the lever pin screw until the semicircular cut in the screw clears the head of the lever pin and allows its removal. Pull the lever out of its joint in the receiver and replace the lever pin in its hole to hold the extractor (22) in place.

3. Draw the breechblock and lever downward until the hole in the left side of the breechblock that gives access to the lever screw (35) can be seen. Remove the lever screw and detach the lever from the breechblock. Push the breechblock up and out through the top of the receiver. Remove the lever pin and take out the extractor.

4. To disassemble the breechblock begin by holding the block, shroud down, against a solid surface. While holding back on the cross pin (6) with the fingers of one hand, press the sear (10), allowing the striker (5) to go forward to the uncocked position and releasing tension on the mainspring (7). Using a drift, drive out the sear pin (11) and remove the sear, taking care not to lose the sear plunger (12) and sear plunger spring (13). Drive out the breech bushing pin (9) and draw the breech bushing (8) out of its seat in the shroud. Remove the mainspring.

Drive the cross pin out of the striker (5) and remove the striker from the breechblock. Remove the breechblock screw (33) and the link (34).

5. To disassemble the trigger mechanism, drive out the trigger pin (16) and the safety lever pin (18). Pull the safety catch (19) to the rear and draw the trigger out of the bottom of the receiver. Push the safety catch forward until it drops out of the receiver along with the safety lever.

6. The right- and left-hand cocking cam plates (36 & 37) should not be removed under normal circumstances.

7. Assembly of the component subassemblies and of the rifle should be done in reverse of the disassembly sequence.

SIMONOV 7.62MM CARBINE

PARTS LEGEND

1. Piston
2. Handguard and gas cylinder
3. Piston extension
4. Piston return spring
5. Front sight
6. Front sight seat
7. Handguard catch
8. Bayonet screw
9. Bayonet assembly
10. Hold open latch pin
11. Hold open latch spring
12. Hold open latch
13. Receiver and barrel assembly
14. Takedown latch
15. Trigger guard latch
16. Latch pin
17. Rear housing
18. Bolt carrier
19. Bolt
20. Firing pin retainer
21. Firing pin
22. Extractor spring
23. Extractor
24. Recoil spring
25. Spring retainer
26. Large spring guide
27. Small spring guide
28. Stock assembly
29. Trigger guard spring
30. Magazine
31. Magazine follower
32. Follower spring
33. Hinge pin
34. Magazine cover
35. Cover latch
36. Latch spring and sear spring
37. Sear
38. Latch stop pin
39. Trigger guard
40. Disconnector hinge pin
41. Trigger pin
42. Safety catch
43. Safety catch spring
44. Trigger
45. Safety catch pin
46. Trigger bar
47. Trigger bar pin
48. Trigger spring
49. Disconnector
50. Rebound disconnector
51. Hammer
52. Hammer strut pin
53. Hammer strut
54. Hammer spring
55. Cleaning rod

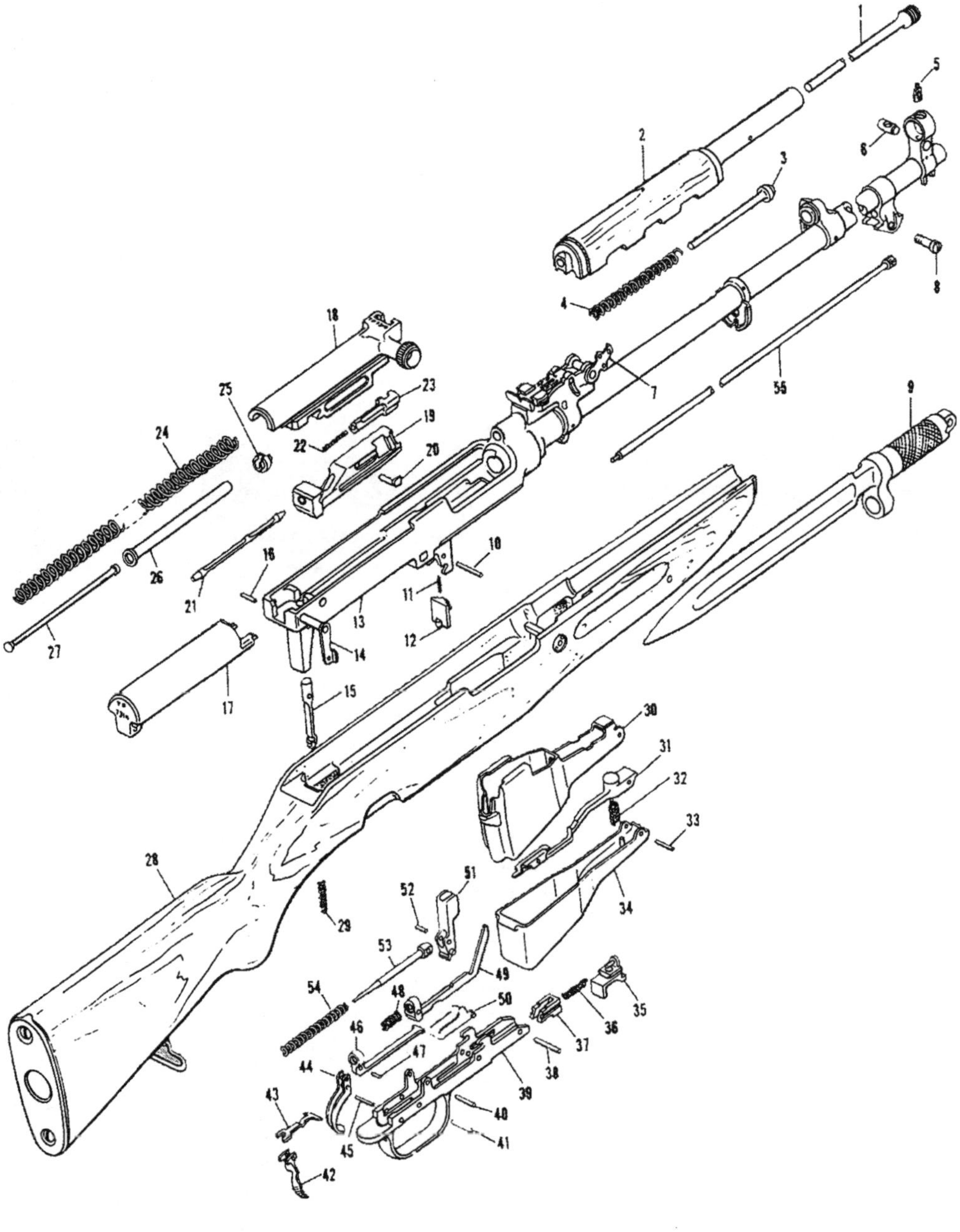

The Russians have used several models of semi-automatic rifles and carbines. They adopted the Simonov rifle in 1936 and the Tokarev rifle in 1938. The Tokarev was used extensively during World War II, but did not prove entirely satisfactory. Shortly after the war, the Simonov carbine was adopted.

The Simonov carbine (also called SKS, standing for Self-Loading Carbine Simonov) is one of three Russian weapons using the 7.62mm., M1943 short rimless cartridge. Gas-operated, it has a fixed, 10-round box magazine and a permanently attached folding bayonet. When it is fired, gas is tapped through a port in top of barrel, and pushes a piston and piston extension rearward. The extension actuates the bolt carrier, which cams rear of bolt upward for unlocking.

This carbine is relatively easy to field strip and maintain, and it functions reliably. It is considered to be effective up to about 400 meters.

The SKS is an excellent weapon and was widely issued among the Soviet block nations and their allies. It was replaced by the 7.62mm., AK assault rifle that better met the tactical requirements of the Russians.

DISASSEMBLY

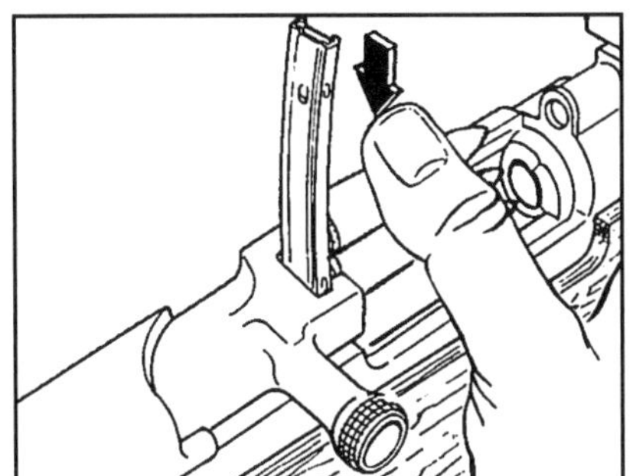

1 The SKS has a fixed box magazine (30). To load, open action by pulling back bolt carrier (18). Insert a loaded stripper clip into clip guides of bolt carrier, and push cartridges down into magazine as shown. The magazine can also be loaded with loose cartridges.

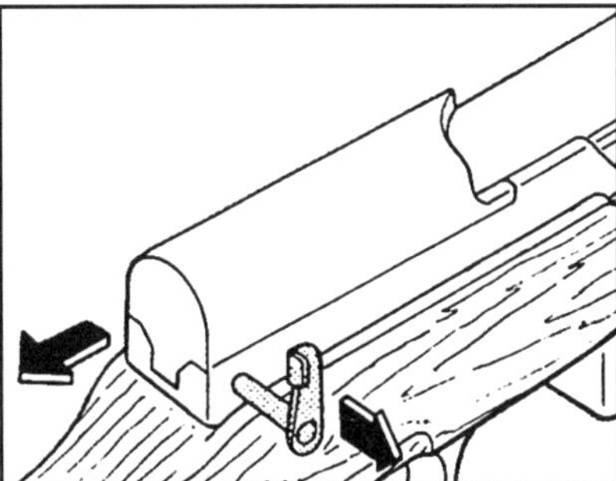

2 To field strip, clear the chamber and unload magazine. Depress follower (31) and ease bolt closed. Swing take-down latch (14) up and pull out. Ease rear housing (17) off. Pull out recoil spring assembly (24-27). Pull bolt carrier (18) and bolt (19) to rear and remove.

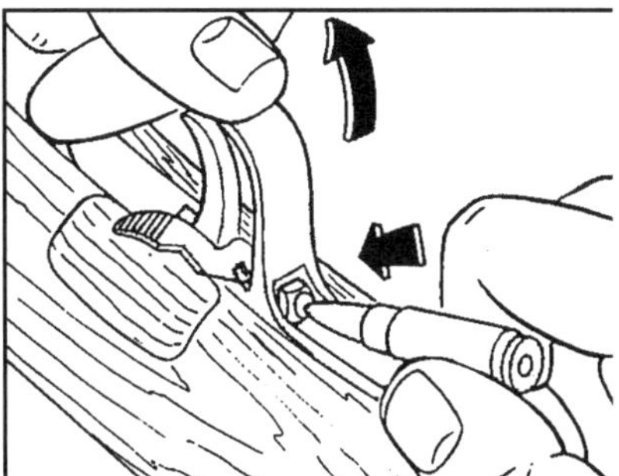

3 For further disassembly, cock hammer and put carbine on safe. Turn carbine upside-down and push in on trigger guard latch (15) with cartridge nose or punch. When latch is pushed in sufficiently, the trigger guard (39) should jump out slightly. Guard can then be pulled free.

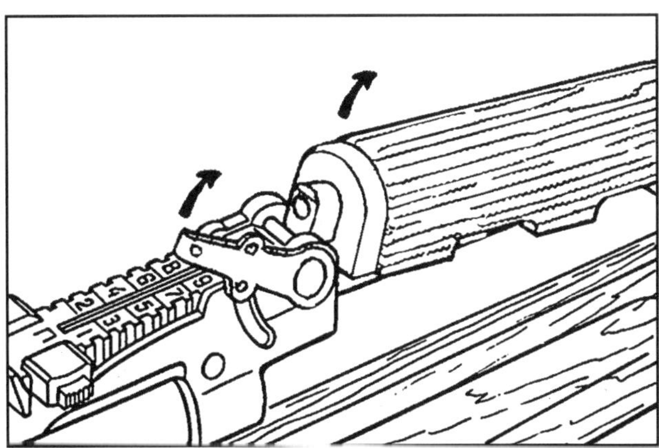

4 Insert point of cartridge into hole of the handguard catch (7) and rotate catch up as shown in illustration. Lift up rear of handguard (2), and pull it free of barrel. Then push piston (1) out of gas cylinder. Pivot bayonet (9) to middle position, and remove cleaning rod (55).

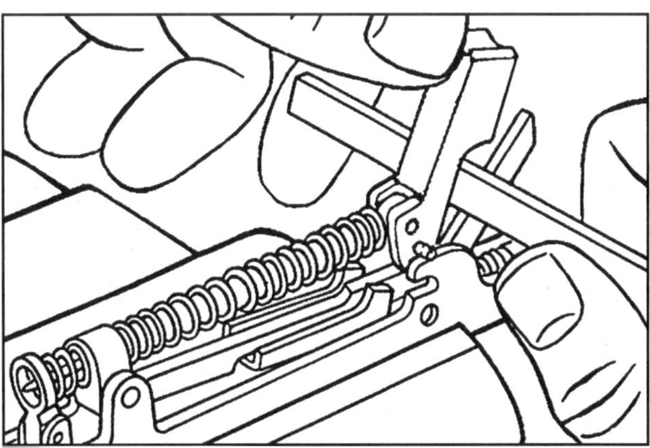

5 To strip trigger guard, place in padded vise. Push down on disconnector (49) and pull trigger (44) to release hammer. NOTE: *Use care; hammer is under heavy spring pressure.* Use metal bar as shown to force hammer out. Remaining parts can be disassembled by driving out pins.

SMITH & WESSON MODEL 3000

PARTS LEGEND

1. Barrel assembly
2. Front sight
3. Barrel ring guide
4. Fore-end cap spring
5. Fore-end cap ball
6. Receiver
7. Ejector
8. Shell stopper plate, left
9. Shell stopper plate pin stopper spring (2)
10. Shell stopper plate, right
11. Shell stopper plate spring (2)
12. Shell stopper pin (2)
13. Magazine tube
14. Magazine follower
15. Magazine spring
16. Magazine spring retainer

17a. Breech bolt assembly

17. Breech bolt
18. Extractor
19. Extractor spring
20. Extractor spring plunger
21. Firing pin
22. Firing pin spring
23. Firing pin retaining pin
24. Locking block
25. Locking block stud
26. Breech bolt base
27. Trigger plate

    27a. Trigger plate assembly

28. Safety button
29. Safety button spring sleeve
30. Safety button spring
31. Safety button spring stopper pin
32. Sear
33. Sear pin
34. Sear spring
35. Trigger
36. Trigger connector plate
37. Trigger connector plate pin
38. Trigger pin
39. Trigger plate pin bushing, large
40. Trigger plate pin stopper spring, large
41. Hammer spring
42. Hammer spring sleeve
43. Hammer
44. Hammer pin
45. Action bar lock
46. Action bar lock spring
47. Carrier
48. Carrier dog
49. Carrier dog washer
50. Carrier dog pin
51. Carrier spring
52. Carrier spring sleeve
53. Trigger plate pin bushing, small
54. Trigger plate pin stopper spring, small
55. Trigger plate, pin, large
56. Trigger plate pin, small
57. Fore-end
58. Fore-end tube
59. Action bar, right
60. Action bar, left
61. Fore-end tube nut
62. Fore-end cap
63. Stock spacer plate
64. Stock
65. Grip cap spacer
66. Grip cap
67. Grip cap screw
68. Grip cap inlay
69. Recoil pad
70. Recoil pad spacer
71. Recoil pad screws (2)
72. Stock retainer washer
73. Stock retainer spring release
74. Stock retainer bolt
75. Magazine plug

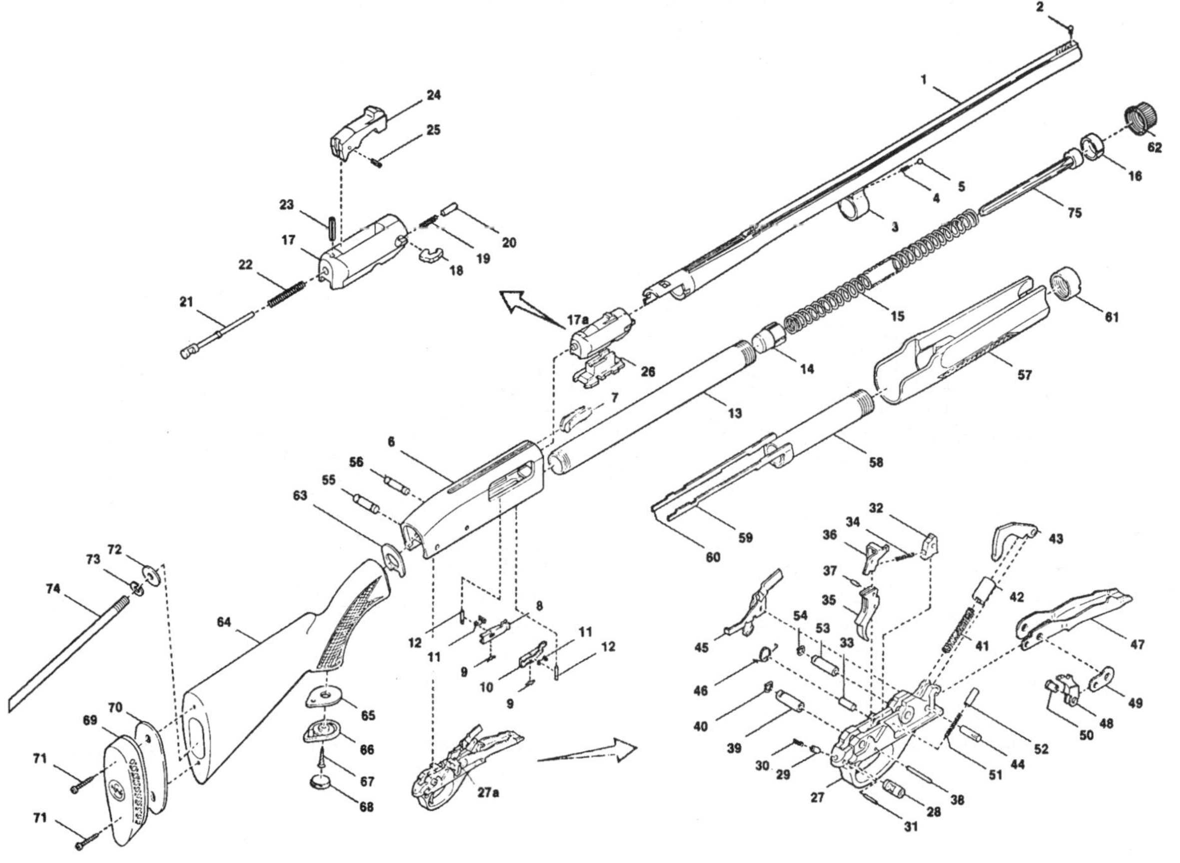

In 1979, following the introduction of its Model 1000 autoloader, Smith & Wesson introduced the Model l000P slide-action shotgun. The 1000P was offered in 12-gauge with either plain or ventilated-rib barrels with 3-inch chambers. In December, 1980, to avoid confusion between their autoloading and slide-action guns, Smith & Wesson changed the model designation of the 1000P to Model 3000.

The Model 3000s were manufactured for Smith & Wesson by Howa Machinery Ltd., of Japan. Similar in design to the Remington 870, the Model 3000 was produced in sporting and police versions. Smith & Wesson exited the shotgun market in the early 1970s and discontinued the Model 3000.

DISASSEMBLY

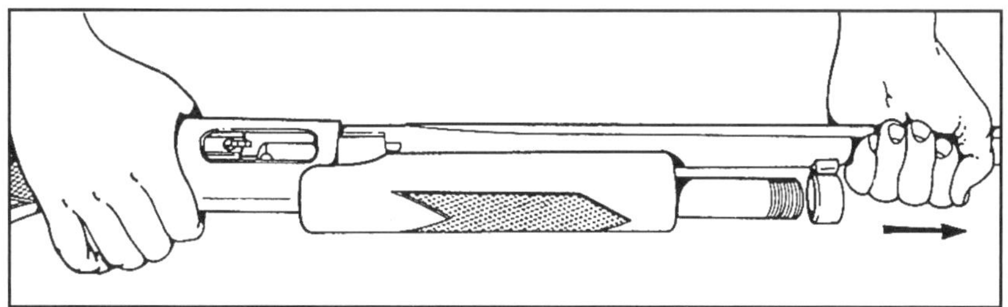

1 Engage the safety. Press upward on the action bar lock (45) and open the action by pulling the fore-end (57) to the rear. Unscrew the fore-end cap (62) and pull the barrel (1) out of the action group and off of the magazine tube (13).

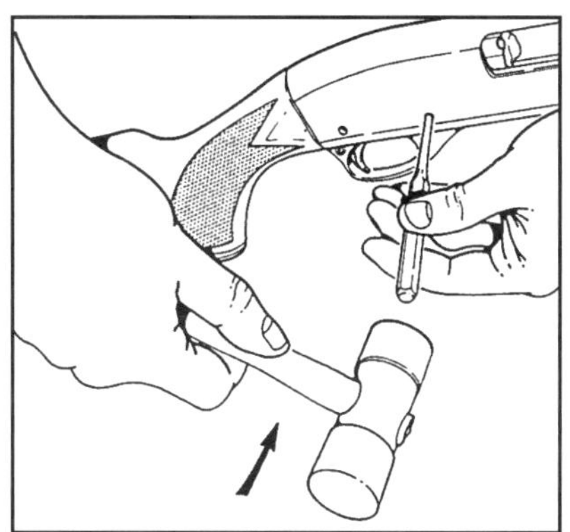

2 With a drift punch, drive out the large (55) and small (56) trigger plate pins to release the trigger plate assembly (27a).

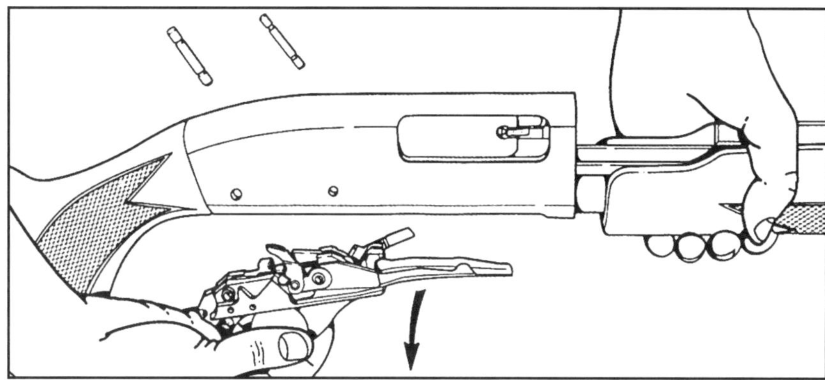

3 Draw the trigger plate (27) downward, out of the receiver (6) using a slight rocking motion to free the slide lock from its engagement.

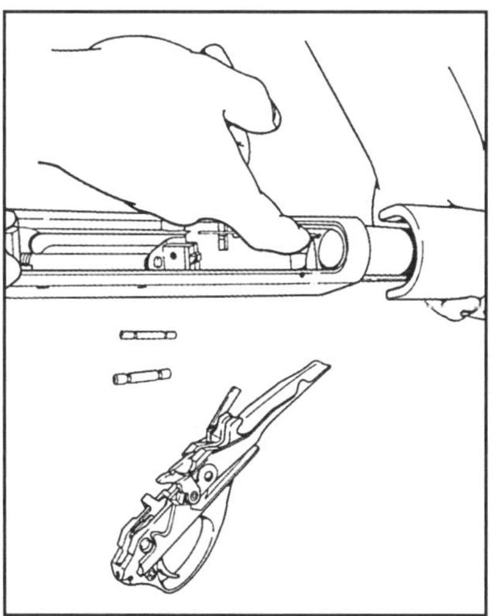

4 Reach into the bottom of the receiver and depress the right shell stopper plate (10) (See Figure 3). Draw the fore-end, fore-end tube (58), action bars (59 & 60), breech bolt base (26), and breech bolt assembly (17a) forward off the magazine tube and out of the receiver. The breech bolt assembly and breech bolt base will lift free of the action slide bars.

NOTE: *Further disassembly, particularly disassembly of the trigger plate and breech bolt assemblies, is not recommended.*

SPRINGFIELD ARMORY M1A1 RIFLE

PARTS LEGEND

1. Barrel
2. Receiver
3. Bolt with roller & clip
4. Firing pin
5. Extractor
6. Extractor spring & plunger
7. Ejector & ejector spring
8. Aperture rear sight
9. Rear sight base
10. Rear sight cover
11. Elevation knob
12. Windage knob
13. Clip guide
14. Clip guide pin
15. Bolt stop pin
16. Bolt stop
17. Bolt stop spring
18. Connector lock
19. Connector lock pin
20. Operating rod guide
21. Operating rod guide pin
22. Barrel band
23. Gas cylinder
24. Spindle valve pin
25. Spindle valve
26. Spindle valve spring
27. Piston
28. Gas cylinder lock
29. Gas cylinder Plug
30. Castle nut
31. Front sight set screw
32. Front sight
33. Castle nut set screw
34. Flash suppressor
35. Operating rod spring guide
36. Operating rod spring
37. Operating rod
38. Buttplate assembly
39. Buttplate wood screw
40. Buttplate machine screw
41. Rear swivel
42. Stock liner screw
43. Stock liner
44. Stock
45. Trigger & sear assembly
46. Hammer spring housing
47. Hammer spring
48. Hammer spring plunger
49. Hammer
50. Trigger housing
51. Safety spring
52. Trigger pin
53. Safety
54. Trigger guard
55. Hammer pin
56. Magazine catch
57. Magazine catch spring
58. Magazine catch pin
59. Handguard
60. Front swivel with rivet & washer
61. Front ferrule
62. Handguard clip

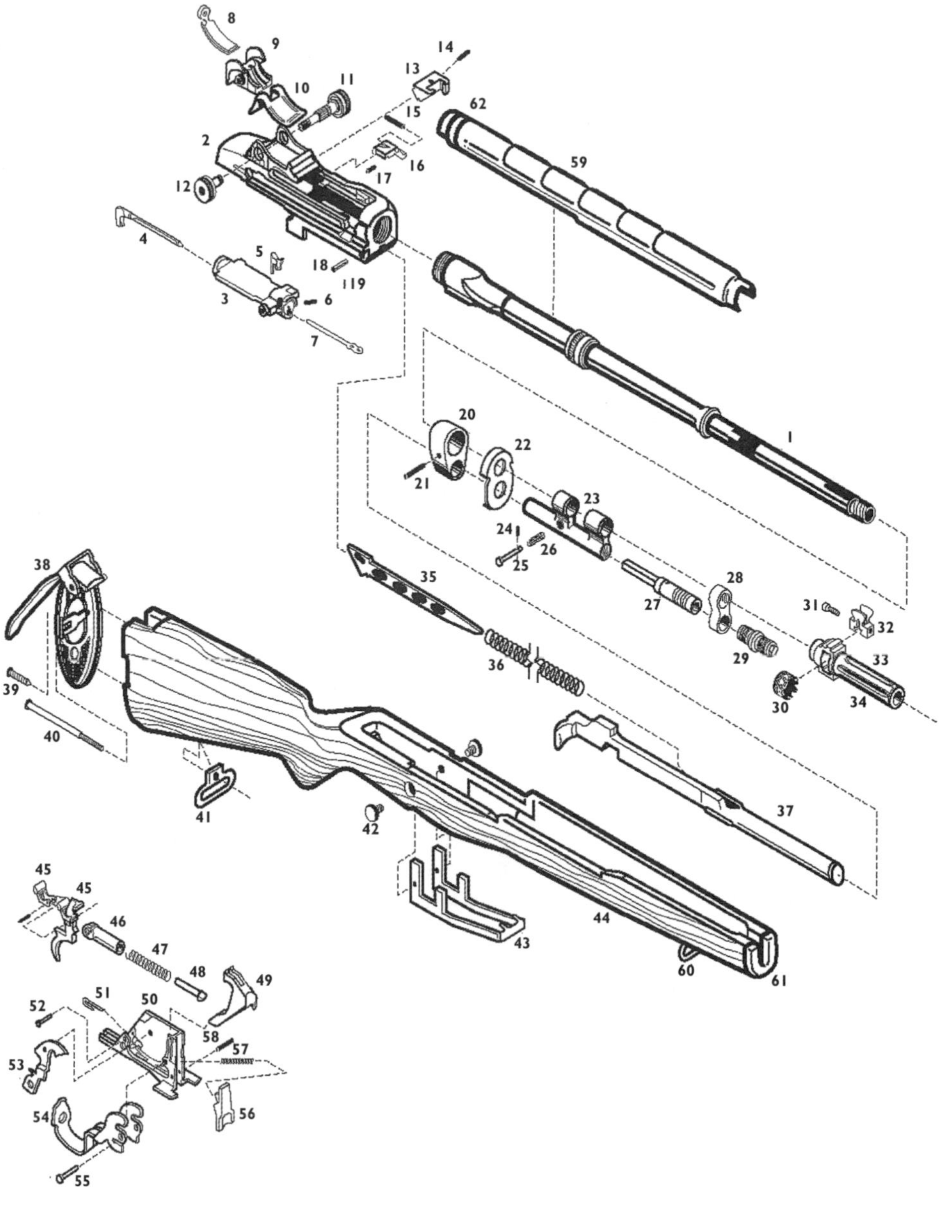

SPRINGFIELD

The M1A1 rifle is manufactured by Springfield Armory Inc. of Geneseo, Illinois. It is a civilian version of the United States military M14 rifle. Despite the name, the Springfield Armory, Inc. is not associated with the federal Springfield Armory in Massachusetts which closed in 1968. Springfield Armory, Inc. was founded in Devine, Texas by Elmer C. Balance who sold the firm and the rights to manufacture the "M1A" to Bob Reese in 1974. Springfield Armory currently offers a variety of M14 pattern rifles including National Match models with glass-bedded receivers and heavy match grade barrels.

First manufactured by Springfield in 1974, the M1A1 is designed for semi-automatic fire only and cannot be modified to fully-automatic. Springfield Armory M1A1 rifles are nearly identical to the M14 but the M1A1's receiver is manufactured by investment casting unlike the drop-forged receivers of the M14s. M1A1s produced by the Springfield Armory retained the M14's cutout for the selector until the late 1990s. In 1994 the passage of the Assault Weapons Ban outlawed bayonet attachments on new manufactured civilian firearms and the M1A1 is no longer produced with a bayonet lug.

M1A1 Rifles are available with fiberglass or walnut stocks. The rifles are chambered for 7.62mm caliber NATO (.308 Win.) ammunition with 10-Round Box magazines. The M1A1's average a little more than 9 lbs. in weight.

DISASSEMBLY

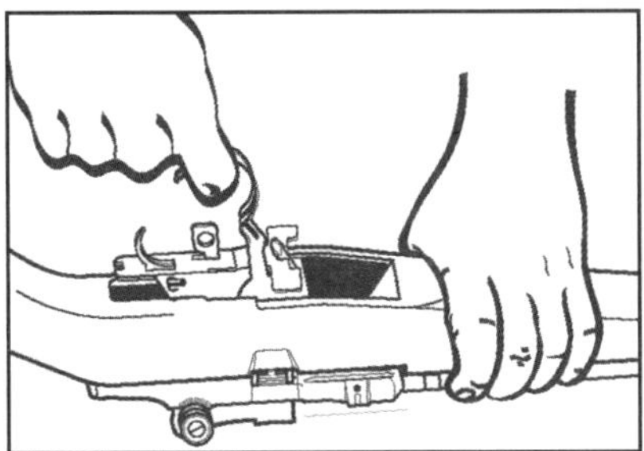

1 Be sure that the rifle is unloaded, remove the magazine and close the bolt by pulling back on the operating rod handle to allow the bolt to close. To remove the trigger-housing group (50), place the rifle upside down. Hold the fore-end with your left hand. Grasp the rear of the trigger guard with the thumb and forefinger of your right hand and pull upward and outward until the mechanism is released and lift out the trigger housing group.

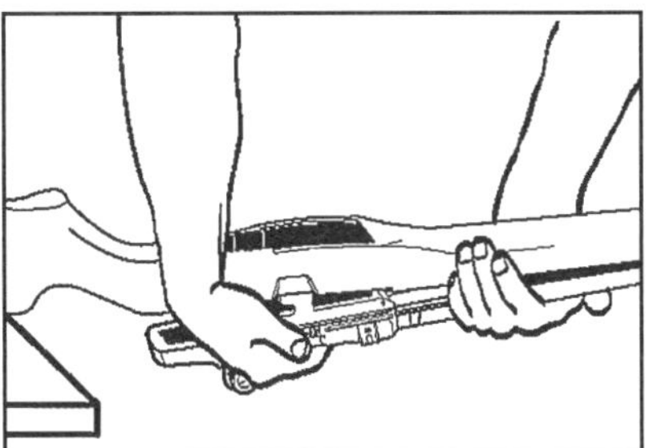

2 To remove the barrel and receiver from the stock, lay the rifle on a flat surface with the sights down and muzzle to the left. Grasp the top (handguard 59) of the fore-end with the left hand and with right hand grasp the rear sights/receiver and pull down.

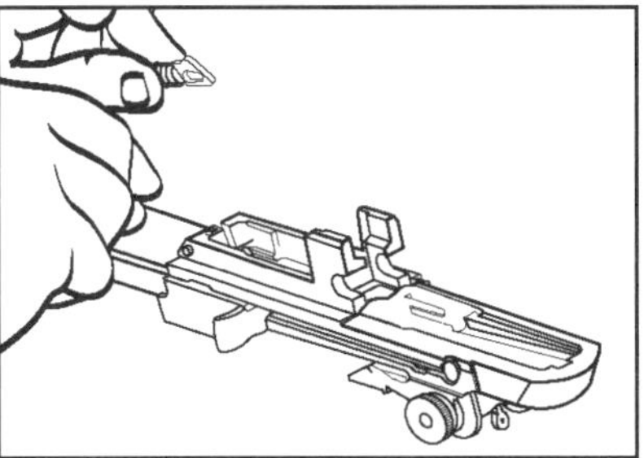

3 Disassembly of barrel and receiver group: CAUTION: The operating rod spring (36) is under tension and will eject the operating spring guide (35). To remove the operating rod spring and Operating rod spring guide, place the barrel and receiver group on a flat surface, sights down, muzzle to the left. With your left hand, pull toward the muzzle on the operating rod spring and spring guide to relieve pressure on the connector lock (18). With your right forefinger pull the connector lock toward the operating rod handle side of the rifle. Allowing the operating rod spring to expand slowly, disconnect and remove the operating rod spring and operating rod spring guide. Separate these two parts.

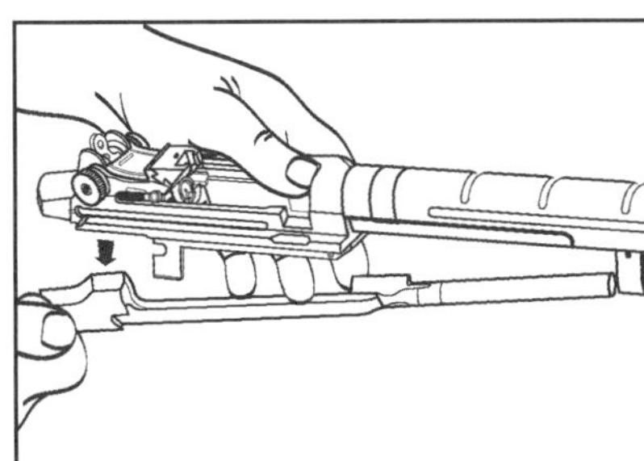

4 To remove the operating rod: Turn the barrel and receiver group so the sights are up and the muzzle is pointing away from you. Pull back the operating rod handle until the guide lug in its inside surface is aligned with the disassembly notch on the right side of the receiver. Rotate the operating rod upward and outward, then pull it to the rear disengaging it from the operating rod guide.

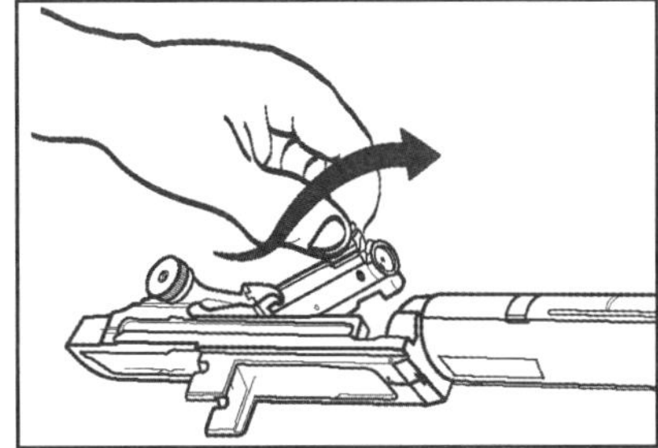

5 To Removing the bolt: Grasp the bolt roller (3) and, while sliding it forward, lift it upward and outward to the right front with a slight counterclockwise rotating motion.

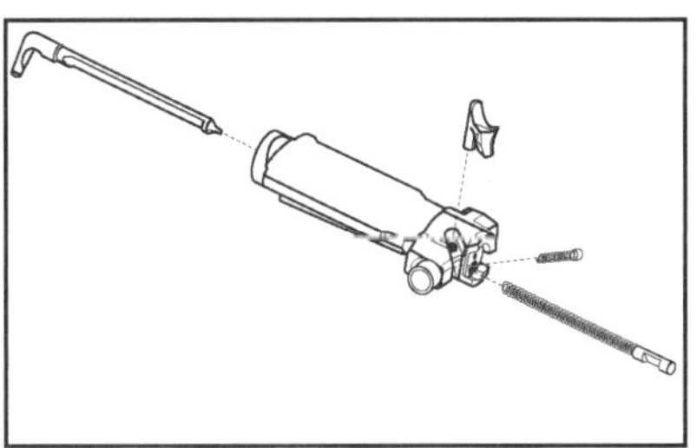

6 Exploded view of bolt. The bolt requires a special disassembly tool and should only be disassembled by a trained gunsmith.

STEVENS NO. 26 CRACK SHOT RIFLE

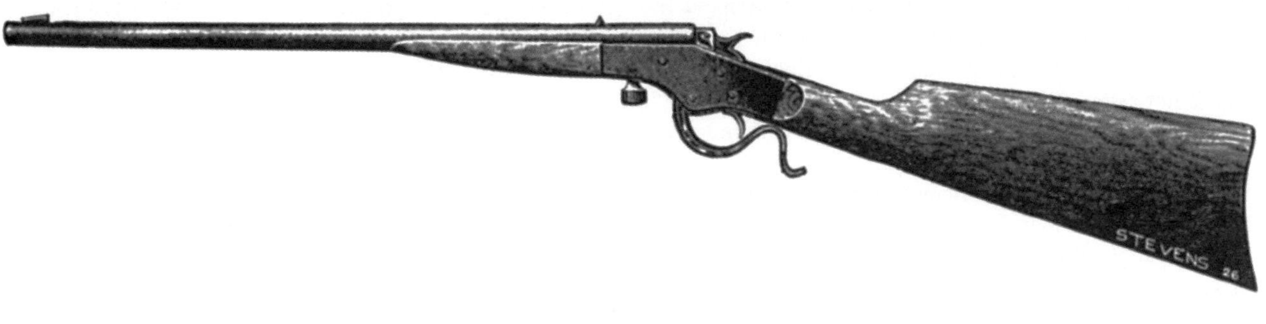

PARTS LEGEND

(Early Version)
1. Hammer
2. Mainspring
3. Main spring plunger
4. Main spring plunger guide
5. Firing pin
6. Firing pin retainer
7. Trigger screw
8. Hammer screw
9. Finger lever lock screw
10. Lock screw roller
11. Breechblock screw
12. Breechblock
13. Extractor
14. Extractor retainer pin
15. Extractor plunger
16. Extractor plunger spring
17. Barrel
18. Barrel lug
19. Rear sight
20. Front sight
21. Receiver
22. Fore-end
23. Fore-end screw
24. Fore-end screw escutcheon
25. Finger lever
26. Finger lever pin
27. Take-down screw
28. Trigger
29. Trigger spring
30. Stock bolt
31. Stock bolt nut
32. Buttstock
33. Buttplate
34. Buttplate screws (2)

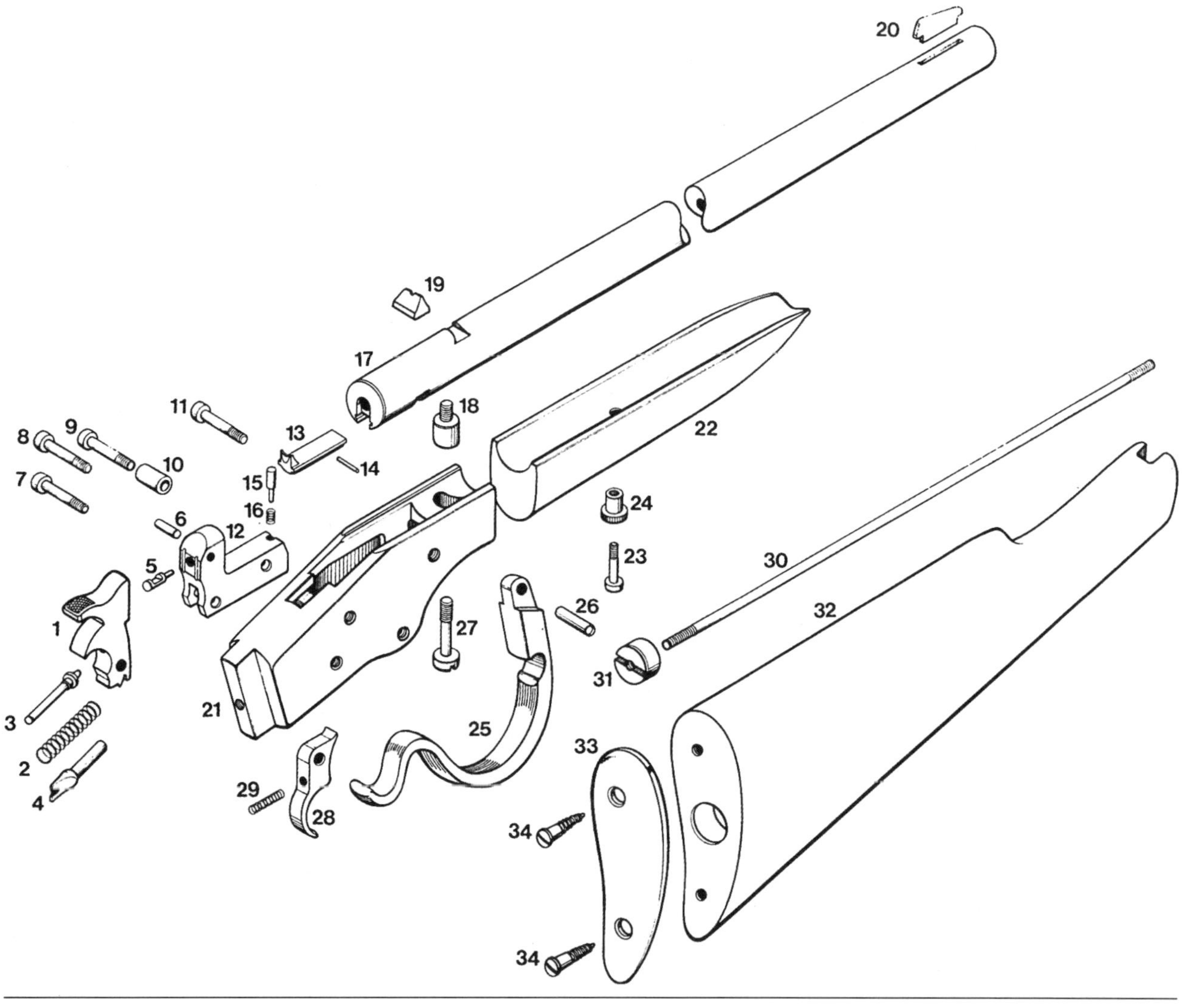

STEVENS

When the J. Stevens Arms Co., introduced its No. 26 Crack Shot rifle in 1913, it had already used and discontinued the Crack Shot name on rifles with break-open ("tip-up"), and rolling block mechanisms; it was to use it finally, in one-word form, for the relatively expensive dropping block Savage/ Stevens Model 72 Crackshot rifle of 1972.

The No. 26 Crack Shot of 1913 became one of the most popular "boys rifles" of its day and was first made with an 18-inch round barrel chambered for either the .22 Long Rifle or .32 Long rimfire cartridge. Its blued, malleable iron action was fitted with a swinging breech operated by an open under-lever. Its smoothbored running mate, the No. I 26 ½, was used with .22 or .32 rimfire shotshells and was often referred to as a "rat gun."

By 1924 the barrels were lengthened to 20 inches ; in 1931 the rifle was also being cataloged in .25 Stevens rimfire caliber, and in the next year all barrels were listed in 22-inch length.

The .25 caliber version was dropped around 1937 when the receiver came to be color-casehardened, and the 1939 catalog introduced the Nos. 26 and 26½ with larger fore-ends, pistol-gripped stocks, adjustable sights and pins replacing the receiver screws. None of the Nos. 26 or 26½ was serial numbered, and the last few were sold in 1943.

DISASSEMBLY

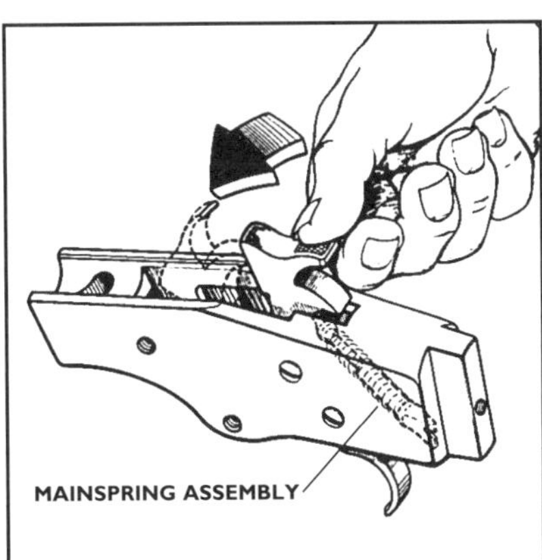

Lower the finger lever and check the chamber to ensure that the gun is not loaded and is safe to service. Unscrew the buttplate screws (34) and remove the buttplate (33). Remove the stock nut (31). (This may require a spanner type blade if the stock bolt protrudes through the nut.) With the stock nut removed, draw the butt- stock (32) off to the rear and remove the stock bolt (30) from the receiver (21).

Lower the finger lever (25) to disengage the finger lever pin (26) and turn out the take-down screw (27). Separate the barrel and forearm assembly from the receiver. Turn out the fore-end screw (23) to remove the fore-end (22). Drift out the extractor retaining pin (14) and remove the extractor (13) from its recess in the barrel. If required, the barrel lug (18) may be unscrewed. (On later versions this lug may be pressed in a dovetail.)

With the lever (25) partly lowered and the hammer (1) in the half cock position, turn out the finger lever lock screw (9) and remove the roller (10). Unscrew the breechblock screw (11) and remove the lever (25) and breechblock assembly through the top of the receiver. Drift out the firing pin retainer (6) to remove the firing pin (5). (Remove the extractor plunger and its spring (15 & 16) only if repair or replacement is required. This may be accomplished by drifting out the plunger from the bottom side of the breechblock. This operation swages the expanded base through the cylindrical cavity, reducing the diameter of the flared plunger as it is drifted out.)

Pull the trigger (28) and slowly lower the hammer (1) to remove the mainspring, plunger and guide (2, 3 & 4) from the receiver (above left). Both the hammer and trigger (1 & 28) may now be detached by turning out their respective screws (7 & 8). Exercise caution when removing the trigger to avoid accidentally displacing its spring (29).

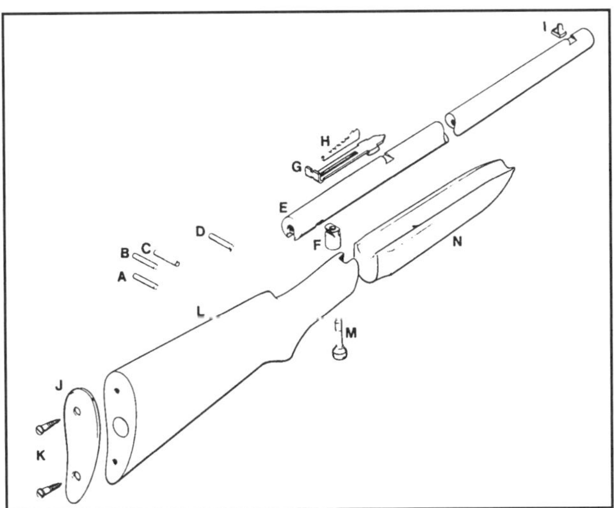

PART LEGEND

(Late Version)
A. Trigger pin
B. Hammer pin
C. Finger lever lock pin
D. Breech block pin
E. Barrel
F. Barrel lug
G. Rear sight
H. Rear sight elevator
I. Front sight
J. Buttplate
K. Buttplate screws (2)
L. Buttstock
M. Takedown screw
N. Fore-end

STEVENS VISIBLE LOADER RIFLE

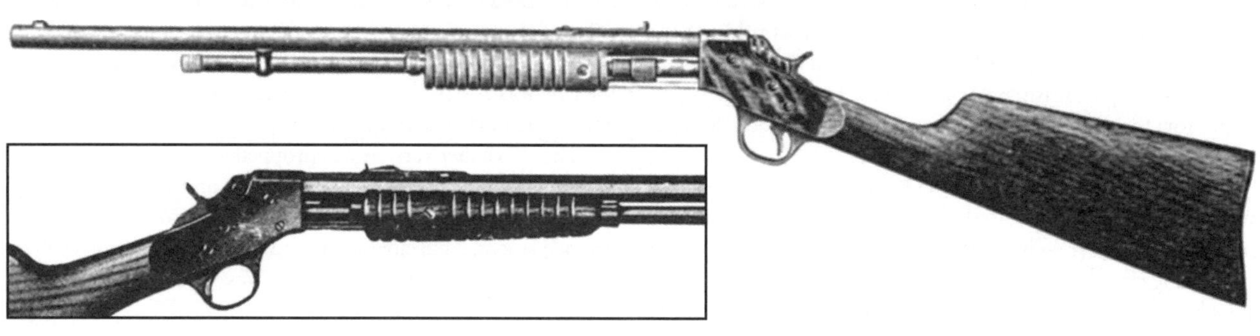

PARTS LEGEND

1. Receiver
2. Stock
3. Breechblock
4. Upper stock screw
5. Lower stock screw
6. Buttplate
7. Buttplate screws (2)
8. Forearm
9. Forearm escutcheons (2)
10. Forearms screws (2)
11. Magazine tube assembly
12. Plug screw
13. Barrel pin screw
14. Barrel pin
15. Outer magazine tube
16. Action bar
17. Action lock
18. Lock seat sleeve
19. Hammer
20. Trigger
21. Mainspring
22. Mainspring shoe
23. Mainspring retainer
24. Hammer strut
25. Hammer or lever post (2)
26. Post screw head (2)
27. Hammer block lever
28. Block lever spring
29. Trigger pin
30. Trigger spring
31. Trigger spring screw
32. Elevator
33. Rear sight
34. Front sight
35. Barrel
36. Front tube ring
37. Rear tube ring
38. Carrier
39. Firing pin
40. Carrier pin
41. Extractor, right
42. Extractor, left
43. Extractor, spring
44. Extractor screws (2)

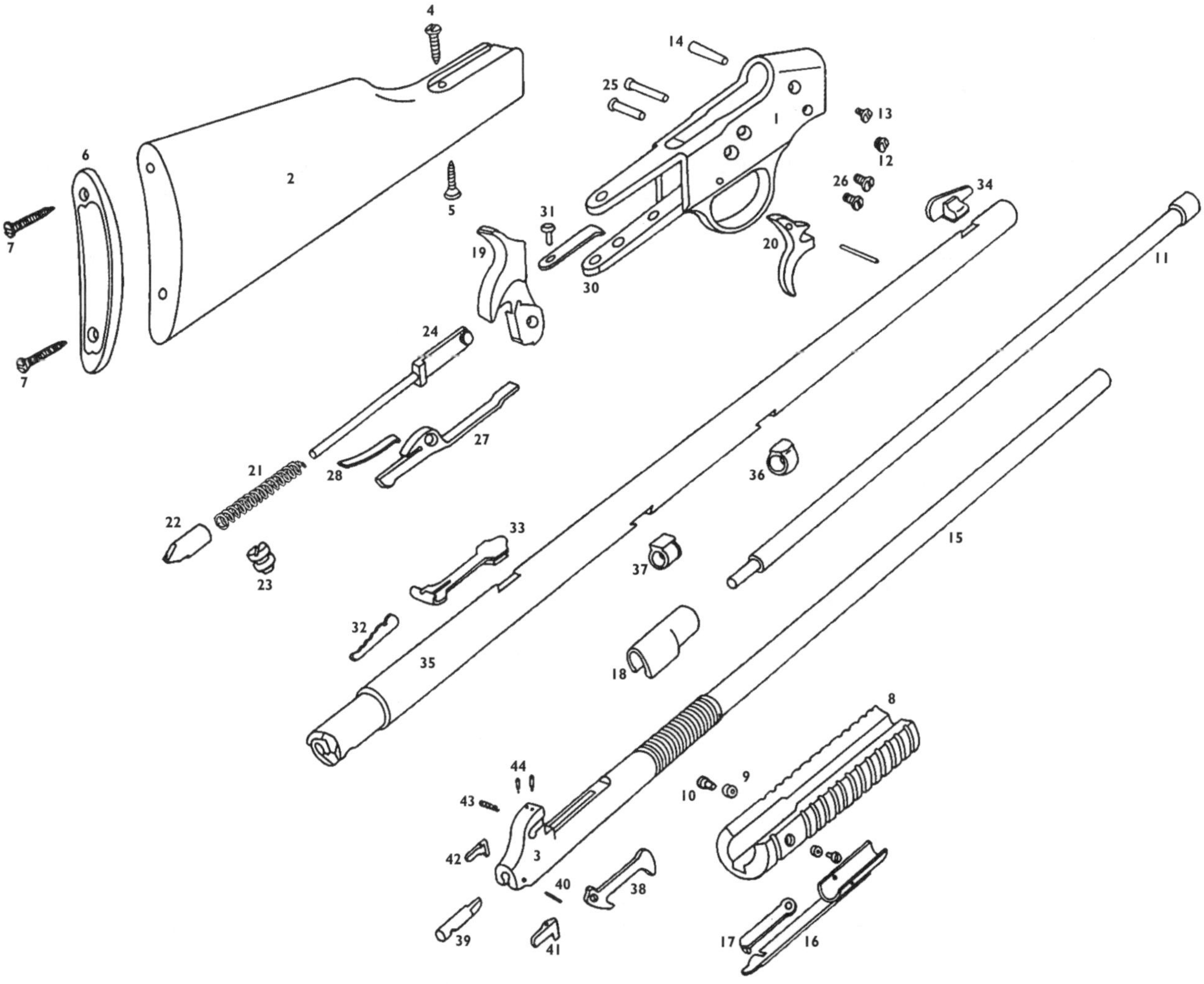

In 1908, the J. Stevens Arms and Tool Co. brought out a novel pump-action .22 rifle, the "Visible Loading Repeater." It was cataloged as the Visible Loading No. 70, and was offered in .22 Short/Long/Long Rifle or .22 Short (Model 70½) versions through Savage's takeover of Stevens begining in 1920.

In the mid-1920s, the rifle's name was changed to "Visible Loader," and so it remained until 1931 when it was replaced with the Visible Loader No. 71 with a pistol-grip stock and 24-inch octagonal barrel. All fired Shorts, Longs and Long Rifles interchangeably, in "regular loadings." Thus modern high speed cartridges should not be used in any of these rifles.

The "visible loading" feature of the rifles is that cartridges are fed straight up from the magazine into the twin extractors on the breech face where they are readily visible. There is no ejector, an empty case is either pushed up and out by the following round or by manual removal.

Perhaps 100,000 rifles were produced over a 26-year span with the last rifle produced in 1934.

DISASSEMBLY

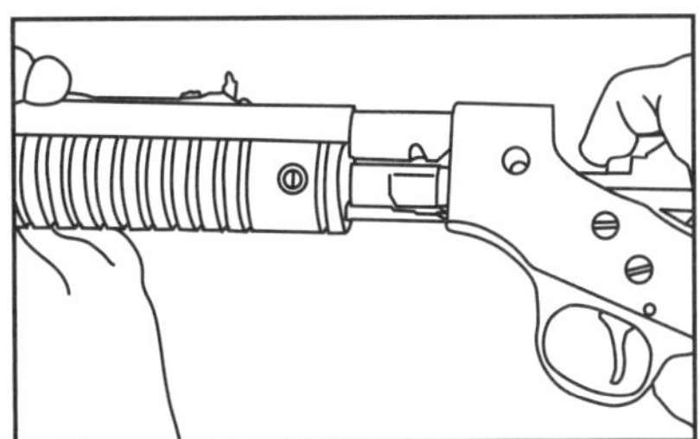

1 Retract the forearm (8) and inspect the open breechblock (3) and inner action area to assure no cartridge is present.

Turn and withdraw the inner magazine tube assembly (11). Remove upper and lower stock screws (4 & 5) from receiver tangs and pull stock to rear.

Remove barrel pin screw (13), and in its cavity place a small punch to drift out the tapered barrel pin (14). Note that the flat of this pin faces down. Firmly hold together the retracted breech-block and receiver in one hand and, with the other, work the barrel forward out of the receiver and off the outer magazine tube (15).

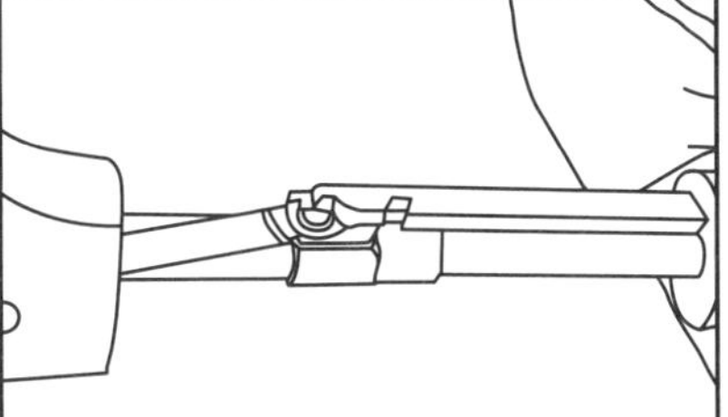

2 With the trigger guard facing up, slowly move the forearm forward to close the breechblock. Note the position and function of the forearm's action bar (16), the action lock (17) under it and the action lock seat (18) that is a sleeve, fine-threaded over the outer magazine tube.

The forearm assembly may now be fully removed. The action lock will drop from its seat. To remove the outer magazine tube/ breechblock assembly, it is necessary to unscrew the action lock seat; around 30 complete turns are required for removal.

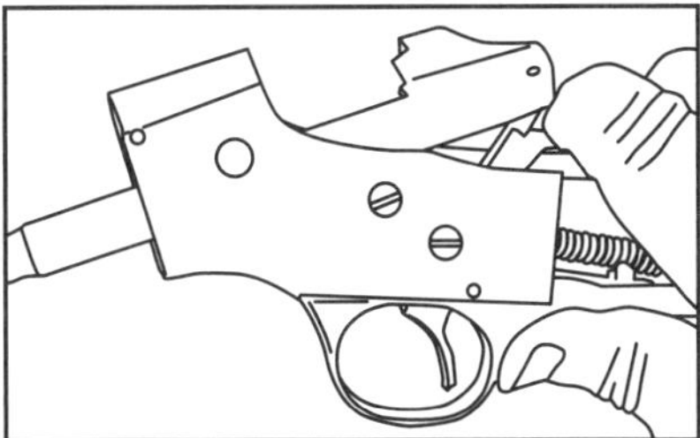

3 After pushing the hammer (19) back fully past the normal cocked position, the breechblock/tube assembly can be angled and slightly rotated back past the hammer and out of the receiver.

Restrain the cocked hammer with the thumb, pull the trigger (20) and allow the hammer to go fully forward.

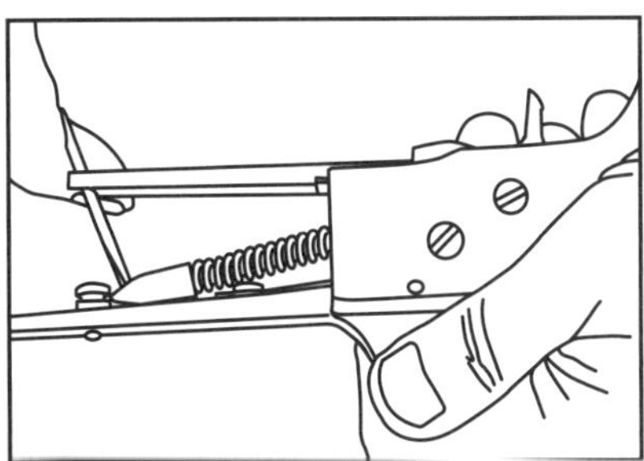

4 Now, with care because of the stored energy of the mainspring (21), insert a thin-bladed screwdriver through the action's upper tang screw hole and pry the main-spring shoe (22) away from the mainspring retainer (23). (Fig. 4) Note the position of the mainspring guide rod assembly, the forward end of which keys into the left rear of the hammer forming the hammer strut (24) A post screw (25) with separate threaded head (26) serves as the hammer pivot and removing it frees the hammer. An identical post screw and head, when removed, frees the hammer block lever (27) and its spring (28).

The trigger pin (29) can now be drifted out and the trigger will fall free. Removal of the trigger spring (30) and its screw (31) are obvious, but will require an offset screwdriver.

If the barrel is to be stripped of its parts, a brass mallet and/or punch is required. With the barrel upright, and muzzle facing forward, remove the rear sight elevator (32) and drive the rear sight (33) and also the front sight (34) from left to right.

With the barrel inverted and muzzle forward, the front (36) and rear (37) magazine tube rings are drifted out from right to left. Note that the beveled edge of the rear ring faces forward.

The breechblock (3) is easily stripped of its parts, but no attempt should be made to remove the thin walled outer magazine tube. With the carrier (38) hanging down, the firing pin (39) may be withdrawn from the block. A punch will remove the carrier pin (40) and the carrier itself.

The right (41) and left (42) extractors are powered by a single coil spring (43) and held in the block by twin screws (44).

Another set of twin screws (10) holds the riveted action bar assembly in the forearm. Their removal completes disassembly..

STEYR MANNLICHER MODEL M

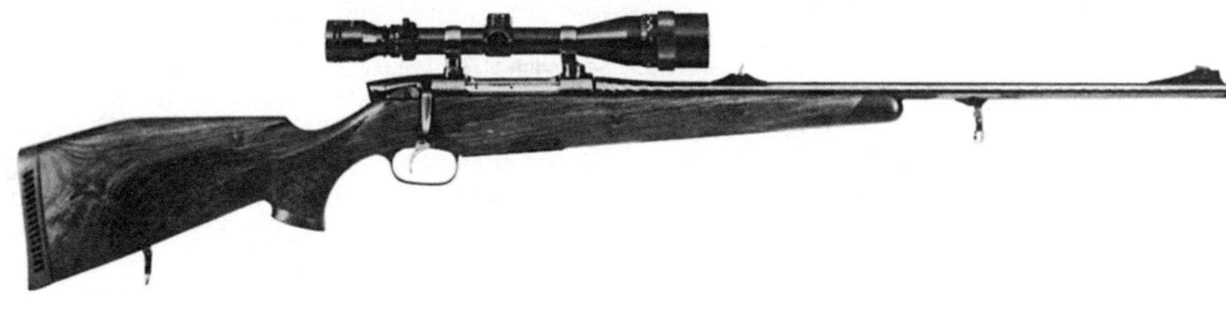

PARTS LEGEND

1. Barrel
2. Front sight ramp
3. Front sight
4. Front sight hood
5. Spring
6. Front sight pin
7. Nut
   7a. Nut
8. Rear sight base
9. Rear sight
10. Rear sight
11. Clamp ring
12. Mainspring
13. Receiver
14. Screw blanking
15. Bolt stop
16. Bolt stop spring
17. Safety catch detent
18. Safety catch detent spring
19. Retaining screw
20. Trigger guard
21. Sear
22. Sear spring
23. Pin
24. Safety catch slide
25. Trigger return spring
26. Slide leaf
27. Trigger housing pin
28. Trigger housing pin
29. Set trigger sear lever
30. Set trigger sear lever pin
31. Circlip
32. Trigger stop pin
33. Trigger pin
34. Trigger housing
35. Adjusting screw
36. Trigger
37. Set trigger
38. Coupling link
39. Internal set trigger spring
40. External set trigger spring
41. Disk
42. Locking screw
43. Trigger pin
44. Insert for set trigger
45. Bolt
46. Bolt handle
47. Bolt handle pin
48. Pin
49. Firing pin
50. Bolt cap
51. Bolt cap pin
52. Spring
53. Locking pin
54. Locking piece
55. Screw blanking
56. Sleeve
57. Disk
58. Circlip
59. Extractor
60. Ejector
61. Ejector spring
62. Spring sleeve
63. Magazine
64. Transparent magazine wall
65. Magazine wall screw
66. Magazine rotor axis pin
67. Magazine follower spring
68. Magazine catch screw
69. Left magazine catch
70. Right magazine catch
71. Magazine carrier
72. Front trigger guard screw
73. Rear trigger guard screw
74. Front bushing
75. Rear bushing
76. Stock

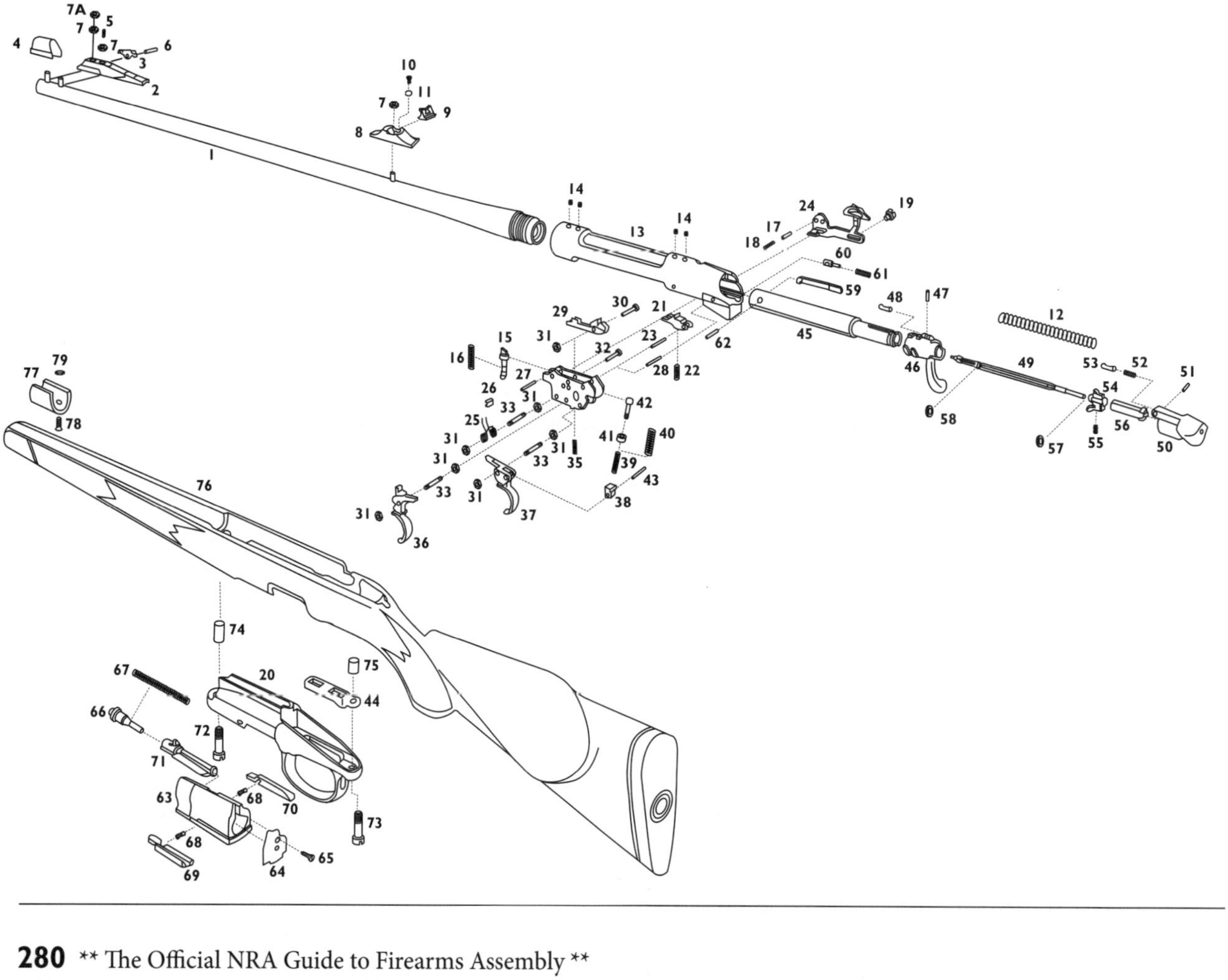

One name stands above all others in the annals of Austrian armsmaking: Ferdinand Ritter von Mannlicher (1848-1903). Mannlicher's talents were second only to those of Paul Mauser in the early years of bolt-action rifle development. He was responsible for such innovations as the *en bloc* clip, the rotary magazine and several turnbolt and straight-pull designs.

Mannlicher teamed up with Otto Schoenauer to produce the Model 1903 rifle, which combined the split-bridge Mannlicher action with a refined, 5-round rotary magazine. The rifle was a failure as a military export arm: only Greece adopted it in 6.5mm. But it had a long and successful career as sporting arm before it was discontinued in 1971.

The Steyr-Mannlicher Model M, introduced in 1967, retained the rotary magazine, but otherwise owed little to earlier Mannlicher designs. The Model M featured a rear-locking turnbolt with a solid bridge. It was offered in 28 different standard, magnum and European calibers, and barrel lengths, and was available with single or double-set triggers. The Model M was manufactured in several different stock designs including a European style full-stocked carbine. The Model M was discontinued in 1996.

DISASSEMBLY

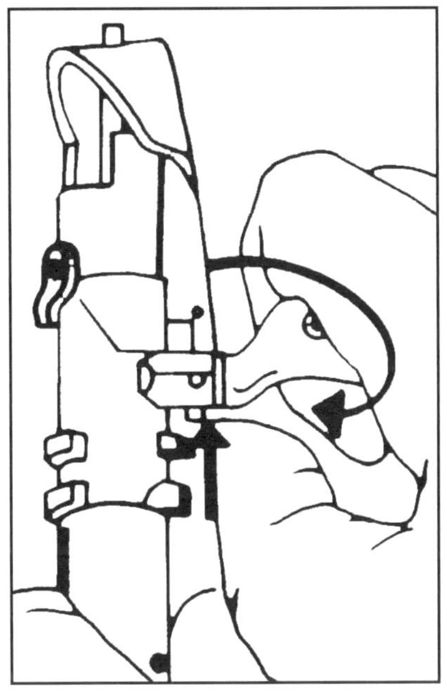

1 Remove the magazine (63) and set it aside. Open the rifle's bolt and insure that no cartridges are present. The barrel/action assembly is detached from the stock by removing the screw (73) at the rear of the trigger guard and a second screw (72) forward of the magazine opening.

To remove the bolt, turn the bolt handle up and to the left at a 60-degree angle and move the bolt to the rear. At the same time, pull the trigger (the forward trigger on double- set trigger guns) and remove the bolt from the action.

Disassembly of the bolt is not necessary under normal conditions, since it is permanently lubricated at the factory. Should disassembly be necessary, start by pressing in the small pin (48) at the base of the bolt handle with the thumb. Then turn the bolt handle clockwise (counterclockwise on left-handed rifles). The locking piece (54) will visibly slide forward along the cocking curve, uncocking the firing pin (49).

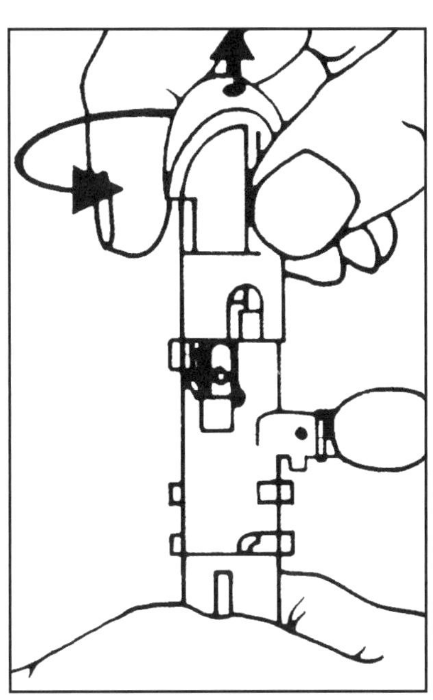

2 The bolt cap (50) can now be turned to the left and removed.

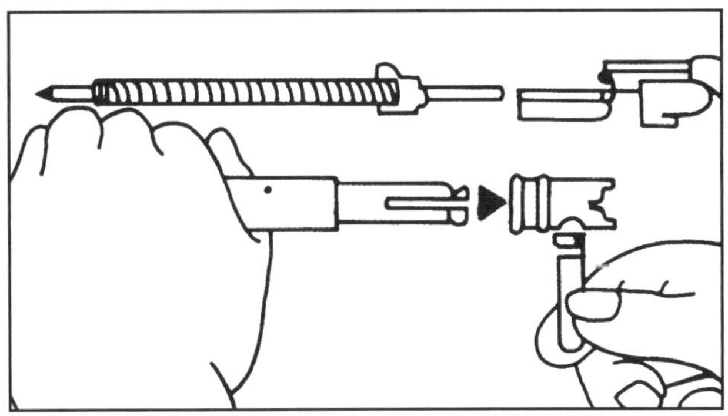

3 The firing pin, bolt handle and locking piece (54) can be removed and the sleeve (56) removed from the firing pin. After cleaning and oiling, reverse the procedure to reassemble the rifle. When replacing the bolt, the bolt handle should point out at about 90 degrees to the rifle and the cocking piece should point straight downward. In this position, the bolt stop snaps automatically into the bolt notch at the bottom of the receiver.

SWISS MODEL 1889 RIFLE

PARTS LEGEND

1. Cocking piece
2. Bolt plug
3. Bolt knob screw
4. Upper bolt knob
5. Bolt cam follower rod
6. Lower bolt knob
7. Knob nut
8. Firing pin spring
9. Firing pin
10. Bolt locking sleeve
11. Bolt
12. Extractor
13. Receiver
14. Sear hinge pin
15. Ejector lock screw
16. Ejector
17. Barrel
18. Bolt stop
19. Bolt stop spring
20. Bolt stop pin
21. Trigger spring
22. Sear arm
23. Trigger pin
24. Trigger
25. Upper handguard
26. Stock
27. Front band
28. Rear band
29. Band screw
30. Trigger and magazine plate
31. Front plate screw
32. Magazine
33. Magazine cut-off
34. Magazine cut-off screw
35. Middle plate screw
36. Rear plate screw
37. Trigger plate screw
38. Trigger guard

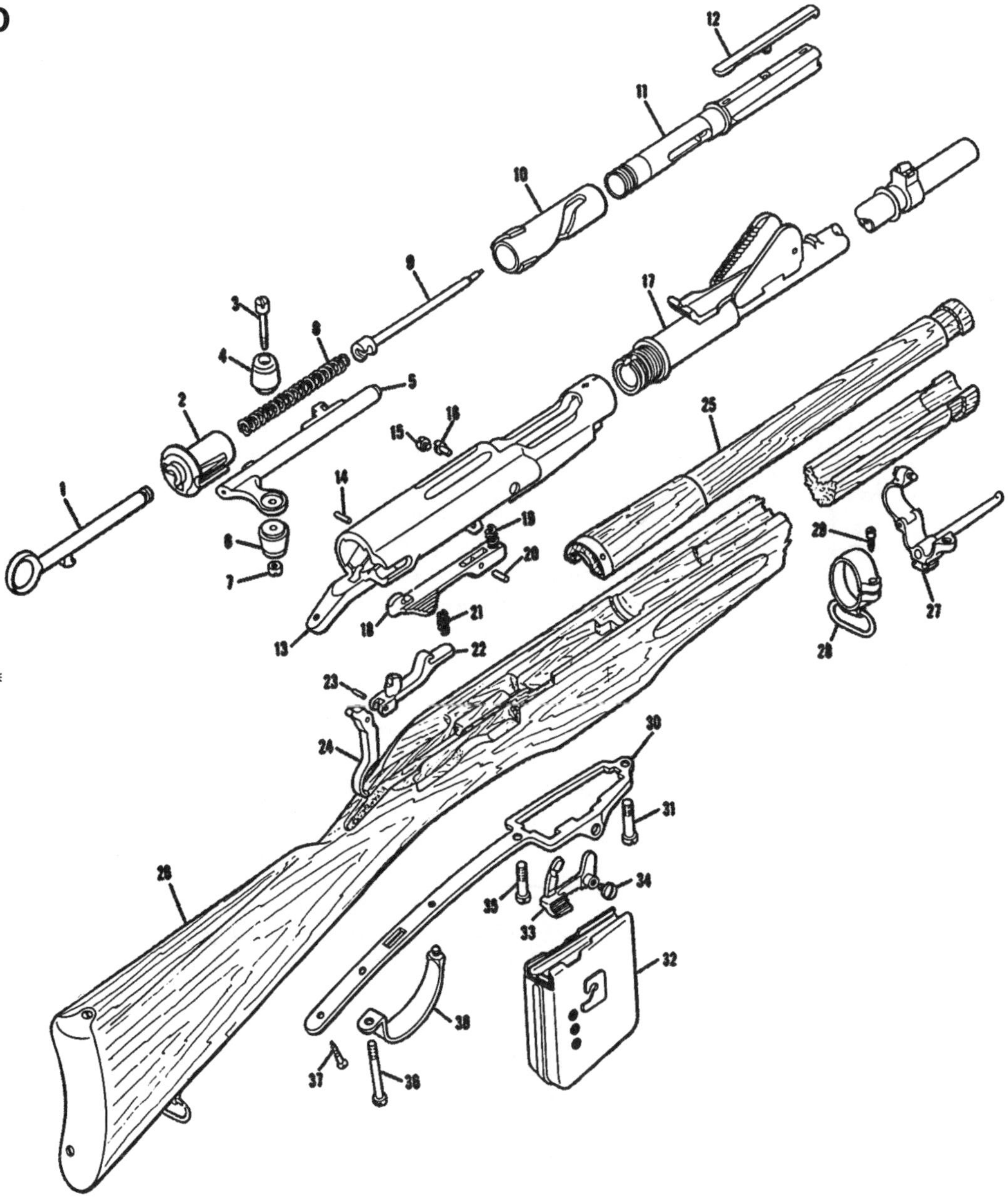

The Swiss adopted their first 7.5mm. Service rifle in 1889. Designated the Swiss Repeating Rifle Model 1889, it was chambered for the Model 90 rimless bottleneck cartridge. The Model 90 cartridge was loaded with a 211-grain, paper-patched, steel-capped, hollow-base lead bullet and a compressed charge of semi-smokeless powder. Muzzle velocity was 1,968 feet per second (f.p.s.). This cartridge was designed by Col. Eduard Rubin, who was Director of the Swiss Federal Ammunition Factory.

Col. Rudolph Schmidt, director of the Federal Arms Factory, was responsible for design of the rifle, which followed the then-accepted ideas of what a military rifle should be. It had a straight-pull action which afforded greater rapidity of fire than was possible with turn-bolt action designs then current. It had a magazine cut-off so that it could be fired by single loading, with the full magazine of 12 rounds held in reserve.

The Model 1889 Schmidt-Rubin's straight-pull design is by far the longest and clumsiest of any military rifle. The receiver is about 1⅓ times as long as that of the Model 98 Mauser. The Model 1889 rifle underwent a series of design changes in 1896, 1911, and 1931, resulting in a more compact and effective arm. The original cartridge was improved, resulting in the Model 1911 ball cartridge with 174-grain bullet.

DISASSEMBLY

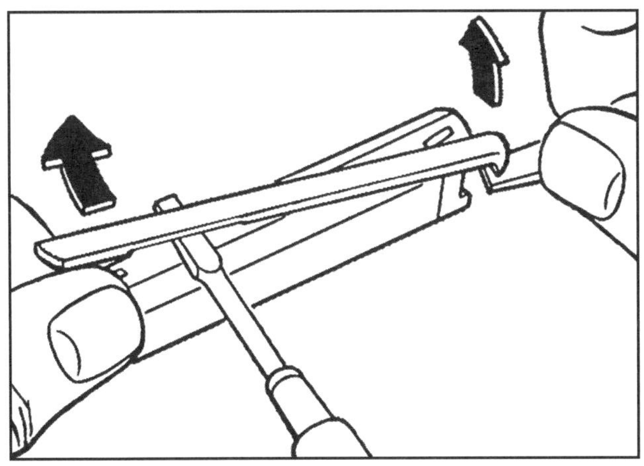

1 To remove bolt, press down on bolt stop (18) and pull bolt free of gun. To remove extractor (12), wedge up extractor tail to free it from its notch in the bolt. Pry up claw and rotate extractor clockwise until it is free of bolt.

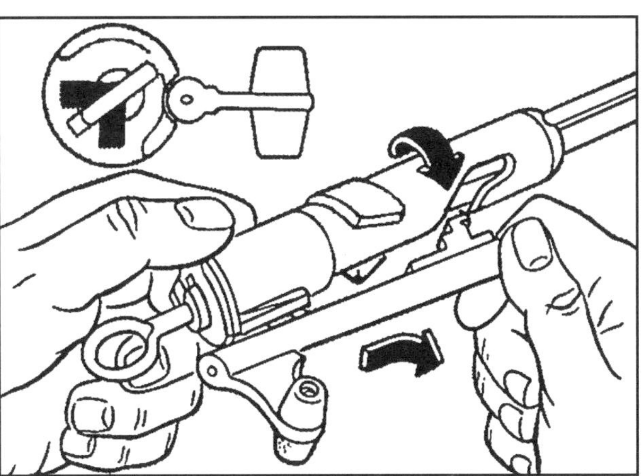

2 To disassemble bolt, pull back cocking piece (1) and bring it to rest between 2 square cutouts in bolt plug (2) as shown. Rotate locking sleeve (10) clockwise until cam rod (5) can be pulled clear of sleeve. Then slide cam rod (5) forward until its rear end is free of dovetail slot in bolt plug (2). Unscrew bolt plug (2) from bolt (11) and remove bolt locking sleeve (10).

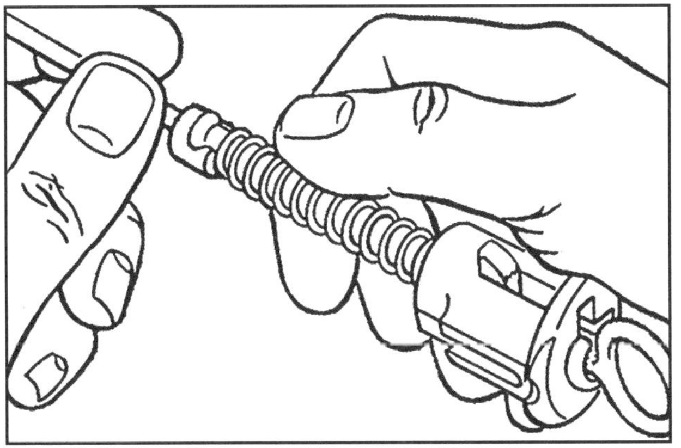

3 The firing pin (9) is retained something like those in the Springfield or Krag. To remove the pin, first be sure cocking piece is all the way forward in its notch. This will relieve firing pin spring (8) tension. Then pull back spring and slide firing pin off cocking piece (1).

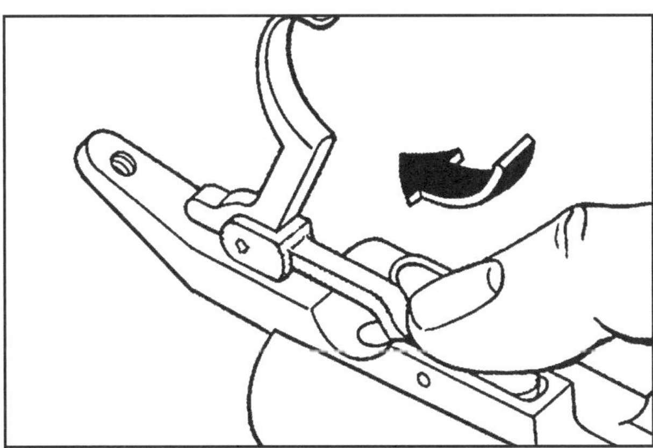

4 To remove the trigger assembly, push sear arm (22) in hard and back as shown, until it can't go any further. Then pull trigger (24) and entire trigger and sear assembly will drop free.

TIKKA T-3 RIFLE

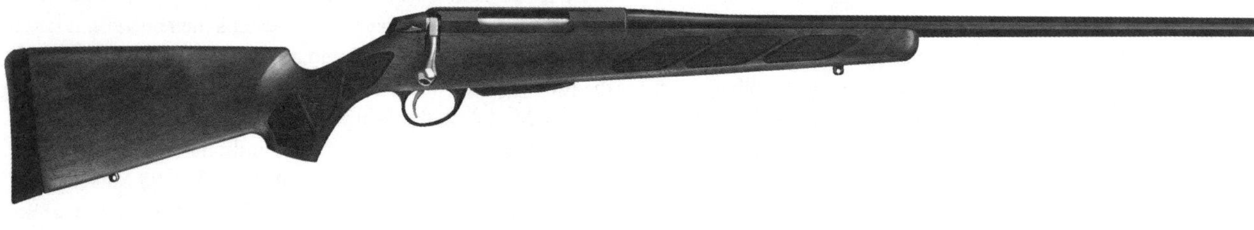

PARTS LEGEND

1. Receiver
2. Barrel
3. Bolt body
4. Stock
5. Trigger mechanism
6. Fastening screw
7. Trigger spring
8. Trigger spring set screw
9. Trigger sear spring
10. Safety lever spring
11. Safety silencer
12. Magazine ejector
13. Set trigger spring
14. Set trigger set screw
15. Firing pin assembly
16. Extractor
17. Extractor plunger
18. Extractor spring
19. Ejector
20. Ejector spring
21. Pin 2.5x6
22. Bolt shroud
23. Bolt handle
24. Bolt release
25. Pin for bolt release
26. Spring for bolt release
27. Trigger guard assembly
28. Magazine catch
29. Magazine catch spring
30. Pin 2x12
31. Magazine
32. Recoil block
33. Recoil pad
34. Mounting screws
35. Straight butt spacer
36. Pistol grip cap
37. Swivel screws
38. Swivels
39. Rear sight base
40. Mounting screw
41. Blade 9.5mm.
41. Blade 12mm.
42. Mounting washer for blade
43. Mounting screw for blade
44. Rear sight base
45. Rear mounting screw for base
46. Front mounting screw for base
47. Blade complete
48. Mounting screws for blade (2)
49. Front sight base
50. Front mounting screw for base
51. Rear mounting screw for base
52. Bead
53. Front sight hood
54. Front fastening screw
55. Rear fastening screw
56. Plug screws for receiver
57. Plug screws for barrel

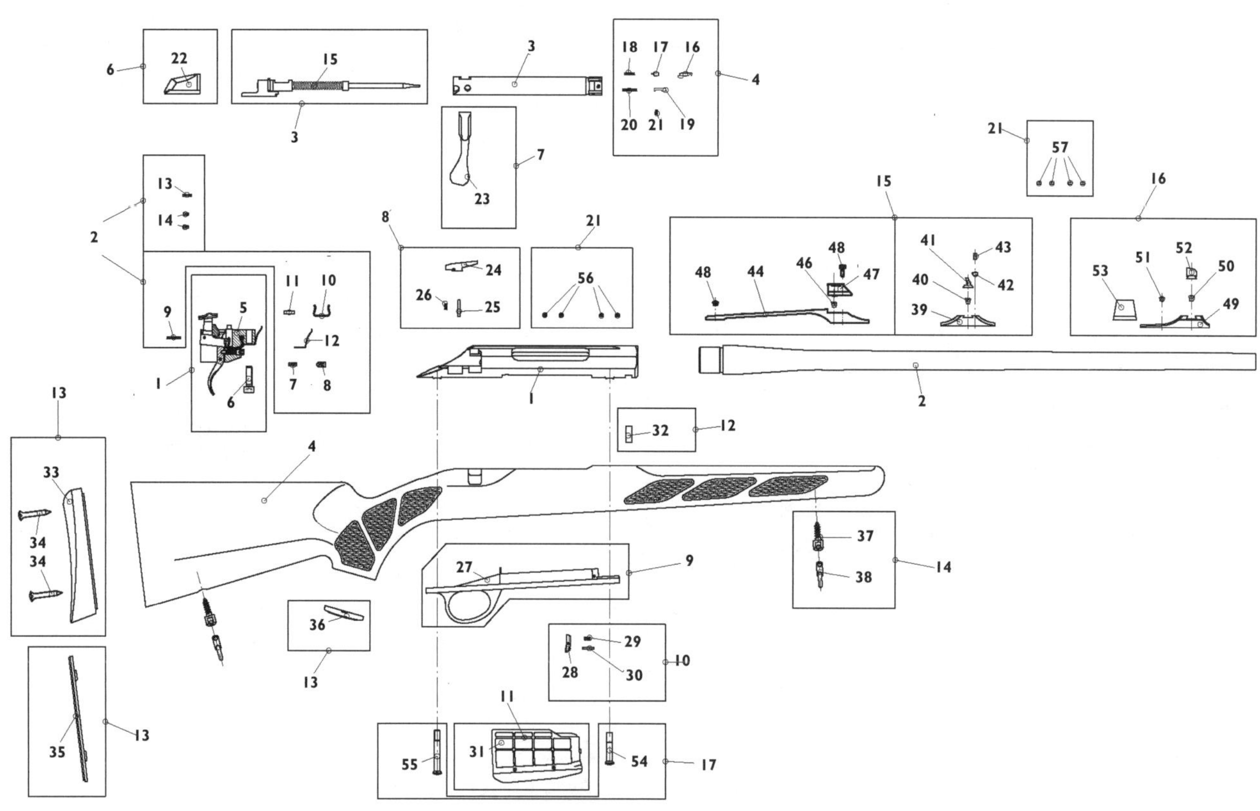

TIKKA

Tikka is a brand of SAKO, Limited, (Suojeluskuntain Ase-ja Konepaja Oy — Civil Guard Gun and Machineworks Ltd.) a firearm manufacturer with factories located in Riihimäki and Jyväskylä, Finland. SAKO, founded in 1927, merged with the state-owned Valmet corpoation of Tourula in 1987 to create SAKO-VALMET. The name was eventually changed to SAKO. The company was aquired by Beretta Holdings in 2000 and Beretta became the sole importer of SAKO and Tikka rifles to the United States.

Imported beginning in 2003, the T-3 was designed by the Italian firm of Giugiaro Design. Part of the "third generation" of Tikka rifles, the T-3 Hunter features a free-floating, cold hammer-forged blued, or stainless barrel, adjustable trigger and detachable polymer magazine that holds anywhere from three to five cartridges depending on caliber. All rifles in the series feature integral scope rails. T-3s come in wood- and synthetic-stocked versions. The rifles are pillar bedded on a recoil lug that is permanently set in the stock. This fits tightly into a groove on the receiver.

T-3 rifles are chambered for: .22-250 Rem, .223 Rem, .243 Win, .25-06 Rem, .270 Win, .270 WSM, .30-06 Sprg, .300 Win Mag, .300 WSM, .308 Win, .338 Win Mag, 6.5mm x 55, 7mm Rem Mag, 7mm-08 Rem. Tikka T-3 versions include the T-3 Hunter and T-3 Lite.

DISASSEMBLY

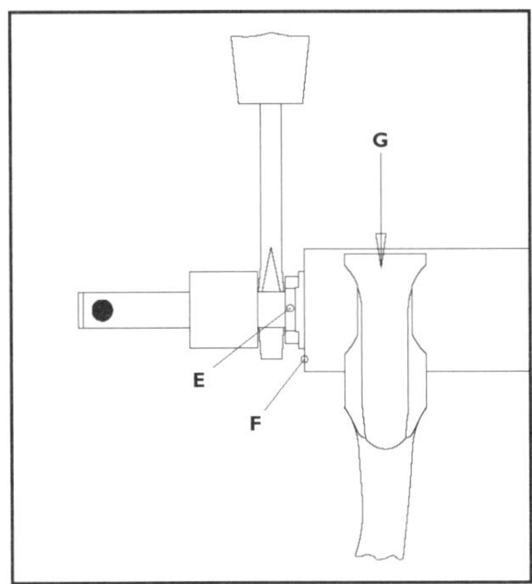

1 Bolt Disassembly and Reassembly: Carefully check that the rifle is unloaded and remove the bolt from the rifle by pressing the bolt-release lever on the left side of the receiver and simultaneously pulling the bolt backwards out of the receiver. Remove the bolt shroud by turning it clockwise until it stops and pulling it away from the bolt.

Insert the tip of a screwdriver (approx. 3mm wide) into the gap between the cocking piece and the bolt handle retainer bushing. IMPORTANT! Do not remove the screwdriver tip from this location until you are ready to reassemble the bolt shroud.

Disengage the firing pin assembly by turning the screwdriver counterclockwise. Push the firing pin assembly forward until the locking cam (E) of the handle retainer bushing touches the bolt's rear surface.

Release the bolt handle from the bolt body. If the bolt handle feels stiff and does not immediately pull out, you can tap it with a plastic mallet at the receiver end (arrow G). Remove the firing pin assembly from the bolt.

The bolt should not require any further disassembly for cleaning purposes. In order to reassemble the bolt after cleaning, reverse the order.

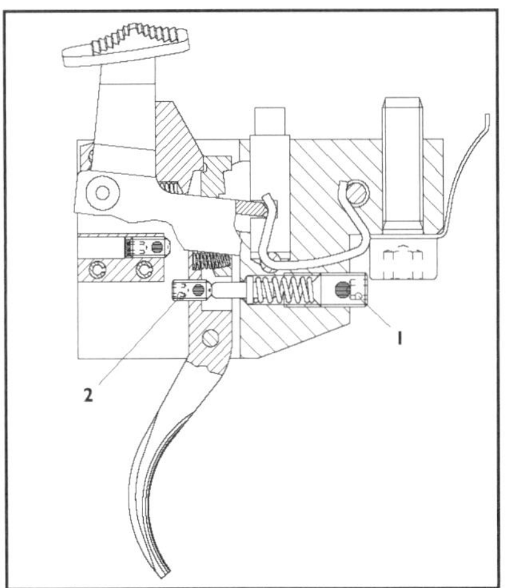

2 Standard Trigger Mechanism: Both the sear engagement and safety are set at the factory and need no adjustment of any kind. CAUTION! The sear engagement, safety and other components of the action are precision mechanisms, which were properly adjusted at the factory. They should not be altered, modified or changed. Modifications to the firearm may decrease its safety and increase the risk of serious injury.

If you alter the trigger pressure, the safest way is to detach the stock first. To do this, remove the trigger guard fastening screws. Trigger pressure can also be adjusted, with a proper tool, through the magazine opening.

Trigger adjustment: The single-stage trigger is adjustable for weight of pull between 2 and 4 lbs. The factory sets the trigger pull at 3 lbs. In order to ensure smooth performance and functioning, you should not increase trigger-pull weight.

Adjust the trigger-pull weight by turning the screw (1) with an Allen wrench. Lighten the trigger by turning counterclockwise. NOTE! Screw (1) is self-locking and can only be turned with a proper tool. NOTE: for safety reasons do not attempt to reduce trigger pressure below 2 lbs. When reassembling the stock, always remember to reinstall the aluminum recoil block into its place in the stock.

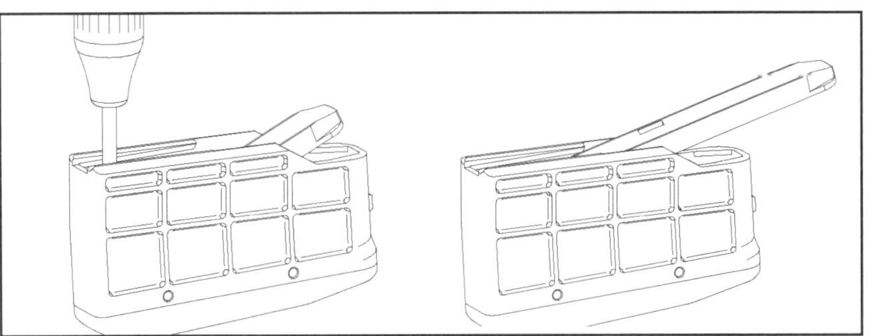

3 Magazine Disassembly & Reassembly: Remove the magazine follower and spring. Depress the rear part of the follower with a screwdriver or a similar tool so that the follower's front end is released. Pull out the follower and spring from the magazine box. Do not detach the magazine floorplate.

TOKAREV MODELS 38 & 40 RIFLES

PARTS LEGEND

1. Front sight
2. Muzzle extension
3. Gas regulator
4. Muzzle extension key
5. Gas cylinder
6. Gas piston
7. Piston rod
8. Piston rod extension
9. Piston spring
10. Bolt cover
11. Bolt carrier
12. Extractor
13. Extractor plunger
14. Extractor spring
15. Bolt
16. Firing pin retainer
17. Firing pin spring
18. Firing pin
19. Rear spring guide
20. Rear recoil spring
21. Middle spring guide
22. Forward recoil spring
23. Barrel and receiver
24. Hold-open latch
25. Hold-open latch spring
26. Ejector
27. Disconnector
28. Ejector pin
29. Trigger guard latch plunger
30. Detent spring
31. Detent
32. Plunger lock
33. Trigger guard latch pin
34. Trigger guard latch
35. Trigger guard latch spring
36. Buttstock
37. Split cross pin
38. Forestock
39. Upper handguard
40. Piston cover
41. Front band
42. Rear band
43. Cleaning rod
44. Magazine
45. Hammer
46. Hammer spring guide
47. Hammer spring
48. Sear
49. Trigger bar
50. Trigger
51. Trigger spring
52. Disconnector operated sear
53. Sear spring
54. Magazine catch spring
55. Magazine catch
56. Magazine catch an sear pins (2)
57. Trigger spring and trigger pins (2)
58. Safety catch
59. Trigger guard
60. Spring cover
61. Safety catch detent
62. Detent spring

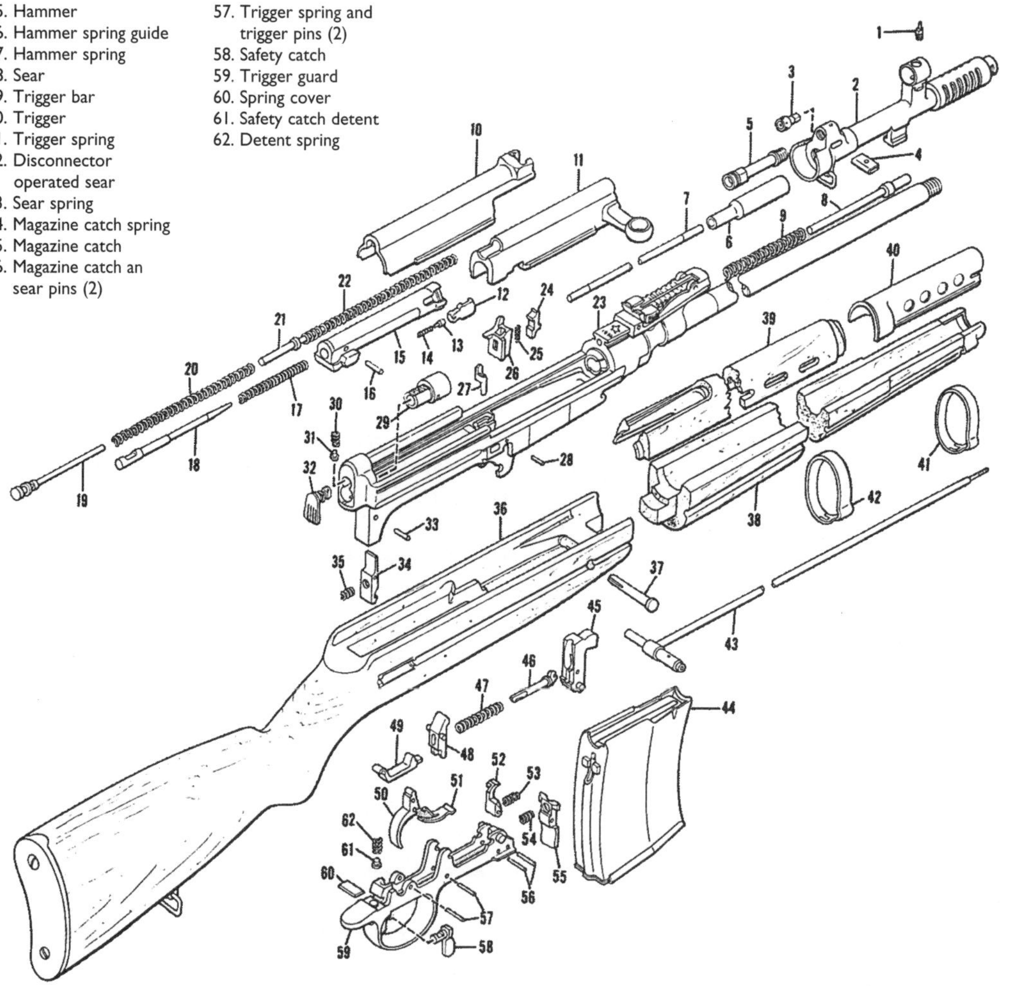

Russia adopted the Tokarev Model 38 semi-automatic rifle in 1938. It replaced the Simonov Model 1936 rifle which had proved unsatisfactory. The Russo-Finnish War of 1940 found the Model 38 wanting and it was slightly modified to become the Model 40. The rifle was shortened and made about ¼ lb. lighter and the 2-piece stock was replaced by a one-piece type. Most parts were interchangeable between the two rifles. A selective-fire model and a carbine were also produced.

The Tokarev rifles contained a number of interesting features. The gas port is adjustable allowing the rifleman to compensate for the varying weather conditions and the uneven quality of Soviet wartime ammunition.

The Tokarevs were manufactured with fluted chambers, a number of thin longitudinal grooves cut into the forward part of the chamber to allow some gas from the cartridge to enter the flutes and aid in preventing stuck cases.

In spite of clever design features, considerable difficulty was experienced in the repair and maintenance of these weapons during World War II. They were dropped during the latter part of the war and replaced by the old but reliable bolt-action rifle.

DISASSEMBLY

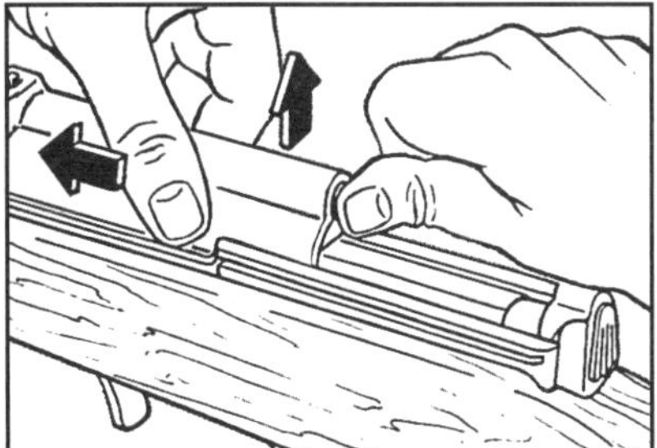

1 To field strip the Tokarev, remove the magazine (44), and retract the bolt fully to cock the hammer and clear the chamber. Next, pull the bolt cover (10) as far forward as it will go. Place the thumb over end of the rear spring guide (19) and while holding it forward, lift bolt cover from receiver. Ease rear spring guide to rear and at same time elevate its rear end and withdraw recoil spring assembly (19), (20), (21), (22) from bolt carrier (11). Removal of this assembly is eased if the forward recoil spring (22) is pulled hard to the rear as the assembly is withdrawn from the bolt carrier.

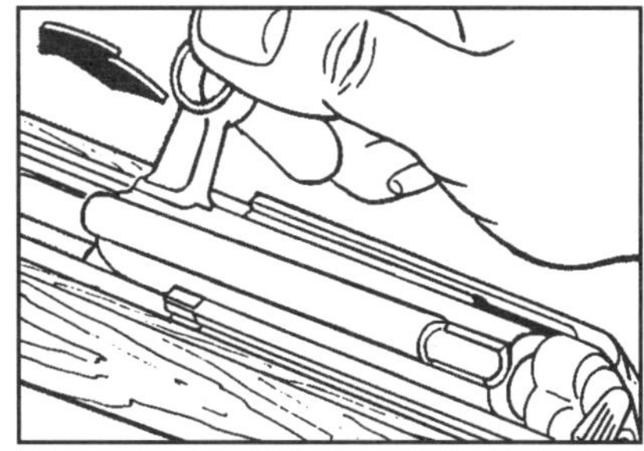

2 To remove the bolt assembly, pull bolt carrier all the way to the rear. Then, while lifting upward on handle, ease bolt carrier forward until it unlocks from receiver. Withdraw bolt carrier forward and free of receiver. Remove the bolt (15) from the bolt carrier.

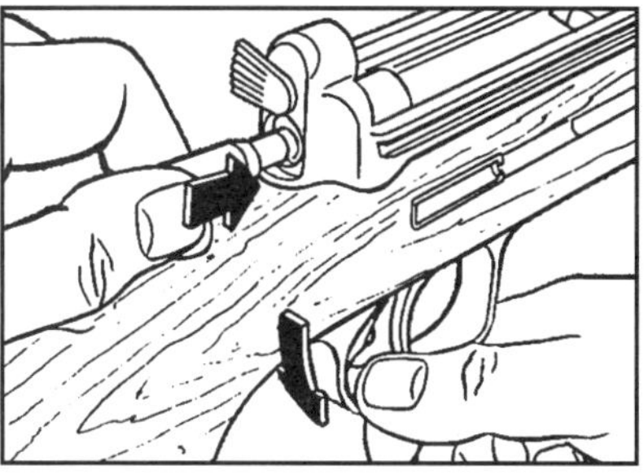

3 To remove the trigger guard assembly, rotate the serrated plunger lock (32) ¼-turn clockwise. Then, with a screwdriver or cartridge push trigger guard latch plunger (29) in as far as possible until it releases the rear of the trigger guard (59). Pull downward on trigger guard loop and withdraw trigger guard assembly from rifle. Lock mechanism should be removed prior to removing trigger guard assembly from rifle.

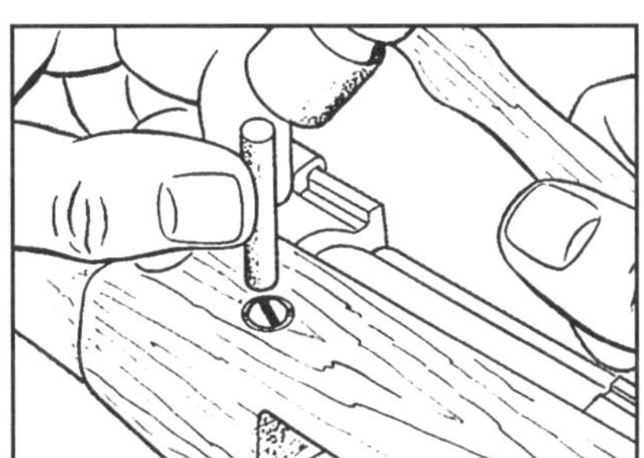

4 To disassemble barrel and receiver from stock, remove barrel bands, upper handguards, and cleaning rod. Cleaning rod of Model 38 rifle is released by inserting bullet tip in rear end of handle and pushing forward until handle plunger is released from its detent. Lift rod handle upward and withdraw rod clear of rifle. In Model 38 rifle the barreled action is retained by a split cross pin (37) which is removed by drifting it out from left to right. Cross pin in Model 40 rifle is a screw removed from right side of stock. Seperate barreled action from stock. Fore-stock portion of the Model 38 rifle stock must be pulled to rear slightly to free it from barrel.

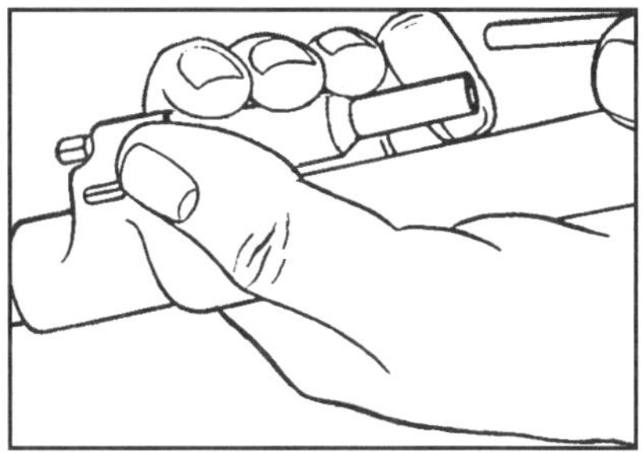

5 To disassemble operating rod assembly, hold gas piston (6) forward and pull piston rod (7) to rear until its upper end clears gas piston. Swing piston rod aside and withdraw it and accompanying piston rod extension (8) and piston spring (9) from its seat. Gas piston can now be pulled down and off gas cylinder (5).

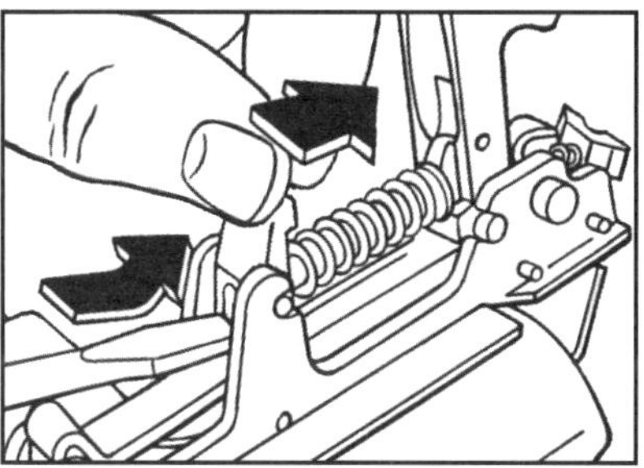

6 To disassemble the trigger mechanism, the hammer (45) must be uncocked. First, push down on the disconnector sear (52) until it clicks, and pull the trigger. To remove the sear (48), first clamp the trigger guard in a vise. Grasp the upper portion of the sear and push the lower end with a large screwdriver. Push the sear out and forward against the hammer spring (47) until it is free of its seat in the guard. Reassemble in the same manner. Use a Russian 7.62mm cartridge to retain the recoil spring assembly in forward position when replacing the bolt cover. Push the bolt carrier assembly all the way forward and slip a cartridge between receiver abutment and end of rear spring guide (19). Fit bolt cover (10) over the rear spring guide.

U.S. KRAG MODEL 1896 RIFLE

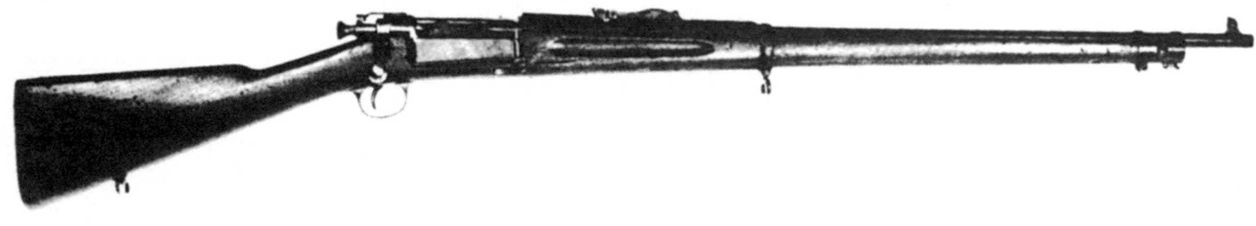

PARTS LEGEND

A. Firing pin assembly
B. Safety lock
C. Sleeve
D. Extractor rivet
E. Extractor
F. Mainspring
G. Striker
H. Bolt
I. Bolt assembly
J. Cutoff
K. Side-plate screw
L. Side-plate
M. Ejector
N. Ejector pin
0. Barrel and receiver assembly
P. Hinge bar
Q. Gate
R. Magazine spring
S. Carrier and follower assembly
T. Sear spring
U. Sear
V. Trigger pin
W. Trigger
X. Front band
Y. Carbine stock Mod. 1896 ass'y
Z. Handguard

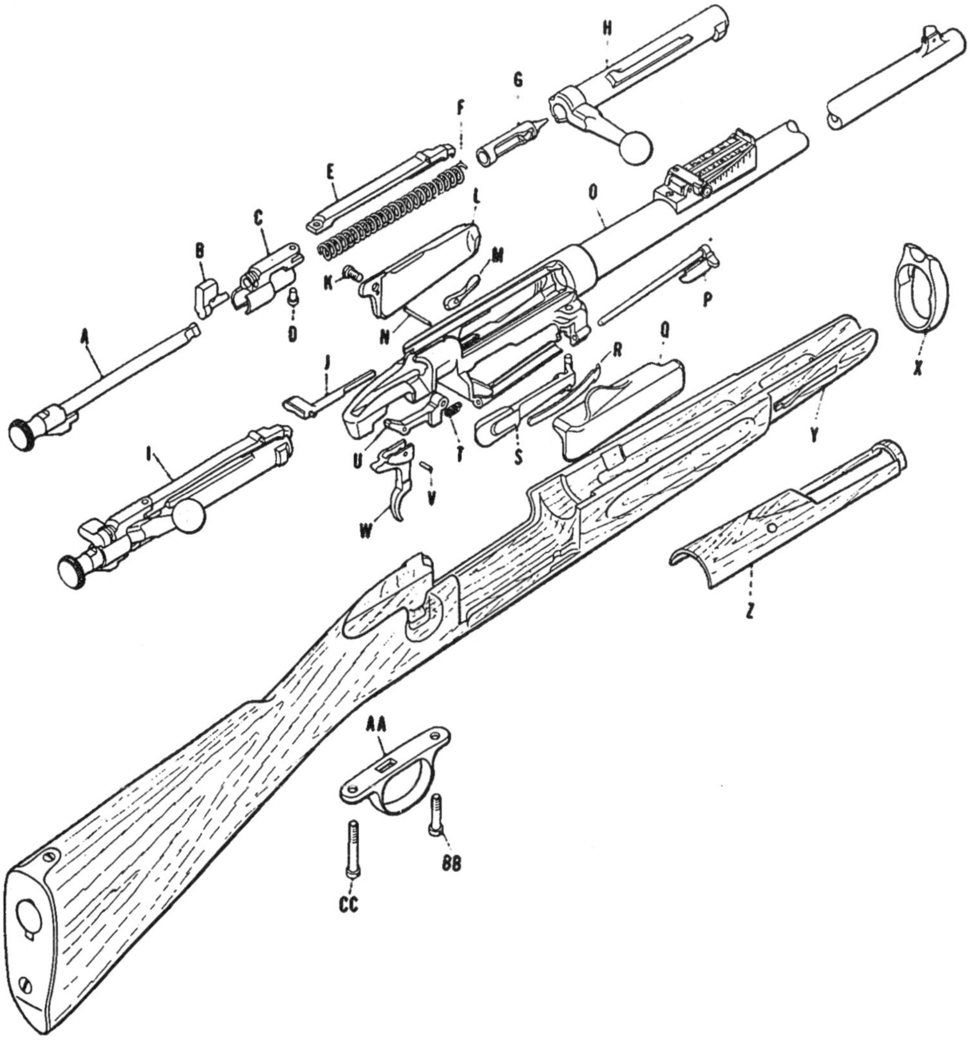

The Krag-Jorgensen rifle, adopted by the Army in 1892, was the first U.S. service arm designed for smokeless powder. The Krag-Jorgensen, familiarly known as the Krag, was a joint development of Captain Ole H. J. Krag and Erik Jorgensen, both Norwegians. Military rifles of their design had been adopted by Denmark in 1889 and Norway in 1894.

Production of the Model 1892 Krag rifle was instituted at Springfield Armory, and the first issue of rifles was made in the fall of 1894. The Service cartridge for these rifles, designated the .30 caliber U. S. Army (.30-40 Krag), was a rimmed type, loaded with a 220-grain round-nose bullet.

The new Krag was not well received by the Army. Early manufacture ammunition was inaccurate, and the quality of early barrels was erratic. The Krag rifle was modified in 1896 and again in 1898. During this period Springfield Armory produced 3 Krag carbines, the Models 1896, 1898, and 1899.

The Krag gave a good account of itself in the Spanish-American War, Philippine Insurrection, and the Boxer Rebellion and later proved popular with sportsmen. The Army, however, felt the need for a magazine system which would eliminate the necessity of handling loose rounds.

Several attempts were made to adapt the Krag for charger loading, but none was successful. The Krag was abandoned in favor of a clip-loaded Mauser-type rifle, the Model 1903 Springfield.

DISASSEMBLY

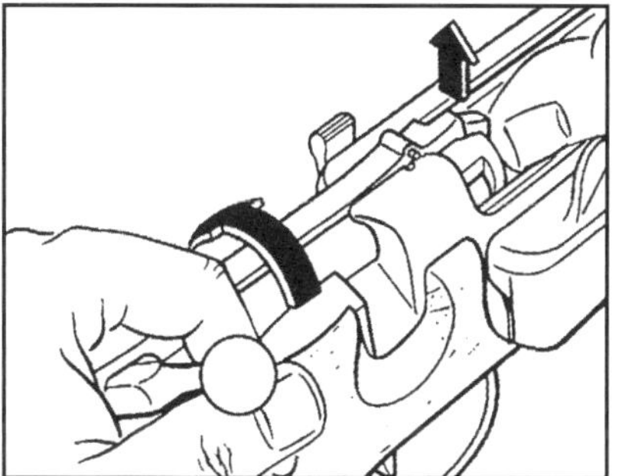

1 To remove bolt, open it and pull it all the way to the rear. Press up on end of extractor (E) and at same time turn bolt counterclockwise. Extractor will snap free of receiver and bolt can be withdrawn.

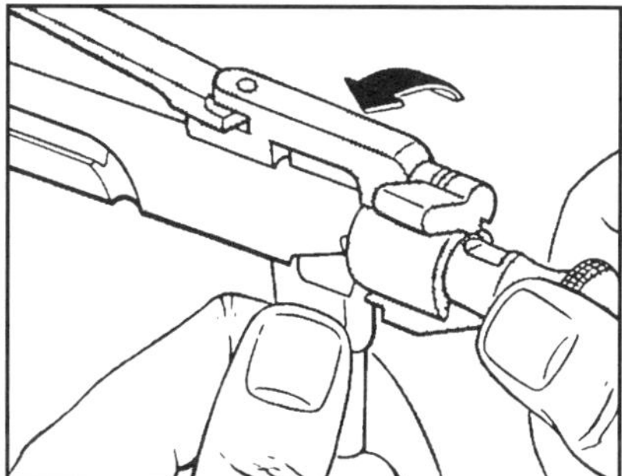

2 To Strip bolt, hold as shown. Pull back on cocking piece knob and rotate entire assembly. Bridge-like section of sleeve will rotate off shoulder on bolt, and whole assembly will snap free.

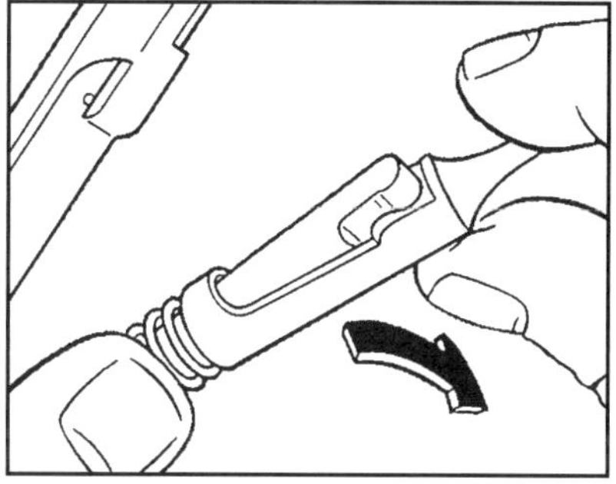

3 To remove striker (G), simply snap it off firing pin rod (A) as shown. Keep a strong grip on striker when it releases from firing pin rod as it is under heavy spring pressure and can fly off hazardously.

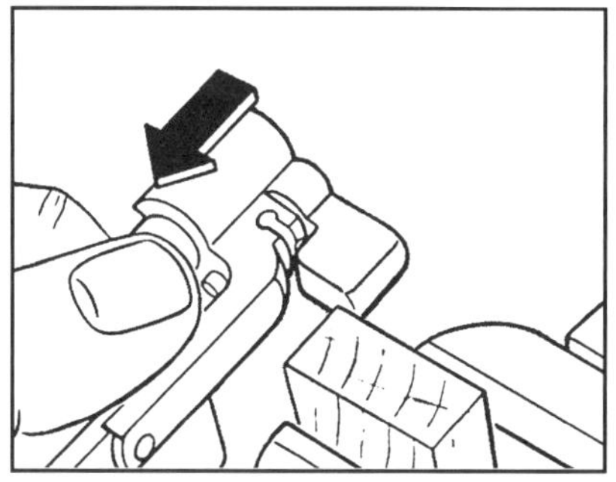

4 After striker (G) and firing pin assembly (A) have been removed, safety lock (B) can be worked loose. Place thumb-piece in vertical position as shown, and hook it over a block of wood and pull sleeve (C) back. Safety lock will then snap free.

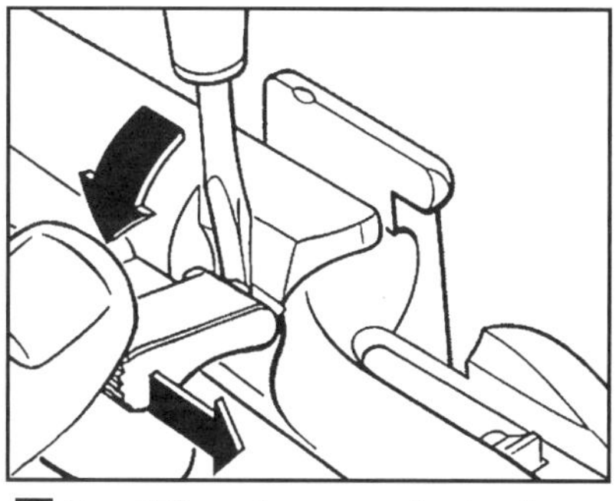

5 Cutoff (J) can be removed only when detent pin is pushed in. To do this, insert a thin screwdriver behind cutoff when it is in vertical position. Push cutoff down to a horizontal position and detent will climb screwdriver blade. Pull cutoff free.

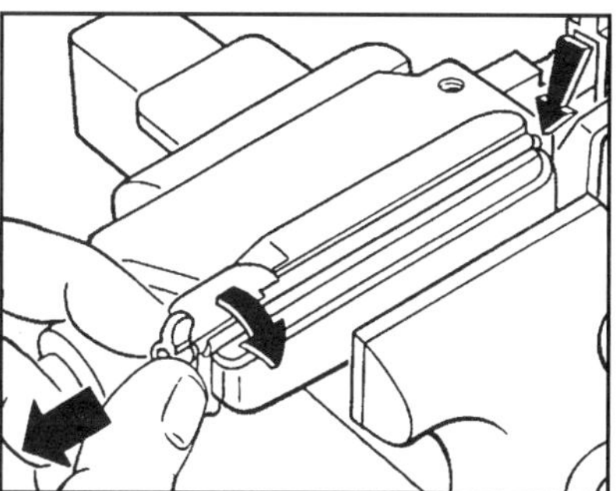

6 Hinge bar (P) is often deformed by improper removal. Hold receiver in a vise, or clamp, to relieve pressure on hinge bar. Rotate the spring and pull hinge bar free. It may be necessary to tap pin at front end (shown by arrow) to start it moving.

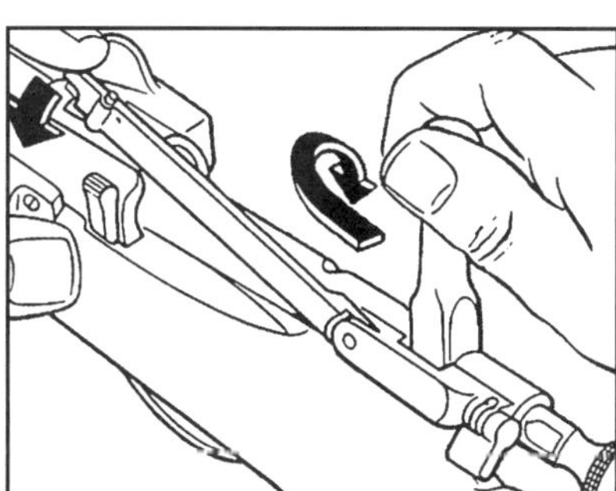

7 To replace bolt, insert it far enough for locking lug to clear receiver wall. Push extractor down into slotted portion of receiver bridge and rotate bolt clockwise. Extractor will snap into position.

U.S. M1 CARBINE

PARTS LEGEND

1. Receiver
2. Rear sight assembly
3. Barrel (with integral gas cylinder lug)
4. Front band assembly
   4A. Front band lock spring (contained in forward end of stock—not shown)
5. Front band screw
6. Front sight assembly
7. Piston
8. Piston nut
9. Operating slide spring
10. Operating slide spring guide
11. Operating slide
12. Operating slide stop pin
13. Operating slide stop spring
14. Trigger housing assembly
15. Trigger housing retaining pin
16. Bolt assembly
17. Handguard assembly
18. Recoil plate
19. Recoil plate screw
20. Recoil plate screw escutcheon (contained in underside of stock)
21. Magazine assembly

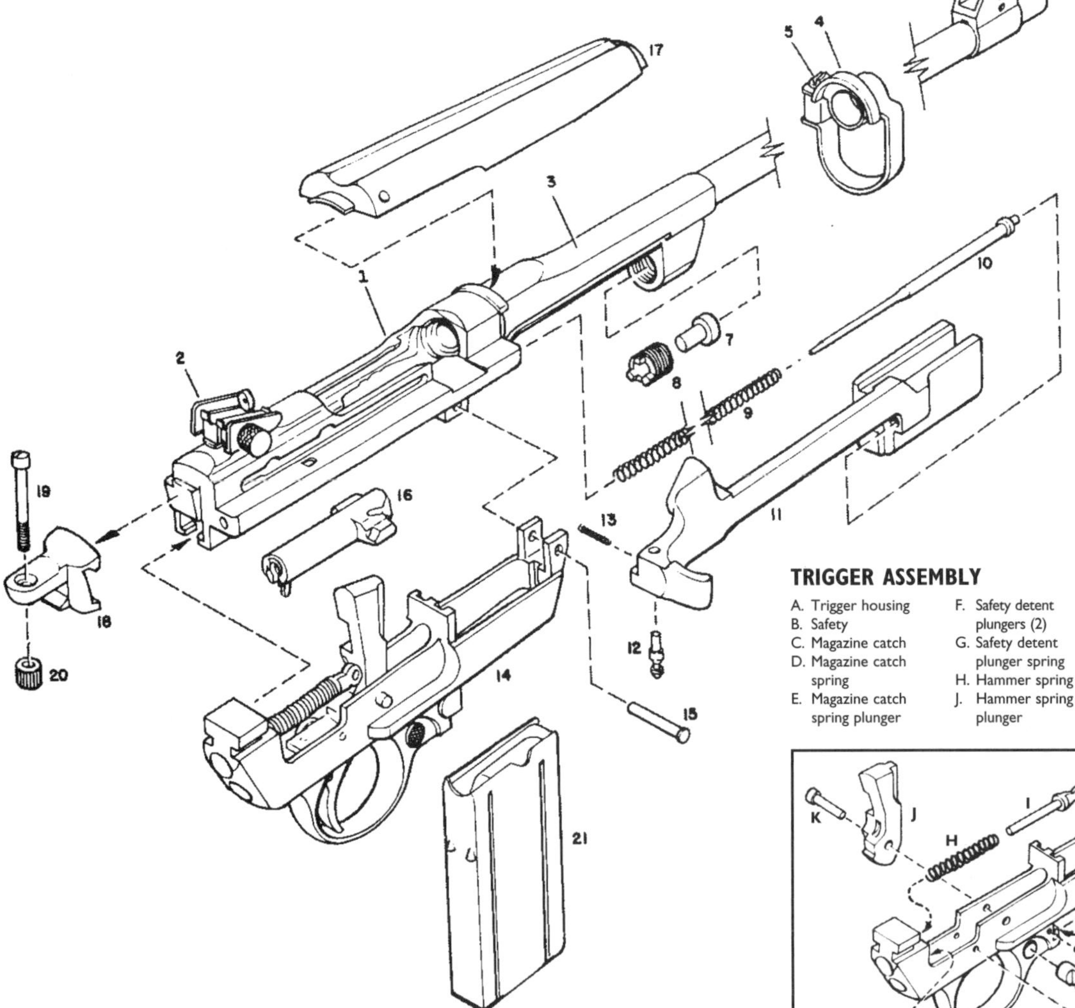

TRIGGER ASSEMBLY

A. Trigger housing
B. Safety
C. Magazine catch
D. Magazine catch spring
E. Magazine catch spring plunger
F. Safety detent plungers (2)
G. Safety detent plunger spring
H. Hammer spring
J. Hammer spring plunger
K. Hammer
L. Hammer pin
M. Trigger
N Trigger spring
O Sear
P. Sear spring
Q. Trigger pin

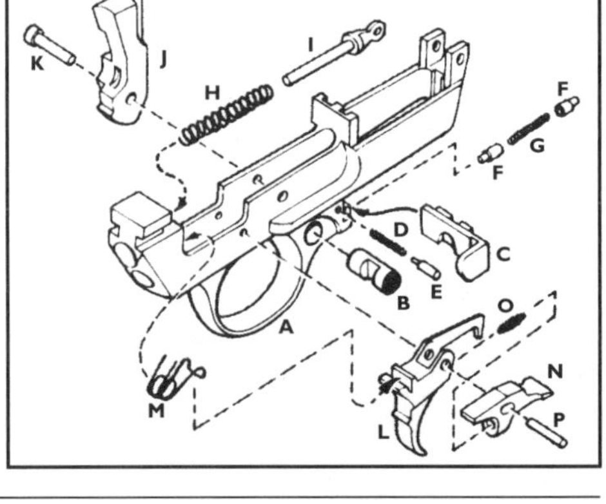

The U.S. Carbine, Cal. .30 M1 was developed by Winchester Repeating Arms and adopted for service use in 1941. It is a semi-automatic, gas-operated, air-cooled, shoulder weapon fed by a detachable box magazine holding 15 rounds.

A modification of the M1 Carbine, designated M1A1, was standardized in May 1942 for airborne troops. The M1A1 Carbine has a folding metal stock, but its barrel and action assembly is identical to that of the M1 version.

New variants, the M2 and M3 Carbines, were standardized in September 1944 and August 1945 respectively. They were fitted with a selector switch permitting either semi- or full-automatic fire. They were regularly issued with a 30-round box magazine.

Contractors producing M1 Carbines included: Winchester Repeating Arms Co.; Inland Division, General Motors Corp.; Rock-Ola Corp.; National Postal Meter Co.; International Business Machines Corp.; Underwood Elliott Fisher Co.; Saginaw Steering Gear Div., General Motors Corp.; Standard Products Corp. and Quality Hardware & Machine Corp.

The basic service ammunition for use in the Carbine was a ball cartridge with full-jacketed, semi-round-nosed, flat-based bullet with a nominal weight of either 108 or 111 grains. A 108-grain cup-based bullet was manufactured prior to February 1942 . The average muzzle velocity is 1970 fps. Muzzle energy with the 108-grain bullet is 930 ft-lbs. Muzzle energy with 111-grain bullet is 956 ft.-lbs.

DISASSEMBLY

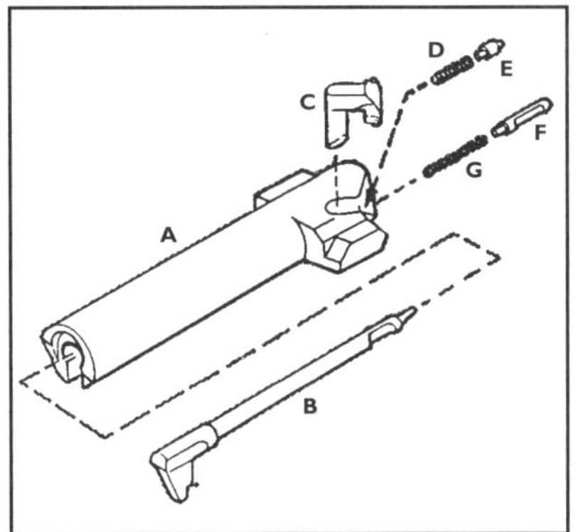

1 To disassemble bolt, press in extractor spring plunger (E) with small screwdriver blade or similar tool and push extractor (C) up out of bolt (A) from bottom, taking care to prevent forcible ejection of compressed spring (D). Remove ejector and spring (O & F) and firing pin (B).

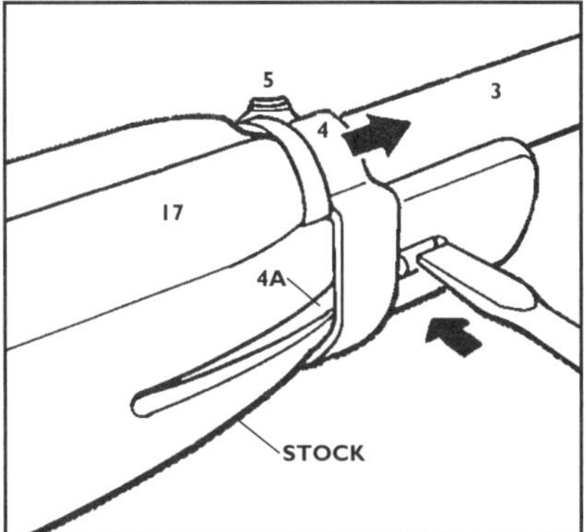

2 Before removing front band (4), front band lock spring (4A) must be depressed as shown using tip of screwdriver blade or small punch. Slide the band forward until it is clear of the stock and of the handguard (17).

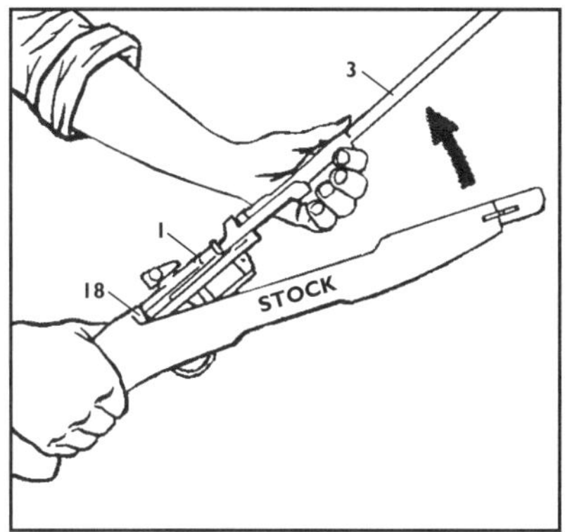

3 To separate barrel and receiver from stock, grasp stock in right hand as shown and lift front of barrel upward until the rear end of the receiver is free of the recoil plate (18) in the stock.

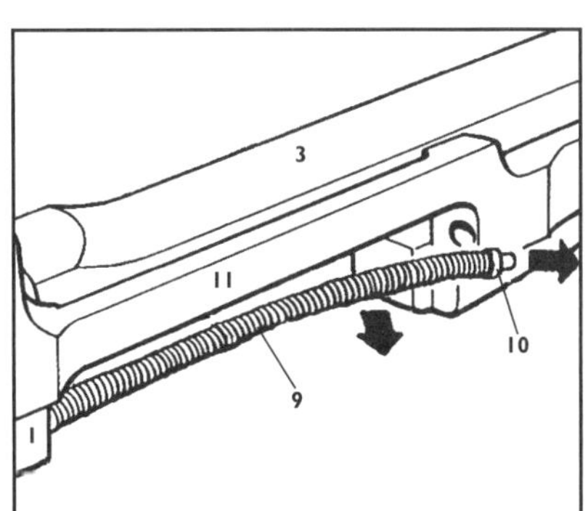

4 A Pull operating slide spring (9) and guide (10) to rear slightly until guide is clear of hole in slide (11). Move guide and spring to right as shown in order to clear slide and withdraw guide and spring to front, pulling spring out of its hole in the front end of the receiver.

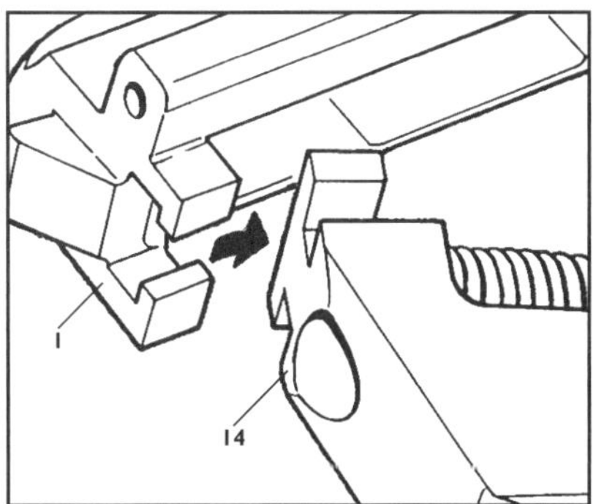

5 After removing trigger housing retaining pin (15), trigger housing (14) must be pushed forward until lugs at rear of housing are clear of slots in underside of receiver as shown.

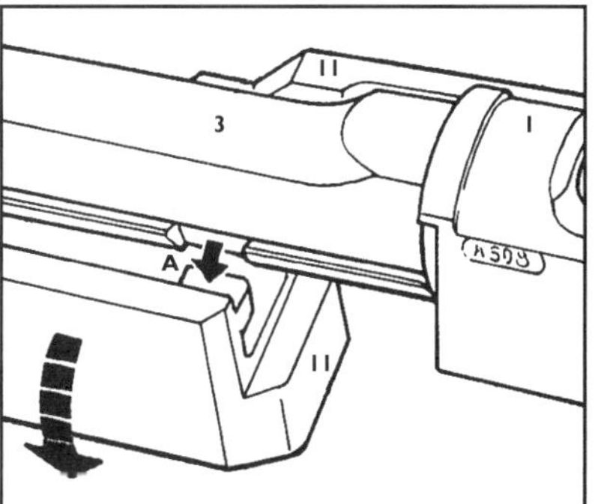

6 After disengaging lug at rear of operating slide (11) from retaining groove at right of receiver, move slide forward to position shown and rotate counterclockwise to disengage the lugs at the front of slide from the grooves in barrel as shown at A.

U.S. M1 RIFLE - GARAND

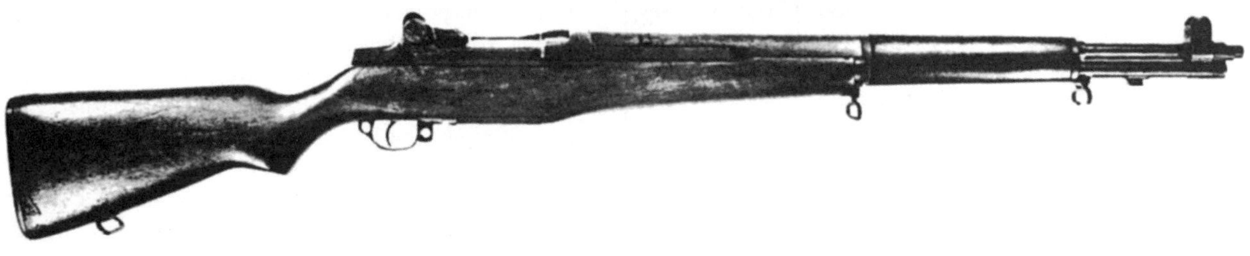

PARTS LEGEND

1. Barrel
2. Lower band
3. Lower band pin
4. Rear handguard
5. Rear handguard band
6. Front sight
7. Front sight screw
8. Gas cylinder
9. Clip latch pin
10. Clip latch
11. Clip latch spring
12. Receiver
13. Ejector
14. Ejector spring
15. Extractor
16. Extractor spring
17. Extractor plunger
18. Firing pin
19. Bolt
20. Safety
21. Trigger housing
22. Trigger pin
23. Trigger guard (old style)
24. Clip ejector
25. Hammer pin
26. Trigger/sear (old style)
27. Hammer spring housing
28. Hammer
29. Slide and follower
30. Operating rod
31. Bullet guide
32. Follower rod
33. Hammer spring plunger
34. Hammer spring
35. Buttplate screw, short
36. Buttplate screw, long
37. Buttplate
38. Stock ferrule swivel
39. Stock ferrule swivel screw
40. Stock ferrule
41. Butt swivel
42. Front handguard spacer
43. Front handguard ferrule
44. Front handguard
45. Accelerator pin
46. Operating rod catch
47. Accelerator
48. Follower arm
49. Operating rod spring
50. Follower arm pin
51. Gas cylinder lock
52. Gas cylinder lock screw/valve
53. Rear sight
54. Stacking swivel
55. Stacking swivel screw

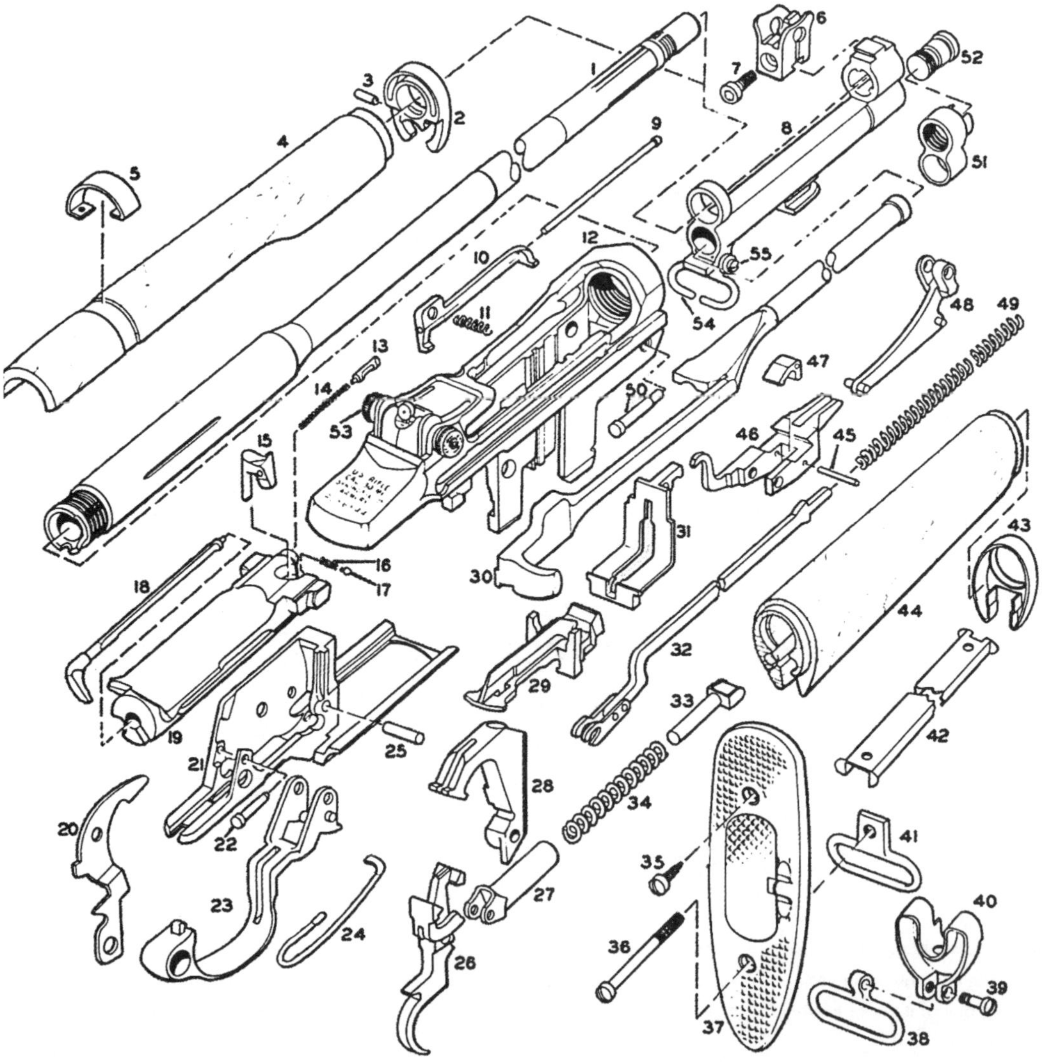

On Jan. 9, 1936, the U.S. Army adopted a semi-automatic rifle to replace the Model 1903 bolt-action Springfield which had been the standard U.S. Service rifle since 1903. The new rifle, designated U.S. Rifle, Cal. .30, M1, was also adopted shortly afterward by the U.S. Navy and the Marine Corps.

The M1 rifle was invented and developed at Springfield Armory by Canadian-born John C. Garand, a civilian engineer who had been employed at the Armory since 1919. Garand's experience in the field of design and production was extensive. His initial design was a primer-actuated light machine gun which he developed at the National Bureau of Standards shortly after World War I. This gun showed such promise that Garand was transferred to Springfield Armory to work on development of a primer-actuated semi-automatic shoulder rifle. He subsequently designed a series of such rifles, but the one finally adopted in 1936 was gas-operated rather than primer-actuated.

Initial delivery of machine-made M1 rifles from Springfield Armory began in September 1937. As might be expected, early production rifles did not perform well in service but the majority of defects noted were due to slight but critical dimensional differences, not in accordance with the design, between the Service test models and the machine-made guns. These troubles were eventually corrected and it is a matter of record that the Ordnance Department during this period endured criticism which was often partisan, to say the least.

Entrance of the United States in World War II resulted in accelerated production of the M1 rifle at Springfield Armory with corollary production by Winchester Repeating Arms Co. beginning in January 1941. By V-J Day (August 14. 1945) a total of 4,028,395 M1 rifles had been produced, of which Winchester manufactured 513,582. During the Korean War additional large numbers of M1 rifles were produced by Springfield Armory, International Harvester Co. and Harrington & Richardson, Inc.

That the M1 rifle gave a good account of itself in every theater of combat in World War 11 is an accepted fact. Subsequent performance in the Korean War only emphasized its general excellence as a battle rifle.

Target shooting activities in the years since the Korean War have shown the M1 to be a superior target rifle as evidenced by comparison of scores fired at all ranges with the 1903 Springfield and the fine National Match M1s and accurized Service rifles in use today.

The M1 does have certain limitations which were emphasized during the Korean War. A primary criticism is its weight, which sometimes exceeds 10 lbs. when the stock is of dense wood. The system of *en bloc* loading with an 8-round clip is also open to criticism since a partially expended clip cannot be conveniently refilled during a lull in battle. Also the infantryman often needed greater magazine capacity when confronted with massed infantry attacking at close range, especially at night when aimed fire was impossible.

To meet the dual requirements of reasonable weight and increased magazine capacity, the Ordnance Dept. developed the M14 rifle which was adopted in 1957.

DISASSEMBLY

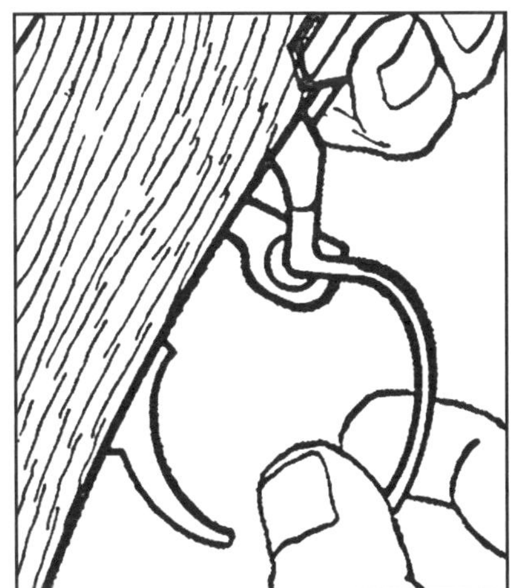

1 Disassembly of the Ml rifle is accomplished by first pulling rearward on the trigger guard (23) and then out and away from stock. Entire trigger housing (21) and assembly will separate from rifle. Lift receiver (12) and assembly away from stock,

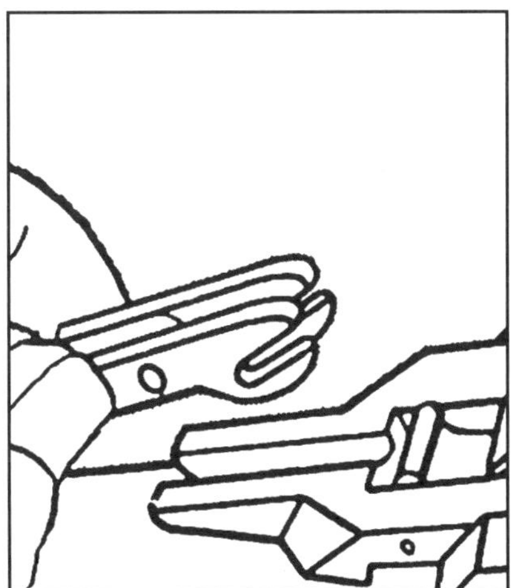

2 Disengage follower rod (32) from follower arm (48) by moving rod toward muzzle end. Remove follower rod and operating rod spring (49). Next push out follower arm pin (50) from left side of receiver.

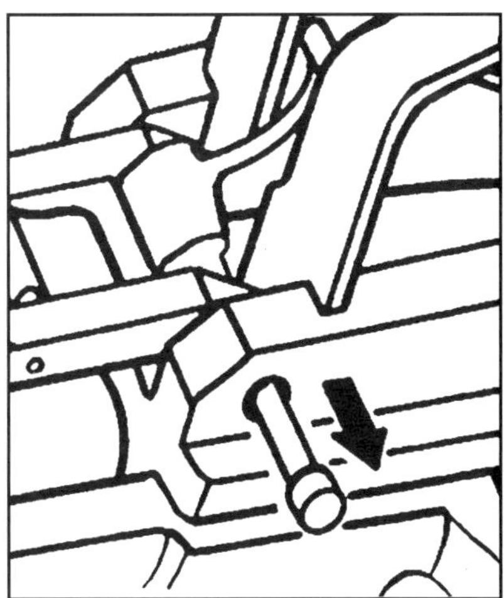

3 Next push out follower arm pin (50) from the left side of receiver.

U.S. M1 RIFLE - GARAND

DISASSEMBLY CONTINUED

4 Lift away bullet guide (31), follower arm, and operating rod catch (46),

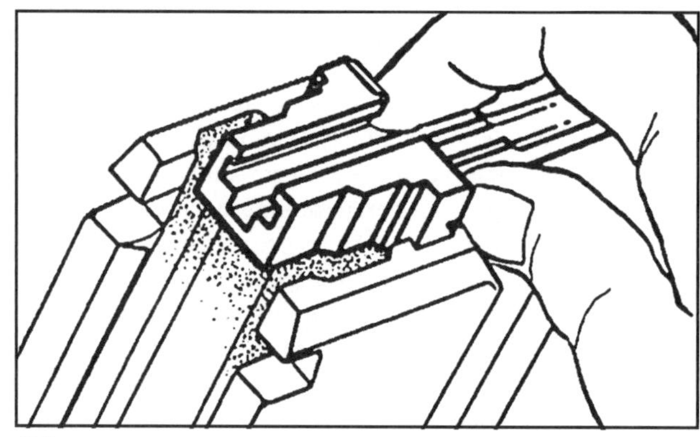

5 Reach down into receiver and lift out slide and follower (29).

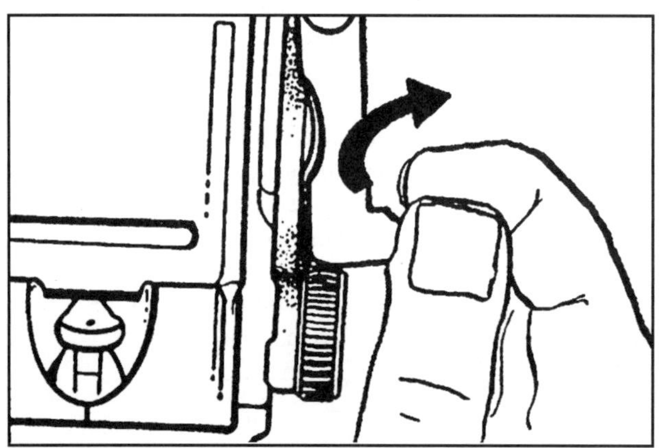

6 Continue disassembly by pulling operating rod (30) to rear until rear surface of handle is directly under forward edge of windage knob on rear sight. Disengage guide lug on operating rod through dismount notch on receiver, with an upward and outward pressure on handle of operating rod. Remove bolt (19) by first grasping it by operating lug and then sliding it forward while lifting upward and outward with a rotating motion.

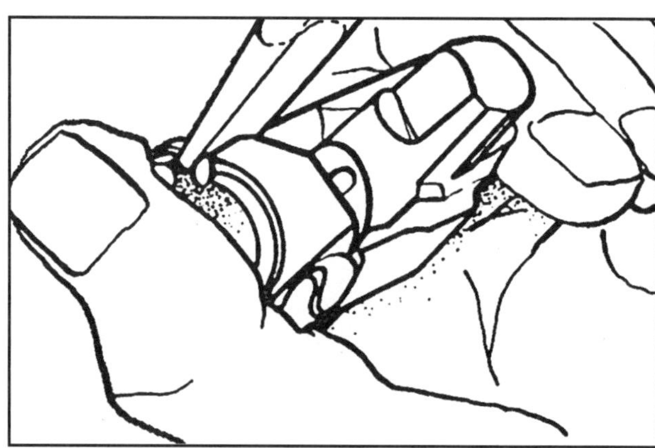

7 Hold bolt in left hand so that left thumb is over ejector (13). Insert blade of a screwdriver between extractor (15) and lower cartridge seat flange. Twist blade against extractor and unseat it. Ejector will snap up against left thumb. Remove extractor, extractor spring (16), and extractor plunger (17).

8 Lift out ejector and ejector spring (14). Do not separate these parts. Remove firing pin (18) from rear of bolt.

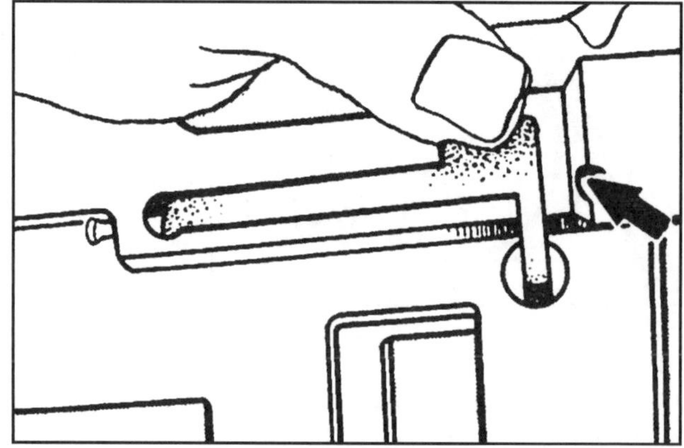

9 To remove clip latch (10), first depress it to remove tension of clip latch spring (II). Using a drift, push forward on clip latch pin (9, arrow) to unseat it. Withdraw pin and remove clip latch and clip latch spring.

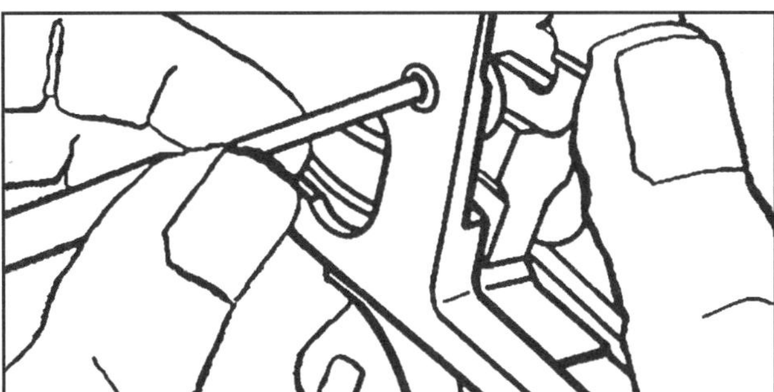

10 Trigger housing assembly is disassembled by first closing and latching trigger guard. Squeeze trigger (26) to permit hammer to go forward. With index finger on trigger and right thumb pushing against sear portion of trigger, drift out trigger pin (22). Lift out trigger and remove hammer spring plunger (33), hammer spring (34), and hammer spring housing (27).

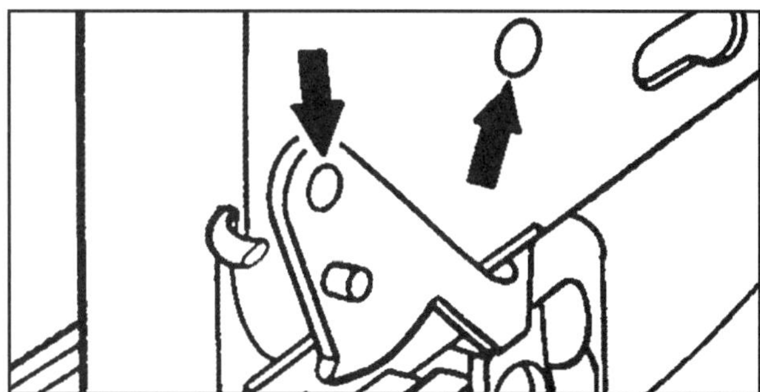

11 Drift out hammer pin (25, left arrow) and lift out hammer (28). Unlatch trigger guard. Using a small drift or punch, push safety stud from its hole (right arrow). Remove safety (20) from trigger housing (21). Swing trigger guard down to open position and slide it rearward until wings are aligned with safety stud hole. Rotate it right and upward until hammer stop inside the right wing clears trigger housing base. Remove trigger guard. Place a screwdriver through lower hole in left side of trigger housing and pry clip ejector (24) upward and out.

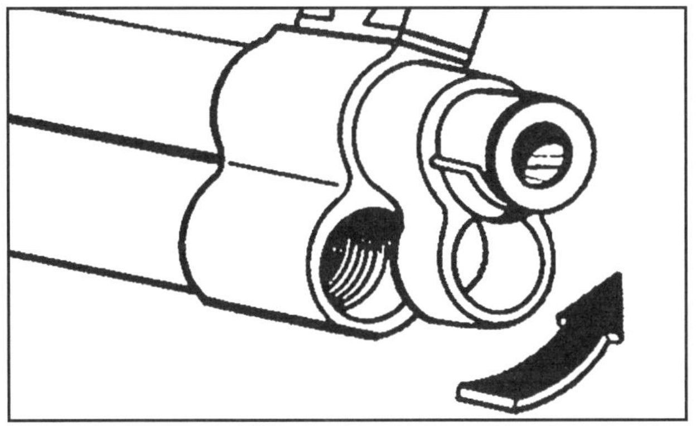

12 With a blunt screwdriver, unscrew and remove the gas cylinder lock screw (52). Unscrew and remove gas cylinder lock (51). Next, remove gas cylinder (8) by tapping it lightly forward on bayonet stud with a piece of soft wood. Do not burr or damage the internal splines. On rifles with gas cylinders modified by a cut extending from front sight base dovetail downward to lower splines, it is necessary to loosen front sight screw before removing gas cylinder to prevent damage to barrel and gas cylinder.

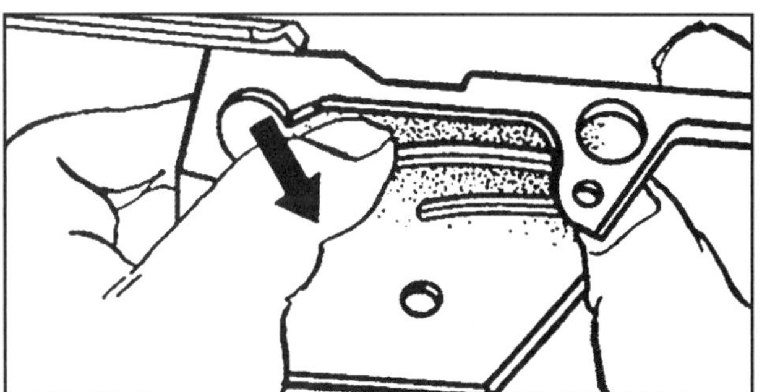

13 Reassemble the rifle in reverse order. To reassemble trigger housing, first place clip ejector in position in trigger housing with short arm facing up and long arm in its slot at front end of housing. Position loop of clip ejector on top of its stud and hold it there. Hold long arm up in its slot and exert downward pressure on rear part of spring. Long arm will snap into notch on trigger housing base.

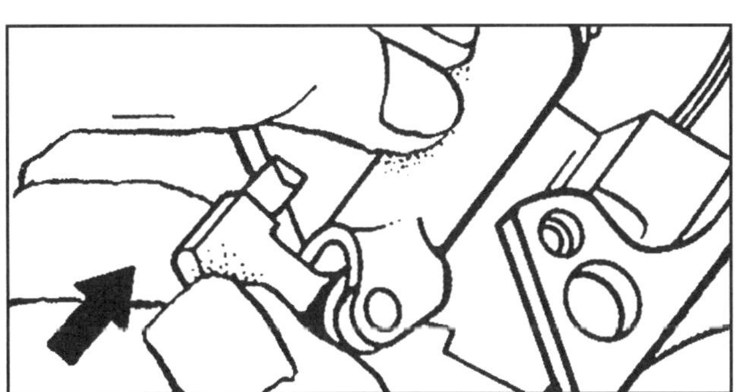

14 Replace trigger guard, safety, hammer, and hammer pin. Assemble hammer spring housing, spring, and plunger as a unit. Place the plunger in its seat on hammer. Make sure that open side of spring housing is toward safety. Hold these parts in a raised position with left thumb and fingers. Insert trigger and trigger pin. Press forward on seal, and seat pin by pressing on its head.

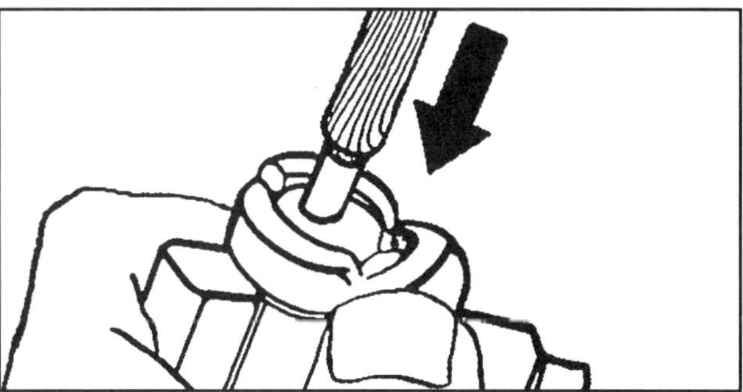

15 When reassembling bolt, first insert firing pin and then, with bolt face upward, place ejector and ejector spring into hole in face of bolt. Replace extractor spring and plunger. Put stud of extractor into its hole in bolt. Exert thumb pressure on extractor and, using a piece of hardwood dowel, depress ejector into face of bolt until extractor seats with an audible click.

U.S. MODEL 1917 RIFLE (ENFIELD)

PARTS LEGEND

1. Receiver
2. Barrel
3. Front sight blade
4. Front sight carrier
5. Front sight spline
6. Front sight pin
7. Upper band
   7a. Upper band screw
8. Stacking swivel
9. Stacking swivel screw
10. Lower band
11. Lower band swivel
12. Lower band swivel screw
13. Handguard ring
14. Rear sight assembly
15. Rear sight base spring
16. Rear sight base spring screw
17. Rear sight joint bolt
18. Rear sight joint bolt nut
19. Bolt stop
20. Ejector
21. Bolt stop screw
22. Bolt stop spring
23. Bolt stop spring rest
24. Bolt
25. Extractor collar
26. Extractor
27. Striker
28. Mainspring
29. Cocking piece
30. Sleeve
31. Safety-lock
32. Safety-lock holder
33. Safety-lock holder screw
34. Safety-lock plunger
35. Safety-lock plunger spring
36. Sear spring
37. Sear
38. Sear pin (Enters receiver from left side — shown on right here for clarity)
39. Trigger pin
40. Trigger
41. Trigger guard
42. Floorplate catch
43. Floorplate catch spring
44. Floorplate catch pin
45. Front guard screw
46. Rear guard screw
47. Floorplate
48. Magazine
49. Magazine spring
50. Follower

NOTE: The following parts are omitted in the drawing: Buttstock, buttplate, buttplate screws (2), butt swivel, swivel screws (2), rear band pin, front and rear handguards, stock bolt and nut, front and rear guard screw bushings

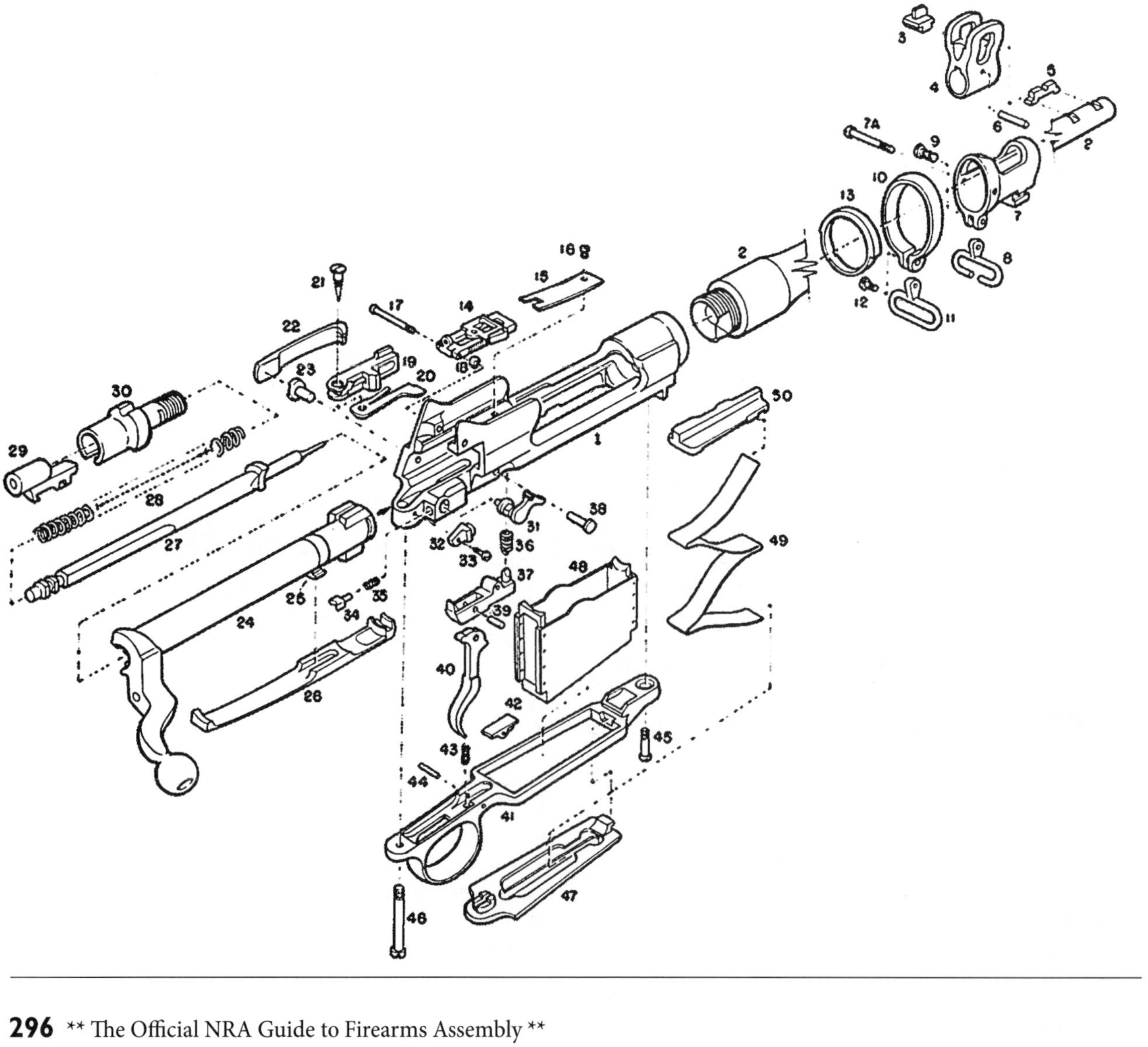

The U.S. Rifle, Caliber .30, Model of 1917, is a Mauser-style bolt-action rifle with dual front locking lugs and a staggered column box magazine. It was developed during World War I as a modification of the British Pattern 1914 Rifle.

In 1913 British Ordnance developed an experimental bolt-action rifle chambered for a .276 caliber rimless cartridge as a potential replacement for the .303 caliber Lee-Enfield service rifle. Only a small number of .276 rifles had been manufactured prior to World War I, at which time the British decided to alter the new rifle to accept the .303 rimmed cartridge.

In 1914, Great Britain turned to several U.S. firms, Winchester, Remington-Union Metallic Cartridge, and Remington Arms to manufacture the new, "Pattern 1914" rifle. Remington Arms Co. operated the Eddystone Arsenal, owned by the Baldwin Locomotive Works. On September 21, 1916, after a considerable number of rifles had been delivered, these contracts were canceled by the British government, due to the fact that British arsenals and factories had been able to achieve adequate production of the Lee-Enfield.

When the United States entered the war in 1917, the supply of Model 1903 Springfield rifles was relatively small and production facilities of Rock Island Arsenal and Springfield Armory were not adequate to produce them in the quantities necessary to equip the rapidly expanding American army. The little time for American firms to tool up for production of the Model 1903 rifle and equipping U. S. troops with the .303 caliber Pattern 1914 rifle would have complicated ammunition supply. The solution was to modify the Pattern 1914 rifle to handle the .30-06 cartridge. After considerable difficulty in standardizing the modified rifle, designated U.S. Rifle, Caliber .30, Model of 1917, initial deliveries were made by Winchester, Eddystone Arsenal and Remington by the summer and fall of 1917. A total of 2,193,429 Model 1917 Enfields were produced by November 1918.

Early in World War II large numbers of the Model 1917 rifles were sold or lend-leased to the Allies. As a result, it was found necessary to produce additional barrels and these were made by the High Standard Manufacturing Corp., (4-groove) and Johnson Automatics, (2-groove), to 1903 Springfield rifling specifications.

DISASSEMBLY

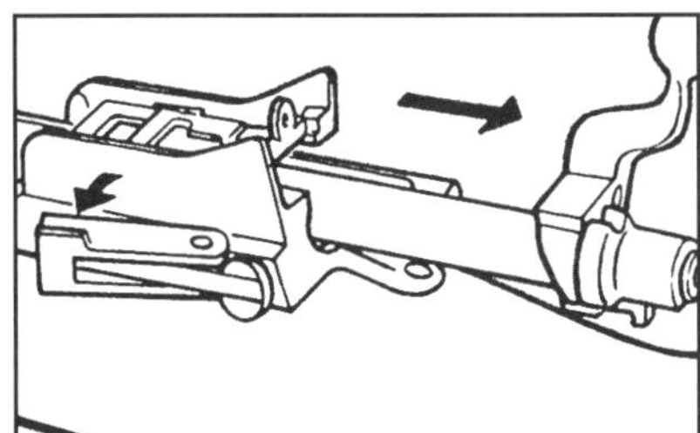

1 To remove bolt, hold bolt stop (19) out as shown at "A" and pull bolt straight out to the rear.

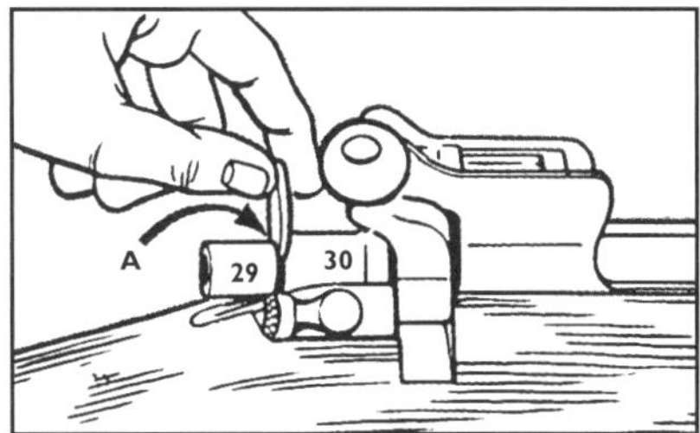

2 To disassemble bolt, open bolt and engage safety. Close bolt, then elevate bolt handle as shown and insert a nickel between end of cocking piece and bolt sleeve so that coin is trapped between these parts as shown.

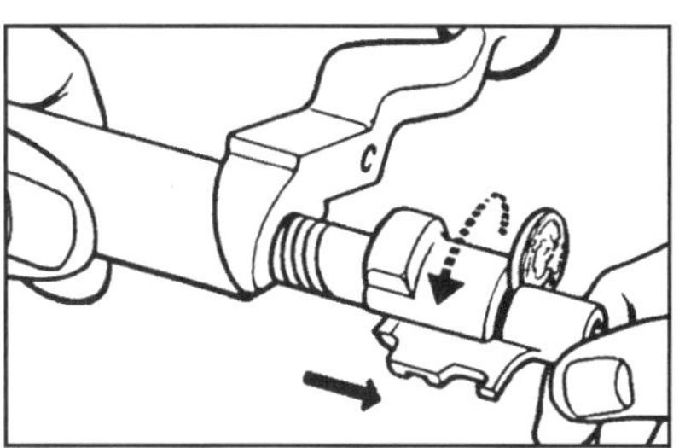

3 Remove bolt and unscrew percussion assembly as shown.

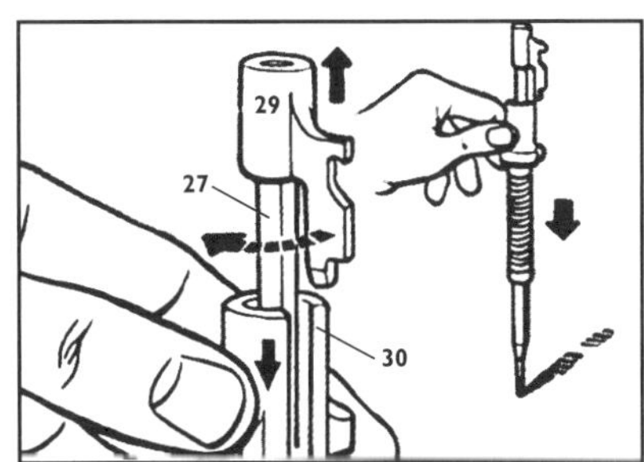

4 With striker point resting on wood surface, force sleeve (30) down. Remove coin and continue forcing sleeve down, compressing mainspring (28) until cocking piece lug clears lug slot in sleeve. Turn cocking piece ¼ turn right or left, disengaging it from striker, and draw cocking piece off to rear. Relieve mainspring pressure gradually and draw off sleeve.

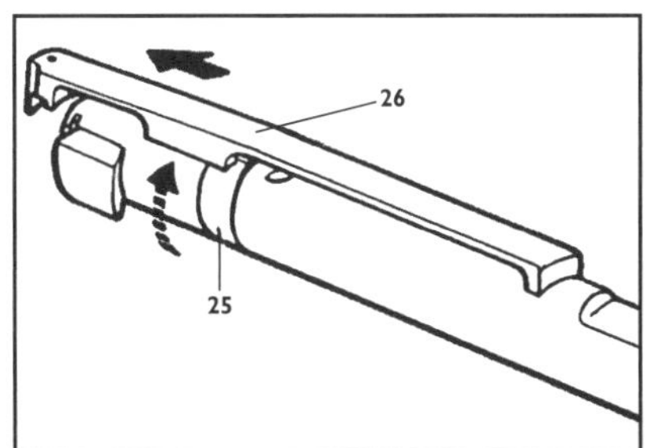

5 Turn extractor (26) to cover gas escape holes in bolt and push forward on extractor until it is free of extractor collar (25). Reassemble bolt in reverse order.

U.S. SPRINGFIELD 1861 RIFLE-MUSKET

PARTS LEGEND

1. Barrel
2. Rear sight
3. Rear sight base screw
4. Cone
5. Cone seat
6. Cone-seat screw
7. Ramrod
8. Upper band
9. Band spring (3)
10. Middle band
11. Lower band
12. Tip screw
13. Tip
14. Guard nut (2)
15. Guard plate
16. Guard bow
17. Trigger pin
18. Trigger
19. Guard plate screws (2)
20. Swivel screw
21. Rod spring pin (M1863)
22. Rod spring (MI863)
23. Hammer screw
24. Hammer
25. Lockplate
26. Mainspring
27. Mainspring swivel
28. Tumbler pin
29. Tumbler
30. Sear spring screw
31. Sear spring
32. Sear
33. Bridle
34. Bridle screw
35. Sear screw
36. Stock (partial)
37. Side screw (2)
38. Breech screw
39. Tang screw
40. Buttplate screw (2)
41. Buttplate
42. Front swivel
43. Side screw washer (2)

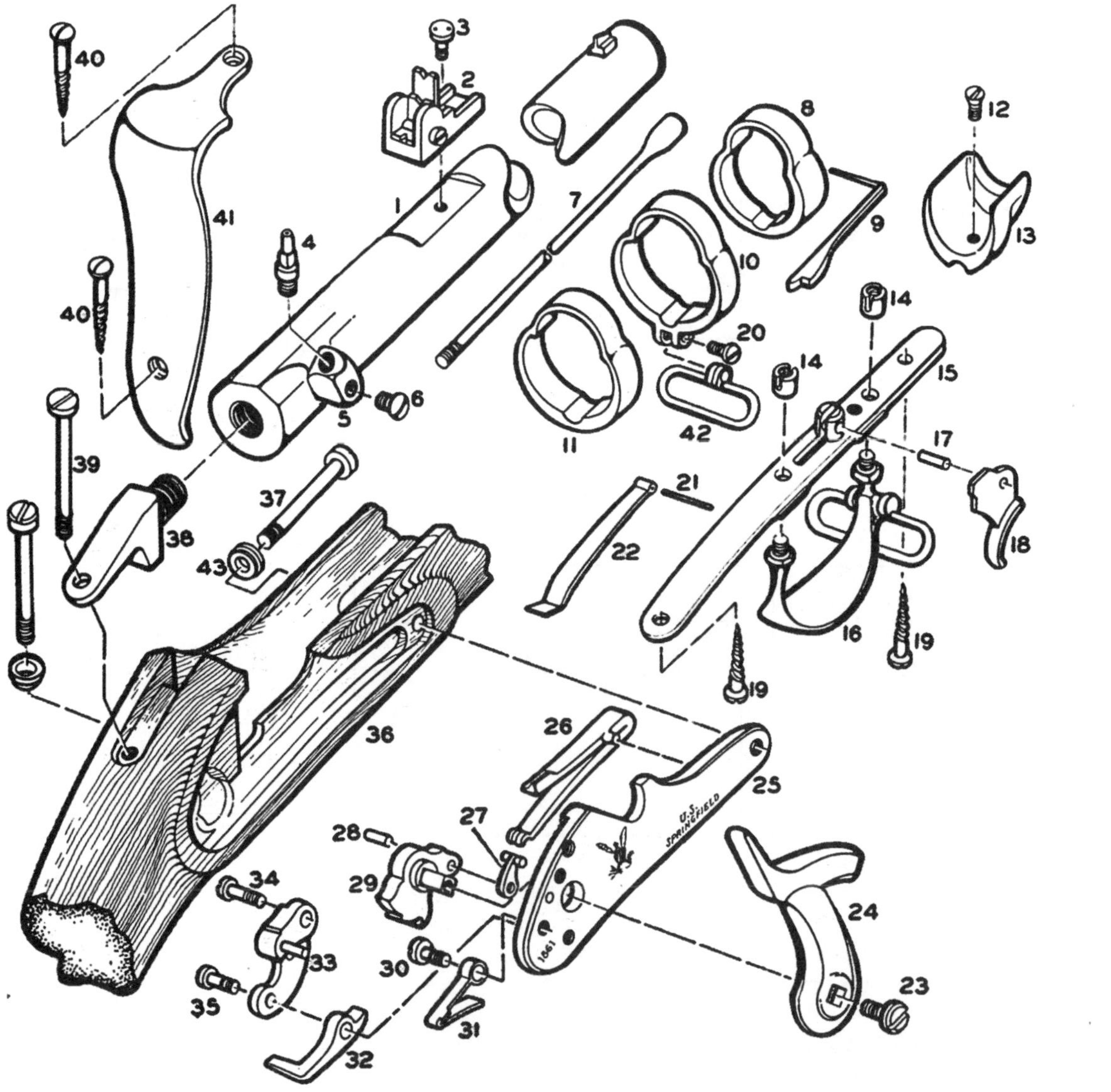

A total of 265,129 .58 caliber Model 1861 Springfield Rifle-Muskets were produced at Springfield Armory and this arm was also the pattern for civilian contractors furnishing muskets to the government. It is quite similar to the Model 1863, and there is a high degree of parts interchangeability between these models. A total of 273,265 Model 1863 Rifle-Muskets were produced at Springfield Armory.

Present-day collectors are often hard put to determine the exact model at hand as the date on the lockplate is not always correct when compared with other parts or features of the arm. This situation stems from the interchanging of parts after manufacture.

The Model 1863 differs from the Model 1861 in the following particulars:

1. Does not have band springs.
2. Cone seat reduced in length and cone-seat screw omitted.
3. Ramrod swell omitted.
4. Spring provided to hold ramrod in place.
5. Open oval bands with screws rather than flat, solid bands.
6. Muzzle crowned, not flat.
7. Lock casehardened in colors, not polished bright.
8. Bands, swivels, rear sight, and guard blued, not polished bright.
9. Different hammer form.

In effect, differences between the Model 1861 and the Model 1863 are minor, and basic disassembly procedures are therefore similar.

DISASSEMBLY

To disassemble Model 1861 Springfield, first place hammer (24) at half cock and withdraw ramrod (7). Remove side screws (37) and separate entire lock assembly from stock (36). Disassemble lock by first applying a mainspring vise to mainspring (26) and then unseating spring from lock-plate (25). Remove sear screw (35) and sear (32) will drop away. Remove bridle screw (34) and bridle will drop away. Next, remove hammer screw (23) and hammer (24). Remove sear spring screw (30) and sear spring (31). Tap tumbler (29) out from exterior of lockplate [see Panel 2]. Continue by removing tang screw (39). Depress band spring (9) for each of the upper, middle, and lower hands (8, 10, & 11) and remove bands. Separate barrel (1) from stock.

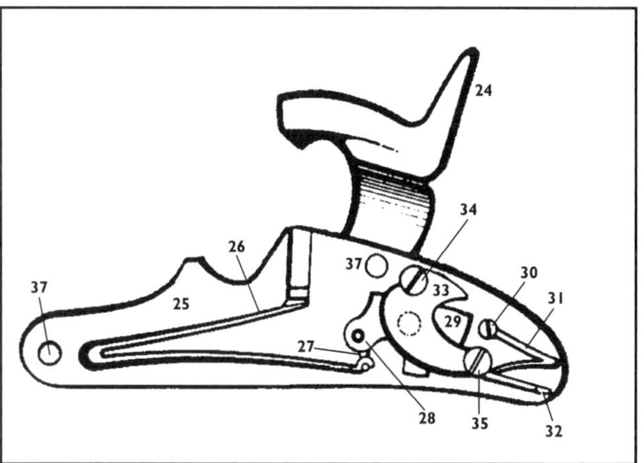

This diagram shows the interior assembly of the lock and relative position of its parts. This diagram can be used for most of the Springfield percussion arms as well as for contract rifle-muskets of the 1961 pattern.

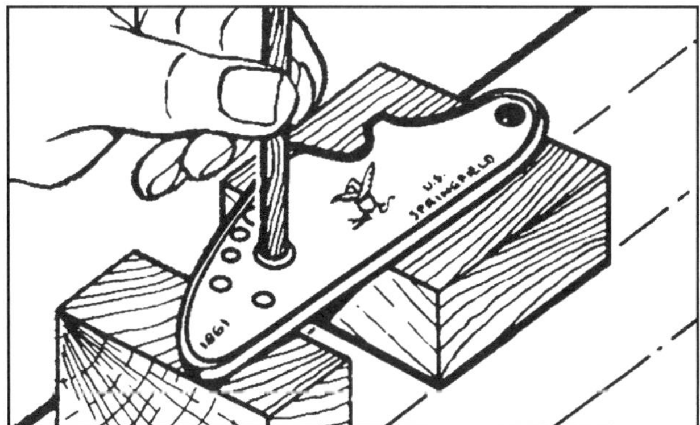

1 Removal of the tumbler (29) may be facilitated by placing the lock-plate (25) face up on a piece of wood and centering a hardwood dowel over the tumbler flange. Tap the dowel lightly with a hammer.

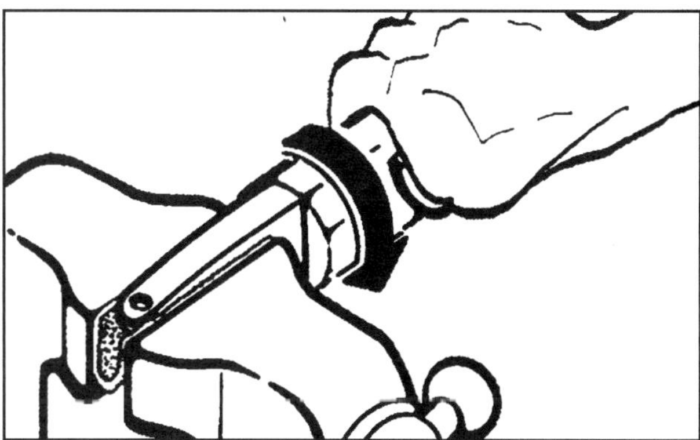

2 Removal of the breech screw (38) is accomplished as follows: Place parallel sides of the breech screw in felt-padded vise jaws and attempt to unscrew the barrrel by hand. If this part is rusted in place, apply penetrating oil for several days and try again. A good grip on the barrel may be had with the use of rubber gloves. Never use a pipe wrench or similar device on the barrel.

U.S. SPRINGFIELD MODEL 1873 RIFLE

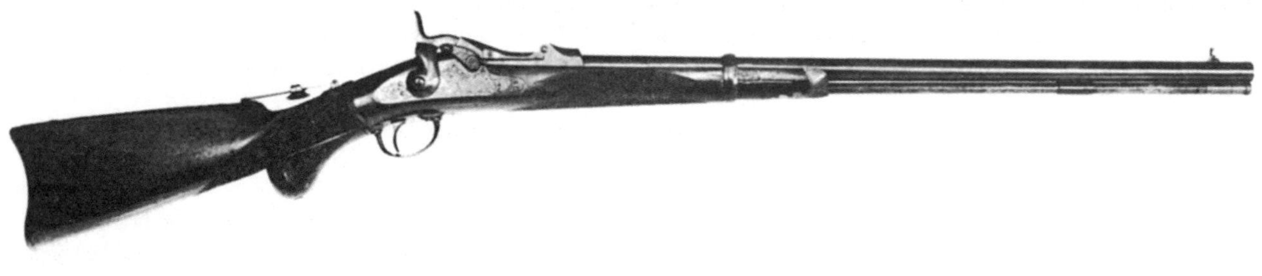

PARTS LEGEND

1. Breech
2. Barrel
3. Rear sight assembly
4. Front sight blade
5. Front sight pin
6. Ejector stud
7. Extractor
8. Ejector spring
9. Spindle
10. Hinge pin
11. Breechblock
12. Firing pin
13. Firing pin screw
14. Cam latch spring
15. Cam latch
16. Breechblock cap
17. Breechblock cap screw
18. Thumb-piece
19. Breech screw
20. Tang screw
21. Side screws (2)
22. Side screw washers (2)
23. Buttplate screws (2)
24. Buttplate
25. Buttstock (shown partially)
26. Lower band
27. Upper band
28. Ramrod stop
29. Band springs (2)
30. Stock tip
31. Stock tip screw
32. Ramrod
33. Lock assembly
34. Guard plate
35. Guard screws (2)
36. Guard bow
37. Guard bow nuts (2)
38. Guard bow swivel
39. Guard bow swivel screw
40. Trigger
41. Trigger screw

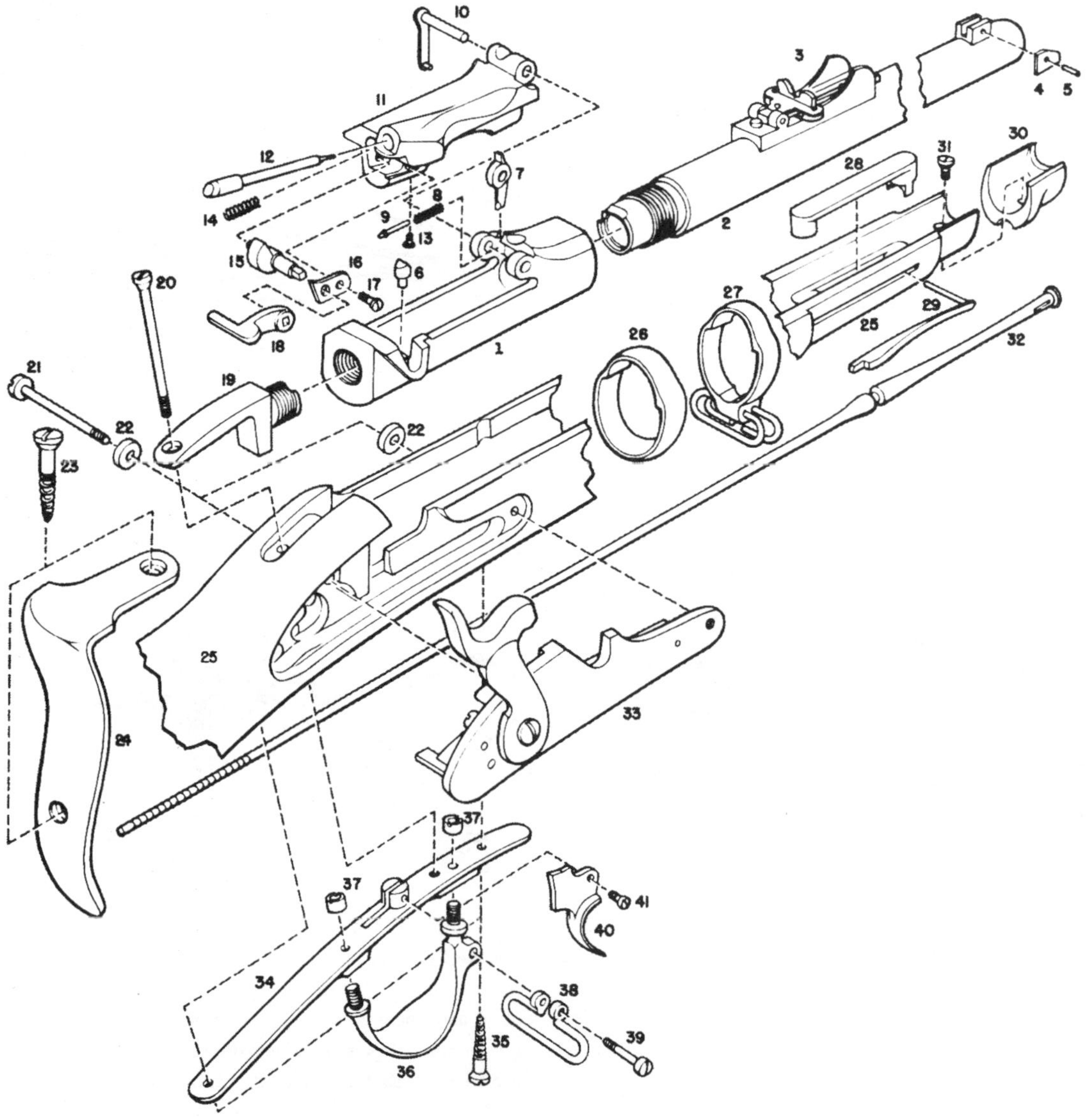

During the latter part of the Civil War, Brigadier General A. B. Dyer, U.S. Chief of Ordnance, commissioned Erskine S. Allin, Master Armorer at Springfield Armory, to develop a breech mechanism that permited the economical conversion of .58 caliber muzzle-loading percussion rifles to breech-loaders using a self-contained metallic cartridge.

Allin accomplished the assigned task, obtaining a patent covering his breech mechanism which was adopted by the Ordnance Board of 1865. Many modifications were made before the design, the Model 1866 rifle, was approved. The .58-caliber barrels were to be altered to accept .50-caliber rifled liners. In fact the final version, the Model 1868, was largely made with new steel barrels rather than relined barrels.

The Model 1870 Springfield was similar to the Model 1868 except for changes in the receiver, barrel, breechblock and sights. It was manufactured in both rifle and carbine form.

The services, however, were dissatisfied with performance of the 1870 rifle and its .50-70 cartridge and a new Ordnance Board convened in 1872. The board examined a total of 99 American and 9 foreign breech-loading designs, including several modifications of the Allin system. Their choice was rifle No. 99, an Allin rifle submitted by Springfield Armory.

The new rifle, designated the Model 1873, was chambered for a .45-caliber, center-fire cartridge loaded with 70 grains of blackpowder and a 405-grain bullet. The carbine cartridge was loaded with 55 grains of blackpowder and a 405-grain bullet.

The Model 1873 was made in regulation, cadet and carbine sizes and remained the basic U. S. service arm until it was superseded by the Krag-Jorgensen repeating rifle in 1892. Numerous changes were made during this period, and subsequent models included the Model 1875 Officer's Model, the Model 1877 Carbine, and the Model 1884 Rifle and Carbine.

DISASSEMBLY

Remove ramrod (32) and tang screw (20). Pull hammer to half-cock and remove 2 side screws (21). Remove lock assembly from stock. Press in on band springs (29) and slide off both upper and lower bands (26-27). Barrel and breech assembly can now be removed from butt-stock (25).

To disassemble breech assembly, remove hinge pin (10) and withdraw breechblock assembly (11). Take care to prevent compressed ejector spring (8), spindle (9), and extractor (7) from escaping. Remove breechblock cap screw (17) and remove cam latch (15) with thumbpiece (18) and breechblock cap (16) together. Remove cam latch spring (14). Firing pin (12) is removed by unscrewing firing pin screw (13) from underside of breechblock.

Trigger mechanism in trigger guard, butt-plate, stock tip, and remaining stock parts are easily removed for repair or replacement of parts. Reassemble rifle in reverse order.

To disassemble lock mechanism, compress mainspring (D) with a Springfield or other suitable mainspring vise or heavy pliers and remove from lockplate (C). Remove sear spring screw (J) and sear spring (H) from lockplate. Remove sear screw (L) and sear (K). Remove bridle screw (N) and bridle (M). Remove tumbler screw (B) from hammer (A). Tumbler (E) may be driven from its seat in hammer with a large punch or brass drift pin. Reassemble lock in reverse order.

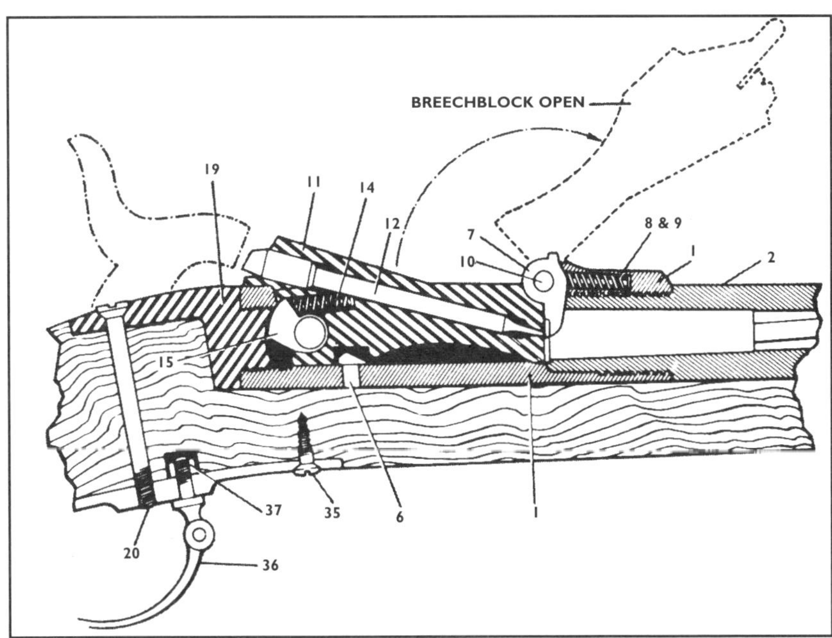

The longitudinal section through the action shows the proper relationship of interior parts

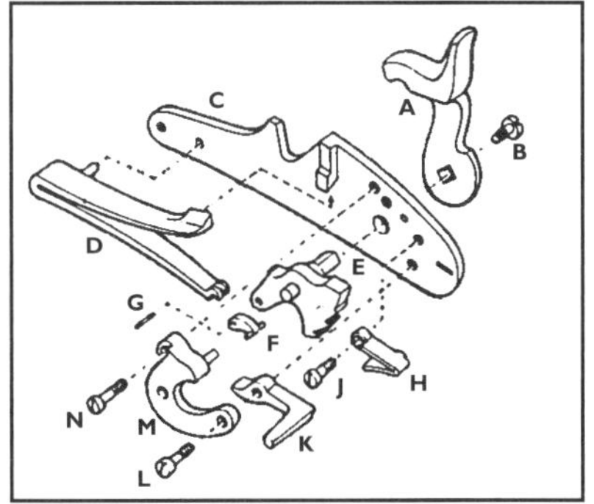

LOCK PARTS

A. Hammer
B. Tumbler screw
C. Lockplate
D. Mainspring
E. Tumbler
F. Mainspring swivel
G. Mainspring swivel pin
H. Sear spring
J. Sear spring screw
K. Sear
L. Sear screw
M. Bridle
N. Bridle screw

U.S. SPRINGFIELD M1903 RIFLE

PARTS LEGEND

1. Receiver
2. Barrel
3. Front sight (complete)
4. Front sight cover
5. Cut-off
6. Cut-off screw
7. Cut-off plunger spring
8. Cut-off plunger
9. Ejector
10. Ejector pin
11. Cut-off spindle
12. Sear pin
13. Sear spring
14. Sear
15. Trigger pin
16. Trigger
17. Floorplate catch
18. Floorplate catch spring
19. Floorplate catch pin
20. Trigger guard
21. Rear guard screw
22. Front guard screw
23. Magazine follower
24. Magazine spring
25. Floorplate
26. Rear sight assembly
27. Bolt
28. Extractor collar
29. Extractor
30. Firing pin
31. Firing pin sleeve
32. Firing pin spring
33. Bolt sleeve
34. Firing pin guide
35. Safety lock assembly
36. Bolt sleeve lock spring
37. Bolt sleeve lock
38. Bolt sleeve lock pin
39. Buttplate
40. Lower buttplate screw
41. Upper buttplate screw
42. Rear swivel
43. Rear swivel screws (2)
44. Rear stock band
45. Rear stock band swivel
46. Rear stock band screw
47. Front stock band
48. Front stock band swivel
49. Front swivel screw
50. Front stock band screw

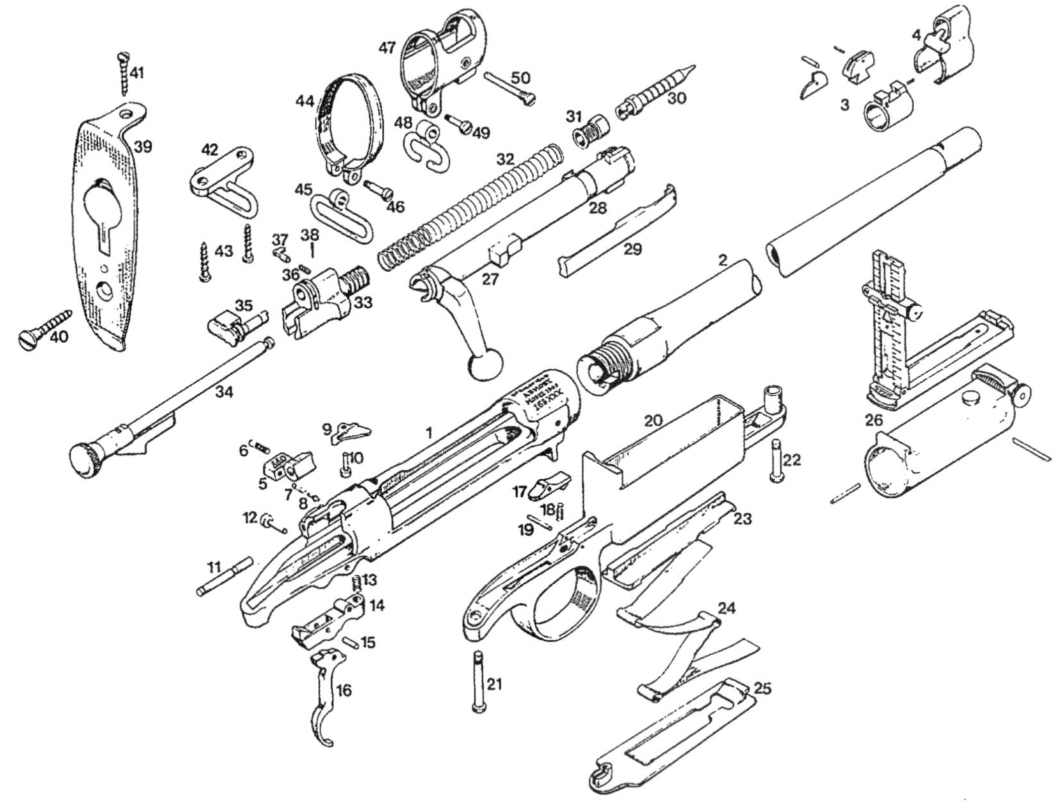

The Model 1903 or M1903 Springfield is probably most often called simply the '03 and was developed by Springfield Armory and made there and at Rock Island Arsenal beginning in 1903 to replace the Krag rifle then in U.S. service.

The M1903 rifles were all based on the Mauser 98 pattern, being 5-shot, fixed box-magazine, clip fed turnbolts with dual opposed locking lugs and full length claw extractors. From 1903 to 1906 the '03 was chambered for the bluntbulleted .30-03 cartridge. In 1906 the now-familiar .30-06 cartridge was standardized, and most .30-03 rifles were recalled and adapted to it as were subsequent M1903s.

In one form or another the Model 1903 rifle served the United States military well for a half-century and, though it began to be replaced by the semi-automatic M1 Garand rifle in 1937, was retired only after the Korean conflict.

Springfield serial numbers to 800000 and Rock Island numbers to 285507 should not be fired as they lack the heat treatment mandated in 1918 due to fractures in brittle receivers.

DISASSEMBLY

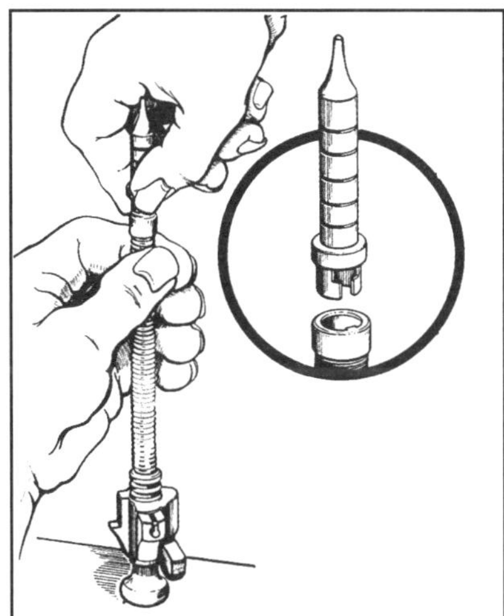

1 Check chamber and magazine to ensure that the rifle is unloaded. Set the cut-off (5) to center notch and close the bolt. With the striker cocked, set the safety (35) in a vertical position; then open the bolt and draw it out. Depress the bolt sleeve lock (37) and unscrew the bolt sleeve (33) counterclockwise.

With the striker cocked and the safety on, remove the sleeve and striker assembly to the rear. While holding the firing pin (30) draw the firing pin guide (34) to the rear and rotate the safety to a "Ready" position to relieve the spring pressure.

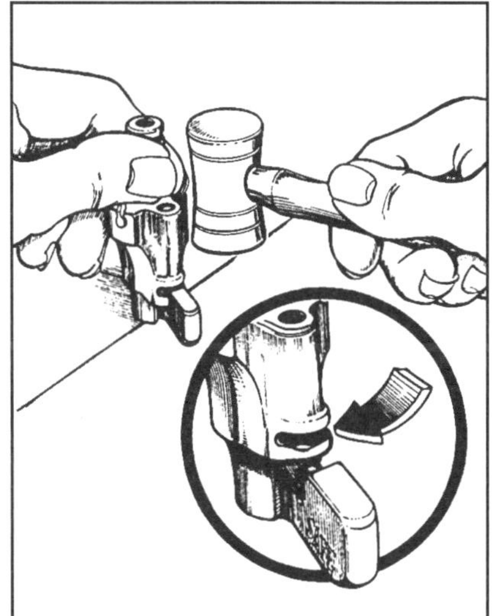

2 Slide the bolt sleeve (33) off the firing pin guide (34) and position on a solid surface. Rotate the safety (35) to the dismounting position (indicated by arrow) and strike the thumbpiece to disengage.

Rotate the extractor (29) to clear the groove in the front of the bolt and slide it forward off the extractor collar (28).

With a small drift punch depress the floor plate catch (17) to remove the floorplate (25), magazine spring (24) and follower (23). Remove the front stock-band screw (50) and slide the front stock-band (47) off the stock. (NOTE: It is necessary to remove the front sight blade before the front stock band can be removed from the barrel). Depress the lock spring (not shown) to remove the rear stock band (44) and upper hand guard. Invert the rifle and remove the front and rear guard screws (22 & 21) to separate the barrelled action, stock and trigger guard.

Remove the cut-off screw (6) from the thumbpiece to disengage the groove in the cut-off spindle (11). Support the cut-off (5) to avoid loss of the spring and plunger (7 & 8) while drawing out the spindle. Drift out the ejector pin (10) from the upper side and remove the ejector. (NOTE: this pin has a slotted head but is not a screw). Drift out the sear pin (12) from right to left and remove the sear (14), spring (13) and the trigger (16) as an assembly.

Reassembly Note: Reassemble in the reverse order ensuring that the pin in the sight slide insert properly engages the groove in the cap as it is installed in the elevation slide. To replace the safety lock assembly in the bolt sleeve use a small lever or screwdriver to depress the plunger and spring during assembly. When installing the bolt group in the receiver, the striker must be cocked and the safety should be in a vertical position.

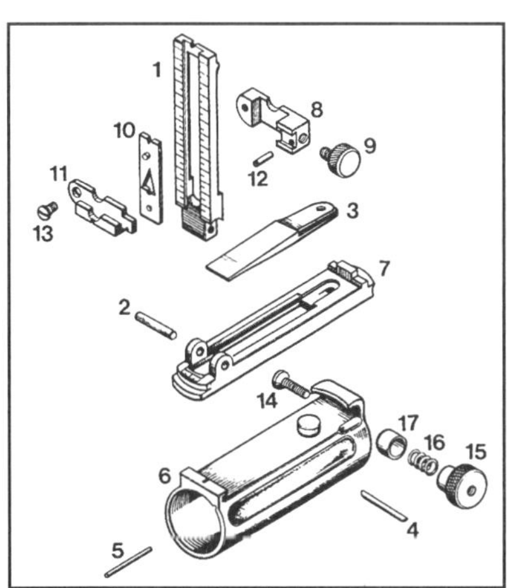

REAR SIGHT GROUP DETAIL

1. Elevation leaf
2. Elevation leaf hinge pin
3. Elevation leaf spring
4. Fixed base cross pin
5. Fixed base spline pin
6. Fixed base sleeve
7. Sight base
8. Slide base
9. Slide blade tension screw
10. Slide insert
11. Slide sight cap
12. Slide sight cap pin
13. Slide sight cap screw
14. Windage screw
15. Windage screw knob
16. Windage spring
17. Windage spring collar

3 Rear Sight Disassembly: Remove the rear sight assembly by turning the windage knob (15) to disengage the sight base (7) from the windage screw (14) and to clear the undercut of the base sleeve. The rear sight subassembly may now be lifted off the pivot lug for field cleaning. (Fig. 3). Further disassembly should be completed in a shop environment as follows: Pivot the elevation leaf (1) forward and drift out the hinge pin (2) while depressing the leaf spring (3). Removal of this spring is facilitated by inserting a pin punch in the small hole in the spring body and sliding it forward to clear the mortise in the base. Remove the slide sight cap screw (13) and drift out the slide sight cap pin (12). Remove the slide blade tension screw (9) and press out the slide sight cap (11) from left to right. This disengages the slide base (8) from the elevation leaf and permits the slide insert (10) to be removed from its groove in the graduated sight leaf. The windage collar (17), knob (15), screw (14) and spring (16) should be removed from the fixed base as an assembly. This may be accomplished by depressing the collar and spring to free the assembly to be drifted from its seat. The fixed base sleeve (6) may be removed by drifting out the lower cross pin (4) and driving the base forward off the spline pin (5). Removal of this base is generally not required except when sporterizing or installing custom sights

U.S. SPRINGFIELD M1903A3 RIFLE

PARTS LEGEND

1.Receiver
2. Handguard ring
3. Barrel
4. Front sight base
5. Front sight
6. Front sight pin
7. Front sight base pin
8. Front sight base key
9. Upper band
10. Upper band screw
11. Stacking swivel assembly
12. Upper swivel assembly
13. Bolt
14. Extractor collar
15. Extractor
16. Striker
17. Striker sleeve
18. Mainspring
19. Bolt sleeve
20. Safety lock assembly
21. Bolt sleeve lock spring
22. Bolt sleeve lock
23. Bolt sleeve lock pin
24. Firing pin rod
25. Aperture spring screw
26. Aperture spring
27. Aperture
28. Windage yoke
29. Windage yoke spring
30. Windage yoke plunger
31. Rear sight base screw
32. Windage index knob screw
33. Windage index knob
34. Windage index knob spring
35. Rear sight base
36. Windage yoke screw
37. Ejector
38. Ejector pin
39. Cut-off plunger
40. Cut-off plunger spring
41. Cut-off
42. Cut-off screw
43. Sear retaining pin
44. Spindle
45. Trigger pin
46. Sear spring
47. Sear
48. Trigger
49. Magazine follower
50. Magazine spring
51. Rear guard screw
52. Front guard screw
53. Trigger guard
54. Stock group
55. Handguard assembly

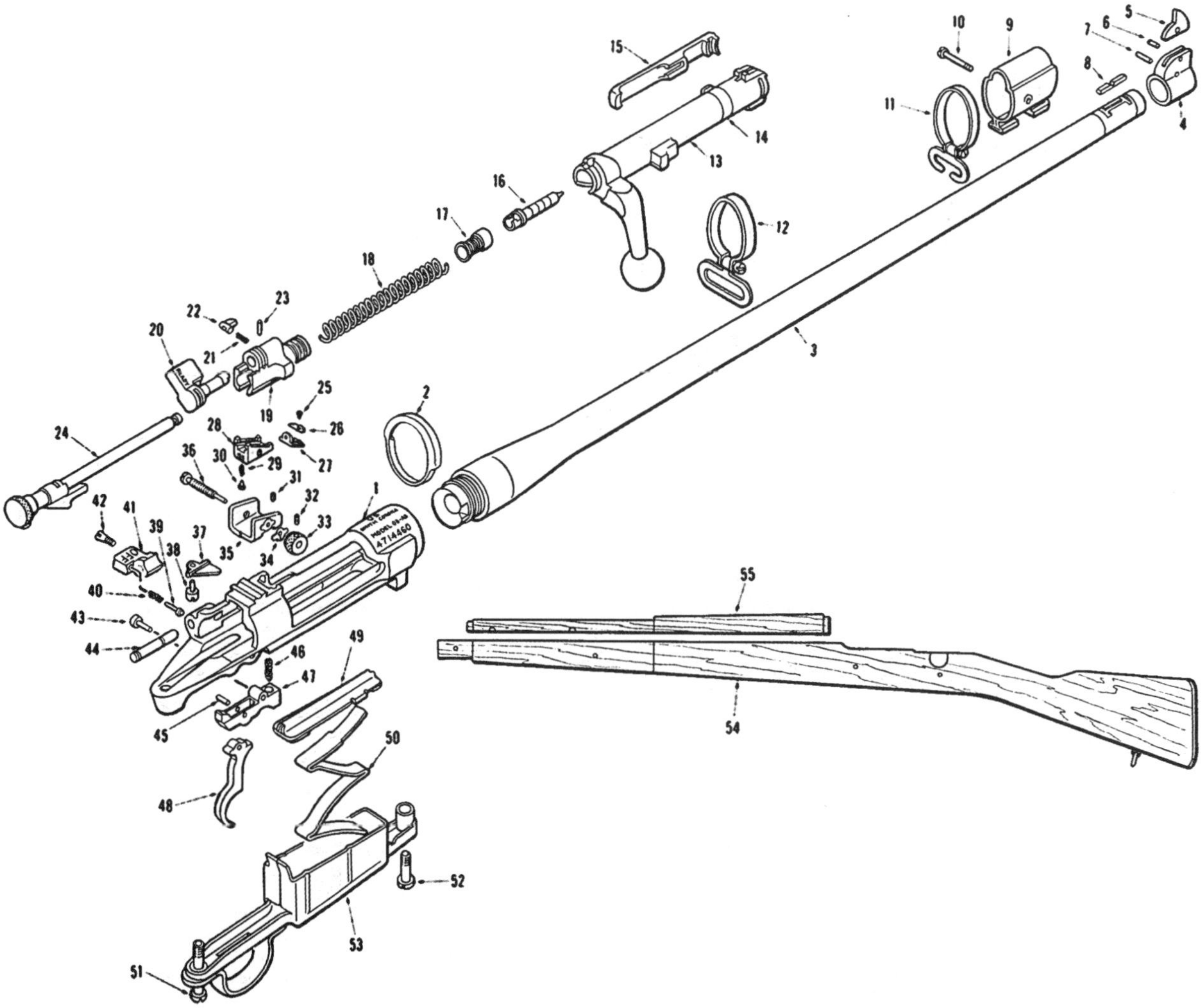

In September of 1941, some months after the United States entry into World War II, Remington Arms began production of the M1903 rifle using old machine tools from the Rock Island Arsenal. With production complicated by worn out tooling, Remington requested Army approval to redesign parts and simplify production.

Milled parts were replaced with stamped parts and eventually the Army designated the revised '03 as the M1903A3. Finger grooves were eliminated from the stock and all stock furniture was produced in stamped metal. The barrel-mounted rear sight was replaced with a simpler peep sight mounted on the rear of the receiver. In early 1942 Smith/Corona Typewriter Company also began production of the M1903A3. Rifles manufactured by Remington and Smith/Corona were finished with a dark gray/black and were Parkerized by late 1943.

The M1903A3 rifle was used as an auxiliary combat weapon and saw extensive use and action Europe, North Africa, and the Pacific. It remained a standard sniper rifle (the M1903A4 fitted the scope over the action) and was issued to grenadiers fitted with a spigot-type rifle-grenade launcher.

DISASSEMBLY

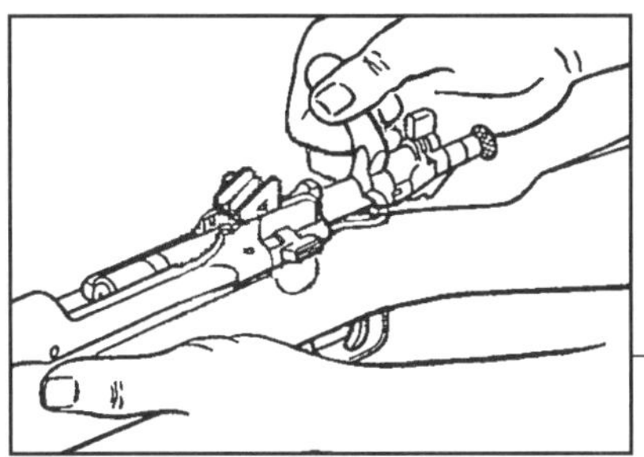

1 To remove bolt assembly cock rifle and then turn safety lock (20) until thumbpiece is vertical. Rotate cut-off (41) to center notch position and pull bolt assembly to rear and out of receiver.

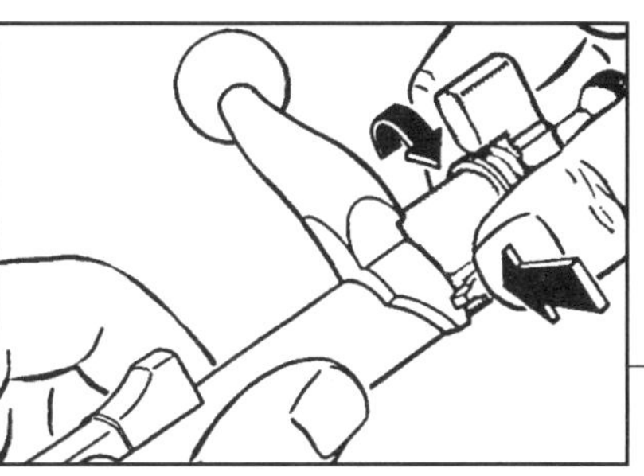

2 To remove firing pin mechanism from bolt depress bolt sleeve lock (22) with thumbnail and unscrew bolt sleeve (19) with firing pin mechanism from bolt (13).

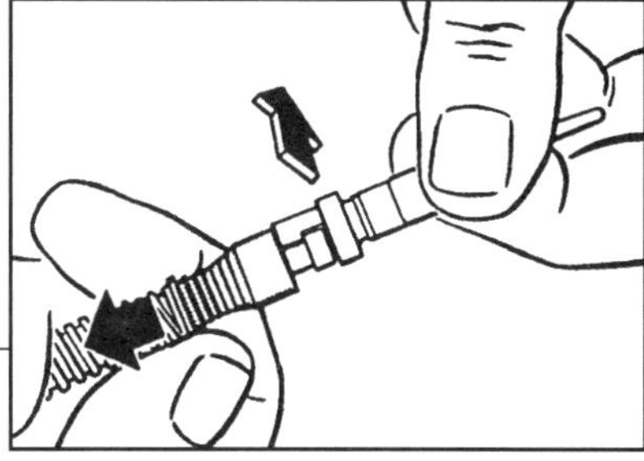

3 Disassemble firing pin mechanism by rotating safety lock (20) to "Ready" position. Place cocking knob of firing pin rod (24) against bench top and pull striker sleeve (17) to rear until striker (16) can be pulled away from end of firing pin rod.

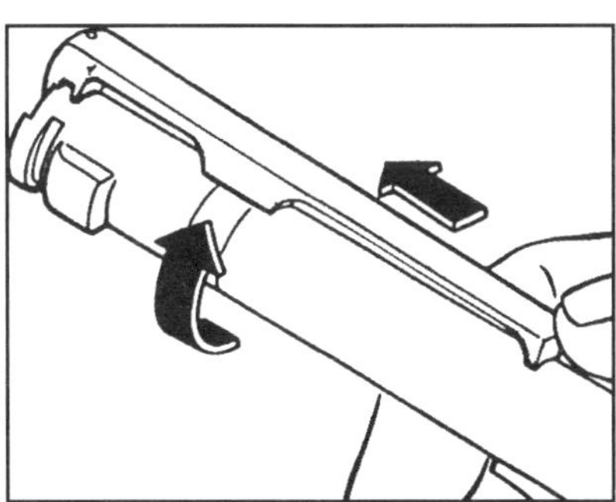

4 To remove extractor (15) from bolt (13), turn it to right, forcing its tongue out of its groove in front of bolt. Then force extractor forward and off bolt.

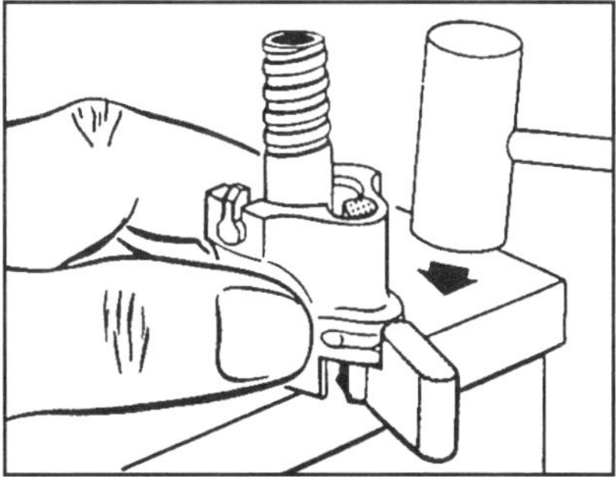

5 To remove safety lock assembly (20) from bolt sleeve (19) turn safety lock to dismounting bevel position on bolt sleeve halfway between the "Ready" and vertical position. Then tap front face of thumbpiece with plastic hammer or block of wood to disengage it from bolt sleeve.

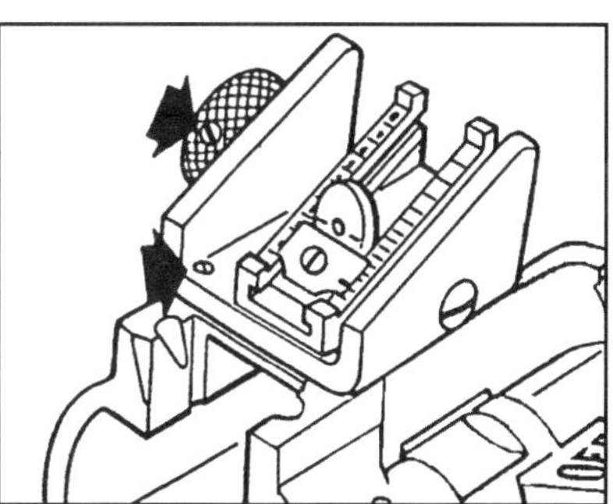

6 To remove rear sight assembly loosen windage index knob screw (32) far enough to free windage index knob (33) from windage yoke screw (36). Turn out windage yoke screw from base and lift windage yoke (28) and attached parts from sight base. Turn out rear sight base screw (31) and drive base from receiver with drift and hammer.

U.S. SPRINGFIELD MODEL 1922 M2

PARTS LEGEND

1. Barrel
2. Receiver
3. Rear sight
4. Ejector stop
5. Ejector stop screw
6. Sear retaining pin
7. Ejector stop plunger spring
8. Ejector stop plunger
9. Spindle
10. Trigger pin
11. Sear spring
12. Sear
13. Trigger
14. Magazine retaining spring
15. Rear guard screw
16. Trigger guard
17. Floorplate catch pin
18. Floorplate catchspring
19. Floorplate catch
20. Front guardscrew
21. Floorplate
22. Magazine
23. Butt swivel screw (2)
24. Butt swivel
25. Lower buttplate screw
26. Buttplate
27. Top buttplate screw
28. Front swivel
29. Front swivel screw
30. Front band
31. Front band retaining pin
32. Sight base screw
33. Front sight
34. Front sight pin
35. Movable stud
36. Firing pin nut
37. Firing pin nut locking spring
38. Cocking piece
39. Bolt sleeve
40. Safety lock
41. Safety lock plunger spring
42. Safety lock plunger
43. Bolt sleeve lock pin
44. Mainspring
45. Firing pin
46. Bolt handle
47. Bolt head
48. Ejector retaining pin
49. Extractor
50. Ejector
51. Ejector spring
52. Bolt sleeve lock
53. Bolt sleeve lock spring
54. Stock

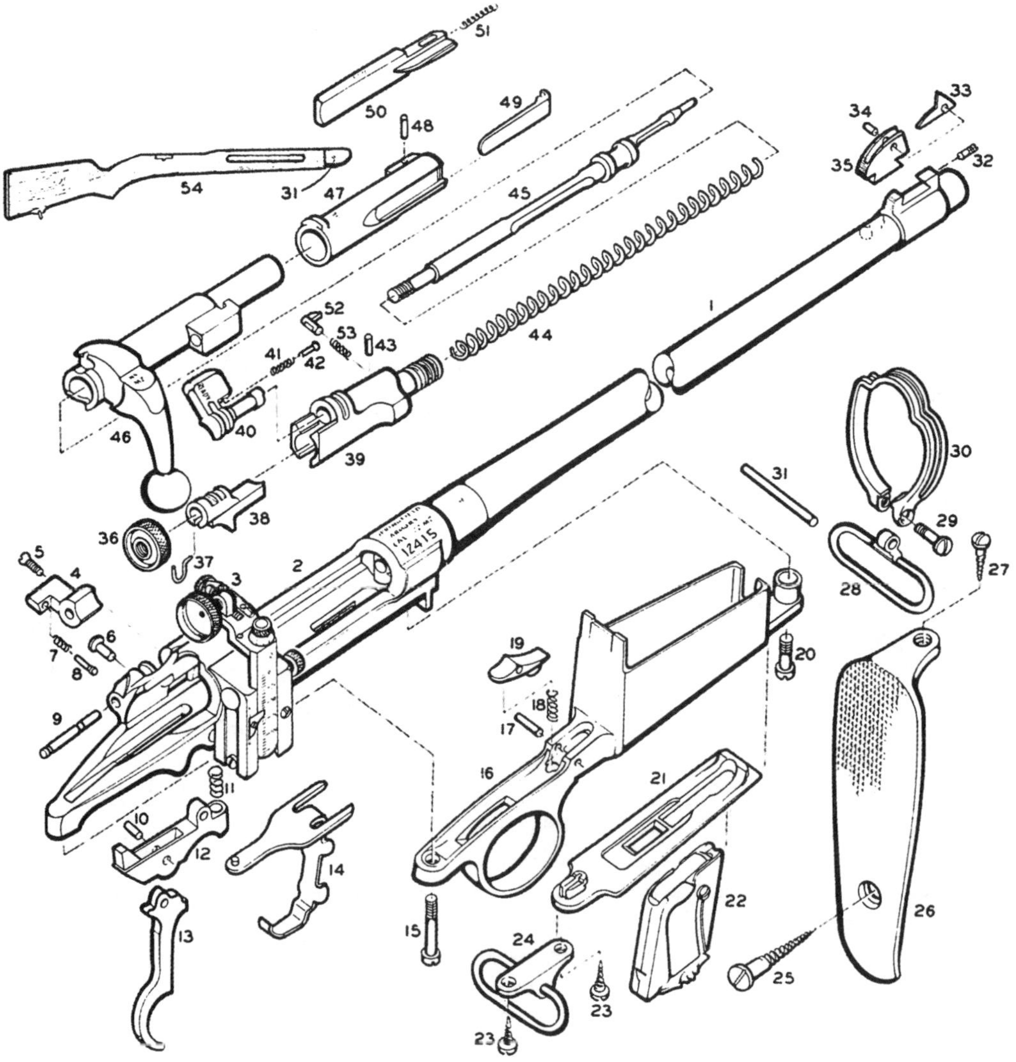

The U.S. M1922 M2 rifle, chambered for the .22 Long Rifle cartridge, was the last in a series of .22 caliber target rifles manufactured at Springfield Armory. It was issued for training and was furnished to high schools and colleges for marksmanship training. M1922s were also sold to NRA members through the office of the Director of Civilian Marksmanship (DCM). Manufacture was discontinued during World War II, but repair functions were continued for several years. The M1922 M2 rifle is now obsolete.

The M1922 M2 is a modification of the M1922 M1 which was in turn developed from the Model 1922 rifle first made in that year. Significant features of the M1922 M2 rifle, in comparison with earlier models, are its shortened striker fall, shortened bolt travel and provision for headspace adjustment within the bolt handle assembly (final version). The M1922 M1 rifle was converted to M2-type by installing the later M2 bolt.

Receiver markings on M1922 M2 rifles are somewhat confusing since arsenal modifications of earlier models to M2-type took place after design of the M2 version had been standardized and its manufacture begun.

The model designations of modified rifles were changed to indicate that an alteration had been performed and several receiver markings will be found on M2 rifles. Rifles with the letters A or B following the serial number are modified arms.

DISASSEMBLY

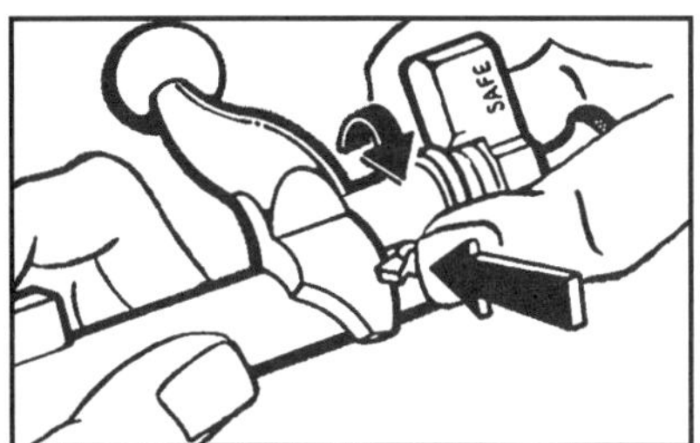

1 Remove bolt assembly by cocking rifle and turning safety lock (40) until thumbpiece is vertical. Rotate ejector stop (4) to center notch position and withdraw bolt assembly. Remove firing pin mechanism from bolt assembly by depressing bolt sleeve lock (52) with thumbnail. Then unscrew bolt sleeve (39) ¼ turn until bolt head can be pulled forward and away from bolt handle. Then unscrew firing pin mechanism from bolt handle.

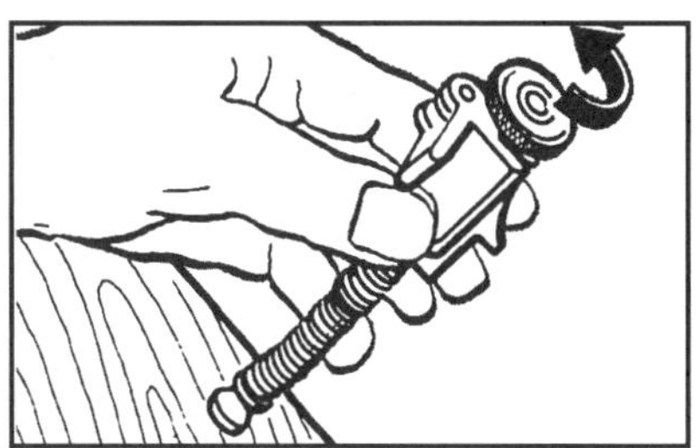

2 Release safety lock and insert striker end of firing pin (45) into a ¼-inch hole in workbench and push inward on bolt sleeve to compress mainspring (44). Unscrew firing pin nut (36) and slowly release tension on mainspring until cocking piece (38) and bolt sleeve separate from firing pin. Then remove the mainspring from firing pin.

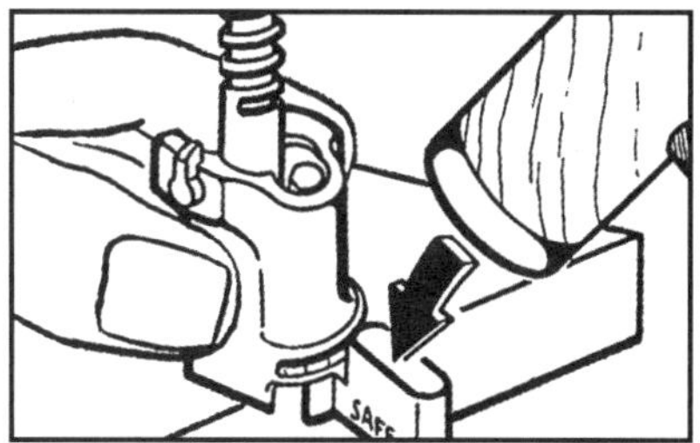

3 Remove safety lock (40) from bolt sleeve by turning it to dismounting bevel position on bolt sleeve halfway between the ready and vertical position. Tap front face of thumbpiece with plastic hammer to disengage it from bolt sleeve.

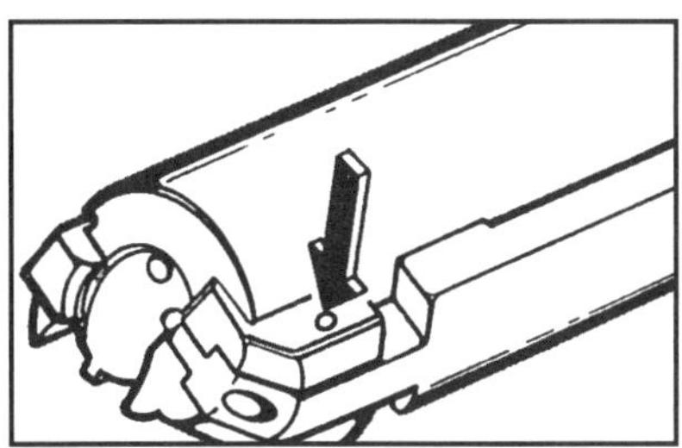

4 Remove ejector (50) by drifting out ejector retaining pin (48). Ejector and ejector spring (51) may be withdrawn from face of bolt head (47).

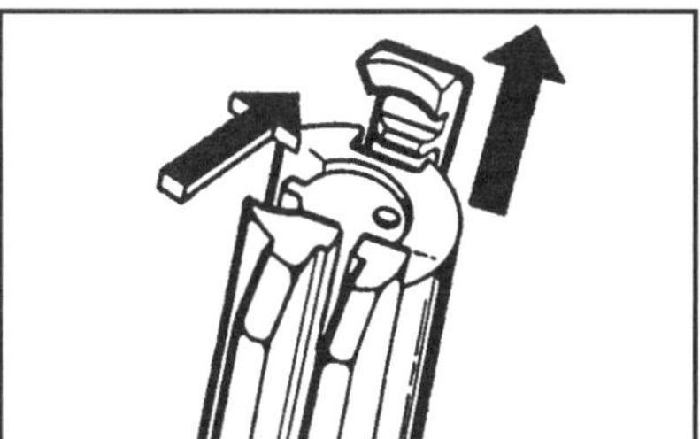

5 Extractor (49) may be removed by forcing lip end away from bolt head face and disengaging its tongue from slot in bolt head and simultaneously forcing it forward and off bolt head.

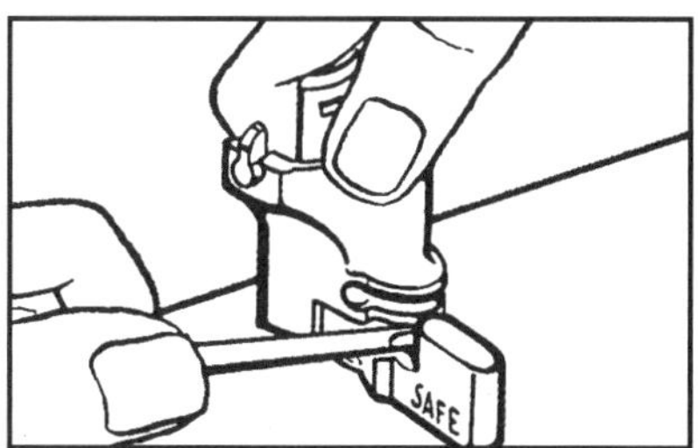

6 Other disassembly is readily apparent. Reassemble rifle in reverse order. To assemble safety lock and bolt sleeve, insert spindle of the safety lock into bolt sleeve hole. Then, with thumbpiece vertical, insert small screwdriver blade between safety lock spindle and safety lock plunger (42), forcing it into thumbpiece until it slips over the edge of sleeve. Continued pressure on safety lock thumbpiece together with withdrawal of screwdriver completes assembly.

VALMET

VALMET MODEL 412 SHOTGUN

PARTS LEGEND

1. Locking bolt
2. Top snap
3. Top snap plunger
4. Top snap plunger washer
5. Top snap spring
6. Safety button
7. Safety pin
8. Safety spring
9. Indicator (2)
10. Top snap pin
11. Top slide trip
12. Top slide trip spring
13. Top slide trip pin
14. Frame assembly
15. Striker (2)
16. Firing pin (2)
17. Firing pin spring (2)
18. Striker pin
19. Screw
20. Ejector operating pin
21. Ejector operating pin spring
22. Cocking crank, right
23. Cocking crank, left
24. Cocking slide spring
25. Hammer, right
26. Hammer, left
27. Support plate
28. Mainspring plunger, left
29. Mainspring plunger, right
30. Mainspring (2)
31. Sear (2)
32. Trigger Pin (2)
33. Sear spring
34. Inertia block
35. Trigger
36. Selector Button
37. Selector cam
38. Selector cam spring
39. Cocking slide
40. Striker pin
41. Ejector spring plunger (2)
42. Ejector spring (2)
43. Barrels
44. Front sight bead
45. Rear sight bead
46. Ejector operating rod, right
47. Ejector operating rod, left
48. Ejector trip
49. Ejector trip spring
50. Covering plate
51. Covering plate screw
52. Fore-end iron
53. Fore-end screw
54. Fore-end wood
55. Fore-end wood (Model Vainio)
56. Fore-end snap spring
57. Fore-end snap assembly
58. Stock bolt washer
59. Fore-end screw
60. Stock
61. Snap pin
62. Stock bolt
63. Butt plate spacer
64. Rubber butt pad
65. Buttpad screw
66. Buttplate
67. Rear trigger
68. Front trigger
69. Trigger spring
70. Screw
71. Buttplate (wood)
72. Safety button
73. Screw
74. Safety spring
75. Ejector, right
76. Ejector, left
77. Barrels (extractor)
78. Extractor
79. Screw
80. Screw
81. Extractor
82. Barrels (combination)
83. Sight plate
84. Spring
85. Crank pin (not shown)
86. Sight bead
87. Sight bead
88. Barrels (rifle)
89. Barrels (side extractor)
90. Extractor
91. Extractor, right
92. Extractor, left
93. Spring pin
94. Rear swivel bow body
95. Front swivel bow body
96. Swivel bow
97. Cocking crank pin
98. Hammer pin
99. Front swivel bow body
100. Trigger adjusting screw
101. Trigger adjusting screw

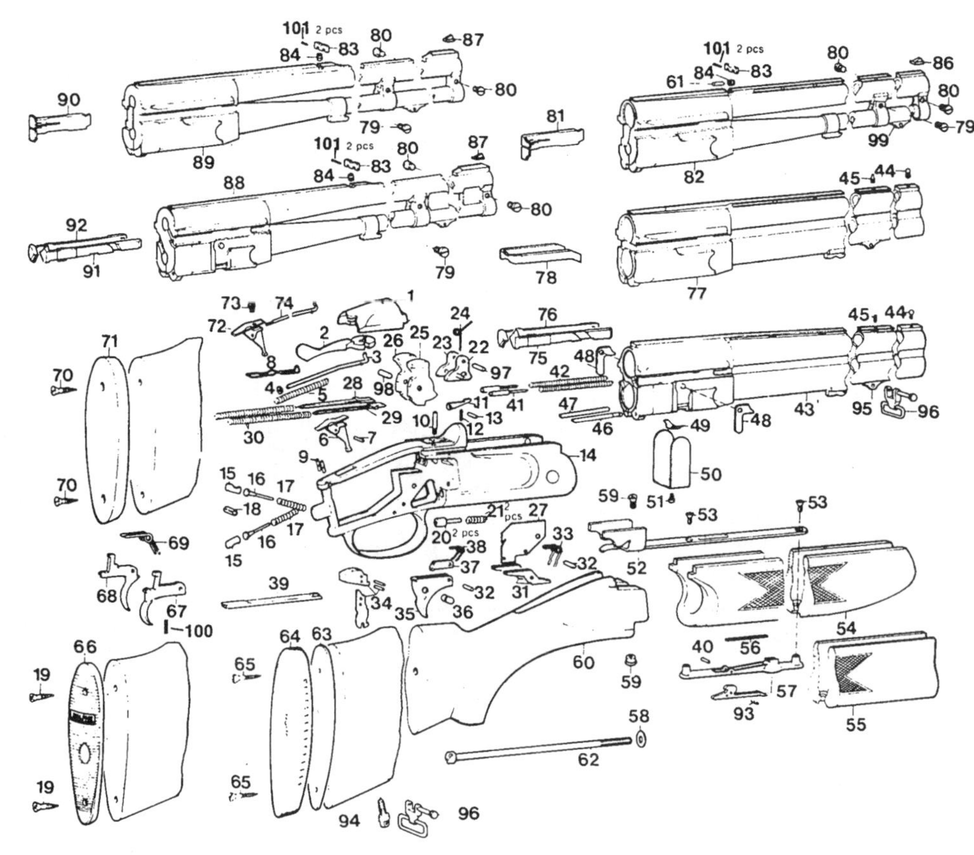

The Valmet over-under shotgun was manufactured the Tourula Works in Finland and first imported into the United States in 1952. The original model, imported by Firearms International, had a plain extractor, no sighting or side ribs, and was bolted by a sliding top lock. Its single trigger mechanism was mounted on a detachable plate.

Beginning in 1969, the Valmet gun was sold under the Savage Arms name. The Savage Model 330 differed from the original version in a number of details. The Model 333, introduced in 1972, had automatic ejectors and a ventilated rib. Its mechanism was different from earlier versions and few parts are interchangeable. The Model 2400 is a combination rifle/shotgun with a 12-gauge top barrel and .222 Rem. or .308 Win. lower barrel. Savage-Valmet guns were discontinued in 1979.

The Model 412, imported by Valmet USA in 1980, resembles the Model 333, but differs in that it accepts several barrel sets on one frame. Shotgun, rifle and combination sets are interchangable without special fitting.

In 1987 Valmet merged with Sako and firearms production under the Valmet name was discontinued by the mid 1990s. A version of the Valmet 412 combination gun, now discontinued, was produced as the Tikka 512.

DISASSEMBLY

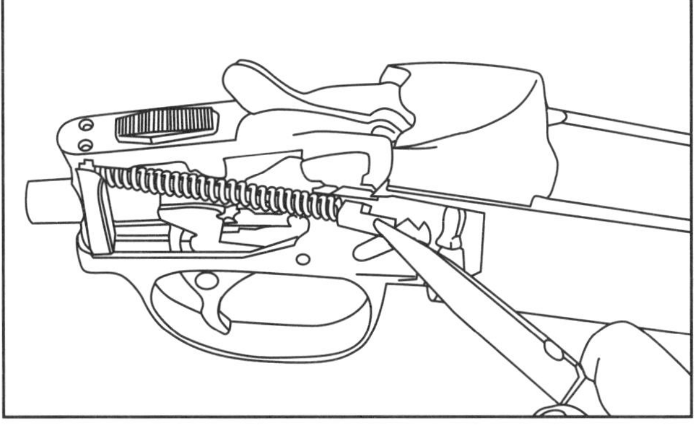

1 Disassemble the forearm and barrels from the frame. Remove the stock by taking out the two screws which hold the buttpad and unscrewing the stock bolt (62). Press the top slide trip (11) and pull the trigger twice to lower the hammers. Remove the mainsprings (30) and plungers (28 and 29) by lifting upward on the front of the plungers.

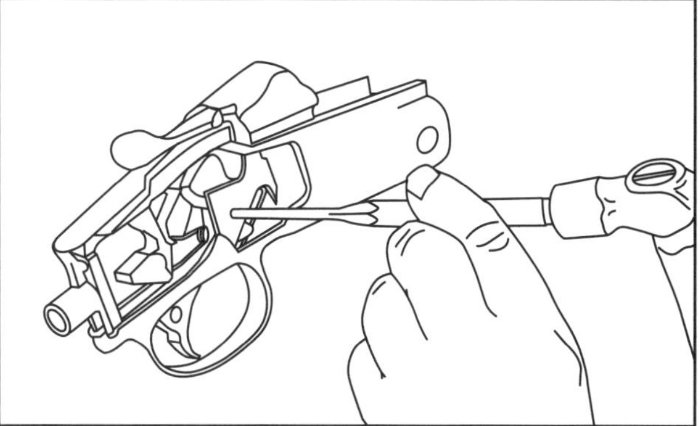

2 Drift out the hammer pin (98) (Figure B) and the sear and trigger pins (32). The support plate (27) will come out with the hammers (25 and 26) and sears (31). Drift out the safety pin (7) and remove the safety button (6) and spring (8) and cocking indicators (9). Also, the top snap plunger (3), washer (4) and spring (5).

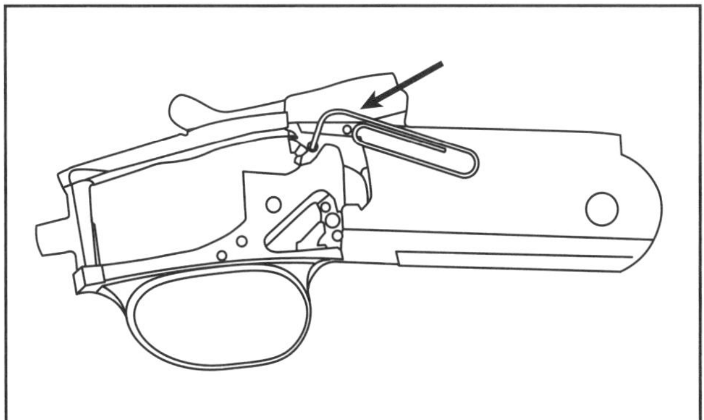

3 Insert a paper clip (Figure C, arrow) and carefully rotate the top snap pin (10) ½ turn and then pull it downward. Slide the locking bolt (1) and top snap (2) off the frame. Drift out the striker pin (18) to free the strikers (15), firing pins (16) and springs (17). Drift out the hammer pin (98) (Figure B) and the sear and trigger pins (32). The support plate (27) will come out with the hammers (25 and 26) and sears (31). Drift out the safety pin (7) and remove the safety button (6) and spring (8) and cocking indicators (9) also, the top snap plunger (3), washer (4) and spring (5).

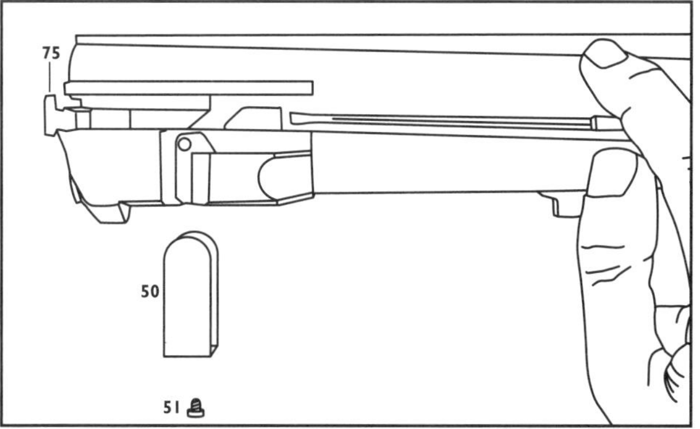

4 To take out the ejectors, remove the covering plate screw (51) and slide the covering plate (50) downward. Lift up on the front end of each ejector (Figure D). The ejectors (75 and 76), plungers (41) and springs (42) will slide out to the rear. When possible, avoid removing the ejector cocking mechanism as it is not easily reassembled.

WEATHERBY MARK V RIFLE

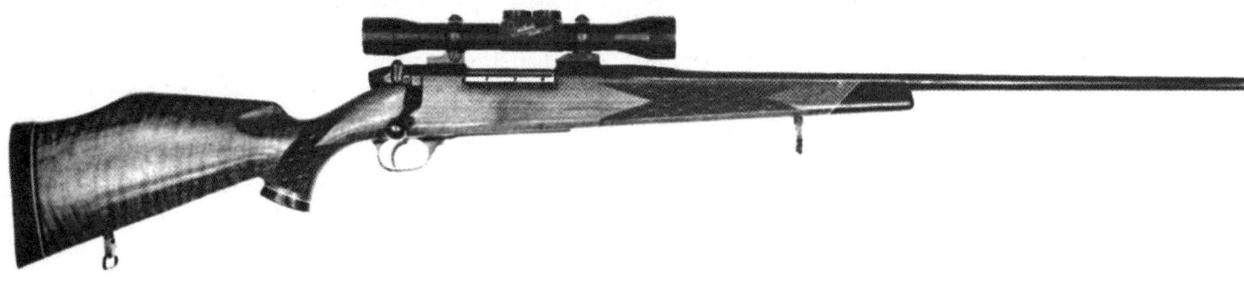

PARTS LEGEND

1. Barrel
2. Filler screw (4)
3. Receiver
4. Bolt
5. Extractor spring
6. Extractor
7. Extractor pin
8. Ejector pin
9. Ejector
10. Ejector spring
11. Firing pin
12. Firing pin spring
13. Bolt sleeve
14. Firing pin retaining ball
15. Cocking piece
16. Safety lever
17. Safety hook screw
18. Safety hook spring
19. Safety hook
20. Magazine box
21. Magazine floorplate release pin
22. Trigger guard
23. Rear trigger guard screw
24. Floorplate catch spring
25. Magazine floorplate catch
26. Magazine floorplate
27. Magazine follower
28. Follower spring
29. Front trigger guard screw
30. Floorplate pin
31. Trigger
32. Trigger release pin
33. Stop screw (3)
34. Bolt release
35. Bolt release pin
36. Tru-arc-ring (3)
37. Side plate
38. Sear
39. Sear lock pin
40. Sear torsion spring
41. Sear pin
42. Sear torsion spring pin
43. Trigger housing
44. Trigger spring
45. Bolt stop
46. Bolt stop spring
47. Trigger housing pin
48. Trigger pin
49. Swivel assembly (2)
50. Stock
51. Buttplate

* Permanently bonded to stock

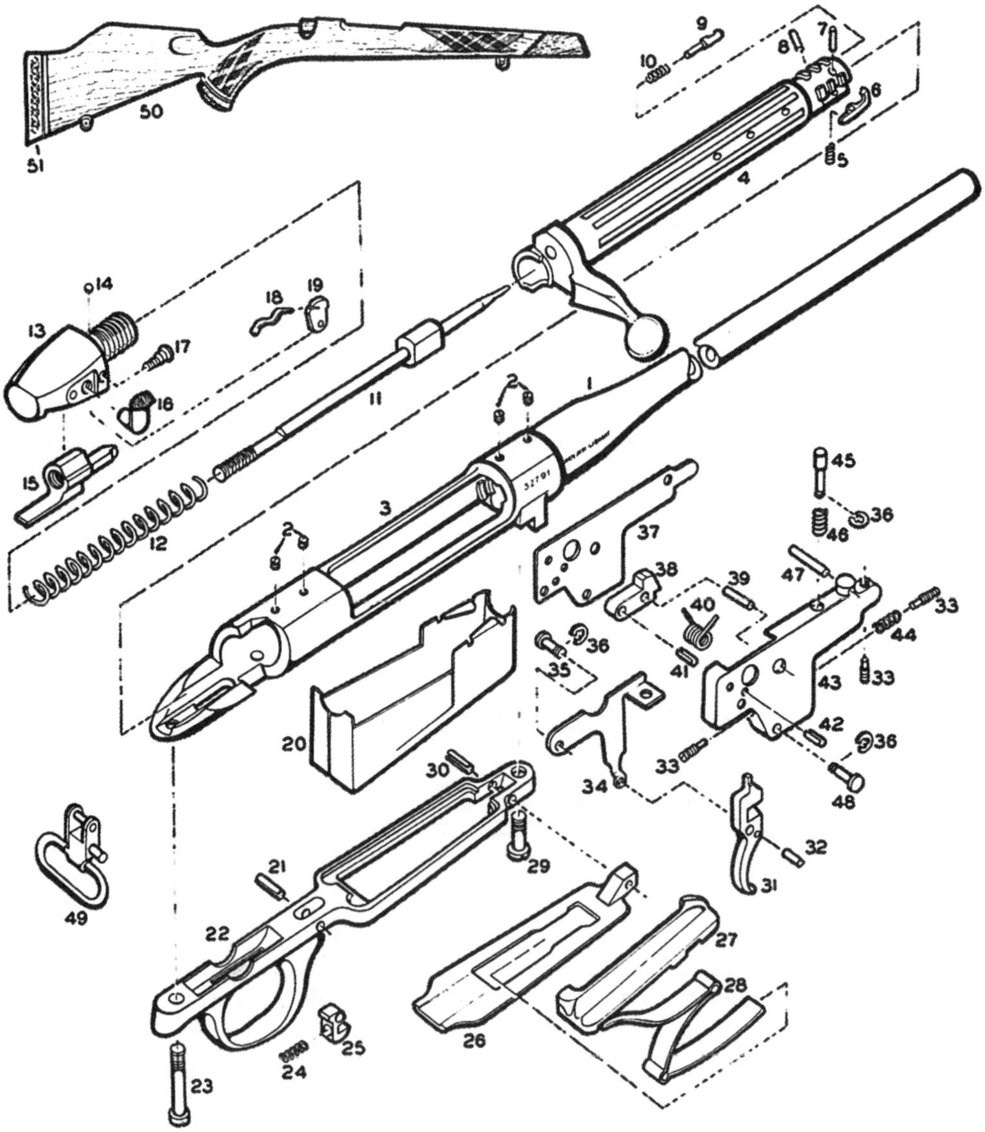

The Weatherby Mark V bolt-action center-fire rifle was introduced in 1958. Its action features locking lugs on the forepart of the bolt engaging locking recesses in the receiver ring. The lug portion of the bolt head is the same diameter as the body eliminating the need for locking lug raceways in the receiver. Cocking is done on opening of the bolt.

An interesting feature in this action is the deep counterbore in the face of the bolt which shrouds the cartridge head. The breech face is counterbored to enclose the bolt head provideing maximum support for the head of the cartridge case.

The Mark V rifle was initially made with major action parts machined from investment castings, but forgings are now used. In later models the safety was moved from the right of the receiver tang to the bolt sleeve. The bolt body has also been fluted to reduce friction and act as troughs for dust and grit.

DISASSEMBLY

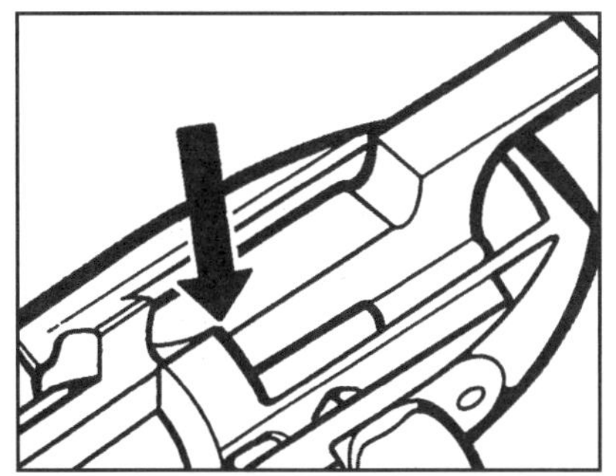

1 Commence disassembly by opening bolt and withdrawing rearward. Pull trigger (31) as far as possible and remove bolt from receiver (3). Engage step of cocking piece (15) on edge of bench and move it rearward approximately ⅛. Rotate cocking piece onto its engaging shoulder in bolt sleeve (13, arrow)..

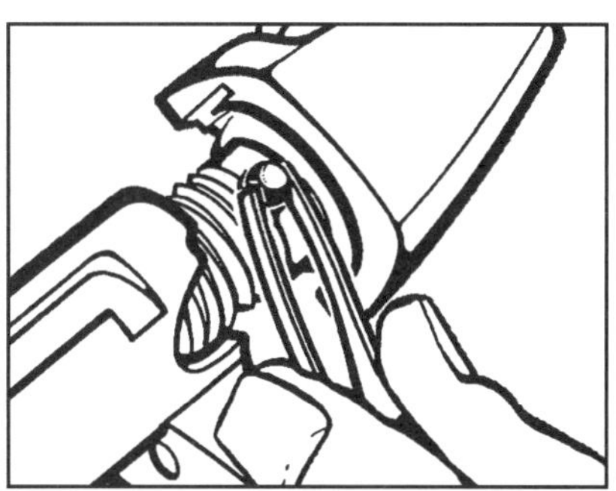

2 Unscrew the bolt (4) from the firing pin assembly. After one or two turns of the bolt, remove firing pin retaining ball (14) through helical opening in bolt. Use tweezers to facilitate this.

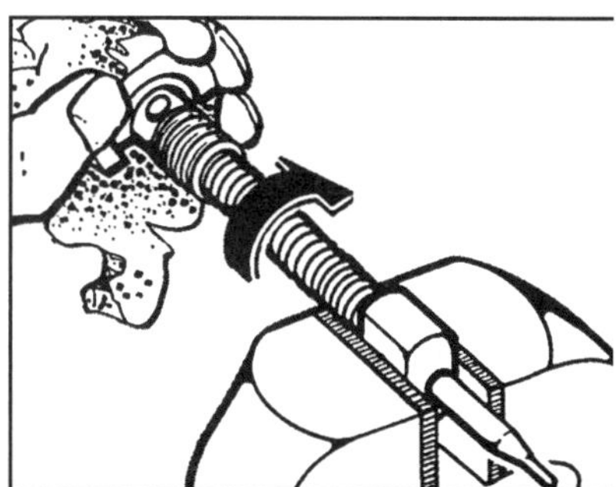

3 With bolt removed from firing pin assembly, release cocking piece from its engaging shoulder. It will move forward into slot in bolt sleeve. Place lug of firing pin (11) in vise with padded jaws and unscrew bolt sleeve from firing pin, maintaining a steady pressure against firing pin spring (12) to prevent parts from flying when firing pin disengages from cocking piece. When reassembling, be sure that the retaining ball (14) lies on the flat of firing pin.

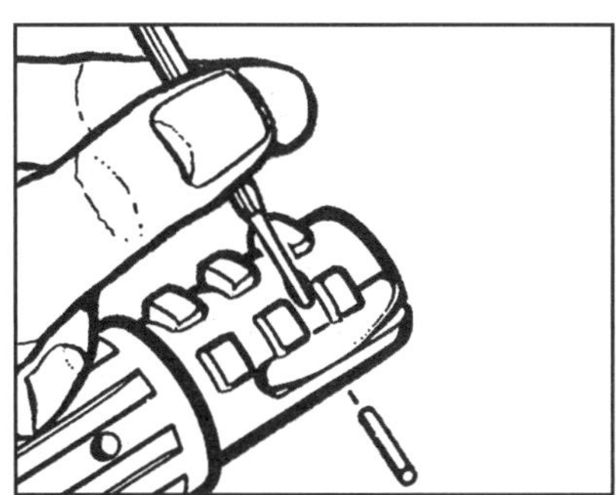

4 Remove extractor (6), or ejector (9), by first drifting out extractor (ejector) pin (7 or 8). Leave drift punch in hole.

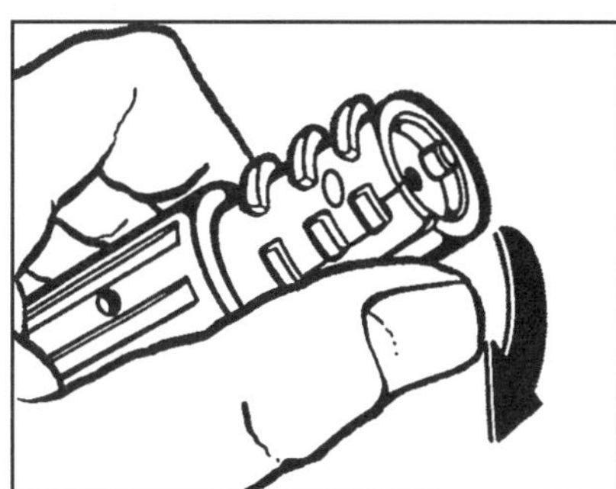

5 Compress extractor (ejector) with thumb and remove drift punch. Release extractor (ejector) slowly until spring (5 or 10) is no longer loaded. Remove spring by tapping on wood surface. It will fall out.

6 Remove front and rear trigger guard screws (29 & 23), trigger guard assembly, and barrel assembly from stock (50). Loosen stop screw (33, lower arrow). Drift out trigger housing pin (47, upper arrow) and remove trigger assembly from bottom of receiver. Further disassembly of trigger housing is not recommended. Reassemble in reverse order.

WEATHERBY MARK XXII RIFLE

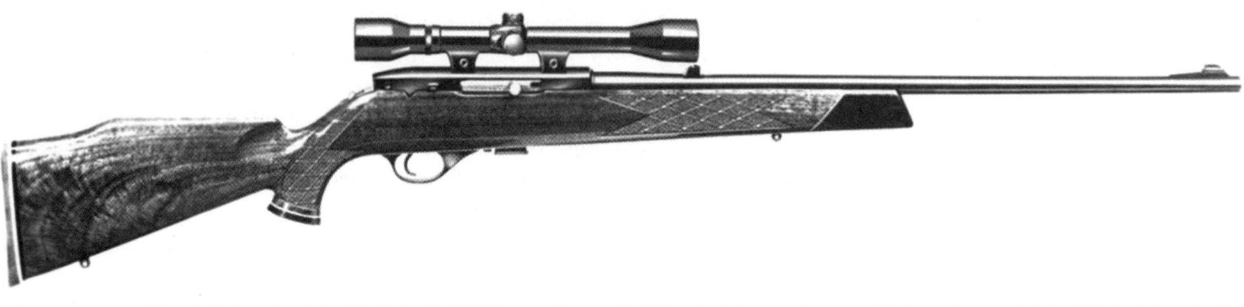

PARTS LEGEND

1. Magazine (10-shot)
2. Mag. (five-shot) not shown
3. Front trigger guard screw
4. Rear trigger guard screw
5. Trigger guard
6. Stock
7. Sling swivel
8. Buttpad & screws
9. Takedown pin & spring
10. Receiver
11. Locating pin
12. Barrel pin
13. Barrel
14. Front sight
15. Front sight ramp screw
16. Front sight ramp
17. Rear sight
18. Operating handle
19. Extractor
20. Extractor plunger
21. Extractor spring
22. Operating handle plunger
23. Firing pin retaining pin
24. Firing pin
25. Firing pin spring
26. Bolt (not shown)
27. Recoil spring guide
28. Recoil spring
29. Pins for 31, 34, 39
30. Stop pins for 31, 39, 41
31. Hammer
32. Hammer spring guide
33. Hammer spring
34. Trigger
35. Trigger spring
36. Disconnector pin
37. Disconnector
38. Disconnector spring
39. Sear
40. Magazine release spring
41. Magazine release
42. Safety tang plate
43. Safety slide
44. Safety button
45. Safety lever pin
46. Safety lever
47. Safety lever spring
48. Selector stud ring
49. Selector lever
50. Selector lever pin ring
51. Selector lever plate pin
52. Selector stud lock ring
53. Selector stud
54. Selector lever plate
55. Trigger assembly screw
56. Selector spring
57. Bolt lock pin ring
58. Bolt lock pin
59. Bolt lock lever
60. Bolt lock spring
61. Tension screw
62. Trigger frame assembly

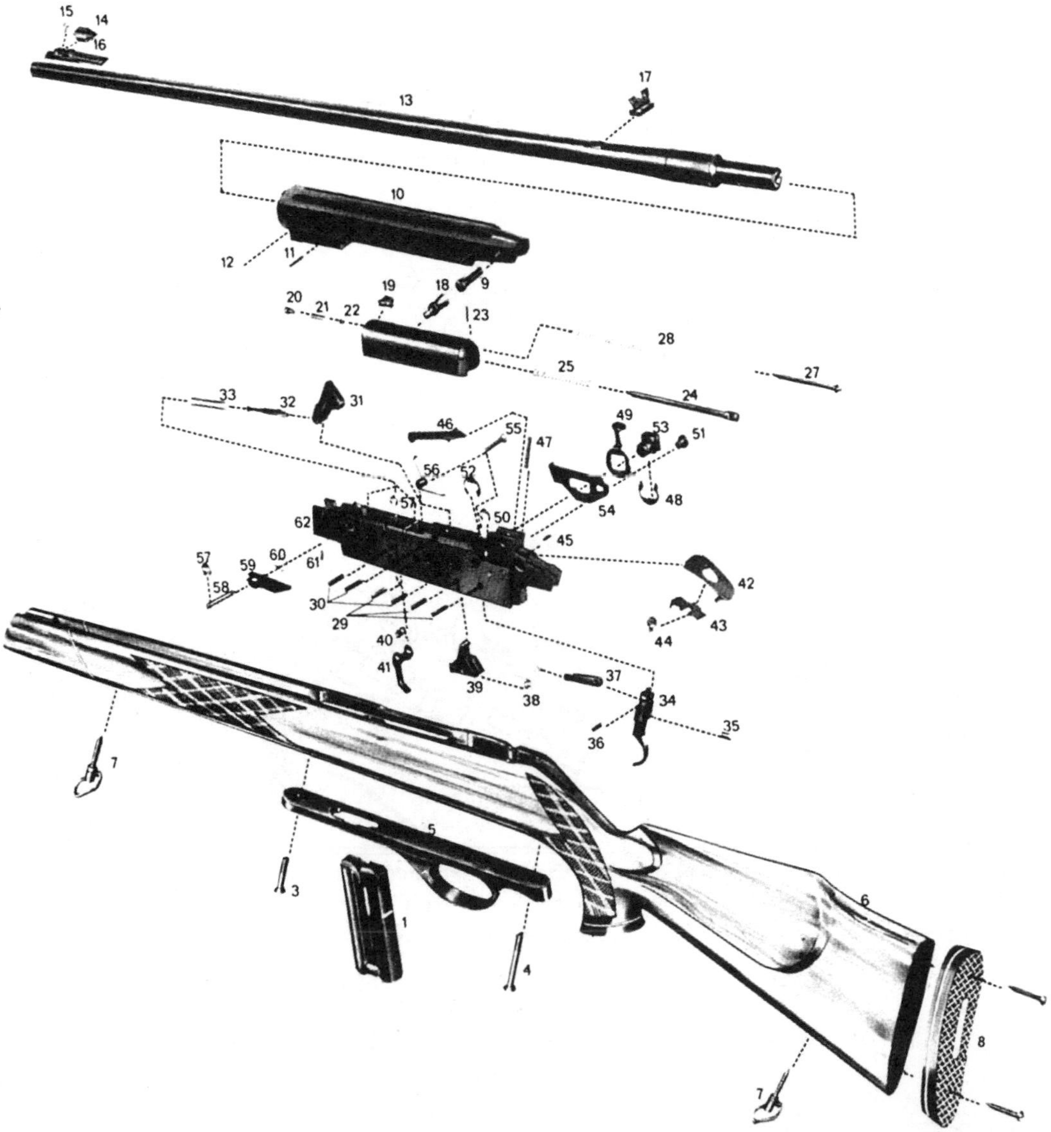

In 1963, Weatherby introduced the Mark XXII rifle chambered for the .22 Long Rifle cartridge. The Mark XXII incorporates a change lever system which permits the shooter to choose semi-automatic or single-shot fire. A single-pin takedown feature permits quick removal of the barreled action from the stock. The takedown feature and no-tool field stripping provide quick access to the breech area for cleaning.

The Mark XXII has a 24-inch contoured barrel and full-length walnut stock. The rifle comes with a 10-shot detachable magazine and 5-shot magazines are available. A tubular magazine version of the rifle was developed in 1972.

The original rifle design was produced by Beretta in Italy. The rifle was sold in Europe under the name Weatherby-Beretta. In 1967, Weatherby transferred production to Japan, but Beretta continued to produce and market the rifle until 1972, when Weatherby established its own marketing programs in Europe. Serial numbers on the rifles without a prefix were manufactured by Beretta. Numbers with a prefix of "J," "N" or "T" were manufactured in Japan.

Current models are available in .22 and .17 HMR caliber with an 8-groove, target grade barrel, Monte Carlo stock and adjustable trigger.

DISASSEMBLY

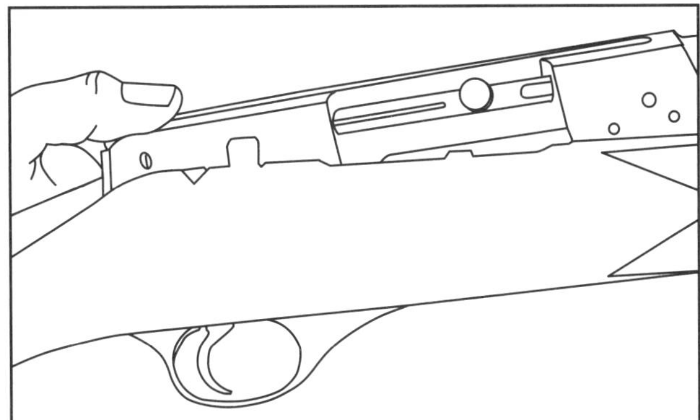

1 Remove magazine and check action to be sure rifle is unloaded. Remove takedown pin (9) at the rear of receiver by pushing it from right to left. With one hand pull forward on barrel and with the other thumb push gently on the top rear of receiver until barrel and receiver assembly move forward about 1/8 inch. The barrel and receiver assembly will now lift out of the stock.

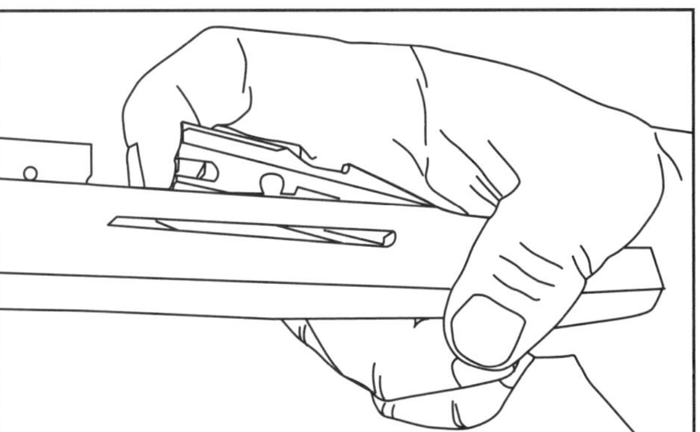

2 To remove bolt assembly from receiver, pull bolt halfway to rear and grasp front of bolt with index finger. Remove operating handle (18) by pulling it out of bolt. Rotating while pulling will help. Carefully lift the front of bolt and ease it upward and forward out of the receiver CAUTION: Recoil spring is under compression. Recoil spring (28) and recoil spring guide (27) will come out with bolt. Reassemble in reverse order making sure recoil spring guide is seated into its recess in the rear wall of receiver.

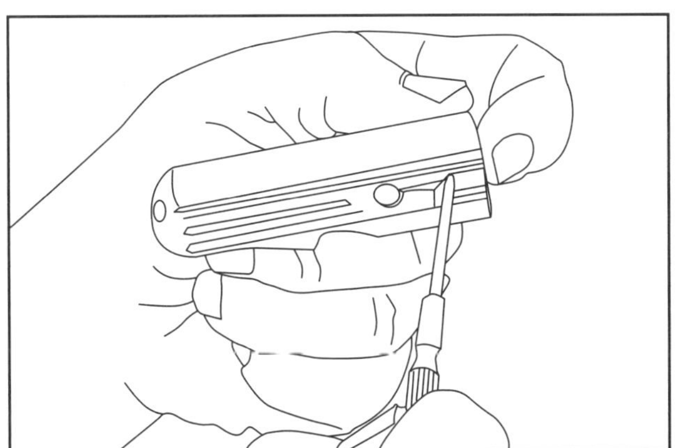

3 To remove extractor (19), insert a small screwdriver between extractor and extractor plunger (20). Push plunger toward the rear of bolt and remove extractor. Reassemble by pushing the extractor tail section against the plunger and seating the extractor into its recess. The plunger will lock the extractor into place.

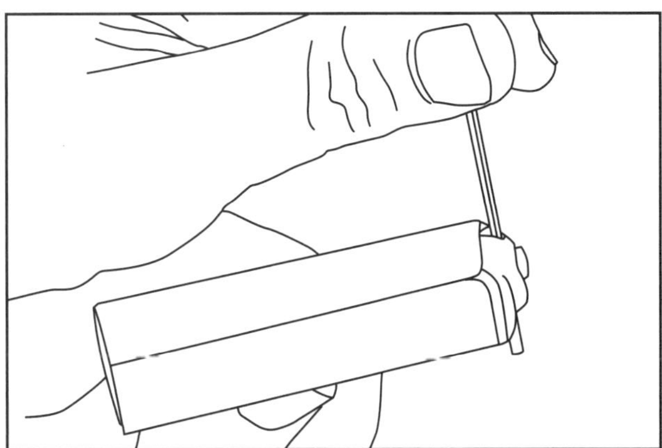

4 To remove firing pin (24), use a small punch to remove retaining pin (23) at rear of bolt. It is not necessary to drive retaining pin out of bolt completely. When removing punch, hold rear of firing pin to prevent it from flying out. Firing pin spring (25) will come out with firing pin. Further disassembly is not recommended.

WINCHESTER MODEL 12 REPEATING

PARTS LEGEND

1. Receiver
2. Receiver shank
3. Buttstock bolt washer
4. Buttstock bolt
5. Barrel chamber ring
6. Barrel chamber ring screw
7. Adjusting sleeve
8. Receiver extension
9. Adjusting sleeve lock
10. Adjusting sleeve lock screw
11. Barrel
12. Magazine band bushing Screws (2)
13. Magazine band bushing
14. Magazine band
15. Action slide handle retaining spring
16. Magazine plug stop
17. Magazine plug
18. Magazine plug screws (2)
19. Magazine locking pin
20. Magazine locking pin spring
21. Magazine tube
22. Magazine spring
23. Magazine follower
24. Three-shell wooden plug
25. Action slide
26. Action slide spring
27. Action slide sleeve screw cap
28. Action slide handle
29. Cartridge cutoff
30. Ejector and ejector spring
31. Breech bolt
32. Firing pin
33. Breech bolt retaining lever
34. Breech bolt retaining lever pin
35. Firing pin retractor
36. Firing pin retractor spring
37. Firing pin retractor screw
38. Extractor—left-hand
39. Extractor spring—left-hand
40. Extractor pin—left-hand
41. Extractor—right-hand
42. Extractor spring plunger—right-hand
43. Extractor spring—right-hand
44. Guard
45. Guard—complete assembly
46. Guard screw
47. Buttstock
48. Buttplate
49. Buttplate screws (2)
50. Hammer
51. Hammer spring and guide rod
52. Hammer spring guide rod pin
53. Hammer pin
54. Trigger lock assembly
55. Trigger
56. Trigger pin
57. Trigger spring (not shown in drawing)
58. Action slide lock and spring
59. Action slide lock pivot
60. Carrier
61. Carrier plunger
62. Carrier plunger spring
63. Carrier plunger screw
64. Carrier pivot
65. Carrier spring

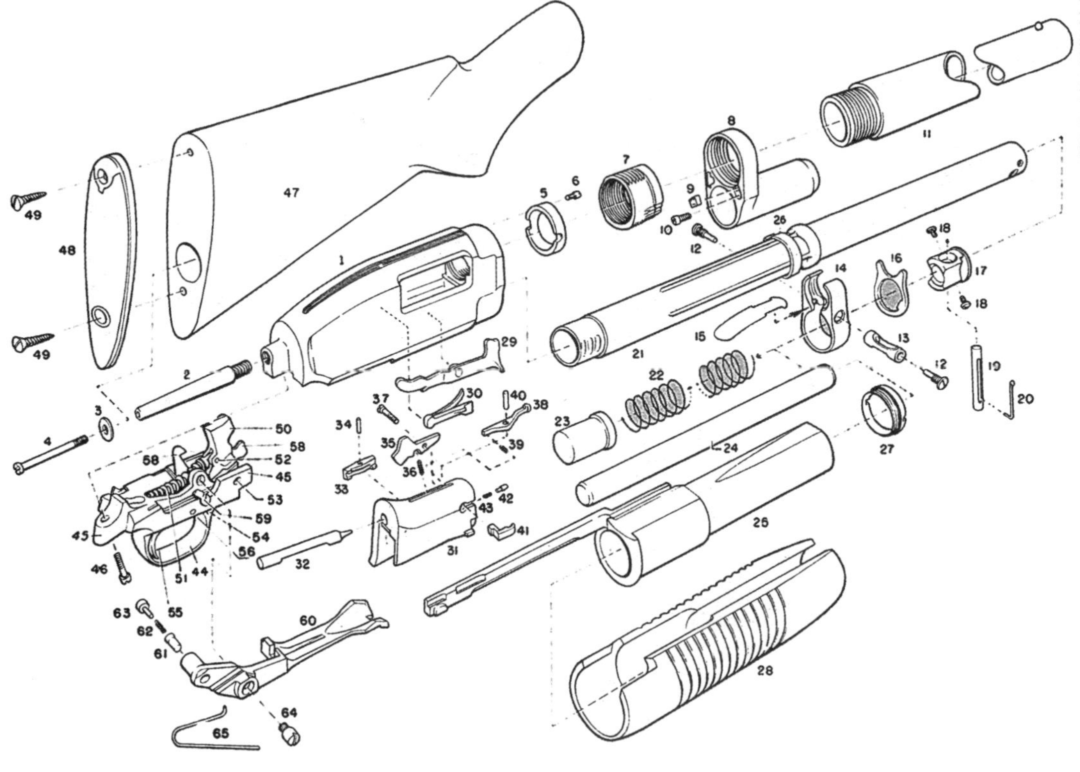

Few repeating shotguns have enjoyed the long-time popularity accorded the Model 12 Winchester since its introduction in 1912. Developed by Thomas C. Johnson, the Model 12 (originally the Model 1912) was initially offered in 20-gauge as the first Winchester shotgun of that gauge and the first hammerless slide-action repeating shotgun to bear the Winchester brand. By 1914 it was available in 12- and 16-gauge, with a 28-gauge version introduced in 1934.

The 12-gauge Model 1912 Trench gun, with 20-inch cylinder-bore barrel, perforated sleeve and bayonet lug was introduced in 1917. Without bayonet and sleeve it was listed in the Winchester catalog as the Model 12 Guard and Riot gun.

The Model 12 Winchester has been offered in a wide array of styles and grades including field, trap and skeet models.

DISASSEMBLY

Remove guard screw (46) and drop complete guard assembly (45) from bottom of receiver (1). It is suggested that action be placed in a properly padded vise with trigger guard up to facilitate disassembly of action. Note that carrier assembly (60-65) may be removed from guard by unscrewing carrier pivot (64) which has a left-hand thread. Further disassembly of parts contained within guard assembly should definitely not be attempted and replacement of parts 50 through 59 should be made by Winchester factory only. Drop cartridge cutoff (29) out of receiver.

The breech bolt (31) may be removed as follows: with breech bolt in its full forward position, gently pry stud of ejector (30) from its seat in the inside of receiver wall and slide ejector to rear and out from under breech bolt and thence out of receiver. Before attempting to remove breech bolt be sure action slide is disengaged from breech bolt. Depress rearmost arms of breech bolt retaining lever (33) and slide breech bolt almost all the way to its rearmost position. Then, lifting breech bolt by its back end first, guide left-hand and right-hand extractors up through vertical slots on inside of receiver walls.

Although not normally necessary, buttstock (47) may be removed by unscrewing buttplate screws (49) and removing buttplate (48), after which buttstock bolt (4) can be unscrewed with a long screwdriver and buttstock pulled away from receiver.

To disassemble breech bolt, remove firing pin retractor screw (37) and lift firing pin retractor (35) out of its seat. Pull firing pin retractor spring (36) out of its hole. The left-hand extractor (38) and spring (39) and breech bolt retaining lever (33) are removed by drifting out their respective retaining pins (40 and 34). Remove right-hand extractor (41) by slipping blade of a small screwdriver between plunger (42) and extractor (41) and easing extractor up out of its hole in side of breech bolt. Remove spring (43) and plunger (42) toward front.

To take down barrel assembly, depress magazine locking pin spring (20) with blade of a small screwdriver and remove magazine locking pin (19) from magazine tube (21). Remove the magazine plug screws (18) while holding front of magazine plug (17) to prevent its sudden ejection. Allow magazine plug and magazine spring (22) to extend slowly to spring's full length and lift spring and wood three-shot plug (24) out of magazine tube (21). Magazine follower (23) may be dropped out of front end of magazine tube.

Remove both magazine band bushing screws (12). Pull magazine tube away from barrel (11) just enough to allow magazine band (14) to clear lug on underside of barrel. The magazine tube, magazine band, action slide handle retaining spring (15), and action slide handle assembly (25-28) may be withdrawn toward front of barrel. The magazine band (14) and magazine band bushing (13) may now be removed from magazine tube. Ordinarily, disassembly of action slide (25) from action slide handle (28) and magazine tube (21) is not recommended and is seldom necessary. To separate these parts, action slide sleeve screw cap (27) must first be removed with a special spanner wrench.

Removal of receiver extension (8) should not be attempted. Remove adjusting sleeve lock screw (10) and slide adjusting sleeve lock (9) away from adjusting sleeve (7) and unscrew adjusting sleeve from barrel. The barrel chamber ring (5) may be removed by unscrewing barrel chamber ring screw (6).

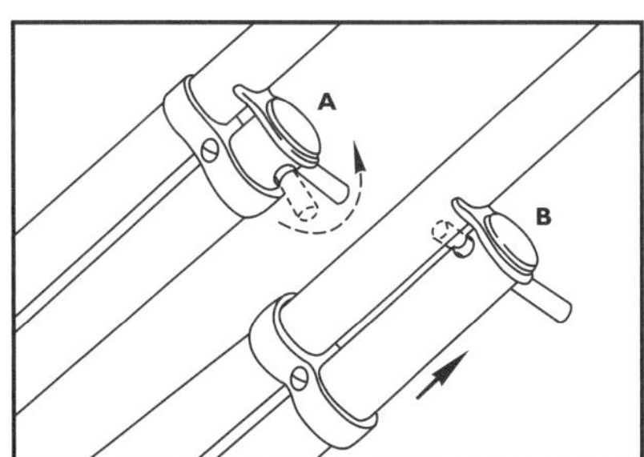

1 Pull slide handle fully rearward and push magazine downward as far as it will go. Push out magazine locking pin as shown at A. Using pin as a lever, turn magazine one-quarter turn clockwise as shown at B. Pin will not rotate unless magazine is at full depth in receiver. Push magazine locking pin back into magazine tube. Threaded end of tube is now engaged with receiver and locked. Bring action slide handle fully forward. Arrows stamped on underside of magazine tube and receiver extension should coincide. Gun is now ready to fire. Take down in reverse order

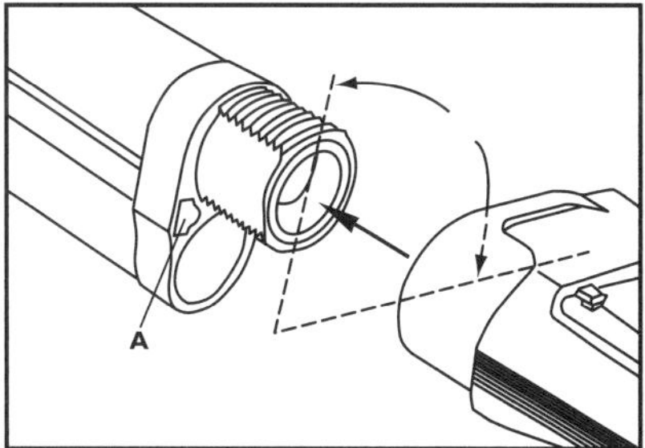

2 To assemble barrel to receiver pull trigger and be sure action slide handle is fully forward and slide is flush with receiver extension as shown at A to prevent slide bar marring receiver.

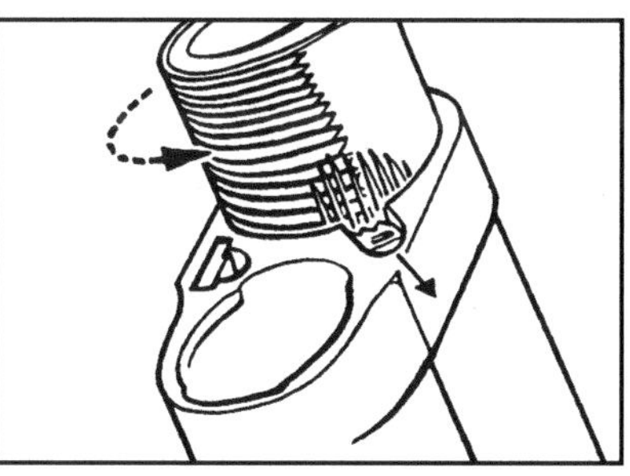

3 Hold receiver and barrel assemblies at right angles to each other, insert threaded barrel shank into receiver, and turn barrel assembly clockwise until contours of receiver and receiver extension coincide as shown.

WINCHESTER MODEL 21 SHOTGUN

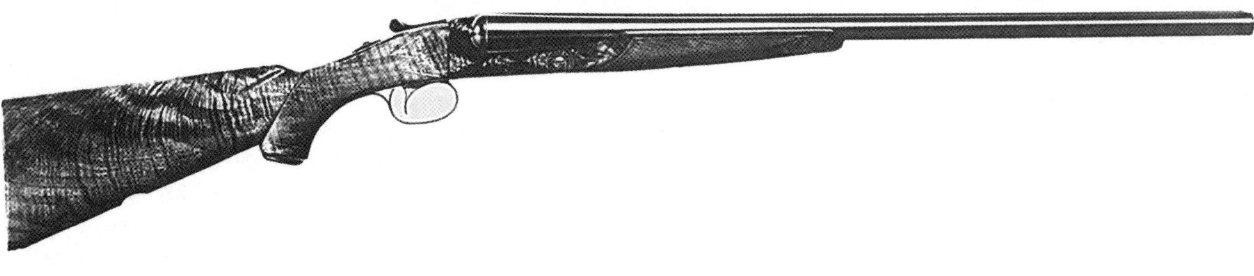

PARTS LEGEND

1. Frame
2. Top-lever
3. Upper tang screw
   3a. Upper tang screw bushing
4. Safety slide
5. Safety slide spring stop pin
6. Safety slide spring
7. Top-lever plunger
8. Top-lever spring
9. Locking bolt
10. Locking bolt lever
11. Locking bolt lever screw
12. Sear, left
13. Sear, right
14. Sear pin
15. Sear spring, right
16. Sear spring, left
17. Sear spring screws (2)
18. Locking bolt catch
19. Locking bolt catch spring
20. Locking bolt catch spring plunger
21. Hammer, left
22. Hammer, right
23. Hammer pin
24. Cocking lever screw
25. Cocking lever, right
26. Joint pin
27. Cocking lever, left
28. Cocking lever screw nut
29. Cocking rod, left
30. Cocking rod, right
31. Hammer springs (2)
32. Trigger plate
33. Trigger plate tang screw
34. Trigger plate screw
35. Safety lever
36. Safety lever operating rod pin
37. Safety lever operating rod
38. Safety lever operating rod returning spring
39. Safety lever operating rod returning spring pin
40. Safety lever pivot pin
41. Timing weight
42. Timing weight pin
43. Timing weight plunger spring
44. Timing weight plunger
45. Trigger (shown assembled—comprises trigger, trigger blade and pin)
46. Shift lever spring
47. Trigger pin
48. Shift lever and shift lever button (shown assembled)
49. Trigger spring
50. Trigger spring plunger
51. Guard bow
52. Guard bow screws (2)
   52a. Buttstock
53. Forearm shoe
54. Ejection sear pin
55. Ejection hammer roll pin
56. Forearm retainer pin
57. Forearm catch pin
58. Ejection hammer roll
59. Ejection sear spring (2)
60. Forearm retainer
61. Forearm retainer spring
62. Forearm catch
63. Ejection hammer, right
64. Ejection hammer, left
65. Ejection hammer springs (2)
66. Ejection hammer spring guide rods (2)
67. Ejection sear, left
68. Ejection sear, right
69. Forearm recoil abutment
70. Forearm recoil screw
71. Forearm catch plate
72. Rear forearm screw
73. Front forearm screw
74. Forearm catch spring
75. Forearm
76. Barrels
77. Extractor, left
78. Extractor, right
79. Locking bolt stop screw
80. Extractor stop screw
81. Barrel stop
82. Barrel stop spring
83. Barrel stop screw
84. Extractor plunger stop pin
85. Extractor plunger
86. Front sight
87. Rear sight

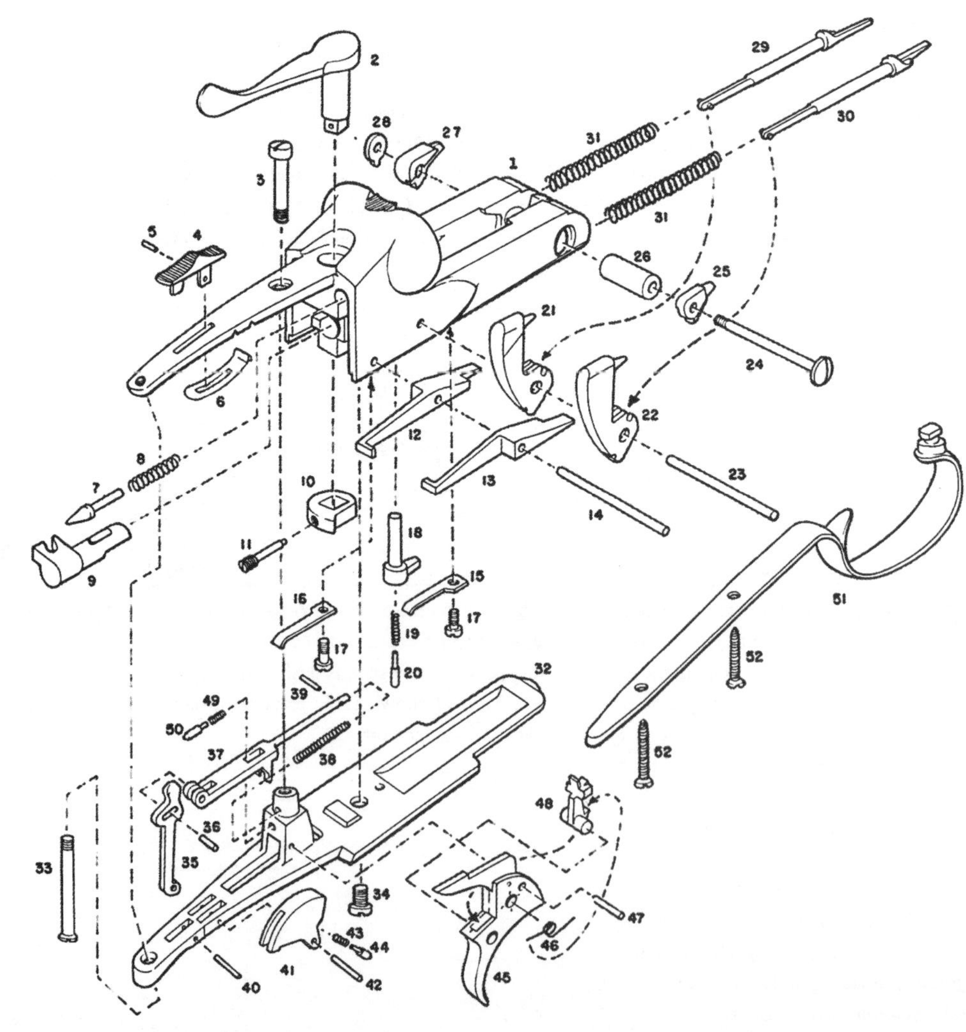

The Winchester Model 21 hammerless double-barrel shotgun, introduced in 1931, was the first arm of this type manufactured by Winchester. Earlier double-barrel shotguns bearing the Winchester name were made in England and were sold in the Winchester store in New York from 1879 until 1884.

The frame of the Model 21 shotgun is of one-piece, forged construction. The barrels are mechanically interlocked by dovetail half-lugs on each barrel. Coil springs are used to operate the hammers and selective ejectors and a floating barrel stop on the forward part of the lug protects the hinge. The Model 21 was produced initially with double trigger, but the single-trigger version followed shortly.

The Model 21 was offered in a variety of standard styles covering every conceivable taste and style in shooting. Custom-built guns were also offered, but even the standard style guns were furnished with special dimensional socks (within certain limits) at no extra charge. Manufacture of the Model 21 with plain extractors was discontinued in 1941 and the double trigger version was discontinued in 1944. After January 1, 1950, the Model 21 was produced in single trigger, selective ejection style only.

Manufacture of the standard-grade gun was discontinued in 1959 and was resumed on a custom basis only beginning in the following year. Custom-built guns were offered in three basic grades — Custom Grade, Pigeon Grade and Grand American Grade — in 12, 16 and 20 gauge only. The Winchester Custom Shop produced about 1,000 Model 21s between 1960 and 1993.

DISASSEMBLY

Basic takedown is shown in Figs. 6, 7, 8, and 9. With the arm dismantled into its major components as shown in Fig. 2, disassembly of the action and frame assembly may be accomplished.

Remove guard bow screws (52) from underside of guard bow (51). Lift rear end of guard bow free of stock and turn guard bow 900, withdrawing it from bottom of trigger plate (32). Remove upper tang screw (3), trigger plate tang screw (33), and trigger plate screw (34). Rap frame sharply with a wooden or plastic hammer to loosen trigger plate and remove it from bottom of frame (1). Disassembly of trigger mechanism contained in trigger plate is not recommended. (See Fig. 4.)

With trigger plate removed, buttstock (52a) may be drawn away from frame to rear. Remove sear spring screws (17) and right and left sear springs (15, 16) from underside of frame and withdraw locking bolt catch spring (19) and plunger (20) from locking bolt catch (18). Trip sears so hammers are in fired position and drift out sear pin (14).

Remove left and right sears (12, 13).

Remove locking bolt lever screw (11) and pull top-lever (2) out top of frame. Remove locking bolt catch (18) and remove locking bolt lever (10), taking care to prevent forcible ejection of top-lever plunger (7) and spring (8). Remove cocking lever screw (24) and nut (28), dropping right and left cocking levers (25, 27) out front of frame.

Hammer springs are difficult to remove and disassembly of hammers (21, 22), hammer springs (31) and left and right cocking rods (29, 30) should only be undertaken by a competent gunsmith. Reassemble in reverse.

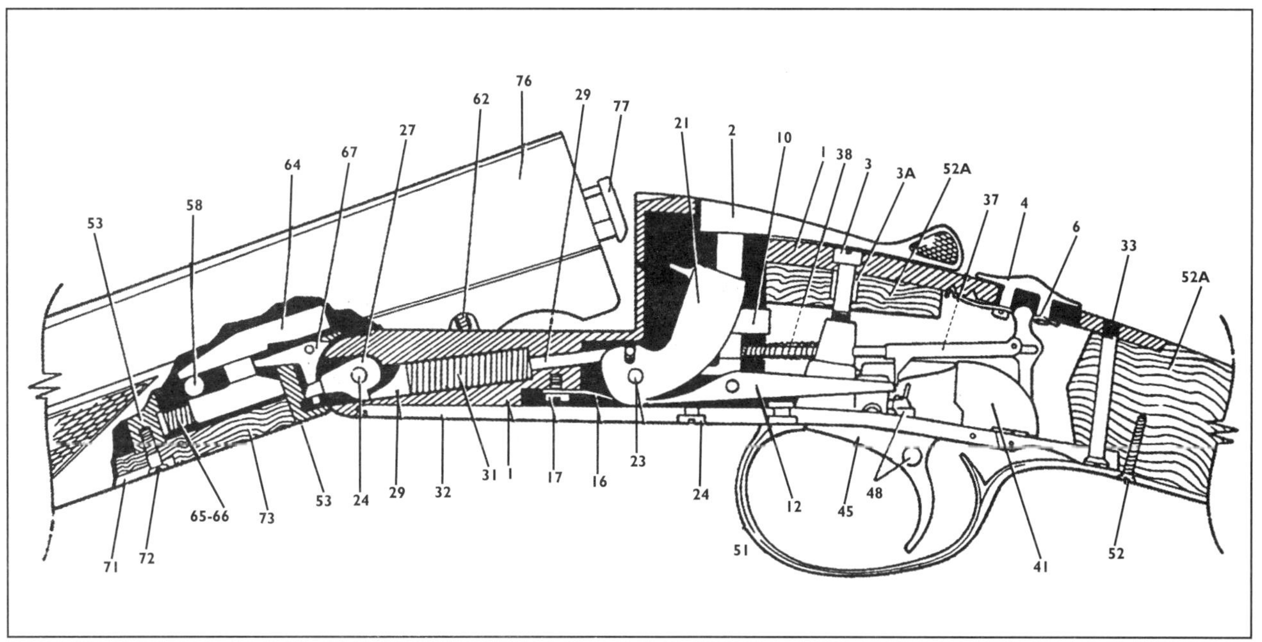

WINCHESTER MODEL 21 SHOTGUN

DISASSEMBLY CONTINUED

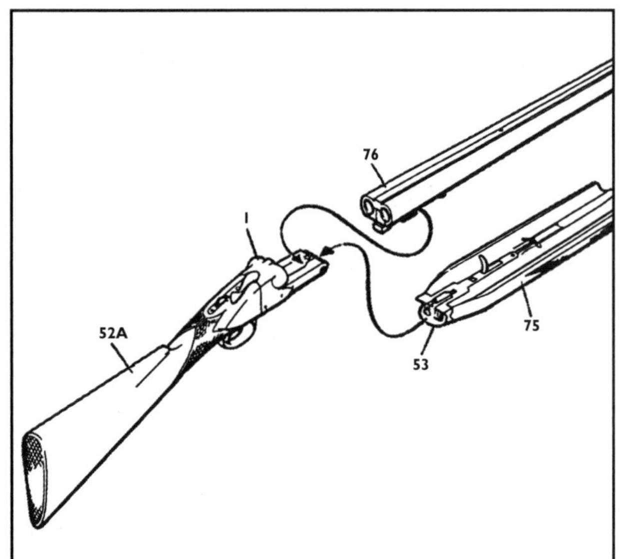

1 Major components. The major components of the arm after basic takedown are shown here. For everyday, normal cleaning, disassembly beyond this point should seldom, if ever, become necessary.

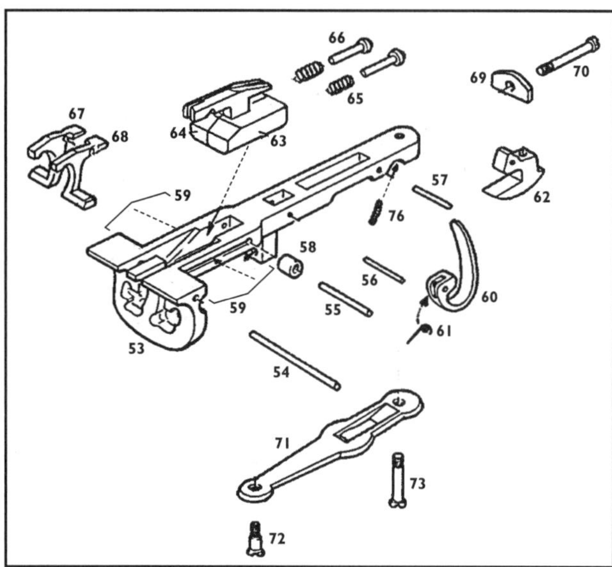

2 Forearm assembly. Remove rear and front fore-arm screws (72, 73) from forearm catch plate (71) on underside of forearm (75). Remove forearm recoil screw (70) and abutment (69). Forearm shoe (53) may be separated from forearm. Further disassembly of shoe is not recommended and seldom necessary.

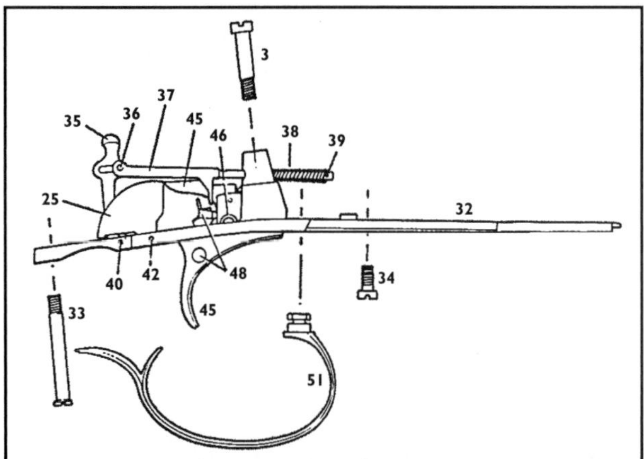

3 Trigger assembly. The assembled trigger mechanism contained in the trigger plate (32) is shown here to illustrate proper relationship of parts. Trigger mechanism should be disassembled only by a competent gunsmith when necessary for replacement or repair of parts. Take care when reassembling trigger plate and trigger mechanism to underside of frame that locking bolt catch spring plunger (20) is properly seated in its hole in top side of trigger plate.

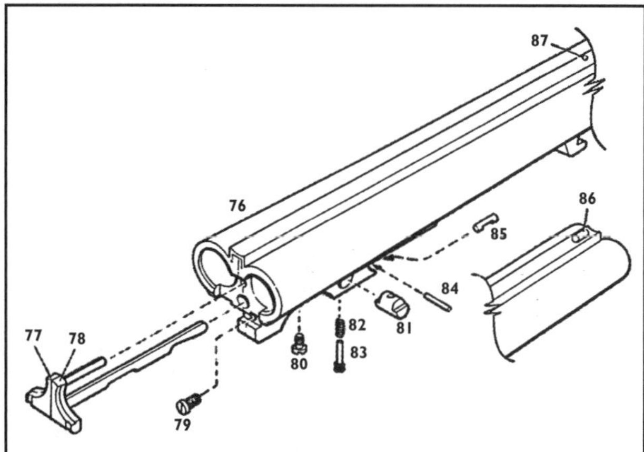

4 Barrel assembly. With barrel separated from frame (1) and wood forearm (75), remove extractor stop screw (80) and locking bolt stop screw (79) from barrel lug. Remove barrel stop screw (83) and spring (82). Remove left and right extractors (77, 78) and barrel stop (81). Drift out extractor plunger stop pin (84) and remove extractor plunger (85) from front end of barrel lug).

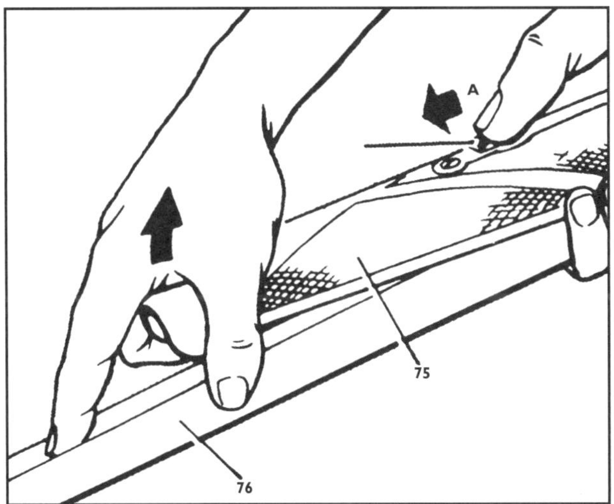

5 To take down the assembled arm, push top-lever (2) over to right swing — hold gun inverted and push forearm catch (62) forward as shown at A while lifting up and off frame (1), lifting up on front end of forearm (75). Separate forearm from barrels (76).

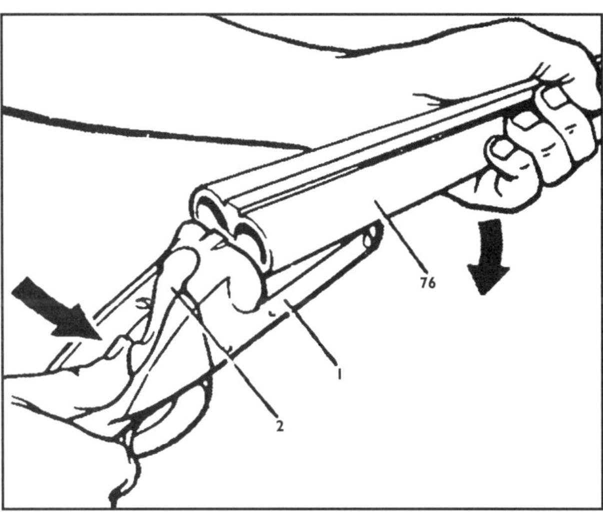

6 Push top-lever(2) over to right swinging breech end of barrels upward. Lift barrels (76) up and off frame (1).

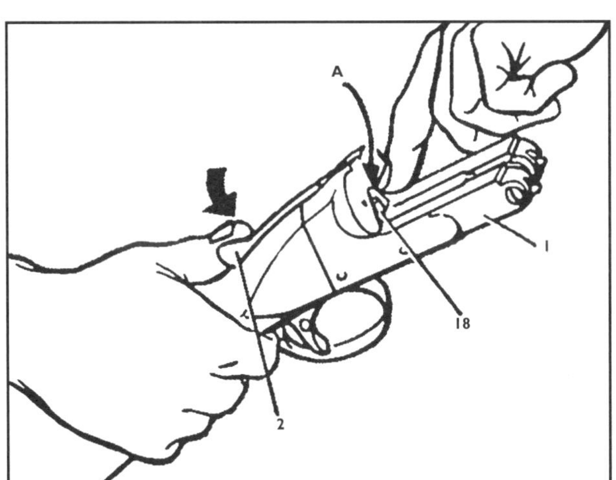

7 With barrels off, push top-lever (2) to right and press down on locking bolt catch (18) as shown at A in order to release locking bolt. Release top-lever.

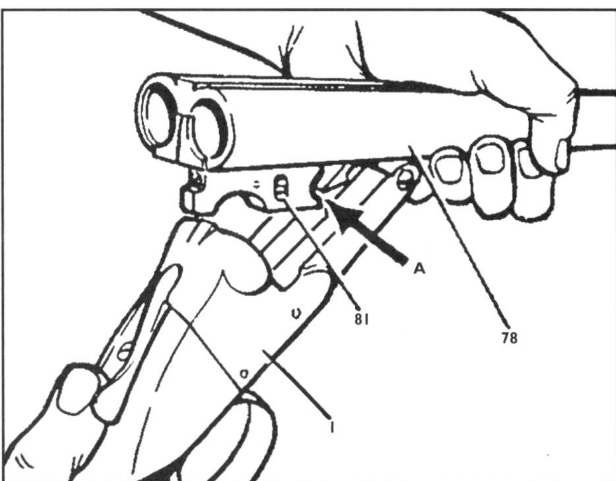

8 In reassembling barrels (76) to frame (1), push top-lever (2) to right until it catches. Hold gun as shown. Notch in front of barrel lug at A must engage joint pin (26) in frame. Note that barrel stop (81) must be in seat in floor of frame before breech can be closed. Swing barrels up and lock. Place forearm against barrels with rear end of shoe (53) engaging cocking levers (25, 27) at front of frame. Press front end of forearm against barrels until forearm assembly locks into place, completing reassembly.

WINCHESTER MODEL 25 SHOTGUN

PARTS LEGEND

1. Barrel *
2. Front sight *
3. Magazine band screw
4. Magazine band
5. Magazine lock screw
6. Magazine lock
7. Receiver
8. Magazine
9. Action slide spring
10. Magazine plug
11. Magazine plug screw (2)
12. Magazine spring
13. Magazine follower
14. Breechbolt
15. Firing pin stop pin
16. Left extractor pin
17. Left extractor
18. Left extractor spring
19. Right extractor spring
20. Right extractor spring plunger
21. Right extractor
22. Firing pin spring
23. Firing pin striker
24. Firing pin
25. Buttplate
26. Buttplate screw (2)
27. Receiver shank *
28. Buttstock bolt
29. Buttstock bolt washer
30. Cartridge cutoff
31. Ejector
32. Ejector spring
33. Action slide
34. Action slide sleeve screw cap
35. Guard
36. Guard screw
37. Action slide lock *
38. Action slide lock screw *
39. Action slide lock pivot *
40. Action slide lock spring *
41. Carrier plunger screw
42. Carrier plunger spring
43. Carrier plunger
44. Carrier
45. Cartridge guide
46. Cartridge guide pivot *
47. Carrier spring
48. Carrier pivot
49. Trigger lock
50. Trigger lock plunger spring
51. Trigger lock plunger
52. Hammer pin
53. Trigger pin
54. Trigger
55. Trigger spring
56. Hammer spring
57. Hammer spring guide rod
58. Hammer spring guide pin
59. Hammer
60. Buttstock
61. Action slide handle

* Factory assembly to other major part. Do not disassemble.

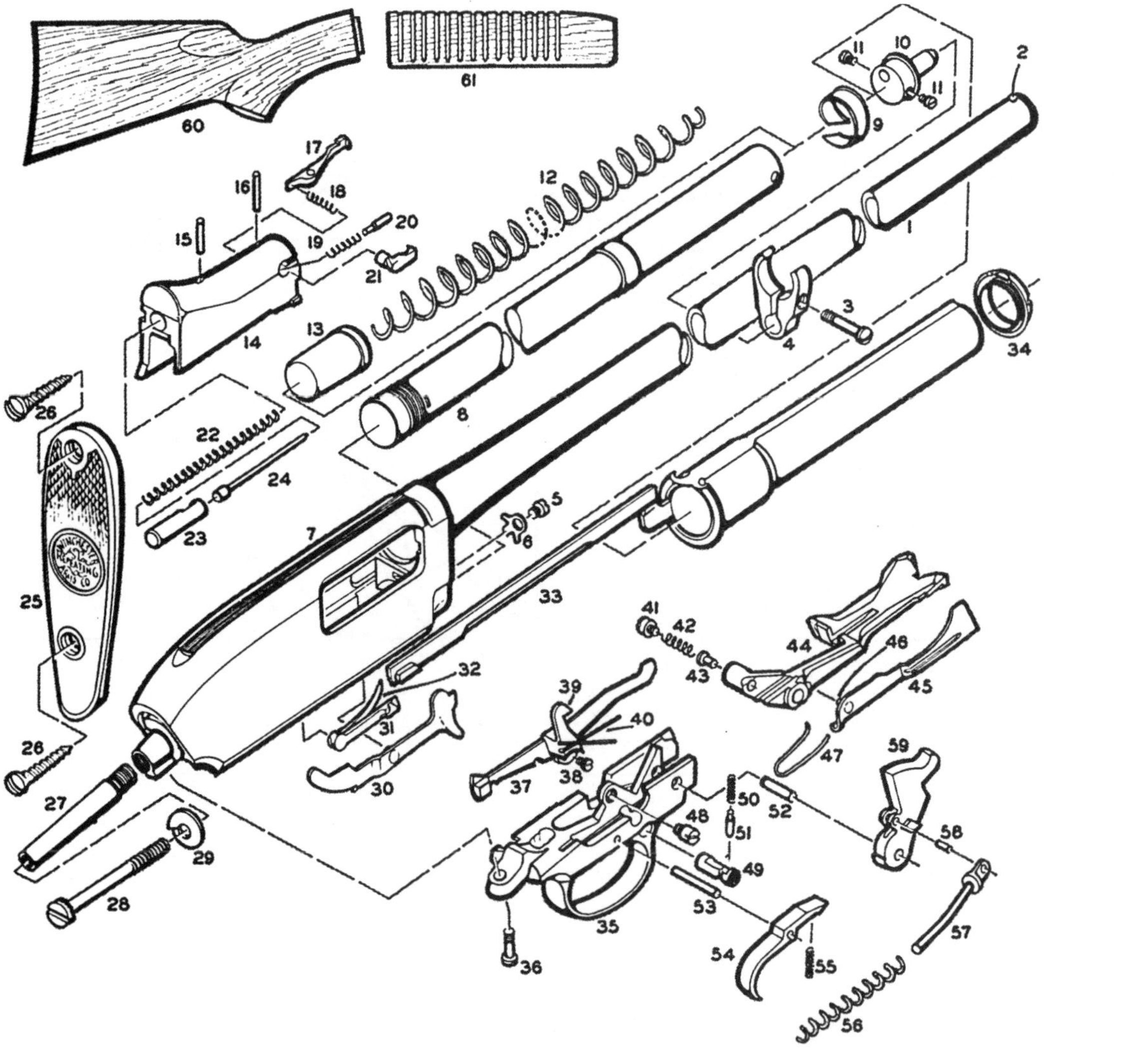

The Winchester Model 25 hammerless slide-action solid-frame shotgun was introduced in 1950. It was made in 12 gauge only, for 2¾-inch shells, and was essentially a moderately priced version of the Winchester Model 12 takedown shotgun. The Model 25 was offered in either 26- or 28-inch barrel lengths with an option of full or modified choke in the 28-inch length, or improved cylinder boring in the 26-inch length. The magazine capacity is 4 shells and a wooden plug was furnished to reduce the capacity to 2 shells. The weight of the gun with a 28-inch barrel is approximately 8 lbs. and the overall length is 47¼ inches.

Winchester discontinued the Model 25 shotgun in 1957.

WINCHESTER

DISASSEMBLY

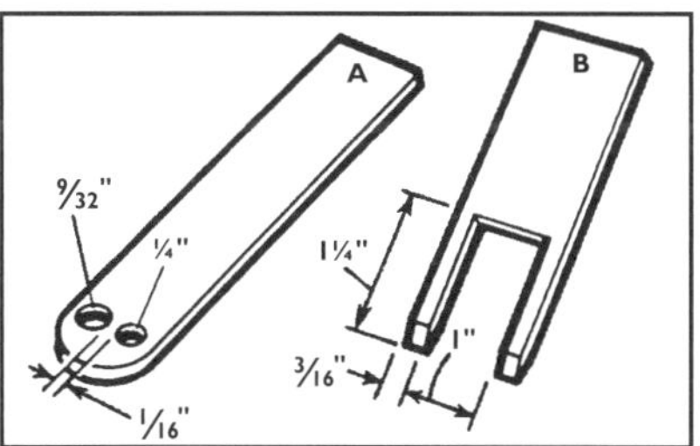

1 To properly disassemble Model 25 it is necessary to fabricate 2 special tools. Make Tool A from 6- or 8-inch bar of ¾ x 3/16 inch cold-rolled steel stock. Drill and shape end as shown. The holes should be slightly chamfered and all edges deburred.

Make Tool B from an 8-inch length of tempered steel dimensioned as shown. An old reciprocating hacksaw blade is excellent. Grind or file the double end to form the screwdrivers.

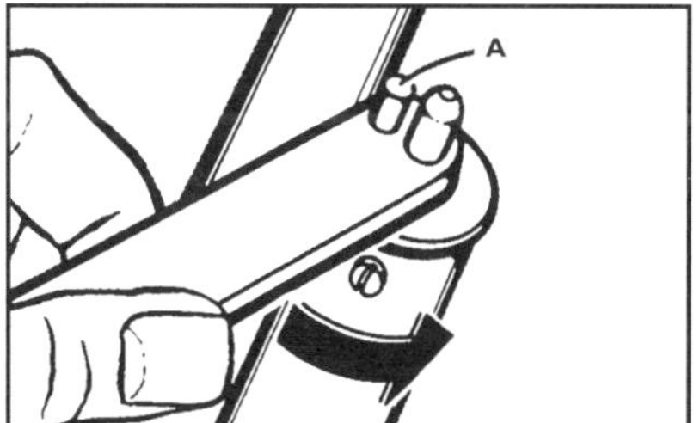

2 Remove magazine band screw (3) and slide magazine band (4) forward on barrel (l). Remove magazine lock screw (5) and magazine lock (6) in face of receiver (7). Apply Tool A to lug in front of magazine plug (10) aligning ¼-inch hole in tool with hole in plug. Insert short piece of ¼-inch drill rod (A) and turn out magazine (8) approximately 150 degrees. Tool is necessary to "break" tight screw fit of magazine to receiver. Unscrew magazine, with action slide handle (61) attached, from receiver. Pull entire assembly straight forward and free of gun.

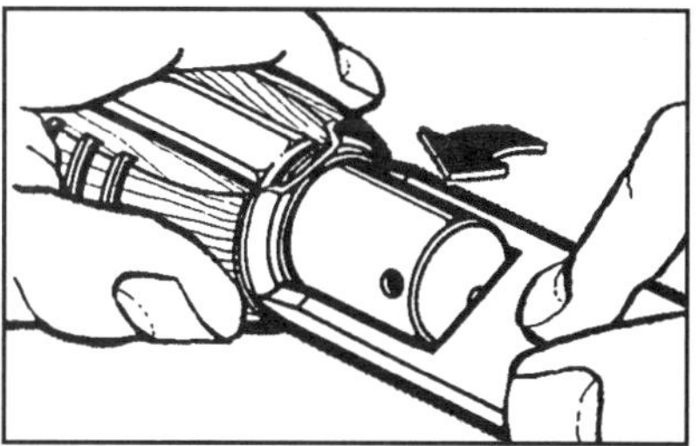

3 Unscrew magazine plug screws (11), holding magazine plug in place with thumb. Slowly remove magazine plug and grasp magazine spring (12) to prevent its escape. Remove spring and follower (13).

Apply Tool B to action slide sleeve screw cap (34) as shown and unscrew it. Pull off action slide handle and withdraw magazine from action slide (33). Remove action slide spring (9). When reassembling, be sure this spring is on rear side of stop collar on magazine.

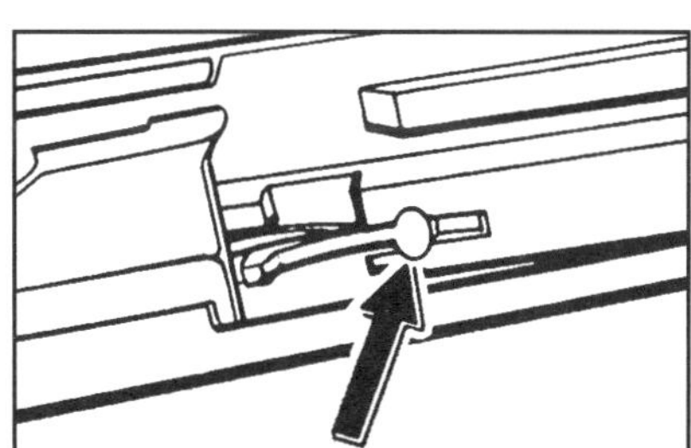

4 Remove guard screw (36) and swing guard (35) down out of receiver (inside left wall of receiver shown). Lift out cartridge cutoff (30). With small screwdriver, pry out ejector (31 — arrow) at rear of breechbolt (14) in receiver. Slide breechbolt fully rearward and lift out.

Remove buttplate screws (26), buttplate (25), buttstock bolt (28), and washer (29). Pull off buttstock (60). In reassembly, replace buttstock after replacing guard.

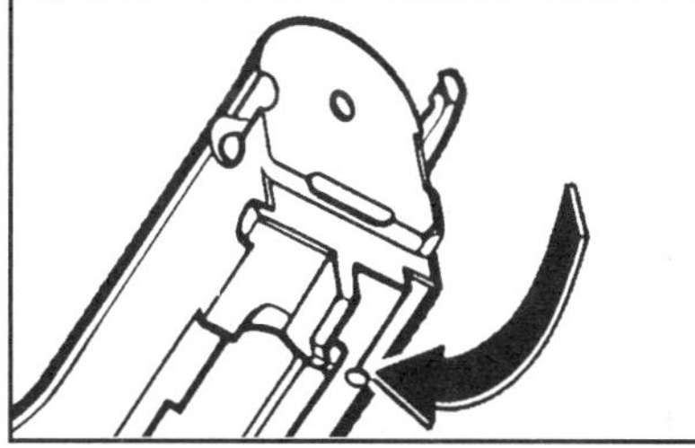

5 Push back right extractor plunger (20) with small screwdriver and lift out right extractor (21) together with plunger and spring (19). Drift out left extractor pin (16, arrow) from bottom of breechbolt and lift away left extractor (17) and spring (18). Drift out firing pin stop pin (15) and remove firing pin striker (23), firing pin (24), and firing pin spring (22). Reassemble bolt in reverse order.

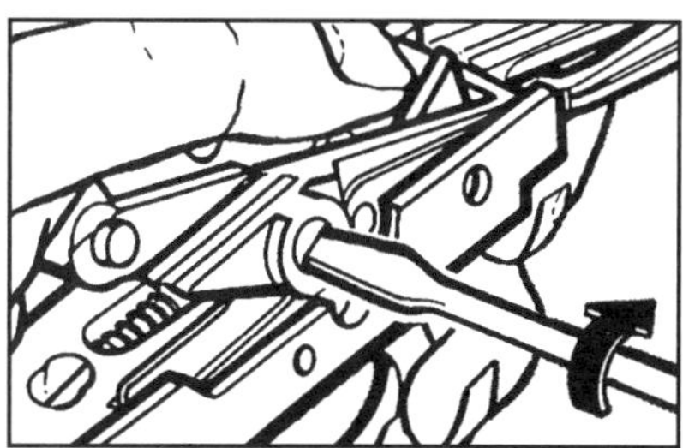

6 Unscrew carrier pivot (48) (left thread — unscrews right). Remove carrier (44) with carrier spring (47) with cartridge guide (45). Lower hammer (59) and drift out hammer pin (52) from the left. Remove hammer, hammer spring (56) and hammer spring guide rod (57).

Drift out trigger pin (53) and remove trigger (54) and trigger spring (55). Do not disassemble action slide lock (37) assembly from guard, lock screw (38) is "staked" to lock pivot (39).

Remove trigger lock (49) by inserting small pin into hole in lock, turn ¼ turn while pushing trigger lock out from left to right. Reassemble in reverse.

WINCHESTER MODEL 43 RIFLE

PARTS LEGEND

1. Barrel
2. Breechbolt body
3. Breechbolt cocking sleeve
4. Breechbolt plug
5. Breechbolt sleeve
6. Breechbolt sleeve pin
7. Buttplate
8. Buttplate screws (2)
9. Extractor, left
10. Extractor, right
11. Extractor pins (2)
12. Extractor spring, left
13. Extractor spring, right
14. Firing pin
15. Firing pin spring
16. Firing pin stop pin
17. Forearm swivel
18. Front sight
19. Front sight cover
20. Guard
21. Guard screw, front
22. Guard screw, rear
23. Magazine
24. Magazine base
25. Magazine catch
26. Magazine catch pin
27. Magazine catch spring
28. Magazine catch stud
29. Magazine follower
30. Magazine housing
31. Magazine housing pin
32. Magazine housing screw
33. Magazine spring
34. Pistol grip cap
35. Pistol grip cap screw
36. Rear sight
37. Rear sight elevator
38. Receiver
39. Receiver plug screws (6)
40. Safety lever
41. Safety lever stop pin
42. Safety lockplate
43. Safety lock plunger
44. Safety lock plunger spring
45. Safety lock screw
46. Stock
47. Stock swivel
48. Stock stud
49. Stock stud screw
50. Stock stud escutcheon
51. Trigger
52. Trigger base
53. Trigger pin
54. Trigger spring
55. Trigger spring adjusting screw

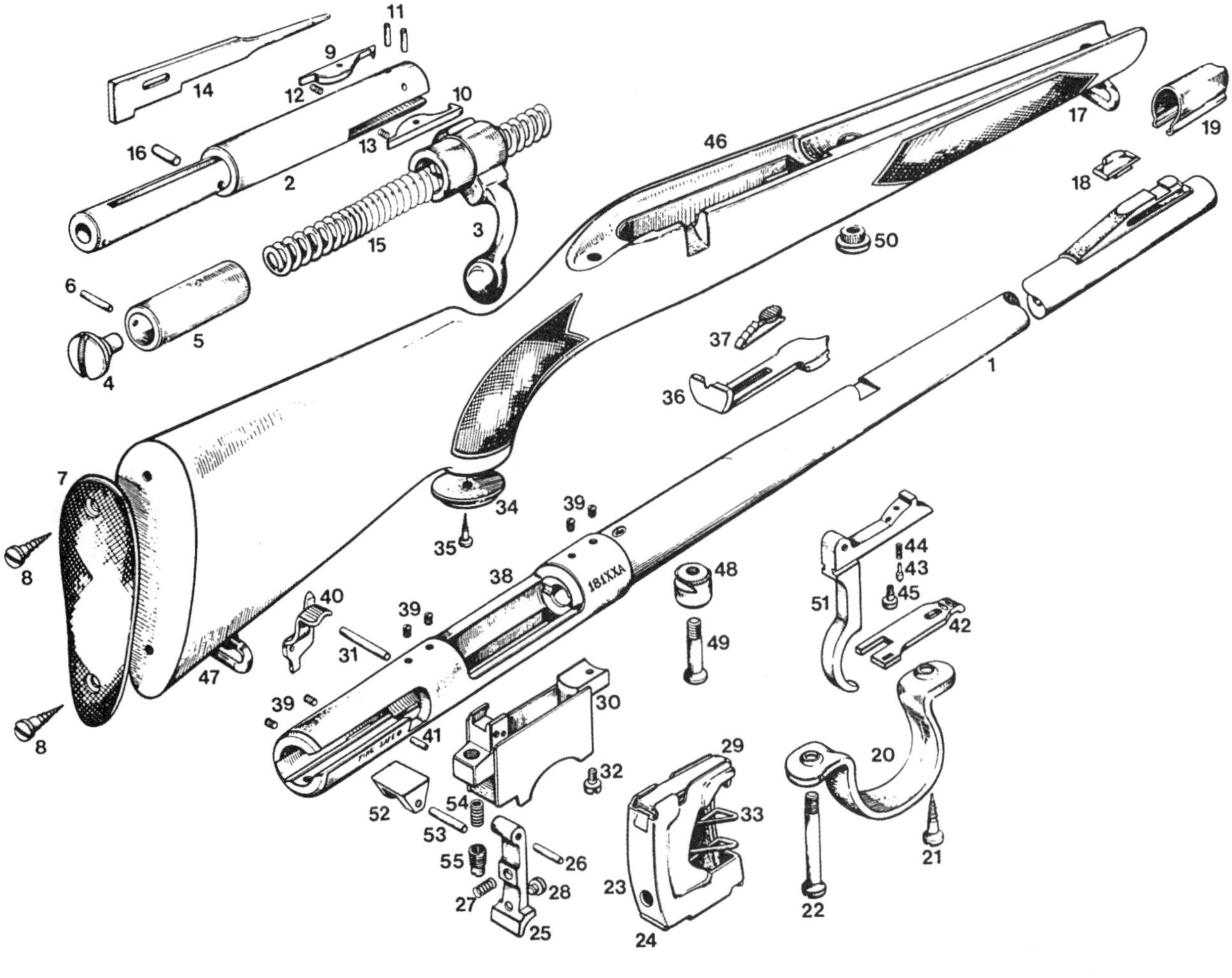

The Model 43 was planned by Winchester in 1944 while the company was still involved in World War II military arms production. The new center-fire, bolt-action repeating rifle was developed as an intermediate action to fill the void between the larger Model 70 and the smaller rimfire offerings such as the Model 75 and the venerable Model 52. Development of the Model 43 required nearly five years and the first production model was offered for sale in 1949.

Early Winchester catalogs advertised the Model 43 as a bolt-action repeater suitable for small game and pest control. A steel receiver was coupled with a twin locking lug bolt with dual extractors. The "speed lock" assembly cocked on opening and the rifle was fitted with a 24-inch round, tapered barrel chambered for .22 Hornet, .218 Bee, .25-20 or the .32-20.

A Standard Model was offered with an uncheckered, pistol grip American walnut stock. The 43 Special Model had a checkered pistol grip and forearm and was offered with either standard open or receiver sight options. The front sight on both models was dovetailed into an integral forged ramp and equipped with a hood. The rifle was equipped with a side lever safety and detachable box magazine. The Model 43 was manufactured by Winchester until 1957, reaching a total production of more than 62,600.

DISASSEMBLY

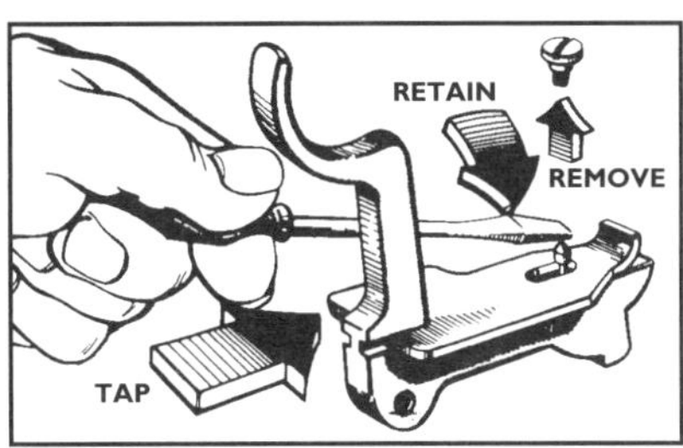

1 Open the bolt and check both the chamber and magazine to ensure that the gun is not loaded and is safe to service. With the action open, depress the trigger (51) and withdraw the bolt to the rear. Depress the magazine catch (25) and remove the magazine (23). Remove the front and rear guard screws (21 & 22) to detach the trigger guard (20). Unscrew the stock stud screw (49) to separate the stock (46) from the action. The stock stud screw escutcheon (50) will remain in the forearm. Drift out the magazine housing pin (31) and remove the magazine housing screw (32) to detach the magazine housing (30) from the receiver (38).

Exercise caution to avoid losing the exposed trigger spring (54). If repair or replacement is required, this spring and the adjusting screw (55) located below it may be easily removed from the housing. If removal is necessary, note the relative position of the screw to facilitate adjustment during reassembly. The magazine catch (25) and its spring (27) may be detached by drifting out the magazine catch pin (26). Push out the trigger pin (53) to disengage both the safety lever (40) and the trigger assembly from the receiver. This pin usually exhibits an expanded head to insure that it remains intact and should be drifted out from the opposite side of the trigger base (52). If further disassembly of this sub-group is required, the safety lockplate (42) may by removed by threading out the safety lock screw (45) and sliding the safety lockplate forward to clear the grooves in the trigger.

There are two detent notches on the lower side of the lockplate. A light tap on the rear of this plate may be required to initiate movement. Retain safety lock plunger (43) and its spring (44) as they protrude through elongated hole in the lockplate as it slides forward. These components are under spring pressure and may be ejected and lost if not retained. To free the safety lockplate for removal, invert the trigger assembly to displace both the plunger and spring from their recess.

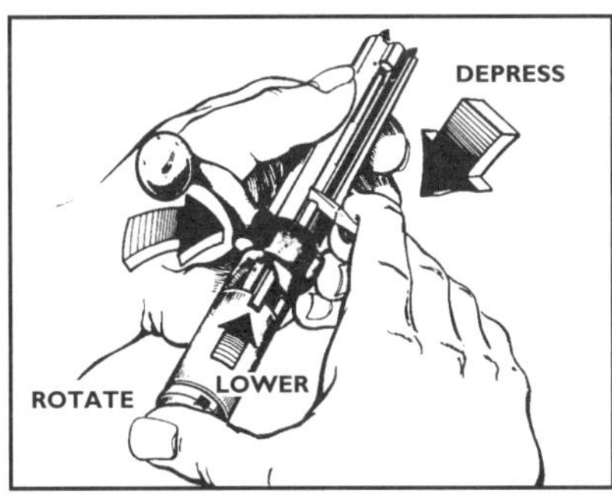

2 To disassemble the breechbolt, release the spring tension by using a screwdriver to depress the firing pin (14) at the sear notch (Fig. 2). This will allow the bolt cocking sleeve (3) to be rotated in order to lower the firing pin to a fired position. Retain the breechbolt plug (4) while drifting out the breechbolt sleeve pin (6) to release both the firing pin spring (15) and the bolt plug (4).

Exercise caution when withdrawing the drift because these components are still under spring pressure. Slide the bolt sleeve (5) off the bolt body (2) to the rear. Move the breechbolt cocking sleeve (3) rearward to expose and drift out the firing pin stop pin (16).

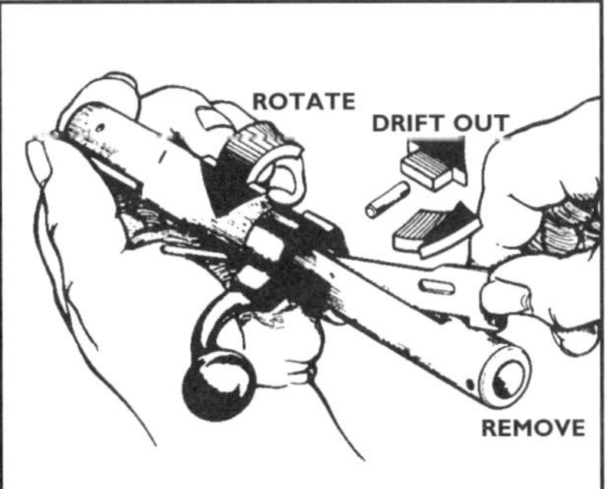

3 The firing pin (14) may now be removed from the top of the bolt body by rotating the cocking sleeve to expose as much of the top slot as possible.

It is a common mistake to attempt to remove the firing pin through the longer slot in the bottom of the bolt body. Persistence in this matter often results in frustration leading to forceful attempts at removal which frequently cause damage to the components. The extractors (9 & 10) with their respective springs (12 & 13) may be removed by drifting out the two extractor pins (11). This procedure is facilitated by the access provided by two smaller diameter "poke holes" located immediately below the extractor pins on the bottom of the bolt. The front and rear sights (18 & 36), the stock stud (48) and trigger base (52) may be drifted from their respective dovetails from left to right to complete disassembly.

WINCHESTER MODEL 50 SHOTGUN

PARTS LEGEND

1. Barrel
2. Bolt
3. Buffer plug
4. Buffer lock
5. Buttplate
6. Buttplate screws (2)
7. Buttstock
8. Carrier
9. Carrier lock
10. Carrier lock screw
11. Carrier lock spring
12. Carrier spring
13. Chamber
14. Chamber plug
15. Chamber plug spring
16. Closing spring tube
17. Closing spring
18. Ejector
19. Ejector spring
20. Extractor
21. Extractor pin
22. Extractor spring
23. Firing pin
24. Firing pin stop pin
25. Firing pin spring
26. Fore-end
27. Front sight
28. Guard
29. Guard pin
30. Hammer
31. Hammer catch
32. Hammer catch spring
33. Hammer pin
34. Hammer spring
35. Inertia rod
36. Link
37. Link pin
38. Magazine follower
39. Magazine plug
40. Magazine plug pin
41. Magazine spring
42. Magazine tube
43. Pawl
44. Pawl pin
45. Receiver
46. Receiver extension tube
47. Safety
48. Safety plunger
49. Safety plunger spring
50. Slide, right
51. Slide, left
52. Slide pin
53. Takedown screw bushing
54. Takedown retaining ring
55. Takedown screw
56. Takedown lock washer
57 Trigger
58. Trigger pin

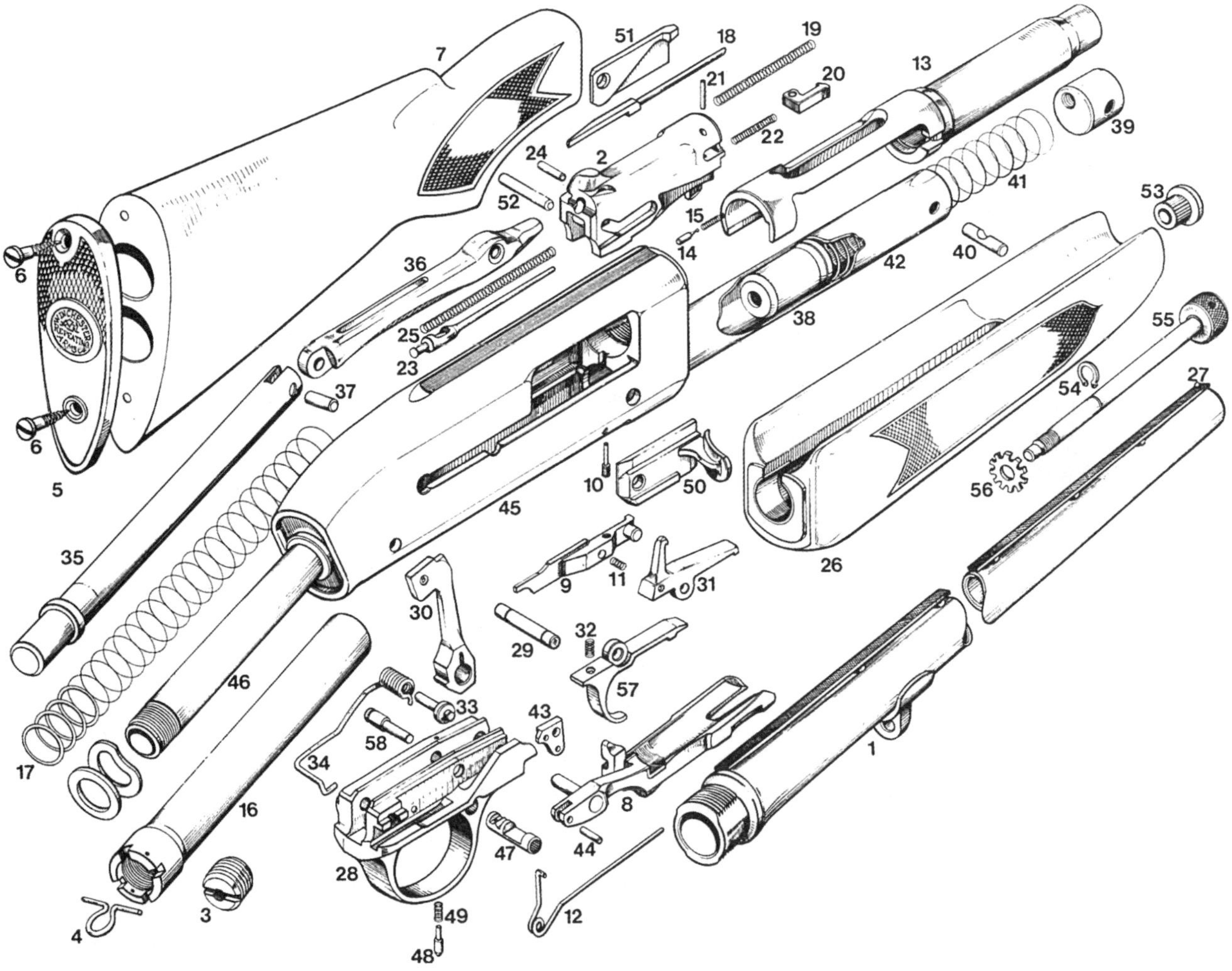

In 1905, Winchester had ended its long association with John M. Browning by turning down the gun that became the very successful Auto-5. The firm brought out its own long-recoil autoloader, the barrel-cocking Model 1911.

The 1911 was produced until 1925, and Winchester got along without an automatic for 15 years, until the introduction of the Model 40. Although it sported one of the first curved receivers, the Model 40 was less successful than the Model 1911 and production was cut off by World War II.

Winchester engineer A.W. "Gus" Swebelius began work on a new self-loading shotgun in 1934, but his efforts were interrupted by the war. In 1945, Swebelius altered a Model 12 to function with inertia weights in combination with the so-called "floating chamber" developed by David M. "Carbine" Williams.

Almost a decade of testing followed before the new gun was introduced in 1954. It caused a stir because, before the Model 50, autoloaders like the Auto-5 and Remington 11-48 used long-recoil operation. While this system was fairly reliable and well-proven, it had several disadvantages. Because the barrel recoiled, full-length ventilated ribs could not be used.

Winchester's "floating chamber" system eliminated these problems by using a fixed barrel. The floating chamber recoiled rearward about .09 inch, transferring its energy to an inertia rod in the buttstock. This, in turn, pulled the bolt to the rear and down, unlocking it from the floating chamber. Once unlocked, the bolt was free to recoil fully rearward, ejecting the spent shell and picking up another round.

The earliest Model 50s could be fired without the barrel attached. Treasury Department officials ruled this constituted a sawed-off shotgun, and Winchester was required to recall the guns and make an engineering change that precluded firing without the barrel installed.

The Model 50 was made in 12- and 20-gauge versions, with field, skeet and trap models available. In 1958, Winchester introduced a Featherweight version with an aluminum receiver. This, in turn, led to the innovative but ill-fated Model 59, which combined the aluminum receiver with a steel-lined glass fiber barrel (below left).

Both the Models 50 and 59 were doomed by the advent of gas operated shotguns, and the Model 50 was discontinued in 1961 with more than 196,000 made, while the Model 59 lasted through 1965, with 82,085 guns made.

The Model 50 suffered from several common malfunctions. One, attributable to "over engineering," was misfiring caused by a light trigger pull. To help prevent doubling, a secondary sear notch was cut in the hammer. A light trigger pull could allow the sear to re-engage the hammer. Winchester attempted to correct the situation by issuing a Model 50 "Blue Book" for gunsmiths with a fix for the problem (below right).

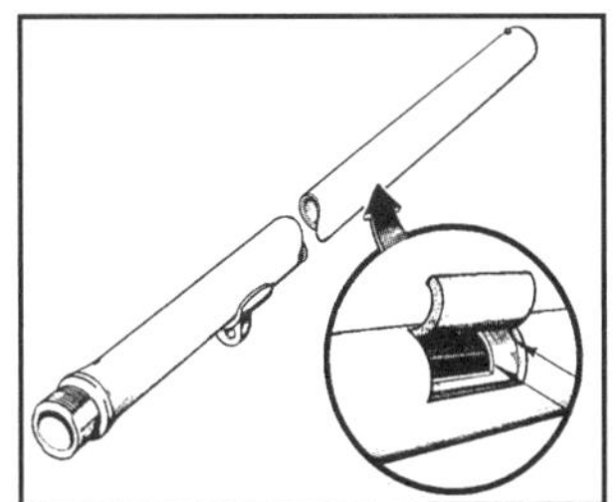

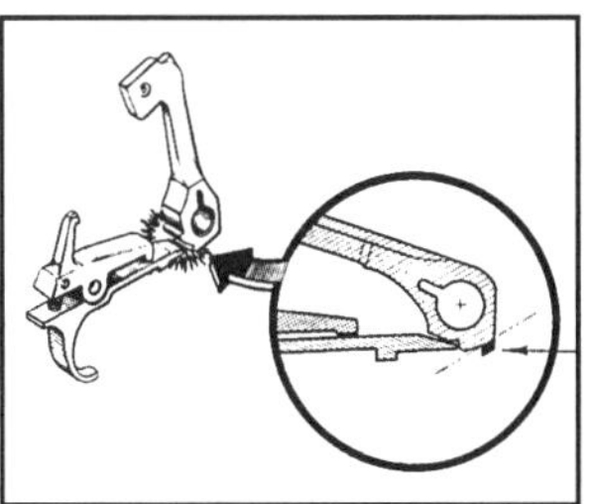

DISASSEMBLY

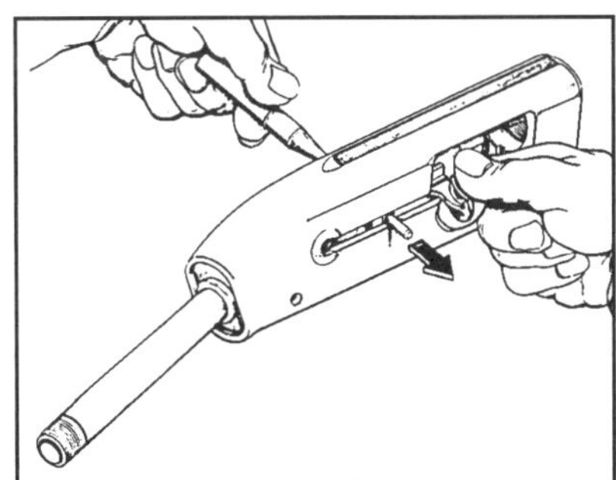

First clear the firearm and check both the chamber and magazine to ensure that the gun is not loaded and is safe to service. Return the bolt to a closed and locked position and engage the safety.

Next loosen the take-down screw (55) to free the fore-end (26) to be removed to the front and off the magazine tube (42). Now grasp the barrel (1), and while exerting pressure toward the receiver (45), rotate it a quarter-turn in either direction to disengage the interrupted locking rings and remove the barrel to the front.

Note: Both the Winchester Models 50 and 59 have floating chambers and special care must be taken during disassembly. To remove the chamber (13) support it with one hand while drawing the operating handle on the right slide (50) to the rear midway of the ejection port to disengage the bolt (2) to release the chamber for removal to the front and out. This chamber sleeve contains a chamber plunger and spring (14 & 15). Note that they are in place, however, there is little danger of them falling free. Now slowly lower the bolt to a closed position.

To remove the trigger group, drift out the guard pin (29) and depress the carrier lock (9) button to clear the carrier and lift the guard (28) out the bottom of the receiver to the rear.

To remove the bolt group, draw the operating handle on the right slide (50) to the rear to align the slide pin (52) with the circular notches in the take-down slot. This aligns the slide pin with a small poke hole In the left side of the receiver. Insert a small drift through this poke hole and push out the slide pin halfway to engage the receiver (45) (left). This retains the bolt group in position.

Next, with access through the bottom of the receiver, insert a screwdriver in front of the link (36) and depress it to the rear to relieve tension of the slide pin (52). While retaining the link, withdraw the slide pin (52) to disconnect the link from the bolt group. Now while slowly releasing the spring tension, raise the link (36) to a vertical position out the bottom of the receiver. The right slide (50) may now be removed out through the ejection port and the bolt (2) with the left slide (51) may be lifted out through the bottom of the receiver. No further disassembly is required for general service and cleaning. Assembly is accomplished in the reverse order.

WINCHESTER MODEL 52C RIFLE

PARTS LEGEND

1. Receiver
2. Receiver sight base plug screw (2)
3. Breech bolt guide
4. Barrel
5. Telescope sight rear mount base
6. Telescope sight rear mount base screw (2)
7. Telescope sight front mount base
8. Telescope sight front mount base screw (2)
9. Front sight base plug screw (2)
10. Barrel band
11. Barrel band lug
12. Barrel band screw
13. Barrel band screw escutcheon
14. Tang screw 44.
15. Tang screw escutcheon
16. Housing screw
17. Breech bolt handle locking plunger
18. Breech bolt handle locking plunger spring
19. Breech bolt handle locking plunger pin
20. Housing (complete assembly)
21. Housing retaining pin
22. Safety lever
23. Safety lever spring
24. Breech bolt lock
25. Breech bolt (complete assembly)
26. Magazine holder
27. Magazine holder screw, rear
28. Magazine holder screw, front
29. Magazine catch
30. Magazine catch pin
31. Magazine catch spring
32. Magazine
33. Stock
34. Resilient spacer (3)
35. Magazine release plunger
36. Magazine release plunger escutcheon
37. Stock abutment plate
38. Stock screw bushing
39. Stock screw
40. Guard
41. Guard plate
42. Guard screw
43. Forearm adjustment base
44. Forearm adjustment front swivel bow & screw
45. Forearm adjusting swivel base
46. Forearm adjusting swivel bow base screw
47. Forearm adjusting swivel bow
48. Forearm adjustment base screw (rear)
49. Forearm adjustment base screw escutcheon
50. Forearm adjusting bow screw escutcheon
51. Buttplate
52. Buttplate screw (2)
53. Stock swivel
54. Stock swivel screw (2)

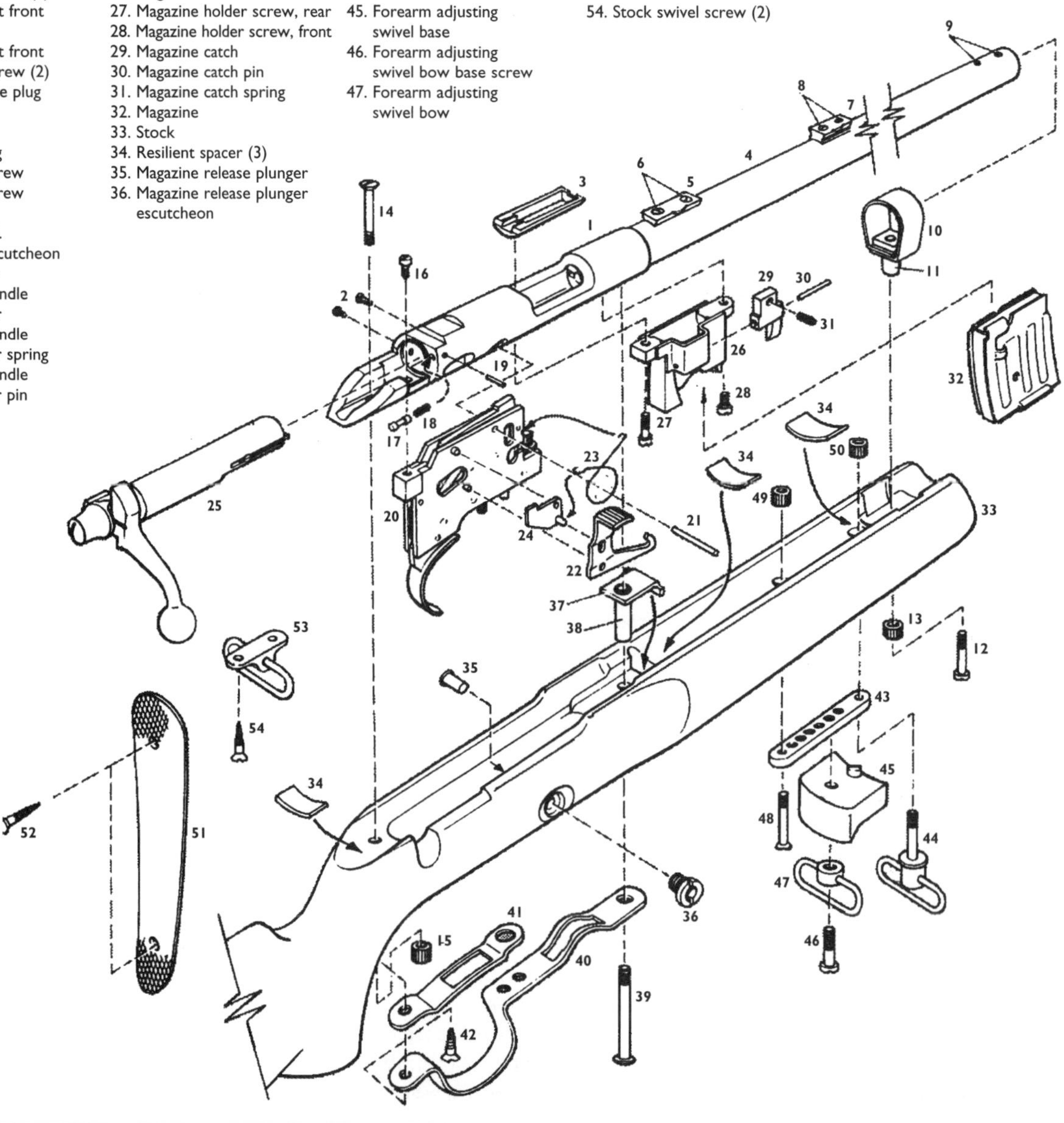

During the 1919 National Matches at Caldwell, New Jersey, Winchester Repeating Arms introduced prototypes of a new .22 caliber bolt-action smallbore target rifle which bore the factory code number G52R. Winchester employee Thomas C. Johnson had been issued patents on both the rifle and the its curved 5-shot box-magazine to which it was adapted. Designated Model 52, first commercial production was in 1920. In 1924 an improved model was introduced which incorporated a better stock design, but with no changes in action or barrel. The Model 52 was first made with a heavy barrel in 1927.

In 1929, a much-improved version was offered featuring speed-lock ignition, improved sights, and improved stock with semi-beavertail fore-end. Shortly thereafter parts kits were made available to modernize the original "slow-lock" action to the newer "speed-lock" type.

The Model 52 Sporting rifle with lightweight barrel and sporting stock was authorized in 1934. This model was discontinued in 1959.

The Model 52B rifle was introduced in 1937. It incorporated several changes, including re-designed trigger, pivoted safety lock on right side of receiver forward of bolt handle, and a new speed-lock mechanism. Stock for the standard-barrel model was re-designed, and the heavy-barrel model was furnished with the new style Marksman stock.

In 1951 the Model 52B was superseded by the Model 52C with new Micro-Motion trigger, improved Marksman stock, and improved barrel band. General specifications were the same as the Model 52B. As a matter of interest, serial numbers of the Model 52C began with gun #75,550. Production of the Model 52C was discontinued in 1961 at which time it was replaced with the Model 52D that lasted until 1978.

DISASSEMBLY

To remove bolt, check to be sure chamber is empty, then close bolt and pull trigger. Push forward on trigger and draw bolt rearward out of receiver. When withdrawing bolt, lift rear of bolt up slightly to clear comb of stock.

To reassemble bolt to receiver, slide bolt into receiver with flat side down. Align lug on underside of bolt handle with slot in receiver. While holding trigger back, push bolt all the way forward into receiver.

To disassemble barrel and receiver from stock, remove barrel band screw (12), tang screw (14), and stock screw (39). Lift barrel and receiver up out of stock (33).

Magazine holder (26) is removed by unscrewing magazine holder screws (27 & 28). Remove breech bolt guide (3) from top of receiver. To remove complete trigger housing assembly (20), unscrew housing screw (16) from top of receiver and drift out housing retaining pin (21). Drop housing down out of bottom of receiver. Safety lever spring (23) is easily removed from housing by lifting its front end out of slot at front edge of housing. Safety lever (22) and breech bolt lock (24) can be lifted up off pins in housing. Reassemble in reverse order.

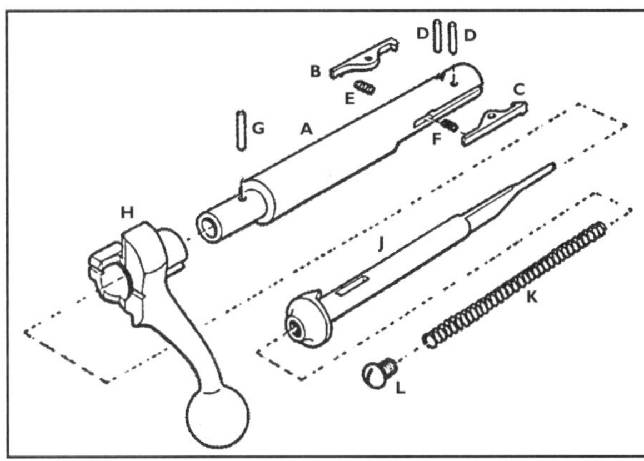

PARTS WINCHESTER 52C BREECH BOLT ASSEMBLY

A. Breech bolt
B. Extractor, left
C. Extractor, right
D. Extractor pin
E. Extractor spring, left
F. Extractor spring, right
G. Firing pin guide pin
H. Breech bolt handle
J. Firing pin
K. Firing pin spring
L. Firing pin plug

Breech bolt can be disassembled by clamping the body of breech bolt (A) firmly in a vise. Breech bolt handle (H) is drawn back far enough to expose firing pin gide pin (G). Drift out pin with a punch, leaving pin in place through hole. Remove firing pin plug (L). Spring (K) may be released by removing punch, but care should be taken to prevent forcible expulsion of spring from firing pin. Remove firing pin and breech bolt handle (H) to rear. In reassembly, firing pin spring (K) must be forced forward of pin hole in breech bolt with blade of screwdriver or similar tool to permit re-entry of pin.

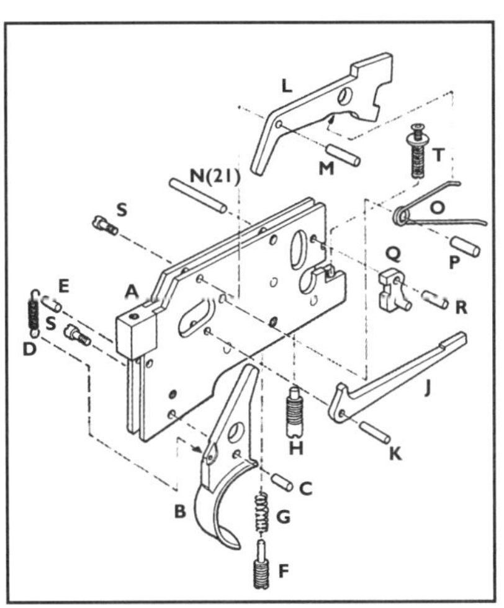

NOTE: All trigger housing parts are sold for factory installation only. The disassembly of this component is not recommended and should only be undertaken by a qualified gunsmith.

PARTS WINCHESTER 52C TRIGGER HOUSING ASSEMBLY

A. Housing
B. Trigger
C. Trigger pin
D. Trigger spring
E. Trigger spring pin
F. Trigger pull adjusting screw
G. Trigger pull adjusting spring
H. Overtravel adjusting screw
J. Trigger lever
K. Trigger lever pin
L. Sear
M. Sear pivot pin
N. Housing retaining pin (21)
O. Sear spring
P. Sear spring pin
Q. Rocker
R. Rocker pin
S. Adjustment locking screw
T. Engagement adjusting screw assembly

WINCHESTER MODEL 54 RIFLE

PARTS LEGEND

1. Barrel
2. Breech bolt
3. Breech bolt sleeve
4. Breech bolt sleeve lock
5. Bolt sleeve lock spring
6. Bolt sleeve lock pin
7. Buttstock
8. Buttplate
9. Buttplate screws (2)
10. Extractor
11. Extractor ring
12. Ejector
13. Ejector pin
14. Ejector spring
15. Firing pin spring
16. Firing pin sleeve
17. Firing pin
18. Forearm stud
19. Forearm stud screw
20. Stud screw escutcheon
21. Guard
22. Guard plate
23. Guard screw, front
24. Guard screw, rear
25. Guard screw, center
26. Magazine box
27. Magazine spring
28. Magazine follower
29. Receiver
30. Safety lock
31. Sear
32. Sear pin
33. Sear spring
34. Swivel bows (2)
35. Trigger
36. Trigger pin
37. Trigger spring
38. Sight, front
39. Sight blank, rear
40. Sight receiver (optional item)

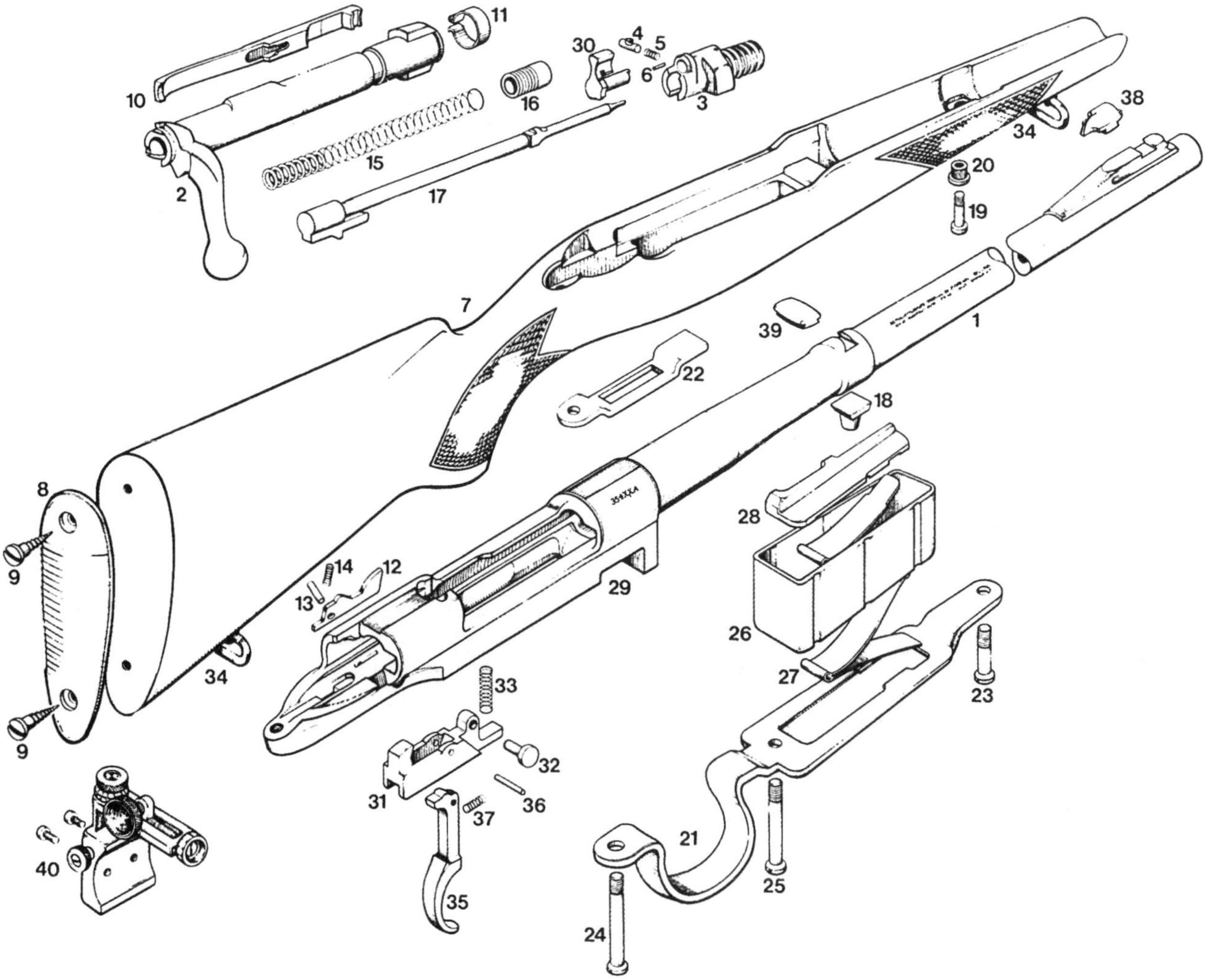

When Winchester Repeating Arms Co. introduced its new sporting rifle in 1925, the influence of the M1903 Springfield was evident in the basic coned breech turnbolt design and in details such as the clip guide in the receiver's bridge and the two-piece firing pin that was changed to a single piece in 1932.

Only two chamberings were initially offered, Springfield's .30-06 and the then-new .270 Win.

The Model 54's receiver was milled from a bar of nickel steel, and the bolt, with its dual, front-mounted locking lugs, was a one-piece forging with integral handle. It was similar, then, to the Springfield, but was lacking the ejector slot in the left locking lug.

The familiar claw extractor common to the Mauser and Springfield was employed, but instead of the Springfield's huge safety lug, the Model 54 used a backup flange by the bolt handle root and a guide lug near the center of the bolt body. While the receiver's smooth appearance was a plus, the stamped steel trigger guard and the use of the trigger as the bolt stop were among the design's criticized features.

The Model 54 did not prove to be dramatically popular, as sporterized and as-issued Springfields and Mausers were readily available at relatively low prices and the Great Depression was soon to come.

Nevertheless the Model 54's caliber choices were expanded to include .22 Hornet, .220 Swift, .250-3000 Savage, .257 Roberts, .30-30 Win, and 7mm. 7.65mm and 9mm Mauser.

The standard rifle's checkered stock was first made with a slim, schnabel-tipped forearm but was later changed to the "NRA Type" with oval forearm. Barrels of 20" or 24" were available, and an uncheckered 20-inch barrelled carbine.

In addition, a Super Grade version of the sporter was made, as were various target models, including the so-called Sniper's Rifle, Sniper's Match, Heavy Barrel, Target Model and National Match.

In 1937, with about 50,000 Model 54s having been produced, the rifle was made all but obsolete by the market appearance of the greatly improved Winchester Model 70.

DISASSEMBLY

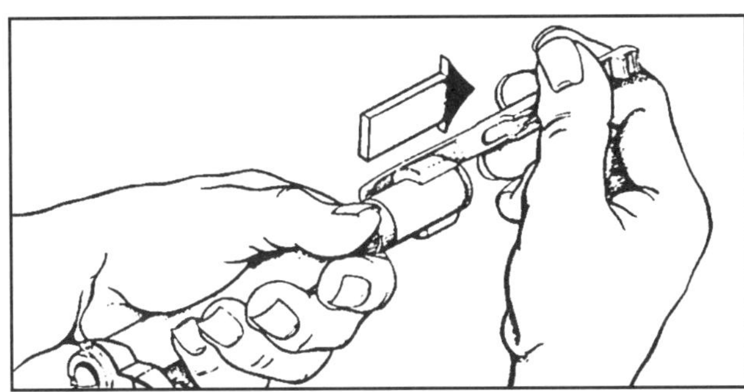

1 Open the bolt and check both chamber and magazine to ensure that the gun is not loaded. Close the bolt and, with the gun cocked, turn the safety lock (30) to a vertical position. Depress the trigger (35), raise the bolt handle and remove the breech bolt (2) from the rear of the action. Rotate the extractor (10) counterclockwise until its retaining rib clears the groove on the front of the bolt. Now the extractor may be pushed forward to disengage the extractor ring (11).

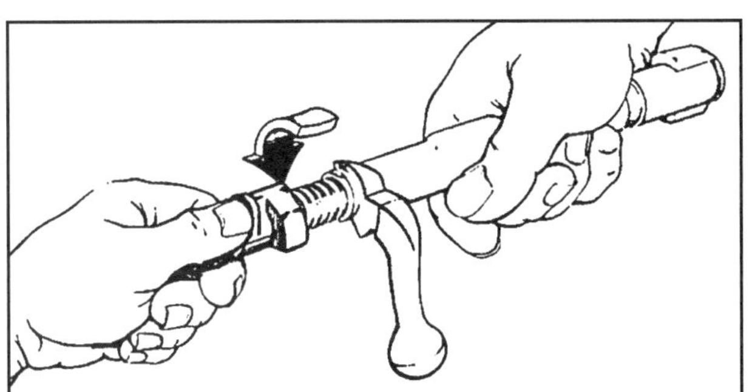

2 NOTE: Do not remove the extractor ring unless replacement is required. Depress the breech bolt sleeve lock (4) and unscrew the breech bolt sleeve (3) counterclockwise to remove the sleeve and firing pin assembly.

Further disassembly of this sub-group requires that the firing pin assembly be supported while rotating the safety lock (30) to allow the firing pin (17)to move forward. Now draw back the firing pin sleeve (16) and rotate it one quarter turn to release the spring compression and remove the sleeve (16) and spring (15) to the front. Now withdraw the firing pin (17) from the bolt sleeve assembly. Rotate the safety lock (30) counterclockwise to align with the disassembly notch and remove to the rear. Next restrain the breech bolt sleeve lock (4) while drifting out the lock pin (6) to the front to remove lock (4) and spring (5).

Remove the three guard screws (23, 24 & 25) and, while supporting the stock, pull rearward on the guard bow and lift the guard (21) from the stock, front end first. Next slide the magazine spring (27) out of the retaining slot in the guard (21) and remove the follower (28) from the other spring leg. The guard plate (22) may now be removed from the stock. Note: This plate is inletted with an interference fit and must be removed carefully to avoid damage to either the stock or its finish. Next remove the forearm stud screw (19) and lift the barrel (1) and receiver (29) out of the stock (7).

The magazine box (26) may now be removed from the bottom of the receiver. Now drift out the headed sear pin (32) from left to right to remove the trigger (35), sear (31) and sear spring (33). If required, the trigger pin (36) may be drifted out to remove the trigger (35) and its spring (37). Next drift out the ejector pin (13) from below to remove both the ejector (12) and the ejector spring (14) to complete disassembly.

WIN. MODEL 55 SINGLE-SHOT RIFLE

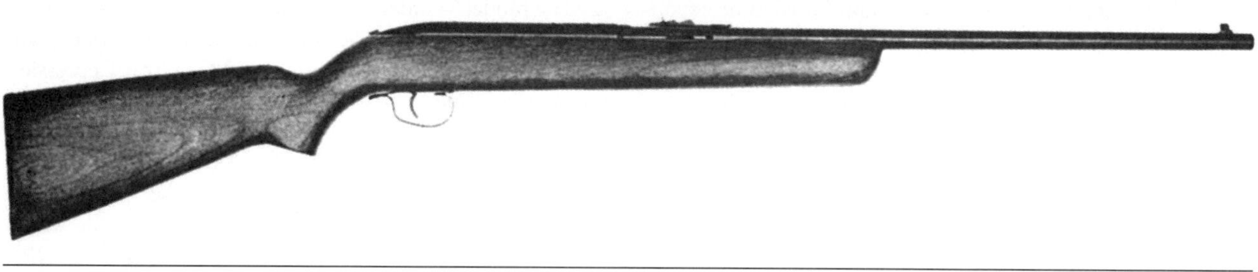

PARTS LEGEND

1. Receiver
2. Cover
3. Cover pin
4. Barrel locating pin
5. Barrel
6. Action slide stop pin
7. Rear sight
8. Front sight
9. Action slide
10. Extractor
11. Extractor spring
12. Extractor pin
13. Action slide spring
14. Buffer washer
15. Washer
16. Safety rod spring
17. Safety rod
18. Mainspring
19. Bolt
20. Safety
21. Sear
22. Sleeve
23. Safety plunger spring
24. Safety plunger
25. Trigger spring plunger
26. Trigger spring
27. Trigger top
28. Trigger
29. Trigger pin
30. Receiver stud
31. Escutcheon
32. Stock stud screw
33. Guard
34. Guard bow screws (2)

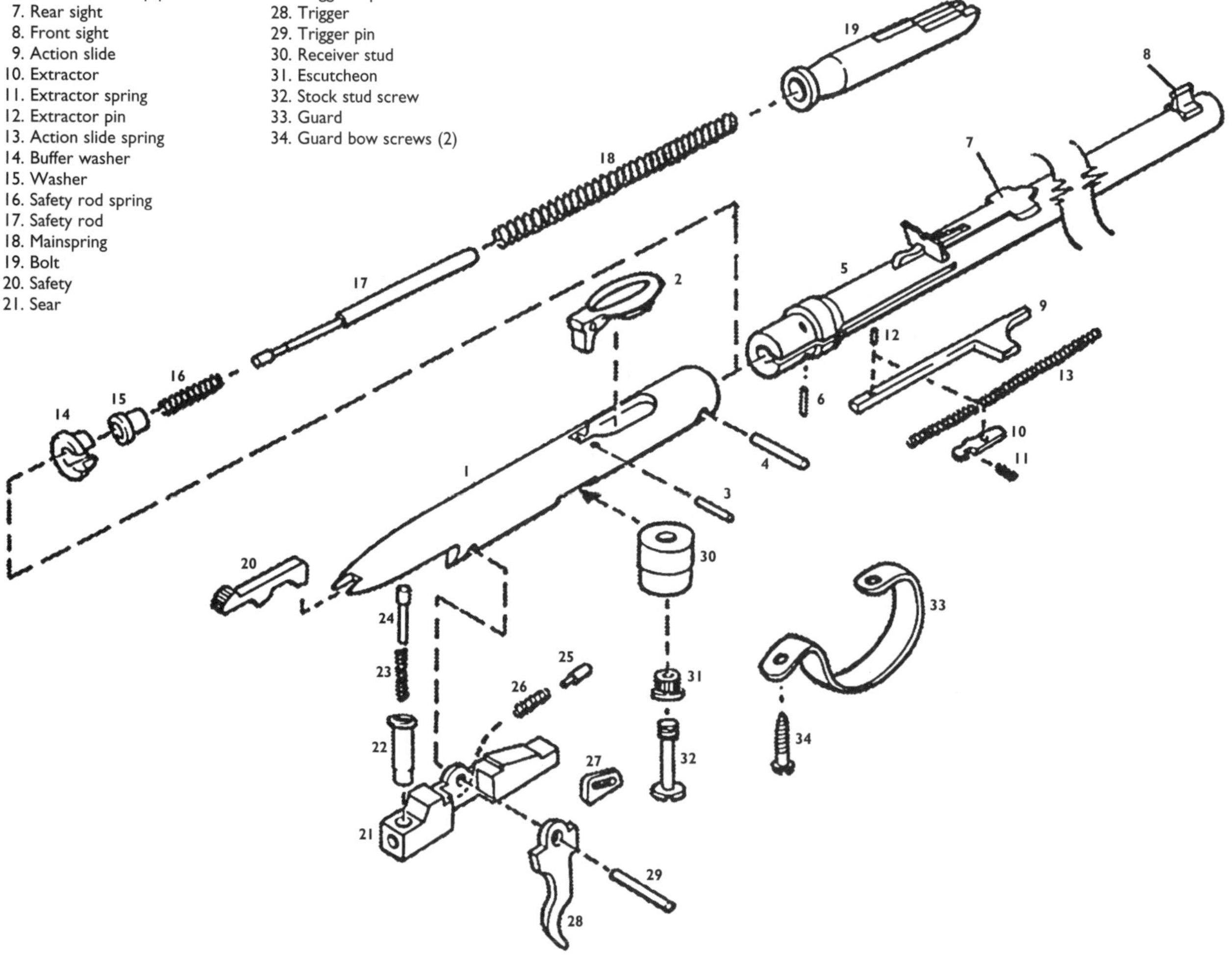

The Winchester Model 55 single-shot rifle introduced in 1958 is chambered for the .22 Short, Long, and Long Rifle rimfire cartridges. It was made in 22-inch barrel length only. Weight is 5½ lbs. Its blowback-operated action is designed to fire from open bolt position.

The action is cocked by retracting the action slide on the right side of the receiver. A cartridge is then inserted in the breech by pressing the bullet nose against the hinged plastic loading chute in the top of the receiver and chambering the round with the finger tip until the rim engages the extractor. The loading chute then rises into closed position. The act of loading automatically engages the safety. Disengagement of the safety readies the gun for firing.

When the trigger is pulled the bolt moves forward, firing the cartridge. The empty case is ejected through the bottom of the receiver as the bolt recoils to the rear or cocked position. After reloading and disengaging the safety, the gun is ready to fire.

The Winchester Model 55 rifle was discontinued in 1961.

DISASSEMBLY

Check action to be sure rifle is unloaded. Cock rifle and put safety (20) in safe position. Loosen stock stud screw (32) in underside of stock and lift the barrel (5) and the receiver (1) assembly out of the stock. Drift out barrel locating pin (4) and slide barrel (5) out of receiver to front. Drift out cover pin (3), depress cover (2), and remove from receiver.

Place front end of receiver against a flat wood surface, release safety (20), and pull trigger. Exercise care to keep fingers clear of receiver openings during this operation. Draw bolt out of receiver to front.

In reassembling, replace bolt in receiver and push all the way in until it catches. Place safety in "Safe" position. Replace cover in top loading port of receiver with front end first and foot of cover in groove of bolt, sliding backward until the front end of cover is flush with the receiver. Replace the cover pin.

Replace barrel in receiver and replace barrel locating pin. Replace barrel and receiver assembly in stock and tighten the stock stud screw.

Trigger mechanism may be disassembled if necessary by drifting out trigger pin (29), taking care not to allow springs (23 & 26) to escape forcibly.

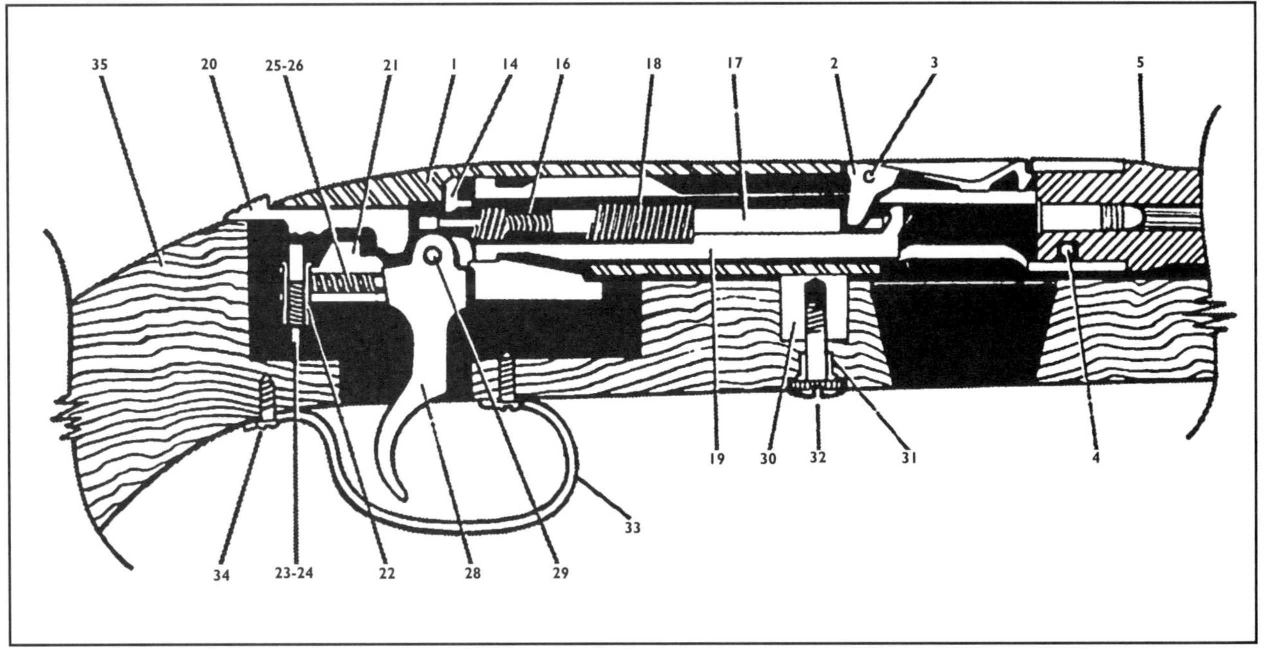

WINCHESTER MODEL 61 RIFLE

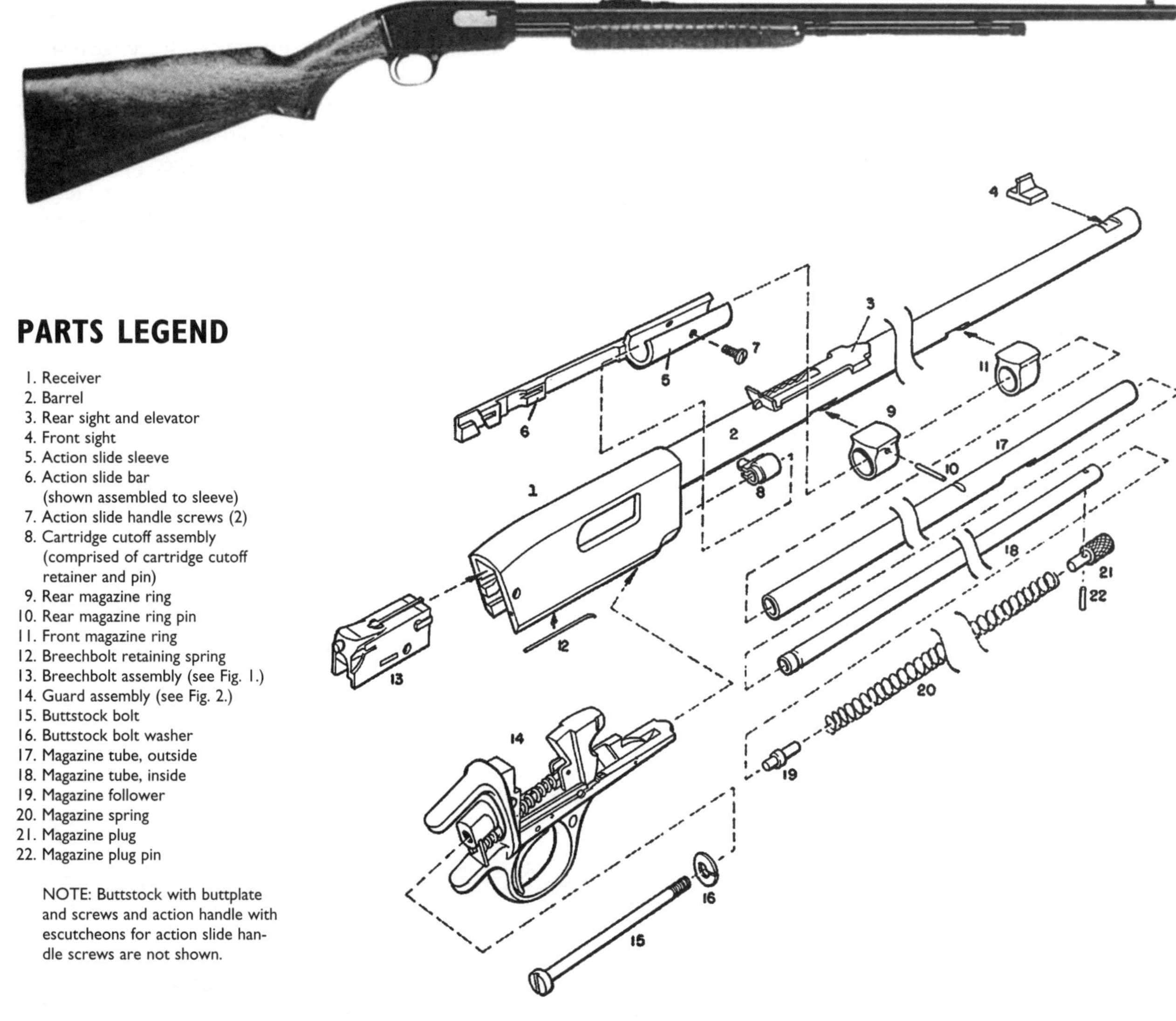

PARTS LEGEND

1. Receiver
2. Barrel
3. Rear sight and elevator
4. Front sight
5. Action slide sleeve
6. Action slide bar (shown assembled to sleeve)
7. Action slide handle screws (2)
8. Cartridge cutoff assembly (comprised of cartridge cutoff retainer and pin)
9. Rear magazine ring
10. Rear magazine ring pin
11. Front magazine ring
12. Breechbolt retaining spring
13. Breechbolt assembly (see Fig. 1.)
14. Guard assembly (see Fig. 2.)
15. Buttstock bolt
16. Buttstock bolt washer
17. Magazine tube, outside
18. Magazine tube, inside
19. Magazine follower
20. Magazine spring
21. Magazine plug
22. Magazine plug pin

NOTE: Buttstock with buttplate and screws and action handle with escutcheons for action slide handle screws are not shown.

DISASSEMBLY

Check action to be sure rifle is unloaded. Loosen takedown screw at left rear of receiver and pull takedown screw (2A, Fig. 2.) out as far as it will go. Pull buttstock and guard (14) to rear away from receiver (1).

To remove breechbolt assembly (13) from receiver, hold receiver inverted and slide breechbolt to rear. With a small screwdriver or other suitable tool, pry breech-bolt forward and upward gently so cam lug on breechbolt comes out of inclined cam cut in side of action slide bar (6). Slide breechbolt backward out of receiver.

Turn inner magazine tube by knurled magazine plug (21) until locking pin is free of notch in outer magazine tube (17) and withdraw inner magazine tube (18) toward muzzle. To disassemble inner magazine tube, drift out magazine plug pin (22) and withdraw plug (21), spring (20), and follower (19). To remove outside magazine tube (17), drift out rear magazine ring pin (10) and draw tube toward muzzle and out of rings (9 & 11).

With receiver held inverted, grasp action slide handle and move action slide bar (6) all the way forward. Pull handle to right and roll it off barrel so action slide bar comes out of slot in receiver to right. Remove action slide handle screws (7) and pull wooden handle off sleeve (5). Remove slide bar (6) from sleeve.

Remove cartridge cutoff assembly (8) from slot at forward end of left side of receiver with fingers, or by drifting out gently.

Further disassembly of cartridge cutoff assembly is not recommended nor is removal of breechbolt retaining spring (12). Remove magazine rings (9 & 11) from barrel (2) by turning rings counterclockwise out of dovetails in barrel. Use a piece of wood dowel to accomplish this.

Remove buttplate screws and buttplate (not shown in exploded drawing) and remove buttstock bolt (15) and washer (16) through hole in rear of buttstock. Pull buttstock off guard assembly to rear. Reassemble in reverse.

The Winchester Model 61 .22 caliber slide-action rifle was introduced in 1932. A hammerless, tubular magazine design, it was available initially with both round and octagonal barrels. The basic model with 24-inch round barrel was chambered for the .22 Short, Long, and Long Rifle cartridges. The 24-inch octagonal barrel was chambered for the .22 Short, .22 Long Rifle, and .22 WRF cartridges.

In 1939 a version of the Model 61 was offered with a smoothbore barrel chambered for the .22 Long Rifle Shot cartridge. The version of the Model 61 with the octagonal barrel was discontinued after World War II and the .22 WRF chambering was then offered in the 24-inch round barrel. The .22 Short chambering was discontinued. In 1960, the rifle was chambered for the .22 Winchester Magnum Rimfire cartridge. This involved redesigning and strengthening components.

In 1963 the basic Model 61, in .22 Short, Long, and Long Rifle chamberings was discontinued on the introduction of the Winchester Model 270 slide-action rifle.

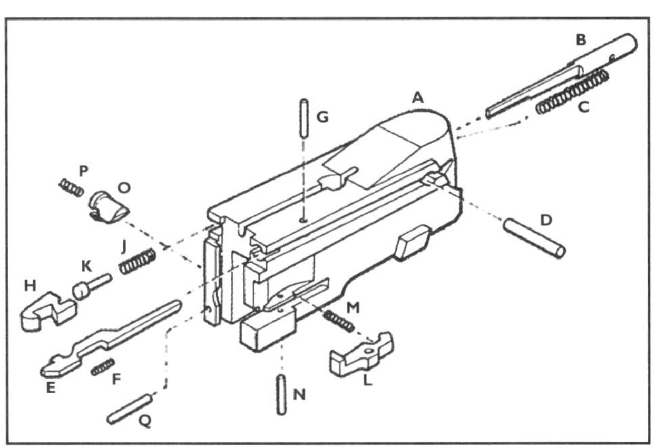

BREECH TAKEDOWN

A. Breechbolt
B. Firing pin
C. Firing pin retracting spring
D. Firing pin stop pin
E. Ejector
F. Ejector spring
G. Ejector pin
H. Upper extractor
J. Upper extractor spring
K. Upper extractor spring plunger
L.. Lower extractor
M. Lower extractor spring
N. Lower extractor pin
O. Carrier plunger
P. Carrier plunger spring
Q. Carrier plunger pin

Drift out ejector pin (G) and withdraw ejector (E) and spring (F) from front of breechbolt (A). Drift out firing pin stop pin (D) and remove firing pin (B) and spring (C) from rear end of breechbolt. To remove upper extractor, place a thin screwdriver between extractor (H) and spring plunger (K), pulling plunger back with screwdriver.

Rock extractor upward and out of breechbolt. Remove plunger (K) and spring (J) from front of breechbolt. Drift out lower extractor pin (N) and remove lower extractor (L) and spring (M), taking care not to allow spring to escape forcibly. Drift out carrier plunger pin (Q) and remove carrier plunger (0) and spring (P) from right side of breechbolt. Reassemble in reverse order.

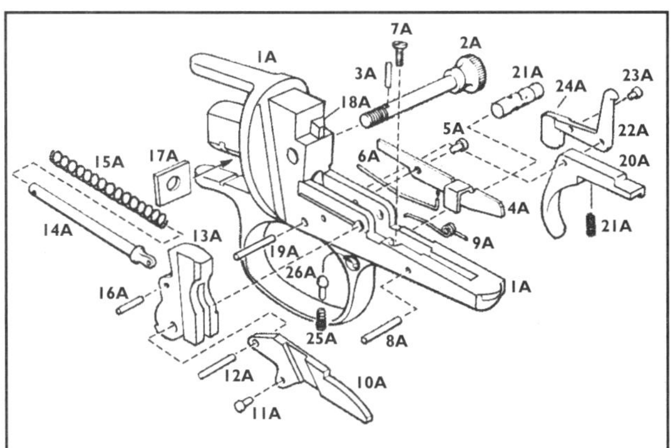

GUARD TAKEDOWN

1A. Guard
2A. Takedown screw
3A. Takedown screw stop pin
4A. Action slide lock
5A. Action slide lock pivot
6A. Action slide lock spring
7A. Carrier stop screw
8A. Carrier spring pin
9A. Carrier spring
10A. Carrier
11A. Carrier stop pin
12A. Hammer pin
13A. Hammer
14A. Hammer spring guide rod
15A. Hammer spring
16A. Hammer spring guide rod pin
17A. Hammer spring abutment
18A. Ejector stop
19A. Trigger pin
20A. Trigger
21A. Trigger spring
22A. Hammer catch
23A. Hammer catch stud
24A. Trigger lock
25A. Trigger lock plunger spring
26A. Trigger lock plunger

Drift out takedown screw stop pin (3A) and remove take-down screw (2A) from guard (lA). Drift out action slide lock pivot (5A) from right to left. Remove action slide lock spring (6A) from hole in lower edge of action slide lock (4A). Lift action slide lock upward and out of guard. Remove carrier stop screw (7A).

Drift out carrier spring pin (8A) and lift carrier upward to allow removal of carrier spring (9A). Drift out hammer pin (12A). Remove hammer (13A) with carrier (10A), and hammer spring (l5A) and guide rod (14A) intact. These parts can now be separated.

Drift out hammer spring abutment (17A) from left to right. Drift out trigger pin (l9A) and remove trigger (20A) and spring (2lA) upward out of guard. Hammer catch (22A) may now be lifted out of guard.

Place trigger lock (24A) in "off" position. Place a small drift or other suitable tool in small hole in lock visible through top of guard and turn lock clockwise (viewed from right side of guard) by moving drift forward. This will disengage plunger (26A) from detent slot in lock.

Drift lock out of guard to left, remove plunger (26A) and spring (25A) from hole inside lock hole. Removal of ejector stop (l8A) is accomplished by drifting out from rear of guard toward front. Reassemble in reverse.

WINCHESTER MODEL 62A RIFLE

PARTS LEGEND

1. Receiver
2. Barrel
3. Buttstock
4. Guard
5. Hammer
6. Trigger
7. Carrier
8. Carrier lever
9. Cartridge stop
10. Cartridge stop pin
11. Carrier lever spring
12. Carrier lever spring screw
13. Carrier lever pin
14. Trigger spring
15. Assembling screw bushing
16. Hammer spring abutment pin
17. Trigger pin
18. Upper tang screw
19. Hammer spring abutment guide rod
20. Hammer spring
21. Hammer spring abutment
22. Action slide handle
23. Action slide handle screw (2)
24. Action slide handle escutcheon (2)
25. Action slide
26. Magazine inside tube
27. Magazine spring
28. Magazine follower
29. Magazine plug
30. Magazine plug pin
31. Magazine outside tube
32. Magazine ring, front
33. Magazine ring pin, rear
34. Magazine ring ping,rear
35. Front sight
36. Rear sight
37. Elevator
38. Slide cover
39. Slide cover stop screw
40. Assembling screw
41. Assembling screw stop pin
42. Breech bolt
43. Extractor
44. Firing pin stop pin (2)
45. Firing pin stop pin (2)
46. Extractor pin
47. Firing pin
48. Firing pin spring
49. Buttplate
50. Buttplote screw (2)

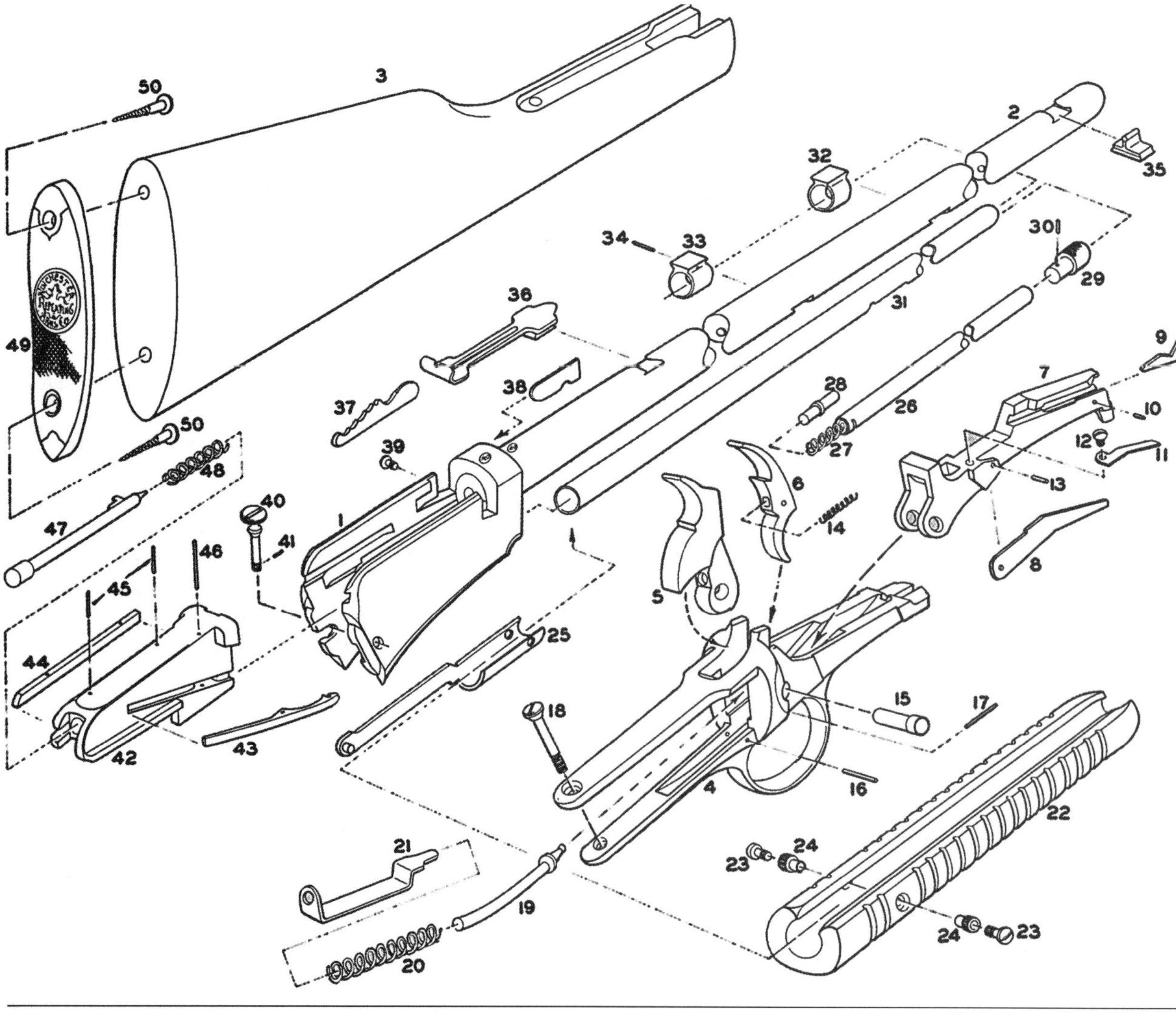

The Winchester Model 62A, .22 caliber tubular magazine rimfire rifle, is a development of the Winchester Model 1890 introduced in that year. In 1932 the Model 1890 was superceded by the Model 62. In the original Model 62, the locking system was so designed that the slide handle moved approximately ¼-inch to the rear before opening movement of the bolt commenced. On May 12, 1938, a change in the locking system was authorized to the one formerly used in the Model 1890, wherein initial movement of the slide handle starts the opening movement of the bolt. The actual designation of the rifle as the Model 62A occurred in 1939, when the forearm was changed from 6- to 8⅜-inches long, and the number of circular grooves on it was increased from 10 to 17. In 1949 the forearm was changed, to a semi-beavertail type.

The Model 62A was also offered in a .22 Short version, primarily intended for use in shooting galleries, and a standard version that handled Short, Long or Long Rifle cartridges interchangeably. The Model 62A was discontinued in 1959.

DISASSEMBLY

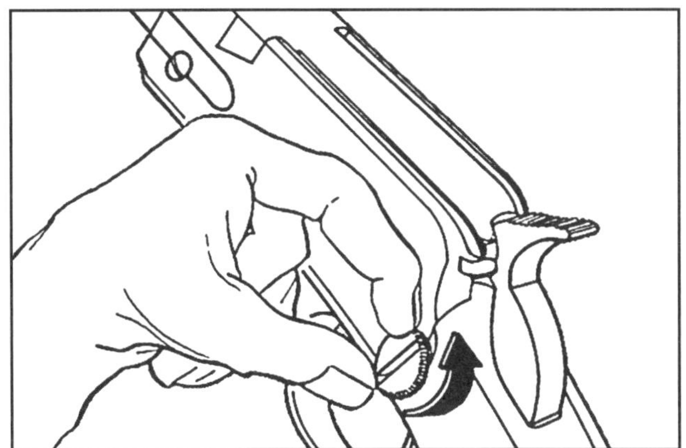

1 Takedown of the Model 62A is accomplished by unscrewing the assembly screw (40) and pulling it out until it clears the corresponding hole on the right rear of the receiver (1). Grasp stock and action assembly and barrel-receiver group firmly, and pull them apart. This disassembly is sufficient for cleaning the rifle.

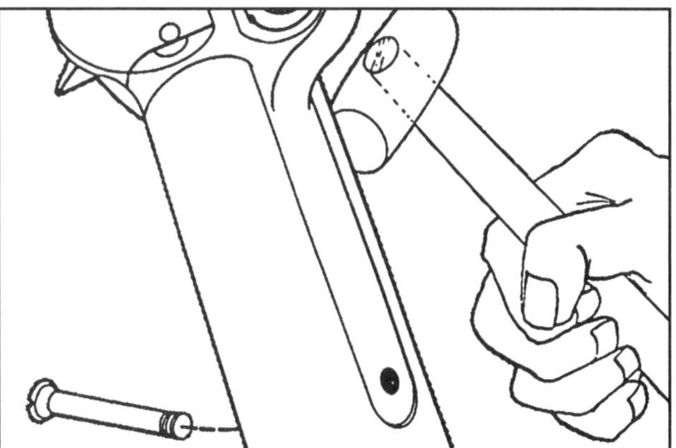

2 To remove or replace stock, unscrew upper tang screw (18) and remove it from rifle. Pull stock (3) away from guard (4). A light tapping at rear of trigger guard with a plastic hammer may be necessary because inletting of stock to guard is often very tight. Further disassembly of this rifle is not recommended, except by a competent gunsmith, due to the manner in which key parts are stake-pinned in place, and special tools are needed.

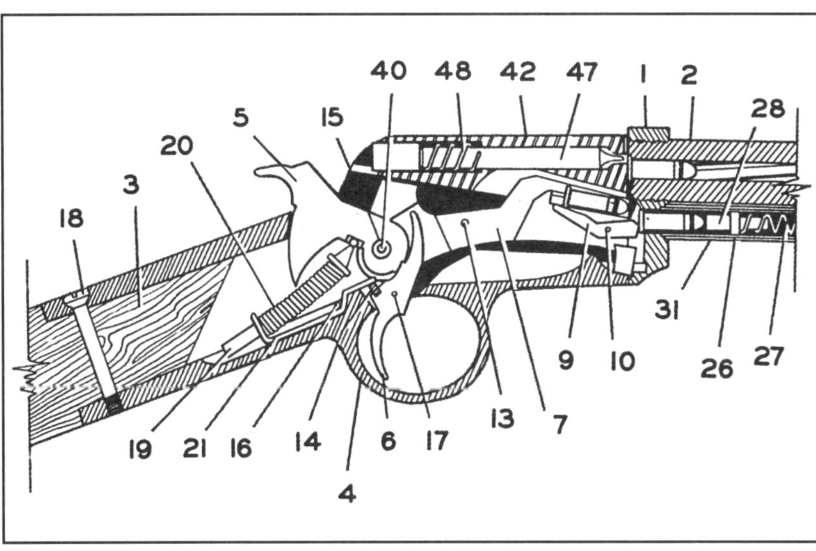

3 This sectional drawing shows the Model 62A action closed and locked prior to firing. The cartridge in the carrier holds the cartridge stop (9) in up position retaining next round in magazine. After discharge, rear movement of the action slide handle (22) and action slide (25) cams breech bolt (42) from locking notches in either side of receiver (1). (Parts 22 and 25 not shown here.) Further rearward movement of the action slide draws back the breech bolt, ejects spent case, and cocks hammer (5). When slide handle is at rearmost position, carrier moves up, placing fresh cartridge in front of bolt which carries it into chamber. During this closing action the bolt also presses carrier downward, permitting another round to be moved into carrier, repeating the cycle. Action must be fully closed and locked before firing pin (47) can strike rim of cartridge.

WINCHESTER MODEL 63 RIFLE

PARTS LEGEND

1. Receiver
2. Barrel
3. Rear sight
4. Front sight
5. Forearm tip tenon
6. Takedown screw bushing
7. Ejector
8. Ejector screw
9. Operating sleeve
10. Operating sleeve tip pin
11. Operating sleeve tip
12. Operating sleeve spring
13. Bolt guide rod
14. Forearm tip
15. Forearm tip screws (2)
16. Bolt
17. Firing pin
18. Firing pin spring
19. Firing pin stop pin
20. Extractor
21. Extractor plunger
22. Extractor plunger spring
23. Extractor plunger stop screw
24. Bolt spring
25. Tang
26. Takedown screw
27. Takedown screw stop pin
28. Takedown screw lock plunger
29. Takedown screw lock plunger spring
30. Takedown screw lock plunger stop pin
31. Trigger spring
32. Trigger lock plunger
33. Trigger lock plunger spring
34. Trigger lock
35. Hammer
36. Hammer pin
37. Hammer spring guide rod
    37A. Slave pin (for guide rod disassembly)
38. Hammer spring
39. Hammer spring abutment
40. Hammer spring guide rod pin
41. Hammer spring abutment pin
42. Trigger
43. Trigger pin
44. Sear
45. Sear spring
46. Buttplate
47. Buttplate screws (2)
48. Buttstock nut
49. Buttstock nut washer
50. Magazine tube, outer
51. Magazine tube, inner
52. Magazine plug pin
53. Magazine spring
54. Magazine follower
55. Magazine plug
56. Cartridge cutoff
57. Cartridge cutoff pin
58. Cartridge cutoff spring
59. Throat pin

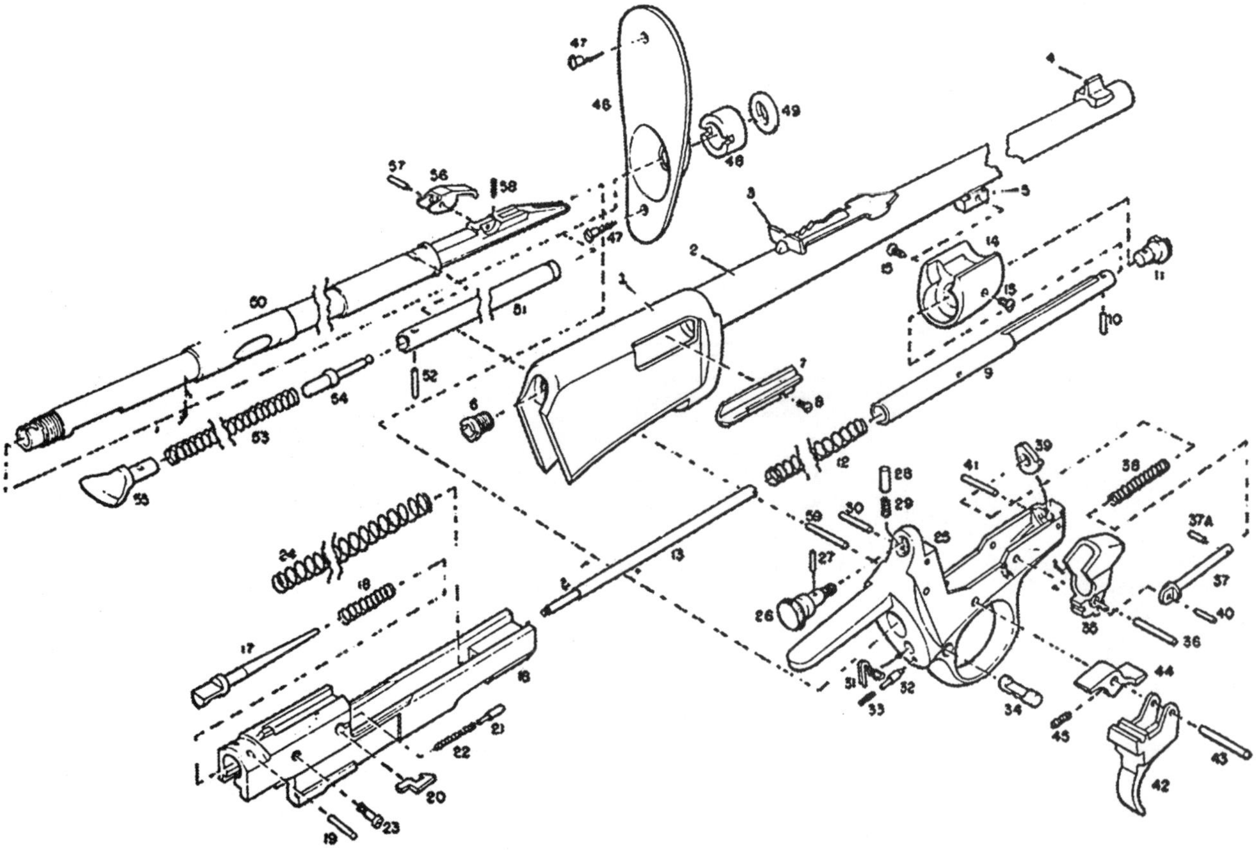

The Winchester Model 63 semi-automatic rifle, in .22 Long Rifle, was introduced in 1933. It was a revamped version of the Winchester Model 1903 rifle chambered for the .22 Winchester Automatic cartridge, a special inside-lubricated type which is not interchangeable with the .22 Long Rifle cartridge.

The Model 63 was made initially with a 20-inch round barrel. A change to 23-inch round barrel was authorized in 1934. Early production rifles were fitted with the same takedown screw locking device as that used on the Winchester Model 1903 rifle. It was necessary to depress the takedown screw lock through a slot in the tang before the takedown screw could be turned. This locking feature was eliminated in later production models. Manufacture of the Model 63 rifle was discontinued by Winchester in 1959.

DISASSEMBLY

To take down barrel and receiver group from tang and stock group, unscrew takedown screw (26) as shown in Fig. 1. Pull receiver (1) from tang (25) in a straight line. Remove both forearm tip screws (15) and forearm tip (14) containing operating sleeve (9) and spring (12) toward muzzle. Hold operating sleeve spring to avoid its forcible ejection during this operation. Operating sleeve tip (11) can be removed by drifting out pin (10). Forearm tip tenon (5) can be driven out of its dovetail in underside of barrel from left to right. Slide forearm forward off receiver.

To remove bolt guide rod (13) and bolt spring (24), hold receiver assembly inverted and, with a long screwdriver, loosen bolt spring guide rod in receiver. Remove bolt spring guide rod while holding spring to prevent its forcible ejection. Reassembly is shown in Fig. 5. Lift rear end of bolt (16) free of receiver and draw bolt out of receiver to rear.

To remove ejector (7) from receiver, unscrew ejector screw (8) through port at right side of receiver. Slide ejector back out of its dovetail and remove from receiver. Reassemble in reverse order.

Extractor (20) can be removed from bolt (16) by unscrewing extractor plunger stop screw (23) from right side of bolt. With a sharp tool inserted between extractor plunger (21) and extractor, compress plunger and roll extractor out of bolt toward front. Remove plunger with spring (22) from front of bolt. Firing pin (17) and spring (18) are removed from rear of bolt after drifting out firing pin stop pin (19). Reassemble bolt in reverse order.

To take down tang and buttstock group, remove inner magazine tube by turning magazine plug (55) to left to free locking pin (52) in inner tube from cam lock cut in end of outer magazine tube (50). Pull inner magazine tube from stock to rear. Remove buttplate screws (47) and buttplate (46). Remove nut (48) and stock as shown in Fig. 4. Remove trigger lock plunger (32) and spring (33) from rear end of tang (25) after withdrawing stock. Hammer and spring assembly is removed from tang as detailed in Figs. 2 & 3.

Drift out trigger pin (43) and remove trigger (42) and sear (44) from tang, taking care not to lose sear spring (45). Trigger lock (34) may be pushed out of tang from left to right. Trigger spring (31) can be pushed out of tang to rear. Reassembly of the trigger spring in the tang is shown in Fig. 6.

Cartridge cutoff (56) can be removed from throat of outer magazine tube (50) by drifting out pin (57), taking care not to allow escape of spring (58). Removal of takedown screw (26) is accomplished by drifting out pin (30). After removing take down screw to rear of tang, remove plunger (28) and spring (29) from hole at rear of tang inside takedown screw hole. Removal of outer magazine tube and throat from tang is not recommended.

WINCHESTER MODEL 63 RIFLE

DISASSEMBLY CONTINUED

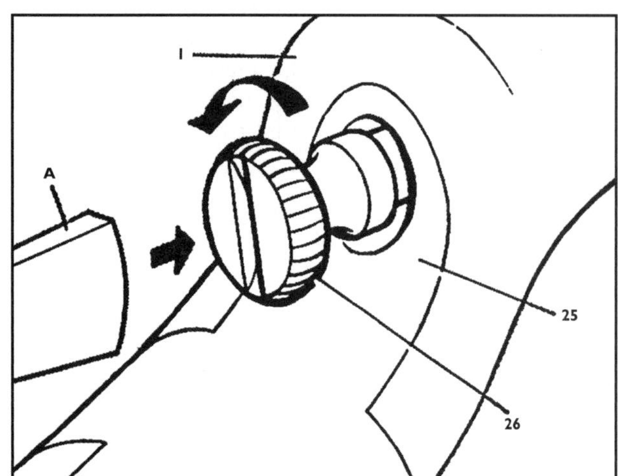

1 To avoid damage, a specially shaped screwdriver should be used as shown above to fit the curved slot in the head of the take-down screw.

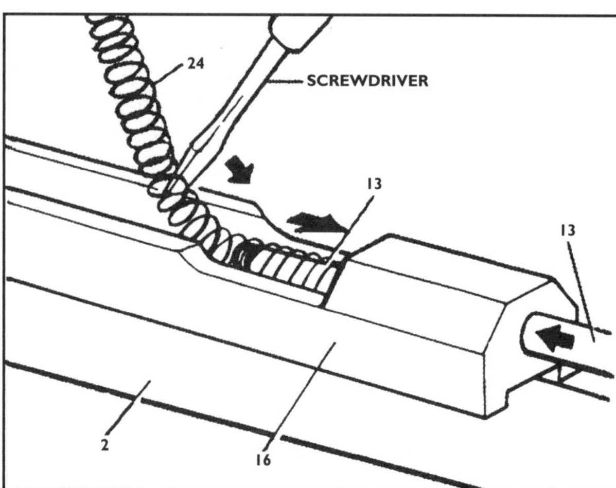

2 To reassemble bolt spring and bolt guide rod to bolt, hold bolt assembly inverted and insert guide rod through front end of bolt, threaded end first. Start spring onto threaded end of guide rod. Slide spring onto rod a few coils at a time with blade of screw-driver as shown, while sliding guide rod back into bolt. When spring is on rod, slide rod back until threaded end engages threads in front end of receiver. Screw guide rod firmly in place.

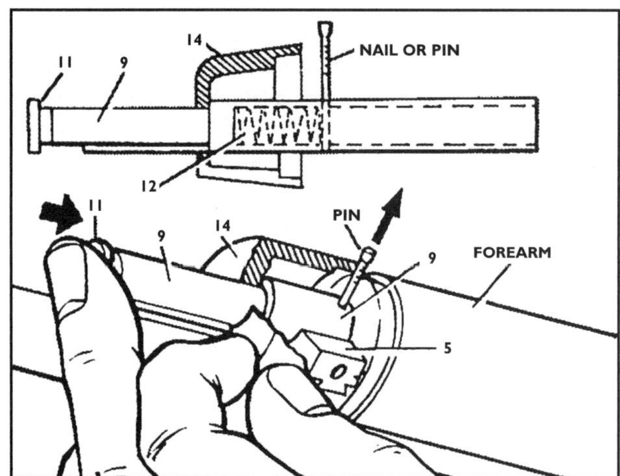

3 Insert operating sleeve spring in open end of operating sleeve. Compress spring with rod or wood dowel until end of the rod can be seen through hole in operating sleeve. Insert a small pin through hole in operating sleeve to hold spring compressed and remove dowel. Push operating sleeve assembly back inside forearm as shown until pin holding operating sleeve spring compressed is against front end of forearm and rim of forearm tip is against pin. Remove pin while pressing on operating sleeve and forearm tip. Spring should snap back against end of bolt guide rod and allow operating sleeve to slide back into forearm and over bolt guide rod. Replace forearm tip screws. Operating sleeve must slide back and forth freely without binding when cocking hammer. Sleeve should lock easily when it is turned so that the rib contacts inside of fore-arm tip at points other than groove for rib on operating sleeve.

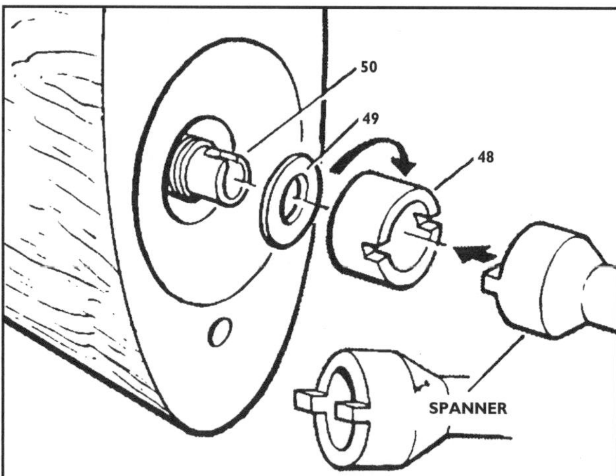

4 Using a suitable spanner as shown, remove buttstock nut and washer. Slide buttstock to rear and off tang and outer magazine tube. In replacing nut, turn it in direction indicated.

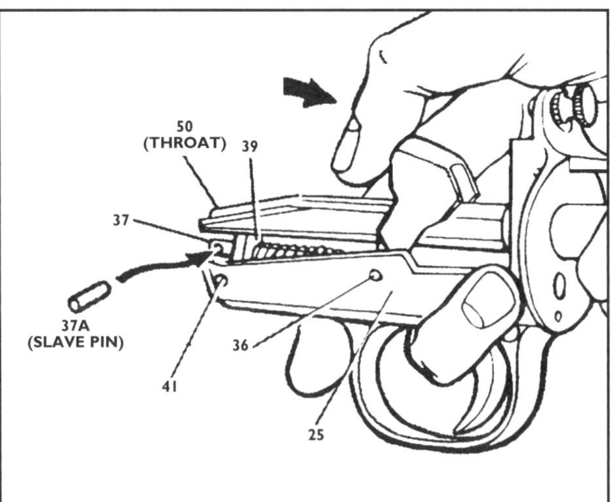

5 Before removing hammer spring abutment and hammer assembly from tang, pull hammer rearward, compressing hammer spring. Insert a small slave pin as shown through hammer spring guide rod where it protrudes through abutment. Release hammer.

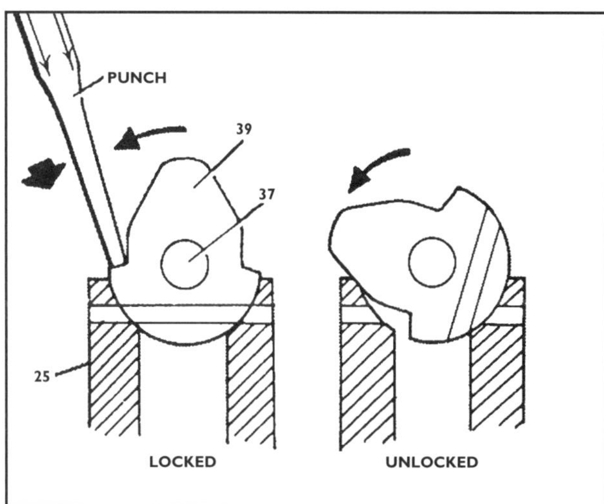

6 To remove hammer spring abutment, drift out pin (41) and place tang in vise, right side up. Use a suitable drift or punch at right of abutment in groove in tang. Tap abutment around out of groove as shown. Drift out the hammer pin and then remove the hammer and spring assembly from the tang.

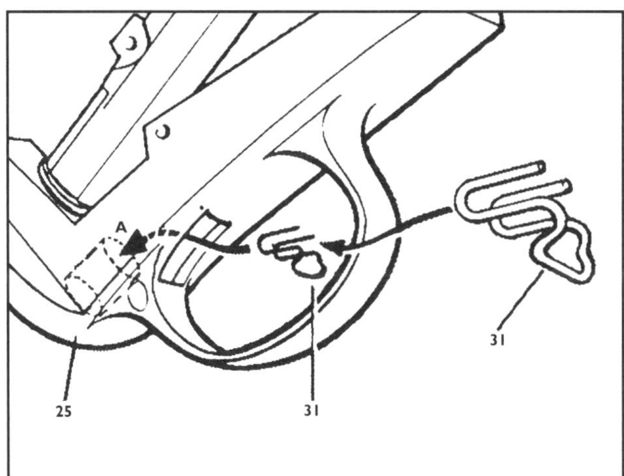

7 Replace trigger spring through guard into trigger hole in underside of tang in the position that is shown at "A." Press spring firmly into hole in rear of tang with the blade of a screwdriver inserted through guard into tang.

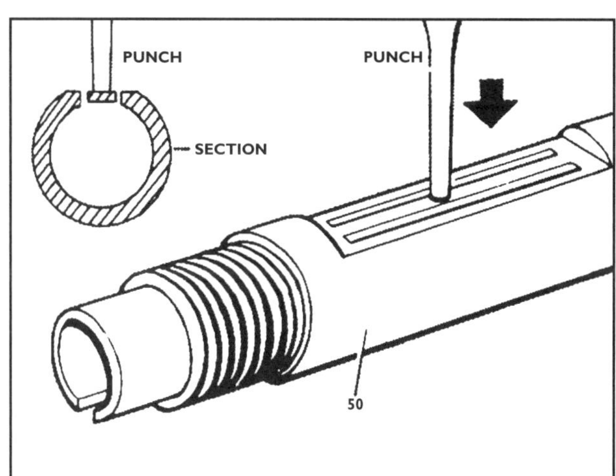

8 Outer magazine is made with fine saw cuts through flattened portion of tube at rear. Grip of outer magazine tube on inner tube is regulated by depressing area between these saw cuts slightly with a punch as shown.

WINCHESTER MODEL 69A RIFLE

PARTS LEGEND

1. Barrel
2. Front sight
3. Rear sight
4. Rear sight elevator
5. Receiver
6. Ejector
7. Trigger base
8. Safety lever stop pin
9. Trigger
10. Safety lock plunger
11. Safety lock plunger spring
12. Safety lock screw
13. Safety lock
14. Safety lever
15. Trigger pin
16. Breechbolt, complete
17. Magazine release plunger
18. Magazine release plunger stop
19. Magazine release plunger spring
20. Magazine release plunger escutcheon
21. Magazine holder
22. Magazine catch
23. Magazine catch screw
24. Magazine holder screws (2)
25. Trigger spring adjusting screw
26. Trigger spring
27. Buttstock
28. Stock stud screw escutcheon
29. Stock stud screw
30. Stock stud
31. Magazine plate
32. Magazine plate screws (2)
33. Magazine
34. Guard bow
35. Guard bow screws (2)
36. Buttplate
37. Buttplate screws (2)

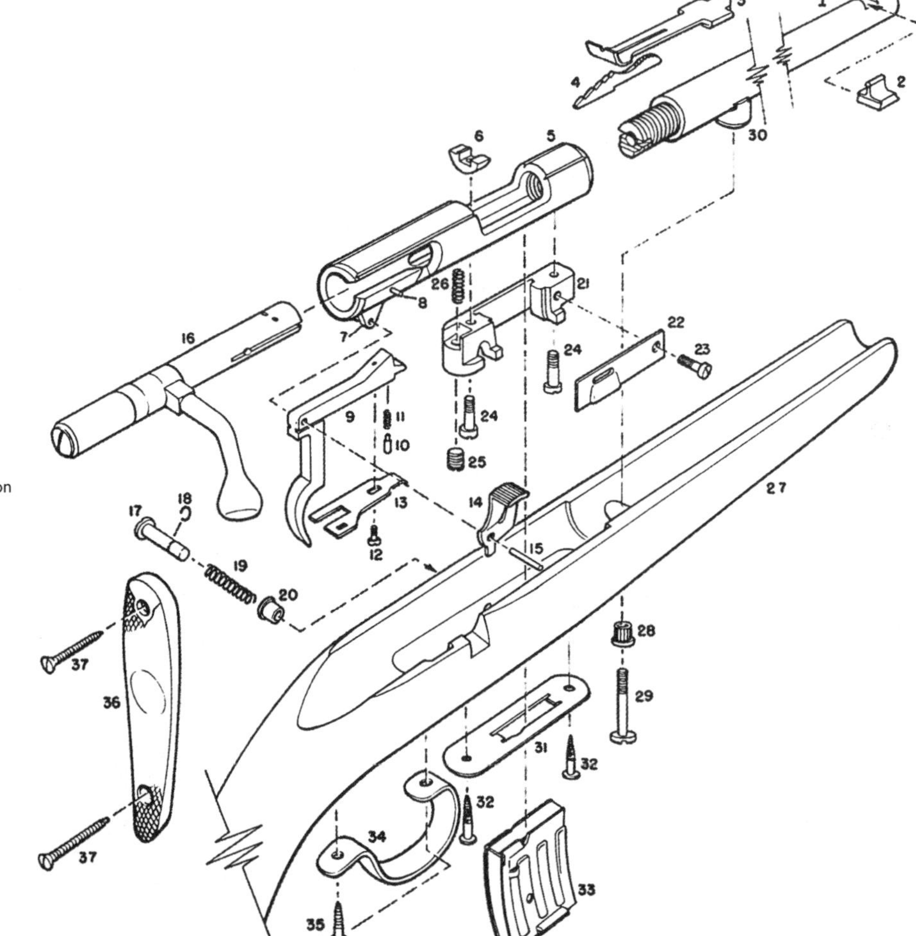

PARTS LEGEND FOR BREECHBOLT ASSEMBLY

A. Breechbolt
B. Extractor, left
C. Extractor, right
D. Extractor springs (2)
E. Extractor pins (2)
F. Firing pin
G. Firing pin stop pin
H. Breechbolt handle and cocking sleeve
J. Firing pin spring
K. Breechbolt sleeve
L. Breechbolt sleeve pin
M. Breechbolt plug

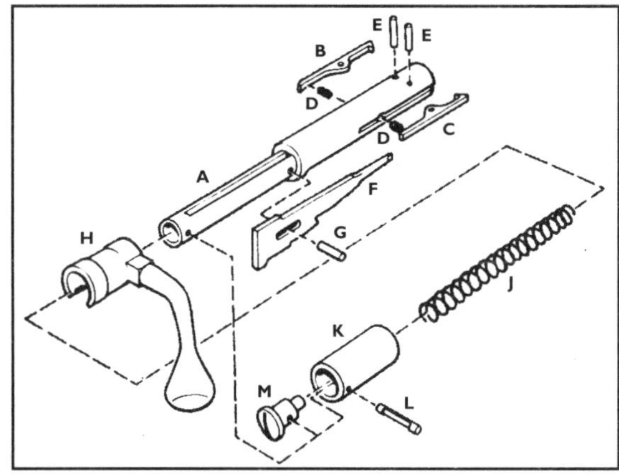

The Winchester Model 69, .22 caliber bolt-action repeating rifle was first announced in January 1935, and initial deliveries were made in March of that year. The Model 69 was an adult-sized rifle with 25-inch barrel and detachable clip-magazine. The action was a speed-lock type with short striker fall and an adjustable trigger. It was regularly furnished with a 5-shot magazine, but 10-shot magazines were available as an accessory item. Sporting, target and match rifle versions were offered. In late 1937 the bolt mechanism was altered to cock on opening rather than closing motion of the bolt. The designation of this rifle was then changed to Model 69A.

From 1937 until 1941, telescopic sights of 2¾X or 4X were offered as accessory items with this rifle, but this practice was not resumed after World War II. Receivers of late production rifles are grooved for popular commercial tip-off scope mounts. A variety of front and rear sights have been furnished for the Model 69 and 69A rifles, and there have been several minor changes in the furniture. None of these has been of significance from the standpoint of disassembly procedure.

When it was discontinued in 1963, the Model 69A had been offered in sporting type and in a target style designated the Junior Target Shooter's Special. The sporting rifle was fitted with a bead front sight and open notch rear. The receiver is tapped for commercial micrometer rear sights. The target version had a Patridge-style front blade and Lyman 57 micrometer rear sights.

DISASSEMBLY

To remove bolt (16) open breech, pull trigger, and slide bolt out to rear. Press in magazine release plunger (17) and pull magazine (33) out bottom of stock.

Unscrew stock stud screw [takedown screw] (29) and lift barrel and receiver assembly up out of stock.

To disassemble trigger mechanism, remove magazine holder screws (24) and drop magazine holder (21) from bottom of receiver, taking care not to lose trigger spring (26). Remove ejector (6) from top of receiver. Drift out trigger pin (15) and remove trigger (9) and safety lock parts (10, 11, 12, 13, 14) intact.

Reassemble in reverse order. The accompanying illustrations describe breechbolt disassembly in detail.

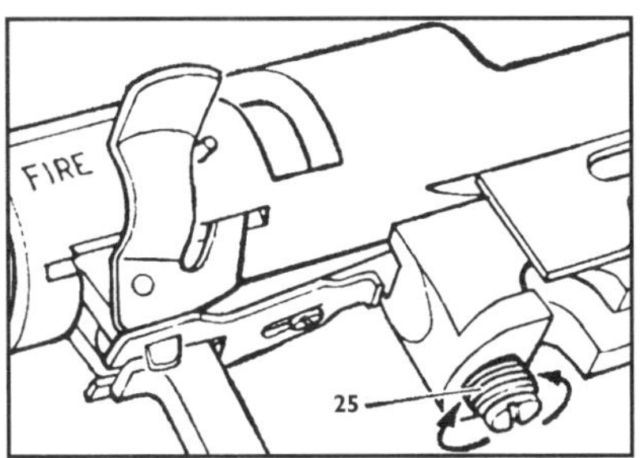

1 To adjust the trigger pull, turn the trigger spring adjusting screw (25) in (or clockwise) for a heavier pull and out (or counterclockwise) for a lighter pull.

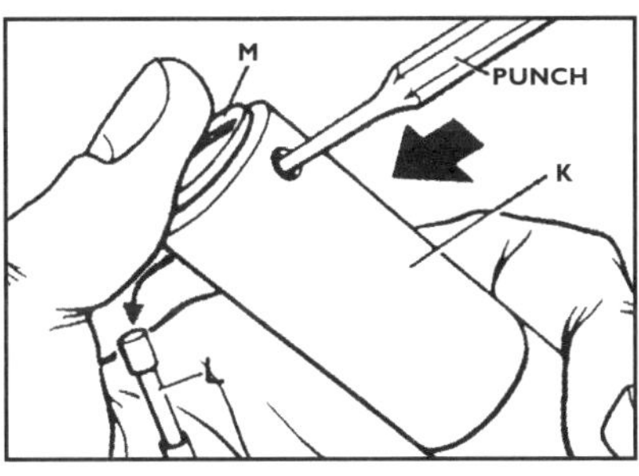

2 To disassemble bolt, drift out breechbolt sleeve pin (L) while holding breechbolt plug (M) in as shown, to prevent escape of spring. Remove plug and firing pin spring (J) from breechbolt (A). Slide breechbolt sleeve (K) off to rear.

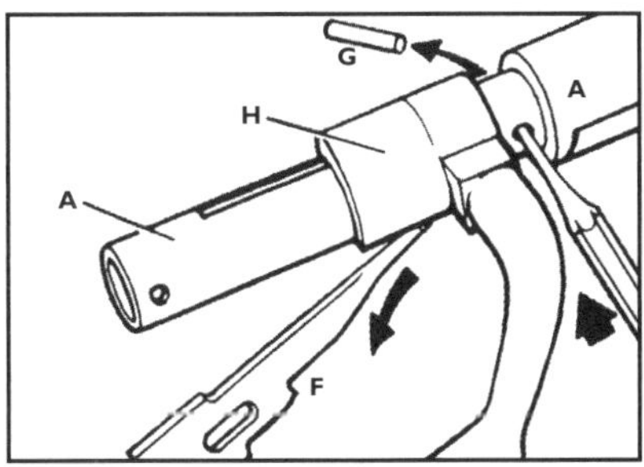

3 Move breechbolt handle and cocking sleeve (H) to rear to expose firing pin stop pin (G) as shown. Drift out pin (O) and drop firing pin (F) out bottom of breechbolt and to rear as shown. Breechbolt handle and cocking sleeve (H) can be removed to rear. Extractors (B & C) and springs (D) can be removed from breechbolt by drifting out pins (E). Reassemble in reverse order.

WINCHESTER "PRE- '64" MODEL 70

PARTS LEGEND

1. Receiver
2. Receiver plug screws
   2a. Metallic sight base plug screws (in left of receiver,not shown here)
3. Barrel
4. Forearm stud
5. Forearm stud screw
6. Rear sight assembly (Lyman shown here, various types available)
7. Front sight (various types available)
8. Breech bolt
9. Extractor ring
10. Extractor
11. Firing pin spring
12. Firing pin sleeve
13. Firing pin
14. Breech bolt sleeve
15. Safety lock (old style)
16. Breech bolt sleeve lock
17. Breech bolt sleeve lock spring
18. Breech bolt sleeve lock pin
19. Firing pin stop screw
20. Safety lock plunger
21. Safety lock plunger spring
22. Safety lock stop pin
23. Ejector
24. Ejector spring
25. Ejector pin
26. Bolt stop plunger
27. Bolt stop plunger spring
28. Bolt stop
29. Trigger pin
30. Trigger
31. Trigger stop screw nut
32. Trigger stop screw
33. Trigger spring
34. Trigger spring adjusting nuts (2)
35. Sear
36. Sear spring
37. Sear pin
38. Magazine
39. Magazine follower
40. Magazine spring
41. Magazine cover
42. Magazine cover hinge plate
43. Magazine cover hinge pin
44. Magazine cover hinge plate screw
45. Guard bow
46. Magazine cover catch
47. Magazine cover catch spring
48. Magazine cover catch pin
49. Front guard bow screw
50. Rear guard bow screw

Note: Buttstock, buttplate, screws, various sling swivels available, and remaining standard buttstock fittings are omitted for clarity

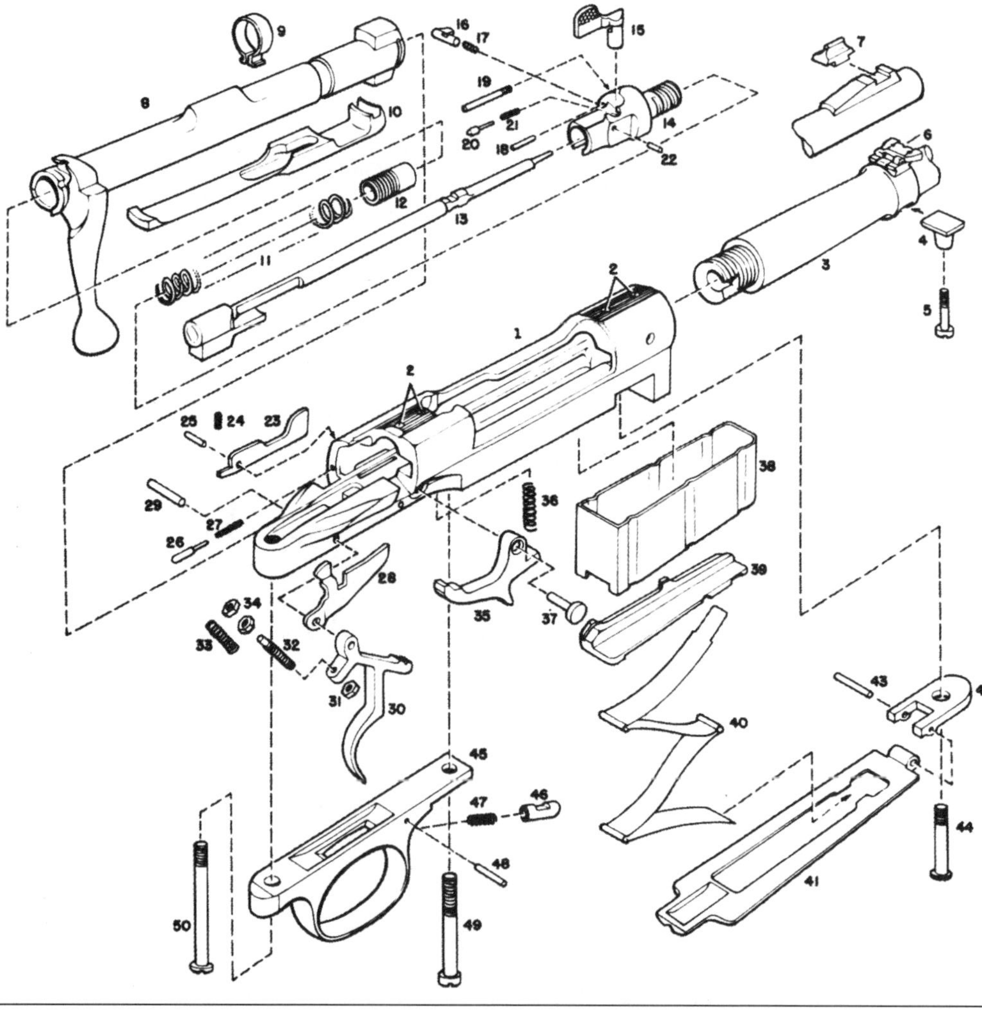

In 1925, the Winchester Repeating Arms Co., of New Haven, Connecticut, announced production of the Winchester Model 54 bolt-action rifle, chambered for the revolutionary .270 WCF cartridge. Both rifle and cartridge were immediately successful. The action design of the Model 54 was basically that of the Mauser 98. It had a one-piece bolt with dual front locking lugs, cock-on-opening action and a Mauser-type staggered-column, integral box-magazine. The Model 54 was made in several grades and chamberings, and in both sporting and target styles.

In 1937 the Model 54 was displaced by the Model 70 bolt-action rifle incorporating several improvements, including an independent bolt stop, hinged floorplate, speed-lock ignition, forged-steel trigger guard, and a better stock design. The Model 70 also featured a safety permitting installation of low-mounted scope sights, and a single-stage trigger of superior design. The bolt handle was redesigned for lowest possible scope mounting and the knob positioned opposite the trigger for maximum effectiveness in rapid-fire.

Since its introduction the Model 70 has achieved an enviable reputation throughout the world. Many consider it to be the finest factory-made bolt-action rifle. It has been produced in a variety of styles for target and sporting purposes. The list of chamberings ranges from the tiny .22 Hornet through the .458 Winchester Magnum.

After World War II, the "Featherweight" model was introduced with an aluminum-alloy trigger guard, magazine floorplate and buttplate, and a lightened barrel and stock.

By the end of 1964, with production at well over a half-million, production of the then-current Model 70 was terminated and the model number applied to a vastly different (in terms of mechanical sophistication and economy of production) Model 70 that has since come to be called the "Post-64" model. The last serial number reported for the "old" (or "Pre-64") rifles is 581471. Serial numbers for the new (or "Post-64") Model 70 rifles began with serial number 700000.

DISASSEMBLY

Check action to he sure rifle is unloaded. Remove breech bolt assembly from receiver. Breech bolt disassembly is shown in detail in illustrations at right.

To remove receiver (l) and barrel (3) from buttstock, remove forearm stud screw (5), magazine cover hinge plate screw (44), magazine cover assembly complete with magazine spring (40) and follower (39), and front and rear guard bow screws (49 & 50). Lift receiver and barrel out of buttstock carefully. Remove guard bow (45) from buttstock.

Receiver parts—ejector (23) bolt stop (28), trigger (30), sear (35) with respective springs—are all easily removed from receiver by drifting out their appropriate pins. Bolt stop plunger (26) and spring (27) are removed from hole at left rear of receiver after removing bolt stop. Assembly is accomplished in reverse order. To facilitate correct reassembly, care should be taken to keep springs and pins in order.

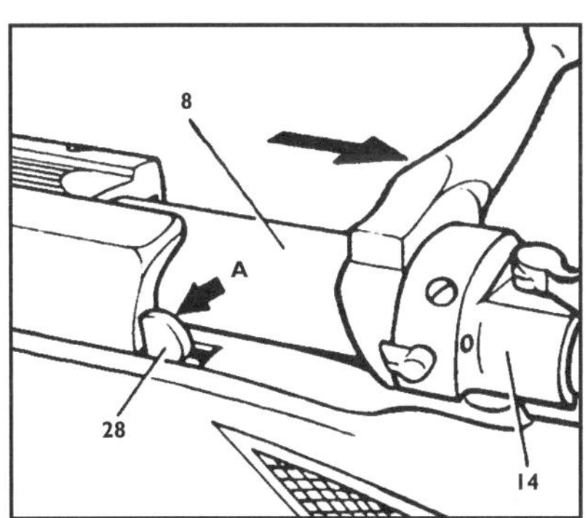

1 To remove breech bolt assembly, depress bolt stop (28) as shown at A and draw bolt to rear and out of receiver.

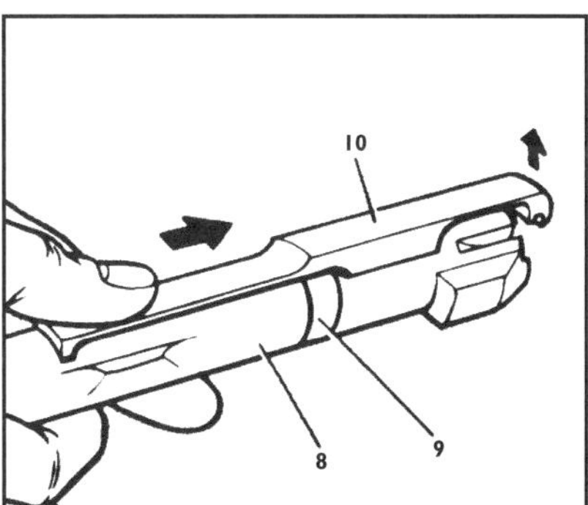

2 Turn extractor (10) to position shown and push forward, releasing extractor from lips of extractor ring (9).

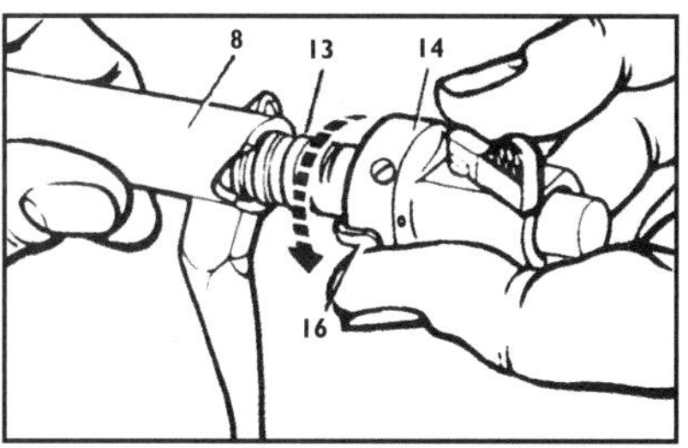

3 With rifle cocked, move safety lock (15) to intermediate position between "safe" and "fire." Then remove the bolt, depress breech bolt sleeve lock (16), and unscrew percussion assembly from the breech bolt and move the safety lock to fire position.

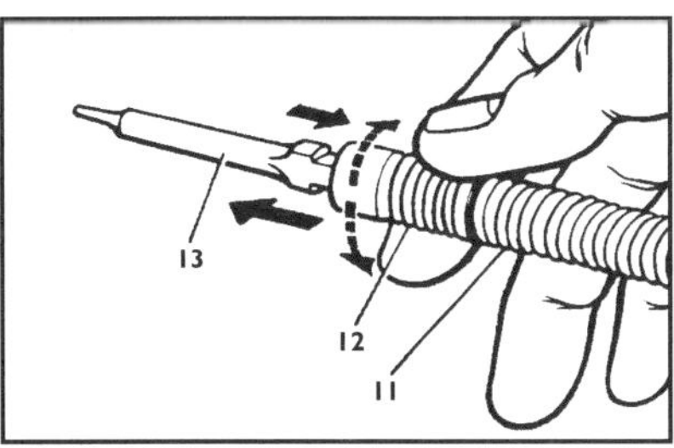

4 To remove firing pin spring (11), grasp firing pin sleeve (12) and pull to rear slightly. Turn firing pin sleeve ¼ turn in either direction as shown and allow sleeve (12) and spring (11) to come forward, taking care to avoid letting the tightly compressed spring get away. Remove spring and sleeve from firing pin. Breech bolt sleeve (14) can be removed from firing pin by unscrewing firing pin stop screw (19). Reassemble in reverse order.

WINCHESTER "POST- '64" MODEL 70

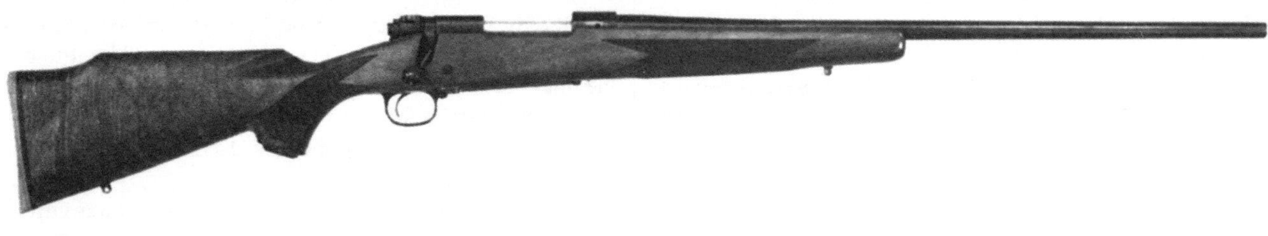

PARTS LEGEND

1. Barrel
2. Breech bolt
3. Breech bolt sleeve
4. Breech bolt sleeve cap
5. Breech bolt sleeve cap pin
6. Breech bolt sleeve lock
7. Breech bolt sleeve lock pin
8. Breech bolt sleeve lock spring
9. Breech bolt stop
10. Breech bolt stop spring
11. Ejector
12. Elector pin
13. Ejector spring
14. Extractor
15. Extractor plunger
16. Extractor spring
17. Firing pin
18. Firing pin spring
19. Firing pin spring retainer
20. Firing pin spring washer
21. Forearm swivel stud screw
22. Forearm swivel stud screw washer
23. Escutcheon
24. Forearm tip w/spacer
25. Magazine
26. Magazine cover
27. Magazine cover catch
28. Magazine cover catch pin
29. Magazine cover catch spring
30. Magazine cover hinge plate
31. Magazine cover hinge plate pin
32. Magazine cover hinge plate screw
33. Magazine follower
34. Magazine spring
35. Pistol grip cap
36. Pistol grip cap spacer
37. Quick detachable swivels(2)
38. Receiver
39. Recoil pad w/spacer
40. Recoil pad screws (2)
41. Safety
42. Safety pin
43. Safety plunger
44. Safety plunger spring
45. Sear
46. Sear pin
47. Sear spring
48. Sight, front
49. Sight cover
50. Sight ramp
51. Sight ramp screw (long)
52. Sight ramp screw (short)
53. Sight, rear (complete)
54. Sight, rear screws (2)
55. Stock
56. Stock swivel stud screw
57. Telescope sight base plug screws (6)
58. Trigger
59. Trigger guard
60. Trigger guard screw (front)
61. Trigger guard screw (rear)
62. Trigger pin
63. Trigger spring
64. Trigger stop screw
65. Trigger stop screw nuts (3)

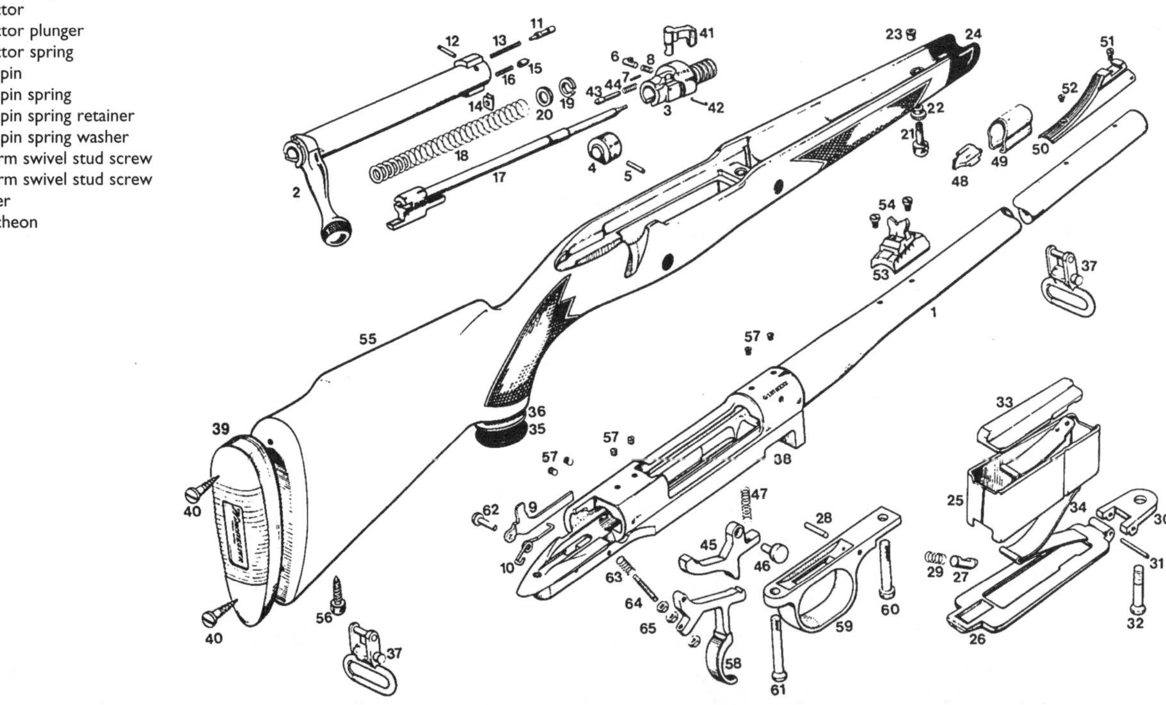

The term "Post-1964" was coined in response to Winchester's introduction of a redesigned Model 70 rifle in 1964. The first rifle featured a redesigned stock with Monte Carlo comb, high-gloss finish and impressed checkering. An engine turned bolt featured a recessed face with an internal extractor and the new swaged barrel was free floated. The "64" rifle was produced for two years, with a serial number range of 700000-818500.

The 1966 version (serial numbers 818501-873694), had a higher, but shortened Monte Carlo stock with a reversed comb profile and cross bolts were added to strengthen the stock around the magazine. A new bolt design featured a red cocking indicator.

The third version, in 1968, is identified by an "anti-bind" device to prevent bolt over-rotation. Additional features included a forged-steel action and stainless steel follower. This version, produced from 1968 to 1971, has "G" prefix serial numbers ranging from G873695 to G1041884.

The 1974 version had a satin-finished, Monte Carlo stock with a pronounced pistol grip with cut checkering. The DeLuxe Model, with additional cosmetics, was renamed the "New Super Grade." Beginning in 1981, the rifle was manufactured under license by U.S. Repeating Arms Co. at the old Winchester plant in New Haven. Olin's Winchester Group ceased production of the Model 70 in 2006.

DISASSEMBLY

First set the three-position safety in the center position to open the bolt and check both the chamber and magazine to ensure that the firearm is not loaded and is safe to service. Depress the bolt stop (9) and withdraw the breech bolt (2) from the action. To further disassemble the bolt group, depress the breech bolt sleeve lock (6) and rotate the breech bolt sleeve (3) and striker assembly counterclockwise and remove. Next support the rear portion of the striker on a non-skid surface and depress the firing pin spring to remove the retainer (19), washer (20) and spring (18) (Fig. 2). Now drift out the breech bolt sleeve cap pin (5) from left to right and remove the cap (4) and striker assembly. The hole in the left side of this cap is marginally smaller, which provides an interference fit to retain the cap pin.

Next drift out the breech bolt sleeve lock pin (7) to remove the lock and spring (6 & 8). Rotate the safety to the fire position to drift out the safety pin (42). Now turn the safety to the rear to clear the detent notches and lift it from its seat to free the safety spring and plunger (44 & 43). Note: This spring is compressed and must be retained during disassembly. Depress the ejector (11) with a fired cartridge case or large drift punch to free the ejector pin (12) to be pushed out (Fig. 3). Now slowly release the ejector (11) and spring (13) for removal.

Using a drift punch, depress the extractor plunger (15) accessible through the small hole in the face of the extractor. With the plunger depressed, slide the extractor(14) out of its slot in the bolt lug. The extractor spring (16) and plunger (15) must be retained as you remove the extractor.

Invert the firearm and depress the magazine cover catch (27) to release the magazine cover (26). Next remove the front and rear trigger guard screws (60 & 61) and magazine cover hinge plate screw (32) to remove both the trigger guard (59) and magazine cover assembly (26). Now the stock (55) and barrelled action may be separated. The magazine spring (34) and follower (33) can now be removed from the cover plate by lifting the rear of the spring and sliding it from its recess. If required, both the magazine cover catch and spring (27 & 29) may be removed from the trigger guard by drifting out the magazine cover catch pin (28).

Renove the magazine box (25) from the bottom of the action. The headed trigger pin (62) must be partially drifted out to the left to release the trigger assembly. The bolt stop (9) and its spring (10) are retained on the outside of the action and may be removed by completely withdrawing the trigger pin. Finally, the headed sear pin (46) is drifted out to the right to release both the sear (45) and its spring (47) to complete disassembly.

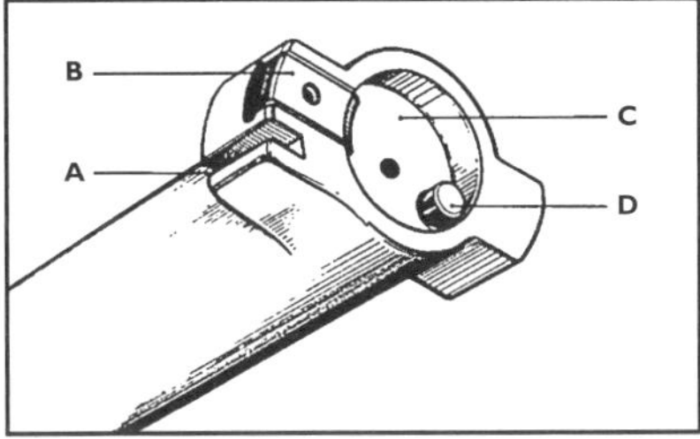

1 The front view of the new bolt design reveals the anti-bind device to be a keyway (A) formed by a secondary lug housing the new extractor (B). Located in the recessed bolt face (C) directly opposed to the keyway is the redesigned ejector (D).

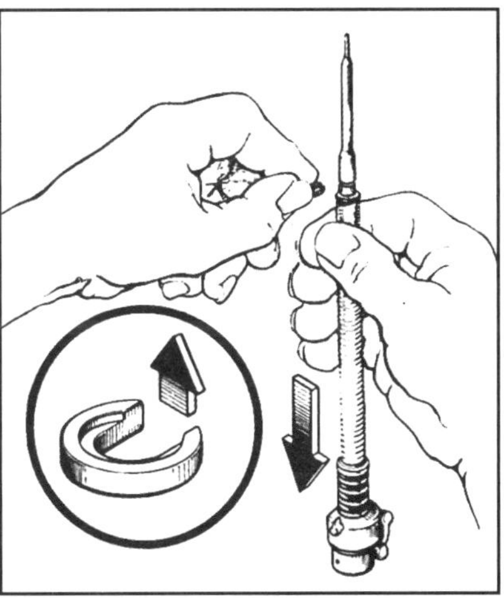

2 Exercise caution during this operation and remove the slotted retainer carefully while releasing gradually the heavy spring pressure. Also note that the recess in the top of this retainer engages the striker and functions as a lock. Ensure that it is in the position shown on reassembly.

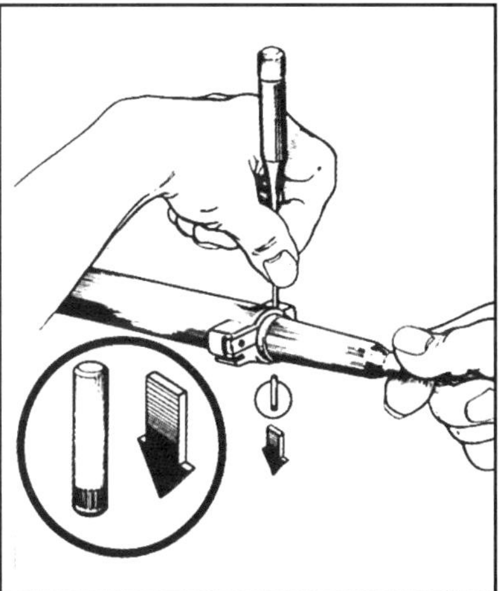

3 The ejector pin is often knurled or serrated on one end to provide a positive friction fit to ensure that it remains in a fixed position. This makes it a one-way pin, and it should not be driven through. Because of the age of these firearms and due to previous repairs or service incorrectly performed, these pins have been found inadvertently installed in an inverted position. If much resistance is encountered when pushing out this pin, particularly with the ejector depressed, reverse the direction and push the pin toward the least amount of resistance.

WINCHESTER MODEL 71 RIFLE

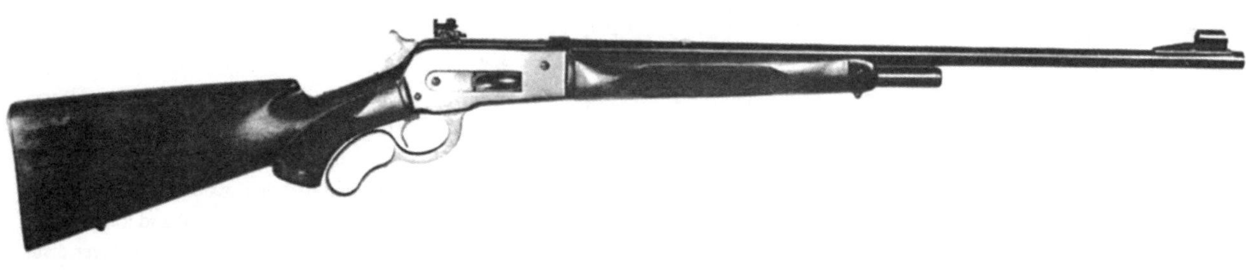

PARTS LEGEND

1. Barrel
2. Front sight
3. Front sight cover
4. Rear sight
5. Rear sight blank
6. Receiver
7. Cartridge stop
8. Cartridge stop screw
9. Cartridge guide
10. Cartridge guide screw
11. Cartridge guide screw bushing
12. Spring cover base
13. Spring cover leaf
14. Spring cover base screw
15. Spring cover leaf pin
16. Spring cover spring
17. Spring cover stop pin
18. Upper tang screw
19. Breechbolt
20. Ejector
21. Ejector spring
22. Ejector collar
23. Finger lever connecting pin
24. Extractor
25. Extractor pin
26. Firing pin
27. Firing pin stop pin
28. Hammer
29. Hammer screw bushing
30. Hammer screw
31. Hammer spring guide rod
32. Hammer spring guide rod pin
33. Hammer spring
34. Hammer spring abutment
35. Hammer spring abutment pin
36. Lower tang
37. Trigger
38. Trigger pin
39. Trigger spring
40. Finger lever
41. Friction stud
42. Friction stud spring
43. Friction stud stop pin
44. Locking bolt, right
45. Locking bolt, left
46. Finger lever bushing pin
47. Finger lever bushing
48. Carrier
49. Carrier plunger
50. Carrier plunger spring
51. Carrier plunger pin
52. Magazine tube
53. Magazine spring
54. Magazine follower
55. Magazine plug
56. Magazine plug screw
57. Forearm tip
58. Forearm tip screws (2)
59. Forearm tip tenon
60. Buttplate
61. Buttplate screws (2)

Note: Stock and forearm not shown

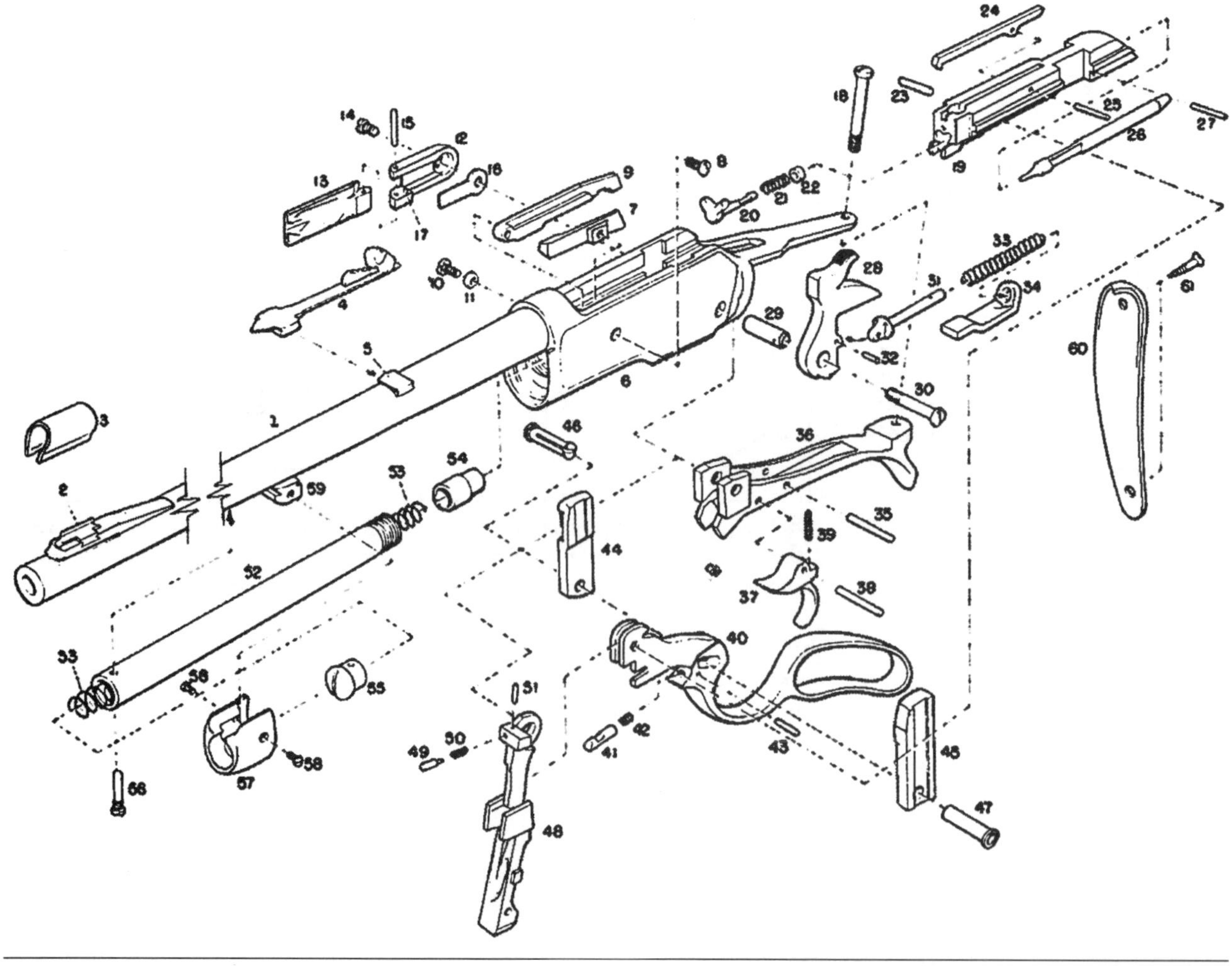

The Winchester Model 71 lever-action rifle was first announced in January 1936. Of solid-frame construction, the Model 71 was essentially a revamped version of Winchester's famous, Browning-designed Model 1886 rifle.

The rimmed, .348 Winchester cartridge was designed especially for the Model 71 and was offered in 150-, 200-, and 250- grain loadings to provide a range of power adequate for virtually all North American big game species. At the time, no other commercial rifle was chambered for this cartridge.

The Model 71 was initially furnished with both 20- and 24-inch barrels, but the 20-inch barrel model was discontinued in 1947. A Deluxe model was stocked in selected American walnut. Both the pistol grip and fore-end were checkered and the pistol grip was capped with hard rubber. The Model 71 was fitted with quick-detachable sling swivels and a 1-inch leather sling as standard acccessories.

The lower-priced Standard model had a plain walnut stock, with no swivels or sling. Both Deluxe and Standard models were available with aperture or open rear sights.

Remington discontinued the Model 71 in 1958.

DISASSEMBLY

Lower lever (40) and check action to be sure rifle is unloaded.

To disassemble the magazine assembly, unscrew magazine plug screw (56) and remove the magazine plug (55), withdrawing magazine spring (53) and follower (54) at same time. Remove forearm tip screws (58) and slide the forearm tip (57) up on the magazine tube slightly. Using a punch or similar tool through magazine plug screw holes at front end of magazine tube, unscrew tube from receiver. Remove magazine tube and forearm from receiver.

To disassemble the action, remove upper tang screw (18) and pull buttstock off receiver to rear. Buttstock may require sharp rap with the hand to loosen it. Remove spring cover base screw (14) and lift spring cover assembly (parts 12, 13, 15, 16, and 17) up out of receiver. Drift out hammer spring abutment pin (35), taking care not to allow abutment to escape under tension of hammer spring. Remove hammer spring abutment (34) and lift small spring (39) out top of trigger (37). Remove hammer screw (30) and hammer screw bushing (29) and lift hammer (28) with hammer spring (33) and guide rod (31) out of the top of the receiver.

The lower tang (36) may he knocked out bottom of receiver to rear. Drift out finger lever bushing pin (46) from left to right and remove finger lever hushing (47). Note that finger lever bushing pin is a slotted pin and should not he mistaken for a screw. Remove right and left locking bolts (44 and 45) from bottom of receiver. Lower finger lever, moving breechbolt back out of receiver until finger-lever connecting pin (23) is exposed. Drift out pin (23) with a punch and remove breechbolt (19) to rear, taking care not to allow ejector (20), spring (21), or collar (22) to escape. Drop finger lever (40) and carrier (48) out bottom of receiver. Remove cartridge guide screw (10) and bushing (II) from right side of receiver and drop cartridge guide (9) out of receiver. Remove cartridge stop screw (8) from left side of receiver and drop cartridge stop (7) out of receiver.

Reassemble in reverse order. Install breechbolt and finger lever, carrier, and locking bolts before attempting to replace cartridge guide. The cartridge guide can be replaced through the spring cover hole in the right side of receiver with rear end of cartridge guide in place in right locking bolt.

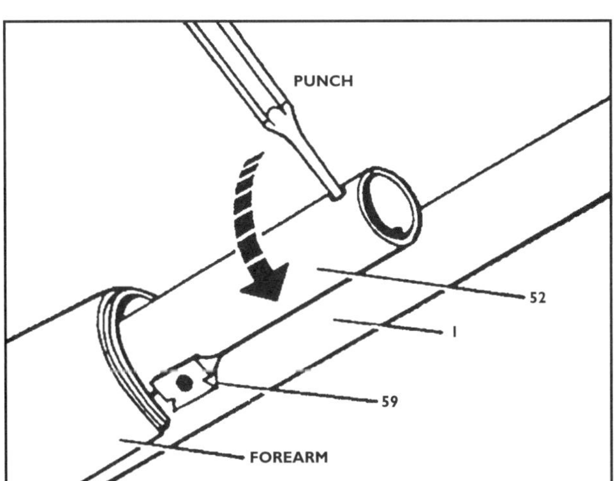

1 After removing magazine plug screw (56), magazine plug (55), spring (53), and follower (54), unscrew magazine tube (52) as shown, using a punch or similar tool through the plug screw holes at front end of magazine tube.

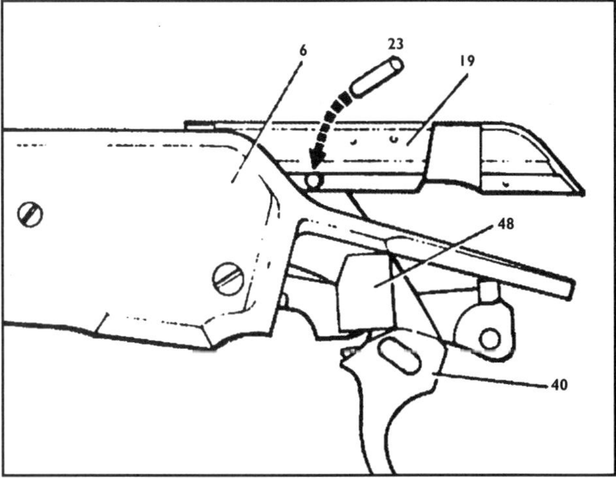

2 When reassembling breechbolt (19), finger lever (40), and carrier (48), the parts should be replaced in receiver as shown. When replacing finger-lever connecting pin (23) through bolt and top of finger lever, be sure ejector (20) is pushed as far back into bolt as possible.

WINCHESTER MODEL 74 SEMI-AUTO

PARTS LEGEND

1. Receiver
2. Barrel
3. Stock (not shown)
4. Bolt
5. Firing pin
6. Firing pin spring
7. Bolt stop
8. Bolt spring rod
9. Bolt spring
10. Operating slide
11. Operating slide pin
12. Sear
13. Sear spring
14. Sear pin
15. Bolt stop plunger
16. Bolt stop plunger spring
17. Bolt stop plunger pin
18. Extractor
19. Extractor spring
20. Extractor pin
21. Safety lock
22. Timing rocker spring
23. Timing rocker
24. Timing rocker guide screw
25. Timing rocker pin
26. Cartridge guide pin
27. Cartridge guide
28. Magazine throat
29. Cartridge Cutoff, right hand
30. Cartridge cutoff, left hand
31. Magazine lifting spring
32. Magazine throat pin
33. Trigger
34. Trigger spring
35. Trigger pin
36. Trigger guard bow
37. Trigger guard screws (20)
38. Shell deflector
39. Stock stud
40. Stock stud screw
41. Rear sight
42. Rear sight elevation bar
43. Front sight
44. Magazine sleeve nut
45. Magazine sleeve
46. Buttplate
47. Buttplate screws (2)
48. inside magazine tube assembly

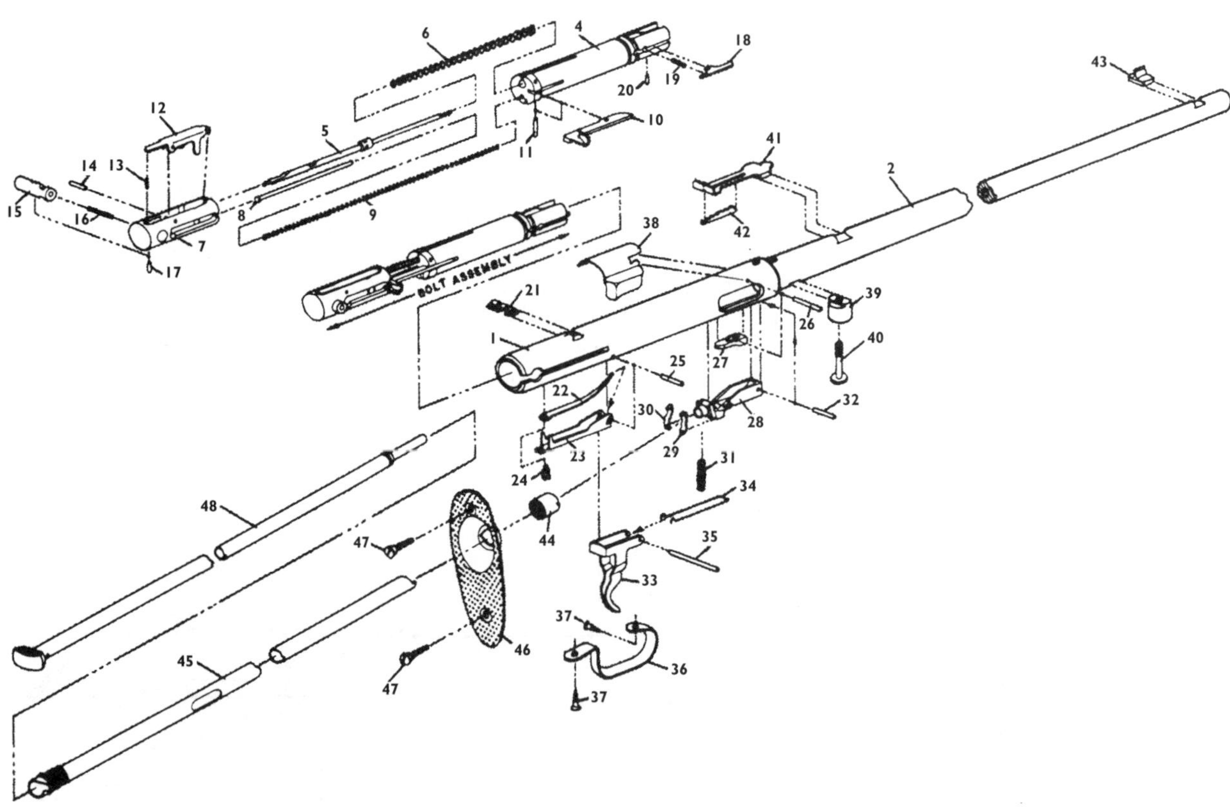

Winchester introduced its Model 74 Automatic rifle in 1939. The Model 74 was designed as a medium-priced, high-quality, self-loading rifle for either standard or high velocity .22 Short or Long Rifle cartridges. Winchester hoped to satisfy consumer demand for a reliable self-loading rifle, chambered for .22 caliber rimfire ammunition. Winchester's earlier attempts to enter this market were the Models 1903 and 63 rifles. As with the '03 and '63, the tubular magazine of the Model 74 is contained in the butt. A special feature of the Model 74 is that the bolt can be easily removed as a separate assembly, for cleaning and inspection.

A Gallery Special (.22 Short) version of the Model 74 was also offered. Gallery rifles were furnished with chromium-plated trimmings, on special order and at extra cost. This variation was discontinued in 1952.

The Model 74 was discontinued in 1955 after approximately 406,570 had been manufactured.

DISASSEMBLY

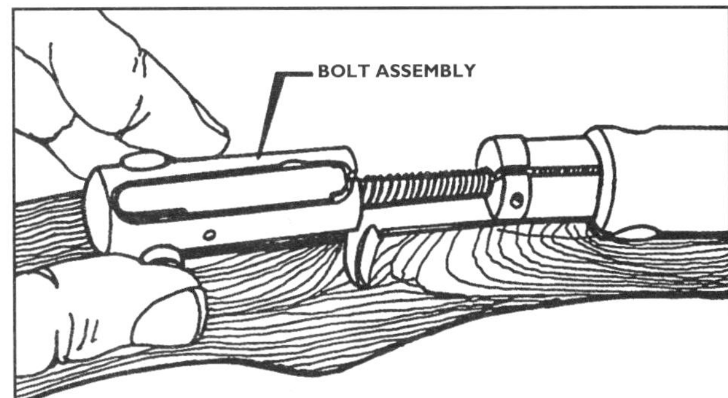

1 Remove the inside magazine tube assembly (48), pull the operating slide (10) rearward, and check that the chamber is clear. Allow the bolt (4) to move forward and pull the trigger (33). Note: Do not put safety lock (21) on "Safe" position. Remove the bolt by pressing the bolt stop plunger (15), see Fig. A, and pulling the bolt out of the receiver (1). Press the trigger in order for bolt assembly to clear timing rocker (23).

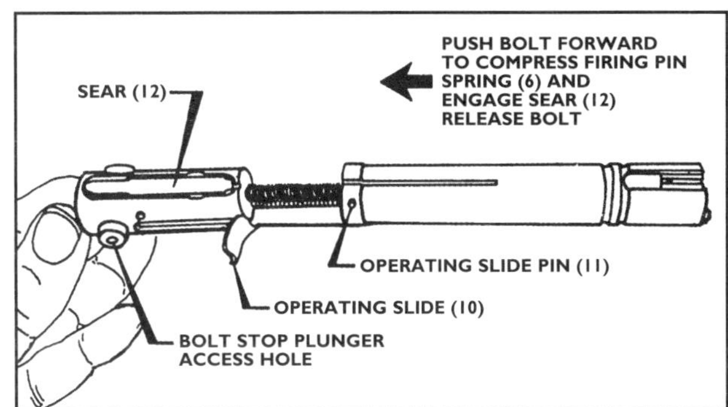

2 To disassemble the bolt, push back so that the notch on the firing pin (5) engages the sear (12) and compresses the firing pin spring (6). Allow bolt to move forward. Again push bolt (4) slightly rearward, drive out operating slide pin (11) and lift out operating slide (10). Carefully allow the bolt to move forward and free of the firing pin. Lift out the bolt spring (9) and bolt spring rod (8). Drive out the extractor pin (20) and remove the extractor (18) and extractor spring (19). Press the rear of the sear to allow the firing pin to move forward. Care should be taken to prevent the firing pin from flying out under pressure of the firing pin spring. Drive out the sear pin (14) and lift out the sear and sear spring (13). From the access hole in the bottom of the machined slot which contained the sear, drive out the bolt stop plunger pin (17) and remove the bolt stop plunger (15) and bolt stop plunger spring (16).

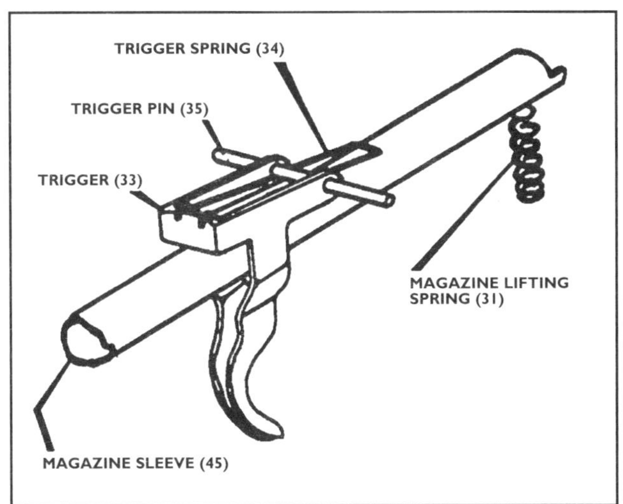

3 Remove the stock stud screw (40), lift out the assembled barrel and receiver. Remove the buttplate screws (47) and the buttplate/magazine tube assembly. Note: Care should be taken to ensure that the trigger spring (34) does not fly out of position, see Fig. D. Drive out the trigger pin (35) and lift out the trigger (33).

Drive out the timing rocker pin (25) and remove the timing rocker guide screw (24). Check orientation of the timing rocker spring (22) with respect to the timing rocker (23) before removing them from the receiver.

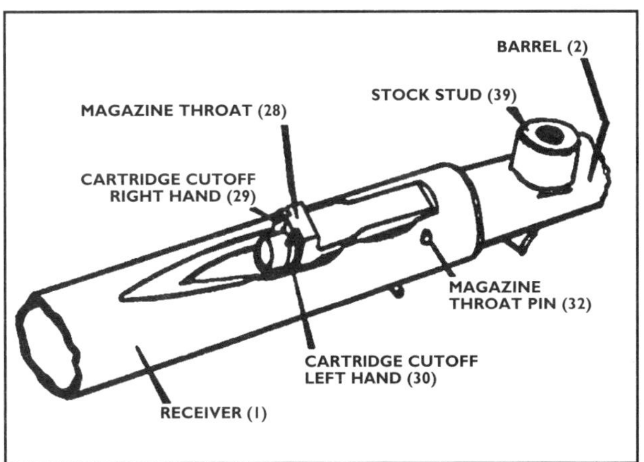

4 Drive out the magazine throat pin (32) and lift out the magazine throat assembly (28), see Fig. E. To remove the cartridge cutoffs, both right and left hand, rotate the cartridge cutoffs off of the pin extensions on the magazine throat (28). Before removing the cartridge guide (27), note orientation of this part with respect to the receiver, drive out the cartridge guide pin (26) and lift out the cartridge guide (27). To remove the safety lock (21), insert the blade of a small screwdriver at the rear of the receiver and lift the safety retaining spring from the base of safety lock (21). The safety retaining spring is staked to wall of receiver; do not attempt to remove it. Slide out the safety lock (21). All other parts are readily disassembled.

WINCHESTER MODEL 75 TARGET

PARTS LEGEND

1. Barrel
2. Front sight assembly
3. Barrel band
4. Barrel band screw
5. Barrel band screw bushing
6. Barrel band screw escutcheon
7. Stock stud
8. Stock stud screw
9. Breech bolt
10. Breech bolt handle and cocking sleeve
11. Breech bolt sleeve
12. Breech bolt sleeve pin
13. Firing pin spring
14. Breech bolt plug
15. Firing pin
    15a. Firing pin stop pin
16. Left-hand extractor
17. Extractor springs (2)
18. Right-hand extractor
19. Extractor pins (2)
20. Ejector
21. Receiver
22. Safety lever stop pin
23. Trigger base
24. Trigger
25. Trigger pin
26. Safety lock plunger spring
27. Safety lock plunger
28. Safety lock
29. Safety lock screw
30. Magazine holder
31. Magazine catch
32. Magazine catch screw
33. Magazine holder screws (2)
34. Trigger spring
35. Trigger spring adjusting screw
36. Safety lever
37. Magazine assembly
38. Guard bow
39. Guard bow screws (2)
40. Buttstock
41. Buttplate
42. Buttplate screws (2)
43. Magazine release plunger
    43a. Magazine release plunger stop
44. Magazine release plunger spring
45. Magazine release plunger escutcheon
46. Forearm adjustment base assembly
47. Forearm adjustment base screws (2)
48. Stock swivel base assembly
49. Stock swivel base assembly screws (2)
50. Receiver sight assembly (Redfield 75 HW)

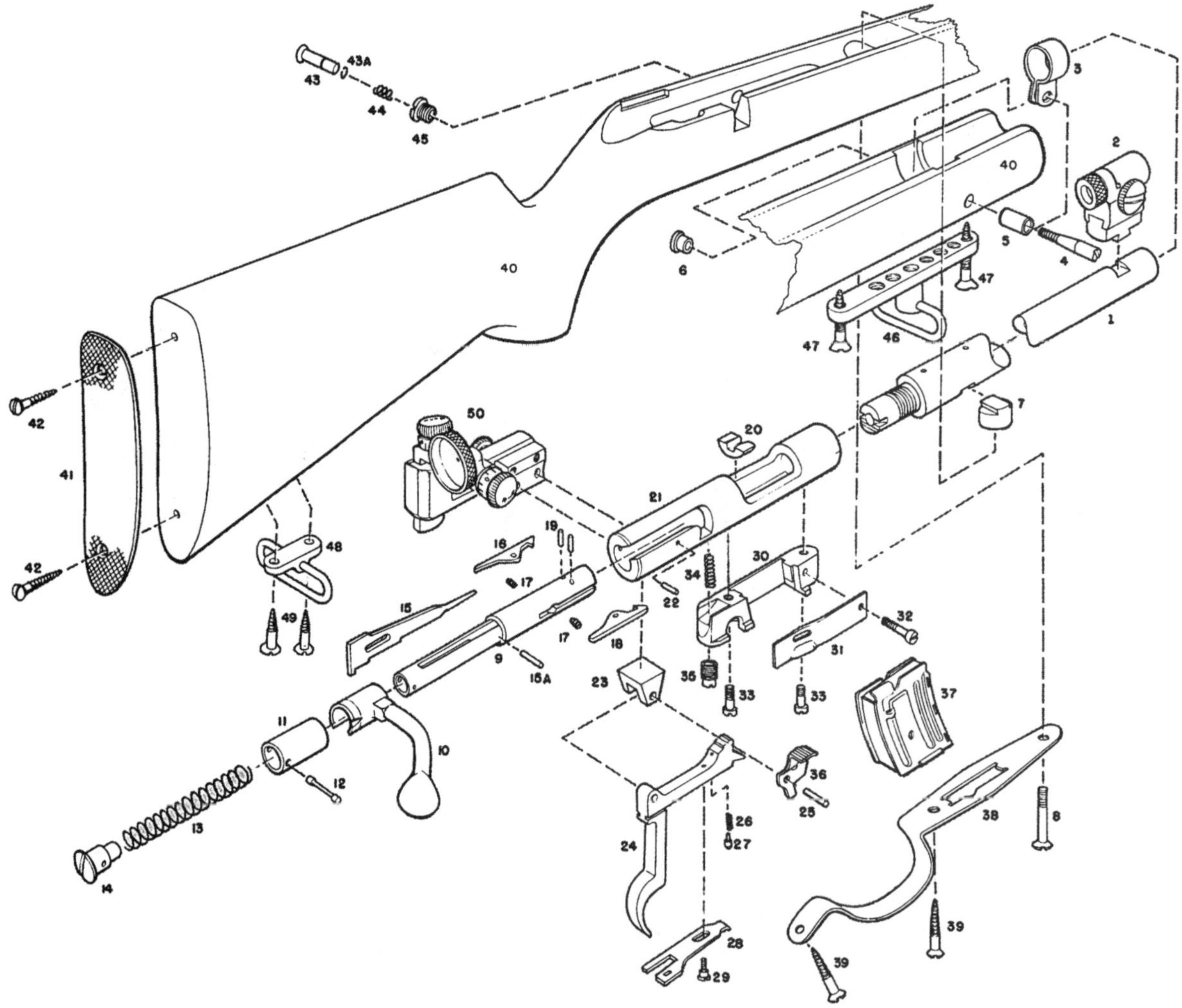

First announced in 1939 as a moderately-priced companion piece to the more expensive Model 52 rifle, the Winchester Model 75, chambered for the .22 Long Rifle cartridge, soon earned an enviable reputation for fine accuracy and reliability. The Model 75 has a speed lock and features a detachable-clip magazine, and like the Model 52 is offered in both target and sporting versions.

The Model 75 Sporter was offered with two sighting combinations, including open rear and bead front sight or Lyman 57E aperture receiver sight and bead front sight. The barrel length is 24 inches. Both pistol grip and forearm are checkered. Weight of the Model 75 is about 5¾ pounds.

The Model 75 Target rifle has a 28-inch barrel and weighs about 8½ pounds. Its beavertail stock is relatively straight to facilitate shooting in the prone position and is factory equipped with a metal base adjustment swivel allowing various adjustments of the sling strap. The Model 75 Target is furnished without sights for those who wish to select and install their own, or is available with Redfield 75 HW aperture receiver sight and Winchester 105A front sight. This model was at one time offered with an eight-power telescopic sight of Winchester make, since discontinued.

During World War II, the Armed Forces purchased large numbers of Model 75s for marksmanship training. Following the war many of these same rifles were issued to D.C.M. rifle clubs. The Model 75 was dropped from production in 1958.

DISASSEMBLY

Turn the bolt handle (10) upward and, holding the trigger (24) back, withdraw the bolt to the rear. Remove the magazine (37) and unscrew the barrel band screw (4) from the fore-end. After removing the stock stud screw (8), the barrel (1) and receiver assembly can be removed from the stock (40). For all normal cleaning purposes, this is sufficient disassembly.

To take down the bolt, gently drift out the breech bolt sleeve pin (12) taking care not to allow, the breech bolt plug (14) and firing pin spring (13) to escape when withdrawal of the sleeve pin releases the compressed spring. In drifting out the sleeve pin, the punch or drift used should fit the sleeve pin hole and will serve to prevent the forceful ejection of the plug and spring. Drift out the firing pin stop pin (15a). With the breech bolt handle and cocking sleeve (10) all the way forward in the position shown in Fig. 2, the firing pin (15) can be withdrawn from the bolt toward the rear. The bolt handle and cocking sleeve (10) can now be slid off the rear of the bolt proper. The left- and right-hand extractors (16 & 18) may be removed by drifting out their retaining pins (19), using care to prevent the loss of the small extractor springs (17). For ordinary cleaning purposes, disassembly of the bolt is not recommended and should only be undertaken by an experienced person when necessary for repair or replacement of broken parts.

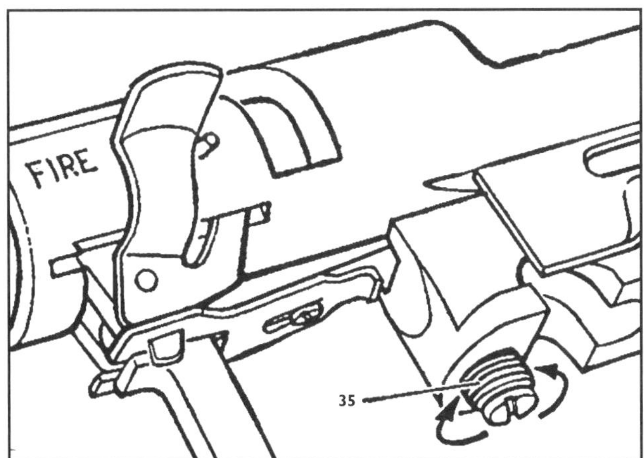

1 To adjust the trigger pull, remove the barrel and receiver assembly from the stock. Turn the trigger spring adjusting screw (35) in (or clockwise) for a heavier pull and out (or counterclockwise) for a lighter pull.

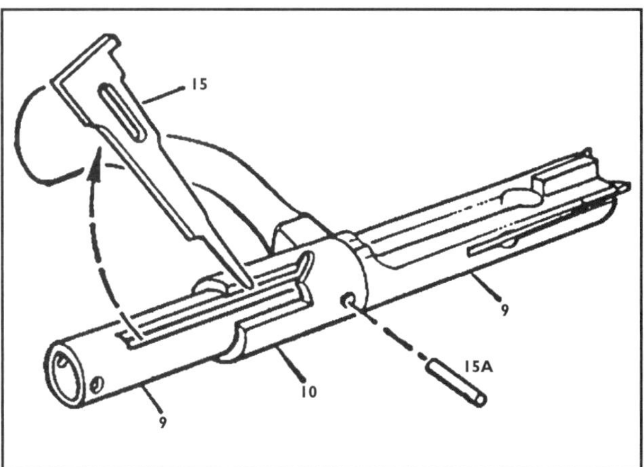

2 The correct relative position of the breech bolt (9) and breech bolt handle and cocking sleeve (10) to allow removal of the firing pin (15).

WINCHESTER

WINCHESTER MODEL 77 RIFLE

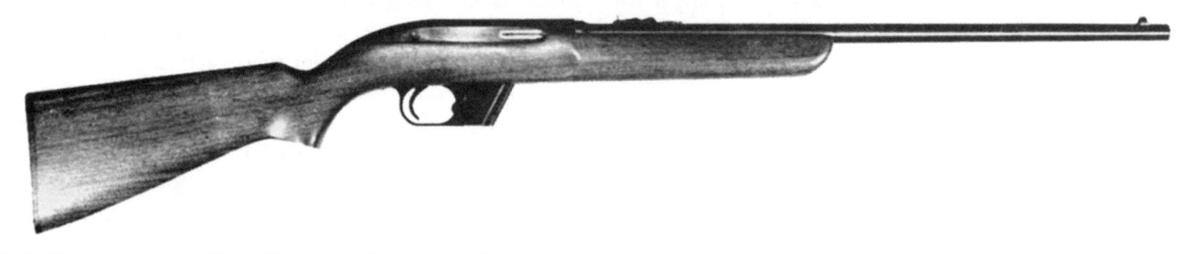

PARTS LEGEND – TUBULAR MAGAZINE MODEL

1. Receiver
2. Barrel
3. Rear sight
4. Front sight
5. Barrel locating pin
6. Receiver stud
7. Magazine ring
8. Magazine ring pin
9. Bolt assembly, complete
10. Safety assembly, complete
11. Trigger
12. Operating slide
13. Throat
14. Carrier
15. Carrier pin
16. Carrier spring
17. Cartridge cutoff pin and washer
18. Mainspring
19. Magazine tube, outside
20. Magazine tube assembly, inside
21. Guard
22. Guard screw (with nut)
23. Receiver stud screw
24. Receiver stud screw escutcheon
25. Recoil block screw

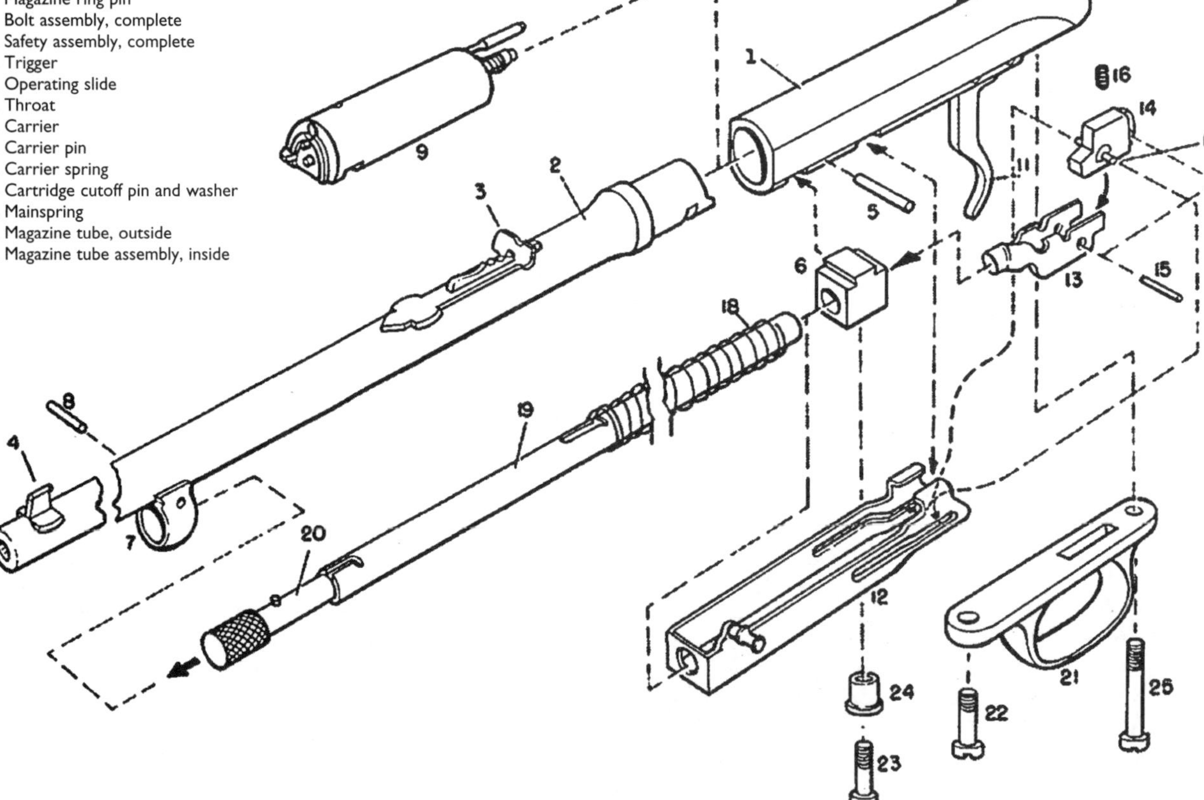

DISASSEMBLY

TUBULAR MAGAZINE MODEL: Remove inside magazine tube (20) and check chamber to ensure it is unloaded. Check throat (13) to ensure that it is unloaded. (If magazine follower can be seen in throat through ejection port at right side of receiver, throat is unloaded.) Cock gun and pull trigger. Hold gun inverted and remove guard screw (22) and recoil block screw (25). Lift barrel and action assembly out of stock.

Barrel, with mainspring (18) and outside magazine tube, are separated from receiver in same manner as in clip magazine model described. Throat (13) is disengaged from operating slide (12) by spreading sides of slide apart and freeing pins in carrier (14) which engage cams in operating slide. Ends of operating slide should be in clearance cuts in receiver during this operation.

Holding action inverted, push throat into receiver stud (6), freeing ears on rear end of throat from recess in receiver. Lift throat assembly upward and toward rear, out of receiver. Operating slide (12) is removed as described for clip magazine model.

Trigger mechanism and bolt assembly are both disassembled in same manner described for clip magazine model. Reassemble in reverse order.

The Winchester Model 77 self-loading rifle, chambered for the .22 caliber Long Rifle cartridge, was introduced in 1955. Both tubular magazine and detachable clip versions were offered under the same model number designation.

The Model 77 fires from a closed breech and ejects empty cases from a port in the right side of the receiver. The trigger guard is of nylon plastic. The receiver is grooved for tip-off scope mounts. The thumb-operated safety on the right side blocks the trigger. There is no hold-open device in the bolt and single loading through the ejection port is not practicable.

The Model 77 weighs about 5½ lbs. Standard barrel length is 22 inches. Cartridge capacity of the detachable clip is 8 rounds; capacity of the tubular magazine is 15 rounds.

Discontinued in 1963, the Model 77 was a well engineered, adult-size rifle designed for small-game hunting and informal target shooting or plinking.

PARTS LEGEND – CLIP MAGAZINE MODEL

1. Receiver
2. Barrel
3. Rear sight
4. Front sight
5. Barrel locating pin
6. Operating slide guide assembly
7. Trigger stop screw
8. Trigger stop screw nut
9. Trigger
10. Trigger pin
11. Disconnector spring
12. Disconnector
13. Sear
14. Sear spring
15. Safety lever
16. Safety lever retaining washer
17. Safety spring
18. Bolt
19. Extractor
20. Extractor spring
21. Extractor pin
22. Timing rod
23. Timing rod spring
24. Timing rod collar
25. Timing rod retaining ring
26. Firing pin
27. Firing pin retracting spring (blued color)
28. Ejector
29. Ejector spring pin
30. Ejector spring
31. Firing pin striker
32. Firing pin striker spring
33. Operating slide assembly
34. Mainspring
35. Guard
36. Recoil block screw
37. Stock stud screw
38. Guard screw escutcheon
39. Guard screw
40. Magazine lock pin
41. Magazine lock
42. Magazine lock spring
43. Magazine

Note: Buttplate, buttplate screws, and buttstock are not shown.

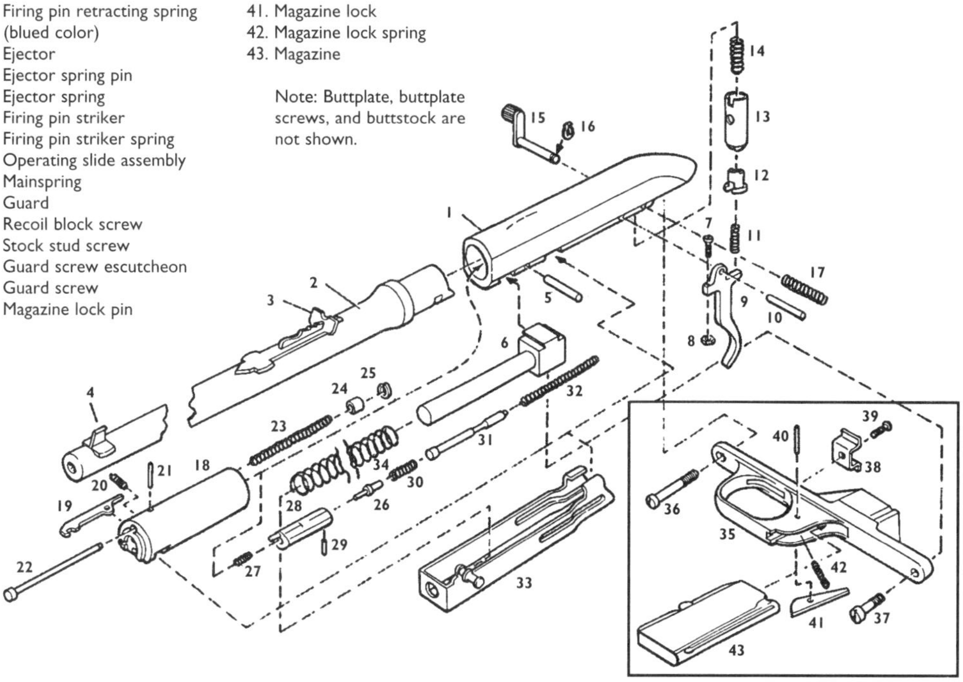

DISASSEMBLY

CLIP MAGAZINE MODEL: Remove magazine (43) and check chamber to ensure gun is not loaded. Cock action and pull trigger to release tension on springs so striker in bolt will not be ejected forcibly during disassembly. Hold gun upside-down and remove stock stud screw (37) and recoil block screw (36). Stock may now be separated from barrel and action assembly.

Barrel (2) is removed from receiver (1) by drifting out barrel locating pin (5) and pulling receiver straight back off barrel.

Take care not to twist receiver on barrel during removal. To remove operating slide assembly (33), hold receiver inverted and press sides of slide apart, disengaging lugs on rear end of slide from T-slots on either side of bolt (18). Enclose operating slide with hand during removal to prevent escape of compressed mainspring (34). Lift rear end of slide (with tugs) upward out of bolt and receiver through clearance slots in receiver and slide operating slide forward and off operating slide guide assembly (6), freeing slide and spring.

Bolt (18) is removed by holding receiver inverted and pushing bolt forward out of receiver with help of screwdriver blade inserted in slots in bottom of receiver just behind bolt.

Trigger assembly is removed from receiver by drifting out trigger pin (10) while holding trigger to prevent escape of compressed sear spring (14). Remove trigger and note positions and relation of disconnector (12), sear (13), sear spring (14), and disconnector spring (11) before removing them from hole in underside of receiver. Safety lever (15) is removed by removing retaining washer (16) from end of safety lever and withdrawing lever to right side of receiver. Spring (17) may be drawn out from left side of receiver.

To disassemble bolt (18), draw striker (31) and spring (32) out of bolt to rear. Grasp timing rod collar (24) and pull it toward front of bolt compressing spring (23). While holding spring compressed, remove retaining ring (25) and remove timing rod (22) from front of bolt and spring (23) and collar (24) from rear of bolt. Extractor (19) and firing pin assembly (26 through 30) are removed by drifting out extractor pin (21). Firing pin assembly is disassembled by drifting out ejector spring pin (29). To avoid confusing extractor spring (20) and firing pin retracting spring (27), note that firing pin retracting spring (27) is colored blue. The gun will not function properly if these 2 springs are interchanged. Reassemble in the reverse order.

WINCHESTER MODEL 88 RIFLE

PARTS LEGEND

1. Receiver
2. Barrel
3. Rear sight (Lyman 16A)
4. Front sight
5. Front sight cover
6. Front & rear mount base and sight plug screws (6)
7. Forearm stud
8. Bolt assembly (See Fig. 1.)
9. Front link pin
10. Front link, left
11. Front link, right
12. Guard
13. Safety
14. Safety spring
15. Safety spring plunger
16. Finger lever pin
17. Finger lever
18. Finger lever spring
19. Trigger
20. Trigger pin
21. Hammer lock
22. Trigger spring
23. Hammer
24. Hammer pin
25. Hammer spring
26. Hammer spring guide rod
27. Hammer spring guide rod pin
28. Hammer spring guide
29. Rear link, left
30. Rear link, right
31. Guard latch
32. Guard latch spring
33. Hammer catch
34. Hammer catch pin
35. Hammer catch spring
36. Guard latch, spring abutment
37. Rear link pin
38. Magazine lock housing
39. Magazine lock
40. Magazine lock pin
41. Magazine lock spring
42. Magazine assembly
43. Stock
44. Forearm swivel screw
45. Forearm swivel screw escutcheon
46. Forearm escutcheon
47. Forearm screw
48. Pistol grip cap
49. Pistol grip cap screw
50. Stock swivel screw
51. Buttplate
52. Buttplate screws
53. Recoil block
54. Recoil block screw
55. Recoil block screw washer
56. Receiver spacer
57. Receiver spacer screw (2)

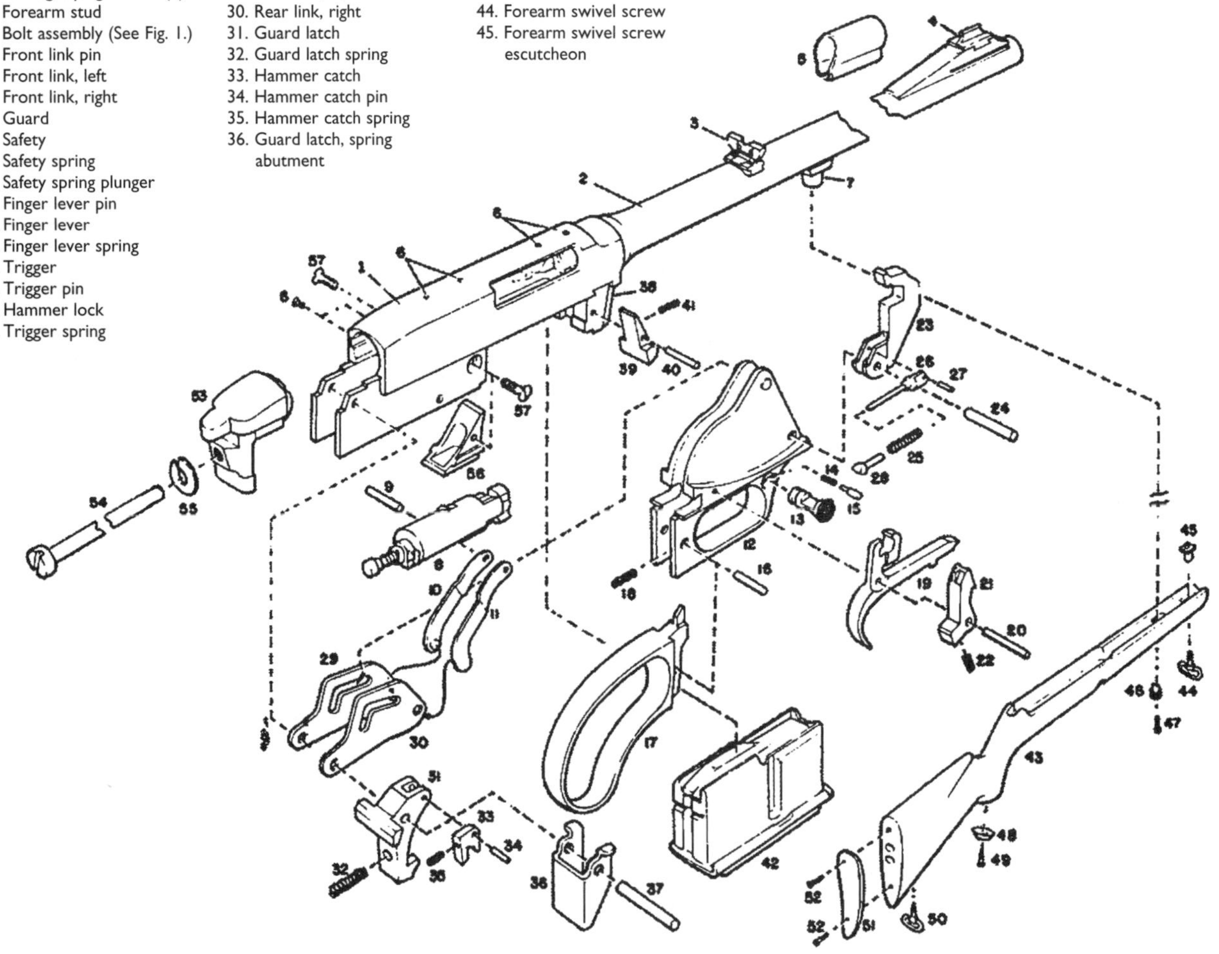

The Winchester Model 88 hammerless, lever-action rifle was introduced in 1955. In design, it represented a radical departure from that of previous Winchester lever-action rifles.

The high pressure levels of modern sporting cartridges dictated a secure breeching system which was provided in the Model 88 by a rotating bolt with triple locking lugs engaging the receiver close to the cartridge head. Other significant design features are its enclosed receiver, detachable box-magazine, one-piece stock, and side ejection port which permits mounting of scope sights directly over the bore.

The Model 88 was chambered for the .243, .308, and .358 Winchester It was discontinued in 1975.

DISASSEMBLY

To disassemble rifle, remove magazine (42) and open action, checking chamber to be sure it is unloaded. Hold gun inverted with lever upward and remove forearm screw (47). Lift barrel and action out of stock, pivoting rear of receiver against recoil block (53). Recoil block may be removed from stock by removing buttplate (51) and unscrewing recoil block screw (54) through hole in butt.

Action is removed intact from receiver as shown in Fig. 2. Remove front ends of rear links from pins in ears of guard. Guard latch assembly (31, 32, 33, 34, 35, 37) is removed by drifting out slave pin used to replace rear link pin (37). Hammer (23) with spring (25) and associated hammer parts (26, 27, 28) are removed by drifting out slave pin used to replace hammer pin (24). Trigger (19) and hammer lock (21) with spring (22) are removed by drifting out trigger pin (20).

Safety (13) can be removed from guard (12) by rotating safety 90 degrees in either direction and pushing it out, taking care not to allow compressed safety plunger spring (14) or plunger (15) to escape. Finger lever (17) is removed by drifting out finger lever pin (16), taking care not to lose compressed spring (18) in guard. Receiver spacer may be removed from receiver by unscrewing receiver spacer screws (57). Magazine lock (39) can be removed from housing (38) by drifting out pin (40), taking care not to lose spring (41).

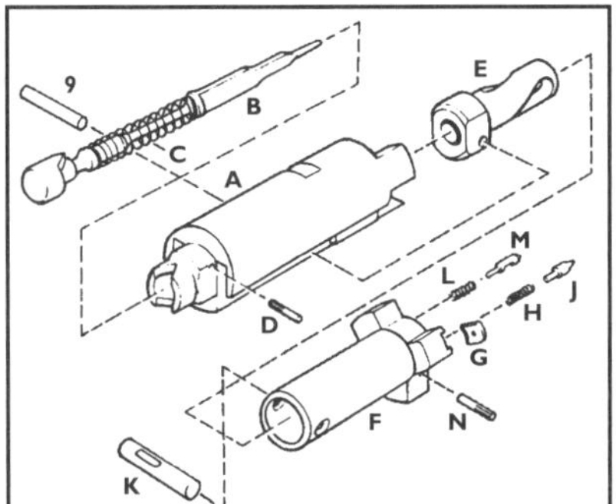

A. Bolt sleeve
B. Firing pin
C. Firing pin spring
D. Firing pin retaining pin
E. Bolt sleeve lock
F. Bolt
G. Extractor
H. Extractor spring
J. Extractor plunger
K. Bolt sleeve lock pin
L. Ejector spring
M. Ejector
N. Ejector pin

1 Bolt is removed from front links (10, II) by removing front link pin (9). Drift out firing pin retaining pin (D), taking care not to force grooved end of pin through hole. Remove firing pin (B) and spring (C) to rear. Remove bolt sleeve cam lock pin (K) and bolt sleeve lock (E) and bolt (F) from bolt sleeve (A). Extractor (G) can be removed by depressing point of plunger (J) with punch and sliding extractor inward and out of dovetail, into counterbore in face of bolt. Ejector (M) can be removed by drifting out ejector pin (N), grooved end first.

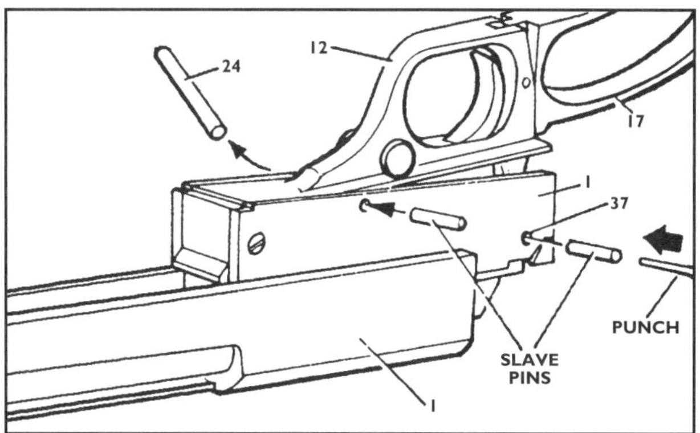

2 To remove action from receiver, 2 slave pins, the same diameter as rear link pin (37) and hammer pin (24) and about ¾ inch long (distance between receiver side-plates), must be used. Tap out hammer pin and rear link pin using slave pins. Remove the action as a unit from the rear end of the receiver.

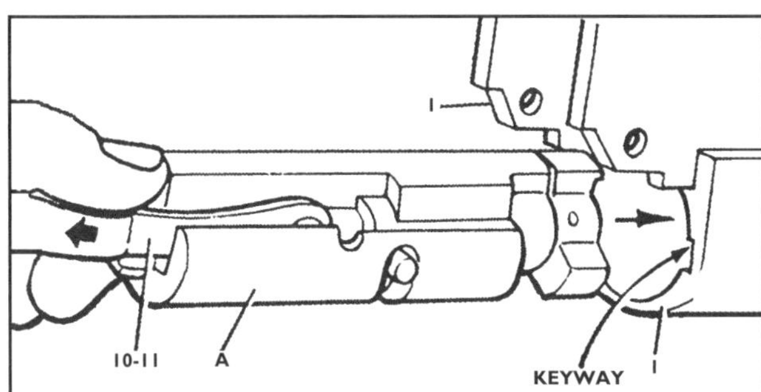

3 To reassemble bolt in receiver, grasp 2 front links as shown until bolt sleeve lock pin (K) is near top of its slot (when gun is held inverted as shown). Insert bolt sleeve in bolt hole in rear of receiver. Pin should enter keyway in rear of receiver. Push bolt sleeve assembly into receiver, swinging links up vertically between receiver side-plates close to receiver spacer. Grasp guard assembly (12) with finger lever up and connect rear ends of front links (10, 11) to front end of rear links (29 & 30), one at a time. Place guard into position in receiver.

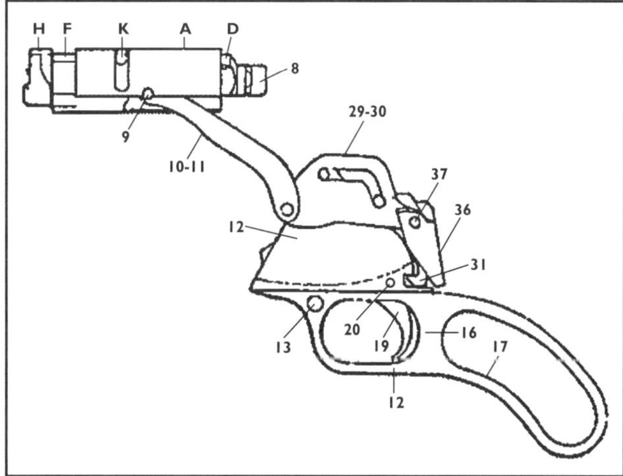

4 Showing relationship of all parts of action assembled. After replacing action in position in receiver, replace hammer pin (24) and rear link pin (37), drifting out slave pins that were used to hold action while it was out of receiver.

WINCHESTER MODEL 94 CARBINE

PARTS LEGEND

1. Barrel with ramp
2. Front sight
3. Front sight cover
4. Rear sight
5. Rear sight elevator
6. Magazine follower
7. Magazine spring
8. Magazine plug
   8a. Magazine tube
9. Magazine plug screw
10. Receiver
11. Cartridge guide, right hand
12. Cartridge guide, left hand
13. Cartridge guide screws (2)
14. Finger lever pin
15. Finger lever pin stop screw
16. Breech bolt
17. Firing pin stop pin
18. Extractor pin
19. Extractor
20. Ejector
21. Ejector spring
22. Ejector stop pin
23. Firing pin
24. Hammer screw
25. Hammer
26. Hammer stirrup
27. Hammer stirrup pin
28. Upper tang screw
29. Carrier screws (2)
30. Carrier
31. Carrier spring
32. Carrier spring screw
33. Link
34. Link pin
35. Link pin stop screw
36. Friction stud
37. Friction stud spring
38. Friction stud stop pin
39. Finger lever
40. Locking bolt
41. Firing pin striker
42. Firing pin striker stop pin
43. Finger lever link screw
44. Lower tang
45. Safety catch
46. Sear and safety catch spring
47. Sear and safety catch spring screw
48. Safety catch pin
49. Mainspring
50. Mainspring screw
51. Mainspring strain screw
52. Trigger
53. Sear
54. Sear pin
55. Spring cover
56. Spring cover screw
57. Peep sight plug screw
58. Rear band
59. Rear band screw
60. Front band
61. Front band screw
62. Buttplate
63. Buttplate screws (2)
64. Buttstock (not shown)
65. Forearm (not shown)

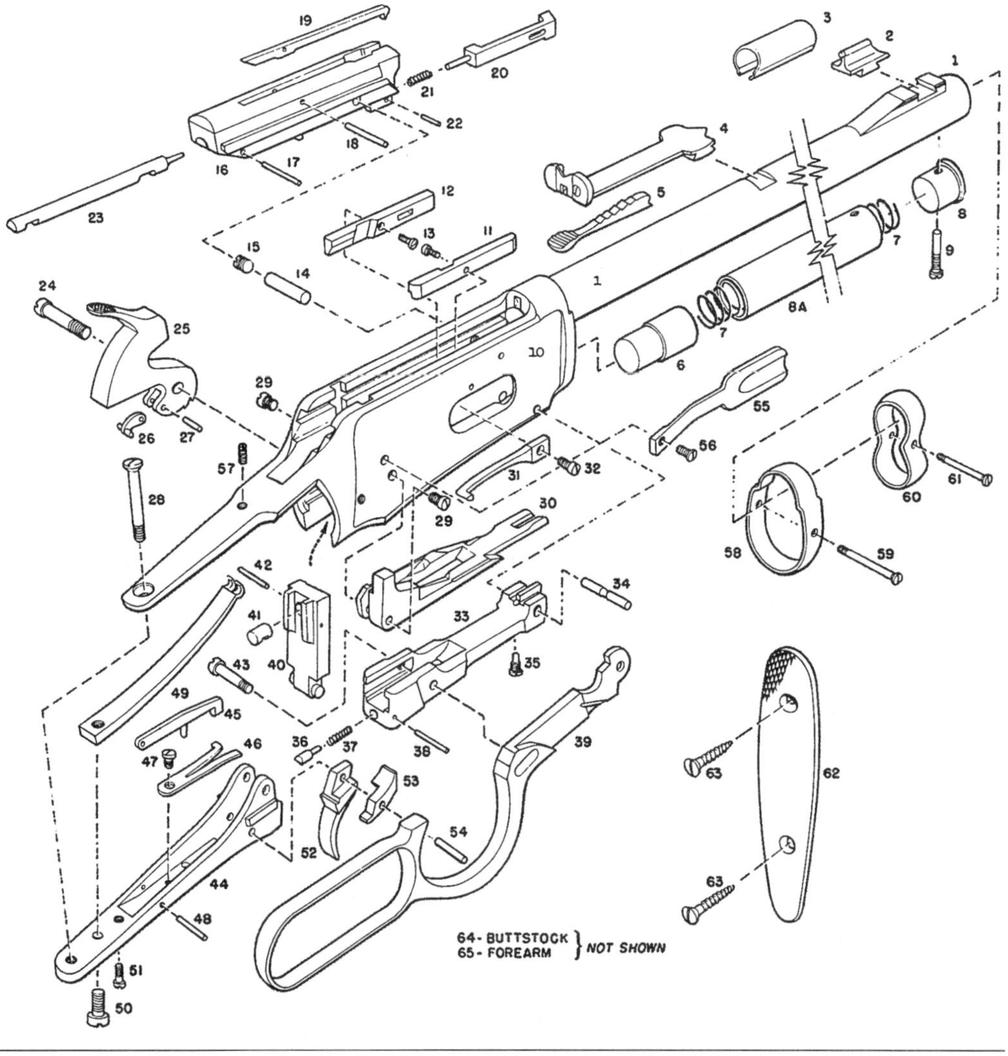

64- BUTTSTOCK
65- FOREARM } NOT SHOWN

The Winchester Model 1894 rifles and carbines have been in continuous production for more than 60 years with only a few minor changes. The Winchester Model 1894 was the first American rifle of sporting type specifically constructed for smokeless powder cartridges. Initial rifles were offered in .32-40 and .38-55 Winchester blackpowder calibers.

Early in 1895 Winchester offered the Model 1894 with nickel steel barrels, chambered for the new .30-30 and .25-35 Winchester smokeless powder cartridges. The .30-30 soon became popular in the West and was offered in .32 Winchester Special chambering in June 1902. A wide variety of carbines and rifles, including takedown models, have been offered over the years. Winchester ceased production of the Model 94 in 2006 with the closing of the historic New Haven factory.

DISASSEMBLY

Unscrew upper tang screw (28) and remove buttstock. Remove finger lever pin stop screw (15) from left-hand side of receiver and drift out finger lever pin (14) through hole at right-hand side of receiver as shown in Fig. 1. Remove link pin stop screw (35) and drift out link pin (34). Finger lever (39) and link (33) may now be removed from bottom of receiver. Separate these parts by removing finger lever link screw (43).

Remove carrier screws (29) from right and left sides of receiver and drop carrier (30) out bottom of receiver.

With hammer let all the way down, remove mainspring screw (50) and mainspring (49). Do not move mainspring strain screw (51) as this will change hammer blow and trigger pull. Remove hammer screw (24) and, while holding safety catch (45) up, pull back on trigger and remove hammer as shown in Fig. 2. Drive out lower tang (44) toward rear of receiver using a brass rod or wood mallet. Locking bolt (40) and breech bolt (16) may now be removed from receiver.

Remove spring cover screw (56) from right side of receiver and remove spring cover (55). Remove carrier spring screw (32) and carrier spring (31) from receiver. Removal of cartridge guides (11 & 12) is not recommended since poorly installed guides will result in improper feeding. The cartridge guides can be easily cleaned while in place within receiver.

While not necessary for normal cleaning purposes, magazine assembly is easily removed. Remove magazine plug screw (9) and magazine plug (8) from front of magazine tube (8a). Withdraw the magazine spring (7) and follower (6) from front of magazine tube. Remove front and rear band screws (59 & 61). Slide forearm (65) and rear band up on barrel and loosen rear band from forearm. Pull magazine tube free of receiver and withdraw to front.

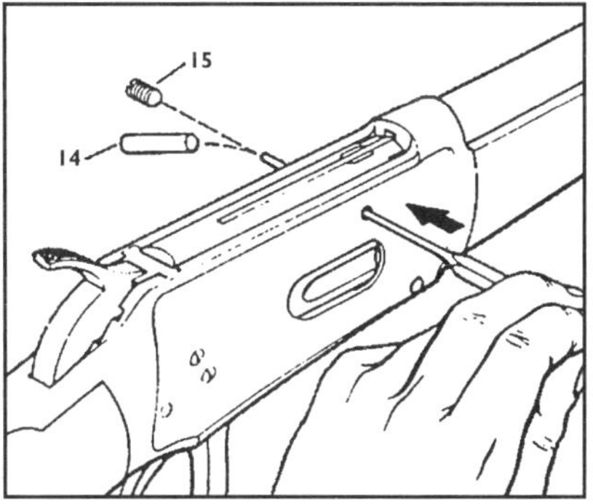

1 Unscrew finger lever pin stop screw (15) and remove from left side of receiver. Drift out finger lever pin (14) as shown with a small punch inserted in hole provided for this purpose in right-hand side of receiver. Remove link pin screw (35) from link and drift out link pin (34) from either side. Draw out and disengage link from trunnion in lower end of locking bolt (40). (Rifle should be held in vise with padded jaws).

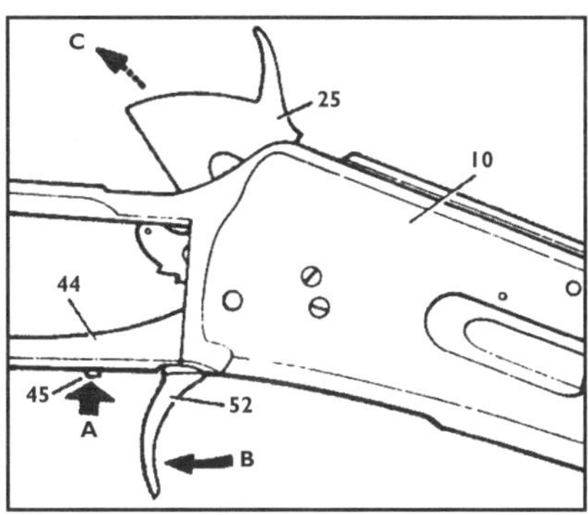

2 Remove mainspring screw and mainspring. Remove hammer screw. While pressing upward an safety catch (45) as shown at A, pull back on trigger B and pull hammer (25) upward and backward out of receiver as shown at C. Reverse this procedure when reinstalling hammer.

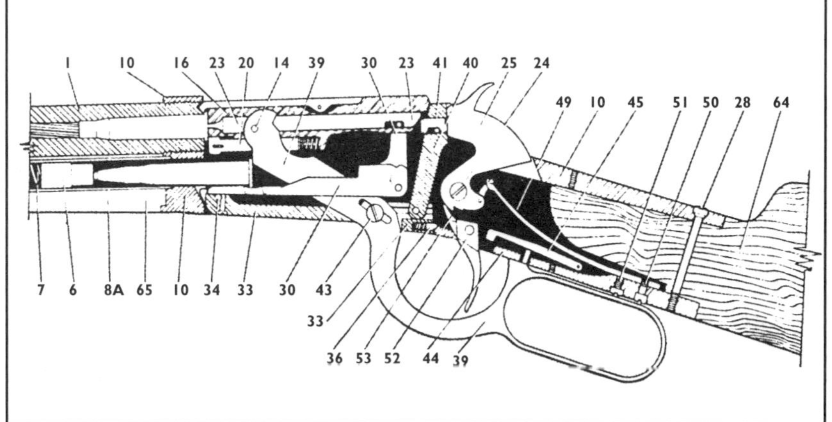

3 This sectional drawing shows the Model 94 action closed and lacked after firing. When lever (39) is pulled down, link (33) drops down, allowing the next cartridge to be moved bock onto carrier (30) by the magazine spring (7). Dropping the lever also lowers the locking bolt (40) and firing pin striker (41), and draws back breech bolt (16), ejects spent cartridge, and cocks hammer (25). When lever is almost to its lowest position, the carrier is moved up, placing cartridge in front of bolt, which carries it into chamber.

WINCHESTER MODEL 100 RIFLE

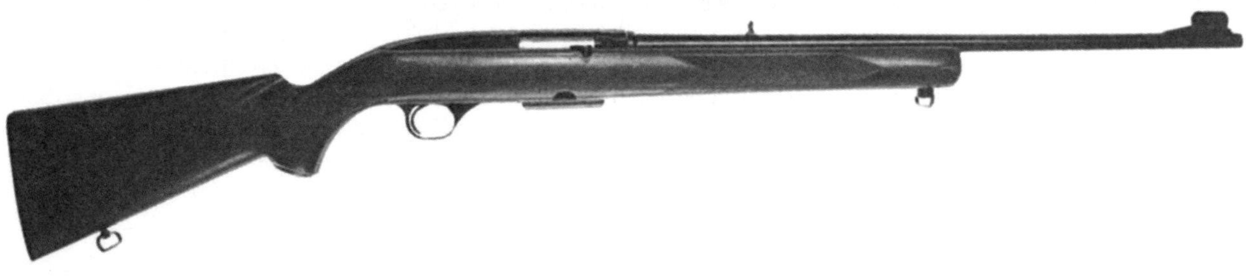

PARTS LEGEND

1. Receiver
2. Telescope and metallic sight base screws (6)
3. Barrel
   3a. Gas cylinder housing (integral with barrel)
4. Rear sight (not shown)
5. Forearm stud
6. Front sight
7. Front sight cover
8. Recoil block
9. Recoil block screw
10. Recoil block screw washer
11. Bolt assembly, complete (see Fig. 1.)
    11a. Bolt sleeve pin (see Fig. 1.)
12. Operating slide guide assembly
    12a. Piston
13. Operating slide pin
14. Gas cylinder
15. Gas cylinder cap
16. Gas cylinder plug (Staked to cap. Removal not recommended.)
17. Retainer
18. Guard housing pin
19. Guard screw
20. Guard housing assembly
21. Operating slide spring guide
22. Operating slide spring guide ring
23. Operating slide spring, inner
24. Operating slide spring, outer
25. Magazine assembly
26. Stock
27. Buttplate
28. Buttplate screws (2)
29. Pistol grip cap & key
30. Pistol grip cap screw
31. Stock swivel
32. Forearm bushing
33. Forearm swivel
34. Forearm screw

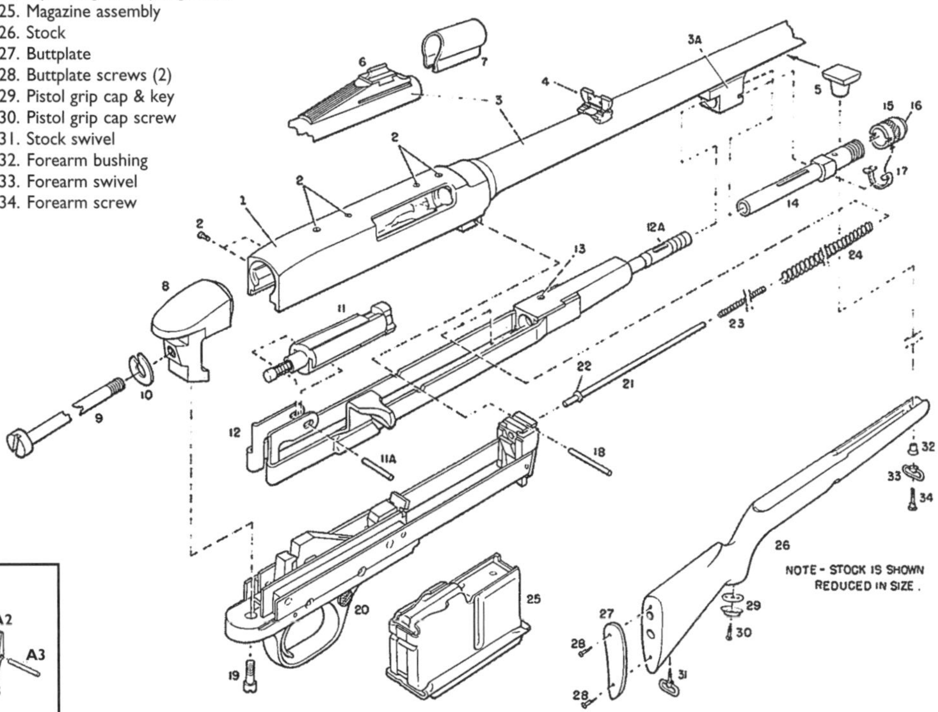

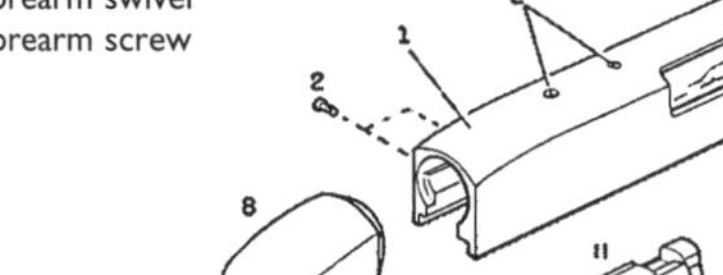

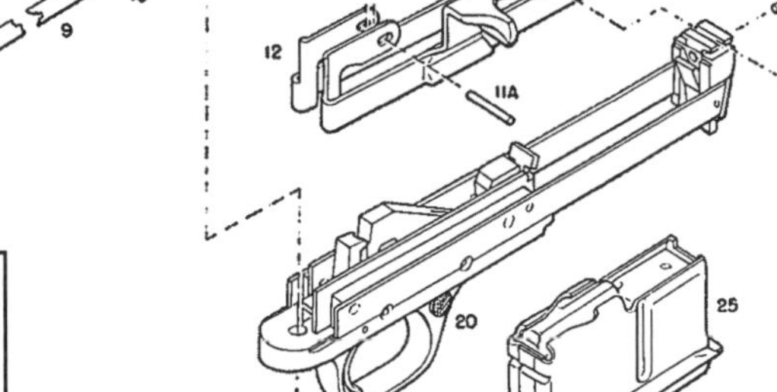

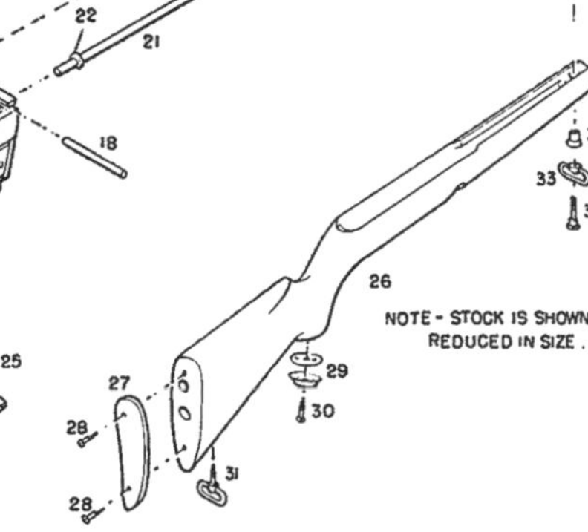

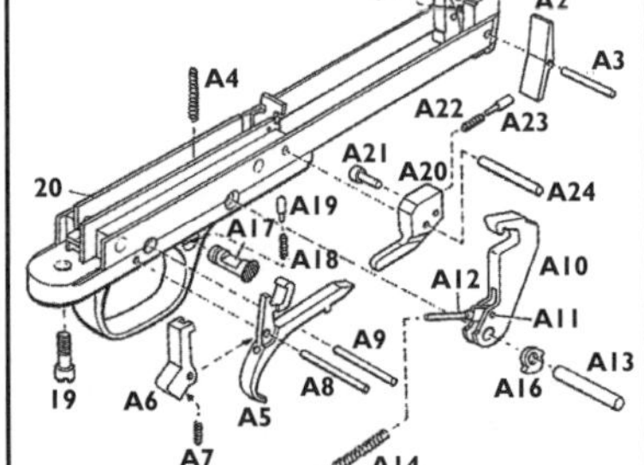

GUARD HOUSING ASSEMBLY

A1. Magazine lock spring
A2. Magazine lock
A3. Magazine lock pin
A4. Trigger spring
A5. Trigger
A6. Hammer lock
A7. Hammer lock spring
A8. Trigger pin
A9. Hammer spring guide pin
A10. Hammer
A11. Hammer spring guide rod pin
A12. Hammer spring guide rod
A13. Hammer pin
A14. Hammer spring
A15. Hammer spring guide
A16. Trigger lock
A17. Safety
A18 Safety spring
A19. Safety spring plunger
A20. Trigger lock lever
A21. Trigger lock lever pin
A22. Trigger lock plunger spring
A23. Trigger lock plunger
A24. Trigger lock lever pivot pin

The Winchester Model 100 self-loading rifle was introduced in 1960 and remained in production until 1975. Initial production was in .308 Win., with .243- and .284 Win. added later on. The standard rifle had a 22-inch barrel. A 19-inch barrel carbine was offered from 1967 to 1973.

The Model 100 was a gas operated arm, fed from a 5-shot detachable box magazine. The rotating bolt had three locking lugs. Ejection of fired cases was to the right.

The gas system of the Model 100 was like that used in the U.S. M14 service rifle. An expansion chamber in the gas piston allowed gradual build-up of pressure against the piston giving a smoother push to the operating parts than is the case when the gas acts directly against the face of the piston as it does in the Ml rifle. No adjustment of the Model 100 gas system was needed to change from one bullet weight to another and the rifle functioned quite well with handloaded ammunition of adequate power.

Its short barrel and good balance earned the Winchester Model 100 high marks for its handling qualities.

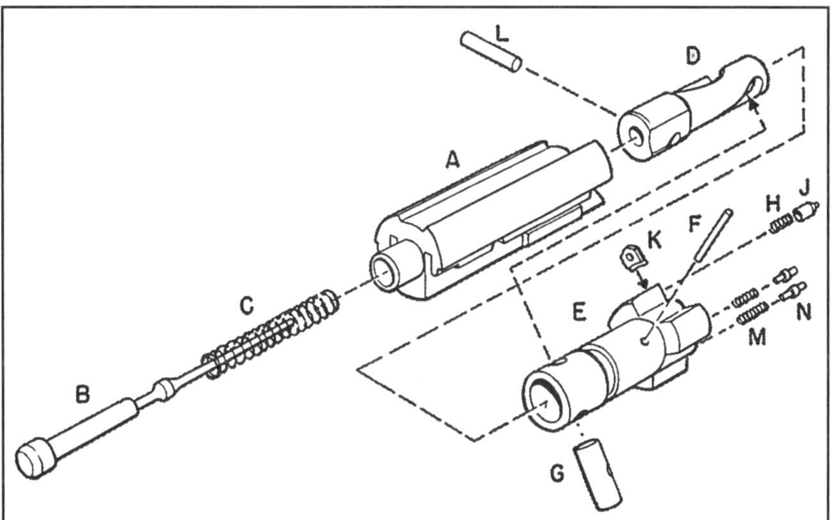

1 To disassemble bolt assembly after removing bolt sleeve pin (L) and withdrawing bolt assembly from operating slide guide assembly, withdraw firing pin (B) and spring (C) from bolt sleeve (A) to rear. Draw bolt (E) and bolt sleeve lock (D) forward out of sleeve. Drift out bolt sleeve lock pin (G) and pull bolt forward out of lock (D). Reassemble in reverse. (See Fig. 5).

BOLT ASSEMBLY

A. Bolt sleeve
B. Firing pin
C. Firing pin Spring
D. Bolt sleeve lock
E. Bolt
F. Ejector pin
G. Bolt sleeve lock pin
H. Extractor spring
J. Extractor plunger
K. Extractor
L. Bolt sleeve pin
M. Ejector springs (2)
N. Ejectors (2)

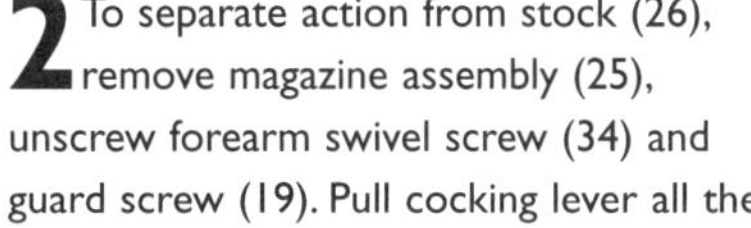

2 To separate action from stock (26), remove magazine assembly (25), unscrew forearm swivel screw (34) and guard screw (19). Pull cocking lever all the way back and hold in this position. Grasp forearm and push barrel up, pivoting rear of receiver against recoil block (8) and lift action up out of stock.

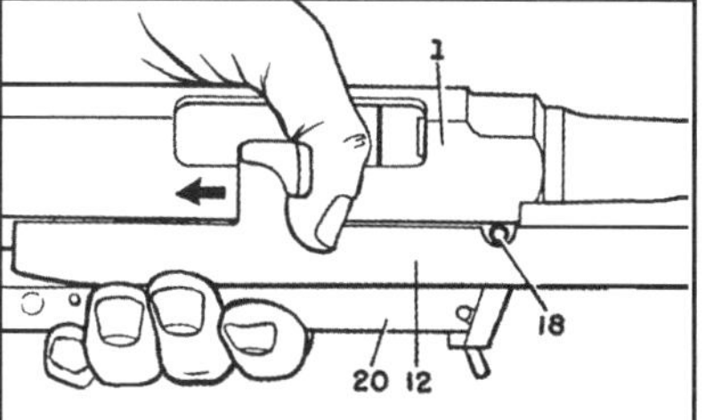

3 Remove trigger guard (20) by pulling cocking handle back until U-shaped notch in slide arm lines up with guard housing pin (18) in receiver as shown here. Drift out pin and draw guard from receiver to rear with operating slide spring guide and springs (21, 23, 24).

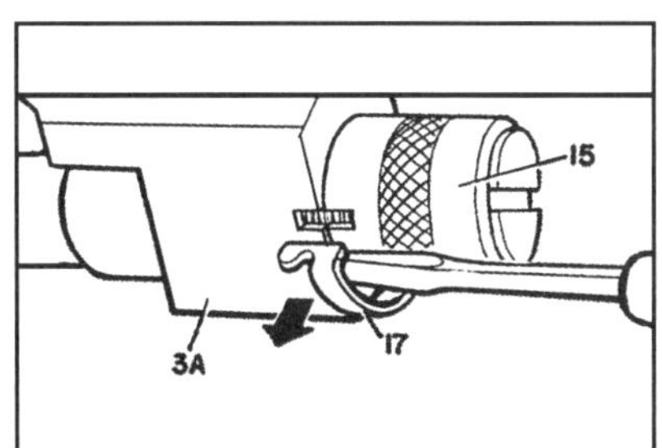

4 Remove retainer (17) using the tip of a screwdriver as shown. Unscrew gas cylinder cap (15) and pull operating slide guide assembly (12) to rear. Draw gas cylinder (14) forward off piston (12a). Slide guide assembly (12) with bolt assembly (11) can be drawn off receiver to rear. Remove the bolt from slide by drifting out bolt-sleeve pin (11A).

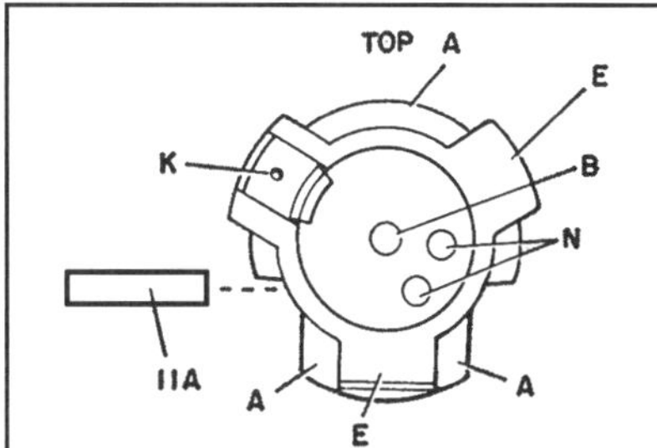

5 If bolt has been disassembled, take care in reassembling that bolt (E) is replaced in sleeve (A) in proper position as shown by this front view. Replace the pin (11a) through the slide guide assembly (12) and the bolt sleeve lock (D).

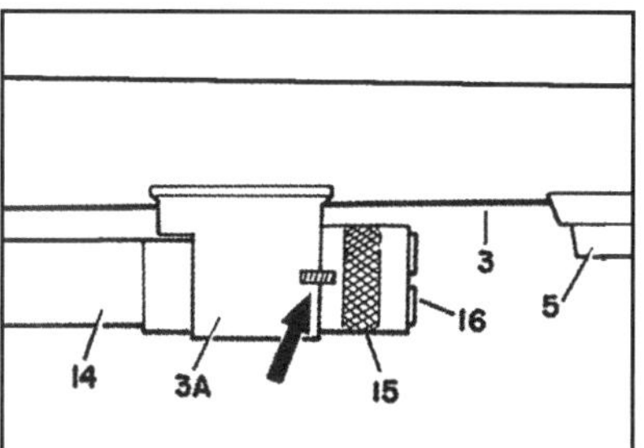

6 When replacing gas cylinder cap (15) screw back on cylinder (14) and tighten. Then loosen cap only sufficiently to line up notches in cap and gas cylinder housing (3a) as shown by arrow. Replace retainer (17), reversing procedure followed in Fig. 4.

WIN. MODEL 1200 SLIDE-ACTION

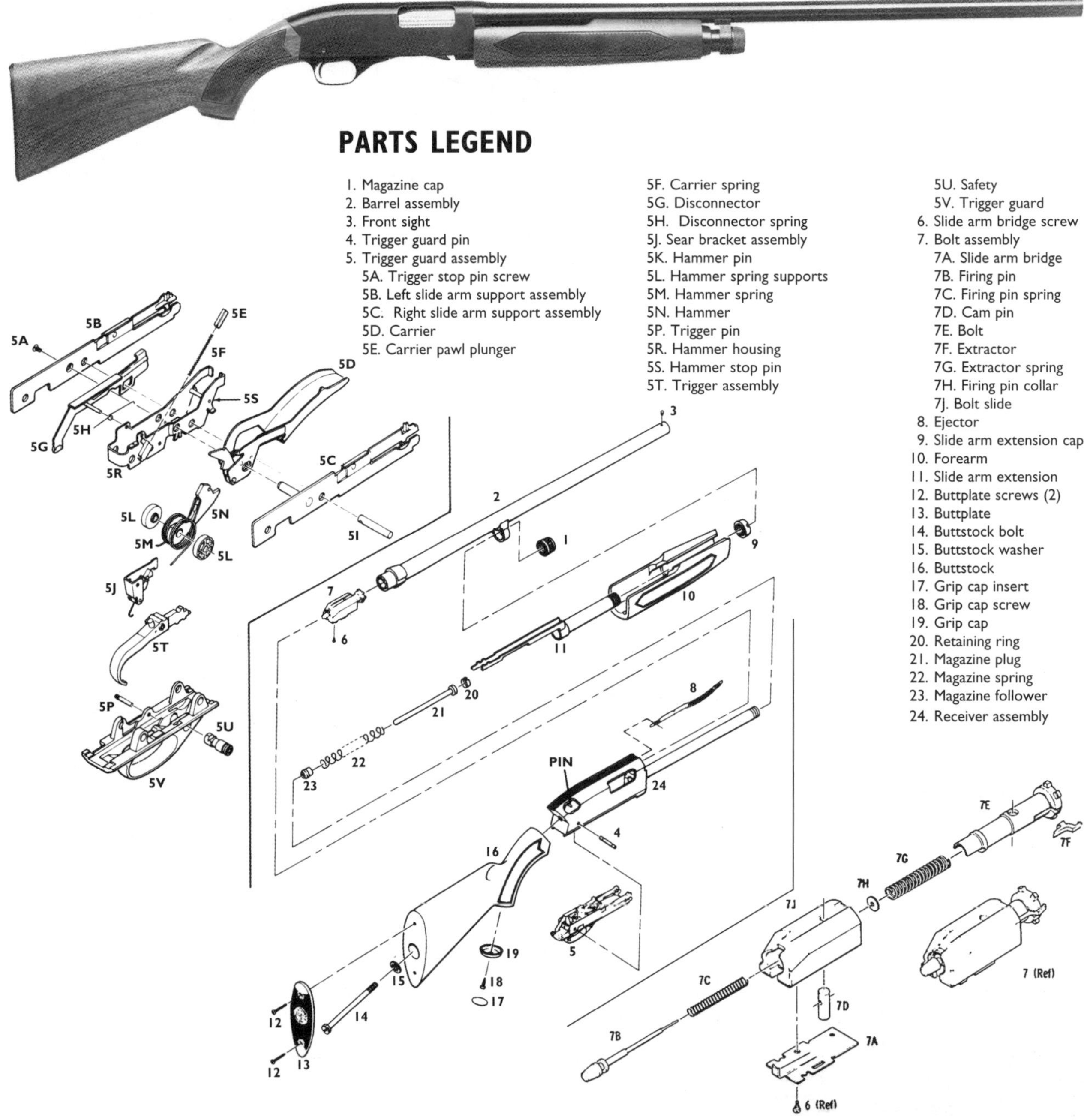

PARTS LEGEND

1. Magazine cap
2. Barrel assembly
3. Front sight
4. Trigger guard pin
5. Trigger guard assembly
   - 5A. Trigger stop pin screw
   - 5B. Left slide arm support assembly
   - 5C. Right slide arm support assembly
   - 5D. Carrier
   - 5E. Carrier pawl plunger
   - 5F. Carrier spring
   - 5G. Disconnector
   - 5H. Disconnector spring
   - 5J. Sear bracket assembly
   - 5K. Hammer pin
   - 5L. Hammer spring supports
   - 5M. Hammer spring
   - 5N. Hammer
   - 5P. Trigger pin
   - 5R. Hammer housing
   - 5S. Hammer stop pin
   - 5T. Trigger assembly
   - 5U. Safety
   - 5V. Trigger guard
6. Slide arm bridge screw
7. Bolt assembly
   - 7A. Slide arm bridge
   - 7B. Firing pin
   - 7C. Firing pin spring
   - 7D. Cam pin
   - 7E. Bolt
   - 7F. Extractor
   - 7G. Extractor spring
   - 7H. Firing pin collar
   - 7J. Bolt slide
8. Ejector
9. Slide arm extension cap
10. Forearm
11. Slide arm extension
12. Buttplate screws (2)
13. Buttplate
14. Buttstock bolt
15. Buttstock washer
16. Buttstock
17. Grip cap insert
18. Grip cap screw
19. Grip cap
20. Retaining ring
21. Magazine plug
22. Magazine spring
23. Magazine follower
24. Receiver assembly

In 1964, Winchester-Western replaced the field grade Model 12 with a lower cost slide-action repeater, the Model 1200.

The Model 1200 is made in 12, 16 and 20 gauge for field use, 12 and 20 gauge for skeet, and 12gauge for trap shooting. There is also a 12-gauge 3-inch magnum field version, and a deer version designed to fire slug loads. While this gun is generally similar to the Model 12 in appearance and operation, it differs considerably in mechanical design.

Among several striking features of the Model 1200 is its bolting system. A short breech ring screwed to the barrel has locking shoulders which are engaged by four locking lugs on the rotary bolt head. This system is extremely strong.

Another important feature is a disconnector which makes it necessary for the shooter to release the trigger before pulling it for another shot. This is desirable for safety reasons. There is no inertia slide release. This device in the Model 12 requires that the slide be pushed forward slightly before opening the gun without firing. It is intended to prevent premature opening of the action in the event of a hangfire, but is rarely necessary with reliable modern ammunition.

By 1974, trap and skeet versions of the Model 1200 had been dropped from the Winchester line, as had guns in 16-gauge Later still the Model 1200 was replaced by the mechanically similar "Defender" model.

DISASSEMBLY

After disassembly steps 1 thru 6 have been completed, pull forearm/slidearm/extension group off the end of the magazine tube and use a spanner wrench to remove slide arm extension cap (9). Pull forearm (10) off the slide arm extension (11). Remove buttplate screws(12) and lift off buttplate (13). Use thin-walled socket (½ nut outside flat dimension) or suitable screwdriver to remove buttstock bolt(14), buttstock washer (15) and buttstock (16). CAUTION: If a screwdriver is used be sure blade is properly engaging slot in stockbolt before applying pressure or the buttstock may be damaged. If removal of the grip cap is desired use thin bladed knife to pry up grip cap insert (17), unscrew grip cap screw (18) and remove grip cap (19). To remove magazine tube components, insert a suitable screwdriver into the end of the magazine tube and pry out the magazine tube plug and withdraw plug (21), magazine spring (22), and magazine follower (23). Further disassembly should not be attempted. Trigger guard assembly takedown (Fig. 2).

emove trigger stop pin screw (5A) and pull off left slide arm support assembly (5B). While restraining carrier use a suitable punch to push out the right slide arm support assembly (5C), remove carrier (5D), carrier pawl plunger (SE), and carrier spring (5F). Disengage safety and ease down hammer while depressing trigger. Rotate disconnector to remove tension on disconnector spring, restrain the sear bracket assembly, pull out the disconnector (5G) and remove disconnector spring (5H) and sear bracket assembly (5J). Use a suitable punch to drive out the hammer pin (5K) from left to right and lift out and disassemble the grouping consisting of: two hammer spring supports (5L), hammer spring (5M), and hammer (5N). Punch out knurled trigger stop pin (5P) from right to left and lift off hammer housing (5R). If desired hammer support pin (5S) can be removed by spreading housing slightly. Remove trigger assembly (5T) and safety (5U) from trigger guard (5V). Bolt assembly takedown procedure (Fig. 3).

Compress firing pin and spring slightly and lift oft slide arm bridge (7A), remove firing pin (7B) and firing pin spring (7C). Rotate bolt so that hole in bolt slide is directly over the top of the cam pin. Insert a punch into bolt slide hole and drive out cam pin (7D). Place rear end of bolt slide on flat surface and remove punch. Remove bolt (7E), extractor (7F), extractor spring (7G), and extractor collar (7H) from bolt slide (7J). To reassemble, reverse sequence.

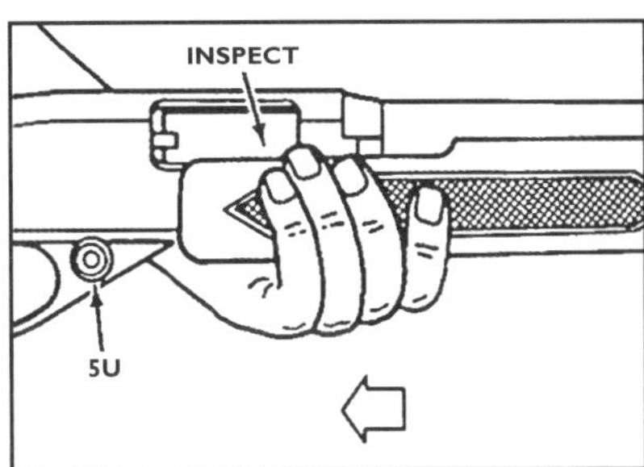

1 Depress disconnector (5G) and pull forearm back to unlock and open action, Inspect chamber, carrier and magazine follower to ascertain that gun is not loaded. Close action and engage safety (5U).

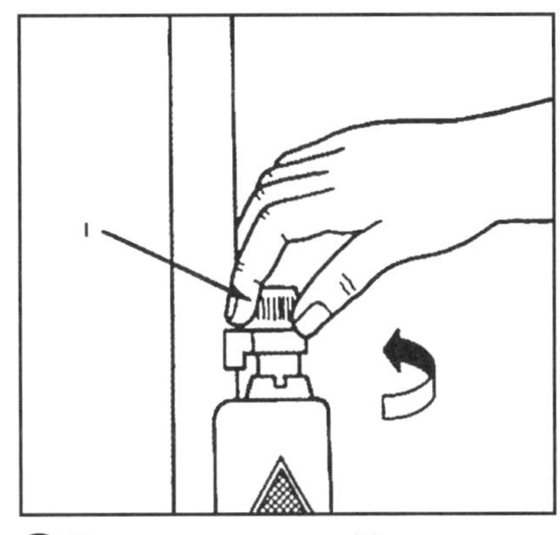

2 Unscrew magazine cap (1).

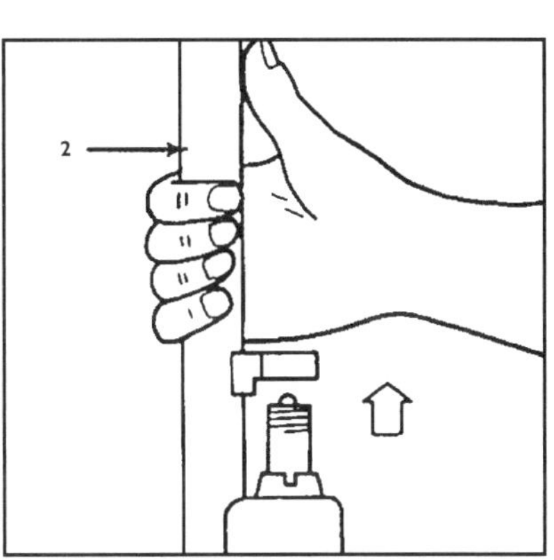

3 Pull barrel assembly (2) from receiver.

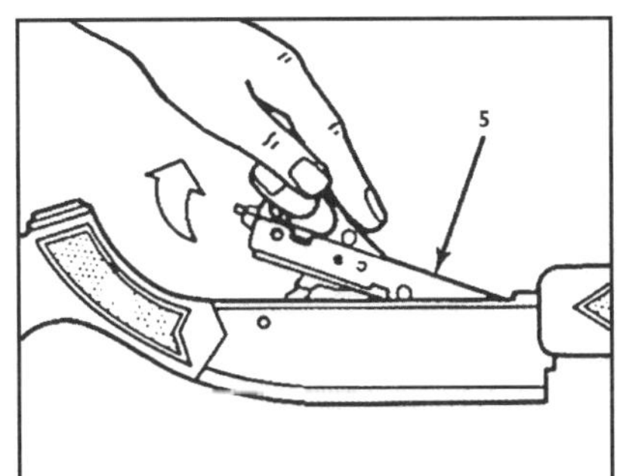

4 Position gun with trigger pointing up and punch out trigger guard pin (4) from left to right. Lift up on trigger guard assembly (5) and withdraw from receiver. For trigger guard assembly takedown procedure see Figure 2.

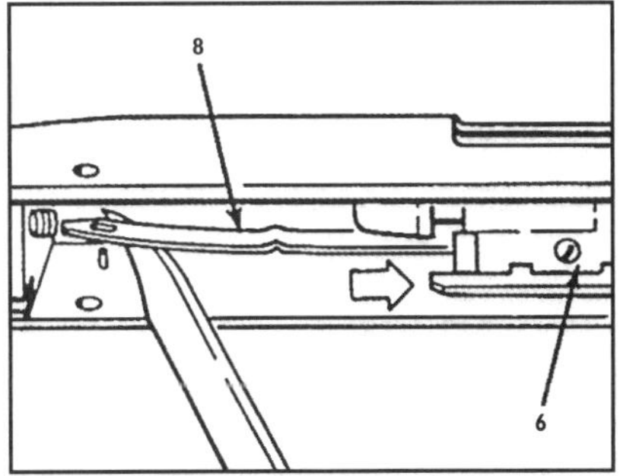

5 Remove slide arm bridge screw (6). Remove ejector (8) by using thin bladed knife to lift it off the retaining pin on inside of receiver and pulling it out the front of the receiver.

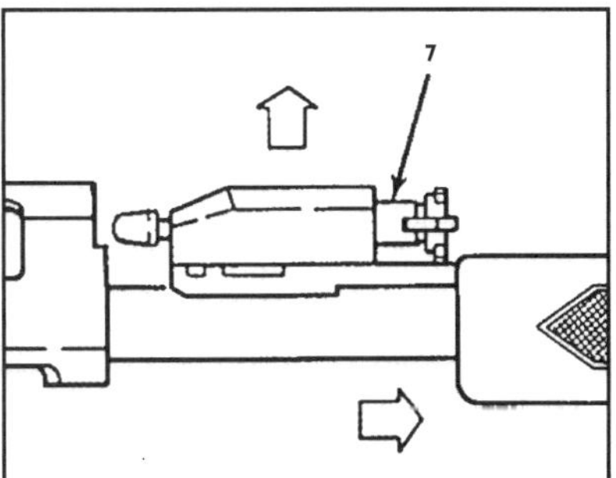

6 Slide forearm forward until bolt assembly (7) exits the front of the receiver and can be lifted from slide arm extension. For bolt assembly takedown procedure see Figure 3.

WINCHESTER MODEL 1300 SHOTGUN

PARTS LEGEND

1. Barrel assembly
2. Breech bolt
3. Breech bolt slide
4. Breech bolt
5. Buttstock assembly
6. Buttstock bolt & washer
7. Cam pin
8. Carrier assembly
9. Carrier plunger
10. Carrier spring
11. Disconnector assembly
12. Disconnector spring
13. Ejector retainer
14. Ejector retainer screw
15. Ejector spring
16. Ejector
17. Extractor spring
18. Extractor
19. Firing pin collar
20. Firing pin spring
21. Firing pin
22. Forearm
23. Hammer
24. Hammer housing
25. Hammer pin
26. Hammer spring supports
27. Hammer spring
28. Hammer stop pin
29. Magazine cap retainer
30. Magazine cap
31. Magazine follower
32. Magazine spring retainer
33. Magazine spring
34. Magazine throat lower
35. Magazine throat upper
36. Magazine throat
37. Magazine tube
38. Shell plug (not shown)
39. Receiver
40. Recoil pad screws
41. Recoil pad
42. Safety
43. Sear assembly
44. Slide arm bridge
45. Slide arm cap
46. Slide arm extension assembly
47. Slide arm extension cap ring
48. Slide support with cutoff
49. Slide support with cutoff
50. Trigger
51. Trigger assembly
52. Trigger guard pin
53. Trigger guard
54. Trigger pin
55. Front sight bead

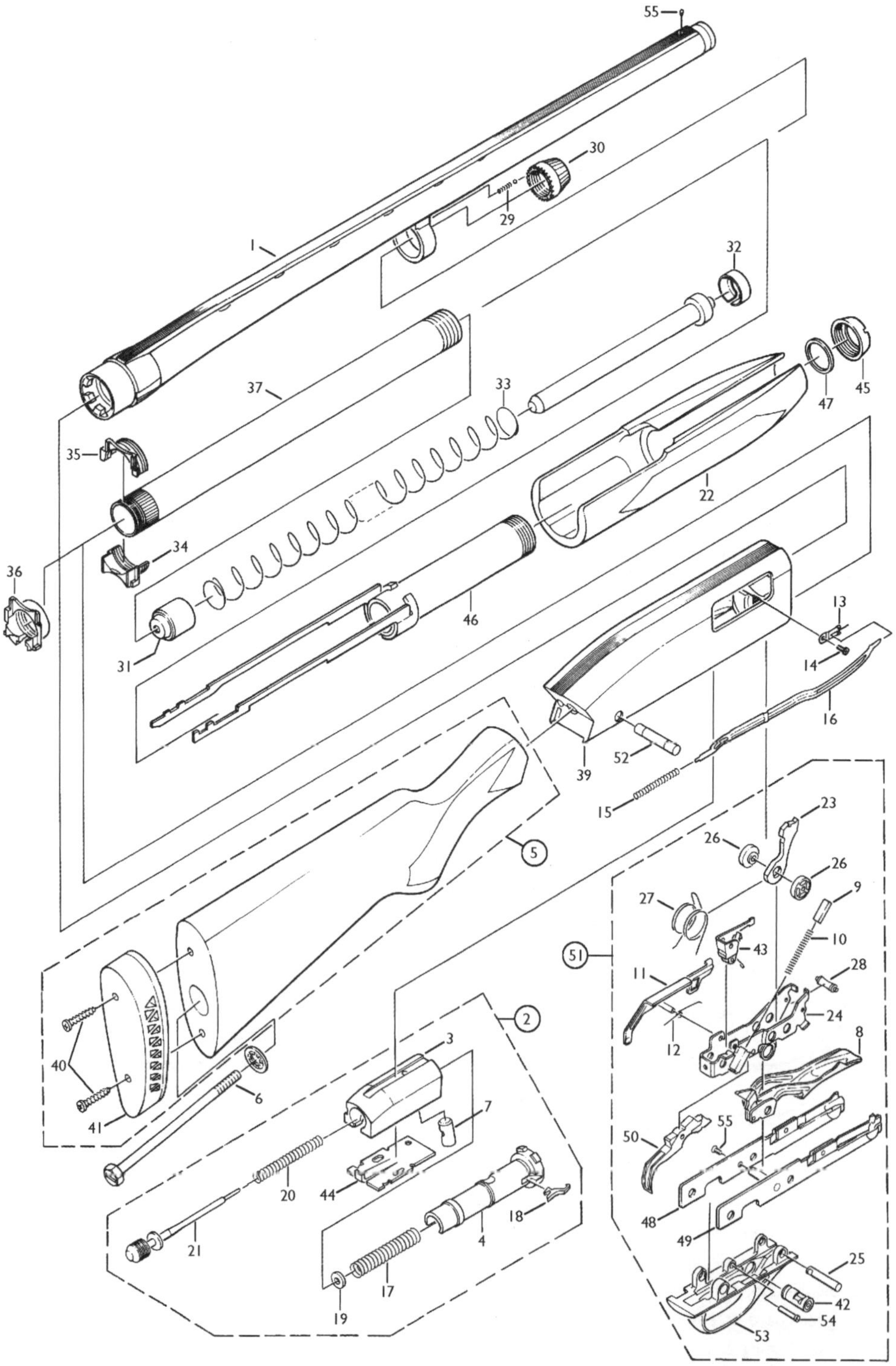

Manufactured at the Winchester factory in New Haven, Connecticut, the Winchester Model 1300 slide-action shotgun was introduced in 1978. The Model 1300 Featherweight, in 12 and 20 gauge, was introduced in 1984. The Model 1300 features a four-lug rotary bolt similar to the AR-15 rifle. The bolt engages the barrel extension instead of the top of the receiver. Field models feature a floating ventilated rib that allows the rib to move without distorting the sight plane.

Model 1300s have been produced in a wide variety of models including guns with ventilated rib barrels, rifled slug barrels with rifle sights, smoothbore barrels with rifle sights and smoothbore barrels with the WinChoke screw-in choke system. The safety is a cross bolt trigger lock. The magazine, without a plug, can hold seven 2¼-inch shells. The stocks are either wood or black plastic for full-length versions and black plastic for the pistol grip model. Models are also available with a pistol grip.

In 2006 the U.S. Repeating Arms Company closed Winchester's historic New Haven factory ending production of the Model 1300 shotguns.

DISASSEMBLY

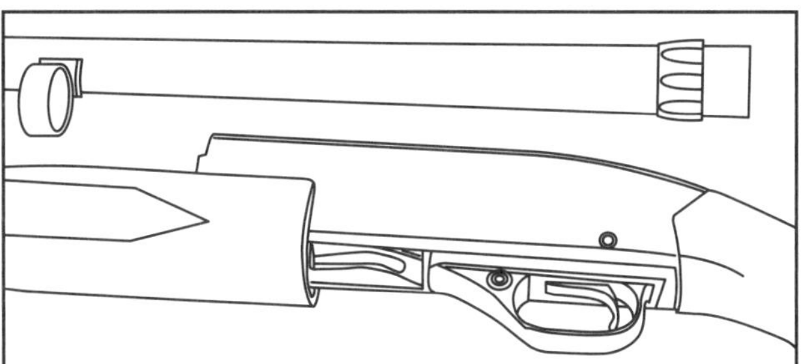

1 Removal of the barrel: Open the action and make sure the gun is unloaded. Close the action and place the safety in the "on safe" position. Unscrew and remove the magazine cap (30). Slide the barrel (1) forward, withdrawing the barrel from the receiver (39) and disengage the barrel bracket from the front end of the magazine. Replace the magazine cap.

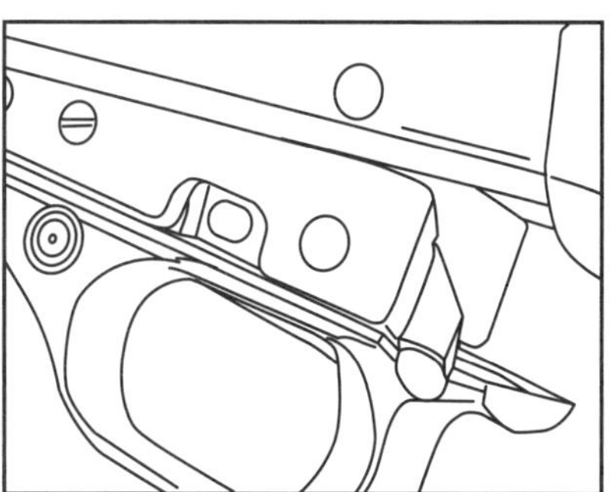

2 Close the action and drive out the trigger guard pin (52) toward either side. Pull the rear of the trigger guard (53) out and then remove it downward toward the rear.

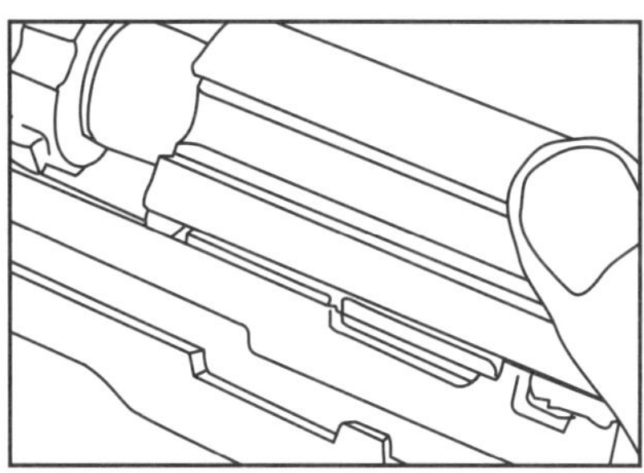

3 Disassembly of the slide and breech-bolt: With the action slide arms (46) still attached to the slide arm bridge (44), simultaneously slide both assemblies forward and out of the front of the receiver. Note that as the breech bolt assembly (2) passes by the ejection port, there may be some resistance from the ejector spring (15). Carefully work it past the resistance.

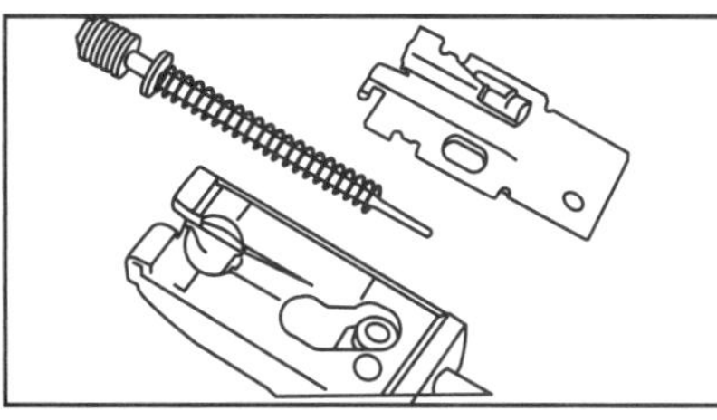

4 Removal of the firing pin: Grasp the breech-bolt assembly, bottom side up (flat side) and push the rear of the firing pin (21) forward with your forefinger. While holding the firing pin in this position, take your other hand and tilt the front end of the slide arm bridge and move it slightly forward. Lift up on the slide arm bridge and disengage the curved tongue on the slide arm bridge from the groove in the firing pin. This will detach the slide arm bridge from the breech bolt slide (3). CAUTION: The firing pin is under spring tension. Control the pin as you remove the firing pin and spring.

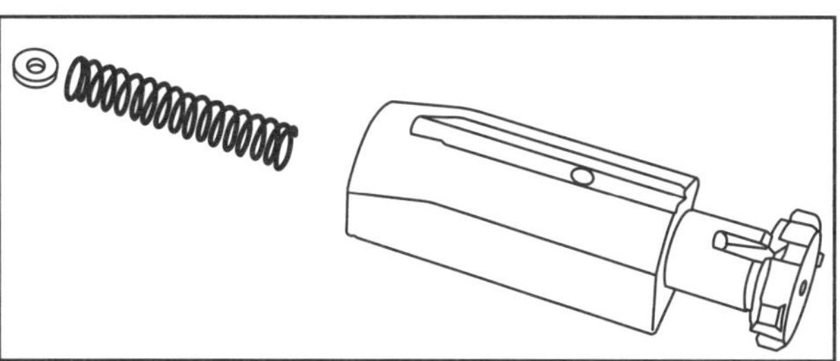

5 Removal of the trigger guard group: Place your gun with the trigger guard facing up on a suitable surface. Remove the trigger guard pin (52) by pushing it out from the left side of the receiver, the side opposite the ejection port. Any sturdy pushing tool that is smaller in diameter than the pin is acceptable. Push the pin through sufficiently until it can be pulled the rest of the way out. With the pin removed, lift the trigger guard group out of the receiver by lifting upward and pulling rearward.

WINCHESTER MODEL 1873 RIFLE

PARTS LEGEND

1. Receiver
2. Barrel
3. Side plate, left
4. Side plate, right
5. Side plate screw
6. Spring cover
7. Spring cover screw
8. Mortise cover (dust cover)
9. Mortise cover stop
10. Mortise cover stop screw
11. Mortise cover spring
12. Mortise cover spring screw
13. Finger lever spring
14. Finger lever spring screw
15. Carrier lever spring
16. Carrier lever spring screw
17. Side tang screws (2)
18. Finger lever screw
19. Rear link pin
20. Breech pin piston (firing pin)
21. Breech pin base
22. Extractor
23. Extractor pin
24. Front link pin
25. Firing pin retractor
26. Upper tang screw
27. Lower tang
28. Hammer
29. Hammer pivot pin
30. Stirrup
31. Stirrup pin
32. Trigger
33. Trigger pivot pin
34. Mainspring
35. Mainspring screw
36. Mainspring tension screw
37. Safety catch
38. Safety catch pin
39. Trigger spring
40. Safety catch spring
41. Trigger & safety catch spring screw
42. Lever latch
43. Lever latch spring
44. Lever latch pin
45. Lower tang screw
46. Finger lever
47. Carrier lever
48. Carrier block
49. Link assembly, right
50. Link assembly, left

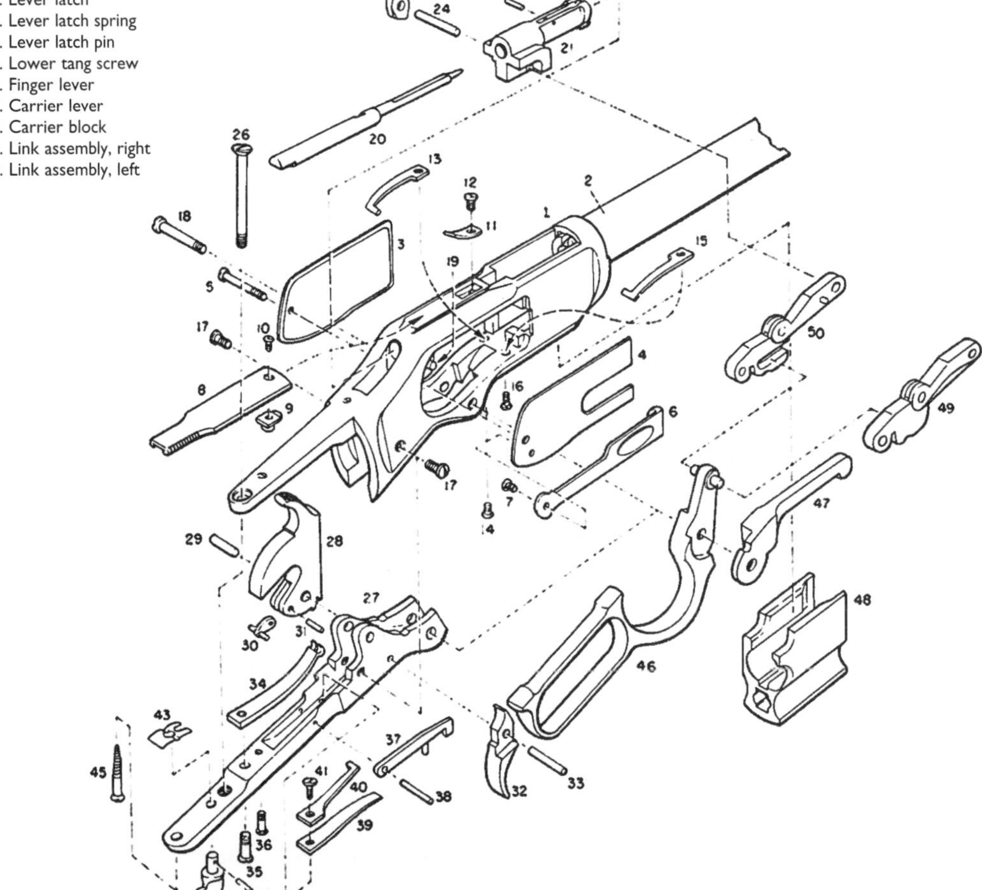

The Winchester Model 1873 lever-action repeating rifle was introduced in 1873 and was first offered in .44-40 Winchester (.44 WCF). The .38-40 Winchester (.38 WCF) chambering was first offered in 1879, followed by the .32-20 (.32 WCF) in 1882. All of these cartridges were loaded with blackpowder as Winchester did not introduce a smokeless powder cartridge until 1894. The .44, .38 and .32 WCF cartridges were also adapted for use in revolvers of the period and this dual purpose utility enhanced their popularity on the frontier.

In 1884 the Model 1873 rifle was offered in .22 Short and .22 Long with a takedown system in which a removable tapered pin secured the frame and stock assembly to the barrel assembly. This system proved unsatisfactory and was later changed to the threaded-shank system used on center-fire rifles of this model. A few Model 1873 rifles were chambered on special order for the .22 Extra Long rimfire.

The Model 1873 was the first repeating rifle made in this country for the .22 rimfire cartridge and was the first rifle made by Winchester for a center- fire cartridge. The receivers were made originally of forged iron, later changed to steel. Standard barrel lengths were 20 , 24 , and 30 , but other barrel lengths were available on special order.

The Model 1873 was an eminently successful rifle and remained in production until 1919.

DISASSEMBLY

Open the rifle action to be sure chamber, carrier block, and magazine are unloaded. With magazine assembly and buttstock removed as outlined in Figs. 1 and 2 proceed as follows:

Remove side plate screw (5) and remove right and left hand side plates (3 & 4) from sides of receiver (1). Lift right and left link assemblies (49 & 50) off link pins (19 & 24) and out of receiver. Drift out front link pin (24) and remove firing pin retractor (25) from underside of breech pin base (21). With hammer at full cock, breech pin piston (firing pin, 20) may be drawn to rear out of breech pin base (21) and out of receiver (1). Remove breech pin base from receiver. Remove finger lever spring screw (14) and carrier lever spring screw (16) from underside of receiver and remove finger lever spring (13) and carrier lever spring (15) from receiver.

Place hammer in fired position and unscrew finger lever screw (18) and 2 side tang screws (17). Pull rear end of lower tang (27) downward and remove tang from underside of receiver along with finger lever (46) and carrier lever (47). Note that forward end of carrier lever fits into slot through bottom portion of carrier block (48). Drop carrier block out bottom of receiver.

Lower tang parts, hammer (28), mainspring (34), safety catch (37), etc., are easily disassembled by drifting out respective pivot pins and removing screws which retain springs. Mortise cover is removed by removing mortise cover stop screw (10) and sliding cover rearward and separating it from mortise cover stop (9).

Reassembly is accomplished in reverse. When replacing assembled lower tang (27) keep hammer (28) in full forward position and place carrier lever (47) inside receiver with its front end in place in slot in carrier block (48). Assemble the tang with finger lever (46) in place into bottom of the receiver.

BARREL AND BUTTSTOCK ASSEMBLY

2. Barrel
51. Rear sight
52. Rear sight elevator
53. Front sight
54. Forearm tip tenon
55. Magazine ring
56. Magazine ring pin
57. Magazine tube
58. Magazine plug
59. Magazine plug screw
60. Magazine spring
61. Magazine follower
62. Fore-end (wood)
63. Fore-end tip
64. Fore-end tip screws (2)
65. Buttstock (wood)
66. Buttplate
67. Buttplate screws (2)
68. Buttplate slide
69. Buttplate slide spring
70. Buttplate slide spring screw

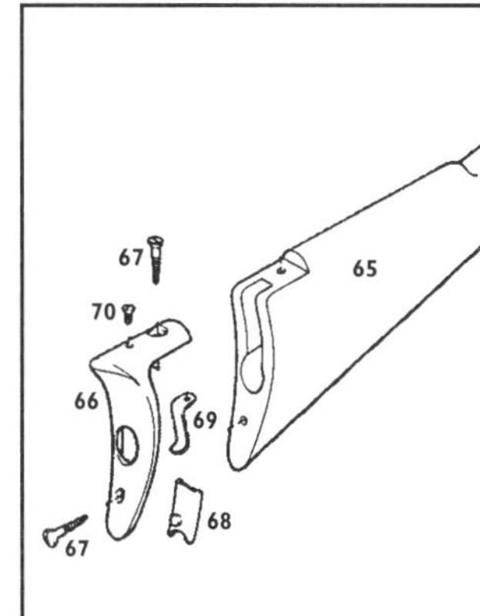

1 To disassemble magazine assembly from barrel, remove magazine plug screw (59) and magazine plug (58). Withdraw magazine spring (60) and follower (61) from magazine tube to front. Drift out magazine ring pin (56) and draw magazine tube (57) out of receiver and fore-end to front. Remove 2 fore-end tip screws (64) and remove fore-end tip. Remove forearm tip tenon (54) and fore-end (62). Reassemble in reverse.

2 To remove buttstock assembly from receiver, remove upper tang screw (26) and lower tang screw (45). Pull buttstock off rear of receiver. Buttplate is removed by unscrewing buttplate screws (67). Buttplate slide (68) is removed by unscrewing buttplate slide spring screw (70) and removing spring (69). Reassemble in reverse.

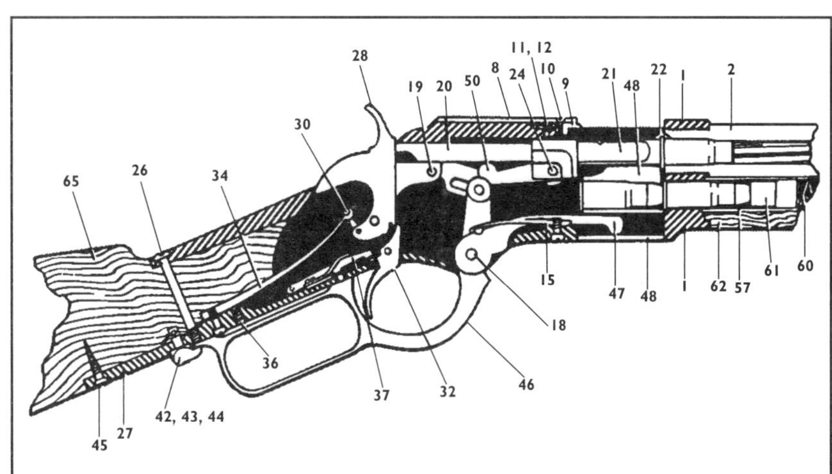

3 This longitudinal section through the rifle shows all parts of the action in proper relationship. The rifle is shown here just after firing with an empty cartridge in the chamber and next cartridge ready in carrier block (48). Lowering lever (46) pulls link assembly (50) down, drawing breech pin piston (20) and breech pin base (21) backward while carrier lever (47) raises the carrier block with next cartridge up to the chamber as empty cartridge is ejected through top of the receiver.

WIN. MODEL 1886 TAKEDOWN

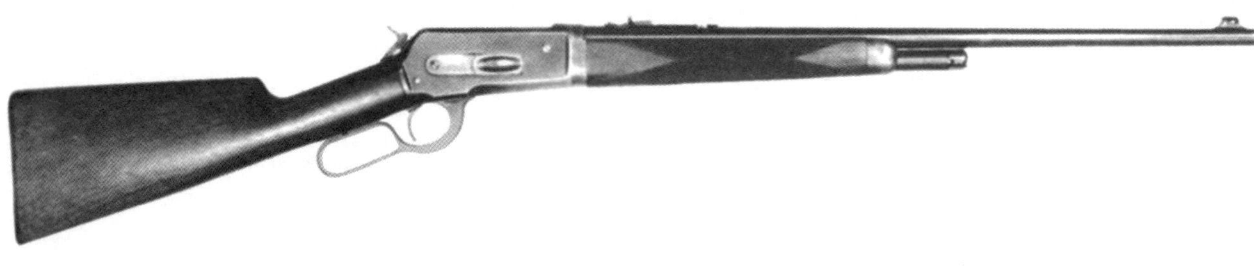

PARTS LEGEND

1. Barrel
2. Breechblock
3. Buttplate
4. Buttplate screws (2)
5. Buttstock
6. Carrier
7. Carrier hook
8. Carrier stop
9. Carrier stop screw
10. Cartridge guide
11. Cartridge guide screw
12. Cartridge stop
13. Cartridge stop screw
14. Ejector
15. Ejector collar
16. Ejector spring
17. Takedown extension
18. Takedown extension screws (3)
19. Extractor
20. Extractor pin
21. Finger lever
22. Finger lever bushing
23. Finger lever bushing pin
24. Lever & breechblock pin
25. Firing pin
26. Firing pin stop pin
27. Fore-end
28. Fore-end tip
29. Fore-end tip screws (2)
30. Fore-end tip tenon
31. Friction stud
32. Friction stud spring
33. Friction stud pin
34. Front sight
35. Hammer
36. Receiver/hammer screw
37. Hammer stirrup
38. Hammer stirrup pin
39. Locking bolt, left
40. Locking bolt, right
41. Lower tang
42. Lower tang screw
43. Magazine follower
44. Magazine lever
45. Magazine lever screw
46. Magazine plunger
47. Magazine plunger spring
48. Magazine plug
49. Magazine plug screw
50. Magazine spring
51. Magazine tube
52. Mainspring
53. Mainspring strain screw
54. Rear sight
55. Rear sight adjustable notch
56. Rear sight notch screw
57. Rear sight elevator
58. Elevator plug screw
59. Receiver
60. Spring cover base
61. Spring cover base screw
62. Spring cover leaf
63. Spring cover leaf spring
64. Spring cover leaf pin
65. Spring cover stop pin
66. Trigger
67. Trigger pin
68. Trigger spring
69. Trigger spring screw
70. Upper tang screw
71. Peep-sight plug screw (not numbered on drawing)

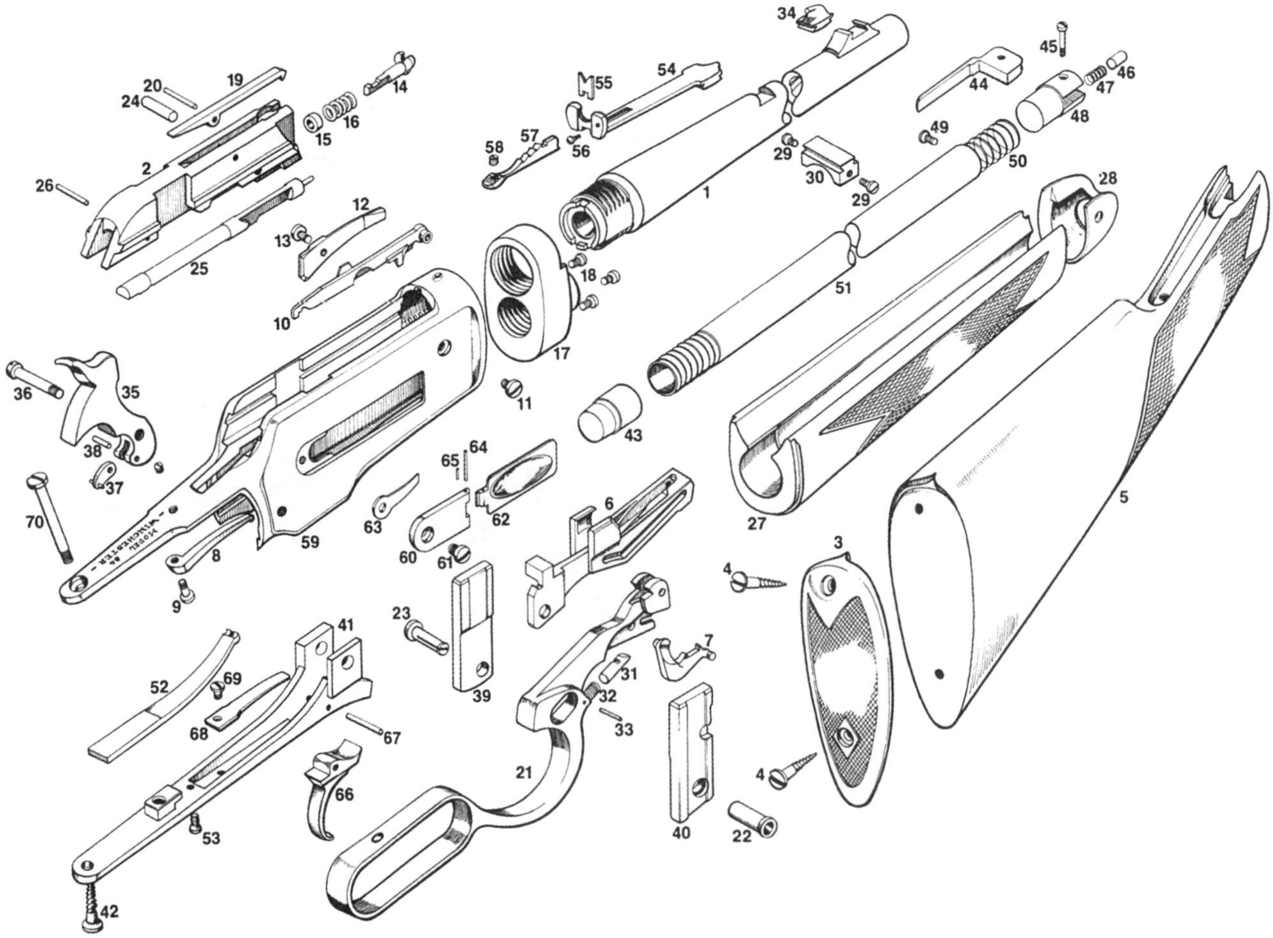

Winchester's takedown system for lever-action rifles was announced in late 1893 for the relatively new Model 1892 rifle. By early 1894, the Model 1886 rifle could be ordered in take-down version, and the following year the Model 1894 rifle was offered with the same option. In 1910 similar takedown systems were offered for the Winchester Model 1895 repeater and for Winchester's Single-Shot Rifle.

The takedown system permitted adjusting the receiver/barrel assembly joint. Adjustment entailed tightening three screws just enough to slightly bulge out part of the extension face opposite the screws. Usually a one-eighth turn of each screw was all that was necessary. Many of these old rifles, however, were "over-adjusted" to the point where the screws were forced through the face of the takedown extension.

TAKEDOWN

Lower finger lever (21) and check chamber and magazine to make sure rifle is unloaded. With breechlock open, extend magazine lever (44) and unscrew magazine tube (51) from the extension (17); this lever will have to be worked back and forth on opposite side of the tube to clear the barrel as it is being turned. When threads disengage, pull magazine tube assembly forward, enough to clear receiver (59). Twist barrel assembly ¼-turn counterclockwise and pull barrel assembly forward out of receiver. CAUTION: Make sure action is partially open so that extractor clears slot in barrel before twisting barrel assembly.

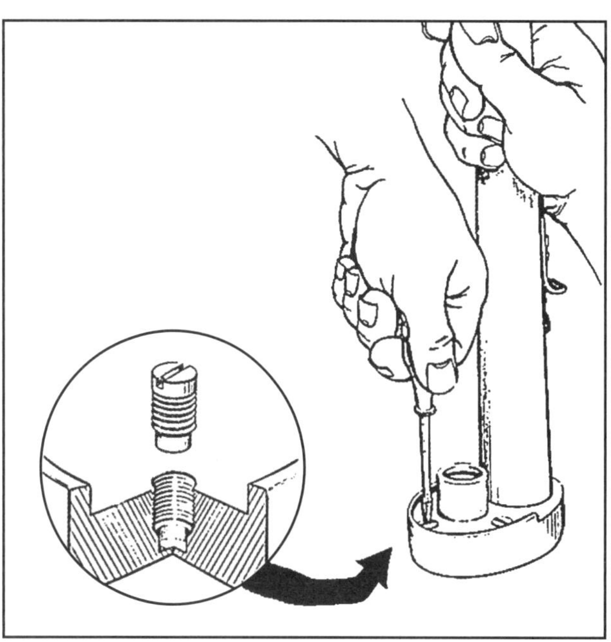

DISASSEMBLY

Buttstock: Remove upper tang screw (70) and lower tang wood screw (42) before removing the buttstock (5) by pulling rearward. If the stock does not slide off the tangs easily, secure the gun by the receiver in a padded vise and pull stock to the rear while striking it at the neck, just ahead of the comb, with the palm and heel of your hand. Remove buttplate screws (4) and buttplate (3).

Magazine: Merely pull entire magazine assembly forward out of fore-end (27). Further disassembly of the magazine tube assembly is accomplished by removing magazine plug screw (49) while keeping thumb pressure on plug so that magazine spring (50) does not fly out. Remove magazine plug (48) while retaining magazine spring until compression is relieved; then withdraw spring and magazine follower (43).

Continue by removing magazine lever screw (45), keeping thumb pressure on the magazine lever to keep from losing its plunger (46) and spring (47).

Fore-end: Remove fore-end tip screws (29), fore-end tip (28) and fore-end (27). Then drift fore-end tenon (30) out from left to right.

Sight: Lift rear-sight tang (54) and remove elevator (57). Drift rear sight from dovetail (l.-r.) with a non-marring punch. To remove front sight (34) on later models with an integral ramp, use a sight press when and where possible, or a drift punch may be used as with the rear sight. However, be careful not to deform or ruin the front sight. On some types of Model 86 sights, a retaining screw must be loosened before drifting out the sight from its dovetail; others merely drift out from left to right.

Receiver: Remove spring-cover screw (61), base (60), and leaf (62). To disassemble, drift out spring cover leaf pin (64) and separate leaf and base. Drift out cover-spring stop pin (65) and lift out spring (63) Note: this spring fits into a recess in the base and may require a lever for removal; if so, proceed carefully to avoid breakage.

WIN. MODEL 1886 TAKEDOWN

DISASSEMBLY CONTINUED

1 Remove mainspring strain screw (53) from lower tang (41); lower hammer (35) and check to see that the mainspring (52) clears the mortise in the lower tang; if not, lever mainspring up to clear and drift out from under retainer.

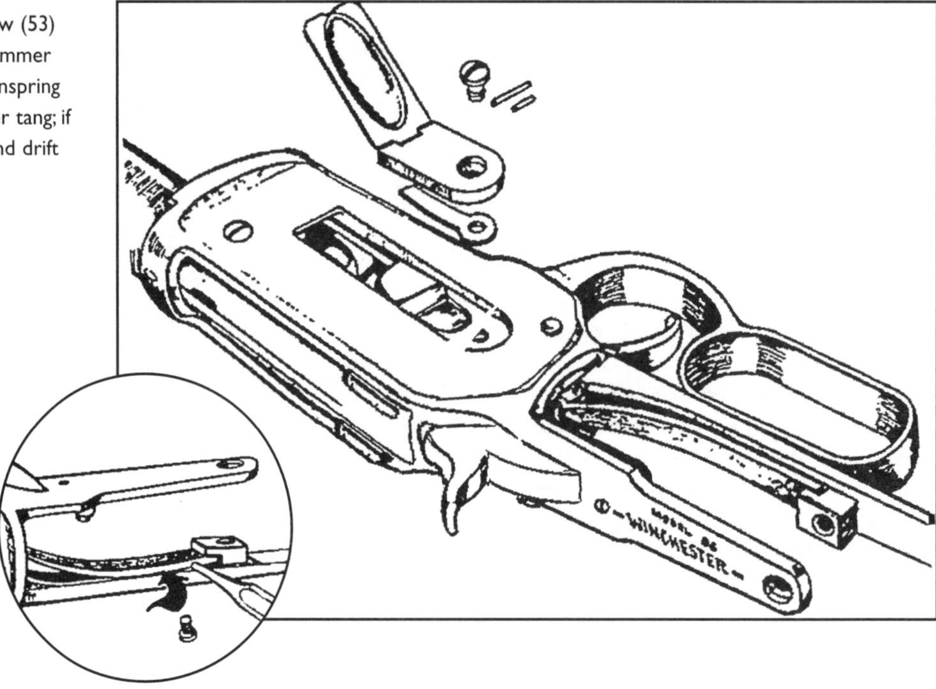

2 Remove hammer screw (36) and lift out hammer through upper tang. If necessary, drift out stirrup pin (38) and remove stirrup (37). The lower tang (41) with trigger assembly can then be pulled from the receiver towards the rear. If much resistance is felt, use a non-marring punch, and tap the lower tang at the receiver end to move it backward. Remove carrier-stop screw (9) and carrier stop (8).

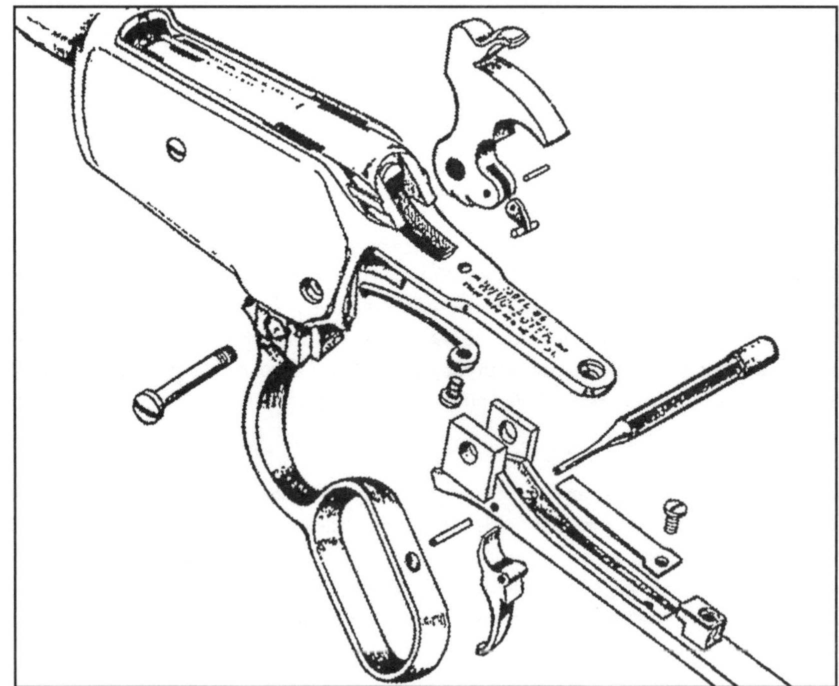

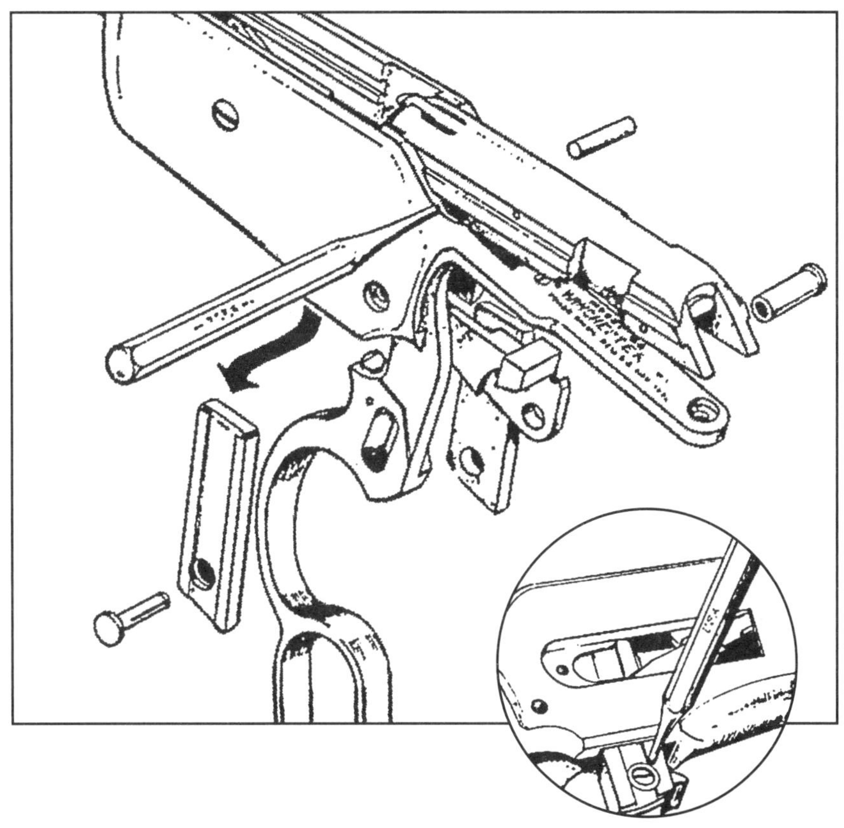

3 Drift out finger-lever bushing pin (23) as shown. NOTE: Split pin has the appearance of a screw, and because its head has the same dimensions as the bushing flange, it may be inverted and consequently the "split pin" may appear on either side of the bolt locking blocks (Fig. 3). Therefore, drift the pin out from the split pin side and remove finger lever bushing

Remove left and right locking blocks (39 & 40). Move breechblock (2) to the rear by lowering the finger lever to expose finger lever connecting pin (24). Drift out connecting pin from left to right. Remove breechblock assembly to the rear; then remove finger lever (21), carrier (6), and carrier hook (7) as an interlocked assembly to the rear and out of the bottom of the receiver.

Remove cartridge stop screw (13) and cartridge stop (12) along with cartridge guide screw (11) and cartridge guide (10).

4 Breechblock and finger lever disassembly: Move ejector (14), ejector spring (16) and ejector collar (15) forward out of the face of the breechblock (2). Drift out extractor pin (20) and lift extractor (19) up and out. Drift out firing pin stop pin (26) and remove firing pin (25) from the rear (Fig. 4).

Drift out friction stud stop pin (33) and remove friction stud (31) and spring (32) from finger lever (Fig. 4, Inset). NOTE: On early models, this friction stud is on the side of the finger lever.

Reassemble in reverse order.

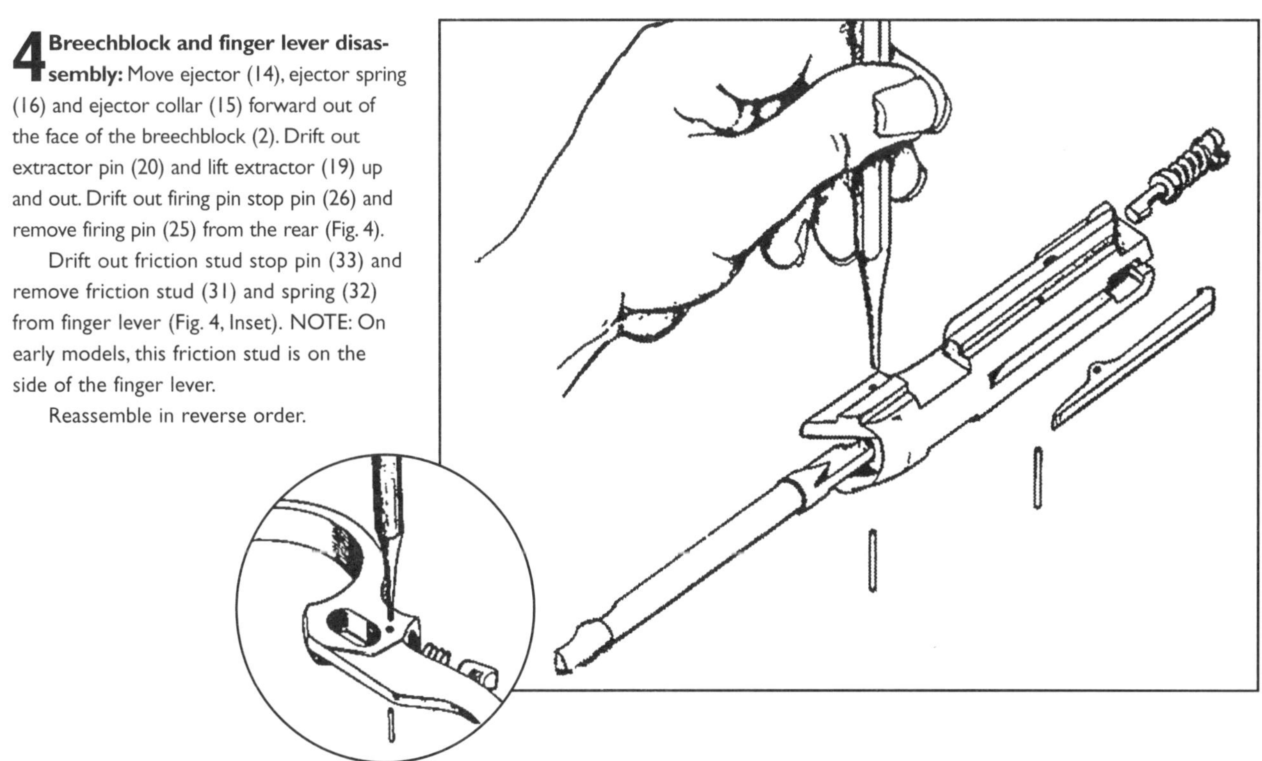

WINCHESTER MODEL 1892 RIFLE

PARTS LEGEND

1. Receiver
2. Barrel
3. Rear sight assembly
4. Front sight
5. Front sight screw
6. Upper tang plug screw
7. Forearm tip tenon
8. Magazine ring
9. Magazine ring pin
10. Forearm tip
11. Forearm tip screws (2)
12. Magazine tube
13. Magazine spring
14. Magazine plug
15. Magazine plug screw
16. Magazine follower
17. Spring cover
18. Spring cover screw
19. Cartridge guide, left
20. Cartridge stop
21. Cartridge stop joint pin
22. Cartridge stop spring
23. Cartridge guide
24. Cartridge guide, right
25. Upper tang screw
26. Breechbolt assembly (see Fig. 1)
27. Lever & breechbolt pin
28. Hammer
29. Stirrup
30. Stirrup pin
31. Hammer screw
32. Lower tang
33. Trigger spring
34. Trigger spring screw
35. Trigger
36. Trigger pin
37. Mainspring
38. Mainspring screw
39. Mainspring strain screw
40. Locking bolt, right
41. Locking bolt, left
42. Locking bolt pin
43. Locking bolt pin stop screw
44. Finger lever
45. Friction stud
46. Friction stud spring
47. Friction stud stop pin
48. Carrier
49. Carrier stop
50. Carrier stop spring
51. Carrier stop pin
52. Carrier screws (2)
53. Lever & breechblock pin hole plug screw

Note: Buttstock, buttplate & screws, and forearm are not shown.

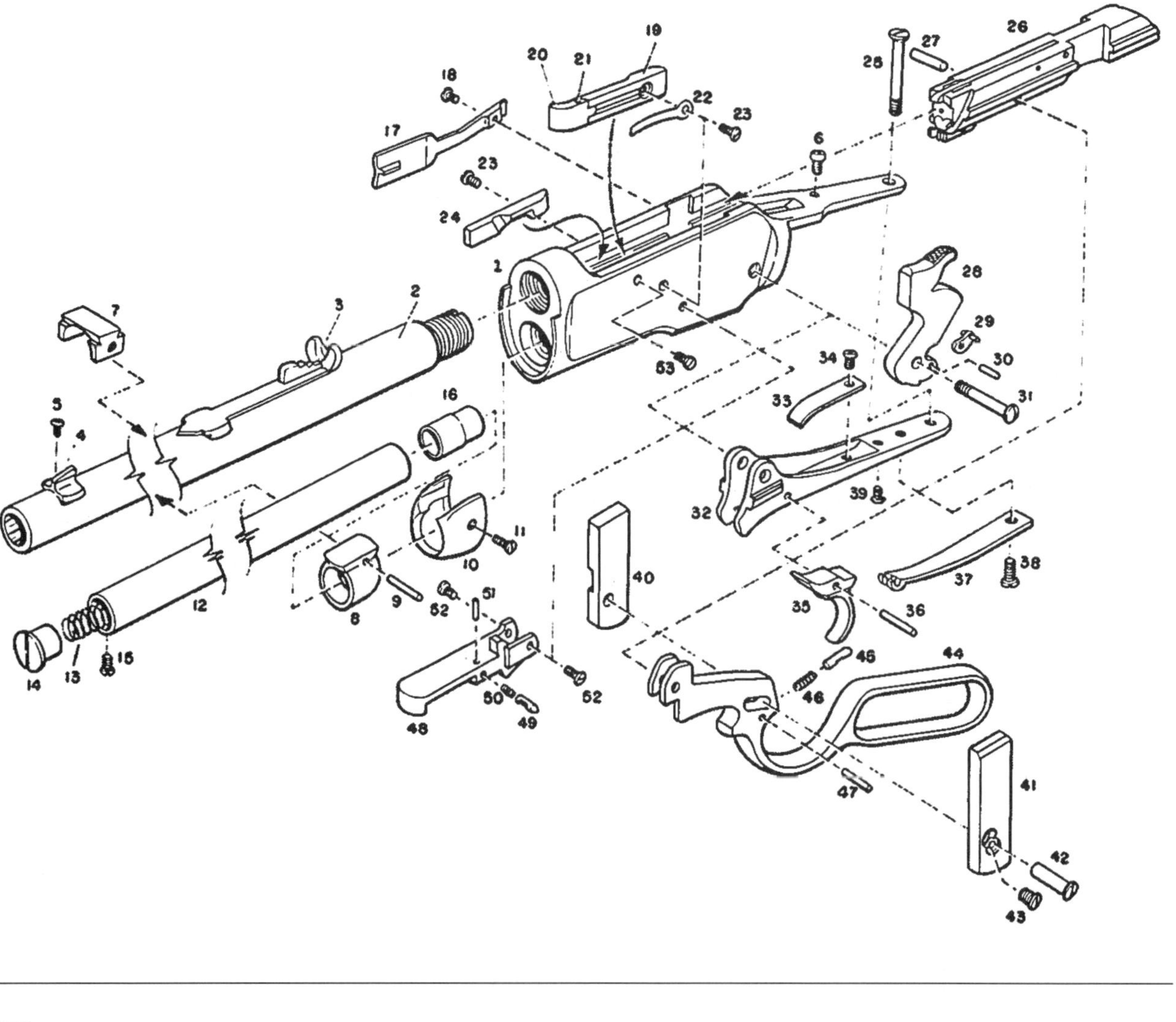

The Winchester Model 1892 lever-action rifle was designed by John M. Browning. It is essentially a scaled-down and somewhat simplified version of the Winchester Model 1886 rifle, also invented by Browning. The Model 1892 was manufactured in sporting rifle, carbine, and musket styles and was chambered for the .44-40, .38-40, .32-20, and .25-20 Winchester center-fire cartridges. The takedown version was first offered in 1893. Set triggers (single-set or double-set) could be had on special order. Extras, including longer than standard barrels, shotgun buttstock, pistol grip stock, etc., were also furnished at extra cost.

Despite the relatively low power of the cartridges for which it was chambered, the Model 1892 proved extremely popular. About 735,000 of this model had been sold by the end of 1914. Near the end of its manufacture it was redesignated Model 92. Manufacture of the Model 1892 in rifle form was discontinued in 1932, but it was made in carbine version until 1941.

DISASSEMBLY

Check action to be sure rifle is unloaded. Remove upper tang screw (25) and remove buttstock to rear by rapping it sharply with heel of hand to loosen. Unscrew magazine plug screw (15) and pull magazine plug (14) out front end of magazine tube (12). Draw magazine spring (13) and follower (16) out front of magazine tube. Remove forearm tip screws (11) from both sides of forearm tip (10). Drift magazine ring pin (9) out of magazine ring (8). Draw magazine tube (12) away from receiver to front, separating magazine tube and wooden forearm and removing forearm tip from tube.

To disassemble action, open finger lever (44) and remove mainspring screw (38) and mainspring (37). Remove hammer screw (31) and remove hammer (28) from top of receiver (1). Lower tang (32) may be slid out of its grooves to rear.

With finger lever (44) partially opened. Remove slocking bolt pin stop screw (43) and drift locking bolt pin (42) out of locking bolts from right to left. Draw right and left locking bolts (40, 41) down out of receiver. With finger lever closed and bolt in its foremost locked position, remove plug screw (53) from left side of receiver and drift lever and breechbolt pin (27) out of breechbolt (26) from right to left using a suitable punch inserted through hole in right side of receiver. Remove finger lever (44) and draw breechbolt assembly (26) out of receiver to rear.

Remove carrier screws (52) from either side of receiver. Slide carrier (48) to rear and down out of receiver.

Cartridge guides (24, 19) can be removed from inside walls of receiver by unscrewing cartridge guide screws (23). Spring cover is removed by removing cover screw (18) from right of receiver.

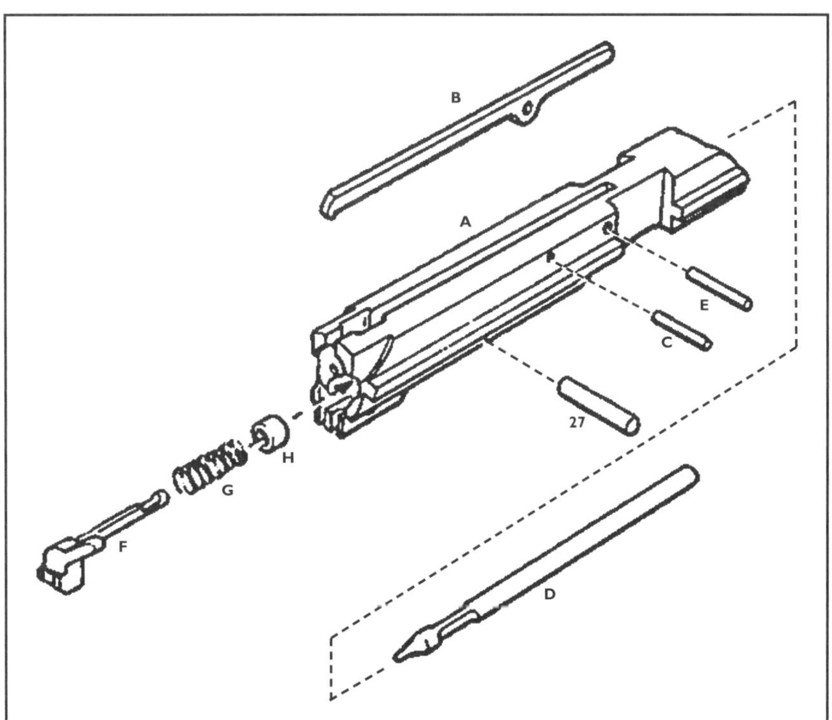

A. Breechbolt
B. Extractor
C. Extractor pin
D. Firing pin
E. Firing pin stop pin
F. Ejector
G. Ejector spring
H. Ejector collar

Note: The ejector guide and ejector guide pins are not shown as separate parts. They are contained on the underside of the breechbolt at its front end. Disassembly of ejector guide is seldom necessary and is not recommended.

Bolt assembly: After removing breech bolt from receiver, disassembly of all components is accomplished by removing the pins C and E. Ejector parts are pulled forward out of breechbolt after removing breechbolt from receiver.

WINCHESTER MODEL 1895 RIFLE

PARTS LEGEND

1. Rear sight elevator
2. Rear sight
3. Barrel
4. Bead front sight
5. Forearm stud
6. Forearm
7. Forearm screw
8. Breechbolt
9. Ejector pin
10. Extractor
11. Ejector
12. Ejector spring
13. Firing lever pin
14. Extractor pin
15. Firing pin recoil lock spring
16. Firing pin recoil lock spring screw
17. Firing pin
18. Firing pin recoil lock
19. Firing pin lock
20. Firing pin lock pin
21. Receiver
22. Carrier screw
23. Sear spring
24. Mainspring
25. Hammer
26. Hammer roller pin
27. Hammer roller
28. Mainspring screw
29. Sear spring screw
30. Sear
31. Sear pin
32. Magazine tip screw(s)
33. Carrier spring
34. Carrier
35. Carrier cam lever
36. Carrier cradle
37. Carrier cradle pin
38. Carrier cam lever pin
39. Locking bolt
40. Cartridge stop
41. Cartridge stop pins (2)
42. Finger lever catch
43. Finger lever catch plunger
44. Finger lever catch plunger spring
45. Trigger
46. Finger lever catch pin
47. Trigger pin
48. Link
49. Magazine
50. Carrier stop pin
51. Finger lever
52. Finger lever link pin
53. Finger lever lock joint pin
54. Finger lever lock plunger spring
55. Finger lever lock plunger
56. Finger lever lock
57. Buttstock
58. Buttplate
59. Buttplate screws (2)
60. Mainspring strain screw
61. Tang screw
62. Hammer screw

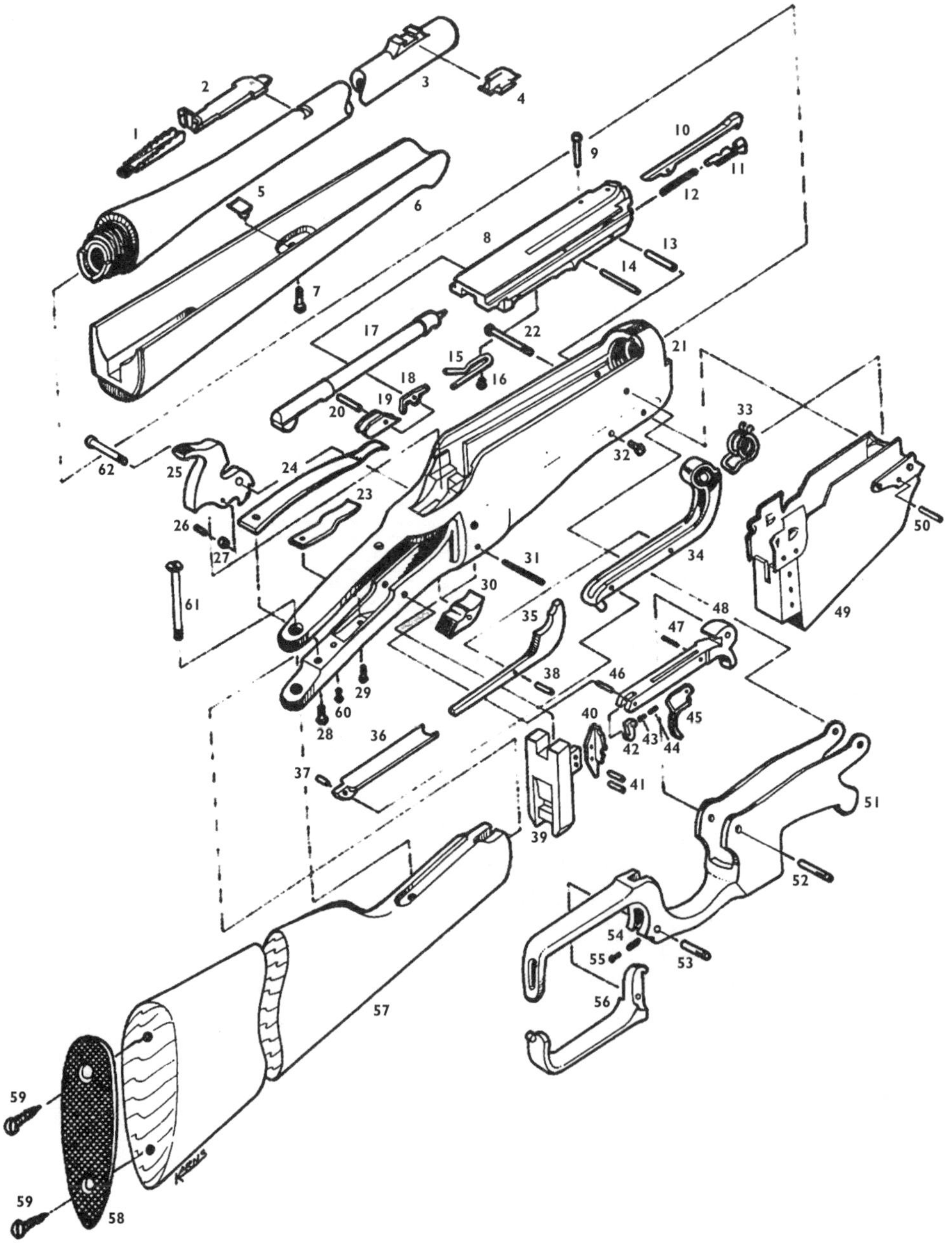

The Winchester Model 95 was first manufactured in February, 1896, and was the first lever-action rifle using a non-detachable box magazine that was designed to handle jacketed, sharp-nosed bullets. It is loaded by pushing the cartridges into the box magazine from the top. The cartridges are held in single column in the magazine and are raised to loading position by spring pressure under the magazine follower.

In the December, 1896, Winchester Repeating Arms Co. catalog, the Model 95 was offered in sporting rifle, carbine and military musket versions, chambered for the .30 U.S. Army (.30- 40 Krag), .38-72 or .40-72 cartridges. A .236 U.S. Navy (6mm) chambered musket was also listed, but apparently was never actually manufactured.

About 5000 early models differed from later models in that they had flat-sided receivers, one-piece finger levers and other minor differences such as V carrier springs instead of the coil type found in later models. In addition to the calibers listed above, the Model 95 eventually was made in .35 Win., .405 Win., .30-03, .30-06, .303 British and 7.62 mm Russian cals.

The .30-06 chambering was discontinued shortly after World War I due to rumors that the action was not strong enough to handle this cartridge. Winchester's investigations, however, suggested that the wrecked rifles examined failed from firing war souvenir 8mm Mauser cartridges in the .30-06-chambered rifles.

The Winchester Model 95 in solid frame and takedown versions were favorite hunting arms among both North American and African big game hunters, and President Theodore Roosevelt especially liked it for lions. Its greatest use, however, was by the Imperial Russian government, for which Winchester made over a quarter of a million 7.62mm muskets in 1915-16. These were equipped with clip guide slots and Winchester-made bayonets.

Final production of the Model 95 took place in 1931, though some guns were sold as late as 1938. Including the Russian order, more than 425,000 model 95s were manufactured.

DISASSEMBLY

Remove the forearm screw (7) and the forearm (6). Remove tang screw (61) and buttstock (57). Open the finger lever (51) and remove the carrier screw (22) and magazine tip screw (32) from the forward end of the frame (21). Remove the magazine (49) with its enclosed carrier (34) and take out the mainspring strain screw (60). Then, remove the mainspring screw (28) and mainspring (24). Close the lever (51), and then remove the hammer screw (62) and finally the hammer (25).

Remove the pin stop screw (not shown) from upper left side of receiver and drive out (from right to left) the finger lever pin (13) from the forward hole in the right side of the frame. Remove finger lever link pin (52) and the link pin (46) (finger lever catch pin on later models); this is the pin that connects the link and the lower tang and also serves to hold the finger lever catch in place. The finger lever (51), link (48) and trigger (45) can then be removed together.

Unscrew the sear spring screw (29) — the forward screw on the bottom of the tang — and drift out (l. to r.) the sear pin (31). Next remove the locking bolt (39) and the breechbolt (8). Further disassembly is not usually necessary or recommended.

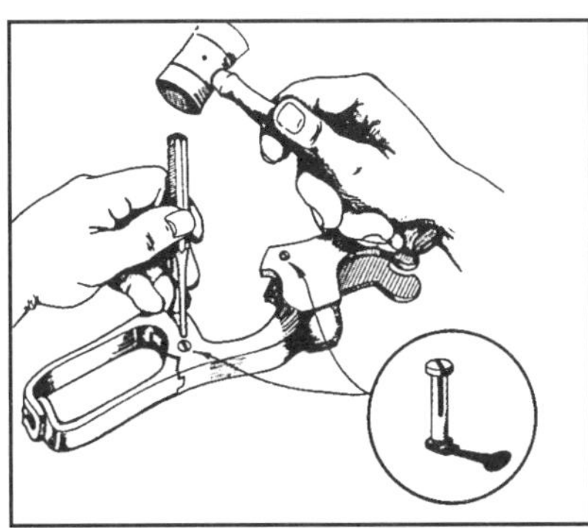

The finger lever link pin (52) and the finger lever lock joint pin (53) may look like screw heads, but they require a punch for removal.

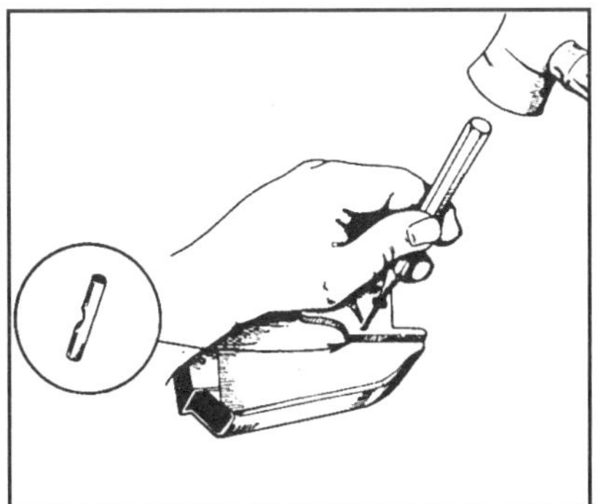

The carrier stop pin (50) holds the carrier assembly in place. It must be punched out to permit removal of internal magazine pieces.

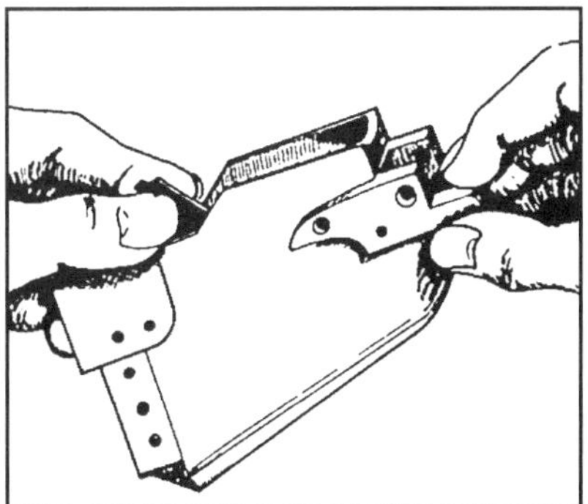

The magazine carrier simply lifts out after removing the stop pin (50). Some rifles use a V carrier spring and don t include this pin.

WINCHESTER MODEL 1897 SHOTGUN

PARTS LEGEND

1. Barrel
2. Magazine band bushing
3. Magazine band bushing screw (2)
4. Magazine band
5. Extension
6. Adjusting sleeve
7. Barrel chamber ring
8. Adjusting sleeve lock screw
9. Adjusting sleeve lock
10. Magazine plug screw (2)
11. Magazine plug
12. Magazine locking pin
13. Magazine locking pin spring
14. Magazine plug stop
15. Action slide sleeve screw cap
16. Action slide spring
17. Action slide
18. Magazine tube
19. Magazine follower
20. Magazine spring
21. Action slide lock release plunger pin spring
22. Action slide lock release plunger pin
23. Cartridge guide stop screw
24. Trigger pin
25. Cartridge stop spring (2)
26. Left cartridge stop
27. Right cartridge stop
28. Cartridge stop screw, left
29. Cartridge stop screw, right
30. Action slide hook
31. Firing pin lock screw
32. Extractor, left
33. Extractor pin, left
34. Extractor plunger, right
35. Extractor plunger spring, right
36. Extractor, right
37. Action slide hook screw
38. Firing pin lock spring
39. Firing pin stop pin
40. Breech bolt
41. Firing pin
42. Firing pin lock
43. Trigger
44. Guard bow
45. Trigger stop screw
46. Trigger spring
47. Buttstock bolt
48. Buttstock bolt washer
49. Receiver shank
50. Carrier pin
51. Receiver
52. Ejector spring
53. Ejector spring screw
54. Barrel chamber ring retaining screw (2)
55. Sear spring screw
56. Sear spring
57. Cartridge guide rivet
58. Cartridge guide
59. Mainspring
60. Mainspring pin
61. Cartridge guide friction spring
62. Hammer pin
63. Action slide lack release plunger
64. Sear pin
65. Sear
66. Hammer stirrup pin
67. Hammer stirrup
68. Carrier
69. Carrier pin stop screw
70. Action slide lock spring
71. Action slide lock
72. Action slide lock joint pin stop screw
73. Action slide lack joint pin
74. Action slide lock spring screw
75. Mainspring strain screw
76. Ejector pin
77. Extension stop screw
78. Front sight
79. Buttplate screw (2)
80. Buttplate
81. Hammer

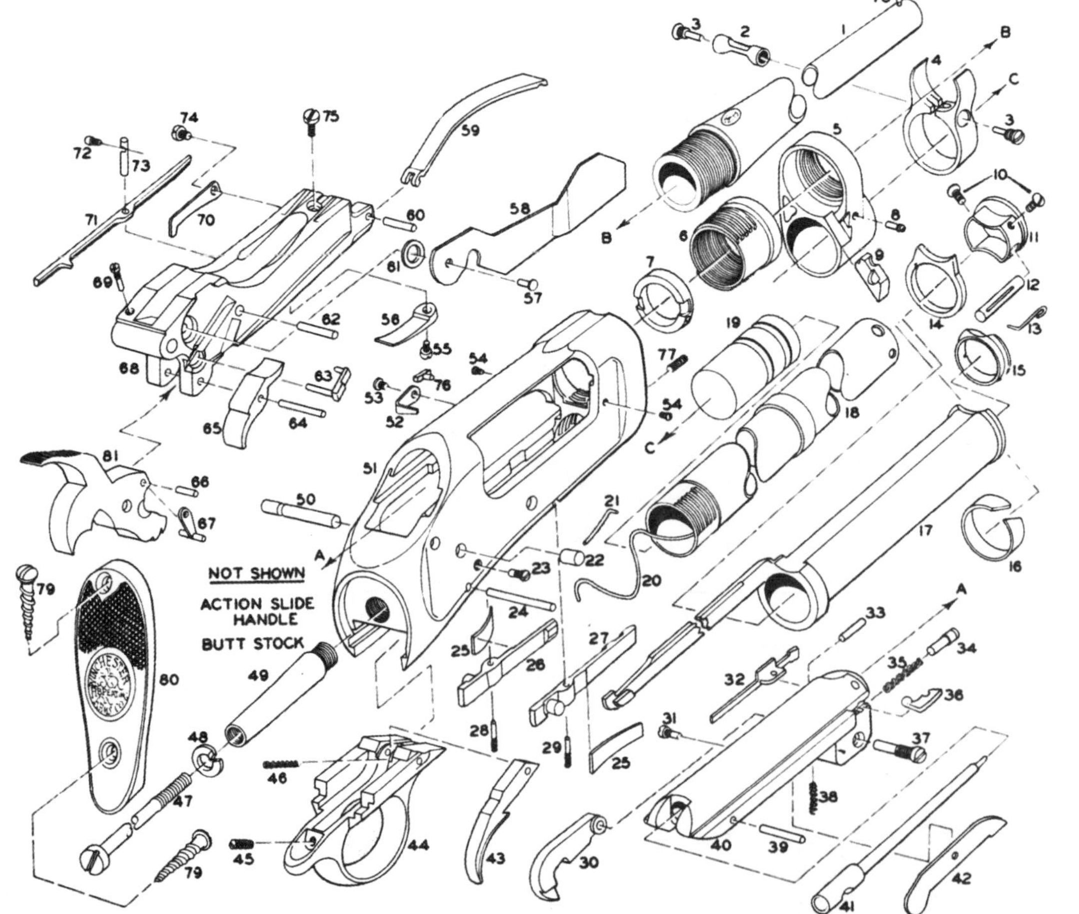

In 1890 Winchester Repeating Arms purchased a patent from the Browning brothers, covering a slide-action shotgun with visible hammer and side ejection. In June 1893 this shotgun was marketed as the Winchester Repeating Shotgun Model 1893. The Model 1893 proved unsatisfactory for use with smokeless powder shells and was discontinued in 1897.

In November 1897 Winchester offered an improved version of this shotgun designated Model 1897. Initial offering was in 12-gauge, solid frame only. The takedown model in 12-gauge was added in 1898, followed by a 16-gauge takedown in 1900. Various other grades and types were introduced, including the 12-gauge "Trench" or combat shotgun issued to U.S. troops during World War I. This unique 20-inch barrel shotgun had a perforated metal barrel jacket and was adapted for a bayonet.

Until 1914 Damascus barrels were available at extra cost for the Model 1897. Serial numbers were a continuation of the Model 1893 series, with the first Model 1897 gun bearing the number 34151. Manufacture of the Model 1897 was discontinued in 1957 with serial number 1024700.

DISASSEMBLY

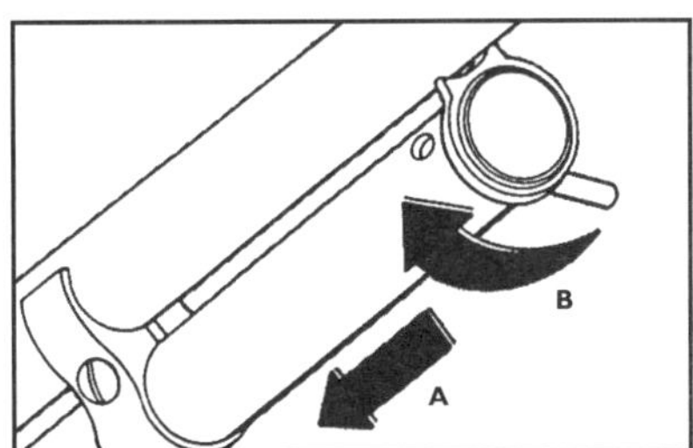

1 Push (A) the magazine locking pin (12) through the magazine tube (18) and pull it out until it stops. Using the magazine locking pin, rotate the magazine tube about 90° left until it stops. Pull out the magazine tube toward the front until it stops (B).

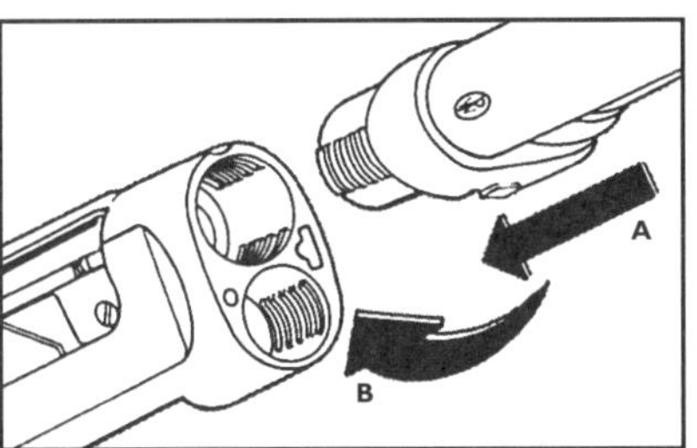

2 Move the action slide assembly (17) forward until it stops and rotate the barrel (1) and magazine tube (18) 90° left until it stops (A). Interrupted screw threads will disengage and release the barrel assembly from the receiver assembly. Remove the barrel, magazine and action slide assembly toward the front (B).

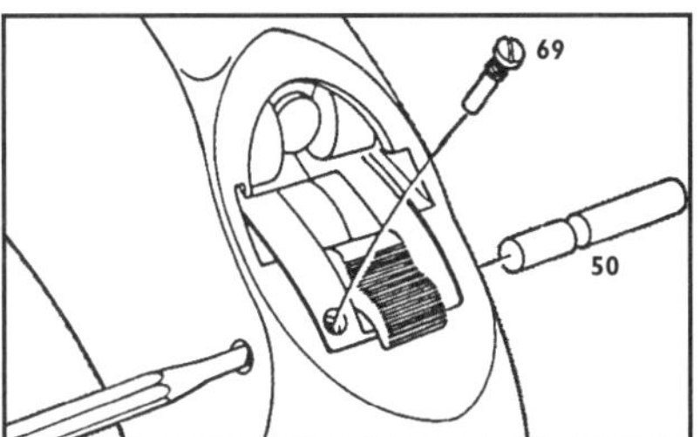

3 To continue disassembly remove carrier pin stop screw (69), dropping hammer, and pushing down carrier. Cock hammer, and drift out carrier pin 150). Remove cartridge guide stop screw (23), and entire carrier assembly may be lifted away from bottom of receiver.

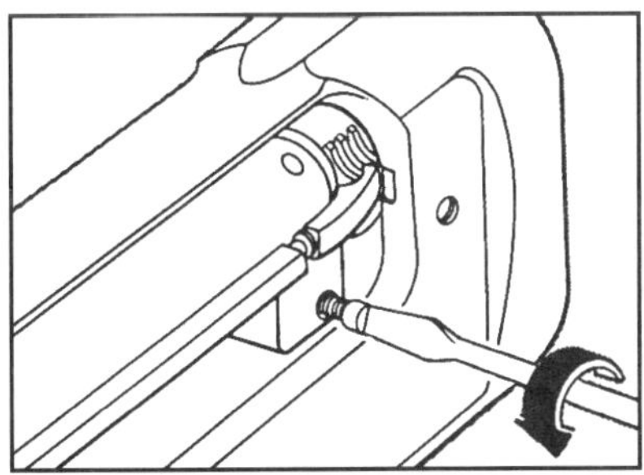

4 Disengage breech bolt (40) from action slide hook (30) by unscrewing action slide hook screw (37). Breech bolt together with action slide hook may now be removed, breech bolt from rear of receiver and hook from side or bottom.

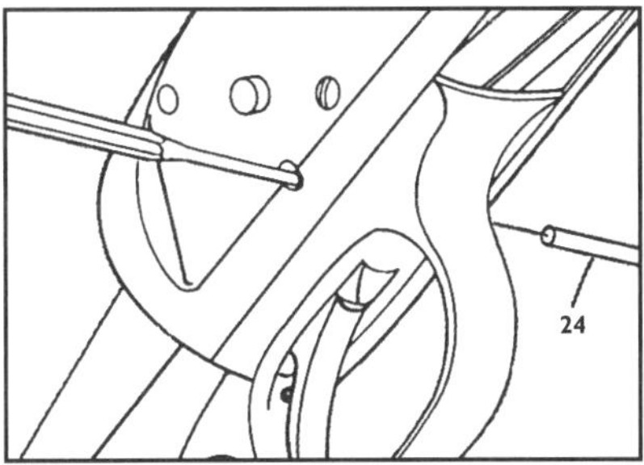

5 Remove 2 buttplate screws (79) and buttplate (80). Using a long-shanked screwdriver, remove buttstock bolt (47) and buttstock boltwasher (48). Then, with a flat-nosed punch, drift out trigger pin (24). Remove guard bow (44) and assembly from back end of receiver.

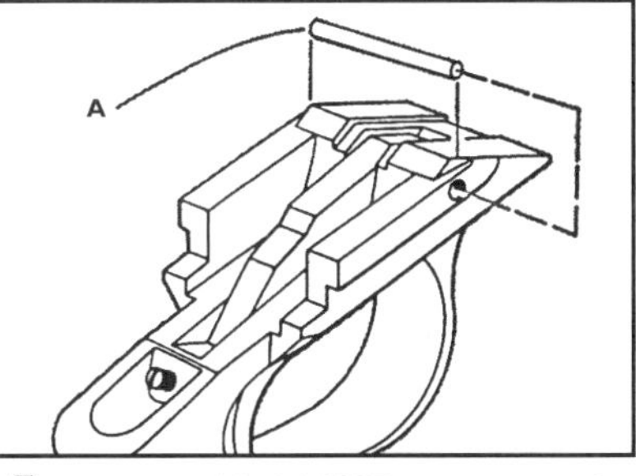

6 Reassemble Model 1897 in reverse order. When reassembling trigger (43) and trigger spring (46), use a piece of smooth nail (A) as a temporary trigger pin. Cut it to width of guard bow as shown. When this assembly is replaced in receiver and trigger pin reinserted, it will drive out slave pin. This reassembly knack will facilitate operation.

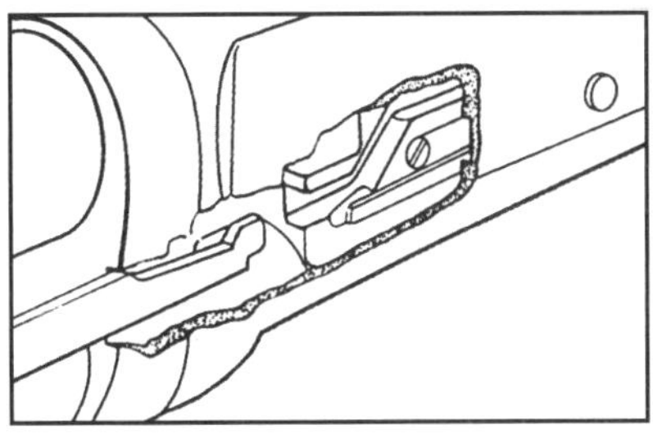

7 Assembly of Model 1897 from fieldtakedown is a bit more tricky than disassembly. First insure that breech bolt (40) is in battery and carrier (68) is fully up. This will align actuating grave an left side of carrier with corresponding notch an arm of action slide (17). Cutaway shows action slide arm just prior to engaging groove.

WINCHESTER MODEL 1904 RIFLE

PARTS LEGEND

1. Receiver/barrel
2. Bolt body
3. Firing pin
4. Mainspring
5. Bolt cocking knob
6. Bolt head pin
7. Bolt body pin
8. Sear/extractor
9. Trigger
10. Trigger pin
11. Sear spring
12. Barrel/stock mounting stud
13. Stock
14. Barrel/stock screw
15. Stock bushing
16. Trigger guard
17. Trigger guard screws
18. Rear sight
19. Rear sight elevation screw
20. Front sight
21. Buttplate
22. Buttplate screws (2)
23. Buttstock sling stud
24. Barrel sling stud

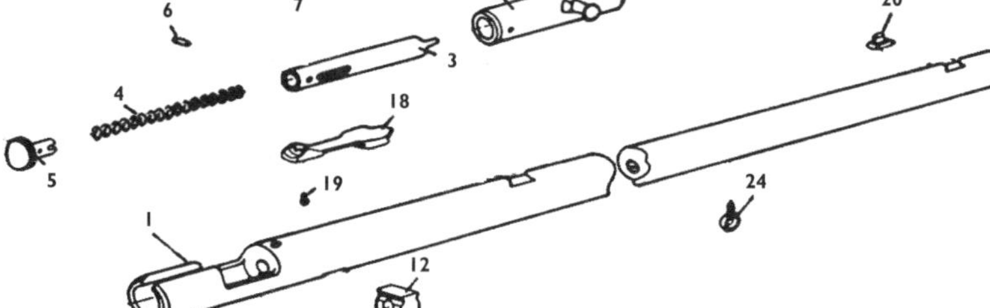

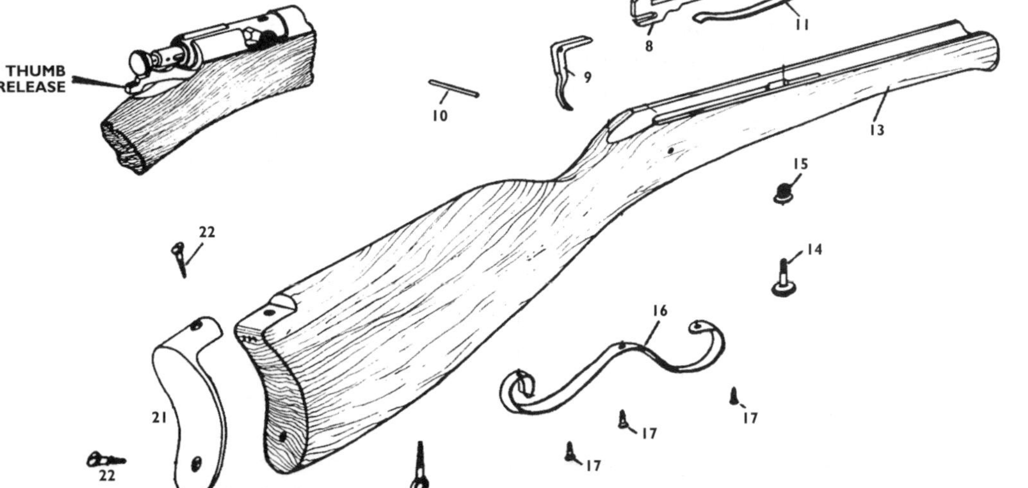

The Model 1900, a John M. Browning design, was Winchester's first venture into the low-priced .22 rimfire market. In the course of manufacture, Browning's design was modified to reduce costs. The Model 1900 is a simple bolt-action rifle, cocked by pulling back on the firing pin head. It was only moderately successful, being too light and lacking the quality to compete on the market. Just over 100,000 were sold.

Winchester redesigned and upgraded the basic components and reintroduced this design as the Model 1902. This model was a great improvement over the Model 1900 and was met with considerably more acceptance. The 1902 was discontinued in 1931 after a production of approximately 640,300.

The final variation, the Winchester Model 1904, was introduced between 1904 and 1931 with 302,850 rifles produced.

An interesting variation was the introduction in 1904 of the Model 99 "Thumb Trigger," (see insert in exploded view). The trigger, including the sear and extractor, was extended rearward beneath the head of the firing pin. The rifle could be fired by pressing the knurled trigger top with the thumb. It was claimed that with this style of trigger the shooter would not throw the gun off target. This model was discontinued in 1923 with approximately 75,400 produced.

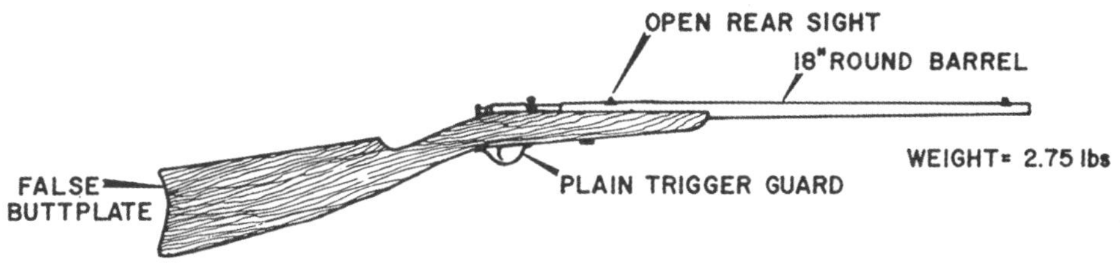

OPEN REAR SIGHT
18" ROUND BARREL
WEIGHT= 2.75 lbs
FALSE BUTTPLATE
PLAIN TRIGGER GUARD

WINCHESTER Model 1900, Cal. .22 Short & .22 Long, Discontinued 1902

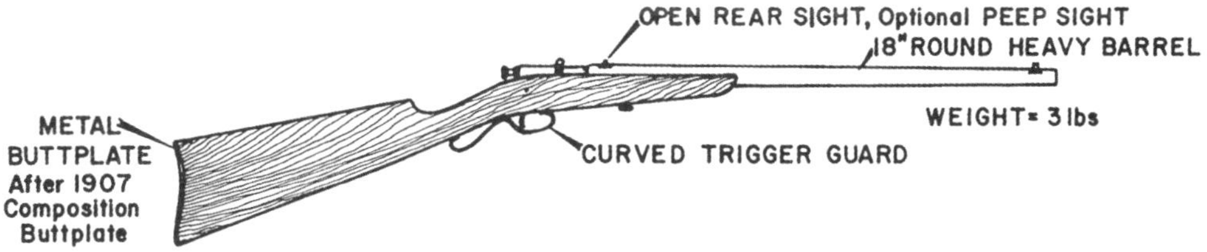

OPEN REAR SIGHT, Optional PEEP SIGHT
18" ROUND HEAVY BARREL
WEIGHT= 3 lbs
METAL BUTTPLATE After 1907 Composition Buttplate
CURVED TRIGGER GUARD

WINCHESTER Model 1902, Cal. .22 S, .22 L, .22 L.R, Discontinued 1931

OPEN REAR SIGHT W/Elevation Screw
21" ROUND HEAVY BARREL
KNOB FORE ARM
METAL BUTTPLATE After 1925 Hard Rubber Buttplate
FULL PISTOL GRIP TRIGGER GUARD
WEIGHT= 4 lbs
CURVED STOCK– BUTT

WINCHESTER Model 1904, Cal. .22S, .22L, .22L.R, Discontinued 1931

DISASSEMBLY

1 Check rifle to ensure that it is unloaded. Loosen barrel stock screw (14), lift barrel-receiver assembly up and forward from stock, and remove.

Pull Barrel Assembly Up And Out Of Stock
Loosen Barrel-Stock Screw

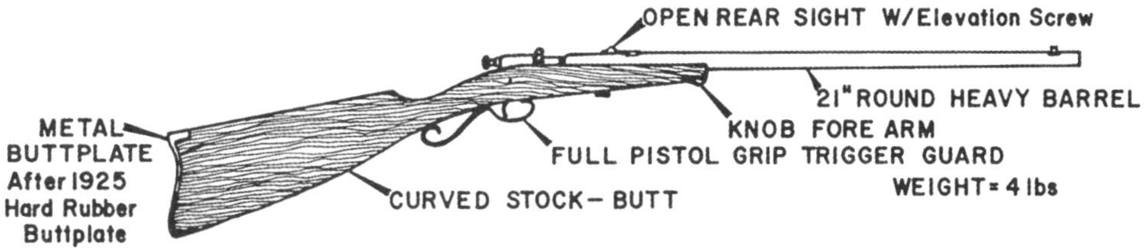

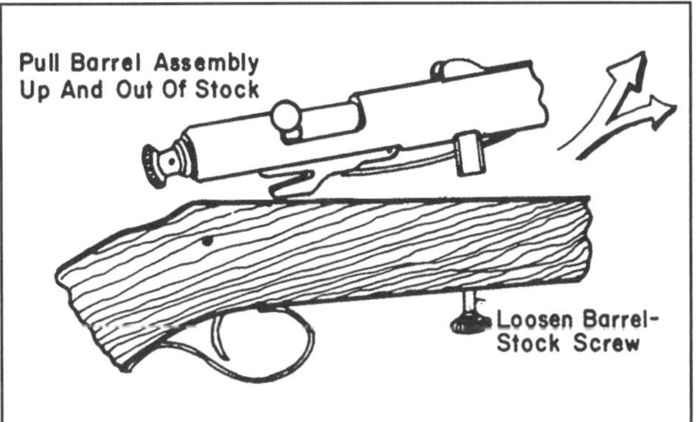

2 Lift bolt handle and slide bolt halfway from receiver; pull down sear extractor (8), and pull bolt assembly rearward and out of receiver section.

Pull Out Bolt Assembly
Pull Down Sear-Extractor

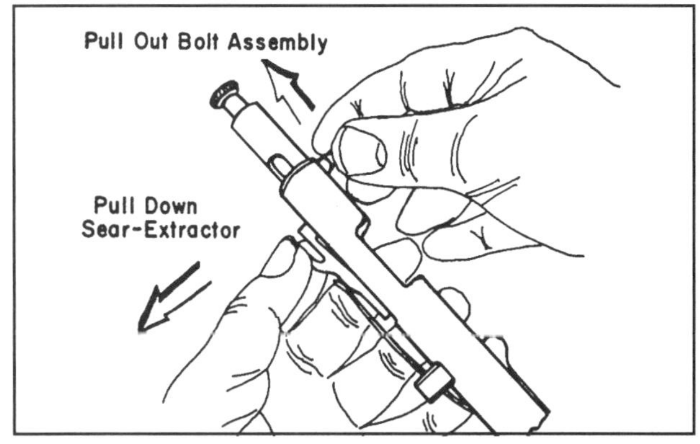

To disassemble bolt, drive out pin (7) from bolt body; remove firing pin assembly. Drive out pin (6) to remove bolt head (5) and mainspring (4).

To remove sear extractor (8), lift up sear spring (11) and pull out sear extractor (8). Slide out sear spring (11) from barrel stud (12).

To remove trigger (9), drive out trigger pin (10) from stock (13), lift out trigger. All other parts are readily dissasembled.

WINCHESTER MODEL 1905 RIFLE

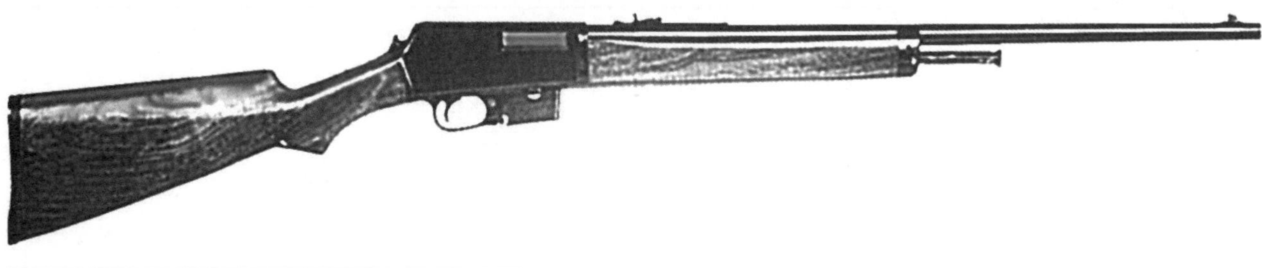

PARTS LEGEND

1. Front sight
2. Barrel
3. Rear sight
4. Sight elevator
5. Ejector
6. Receiver
7. Steel buffer washers
8. Fiber buffer washers
9. Bolt guide rod
10. Recoil spring
11. Operating sleeve tip
12. Tip pin
13. Operating sleeve
14. Forearm screw
15. Forearm tip
16. Operating sleeve spring
17. Bolt
18. Extractor
19. Extractor Plunger Stop screw
20. Forearm
21. Extractor spring
22. Extractor plunger
23. Firing pin retainer pin
24. Firing pin spring
25. Firing pin
26. Hammer
27. Hammer strut pin
28. Hammer strut
29. Hammer spring
30. Buttstock
31. Butt cap
32. Buttstock bolt and washer
33. Buttplate
34. Takedown screw
35. Screw Stop pin
36. Take down screw lock
37. Trigger mechanism housing
38. Trigger spring
39. Magazine
40. Safety catch
41. Trigger pin
42. Disconnector
43. Sear
44. Trigger
45. Sear spring
46. Hammer pin
47. Magazine catch spring
48. Safety catch plunger
49. Plunger spring
50. Disconnector spring retainer
51. Disconnector spring
52. Magazine catch screw
53. Magazine catch

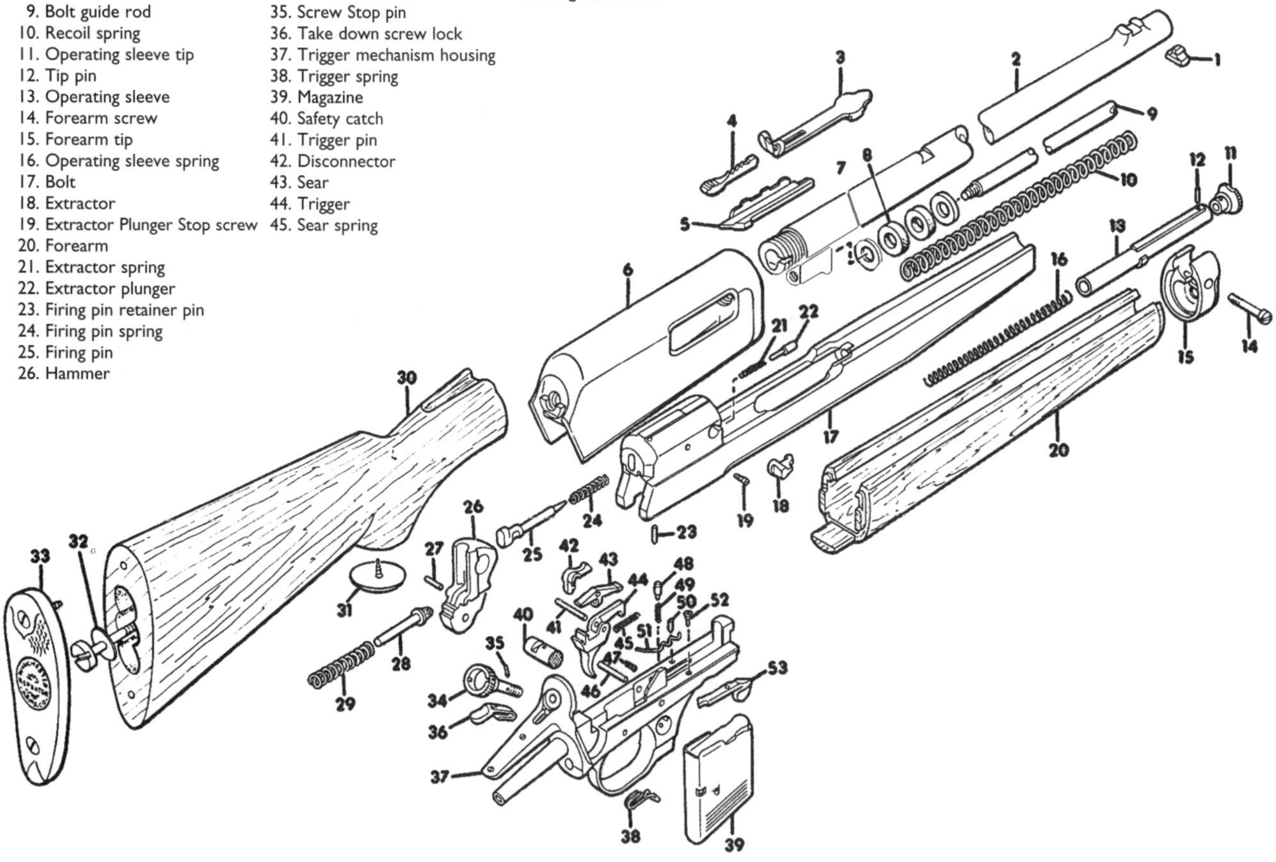

Introduced in 1905, the Winchester Model 1905 self-loading rifle was developed by Thomas C. Johnson, a Winchester engineer. Featuring a simple, blowback-operated mechanism, the Model 1905 was designed for the .32 and .35 Winchester self-loading smokeless cartridges.

The Model 1905 rifle was discontinued in 1920 after more than 29,000 had been manufactured. A 22-inch round barrel was standard on this rifle and both 5-shot and 10-shot detachable box magazines were available. The Model 1905 was the first Winchester rifle of self-loading type to be chambered for center-fire cartridges, and was also the first Winchester rifle to feature a detachable box magazine.

DISASSEMBLY

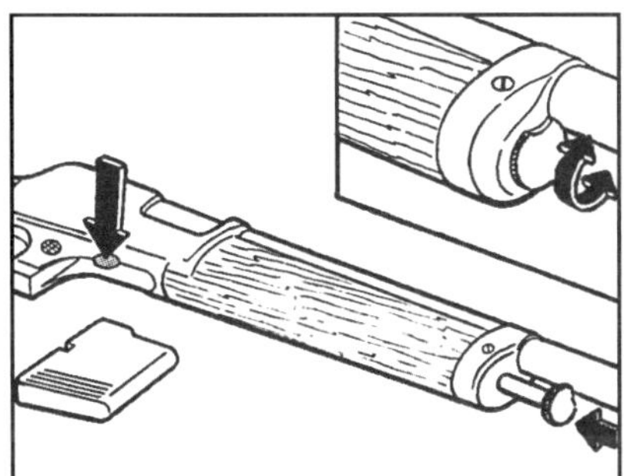

1 To disassemble the Model 1905, first remove the magazine (39). Then push back on the operating sleeve (13) projecting from the end of the forearm. This clears the chamber and cocks the hammer (26). Ease the operating sleeve forward to close the bolt (17). If the gun is to be cleaned, turn the operating sleeve tip (11) either left or right while the sleeve is depressed. This locks the bolt open.

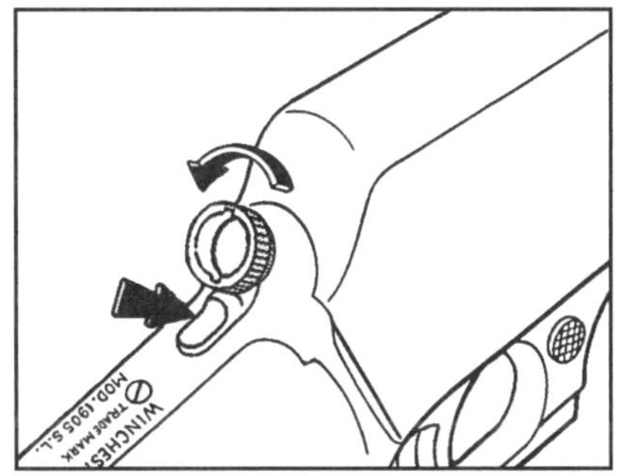

2 To further disassemble, press on the takedown screw lock (36) and turn the takedown screw (34) in the direction shown. When it is free of the threads, pull the barrel and frame straight forward and the buttstock and trigger assembly then pulls away from the barrel and receiver. The hammer should be cocked when reassembling the butt section to the receiver.

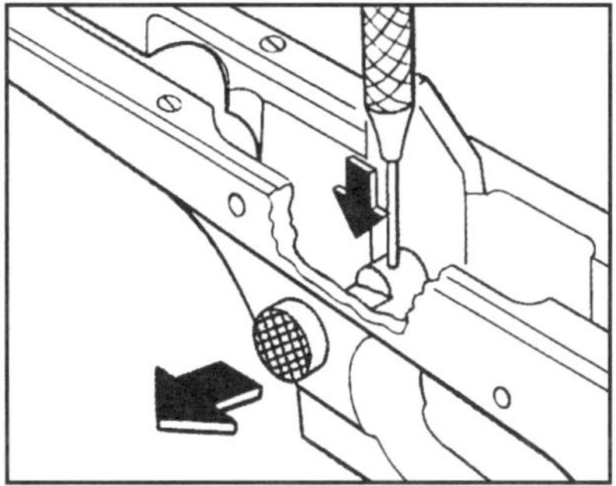

3 The safety catch (40) is retained by the plunger spring (49) and safety catch plunger (48). To remove the safety catch, insert a punch or nail in the hole in the safety catch. Press the safety catch plunger downward and at the same time push the safety catch out from right to left. All other pins must be driven out from left to right.

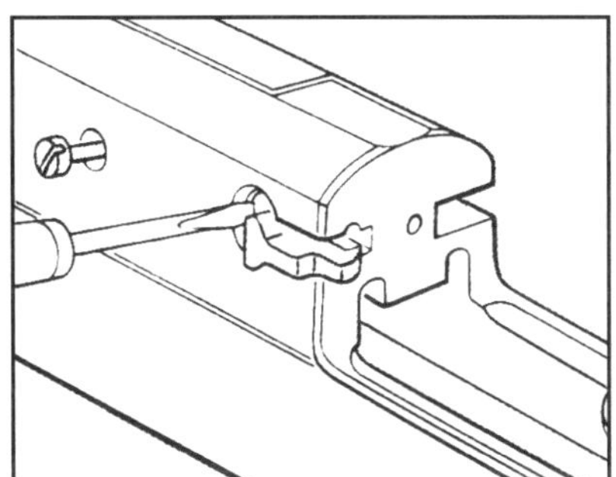

4 The extractor is retained by the extractor spring (21) and extractor plunger (22). To remove the extractor, first take out the extractor plunger stop screw (19). Then insert a thin screwdriver between the extractor and extractor plunger. Push back the extractor plunger as far as possible and lift out the extractor (18).

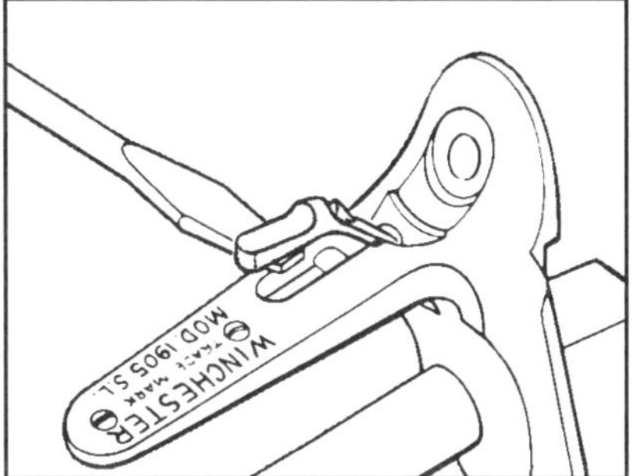

5 To remove the takedown screw (34), drive out the screw stop pin (35) just above the threads on the takedown screw and remove it from the trigger mechanism housing (37). Takedown screw lock (36) can then be removed by prying it out carefully, as shown, with a screwdriver.

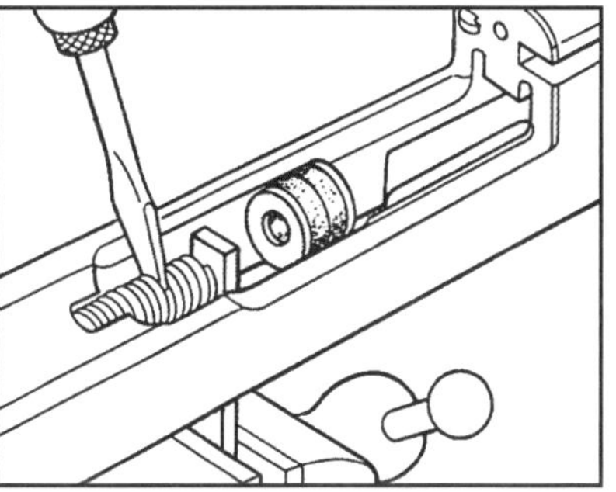

6 Do not remove the recoil spring (10) and bolt guide rod (9) from the buffer assembly unless it is necessary. If removed, reassemble by first inserting the recoil spring and bolt guide rod in the bolt (17). Clamp a rectangular piece of steel in a vise and push back on the recoil spring and bolt guide rod. Insert the buffers with steel washers (7) on the outside. Ease the recoil spring and bolt guide rod up to the washers. Be sure the bolt guide rod is up against the steel bar so the recoil spring does not slip off the bolt guide rod and kink. Hold back the recoil spring with a screwdriver and ease out the steel bar. When the recoil spring is against the washers, push the bolt guide rod through the buffers and screw into place.

WINCHESTER MODEL 1907 RIFLE

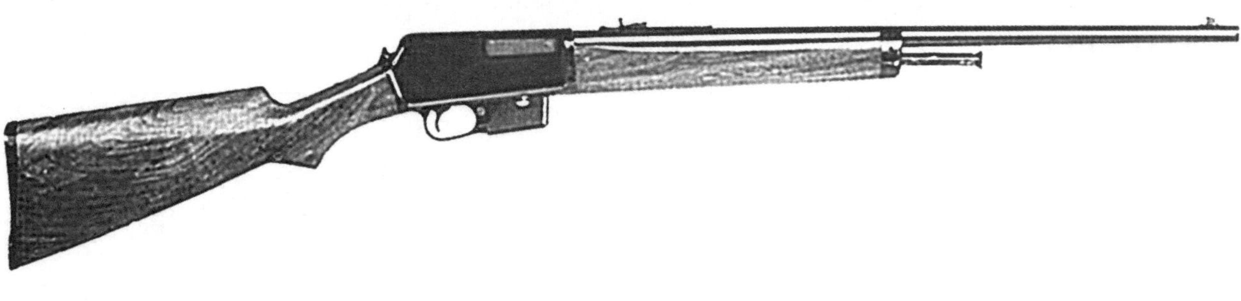

PARTS LEGEND

1. Receiver
2. Barrel
3. Rear sight assembly
4. Forearm tip key
5. Front sight
6. Forearm tip (with bow)
7. Forearm tip nut plunger and spring
8. Forearm tip nut
9. Operating sleeve spring
10. Operating sleeve
11. Operating sleeve tip
12. Operating sleeve tip pin
13. Buffer washers
14. Buffer
15. Bolt spring
16. Bolt guide rod
17. Bolt assembly (see Fig. 2.)
18. Guard assembly (see Fig. 1.)
19. Magazine
20. Ejector
21. Takedown screw bushing
22. Takedown screw
23. Buttstock bolt
24. Buttstock bolt washer

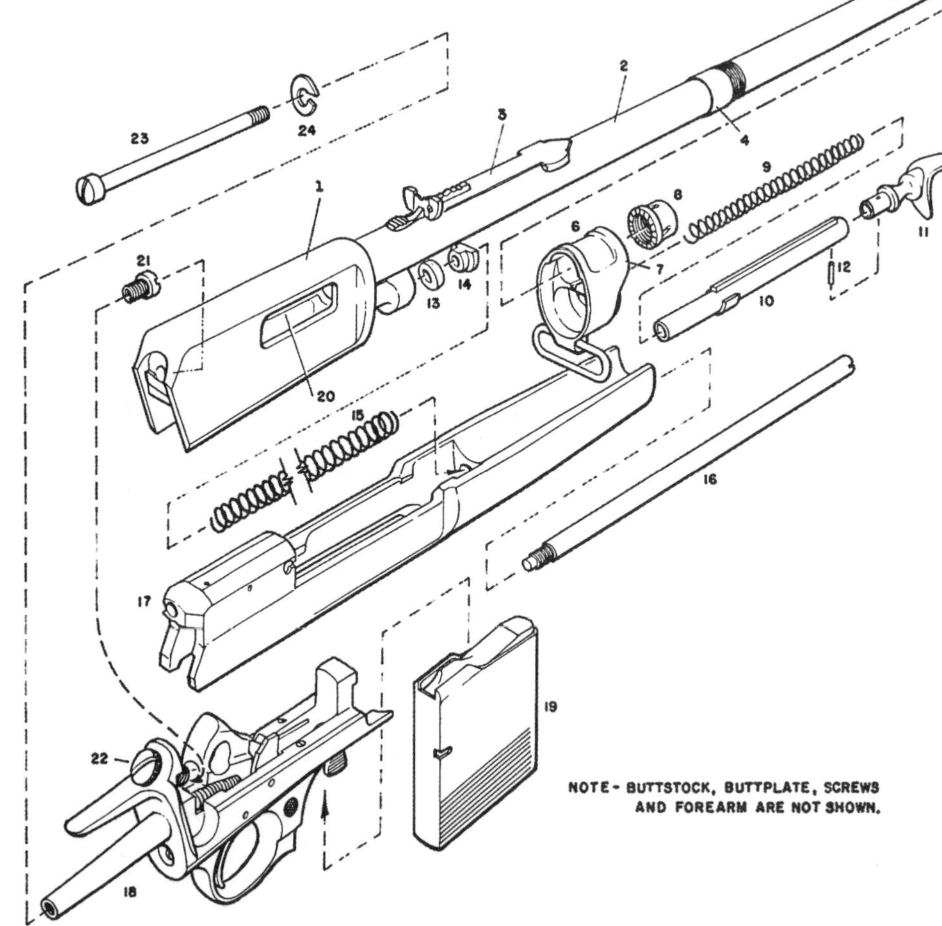

The Winchester Model 1907 Self-Loading rifle, later called Model 07, was introduced in 1907 and was essentially an improved model of the earlier Model 1905. The Model 1907 rifle is blowback operated and chambered for the .351 Winchester Self-Loading cartridge, a cartridge made for use in this arm only. It fires a 180-grain bullet at a muzzle velocity of 1856 feet per second and muzzle energy of 1378 foot-pounds. The Model 1907 breech mechanism is a "balanced type" where the breechbolt assembly is weighted in proportion to the weight and velocity of the bullet. This kept the breech sufficiently closed until the bullet had left the barrel. A 20-inch barrel and 5-shot detachable box magazine were standard for the 1907 and a 10-shot magazine was offered in 1911.

The Model 1907 Police rifle was authorized in 1934 with a 1¼-inch sling strap and optional knife bayonet. The Police rifle was discontinued in 1937, and the sporting rifle in 1957.

DISASSEMBLY

Check action to be sure rifle is unloaded. Press in magazine lock (D, Fig. 1) and withdraw magazine (19) from bottom of receiver and guard assembly (1 & 18). Cock hammer, loosen takedown screw (22), and separate guard and buttstock assembly from receiver and barrel assembly. Buttstock can be removed from guard assembly by removing buttplate (not shown) and unscrewing buttstock bolt (23) through hole in rear of buttstock. Buttstock may be drawn off the tang of the guard assembly to the rear.

Unscrew forearm tip nut (8) using a suitable spanner. Slide nut forward on barrel. Tap forearm tip (6) forward off forearm, and draw tip with operating sleeve (10) and operating sleeve spring (9) intact forward on barrel. Remove spring (9) from sleeve. Note that operating sleeve is pinned to operating sleeve tip (11) and cannot be separated from forearm tip (6) without first removing pin (12) and tip from sleeve. Pull wooden forearm (not shown) forward away from front edge of receiver (1) and off front end of bolt.

Bolt spring (15) can be removed by unscrewing bolt guide rod (16) from front end of bolt while holding bolt (17) in its rearmost position. Withdraw bolt guide rod and draw bolt forward. Remove bolt spring (15) through opening in bottom of bolt, taking care not to allow compressed spring to escape forcibly.

NOTE: Since reassembly of bolt spring (15), guide rod (16), buffer washers and buffer (13 & 14), and bolt (17) cannot be accomplished without factory tools, disassembly of the bolt is not recommended and should only be attempted by a skilled gunsmith with the proper tools at hand. Disassembly of the bolt is seldom if ever necessary for normal cleaning purposes and maintenance. Reassemble in reverse.

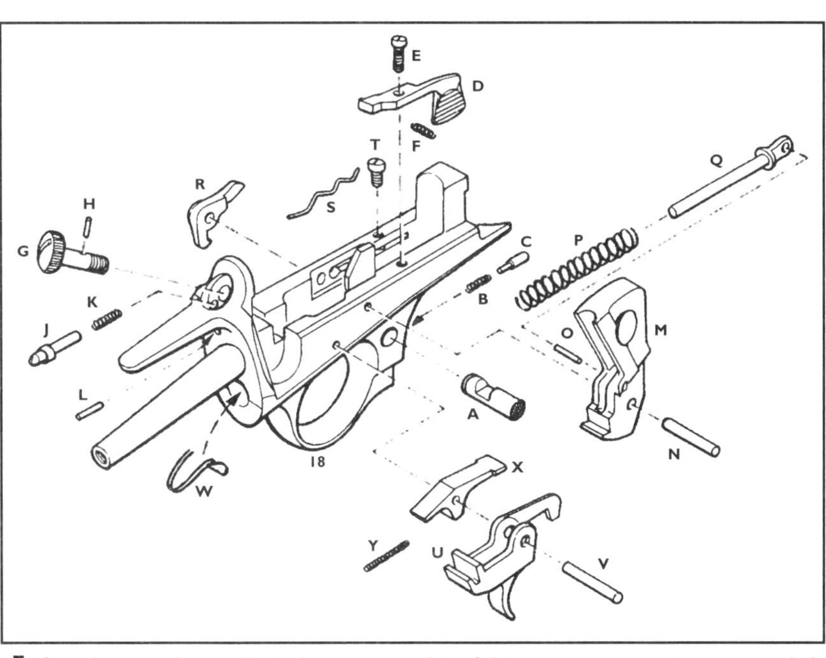

1 Complete guard assembly is shown here. Since the respective retaining pins are staked in place at the factory, disassembly of this component is not recommended and should only be undertaken by a competent gunsmith.

GUARD ASSEMBLY

A. Trigger lock
B. Trigger lock plunger spring
C. Trigger lock plunger
D. Magazine lock
E. Magazine lock screw
F. Magazine lock spring
G. Takedown screw (No. 22)
H. Takedown screw stop pin
J. Takedown screw lock
K. Takedown screw lock spring
L. Takedown screw lock pin
M. Hammer
N. Hammer pin
O. Hammer spring guide rod pin
P. Hammer spring
Q. Hammer spring guide rod
R. Timing lever
S. Timing lever spring
T. Timing lever spring screw
U. Trigger
V. Trigger pin
W. Trigger spring
X. Sear
Y. Sear spring

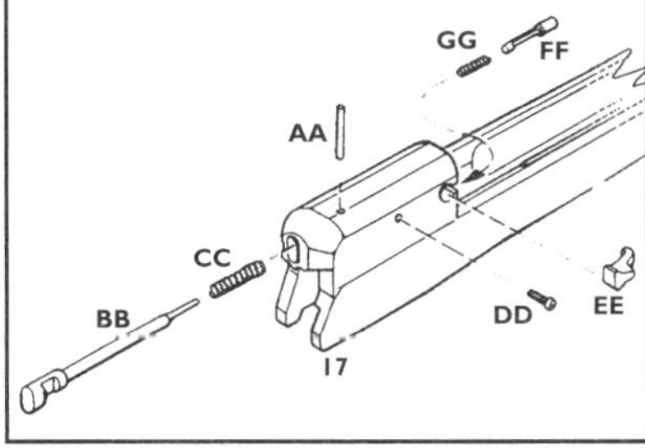

2 The bolt assembly is shown disassembled here. Firing pin (BB) and spring (CC) are removed by drifting out pin (AA). Extractor (EE), spring (GG), and plunger (FF) are removed by unscrewing the screw (DD).

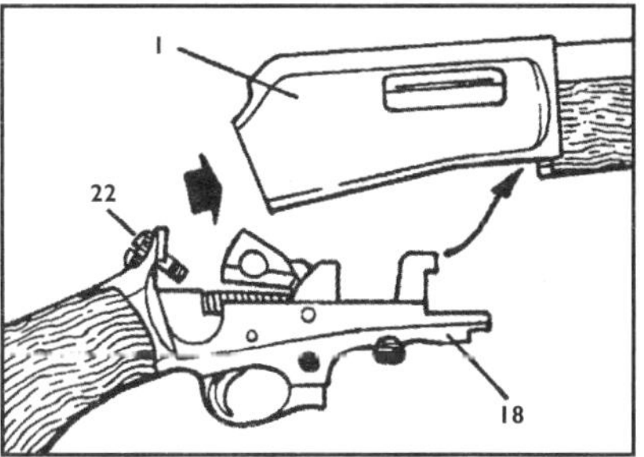

3 After loosening takedown screw (22), pull receiver and barrel straight forward slightly to disengage lug at forward end of guard (18) from corresponding groove in front end of receiver (1). Lift barrel and receiver assembly from guard and buttstock assembly.

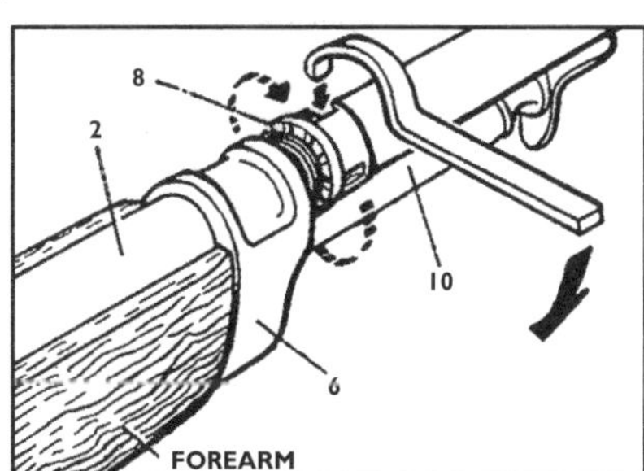

4 When removing forearm tip nut (8), a suitable type of spanner wrench should be used as shown to prevent damaging nut. After unscrewing nut, slide it forward on barrel to allow forearm tip (6) to be moved forward, away from front edge of wood forearm.

WINCHESTER MODEL 1911 SHOTGUN

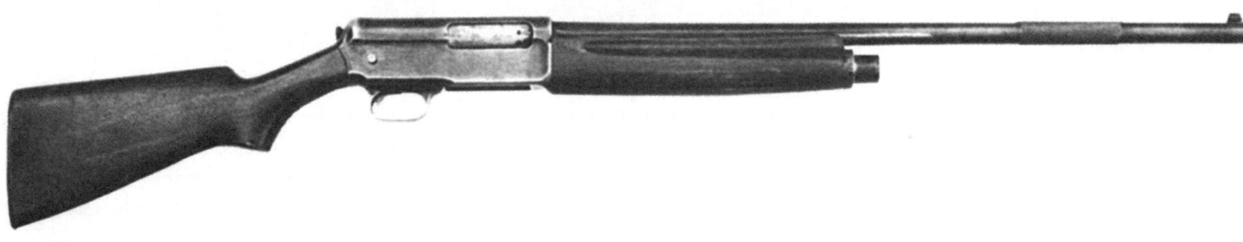

PARTS LEGEND

1. Barrel
2. Barrel buffer (2)
3. Barrel buffer nut
4. Barrel buffer nut stop
5. Barrel buffer washer
6. Barrel extension
7. Barrel spring
8. Bolt buffer
9. Bolt
10. Bolt catch
11. Bolt catch cap
12. Bolt catch spring
13. Bolt spring
14. Bolt spring follower
15. Bolt spring follower rod
    a. Cap
    b. Washer
16. Bolt stop
17. Bolt stop spring
18. Buttstock
19. Buttplate
20. Buttplate screws (2)
21. Carrier
22. Carrier screw
23. Carrier cam
24. Carrier cam plunger
25. Carrier cam plunger spring
26. Carrier roll
27. Carrier roll pin
28. Carrier spring
29. Cartridge cutoff
30. Cartridge cutoff spring
31. Cartridge stop
32. Cartridge stop plunger
33. Cartridge stop plunger spring
34. Extractor
35. Extractor pin
36. Extractor spring
37. Ejector
38. Ejector rivet
39. Firing pin
40. Firing pin spring
41. Forearm
42. Trigger guard
43. Hammer
44. Hammer spring guide rod
45. Hammer spring guide rod pin
46. Hammer spring
47. Hammer pin
48. Locking block
49. Locking block operating rod
50. Locking block operating rod pin
51. Magazine tube
52. Magazine cap
53. Magazine follower
54. Magazine spring
55. Magazine friction plunger
56. Magazine friction plunger escutcheon
57. Magazine friction plunger spring
58. Receiver
59. Soar
60. Sear spring
61. Takedown screw
62. Takedown screw bushing
63. Takedown screw stop
64. Takedown screw lock
65. Takedown screw lock spring
66. Tang screw
67. Tang screw friction plunger
68. Tang screw friction plunger spring
69. Timing rod
70. Timing rod operating lever
71. Timing rod operating lever spring
72. Timing rod operating lever pin
73. Timing rod pin
74. Trigger
75. Trigger lock (safety)
76. Trigger lock plunger
77. Trigger lock plunger spring
78. Trigger pin
79. Trigger spring
80. Trigger spring plunger

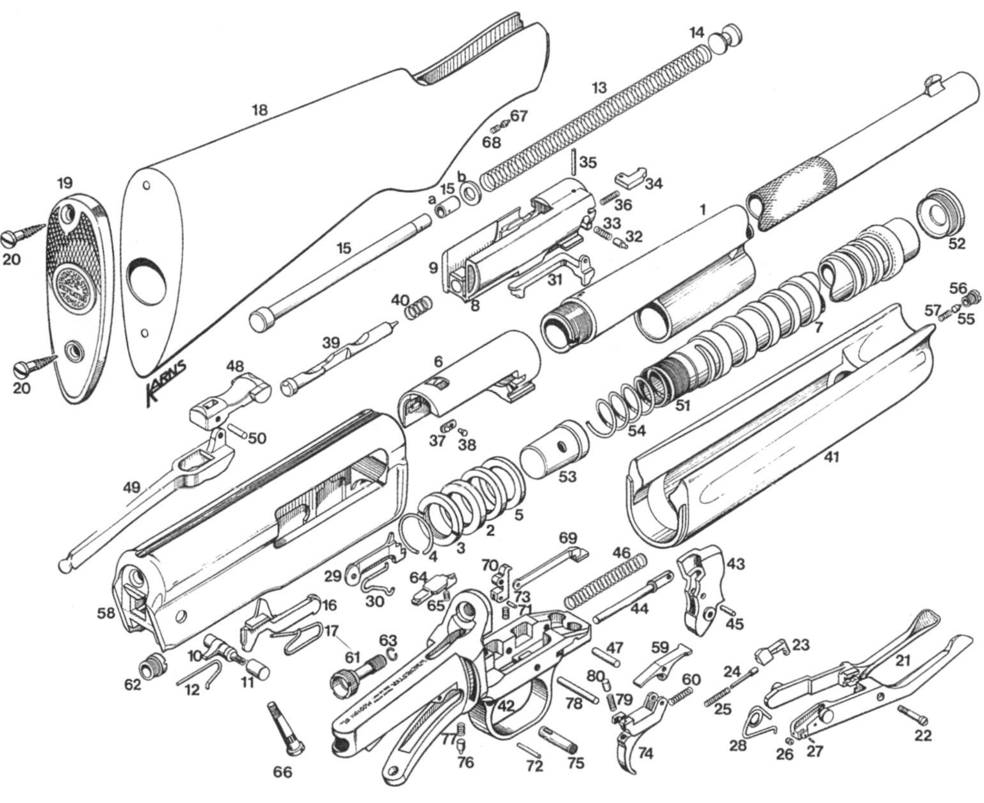

The Model 1911 was Winchester's first self-loading, concealed-hammer shotgun. It featured an action that was manually cycled by pulling backwards on a knurled portion of the barrel. The Model 1911's breechblock and barrel remained locked together during recoil. Downward pressure exerted on the locking rod as the breechblock/barrel unit recoiled unlocked the locking block, allowing the barrel to be returned by the barrel spring. Subsequent cartridges were chambered and fired in a conventional, semi-automatic mode. Only the first round required manual chambering.

Both plain and fancy grades were offered and standard barrels were offered in both 26- and 28-inch lengths in either full, modified, or cylinder choke. Trap and Pigeon grades were introduced in 1913 with fancy grade, heavy walnut stocks. The standard buttstock offered with part of the production of the Winchester 1911 was unusual in that it was constructed of three pieces of laminated birch. The fore-end was also birch, but with a reinforced rock elm insert.

Production of the Winchester Model 1911 shotgun began in 1911 and continued until 1925, with a total number of 82,774.

DISASSEMBLY

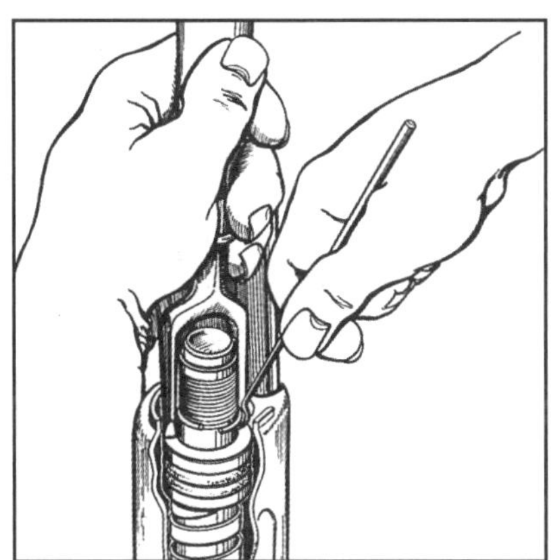

1 Note that all pins are drifted out from left to right as viewed from above.

First make certain the gun is unloaded, then press down on the takedown screw lock (64) while loosening the takedown screw (61) at the rear of the receiver. Separate the rear stock and firing mechanism from the front receiver/barrel before pressing the bolt catch (10) from right to left. Rest rear of receiver (58) on a solid bench; grab the knurled section of the barrel (1) and "pump" the barrel rearward. Raise the locking block operating rod (49) to release the barrel and allow it to move forward away from the locking block. Unscrew magazine tube (51) and remove magazine and barrel.

With the barrel held in a padded vise, remove the barrel buffer nut stop (4) and nut (3), being careful not to let the barrel spring fly out.

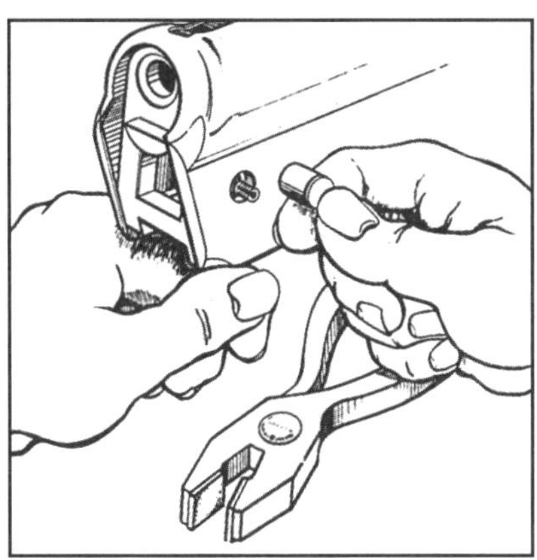

2 Remove the two barrel buffers (2) and the barrel buffer washer (5). Remove the barrel spring (7) and forearm (41), then magazine cap (52), magazine spring (54), and magazine follower (53).

To disassemble the receiver, press the bolt catch (10) from left to right. Remove the cartridge cutoff spring (30) and cartridge cutoff (29). Press down on the bolt stop (16) while pressing the bolt (9) forward. Gently pry out the carrier (21) from the left side of the receiver. Remove the carrier screw (22). Press the cartridge stop plunger (32), at the right side of the breechblock, and remove cartridge stop (31), cartridge stop plunger (32), and cartridge stop plunger spring (33), being careful to restrain the spring.

Remove the bolt (9) from the receiver. Both the bolt stop (16) and bolt stop spring (17) can be removed from the receiver. Remove the carrier spring (28), bolt catch (10) and bolt catch spring (12). Note: bolt catch is made in two pieces; the cap (11) unscrews.

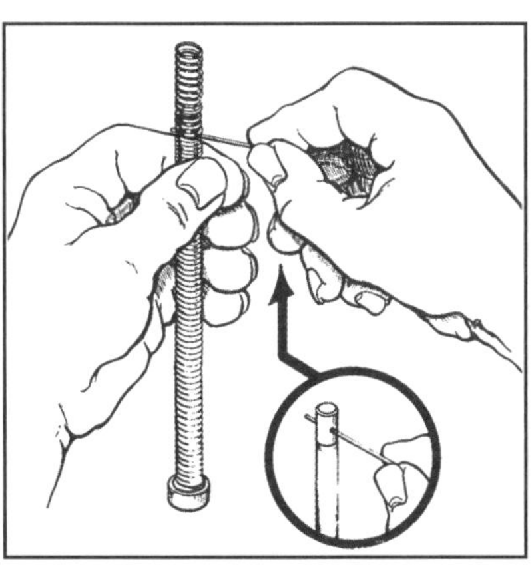

3 **Assembly Notes:** The carrier screw (22) must be staked into position. Place bolt spring follower rod (15) on a non-slip surface and insert the bolt spring, compressing the spring to about an inch and a half. Holding the spring in this position, insert a small pin into the hole in the rod's cap (15a) to retain the compressed spring

To install the guide and spring as an assembly, slide the buttstock into place and remove the retaining pin, keeping pressure on the buttstock until the tang screw (66) is installed.

To disassemble breechblock further: press in on the firing pin (39), then lift the bolt stop (16) and remove it from the bolt. The firing pin and spring can then be removed. Drift out the extractor pin (35), then remove the extractor (34) and its spring (36).

To remove the carrier cam (23), pull out on the carrier cam plunger (24). Cam will fall out. Carefully release carrier cam plunger.

Disassemble the buttstock and trigger guard group by unscrewing the tang screw (66). Grasp buttstock at the grip area, remove bolt spring (13) and bolt spring follower stop rod (15). Remove bolt spring follower (14) from the upper tang of the trigger guard (42).

Drive out hammer pin (47) before removing hammer (43) and hammer spring (46). Drive out the trigger pin (78), then remove the sear (59) and sear spring (60). Remove the trigger (74), trigger spring (79) and trigger spring plunger (80). Remove timing rod pin (73), timing rod (69), timing rod operating lever (70) and spring (71).

Remove the takedown screw bushing (62) and takedown screw (61). The takedown screw lock (64) and spring (65) will fall out. Push the trigger lock (safety) (75) to "SAFE," then press in on the trigger lock plunger (76) and turn the trigger lock (safety) sideways to remove. Take out the trigger lock plunger (76) and its spring (77).

WIN. HOTCHKISS MODEL 1879

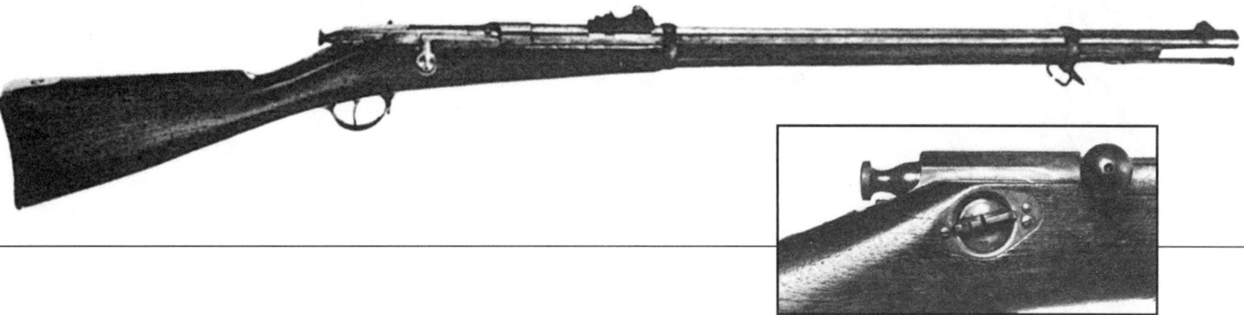

Combined magazine cutoff and safety button in the right side of the stock is the distinguishing feature of the early version.

PARTS LEGEND

1. Barrel
2. Receiver
3. Stock (not shown)
4. Cocking piece
5. Bolt
6. Mainspring
7. Striker
8. Bolt head
9. Extractor
10. Striker locking screw
11. Trigger
12. Cartridge stop and trigger bar
13. Trigger spring
14. Trigger pin
15. Trigger bar pin
16 .Bolt and trigger lock
17. Bolt and trigger lock pin
18. Trigger spring screw
19. Trigger guard
20. Front guard screw
21. Rear trigger guard screw
22. Side screw
23. Saddle ring mounting assembly Plate
24 .Stock bushing — cut-off mounting plate
25. Magazine cut-off mounting plate
26. Magazine cut-off mounting plate screws (2)
27. Magazine cut-off and safety
28. Recoil plate (omitted on earlier models)
29. Recoil plate screw escutcheon (contained in underside of stock)
30. Recoil plate screw
31. Rear sight
32. Rear sight mounting screws (2)
33. Front sight
34. Front sight pin
35. Magazine tube
36. Magazine spring
37. Magazine follower
38. Buttplate
39. Buttplate screws (2)
40. Band
41. Bandspring

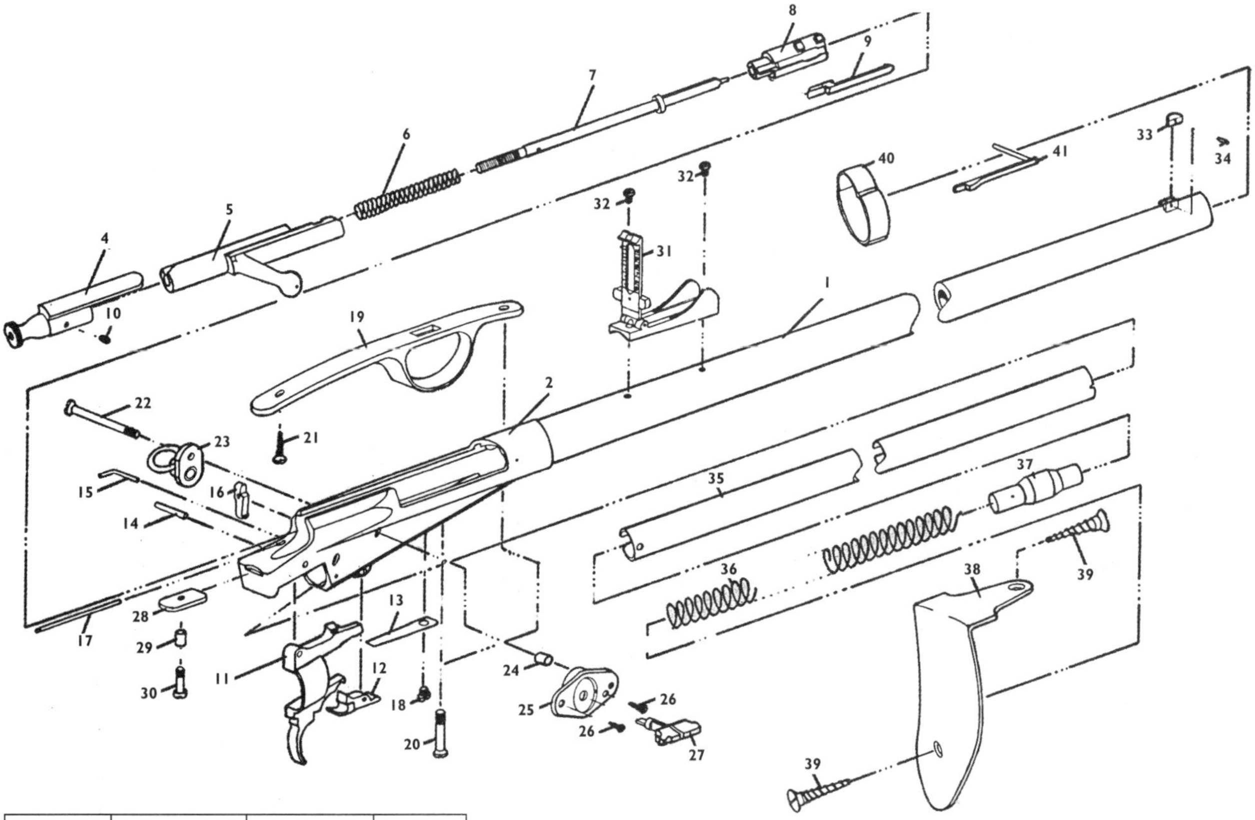

	Barrel length	Total length	Weight
MUSKET	32" round	48⅝"	9 lbs.
CARBINE	24" round	44"	8½ lbs.

Winchester's first bolt-action rifle was manufactured on patent rights purchased from Benjamin B. Hotchkiss. Announced in 1878, the Winchester Hotchkiss rifle has a tubular magazine in the buttstock. The .45-70 cartridges are fed forward by the magazine spring and follower. Pulling the trigger depresses the lower cartridge stop below the magazine tube, and the lead cartridge, under pressure from the magazine spring, moves forward to bear against the underside of the bolt. Pulling the bolt rearward releases the cartridge, and spring pressure moves it toward the chamber. Closing the bolt chambers the round, while the upper stop prevents a second cartridge from being released.

In the first style rifle, the magazine cutoff and safety were contained in a single button located on the right side of the one-piece stock. Rotating the magazine cutoff 270 degrees clockwise locked the cartridges in the magazine tube from moving forward. The rifle can then be used as a single shot, keeping in reserve five rounds in the magazine. Rotating the magazine cutoff clockwise 90 degrees from horizontal locks the bolt and trigger, acting as a safety. In the second style, the magazine cutoff is on the right side of the receiver while the safety is on the left. The changes are said to have resulted from tests made at Springfield Armory. The rifle was considered by the U.S. Ordnance Department. It is recorded that the United States Navy ordered 2500 for possible use. Sale of the Winchester Hotchkiss as a sporting arm was very limited. About 22,500 of these one-piece-stock Winchester Hotchkiss rifles had been produced when manufacture ceased in 1883.

DISASSEMBLY

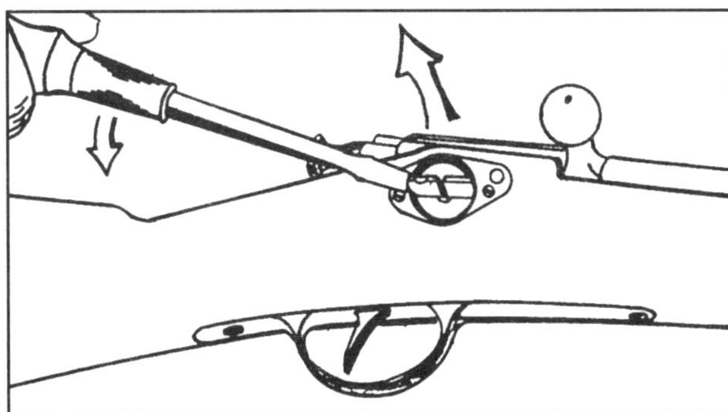

1 Compress sides of the magazine cutoff and safety (27) and lift out. Remove buttplate screws (39), buttplate (38), magazine spring (36) and follower (37). Insert drift pin in the hole at the right side of magazine tube (35) and slide it out from stock. Depress bandspring (41), slide off band (40). Remove side screw (22) and front guard screw (20). Lift the barrel and receiver assembly from the stock.

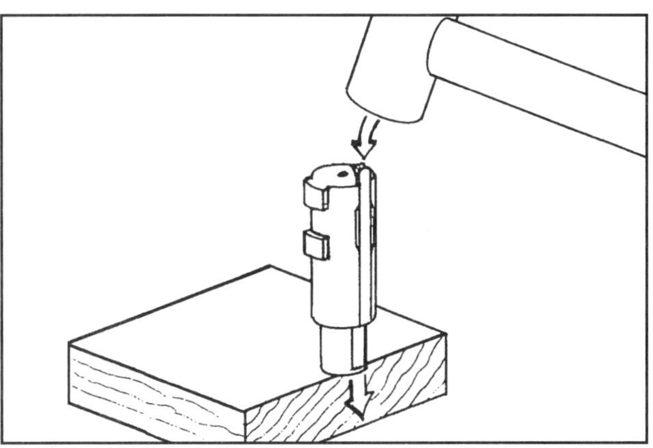

2 Press the trigger (11) and remove bolt assembly. Relieve mainspring (6) by rotating cocking piece (4) counterclockwise and allow it to move forward. Rotate bolt head (8) and remove it from bolt (5). Place the bolt head on a wood block and tap extractor (9) out with a plastic hammer.

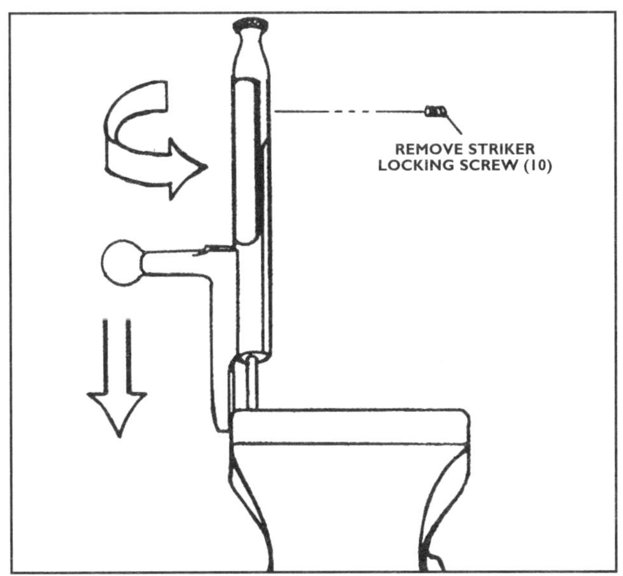

3 Place the striker (7) in vise or clamp and unscrew striker locking screw (10) from cocking piece (4) (Figure C). Push down on bolt handle and rotate cocking piece (4) counterclockwise. When compression is relieved, lift out striker (7) and mainspring (6). Other disassembly is readily apparent.

When reassembling cocking piece to striker, align indexing notch on striker with threaded hole for striker locking screw. When installing magazine cutoff and safety, be sure that the cutoff is parallel to the axis of the barrel and indexing notch is to the left, or toward butt of stock.

WIN. HOTCHKISS MODEL 1883

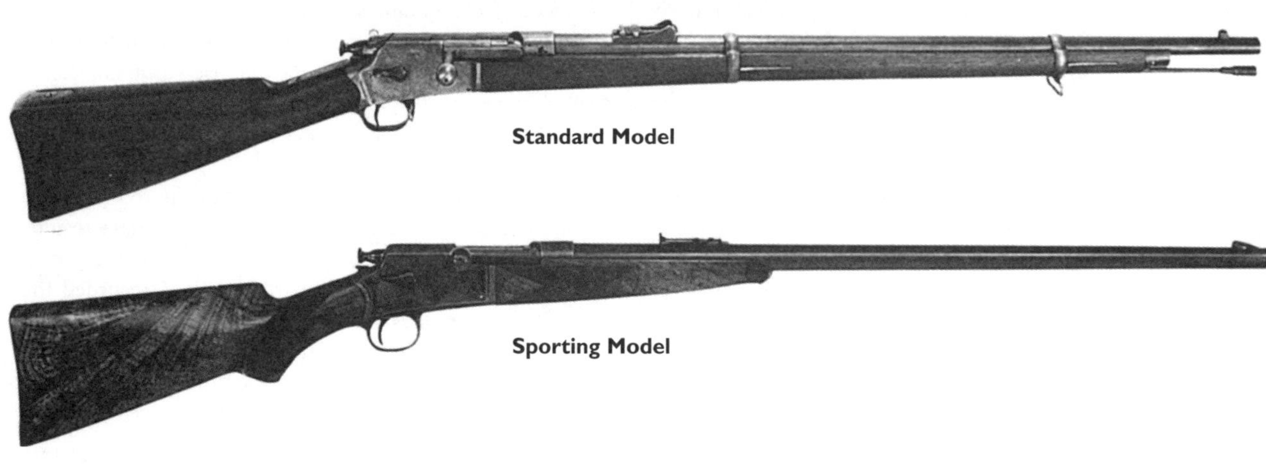

Standard Model

Sporting Model

PARTS LEGEND

1. Barrel
2. Receiver
3. Buttstock (not shown)
   3a. Fore-end (not shown)
4. Cocking piece
5. Bolt
6. Mainspring
7. Striker
8. Bolt Head
9. Extractor
10. Striker locking screw
11. Trigger
12. Trigger/cartridge stop spring
13. Trigger spring roller
14. Trigger spring roller pin
15. Trigger spring screw
16. Trigger spring retaining pin
17. Trigger guard
18. Receiver/trigger guard screws(2)
19. Trigger screw
20. Tang screw
21. Tang screw bushing
22. Trigger guard front screw
23. Trigger guard rear screw
24. Magazine cutoff lever
25. Safety lever
26. Cartridge guide screw
27. Cutoff lever retaining spring
28. Safety lever retaining spring
29. Retaining spring screws (2)
30. Rear sight
31. Rear sight screws (2)
32. Front sight
33. Front sight pin
34. Upper band (with sling swivel)
35. Band springs (2)
36. Lower band
37. Nose cap
38. Nose cap screw
39. Magazine cap
40. Magazine tube retaining ring
41. Magazine tube
42. Magazine spring
43. Magazine follower
44. Buttplate
45. Buttplate screws (2)
46. Ramrod

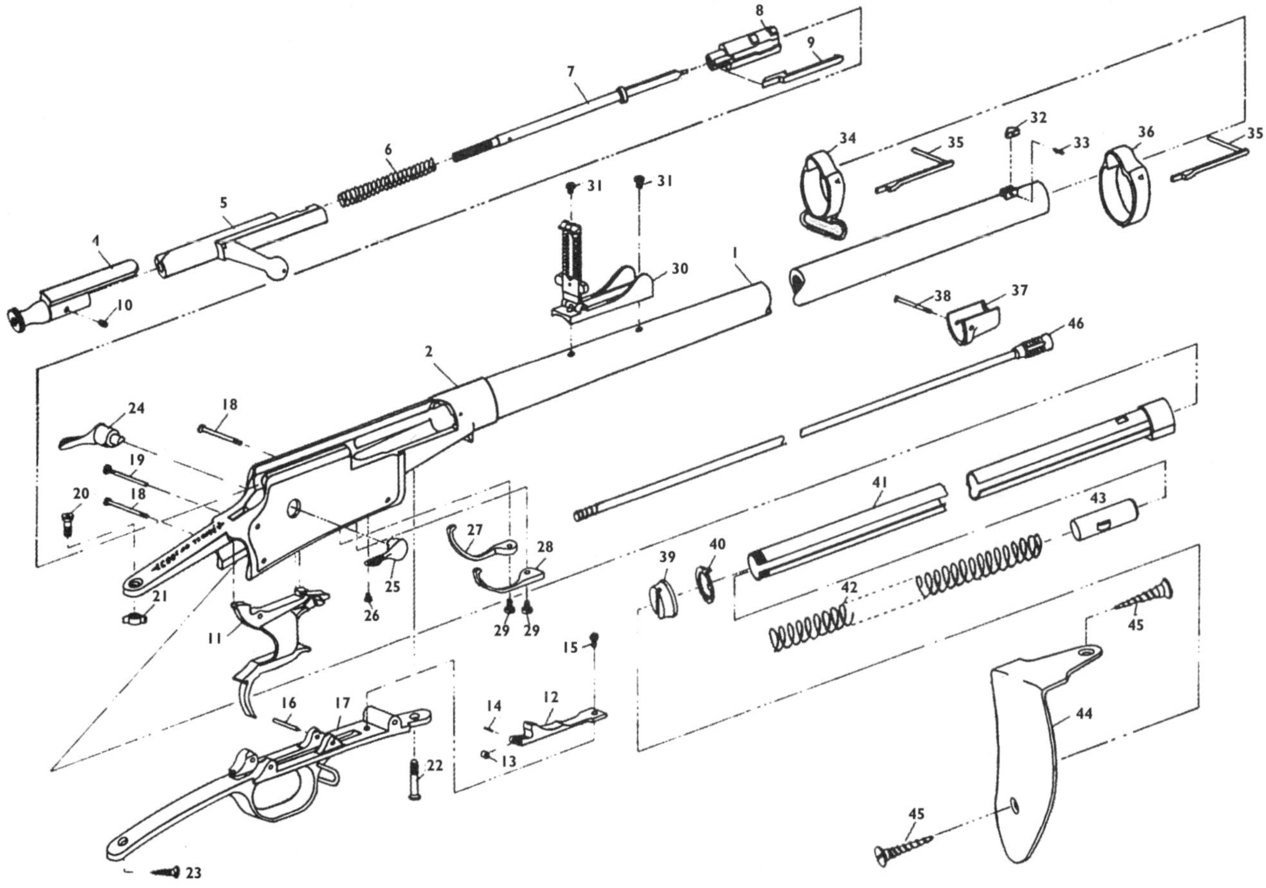

The Hotchkiss Magazine Rifle Model 1883 was Winchester's second attempt at marketing a bolt-action repeating rifle. More than a cosmetic change from the Model 1879 Hotchkiss, the Model 1883 design represented a major effort to remedy weaknesses of the 1879 and 1880 Hotchkiss repeaters.

The receiver was redesigned to include side panels to strengthen the receiver. These imitated the appearance of the widely accepted lever-action frame. A two-piece stock accomodated the side panels. The combination magazine cutoff/safety switch was replaced by two separate levers mounted on opposite sides of the receiver. The cutoff lever locks the magazine tube at the case rim blocking the passage of the cartridge. This permits the use of the rifle as a single-shot. The 1883 loads with a 5-round tubular magazine that runs obliquely to the axis of the bore and into the buttstock. The safety lever can only be engaged when the rifle is cocked.

From 1883 until 1899, nearly 62,000 Model 1883 Winchester rifles were manufactured at the New Haven factory. Most, including 750 sold to the U.S. Army for trials, were military arms in .45-70. A limited number of sporting rifles and carbines, also in .45-70, were also sold. The Hotchkiss was never a real success and was discontinued in 1899.

DISASSEMBLY

Make sure the chamber and magazine of the rifle are clear. The following cautions apply when removing the magazine tube and cap. The threads on the magazine tube are very fine and the brass magazine cap fragile. To preclude damage, use of a solvent to loosen accumulated dirt and corrosion is recommended prior to attempting to remove the magazine cap. Note that the magazine retaining ring is captive in the buttstock and should be removed, as a unit, with the buttstock. A sharp blow of the heel of the hand may be needed to start the buttstock moving off the magazine tube.

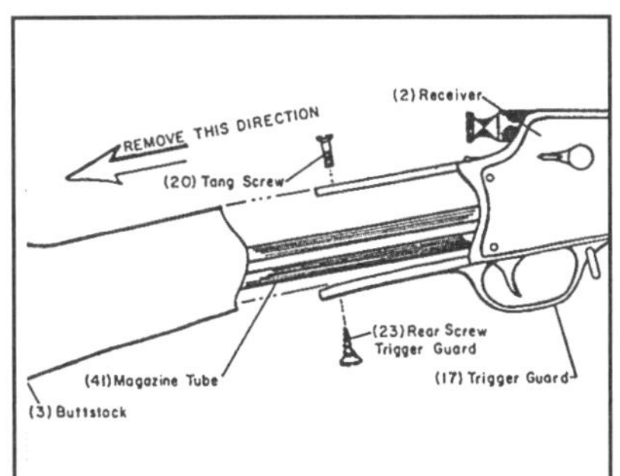

1 Remove the buttplate screws (45) and the buttplate (44) from the buttstock (3). Unscrew and remove the magazine cap (39) from the magazine tube (41), releasing the tension on the magazine spring (42). Next remove the tang screw (20) and rear trigger guard screw (23) and slide the buttstock to the rear, off the magazine tube. Withdraw the magazine spring and follower (43) from the magazine tube.

Invert the receiver (2). Remove the front trigger screw (22) and receiver trigger guard screws (18) and lift the trigger guard (17) out of the receiver. Depress the band springs (35) and slide the upper band (34) and lower band (36) off the fore-end (3a). Lift the fore-end away from the barrel (1) and receiver.

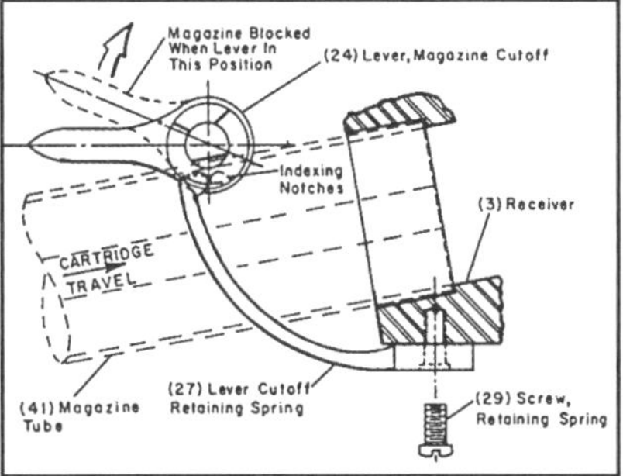

2 Remove the cutoff and safety retaining spring screws (29) and lift the cutoff lever retaining spring (27) and safety lever retaining spring (28) out of the receiver. Remove the cutoff lever (24) and safety lever (25) from the receiver side panels. It is important, in step 6, to record the position of the hands on the retaining springs with respect to the positions of the levers. This relationship must be duplicated when reassembling the rifle.

Remove the trigger screw (19) from the left receiver side panel and slide the magazine tube (41) and trigger (11) Out of the rear of the receiver. Withdraw the bolt (5) from the receiver.

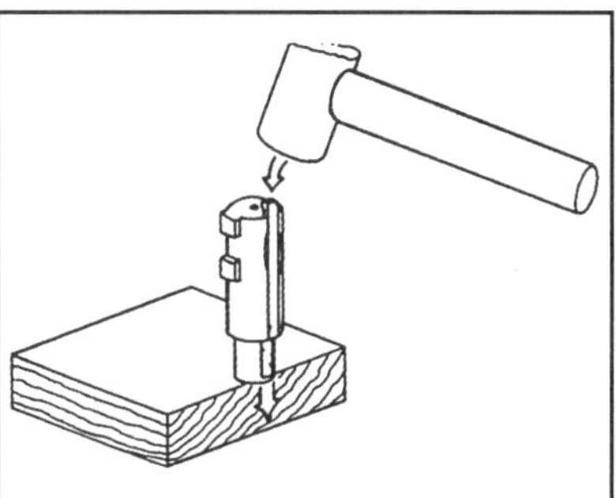

3 **To disassemble the bolt:** Relieve tension on the mainspring (6) by rotating the cocking piece (4) counterclockwise and allowing it to move forward. Slide the bolt head (8) forward to disengage it from the bolt.

To remove the extractor (9), place the bolt head, extractor up, on a wood block and use a soft-faced hammer to drive the extractor from the bolt head.

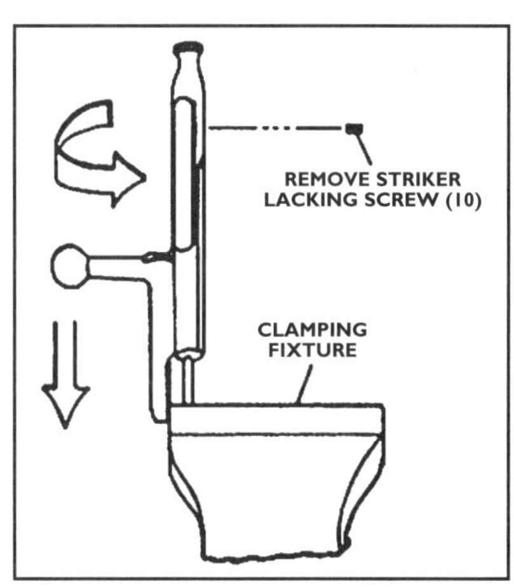

4 Clamp the striker vertically in a vise. Unscrew the striker locking screw (10) from the cocking piece. Push downward on the bolt handle to compress the mainspring and rotate the cocking piece counterclockwise until the cocking piece is removed from the striker. Lift the bolt body off the striker and remove the mainspring. Further disassembly is not recommended. Reassemble in reverse order.

WIN.-LEE STRAIGHT PULL RIFLE

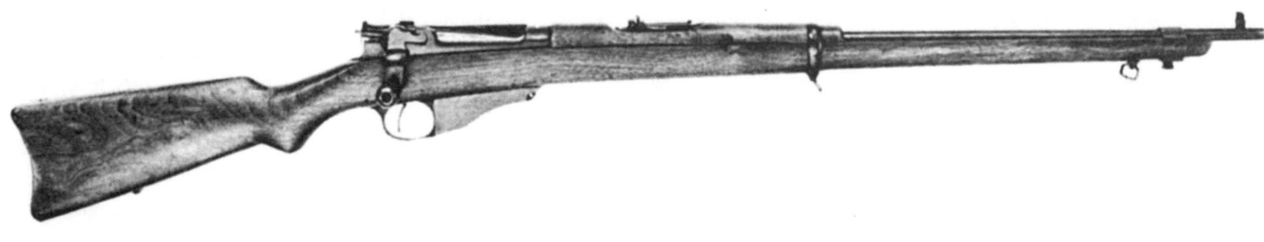

PARTS LEGEND

1. Receiver
2. Barrel
3. Stock (not shown)
   3a. Handguard (not shown)
4. Bolt
5. Striker spring
6. Striker
7. Striker collar
8. Cam lever (bolt handle) assembly
9. Extractor
10. Extractor spring and pin
11. Firing pin lock assembly
12. Bolt release
13. Bolt stop assembly
14. Lock pin
15. Trigger guard assembly
16. Follower assembly
17. Elevator spring assembly
18. Clip guide
19. Clip guide pins (2)
20. Sear
21. Sear pin
22. Sear fly
23. Sear spring
24. Trigger
25. Trigger spring
26. Trigger pin
27. Trigger spring screw
28. Trigger guard screw
29. Receiver tang screw
30. Tang screw bushing
31. Rear sight assembly
32. Rear sight screws (2)
33. Front sight blade
34. Front sight pin
35. Front sight cover
36. Front sight cover screws
37. Upper band with stacking swivel
38. Upper band screw
39. Middle band with sling swivel
40. Sling swivel tension clip
41. Lower band screw
42. Lower swivel assembly
43. Lower swivel screws (2)
44. Buttplate
45. Buttplate screws (2)
46. Buttplate slide
47. Buttplate slide spring
48. Buttplate slide spring screw

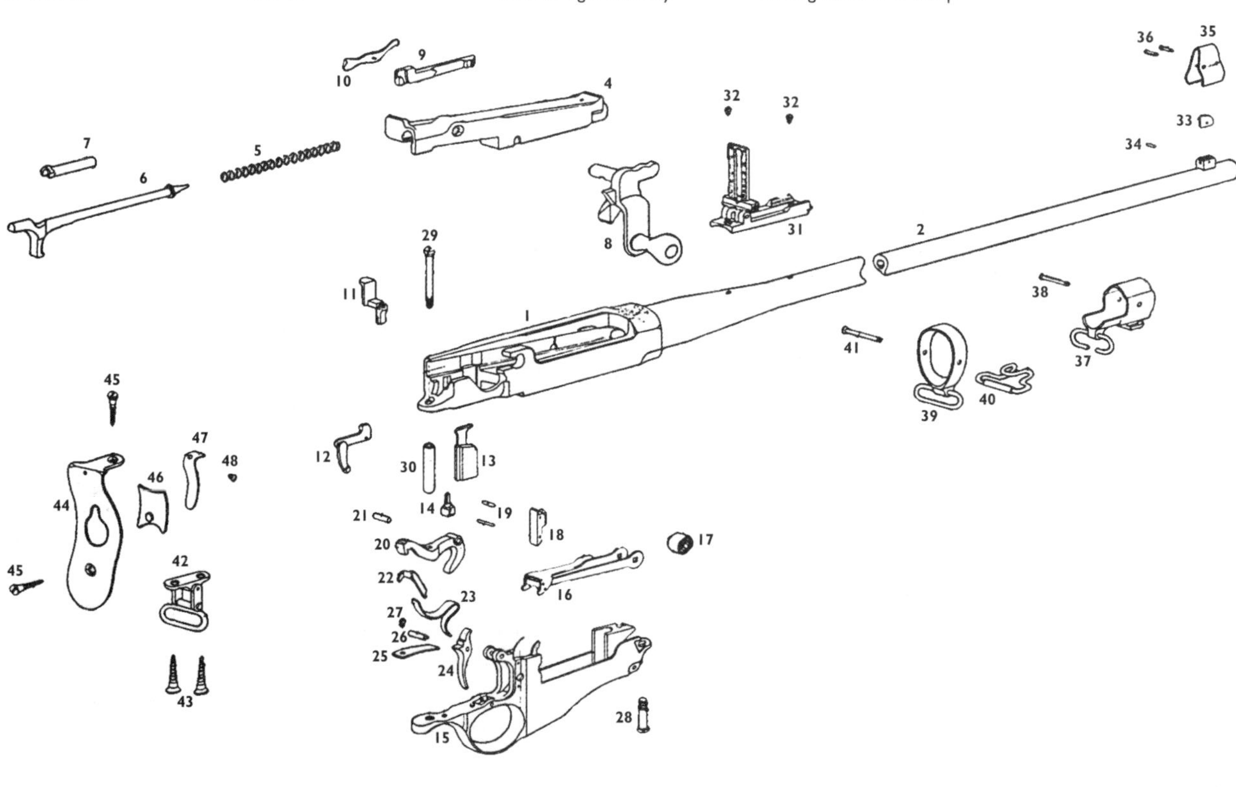

Shortly before the Spanish-American War, the U.S. Navy selected the Winchester-Lee Model 1895 rifle and purchased some 15,000 Lees from Winchester, who held manufacturing rights from the Lee Arms Co.

Devised by James P. Lee of Lee-Enfield fame, the Model 1895 Winchester-Lee was a manually operated straight-pull bolt-action repeater. Locking and unlocking were handled by a wedge machined integral with the bolt and cammed into and out of a locking seat in the receiver by the action of the bolt handle. The Lee cartridge fired a 6mm (.244 caliber), ½-grain, round-nosed bullet at an unheard of 2,550 f.p.s. The rifle had an integral 5-round box magazine that could be loaded singly or using a 5-round clip.

Winchester also added the Lee to its catalog both as a sporting modle and a military-style "musket." The Lee military rifles were full stocked and had 28-inch barrels fitted for a knife bayonet while the sporting rifles, of which some 1,700 were made, had 24-inch barrels without handguards.

The Winchester-Lee was not a commercial success and production ceased in 1902, after about 20,000 units had been built.

DISASSEMBLY

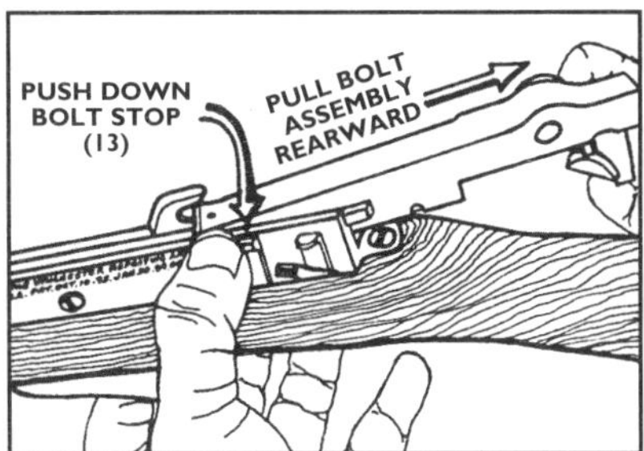

1 Begin disassembly by opening the bolt — depress the bolt release (12) to unlock a cocked bolt, or simply pull the cam lever (8) of an uncocked bolt straight to the rear. Check the magazine and chamber to make sure the rifle is unloaded.

Remove the bolt assembly (4) by pressing the top of the bolt stop (13) outward to clear the sidewall of the receiver (1) and down. Draw the bolt assembly to the rear out of the receiver, taking care not to drop the assembled extractor (9) and extractor spring and pin (10).

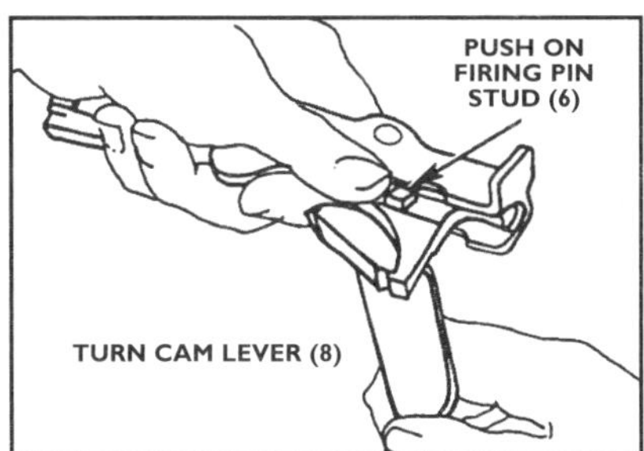

2 To remove the striker assembly from the bolt, grasp the bolt in the left hand, left side up. Place the left thumb against the square stud on the side of the striker rod (6). With the right hand, rotate the cam lever as far toward the rear as possible (see Figure B). Hold the striker rod to the rear by applying thumb pressure to the square stud and rotate the cam lever forward until it is clear of the sear nose. Let the striker rod ride forward under pressure of the striker spring (5). Now, position the cam lever so that the lever is perpendicular to the bolt and draw downward on the lever, pulling the cam lever free of the bolt. Remove the striker rod and assembled collar (7) and striker spring from the rear of the bolt.

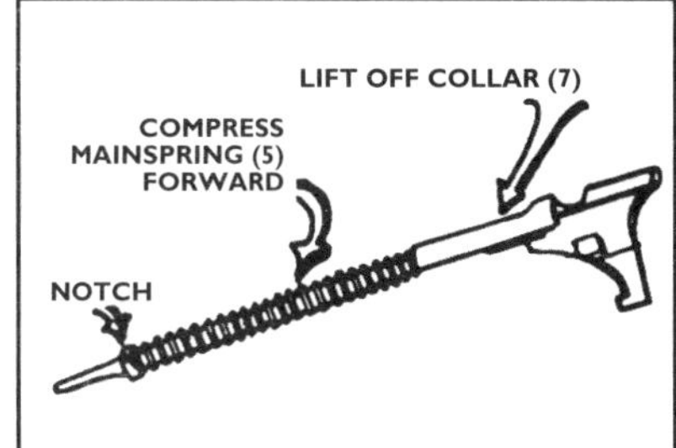

3 To disassemble the striker assembly, press the collar forward, compressing the striker spring, and lift the rear of the collar clear of the striker rod. The striker spring may be removed by aligning the wire end of the spring with the notch in the striker rod bushingand "unscrewing" the striker spring.

NOTE: On some models of the Winchester-Lee rifle the firing pin is integral with the striker rod, as shown in the drawing. On others, the firing pin is separate and is mounted in the bolt along with a retraction spring, held in place by a cross pin.

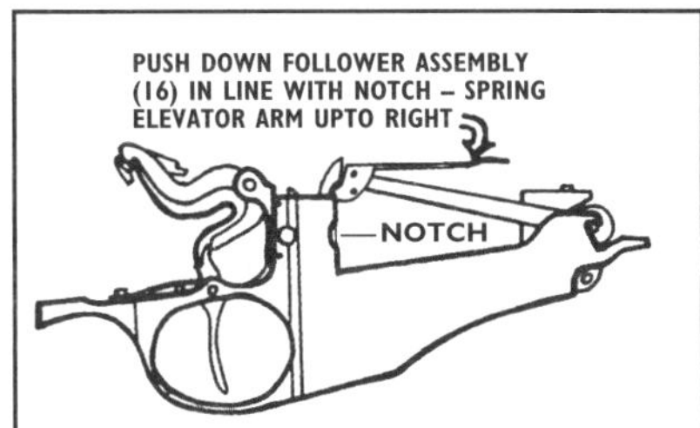

4 Disassembly of receiver and magazine assembly: Remove the upper (38) and middle (41) band screws and slide or drift the upper (37) and middle (39) bands off the stock. Remove the handguard (3a) by raising the rear sight elevation ladder to the vertical position. Slide the elevation slide to the top of the ladder. Push the handguard forward to get it clear of the mortise in the rear sight base, then lift it clear of the barrel (2) and base. Turn the handguard 90 degrees to clear the elevation slide and lift it off the rifle.

Remove the receiver tang screw (29) and the trigger guard screw (28). Lift the stock and captive trigger guard assembly (15) away from the barrel and receiver. Lift the trigger guard assembly out of its mortise in the stock. To release tension on the magazine follower assembly (16), press the rear of the follower down until the guides on the follower are aligned with the disassembly notch in the trigger guard housing and lift the follower and elevator arm out of the track in the housing. Rotate the follower and elevator arm as far clockwise as they will go. Remove the clockspring-like elevator spring assembly (17) by inserting the blade of a small screwdriver between the spring and the trigger guard housing and prying the spring off its retaining stud. Lift the follower, elevator arm, and spring assembly out of the trigger guard.

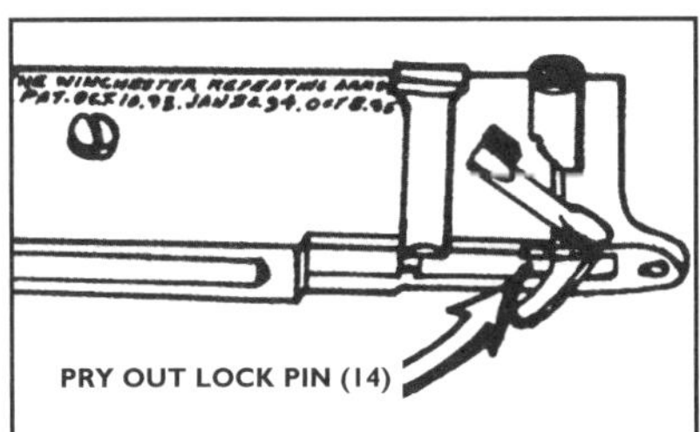

5 Detailed disassembly of the receiver is begun by pushing down on the thumb-piece of the bolt stop assembly until the assembly drops free of the receiver. (Use a soft-faced hammer, if necessary, to drive the assembly downward).

Invert the receiver and gently pry or drift the lock pin (14) from its mortise in the receiver. Pry gently upward on the bolt release thumbpiece until it clears its locking slot in the receiver. Then, holding the thumbpiece clear, rotate the bolt release counterclockwise and out of the receiver. Pull the firing pin lock assembly (11) as far out of the bottom of the receiver as it will go. Then push the bottom of the assembly toward the center of the receiver and lift it out of its clearance hole.

NOTE: The trigger mechanism of the Lee rifle is assembled with pins that are staked in place. Disassembly is not recommended. Reassemble the rifle in reverse order.

WINCHESTER LEVER-ACTION

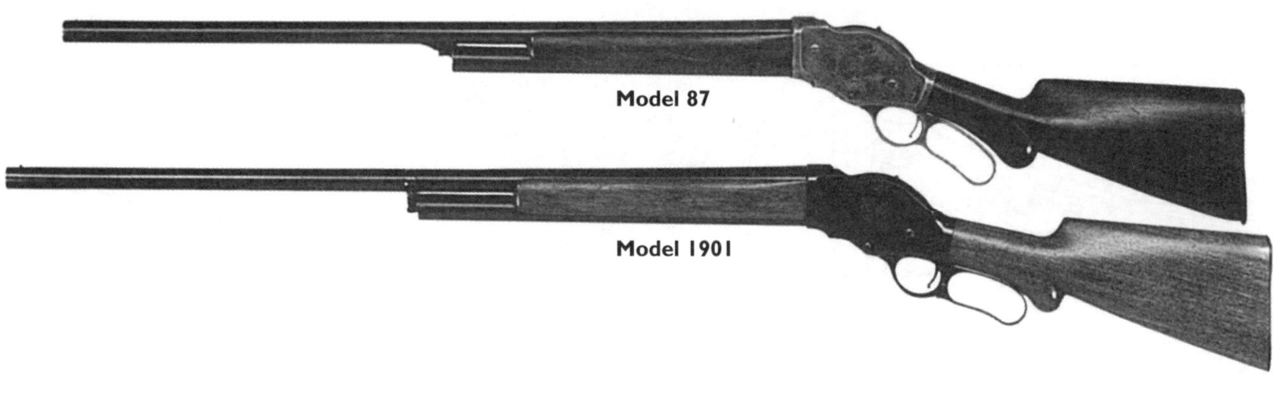

Model 87

Model 1901

PARTS LEGEND

1. Receiver
2. Tang screw
3. Trigger spring screw
4. Sear pin
5. Carrier screw (2)
6. Breechblock pin
7. Trigger Spring
8. Breechblock stud screw
9. Left-hand carrier
10. Cartridge Lifter
11. Right-hand carrier
12. Left-hand extractor
13. Extractor spring & pin
14. Breechblock stud
15. Right-hand extractor spring & pin
16. Right-hand extractor
17. Firing pin stop pin
18. Carrier stop screws
19. Firing pin spring
20. Firing Pin
21. Trigger & sear
22. Breechblock
23. Hammer
24. Mainspring
25. Buttstock
26. Buttplate
27. Buttplate screws (2)
28. Cartridge lifter pin
29. Cartridge ifter stop screw
30. Barrel
31. Front sight
32. Magazine tube
33. Magazine plug
34. Magazine plug screw
35. Magazine spring
36. Magazine follower
37. Magazine band
38. Magazine band screw
39. Forearm (2 parts)
40. Forearm screws & grommets

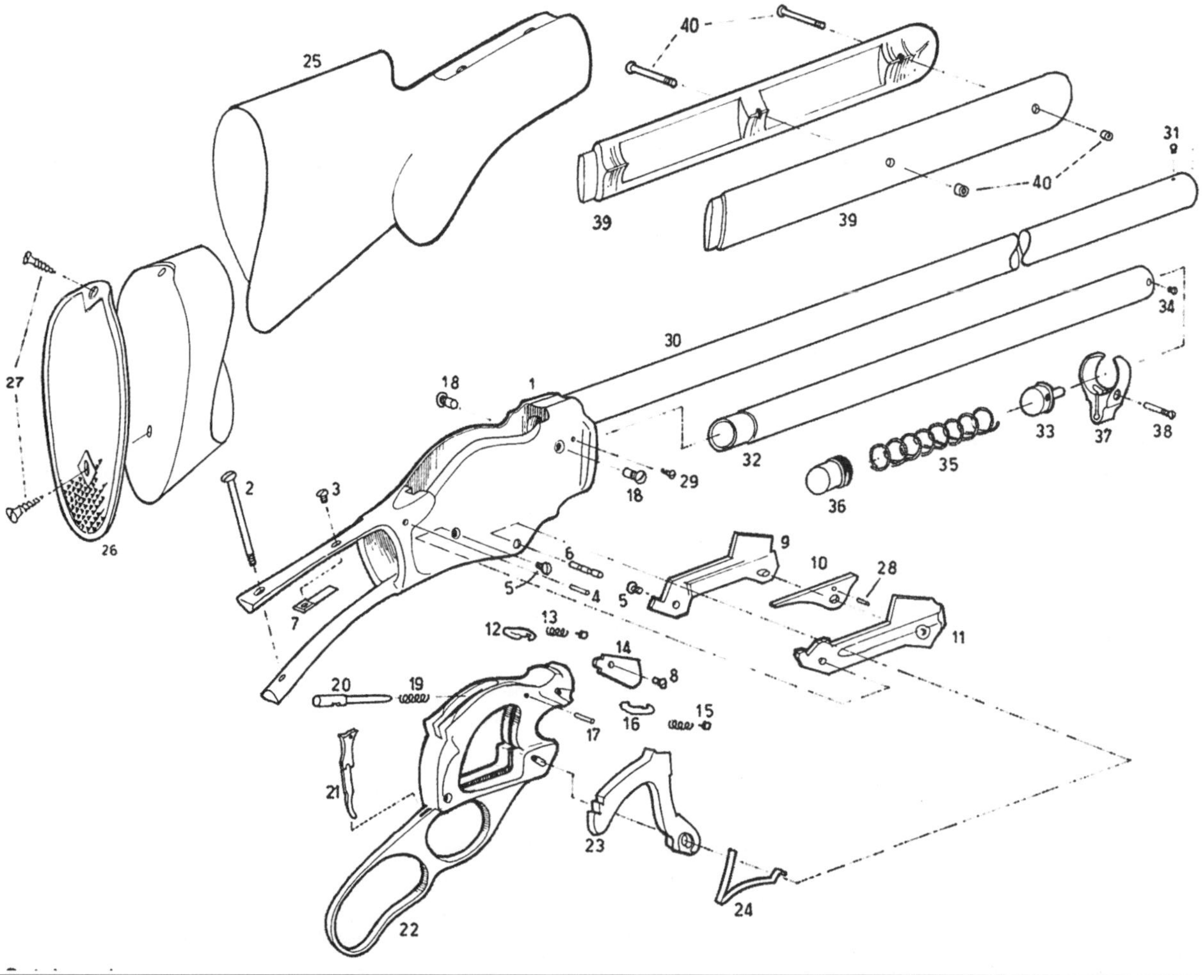

In 1885, Winchester purchased the patents for a lever-action repeating shotgun designed by the Browning brothers to replace the English-made Winchester double-barrel shotgun discontinued in 1884. This was the first lever-action repeating shotgun made in the United States, and it was first announced in 1887 by Winchester as the Model 1887 Shotgun, a hammer-type repeater with solid frame and tubular magazine.

The action was simple and rugged and the gun was popular in its day. Earlier guns were made with one left side extractor and can be recognized by the flat-head screw on the right side that secures the breechblock stud. In 1889, however, Winchester began using double extractors — one on each side of the breechblock.

The Model 87 was made in both 12- and 10-gauge models; the 12-gauge weighs approximately 8 lbs., while the 10-gauge is slightly over 9 lbs. More than 65,000 of these guns were manufactured from 1887 to 1901, when it was modified (a two-peice lever, for example) and reissued as the Model 1901 in 10-gauge only. The Model 1901 (introduced in 1902), continued in production until 1920.

DISASSEMBLY

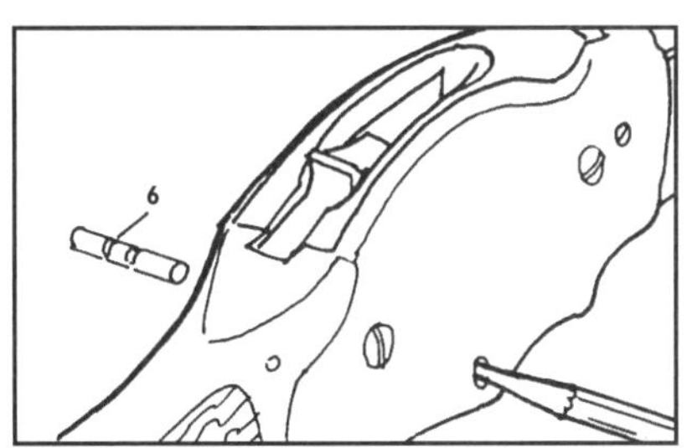

1 Unscrew the tang screw (2) and pull stock (25) away from receiver (1), being careful to pull it straight to the rear to avoid splitting the wood around the receiver tangs. It my be necessary to tap the rear of the receiver with a plastic hammer at a point about where the sear pin (4) enters the receiver, to loosen the buttstock.

Open the action by moving the lever (22) down and forward. At this point, all working parts are exposed and accessible for cleaning, lubrication, etc. Use a pair of pliers or mainspring vise to compress the mainspring (24), and draw it backward through the hammer slot in the breech-block.

Remove the right and left carrier screws (5) and lift the carrier assembly (8, 10, 11) out through the top of the receiver.

Use a drift punch and push out the breechblock pin (6), which will free the hammer (23) and breechblock (22) from the receiver. Remove them through the bottom of the receiver. The hammer then slips out through the top-rearward slot in the breechblock.

To remove the extractors (12 and 16), use your thumb to push the extractor against the lower edge of its slot and then push back the extractor pin and spring (13 and 15) with the point of a knife, and push the extractor hook towards the breech-block stud (14); the extractors will lift out. CAUTION: Be careful that the extractor spring and pins do not fly out and become lost.

The firing pin (20) and firing pin spring (19) are removed by taking out the firing pin stop screw (17), keeping a finger on the rear of the firing pin to keep it from flying backward. The firing pin and its spring are then removed from the breechblock (22).

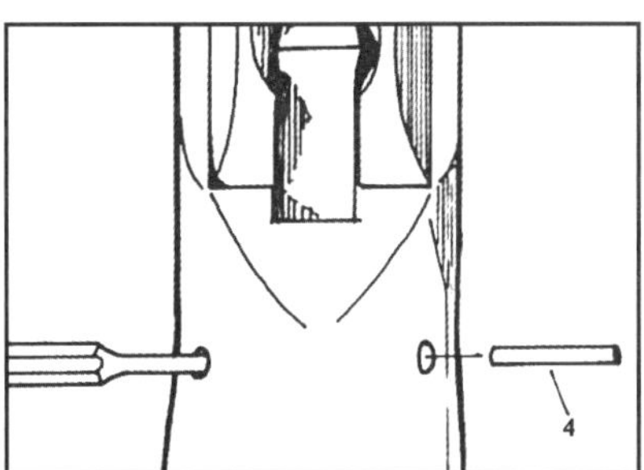

2 To remove the trigger and sear, unscrew the trigger spring screw (3) and remove both the screw and spring (7) from the receiver. Drive out the sear pin (4) with a drift punch and remove the trigger (21) through the bottom of the receiver (Figure 2).

Remove the two forearm screws (40), and remove the two-piece forearm (39) from the gun. Be careful not to split the tenons that fit into the action in doing so.

Remove magazine band screw (38) from the magazine band (37) and then slip the magazine band away from the magazine plug (33) and off the barrel.

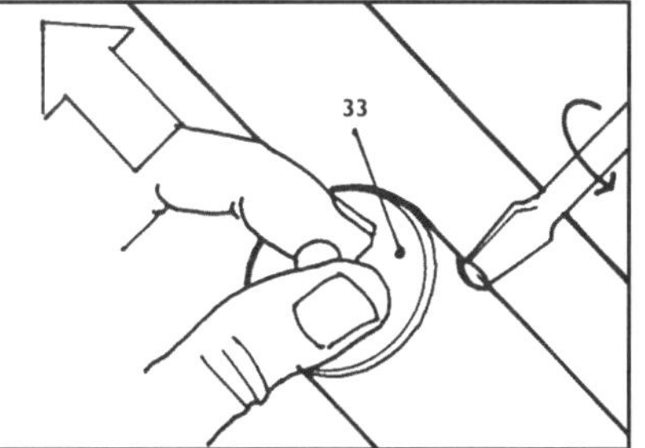

3 Remove magazine plug screw (34) from magazine plug (33), holding your thumb over the end of the plug so it and the magazine spring do not fly out when the retaining screw is removed. Then, carefully work the magazine plug out of the magazine tube (32), allowing the magazine spring (35) to follow it out. The magazine tube may then be removed by pulling it straight forward out of the receiver. By tipping this tube downward (the end towards the muzzle), the magazine follower (36) should fall out.

Reassemble in reverse order, observing the following hints: Replace the sear spring (7) and sear spring screw (3) partially; do not tighten the screw at first. Replace the trigger and sear (21) and the sear pin (4). Tighten the sear spring screw. Insert the hammer into the breechblock and, while together, pass them into the receiver from below. Insert the breechblock pin. Hold back the trigger to facilitate placing the hammer in its proper position.

Lay the right- and left-hand carriers (9 & 11) together with the carrier lifter (10) and slip the assembly into the receiver from above. Replace right and left carrier screws (5); these screws are readily replaced with the breechblock in the nearly closed position.

Slip in the mainspring through the hammer slot in the breechblock. Compress it and slip it into place, making sure that the hooking end of the mainspring lies around the breechblock pin, and that the short end of the mainspring lies against the hammer.

WINCHESTER SINGLE-SHOT RIFLE

PARTS LEGEND

1. Front sight
2. Barrel
3. Rear sight
4. Mainspring base
5. Mainspring
6. Mainspring screw
7. Forearm screw
8. Receiver
9. Sear spring screw
10. Sear spring
11. Sear
12. Sear pin
13. Lower tang screw
14. Side tang screws (2)
15. Tang
16. Knock-off spring screw
17. Knock-off spring
18. Knock-off
19. Knock-off pin
20. Trigger
21. Trigger pin
22. Upper tang screw
23. Breechblock
24. Firing pin
25. Extractor
26. Firing pin stop pin
27. Hammer
28. Hammer pin
29. Link
30. Link pin, long
31. Link pin, short
32. Finger lever
33. Finger lever pin
34. Finger lever pin stop screw
35. Buttplate
36. Buttplate screws (2)

NOTE: Buttstock and forearm not shown.

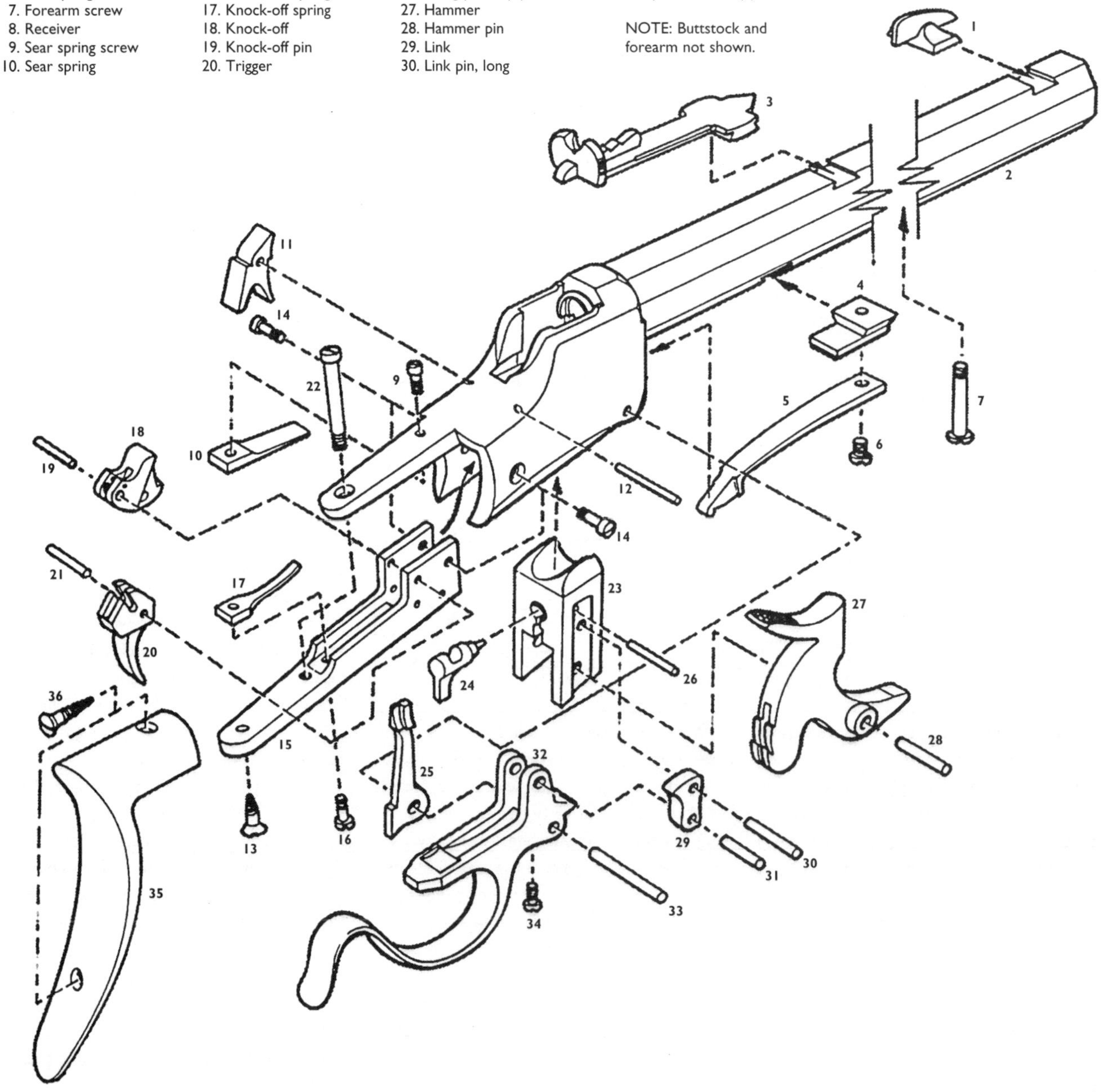

The Winchester lever-action single-shot rifle was manufactured from 1885 until 1920, and at one time or another during this period was available in 3 sizes of frame and in 6 barrel weights. It was chambered for a great many rimmed cartridges, ranging in caliber from the .22 Short rimfire through and including the .50 Eley center-fire. There was limited production in rimless calibers, including 7mm Mauser, 7.65mm Mauser, and .30-06. This dropping-block action was also used for a 20-ga. shotgun first made in 1914 and the shotgun was offered in both solid-frame and take-down styles.

The actions of Winchester single-shot rifles were casehardened in colors until August 1901, but those manufactured in following years were heat-treated and given a blued finish. Color case-hardening was obtainable on special order following institution of the improved heat treatment method. The Winchester firm would at one time reheat-treat the older casehardened actions, but this service is no longer offered by that company.

Plain triggers were standard on most versions of this rifle, but set triggers could be furnished on special order.

The single-shot rifle in takedown version was first offered in 1910. The development of this system necessitated a change in the design of the mainspring. The flat mainspring of the solid-frame rifle was attached to a base on the barrel, but in the takedown type the mainspring of music wire was fitted around the hammer assembly. This latter action is commonly called the coiled-spring type, and it eventually became standard for both takedown and solid-frame rifles.

The final version of the Winchester single-shot rifle was the Model 87 musket introduced in 1918 in cal. 22 rim-fire. Large numbers of this model were purchased by the U.S. government for troop training purposes during World War I and were later issued to shooting clubs through the Director of Civilian Marksmanship. This rifle was the first of the series to be given a model number. Until that time this basic rifle was merely listed as the Winchester Single-Shot, without the customary model number applied to other Winchester rifles and shotguns.

The design of the Winchester Single-Shot rifle was based upon a patent granted to John M. Browning in 1879. The Browning firm produced nearly 600 of these rifles in their Ogden, Utah shop, but sold the manufacturing and sales rights to the Winchester firm in 1883. Winchester engineers made only minor design changes in tooling up for its manufacture.

DISASSEMBLY

Drop finger lever (32) and check action to be sure rifle is not loaded. Unscrew forearm screw (7) and remove wood forearm to expose mainspring (5). Unscrew mainspring screw (6) and remove mainspring. Loosen finger lever pin stop screw (34) and drift out finger lever pin (33) with a suitable punch. Pull breechblock (23) with firing pin (24) and hammer (27) attached out bottom of receiver by finger lever (32). Extractor (25) will drop out bottom of receiver after removing breechblock. Above parts may all be separated by drifting out their respective pins.

To disassemble trigger mechanism, unscrew upper and lower tang screws (22 & 13) and remove buttstock to rear. Unscrew side tang screws (14) from left and right sides of receiver and remove tang (15). Remove knock-off spring screw (16) from underside of tang and remove knock-off spring (17). Trigger (20) and knock-off (18) can be removed by drifting out their respective retaining pins (21 & 19). Unscrew sear spring screw (9) from top of receiver tang and drop out sear spring (10). Drift out sear pin (12) and remove sear (11) from receiver. Reassemble in reverse (see Fig. 2).

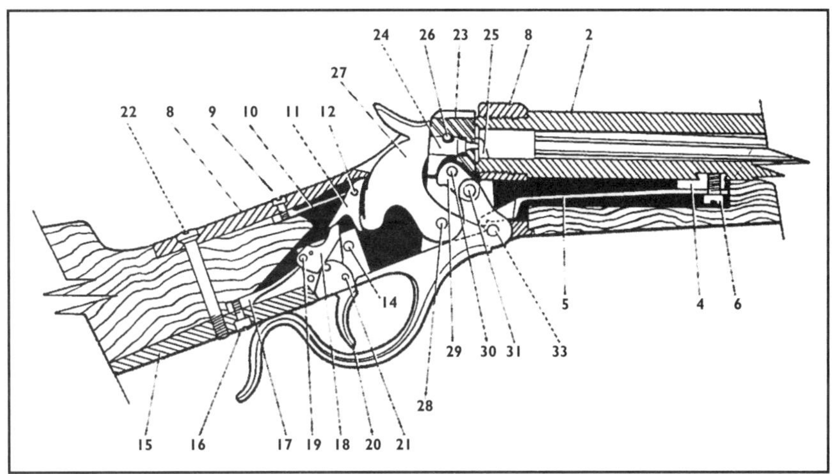

1 The cutaway section of the rifle shows all parts assembled properly.

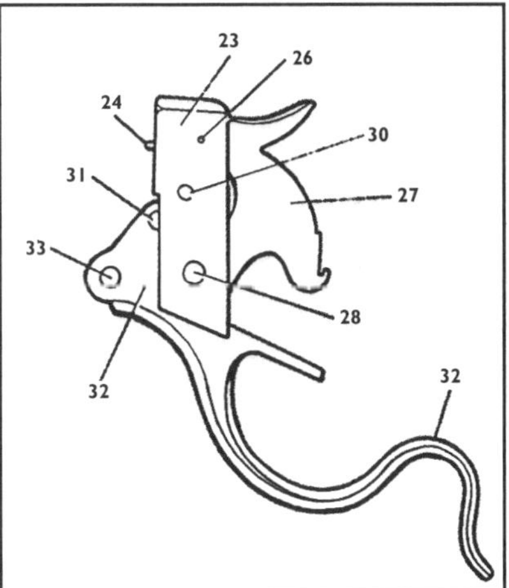

2 To reassemble breechblock (23), hammer (27), and finger lever (32) in receiver, place them assembled in the position shown and push them partly into position from underside of receiver. Replace extractor (25) in receiver and push breech block, hammer, and finger lever up into position, aligning front hole of finger lever with its corresponding hole in receiver. Replace finger lever pin (33) and tighten finger lever pin stop screw (34).

APPENDIX

When setting out to disassemble a firearm, its owner is often challenged to find instructions for the procedure as it applies to the particular gun in question. As a partial solution to this problem, the list that follows contains the brand names and model designations of many rifles and shotguns, represented generally, but not specifically, in this book. These firearms are listed alphabetically with the page number in the book on which a mechanically and operationally similar firearm is described.

Keep in mind, when applying the directions for one firearm to the disassembly of another similar gun, that differences will exist and procedures may need adaptation if disassembly and reassembly are to be done successfully. Discretion, in this instance, may save an embarrassing trip to one's local gunsmith.

INDEX

INDEX

INDEX